Lecture Notes in Artificial Intelligence   6803

Edited by R. Goebel, J. Siekmann, and W. Wahlster

Subseries of Lecture Notes in Computer Science

W0193327

Nikolaj Bjørner
Viorica Sofronie-Stokkermans (Eds.)

Automated Deduction – CADE-23

23rd International Conference on Automated Deduction
Wrocław, Poland, July 31 - August 5, 2011
Proceedings

 Springer

Series Editors

Randy Goebel, University of Alberta, Edmonton, Canada
Jörg Siekmann, University of Saarland, Saarbrücken, Germany
Wolfgang Wahlster, DFKI and University of Saarland, Saarbrücken, Germany

Volume Editors

Nikolaj Bjørner
Microsoft Research
One Microsoft Way, Redmond, WA 98052-6399, USA
E-mail: nbjorner@microsoft.com

Viorica Sofronie-Stokkermans
Max-Planck-Institut für Informatik
Campus E 1.4, 66123, Saarbrücken, Germany
E-mail: sofronie@mpi-inf.mpg.de

ISSN 0302-9743   e-ISSN 1611-3349
ISBN 978-3-642-22437-9   ISBN 978-3-642-22438-6   (eBook)
DOI 10.1007/978-3-642-22438-6
Springer Heidelberg Dordrecht London New York

Library of Congress Control Number: 2011931516

CR Subject Classification (1998): I.2.3, I.2, F.4.1, F.3, F.4, D.2.4

LNCS Sublibrary: SL 7 – Artificial Intelligence

Typesetting: Camera-ready by author, data conversion by Scientific Publishing Services, Chennai, India

Printed on acid-free paper

Springer is part of Springer Science+Business Media (www.springer.com)

Preface

This volume contains the papers presented at the 23rd International Conference on Automated Deduction (CADE 23), held between July 31 and August 5, 2011 in Wrocław, Poland. CADE is the major forum for the presentation of research in all aspects of automated deduction.

The Program Committee decided to accept 28 regular papers and 7 system descriptions from a total of 80 submissions. Each submission was reviewed by at least three Program Committee members and external reviewers. We would like to thank all the members of the Program Committee for their careful and thoughtful deliberations. Many thanks to Andrei Voronkov for providing the EasyChair system which greatly facilitated the reviewing process, the electronic Program Committee meeting, and the preparation of the proceedings. In addition to the contributed papers, the program included four invited lectures by Koen Claessen, Byron Cook, Xavier Leroy, and Aarne Ranta. We thank the invited speakers not only for their presentations, but also for contributing abstracts, extended abstracts, or full papers to the proceedings.

In addition, on the days preceding CADE a diverse range of affiliated events took place. Six workshops:

- *BOOGIE 2011:* The First International Workshop on Intermediate Verification Languages
- *Thedu 11:* CTP Components for Educational Software
- *PSATTT11:* International Workshop on Proof Search in Axiomatic Theories and Type Theories
- *PxTP:* Workshop on Proof eXchange for Theorem Proving
- *ATE 2011:* The First Workshop on Automated Theory Engineering
- *UNIF:* The International Workshop on Unification

Six tutorials:

- First-Order Theorem Proving and Vampire
- Grammatical Framework: A Hands-On Introduction
- Model Checking Modulo Theories: Theory and Practice
- Practical Computer Formalization of Mathematics Using Mizar
- Practical Reasoning with Quantified Boolean Formulas
- Computational Logic and Human Thinking

The CADE ATP System Competition (CASC) was also held. All this helped to make the conference a success.

During the conference, the Herbrand Award for Distinguished Contributions to Automated Reasoning was presented to Nachum Dershowitz in recognition of his ground-breaking research on the design and use of well-founded orderings in term rewriting and automated deduction. The Selection Committee for the Herbrand Award consisted of the CADE-23 Program Committee members, the trustees of CADE Inc., and the Herbrand Award winners of the last ten years. The Herbrand Award ceremony and the acceptance speech by Nachum Dershowitz were part of the conference program. In addition, the conference program also contained a lecture dedicated to the memory of William McCune.

Many people helped to make CADE 23 a success. We are very grateful to Hans de Nivelle (CADE General Chair), Katarzyna Wodzyńska and Arkadiusz Janicki (local organization) for the tremendous effort they devoted to the organization of the conference. We thank Aaron Stump (Workshop Chair), Carsten Schürmann (Publicity Chair), Geoff Sutcliffe (CASC Chair), all the individual workshop organizers, and all the tutorial speakers. Last, but not least, we thank all authors who submitted papers to CADE 23, and all participants of the conference.

CADE 23 received support from the Department of Computer Science at the University of Wrocław toward the Woody Bledsoe Awards, the University of Wrocław, and Microsoft Research.

May 2011

Nikolaj Bjørner
Viorica Sofronie-Stokkermans

Organization

Program Chairs

Nikolaj Bjørner   Microsoft Research, USA
Viorica Sofronie-Stokkermans   Max Planck Institute for Informatics, Germany

Program Committee

Alessandro Armando   University of Genoa and FBK-IRST, Italy
Franz Baader   TU Dresden, Germany
Peter Baumgartner   National ICT, Australia
Bernhard Beckert   Karlsruhe Institute of Technology, Germany
Nikolaj Bjørner   Microsoft Research, USA
Maria Paola Bonacina   Università degli Studi di Verona, Italy
Alessandro Cimatti   FBK-IRST, Italy
Leonardo de Moura   Microsoft Research, USA
Hans de Nivelle   University of Wrocław, Poland
Stephanie Delaune   LSV, CNRS, ENS Cachan, and INRIA Saclay,
                              France
Bruno Dutertre   SRI International, USA
Ulrich Furbach   University of Koblenz, Germany
Silvio Ghilardi   Università degli Studi di Milano, Italy
Jürgen Giesl   RWTH Aachen, Germany
Rajeev Goré   The Australian National University, Australia
John Harrison   Intel Corporation, USA
Ullrich Hustadt   University of Liverpool, UK
Reiner Hähnle   Chalmers University of Technology, Sweden
Deepak Kapur   University of New Mexico, USA
Viktor Kuncak   EPFL, Switzerland
Alexander Leitsch   Vienna University of Technology, Austria
Christopher Lynch   Clarkson University, USA
Claude Marché   INRIA Saclay, France
Aart Middeldorp   University of Innsbruck, Austria
Tobias Nipkow   Technische Universität München, Germany
Albert Oliveras   Technical University of Catalonia, Spain
Lawrence Paulson   University of Cambridge, UK
Frank Pfenning   Carnegie Mellon University, USA
Brigitte Pientka   McGill University, Canada
David Plaisted   University of North Carolina-Chapel Hill, USA
Michael Rusinowitch   INRIA Nancy Grand Est, France

Renate A. Schmidt   The University of Manchester, UK
Carsten Schürmann   IT University of Copenhagen, Denmark
Roberto Sebastiani   University of Trento, Italy
Gert Smolka   Saarland University, Germany
Viorica Sofronie-Stokkermans   Max Planck Institute for Informatics, Germany
Aaron Stump   The University of Iowa, USA
Geoff Sutcliffe   University of Miami, USA
Cesare Tinelli   The University of Iowa, USA
Andrei Voronkov   The University of Manchester, UK
Christoph Weidenbach   Max Planck Institute for Informatics, Germany
Frank Wolter   University of Liverpool, UK

Conference Chair

Hans De Nivelle   University of Wrocław, Poland

Workshops Chair

Aaron Stump   The University of Iowa, USA

Publicity Chair

Carsten Schürmann   IT University of Copenhagen, Denmark

System Competition

Geoff Sutcliffe   University of Miami, USA

Additional Reviewers

Besson, Frédéric   Calvanese, Diego   Griggio, Alberto
Biere, Armin   Denman, William   Jacobs, Swen
Bormer, Thorsten   Enache, Ramona   Jobstmann, Barbara
Bozzano, Marco   Falke, Stephan   Johansson, Moa
Brotherston, James   Felgenhauer, Bertram   Kaminski, Mark
Brown, Chad   Fiorentini, Camillo   Klop, Jan Willem
Bruns, Daniel   Gladisch, Christoph   Kneuss, Etienne
Bruttomesso, Roberto   Glimm, Birte   Kohlhase, Michael
Böhme, Sascha   Gofman, Mikhail I.   Konev, Boris

Kusakari, Keiichirou
Lange, Martin
Leroux, Jérôme
Losa, Giuliano
Ludwig, Michel
Lukasiewicz, Thomas
Mastroeni, Isabella
Momigliano, Alberto
Moser, Georg
Möller, Ralf
Narasamdya, Iman
Neurauter, Friedrich
Nguyen, Phuong
Nieuwenhuis, Robert
Noschinski, Lars
Oostrom, Vincent van
Otop, Jan
Palmigiano, Alessandra
Papacchini, Fabio

Paskevich, Andrei
Peñaloza, Rafael
Piskac, Ruzica
Ranise, Silvio
Ridgeway, Jeremy
Riesco, Adrian
Roveri, Marco
Rümmer, Philipp
Schaafsma,
  Bastiaan Joost
Schmitt, Peter
Schneider, Michael
Schneider, Thomas
Schulz, Stephan
Schwoon, Stefan
Sternagel, Christian
Suda, Martin
Suter, Philippe
Tacchella, Armando

Teige, Tino
Thiemann, René
Tiu, Alwen
Tobies, Stephan
Tomasi, Silvia
Tonetta, Stefano
Turuani, Mathieu
Urbain, Xavier
Vescovi, Michele
Vrijer, Roel de
Waaler, Arild
Waldmann, Uwe
Weiß, Benjamin
Weller, Daniel
Widmann, Florian
Wischnewski, Patrick
Witkowski, Piotr
Wolter, Diedrich
Zankl, Harald

Table of Contents

The Anatomy of Equinox – An Extensible Automated Reasoning Tool for First-Order Logic and Beyond
(Talk Abstract)

Koen Claessen

Chalmers University of Technology, Gothenburg, Sweden
koen@chalmers.se

Equinox is an automated reasoning tool for first-order logic. It is also a framework for building highly targeted automated reasoning tools for specific domains.

The aim behind Equinox is to obtain an automated reasoning tool with a modular and extensible architecture. SAT modulo theory (SMT) solvers have the same aim. However, the way in which this aim is realized in Equinox is quite different from the way this is done traditional SMT solvers.

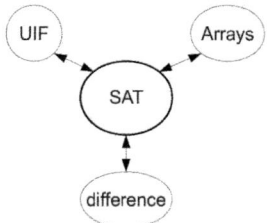

Fig. 1. Traditional architecture of an SMT-solver

Fig. 1 shows the architecture of a traditional SMT solver. In the middle sits the SAT-solver, which is the main responsible for all primitive logical (boolean) reasoning. Around the SAT-solver sit the theories with which the SAT-solver is extended. They communicate with the SAT-solver in a language which both understand; namely SAT literals and constraints over those literals. The picture shows three different commonly used theories: uninterpreted functions (UIF), arrays, and difference logic. Each theory is supposed to express which situations they allow and disallow in terms of literals and constraints over these literals.

Equinox employs a different approach, which we call the *layered approach*. It is depicted in Fig. 2. The reasoning tool is organized in layers, each of which implement a full logic of their own. Such a logic consists of syntax, constraints, and models. The intention is that the logic associated with a certain layer is more expressive than the logic associated with the layer below. Thus, a layer can extend a logic's syntax and constraints, and consequently augment the notion of model associated with that logic. A layer can express what it allows and

N. Bjørner and V. Sofronie-Stokkermans (Eds.): CADE 2011, LNAI 6803, pp. 1–3, 2011.

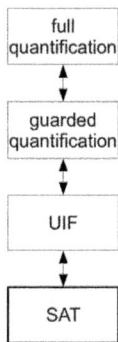

Fig. 2. The layered approach

disallows in terms of the full language of the layer below. By building more and more layers on top of each other, we can support more and more complex logics.

The bottom layer of Equinox consists of a SAT-solver, with propositional logic as its associated logic. The layer directly above it implements uninterpreted functions and equality. The language with which the two layers communicate with each other is their common language, namely propositional logic. The layers above that add universal quantification to the logic. (Equinox supports first-order quantification in two tiers; first a form of guarded quantification is added, then full quantification is added.) The quantification layer communicates with the UIF layer in terms of their common language, namely quantifier-free first-order logic, with finite first-order models.

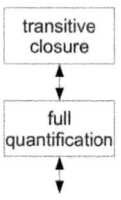

Fig. 3. Extending with a layer at the top

The advantage of the layered approach becomes clear once we want to augment the existing logic (in this case full first-order logic) with a more expressive logic. Fig. 3 shows that we can add a layer implementing transitive closure. The language that is used to communicate between the top two layers is full first-order logic. In other words, the top layer can add constraints which are full first-order logic axioms to the layer below. (Because first-order logic is not decidable, we have to slightly adapt the concept of model in order for this to work).

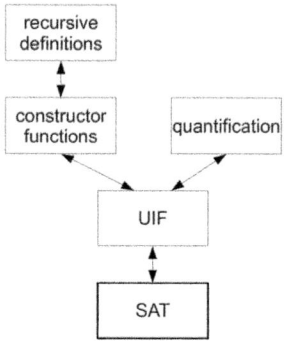

Fig. 4. Extending with layers sideways

Many imaginable extensions to an exisiting logic do not require adding a layer at the very top, because those extensions are implementable using simpler layers that occur lower in the hierarchy. In order to support modularity, Equinox allows the addition of *sideways layers*, depicted in Fig. 4. An example of a sideways layer is adding the concept of "constructor function" to first-order logic. A constructor function is an injective function, whose results are not equal to the results of any other constructor function. Constructor functions commonly occur when modelling algebraic datatypes or functional programs with pattern matching.

Constructor functions are axiomatizable using first-order logic axioms, but much more efficient is implementing them as a layer that directly talks to the UIF layer. This poses a problem for modularity, since we change the logic by adding a layer. What happens to the layer above? A sideways layer allows the extension of a logic with new features, but it can still mimic the underlying logic, so any layer extending the underlying logic will not be affected by the extension.

This design allows for a very modular construction of domain-specific reasoning tools. In the talk, we will see a number of examples of logics for which we can build reasoning tools in this way, in particular (1) first-order logic, (2) first-order logic with transitive closure, (3) constructor functions recursive functional programs, and (4) separation logic.

Advances in Proving Program Termination and Liveness

Byron Cook

Microsoft Research and Queen Mary, University of London

Abstract. Because the halting problem is undecidable, many have considered the dream of automatically proving termination (and other liveness properties) to be impossible. While not refuting Turing's original result of undecidability, recent research now makes this dream a practical reality. I will describe this recent work and its application to industrial software and models of biological systems. I will also describe recent adaptations of these new technologies to the problem of proving temporal properties in logics such as CTL and LTL.

N. Bjørner and V. Sofronie-Stokkermans (Eds.): CADE 2011, LNAI 6803, p. 4, 2011.
© Springer-Verlag Berlin Heidelberg 2011

Translating between Language and Logic: What Is Easy and What Is Difficult

Aarne Ranta

Department of Computer Science and Engineering
Chalmers University of Technology and University of Gothenburg

Abstract. Natural language interfaces make formal systems accessible in informal language. They have a potential to make systems like theorem provers more widely used by students, mathematicians, and engineers who are not experts in logic. This paper shows that simple but still useful interfaces are easy to build with available technology. They are moreover easy to adapt to different formalisms and natural languages. The language can be made reasonably nice and stylistically varied. However, a fully general translation between logic and natural language also poses difficult, even unsolvable problems. This paper investigates what can be realistically expected and what problems are hard.

Keywords: Grammatical Framework, natural language interface.

1 Introduction

Mature technology is characterized by *invisibility*: it never reminds the user of its existence. Operating systems are a prime example. Still a decade ago, you'd better be a Unix hacker to do anything useful with a Unix computer. Nowadays Unix is hidden under a layer of Mac OS or Ubuntu Linux, and it works so well that the layman user hardly ever notices it is there.

When will formal proof systems mature? Decades of accumulated experience and improvements have produced many systems that are sophisticated, efficient, and robust. But using them is often an expert task—if not for the same experts as the ones who developed the systems, then at least for persons with a special training. One reason (not always the only one, of course) is that the systems use formalized proof languages, which have to be learnt. The formalized language, close to the machine language of the underlying proof engine, constantly reminds the user of the existence of the engine.

Let us focus on one use case: a student who wants to use a proof system as an infatigable teaching assistant, helping her to construct and verify proofs. This case easily extends to a mathematician who needs help in proving new theorems, and to an engineer who needs to verify software or hardware systems with respect to informal specifications. Now, the student must constantly perform manual conversions between the informal mathematical language of her textbooks and the formalism used by the proof system.

We can imagine this to be otherwise. Computer algebra systems, such as Mathematica [1], are able to manipulate normal mathematical notations, for instance, $\sqrt{x}$ instead

N. Bjørner and V. Sofronie-Stokkermans (Eds.): CADE 2011, LNAI 6803, pp. 5–25, 2011.

of its formalized representation `Sqrt[x]`. The support for normal mathematical language is one (although not the only one) of the reasons why computer algebras, unlike formal proof systems, have become main-stream tools in mathematics education.

Now, what is the proof-system counterpart of algebraic formulas in computer algebra? It is mathematical text, which is a mixture of natural language and algebraic formulas. The natural language part cannot be replaced by formulas. Therefore it is only by allowing input and output in text that proof system can hide their internal technology and reach the same level of maturity as computer algebras.

The importance of informal language for proof systems has of course been noticed several times. It has motivated systems like STUDENT [2], Mathematical Vernacular [3], Mizar [4], OMEGA [5], Isar [6], Vip [7], Theorema [8], MathLang [9], Naproche [10], and FMathL [11]. These systems permit user interaction in a notation that resembles English more than logical symbolisms do. The notations are of course limited, and far from a full coverage of the language found in mathematics books. Their development and maintenance has required considerable efforts. What we hope to show in this paper is that such interfaces are now easy to build, that they can be ported to other languages than English, and that their language can be made fairly sophisticated.

In Section 2, we will give a brief overview of the language of mathematics. In Section 3, we will introduce GF, Grammatical Framework [12,13], as a tool that enables the construction of translation systems with the minimum of effort. Section 4 defines a simple predicate logic interface, which, while satisfying the grammar rules of natural language, is easy to build and to port to different notations of formal logic and to different natural languages. In this interface, the formula

$$(\forall x)(Nat(x) \supset Even(x) \vee Odd(x))$$

gets translated to English, German, French, and Finnish in the following ways:

> *for all x, if x is a natural number then x is even or x is odd*
> *für alle x, wenn x eine natürliche Zahl ist, dann ist x gerade oder x ist ungerade*
> *pour tour x, si x est un nombre entier alors x est pair ou x est impair*
> *kaikille x, jos x on luonnollinen luku niin x on parillinen tai x on pariton*

In Section 5, we will increase the sophistication of the language by well-known techniques from linguistics and compiler construction. For instance, the above formula then gets the translations

> *every natural number is even or odd*
> *jede natürliche Zahl ist gerade oder ungerade*
> *tout nombre entier est pair ou impair*
> *jokainen luonnollinen luku on parillinen tai pariton*

and the translation still works in both directions between the formula and the sentences. In Section 6, we will discuss some problems that are either open or positively undecidable. Section 7 summarizes some natural language interfaces implemented in GF, and

Section 8 concludes. The associated web page [14] contains the complete code referred to in this paper, as well as a live translation demo.

Throughout this paper, we will use the terms *easy* and *difficult* in a special way. *Easy* problems are ones that can be solved by well-known techniques; this doesn't mean that it was easy to develop these techniques in the first place. Thus the *easy* problems in natural language interfaces don't require training in GF or linguistics but can reuse existing components and libraries. For the *difficult* problems, no out-of-the-box solution exists. This relation between easy and difficult has parallels in all areas of technology. For instance, in automatic theorem proving itself, some classes of formulas are easy to decide with known techniques; some classes are easy for humans but still impossible for computers; and some classes will remain difficult forever. An important aspect of progress in both natural language processing and automatic reasoning has been to identify and extend the classes of easy problems, instead of getting paralyzed by the impossibility of the full problem.

2   The Language of Mathematics

What is the ideal language for interaction with proof systems? If we take mathematic books as the starting point, the answer is clear: it is a natural language, such as English or Polish or French, containing some mathematical formulas as parts of the text and structured by headers such as "definition" and "lemma". There can also be diagrams, linked to the text in intricate ways; for instance, a diagram showing a triangle may "bind" the variables used for its sides and angles in the text.

Ignoring the diagrams and the structuring headers for a moment, let us concentrate on the text parts. Mathematical texts consist of two kinds of elements, *verbal* (natural language words) and *symbolic* (mathematical formulas). The distribution of these elements is characterized by the following principles:

- Each sentence is a well-formed natural language sentence.
- A sentence may contain symbolic parts in the following roles:
  - noun phrases, as in x^2 *is divisible by* $\sqrt{x}$;
  - subsentences formed with certain predicates, as in *we conclude that* $x^2 > \sqrt{x}$.
- A symbolic part may not contain verbal parts (with some exceptions, for instance, the notation for set comprehension).

Of particular interest here is that logical constants are never (at least in traditional style) expressed by formulas. Also most logically atomic sentences are expressed by informal text, and so are many noun phrases corresponding to singular terms. The last rule may mandate the use of verbal expression even when symbolic notation exists. For instance, the sentence *the square of every odd number is odd* could not use the symbolic notation for the square, because it would then contain the verbal expression *every odd number* as its part. The conversion to symbolic notation is a complex procedure, as it involves the introduction of a variable: *for every odd number x,* x^2 *is odd*. For this example, the purely verbal expression is probably the better one.

3   GF in a Nutshell

3.1   Abstract and Concrete Syntax

GF is based on a distinction between *abstract syntax* and *concrete syntax*. An abstract syntax defines a system of *trees*, and a concrete syntax specifies how the trees are realized as *strings*. This distinction is only implicit in context-free (BNF, Backus-Naur Form) grammars. To give an example, the BNF rule for multiplication expressions

```
Exp  ::= Exp "*" Exp
```

is in GF analysed into a pair of rules,

```
fun EMul : Exp -> Exp -> Exp
lin EMul x y = x ++ "*" ++ y
```

The first rule belongs to abstract syntax and defines a *function* EMul for constructing trees of the form (EMul x y). The second rule belongs to concrete syntax and defines the *linearization* of trees of the forms (EMul x y): it is the linearization of x concatenated (++) with the token * followed by the linearization of y.

GF grammars are *reversible*: they can be used both for linearizing trees into strings and for *parsing* strings into trees. They may be *ambiguous*: the string x * y * z results in two trees, (EMul (EMul x y) z) and (EMul x (EMul y z)).

3.2   Parametrization

Avoiding ambiguity may or may not be a goal for the grammar writer. In the rule above, a natural way to avoid ambiguity is to *parametrize* the linearization on *precedence*. Each expression has a precedence number, which can be compared to an expected number; parentheses are used if the given number is lower than the expected number. Rather than showing the low-level GF code for this, we use the GF library function infixl (left associative infix). Then we get the correct use of parentheses and the precedence level 2 by writing

```
lin EMul x y = infixl 2 "*" x y
```

Since GF is a functional programming language, we can be even more concise by using *partial application*,

```
lin EMul = infixl 2 "*"
```

This rule is similar to a precedence declaration in languages like Haskell [15],

```
infixl 2 *
```

Thus syntactic conventions such as precedences are a special case of GF's concrete syntax rules, which also cover parameters used in natural languages (see 3.3). What is important is that concrete syntax can be parametrized in different ways without changing the abstract syntax.

3.3   Multilinguality

The most important property of GF in most applications is its *multilinguality*: one abstract syntax can be equipped with many concrete syntaxes. Thus the function `EMul` can also be given the linearization

```
lin EMul x y = x ++ y ++ "imul"
```

which generates the reverse Polish notation of Java Virtual Machine. Now, combining the parsing of x * y with linearization into x y imul makes GF usable as a *compiler*. Since the number of concrete syntaxes attached to an abstract syntax is unlimited, and since all grammars are reversible, GF can be seen as a framework for building *multi-source multi-target compiler-decompilers*.

Yet another aspect of GF is the expressive power of its concrete syntax, reaching beyond the context-free: GF is equivalent to *Parallel Multiple Context-Free Grammars* (PMCFG, [16]). Therefore GF is capable of dealing with all the complexities of natural languages. Sometimes this extra power is not needed; for instance, an English rule for `EMul` can be simply written

```
lin EMul x y = "the product of" ++ x ++ "and" ++ y
```

But in German, the equivalent phrase has to *inflect* in different cases; in particular, the operands have to be in the dative case required by the preposition *von*. This is written

```
lin EMul x y = \\c => defArt Neutr c ++ Produkt_N ! c ++
                        "von" ++ x ! Dat ++ "und" ++ y ! Dat
```

where a case variable c is passed to the definite article (`defArt`), which in the neuter form produces *das*, *dem* or *des* as function of the case. The noun *Produkt* ("product") likewise depends on case.

Without going to the details of the notation, let alone German grammar, we notice that case belongs to the concrete syntax of German without affecting the abstract syntax. French has a different parameter system, involving gender (*le produit* vs. *la somme*) and article-preposition contractions (*le produit du produit*), etc. All these variations can be defined in GF, which enables the use of one and the same abstract syntax for a wide variety of languages.

3.4   Grammar Engineering

That the expressive power of GF is sufficient for multilingual grammars does not yet mean that it is *easy* to write them. The German `EMul` rule above is really the tip of an iceberg of the complexity found in natural languages. Writing formal grammars of natural language from scratch is *difficult* and laborious. To this end, a considerable part of the GF effort has gone to the development of *libraries* of grammars, which encapsulate the difficulties [17]. The *GF Resource Grammar Library*, RGL [18] is a collaborative project, which has produced implementations of 18 languages ranging from English, German, and French to Finnish, Arabic, and Urdu.

The RGL function app builds noun phrases (NP) as function applications with relational nouns (N2). It has several overloaded instances, for example,

```
app : N2 -> NP -> NP          -- the successor of x
app : N2 -> NP -> NP -> NP -- the sum of x and y
```

We use app to write the linearization rules of EMul for English, German, French, and Finnish as follows (hiding the variables by partial application):

```
lin EMul = app (mkN2 (mkN "product"))
lin EMul = app (mkN2 (mkN "Produkt" "Produkte" Neutr))
lin EMul = app (mkN2 (mkN "produit"))
lin EMul = app (mkN2 (mkN "tulo"))
```

In most of these cases, it is enough to write just the dictionary form of the word equivalent to *product*; the RGL function mkN infers all grammatical properties from this form. In German, however, the plural form and the gender need to be given separately. The syntactic construction is the same in all languages, using the function app, which yields equivalents of *the product of x and y*.

The RGL enables a *division of labour* between two kinds of grammar writers: *linguists*, who write the resource grammar libraries, and *application programmers*, who use the libraries for their specific purposes. An application programmer has an access to the RGL via its API (*Application Programmer's Interface*), which hides the linguistic complexity and details such as the passing of parameters. What the application programmer has to know is the vocabulary of her domain. For instance, the translation of *product* as *tulo* in Finnish is specific to mathematics; in many other contexts the translation is *tuote*. This kind of knowledge may be beyond the reach of the linguist, which shows that also the application programmer's knowledge makes an essential contribution to the quality of a translation system.

4   Baseline Translation for the Core Syntax of Logic

Let us start with a simple but complete *core syntax* of predicate logic, specified by the following table:

construction	symbolic	verbal
negation	$\sim P$	*it is not the case that P*
conjunction	$P \mathbin{\&} Q$	*P and Q*
disjunction	$P \vee Q$	*P or Q*
implication	$P \supset Q$	*if P then Q*
universal quantification	$(\forall x)P$	*for all x, P*
existential quantification	$(\exists x)P$	*there exists an x such that P*

How to write the grammar in GF is described below, with full details for the abstract syntax (4.1) and the concrete syntax of natural language (4.2). The "verbal" column is generalized from English string templates to RGL structures, which work for all RGL languages. The formation of atomic sentences is described in 4.3, and Section 4.4 improves the grammar by eliminating the ambiguities of the verbalizations.

4.1   Abstract Syntax

The abstract syntax of predicate calculus can be written as follows:

```
cat Prop ; Ind ; Var
fun
   And, Or, If   : Prop -> Prop -> Prop
   Not           : Prop -> Prop
   Forall, Exist : Var  -> Prop -> Prop
   IVar          : Var  -> Ind
   VStr          : String -> Var
```

This abstract syntax introduces three *categories* (types of syntax trees); Prop (proposition), Ind (individual), and Var (variable); the category String is a built-in category of GF. It addresses pure predicate calculus. It can be extended with domain-specific functions. For instance, in arithmetic such functions may include the use of built-in integers (Int), addition and multiplication, and the predicates *natural number*, *even*, *odd*, and *equal*:

```
fun
   IInt            : Int -> Ind
   Add, Mul        : Ind -> Ind -> Ind
   Nat, Even, Odd  : Ind -> Prop
   Equal           : Ind -> Ind -> Prop
```

Now the sentence

for all x, if x is a natural number then x is even or x is odd

can be expected to have the abstract syntax

```
Forall (VStr "x") (If (Nat (IVar (VStr "x")))
    (Or (Even (IVar (VStr "x"))) (Odd (IVar (VStr "x")))))
```

4.2   Concrete Syntax

When the RGL library is used, the first step in concrete syntax is to define the linguistic categories used for linearizing the categories of the application grammar. In the case at hand, propositions come out as sentences (S) and individuals and variables as noun phrases (NP). Thus we set

```
lincat Prop = S ; Ind, Var = NP
```

and can then define

```
lin
   And = mkS and_Conj
   Or  = mkS or_Conj
   If p q = mkS (mkAdv if_Subj p) (mkS then_Adv q)
```

```
Not = negS
Forall x p = mkS (mkAdv for_Prep (mkNP all_Predet x)) p
Exist  x p = mkS (existS (mkNP x (mkRS p)))
IVar x = x
VStr s = symb s
```

We refer to the on-line RGL documentation for the details of the API functions used here. All of them are general-purpose functions readily available for all RGL languages, except negS and existS, which are constructed by using the RGL in different ways in different languages. Thus a straightforward implementation for the negation in English is *it is not the case that P*, obtained by

```
negS p = mkS negative_Pol
    (mkCl it_NP (mkNP the_Det (mkCN (mkN "case") p)))
```

and similarly for German (*es ist nicht der Fall, dass P*) and French (*il n' est pas le cas que P*). This form of negation works for all kinds of propositions, complex and atomic alike. We will show later how to optimize this for atomic propositions and produce *x is not odd* instead of *it is not the case that x is odd*. Existence can likewise be straightforwardly linearized as *there exists x such that P* and its equivalents.

At the other end of the translation, we need a grammar for the symbolic notation of logic. By using precedences in the way shown in Section 3.2, this is straighforward for some notations; some others, however, may use devices such as lists (many-place conjunctions rather than binary ones) and domain-restricted quantifiers. We will return to these variations in Section 5.

4.3   The Lexicon

To extend the concrete syntax to arithmetic constants, we can write

```
lin
  IInt  = symb
  Add   = app  (mkN2 (mkN "sum"))
  Mul   = app  (mkN2 (mkN "product"))
  Nat   = pred (mkCN (mkA "natural") (mkN "number"))
  Even  = pred (mkA "even")
  Odd   = pred (mkA "odd")
  Equal = pred (mkA "equal")
```

and similarly in other languages, varying the adjectives and nouns used. A particularly useful RGL function for this purpose is pred, which is an overloaded function covering different kinds of predication with adjectives, nouns, and verbs:

```
pred : A   -> NP -> S        -- x is even
pred : A   -> NP -> NP -> S  -- x and y are equal
pred : CN -> NP -> S         -- x is a number
pred : V   -> NP -> S        -- x converges
pred : V2  -> NP -> NP -> S  -- x includes y
```

Since the main part of work in natural language interfaces has to do with the non-logical vocabulary, the main devices needed by most programmers will be the functions `app` (Section 3.4) and `pred`, as well as lexical functions such as `mkN` and `mkA`.

The lexical work can be further reduced by using a general-purpose multilingual mathematical lexicon. Such a lexicon was built for six languages within the WebALT project [19] to cover the content lexicons in the OpenMath project [20]. The WebALT lexicon is extended and ported to more languages in the MOLTO project [21].

4.4 Ambiguity

The baseline grammar of predicate logic has a narrow coverage and produces clumsy language. Its worst property, however, is that the language is ambiguous. As there is no concept of precedence, we have the following ambiguities:

P and Q or R : $\qquad\qquad\qquad (P\&Q) \vee R$ vs. $P\&(Q \vee R)$
it is not the case that P *and* Q : $(\sim P)\&Q$ vs. $\sim (P\&Q)$
for all x, P and Q : $\qquad\quad ((\forall x)P)\&Q$ vs. $(\forall x)(P\&Q)$

Introducing a precedence order by stipulation would not solve the problem. For instance, stipulating that *and* binds stronger than *or* would simply make $P\&(Q \vee R)$ inexpressible! Moreover, stipulations like this would cause the language no longer to be a real fragment of natural language, since the user would have to learn the artificial precedence rules separately in order really to understand the language.

The ambiguity problem will be revisited in Section 5, using techniques from natural language generation (NLG) to reduce ambiguities in optimized ways. However, even in the simple interface we can solve the problem by parametrizing the concrete syntax. We just need a Boolean parameter that indicates whether a proposition is complex (i.e. formed by a connective). Such parameters can in GF be attached to expressions by using *records*. Thus the linearization type of propositions becomes

```
lincat Prop = {s : S ; isCompl : Bool}
```

Following an idea from [22], we can use bulleted lists to structure sentences—a device that is more natural-language-like than parentheses would be. Thus we have the following unambiguous variants of *P and Q or R*:

$(P\&Q) \vee R$	$P\&(Q \vee R)$
either of the following holds:	both of the following hold:
• P and Q	• P
• R	• Q or R

The rule for generating this says that, if *none* of the operands is complex, the sentence conjunction can be used; otherwise, the bulleted structure must be used:

```
lin And p q = case <p.isCompl, q.isCompl> of {
  <False,False>
    => {s = mkS and_Conj p.s and q.s ; isCompl = True} ;
  _ => {s = bulletS Pl "both" p.s q.s ; isCompl = False}
  }
```

Unfortunately, it is not decidable whether a GF grammar (or even a context-free grammar) is ambiguous. Working on the high abstraction level of RGL can make it difficult even to see the effect of individual rules. Therefore, the only certain procedure is to test with the parser. When generating natural language from logic, the parser test can be applied to a set of alternative equivalent expressions to select, for instance, the shortest unambiguous one. The next section will show how such equivalent expressions are generated.

In general, syntactic disambiguation may be based on semantic considerations, which makes it *difficult* (Section 6.1). But one semantic method is *easy* to implement for fragment at hand: *binding analysis*. Thus, when parsing the sentence *for all x, x is even or x is odd*, the interpretation $((\forall x)Even(x)) \vee Odd(x)$ can be excluded, because it contains an unbound variable. A general and powerful approach to semantics-based disambiguation uses *dependent types* and *higher-order abstract syntax* ([13], Chapter 6). For instance, the universal quantifier can be declared

```
fun Univ : (A : Dom) -> (Var A -> Prop) -> Prop
```

The body of quantification now depends on a variable, which moreover is typed with respect to a domain. In this way, both binding analysis and the well-typedness of predicate applications with respect to domains is defined in GF, in a declarative way. However, this method is *difficult* (though not impossible) to scale up to the syntax extensions discussed in the next section.

5   Beyond the Baseline Translations: Easy Improvements

In this section, we will extend the abstract syntax of logic with structures available in natural language but not in standard predicate logic (Section 5.1). This extended syntax is still a conservative extension of the core syntax and can easily be translated to it (5.2). The most challenging part is the reverse: given a core syntax tree, find the best tree in the extended syntax. In addition to better style, the extended syntax provides new ways to eliminate ambiguity (5.3). Finally, Section 5.4 will show how to optimally divide the expressions into verbal and symbolic parts, as specified in Section 2.

For reasons of space and readability, we will no longer give the explicit GF code. Instead, we use a logical formalism extended with constructs that correspond to the desired natural language structures. At this point, and certainly with help from GF documentation, the reader should be able easily to reconstruct the GF code. The full code is shown on the associated web page [14], including a concrete syntax using RGL, and the conversions of Sections 5.2 and 5.3.

The core-to-extension conversions of Section 5.3 could not be implemented as linearization rules of core syntax. The reason is *compositionality*: every linearization rule is a mapping * such that

$$(f\, t_1 \ldots t_n)^* = h\, t_1^* \ldots t_n^*$$

where the function h operates on the *linearizations* of the immediate subtrees t_i. Thus it cannot analyse the subtrees t_i, as the conversions of Section 5.3 have to do. When two languages are related by an abstract syntax and compositional linearizations, they are in a part-to-part correspondance; this is no longer true for core syntax formulas and their optimal natural language expressions.

Even though the conversions cannot be defined as linearizations, they could in principle be written in GF as *semantic actions* ([13], Chapter 6). But this would require advanced GF hackery and therefore be *difficult*; GF is a special-purpose language designed for multilingual grammars, and lacks the program constructs and libraries needed for non-compositional translations, such as list processing, state management, and so on. The conversions in [14] are therefore written in Haskell. This is an illustration of the technique of *embedded grammars*, where a GF grammars can be combined with host language programs ([13], Chapter 7). Thus the overall system written in Haskell provides linearization and parsing via the GF grammar, and abstract syntax trees can be manipulated as Haskell data objects. In particular, the technique of *almost compositional functions* [23] is available, which makes it *easy* for Haskell programmers to implement conversions such as the ones in Section 5.3. The same technique is available for Java as well, and provides the *easy* way for Java programmers to use GF for building natural language interfaces to Java programs.

5.1   Extended Abstract Syntax

The core logical language addressed in Section 4 has a minimal set of categories and one function for each logical constant. The extended language has a more fine-grained structure. The following table gives the extensions in symbolic logic and English examples:

construction	symbolic	verbal (example)
atom negation	$\overline{A}$	*x is not even*
conjunction of proposition list	$\&[P_1, \ldots, P_n]$	*P, Q and R*
conjunction of predicate list	$\&[F_1, \ldots, F_n]$	*even and odd*
conjunction of term list	$\&[a_1, \ldots, a_n]$	*x and y*
bounded quantification	$(\forall x_1, \ldots, x_n : K)P$	*for all numbers x and y, P*
in-situ quantification	$F(\forall K)$	*every number is even*
one-place predication	$F^1(x)$	*x is even*
two-place predication	$F^2(x, y)$	*x is equal to y*
reflexive predication	$\mathrm{Refl}(F^2)(x)$	*x is equal to itself*
modified predicate	$\mathrm{Mod}(K, F)(x)$	*x is an even number*

All constructs with $\&$ also have a variant for $\vee$, and so have the constructs with $\forall$ for $\exists$.

The new forms of expression involve some new categories. Obviously, we need categories of *lists* of propositions, predicates, variables, and individual terms. But we also introduce separate categories of one- and two-place predicates, and it is useful to have a separate category of atomic propositions.

It is moreover useful to distinguish a category of *kind predicates*, typically used for restricting the domain of quantification (the variable K in the table above). For instance, *natural number* is a kind predicate, as opposed to *odd*, which is an "ordinary" predicate. But we will also allow the use of K in a predication position, to say *x is a natural number*. Modified predicates combine a kind predicate with another predicate into a new kind predicate. Very typically, kind predicates are expressed with nouns and other one-place predicates with adjectives (cf. [9]); but this need not be assumed for all predicates and all languages.

The new syntax is a proper extension of the core syntax of Section 4. It is, in particular, not necessary to force all concepts into the categories of one- or two-place predicates: they can still be expressed by "raw" propositional functions. But reclassifying the arithmetic lexicon with the new categories will give opportunities for better language generation via the extended syntax. Thus *Even* and *Odd* can be classified as one-place predicates, *Equal* as a two-place predicate, and *Nat* as a kind predicate. We can then obtain the sentence

every natural number is even or odd

as a compositional translation of the formula

$$\vee[Even, Odd](\forall Nat)$$

It remains to see how this formula is converted to a core syntax formula (easy), and how it can be obtained as an optimization of the core formula (more tricky).

5.2   From Extended Syntax to Core Syntax

Mapping the extended syntax into the core syntax can be seen as *denotational semantics*, where the core syntax works as a *model* of the extended syntax. The semantics follows the ideas of Montague [24], which focused particularly on in-situ quantification. The question of quantification has indeed been central in linguistic semantics (see e.g. [25]); what we use here is a small, *easy* part of the potential, carefully avoiding usages that lead to ambiguities and other *difficult* problems.

The crucial rule is in-situ quantification. It requires that trees of type Ind are interpreted, not as individuals but as quantifiers, that is, as functions from propositional functions to propositions. Thus the type of the interpretation is

$$(\forall K)^* : (Ind \rightarrow Prop) \rightarrow Prop$$

The interpretation is defined by specifying how this function applies to a propositional function F (which need not be an atomic predicate):

$$(\forall K)^* F = (\forall x : K^*)(F x)$$

The rule introduces a bound variable x, which must be fresh in the context in which the rule is applied. Notice that we define the result as a proposition still in the extended syntax. It can be processed further by moving the kind K to the body, using the rule

$$((\forall x_1, \ldots, x_n : K)P)^* = (\forall x_1) \cdots (\forall x_n)((K^* x_1) \& \ldots \& (K^* x_n) \supset P^*)$$

But the intermediate stage is useful if the target logic formalism supports domain-restricted quantifiers. In general, various constructs of the extended syntax are available in extensions of predicate logic, such as TFF and THF [26].

Conjunctions of individuals are likewise interpreted as functions on propositional functions,

$$\&[a_1, \ldots, a_n]^* F = \&[a_1^* F, \ldots, a_n^* F]$$

The interpretation of predication is "reversed": now it is the argument that is applied to the predicate, rather then the other way round (interestingly, this shift of point of view was already known to Frege [27], §10: "one can conceive $\Phi(A)$ as a function of the argument Φ"!). Two-place predication requires lambda abstraction.

$$(F(a))^* \;=\; a^* F^*$$
$$(F(a,b))^* \;=\; a^*((\lambda x)b^*((\lambda y)(F^* x\, y)))$$

Atomic predicates, including simple kind predicates, can be interpreted as themselves, whereas the conjunction of predicates is a propositional function forming a conjunction of propositions:

$$\&[F_1,\ldots,F_n]^*\, x \;=\; \&[(F_1^* x),\ldots,(F_n^* x)]$$

Reflexive predicates expand to repeated application, whereas modified kind predicates are interpreted as conjunctions:

$$(Refl(F))^* x \;=\; F^* x\, x$$
$$(Mod(K,F))^*\, x \;=\; (K^* x)\&(F^* x)$$

The elimination of list conjunctions is simple folding with the binary conjunction:

$$\&[P_1,\ldots,P_n]^* \;=\; P_1^*\&\ldots\&P_n^*$$

Now we can satisfy one direction of the desired conversion: we can parse *every natural number is even or odd* and obtain the formula

$$\vee[Even, Odd](\forall\, Nat)$$

whose interpretation in the core syntax is

$$(\forall x)(Nat(x) \supset Even(x) \vee Odd(x))$$

whose compositional translation is *for all x, if x is a natural number then x is even or x is odd*.

5.3   From Core Syntax to Extended Syntax

Finding extended syntax equivalents for core syntax trees is trickier than the opposite direction. It is a problem of *optimization*: find the "best" possible tree to express the same proposition as the original. Now, the "sameness" of propositions is defined by the interpretation shown in Section 5.2. But what does the "best" mean? Let us consider some conversions that clearly improve the proposition.

1. **Flattening.** Nested binary conjunctions can be flattened to lists, to the effect that *P and Q and R* becomes *P, Q and R*. This has many good effects: a syntactic ambiguity is eliminated; bullet lists become arbitrarily long and thus more natural; and opportunities are created for the next operation, aggregation.

2. **Aggregation.** This is a standard technique from NLG [28]. For the task at hand, its main usage is to share common parts of predications, for instance, to convert *x is even or x is odd* to *x is even or odd*. Thus the subject-sharing aggregation rule has the effect

$$\&[F_1(a),\ldots,F_n(a)] \;\Longrightarrow\; \&[F_1,\ldots,F_n](a)$$

The predicate-sharing aggregation rule is, dually,

$$\&[F(a_1), \ldots, F(a_n)] \implies F(\&[a_1, \ldots, a_n])$$

Aggregation can be further strengthened by sorting the conjuncts by the predicate or the argument, and then grouping maximally long segments. Notice that aggregation reduces ambiguity: *x is even or x is odd and y is odd* is ambiguous, but the two readings are captured by *x is even or odd and y is odd* and *x is even or x and y are odd*.

3. **In-situ quantification.** The schematic rule is to find an occurrence of the bound variable in the body of the sentence and replace it with a quantifier phrase:

$$(\forall x : K)P \implies P((\forall K)/x)$$

If the starting point is a formula with domainless quantification, the pattern must first be found by the rules

$(\forall x)(K(x) \supset P) \implies (\forall x : K)P$
$(\exists x)(K(x)\&P) \implies (\exists x : K)P$

The in-situ rule is restricted to cases where P is atomic and has exactly one occurrence of the variable. Thus aggregation can create an opportunity for in-situ quantification:

for all natural numbers x, x is even or x is odd
$\implies$ *for all natural numbers x, x is even or odd*
$\implies$ *every natural number is even or odd*

This chain of steps shows why in-situ quantification is restricted to propositions with a single occurrence of the variable: perfoming it *before* aggregation would form the sentence *every number is even or every number is odd*, which has a different meaning.

4. **Verb negation**

$$\sim A \implies \overline{A}$$

This has the effect of transforming *it is not the case that x is even* to *x is not even*. Verb negation is problematic if in-situ quantifiers are present, since for instance *every natural number is not even* has two parses, where either the quantifier or the negation has wider scope. If in-situ quantification is restricted to atomic formulas, the only interpretation is $\sim (\forall x : Nat)Even(x)$. But relying on this is better avoided altogether, to remain on the safe side—and thus create verb negation only for formulas without in-situ quantifiers.

5. **Reflexivization**

$$F(x, x) \implies Refl(F)(x)$$

which has the effect of converting *x is equal to x* to *x is equal to itself*. This can again create an opportunity for in-situ quantification: *every natural number is equal to itself*.

6. **Modification**, combining a kind and a modifying predicate into a complex kind predicate

$$K(x)\&F(x) \implies Mod(K, F)(x)$$

which has the effect of converting *x is a number and x is even* to *x is an even number*. As the number of occurrences of x is reduced, there is a new opportunity for in-situ quantification: *some even number is prime*.

5.4 Verbal vs. Symbolic

In Section 2, we suggested that symbolic expressions are preferred in mathematical text, whenever available. This creates a tension with the conversions of Section 5.3, which try to minimize the use of symbols. But there is no contradiction here: the conversions minimize the use of symbols for expressing the *logical structure*, whereas Section 2 suggests it should be maximized in *atomic formulas*. The symbols needed for logical structure are the bound variables, which are replaced by in-situ quantification whenever possible without introducing ambiguity.

Hence, the strategy is to perform the conversions of 5.3 first, and then express symbolically whatever is possible. Here are two examples of the two-step procedure, leading to different outcomes:

> *for all x, if x is a number and x is odd, then x^2 is odd*
> $\implies$ *(every odd number)^2 is odd* (**incorrect!**)
> $\implies$ *the square of every odd number is odd*

> *for all x, if x is a number and x is odd, then the sum of x and the square of x is even*
> $\implies$ *for all odd numbers x, the sum of x and the square of x is even*
> $\implies$ *for all odd numbers x, $x + x^2$ is even*

The latter could be improved by using pronouns to eliminate the variable: *the sum of every odd number and its square is even*. However, the analysis and synthesis of (non-reflexive) pronouns belongs to the problems we still consider *difficult*.

The choice between verbal and symbolic expressions is easy to implement, since it can be performed by linearization. All that is needed is a Boolean parameter saying whether an expression is symbolic. If all arguments of a function are symbolic, the application of the function to them can be rendered symbolically; if not, the verbal expression is chosen. For example, using strings rather than RGL to make the idea explicit, the square function becomes

```
lin Square x = {
  s = case x.isSymbolic of {
        True  => x.s ++ "^2" ;
        False => "the square of" ++ x.s
        } ;
  isSymbolic = x.isSymbolic
  }
```

Thus the feature of being symbolic is inherited from the argument. Variables and integers are symbolic, whereas in-situ quantifiers are not.

6 The Limits of Known Techniques

6.1 The Dynamicity of Language

The Holy Grail of theorem proving in natural language is a system able to formalize any mathematical text automatically. In one sense, this goal has already been reached. The

Boxer system [29] is able to parse *any* English sentence and translate it into a formula of predicate calculus. Combined with theorem proving and model checking, Boxer can moreover solve problems in open-domain textual entailment by formal reasoning [30].

The problem that remains with Boxer is that the quality of formalization and reasoning is far from perfect. It is useful for information retrieval that goes beyond string matching, but not for the precision task of checking mathematical proofs. While the retrieval aspect of reasoning is an important topic, no-one seriously claims that the technique would reach the precision needed for mathematics. What we have here is the classical trade-off in natural language processing: we cannot maximize both *coverage* and *precision* at the same time, but have to choose.

Our target in this paper has obviously been to maintain precision while extending the coverage step by step. What is more, our perspective has mainly been that of *generation*: we have started from an abstract syntax of predicate calculus and seen how it is reflected in natural language. The opposite perspective of *analysis* is only implicit, via the reversibility of GF grammars. If our grammar does manage to parse a sentence from a real text, it happens more as a lucky coincidence than by design. (This is not so bad as it might sound, since parsing in GF is *predictive*, which means that the user input is guided by word suggestions and completions; see [31].)

The task of formalizing real mathematical texts is thoroughly analysed by Ganesalingam [32]. With samples of real texts as starting point, he shows that mathematical language is not only complex but also *ambiguous* and *dynamically changing*. Even things like operator precedence can be ambiguous. For instance, addition binds stronger than equality in formulas like $2 + 2 = 4$. But [32] cites the expression

$$\lambda + K = S$$

which in [33] stands for the theory λ enriched with the axiom $K = S$, and should hence be parsed $\lambda + (K = S)$. The solution to this ambiguity is to look at the *types* of the expression. The $+$ and $=$ operators are *overloaded*: they work for different types, including numbers and theories. Not only does their semantics depend on the type, which is common in programming languages, but also their syntactic properties.

Because of the intertwining of parsing and type checking, the usual pipe-lined techniques are insufficient for automatically formalizing arbitrary mathematical texts. This is nothing new for natural language: overload resolution is, basically, just an instance of *word sense disambiguation*, which is needed in tasks like information retrieval and machine translation. One thing shown in [32] is that, despite its believed exactness, the informal language of mathematics inherits many of the general problems of natural language processing.

As suggested in Section 4.4, parsing intertwined with type checking can be theoretically understood via the use of *dependent types* (cf. also [34,35]). It is also supported by GF. But it is not yet a piece of technology that can be called *easy*; building a natural language interface that uses GF's dependent types is still a research project. [36] and [37] are pioneering examples. They also use dependent types to deal with pronouns and definite descriptions, as suggested in [34].

6.2   The Structure of Proof Texts

Given that the analysis of arbitrary mathematical text is beyond the reach of current technology, how is it with generation? The task of *text generation from formal proofs* has a great potential, for instance, in industry, where theorem provers are used for verifying large systems. The users are not always happy with just the answer "yes" or "no", but want to understand why. [38] was a pioneering work in generating text from Coq proofs. Even though it worked reasonably for small proofs, the text generated from larger proofs turned out to be practically unreadable.

The problems in proof generation are analogous to the problems in sentence generation: the structure has to be changed by techniques such as aggregation (Section 5.3). Some such techniques, inspired by code generation in compilers, were developed in [39]. But there is also another aspect: the hiding of uninteresting steps. Natural proofs typically take much longer steps than formalized proofs. Thus we also have the question which steps to show. [40] suggests a promising approach, trying to identify the decisive branching points in proofs as the ones worth showing. This idea resembles the methods of *dataflow analysis* in compiler construction [41], in particular the technique of *basic blocks*. But, in analogy to the "full employment theorem for compiler writers", which Appel [41] attributes to Rice [42], it seems that text generation involves undecidable optimization problems that have no ultimate automatic solution.

Even though the techniques shown in this paper don't scale up to proof texts, they do easily extend beyond individual propositions. [43] shows that texts consisting of definition and theorem block can be made natural and readable. [36] likewise succeeds with software specifications where the texts describe invariants and pre- and postconditions.

7   Projects

GF was first released in 1998, in a project entitled "Multilingual Document Authoring" at Xerox Research Centre Europe in Grenoble [44]. The project built on earlier work on natural language proof editors in [45,46]. The earlier work had focused on the multilingual rendering of formal mathematics, based on constructive type theory [47] and the ALF system [48]. The Xerox project shifted the focus from mathematics to more "layman" applications such as user manuals, tourist phrasebooks, and spoken dialogue systems (see [13] for a survey). But the translation between logic and language has been a recurring theme in GF projects. Here are some of them:

- **Alfa**, a type-theoretical proof editor was equipped with a GF grammar and a system of annotations for defining a multilingual mathematical lexicon [43]. The system was aimed to be portable to different applications, due to the generality of Alfa itself. As an early design choice, dependent types were not employed in GF, but type checking was left to Alfa. The lack of resource grammars made it difficult to define the translations of new concepts.
- **KeY**, a software verification system [49] was equipped with a translation of specifications between OCL (Object Constraint Language, [50]), English, and German [36]. Dependent types were used to guide the author to write meaningful specifications. This was the first large-scale application of the resource grammar library.

- **FraCaS** [51], a test suite of textual entailment in English, was parsed with an extension of RGL, translated to the TPTP format, and fed to automated reasoning tools [52].
- **WebALT** (Web Advanced Learning Technology), a European project aiming to build a repository of multilingual math exercises [19] using formalizations from the OpenMath project [20]. The work is continued in the MOLTO project [21], and the lexicon is used in the web demo of this article [14]
- **Attempto** (Attempto Controlled English), a natural language fragment used for knowledge representation and reasoning [53]. The fragment was implemented in GF and ported to five other languages using the RGL [54].
- **OWL** (Web Ontology Language, [55]), interfaced with English and Latvian via Attempto [53], but without a previously existing Latvian RGL [56].
- **SUMO** (Suggested Upper Merged Ontology, [57]). This large knowledge base and lexicon was reverse-engineered in GF, with improved natural language generation for three languages using RGL [37]. The abstract syntax uses dependent types to express the semantics of SUMO.
- **MathNat**. An educational proof system implemented in GF and linked to theorem proving in the TPTP format [58].
- **Nomic**. A computer game where new rules can be defined by the players in English [59]. Aimed as a pilot study for a controlled natural language for contracts.
- **MOLTO KRI** (Knowledge Representation Infrastructure). A query language with a back end in ontology-based reasoning [60].

8 Conclusion

Accumulated experience, the growth of the resource grammar libraries, and the improvement of tools make it *easy* to build translators between formal and informal languages in GF. The translators can produce reasonably understandable language and are portable to all languages available in the grammar library (currently 18). The effort can be brought down to the level of a few days' engineering or an undergraduate project; still some years ago, it was a research project requiring at least a PhD student.

The scope for improvements is endless. Parsing natural language is still restricted to very small fragments. Increasing the coverage is not just the matter of writing bigger grammars, but new ideas are needed for disambiguation. Generating natural language, especially from complex formal proofs, still tends to produce texts that are unreadable in spite of being grammatically correct. New ideas are needed even here.

Acknowledgements. I am grateful to Wolfgang Ahrendt, Olga Caprotti, Ramona Enache, Reiner Hähnle, Thomas Hallgren, and Jordi Saludes for suggestions and comments. The research leading to these results has received funding from the European Union's Seventh Framework Programme (FP7/2007-2013) under grant agreement n:o FP7-ICT-247914.

References

1. Wolfram Research, I.: Mathematica Homepage (2000), http://www.wolfram.com/products/mathematica/
2. Bobrow, D.G.: Natural Language Input for a Computer Problem Solving System. PhD thesis, Massachusetts Institute of Technology (1964)
3. de Bruijn, N.G.: Mathematical Vernacular: a Language for Mathematics with Typed Sets. In: Nederpelt, R. (ed.) Selected Papers on Automath, pp. 865–935. North-Holland Publishing Company, Amsterdam (1994)
4. Trybulec, A.: The Mizar Homepage (2006), http://mizar.org/
5. Benzmüller, C., Cheikhrouhou, L., Fehrer, D., Fiedler, A., Huang, K.M., Kohlhase, M., Konrad, K., Melis, E., Meier, A., Schaarschmidt, W., Siekmann, J., Sorge, V.: Omega: Towards a mathematical assistant. In: McCune, W. (ed.) CADE 1997. LNCS, vol. 1249, Springer, Heidelberg (1997)
6. Wenzel, M.: Isar - a generic interpretative approach to readable formal proof documents. In: Bertot, Y., Dowek, G., Hirschowitz, A., Paulin, C., Théry, L. (eds.) TPHOLs 1999. LNCS, vol. 1690, pp. 167–184. Springer, Heidelberg (1999)
7. Zinn, C.: Understanding Informal Mathematical Discourse. PhD thesis, Department of Computer Science, University of Erlangen-Nürnberg (2010)
8. Buchberger, B., Craciun, A., Jebelean, T., Kovács, L., Kutsia, T., Nakagawa, K., Piroi, F., Popov, N., Robu, J., Rosenkranz, M.: Theorema: Towards computer-aided mathematical theory exploration. J. Applied Logic 4(4), 470–504 (2006)
9. Kamareddine, F., Wells, J.B.: Computerizing Mathematical Text with MathLang. Electr. Notes Theor. Comput. Sci. 205, 5–30 (2008)
10. Cramer, M., Fisseni, B., Koepke, P., Kühlwein, D., Schröder, B., Veldman, J.: The Naproche Project Controlled Natural Language Proof Checking of Mathematical Texts. In: Fuchs, N.E. (ed.) CNL 2009. LNCS, vol. 5972, pp. 170–186. Springer, Heidelberg (2010)
11. Neumaier, A.: FMathL - Formal Mathematical Language (2009), http://www.mat.univie.ac.at/~neum/FMathL.html
12. Ranta, A.: Grammatical Framework: A Type-Theoretical Grammar Formalism. The Journal of Functional Programming 14(2), 145–189 (2004), http://www.cse.chalmers.se/~aarne/articles/gf-jfp.pdf
13. Ranta, A.: Grammatical Framework: Programming with Multilingual Grammars. CSLI Publications, Stanford (2011) ISBN-10: 1-57586-626-9 (Paper), 1-57586-627-7 (Cloth)
14. Ranta, A.: Grammatical Framework: A Hands-On Introduction. CADE-23 Tutorial, Wroclaw (2011), http://www.grammaticalframework.org/gf-cade-2011/
15. Peyton Jones, S.: Haskell 98 language and libraries: the Revised Report (2003), http://www.haskell.org/haskellwiki/Language_and_library_specification
16. Seki, H., Matsumura, T., Fujii, M., Kasami, T.: On multiple context-free grammars. Theoretical Computer Science 88, 191–229 (1991)
17. Ranta, A.: Grammars as Software Libraries. In: Bertot, Y., Huet, G., Lévy, J.J., Plotkin, G. (eds.) From Semantics to Computer Science. Essays in Honour of Gilles Kahn, pp. 281–308. Cambridge University Press, Cambridge (2009), http://www.cse.chalmers.se/~aarne/articles/libraries-kahn.pdf
18. Ranta, A.: The GF Resource Grammar Library. Linguistics in Language Technology 2 (2009), http://elanguage.net/journals/index.php/lilt/article/viewFile/214/158
19. Caprotti, O.: WebALT! Deliver Mathematics Everywhere. In: Proceedings of SITE 2006, Orlando, March 20-24 (2006), http://webalt.math.helsinki.fi/content/e16/e301/e512/PosterDemoWebALT_eng.pdf

20. Abbott, J., Díaz, A., Sutor, R.S.: A report on OpenMath: a protocol for the exchange of mathematical information. SIGSAM Bull 30, 21–24 (1996)
21. Saludes, J., Xambó, S.: MOLTO Mathematical Grammar Library (2010), http://www.molto-project.eu/node/1246
22. Burke, D.A., Johannisson, K.: Translating Formal Software Specifications to Natural Language / A Grammer-Based Approach. In: Blache, P., Stabler, E.P., Busquets, J.V., Moot, R. (eds.) LACL 2005. LNCS (LNAI), vol. 3492, pp. 51–66. Springer, Heidelberg (2005), http://www.springerlink.com/content/?k=LNCS+3492
23. Bringert, B., Ranta, A.: A Pattern for Almost Compositional Functions. The Journal of Functional Programming 18(5-6), 567–598 (2008)
24. Montague, R.: Formal Philosophy. Yale University Press, New Haven (1974); Collected papers edited by Richmond Thomason
25. Barwise, J., Cooper, R.: Generalized quantifiers and natural language. Linguistics and Philosophy 4(2), 159–219 (1981)
26. Sutcliffe, G., Benzmüller, C.: Automated Reasoning in Higher-Order Logic using the TPTP THF Infrastructure. Journal of Formalized Reasoning 3 (2010)
27. Frege, G.: Begriffsschrift. Louis Nebert, Halle A/S (1879)
28. Reiter, E., Dale, R.: Building Natural Language Generation Systems. Cambridge University Press, Cambridge (2000)
29. Bos, J., Clark, S., Steedman, M., Curran, J.R., Hockenmaier, J.: Wide-Coverage Semantic Representations from a CCG Parser. In: Proceedings of the 20th International Conference on Computational Linguistics (COLING 2004), Geneva, Switzerland, pp. 1240–1246 (2004)
30. Bos, J., Markert, K.: Recognising Textual Entailment with Robust Logical Inference. In: Quiñonero-Candela, J., Dagan, I., Magnini, B., d'Alché-Buc, F. (eds.) MLCW 2005. LNCS (LNAI), vol. 3944, pp. 404–426. Springer, Heidelberg (2006)
31. Angelov, K.: Incremental Parsing with Parallel Multiple Context-Free Grammars. In: Proceedings of EACL 2009, Athens (2009)
32. Ganesalingam, M.: The Language of Mathematics. PhD thesis, Department of Computer Science, University of Cambridge (2010), http://people.pwf.cam.ac.uk/mg262/
33. Barendregt, H.: The Lambda Calculus. Its Syntax and Semantics. North-Holland, Amsterdam (1981)
34. Ranta, A.: Type Theoretical Grammar. Oxford University Press, Oxford (1994)
35. Ljunglöf, P.: The Expressivity and Complexity of Grammatical Framework. PhD thesis, Dept. of Computing Science, Chalmers University of Technology and Gothenburg University (2004), http://www.cs.chalmers.se/~peb/pubs/p04-PhD-thesis.pdf
36. Johannisson, K.: Formal and Informal Software Specifications. PhD thesis, Dept. of Computing Science, Chalmers University of Technology and Gothenburg University (2005)
37. Angelov, K., Enache, R.: Typeful Ontologies with Direct Multilingual Verbalization. In: Fuchs, N., Rosner, M. (eds.) CNL 2010, Controlled Natural Language (2010)
38. Coscoy, Y., Kahn, G., Thery, L.: Extracting text from proofs. In: Dezani-Ciancaglini, M., Plotkin, G. (eds.) TLCA 1995. LNCS, vol. 902, pp. 109–123. Springer, Heidelberg (1995)
39. Coscoy, Y.: Explication textuelle de preuves pour le calcul des constructions inductives. PhD thesis, Université de Nice-Sophia-Antipolis (2000)
40. Wiedijk, F.: Formal Proof Sketches. In: Berardi, S., Coppo, M., Damiani, F. (eds.) TYPES 2003. LNCS, vol. 3085, pp. 378–393. Springer, Heidelberg (2004)
41. Appel, A.: Modern Compiler Implementation in ML. Cambridge University Press, Cambridge (1998)

42. Rice, H.G.: Classes of recursively enumerable sets and their decision problems. Transactions of the American Mathematical Society 74(2), 358–366 (1953)
43. Hallgren, T., Ranta, A.: An Extensible Proof Text Editor. In: Parigot, M., Voronkov, A. (eds.) LPAR 2000. LNCS (LNAI), vol. 1955, pp. 70–84. Springer, Heidelberg (2000), http://www.cse.chalmers.se/~aarne/articles/lpar2000.pdf
44. Dymetman, M., Lux, V., Ranta, A.: XML and multilingual document authoring: Convergent trends. In: Proc. Computational Linguistics COLING, Saarbrücken, Germany, pp. 243–249. International Committee on Computational Linguistics (2000)
45. Ranta, A.: Context-relative syntactic categories and the formalization of mathematical text. In: Berardi, S., Coppo, M. (eds.) TYPES 1995. LNCS, vol. 1158, pp. 231–248. Springer, Heidelberg (1996)
46. Ranta, A.: Structures grammaticales dans le français mathématique. Mathématiques, informatique et Sciences Humaines 138/139, 5-56–5-36 (1997)
47. Martin-Löf, P.: Intuitionistic Type Theory. Bibliopolis, Napoli (1984)
48. Magnusson, L., Nordström, B.: The ALF proof editor and its proof engine. In: Types for Proofs and Programs, pp. 213–237. Springer, Heidelberg (1994)
49. Beckert, B., Hähnle, R., Schmitt, P.H. (eds.): Verification of Object-Oriented Software. LNCS, vol. 4334. Springer, Heidelberg (2007)
50. Warmer, J., Kleppe, A.: The Object Constraint Language: Precise Modelling with UML. Addison-Wesley, London (1999)
51. Kamp, H., Crouch, R., van Genabith, J., Cooper, R., Poesio, M., van Eijck, J., Jaspars, J., Pinkal, M., Vestre, E., Pulman, S.: Specification of linguistic coverage. FRACAS Deliverable D2 (1994)
52. Bringert, B.: Semantics of the GF Resource Grammar Library. Report, Chalmers University (2008), http://www.cse.chalmers.se/alumni/bringert/darcs/mosg/
53. Fuchs, N.E., Kaljurand, K., Kuhn, T.: Attempto Controlled English for Knowledge Representation. In: Baroglio, C., Bonatti, P.A., Małuszyński, J., Marchiori, M., Polleres, A., Schaffert, S. (eds.) Reasoning Web. LNCS, vol. 5224, pp. 104–124. Springer, Heidelberg (2008)
54. Angelov, K., Ranta, A.: Implementing Controlled Languages in GF. In: Fuchs, N.E. (ed.) CNL 2009. LNCS, vol. 5972, pp. 82–101. Springer, Heidelberg (2010)
55. Dean, M., Schreiber, G.: OWL Web Ontology Language Reference (2004), http://www.w3.org/TR/owl-ref/
56. Gruzitis, N., Barzdins, G.: Towards a More Natural Multilingual Controlled Language Interface to OWL. In: 9th International Conference on Computational Semantics (IWCS), pp. 335–339 (2011), http://www.aclweb.org/anthology/W/W11/W11-0138.pdf
57. Niles, I., Pease, A.: Towards a standard upper ontology. In: Proceedings of the International Conference on Formal Ontology in Information Systems (FOIS 2001), vol. 2001, pp. 2–9. ACM, New York (2001)
58. Humayoun, M., Raffalli, C.: MathNat - Mathematical Text in a Controlled Natural Language. Journal on Research in Computing Science 66 (2010)
59. Camilleri, J.J., Pace, G.J., Rosner.: In: Playing Nomic Using a Controlled Natural Language (2010), http://sunsite.informatik.rwth-aachen.de/Publications/CEUR-WS/Vol-622/paper7.pdf
60. Mitankin, P., Ilchev, A.: Knowledge Representation Infrastructure, MOLTO Deliverable D4.1(2010)http://www.molto-project.eu/sites/default/files/D4.1_0.pdf

ASASP: Automated Symbolic Analysis of Security Policies

Francesco Alberti[1], Alessandro Armando[2,3], and Silvio Ranise[3]

[1] Università della Svizzera Italiana, Lugano (Svizzera)
[2] Università degli Studi di Genova (Italia)
[3] FBK-Irst, Trento (Italia)

Abstract. We describe ASASP, a symbolic reachability procedure for the analysis of administrative access control policies. The tool represents access policies and their administrative actions as formulae of the Bernays-Shönfinkel-Ramsey class and then uses a symbolic reachability procedure to solve security analysis problems. Checks for fix-point—reduced to satisfiability problems—are mechanized by Satisfiability Modulo Theories solving and Automated Theorem Proving. ASASP has been successfully applied to the analysis of benchmark problems arising in (extensions of) the Role-Based Access Control model. Our tool shows better scalability than a state-of-the-art tool on a significant set of instances of these problems.

1 Introduction

Access control is one of the key ingredients to ensure the security of software systems where several users may perform actions on shared resources. To guarantee flexibility and scalability, access control is managed by several security officers that may delegate permissions to other users that, in turn, may delegate others. Indeed, such chains of delegation may give rise to unexpected situations where, e.g., untrusted users may get access to a sensitive resource. Thus, security analysis is critical for the design and maintenance of access control policies.

In this paper, we describe the *Automated Symbolic Analysis of Security Policies* (ASASP) tool, based on the model checking modulo theories approach of [2]. Security analysis is reduced to repeatedly checking the satisfiability of formulae in the Bernays-Schönfinkel-Ramsey class [6] by hierarchical combination of Satisfiability Modulo Theories (SMT) solving and Automated Theorem Proving (ATP). The use of an SMT solver allows us for quick and incremental—but incomplete—satisfiability checks while (refutation) complete and computationally more expensive checks are performed by the theorem prover only when needed. A *divide and conquer* heuristics for splitting complex access control queries into simpler ones is key to the scalability of ASASP on a set of benchmark problems arising in the security analysis of (extensions of) Administrative Role-Based Access Control (ARBAC) policies [1].

Theoretically, the techniques underlying ASASP are developed in the context of the model checking modulo theories approach [2]. In practice, it is difficult—or even impossible—to use the available implementation [3], called MCMT, for

N. Bjørner and V. Sofronie-Stokkermans (Eds.): CADE 2011, LNAI 6803, pp. 26–33, 2011.
© Springer-Verlag Berlin Heidelberg 2011

the security analysis of access control policies. There are two reasons for this. First, the satisfiability problems for fix-point tests of access control policies seem easier to solve as they fall in the Bernays-Shönfinkel-Ramsey (BSR) class for which specialized tools exist. In MCMT instead, *ad hoc* instantiation techniques have been designed and implemented [3] to integrate the handling of universal quantifiers with quantifier-free reasoning in rich background theories. These are needed to model the data structures manipulated by systems [2]. Second, MCMT permits only mono-dimensional arrays [3] while access control policies routinely uses binary relations for which at least bi-dimensional arrays are needed to represent their characteristic functions. An encoding of multidimensional arrays by mono-dimensional arrays indexed by tuples is possible, although it makes it useless some heuristics of MCMT with an unacceptable degradations of its performances. Another limitation of MCMT concerns the number of existentially quantified variables in formulae representing transitions which is bounded to at most two (although this is sufficient to specify several different classes of systems as shown in [2]) while administrative actions usually require many more of such variables. An extensive discussion of the related work about the techniques underlying ASASP can be found in [1].

2   Background on Administrative Access Control

Although ASASP can be used for the automated analysis of a more general class of administrative access control policies [1], here—for lack of space—we consider only a sub-class.

Role-Based Access Control (RBAC) regulates access through roles. Roles in a set R associate permissions in a set P to users in a set U by using the following two relations: $UA \subseteq U \times R$ and $PA \subseteq R \times P$. Roles are structured hierarchically so as to permit permission inheritance. Formally, a role hierarchy is a partial order $\succeq$ on R, where $r_1 \succeq r_2$ means that r_1 is *more senior than* r_2 for $r_1, r_2 \in R$. A user u is an *explicit* member of role r when $(u, r) \in UA$ while u is an *implicit* member of r if there exists $r' \in R$ such that $r' \succeq r$ and $(u, r') \in UA$. Given UA and PA, a user u *has permission* p if there exists a role $r \in R$ such that $(p, r) \in PA$ and u is a member of r, either explicit or implicit. A *RBAC policy* is a tuple $(U, R, P, UA, PA, \succeq)$.

Administrative RBAC (ARBAC). Usually (see, e.g., [10]), administrators may only update the relation UA while PA is assumed constant; so, a RBAC policy $(U, R, P, UA, PA, \succeq)$ will be abbreviated by UA. To be able to specify administrative actions, we need to preliminarily specify the pre-conditions of such actions. A *pre-condition* is a finite set of expressions of the forms r or $\bar{r}$ (for $r \in R$), called *role literals*. In a RBAC policy UA, a user $u \in U$ *satisfies* a pre-condition C if, for each $\ell \in C$, u is a member of r when ℓ is r or u

is not a member of r when ℓ is $\bar{r}$ for $r \in R$. Permission to assign users to roles is specified by a ternary relation can_assign containing tuples of the form (C_a, C, r). Permission to revoke users from roles is specified by a binary relation can_revoke containing tuples of the form (C_a, r). We say that C_a is the *administrative pre-condition*, a user u_a satisfying C_a is the *administrator*, and C is a *(simple) pre-condition*. The relation can_revoke is only binary because it has been observed that simple pre-conditions are useless when revoking roles (see, e.g., [10] for a discussion on this point). The semantics of the administrative actions in $\psi :=$ (can_assign, can_revoke) is given by a transition system whose states are the RBAC policies and a state change is specified by a binary relation $\rightarrow_\psi$ on pair of RBAC policies as follows: $UA \rightarrow_\psi UA'$ iff either (i) there exists $(C_a, C, r) \in can\_assign$, u_a satisfying C_a, u satisfying C, and $UA' = UA \cup \{(u, r)\}$ or (ii) there exists $(C_a, r) \in can\_revoke$, u_a satisfying C_a, and $UA' = UA \setminus \{(u, r)\}$.

A simple example. We consider the access control system of a small company as depicted in Figure 1, where a simple line between a user u—on the left—and a role r—in the middle—(resp. permission p—on the right) indicates that $(u, r) \in UA$ (resp. $(p, r) \in PA$) and an arrow from a role r_1 to a role r_2 that $r_1 \succeq r_2$. For example, B is an implicit member of role Em because M is more senior than Em and A is an explicit member of role EM; thus, both A and B have permission E. Figure 1 also contains two administrative actions: the tuple in can_assign says that a member of role HR (the administrator) can add the role PT to a user who is a member of Em and is not member of FT while the pair in can_revoke says that a member of role M can revoke the role membership of a user of the role FT. For instance, it is easy to see that user A satisfies pre-condition $\{Em, \overline{FT}\}$ of the triple in can_assign and that user C can be the administrator, so that the application of the action is the RBAC policy $UA' := UA \cup \{(A, PT)\}$. In UA', user A may get permission R besides E.

RBAC policy

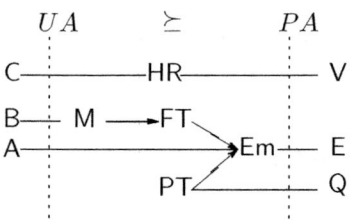

Administrative actions
($\{HR\}, \{Em, \overline{FT}\}, PT) \in can\_assign$
($\{M\}, FT) \in can\_revoke$

Fig. 1. An ARBAC policy

User-role reachability problem. A pair (u_g, R_g) is called an *(RBAC) goal* for $u_g \in U$ and R_g a finite set of roles. The cardinality $|R_g|$ of R_g is the *size* of the goal. Given a set S_0 of (initial) RBAC policies, a goal (u_g, R_g), and administrative actions $\psi = (can\_assign, can\_revoke)$, (an instance of) the *user-role reachability problem* [10] consists of establishing if there exist $UA_0 \in S_0$ and UA_f such that $UA_0 \rightarrow_\psi^* UA_f$ and u_g is member of each role of R_g in UA_f, where $\rightarrow_\psi^*$ denotes the reflexive and transitive closure of $\rightarrow_\psi$.

3   ASASP: Architecture, Implementation, and Experiments

By using standard techniques [1], we can symbolically represent sets of policies and related administrative actions as BSR formulae and—along the lines of [2]—a backward reachability procedure may solve the user-role reachability problem. The binary predicate ua and its primed version ua' denote an RBAC policy UA immediately before and after, respectively, of the execution of an administrative action.

An example of formalization. We briefly sketch how to represent the AR-BAC policy in Figure 1 with BSR formulae. Let $User, Role$, and $Perm$ be sort symbols, ua : $User, Role$, pa : $Role, Perm$, and $\succeq$: $Role, Role$ be predicate symbols (constants symbols will be written in sanserif, as those in Figure 1 and implicitly assumed to be of appropriate sort). The fact that we have only three permissions E, V, and Q can be axiomatized by the following sentences: $E \neq V$, $E \neq Q$, $V \neq Q$, and $\forall p.(p = E \vee p = V \vee p = Q)$, for p variable of sort $Perm$. The fact that there are only five roles can be formalized similarly while the role hierarchy of Figure 1 is formalized by adding $M \succeq FT$, $FT \succeq Em$, and $PT \succeq Em$ to the BSR sentences for reflexivity, antisymmetry, and transitivity of $\succeq$ (constraining it to be a partial order). The (initial) relation UA of Figure 1 can be specified as the following formula in the BSR class: $\forall u, r.(ua(u,r) \Leftrightarrow (u = C \wedge r = HR) \vee (u = B \wedge r = M) \vee (u = A \wedge r = Em))$; and the relation PA as $\forall p, r.(pa(r,p) \Leftrightarrow ((r = HR \wedge p = V) \vee (r = Em \wedge p = E) \vee (r = PT \wedge p = Q)))$, where u, p, r are variables of sorts $User, Perm, Role$, respectively. The goal $(A, \{PT\})$ can be represented by the following formula in the BSR class: $\exists u, r.(u = A \wedge r \succeq PT \wedge ua(u,r))$. The administrative action $(\{HR\}, \{Em, \overline{FT}\}, PT) \in can\_assign$ of Figure 1 can be represented as

$$\exists u_a, u, r_a, r_1. \begin{pmatrix} r_a \succeq HR \wedge ua(u_a, r_a) \wedge \\ r_1 \succeq Em \wedge ua(u, r_1) \wedge \neg \exists r_2.(r_2 \succeq FT \wedge ua(u, r_2)) \wedge \\ \forall x, y.(ua'(x,y) \Leftrightarrow ((x = u \wedge y = PT) \vee ua(x,y))) \end{pmatrix}. \quad (1)$$

The tuple in can_revoke can be represented similarly. Notice the presence of the (implicit) universal quantification in the sub-formula $\neg \exists r_2.(r_2 \succeq FT \wedge ua(u, r_2))$ of (1). This may be problematic to guarantee closure under pre-image computation in the backward reachability procedure (see the discussion below). Fortunately, since there are only five roles (as shown in Figure 1), the universal quantifier can be replaced by the logically equivalent quantifier-free formula $\neg ua(u, FT) \vee \neg ua(u, M)$, thereby avoiding problems for pre-image computation. ***The core algorithm*** of ASASP[1] consists of iteratively computing the symbolic representation $\mathcal{R}(ua)$ of the set of backward reachable states as follows: $\mathcal{R}_0(ua) := G(ua)$ and $\mathcal{R}_{i+1}(ua) := \mathcal{R}_i(ua) \vee Pre(\mathcal{R}_i, T)$ for $i \geq 0$, where G is the symbolic representation of a RBAC goal, $T(ua, ua')$ is the symbolic representation of ψ, and $Pre(\mathcal{R}_i, T) := \exists ua'.(\mathcal{R}_i(ua') \wedge T(ua, ua'))$ is the *pre-image*

---

[1] The sources of the tool, the benchmark problems discussed below, and some related papers are available at http://st.fbk.eu/ASASP.

of $\mathcal{R}_i$. To mechanize this, there are two issues to address. First, it should be possible to find a BSR formula which is logically equivalent to the second-order formula $Pre(\mathcal{R}_i, T)$, i.e. we have closure under pre-image computation. Second, there should exist decidable ways to stop computing formulae in the sequence $\mathcal{R}_0, \mathcal{R}_1, \mathcal{R}_2, \dots$ This is done by performing either a *safety check*, i.e. test the satisfiability of $\mathcal{R}_i(ua) \wedge I(ua)$ where $I(ua)$ characterizes the set S_0 of initial policies or a *fix-point check*, i.e. test the validity of $\mathcal{R}_{i+1}(ua) \Rightarrow \mathcal{R}_i(ua)$. Both logical problems should be decidable. In case the safety check is positive, ASASP concludes that the reachability problem has a solution, i.e. a sequence of administrative actions transforming one of the policies in I into one satisfying the goal G, and returns it. If the safety check is negative and the fix-point check is positive, ASASP returns that there is no solution. Following [2], restrictions on the shape of I, G, and T can be identified to guarantee the full automation of the procedure—i.e. the two requirements mentioned above and termination [1].

Architecture and refinements. The following three refinements of the core algorithm described above are crucial for efficiency. First, since $Pre(\mathcal{R}_i, \bigvee_{j=1}^{n} t_j)$ is equivalent to $\bigvee_{j=1}^{n} Pre(\mathcal{R}_i, t_j)$ when t_j is of a suitable form (e.g., that obtained when representing the administrative actions of ARBAC), it is possible to store the formula representing the set of backward reachable states by using a labelled tree, whose root node is labelled by the goal G, its children by $Pre(G, t_j)$, the edge connecting each child with the root by t_j, and so on (recursively) for $j = 1, \dots, n$ (see [1] for details). It is easy to see that, by taking the disjunction of the formulae labelling all the nodes of a tree of depth k, we obtain a formula which is logically equivalent to $\mathcal{R}_k$ above. A key advantage of this data structure is to allow for an easy computation of the sequence of administrative actions leading from an initial policy to one satisfying the goal of a user-role reachability problem by simply collecting the labels of the edges from a leaf (whose label denotes a set of states with a non-empty intersection with the initial states) to the root node. This information is crucial for administrators to fix bugged policies. Another advantage consists in the possibility, without loss of precision, of deleting a node that would be labelled by an unsatisfiable preimage $Pre(\mathcal{R}_i, t_j)$, thereby reducing the size of the formula representing the set of backward reachable states and reducing the burden for SMT solvers and ATPs when checking for safety or fix-point. A similar approach for the elimination of redundancies in $\mathcal{R}_i$ has already been found extremely useful in MCMT [3,2]. To furtherly eliminate redundancy, after $Pre(\mathcal{R}_i, t_j)$ is found satisfiable, we check if $Pre(\mathcal{R}_i, t_j) \Rightarrow \mathcal{R}_{i-1}$ is valid and if so, $Pre(\mathcal{R}_i, t_j)$ is discarded. This can be seen as a simplified, and computationally cheap version, of the fix-point check, which is performed afterwards. Second, when checking for satisfiability, we first invoke an SMT solver and if this returns 'unknown,' we resort to an ATP (we call this a hierarchical combination). This is so because SMT solvers natively support (stack-wise) incrementality but, in many cases, approximate satisfiability checks for BSR, while ATPs are refutation complete and perform very well on formulae belonging to the BSR class but do not support incremental satisfiability checks. This is crucial to obtain a good trade-off between efficiency and precision. Third, the size of the goal critically affects the complexity of the security analysis problem for RBAC policies (see, e.g., [10]). In order to mitigate the problem, we incorporated a *divide et impera* heuristic: we generate a reachability problem for each role in the set R_g of roles in the goal. If (at least) one of the $k = |R_g|$ sub-goals is unreachable, ASASP concludes that the original goal is also so. Otherwise, if each sub-goal $j = 1, ..., k$ is reachable with a certain sequence σ_j for administrative actions, then ASASP tries to solve an additional problem composed by the original goal with the transitions in $\bigcup_{j=1}^{k} \sigma_j$ (regarding σ_j as a set), that is hopefully smaller than the original set of administrative actions. If the last problem does not admit a solution (because some transitions may interfere), we can iterate again the process by selecting some other solutions (if any) to one or more of the k sub-problems and try to solve again the original problem.

Implementation. ASASP is based on a client-server architecture, where the client (implemented in C) computes pre-images and generates the formulae encoding tests for safety and fix-point and the server consists of a hierarchic combination of the SMT solver Z3 (version 2.11) [12] and two ATPs, the latest versions of SPASS [9] and iProver [5]. To facilitate the integration of new satisfiability solving techniques, ASASP uses the new version (2.0) of the SMT-LIB format [8] for the on-line invocation of SMT solvers and the TPTP format [11] when using ATPs.

Experiments. We evaluated ASASP on a set of significant benchmarks and the results clearly demonstrate its scalability. We consider three classes of problems of increasing difficulty: (a) the synthetic benchmarks described in [10] for the ARBAC model without role hierarchy, (b) the same problems considered in (a) augmented with randomly generated role hierarchies, and (c) a new set of synthetic benchmarks—derived from (b)—for the administration of a simple instance of the policies introduced in [1]. Each class consists of randomly generated user-role reachability problems which are classified w.r.t. the size of their goal, that was shown [7] to be the parameter characterizing the computational difficulty. All the experiments were conducted on an Intel(R) Core(TM)2 Duo CPU

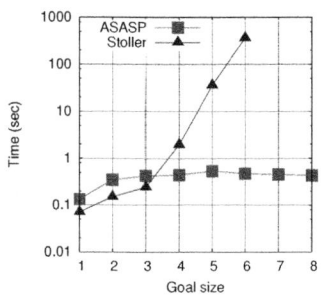

Fig. 2. ASASP vs. *Stoller*

T5870, 2 GHz, 3 GB RAM, running Linux Debian 2.6.32. Figure 2 shows the plots of the median time (logarithmic scale) of ASASP and the tool—using backward search—described in [10],[2] called *Stoller* here, to solve the problems in

---

[2] In [10], an algorithm based on forward reachability is also presented, which is evaluated on two classes of benchmarks whose goals are never reachable by construction. This corresponds to the worst-case choice for a forward search since it requires the exploration of the whole state space. For our tool—based on backward reachability— they are too easy and thus not considered here.

the benchmark class (a) for increasing values of the goal size (for the results on the other two benchmark classes, see [1]). For small goal sizes, ASASP is slower than *Stoller* since it incurs in the overhead of invoking general purpose reasoning systems for safety and fix-point checks instead of the *ad hoc* algorithms used by *Stoller*. However, the time taken by *Stoller* grows quickly as the size of the goal increases and for goal size larger than 6, we do not report the median value as *Stoller* solves less than 50% of the instance problems in the given time-out (set to 1, 800 sec). There is a "cut-off effect" for goal sizes larger than 5 when problem instances become over-constrained (as it is unlikely that more and more goal roles are reachable). ASASP outperforms *Stoller* for larger values of the goal size; the key to obtain such a nice asymptotic behavior for ASASP is the third refinement described above. Similar observations also hold for the behavior of ASASP and *Stoller* on benchmark class (b). The results on benchmark class (c) show a similar asymptotic behavior for ASASP; a comparison with *Stoller* on these problems is impossible given its restrictions in the input format.

4   Conclusions and Future Work

We have presented ASASP, a tool for the symbolic analysis of security policies based on the model checking modulo theories approach of [3,2]. ASASP shows better scalability than the state-of-the-art tool in [10] on a significant set of instances of benchmarks. An interesting line of future work is to extend our approach to perform incremental analysis, i.e. incrementally updating the result of the analysis when the underlying policy changes as it is common in real-world applications [4].

Acknowledgements. This work was partially supported by the "Automated Security Analysis of Identity and Access Management Systems (SIAM)" project funded by Provincia Autonoma di Trento in the context of the "team 2009 - Incoming" COFUND action of the European Commission (FP7).

References

1. Alberti, F., Armando, A., Ranise, S.: Efficient Symbolic Automated Analysis of Administrative Role Based Access Control Policies. In: ASIACCS (2011)
2. Ghilardi, S., Ranise, S.: Backward Reachability of Array-based Systems by SMT solving: Termination and Invariant Synthesis. In: LMCS, vol. 6(4) (2010)
3. Ghilardi, S., Ranise, S.: MCMT: A Model Checker Modulo Theories. In: Giesl, J., Hähnle, R. (eds.) IJCAR 2010. LNCS, vol. 6173, pp. 22–29. Springer, Heidelberg (2010)
4. Gofman, M.I., Luo, R., Yang, P.: User-Role Reachability Analysis of Evolving Administrative Role Based Access Control. In: Gritzalis, D., Preneel, B., Theoharidou, M. (eds.) ESORICS 2010. LNCS, vol. 6345, pp. 455–471. Springer, Heidelberg (2010)
5. iProver, http://www.cs.man.ac.uk/~korovink/iprover

6. Ramsey, F.P.: On a problem in formal logic. Proc. of the London Mathematical Society, 264–286 (1930)
7. Sasturkar, A., Yang, P., Stoller, S.D., Ramakrishnan, C.R.: Policy analysis for administrative role based access control. In: 19th CSF Workshop. IEEE, New York (2006)
8. SMT- LIB: http://www.smt-lib.org
9. SPASS, http://www.spass-prover.org
10. Stoller, S.D., Yang, P., Ramakrishnan, C.R., Gofman, M.I.: Efficient policy analysis for administrative role based access control. In: ACM CCS (2007)
11. TPTP, http://www.cs.miami.edu/~tptp
12. Z3, http://research.microsoft.com/projects/z3/

Backward Trace Slicing for Rewriting Logic Theories[*]

María Alpuente[1], Demis Ballis[2], Javier Espert[1], and Daniel Romero[1]

[1] DSIC-ELP, Universidad Politécnica de Valencia
Camino de Vera s/n, Apdo 22012, 46071 Valencia, Spain
{alpuente,jespert,dromero}@dsic.upv.es
[2] Dipartimento di Matematica e Informatica
Via delle Scienze 206, 33100 Udine, Italy
demis.ballis@uniud.it

Abstract. Trace slicing is a widely used technique for execution trace analysis that is effectively used in program debugging, analysis and comprehension. In this paper, we present a backward trace slicing technique that can be used for the analysis of Rewriting Logic theories. Our trace slicing technique allows us to systematically trace back rewrite sequences modulo equational axioms (such as associativity and commutativity) by means of an algorithm that dynamically simplifies the traces by detecting control and data dependencies, and dropping useless data that do not influence the final result. Our methodology is particularly suitable for analyzing complex, textually-large system computations such as those delivered as counter-example traces by Maude model-checkers.

1 Introduction

The analysis of execution traces plays a fundamental role in many program manipulation techniques. Trace slicing is a technique for reducing the size of traces by focusing on selected aspects of program execution, which makes it suitable for trace analysis and monitoring [7].

Rewriting Logic (RWL) is a very general *logical* and *semantic framework*, which is particularly suitable for formalizing highly concurrent, complex systems (e.g., biological systems [5,17] and Web systems [3,4]). RWL is efficiently implemented in the high-performance system Maude [9]. Roughly speaking, a *rewriting logic theory* seamlessly combines a *term rewriting system* (TRS) together with an *equational theory* that may include sorts, functions, and algebraic laws (such as commutativity and associativity) so that rewrite steps are applied *modulo* the equations. Within this framework, the system states are typically represented as elements of an algebraic data type that is specified by the equational theory, while the system computations are modeled via the rewrite rules, which describe transitions between states.

---

[*] This work has been partially supported by the EU (FEDER) and the Spanish MEC TIN2010-21062-C02-02 project, by Generalitat Valenciana PROMETEO2011/052, and by the Italian MUR under grant RBIN04M8S8, FIRB project, Internationalization 2004. Daniel Romero is also supported by FPI–MEC grant BES–2008–004860.

N. Bjørner and V. Sofronie-Stokkermans (Eds.): CADE 2011, LNAI 6803, pp. 34–48, 2011.
© Springer-Verlag Berlin Heidelberg 2011

Due to the many important applications of RWL, in recent years, the debugging and optimization of RWL theories have received growing attention [2,14,15]. However, the existing tools provide hardly support for execution trace analysis. The original motivation for our work was to reduce the size of the counterexample traces delivered by Web-TLR, which is a RWL-based model-checking tool for Web applications proposed in [3,4]. As a matter of fact, the analysis (or even the simple inspection) of such traces may be unfeasible because of the size and complexity of the traces under examination. Typical counterexample traces in Web-TLR are 75 Kb long for a model size of 1.5 Kb, that is, the trace is in a ratio of 5.000% w.r.t. the model.

To the best of our knowledge, this paper presents the first trace slicing technique for RWL theories. The basic idea is to take a trace produced by the RWL engine and traverse and analyze it backwards to filter out events that are irrelevant for the rewritten task. The trace slicing technique that we propose is fully general and can be applied to optimizing any RWL-based tool that manipulates rewrite logic traces. Our technique relies on a suitable mechanism of backward tracing that is formalized by means of a procedure that labels the calls (terms) involved in the rewrite steps. This allows us to infer, from a term t and positions of interest on it, positions of interest of the term that was rewritten to t. Our labeling procedure extends the technique in [6], which allows descendants and origins to be traced in orthogonal (i.e., left-linear and overlap-free) term rewriting systems in order to deal with rewrite theories that may contain commutativity/associativity axioms, as well as nonleft-linear, collapsing equations and rules.

Plan of the paper. Section 2 summarizes some preliminary definitions and notations about term rewriting systems. In Section 3, we recall the essential notions concerning rewriting modulo equational theories. In Section 4, we formalize our backward trace slicing technique for elementary rewriting logic theories. Section 5 extends the trace slicing technique of Section 4 by considering extended rewrite theories, i.e., rewrite theories that may include collapsing, nonleft-linear rules, associative/commutative equational axioms, and built-in operators. Section 6 describes a software tool that implements the proposed backward slicing technique and reports on an experimental evaluation of the tool that allows us to assess the practical advantages of the trace slicing technique. In Section 7, we discuss some related work and then we conclude. More details and missing proofs can be found in [1].

2   Preliminaries

A many-sorted signature (Σ, S) consists of a set of sorts S and a $S^* \times S$-indexed family of sets $\Sigma = \{\Sigma_{\bar{s} \times s}\}_{(\bar{s},s) \in S^* \times S}$, which are sets of *function symbols* (or operators) with a given string of argument sorts and result sort. Given an S-sorted set $\mathcal{V} = \{\mathcal{V}_s \mid s \in S\}$ of disjoint sets of variables, $T_\Sigma(\mathcal{V})_s$ and $T_{\Sigma s}$ are the sets of terms and ground terms of sorts s, respectively. We write $T_\Sigma(\mathcal{V})$ and T_Σ for the corresponding term algebras. An *equation* is a pair of terms of the form $s = t$, with $s, t \in T_{\Sigma}(\mathcal{V})_s$. In order to simplify the presentation, we often disregard sorts when no confusion can arise.

Terms are viewed as labelled trees in the usual way. Positions are represented by sequences of natural numbers denoting an access path in a term. The empty sequence Λ denotes the root position. By $root(t)$, we denote the symbol that occurs at the root position of t. We let $\mathcal{P}os(t)$ denote the set of positions of t. By notation $w_1.w_2$, we denote the concatenation of positions (sequences) w_1 and w_2. Positions are ordered by the prefix ordering, that is, given the positions $w_1, w_2, w_1 \leq w_2$ if there exists a position x such that $w_1.x = w_2$. $t_{|u}$ is the subterm at the position u of t. $t[r]_u$ is the term t with the subterm rooted at the position u replaced by r. A substitution σ is a mapping from variables to terms $\{x_1/t_1, \ldots, x_n/t_n\}$ such that $x_i\sigma = t_i$ for $i = 1, \ldots, n$ (with $x_i \neq x_j$ if $i \neq j$), and $x\sigma = x$ for any other variable x. By ε, we denote the *empty* substitution. Given a substitution σ, the *domain* of σ is the set $Dom(\sigma) = \{x | x\sigma \neq x\}$. By $Var(t)$ (resp. $FSymbols(t)$), we denote the set of variables (resp. function symbols) occurring in the term t.

A *context* is a term $\gamma \in T_{\Sigma \cup \{\square\}}(\mathcal{V})$ with zero or more holes $\square$[1], and $\square \notin \Sigma$. We write $\gamma[\,]_u$ to denote that there is a hole at position u of γ. By notation $\gamma[\,]$, we define an arbitrary context (where the number and the positions of the holes are clarified *in situ*), while we write $\gamma[t_1, \ldots t_n]$ to denote the term obtained by filling the holes appearing in $\gamma[\,]$ with terms $t_1, \ldots, t_n$. By notation $t^{\square}$, we denote the context obtained by applying the substitution $\sigma = \{x_1/\square, \ldots, x_n/\square\}$ to t, where $Var(t) = \{x_1 \ldots, x_n\}$ (i.e., $t^{\square} = t\sigma$).

A *term rewriting system* (TRS for short) is a pair (Σ, R), where Σ is a signature and R is a finite set of reduction (or rewrite) rules of the form $\lambda \rightarrow \rho$, $\lambda, \rho \in T_{\Sigma}(\mathcal{V})$, $\lambda \notin \mathcal{V}$ and $Var(\rho) \subseteq Var(\lambda)$. We often write just R instead of (Σ, R). A rewrite step is the application of a rewrite rule to an expression. A term s *rewrites* to a term t via $r \in R$, $s \xrightarrow{r}_R t$ (or $s \xrightarrow{r,\sigma}_R t$), if there exists a position q in s such that λ *matches* $s_{|q}$ via a substitution σ (in symbols, $s_{|q} = \lambda\sigma$), and t is obtained from s by replacing the subterm $s_{|q} = \lambda\sigma$ with the term $\rho\sigma$, in symbols $t = s[\rho\sigma]_q$. The rule $\lambda \rightarrow \rho$ (or equation $\lambda = \rho$) is *collapsing* if $\rho \in \mathcal{V}$; it is *left-linear* if no variable occurs in λ more than once. We denote the transitive and reflexive closure of $\rightarrow$ by $\rightarrow^*$.

Let $r : \lambda \rightarrow \rho$ be a rule. We call the context $\lambda^{\square}$ (resp. $\rho^{\square}$) *redex pattern* (resp. *contractum pattern*) of r. For example, the context $f(g(\square, \square), a)$ (resp. $d(s(\square), \square)$) is the redex pattern (resp. contractum pattern) of the rule $r : f(g(x, y), a)) \rightarrow d(s(y), y)$, where a is a constant symbol.

3   Rewriting Modulo Equational Theories

An *equational theory* is a pair (Σ, E), where Σ is a signature and $E = \Delta \cup B$ consists of a set of (oriented) equations Δ together with a collection B of equational axioms (e.g., associativity and commutativity axioms) that are associated

---

[1] Actually, when considering types, we assume to have a distinct $\square_s$ symbol for each sort $s \in S$, and by abuse we simply denote $\square_s$ by $\square$.

with some operator of Σ. The equational theory E induces a least congruence relation on the term algebra $T_\Sigma(\mathcal{V})$, which is usually denoted by $=_E$.

A *rewrite theory* is a triple $\mathcal{R} = (\Sigma, E, R)$, where (Σ, E) is an equational theory, and R is a TRS. Examples of rewrite theories can be found in [9].

Rewriting modulo equational theories [14] can be defined by lifting the standard rewrite relation $\rightarrow_R$ on terms to the E-congruence classes induced by $=_E$. More precisely, the rewrite relation $\rightarrow_{R/E}$ for rewriting modulo E is defined as $=_E \circ \rightarrow_R \circ =_E$. A computation in $\mathcal{R}$ using $\rightarrow_{R\cup\Delta,B}$ is a *rewriting logic deduction*, in which the *equational simplification* with Δ (i.e., applying the oriented equations in Δ to a term t until a canonical form $t\downarrow_E$ is reached where no further equations can be applied) is intermixed with the rewriting computation with the rules of R, using an *algorithm of matching modulo*[2] B in both cases. Formally, given a rewrite theory $\mathcal{R} = (\Sigma, E, R)$, where $E = \Delta \cup B$, a *rewrite step modulo* E on a term s_0 by means of the rule $r : \lambda \rightarrow \rho \in R$ (in symbols, $s_0 \xrightarrow{r}_{R\cup\Delta,B} s_1$) can be implemented as follows: (i) apply (modulo B) the equations of Δ on s_0 to reach a canonical form $(s_0 \downarrow_E)$; (ii) rewrite (modulo B) $(s_0 \downarrow_E)$ to term v by using $r \in R$; and (iii), apply (modulo B) the equations of Δ on v again to reach a canonical form for v, $s_1 = v \downarrow_E$.

Since the equations of Δ are implicitly oriented (from left to right), the equational simplification can be seen as a sequence of (equational) rewrite steps $(\rightarrow_{\Delta/B})$. Therefore, a *rewrite step modulo* E $s_0 \xrightarrow{r}_{R\cup\Delta,B} s_1$ can be expanded into a sequence of rewrite steps as follows:

$$\overbrace{s_0 \rightarrow_{\Delta/B} \cdots \rightarrow_{\Delta/B} s_0\downarrow_E}^{\substack{\text{equational}\\\text{simplification}}} =_B \overbrace{u \xrightarrow{r}_R v}^{\substack{\text{rewrite}\\\text{step}/B}} \overbrace{\rightarrow_{\Delta/B} \cdots \rightarrow_{\Delta/B} v\downarrow_E}^{\substack{\text{equational}\\\text{simplification}}} = s_1$$

Given a finite rewrite sequence $\mathcal{S} = s_0 \rightarrow_{R\cup\Delta,B} s_1 \rightarrow_{R\cup\Delta,B} \cdots \rightarrow s_n$ in the rewrite theory $\mathcal{R}$, the *execution trace* of $\mathcal{S}$ is the rewrite sequence $\mathcal{T}$ obtained by expanding all the rewrite steps $s_i \rightarrow_{R\cup\Delta,B} s_{i+1}$ of $\mathcal{S}$ as is described above.

In this work, a rewrite theory $\mathcal{R} = (\Sigma, B \cup \Delta, R)$ is called *elementary* if $\mathcal{R}$ does not contain equational axioms $(B = \emptyset)$ and both rules and equations are left-linear and not collapsing.

4 Backward Trace Slicing for Elementary Rewrite Theories

In this section, we formalize a backward trace slicing technique for *elementary rewrite theories* that is based on a term labeling procedure that is inspired by [6]. Since equations in Δ are treated as rewrite rules that are used to simplify terms, our formulation for the trace slicing technique is purely based on standard rewriting.

---

[2] A subterm of t matches l (*modulo B*) via the substitution σ if $t =_B u$ and $u_{|q} = l\sigma$ for a position q of u.

4.1   Labeling Procedure for Rewrite Theories

Let us define a labeling procedure for rules similar to [6] that allows us to trace symbols involved in a rewrite step. First, we provide the notion of labeling for terms, and then we show how it can be naturally lifted to rules and rewrite steps.

Consider a set $\mathcal{A}$ of *atomic labels*, which are denoted by Greek letters $\alpha, \beta, \ldots$. *Composite labels* (or simply *labels*) are defined as finite sets of elements of $\mathcal{A}$. By abuse, we write the label $\alpha\beta\gamma$ as a compact denotation for the set $\{\alpha, \beta, \gamma\}$.

A *labeling* for a term $t \in T_{\Sigma \cup \{\Box\}}(\mathcal{V})$ is a map L that assigns a label to (the symbol occurring at) each position w of t, provided that $root(t_{|w}) \neq \Box$. If t is a term, then t^L denotes the labeled version of t. Note that, in the case when t is a context, occurrences of symbol $\Box$ appearing in the labeled version of t are not labeled. The *codomain* of a labeling L is denoted by $Cod(L) = \{l \mid (w \mapsto l) \in L\}$.

An *initial labeling* for the term t is a labeling for t that assigns distinct fresh atomic labels to each position of the term. For example, given $t = f(g(a, a), \Box)$, then $t^L = f^\alpha(g^\beta(a^\gamma, a^\delta), \Box)$ is the labeled version of t via the initial labeling $L = \{\Lambda \mapsto \alpha, 1 \mapsto \beta, 1.1 \mapsto \gamma, 1.2 \mapsto \delta\}$. This notion extends to rules and rewrite steps in a natural way as shown below.

Labeling of Rules. The labeling of a rewriting rule is formalized as follows:

Definition 1. *(rule labeling) [6] Given a rule $r : \lambda \to \rho$, a labeling L_r for r is defined by means of the following procedure.*

r_1. *The redex pattern $\lambda^\Box$ is labeled by means of an initial labeling L.*
r_2. *A new label l is formed by joining all the labels that occur in the labeled redex pattern $\lambda^\Box$ (say in alphabetical order) of the rule r. Label l is then associated with each position w of the contractum pattern $\rho^\Box$, provided that $root(\rho^\Box_{|w}) \neq \Box$.*

The labeled version of r w.r.t. L_r is denoted by r^{L_r}. Note that the labeling procedure shown in Definition 1 does not assign labels to variables but only to the function symbols occurring in the rule.

Labeling of Rewrite Steps. Before giving the definition of labeling for a rewrite step, we need to formalize the auxiliary notion of substitution labeling.

Definition 2. *(substitution labeling) Let $\sigma = \{x_1/t_1, \ldots, x_n/t_n\}$ be a substitution. A labeling L_σ for the substitution σ is defined by a set of initial labelings $L_\sigma = \{L_{x_1/t_1}, \ldots, L_{x_n/t_n}\}$ such that (i) for each binding (x_i/t_i) in the substitution σ, t_i is labeled using the corresponding initial labeling L_{x_i/t_i}, and (ii) the sets $Cod(L_{x_1/t_1}), \ldots, Cod(L_{x_n/t_n})$ are pairwise disjoint.*

By using Definition 2, we can formulate a labeling procedure for rewrite steps as follows.

Definition 3. *(rewrite step labeling) Let $r : \lambda \to \rho$ be a rule, and $\mu : t \xrightarrow{r, \sigma} s$ be a rewrite step using r such that $t = C[\lambda\sigma]_q$ and $s = C[\rho\sigma]_q$, for a context C*

and position q. Let $\sigma = \{x_1/t_1, \ldots, x_n/t_n\}$. *Let* L_r *be a labeling for the rule* r, L_C *be an initial labeling for the context* C, *and* $L_\sigma = \{L_{x_1/t_1}, \ldots, L_{x_n/t_n}\}$ *be a labeling for the substitution* σ *such that the sets* $Cod(L_C)$, $Cod(L_r)$, *and* $Cod(\sigma)$ *are pairwise disjoint, where* $Cod(\sigma) = \bigcup_{i=1}^{n} Cod(L_{x_i/t_i})$.

The rewrite step *labeling* L_μ *for* μ *is defined by successively applying the following steps:*

s_1. *First, positions of* t *or* s *that belong to the context* C *are labeled by using the initial labeling* L_C.

s_2. *Then positions of* $t_{|q}$ *(resp.* $s_{|q}$*) that correspond to the redex pattern (resp. contractum pattern) of the rule* r *rooted at the position* q *are labeled according to the labeling* L_r.

s_3. *Finally, for each term* t_j, $j = \{1, \ldots, n\}$, *which has been introduced in* t *or* s *via the binding* $x_j/t_j \in \sigma$, *with* $x_j \in Var(\lambda)$, t_j *is labeled using the corresponding labeling* $L_{x_j/t_j} \in L_\sigma$

The labeled version of a rewrite step μ w.r.t. L_μ is denoted by μ^{L_μ}. Let us illustrate these definitions by means of a rather intuitive example.

Example 1. Consider the rule $r : f(g(x,y),a)) \rightarrow d(s(y),y)$. The labeled version of rule r using the initial labeling $L = \{(\Lambda \mapsto \alpha, 1 \mapsto \beta, 2 \mapsto \gamma\}$ is as follows:

$$f^\alpha(g^\beta(x,y),a^\gamma) \rightarrow d^{\alpha\beta\gamma}(s^{\alpha\beta\gamma}(y),y)$$

Consider a rewrite step $\mu : C[\lambda\sigma] \xrightarrow{r} C[\rho\sigma]$ using r, where $C[\lambda\sigma] = d(f(g(a,h(b)),a),a)$, $C[\rho\sigma] = d(d(s(h(b)),h(b)),a)$, and $\sigma = \{x/a, y/h(b)\}$. Let $L_C = \{\Lambda \mapsto \delta, 2 \mapsto \epsilon\}$, $L_{x/a} = \{\Lambda \mapsto \zeta\}$, and $L_{y/h(b)} = \{\Lambda \mapsto \eta, 1 \mapsto \theta\}$ be the labelings for C and the bindings in σ, respectively. Then, the corresponding labeled rewrite step μ^L is as follows

$$\mu^L : d^\delta(f^\alpha(g^\beta(a^\zeta,h^\eta(b^\theta)),a^\gamma),a^\epsilon) \rightarrow d^\delta(d^{\alpha\beta\gamma}(s^{\alpha\beta\gamma}(h^\eta(b^\theta)),h^\eta(b^\theta)),a^\epsilon)$$

4.2   Backward Tracing Relation

Given a rewrite step $\mu : t \xrightarrow{r} s$ and the labeling process defined in the previous section, the *backward tracing relation* computes the set of positions in t that are origin for a position w in s. Formally,

Definition 4. *(origin positions) Let* $\mu : t \xrightarrow{r} s$ *be a rewrite step and* L *be a labeling for* μ *where* L_t *(resp.* L_s*) is the labeling of* t *(resp.* s*). Given a position* w *of* s, *the set of origin positions of* w *in* t *w.r.t.* μ *and* L *(in symbols,* $\triangleleft_\mu^L w$*) is defined as follows:*

$$\triangleleft_\mu^L w = \{v \in \mathcal{P}os(t) \mid \exists p \in \mathcal{P}os(s), (v \mapsto l_v) \in L_t, (p \mapsto l_p) \in L_s \text{ s.t. } p \le w \text{ and } l_v \subseteq l_p\}$$

Note that Definition 4 considers all positions of s in the path from its root to w for computing the origin positions of w. Roughly speaking, a position v in t is an origin of w, if the label of the symbol that occurs in t^L at position v is contained in the label of a symbol that occurs in s^L in the path from its root to the position w.

Example 2. Consider again the rewrite step $\mu^L : t^L \to s^L$ of Example 1, and let w be the position 1.2 of s^L. The set of labeled symbols occurring in s^L in the path from its root to position w is the set $z = \{h^\eta, d^{\alpha\beta\gamma}, d^\delta\}$. Now, the labeled symbols occurring in t^L whose label is contained in the label of one element of z is the set $\{h^\eta, f^\alpha, g^\beta, a^\gamma, d^\delta\}$. By Definition 4, the set of origin positions of w in μ^L is $\triangleleft^L_\mu w = \{1.1.2, 1, 1.1, 1.2, \Lambda\}$.

4.3   The Backward Trace Slicing Algorithm

First, let us formalize the slicing criterion, which basically represents the information we want to trace back across the execution trace in order to find out the "origins" of the data we observe. Given a term t, we denote by $\mathcal{O}_t$ the set of *observed* positions of t.

Definition 5. *(slicing criterion) Given a rewrite theory $\mathcal{R} = (\Sigma, \Delta, R)$ and an execution trace $\mathcal{T} : s \to^* t$ in $\mathcal{R}$, a slicing criterion for $\mathcal{T}$ is any set $\mathcal{O}_t$ of positions of the term t.*

In the following, we show how backward trace slicing can be performed by exploiting the backward tracing relation $\triangleleft^L_\mu$ that was introduced in Definition 4. Informally, given a slicing criterion $\mathcal{O}_{t_n}$ for $\mathcal{T} : t_0 \to t_2 \to \ldots \to t_n$, at each rewrite step $t_{i-1} \to t_i$, $i = 1, \ldots, n$, our technique inductively computes the backward tracing relation between the relevant positions of t_i and those in t_{i-1}. The algorithm proceeds backwards, from the final term t_n to the initial term t_0, and recursively generates at step i the corresponding set of relevant positions, $P_{t_{n-i}}$. Finally, by means of a removal function, a simplified trace is obtained where each t_j is replaced by the corresponding *term slice* that contains only the relevant information w.r.t. P_{t_j}.

Definition 6. *(sequence of relevant position sets) Let $\mathcal{R} = (\Sigma, \Delta, R)$ be a rewrite theory, and $\mathcal{T} : t_0 \overset{r_1}{\to} t_1 \ldots \overset{r_n}{\to} t_n$ be an execution trace in $\mathcal{R}$. Let L_i be the labeling for the rewrite step $t_i \to t_{i+1}$ with $0 \le i < n$. The sequence of relevant position sets in $\mathcal{T}$ w.r.t. the slicing criterion $\mathcal{O}_{t_n}$ is defined as follows:*

$$relevant\_positions(\mathcal{T}, \mathcal{O}_{t_n}) = [P_0, \ldots, P_n]$$
$$where \begin{cases} P_n = \mathcal{O}_{t_n} \\ P_j = \bigcup_{p \in P_{j+1}} \triangleleft^{L_j}_{(t_j \to t_{j+1})} p, \text{ with } 0 \le j < n \end{cases}$$

Now, it is straightforward to formalize a procedure that obtains a term slice from each term t in $\mathcal{T}$ and the corresponding set of relevant positions of t. We introduce the fresh symbol $\bullet \notin \Sigma$ to replace any information in the term that is not relevant, hence does not affect the observed criterion.

Definition 7. *(term slice) Let $t \in T_\Sigma$ be a term and P be a set of positions of t. A term slice of t with respect to P is defined as follows:*

$$slice(t, P) = sl\_rec(t, P, \Lambda), \text{ where}$$

$$sl\_rec(t, P, p) = \begin{cases} f(sl\_rec(t_1, P, p.1), \ldots, sl\_rec(t_n, P, p.n)) \\ \quad \textit{if } t = f(t_1, \ldots, t_n) \textit{ and there exists } w \textit{ s.t. } (p.w) \in P \\ \bullet \quad \textit{otherwise} \end{cases}$$

In the following, we use the notation $t^\bullet$ to denote a term slice of the term t. Roughly speaking, the symbol $\bullet$ can be thought of as a variable, and we denote by $[t^\bullet]$ the term that is obtained by replacing all occurrences of $\bullet$ in $t^\bullet$ with fresh variables. Then, we say that t' is a concretization of $t^\bullet$ (in symbols, $t^\bullet \propto t'$) , if $[t^\bullet]\sigma = t'$, for some substitution σ. Let us define a *sliced rewrite step* between two term slices as follows.

Definition 8. *(sliced rewrite step) Let $\mathcal{R} = (\Sigma, \Delta, R)$ be a rewrite theory and r a rule of $\mathcal{R}$. The term slice $s^\bullet$ rewrites to the term slice $t^\bullet$ via r (in symbols, $s^\bullet \xrightarrow{r} t^\bullet$) if there exist two terms s and t such that $s^\bullet$ is a term slice of s, $t^\bullet$ is a term slice of t, and $s \xrightarrow{r} t$.*

Finally, using Definition 8, backward trace slicing is formalized as follows.

Definition 9. *(backward trace slicing) Let $\mathcal{R} = (\Sigma, \Delta, R)$ be a rewrite theory, and $\mathcal{T} : t_0 \xrightarrow{r_1} t_1 \ldots \xrightarrow{r_n} t_n$ be an execution trace in $\mathcal{R}$. Let $\mathcal{O}_{t_n}$ be a slicing criterion for $\mathcal{T}$, and let $[P_0, \ldots, P_n]$ be the sequence of the relevant position sets of $\mathcal{T}$ w.r.t. $\mathcal{O}_{t_n}$. A trace slice $\mathcal{T}^\bullet$ of $\mathcal{T}$ w.r.t. $\mathcal{O}_{t_n}$ is defined as the sliced rewrite sequence of term slices $t_i^\bullet = slice(t_i, P_i)$ which is obtained by gluing together the sliced rewrite steps in the set*

$$\mathcal{K}^\bullet = \{t_{k-1}^\bullet \xrightarrow{r_k} t_k^\bullet \mid 0 < k \leq n \ \wedge \ t_{k-1}^\bullet \neq t_k^\bullet\}.$$

Note that in Definition 9, the sliced rewrite steps that do not affect the relevant positions (i.e., $t_{k-1}^\bullet \xrightarrow{r_k} t_k^\bullet$ with $t_{k-1}^\bullet = t_k^\bullet$) are discarded, which further reduces the size of the trace.

A desirable property of a slicing technique is to ensure that, for any concretization of the term slice $t_0^\bullet$, the trace slice $\mathcal{T}^\bullet$ can be reproduced. This property ensures that the rules involved in $\mathcal{T}^\bullet$ can be applied again to every concrete trace $\mathcal{T}'$ that we can derive by instantiating all the variables in $[t_0^\bullet]$ with arbitrary terms.

Theorem 1. *(soundness) Let $\mathcal{R}$ be an elementary rewrite theory. Let $\mathcal{T}$ be an execution trace in the rewrite theory $\mathcal{R}$, and let $\mathcal{O}$ be a slicing criterion for $\mathcal{T}$. Let $\mathcal{T}^\bullet : t_0^\bullet \xrightarrow{r_1} t_1^\bullet \ldots \xrightarrow{r_n} t_n^\bullet$ be the corresponding trace slice w.r.t. $\mathcal{O}$. Then, for any concretization t_0' of $t_0^\bullet$, it holds that $\mathcal{T}' : t_0' \xrightarrow{r_1} t_1' \ldots \xrightarrow{r_n} t_n'$ is an execution trace in $\mathcal{R}$, and $t_i^\bullet \propto t_i'$, for $i = 1, \ldots, n$.*

The proof of Theorem 1 relies on the fact that redex patterns are preserved by backward trace slicing. Therefore, for $i = 1, \ldots, n$, the rule r_i can be applied to any concretization t_{i-1}' of term $t_{i-1}^\bullet$ since the redex pattern of r_i does appear in $t_{i-1}^\bullet$, and hence in t_{i-1}'. A detailed proof of Theorem 1 can be found in [1].

Note that our basic framework enjoys neededness of the extracted information (in the sense of [18]), since the information captured by every sliced rewrite step in a trace slice is all and only the information that is needed to produce the data of interest in the reduced term.

5   Backward Trace Slicing for Extended Rewrite Theories

In this section, we consider an extension of our basic slicing methodology that allows us to deal with extended rewrite theories $\mathcal{R} = (\Sigma, E, R)$ where the equational theory (Σ, E) may contain associativity and commutativity axioms, and R may contain collapsing as well as nonleft-linear rules. Moreover, we also consider the built-in operators, which are not equipped with an explicit functional definition (e.g., Maude arithmetical operators). It is worth noting that all the proposed extensions are restricted to the labeling procedure of Section 4.1, keeping the backbone of our slicing technique unchanged.

5.1   Dealing with Collapsing and Nonleft-Linear Rules

Collapsing Rules. The main difficulty with collapsing rules is that they have a trivial contractum pattern, which consists in the empty context $\square$; hence, it is not possible to propagate labels from the left-hand side of the rule to its right-hand side. This makes the rule labeling procedure of Definition 1 completely unproductive for trace slicing.

In order to overcome this problem, we keep track of the labels in the left-hand side of the collapsing rule r, whenever a rewrite step involving r takes place. This amounts to extending the labeling procedure of Definition 3 as follows.

Definition 10. *(rewrite step labeling for collapsing rules) Let $\mu : t \xrightarrow{r,\sigma} s$ be a rewrite step s.t. $\sigma = \{x_1/t_1, \ldots, x_n/t_n\}$, where $r : \lambda \to x_i$ is a collapsing rule. Let L_r be a labeling for the rule r. In order to label the step μ, we extend the labeling procedure formalized in Definition 3 as follows:*

s_4. *Let t_i be the term introduced in s via the binding $x_i/t_i \in \sigma$, for some $i \in \{1, \ldots, n\}$. Then, the label l_i of the root symbol of t_i in s is replaced by a new composite label $l_c l_i$, where l_c is formed by joining all the labels appearing in the redex pattern of r^{L_r}.*

Nonleft-linear Rules. The trace slicing technique we described so far does not work for nonleft-linear TRS. Consider the rule: $r : f(x, y, x) \to g(x, y)$ and the one-step trace $\mathcal{T} : f(a, b, a) \to g(a, b)$. If we are interested in tracing back the symbol g that occurs in the final state $g(a, b)$, we would get the following trace slice $\mathcal{T}^\bullet : f(\bullet, \bullet, \bullet) \to g(\bullet, \bullet)$. However, $f(a, b, b)$ is a concretization of $f(\bullet, \bullet, \bullet)$ that cannot be rewritten by using r. In the following, we augment Definition 10 in order to also deal with nonleft-linear rules.

Definition 11. *(rewrite step labeling for nonleft-linear rules) Let $\mu : t \xrightarrow{r,\sigma} s$ be a rewrite step s.t. $\sigma = \{x_1/t_1, .., x_n/t_n\}$, where r is a nonleft-linear rule. Let $L_\sigma = \{L_{x_1/t_1}, .., L_{x_n/t_n}\}$ be a labeling for the substitution σ. In order to label the step μ, we further extend the labeling procedure formalized in Definition 10 as follows:*

s_5. *For each variable x_j that occurs more than once in the left-hand side of the rule r, the following steps must be followed:*
- *we form a new label l_{x_j} by joining all the labels in $Cod(L_{x_j/t})$ where $L_{x_j/t} \in L_\sigma$;*

- *let l_s be the label of the root symbol of s. Then, l_s is replaced by a new composite label $l_{x_j} l_s$.*

Note that, whenever a rewrite step μ involves the application of a rule that is both collapsing and non left-linear, the labeling for μ is obtained by sequentially applying step s_4 of Definition 10 and step s_5 of Definition 11 (over the labeled rewrite step resulting from s_4).

Example 3. Consider the labeled, collapsing and nonleft-linear rule $f^\beta(x, y, x) \to y$ together with the rewrite step $\mu : h(f(a, b, a), b) \to h(b, b)$, and matching substitution $\sigma = \{x/a, y/b\}$. Let $L_{h(\square, b)} = \{\Lambda \mapsto \alpha, 2 \mapsto \epsilon\}$ be the labeling for the context $h(\square, b)$. Then, for the labeling $L_\sigma = \{L_{x/a}, L_{y/b}\}$, with $L_{x/a} = \{\Lambda \mapsto \gamma\}$ and $L_{y/b} = \{\Lambda \mapsto \delta\}$, the labeled version of μ is $h^\alpha(f^\beta(a^\gamma, b^\delta, a^\gamma), b^\epsilon) \to h^\alpha(b^{\beta\gamma\delta}, b^\epsilon)$. Finally, by considering the criterion $\{1\}$, we can safely trace back the symbol b of the sliced final state $h(b, \bullet)$ and obtain the following trace slice

$$h(f(g(a), b, g(a)), \bullet) \to h(b, \bullet).$$

5.2   Built-in Operators

In practical implementations of RWL (e.g., Maude [9]), several commonly used operators are pre-defined (e.g., arithmetic operators, if-then-else constructs), which do not have an explicit specification. To overcome this limitation, we further extend our labeling process in order to deal with built-in operators.

Definition 12. *(rewrite step labeling for built-in operators) For the case of a rewrite step $\mu : C[op(t_1, \ldots, t_n)] \to C[t']$ involving a call to a built-in, n-ary operator op, we extend Definition 11 by introducing the following additional case:*

s_6. *Given an initial labeling L_{op} for the term $op(t_1, \ldots, t_n)$,*
- *each symbol occurrence in t' is labeled with a new label that is formed by joining the labels of all the (labeled) arguments $t_1, \ldots, t_n$ of op;*
- *the remaining symbol occurrences of $C[t']$ that are not considered in the previous step inherit all the labels appearing in $C[op(t_1, \ldots, t_n)]$.*

For example, by applying Definition 12, the addition of two natural numbers implemented through the built-in operator $+$ might be labeled as $+^\alpha(7^\beta, 8^\gamma) \to 15^{\beta\gamma}$.

5.3   Associative-Commutative Axioms

Let us finally consider an extended rewrite theory $\mathcal{R} = (\Sigma, \Delta \cup B, R)$, where B is a set of associativity (A) and commutativity (C) axioms that hold for some function symbols in Σ. Now, since B only contains associativity/commutativity (AC) axioms, terms can be represented by means of a single representative of their AC congruence class, called *AC canonical form* [11]. This representative is obtained by replacing nested occurrences of the same AC operator by a flattened argument list under a variadic symbol, whose elements are sorted by means of some linear ordering [3]. The inverse process to the flat transformation is the unflat transformation, which is nondeterministic (in the sense that it generates all the unflattended terms that are equivalent (modulo AC) to the flattened term [4]).

For example, consider a binary AC operator f together with the standard lexicographic ordering over symbols. Given the B-equivalence $f(b, f(f(b, a), c)) =_B f(f(b, c), f(a, b))$, we can represent it by using the "internal sequence" $f(b, f(f(b, a), c)) \to^*_{flat_B} f(a, b, b, c) \to^*_{unflat_B} f(f(b, c), f(a, b))$, where the first one corresponds to the *flattening* transformation sequence that obtains the AC canonical form, while the second one corresponds to the inverse, unflattening one.

The key idea for extending our labeling procedure in order to cope with B-equivalence $=_B$ is to exploit the flat/unflat transformations mentioned above. Without loss of generality, we assume that flat/unflat transformations are stable w.r.t. the lexicographic ordering over positions $\sqsubseteq$[5]. This assumption allows us to trace back arguments of commutative operators, since multiple occurrences of the same symbol can be precisely identified.

Definition 13. *(AC Labeling.) Let f be an associative-commutative operator and B be the AC axioms for f. Consider the B-equivalence $t_1 =_B t_2$ and the corresponding (internal) flat/unflat transformation $\mathcal{T} : t_1 \to^*_{flat_B} s \to^*_{unflat_B} t_2$. Let L be an initial labeling for t_1. The labeling procedure for $t_1 =_B t_2$ is as follows.*

1. *(flattening) For each flattening transformation step $t_{|v} \to_{flat_B} t'_{|v}$ in $\mathcal{T}$ for the symbol f, a new label l_f is formed by joining all the labels attached to the symbol f in any position w of t^L s.t. $w = v$ or $w \geq v$, and every symbol on the path from v to w is f; then, label l_f is attached to the root symbol of $t'_{|v}$.*
2. *(unflattening) For each unflattening transformation step $t_{|v} \to_{unflat_B} t'_{|v}$ in $\mathcal{T}$ for the symbol f, the label of the symbol f in the position v of t^L is attached to the symbol f in any position w of t' such that $w = v$ or $w \geq v$, and every symbol on the path from v to w is f.*
3. *The remaining symbol occurrences in t' that are not considered in cases 1 or 2 above inherit the label of the corresponding symbol occurrence in t.*

Example 4. Consider the transformation sequence

$$f(b, f(b, f(a, c))) \to^*_{flat_B} f(a, b, b, c) \to^*_{unflat_B} f(f(b, c), f(a, b))$$

by using Definition 13, the associated transformation sequence can be labeled as follows:

---

[3] Specifically, Maude uses the lexicographic order of symbols.

[4] These two processes are typically hidden inside the B-matching algorithms that are used to implement rewriting modulo B. See [9] (Section 4.8) for an in-depth discussion on matching and simplification modulo AC in Maude.

[5] The lexicographic ordering $\sqsubseteq$ is defined as follows: $\Lambda \sqsubseteq w$ for every position w, and given the positions $w_1 = i.w'_1$ and $w_2 = j.w'_2$, $w_1 \sqsubseteq w_2$ iff $i < j$ or ($i = j$ and $w'_1 \sqsubseteq w'_2$). Obviously, in a practical implementation of our technique, the considered ordering among the terms should be chosen to agree with the ordering considered by flat/unflat transformations in the RWL infrastructure.

$$f^\alpha(b^\beta, f^\gamma(b^\delta, f^\epsilon(a^\zeta, c^\eta))) \rightarrow^*_{flat_B} f^{\alpha\gamma\epsilon}(a^\zeta, b^\beta, b^\delta, c^\eta) \rightarrow^*_{unflat_B}$$
$$f^{\alpha\gamma\epsilon}(f^{\alpha\gamma\epsilon}(b^\beta, c^\eta), f^{\alpha\gamma\epsilon}(a^\zeta, b^\delta))$$

Note that the original order between the two occurrences of the constant b is not changed by the flat/unflat transformations. For example, in the first term, b^β is in position 1 and b^δ is in position 2.1 with $1 \sqsubseteq 2.1$, whereas, in the last term, b^β is in position 1.1 and b^δ is in position 2.2 with $1.1 \sqsubseteq 2.2$.

Finally, note that the methodology described in this section can be easily extended to deal with other equational attributes, e.g., identity (U), by explicitly encoding the internal transformations performed via suitable rewrite rules.

Soundness of the backward trace slicing algorithm for the extended rewrite theories is established by the following theorem which properly extends Theorem 1. The proof of such an extension can be found in [1].

Theorem 2. *(extended soundness) Let $\mathcal{R} = (\Sigma, E, R)$ be an extended rewrite theory. Let $\mathcal{T}$ be an execution trace in the rewrite theory $\mathcal{R}$, and let $\mathcal{O}$ be a slicing criterion for $\mathcal{T}$. Let $\mathcal{T}^\bullet : t_0^\bullet \xrightarrow{r_1} t_1^\bullet \ldots \xrightarrow{r_n} t_n^\bullet$ be the corresponding trace slice w.r.t. $\mathcal{O}$. Then, for any concretization t_0' of $t_0^\bullet$, it holds that $\mathcal{T}' : t_0' \xrightarrow{r_1} t_1' \ldots \xrightarrow{r_n} t_n'$ is an execution trace in $\mathcal{R}$, and $t_i^\bullet \propto t_i'$, for $i = 1, \ldots, n$.*

6   Experimental Evaluation

We have developed a prototype implementation of our slicing methodology that is publicly available at `http://www.dsic.upv.es/~dromero/slicing.html`. The implementation is written in Maude and consists of approximately 800 lines of code. Maude is a high-performance, reflective language that supports both equational and rewriting logic programming, which is particularly suitable for developing domain-specific applications [12]. The reflection capabilities of Maude allow metalevel computations in RWL to be handled at the object-level. This facility allows us to easily manipulate computation traces of Maude itself and eliminate the irrelevant contents by implementing the backward slicing procedures that we have defined in this paper. Using reflection to implement the slicing tool has one important additional advantage, namely, the ability to quickly integrate the tool within the Maude formal tool environment [10], which is also developed using reflection.

In order to evaluate the usefulness of our approach, we benchmarked our prototype with several examples of Maude applications, namely: *War of Souls* (WoS), a role-playing game that is modeled as a nontrivial producer/consumer application; *Fault-Tolerant Communication Protocol* (FTCP), a Maude specification that models a fault-tolerant, client-server communication protocol; and Web-TLR, a software tool designed for model-checking real-size Web applications (e.g., Web-mailers, Electronic forums), which is based on rewriting logic.

We have tested our tool on some execution traces that were generated by the Maude applications described above by imposing different slicing criteria. For

Table 1. Summary of the reductions achieved

Example	Example trace	Original trace size	Slicing criterion	Sliced trace size	% reduction
WoS	WoS.$\mathcal{T}_1$	776	WoS.$\mathcal{T}_1.O_1$	201	74.10%
			WoS.$\mathcal{T}_1.O_2$	138	82.22%
	WoS.$\mathcal{T}_2$	997	WoS.$\mathcal{T}_2.O_1$	404	58.48%
			WoS.$\mathcal{T}_2.O_2$	174	82.55%
FTCP	FTCP.$\mathcal{T}_1$	2445	FTCP.$\mathcal{T}_1.O_1$	895	63.39%
			FTCP.$\mathcal{T}_1.O_2$	698	71.45%
	FTCP.$\mathcal{T}_2$	2369	FTCP.$\mathcal{T}_2.O_1$	364	84.63%
			FTCP.$\mathcal{T}_2.O_2$	707	70.16%
Web-TLR	Web-TLR.$\mathcal{T}_1$	31829	Web-TLR.$\mathcal{T}_1.O_1$	1949	93.88%
			Web-TLR.$\mathcal{T}_1.O_2$	1598	94.97%
	Web-TLR.$\mathcal{T}_2$	72098	Web-TLR.$\mathcal{T}_2.O_1$	9090	87.39%
			Web-TLR.$\mathcal{T}_2.O_2$	7119	90.13%

each application, we considered two execution traces that were sliced using two different criteria. As for the WoS example, we have chosen criteria that allow us to backtrace both the values produced and the entities in play — e.g., the criterion WoS.$\mathcal{T}_1.O_2$ isolates players' behaviors along the trace $\mathcal{T}_1$. Execution traces in the FTCP example represent client-server interactions. In this case, the chosen criteria aim at isolating a server and a client in a scenario that involves multiple servers and clients (FTCP.$\mathcal{T}_2.O_1$), and tracking the response generated by a server according to a given client request (FTCP.$\mathcal{T}_1.O_1$). In the last example, we have used Web-TLR to verify two LTL(R) properties of a Webmail application. The considered execution traces are much bigger for this program, and correspond to the counterexamples produced as outcome by the built-in model-checker of Web-TLR. In this case, the chosen criteria allow us to monitor the messages exchanged by the Web browsers and the Webmail server, as well as to focus our attention on the data structures of the interacting entities (e.g., browser/server sessions, server database).

Table 1 summarizes the results we achieved. For each criterion, Table 1 shows the size of the original trace and of the computed trace slice, both measures as the length of the corresponding string. The *%reduction* column shows the percentage of reduction achieved. These results are very encouraging, and show an impressive reduction rate (up to $\sim 95\%$). Actually, sometimes the trace slices are small enough to be easily inspected by the user, who can restrict her attention to the part of the computation she wants to observe getting rid of those data that are useless or even noisy w.r.t. the considered slicing criterion.

7   Conclusion and Related Work

We have presented a backward trace-slicing technique for rewriting logic theories. The key idea consists in tracing back —through the rewrite sequence— all the relevant symbols of the final state that we are interested in. Preliminary experiments demonstrate that the system works very satisfactorily on our benchmarks —e.g., we obtained trace slices that achieved a reduction of up to almost 95% in reasonable time (max. 0.5s on a Linux box equipped with an Intel Core 2 Duo 2.26GHz and 4Gb of RAM memory).

Tracing techniques have been extensively used in functional programming for implementing debugging tools [8]. For instance, Hat [8] is an interactive debugging system that enables exploring a computation backwards, starting from the program output or an error message (with which the computation aborted). Backward tracing in Hat is carried out by navigating a redex trail (that is, a graph-like data structure that records dependencies among function calls), whereas tracing in our approach does not require the construction of any auxiliary data structure.

Our backward tracing relation extends a previous tracing relation that was formalized in [6] for orthogonal TRSs. In [6], a label is formed from atomic labels by using the operations of sequence concatenation and underlining (e.g., a, b, ab, $\underline{abcd}$, are labels), which are used to keep track of the rule application order. Collapsing rules are simply avoided by coding them away. This is done by replacing each collapsing rule $\lambda \to x$ with the rule $\lambda \to \varepsilon(x)$, where ε is a unary dummy symbol. Then, in order to lift the rewrite relation to terms containing ϵ occurrences, infinitely many new extra-rules are added that are built by saturating all left-hand sides with $\varepsilon(x)$. In contrast to [6], we use a simpler notion of labeling, where composite labels are interpreted as sets of atomic labels, and in the case of collapsing as well as nonleft-linear rules we label the rewrite steps themselves so that we can deal with these rules in an effective way.

The work that is most closely related to ours is [13], which formalizes a notion of dynamic dependence among symbols by means of contexts and studies its application to program slicing of TRSs that may include collapsing as well as nonleft-linear rules. Both the *creating* and the *created* contexts associated with a reduction (i.e., the minimal subcontext that is needed to match the left-hand side of a rule and the minimal context that is "constructed" by the right-hand side of the rule, respectively) are tracked. Intuitively, these concepts are similar to our notions of redex and contractum patterns. The main differences with respect to our work are as follows. First, in [13] the slicing is given as a context, while we consider term slices. Second, the slice is obtained only on the first term of the sequence by the transitive and reflexive closure of the dependence relation, while we slice the whole execution trace, step by step. Obviously, their notion of slice is smaller, but we think that our approach can be more useful for trace analysis and program debugging. An extension of [6] is described in [18], which provides a generic definition of labeling that works not only for orthogonal TRSs as is the case of [6] but for the wider class of all left-linear TRSs. The nonleft-linear case is not handled by [18]. Specifically, [18] describes a methodology of static and dynamic tracing that is mainly based on the notion of *sample of a traced proof term* —i.e., a pair (μ, P) that records a rewrite step $\mu = s \to t$, and a set P of reachable positions in t from a set of observed positions in s. The tracing proceeds forward, while ours employs a backward strategy that is particularly convenient for error diagnosis and program debugging. Finally, [13] and [18] apply to TRSs whereas we deal with the richer framework of RWL that considers equations and equational axioms, namely rewriting modulo equational theories.

References

1. Alpuente, M., Ballis, D., Espert, J., Romero, D.: Backward trace slicing for RWL rewriting logic theories (Technical Report), http://hdl.handle.net/10251/10770
2. Alpuente, M., Ballis, D., Baggi, M., Falaschi, M.: A Fold/Unfold Transformation Framework for Rewrite Theories extended to CCT. In: Proc. PEPM 2010, pp. 43–52. ACM, New York (2010)
3. Alpuente, M., Ballis, D., Espert, J., Romero, D.: Model-Checking Web Applications with WEB-TLR. In: Bouajjani, A., Chin, W.-N. (eds.) ATVA 2010. LNCS, vol. 6252, pp. 341–346. Springer, Heidelberg (2010)
4. Alpuente, M., Ballis, D., Romero, D.: Specification and Verification of Web Applications in Rewriting Logic. In: Cavalcanti, A., Dams, D.R. (eds.) FM 2009. LNCS, vol. 5850, pp. 790–805. Springer, Heidelberg (2009)
5. Baggi, M., Ballis, D., Falaschi, M.: Quantitative pathway logic for computational biology. In: Degano, P., Gorrieri, R. (eds.) CMSB 2009. LNCS, vol. 5688, pp. 68–82. Springer, Heidelberg (2009)
6. Bethke, I., Klop, J.W., de Vrijer, R.: Descendants and origins in term rewriting. Inf. Comput. 159(1-2), 59–124 (2000)
7. Chen, F., Roşu, G.: Parametric trace slicing and monitoring. In: Kowalewski, S., Philippou, A. (eds.) TACAS 2009. LNCS, vol. 5505, pp. 246–261. Springer, Heidelberg (2009)
8. Chitil, O., Runciman, C., Wallace, M.: Freja, hat and hood - a comparative evaluation of three systems for tracing and debugging lazy functional programs. In: Mohnen, M., Koopman, P. (eds.) IFL 2000. LNCS, vol. 2011, pp. 176–193. Springer, Heidelberg (2001)
9. Clavel, M., Durán, F., Eker, S., Lincoln, P., Martí-Oliet, N., Bevilacqua, V., Talcott, C.: All About Maude - A High-Performance Logical Framework. LNCS, vol. 4350. Springer, Heidelberg (2007)
10. Clavel, M., Durán, F., Hendrix, J., Lucas, S., Bevilacqua, V., Ölveczky, P.C.: The Maude Formal Tool Environment. In: Mossakowski, T., Montanari, U., Haveraaen, M. (eds.) CALCO 2007. LNCS, vol. 4624, pp. 173–178. Springer, Heidelberg (2007)
11. Eker, S.: Associative-Commutative Rewriting on Large Terms. In: Nieuwenhuis, R. (ed.) RTA 2003. LNCS, vol. 2706, pp. 14–29. Springer, Heidelberg (2003)
12. Eker, S., Bevilacqua, V., Sridharanarayanan, A.: The maude LTL model checker and its implementation. In: Ball, T., Rajamani, S.K. (eds.) SPIN 2003. LNCS, vol. 2648, pp. 230–234. Springer, Heidelberg (2003)
13. Field, J., Tip, F.: Dynamic dependence in term rewriting systems and its application to program slicing. In: Penjam, J. (ed.) PLILP 1994. LNCS, vol. 844, pp. 415–431. Springer, Heidelberg (1994)
14. Martí-Oliet, N., Meseguer, J.: Rewriting Logic: Roadmap and Bibliography. Theoretical Computer Science 285(2), 121–154 (2002)
15. Riesco, A., Verdejo, A., Martí-Oliet, N.: Declarative Debugging of Missing Answers for Maude Specifications. In: Proc. RTA 2010, LIPIcs, vol. 6, pp. 277–294 (2010)
16. Rosu, G., Havelund, K.: Rewriting-Based Techniques for Runtime Verification. Autom. Softw. Eng. 12(2), 151–197 (2005)
17. Talcott, C.: Pathway logic. Formal Methods for Computational Systems Biology 5016, 21–53 (2008)
18. TeReSe (ed.): Term Rewriting Systems. Cambridge University Press, Cambridge (2003)

Deciding Security for Protocols with Recursive Tests[*]

Mathilde Arnaud[1,2], Véronique Cortier[2], and Stéphanie Delaune[1]

[1] LSV, ENS Cachan & CNRS & INRIA Saclay Île-de-France, France
[2] LORIA, CNRS, France

Abstract. Security protocols aim at securing communications over public networks. Their design is notoriously difficult and error-prone. Formal methods have shown their usefulness for providing a careful security analysis in the case of standard authentication and confidentiality protocols. However, most current techniques do not apply to protocols that perform recursive computation *e.g.* on a list of messages received from the network.

While considering general recursive input/output actions very quickly yields undecidability, we focus on protocols that perform *recursive tests* on received messages but output messages that depend on the inputs in a standard way. This is in particular the case of secured routing protocols, distributed right delegation or PKI certification paths. We provide NPTIME decision procedures for protocols with recursive tests and for a bounded number of sessions. We also revisit constraint system solving, providing a complete symbolic representation of the attacker knowledge.

1 Introduction

Security protocols are communication programs that aim at securing communications over public channels like the Internet. It has been recognized that designing a secure protocol is a difficult and error-prone task. Indeed, protocols are very sensitive to small changes in their description and many protocols have been shown to be flawed several years after their publication (and deployment). Formal methods have been successfully applied to the analysis of security protocols, yielding the discovery of new attacks like the famous man-in-the-middle attack in the Needham-Schroeder public key protocol [17] or, more recently, a flaw in Gmail [4]. Many decision procedures have been proposed (*e.g.* [18,20]) and efficient tools have been designed such as ProVerif [8] and AVISPA [3].

While formal methods have been successful in the treatment of security protocols using standard primitives like encryption and signatures, there are much fewer results for protocols with recursive primitives, that is, primitives that involve iterative or recursive operations. For example, in group protocols, the server

---

[*] This work has been partially supported by the project ANR-07-SESU-002 AVOTÉ. The research leading to these results has also received funding from the European Research Council under the European Union's Seventh Framework Programme (FP7/2007-2013) / ERC grant agreement number 258865 (ERC ProSecure project).

N. Bjørner and V. Sofronie-Stokkermans (Eds.): CADE 2011, LNAI 6803, pp. 49–63, 2011.

or the leader typically has to process a request that contains the contributions of each different agent in the group and these contributions are used to compute a common shared key (see *e.g.* the Asokan-Ginzboorg group protocol [6]). Secured versions of routing protocols [9,14,12] also require the nodes (typically the node originating the request) to check the validity of the route they receive. This is usually performed by checking that each node has properly signed (or MACed) some part of the route, the whole incoming message forming a chain where each component is a contribution from a node in the path. Other examples of protocols performing recursive operations are certification paths for public keys (see *e.g.* X.509 certification paths [13]) and right delegation in distributed systems [7].

Recursive operations may yield complex computations. Therefore it is difficult to check the security of protocols with recursive primitives and very few decision procedures have been proposed for recursive protocols. One of the first decidability results [16] holds when the recursive operation can be modeled using tree transducers, which forbids any equality test and also forbids composed keys and chained lists. In [21] recursive computation is modeled using Horn clauses and an NEXPTIME procedure is proposed. This is extended in [15] to include the Exclusive Or operator. This approach however does not allow composed keys nor list mapping (where the same operation, *e.g.* signing, is applied to each element of the list). To circumvent these restrictions, another procedure has been proposed [10] to handle list mapping provided that each element of the list is properly tagged. No complexity bound is provided. All these results hold for rather limited classes of recursive operations (on lists of terms). This is due to the fact that even a single input/output step of a protocol may reveal complex information, as soon as it involves a recursive computation. Consequently, recursive primitives very quickly yield undecidability [16].

Our contributions. The originality of our approach consists in considering protocols that perform standard input/output actions (modeled using usual pattern matching) but that are allowed to perform *recursive tests* such as checking the validity of a route or the validity of a chain of certificates. Indeed, several families of protocols use recursivity only for performing sanity checks at some steps of the protocol. This is in particular the case of secured routing protocols, distributed right delegation, and PKI certification paths.

For checking security of protocols with recursive tests (for a bounded number of sessions), we reuse the setting of constraint systems [18,11] and add tests of membership to recursive languages. As a first contribution, we revisit the procedure of [11] for solving constraint systems and obtain a complete symbolic representation of the knowledge of the attacker, in the spirit of the characterization obtained in [1] in the passive case (with no active attacker). This result holds for general constraint systems and is of independent interest.

Our second contribution is the proposition of (NPTIME) decision procedures for two classes of recursive languages (used for tests): *link-based recursive languages* and *mapping-based languages*. A link-based recursive language contains chains of links where consecutive links have to satisfy a given relation. A typical example is X.509 public key certificates [13] that consist in a chain of signatures of the form: $[\llbracket \langle A_1, \mathsf{pub}(A_1) \rangle \rrbracket_{\mathsf{sk}(A_2)}; \llbracket \langle A_2, \mathsf{pub}(A_2) \rangle \rrbracket_{\mathsf{sk}(A_3)}; \cdots ; \llbracket \langle A_n, \mathsf{pub}(A_n) \rangle \rrbracket_{\mathsf{sk}(S)}]$. The purpose of this chain is to authenticate the public key of A_1. The chain begins with the certificate $\llbracket \langle A_1, \mathsf{pub}(A_1) \rangle \rrbracket_{\mathsf{sk}(A_2)}$, and each certificate in the chain is signed by the entity identified by the next certificate in the chain. The chain terminates with a certificate signed by a trusted party S.

A mapping-based language contains lists that are based on a list of names (typically names of agents involved in the protocol session) and are uniquely defined by it. Typical examples can be found in the context of routing protocols, when nodes check for the validity of the route. For example, in the SMNDP protocol [12], a route from the source A_0 to the destination A_n is represented by a list $l_{route} = [A_n; \ldots; A_1]$. This list is accepted by the source node A_0 only if the received message is of the form:

$$[\llbracket \langle A_n, A_0, l_{route} \rangle \rrbracket_{\mathsf{sk}(A_1)}; \llbracket \langle A_n, A_0, l_{route} \rangle \rrbracket_{\mathsf{sk}(A_2)}; \ldots ; \llbracket \langle A_n, A_0, l_{route} \rangle \rrbracket_{\mathsf{sk}(A_n)}].$$

Note that a link $\llbracket \langle A_n, A_0, l_{route} \rangle \rrbracket_{\mathsf{sk}(A_i)}$ both depends on the list l_{route} and on its i-th element.

For each of these two languages, we show that it is possible to bound the size of a minimal attack (bounding in particular the size of the lists used in membership tests), relying on the new characterization we have obtained for solutions of constraint systems. As a consequence, we obtained two new NP decision procedures for two classes of languages that encompass most of the recursive tests involved in secured routing protocols and chain certificates. We illustrate our results with several examples of relevant recursive languages. Detailed proofs of our results can be found in [5].

2 Models for Security Protocols

2.1 Messages

As usual, messages are represented using a term algebra. We consider the *sorted signature* $\mathcal{F} = \{\mathsf{senc}, \mathsf{aenc}, \llbracket \_ \rrbracket \_, \langle \_, \_ \rangle, \mathsf{h}, ::, [], \mathsf{pub}, \mathsf{priv}, \mathsf{vk}, \mathsf{sk}\}$ with corresponding arities:

- $ar(\mathsf{f}) = \mathsf{Msg} \times \mathsf{Msg} \to \mathsf{Msg}$ for $\mathsf{f} \in \{\mathsf{senc}, \mathsf{aenc}, \llbracket \_ \rrbracket \_, \langle \_, \_ \rangle\}$,
- $ar(\mathsf{h}) = \mathsf{Msg} \to \mathsf{Msg}$,
- $ar(::) = \mathsf{Msg} \times \mathsf{List} \to \mathsf{List}$, and $ar([]) = \mathsf{List}$,
- $ar(\mathsf{f}) = \mathsf{Base} \to \mathsf{Msg}$ for $\mathsf{f} \in \mathcal{F}_s = \{\mathsf{pub}, \mathsf{priv}, \mathsf{vk}, \mathsf{sk}\}$.

The sort Msg is a supersort of List and Base. The symbol $\langle\rangle$ represents the pairing function, $::$ is the list constructor, and $[]$ represents the empty list. For the sake of clarity, we write $\langle u_1, u_2, u_3 \rangle$ for the term $\langle u_1, \langle u_2, u_3 \rangle \rangle$, and $[u_1; u_2; u_3]$ for $u_1::(u_2::(u_3::[]))$. The terms $\mathsf{pub}(A)$ and $\mathsf{priv}(A)$ represent respectively the public and private keys associated to an agent A, whereas the terms $\mathsf{sk}(A)$ and $\mathsf{vk}(A)$ represent respectively the signature and verification keys associated to an agent A. The function symbol senc (resp. aenc) is used to model symmetric (resp.

asymmetric) encryption whereas the term $[\![m]\!]_{\mathsf{sk}(A)}$ represents the message m signed by the agent A.

We consider an infinite set of *names* $\mathcal{N} = \{Rep, Req, N, K, A, S, D, Id \ldots\}$ having Base sort. These names typically represent constants, nonces, symmetric keys, or agent names. Moreover, we assume that we have three disjoint infinite sets of variables, one for each sort, denoted $\mathcal{X}_{\mathsf{Base}}$, $\mathcal{X}_{\mathsf{List}}$, and $\mathcal{X}_{\mathsf{Msg}}$ respectively. We write $vars(u)$ for the set of variables occurring in u. A term is *ground* if it has no variables.

We write $st(u)$ for the set of *subterms* of a term u. This notion is extended as expected to sets of terms. *Substitutions* are written $\sigma = \{x_1 \mapsto t_1, \ldots, x_n \mapsto t_n\}$ with $dom(\sigma) = \{x_1, \ldots, x_n\}$. They are assumed to be well-sorted substitutions, that is the sort of each x_i is a supersort of the sort of t_i. Such a substitution σ is *ground* if all the t_i are ground terms. The application of a substitution σ to a term u is written $u\sigma$. A most general unifier of terms u_1 and u_2 is a substitution (when it exists) denoted by $mgu(u_1, u_2)$.

2.2   Intruder Capabiblities

The ability of the intruder is modeled by a deduction system described below and corresponds to the usual rules representing attacker abilities (often called Dolev-Yao rules).

$$\frac{u_1 \quad \cdots \quad u_n}{\mathsf{f}(u_1, \ldots, u_n)}\ \mathsf{f} \in \mathcal{F} \smallsetminus \mathcal{F}_s \qquad \frac{\langle u_1, u_2 \rangle}{u_i}\ i \in \{1,2\} \qquad \frac{u_1 :: u_2}{u_i}\ i \in \{1,2\}$$

$$\frac{\mathsf{senc}(u_1, u_2) \quad u_2}{u_1} \qquad \frac{\mathsf{aenc}(u_1, \mathsf{pub}(u_2)) \quad \mathsf{priv}(u_2)}{u_1} \qquad \frac{[\![u_1]\!]_{\mathsf{sk}(u_2)}}{u_1}\ \textit{(optional)}$$

The first inference rule describes the *composition rules*. The remaining inference rules describe the *decomposition* rules. Intuitively, these deduction rules say that an intruder can compose messages by pairing, building lists, encrypting and signing messages provided he has the corresponding keys. Conversely, he can retrieve the components of a pair or a list, and he can also decompose messages by decrypting provided he has the decryption keys. For signatures, the intruder is also able to *verify* whether a signature $[\![m]\!]_{\mathsf{sk}(a)}$ and a message m match (provided he has the verification key $\mathsf{vk}(a)$), but this does not give him any new message. That is why this capability is not represented in the deduction system. We also consider an optional rule that expresses that an intruder can retrieve the whole message from its signature. This property may or may not hold depending on the signature scheme, and that is why this rule is optional. Our results hold in both cases (that is, when the deduction relation $\vdash$ is defined with or without this rule).

A term u is *deducible* from a set of terms T, denoted by $T \vdash u$, if there exists a *proof*, *i.e.* a tree such that the root is labelled with u, the leaves are labelled with $v \in T$ and every intermediate node is an instance of one of the rules of the deduction system.

2.3 Constraint Systems

Constraint systems are quite common (see *e.g.* [11,18]) in modeling security protocols. A constraint system represents in a symbolic and compact way which trace instances of a protocol are possible once an interleaving of actions has been fixed. They are used, for instance, to specify secrecy preservation of security protocols under a particular, finite scenario. Note that, even if the scenario is fixed, there are still many (actually infinitely many) possible instances of it, because the intruder may affect the content of the messages by intercepting sent messages and forging received messages. The behaviour of the attacker is taken into account relying on the inference system presented in Section 2.2. To enforce the intruder capabilities, we also assume he knows an infinite set of names $\mathcal{I}$ that he might use at his will to mount attacks.

Definition 1 (constraint system). *A* constraint system *is a pair* $(\mathcal{C},\mathcal{I})$ *such that* $\mathcal{I}$ *is a non empty (and possibly infinite) set of names, and* $\mathcal{C}$ *is either* $\perp$ *or a finite conjunction* $\bigwedge_{i=1}^{n} T_i \Vdash u_i$ *of expressions called* deducibility constraints, *where each* T_i *is a finite set of terms, called the* left-hand side *of the constraint and each* u_i *is a term, called the* right-hand side *of the constraint, such that:*

- $T_i \subseteq T_{i+1}$ *for every* i *such that* $1 \leq i < n$;
- *if* $x \in vars(T_i)$ *for some* i *then there exists* $j < i$ *such that* $x \in vars(u_j)$.

Moreover, we assume that $st(\mathcal{C}) \cap \mathcal{I} = \emptyset$.

The second condition in Definition 1 says that each time a new variable is introduced, it first occurs in some right-hand side. The left-hand side of a constraint system usually represents the messages sent on the network, while the right-hand side represents the message expected by the party.

Definition 2 (non-confusing solution). *Let* $(\mathcal{C},\mathcal{I})$ *be a constraint system where* $\mathcal{C} = \bigwedge_{i=1}^{n} T_i \Vdash u_i$. *A* solution *of* $(\mathcal{C},\mathcal{I})$ *is a ground substitution* θ *whose domain is* $vars(\mathcal{C})$ *such that* $T_i\theta \cup \mathcal{I} \vdash u_i\theta$ *for every* $i \in \{1,\ldots,n\}$. *The empty constraint system is always satisfiable whereas* $(\perp,\mathcal{I})$ *denotes an unsatisfiable constraint system. Furthermore, we say that* θ *is* non-confusing *for* $(\mathcal{C},\mathcal{I})$ *if* $t_1 = t_2$ *for any* $t_1, t_2 \in st(T_n)$ *such that* $t_1\theta = t_2\theta$.

In other words, non-confusing solutions do not map two distinct subterms of a left-hand side of the constraint system to the same term. Later on, we will show that we can restrict ourselves to consider this particular case of solutions.

Constraint systems model protocols that perform pattern matching only. In particular, deducibility constraints cannot ensure that some message is a valid chain of certificates since this cannot be checked using a pattern. Therefore, we extend constraint systems with *language constraints* of the form $u \in \mathcal{L}$ where $\mathcal{L}$ can be any language, that is, any set of terms. In particular, $\mathcal{L}$ will typically be a recursively defined set of terms. We provide in Sections 4 and 5 several examples of classes of recursive languages but for the moment $\mathcal{L}$ can be left unspecified.

Definition 3 (language constraint). *Let $\mathcal{L}$ be a language (i.e. a set of terms). An $\mathcal{L}$-language constraint associated to some constraint system $(\mathcal{C}, \mathcal{I})$ is an expression of the form $u_1 \in \mathcal{L} \wedge \ldots \wedge u_k \in \mathcal{L}$ where each u_i is a term such that $vars(u_i) \subseteq vars(\mathcal{C})$ and $st(u_i) \cap \mathcal{I} = \emptyset$.*

A solution of a constraint system $(\mathcal{C}, \mathcal{I})$ and of an $\mathcal{L}$-language constraint $\phi = u_1 \in \mathcal{L} \wedge \ldots \wedge u_k \in \mathcal{L}$ is a ground substitution θ such that θ is a solution of $(\mathcal{C}, \mathcal{I})$ and $u_i \theta \in \mathcal{L}$ for any $1 \leq i \leq k$. We denote $st(\phi) = \{st(u_i) \mid 1 \leq i \leq k\}$.

2.4   Example: the **SMNDP** Protocol

The aim of the SMNDP protocol [12] is to find a path from a source node S towards a destination node D. Actually, nodes broadcast the route request to their neighbors, adding their name to the current path. When the request reaches the destination, D signs the route and sends the reply back over the network.

More formally, if D receives a request message of the form $\langle Req, S, D, Id, l \rangle$, where Id is a name (the identifier of the request) and l is the path built during the request phase, D will compute the signature $s_0 = [\![\langle D, S, D::l \rangle]\!]_{\mathsf{sk}(D)}$ and send back the reply $\langle Rep, D, S, D::l, [s_0] \rangle$. All nodes along the route then have to certify the route by adding their own signature. More precisely, during the reply phase, an intermediate node A_i receiving a message of the form $\langle Rep, D, S, l_{route}, [s_{i-1}, \ldots, s_0] \rangle$ would compute $s_i = [\![\langle D, S, l_{route} \rangle]\!]_{\mathsf{sk}(A_i)}$ and send the message $\langle Rep, D, S, l_{route}, [s_i, \ldots, s_0] \rangle$. The list of signatures expected by S built over the list $l_{route} = [D, A_1, \ldots, A_n]$ is the list $l_{sign} = [s_n, \ldots, s_0]$ where $s_0 = [\![\langle D, S, l_{route} \rangle]\!]_{\mathsf{sk}(D)}$ and $s_i = [\![\langle D, S, l_{route} \rangle]\!]_{\mathsf{sk}(A_i)}$ for $1 \leq i \leq n$. We will denote by $\mathcal{L}_{\mathsf{SMNDP}}$ the set of messages of the form $\langle \langle S, D \rangle, \langle l_{route}, l_{sign} \rangle \rangle$.

Consider the following network configuration, where S is the source node, D is the destination node, X is an intermediate (honest) node, W is a node who has been compromised (*i.e.* the intruder knows the secret key $\mathsf{sk}(W)$), and I is a malicious node, *i.e.* a node controlled by the intruder.

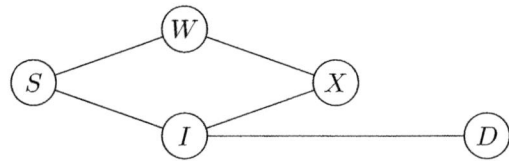

An execution of the protocol where D is ready to answer a request and the source is ready to input the final message can be represented by the following constraint system:

$$\mathcal{C} = \left\{ \begin{array}{l} T_0 \cup \{u_0, u_1\} \Vdash v_1 \\ T_0 \cup \{u_0, u_1, u_2\} \Vdash v_2 \end{array} \right.$$

with $T_0 = \{S, D, X, I, W, \mathsf{sk}(I), \mathsf{sk}(W)\}$ the initial knowledge of the intruder
$u_0 = \langle Req, S, D, Id, [] \rangle$,
$u_1 = \langle Req, S, D, Id, [X, W] \rangle$,
$u_2 = \langle Rep, D, S, D{::}x_l, [[\langle D, S, D{::}x_l \rangle]_{\mathsf{sk}(D)}] \rangle$,
$v_1 = \langle Req, S, D, x_{id}, x_l \rangle$,
$v_2 = \langle Rep, D, S, D{::}x_{route}, x_{sign} \rangle$

Let $\mathcal{I}$ be a non-empty set of names such that $st(\mathcal{C}) \cap \mathcal{I} = \emptyset$. We have that $(\mathcal{C}, \mathcal{I})$ is a constraint system. A solution to $(\mathcal{C}, \mathcal{I}) \wedge \langle \langle S, D \rangle, \langle D{::}x_{route}, x_{sign} \rangle \rangle \in \mathcal{L}_{\mathsf{SMNDP}}$ is e.g. the substitution $\theta = \{x_{id} \mapsto Id, x_l \mapsto [I; W], x_{route} \mapsto [I; W], x_{sign} \mapsto l_{sign}\}$ where:

- $l_{route} = [D, I, W]$, and
- $l_{sign} = [[\langle D, S, l_{route} \rangle]_{\mathsf{sk}(W)}; [\langle D, S, l_{route} \rangle]_{\mathsf{sk}(I)}; [\langle D, S, l_{route} \rangle]_{\mathsf{sk}(D)}]$.

This solution reflects an attack (discovered in [2]) where the attacker sends to the destination node D the message $\langle Req, S, D, Id, l \rangle$ with a false list $l = [I, W]$. Then D answers accordingly by $\langle Rep, D, S, l_{route}, [[\langle D, S, l_{route} \rangle]_{\mathsf{sk}(D)}] \rangle$. The intruder concludes the attack by sending to S the message $\langle Rep, D, S, l_{route}, l_{sign} \rangle$. This yields S accepting W, I, D as a route to D, while it is not a valid route.

3   Constraint Solving Procedure

As a first contribution, we provide a complete symbolic representation of the attacker knowledge, in the spirit of the characterization obtained in [1] in the passive case (that is, when the intruder only eavesdrops on the messages exchanged during the protocol execution). Revisiting the constraint solving procedure proposed in [11], we show that it is possible to compute a finite set $(\mathcal{C}_1, \mathcal{I}), \ldots, (\mathcal{C}_n, \mathcal{I})$ of solved forms whose solutions represent all the solutions of $(\mathcal{C}, \mathcal{I})$. This first result is an easy adaptation of the proof techniques of [11] to our richer term algebra. More importantly, we show that it is sufficient to consider the solutions of $(\mathcal{C}_i, \mathcal{I})$ that are obtained by applying composition rules only.

3.1   Simplification Rules

Our procedure is based on a set of simplification rules allowing a general constraint system to be reduced to some simpler ones, called *solved*, on which satisfiability can be easily decided. A constraint system $(\mathcal{C}, \mathcal{I})$ is said to be solved if $\mathcal{C} \neq \bot$ and if each of its constraints is of the form $T \Vdash x$, where x is a variable. Note that the empty constraint system is solved. Solved constraint systems are particularly simple since they always have a solution. Indeed, let $N_0 \in \mathcal{I}$, the substitution τ defined by $x\tau = N_0$ for every variable x is a solution since $T\tau \cup \mathcal{I} \vdash x\tau$ for any constraint $T \Vdash x$ of the solved constraint system.

The *simplification rules* we consider are the following ones:

R_{ax} : $(\mathcal{C} \wedge T \Vdash u, \mathcal{I}) \rightsquigarrow (\mathcal{C}, \mathcal{I})$ if $T \cup \{x \mid T' \Vdash x \in \mathcal{C}, T' \subsetneq T\} \vdash u$

R_{unif} : $(\mathcal{C} \wedge T \Vdash u, \mathcal{I}) \rightsquigarrow_\sigma (\mathcal{C}\sigma \wedge T\sigma \Vdash u\sigma, \mathcal{I})$ if $\sigma = mgu(t_1, t_2)$
      where $t_1 \in st(T)$, $t_2 \in st(T \cup \{u\})$, and $t_1 \neq t_2$

R_{fail} : $(\mathcal{C} \wedge T \Vdash u, \mathcal{I}) \rightsquigarrow (\bot, \mathcal{I})$ if $vars(T \cup \{u\}) = \emptyset$ and $T \nvdash u$

R_f : $(\mathcal{C} \wedge T \Vdash f(u, v), \mathcal{I}) \rightsquigarrow (\mathcal{C} \wedge T \Vdash u \wedge T \Vdash v, \mathcal{I})$ for $f \in \mathcal{F} \setminus \mathcal{F}_s$

All the rules are indexed by a substitution (when there is no index then the identity substitution is implicitly considered). We write $(\mathcal{C}, \mathcal{I}) \rightsquigarrow_\sigma^* (\mathcal{C}', \mathcal{I})$ if there are $\mathcal{C}_1, \ldots, \mathcal{C}_n$ such that $(\mathcal{C}, \mathcal{I}) \rightsquigarrow_{\sigma_0} (\mathcal{C}_1, \mathcal{I}) \rightsquigarrow_{\sigma_1} \ldots \rightsquigarrow_{\sigma_n} (\mathcal{C}', \mathcal{I})$ and $\sigma = \sigma_n \circ \cdots \circ \sigma_1 \circ \sigma_0$. Our rules are similar to those in [11] except for the rule R_{unif}. We authorize unification with a subterm of u and also with variables.

Soundness and termination are still ensured by [11]. To ensure termination in polynomial time, we consider the strategy $\mathcal{S}$ that consists of applying R_{fail} as soon as possible, R_{unif} and then R_f, beginning with the constraint having the largest right hand side. Lastly, we apply R_{ax} on the remaining constraints. We show that these rules form a complete decision procedure.

Theorem 1. *Let $(\mathcal{C}, \mathcal{I})$ be a constraint system. We have that:*

- *Soundness: If $(\mathcal{C}, \mathcal{I}) \rightsquigarrow_\sigma^* (\mathcal{C}', \mathcal{I})$ for some constraint system $(\mathcal{C}', \mathcal{I})$ and some substitution σ and if θ is a solution of $(\mathcal{C}', \mathcal{I})$ then $\theta \circ \sigma$ is a solution of $(\mathcal{C}, \mathcal{I})$.*
- *Completeness: If θ is a solution of $(\mathcal{C}, \mathcal{I})$, then there exist a constraint system $(\mathcal{C}', \mathcal{I})$ in solved form and substitutions σ, θ' such that $\theta = \theta' \circ \sigma$, $(\mathcal{C}, \mathcal{I}) \rightsquigarrow_\sigma^* (\mathcal{C}', \mathcal{I})$ following the strategy $\mathcal{S}$, and θ' is a non-confusing solution of $(\mathcal{C}', \mathcal{I})$.*
- *Termination: If $(\mathcal{C}, \mathcal{I}) \rightsquigarrow_\sigma^n (\mathcal{C}', \mathcal{I})$ following the strategy $\mathcal{S}$, then n is polynomially bounded in the size of $\mathcal{C}$. Moreover, the number of subterms of $\mathcal{C}'$ is smaller than the number of subterms of $\mathcal{C}$.*

Example 1. Consider our former example of a constraint system (see Section 2.4), we can simplify the constraint system $(\mathcal{C}, \mathcal{I})$ following strategy $\mathcal{S}$:

- R_{unif}: $(\mathcal{C}, \mathcal{I}) \rightsquigarrow_\sigma (\mathcal{C}_1, \mathcal{I})$ with $\mathcal{C}_1 = \mathcal{C}\sigma$ where $\sigma = \{x_{id} \mapsto Id\}$,
- R_f: $(\mathcal{C}_1, \mathcal{I}) \rightsquigarrow^* (\mathcal{C}_2, \mathcal{I})$ with

$$\mathcal{C}_2 = \begin{cases} T_0 \cup \{u_0\sigma, u_1\sigma\} \Vdash Req & \wedge & T_0 \cup \{u_0\sigma, u_1\sigma, u_2\sigma\} \Vdash Rep & \wedge \\ T_0 \cup \{u_0\sigma, u_1\sigma\} \Vdash S & \wedge & T_0 \cup \{u_0\sigma, u_1\sigma, u_2\sigma\} \Vdash D & \wedge \\ T_0 \cup \{u_0\sigma, u_1\sigma\} \Vdash D & \wedge & T_0 \cup \{u_0\sigma, u_1\sigma, u_2\sigma\} \Vdash S & \wedge \\ T_0 \cup \{u_0\sigma, u_1\sigma\} \Vdash Id & \wedge & T_0 \cup \{u_0\sigma, u_1\sigma, u_2\sigma\} \Vdash x_{route} & \wedge \\ T_0 \cup \{u_0\sigma, u_1\sigma\} \Vdash x_l & \wedge & T_0 \cup \{u_0\sigma, u_1\sigma, u_2\sigma\} \Vdash x_{sign} \end{cases}$$

- R_{ax}: $(\mathcal{C}_2, \mathcal{I}) \rightsquigarrow^* (\mathcal{C}', \mathcal{I})$ with

$$\mathcal{C}' = \begin{cases} T_0 \cup \{u_0\sigma, u_1\sigma\} \Vdash x_l & \wedge & T_0 \cup \{u_0\sigma, u_1\sigma, u_2\sigma\} \Vdash x_{route} \\ & \wedge & T_0 \cup \{u_0\sigma, u_1\sigma, u_2\sigma\} \Vdash x_{sign} \end{cases}$$

The constraint system $(\mathcal{C}', \mathcal{I})$ is in solved form, and we have that $\theta = \theta' \circ \sigma$ where $\theta' = \{x_l \mapsto [I; W], x_{route} \mapsto [I; W], x_{sign} \mapsto l_{sign}\}$ is a non-confusing solution of $(\mathcal{C}', \mathcal{I})$.

Compared to [11], we prove in addition that on the resulting solved constraint systems, we can restrict our attention to non-confusing solutions. Intuitively, we exploit the transformation rules such that any possible equality between subterms has already been guessed, thus ensuring that two distinct subterms do not map to the same term. Interestingly, non-confusing solutions of a solved constraint system enjoy a nice characterization.

3.2   A Basis for Deducible Terms

We show that, for any non-confusing solution, any term deducible from the attacker knowledge may be obtained by composition only.

We first associate to each set of terms T the set of subterms of T that may be deduced from $T \cup vars(T)$. Note that on solved constraint systems, these variables are indeed deducible.

$$Sat_v(T) = \{u \in st(T) \mid T \cup vars(T) \vdash u\}$$

Proposition 1. *Let $(\mathcal{C}, \mathcal{I})$ be a constraint system in solved form, θ be a non-confusing solution of $(\mathcal{C}, \mathcal{I})$, T be a left-hand side of a constraint in $\mathcal{C}$ and u be a term such that $T\theta \cup \mathcal{I} \vdash u$. We have that $Sat_v(T)\theta \cup \mathcal{I} \vdash u$ by using composition rules only.*

Proposition 1 states that it is possible to compute from a solved constraint system, a "basis" $Sat_v(T)$ from which all deducible terms can be obtained applying only composition rules. This follows the spirit of [1] but now in the active case.

This characterization is crucial in the remaining of the paper, when considering recursive tests. More generally, we believe that this characterization provides more modularity and could be useful when considering other properties such as checking the validity of a route or authentication properties.

We will also use the notion of *constructive solution* on constraint systems in solved form, which is weaker than the notion of non-confusing solution.

Definition 4 (constructive solution). *Let $(\mathcal{C}, \mathcal{I})$ be a constraint system in solved form. A substitution θ is a* constructive solution *of $(\mathcal{C}, \mathcal{I})$ if for every deducibility constraint $T \Vdash x$ in $\mathcal{C}$, we have that $Sat_v(T)\theta \cup \mathcal{I} \vdash x\theta$ using composition rules only.*

A non-confusing solution of a solved system is a constructive solution, while the converse does not always hold. This notion will be used in proofs as we will transform solutions, preserving the constructive property but not the non-confusing property.

4   Link-Based Recursive Languages

A chain of certificates is typically formed by a list of links such that consecutive links follow a certain relation. For example, the chain of public key certificates

$[[\![\langle A_1, \mathsf{pub}(A_1)\rangle]\!]_{\mathsf{sk}(A_2)}; [\![\langle A_2, \mathsf{pub}(A_2)\rangle]\!]_{\mathsf{sk}(A_3)}; [\![\langle A_3, \mathsf{pub}(A_3)\rangle]\!]_{\mathsf{sk}(S)}]$ is based on the link $[\![\langle x, \mathsf{pub}(y)\rangle]\!]_{\mathsf{sk}(z)}$, and the names occurring in two consecutive links have to satisfy a certain relation. We provide a generic definition that captures such link-based recursive language.

Definition 5 (link-based recursive language). *Let* m *be a term built over variables of sort* Base. *A* link-based recursive language $\mathcal{L}$ *is defined by three terms* w_0, w_1, w_2 *of sort* List *such that* $w_0 = [\mathsf{m}\theta_0^1; \ldots; \mathsf{m}\theta_0^{k_0}]$, $w_i = \mathsf{m}\theta_i^1 :: \ldots :: \mathsf{m}\theta_i^{k_i} :: x^{\mathsf{m}}$ *for* $i = 1, 2$, *and* w_2 *is a strict subterm of* w_1.

Once w_0, w_1, w_2 *are given, the language is recursively defined as follows. A ground term* t *belongs to the language* $\mathcal{L}$ *if either* $t = w_0\sigma$ *for some* σ, *or there exists* σ *such that* $t = w_1\sigma$, *and* $w_2\sigma \in \mathcal{L}$.

Intuitively, w_0 is the basic valid chain while w_1 encodes the desired dependence between the links and w_2 allows for a recursive call.

Example 2. As defined in [13], X.509 public key certificates consist in chains of signatures of the form:

$$[[\![\langle A_1, \mathsf{pub}(A_1)\rangle]\!]_{\mathsf{sk}(A_2)}; [\![\langle A_2, \mathsf{pub}(A_2)\rangle]\!]_{\mathsf{sk}(A_3)}; \cdots ; [\![\langle A_n, \mathsf{pub}(A_n)\rangle]\!]_{\mathsf{sk}(S)}]$$

where S is some trusted server and each agent A_{i+1} certifies the public key $\mathsf{pub}(A_i)$ of agent A_i. These chained lists are all built from the term $\mathsf{m} = [\![\langle x, \mathsf{pub}(y)\rangle]\!]_{\mathsf{sk}(z)}$ with $x, y, z \in \mathcal{X}_{\mathsf{Base}}$. The set of valid chains of signatures can be formally expressed as the m-link-based recursive language $\mathcal{L}_{\mathsf{cert}}$ defined by:

$$\begin{cases} w_0 = [[\![\langle x, \mathsf{pub}(x)\rangle]\!]_{\mathsf{sk}(S)}], \\ w_1 = [\![\langle x, \mathsf{pub}(x)\rangle]\!]_{\mathsf{sk}(y)} :: [\![\langle y, \mathsf{pub}(y)\rangle]\!]_{\mathsf{sk}(z)} :: x^{\mathsf{m}}, \\ w_2 = [\![\langle y, \mathsf{pub}(y)\rangle]\!]_{\mathsf{sk}(z)} :: x^{\mathsf{m}}. \end{cases}$$

Similarly, link-based recursive languages can also describe delegation rights certificates in the context of distributed access-rights management. In [7] for example, the certificate chains delegating authorization for operation O are of the form:

$$[[\![\langle A_1, \mathsf{pub}(A_1), O\rangle]\!]_{\mathsf{sk}(A_2)}; [\![\langle A_2, \mathsf{pub}(A_2), O\rangle]\!]_{\mathsf{sk}(A_3)}; \ldots ; [\![\langle A_n, \mathsf{pub}(A_n), O\rangle]\!]_{\mathsf{sk}(S)}]$$

where S has authority over operation O and each agent A_{i+1} delegates the rights for operation O to agent A_i. These chained lists are all built from the term $\mathsf{m} = [\![\langle x, \mathsf{pub}(y), O\rangle]\!]_{\mathsf{sk}(z)}$ with $x, y, z \in \mathcal{X}_{\mathsf{Base}}$.

Example 3. In the recursive authentication protocol [19], a certificate list consists in a chain of encryptions of the form:

$$[\mathsf{senc}(\langle K_{ab}, B, N_a\rangle, K_a); \mathsf{senc}(\langle K_{ab}, A, N_b\rangle, K_b);$$
$$\mathsf{senc}(\langle K_{bc}, C, N_b\rangle, K_b); \mathsf{senc}(\langle K_{bc}, B, N_c\rangle, K_c); \ldots ; \mathsf{senc}(\langle K_{ds}, S, N_d\rangle, K_d)]$$

where S is a trusted server distributing session keys $K_{ab}, K_{bc}, \ldots, K_{ds}$ to each pair of successive agents via these certificates. These chained lists are all built from the term $\mathsf{m} = \mathsf{senc}(\langle y_1, y_2, y_3 \rangle, z)$ with $y_1, y_2, y_3, z \in \mathcal{X}_{\mathsf{Base}}$. The set of valid chains of encryptions in this protocol can be formally expressed as the m-link-based recursive language $\mathcal{L}_{\mathsf{RA}}$ defined by:

$$
\begin{cases}
w_0 = [\mathsf{senc}(\langle z, S, x \rangle, x_k)], \\
w_1 = \mathsf{senc}(\langle z, x_a, x \rangle, x_{k_b})::\mathsf{senc}(\langle z, x_b, y \rangle, x_{k_a})::\mathsf{senc}(\langle z', x_c, y \rangle, x_{k_a})::x^{\mathsf{m}}, \\
w_2 = \mathsf{senc}(\langle z', x_c, y \rangle, x_{k_a})::x^{\mathsf{m}}.
\end{cases}
$$

We propose a procedure for checking for secrecy preservation for a protocol with link-based recursive tests in NP, for a bounded number of sessions.

Theorem 2. *Let $\mathcal{L}$ be a link-based recursive language. Let $(\mathcal{C}, \mathcal{I})$ be a constraint system and ϕ be an $\mathcal{L}$-language constraint associated to $(\mathcal{C}, \mathcal{I})$. Deciding whether $(\mathcal{C}, \mathcal{I})$ and ϕ has a solution is in NP.*

The proof of Theorem 2 involves three main steps. First, thanks to Theorem 1, it is sufficient to decide in polynomial (DAG) size whether $(\mathcal{C}, \mathcal{I})$ with language constraint ϕ has a non-confusing solution when $(\mathcal{C}, \mathcal{I})$ is a solved constraint system. Then, we show that we can (polynomially) bound the size of the lists in ϕ. This relies partly on Proposition 1, as it shows that a non-confusing solution is a constructive solution.

Proposition 2. *Let $(\mathcal{C}, \mathcal{I})$ be a constraint system in solved form and ϕ be an $\mathcal{L}$-language constraint associated to $(\mathcal{C}, \mathcal{I})$ where $\mathcal{L}$ is a link-based recursive language. Let θ be a constructive solution of $(\mathcal{C}, \mathcal{I})$ and ϕ. Then there exists a constructive solution θ' of $(\mathcal{C}, \mathcal{I})$ and ϕ such that $\phi\theta'$ is polynomial in the size of $\mathcal{C}$, and ϕ.*

Proposition 2 is proved by first showing that there is a solution that uses a bounded number of distinct names. Thus there is a finite number of instances of m used in recursive calls, allowing us to cut the lists while preserving the membership to the recursive language.

The third step of the proof of Theorem 2 consists in showing that we can restrict our attention to solutions θ such that $x\theta$ is either a constant or a subterm of $\phi\theta$, by using Lemma 1. This lemma is a generic lemma that shows how any solution can be transformed by projecting some variables on constants. It will be reused in the next section.

Lemma 1. *Let $\mathcal{L}$ be a language, i.e. a set of terms. Let $(\mathcal{C}, \mathcal{I})$ be a constraint system in solved form and ϕ be an $\mathcal{L}$-language constraint associated to $(\mathcal{C}, \mathcal{I})$. Let θ be a constructive solution of $(\mathcal{C}, \mathcal{I})$ and ϕ. Let N_0 be a name of Base sort in $\mathcal{I}$, and θ' be a substitution such that:*

$$
\begin{cases}
x\theta' = x\theta & \text{if } x\theta \in st(\phi\theta) \\
x\theta' = [] & \text{if } x \in \mathcal{X}_{\mathsf{List}} \text{ and } x\theta \notin st(\phi\theta) \\
x\theta' = N_0 & \text{if } x \notin \mathcal{X}_{\mathsf{List}} \text{ and } x\theta \notin st(\phi\theta)
\end{cases}
$$

The substitution θ' is a constructive solution of $(\mathcal{C}, \mathcal{I})$ and ϕ.

5   Routing Protocols

Routing protocols typically perform recursive checks to ensure the validity of a
given route. However, link-based recursive languages do not suffice to express
these checks. Indeed, in routing protocols, nodes aim at establishing and certifying a successful route (*i.e.* a list of names of nodes) between two given nodes
that wish to communicate. Each node on the route typically contributes to the
routing protocol by certifying that the proposed route is correct, to the best of
its knowledge. Thus each contribution contains a list of names (the route). Then
the final node receives a list of contributions and needs to check that each contribution contains the same list of names, which has also to be consistent with the
whole received message. For example, in the case of the SMNDP protocol [12],
the source node has to check that the received message is of the form:

$$[[\langle D, S, l_{route}\rangle]_{\mathsf{sk}(A_n)}; \ldots; [\langle D, S, l_{route}\rangle]_{\mathsf{sk}(A_1)}; [\langle D, S, l_{route}\rangle]_{\mathsf{sk}(D)}]$$

where $l_{route} = [D; A_1; \ldots; A_n]$.

5.1   Mapping-Based Languages

An interesting property in the case of routing protocols is that (valid) messages
are uniquely determined by the list of nodes $[A_1; \ldots; A_n]$ in addition to some
parameters (*e.g.* the source and destination nodes in the case of SMNDP). We
propose a generic definition that captures any such language based on a list of
names.

Definition 6 (mapping-based language). *Let* b *be a term that contains no
name and no* :: *symbol, and such that:*

$$\{w_1, w_1^p, \ldots, w_m^p\} \subseteq vars(\mathsf{b}) \subseteq \{w_1, w_2, w_3, w_1^p, \ldots, w_m^p\}.$$

The variables $w_1^p, \ldots, w_m^p$ *are the parameters of the language, whereas* w_1, w_2,
and w_3 *are special variables. Let* $\mathcal{P} = \langle P_1, \ldots, P_m \rangle$ *be a tuple of names and*
$\sigma_{\mathcal{P}} = \{w_1^p \mapsto P_1, \ldots, w_m^p \mapsto P_m\}$. *Let* $l = [A_1; \ldots; A_n]$ *be a list of names, the
links are defined over* l *recursively in the following manner :*

$$\mathsf{m}_{\mathcal{P}}(i, l) = (\mathsf{b}\sigma_{\mathcal{P}})\{w_1 \mapsto l, w_2 \mapsto A_i, w_3 \mapsto [\mathsf{m}_{\mathcal{P}}(i-1, l); \ldots; \mathsf{m}_{\mathcal{P}}(1, l)]\}$$

The mapping-based *language (defined by* b*) is the following one:*

$$\mathcal{L} = \{\langle \mathcal{P}, \langle l, l' \rangle\rangle \mid \mathcal{P} = \langle P_1, \ldots, P_m \rangle \text{ is a tuple of names,}$$
$$l = [A_1; \ldots; A_n] \text{ a list of names, } n \in \mathbb{N}, \text{ and } l' = [\mathsf{m}_{\mathcal{P}}(n, l); \ldots; \mathsf{m}_{\mathcal{P}}(1, l)]\}.$$

A mapping-based language is defined by a base shape b. The special variables
w_2 and w_3 are optional and may not occur in b. Each element of the language
is a triple $\langle \mathcal{P}, \langle l, l' \rangle\rangle$ where l' is a list of links entirely determined by the tuple
$\mathcal{P} = \langle P_1, \ldots, P_m \rangle$ and the list l of arbitrary length n. In the list l', each link

contains the same parameters $P_1, \ldots, P_m$ (*e.g.* the source and destination nodes), the list l of n names $[A_1; \ldots; A_n]$ and possibly the current name A_i and the list of previous links, following the base shape b.

We illustrate this definition with two examples of routing protocols.

Example 4 (SMNDP protocol [12]). Recall that in SMNDP, the list of signatures expected by the source node S built over the list $l = [A_1, \ldots, A_n]$ is the list $[s_n, \ldots, s_1]$, where $s_i = [\![\langle D, S, l \rangle]\!]_{\mathsf{sk}(A_i)}$. This language has two parameters, the name of the source w_1^p and the name of the destination w_2^p. The language can be formally described with $\mathsf{b} = [\![\langle w_2^p, w_1^p, w_1 \rangle]\!]_{\mathsf{sk}(w_2)}$.

Example 5 (endairA protocol [9]). The difference between SMNDP and endairA lies in the fact that during the reply phase, the intermediate nodes compute a signature over the partial signature list that they receive. In the endairA protocol, the list of signatures expected by the source node S built over the list of nodes $l = [A_1, \ldots, A_n]$ is the list $l'_s = [s_n, \ldots, s_1]$, where $s_i = [\![\langle D, S, l, [s_{i-1}; \ldots; s_1] \rangle]\!]_{\mathsf{sk}(A_i)}$.

This language has two parameters, the name of the source w_1^p and the name of the destination w_2^p. The language can be formally described with $\mathsf{b} = [\![\langle w_2^p, w_1^p, w_1, w_3 \rangle]\!]_{\mathsf{sk}(w_2)}$.

5.2 Decision Procedure

We propose a procedure for checking for secrecy preservation for a protocol with mapping-based tests in NP, for a bounded number of sessions.

Theorem 3. *Let $\mathcal{L}$ be a mapping-based language. Let $(\mathcal{C}, \mathcal{I})$ be a constraint system and ϕ be an $\mathcal{L}$-language constraint associated to $(\mathcal{C}, \mathcal{I})$.*
Deciding whether $(\mathcal{C}, \mathcal{I}) \wedge \phi$ has a solution is in NP.

The proof of Theorem 3 involves three main steps. First, thanks to Theorem 1, it is sufficient to decide in polynomial (DAG) size whether $(\mathcal{C}, \mathcal{I})$ with language constraint ϕ has a non-confusing solution when $(\mathcal{C}, \mathcal{I})$ is a solved constraint system. Due to Proposition 1, we deduce that it is sufficient to show that deciding whether $(\mathcal{C}, \mathcal{I}) \wedge \phi$ has a constructive solution is in NP, where $(\mathcal{C}, \mathcal{I})$ is a solved constraint system.

The second and key step of the proof consists in bounding the size of a constructive solution. Note that the requirement on the form of ϕ is not a restriction since any substitution satisfying ϕ will necessarily have this shape.

Proposition 3. *Let $\mathcal{L}$ be a mapping-based language. Let $(\mathcal{C}, \mathcal{I})$ be a constraint system in solved form, ϕ be an $\mathcal{L}$-language constraint associated to $(\mathcal{C}, \mathcal{I})$, and τ be a constructive solution of $(\mathcal{C}, \mathcal{I}) \wedge \phi$. We further assume that ϕ is of the form $u_1 \Subset \mathcal{L} \wedge \ldots \wedge u_k \Subset \mathcal{L}$ where $u_j = \langle \langle p_1^j, \ldots, p_m^j \rangle, \langle l_j, l'_j \rangle \rangle$.*
There exists a constructive solution τ' of $(\mathcal{C}, \mathcal{I}) \wedge \phi$ such that, for every j, the length of $l_j \tau'$ is polynomially bounded on the size of $\mathcal{C}$ and ϕ.

For each constraint $\langle \langle p_1^j, \ldots, p_m^j \rangle, \langle l_j, l'_j \rangle \rangle \Subset \mathcal{L}$, the list l_j provides constraints on the last elements of the list l'_j, while l'_j provides constraints on the last elements of the list l_j. The main idea of the proof of Proposition 3 is to show that it is possible to cut the middle of the list l_j, modifying the list l'_j accordingly. This is however not straightforward as we have to show that the new substitution is still a solution of the constraint system $(\mathcal{C}, \mathcal{I})$. In particular, cutting part of the list might destroy some interesting equalities, used to deduce terms. Such cases are actually avoided by considering constructive solutions and by cutting at some position in the lists such that none of the elements are subterms of the constraint, which can be ensured by combinatorial arguments.

Proposition 3 allows us to bound the size of $l_j\theta$ for a minimal solution θ, which in turn bounds the size of $l'_j\theta$. The last step of the proof of Theorem 3 consists in showing that any $x\theta$ is bounded by the size of the lists or can be replaced by a constant, by applying Lemma 1.

6   Conclusion

We have provided two new NP decision procedures for (automatically) analysing confidentiality of security protocols with recursive tests, for a bounded number of sessions. The classes of recursive languages we can consider both encompass chained-based lists of certificates and most of the recursive tests performed in the context of routing protocols. These procedures rely on a new characterization of the solutions of a constraint system, extending the procedure for solving constraint systems. We believe that this new characterization is of independent interest and could be used for other families of protocols.

As further work, we plan to implement our procedure, which will require us to optimize it. We also plan to consider larger classes of recursive languages in order to capture *e.g.* the recursive tests performed in the context of group protocols. It would also be interesting to see whether our techniques could be extended for analysing protocols that use such recursive languages not only for performing tests but also as outputs in protocols.

References

1. Abadi, M., Cortier, V.: Deciding knowledge in security protocols under equational theories. Theoretical Computer Science 387(1-2), 2–32 (2006)
2. Andel, T.R., Yasinsac, A.: Automated security analysis of ad hoc routing protocols. In: Proc. of the Joint Workshop on Foundations of Computer Security and Automated Reasoning for Security Protocol Analysis (FCS-ARSPA 2007), pp. 9–26 (2007)
3. Armando, A., Basin, D., Boichut, Y., Chevalier, Y., Compagna, L., Cuellar, J., Drielsma, P.H., Heám, P.C., Kouchnarenko, O., Mantovani, J., Mödersheim, S., von Oheimb, D., Rusinowitch, M., Santiago, J., Turuani, M., Viganò, L., Vigneron, L.: The AVISPA Tool for the Automated Validation of Internet Security Protocols and Applications. In: Etessami, K., Rajamani, S.K. (eds.) CAV 2005. LNCS, vol. 3576, pp. 281–285. Springer, Heidelberg (2005)

4. Armando, A., Carbone, R., Compagna, L., Cuéllar, J., Tobarra, M.L.: Formal analysis of SAML 2.0 web browser single sign-on: breaking the SAML-based single sign-on for google apps. In: Proc. of the 6th ACM Workshop on Formal Methods in Security Engineering (FMSE 2008), pp. 1–10 (2008)
5. Arnaud, M., Cortier, V., Delaune, S.: Deciding security for protocols with recursive tests. Research Report LSV-11-05, Laboratoire Spécification et Vérification, ENS Cachan, France, p. 46 (April 2011)
6. Asokan, N., Ginzboorg, P.: Key agreement in ad hoc networks. Computer Communications 23(17), 1627–1637 (2000)
7. Aura, T.: Distributed access-rights management with delegation certificates. In: Ryan, M. (ed.) Secure Internet Programming. LNCS, vol. 1603, pp. 211–235. Springer, Heidelberg (1999)
8. Blanchet, B.: An automatic security protocol verifier based on resolution theorem proving (invited tutorial). In: Nieuwenhuis, R. (ed.) CADE 2005. LNCS (LNAI), vol. 3632, Springer, Heidelberg (2005)
9. Buttyán, L., Vajda, I.: Towards Provable Security for Ad Hoc Routing Protocols. In: Proc. of the 2nd ACM workshop on Security of ad hoc and sensor networks (SASN 2004), pp. 94–105. ACM, New York (2004)
10. Chridi, N., Turuani, M., Rusinowitch, M.: Decidable analysis for a class of cryptographic group protocols with unbounded lists. In: Proc. of the 22nd IEEE Computer Security Foundations Symposium (CSF 2009), pp. 277–289 (2009)
11. Comon-Lundh, H., Cortier, V., Zalinescu, E.: Deciding security properties for cryptographic protocols. Application to key cycles. ACM Transactions on Computational Logic (TOCL) 11(4), 496–520 (2010)
12. Feng, T., Guo, X., Ma, J., Li, X.: UC-Secure Source Routing Protocol (2009)
13. Housley, R., Ford, W., Polk, W.: X.509 certificate and CRL profile. IETF standard, RFC 2459 (1998)
14. Hu, Y.-C., Perrig, A., Johnson, D.: Ariadne: A Secure On-Demand Routing Protocol for Ad Hoc Networks. Wireless Networks 11, 21–38 (2005)
15. Küsters, R., Truderung, T.: On the Automatic Analysis of Recursive Security Protocols with XOR. In: Thomas, W., Weil, P. (eds.) STACS 2007. LNCS, vol. 4393, pp. 646–657. Springer, Heidelberg (2007)
16. Küsters, R., Wilke, T.: Automata-Based Analysis of Recursive Cryptographic Protocols. In: Diekert, V., Habib, M. (eds.) STACS 2004. LNCS, vol. 2996, pp. 382–393. Springer, Heidelberg (2004)
17. Lowe, G.: Breaking and fixing the Needham-Schroeder public-key protocol using FDR. In: Margaria, T., Steffen, B. (eds.) TACAS 1996. LNCS, vol. 1055, pp. 147–166. Springer, Heidelberg (1996)
18. Millen, J.K., Shmatikov, V.: Constraint solving for bounded-process cryptographic protocol analysis. In: Proc. of the 8th ACM Conference on Computer and Communications Security (CCS 2001), pp. 166–175 (2001)
19. Paulson, L.C.: Mechanized proofs for a recursive authentication protocol. In: Proc. of the 10th IEEE Computer Security Foundations Workshop, pp. 84–95. IEEE Computer Society Press, Los Alamitos (1997)
20. Rusinowitch, M., Turuani, M.: Protocol insecurity with finite number of sessions is NP-complete. In: Proc. of the 14th Computer Security Foundations Workshop (CSFW 2001), pp. 174–190. IEEE Computer Society Press, Los Alamitos (2001)
21. Truderung, T.: Selecting theories and recursive protocols. In: Abadi, M., de Alfaro, L. (eds.) CONCUR 2005. LNCS, vol. 3653, pp. 217–232. Springer, Heidelberg (2005)

The Matita Interactive Theorem Prover

Andrea Asperti[1], Wilmer Ricciotti[1], Claudio Sacerdoti Coen[1], and
Enrico Tassi[2]

[1] Department of Computer Science, University of Bologna
Mura Anteo Zamboni, 7 — 40127 Bologna, ITALY
{asperti,ricciott,sacerdot}@cs.unibo.it
[2] Microsoft Research - INRIA Joint Centre
enrico.tassi@inria.fr

Abstract. Matita is an interactive theorem prover being developed by
the Helm team at the University of Bologna. Its stable version 0.5.x may
be downloaded at http://matita.cs.unibo.it. The tool originated in
the European project MoWGLI as a set of XML-based tools aimed to
provide a mathematician-friendly web-interface to repositories of formal
mathematical knoweldge, supporting advanced content-based functionalities for querying, searching and browsing the library. It has since then
evolved into a fully fledged ITP, specifically designed as a light-weight,
but competitive system, particularly suited for the assessment of innova-
tive ideas, both at foundational and logical level. In this paper, we give an
account of the whole system, its peculiarities and its main applications.

1   The System

Matita is an interactive proof assistant, adopting a dependent type theory - the
Calculus of (Co)Inductive Constructions (CIC) - as its foundational language for
describing proofs. It is thus compatible, at the proof term level, with Coq [27],
and the two systems are able to check each other's proof objects. Since the two
systems do not share a single line of code, but are akin to each other, it is natural
to take Coq as the main term of comparison, referring to other systems (most
notably, Isabelle and HOL) when some ideas or philosophies characteristic of
these latter tools have been imported into our system.

Similarly to Coq, Matita follows the so called *De Bruijn principle*, stating
that proofs generated by the system should be verifiable by a small and trusted
component, traditionally called *kernel*. Unsurprisingly, the kernel has roughly the
same size in the two tools, in spite of a few differences in the encoding of terms: in
particular, Matita's kernel handles *explicit substitutions* to mimic Coq's Section
mechanism, and can cope with *existential metavariables*, i.e. non-linear placeholders that are Curry-Howard isomorphic to holes in the proofs. Metavariables
cannot be instantiated by the kernel: they are considered as opaque constants,
with a declared type, only equal to themselves.

While this extension does not make the kernel sensibly more complex or fragile, it has a beneficial effect on the size of the type inference subsystem, here

N. Bjørner and V. Sofronie-Stokkermans (Eds.): CADE 2011, LNAI 6803, pp. 64–69, 2011.

called *refiner*. In particular, the refiner can directly call the kernel to check the complex and delicate conditions (guardedness, positivity) needed to ensure the termination of recursive functions and detect erroneous definition of inductive types leading to logical paradoxes. The Matita refiner implements several advanced features like coercive subtyping [16] and subset coercions [24], that allow for some automatic modifications of the user input to fix a type error or annotate simple programs with proof obligations.

The kernel compares types up to conversion, that is a decidable relation involving β-reduction, constant unfolding and recursive function computation. On the contrary, the refiner deals with incomplete terms, and compares types with a higher order unification algorithm in charge of finding an instantiation for metavariables that makes the two types convertible. Higher order unification is in general semi-decidable, and is thus usually implemented as an extension of the usual first order algorithm equipped with some extra heuristics. To avoid the inherent complexity of combining together many heuristics, Matita enables the user to extend unification by means of *unification hints* [4], that give explicit solutions for the cases not handled by the basic algorithm.

Remarkably, many ad-hoc mechanisms studied in the last years for dealing with the formalization of algebraic structures, including Canonical Structures, Type Classes [25,28], and Coercion Pullbacks [21], can be implemented on top of unification hints.

Library. Besides the aforementioned components, that make up the core of all theorem provers, the most important aspect of Matita is its document-centric philosophy. Matita is meant, first of all, as an interface between the user and the mathematical library, storing definitions, theorems and notation. An important consequence of this is that once a concept has been defined and added to the library, it will stay visible unless it is removed or invalidated, with no need for the user to explicitly reference or include a part of the library.

Objects are stored in the library together with metadata, which are used for indexing and searching. The searching facility provided by Matita, that is a key component of the system, has been described in [2].

Disambiguation. A well known, complex problem for interactive provers is that, at a linguistic level, ordinary mathematical discourse systematically overloads symbols and abuses notations in ways that make mechanical interpretation difficult. This originates from various sources, including conflicting parsing rules, implicit information that a human reader can recover from the context, overloading of operators, and so on. The complexity of the problem is due to the fact that the comprehension of the text sometimes requires not just knowledge of the notation and conventions at play but some understanding of the relevant mathematical aspects of the discipline (e.g. the fact that a given set *can be equipped* by a suitable algebraic structure), requiring the system *to dig* into its base of knowledge, in order *to correctly parse* the statement!

Matita was designed keeping in mind that ambiguous notation is not an unfortunate accident, but a powerful tool in the hands of mathematicians. For this reason, the user is allowed the maximum degree of flexibility in defining notation.

To manage ambiguous notation, Matita provides an ambiguous parser (described in [23]) associating to the user input the set of all its possible interpretations (according to the defined notation). While ambiguous parsing is a potentially expensive operation, Matita is able to preserve efficiency by means of a sophisticated algorithm, capable of detecting semantic errors as early as possible, in order to prevent semantic analysis of a multitude of incorrect interpretations. At the end of the process, it is possible that we are left with more than one interpretation: in this case, Matita asks the user to select the correct interpretation, then it stores it into the script to avoid interrogating the user again the next time the script is executed.

2   Proof Authoring

The user interface of Matita was inspired by that of CtCoq [11] and Proof General [9] and is, in our experience, quite easy to learn for newcomers. The main language used to write proof scripts is procedural, in the LCF tradition, and essentially similar to the one used by Coq. In addition to that, Matita features a declarative language ([13]), in the style usually ascribed to Trybulec (the so called Mizar-style [19]), and made popular in the ITP community mostly by the work of Wenzel [29].

Despite many similarities to Coq, Matita departs from it in more than one respect (see [5] for details). The sequent-window is based on a MathML-compliant GTK-widget providing a sophisticated bidimensional rendering and supporting hyperlinks. During proof authoring, *direct manipulation* of terms is available on the generated MathML markup: the user can follow hyperlinks to library objects, visually select semantically meaningful subterms using the mouse, and perform contextual actions on them like copy&paste or tactic application. To textually represent graphical selections Matita adopts *patterns*, that are generated on-the-fly from visual selections and consistently used by all tactics.

Step by step tacticals. LCF-tacticals (operations combining a number of tactics in complex proof strategies), which are used for a better syntactical structuring of proof scripts, are also provided by Matita. Tacticals provide syntax for expressing concepts like branching, mimicking the tree structure of proofs at the script level. Since branches of proof trees usually corresponds to conceptual parts of pen & paper proofs, the branching tactical helps improving script readability.

In other systems, the practical use of these constructs is limited by the need of executing each tactical in a single step, even though it is composed of multiple tactics. Instead, Matita offers the possibility of interrupting the execution of a script at intermediate evaluation steps of a tactical, allowing the user to inspect changes in the status and, if needed, edit the script. This is a notable improvement in the overall user experience. Step by step tacticals – also called *tinycals* – are described in [22].

Automation. Automation is a well known weak point of Coq, only partially compensated by powerful reflexive tactics. Matita was intended to fill this gap, with a particular attention to support the automation of those small logical transformations (*small step* automation) needed to *match* [7] the current goal versus the knowledge bases of already proved results, and which constitute the underlying *glue* [8] of the actual mathematical discourse. A large part of this glue can be expressed in form of rewritings, allowing mathematicians to freely move between different incarnations of the same entity without even mentioning the transformation (sometimes referred to as Poincaré's principle). For this reason, the main component of Matita automation is a powerful *paramodulation tool*[1] able to exploit the *whole library* of known equational *facts* (unit equalities) in order to solve equational goals. Paramodulation is also used to supply matching *up to equational rewriting* between a goal and a given statement, and this in turn is used to support a simple, smooth but effective integration between equational reasoning and a backward-based, Prolog-like resolution procedure. Again, this automation tactic exploits the *whole library* of visible results, adopting a philosophy already advocated and implemented by several successful systems (see e.g. [18]), and contrasting with the approach of Coq, requiring the user to thoroughly select a collection of theorems to be used. On the other side, we are not eager to extend our SLD-approach to a more general resolution technique, since the prolog style, being closer to the LCF backward based procedural approach, allows a better interaction between the user and the application, permitting the user to *drive* the automatic search, e.g. by pruning or reordering the search space [6].

3   Formalizations

In the last years, Matita was successfully used in formalizations of considerable complexity, spanning on the following areas:

Number theory. These formalizations include results about Möbius's μ, Euler's ϕ and Chebyshev's ψ and θ functions, up to a fully arithmetical proof of the property of prime numbers known as Bertrand's postulate ([1,3]).

Constructive analysis. The main result is Lebesgue's dominated convergence theorem in the new, abstract setting of convex uniform spaces [20]. The formalization stresses some features peculiar of Matita, like coercions pullback.

Programming languages metatheory. Comprises the formalization of several different solutions of part 1A of the POPLmark challenge [10], characterized by a different treatment of binding structures.

Hardware formalization. Matita has been used to provide two realistic and executable models of microprocessors for the Freescale 8-bit family and the 8051/8052 microprocessors respectively. The formalization also captures the intensional behaviour, comprising exact execution times.

Software verification. Matita is employed in the FET Open EU Project CerCo (Certified Complexity)[2] [12] for the verification of the first formally

---

[1] Matita paramodulation tool took part in the UEQ category of the 2009 CASC competition ([26]), scoring better than Metis [14], Otter [17], and iProver [15].

[2] The project CerCo acknowledges the financial support of the Future and Emerging Technologies (FET) programme within the Seventh Framework Programme for Research of the European Commission, under FET-Open grant number: 243881.

certified complexity preserving compiler. The compiler, which targets the 8051 microprocessor, annotates the input program (in C) with the exact computational cost of every O(1) program slice. The costs, that are dependent on the compilation strategy, are directly computed from the generated object code. Hence it will be possible to reason on a hard real time program at the C level, knowing that the compiled code will have the same behaviour. The formalization in Matita will include executable formal models of every intermediate languages, a dependently typed implementation of the compiler, and the proof of preservation of extensional and intensional properties.

References

1. Asperti, A., Armentano, C.: A page in number theory. Journal of Formalized Reasoning 1, 1–23 (2008)
2. Asperti, A., Guidi, F., Coen, C.S., Tassi, E., Zacchiroli, S.: A content based mathematical search engine: Whelp. In: Filliâtre, J.-C., Paulin-Mohring, C., Werner, B. (eds.) TYPES 2004. LNCS, vol. 3839, pp. 17–32. Springer, Heidelberg (2006)
3. Asperti, A., Ricciotti, W.: About the formalization of some results by chebyshev in number theory. In: Berardi, S., Damiani, F., de'Liguoro, U. (eds.) TYPES 2008. LNCS, vol. 5497, pp. 19–31. Springer, Heidelberg (2009)
4. Asperti, A., Ricciotti, W., Sacerdoti Coen, C., Tassi, E.: Hints in unification. In: Berghofer, S., Nipkow, T., Urban, C., Wenzel, M. (eds.) TPHOLs 2009. LNCS, vol. 5674, pp. 84–98. Springer, Heidelberg (2009)
5. Asperti, A., Coen, C.S., Tassi, E., Zacchiroli, S.: User interaction with the Matita proof assistant. J. Autom. Reasoning 39(2), 109–139 (2007)
6. Asperti, A., Tassi, E.: An interactive driver for goal directed proof strategies. In: Proc. of UITP 2008. ENTCS, vol. 226, pp. 89–105 (2009)
7. Asperti, A., Tassi, E.: Smart matching. In: Autexier, S., Calmet, J., Delahaye, D., Ion, P.D.F., Rideau, L., Rioboo, R., Sexton, A.P. (eds.) AISC 2010. LNCS, vol. 6167, pp. 263–277. Springer, Heidelberg (2010)
8. Asperti, A., Tassi, E.: Superposition as a logical glue. In: Proc. of TYPES 2009, EPTCS (2010) (to appear)
9. Aspinall, D.: Proof general: A generic tool for proof development. In: Graf, S. (ed.) TACAS 2000. LNCS, vol. 1785, p. 38. Springer, Heidelberg (2000)
10. Aydemir, B.E., Bohannon, A., Fairbairn, M., Foster, J.N., Babu, C. S., Sewell, P., Vytiniotis, D., Washburn, G., Weirich, S., Zdancewic, S.: Mechanized metatheory for the masses: The POPLmark challenge. In: Hurd, J., Melham, T. (eds.) TPHOLs 2005. LNCS, vol. 3603, pp. 50–65. Springer, Heidelberg (2005)
11. Bertot, Y.: The CtCoq system: Design and architecture. Formal Aspects of Computing 11, 225–243 (1999)
12. The CerCo website, http://cerco.cs.unibo.it
13. Coen, C.S.: Declarative representation of proof terms. J. Autom. Reasoning 44(1-2), 25–52 (2010)
14. Hurd, J.: First-order proof tactics in higher-order logic theorem provers. Technical Report NASA/CP-2003-212448, Nasa technical reports (2003)
15. Korovin, K.: iProver – an instantiation-based theorem prover for first-order logic (System description). In: Armando, A., Baumgartner, P., Dowek, G. (eds.) IJCAR 2008. LNCS (LNAI), vol. 5195, pp. 292–298. Springer, Heidelberg (2008)

16. Luo, Z.: Coercive subtyping. J. Logic and Computation 9(1), 105–130 (1999)
17. McCune, W., Wos, L.: Otter - the CADE-13 competition incarnations. J. of Autom. Reasoning 18(2), 211–220 (1997)
18. Meng, J., Quigley, C., Paulson, L.C.: Automation for interactive proof: First prototype. Inf. Comput. 204(10), 1575–1596 (2006)
19. The Mizar proof-assistant, http://mizar.uwb.edu.pl/
20. Coen, C.S., Tassi, E.: A constructive and formal proof of Lebesgue's dominated convergence theorem in the interactive theorem prover Matita. Journal of Formalized Reasoning 1, 51–89 (2008)
21. Sacerdoti Coen, C., Tassi, E.: Working with mathematical structures in type theory. In: Miculan, M., Scagnetto, I., Honsell, F. (eds.) TYPES 2007. LNCS, vol. 4941, pp. 157–172. Springer, Heidelberg (2008)
22. Coen, C.S., Tassi, E., Zacchiroli, S.: Tinycals: step by step tacticals. In: Proc. of UITP 2006. ENTCS, vol. 174, pp. 125–142. Elsevier Science, Amsterdam (2006)
23. Coen, C.S., Zacchiroli, S.: Efficient ambiguous parsing of mathematical formulae. In: Asperti, A., Bancerek, G., Trybulec, A. (eds.) MKM 2004. LNCS, vol. 3119, pp. 347–362. Springer, Heidelberg (2004)
24. Sozeau, M.: Subset coercions in COQ. In: Altenkirch, T., McBride, C. (eds.) TYPES 2006. LNCS, vol. 4502, pp. 237–252. Springer, Heidelberg (2007)
25. Sozeau, M., Oury, N.: First-class type classes. In: Mohamed, O.A., Muñoz, C., Tahar, S. (eds.) TPHOLs 2008. LNCS, vol. 5170, pp. 278–293. Springer, Heidelberg (2008)
26. Sutcliffe, G.: The CADE-22 automated theorem proving system competition - CASC-22. AI Commun. 23, 47–59 (2010)
27. The Coq Development Team. The Coq proof assistant reference manual, http://coq.inria.fr/doc/main.html
28. Wenzel, M.: Type classes and overloading in higher-order logic. In: Gunter, E.L., Felty, A.P. (eds.) TPHOLs 1997. LNCS, vol. 1275, pp. 307–322. Springer, Heidelberg (1997)
29. Wenzel, M.T.: Isar - A generic interpretative approach to readable formal proof documents. In: Bertot, Y., Dowek, G., Hirschowitz, A., Paulin, C., Théry, L. (eds.) TPHOLs 1999. LNCS, vol. 1690, pp. 167–184. Springer, Heidelberg (1999)

Unification in the Description Logic $\mathcal{EL}$ without the Top Concept

Franz Baader[1,*], Nguyen Thanh Binh[2], Stefan Borgwardt[1,*], and
Barbara Morawska[1,*]

[1] TU Dresden, Germany
{baader,stefborg,morawska}@tcs.inf.tu-dresden.de
[2] ETH Zürich, Switzerland
thannguy@inf.ethz.ch

Abstract. Unification in Description Logics has been proposed as a
novel inference service that can, for example, be used to detect redundancies in ontologies. The inexpressive Description Logic $\mathcal{EL}$ is of particular
interest in this context since, on the one hand, several large biomedical
ontologies are defined using $\mathcal{EL}$. On the other hand, unification in $\mathcal{EL}$ has
recently been shown to be NP-complete, and thus of considerably lower
complexity than unification in other DLs of similarly restricted expressive power. However, $\mathcal{EL}$ allows the use of the top concept ($\top$), which
represents the whole interpretation domain, whereas the large medical
ontology SNOMED CT makes no use of this feature. Surprisingly, removing the top concept from $\mathcal{EL}$ makes the unification problem considerably
harder. More precisely, we will show in this paper that unification in $\mathcal{EL}$
without the top concept is PSPACE-complete.

1 Introduction

Description logics (DLs) [4] are a well-investigated family of logic-based knowledge representation formalisms. They can be used to represent the relevant concepts of an application domain using concept terms, which are built from concept
names and role names using certain concept constructors. The DL $\mathcal{EL}$ offers the
constructors conjunction ($\sqcap$), existential restriction ($\exists r.C$), and the top concept
($\top$). From a semantic point of view, concept names and concept terms represent
sets of individuals, whereas roles represent binary relations between individuals.
The top concept is interpreted as the set of all individuals. For example, using
the concept names Male, Female, Person and the role names child, job, the concept of *persons having a son, a daughter, and a job* can be represented by the
$\mathcal{EL}$-concept term   Person $\sqcap$ $\exists$child.Male $\sqcap$ $\exists$child.Female $\sqcap$ $\exists$job.$\top$.

In this example, the availability of the top concept in $\mathcal{EL}$ allows us to state
that the person has some job, without specifying any further to which concept
this job belongs. Knowledge representation systems based on DLs provide their
users with various inference services that allow them to deduce implicit knowledge from the explicitly represented knowledge. For instance, the subsumption

---

* Supported by DFG under grant BA 1122/14-1.

N. Bjørner and V. Sofronie-Stokkermans (Eds.): CADE 2011, LNAI 6803, pp. 70–84, 2011.
© Springer-Verlag Berlin Heidelberg 2011

algorithm allows one to determine subconcept-superconcept relationships. For example, the concept term $\exists$job.$\top$ subsumes (i.e., is a superconcept of) the concept term $\exists$job.Boring since anyone that has a boring job at least has some job. Two concept terms are called *equivalent* if they subsume each other, i.e., if they are always interpreted as the same set of individuals.

The DL $\mathcal{EL}$ has recently drawn considerable attention since, on the one hand, important inference problems such as the subsumption problem are polynomial in $\mathcal{EL}$ [1,3]. On the other hand, though quite inexpressive, $\mathcal{EL}$ can be used to define biomedical ontologies. For example, the large medical ontology SNOMED CT[1] can be expressed in $\mathcal{EL}$. Actually, if one takes a closer look at the concept definitions in SNOMED CT, then one sees that they do not contain the top concept.

Unification in DLs has been proposed in [8] as a novel inference service that can, for example, be used to detect redundancies in ontologies. For example, assume that one knowledge engineer defines the concept of *female professors* as

$$\text{Person} \sqcap \text{Female} \sqcap \exists\text{job.Professor},$$

whereas another knowledge engineer represent this notion in a somewhat different way, e.g., by using the concept term

$$\text{Woman} \sqcap \exists\text{job.}(\text{Teacher} \sqcap \text{Researcher}).$$

These two concept terms are not equivalent, but they are nevertheless meant to represent the same concept. They can obviously be made equivalent by substituting the concept name Professor in the first term by the concept term Teacher $\sqcap$ Researcher and the concept name Woman in the second term by the concept term Person $\sqcap$ Female. We call a substitution that makes two concept terms equivalent a *unifier* of the two terms. Such a unifier proposes definitions for the concept names that are used as variables. In our example, we know that, if we define Woman as Person $\sqcap$ Female and Professor as Teacher $\sqcap$ Researcher, then the two concept terms from above are equivalent w.r.t. these definitions.

In [8] it was shown that, for the DL $\mathcal{FL}_0$, which differs from $\mathcal{EL}$ by offering value restrictions ($\forall r.C$) in place of existential restrictions, deciding unifiability is an ExpTime-complete problem. In [5], we were able to show that unification in $\mathcal{EL}$ is of considerably lower complexity: the decision problem is "only" NP-complete. The original unification algorithm for $\mathcal{EL}$ introduced in [5] was a brutal "guess and then test" NP-algorithm, but we have since then also developed more practical algorithms. On the one hand, in [7] we describe a goal-oriented unification algorithm for $\mathcal{EL}$, in which non-deterministic decisions are only made if they are triggered by "unsolved parts" of the unification problem. On the other hand, in [6], we present an algorithm that is based on a reduction to satisfiability in propositional logic (SAT), and thus allows us to employ highly optimized state-of-the-art SAT solvers for implementing an $\mathcal{EL}$-unification algorithm.

As mentioned above, however, SNOMED CT is not formulated in $\mathcal{EL}$, but rather in its sub-logic $\mathcal{EL}^{-\top}$, which differs from $\mathcal{EL}$ in that the use of the top

---

[1] See http://www.ihtsdo.org/snomed-ct/

Table 1. Syntax and semantics of $\mathcal{EL}$ and $\mathcal{EL}^{-\top}$

Name	Syntax	Semantics	$\mathcal{EL}$	$\mathcal{EL}^{-\top}$
concept name	A	$A^{\mathcal{I}} \subseteq \mathcal{D}_{\mathcal{I}}$	×	×
role name	r	$r^{\mathcal{I}} \subseteq \mathcal{D}_{\mathcal{I}} \times \mathcal{D}_{\mathcal{I}}$	×	×
top-concept	$\top$	$\top^{\mathcal{I}} = \mathcal{D}_{\mathcal{I}}$	×	
conjunction	$C \sqcap D$	$(C \sqcap D)^{\mathcal{I}} = C^{\mathcal{I}} \cap D^{\mathcal{I}}$	×	×
existential restriction	$\exists r.C$	$(\exists r.C)^{\mathcal{I}} = \{x \mid \exists y : (x,y) \in r^{\mathcal{I}} \wedge y \in C^{\mathcal{I}}\}$	×	×
subsumption	$C \sqsubseteq D$	$C^{\mathcal{I}} \subseteq D^{\mathcal{I}}$	×	×
equivalence	$C \equiv D$	$C^{\mathcal{I}} = D^{\mathcal{I}}$	×	×

concept is disallowed. If we employ $\mathcal{EL}$-unification to detect redundancies in (extensions of) SNOMED CT, then a unifier may introduce concept terms that contain the top concept, and thus propose definitions for concept names that are of a form that is not used in SNOMED CT. Apart from this practical motivation for investigating unification in $\mathcal{EL}^{-\top}$, we also found it interesting to see how such a small change in the logic influences the unification problem. Surprisingly, it turned out that the complexity of the problem increases considerably (from NP to PSPACE). In addition, compared to $\mathcal{EL}$-unification, quite different methods had to be developed to actually solve $\mathcal{EL}^{-\top}$-unification problems. In particular, we will show in this paper, that—similar to the case of $\mathcal{FL}_0$-unification—$\mathcal{EL}^{-\top}$-unification can be reduced to solving certain language equations. In contrast to the case of $\mathcal{FL}_0$-unification, these language equations can be solved in PSPACE rather than EXPTIME, which we show by a reduction to the emptiness problem for alternating automata on finite words. Complete proofs of the results presented in this paper can be found in [2].

2   The Description Logics $\mathcal{EL}$ and $\mathcal{EL}^{-\top}$

Starting with a set N_C of concept names and a set N_R of role names, $\mathcal{EL}$-*concept terms* are built using the concept constructors *top-concept* ($\top$), *conjunction* ($C \sqcap D$), and *existential restriction* ($\exists r.C$ for every $r \in N_R$). The $\mathcal{EL}$-concept term C is an $\mathcal{EL}^{-\top}$-*concept term* if $\top$ does not occur in C. Since $\mathcal{EL}^{-\top}$-concept terms are special $\mathcal{EL}$-concept terms, many definitions and results transfer from $\mathcal{EL}$ to $\mathcal{EL}^{-\top}$, and thus we only formulate them for $\mathcal{EL}$. We will explicitly mention it if this is not the case.

The semantics of $\mathcal{EL}$ and $\mathcal{EL}^{-\top}$ is defined in the usual way, using the notion of an interpretation $\mathcal{I} = (\mathcal{D}_{\mathcal{I}}, \cdot^{\mathcal{I}})$, which consists of a nonempty domain $\mathcal{D}_{\mathcal{I}}$ and an interpretation function $\cdot^{\mathcal{I}}$ that assigns binary relations on $\mathcal{D}_{\mathcal{I}}$ to role names and subsets of $\mathcal{D}_{\mathcal{I}}$ to concept terms, as shown in the semantics column of Table 1.

The concept term C *is subsumed by* the concept term D (written $C \sqsubseteq D$) iff $C^{\mathcal{I}} \subseteq D^{\mathcal{I}}$ holds for all interpretations $\mathcal{I}$. We say that C *is equivalent to* D (written $C \equiv D$) iff $C \sqsubseteq D$ and $D \sqsubseteq C$, i.e., iff $C^{\mathcal{I}} = D^{\mathcal{I}}$ holds for all interpretations $\mathcal{I}$.

An $\mathcal{EL}$-concept term is called an *atom* iff it is a concept name $A \in N_C$ or an existential restriction $\exists r.D$. Concept names and existential restrictions $\exists r.D$, where D is a concept name or $\top$, are called *flat atoms*. The set $\mathrm{At}(C)$ of *atoms of an $\mathcal{EL}$-concept term* C consists of all the subterms of C that are atoms. For example, $C = A \sqcap \exists r.(B \sqcap \exists r.\top)$ has the atom set $\mathrm{At}(C) = \{A, \exists r.(B \sqcap \exists r.\top), B, \exists r.\top\}$. Obviously, any $\mathcal{EL}$-concept term C is a conjunction $C = C_1 \sqcap \ldots \sqcap C_n$ of atoms and $\top$. We call the atoms among $C_1, \ldots, C_n$ the *top-level atoms* of C. The $\mathcal{EL}$-concept term C is called *flat* if all its top-level atoms are flat. Subsumption in $\mathcal{EL}$ and $\mathcal{EL}^{-\top}$ can be characterized as follows [7]:

Lemma 1. *Let* $C = A_1 \sqcap \ldots \sqcap A_k \sqcap \exists r_1.C_1 \sqcap \ldots \sqcap \exists r_m.C_m$ *and* $D = B_1 \sqcap \ldots \sqcap B_l \sqcap \exists s_1.D_1 \sqcap \ldots \sqcap \exists s_n.D_n$ *be two $\mathcal{EL}$-concept terms, where* $A_1, \ldots, A_k, B_1, \ldots, B_l$ *are concept names. Then* $C \sqsubseteq D$ *iff* $\{B_1, \ldots, B_l\} \subseteq \{A_1, \ldots, A_k\}$ *and for every* $j \in \{1, \ldots, n\}$ *there exists an* $i \in \{1, \ldots, m\}$ *such that* $r_i = s_j$ *and* $C_i \sqsubseteq D_j$.

In particular, this means that $C \sqsubseteq D$ iff for every top-level atom D' of D there is a top-level atom C' of C such that $C' \sqsubseteq D'$.

Modulo equivalence, the subsumption relation is a partial order on concept terms. In $\mathcal{EL}$, the top concept $\top$ is the greatest element w.r.t. this order. In $\mathcal{EL}^{-\top}$, there are many incomparable maximal concept terms. We will see below that these are exactly the $\mathcal{EL}^{-\top}$-concept terms of the form $\exists r_1. \cdots \exists r_n.A$ for $n \geq 0$ role names $r_1, \ldots, r_n$ and a concept name A. We call such concept terms *particles* . The set $\mathrm{Part}(C)$ of all particles of a given $\mathcal{EL}^{-\top}$-concept term C is defined as

- $\mathrm{Part}(C) := \{C\}$ if C is a concept name,
- $\mathrm{Part}(C) := \{\exists r.E \mid E \in \mathrm{Part}(D)\}$ if $C = \exists r.D$,
- $\mathrm{Part}(C) := \mathrm{Part}(C_1) \cup \mathrm{Part}(C_2)$ if $C = C_1 \sqcap C_2$.

For example, the particles of $C = A \sqcap \exists r.(A \sqcap \exists r.B)$ are $A, \exists r.A, \exists r.\exists r.B$. Such particles will play an important role in our $\mathcal{EL}^{-\top}$-unification algorithm. The next lemma states that particles are indeed the maximal concept terms w.r.t. to subsumption in $\mathcal{EL}^{-\top}$, and that the particles subsuming an $\mathcal{EL}^{-\top}$-concept term C are exactly the particles of C.

Lemma 2. *Let* C *be an $\mathcal{EL}^{-\top}$-concept term and* B *a particle.*

1. *If* $B \sqsubseteq C$, *then* $B \equiv C$.
2. $B \in \mathrm{Part}(C)$ *iff* $C \sqsubseteq B$.

3 Unification in $\mathcal{EL}$ and $\mathcal{EL}^{-\top}$

To define unification in $\mathcal{EL}$ and $\mathcal{EL}^{-\top}$ simultaneously, let $\mathcal{L} \in \{\mathcal{EL}, \mathcal{EL}^{-\top}\}$. When defining unification in $\mathcal{L}$, we assume that the set of concepts names is partitioned into a set N_v of concept variables (which may be replaced by substitutions) and a set N_c of concept constants (which must not be replaced by substitutions). An $\mathcal{L}$-*substitution* σ is a mapping from N_v into the set of all $\mathcal{L}$-concept terms. This mapping is extended to concept terms in the usual way, i.e., by replacing all occurrences of variables in the term by their σ-images. An $\mathcal{L}$-concept term is called *ground* if it contains no variables, and an $\mathcal{L}$-substitution σ is called *ground* if the concept terms $\sigma(X)$ are ground for all $X \in N_v$.

Unification tries to make concept terms equivalent by applying a substitution.

Definition 1. *An $\mathcal{L}$-unification problem is of the form* $\Gamma = \{C_1 \equiv^? D_1, \ldots, C_n \equiv^? D_n\}$, *where* $C_1, D_1, \ldots C_n, D_n$ *are $\mathcal{L}$-concept terms. The $\mathcal{L}$-substitution σ is an $\mathcal{L}$-unifier of Γ iff it solves all the equations $C_i \equiv^? D_i$ in Γ, i.e., iff $\sigma(C_i) \equiv \sigma(D_i)$ for $i = 1, \ldots, n$. In this case, Γ is called $\mathcal{L}$-unifiable.*

In the following, we will use the subsumption $C \sqsubseteq^? D$ as an abbreviation for the equation $C \sqcap D \equiv^? C$. Obviously, σ solves this equation iff $\sigma(C) \sqsubseteq \sigma(D)$.

Clearly, every $\mathcal{EL}^{-\top}$-unification problem Γ is also an $\mathcal{EL}$-unification problem. Whether Γ is $\mathcal{L}$-unifiable or not may depend, however, on whether $\mathcal{L} = \mathcal{EL}$ or $\mathcal{L} = \mathcal{EL}^{-\top}$. As an example, consider the problem $\Gamma := \{A \sqsubseteq^? X, B \sqsubseteq^? X\}$, where A, B are distinct concept constants and X is a concept variable. Obviously, the substitution that replaces X by $\top$ is an $\mathcal{EL}$-unifier of Γ. However, Γ does not have an $\mathcal{EL}^{-\top}$-unifier. In fact, for such a unifier σ, the $\mathcal{EL}^{-\top}$-concept term $\sigma(X)$ would need to satisfy $A \sqsubseteq \sigma(X)$ and $B \sqsubseteq \sigma(X)$. Since A and B are particles, Lemma 2 would imply $A \equiv \sigma(X) \equiv B$ and thus $A \equiv B$, which is not the case.

It is easy to see that, for both $\mathcal{L} = \mathcal{EL}$ and $\mathcal{L} = \mathcal{EL}^{-\top}$, an $\mathcal{L}$-unification problem Γ has an $\mathcal{L}$-unifier iff it has a ground $\mathcal{L}$-unifier σ that uses only concept and role names occurring in Γ,[2] i.e., for all variables X, the $\mathcal{L}$-concept term $\sigma(X)$ is a ground term that contains only such concept and role names. In addition, we may without loss of generality restrict our attention to *flat $\mathcal{L}$-unification problems*, i.e., unification problems in which the left- and right-hand sides of equations are flat $\mathcal{L}$-concept terms (see, e.g., [7]).

Given a flat $\mathcal{L}$-unification problem Γ, we denote by $\mathrm{At}(\Gamma)$ the set of all atoms of Γ, i.e., the union of all sets of atoms of the concept terms occurring in Γ. By $\mathrm{Var}(\Gamma)$ we denote the variables that occur in Γ, and by $\mathrm{NV}(\Gamma) := \mathrm{At}(\Gamma) \backslash \mathrm{Var}(\Gamma)$ the set of all *non-variable atoms* of Γ.

$\mathcal{EL}$-unification by guessing acyclic assignments

The NP-algorithm for $\mathcal{EL}$-unification introduced in [5] guesses, for every variable X occurring in Γ, a set $S(X)$ of non-variable atoms of Γ. Given such an *assignment* of sets of non-variable atoms to the variables in Γ, we say that the variable X *directly depends on* the variable Y if Y occurs in an atom of $S(X)$. Let *depends on* be the transitive closure of *directly depends on*. If there is no variable that depends on itself, then we call this assignment *acyclic*. In case the guessed assignment is not acyclic, this run of the NP-algorithm returns "fail."

---

[2] Without loss of generality, we assume that Γ contains at least one concept name.

Otherwise, there exists a strict linear order $>$ on the variables occurring in Γ such that $X > Y$ if X depends on Y. One can then define the substitution γ^S induced by the assignment S along this linear order:

- If X is the least variable w.r.t. $>$, then $\gamma^S(X)$ is the conjunction of the elements of $S(X)$, where the empty conjunction is $\top$.
- Assume $\gamma^S(Y)$ is defined for all variables $Y < X$. If $S(X) = \{D_1, \ldots, D_n\}$, then $\gamma^S(X) := \gamma^S(D_1) \sqcap \ldots \sqcap \gamma^S(D_n)$.

The algorithm then tests whether the substitution γ^S computed this way is a unifier of Γ. If this is the case, then this run returns γ^S; otherwise, it returns "fail." In [5] it is shown that Γ is unifiable iff there is a run of this algorithm on input Γ that returns a substitution (which is then an $\mathcal{EL}$-unifier of Γ).

Why this does not work for $\mathcal{EL}^{-\top}$

The $\mathcal{EL}$-unifiers returned by the $\mathcal{EL}$-unification algorithm sketched above need not be $\mathcal{EL}^{-\top}$-unifiers since some of the sets $S(X)$ in the guessed assignment may be empty, in which case $\gamma^S(X) = \top$. This suggests the following simple modification of the above algorithm: require that the guessed assignment is such that all sets $S(X)$ are nonempty. If such an assignment S is acyclic, then the induced substitution γ^S is actually an $\mathcal{EL}^{-\top}$-substitution, and thus the substitutions returned by the modified algorithm are indeed $\mathcal{EL}^{-\top}$-unifiers. However, this modified algorithm does not always detect $\mathcal{EL}^{-\top}$-unifiability, i.e., it may return no substitution although the input problem is $\mathcal{EL}^{-\top}$-unifiable.

As an example, consider the $\mathcal{EL}^{-\top}$-unification problem

$$\Gamma := \{A \sqcap B \equiv^? Y, \ B \sqcap C \equiv^? Z, \ \exists r.Y \sqsubseteq^? X, \ \exists r.Z \sqsubseteq^? X\},$$

where X, Y, Z are concept variables and A, B, C are distinct concept constants. We claim that, up to equivalence, the substitution that maps X to $\exists r.B$, Y to $A \sqcap B$, and Z to $B \sqcap C$ is the only $\mathcal{EL}^{-\top}$-unifier of Γ. In fact, any $\mathcal{EL}^{-\top}$-unifier γ of Γ must map Y to $A \sqcap B$ and Z to $B \sqcap C$, and thus satisfy $\exists r.(A \sqcap B) \sqsubseteq \gamma(X)$ and $\exists r.(B \sqcap C) \sqsubseteq \gamma(X)$. Lemma 1 then yields that the only possible top-level atom of $\gamma(X)$ is $\exists r.B$. However, there is no non-variable atom $D \in NV(\Gamma)$ such that $\gamma(D)$ is equivalent to $\exists r.B$. This shows that Γ has an $\mathcal{EL}^{-\top}$-unifier, but this unifier cannot be computed by the modified algorithm sketched above.

The main idea underlying the $\mathcal{EL}^{-\top}$-unification algorithm introduced in the next section is that one starts with an $\mathcal{EL}$-unifier, and then conjoins "appropriate" particles to the images of the variables that are replaced by $\top$ by this unifier. It is, however, not so easy to decide which particles can be added this way without turning the $\mathcal{EL}$-unifier into an $\mathcal{EL}^{-\top}$-substitution that no longer solves the unification problem.

4   An $\mathcal{EL}^{-\top}$-Unification Algorithm

In the following, let Γ be a flat $\mathcal{EL}^{-\top}$-unification problem. Without loss of generality we assume that Γ consists of subsumptions of the form $C_1 \sqcap \ldots \sqcap C_n \sqsubseteq^? D$

for atoms $C_1, \ldots, C_n, D$. Our decision procedure for $\mathcal{EL}^{-\top}$-unifiability proceeds in four steps.

Step 1. If S is an acyclic assignment guessed by the $\mathcal{EL}$-unification algorithm sketched above, then $D \in S(X)$ implies that the subsumption $\gamma^S(X) \sqsubseteq \gamma^S(D)$ holds for the substitution γ^S induced by S. Instead of guessing just subsumptions between variables and non-variable atoms, our $\mathcal{EL}^{-\top}$-unification algorithm starts with guessing subsumptions between arbitrary atoms of Γ. To be more precise, it guesses a mapping $\tau : \mathrm{At}(\Gamma)^2 \to \{0, 1\}$, which specifies which subsumptions between atoms of Γ should hold for the $\mathcal{EL}^{-\top}$-unifier that it tries to generate: if $\tau(D_1, D_2) = 1$ for $D_1, D_2 \in \mathrm{At}(\Gamma)$, then this means that the search for a unifier is restricted (in this branch of the search tree) to substitutions γ satisfying $\gamma(D_1) \sqsubseteq \gamma(D_2)$. Obviously, any such mapping τ also yields an assignment

$$S^\tau(X) := \{D \in \mathrm{NV}(\Gamma) \mid \tau(X, D) = 1\},$$

and we require that this assignment is acyclic and induces an $\mathcal{EL}$-unifier of Γ.

Definition 2. *The mapping* $\tau : \mathrm{At}(\Gamma)^2 \to \{0, 1\}$ *is called a* subsumption mapping *for* Γ *if it satisfies the following three conditions:*

1. *It respects the properties of subsumption in* $\mathcal{EL}$:
    (a) $\tau(D, D) = 1$ *for each* $D \in \mathrm{At}(\Gamma)$.
    (b) $\tau(A_1, A_2) = 0$ *for distinct concept constants* $A_1, A_2 \in \mathrm{At}(\Gamma)$.
    (c) $\tau(\exists r.C_1, \exists s.C_2) = 0$ *for distinct* $r, s \in N_R$ *with* $\exists r.C_1, \exists s.C_2 \in \mathrm{At}(\Gamma)$.
    (d) $\tau(A, \exists r.C) = \tau(\exists r.C, A) = 0$ *for each constant* $A \in \mathrm{At}(\Gamma)$, *role name* r *and variable or constant* C *with* $\exists r.C \in \mathrm{At}(\Gamma)$.
    (e) *If* $\exists r.C_1, \exists r.C_2 \in \mathrm{At}(\Gamma)$, *then* $\tau(\exists r.C_1, \exists r.C_2) = \tau(C_1, C_2)$.
    (f) *For all atoms* $D_1, D_2, D_3 \in \mathrm{At}(\Gamma)$, *if* $\tau(D_1, D_2) = \tau(D_2, D_3) = 1$, *then* $\tau(D_1, D_3) = 1$.
2. *It induces an* $\mathcal{EL}$*-substitution, i.e., the assignment* S^τ *is acyclic and thus induces a substitution* γ^{S^τ}, *which we will simply denote by* γ^τ.
3. *It respects the subsumptions of* Γ, *i.e., it satisfies the following conditions for each subsumption* $C_1 \sqcap \ldots \sqcap C_n \sqsubseteq^? D$ *in* Γ:
    (a) *If* D *is a non-variable atom, then there is at least one* C_i *such that* $\tau(C_i, D) = 1$.
    (b) *If* D *is a variable and* $\tau(D, C) = 1$ *for a non-variable atom* $C \in \mathrm{NV}(\Gamma)$, *then there is at least one* C_i *with* $\tau(C_i, C) = 1$.

Though this is not really necessary for the proof of correctness of our $\mathcal{EL}^{-\top}$-unification algorithm, it can be shown that the substitution γ^τ induced by a subsumption mapping τ for Γ is indeed an $\mathcal{EL}$-unifier of Γ. It should be noted that γ^τ need not be an $\mathcal{EL}^{-\top}$-unifier of Γ. In addition, γ^τ need not agree with τ on every subsumption between atoms of Γ. The reason for this is that τ specifies subsumptions which should hold in the $\mathcal{EL}^{-\top}$-unifier of Γ to be constructed. To turn γ^τ into such an $\mathcal{EL}^{-\top}$-unifier, we may have to add certain particles, and these additions may invalidate subsumptions that hold for γ^τ. However, we will ensure that no subsumption claimed by τ is invalidated.

Step 2. In this step, we use τ to turn Γ into a unification problem that has only variables on the right-hand sides of subsumptions. More precisely, we define $\Delta_{\Gamma,\tau} := \Delta_\Gamma \cup \Delta_\tau$, where

$$\Delta_\Gamma := \{C_1 \sqcap \ldots \sqcap C_n \sqsubseteq^? X \in \Gamma \mid X \text{ is a variable of } \Gamma\},$$

$$\Delta_\tau := \{C \sqsubseteq^? X \mid X \text{ is a variable and } C \text{ an atom of } \Gamma \text{ with } \tau(C,X) = 1\}.$$

For an arbitrary $\mathcal{EL}^{-\top}$-substitution σ, we define

$$S^\sigma(X) := \{D \in \mathrm{NV}(\Gamma) \mid \sigma(X) \sqsubseteq \sigma(D)\},$$

and write $S^\tau \leq S^\sigma$ if $S^\tau(X) \subseteq S^\sigma(X)$ for every variable X. The following lemma states the connection between $\mathcal{EL}^{-\top}$-unifiability of Γ and of $\Delta_{\Gamma,\tau}$, using the notation that we have just introduced.

Lemma 3. *Let Γ be a flat $\mathcal{EL}^{-\top}$-unification problem. Then the following statements are equivalent for any $\mathcal{EL}^{-\top}$-substitution σ:*

1. *σ is an $\mathcal{EL}^{-\top}$-unifier of Γ.*
2. *There is a subsumption mapping $\tau : \mathrm{At}(\Gamma)^2 \to \{0,1\}$ for Γ such that σ is an $\mathcal{EL}^{-\top}$-unifier of $\Delta_{\Gamma,\tau}$ and $S^\tau \leq S^\sigma$.*

Step 3. In this step, we characterize which particles can be added in order to turn γ^τ into an $\mathcal{EL}^{-\top}$-unifier σ of $\Delta_{\Gamma,\tau}$ satisfying $S^\tau \leq S^\sigma$. Recall that particles are of the form $\exists r_1. \cdots \exists r_n.A$ for $n \geq 0$ role names $r_1, \ldots, r_n$ and a concept name A. We write such a particle as $\exists w.A$, where $w = r_1 \cdots r_n$ is viewed as a word over the alphabet N_R of all role names. If $n = 0$, then w is the empty word ε and $\exists \varepsilon.A$ is just A.

Admissible particles are determined by solutions of a system of linear language inclusions. These *linear inclusions* are of the form

$$X_i \subseteq L_0 \cup L_1 X_1 \cup \ldots \cup L_n X_n, \tag{1}$$

where $X_1, \ldots, X_n$ are indeterminates, $i \in \{1, \ldots, n\}$, and each L_i ($i \in \{0, \ldots, n\}$) is a subset of $N_R \cup \{\varepsilon\}$. A *solution* θ of such an inclusion assigns sets of words $\theta(X_i) \subseteq N_R^*$ to the indeterminates X_i such that $\theta(X_i) \subseteq L_0 \cup L_1 \theta(X_1) \cup \ldots \cup L_n \theta(X_n)$.

The unification problem $\Delta_{\Gamma,\tau}$ induces a finite system $\mathcal{I}_{\Gamma,\tau}$ of such inclusions. The indeterminates of $\mathcal{I}_{\Gamma,\tau}$ are of the form X_A, where $X \in N_v$ and $A \in N_c$. For each constant $A \in N_c$ and each subsumption of the form $C_1 \sqcap \ldots \sqcap C_n \sqsubseteq^? X \in \Delta_{\Gamma,\tau}$, we add the following inclusion to $\mathcal{I}_{\Gamma,\tau}$:

$$X_A \subseteq f_A(C_1) \cup \ldots \cup f_A(C_n), \text{ where}$$

$$f_A(C) := \begin{cases} \{r\} f_A(C') & \text{if } C = \exists r.C' \\ Y_A & \text{if } C = Y \text{ is a variable} \\ \{\varepsilon\} & \text{if } C = A \\ \emptyset & \text{if } C \in N_c \setminus \{A\} \end{cases}$$

Since $\Delta_{\Gamma,\tau}$ contains only flat atoms, these inclusion are indeed of the form (1).

We call a solution θ of $\mathcal{I}_{\Gamma,\tau}$ *admissible* if, for every variable $X \in N_v$, there is a constant $A \in N_c$ such that $\theta(X_A)$ is nonempty. This condition will ensure that we can add enough particles to turn γ^τ into an $\mathcal{EL}^{-\top}$-substitution. In order to obtain a substitution at all, only finitely many particles can be added. Thus, we are interested in *finite* solutions of $\mathcal{I}_{\Gamma,\tau}$, i.e., solutions θ such that all the sets $\theta(X_A)$ are finite.

Lemma 4. *Let Γ be a flat $\mathcal{EL}^{-\top}$-unification problem and τ a subsumption mapping for Γ. Then $\Delta_{\Gamma,\tau}$ has an $\mathcal{EL}^{-\top}$-unifier σ with $S^\tau \le S^\sigma$ iff $\mathcal{I}_{\Gamma,\tau}$ has a finite, admissible solution.*

Proof sketch. Given a ground $\mathcal{EL}^{-\top}$-unifier σ of $\Delta_{\Gamma,\tau}$ with $S^\tau \le S^\sigma$, we define for each concept variable X and concept constant A occurring in Γ:

$$\theta(X_A) := \{w \in N_R^* \mid \exists w.A \in \mathrm{Part}(\sigma(X))\}.$$

It can then be shown that θ is a solution of $\mathcal{I}_{\Gamma,\tau}$. This solution is finite since any concept term has only finitely many particles, and it is admissible since σ is an $\mathcal{EL}^{-\top}$-substitution.

Conversely, let θ be a finite, admissible solution of $\mathcal{I}_{\Gamma,\tau}$. We define the substitution σ by induction on the dependency order $>$ induced by S^τ as follows. Let X be a variable of Γ and assume that $\sigma(Y)$ has already been defined for all variables Y with $X > Y$. Then we set

$$\sigma(X) := \prod_{D \in S^\tau(X)} \sigma(D) \sqcap \prod_{A \in N_c} \prod_{w \in \theta(X_A)} \exists w.A.$$

Since θ is finite and admissible, σ is a well-defined $\mathcal{EL}^{-\top}$-substitution. It can be shown that $\sigma(X)$ is indeed an $\mathcal{EL}^{-\top}$-unifier of $\Delta_{\Gamma,\tau}$ with $S^\tau \le S^\sigma$.   □

Step 4. In this step we show how to test whether the system $\mathcal{I}_{\Gamma,\tau}$ of linear language inclusions constructed in the previous step has a finite, admissible solution or not. The main idea is to consider the greatest solution of $\mathcal{I}_{\Gamma,\tau}$.

To be more precise, given a system of linear language inclusions $\mathcal{I}$, we can order the solutions of $\mathcal{I}$ by defining $\theta_1 \subseteq \theta_2$ iff $\theta_1(X) \subseteq \theta_2(X)$ for all indeterminates X of $\mathcal{I}$. Since $\theta_\emptyset$, which assigns the empty set to each indeterminate of $\mathcal{I}$, is a solution of $\mathcal{I}$ and solutions are closed under argument-wise union, the following clearly defines the (unique) greatest solution θ^* of $\mathcal{I}$ w.r.t. this order:

$$\theta^*(X) := \bigcup_{\theta \text{ solution of } \mathcal{I}} \theta(X).$$

Lemma 5. *Let X be an indeterminate in $\mathcal{I}$ and θ^* the maximal solution of $\mathcal{I}$. If $\theta^*(X)$ is nonempty, then there is a finite solution θ of $\mathcal{I}$ such that $\theta(X)$ is nonempty.*

Proof. Let $w \in \theta^*(X)$. We construct the finite solution θ of $\mathcal{I}$ by keeping only the words of length $|w|$: for all indeterminates Y occurring in $\mathcal{I}$ we define

$$\theta(Y) := \{u \in \theta^*(Y) \mid |u| \leq |w|\}.$$

By definition, we have $w \in \theta(X)$. To show that θ is indeed a solution of $\mathcal{I}$, consider an arbitrary inclusion $Y \subseteq L_0 \cup L_1 X_1 \cup \ldots \cup L_n X_n$ in $\mathcal{I}$, and assume that $u \in \theta(Y)$. We must show that $u \in L_0 \cup L_1\theta(X_1) \cup \ldots \cup L_n\theta(X_n)$. Since $u \in \theta^*(Y)$ and θ^* is a solution of $\mathcal{I}$, we have (i) $u \in L_0$ or (ii) $u \in L_i\theta^*(X_i)$ for some $i, 1 \leq i \leq n$. In the first case, we are done. In the second case, $u = \alpha u'$ for some $\alpha \in L_i \subseteq N_R \cup \{\varepsilon\}$ and $u' \in \theta^*(X_i)$. Since $|u'| \leq |u| \leq |w|$, we have $u' \in \theta(X_i)$, and thus $u \in L_i\theta(X_i)$.   □

Lemma 6. *There is a finite, admissible solution of $\mathcal{I}_{\Gamma,\tau}$ iff the maximal solution θ^* of $\mathcal{I}_{\Gamma,\tau}$ is admissible.*

Proof. If $\mathcal{I}_{\Gamma,\tau}$ has a finite, admissible solution θ, then the maximal solution of $\mathcal{I}_{\Gamma,\tau}$ contains this solution, and is thus also admissible.

Conversely, if θ^* is admissible, then (by Lemma 5) for each $X \in \text{Var}(\Gamma)$ there is a constant $A(X)$ and a finite solution θ_X of $\mathcal{I}_{\Gamma,\tau}$ such that $\theta_X(X_{A(X)}) \neq \emptyset$. The union of these solutions θ_X for $X \in \text{Var}(\Gamma)$ is the desired finite, admissible solution.   □

Given this lemma, it remains to show how we can test admissibility of the maximal solution θ^* of $\mathcal{I}_{\Gamma,\tau}$. For this purpose, it is obviously sufficient to be able to test, for each indeterminate X_A in $\mathcal{I}_{\Gamma,\tau}$, whether $\theta^*(X_A)$ is empty or not. This can be achieved by representing the languages $\theta^*(X_A)$ using *alternating finite automata with ε-transitions (ε-AFA)*, which are a special case of two-way alternating finite automata. In fact, as shown in [11], the emptiness problem for two-way alternating finite automata (and thus also for ε-AFA) is in PSPACE.

Lemma 7. *For each indeterminate X_A in $\mathcal{I}_{\Gamma,\tau}$, we can construct in polynomial time in the size of $\mathcal{I}_{\Gamma,\tau}$ an ε-AFA $\mathcal{A}(X, A)$ such that the language $L(\mathcal{A}(X, A))$ accepted by $\mathcal{A}(X, A)$ is equal to $\theta^*(X_A)$, where θ^* denotes the maximal solution of $\mathcal{I}_{\Gamma,\tau}$.*

This finishes the description of our $\mathcal{EL}^{-\top}$-unification algorithm. It remains to argue why it is a PSPACE decision procedure for $\mathcal{EL}^{-\top}$-unifiability.

Theorem 1. *The problem of deciding unifiability in $\mathcal{EL}^{-\top}$ is in PSPACE.*

Proof. We show that the problem is in NPSPACE, which is equal to PSPACE by Savitch's theorem [14].

Let Γ be a flat $\mathcal{EL}^{-\top}$-unification problem. By Lemma 3, Lemma 4, and Lemma 6, we know that Γ is $\mathcal{EL}^{-\top}$-unifiable iff there is a subsumption mapping τ for Γ such that the maximal solution θ^* of $\mathcal{I}_{\Gamma,\tau}$ is admissible.

Thus, we first guess a mapping $\tau : \text{At}(\Gamma)^2 \to \{0, 1\}$ and test whether τ is a subsumption mapping for Γ. Guessing τ can clearly be done in NPSPACE. For a given mapping τ, the test whether it is a subsumption mapping for Γ can be done in polynomial time.

From τ we can first construct $\Delta_{\Gamma,\tau}$ and then $\mathcal{I}_{\Gamma,\tau}$ in polynomial time. Given $\mathcal{I}_{\Gamma,\tau}$, we then construct the (polynomially many) ε-AFA $\mathcal{A}(X,A)$, and test them for emptiness. Since the emptiness problem for ε-AFA is in PSPACE, this can be achieved within PSPACE. Given the results of these emptiness tests, we can then check in polynomial time whether, for each concept variable X of Γ there is a concept constant A of Γ such that $\theta^*(X_A) = L(\mathcal{A}(X,A)) \neq \emptyset$. If this is the case, then θ^* is admissible, and thus Γ is $\mathcal{EL}^{-\top}$-unifiable.   □

5   PSpace-Hardness of $\mathcal{EL}^{-\top}$-Unification

We show PSPACE-hardness of $\mathcal{EL}^{-\top}$-unification by reducing the PSPACE-hard intersection emptiness problem for deterministic finite automata (DFA) [12,9] to the problem of deciding whether a given $\mathcal{EL}^{-\top}$-unification problem has an $\mathcal{EL}^{-\top}$-unifier or not.

First, we define a translation from a given DFA $\mathcal{A} = (Q, \Sigma, q_0, \delta, F)$ to a set of subsumptions $\Gamma_{\mathcal{A}}$. In the following, we only consider automata that accept a nonempty language. For such DFAs we can assume without loss of generality that there is no state $q \in Q$ that cannot be reached from q_0 or from which F cannot be reached. In fact, such states can be removed from $\mathcal{A}$ without changing the accepted language.

For every state $q \in Q$, we introduce a concept variable X_q. We use only one concept constant, A, and define $N_R := \Sigma$. The set $\Gamma_{\mathcal{A}}$ is defined as follows:

$$\Gamma_{\mathcal{A}} := \{ L_q \sqsubseteq^? X_q \mid q \in Q \setminus F \} \cup \{ A \sqcap L_q \sqsubseteq^? X_q \mid q \in F \}, \text{ where}$$

$$L_q := \bigsqcap_{\substack{\alpha \in \Sigma \\ \delta(q,\alpha) \text{ is defined}}} \exists \alpha.X_{\delta(q,\alpha)}.$$

Note that the left-hand sides of the subsumptions in $\Gamma_{\mathcal{A}}$ are indeed $\mathcal{EL}^{-\top}$-concept terms, i.e., the conjunctions on the left-hand sides are nonempty. In fact, every state $q \in Q$ is either a final state or a final state is reachable by a nonempty path from q. In the first case, A occurs in the conjunction, and in the second, there must be an $\alpha \in \Sigma$ such that $\delta(q,\alpha)$ is defined, in which case $\exists \alpha.X_{\delta(q,\alpha)}$ occurs in the conjunction.

The following lemma, which can easily be proved by induction on $|w|$, connects particles occurring in $\mathcal{EL}^{-\top}$-unifiers of $\Gamma_{\mathcal{A}}$ to words accepted by states of the DFA $\mathcal{A}$.

Lemma 8. Let $q \in Q$, $w \in \Sigma^*$, and γ be a ground $\mathcal{EL}^{-\top}$-unifier of $\Gamma_{\mathcal{A}}$ with $\gamma(X_q) \sqsubseteq \exists w.A$. Then $w \in L(\mathcal{A}_q)$, where $\mathcal{A}_q := (Q, \Sigma, q, \delta, F)$ is obtained from $\mathcal{A}$ by making q the initial state.

Together with Lemma 2, this lemma implies that, for every ground $\mathcal{EL}^{-\top}$-unifier γ of $\Gamma_{\mathcal{A}}$, the language $\{ w \in \Sigma^* \mid \exists w.A \in \mathrm{Part}(\gamma(X_{q_0})) \}$ is contained in $L(\mathcal{A})$.

Conversely, we will show that for every word w accepted by $\mathcal{A}$ we can construct a unifier γ_w such that $\exists w.A \in \mathrm{Part}(\gamma_w(X_{q_0}))$.

For the construction of γ_w, we first consider every $q \in Q$ and try to find a word u_q of minimal length that is accepted by $\mathcal{A}_q$. Such a word always exists since we have assumed that we can reach F from every state. Taking arbitrary such words is not sufficient, however. They need to be related in the following sense.

Lemma 9. *There exists a mapping from the states $q \in Q$ to words $u_q \in L(\mathcal{A}_q)$ such that that either $q \in F$ and $u_q = \varepsilon$ or there is a symbol $\alpha \in \Sigma$ such that $\delta(q, \alpha)$ is defined and $u_q = \alpha u_{\delta(q,\alpha)}$.*

Proof. We construct the words u_q by induction on the length n of a shortest word accepted by $\mathcal{A}_q$.

If $n = 0$, then q must be a final state. In this case, we set $u_q := \varepsilon$.

Now, let q be a state such that a shortest word w_q accepted by $\mathcal{A}_q$ has length $n > 0$. Then $w_q = \alpha w'$ for $\alpha \in \Sigma$ and $w' \in \Sigma^*$ and the transition $\delta(q, \alpha) = q'$ is defined. The length of a shortest word accepted by $\mathcal{A}_{q'}$ must be smaller than n, since w' is accepted by $\mathcal{A}_{q'}$. By induction, $u_{q'} \in L(\mathcal{A}_{q'})$ has already been defined and we have $\alpha u_{q'} \in L(\mathcal{A}_q)$. Since $\alpha u_{q'}$ cannot be shorter than $w_q = \alpha w'$, it must also be of length n. We now define $u_q := \alpha u_{q'}$. $\qquad\square$

We can now proceed with the definition of γ_w for a word $w \in L(\mathcal{A})$. The (unique) accepting run of $\mathcal{A}$ on $w = w_1 \ldots w_n$ yields a sequence of states $q_0, q_1, \ldots, q_n$ with $q_n \in F$ and $\delta(q_i, w_{i+1}) = q_{i+1}$ for every $i \in \{0, \ldots, n-1\}$. We define the substitution γ_w as follows:

$$\gamma_w(X_q) := \exists u_q.A \sqcap \bigsqcap_{i \in I_q} \exists w_{i+1} \ldots w_n.A,$$

where $I_q := \{i \in \{0, \ldots, n-1\} \mid q_i = q\}$. For every $q \in Q$, we include at least the conjunct $\exists u_q.A$ in $\gamma_w(X_q)$, and thus γ_w is in fact an $\mathcal{EL}^{-\top}$-substitution.

Lemma 10. *If $w \in L(\mathcal{A})$, then γ_w is an $\mathcal{EL}^{-\top}$-unifier of $\Gamma_{\mathcal{A}}$ and $\gamma_w(X_{q_0}) \sqsubseteq \exists w.A$.*

Proof. Let the unique accepting run of $\mathcal{A}$ on $w = w_1 \ldots w_n$ be given by the sequence $q_0 q_1 \ldots q_n$ of states with $q_n \in F$ and $\delta(q_i, w_{i+1}) = q_{i+1}$ for every $i \in \{0, \ldots, n-1\}$, and let γ_w be defined as above.

We must show that γ_w satisfies the subsumption constraints introduced in $\Gamma_{\mathcal{A}}$ for every state $q \in Q$: $L_q \sqsubseteq^? X_q$ if $q \in Q \setminus F$ and $A \sqcap L_q \sqsubseteq^? X_q$ if $q \in F$, where

$$L_q := \bigsqcap_{\substack{\alpha \in \Sigma \\ \delta(q,\alpha) \text{ is defined}}} \exists \alpha.X_{\delta(q,\alpha)}.$$

To do this, we consider every top-level atom of $\gamma_w(X_q)$ and show that it subsumes the left-hand side of the above subsumption.

- Consider the conjunct $\exists u_q.A$. If $u_q = \varepsilon$, then $q \in F$ and the left-hand side contains the conjunct A. In this case, the subsumption is satisfied. Otherwise, there is a symbol $\alpha \in \Sigma$ such that $q' := \delta(q, \alpha)$ is defined and $u_q = \alpha u_{q'}$. Since $\exists u_{q'}.A$ is a top-level atom of $\gamma_w(X_{q'})$, we have $\gamma(X_{q'}) \sqsubseteq \exists u_{q'}.A$, and thus $\gamma_w(L_q) \sqsubseteq \exists \alpha.\gamma_w(X_{q'}) \sqsubseteq \exists u_q.A$.
- Let $i \in I_q$, i.e., $q_i = q$, and consider the conjunct $\exists w_{i+1} \ldots w_n.A$. Since we have $\delta(q_i, w_{i+1}) = q_{i+1}$ and $\exists w_{i+2} \ldots w_n.A$ is a conjunct of $\gamma_w(X_{q_{i+1}})$,[3] we obtain $\gamma_w(L_q) \sqsubseteq \exists w_{i+1}.\gamma_w(X_{q_{i+1}}) \sqsubseteq \exists w_{i+1}\exists w_{i+2} \ldots w_n.A = \exists w_{i+1} \ldots w_n.A$.

This shows that γ_w is a ground $\mathcal{EL}^{-\top}$-unifier of Γ_A. Furthermore, since $0 \in I_{q_0}$, the particle $\exists w_1 \ldots w_n.A = \exists w.A$ is a top-level atom of $\gamma_w(X_{q_0})$, and thus $\gamma_w(X_{q_0}) \sqsubseteq \exists w.A$.   □

For the *intersection emptiness problem* one considers finitely many DFAs $\mathcal{A}_1, \ldots, \mathcal{A}_k$, and asks whether $L(\mathcal{A}_1) \cap \ldots \cap L(\mathcal{A}_k) \neq \emptyset$. Since this problem is trivially solvable in polynomial time in case $L(\mathcal{A}_i) = \emptyset$ for some $i, 1 \leq i \leq k$, we can assume that the languages $L(\mathcal{A}_i)$ are all nonempty. Thus, we can also assume without loss of generality that the automata $\mathcal{A}_i = (Q_i, \Sigma, q_{0,i}, \delta_i, F_i)$ have pairwise disjoint sets of states Q_i and are reduced in the sense introduced above, i.e., there is no state that cannot be reached from the initial state or from which no final state can be reached. The flat $\mathcal{EL}^{-\top}$-unification problem Γ is now defined as follows:

$$\Gamma := \bigcup_{i \in \{1, \ldots, k\}} \left(\Gamma_{\mathcal{A}_i} \cup \{X_{q_{0,i}} \sqsubseteq^? Y\} \right) ,$$

where Y is a new variable not contained in $\Gamma_{\mathcal{A}_i}$ for $i = 1, \ldots, k$.

Lemma 11. Γ *is unifiable in* $\mathcal{EL}^{-\top}$ *iff* $L(\mathcal{A}_1) \cap \ldots \cap L(\mathcal{A}_k) \neq \emptyset$.

Proof. If Γ is unifiable in $\mathcal{EL}^{-\top}$, then it has a ground $\mathcal{EL}^{-\top}$-unifier γ and there must be a particle $\exists w.A$ with $w \in \Sigma^*$ and $\gamma(Y) \sqsubseteq \exists w.A$. Since $\gamma(X_{q_{0,i}}) \sqsubseteq \gamma(Y) \sqsubseteq \exists w.A$, Lemma 8 yields $w \in L(\mathcal{A}_{i,q_{0,i}}) = L(\mathcal{A}_i)$ for each $i \in \{1, \ldots, k\}$. Thus, the intersection of the languages $L(\mathcal{A}_i)$ is nonempty.

Conversely, let $w \in \Sigma^*$ be a word with $w \in L(\mathcal{A}_1) \cap \ldots \cap L(\mathcal{A}_k)$. By Lemma 10, we have for each of the unification problems $\Gamma_{\mathcal{A}_i}$ an $\mathcal{EL}^{-\top}$-unifier $\gamma_{w,i}$ such that $\gamma_{w,i}(X_{q_{0,i}}) \sqsubseteq \exists w.A$. Since the automata have disjoint state sets, the unification problems $\Gamma_{\mathcal{A}_i}$ do not share variables. Thus, we can combine the unifiers $\gamma_{w,i}$ into an $\mathcal{EL}^{-\top}$-substitution γ by defining $\gamma(Y) := \exists w.A$ and $\gamma(X_q) := \gamma_{w,i}(X_q)$ for each $i \in \{1, \ldots, k\}$ and $q \in Q_i$. Obviously, this is an $\mathcal{EL}^{-\top}$-unifier of Γ since it satisfies the additional subsumptions $X_{q_{0,i}} \sqsubseteq^? Y$.   □

Since the intersection emptiness problem for DFAs is PSPACE-hard [12,9], this lemma immediately yields our final theorem:

---
[3] If $i = n - 1$, then $\exists w_{i+2} \ldots w_n.A = A$.

Theorem 2. *The problem of deciding unifiability in $\mathcal{EL}^{-\top}$ is PSPACE-hard.*

6 Conclusion

Unification in $\mathcal{EL}$ was introduced in [5] as an inference service that can support the detection of redundancies in large biomedical ontologies, which are frequently written in this DL. Motivated by the fact that the large medical ontology SNOMED CT actually does not use the top concept available in $\mathcal{EL}$, we have in this paper investigated unification in $\mathcal{EL}^{-\top}$, which is obtained from $\mathcal{EL}$ by removing the top concept. More precisely, SNOMED CT is a so-called acyclic $\mathcal{EL}^{-\top}$-TBox,[4] rather than a collection of $\mathcal{EL}^{-\top}$-concept terms. However, as shown in [7], acyclic TBoxes can be easily handled by a unification algorithm for concept terms.

Surprisingly, it has turned out that the complexity of unification in $\mathcal{EL}^{-\top}$ (PSPACE) is considerably higher than of unification in $\mathcal{EL}$ (NP). From a theoretical point of view, this result is interesting since it provides us with a natural example where reducing the expressiveness of a given DL (in a rather minor way) results in a drastic increase of the complexity of the unifiability problem. Regarding the complexity of unification in more expressive DLs, not much is known. If we add negation to $\mathcal{EL}$, then we obtain the well-known DL $\mathcal{ALC}$, which corresponds to the basic (multi-)modal logic K [15]. Decidability of unification in K is a long-standing open problem. Recently, undecidability of unification in some extensions of K (for example, by the universal modality) was shown in [18]. These undecidability results also imply undecidability of unification in some expressive DLs (e.g., in $\mathcal{SHIQ}$ [10]).

Apart from its theoretical interest, the result of this paper also has practical implications. Whereas practically rather efficient unification algorithm for $\mathcal{EL}$ can readily be obtained by a translation into SAT [6], it is not so clear how to turn the PSPACE algorithm for $\mathcal{EL}^{-\top}$-unification introduced in this paper into a practically useful algorithm. One possibility could be to use a SAT modulo theories (SMT) approach [13]. The idea is that the SAT solver is used to generate all possible subsumption mappings for Γ, and that the theory solver tests the system $\mathcal{I}_{\Gamma,\tau}$ induced by τ for the existence of a finite, admissible solution. How well this works will mainly depend on whether we can develop such a theory solver that satisfies well all the requirements imposed by the SMT approach.

Another topic for future research is how to actually compute $\mathcal{EL}^{-\top}$-unifiers for a unifiable $\mathcal{EL}^{-\top}$-unification problem. In principle, our decision procedure is constructive in the sense that, from appropriate successful runs of the ε-AFA $\mathcal{A}(X, A)$, one can construct a finite, admissible solution of $\mathcal{I}_{\Gamma,\tau}$, and from this an $\mathcal{EL}^{-\top}$-unifier of Γ. However, this needs to be made more explicit, and we need to investigate what kind of $\mathcal{EL}^{-\top}$-unifiers can be computed this way.

---

[4] Note that the right-identity rules in SNOMED CT [16] are actually not expressed using complex role inclusion axioms, but through the SEP-triplet encoding [17]. Thus, complex role inclusion axioms are not relevant here.

84   F. Baader et al.

References

1. Baader, F.: Terminological cycles in a description logic with existential restrictions. In: Proc. of the 18th Int. Joint Conf. on Artificial Intelligence (IJCAI 2003), pp. 325–330. Morgan Kaufmann, Los Alamitos (2003)
2. Baader, F., Binh, N.T., Borgwardt, S., Morawska, B.: Unification in the description logic $\mathcal{EL}$ without the top concept. LTCS-Report 11-01, TU Dresden, Dresden, Germany (2011), http://lat.inf.tu-dresden.de/research/reports.html
3. Baader, F., Brandt, S., Lutz, C.: Pushing the $\mathcal{EL}$ envelope. In: Proc. of the 19th Int. Joint Conf. on Artificial Intelligence (IJCAI 2005), pp. 364–369. Morgan Kaufmann, Los Alamitos (2005)
4. Baader, F., Calvanese, D., McGuinness, D., Nardi, D., Patel-Schneider, P.F. (eds.): The Description Logic Handbook: Theory, Implementation, and Applications. Cambridge University Press, Cambridge (2003)
5. Baader, F., Morawska, B.: Unification in the Description Logic $\mathcal{EL}$. In: Treinen, R. (ed.) RTA 2009. LNCS, vol. 5595, pp. 350–364. Springer, Heidelberg (2009)
6. Baader, F., Morawska, B.: SAT Encoding of Unification in $\mathcal{EL}$. In: Fermüller, C.G., Voronkov, A. (eds.) LPAR-17. LNCS, vol. 6397, pp. 97–111. Springer, Heidelberg (2010)
7. Baader, F., Morawaska, B.: Unification in the description logic $\mathcal{EL}$. Logical Methods in Computer Science 6(3) (2010)
8. Baader, F., Narendran, P.: Unification of concept terms in description logics. J. of Symbolic Computation 31(3), 277–305 (2001)
9. Garey, M.R., Johnson, D.S.: Computers and Intractability — A guide to NP-completeness. W.H. Freeman and Company, San Francisco (1979)
10. Horrocks, I., Sattler, U., Tobies, S.: Practical reasoning for very expressive description logics. Logic Journal of the IGPL 8(3), 239–264 (2000)
11. Jiang, T., Ravikumar, B.: A note on the space complexity of some decision problems for finite automata. Information Processing Letters 40, 25–31 (1991)
12. Kozen, D.: Lower bounds for natural proof systems. In: Annual IEEE Symposium on Foundations of Computer Science, pp. 254–266 (1977)
13. Nieuwenhuis, R., Oliveras, A., Tinelli, C.: Solving SAT and SAT modulo theories: From an abstract Davis-Putnam-Logemann-Loveland procedure to DPLL(T). J. ACM 53(6), 937–977 (2006)
14. Savitch, W.J.: Relationships between nondeterministic and deterministic tape complexities. Journal of Computer and System Sciences 4(2), 177–192 (1970)
15. Schild, K.: A correspondence theory for terminological logics: Preliminary report. In: Proc. of the 12th Int. Joint Conf. on Artificial Intelligence (IJCAI 1991), pp. 466–471 (1991)
16. Spackman., K.A.: Spackman. Managing clinical terminology hierarchies using algorithmic calculation of subsumption: Experience with SNOMED-RT. Journal of the American Medical Informatics Association (2000); Fall Symposium Special Issue
17. Suntisrivaraporn, B., Baader, F., Schulz, S., Spackman, K.: Replacing SEP-Triplets in SNOMED CT Using Tractable Description Logic Operators. In: Bellazzi, R., Abu-Hanna, A., Hunter, J. (eds.) AIME 2007. LNCS (LNAI), vol. 4594, pp. 287–291. Springer, Heidelberg (2007)
18. Wolter, F., Zakharyaschev, M.: Undecidability of the unification and admissibility problems for modal and description logics. ACM Trans. Comput. Log. 9(4) (2008)

Model Evolution with Equality
Modulo Built-in Theories

Peter Baumgartner[1,*] and Cesare Tinelli[2]

[1] NICTA and Australian National University, Canberra, Australia
[2] The University of Iowa, USA

Abstract. Many applications of automated deduction require reasoning modulo
background theories, in particular some form of integer arithmetic. Developing
corresponding automated reasoning systems that are also able to deal with quantified formulas has recently been an active area of research. We contribute to
this line of research and propose a novel instantiation-based method for a large
fragment of first-order logic with equality modulo a given complete background
theory, such as linear integer arithmetic. The new calculus is an extension of the
Model Evolution Calculus with Equality, a first-order logic version of the propositional DPLL procedure, including its ordering-based redundancy criteria. We
present a basic version of the calculus and prove it sound and (refutationally)
complete under certain conditions[1].

1 Introduction

Many applications of automated deduction require reasoning modulo background theories, in particular some form of integer arithmetic. Developing sophisticated automated
reasoning systems that are also able to deal with quantified formulas has recently been
an active area of research [6,8,10,3,1]. We contribute to this line of research and propose
a novel instantiation-based method for a large fragment of first-order logic with equality
modulo a given complete background theory, such as linear integer arithmetic. The new
calculus, $\mathcal{ME}_E(T)$, is an extension of the Model Evolution calculus with equality [4],
a first-order logic version of the propositional DPLL procedure, including its ordering-
based redundancy criteria as recently developed in [5]. At the same time, $\mathcal{ME}_E(T)$ is a
generalization wrt. these features of the earlier $\mathcal{ME}(LIA)$ calculus [3].

Instantiation based methods, including Model Evolution, have proven to be a successful alternative to classical, saturation-based automated theorem proving methods.
This then justifies attempts to develop theory-reasoning versions of them, even if their
input logic or their associated decidability results are not new. As one of these extensions, we think $\mathcal{ME}_E(T)$ is relevant in particular for its versatility since it combines powerful techniques for first-order equational logic with equality, based on an adaptation of
the Bachmair-Ganzinger theory of superposition, with a black-box theory reasoner. In
this sense, $\mathcal{ME}_E(T)$ is similar to the hierarchic superposition calculus [1,2].

---

[*] NICTA is funded by the Australian Government's *Backing Australia's Ability* initiative.

[1] The full version of this paper, which includes all proofs, is available as a NICTA research
report from http://www.nicta.com.au/research/research_publications.

N. Bjørner and V. Sofronie-Stokkermans (Eds.): CADE 2011, LNAI 6803, pp. 85–100, 2011.
© Springer-Verlag Berlin Heidelberg 2011

$\mathcal{ME}_E(T)$ also relates to DPLL(T) [9], a main approach for theorem proving modulo theories. DPLL(T) is essentially limited to the ground case and resorts to incomplete or inefficient heuristics to deal with quantified formulas [7, e.g.]. In fact, addressing this intrinsic limitation by lifting DPLL(T) to the first-order level is one of the main motivations for $\mathcal{ME}_E(T)$, much like lifting the propositional DPLL procedure to the first-order level while preserving its good properties was the main motivation for Model Evolution.

One possible application of $\mathcal{ME}_E(T)$ is in finite model reasoning. For example, the three formulas $1 \leq a \leq 100$, $P(a)$ and $\neg P(x) \leftarrow 1 \leq x \wedge x \leq 100$ together are unsatisfiable, when a is a constant and T is a theory of the integers. Finite model finders, e.g., need about 100 steps to refute the clause set, one for each possible value of a. Our calculus, on the other hand, can reason directly with integer intervals and allows a refutation in $O(1)$ steps. See Section 7 for further discussion of how this is achieved, variations of the example, and considerations on $\mathcal{ME}_E(T)$ as a decision procedure.

The most promising applications of $\mathcal{ME}_E(T)$ could be in software verification. Quite frequently, proof obligations arise there that require quantified formulas to define data structures with *specific* properties, e.g., ordered lists or ordered arrays, and to prove that these properties are preserved under certain operations, e.g., when an element is inserted at an appropriate position. In the array case, one could define ordered arrays with an axiom of the form "for all i, j with $0 \leq i < j \leq m$, $a[i] \leq a[j]$", where i and j are variables and m is a parameter, all integer-valued. Our calculus natively supports parameters like m and is well suited to reason with bounded quantification like the one above. In general, parameters like m must be additionally constrained to a finite domain for the calculus to be effective, see again Section 7.

The general idea behind our calculus with respect to theory reasoning is to use *rigid* variables to represent individual, but not yet known, elements of the background domain, and instantiate them as needed to carry the derivation forward. As a simple example without parameters, consider the clauses $f(x) \approx g(x) \leftarrow x > 5$ and $\neg(f(y + y) \approx g(8))$. These clauses will be refuted, essentially, by checking satisfiability of the set $\{v_1 = v_2 + v_2, v_1 > 5, v_1 = 8\}$ of constraints over rigid variables and (ordered) paramodulation inferences for reasoning with the equations in these clauses.

2   Preliminaries

We work in the context of standard many-sorted logic with first-order signatures comprised of sorts and operators (i.e., function symbols and predicate symbols) of given arities over these sorts. We rely on the usual notions of structure, (well-sorted) term/formula, satisfiability, and so on. If Σ is a sorted signature and X a set of sorted variables we will call $\Sigma(X)$-*term (resp. -formula)* a well-sorted term (resp. formula) built with symbols from Σ and variables from X. The notation $\Sigma(X_1, X_2)$ is a shorthand for $\Sigma(X_1 \cup X_2)$.

Syntax. For simplicity, we consider here only signatures with at most two sorts: a *background* sort B and a *foreground* sort F. We assume a *background signature* Σ_B having B as the only sort and an at most countable set of operators that includes an (infix) equality predicate symbol $=$ of arity $B \times B$. We will write $s \neq t$ as an abbreviation of $\neg(s = t)$. We fix an infinite set X_B of B-*variables*, variables of sort B.

We assume a complete first-order *background theory* T of signature Σ_B all of whose models interpret $=$ as the identity relation. Since T is complete and we do not extend Σ_B in any essential way with respect to T, we can specify it with no loss of generality simply as a Σ_B-structure. We call the set $|B|$ that T associates to the sort B the *background domain*. We assume, again with no loss of generality, that $|B|$ is at most countably infinite and all of its elements are included in Σ as B-constant symbols.Our running example for T will be the theory of linear integer arithmetic (LIA). For that example, Σ_B's operators are $\leq$, $+$ and all the integer constants, all with the expected arities, T is the structure of the integer numbers with those operators, and $|B| = \{0, \pm 1, \pm 2, \ldots\}$.

We will consider formulas over an expanded signature Σ_B^{Π} and expanded set of variables $X_B \cup V$ where Σ_B^{Π} is obtained by adding to Σ_B an infinite set Π of *parameters*, free constants of sort B, and V is a set of B-variables not in X_B, which we call *rigid variables*. The function and predicate symbols of Σ_B^{Π} are collectively referred to as the *background operators*. We call *(background) constraint* any formula in the closure of the set of $\Sigma_B^{\Pi}(X_B, V)$-atoms under conjunction, negation and existential quantification of variables.[2] A *closed constraint* is a constraint with no free variables (but possibly with rigid variables).

Note that rigid variables always occur free in a constraint. We will always interpret distinct rigid variables in a constraint as distinct elements of $|B|$. Intuitively, in the calculus presented here, a rigid variable v will stand for a specific, but unspecified, background domain element, and will be introduced during proof search similarly to rigid variables in free-variable tableaux calculi. In contrast, parameters will be free constants in input formulas, standing for arbitrary domain values.

The *full signature* Σ for our calculus is obtained by adding to Σ_B^{Π} the foreground sort F, function symbols of given arities over B and F, and one infix equality predicate symbol, $\approx$, of arity $F \times F$. The new function symbols and $\approx$ are the *foreground operators*. As usual, we do not consider additional foreground predicate symbols because they can be encoded as function symbols, e.g., an atom of the form $P(t_1, \ldots, t_n)$ can be encoded as $P(t_1, \ldots, t_n) \approx tt$, where tt is a new, otherwise unused, foreground constant. For convenience, however, in examples we will often write the former and mean the latter. Since $\approx$ will always denote a congruence relation, we will identify $s \approx t$ with $t \approx s$.

Let X_F be an infinite set of F-*variables*, variables of sort F, disjoint from X_B and V, and let $X = X_B \cup X_F$. When we say just "variable" we will always mean a variable in X, not a rigid variable.

The calculus takes as input $\Sigma(X)$-formulas of a specific form, defined later, and manipulate more generally $\Sigma(X, V)$ formulas, i.e., formulas possibly containing rigid variables. We use, possibly with subscripts, the letters $\{x, y\}$, $\{u, v\}$, $\{a, b\}$, and $\{f, e\}$ to denote respectively regular variables (those in X), rigid variables, parameters, and foreground function symbols.

---

[2] The calculus needs a decision procedure only for the validity of the $\forall\exists$-fragment over the class of constraints used in input formulas. When such formulas contain no parameters, a decision procedure for the $\exists$-fragment is sufficient.

To simplify the presentation here, *we restrict the return sort of all foreground function symbols to be* F . This is a true restriction for non-constant function symbols (foreground constant symbols of sort B can be supplied as parameters instead). For example, if Σ is the signature of lists of integers, with T being again LIA and F being the list sort, our logic allows formulas like $cdr(cons(x, y)) \approx y$ but not $car(cons(x, y)) \approx x$, as *car* would be integer-sorted. To overcome this limitation somewhat, one could turn *car* into a predicate symbol and use $car(cons(x, y), x)$ instead, together with the (universal) functionality constraint $\neg car(x, y) \lor \neg car(x, z) \leftarrow y \neq z$. This solution is however approximate as it does not include a totality restriction on the new predicate symbols.

A *term* is a (well-sorted) $\Sigma(X, V)$-term, a *formula* is a (well-sorted) $\Sigma(X, V)$-formula. A *foreground term* is a term with no operators from Σ_B^Π. Foreground atoms, literals, and formulas are defined analogously. An *ordinary foreground clause* is a multiset of foreground literals, usually written as a disjunction. A *background term* is a (well-sorted) $\Sigma_B^\Pi(X_B, V)$-term. Note that background terms are always B-sorted and vice versa. Foreground terms are made of foreground symbols, variables and rigid variables; they are all F-sorted unless they are rigid variables. A *ground term* is a term with no variables and no rigid variables. A *Herbrand term* is a ground term whose only background subterms are background domain elements. Intuitively, Herbrand terms do not contain symbols that need external evaluation, i.e., they contain no parameters, no variables, and no rigid variables. For example, $f(e, 1)$ and 1 are Herbrand terms, but $f(v, 1)$ and $f(a, 1)$ are not.

A *substitution* is a mapping σ from variables to terms that is sort respecting, that is, maps each variable $x \in X$ to a term of the same sort. We write substitution application in postfix form and extend the notation to (multi)sets S of terms or formulas as expected, that is, $S\sigma = \{F\sigma \mid F \in S\}$. The *domain* of a substitution σ is the set $\mathrm{dom}(\sigma) = \{x \mid x \neq x\sigma\}$. We work with substitutions with finite domains only. A *Herbrand substitution* is a substitution that maps every variable to a Herbrand term. We denote by $fvar(F)$ the set of non-rigid variables that occur free in F, where F is a term or formula.

Semantics. An *interpretation* I is any Σ-structure augmented to include an injective, possibly partial, mapping from the set V of rigid variables to the domain of B in I. We will be interested primarily in Herbrand interpretations, defined below.

Definition 2.1 (Herbrand interpretations). *A (T-based) Herbrand interpretation is any interpretation I that (i) is identical to T over the symbols of Σ^B, (ii) interprets every foreground n-ary function symbol f as itself, i.e., $f^I(d_1, \ldots, d_n) = f(d_1, \ldots, d_n)$ for every tuple $(d_1, \ldots, d_n)$ of domain elements from the proper domain, and (iii) interprets $\approx$ as a congruence relation on F-sorted Herbrand terms.*[3]

A *(parameter) valuation* π is a mapping from Π to $|B|$. An *assignment* α is an *injective* mapping from a (finite or infinite) subset of V to $|B|$. The range of α is denoted by $\mathrm{ran}(\alpha)$. Since T is fixed, a Herbrand interpretation I is completely characterized by a congruence relation on the Herbrand terms, a valuation π and an assignment α.

An assignment α is *suitable* for a formula or set of formulas F if its domain includes all the rigid variables occurring in F. Since all the elements of $|B|$ are constants of Σ_B we will often treat assignments and valuations similarly to substitutions. For any Herbrand

---

[3] Note that Condition (*iii*) is well defined because, by Condition (*ii*), the interpretation of the sort F is the set of all F-sorted Herbrand terms.

interpretation I, valuation π and assignment α, we denote by $I[\pi]$ the interpretation that agrees with π on the meaning of the parameters (that is, $a^I = a\pi$ for all $a \in \Pi$) and is otherwise identical to I; we denote by $I[\alpha]$ the interpretation that agrees with α on the meaning of the rigid variables in α's domain and is otherwise identical to I. We write $I[\pi, \alpha]$ as a shorthand for $I[\pi][\alpha]$.

The symbols I, α and π we will always denote respectively Herbrand interpretations, assignments and valuations. Hence, we will often use the symbols directly, without further qualification. We will do the same for other selected symbols introduced later. Also, we will often implicitly assume that α is suitable for the formulas in its context.

Definition 2.2 (Satisfaction of constraints). *Let c be a closed constraint. For all π and all α suitable for c, the pair (π, α) satisfies c, written as $(\pi, \alpha) \models c$, if $T \models c\pi\alpha$ in the standard sense.*[4] *If α is suitable for a set Γ of closed constraints, (π, α) satisfies Γ, written $(\pi, \alpha) \models \Gamma$, iff (π, α) satisfies every $c \in \Gamma$.*

The set Γ above is *satisfiable* if $(\pi, \alpha) \models \Gamma$, for some π and α. Since constraints contain no foreground symbols, for any interpretation $I[\pi, \alpha]$, $I[\pi, \alpha] \models c$ iff $(\pi, \alpha) \models c$.

The satisfiability of arbitrary closed constraints, which may contain rigid variables, reduces in a straightforward way to the satisfiability of Σ_B-constraints without rigid variables, and so can be decided by any decision procedure for the latter. It requires only to read parameters and rigid variables as variables in the usual sense, and to conjoin disequality constraints $u \neq v$ for all distinct rigid variables u and v that occur in c.

Finally, we assume a reduction ordering $>$ that is total on the Herbrand terms.[5] We also require that $>$ is stable under assignments, i.e., if $s > t$ then $s\alpha > t\alpha$, for every suitable assignment α for s and t. The ordering $>$ is extended to literals over Herbrand terms by identifying a positive literal $s \approx t$ with the multiset $\{s, t\}$, a negative literal $\neg(s \approx t)$ with the multiset $\{s, s, t, t\}$, and using the multiset extension of $>$. Multisets of literals are compared by the multiset extension of that ordering, also denoted by $>$.

3   Contexts and Constrained Clauses

Our calculus maintains two data structures for representing Herbrand interpretations: a *foreground context* Λ, a set of foreground literals, for the foreground operators; and a *background context* Γ, a set of closed constraints, for valuations and assignments. The elements of Λ are called *context literals*. We identify every foreground context Λ with its closure under renaming of (regular) variables, and assume it contains a pseudo-literal of the form $\neg x$. A foreground literal K is *contradictory with* Λ if $\overline{K} \in \Lambda$, where $\overline{K}$ denotes the complement of K. Λ itself is *contradictory* if it contains a literal that is contradictory with Λ. We will work only with non-contradictory contexts.

For any foreground literals K and L, we write $K \gtrsim L$ iff L is an instance of K, i.e., iff there is a substitution σ such that $K\sigma = L$. We write $K \sim L$ iff K and L are variants, equivalently, iff $K \gtrsim L$ and $L \gtrsim K$. We write $K \gtrsim L$ iff $K \gtrsim L$ but $L \not\gtrsim K$.

---

[4] Observe that the test $T \models c\pi\alpha$ is well formed because $c\pi\alpha$ is closed and contains neither parameters nor rigid variables.

[5] A *reduction ordering* is a strict, well-founded ordering on terms that is compatible with contexts, i.e., $s > t$ implies $f[s] > f[t]$, and stable under substitutions, i.e., $s > t$ implies $s\sigma > t\sigma$.

Definition 3.1 (Productivity). *Let K, L be foreground literals. We say that K produces L in Λ if (i) $K \gtrsim L$, and (ii) there is no $K' \in \Lambda$ such that $K \gtrsim \overline{K'} \gtrsim L$.*

Since foreground contexts contain the pseudo-literal $\neg x$, it is not difficult to see that Λ produces at least one of K and $\overline{K}$, for every Λ and literal K.

The calculus works with *constrained clauses*, expressions of the form $C \leftarrow R \cdot c$ where R is a multiset of foreground literals, the set of *context restrictions*, C is an ordinary foreground clause, and c is a (background) constraint with $fvar(c) \subseteq fvar(C) \cup fvar(R)$. When C is empty we write it as $\square$. When R is empty, we write the constrained clause more simply as $C \leftarrow c$. The calculus takes as input only clauses of the latter form, hence we call such clauses *input constrained clauses*. Below we will often speak of (input) clauses instead of (input) constrained clauses when no confusion can arise.

We can turn any expression of the form $C \leftarrow c$ where C is an arbitrary ordinary Σ-clause and c a constraint into an input clause by abstracting out offending subterms from C, moving them to the constraint side of $\leftarrow$, and existentially quantifying variables in the constraint side that do not occur in the clause side. For example, $P(a, v, x + 5) \leftarrow x > v$ becomes $P(x_1, v, x_2) \leftarrow \exists x (x > v \wedge x_1 = a \wedge x_2 = x + 5)$. As will be clear later, this transformation preserves the semantics of the original expression.

The variables of input clauses are implicitly universally quantified. Because the background domain elements (such as, e.g., $0, 1, -1, \ldots$) are also background constants, we can define the semantics of input clauses in terms of Herbrand interpretations. To do that, we need one auxiliary definition first.

If γ is a Herbrand substitution and $C \leftarrow c$ an input clause, the clause $(C \leftarrow c)\gamma = C\gamma \leftarrow c\gamma$ is a *Herbrand instance* of $C \leftarrow c$. For example, $(P(v, x, y) \leftarrow x > a)\gamma$ is $P(v, 1, f(1, e)) \leftarrow 1 > a$ if $\gamma = \{x \mapsto 1, y \mapsto f(1, e), \ldots\}$. A Herbrand instance $C \leftarrow c$ can be evaluated directly by an interpretation $I[\alpha]$, for suitable α: we say that $I[\alpha]$ *satisfies* $C \leftarrow c$, written $I[\alpha] \models C \leftarrow c$ if $I[\alpha] \models C \vee \neg c$. For input clauses $C \leftarrow c$ we say that $I[\alpha]$ *satisfies* $C \leftarrow c$ iff $I[\alpha]$ satisfies every Herbrand instance of $C \leftarrow c$.

Definition 3.2 (Satisfaction of sets of formulas). *Let Δ be a set of input clauses and closed constraints. We say that $I[\alpha]$ satisfies Δ, written as $I[\alpha] \models \Delta$, if $I[\alpha] \models F$, for every $F \in \Delta$.*

We say that Δ *is satisfiable* if some $I[\alpha]$ satisfies F. Let G be an input clause or closed constraint. We say that Δ *entails* G, written as $\Delta \models G$, if for every suitable assignment α for Δ and G, every interpretation $I[\alpha]$ that satisfies Δ also satisfies G.

The definition of satisfaction of general constrained clauses $C \leftarrow R \cdot c$, with a non-empty restriction R, is more complex because in our completeness argument for the calculus C is evaluated *semantically*, with respect to Herbrand interpretations induced by a context, whereas R is evaluated syntactically, with respect to productivity in a context. Moreover, constrained clause satisfaction is not definable purely at the ground level but requires a suitable notion of *Herbrand closure*.

Definition 3.3 (Herbrand closure). *Let γ be a Herbrand substitution. The pair $(C \leftarrow R \cdot c, \gamma)$ is a Herbrand closure (of $C \leftarrow R \cdot c$).*

Context restrictions are evaluated in terms of productivity by applying an assignment to the involved rigid variables first. To this end, we will use *evaluated contexts* $\Lambda\alpha = \{K\alpha \mid$

$K \in \Lambda$}. By the injectivity of α, the notions above on contexts apply *isomorphically* after evaluation by α. For instance, K produces L in Λ iff $K\alpha$ produces $L\alpha$ in $\Lambda\alpha$.

Definition 3.4 (Satisfaction of context restrictions). *Let R be a set of context restrictions and γ a Herbrand substitution. The pair (Λ, α) satisfies (R, γ), written as $(\Lambda, \alpha) \models (R, \gamma)$, if*

(i) $R\alpha\gamma$ contains no trivial literals, *of the form $t \approx t$ or $\neg(t \approx t)$, and for every $l \approx r \in R\alpha\gamma$, if $l > r$ then l is not a variable, and*
(ii) for every $K \in R\alpha$ there is an $L \in \Lambda\alpha$ that produces both K and $K\gamma$ in $\Lambda\alpha$.

Point (*i*) makes paramodulation into variables unnecessary for completeness in the calculus.

Definition 3.5 (Satisfaction of Herbrand closures). *A triple (Λ, α, I) satisfies $(C \leftarrow R \cdot c, \gamma)$, written as $(\Lambda, \alpha, I) \models (C \leftarrow R \cdot c, \gamma)$, iff $(\Lambda, \alpha) \not\models (R, \gamma)$ or $I \models (C \leftarrow c)\gamma$.*

We will use Definition 3.5 always with $I = I[\alpha]$. The component Λ in the previous definition is irrelevant for input clauses (where $R = \emptyset$), and satisfaction of Herbrand closures and Herbrand instances coincide then. Formally, $(\Lambda, \alpha, I[\alpha]) \models (C \leftarrow \emptyset \cdot c, \gamma)$ if and only if $I[\alpha] \models (C \leftarrow c)\gamma$.

In our soundness arguments for the calculus a constrained clause $C \leftarrow R \cdot c$ will stand for the Σ-formula $C \vee (\bigvee_{L \in R} \overline{L}) \vee \neg c$. We call the latter the *clause form* of $C \leftarrow R \cdot c$ and denote it by $(C \leftarrow R \cdot c)^c$. If Φ is a set of clauses, $\Phi^c = \{F^c \mid F \in \Phi\}$.

4   Core Inference Rules

The calculus works on sequents of the form $\Lambda \cdot \Gamma \vdash \Phi$, where $\Lambda \cdot \Gamma$ is a context and Φ is a set of constrained clauses. It has five core inference rules: Ref, Para, Pos-Res, Split and Close. In their description, if S is a set and a is an element, we will write S, a as an abbreviation of $S \cup \{a\}$.

The first two inference rules perform equality reasoning at the foreground level.

$$\text{Ref} \ \frac{\Lambda \cdot \Gamma \vdash \Phi}{\Lambda \cdot \Gamma \vdash \Phi, (C \leftarrow R \cdot c)\sigma}$$

if Φ contains a clause $\neg(s \approx t) \vee C \leftarrow R \cdot c$, the *selected clause*, and σ is an mgu of s and t. The new clause in the conclusion is the *derived clause*.

The next inference rule is a variant of ordered paramodulation.

$$\text{Para} \ \frac{\Lambda \cdot \Gamma \vdash \Phi}{\Lambda \cdot \Gamma \vdash \Phi, (L[r] \vee C \leftarrow (R \cup \{l \approx r\}) \cdot c)\sigma}$$

if $l \approx r \in \Lambda$ and Φ contains a clause $L[s] \vee C \leftarrow R \cdot c$, the *selected clause*, such that (*i*) σ is an mgu of l and s, (*ii*) s is neither a variable nor a rigid variable, (*iii*) $r\sigma \not\succeq l\sigma$, and (*iv*) $l \approx r$ produces $(l \approx r)\sigma$ in Λ. The context literal $l \approx r$ is the *selected context equation*, and the new clause in the conclusion is the *derived clause*.

We can afford to not paramodulate into rigid variables s, as these are B-sorted, and the resulting unifier with (an F-sorted variable) l would be ill-sorted. The equation $l \approx r$ is added to R to preserve soundness.

For example, if $\Lambda = \{f(x, y, e) \approx x\}$ then the clause $P(f(x, e, y)) \lor y \approx e \leftarrow \emptyset \cdot x > 5$ paramodulates into $P(x) \lor e \approx e \leftarrow f(x, e, e) \approx x \cdot x > 5$.

Let $C = L_1 \lor \cdots \lor L_n$ be an ordinary foreground clause with $n \geq 0$. We say that a substitution σ is a *context unifier of C against Λ* if there are literals $K_1, \ldots, K_n \in \Lambda$ such that σ is a simultaneous most general unifier of the sets $\{K_1, \overline{L}_1\}, \ldots, \{K_n, \overline{L}_n\}$. We say that σ is *productive* iff K_i produces $\overline{L}_i \sigma$ in Λ, for all $i = 1, \ldots, n$.

For any ordinary foreground clause, let $\overline{C} = \{\overline{L} \mid L \in C\}$.

$$\text{Pos-Res} \quad \frac{\Lambda \cdot \Gamma \vdash \Phi}{\Lambda \cdot \Gamma \vdash \Phi, (\square \leftarrow (R \cup \overline{C}) \cdot c)\sigma}$$

if Φ contains a clause of the form $C \leftarrow R \cdot c$, the *selected clause*, such that (*i*) $C \neq \square$ and C consists of positive literals only, and (*ii*) σ is a productive context unifier of C against Λ. The new clause in the conclusion is the *derived clause*.

For example, if $\Lambda = \{\neg P(e)\}$, from $f(x, y, z) \approx g(y) \lor P(x) \leftarrow \emptyset \cdot y > 5$ one gets $\square \leftarrow \{\neg(f(e, y, z) \approx g(y)), \neg P(e)\} \cdot y > 5$. (Recall that Λ implicitly contains $\neg x$.)

Intuitively, Pos-Res is applied when all literals in the ordinary clause part of a clause have been sufficiently processed by the equality inference rules Para and Ref and turns them into context restrictions. Deriving an empty constrained clause this way does not necessary produce a contradiction, as the clause could be satisfied, in an interpretation that falsifies its context restriction or falsifies its constraint. The Split rule below considers this possibility.

The rule has side conditions that treat context literals as constrained clauses. Formally, let $\Lambda^{(e,n)} = \{K^{(e,n)} \leftarrow \top \mid K \in \Lambda\}$ be the *clause form of Λ*, where $K^{(e,n)}$ is the context literal obtained from K by replacing every foreground variable by a fixed foreground constant e and replacing every background variable by a fixed background domain element n. We say that $(C \leftarrow R \cdot c)\delta$ is a *domain instance* of a clause $C \leftarrow R \cdot c$ if δ moves every B-sorted variable of $fvar(c)$ to a rigid variable and does not move the other variables of $fvar(c)$.

$$\text{Split} \quad \frac{\Lambda \cdot \Gamma \vdash \Phi}{\Lambda, \overline{K} \cdot \Gamma, c \vdash \Phi \qquad \Lambda, K \cdot \Gamma^\star \vdash \Phi}$$

if there is a domain instance $(\square \leftarrow R \cdot c)$ of some clause in Φ such that (*i*) $K \in R$ and neither $\overline{K}$ nor K is contradictory with Λ, (*ii*) for every $L \in R$, Λ produces L, (*iii*) $\Gamma \cup \{c\}$ is satisfiable, and (*iv*) $\Gamma^\star$ is any satisfiable background context such that $\Gamma \cup \{c\} \subseteq \Gamma^\star$ and $(\Lambda \cup \overline{K})^{(e,n)} \cup \Phi^c \cup \Gamma^\star$ is not satisfiable, if such a $\Gamma^\star$ exists, or else $\Gamma^\star = \Gamma \cup \{c\}$. The clause $\square \leftarrow R \cdot c$ is the *selected clause*, and the literal $\overline{K}$ is the *split literal*.

For example, if $\Lambda = \{\neg P(e)\}$ and Φ contains $\square \leftarrow \{\neg(f(e, y, z) \approx g(y)), \neg P(e) \cdot y > 5$, where y is B-sorted and the sort of z is irrelevant, the domain instance could be $\square \leftarrow \{\neg(f(e, v_1, z) \approx g(v_1)), \neg P(e)\} \cdot v_1 > 5$, and the split literal then is $f(e, v_1, z) \approx g(v_1)$.

The set Φ can also be seen to implicitly contain with each clause all its domain instances, and taking one of those as the selected clause for Split.

While splitting is done in a complementary way, as in earlier $\mathcal{ME}$ calculi, background contexts are global to derivations. Moreover, all constraints added to Γ in the course of the further derivation of the left branch need to be present in the right branch as well. This is modeled by Condition (iv). The branch $\Gamma^\star$ can be obtained in a constructive way by trying to extend the left branch to a refutation sub-tree, which, if successful, gives the desired $\Gamma^\star$. If not successful, no matter if finite or infinite, the input clause set is satisfiable, and the derivation need not return to the right branch anyway. We remark that extending background constraints, as done by Split (and Close and Restrict below) causes no soundness problems, as our soundness theorem applies relative to derived background contexts only. See Section 7 for details and how soundness in the usual sense is recovered.

$$\text{Close} \quad \frac{\Lambda \cdot \Gamma \vdash \Phi}{\Lambda \cdot \Gamma, c \vdash \Phi, (\square \leftarrow \emptyset \cdot \top)}$$

if Φ contains a clause $\square \leftarrow R \cdot c$ such that (i) $R \subseteq \Lambda$, and (ii) $\Gamma \cup \{c\}$ is satisfiable. The clause $\square \leftarrow R \cdot c$ is the *selected clause*.

5   Model Construction, Redundancy and Static Completeness

In this section we show how to derive from a sequent $\Lambda \cdot \Gamma \vdash \Phi$ an intended interpretation $I[\Lambda, \pi, \alpha]$ as a canonical candidate model for Φ. Its components π and α will be determined first by Γ, and its congruence relation will be presented by a convergent ground rewrite system $\mathcal{R}_{\Lambda,\alpha}$ extracted from Λ and α. The general technique for defining $\mathcal{R}_{\Lambda,\alpha}$ is borrowed from the completeness proof of the Superposition calculus and the earlier $\mathcal{ME}_E$ calculus.

A *rewrite rule* is an expression of the form $l \to r$ where l and r are F-sorted Herbrand terms. A *rewrite system* is a set of rewrite rules. The rewrite systems constructed below will be ordered, that is, consist of rules of the form $l \to r$ such that $l > r$. For a given Λ and suitable assignment α, we define by induction on the term ordering $>$ sets ϵ_K and $\mathcal{R}_K$ for every ground equation K between F-sorted Herbrand-terms. Assume that ϵ_L has already been defined for all such L with $K > L$. Let $\mathcal{R}_K = \bigcup_{K>L} \epsilon_L$, where

$$\epsilon_{l \approx r} = \begin{cases} \{l \to r\} & \text{if } \Lambda\alpha \text{ produces } l \approx r, l > r, \text{ and } l \text{ and } r \text{ are irreducible wrt } \mathcal{R}_{l \approx r} \\ \emptyset & \text{otherwise} \end{cases}$$

Finally define $\mathcal{R}_{\Lambda,\alpha} = \bigcup_K \epsilon_K$. If $\epsilon_{l \approx r} = l \to r$ we say that $l \approx r$ *generates* $l \to r$ in $\mathcal{R}_{\Lambda,\alpha}$.

For example, if $\Lambda = \{P(x), \neg P(v)\}$ and $\alpha = \{v \mapsto 1\}$ then $\mathcal{R}_{\Lambda,\alpha}$ contains $P(0) \to \text{tt}$, $P(-1) \to \text{tt}$, $P(-2) \to \text{tt}$, $P(2) \to \text{tt}$, $P(-3) \to \text{tt}$, $P(3) \to \text{tt}, \ldots$ but not $P(1) \to \text{tt}$, which is irreducible, but $P(1) \to \text{tt}$ is not produced by $\Lambda\alpha$.

Definition 5.1 (Induced interpretation). *Let Λ be a context, π a valuation, and α a suitable assignment for Λ. The* interpretation induced by Λ, π and α, *written as $I[\Lambda, \pi, \alpha]$, is the Herbrand interpretation $I[\pi, \alpha]$ that interprets foreground equality as $\mathcal{R}_{\Lambda,\alpha}^\star$, the congruence closure of $\mathcal{R}_{\Lambda,\alpha}$ (as a set of equations) over the Herbrand terms.*

The rewrite system $\mathcal{R}_{\Lambda,\alpha}$ is fully reduced by construction (no rule in $\mathcal{R}_{\Lambda,\alpha}$ rewrites any other rule in it). Since $>$ is well-founded on the Herbrand terms, $\mathcal{R}_{\Lambda,\alpha}$ is convergent. It follows from well-known results that equality of Herbrand terms in $\mathcal{R}^\star_{\Lambda,\alpha}$ can be decided by reduction to normal form using the rules in $\mathcal{R}_{\Lambda,\alpha}$.

The rewrite system $\mathcal{R}_{\Lambda,\alpha}$ will also be used to evaluate evaluated context restrictions:

Definition 5.2 (Satisfaction of variable-free foreground literals). *Let R be a set of literals over Herbrand terms. We say that $\mathcal{R}_{\Lambda,\alpha}$ satisfies R, and write $\mathcal{R}_{\Lambda,\alpha} \models R$, iff*

(i) for every $l \approx r \in R$, if $l > r$ then $l \to r \in \mathcal{R}_{\Lambda,\alpha}$, and
(ii) for every $\neg(l \approx r) \in R$, l and r are irreducible wrt. $\mathcal{R}_{\Lambda,\alpha}$.

For example, if $\Lambda = \{f(v) \approx e_2\}$, $\alpha = \{v \mapsto 1\}$, and $f(1) > e_1 > e_2 > 1$ then $\mathcal{R}_{\Lambda,\alpha} = \{f(1) \to e_2\}$ and $\mathcal{R}_{\Lambda,\alpha} \not\models \{\neg(f(1) \approx e_1), e_2 \approx e_1\}$ because the left-hand side of $\neg(f(1) \approx e_1)$ is reducible wrt. $\mathcal{R}_{\Lambda,\alpha}$, and because $e_1 \to e_2$ is not in $\mathcal{R}_{\Lambda,\alpha}$.

Our concepts of redundancy require comparing Herbrand closures. To this end, define $(C_1 \leftarrow R_1 \cdot c_1, \gamma_1) > (C_2 \leftarrow R_2 \cdot c_2, \gamma_2)$ iff $C_1\gamma_1 > C_2\gamma_2$, or else $C_1\gamma_1 = C_2\gamma_2$ and $R_1\gamma_1 > R_2\gamma_2$. Note that even if it ignores constraints, this ordering is not total, as constrained clauses may contain rigid variables.

Definition 5.3 (Redundant clause). *Let $\Lambda \cdot \Gamma \vdash \Phi$ be a sequent, and $\mathcal{D}$ and $(C \leftarrow R \cdot c, \gamma)$ Herbrand closures. We say that $(C \leftarrow R \cdot c, \gamma)$ is redundant wrt $\mathcal{D}$ and $\Lambda \cdot \Gamma \vdash \Phi$ iff (a) there is a $K \in R$ that is contradictory with Λ, (b) $\Gamma \cup \{c\gamma\}$ is not satisfiable, or (c) there exist Herbrand closures $(C_i \leftarrow R_i \cdot c_i, \gamma_i)$ of clauses in Φ, such that all of the following hold:*

(i) for every $L \in R_i$ there is a $K \in R$ such that $L \sim K$ and $L\gamma_i = K\gamma$,
(ii) $\Gamma \cup \{c\gamma\} \models c_i\gamma_i$,
(iii) $\mathcal{D} > (C_i \leftarrow R_i \cdot c_i, \gamma_i)$, and
(iv) $\{C_1\gamma_1, \ldots, C_n\gamma_n\} \models C\gamma$.

We say that a Herbrand closure $(C \leftarrow R \cdot c, \gamma)$ is *redundant wrt $\Lambda \cdot \Gamma \vdash \Phi$* iff it is redundant wrt $(C \leftarrow R \cdot c, \gamma)$ and $\Lambda \cdot \Gamma \vdash \Phi$, and that a clause $C \leftarrow R \cdot c$ is *redundant wrt $\Lambda \cdot \Gamma \vdash \Phi$* iff every Herbrand closure of $C \leftarrow R \cdot c$ is redundant wrt. $\Lambda \cdot \Gamma \vdash \Phi$.

If case (a) or (b) in the previous definition applies then $(C \leftarrow R \cdot c, \gamma)$ is trivially satisfied by $(\Lambda, \alpha, I[\alpha])$, for every suitable α that satisfies Γ and every $I[\alpha]$. Case (c) provides with (ii) and (iv) conditions under which $(C \leftarrow c)\gamma$ follows from the $(C_i \leftarrow c_i)\gamma_i$'s (in the sense of Definition 3.2). The context restrictions are taken into account by condition (i), which makes sure that evaluation of the pairs (R_i, γ_i) in terms of Definition 3.4 is the same as for (R, γ). In condition (iv), entailment $\models$ is meant as entailment in equational clause logic between sets of ordinary ground clauses and an ordinary ground clause.

Given a **Pos-Res**, **Ref** or **Para** inference with premise $\Lambda \cdot \Gamma \vdash \Phi$, selected clause $C \leftarrow R \cdot c$, selected context equation $l \approx r$ in case of **Para**, and a Herbrand substitution γ. If applying γ to $C \leftarrow R \cdot c$, the derived clause, and $l \approx r$ satisfies all applicability conditions of that inference rule, except $(C \leftarrow R \cdot c)\gamma \in \Phi$ and $(l \approx r)\gamma \in \Lambda$, we call the resulting ground inference a *ground instance via γ (of the given inference)*. This is not always the case, as, e.g., ordering constraints could be unsatisfied after application of γ.

Definition 5.4 (Redundant inference). *Let $\Lambda \cdot \Gamma \vdash \Phi$ and $\Lambda' \cdot \Gamma' \vdash \Phi'$ be sequents. An inference with premise $\Lambda \cdot \Gamma \vdash \Phi$ and selected clause $C \leftarrow R \cdot c$ is* redundant wrt *$\Lambda' \cdot \Gamma' \vdash \Phi'$ iff for every Herbrand substitution γ, $(C \leftarrow R \cdot c, \gamma)$ is redundant wrt. $\Lambda' \cdot \Gamma' \vdash \Phi'$ or the following holds, depending on the inference rule applied:*

Pos-Res, Ref, Para: *Applying γ to that inference does not result in a ground instance via γ, or $(C' \leftarrow R' \cdot c', \gamma)$ is redundant wrt. $(C \leftarrow R \cdot c, \gamma)$ and $\Lambda' \cdot \Gamma' \vdash \Phi'$, where $C' \leftarrow R' \cdot c'$ is the derived clause of that inference.*

Split $(C = \square)$: *(a) there is a literal $K \in R$ such that Λ' does not produce K or (b) the split literal is contradictory with Λ'.*

Close $(C = \square)$: $\square \leftarrow \emptyset \cdot \top \in \Phi'$.

Definition 5.5 (Saturated sequent). *A sequent $\Lambda \cdot \Gamma \vdash \Phi$ is* saturated *iff every inference with a core inference rule and premise $\Lambda \cdot \Gamma \vdash \Phi$ is redundant wrt. $\Lambda \cdot \Gamma \vdash \Phi$.*

We note that actually carrying out an inference makes it redundant wrt. the (all) conclusion(s), which already indicates that saturated sequents, although possibly infinite in each of its components, can be effectively computed.

Our first completeness result holds only for saturated sequents with respect to *relevant* closures. We say that a clause $(C \leftarrow R \cdot c, \gamma)$ is *relevant wrt. Λ and α iff $\mathcal{R}_{\Lambda,\alpha} \models R\alpha\gamma$.* All Herbrand closures of input clauses are always relevant.

Theorem 5.6 (Static completeness). *Let $\Lambda \cdot \Gamma \vdash \Phi$ be a saturated sequent, π a valuation and α a suitable assignment for $\Lambda \cdot \Gamma \vdash \Phi$. If $(\pi, \alpha) \models \Gamma$, $\mathrm{ran}(\alpha) = |B|$ and $(\square \leftarrow \emptyset \cdot \top) \notin \Phi$ then the induced interpretation $I[\Lambda, \pi, \alpha]$ satisfies all Herbrand closures of all clauses in Φ that are relevant wrt. Λ and α. Moreover, $I[\Lambda, \pi, \alpha] \models C \leftarrow c$, for every $C \leftarrow c \in \Phi$.*

The stronger statement $I[\Lambda, \pi, \alpha] \models \Phi$ does in general not follow, as $I[\Lambda, \pi, \alpha]$ possibly does not satisfy a *non-relevant* closure of a clause in Φ. See [5] for a discussion why.

6 The $\mathcal{ME}_E(T)$ Calculus

We now turn to the process of deriving saturated sequents. First, we introduce two more inference rules. The first one, Simp, is a generic simplification rule.

$$\text{Simp} \quad \frac{\Lambda \cdot \Gamma \vdash \Phi, C \leftarrow R \cdot c}{\Lambda \cdot \Gamma \vdash \Phi, C' \leftarrow R' \cdot c'}$$

if (1) $C \leftarrow R \cdot c$ is redundant wrt. $\Lambda \cdot \Gamma \vdash \Phi, C' \leftarrow R' \cdot c'$, and (2) $\Gamma \cup \Lambda^{(e,n)} \cup (\Phi \cup \{C \leftarrow R \cdot c\})^c \models (C' \leftarrow R' \cdot c')^c$. The first condition is needed for completeness, the second for soundness.

For example, if Λ contains a ground literal K, then every constrained clause of the form $C \leftarrow (\{\overline{K}\} \cup R) \cdot c$ can be deleted, and every constrained clause of the form $C \leftarrow (\{K\} \cup R) \cdot c$ can be replaced by $C \leftarrow R \cdot c$. The Simp rule encompasses various additional forms of simplification of the literals in C based on rewriting and subsumption, see [5].

$$\text{Restrict} \quad \frac{\Lambda \cdot \Gamma \vdash \Phi}{\Lambda \cdot \Gamma, c \vdash \Phi}$$

if c is a closed constraint such that $\Gamma \cup \{c\}$ is satisfiable.

For example, by 10-fold application of restrict one can construct a background context $\{1 \leq v_1 \leq 10, \ldots, 1 \leq v_{10} \leq 10\}$ that represents the numbers $1, \ldots, 10$ in a "nondeterministic" way. The purpose of Restrict is to construct finitely committed branches, as formally introduced below.

We are now ready to introduce derivation formally. In the following, we will use κ to denote an at most countably infinite ordinal. Let Ψ be a set of input clauses and Γ a satisfiable set of closed constraints, both rigid variable-free. A *derivation from* Ψ *and* Γ is a sequence $((N_i, E_i))_{0 \leq i < \kappa}$ of trees of sequents (called derivation trees) with nodes N_i and edges E_i, such that $\mathbf{T}_0$ consists of the root-only tree whose sequent is $\neg x \cdot \Gamma \vdash \Psi$, and $\mathbf{T}_i$ is obtained by one single application of one of the core inference rules, Simp or Restrict to a leaf of $\mathbf{T}_{i-1}$, for all $1 \leq i < \kappa$.

A *refutation* is a derivation that contains a *refutation tree*, that is, a derivation tree that contains in each leaf a sequent with $\square \leftarrow \emptyset \cdot \top$ in its clauses.

Every derivation determines a possibly infinite *limit tree* $\mathbf{T} = (\bigcup_{i<\kappa} N_i, \bigcup_{i<\kappa} E_i)$. In the following, let $\Lambda_i \cdot \Gamma_i \vdash \Phi_i$ be the sequent labeling the node i in some branch $\mathbf{B}$ with κ nodes of a limit tree $\mathbf{T}$, for all $i < \kappa$. Let

- $\Gamma_{\mathbf{B}} = \bigcup_{i<\kappa} \Gamma_i$ the *limit background context*,
- $\Lambda_{\mathbf{B}} = \bigcup_{i<\kappa} \Lambda_i$ be the *limit foreground context*, and
- $\Phi_{\mathbf{B}} = \bigcup_{i<\kappa} \bigcap_{i \leq j < \kappa} \Phi_j$ be the *persistent clauses*.

The tuple $\Lambda_{\mathbf{B}} \cdot \Gamma_{\mathbf{B}} \vdash \Phi_{\mathbf{B}}$ is the *limit sequent (of $\mathbf{B}$)*. To prove a completeness result, derivations in $\mathcal{ME}_E(\mathbf{T})$ need to construct limit sequents with certain properties:

Definition 6.1 (Exhausted branch). *We say that $\mathbf{B}$ is* exhausted *iff for all $i < \kappa$:*

(i) every Pos-Res, Ref, Para, Split and Close inference with premise $\Lambda_i \cdot \Gamma_i \vdash \Phi_i$ and a persistent selected clause is redundant wrt. $\Lambda_j \cdot \Gamma_j \vdash \Phi_j$ for some j with $i \leq j < \kappa$.
(ii) $(\square \leftarrow \emptyset \cdot \top) \notin \Phi_i$.

While the above notion is similar to the one already used in $\mathcal{ME}_E$, $\mathcal{ME}_E(\mathbf{T})$ has additional requirements on the limit background context $\Gamma_{\mathbf{B}}$, introduced next.

Definition 6.2 (Finitely committed branch). *We say that $\mathbf{B}$ is* finitely committed *iff (a) $\Gamma_{\mathbf{B}}$ is finite or (b) for all $i < \kappa$, there are π_i and α_i such that $(\pi_i, \alpha_i) \models \Gamma_i$, and*

(i) $\bigcup_{i<\kappa} \bigcap_{i \leq j < \kappa} \mathrm{ran}(\alpha_j) = |\mathsf{B}|$,
(ii) for every $n \in |\mathsf{B}|$, the set $\{v \mid \alpha_i(v) = n, \text{ for some } i < \kappa\}$ is finite,
(iii) for every rigid variable v occuring in $\Gamma_{\mathbf{B}}$, the set $\{\alpha_i(v) \mid v \in \mathrm{dom}(\alpha_i), \text{ for some } i < \kappa\}$ is finite, and
(iv) for every parameter a occuring in $\Gamma_{\mathbf{B}}$, the set $\{\pi_i(a) \mid i < \kappa\}$ is finite.

The set in condition (i) consists of those background domain elements that are represented by some (not necessarily the same) rigid variable from some point on forever. The condition requires that this must be the case for all background domain elements. Condition (ii) says that only finitely many rigid variables can be used for that. Condition (iii) says that no rigid variable occuring in $\Gamma_{\mathbf{B}}$ can be assigned infinitely many values as the context evolves. Condition (iv) is similar, but for parameters. (Recall that parameter valuations are total, hence $\pi_i(a)$ is defined for every parameter a.)

The purpose of Definition 6.2 is to make sure that a valuation π and a suitable assignment α for Γ always exists, and moreover, that (π, α) satisfies Γ_B:

Proposition 6.3 (Compactness of finitely committed branches). *If* **B** *is finitely committed then there is a π and an α such that* $\mathrm{ran}(\alpha) = |B|$ *and* $(\pi, \alpha) \models \Gamma_B$.

To see one of the issues that Proposition 6.3 addresses consider $\Gamma_i = \bigcup_{n \leq i} \{v_1 > n\}$, then Γ_B is not satisfiable, although every finite subset is satisfiable. On the other hand, condition (iii) in Definition 6.2 is not satisfied.

With enough Restrict applications finitely committed limit branches can be constructed in a straightforward way if the input background constraints confine every parameter to a finite domain. In the LIA case, e.g., one could "slice" the integers in intervals of, say, 100 elements and enumerate, with Restrict, declarations like $1 \leq v_1 \leq 100, \ldots, 1 \leq v_{100} \leq 100$ before any rigid variable v_i is used for the first time (in Split), and do that for all intervals. In certain cases it is possible to determine *a priori* that limit background contexts will be finite, and then Restrict is not required at all, see Section 7.

Definition 6.4 (Fairness). *A derivation is fair iff it is a refutation or its limit tree has an exhausted and finitely committed branch.*

Theorem 6.5 (Completeness). *Let Ψ be a set of input clauses and Γ a satisfiable set of closed constraints, both rigid variable-free. Suppose a fair derivation from Ψ and Γ that is not a refutation. Let* **B** *be any exhausted and finitely committed branch of its limit tree, and let $\Lambda_B \cdot \Gamma_B \vdash \Phi_B$ be the limit sequent of* **B**.

Then there is a valuation π and a suitable assignment α for Γ_B such that $\mathrm{ran}(\alpha) = |B|$ *and $(\pi, \alpha) \models \Gamma_B$, and it holds $I[\Lambda_B, \pi] \models \Gamma \cup \Psi$, where $I[\Lambda_B, \pi, \alpha]$ is the interpretation induced by Λ_B, π, and α.*

The proof exploits Proposition 6.3 to show that π and α exist as claimed. It then proceeds by showing that $\Lambda_B \cdot \Gamma_B \vdash \Phi_B$ is saturated, as a link with Theorem 6.5.

7   Soundness and Special Cases

Theorem 7.1 (Relative refutational soundness). *Let Ψ be a set of input clauses and Γ a satisfiable set of closed constraints, both rigid variable-free. Suppose a refutation from Ψ and Γ and let Γ_B be its limit background context. Then, $\Gamma_B \supseteq \Gamma$, Γ_B is satisfiable, and $\Gamma_B \cup \Psi$ is not satisfiable.*

Here, by the limit background context Γ_B of a refutation we mean the background context of the sequent in the leaf of the rightmost branch in its refutation tree.

Suppose the conditions of Theorem 7.1 hold, and let $I[\pi, \alpha]$ be such that $(\pi, \alpha) \models \Gamma_B$, as claimed. It follows $I[\pi, \alpha] \not\models \Psi$ and, as Ψ is rigid variable-free, $I[\pi] \not\models \Psi$. (If additionally Ψ is parameter-free then Γ_B and Ψ are independent, and so Ψ alone is not satisfiable.) For example, if $\Psi = \{P(x) \leftarrow x = a, \neg P(x) \leftarrow x = 5\}$ and $\Gamma = \{a > 2\}$ then there is a refutation with, say, $\Gamma_{\mathbf{B}} = \{a > 2, v_1 = a, v_1 = 5\}$. Notice that $(\pi, \alpha) \models \Gamma_{\mathbf{B}}$ entails $\pi = \{a \mapsto 5\}$, and, obviously, $I[\pi] \not\models \Psi$. But of course $\Psi \cup \Gamma$ is satisfiable, take, e.g., $\pi = \{a \mapsto 3\}$. A usual soundness result can thus be not based on *single* refutations, and this is why we call the soundness result above "relative". To fix that, we work with *sequences* of refutations whose limit background contexts collectively cover the initially given Γ. In the example, the next derivation starts with (essentially) $\Gamma = \{a > 2, \neg(a = 5)\}$, which leads to a derivation that provides the expected model.

Define $\mathrm{mods}(\Gamma) = \{\pi \mid (\pi, \alpha) \models \Gamma$, for some suitable $\alpha\}$. Then, the intuition above leads to the following general procedure:

1: $\mathbf{D} \leftarrow$ a fair derivation from Ψ and Γ {both Ψ and Γ assumed rigid-variable free}
2: **while** $\mathbf{D}$ is a refutation **do**
3:     $\Gamma_{\mathbf{B}} \leftarrow$ the limit background context of $\mathbf{D}$
4:     **if** $\mathrm{mods}(\Gamma_{\mathbf{B}}) = \mathrm{mods}(\Gamma)$ **then**
5:         **return** unsatisfiable
6:     **else**
7:         $\Gamma' \leftarrow$ any background context s.t. $\mathrm{mods}(\Gamma') = \mathrm{mods}(\Gamma) \setminus \mathrm{mods}(\Gamma_{\mathbf{B}})$
8:         $\Gamma \leftarrow \Gamma'$; $\mathbf{D} \leftarrow$ a fair derivation from Ψ and Γ
9: **return** satisfiable

At line 4, $\mathrm{mods}(\Gamma)$ is the set of parameter valuations under which the unsatisfiability of Ψ is yet to be established. If the current refutation $\mathbf{D}$ from Ψ and Γ does not further constrain Γ, i.e., if $\mathrm{mods}(\Gamma_{\mathbf{B}}) = \mathrm{mods}(\Gamma)$, then nothing remains to be done. Otherwise $\mathrm{mods}(\Gamma) \setminus \mathrm{mods}(\Gamma_{\mathbf{B}})$ is non-empty, and in the next iteration Γ is taken to stand for exactly those parameter valuations that are not sanctioned by the current refutation, i.e., those that satisfy the current Γ but not $\Gamma_{\mathbf{B}}$. It follows easily with Theorem 7.1 that if the procedure terminates with "unsatisfiable" on line 5 then $\Psi \cup \Gamma$ is indeed unsatisfiable, the desired standard soundness result. If on the other hand $\mathbf{D}$ is not a refutation then the procedure returns "satisfiable", which is sanctioned by Theorem 6.5.

Notice that the test in line 4 can be made operational by checking the validity of the formula $(\exists \bigwedge_{c \in \Gamma} c) \equiv (\exists \bigwedge_{c \in \Gamma_{\mathbf{B}}} c)$, where $\exists F$ denotes the existential quantification over all rigid variables occurring in F. Similarly, Γ' on line 7 can be taken as $\Gamma \cup \{\neg \exists \bigwedge_{c \in \Gamma_{\mathbf{B}}} c\}$. If the background theory admits quantifier elimination (e.g., LIA extended with divisibility predicates) the existential quantifiers can be removed and further simplifications may take place. In the example, the background context Γ' computed in the first iteration is $\Gamma' = \{a > 2, \neg \exists v_1 (a > 2 \wedge v_1 = a \wedge v_1 = 5)\} \equiv \{a > 2, \neg(a = 5)\}$.

The derivation $\mathbf{D}$ might not be finite. In this case the procedure does not terminate, but this is acceptable as by $\Psi \cup \Gamma$ is satisfiable then. Another source of non-termination comes from growing the sets Γ' without bound. This is theoretically acceptable, as our logic is not even semi-decidable. In practice, one could add to Γ finite domain declarations for all parameters involved, such as $1 \leq a \leq 100$. This leads to finitely many Γ' only. Moreover, the sets Γ' can then be computed in a conflict-driven way. For example, if $\Psi = \{P(x) \leftarrow x = a, \neg P(x) \leftarrow 1 \leq x \leq 50\}$ and $\Gamma = \{1 \leq a \leq 100\}$, the procedure will derive in the first iteration a refutation (in $O(1)$ time). The second iteration will then result in a derivation (a non-refutation) that restricts a to the range $[51, 100]$ and the procedure will stop with "satisfiable".

Another special case is when all clauses are of the form $C \leftarrow R \cdot (c \wedge x_1 = t_1 \wedge \cdots \wedge x_n = t_n)$, where $\{x_1, \ldots, x_n\} = fvar(C) \cup fvar(R)$, and c and the t_i's are ground. Such clauses, where initially $R = \emptyset$, are obtained from abstraction of formulas of the form $C \leftarrow c$, where C is an ordinary ground Σ-clause and c is a ground constraint. (This is the fragment over which $\mathcal{M}\mathcal{E}_E(T)$ overlaps with typical SMT methods.) It is not too difficult to argue that all derivable clauses then have that form as well. As a consequence, (i) all split literals are variable-free, and hence so are all derivable foreground contexts, and (ii) there is only one instantiation of the x_i's in Split, since no (satisfiable) background context can contain $v_1 = t$ and $v_2 = t$ for different rigid variables v_1 and v_2. It follows that the limit background contexts are finite *for any input background context*, hence no finite domain declarations for parameters are needed. Moreover, as the set of (non-rigid variable) background terms t_i is fixed a priori, there are only finitely many non-equivalent background contexts. Therefore, the procedure above cannot grow Γ indefinitely. Furthermore, all derivations are guaranteed to be final because context literals are variable-free and can use only finitely-many rigid variables. As a consequence, $\mathcal{M}\mathcal{E}_E(T)$ provides a decision procedure for ground problems in the combination of the background theory and uninterpreted (F-sorted) function symbols with equality.

8 Conclusions

We presented the new $\mathcal{M}\mathcal{E}_E(T)$ calculus, which properly generalizes the essentials of two earlier Model Evolution calculi, $\mathcal{M}\mathcal{E}_E$ [4], and $\mathcal{M}\mathcal{E}(LIA)$ [3], one with equational inference rules but without theory reasoning, and the other with theory reasoning by without equality over non-theory symbols.

Much remains to be done. Further work includes extending the calculus with "universal variables" and additional simplification rules. A further extension, which could be done along the lines of [2], would allow also B-sorted (non-constant) function symbols. Another important question is how to strengthen the model-building capabilities of the calculus, to guarantee termination in more cases of practical relevance.

References

1. Althaus, E., Kruglov, E., Weidenbach, C.: Superposition modulo linear arithmetic SUP(LA). In: Ghilardi, S., Sebastiani, R. (eds.) FroCoS 2009. LNCS, vol. 5749, pp. 84–99. Springer, Heidelberg (2009)
2. Bachmair, L., Ganzinger, H., Waldmann, U.: Refutational theorem proving for hierachic first-order theories. Appl. Algebra Eng. Commun. Comput. 5, 193–212 (1994)
3. Baumgartner, P., Fuchs, A., Tinelli, C.: ME(LIA) - model evolution with linear integer arithmetic constraints. In: Cervesato, I., Veith, H., Voronkov, A. (eds.) LPAR 2008. LNCS (LNAI), vol. 5330, pp. 258–273. Springer, Heidelberg (2008)
4. Baumgartner, P., Tinelli, C.: The Model Evolution Calculus with Equality. In: Nieuwenhuis, R. (ed.) CADE 2005. LNCS (LNAI), vol. 3632, pp. 392–408. Springer, Heidelberg (2005)
5. Baumgartner, P., Waldmann, U.: Superposition and Model Evolution Combined. In: Schmidt, R.A. (ed.) CADE-22. LNCS, vol. 5663, pp. 17–34. Springer, Heidelberg (2009)
6. Ganzinger, H., Korovin, K.: Theory instantiation. In: Hermann, M., Voronkov, A. (eds.) LPAR 2006. LNCS (LNAI), vol. 4246, pp. 497–511. Springer, Heidelberg (2006)

7. Ge, Y., Barrett, C.W., Tinelli, C.: Solving quantified verification conditions using satisfiability modulo theories. In: Pfenning, F. (ed.) CADE 2007. LNCS (LNAI), vol. 4603, pp. 167–182. Springer, Heidelberg (2007)

8. Korovin, K., Voronkov, A.: Integrating linear arithmetic into superposition calculus. In: Duparc, J., Henzinger, T.A. (eds.) CSL 2007. LNCS, vol. 4646, pp. 223–237. Springer, Heidelberg (2007)

9. Nieuwenhuis, R., Oliveras, A., Tinelli, C.: Solving SAT and SAT Modulo Theories: from an Abstract Davis-Putnam-Logemann-Loveland Procedure to DPLL(T). Journal of the ACM 53(6), 937–977 (2006)

10. Rümmer, P.: A constraint sequent calculus for first-order logic with linear integer arithmetic. In: Cervesato, I., Veith, H., Voronkov, A. (eds.) LPAR 2008. LNCS (LNAI), vol. 5330, pp. 274–289. Springer, Heidelberg (2008)

Blocked Clause Elimination for QBF

Armin Biere*, Florian Lonsing, and Martina Seidl

Institute for Formal Models and Verification
Johannes Kepler University, Linz, Austria
http://fmv.jku.at/

Abstract. Quantified Boolean formulas (QBF) provide a powerful framework for encoding problems from various application domains, not least because efficient QBF solvers are available. Despite sophisticated evaluation techniques, the performance of such a solver usually depends on the way a problem is represented. However, the translation to process-able QBF encodings is in general not unique and may either introduce variables and clauses not relevant for the solving process or blur infor-mation which could be beneficial for the solving process. To deal with both of these issues, preprocessors have been introduced which rewrite a given QBF before it is passed to a solver.

In this paper, we present novel preprocessing methods for QBF based on blocked clause elimination (BCE), a technique successfully applied in SAT. Quantified blocked clause elimination (QBCE) allows to simulate various structural preprocessing techniques as BCE in SAT. We have im-plemented QBCE and extensions of QBCE in the preprocessor bloqqer. In our experiments we show that preprocessing with QBCE reduces for-mulas substantially and allows us to solve considerable more instances than the previous state-of-the-art.

1   Introduction

Preprocessing in the context of SAT solving refers to techniques applied on a propositional formula before the actual solving process is started [1,2,6,11]. The intention behind preprocessing is to simplify the formula in such a way that solving time spent on the preprocessed formula together with the time spent on the preprocessing is less than the solving time of the original formula. The term "simplification" denotes the reduction of the formula in size as well as modifications extending the formula. On the one hand, state-of-the-art prepro-cessors apply various techniques which result in safe substitution and removal of single variable occurrences or even of complete clauses. On the other hand, in some situations preprocessors are able to identify information which can be used within the solving process and, consequently, might actually increase formula size. Especially if only formulas in conjunctive normal form (CNF) are consid-ered, the goal is to reconstruct structural information which has been blurred

---

* The 1st author is financially supported by the Austrian Science Foundation (FWF) NFN Grant S11408-N23 (RiSE).

N. Bjørner and V. Sofronie-Stokkermans (Eds.): CADE 2011, LNAI 6803, pp. 101–115, 2011.

by the normal form transformation. The extra effort spent on the preprocessing step is justified by the assumption that the costs of one single application of the implemented techniques is negligible, whereas a dynamic application within the solving process would be too expensive.

Preprocessing has been successfully applied to propositional formulas [1,2,6,11]. As SAT is the prototypical problem for NP, the problem of evaluating QBF (QSAT) is prototypical for PSPACE, offering a powerful framework for important application in artificial intelligence, knowledge representation, verification, and synthesis.

During the last decade, much effort has been spent in the development of efficient QBF solvers, but despite several success stories, the achievements are far from the progress which has been made in SAT solving, particularly when it comes to real applications. Motivated by the impact of preprocessing in SAT, some preprocessors for QBF have recently been presented which implement various kinds of preprocessing techniques and which proved to be advantageous for the evaluation of representative QBF benchmark sets [4,8,15,17,19]. Based on these experiments, we present the preprocessor bloqqer which incorporates several well established preprocessing techniques like (self-subsuming) resolution and expansion-based variable elimination as well as preprocessing techniques novel to QBF based on blocked clause elimination.

This paper is structured as follows. First, we introduce the basic terminology and the concepts used within this paper in Section 2 and we shortly review current preprocessing techniques for QBF in Section 3. In Section 4, we present novel preprocessing techniques based on blocked clause elimination for QBF and discuss the interrelationship with other approaches. We present our implementation bloqqer in Section 5 and compare and discuss the results obtained from various experiments. Finally, we conclude with an outlook to our future work.

2　Preliminaries

A QBF ϕ in prenex conjunctive normal form (PCNF) defined over the set of propositional variables V is an expression of the form $\phi = S_1 \ldots S_k \psi$ where ψ is called the *matrix* and $S_1 \ldots S_k$ is called the *quantifier prefix*.

The *matrix* is a propositional formula in conjunctive normal form, i.e., $\psi = C_1 \wedge \ldots \wedge C_n$ where $C_1, \ldots, C_n$ are clauses. A *clause* is a disjunction of literals, i.e., $C_i = l_1 \vee \ldots \vee l_m$. A *literal* l is either a variable x or a negated variable $\neg x$ with $x \in V$. The function var(l) returns x if l is of the form x or $\neg x$. If $l = x$ then $\bar{l} = \neg x$ else $\bar{l} = x$. If convenient, we consider the matrix as a set of clauses and a clause as a set of literals. Consequently, we also write $\{C_1, \ldots, C_n\}$ for ψ and $\{l_1, \ldots, l_m\}$ for a clause C. A clause C is tautological if $l, \bar{l} \in C$. If not stated otherwise, we assume clauses to be non-tautological in the following.

The *quantifier prefix* $S_1 \ldots S_k$ is an ordered partition of the variables V into scopes S_i. The size of a quantifier prefix $|S_1 \ldots S_k|$ is given by $|S_1| + \ldots + |S_k|$. The function quant(S) associates either an *existential quantifier* (quant(S) = $\exists$) or a *universal quantifier* (quant(S) = $\forall$) with each scope S. For scopes S_i and S_{i+1},

$\mathsf{quant}(S_i) \neq \mathsf{quant}(S_{i+1})$. Alternatively, we also write $Qx_1, \ldots, x_n$ for a scope $S = \{x_1, \ldots, x_n\}$ with $\mathsf{quant}(S) = Q, Q \in \{\forall, \exists\}$. For a clause C, its existential and its universal literals are defined by $L_Q(C) = \{l \in C \mid \mathsf{quant}(l) = Q\}$ with $Q \in \{\forall, \exists\}$. For a literal l with $\mathsf{var}(l) \in S$, $\mathsf{quant}(l) = \mathsf{quant}(S)$ denotes the type of l. For literals l, k with $\mathsf{var}(l) \in S_i$ and $\mathsf{var}(k) \in S_j$, $l \leq k$ if $i \leq j$. The indices i and, resp., j are called the *level* of l and, resp., of k.

Let l be a literal, then $\phi[l]$ denotes the QBF which is obtained by deleting the clauses C with $l \in C$, by removing each occurrence of $\bar{l}$, and by substituting the scope S_i with $\mathsf{var}(l) \in S_i$ by $S_i \backslash \{\mathsf{var}(l)\}$. The truth value of a QBF ϕ is recursively defined as follows.

- If $\psi = \emptyset$ then ϕ is true, if $\emptyset \in \psi$ then ϕ is false.
- If $\mathsf{quant}(S_1) = \forall$ (resp., $\mathsf{quant}(S_1) = \exists$) and $x \in S_1$, then ϕ is true iff $\phi[x]$ and (resp., or) $\phi[\neg x]$ is true.

The *Q-resolvent* $C_1 \otimes C_2$ of two clauses C_1 and C_2 with $l \in C_1$, $\bar{l} \in C_2$, and $\mathsf{quant}(l) = \exists$ is defined as $C_1' \backslash \{l\} \cup C_2' \backslash \{\bar{l}\}$ where

$$C_i' = C_i \backslash \{k \mid k \in C_i, \mathsf{quant}(k) = \forall, \forall k' \in C_i \text{ with } \mathsf{quant}(k') = \exists \ : k > k'\}.$$

The literal l is called *pivot element*. The removal of a universally quantified literal k from a clause which does not contain any existentially quantified variables with a higher level than k is also referred to as *forall reduction*. The construction rule of Q-resolvents enhanced with the forall reduction rule form the quantified resolution calculus which is sound and complete for QBF [5].

A literal l is called *pure* in a QBF $\phi = S_1 \ldots S_n \psi$ if $l \in \bigcup_{C \in \psi}$ and $\bar{l} \notin \bigcup_{C \in \psi}$. Then ϕ is equivalent to $\phi[l]$ if $\mathsf{quant}(l) = \exists$ and equivalent to $\phi[\bar{l}]$ if $\mathsf{quant}(l) = \forall$. An existentially quantified literal l is called *unit* in ϕ if $\{l, k_1, \ldots, k_m\} \in \psi$ with $\mathsf{quant}(k_i) = \forall$ and $l < k_i$. If l is unit in ϕ then ϕ is equivalent to $\phi[l]$. If ϕ contains a non-tautological clause with universally quantified literals only, then ϕ is false.

3   Preprocessing Techniques for QBF

Recently, several preprocessors for QBF have been proposed which implement different techniques to prepare formulas in PCNF for the actual solving process. Only the preprocessor PReDom [15] operates on a circuit-based representation with the aim to identify structural dominators. A node n_1 of a circuit dominates a node n_2 if every path starting from n_1 contains n_2. PReDom reduces dominated subcircuits such that the truth value of the original QBF is preserved.

The preprocessor realized within the logic framework proverbox [4], the preprocessors sQueezeBF [8] and prequel [19], as well as the approach presented in [17], all process formulas in PCNF encoded in the QDIMACS format and implement—among other techniques—unit propagation, forall reduction, and some kind of equality detection and substitution. The former three systems additionally implement pure literal detection and subsumption as well. When these basic simplification techniques are not applicable anymore, the preprocessor presented in [17] performs constant detection. If a literal is implied by the matrix of the given QBF, then it may be added as unit clause. For testing whether this implication holds, a SAT solver is applied. The preprocessor prequel [19] uses hyper binary resolution which—if applicable—resolves a clause of arbitrary length with binary clauses, until the resolvent is binary or even a unit clause. In the preprocessor built upon the framework proverbox [4], universally quantified variables are selectively expanded and consequently eliminated. Furthermore, Q-resolution is integrated in order to reduce duplications introduced by universal expansion. The preprocessor sQueezeBF [8] also implements Q-resolution (cf. [5]), but with the goal to remove existentially quantified variables. Similar to the approach implemented in the QBF solver Quantor [3], an existentially quantified variable may be eliminated from a formula, if all possible resolvents over this variable are added to the formula instead.

All of the previously presented techniques are applied with the intention to eliminate variables, literals, and/or clauses. Only hyper binary resolution is used to uncover hidden information beneficial for the solving process. In the preprocessor sQueezeBF [8], which we consider as the previous state-of-the-art, two rewriting rules have been introduced. These rewrite rules which are applied if the substitution of an equivalence would negatively affect the size of the QBF are defined as follows.

Lemma 1 (RW1: Removed Implication, see [8])

Let $\phi = S_1 \ldots S_n((l \vee \alpha) \wedge (l \Leftrightarrow \gamma) \wedge \psi)$ such that (i) $quant(l) = \exists$, (ii) l does occur neither in ψ, α, nor γ, and (iii) $k \leq l$ forall literals k occurring in γ. Then ϕ is equivalent to the formula $S_1 \ldots S_n((l \vee \alpha) \wedge (l \Rightarrow \gamma) \wedge \psi)$.

This rewriting may be beneficial with respect to two aspects: (i) the formula becomes smaller, and (ii) when α becomes true, l is pure. In the next section, we will argue that quantified blocked clause elimination is able to simulate RW1. In the case that l occurs in two polarities, the following rewrite rule may be applied.

Lemma 2 (RW2: Splitted Equivalence, see [8])

Let $\phi = S_1 \ldots S_i \ldots S_n((l \vee \alpha) \wedge (\bar{l} \vee \beta) \wedge (l \Leftrightarrow \gamma) \wedge \psi)$ such that (i) $quant(l) = \exists$, $var(l) \in S_i$, (ii) l does occur neither in ψ, α, β, nor γ, and (iii) $k \leq l$ forall literals k occurring in γ. Then ϕ is equivalent to the formula

$$S_1 \ldots S_i' \ldots S_n((l \vee \alpha) \wedge (l' \vee \beta) \wedge (l \Rightarrow \gamma) \wedge (l' \Rightarrow \overline{\gamma}) \wedge \psi)$$

where l' is a fresh variable with $quant(l') = \exists$ and the same polarity as l and $S_i' = S_i \cup \{var(l')\}$.

The application of this rewrite rule does not reduce formula size, but it may trigger pure literal elimination. If α (resp., β) becomes true, then $(l \Rightarrow \gamma)$ (resp., $(\gamma \Rightarrow \bar{l'})$) may be removed. At first sight, this rewrite rule affects unit literal propagation adversely, because the original QBF ϕ reduces to $\beta \wedge \gamma \wedge \psi$ if α is false and to $\alpha \wedge \gamma \wedge \psi$ if β is false. Having the rewrite rule applied, we only obtain $(l' \vee \beta) \wedge \gamma \wedge (l' \Rightarrow \overline{\gamma}) \wedge \psi$ in the one case and $(l \vee \alpha) \wedge \neg\gamma \wedge (l \Rightarrow \gamma) \wedge \psi$ in the other case. To overcome this limitation, the *efficiency clause* $(\overline{l} \vee \overline{l'})$ which is obviously entailed by $(l \Rightarrow \gamma) \wedge (l' \Rightarrow \overline{\gamma})$ has to be added to the formula when the rewrite rule is applied.

4   Quantified Blocked Clause Elimination

Originally introduced for restricting worst-case upper bounds for SAT-algorithms [12], *blocked clauses* have proven to be effective for preprocessing in SAT [11,16], because blocked clauses may be eliminated while preserving satisfiability. In the following, we generalize the notion of blocked clauses and blocked clause elimination (BCE) for QBF. We prove that also in the case of QBF under certain restrictions blocked clauses may be omitted. Subsequently, we shortly discuss the integration of quantified BCE (QBCE) with other preprocessing techniques, before we propose extensions for QBCE.

4.1   Definition

Within a resolution proof, blocked clauses of a formula only generate clauses which are tautological. Consequently, blocked clauses may be removed without changing the truth value of a formula. In the following we describe the characteristics which allow the syntactical identification of blocked clauses in QBF.

Definition 1 (Quantified Blocking Literal). *A literal l with* **quant**$(l) = \exists$ *in a clause $C \in \psi$ of a QBF $\phi = S_1 \dots S_n \psi$ is called a* quantified blocking literal *if forall $C' \in \psi$ with $\overline{l} \in C'$, a literal k with $k \leq l$ exists such that $k, \overline{k} \in C \otimes C'$.*

Definition 2 (Quantified Blocked Clause). *A clause is* quantified blocked *if it contains a quantified blocking literal.*

Example 1. Both clauses in $\forall x \exists y((x \vee \neg y) \wedge (\neg x \vee y))$ are quantified blocked clauses, whereas none of the clauses in $\exists x \forall y((x \vee \neg y) \wedge (\neg x \vee y))$ is a quantified blocked clause.

As the following theorem shows, quantified blocked clauses contain redundant information only, and may therefore be removed from the formula.

Theorem 1 (Quantified Blocked Clause Elimination (QBCE)). *Let $\phi = S_1 \dots S_n(\psi \cup C)$ be a QBF and let C be a quantified blocked clause in ϕ with blocking literal l. It holds that $\phi \Leftrightarrow S_1 \dots S_n \psi$.*

Proof. Let C be a quantified blocked clause with the quantified blocking literal l with var$(l) \in S_i$, $i \leq n$. The direction $\phi \Rightarrow S_1 \dots S_n \psi$ trivially holds. We show $S_1 \dots S_n \psi \Rightarrow \phi$ by induction over $q = |S_1 \dots S_{i-1}|$. W.l.o.g. assume $i = n$.

In the base case, we have $q = 0$, i.e., var$(l) \in S_1$ with quant$(S_1) = \exists$. The same argument as in SAT applies: Let σ be a satisfying assignment for ψ, i.e., for each $C' \in \psi$ there exists a literal l' such that $\sigma(l') = \top$. If σ satisfies C, the implication $S_1\psi \Rightarrow \phi$ holds, otherwise we construct a satisfying assignment σ' for $\psi \cup C$ as follows. Let $\sigma'(l') = \sigma(l')$ for $l' \neq l$ and $\sigma'(l) = \top$. σ' satisfies not only C but also all other clauses $C' \in \psi$. If $\bar{l} \in C'$, there exists a literal $k \neq l$ such that $k \in C$ and $\bar{k} \in C'$, with $\sigma(k) = \sigma(C) = \sigma'(k) = \bot$ and thus $\sigma'(C') = \sigma'(\bar{k}) = \top$ [12]. Note that $k \in S_1$ due to the restriction $k \leq l$.

For the induction step, assume $q > 0$. Let h be a literal with $\mathsf{var}(h) = y$ and $y \in S_1$. Note that $\mathsf{var}(l) \neq y$. We show that $S_1\backslash\{y\}\ldots S_n\psi[h] \Rightarrow \phi[h]$. The rest follows from lifting the implication over the conjunction that defines the semantics of universal quantification if $\mathsf{quant}(S_1) = \forall$ and respectively over the disjunction that defines the semantics of the existential quantification if $\mathsf{quant}(S_1) = \exists$. Three cases have to be considered for showing that $C[h]$ is a blocking clause or removed in $\phi[h]$.

1. $h \in C$. Then C is removed from $\phi[h]$.
2. $h \notin C$ and $\bar{h} \notin C$. Consequently, $C[h] = C$. Furthermore, C is still a quantified blocked clause in $\phi[h]$, since h was not used to make a resolvent on l tautological. Then the induction hypothesis is applicable.
3. $\bar{h} \in C$. Consequently, $C[h] = C\backslash\{\bar{h}\}$ which is a quantified blocked clause in $\phi[h]$, because each clause C' with $h, \bar{h} \in C \otimes C'$ is removed from $\phi[h]$ and other clauses C' with $k, \bar{k} \in C \otimes C'$ and $y \neq \mathsf{var}(k)$ still produce tautological resolvents with C on l. Note $l \in C[h]$ since $l \neq \bar{h}$.

For a QBF ϕ in PCNF, quantified blocked clause elimination repeats the removal of quantified blocked clauses from ϕ until fixpoint. The resulting QBF is denoted by $\mathsf{QBCE}(\phi)$.

Theorem 2. *The application of QBCE(ϕ) on a QBF ϕ is confluent.*

Proof. The argument is similar as for propositional logic (cf. [11]). ∎

Note that for the soundness of quantified blocked clause elimination for QBF as stated in Theorem 1, the level of the blocking literal must be equal or higher than the level of the literal making the resolvent tautological as the following example illustrates.

Example 2. As we have seen in Example 1, the QBF

$$\exists x \forall y ((x \vee \neg y) \wedge (\neg x \vee y))$$

contains no blocking clause. If we loosen the criterion and do not consider the quantifier levels of the variables, then all clauses become blocking clauses and according to Theorem 1, they may be removed immediately. Consequently, the formula evaluates to true, what is in contrast to the formula's original truth value. In this formula, a contradiction is directly derivable if forall reduction is applied. An extended example, where forall reduction is not applicable, is given by the formula

$$\exists x \forall y \exists z ((x \vee \neg z) \wedge (\neg x \vee z) \wedge (y \vee \neg z) \wedge (\neg y \vee z))$$

which contains an additional existential variable z which is equivalent to y. The variable z prohibits the application of the forall reduction rule. Furthermore, the first two clauses are not quantified blocked on x and $\neg x$, respectively, because $z < x$ does not hold. If they are removed, the formula evaluates to true.

4.2   Discussion

Quantified blocked clauses as defined above may be eliminated from a formula without changing its truth value, because they contain redundant information only. Hence, quantified blocked clause elimination is applied in order to remove clauses from a QBF which may result in a reduction in the number of variables occurring in the formula too. The following properties established for SAT [11,12], also hold for QBF. For the sake of compactness, we omit the prefix "quantified" if no confusion arises.

1. Formulas which are smaller with respect to their number of clauses potentially contain more blocked clauses. If the matrix of a QBF ϕ_1 is a subset of the matrix of the QBF ϕ_2 then there might be clauses which are blocked in ϕ_1, but not in ϕ_2. If there is a clause C which is blocked in ϕ_2, but not in ϕ_1, then $C \not\in \phi_1$.
2. From the statement above, it follows immediately that QBCE has a unique fixpoint. If a clause C is blocked in a QBF ϕ, then any clause C' with $C \neq C'$ blocked in ϕ is also blocked in $\phi \setminus \{C\}$.
3. If a clause C is subsumed by a blocked clause C', i.e., $C' \subseteq C$, then C is also a blocked clause. Obviously, the other direction does not hold.
4. Clauses containing a pure literal are blocked. The pure literal is the blocking literal. In fact, QBCE may be considered as a generalization of pure literal elimination rule.
5. If the clauses $C_1 \ldots C_n$ are the only clauses of a QBF ϕ which contain the literal l, then a clause C with $\bar{l} \in C$ is blocked if for each clause C_i, the clause C contains a literal k_i with $\bar{k}_i \in C_i$ and $k_i < l$. In particular, if a QBF ϕ contains an equivalence of the form $(l, \bar{k}_1, \ldots, \bar{k}_n), (\bar{l}, k_1), \ldots, (\bar{l}, k_n)$ and l occurs in no other than these clauses, then the equivalence may be removed due to QBCE.

The fifth property indicates that QBCE may be used to eliminate equivalences under certain conditions. In fact, like BCE in SAT [11], QBCE is able to achieve similar simplifications on a formula in PCNF as other techniques directly applied on the original encoding with more structural information (e.g., a circuit-based representation) before the transformation to normal form is performed. Therefore, we show the close connection between QBCE and the rewriting rules RW1 and RW2 given in Definition 1 and Definition 2. As argued by [8], the application of equivalence rewriting together with the application of the pure literal elimination rule show a similar effect than *don't care propagation* performed on the original, non-CNF formula.

Theorem 3. *QBCE subsumes RW1 given in Definition 1.*

Proof. First we argue, that with QBCE the same effect may be obtained as with RW1, and then we provide a QBF which may be simplified by the application of QBCE, but not by the application of RW1.

1. Whenever RW1 is applicable, also QBCE is applicable. Recall that RW1 substitutes the matrix of a QBF of the form $(l \vee \alpha) \wedge (l \Leftrightarrow \gamma) \wedge \psi$ by $(l \vee \alpha) \wedge (l \Rightarrow \gamma) \wedge \psi$ with the restriction that l does occur neither in α, γ, nor ψ and that all literals of γ have a lower level than l. The rule RW1 therefore removes clauses of the form $\bar{\gamma} \vee l$. Since $\bar{l}$ occurs only in the clauses representing the equivalence, the clauses of $\bar{\gamma} \vee l$ are blocked and may be omitted.
2. In some situations, QBCE is applicable, but not RW1. For example, the QBF

$$\forall y \exists x \exists z ((x \vee z) \wedge (\bar{x} \vee \bar{z}) \wedge (z \vee \bar{y} \vee x) \wedge (\bar{z} \vee y \vee \bar{x}))$$

   is reducible by QBCE, but not by RW1. Only if we had applied subsumption first, also RW1 would have been applicable.

Consequently, the application of QBCE has at least the same effects as the application of RW1:

– The number of clauses is reduced. If γ is a disjunction of n literals then n binary clauses are blocked, if γ is a conjunction of n literals then a clause of size $n + 1$ is blocked.
– The application of QBCE may directly trigger the application of other pruning techniques. For example, if a clause $(l \vee \bar{x})$ is removed then x might become pure and, depending on the quantification type of x, either all clauses containing x or all occurrences of x may be removed immediately.
– Other pruning techniques may become applicable during preprocessing or even during the solving process. For example, if QBCE has been applied and α later becomes true, then the literal l becomes pure.

The application of RW1 enables similar optimizations achieved by using the Plaisted-Greenbaum transformation [18] instead of the Tseitin transformation [20]. In this case, the subformula which shall be abbreviated by a freshly introduced variable occurs in one polarity only, therefore one direction of the implication may be omitted. When the subformula occurs in both polarities, then it is possible to treat positive and negative occurrences independently and to introduce two new variables.

The retrospective application of this approach is covered by RW2. The rule RW2 provides no direct simplifications itself and even introduces an extra variable, but after its application, it becomes more likely that (i) more variables become pure and (ii) RW1 or QBCE become applicable. In fact, if RW2 is used during preprocessing, then there exist situations, where the pure literal elimination rule, which is implemented by most state-of-the-art QBF solvers, performs reductions. The same effect can be achieved, if QBCE is applied dynamically during the solving process without applying RW2. Hence, no new variables have to be introduced to achieve the same effects. Consider the following formula. Let $\psi = ((l \vee \alpha) \wedge (\bar{l} \vee \beta) \wedge (l \Leftrightarrow \gamma) \wedge \delta)$ be the matrix of a QBF and let $\psi' = ((l \vee \alpha) \wedge (l' \vee \beta) \wedge (l \Rightarrow \gamma) \wedge (\gamma \Rightarrow \bar{l}') \wedge \delta)$ be the formula obtained after the application of RW2. Then the benefits of RW2 in combination with the pure literal elimination rule identified by [11], can also be obtained by QBCE.

1. If α (resp. β) becomes true in ψ', then l (resp. l') becomes pure and ψ' may be simplified to $((l' \vee \beta) \wedge (\gamma \Rightarrow \bar{l}') \wedge \delta)$ (resp. $((l \vee \alpha \wedge (l \Rightarrow \gamma)) \wedge \delta))$. If α (resp. β) becomes true in ψ then the same reductions may be obtained by the application of QBCE on ψ.
2. If both α and β become true, then ψ' may be reduced to δ because l and l' are pure. Also ψ may be reduced to γ by the application of QBCE if α and β become true.

When combining RW2 and QBCE, the two techniques potentially influence each other as follows:

- The application of RW2 preserves existing blocked clauses and might even uncover new blocked clauses.
- The application of QBCE might limit or even inhibit the application of RW2, namely when one of the clauses forming the equivalence is removed.

These observations indicate that it might be advantageous to apply RW2 before QBCE. As we will see in the next section, our experiments confirm this conjecture.

4.3   Extensions

For SAT, several extensions of BCE and related clause elimination procedures have been proposed. Based on the adoption of BCE for QSAT, also these extensions may be applied for preprocessing QBF. The goal is to add literals to clauses for making them either tautological or for triggering the application of blocked clause elimination. For SAT, covered clauses have been introduced in [9,10]. In the following, we leverage covered clauses from SAT to QBF.

Quantified Blocked Covered Clause Elimination. Covered clauses are clauses which are blocked or tautological when they are enriched with literals contained in any resolvent with pivot element l, the covering literal.

Definition 3 (Quantified Covered Literal). *Let the set of* resolution candidates $R_\phi(C, l) = \{C' \backslash \{\bar{l}\} \mid C' \in \psi, \bar{l} \in C', \not\exists k : \{k, \bar{k}\} \subseteq C \otimes C'\}$ *where* ϕ *is a QBF with matrix* ψ, $C \in \psi$, $l \in C$. *The set of* quantified covered literals $\mathcal{C}_\phi(C, l)$ *with respect to a clause C and a literal l is given by the intersection of the resolution candidates*

$$\mathcal{C}_\phi(C, l) = \bigcap \{C'' \mid C' \in R_\phi(C, l), C'' \subseteq C', \forall k \in C'' : k \leq l\}.$$

A literal l is called *covering literal* if $\mathcal{C}_\phi(C, l) \neq \emptyset$, i.e., l covers the literals in $\mathcal{C}_\phi(C, l)$.

Lemma 3. *The replacement of a clause C in a QBF ϕ by $C \cup \mathcal{C}_\phi(C, l)$ preserves unsatisfiability.*

Proof. Analogous to the proof of Theorem 1.

In the following, $\mathcal{C}_\phi(C)$ denotes the clause C extended with all quantified covered literals, i.e., for all $l \in \mathcal{C}_\phi(C)$ it holds that $\mathcal{C}_\phi(C, l) \subseteq \mathcal{C}_\phi(C)$.

Lemma 4 (Quantified Covered Literal Addition) *The replacement of a clause C in a QBF ϕ by $\mathcal{C}_\phi(C)$ preserves unsatisfiability.*

Proof Iterative application of Lemma 3.

Definition 4 (Quantified Covered Clause). *A clause C in a QBF ϕ is covered if $\mathcal{C}_\phi(C)$ is tautological or blocked w.r.t. ϕ.*

Theorem 4 (Quantified Covered Clause Elimination). *The removal of a covered clause preserves unsatisfiability.*

Proof. According to Lemma 4, each clause may be replaced by the clause $\mathcal{C}_\phi(C)$. If this clause is blocked, it may be removed according to Theorem 1. If it is tautological, it may be removed due to standard rewriting rules.

Example 3. In the QBF $\forall a, b, c \, \exists x, y((x \vee \neg a) \wedge (\neg x \vee y \vee b) \wedge (\neg x \vee y \vee c) \wedge (\neg y \vee a))$ the literal x of the clause $(x \vee \neg a)$ covers the literal y. We therefore may replace this clause by $(x \vee \neg a \vee y)$ which is blocked, and, consequently, can be eliminated.

As discussed in [10] covered clause elimination is confluent and more effective than QBCE.

Quantified Hidden Blocked Clause/Tautology Elimination. Quantified hidden blocked clauses and quantified hidden tautologies are uncovered by the addition of literals which are derivable from implications contained within a QBF. For SAT, these techniques have been presented in [9].

Definition 5 (Quantified Hidden Literal). *Let ϕ be a QBF with matrix ψ. A literal l is called quantified hidden literal w.r.t. a clause $C \in \psi$ if ψ contains a clause $(l_1, \ldots, l_n, \bar{l})$ with $l_i \leq l$ and $l_1, \ldots, l_n \in C$.*

Lemma 5. *The replacement of a clause C in a QBF ϕ with $C \cup \{l\}$ preserves unsatisfiability if l is a quantified hidden literal with respect to C.*

Proof. Analogous to the proof of Theorem 1.

Theorem 5. *Let C' be a clause obtained from a clause $C \in \phi$ by adding hidden literals. If C' is blocked or tautological, the removal of C from ϕ preserves unsatisfiability.*

Proof. Due to the (iterative) application of Lemma 5, C may be replaced by C' in ψ. If C' is blocked, it may be removed according to Theorem 1. If C' is tautological, it may be replaced due to standard rewriting rules.

Table 1. Impact of preprocessors

Family	no preprocessing			bloqqer			sQueezeBF		
	V	C	A	%V	%C	A	%V	%C	A
Abduction	1474	3435	2	-38	-22	-2	-7	-20	-1
Adder	3527	4405	3	-67	266	-1	-26	-37	0
blackbox*	11437	27819	153	-95	-77	-145	4	-81	-145
Blocks	518	6756	2	-44	-47	-1	7	-48	0
BMC	265932	680732	2	-98	-92	-1	-78	-95	0
Chain	3290	19663	2	-100	-100	-2	-100	-100	-2
circuits	1400	1920	2	-61	137	0	0	-40	0
confplan	1285	47890	2	-56	-6	-1	49	-70	0
Connect4	218810	93504	46	-99	-82	-32	-89	-45	-5
Counter	1951	5169	28	-80	-61	-22	1	-1	0
Debug	159502	1036810	2	-3	-15	0	-63	-52	0
evadepursue	7666	74014	9	-40	-54	0	-2	-51	0
FPGA*	65	433	2	332	828	0	1	-5	0
Impl	74	146	36	-100	-100	-36	-100	-100	-36
jmc_quant	508	995	4	25	321	0	0	-68	0
mqm	1724	5060	18	-50	10	-2	0	-14	0
pan	1847	10999	32	-91	-87	-31	38	-40	-11
Rintanen	1871	178750	2	-8	-1	0	7	0	0
Sakallah	44526	29282	2	-81	-50	-1	-79	-76	-1
Scholl-Becker	2758	7712	5	-83	-30	1	34	-43	-1
SortNet	1491	4972	2	-70	-10	0	21	-30	0
SzymanskiP	148973	168917	2	-100	-100	-2	-7	-70	0
tipdiam	5397	15428	2	-91	-79	-1	4	-78	0
tipfixpoint	9103	26407	2	-95	-88	-1	7	-71	0
Toilet	365	3129	2	-52	-100	-2	30	-44	-2
VonNeumann	1040116	1523169	2	-100	-100	-2	-100	-100	-2

5   Experimental Evaluation

Together with variable expansion, equivalence replacement, pure and unit literal elimination as well as with subsumption (cf. Section 3), the previously presented techniques are implemented in the preprocessor bloqqer[1]. To test our implementation, we applied bloqqer on the benchmark set used at the QBF Competition 2010[2] which consists of 568 formulas. For the sake of compactness, we aggregated the 36 families to 26 sets. All experiments were performed on 2.83 GHz

---

[1] Available at http://fmv.jku.at/bloqqer
[2] Available at http://www.qbflib.org

Table 2. Experiments with various solvers

	preprocessor	SOLVED	SAT	UNSAT	UNKN	Σ (10³)	AVG	MEDIAN
		# formulas				runtime (sec)		
DepQBF	sQueezeBF/bloqqer	482	234	248	86	102	180	5
	bloqqer	467	224	243	101	112	198	5
	bloqqer/ sQueezeBF	452	213	239	116	147	258	19
	sQueezeBF	435	201	234	133	131	231	6
	no preprocessing	373	167	206	195	189	332	26
QuBE	sQueezeBF/bloqqer	454	207	247	114	129	227	7
	bloqqer	444	200	244	124	139	246	5
	bloqqer/sQueezeBF	421	183	238	147	174	307	27
	sQueezeBF	406	181	225	162	177	313	31
	no preprocessing	332	135	197	236	242	426	258
Nenofex	bloqqer/sQueezeBF	271	134	137	297	273	482	76
	sQueezeBF/bloqqer	270	136	134	298	277	488	31
	bloqqer	268	132	136	300	276	487	23
	sQueezeBF	246	122	124	322	297	524	88
	no preprocessing	221	107	114	347	319	561	113
Quantor	bloqqer	288	145	143	280	266	468	34
	sQueezeBF/bloqqer	285	147	138	283	268	472	39
	bloqqer/sQueezeBF	270	131	139	298	276	486	34
	sQueezeBF	222	106	116	346	318	561	49
	no preprocessing	206	100	106	362	333	587	38

Intel Core 2 Quad machines each equipped with 8 GB memory and running
Ubuntu 9.04. The time limit and memory limit were set to 900 seconds and 7
GB, respectively. Time spent on the preprocessing is included in the time limit.
If the preprocessor has not terminated after 900 seconds, the preprocessing is
aborted and the formula is considered to be unsolved. In the following evaluation,
sQueezeBF [8] serves as reference preprocessor, because sQueezeBF incorporates
similar features as bloqqer except that bloqqer implements QBCE and sQueezeBF
implements RW1 and RW2. Furthermore, sQueezeBF was shown to be the most
effective state-of-the art preprocessor in [8].

First, we evaluated the impact of bloqqer on the formula size in terms of
number of variables (V), number of clauses (C), and number of quantifier alternations in the prefix (A). Table 1 shows the concrete results for the different
formula sets. The first column (no preprocessing) contains the average values
for the number of variables, number of clauses, and quantifier alternations of

Table 3. # formulas (# satisfiable formulas) solved by DepQBF

Family (set size)	sQueezeBF/ bloqqer	bloqqer/ sQueezeBF	bloqqer	sQueezeBF	no preproc.
Abduction (52)	48 (29)	49 (30)	49 (30)	48 (29)	50 (31)
Adder (15)	3 (3)	4 (3)	4 (3)	1 (1)	0 (0)
blackbox* (61)	52 (2)	45 (2)	46 (2)	55 (2)	43 (0)
Blocks (5)	4 (2)	5 (2)	5 (2)	5 (2)	4 (1)
BMC (18)	14 (5)	16 (6)	15 (5)	13 (5)	12 (5)
Chain (1)	1 (1)	1 (1)	1 (1)	1 (1)	0 (0)
circuits (3)	2 (2)	2 (2)	2 (2)	2 (2)	2 (2)
conf_planning (15)	5 (4)	5 (4)	5 (4)	5 (4)	4 (3)
Connect4 (11)	8 (0)	8 (0)	8 (0)	8 (0)	8 (0)
Counter (4)	3 (3)	3 (3)	4 (4)	2 (2)	2 (2)
Debug (5)	0 (0)	0 (0)	0 (0)	0 (0)	0 (0)
evader-pursuer (22)	17 (7)	11 (2)	11 (3)	10 (3)	10 (3)
FPGA* (3)	3 (1)	3 (1)	3 (1)	3 (1)	3 (1)
Impl (1)	1 (1)	1 (1)	1 (1)	1 (1)	1 (1)
jmc_quant (3)	3 (2)	3 (2)	3 (2)	3 (2)	0 (0)
mqm (136)	136 (66)	123 (58)	136 (66)	136 (66)	136 (66)
pan (80)	75 (41)	76 (41)	76 (41)	44 (22)	26 (15)
Rintanen (1)	1 (0)	1 (0)	1 (0)	1 (0)	1 (0)
Sakallah (19)	11 (10)	13 (11)	15 (13)	10 (9)	0 (0)
Scholl-Becker (24)	15 (5)	14 (4)	14 (4)	13 (5)	11 (4)
Sorting_networks (6)	3 (1)	3 (1)	2 (1)	3 (1)	6 (4)
SzymanskiP (2)	2 (0)	2 (0)	2 (0)	2 (0)	0 (0)
tipdiam (14)	13 (12)	8 (8)	8 (8)	11 (10)	3 (3)
tipfixpoint (24)	19 (10)	13 (4)	13 (4)	16 (7)	9 (0)
Toilet (41)	41 (27)	41 (27)	41 (27)	40 (26)	40 (26)
VonNeumann (2)	2 (0)	2 (0)	2 (0)	2 (0)	2 (0)

the unpreprocessed formulas. The second column (bloqqer) indicates the effects of applying bloqqer on these formulas. For the subcolumns V and C the average increase/decrease in percent w.r.t. the original formulas is shown, whereas for A the number of additional quantifier alternations is given. The third column shows how the application of sQueezeBF effects the formula size. bloqqer decreases the variable number of all but two formula sets by about 70 percent on average. For 21 formulas sets, we observe a decrease of the clause number of about 60 percent. For the majority of formula sets also a reduction of the quantifier prefix is achieved. This decrease of the formula size may be observed although bloqqer implements preprocessing techniques like variable expansion which adds new clauses and variables. QBCE is performed during the existential variable elimination through resolution. Hidden tautologies and hidden blocked clauses are found in the backward subsumption phase after variable elimination. Overall, $116 * 10^4$ blocked clauses, $79 * 10^4$ hidden blocked clauses as well as $196 * 10^4$ hidden tautologies have been detected. The size reduction achieved by sQueezeBF is more moderate (cf. third column of Table 1). bloqqer is able to directly evaluate 148 formulas and has no timeouts, sQueezeBF solves only 39 formulas and does not terminate on 14 formulas.

Second, we evaluated the impact of bloqqer on the runtimes of the four state-of-the-art QBF solvers DepQBF [14], QuBE [7], Nenofex [13], and Quantor [3]. For each solver we considered five preprocessing variants: (1) no preprocessing, (2) preprocessing with bloqqer only, (3) preprocessing with sQueezeBF only, (4) preprocessing with the combination bloqqer/sQueezeBF, and (5) preprocessing with the combination sQueezeBF/bloqqer. The results in Table 2 clearly show the positive impact of preprocessing on the number of solved formulas as well as on the runtime. The time values include a penalty of 900 for each unsolved formula. All solvers have in common that the omission of preprocessing negatively influences the solvers. The experiments also indicate that it might be advantageous not to use sQueezeBF alone, but in combination with bloqqer. Which variant is preferable seems to be solver dependent. The best results are obtained with sQueezeBF/bloqqer and the solver DepQBF. In the benchmark set, some families are represented very prominently compared to other families. Table 3 shows the detailed results when the solver DepQBF is applied. We clearly see that the accumulated results are also valid for the various sets.

Finally, we were interested in the impact of the different preprocessing techniques implemented in bloqqer and therefore we ran bloqqer with various options and passed the formals to DepQBF. Recall that with all options enabled, 467 formulas are solved and that with no preprocessing only 373 formulas are solved. If QBCE only is enabled, then still 403 formulas are solved, if all options except the extensions of QBCE are enabled, then 454 formulas are solved. Due to space limitations, we kindly refer to the web page of bloqqer for more details.

6   Conclusion and Future Work

As blocked clause elimination is an effective simplification technique for SAT, quantified blocked clause elimination is an effective simplification technique for QSAT. With QBCE similar effects can be achieved as with simplifications performed on formulas not in PCNF in combination with the polarity-based Plaisted-Greenbaum transformation. We provide an implementation of QBCE and extended variants together with well established simplification techniques in the preprocessor bloqqer. The application of QBCE results in a considerable reduction of formula size and improved solving time.

For future work, we consider to integrate QBCE and its extensions directly into a QBF solver. During the solving process clauses may become blocked which then may be removed immediately. Furthermore, we will investigate if it is possible to loosen the blocking criterion by taking variable dependencies into account.

References

1. Bacchus, F., Winter, J.: Effective Preprocessing with Hyper-Resolution and Equality Reduction. In: Giunchiglia, E., Tacchella, A. (eds.) SAT 2003. LNCS, vol. 2919, pp. 341–355. Springer, Heidelberg (2004)
2. Le Berre, D.: Exploiting the Real Power of Unit Propagation Lookahead. Electronic Notes in Discrete Mathematics 9, 59–80 (2001)
3. Biere, A.: Resolve and expand. In: Hoos, H.H., Mitchell, D.G. (eds.) SAT 2004. LNCS, vol. 3542, pp. 59–70. Springer, Heidelberg (2005)
4. Bubeck, U., Kleine Büning, H.: Bounded Universal Expansion for Preprocessing QBF. In: Marques-Silva, J., Sakallah, K.A. (eds.) SAT 2007. LNCS, vol. 4501, pp. 244–257. Springer, Heidelberg (2007)
5. Büning, H.K., Karpinski, M., Flögel, A.: Resolution for Quantified Boolean Formulas. Information and Computation 117(1), 12–18 (1995)
6. Eén, N., Biere, A.: Effective Preprocessing in SAT Through Variable and Clause Elimination. In: Bacchus, F., Walsh, T. (eds.) SAT 2005. LNCS, vol. 3569, pp. 61–75. Springer, Heidelberg (2005)
7. Giunchiglia, E., Marin, P., Narizzano, M.: QuBE 7.0. JSAT 7, 83–88 (2010)
8. Giunchiglia, E., Marin, P., Narizzano, M.: sQueezeBF: An Effective Preprocessor for QBFs Based on Equivalence Reasoning. In: Strichman, O., Szeider, S. (eds.) SAT 2010. LNCS, vol. 6175, pp. 85–98. Springer, Heidelberg (2010)
9. Heule, M., Järvisalo, M., Biere, A.: Clause elimination procedures for cnf formulas. In: Fermüller, C.G., Voronkov, A. (eds.) LPAR-17. LNCS, vol. 6397, pp. 357–371. Springer, Heidelberg (2010)
10. Heule, M., Järvisalo, M., Biere, A.: Covered Clause Elimination. CoRR, abs/1011.5202 (2010); Short paper proceedings LPAR-17
11. Järvisalo, M., Biere, A., Heule, M.: Blocked Clause Elimination. In: Esparza, J., Majumdar, R. (eds.) TACAS 2010. LNCS, vol. 6015, pp. 129–144. Springer, Heidelberg (2010)
12. Kullmann, O.: On a Generalization of Extended Resolution. Discrete Applied Mathematics 96, 149–176 (1999)
13. Lonsing, F., Biere, A.: Nenofex: Expanding NNF for QBF solving. In: Kleine Büning, H., Zhao, X. (eds.) SAT 2008. LNCS, vol. 4996, pp. 196–210. Springer, Heidelberg (2008)
14. Lonsing, F., Biere, A.: DepQBF: A Dependency-Aware QBF Solver (System Description). JSAT 7, 71–76 (2010)
15. Mangassarian, H., Le, B., Goultiaeva, A., Veneris, A.G., Bacchus, F.: Leveraging Dominators for Preprocessing QBF. In: Design, Automation and Test in Europe (DATE 2010), pp. 1695–1700. IEEE, Los Alamitos (2010)
16. Ostrowski, R., Grgoire, E., Mazure, B., Saïs, L.: Recovering and Exploiting Structural Knowledge from CNF Formulas. In: Proc. of the 8th Int. Conf. on Princ. and Pract. of Constraint Prog (CP 2002), pp. 199–206. Springer, Heidelberg (2006)
17. Pigorsch, F., Scholl, C.: An AIG-Based QBF-Solver Using SAT for Preprocessing. In: Proc. of the 47th Design Aut. Conf (DAC 2010), pp. 170–175 (2010)
18. Plaisted, D.A., Greenbaum, S.: A Structure-Preserving Clause Form Translation. Journal of Symbolic Computation 2(3), 293–304 (1986)
19. Samulowitz, H., Davies, J., Bacchus, F.: Preprocessing QBF. In: Benhamou, F. (ed.) CP 2006. LNCS, vol. 4204, pp. 514–529. Springer, Heidelberg (2006)
20. Tseitin, G.S.: On the Complexity of Derivation in Propositional Calculus. Studies in Constructive Mathematics and Mathematical Logic 2(115-125), 10–13 (1968)

Extending Sledgehammer with SMT Solvers

Jasmin Christian Blanchette[1,*], Sascha Böhme[1], and Lawrence C. Paulson[2]

[1] Institut für Informatik, Technische Universität München, Germany
[2] Computer Laboratory, University of Cambridge, U.K.

Abstract. Sledgehammer is a component of Isabelle/HOL that employs first-order automatic theorem provers (ATPs) to discharge goals arising in interactive proofs. It heuristically selects relevant facts and, if an ATP is successful, produces a snippet that replays the proof in Isabelle. We extended Sledgehammer to invoke satisfiability modulo theories (SMT) solvers as well, exploiting its relevance filter and parallel architecture. Isabelle users are now pleasantly surprised by SMT proofs for problems beyond the ATPs' reach. Remarkably, the best SMT solver performs better than the best ATP on most of our benchmarks.

1 Introduction

It is widely recognized that combining automated reasoning systems of different types can deliver huge rewards. There have been several attempts to combine interactive theorem provers (which are better at formal modeling than at proving theorems) with a variety of automatic theorem provers (ATPs) [1, 7, 20, 39, 42]. One of the most successful such combinations is Sledgehammer [27, 34], which interfaces Isabelle/HOL [31] with resolution provers for classical first-order logic. Sledgehammer is both effective, solving approximately one third of nontrivial goals arising in interactive proofs [9], and easy to use, since it is invoked with a single mouse gesture. It has become indispensable to Isabelle users and has transformed the way Isabelle is taught to beginners [33].

Given an Isabelle/HOL conjecture, Sledgehammer heuristically selects a few hundred relevant lemmas from Isabelle's libraries, translates them to unsorted first-order logic along with the conjecture, and sends the resulting problem to four theorem provers (Section 2). The provers run in parallel, either locally or remotely via SystemOnTPTP [40]. Users can keep working during the proof search, although most users find it hard to think while automatic provers are active in the background and prefer to wait up to 30 seconds for the responses. Isabelle's built-in prover Metis [21, 34] reconstructs resolution proofs in higher-order logic (HOL).

First-order ATPs are powerful and general, but they can usefully be complemented by other technologies. Satisfiability modulo theories (SMT) is a powerful technology based on combining a satisfiability solver with decision procedures for first-order theories, such as equality, integer and real arithmetic, and bit-vector reasoning. SMT solvers are particularly well suited to discharging large proof obligations arising from program

---

* Research supported by the Deutsche Forschungsgemeinschaft [grant number Ni 491/11-2]. Sledgehammer was originally supported by the U.K.'s Engineering and Physical Sciences Research Council [grant number GR/S57198/01].

N. Bjørner and V. Sofronie-Stokkermans (Eds.): CADE 2011, LNAI 6803, pp. 116–130, 2011.

verification. Although they are automatic theorem provers in a general sense, they rely on techniques entirely different from classical resolution. In this paper, we will find it convenient to reserve the abbreviation ATP for resolution provers.[1]

There have also been several attempts to combine interactive theorem provers with SMT solvers, either as oracles [5, 17, 37] or with proof reconstruction [18, 22, 26]. In previous work, we integrated the SMT solvers CVC3 [4], Yices [16] and Z3 [15] with Isabelle as oracles and implemented step-by-step proof reconstruction for Z3 [10]. The resulting *smt* proof method takes a list of problem-specific facts that are passed to the SMT solver along with the conjecture (Section 3).

While a motivated user can go a long way with the *smt* proof method [8], the need to specify facts and to guess that a conjecture could be solved by SMT makes it hard to use. As evidence of this, the Isabelle formalizations accepted in the *Archive of Formal Proofs* [23] in 2010 and 2011, after *smt* was introduced in Isabelle, contain 7958 calls to the simplifier, 928 calls to the internal tableau prover, 219 calls to Metis (virtually all generated using Sledgehammer), but not even one *smt* call.

Can typical Isabelle users benefit from SMT solvers? We assumed so and took the obvious next step, namely to have Sledgehammer run SMT solvers in parallel with ATPs, reusing the existing relevance filter and parallel architecture (Section 4). This idea seemed promising for a number of reasons:

- ATPs and SMT solvers have complementary strengths. The former handle quantifiers better, whereas the latter excel on large, mostly ground problems.
- The translation of higher-order constructs and types is done differently for the SMT solvers than for the ATPs—differences that should result in more proved goals.[2]
- Users should not have to guess whether a problem is more appropriate for ATPs or SMT solvers. Both classes of prover should be run concurrently.

Such an integration required extensive refactoring of Sledgehammer, a delicate piece of engineering developed by eight people in Cambridge and Munich over a period of seven years. The refactoring seemed worthwhile, especially since it also benefits other provers that we might want to interface with Sledgehammer, such as higher-order ATPs [3, 6].

The Sledgehammer–SMT integration is, to our knowledge, the first of its kind, and we had no clear idea of how successful it would be as we started the implementation work. Would the SMT solvers only prove conjectures already provable using the ATPs, or would they find original proofs? Would the decision procedures be pertinent to typical interactive goals? Would the SMT solvers scale in the face of hundreds of quantified facts translated en masse, as opposed to carefully crafted axiomatizations?

The first results with Z3 were disappointing: Given a few hundred facts, the solver often ran out of memory or crashed. It took some tweaking and help from the Z3 developers to obtain decent results. We eventually added support for CVC3 and Yices, two solvers that, like Z3, support quantifiers via (automatically inferred) "triggers"— patterns that guide quantifier instantiations. Our evaluation on a large benchmark suite shows that SMT solvers add considerable power to Sledgehammer (Section 5).

---

[1] Instantiation-based provers such as Equinox [12] and iProver [24] are promising, but in case of success they currently do not deliver a proof, not even the list of used axioms.

[2] There are also many efficiency, readability, and robustness advantages of obtaining several proofs for the same goal from different sources [41].

2 Sledgehammer

Sledgehammer is Isabelle's subsystem for harnessing the power of first-order ATPs. Its processing steps include relevance filtering, translation to classical first-order logic, parallel ATP invocation, proof reconstruction, and proof minimization.

Relevance Filtering. Sledgehammer employs a simple relevance filter to extract from Isabelle's enormous libraries a few hundred lemmas that appear to be relevant to the problem at hand. The relevance test is based on how many constants (symbols) are shared between the conjecture and each candidate lemma [28]. Although crude, this filter greatly improves Sledgehammer's success rate, because most ATPs perform badly in the presence of thousands of axioms.

Translation into Classical First-Order Logic. Isabelle's formalism, polymorphic higher-order logic [2, 45], is much richer than the ATPs' unsorted first-order logic. Sledgehammer uses various techniques to translate HOL formulas to first-order logic [27]. Many compromises are necessary here. The translation is unsound; the ATP proofs can be trusted only after they have been reconstructed. Higher-order features complicate the translation: λ-abstractions are rewritten to combinators, and curried functions are passed varying numbers of arguments by means of an explicit apply operator.

Parallel ATP Invocation. For a number of years, Isabelle has emphasized parallelism to exploit modern multi-core architectures [46]. Accordingly, Sledgehammer invokes several ATPs in parallel, with great success: Running E [38], SPASS [44], and Vampire [36] in parallel for five seconds solves as many problems as running a single theorem prover for two minutes [9, §8]. Recent versions of Sledgehammer also invoke SInE [19], a wrapper around E that is designed to cope with large axiom bases.

Proof Reconstruction. As in other LCF-style theorem provers, Isabelle theorems can only be generated within a small inference kernel. It is possible to bypass this safety mechanism, generally if some external tool is to be trusted as an oracle, but all oracle inferences are tracked. Sledgehammer performs true proof reconstruction by running Isabelle's built-in resolution prover, Metis, supplying it with the short list of facts used in the proof found by the external ATP.

The Metis call with the identified facts is all that Sledgehammer includes in the Isabelle proof text, which can then be replayed without external provers. Since Metis is given only a handful of facts, it usually succeeds within milliseconds.

Proof Minimization. Proof reconstruction using Metis loses about 10% of ATP proofs, partly because some of the proofs are unsound in a typed setting, but also because Metis times out [9, §3]. Automatic provers frequently use many more facts than are necessary. Sledgehammer's minimization tool takes a set of facts returned by a prover and repeatedly calls it with subsets of the facts to find a minimal set. Depending on the number of initial facts, it relies on either of these two algorithms:

- The naive linear algorithm attempts to remove one fact at a time. This can require as many prover invocations as there are facts in the initial set. A refinement is to inspect the ATP proofs to eliminate more facts at each iteration.

- The binary algorithm recursively bisects the facts [11, §4.3]. It performs best when a small fraction of the facts are actually required [9, §7].

Example. In the Isabelle proof below, taken from a formalization of the Robbins conjecture [43], four of the five subproofs are discharged by a Metis call generated automatically by Sledgehammer using an ATP:

proof −
    let $z =$ "$-(x \sqcup -y)$" **and** $ky =$ "$y \sqcup k \otimes (x \sqcup z)$"
    have "$-(x \sqcup -ky) = z$" **by** (*simp add: copyp0*)
    hence "$-(-ky \sqcup -(-y \sqcup z)) = z$" **by** (*metis assms sup_comm*)
    also have "$-(z \sqcup -ky) = x$" **by** (*metis assms copyp0 sup_comm*)
    hence "$z = -(-y \sqcup -(-ky \sqcup z))$" **by** (*metis sup_comm*)
    finally show "$-(y \sqcup k \otimes (x \sqcup -(x \sqcup -y))) = -y$" **by** (*metis eq_intro*)
qed

The example is typical of the way Isabelle users employ the tool: If they understand the problem well enough to propose some intermediate properties, all they need to do is state a progression of properties in small enough steps and let Sledgehammer or an automatic Isabelle tactic prove each one.

3   The SMT Proof Method

SMT solvers are available in Isabelle through the *smt* proof method. It translates the conjecture and any user-supplied facts to the SMT solvers' many-sorted first-order logic, invokes a solver, and (depending on the solver) either trusts the result or attempts to reconstruct the proof in Isabelle.

Translation into Many-Sorted First-Order Logic. The translation maps HOL equality and arithmetic operators to the corresponding SMT-LIB 1.2 [35] concepts. The theories of arrays, bit vectors, and algebraic datatypes are not yet exploited.

Many-sorted first-order logic's support for sorts would seem to make it more appropriate to encode HOL typing information than classical first-order logic, but it does not support polymorphism. Several solutions have been proposed in the literature [14, 25]. Our current approach is to monomorphize the formulas: Polymorphic formulas are iteratively instantiated with relevant ground instances of their polymorphic constants. This process is iterated a bounded number of times to obtain the monomorphized problem.

Partial applications are translated using an explicit apply operator. In contrast with the combinator approach used by Sledgehammer when communicating with ATPs, the *smt* method lifts λ-abstractions into new rules, thereby introducing fresh constants.

Proof Reconstruction. CVC3 and Z3 provide independently checkable proofs of unsatisfiability. We have implemented proof reconstruction for Z3 and support CVC3 and Yices as oracles. Reconstruction relies extensively on standard Isabelle proof methods such as the simplifier, the classical reasoner, and the arithmetic decision procedures. Certificates make it possible to store Z3 proofs alongside Isabelle formalizations, allowing SMT proof replay without Z3; only if the formalizations change must the certificates be regenerated. Using SMT solvers as oracles requires trusting both the solvers and the *smt* method's translation, so it is generally frowned upon.

Example. The periodic integer recurrence relation $x_{i+2} = |x_{i+1}| - x_i$ has period 9. This property can be proved in Isabelle using the *smt* method as follows:

lemma "$x_3 = |x_2| - x_1 \land x_4 = |x_3| - x_2 \land x_5 = |x_4| - x_3 \land x_6 = |x_5| - x_4 \land$
$x_7 = |x_6| - x_5 \land x_8 = |x_7| - x_6 \land x_9 = |x_8| - x_7 \land x_{10} = |x_9| - x_8 \land$
$x_{11} = |x_{10}| - x_9 \implies x_1 = x_{10} \land x_2 = (x_{11} :: int)$"
by *smt*

SMT solvers prove the formula almost instantly, and proof reconstruction (if enabled) takes a few seconds. In contrast, Isabelle's arithmetic decision procedure requires several minutes to prove the same result. This example does not require any problem-specific facts, but these would have been supplied as arguments in the *smt* call just like for *metis* in the previous section.

4 Combining Sledgehammer and SMT

Extending Sledgehammer with SMT solvers was to a large extent a matter of connecting existing components: Sledgehammer's relevance filter and minimizer with the *smt* method's translation and proof reconstruction. Figure 1 depicts the resulting architecture, omitting proof reconstruction and minimization.

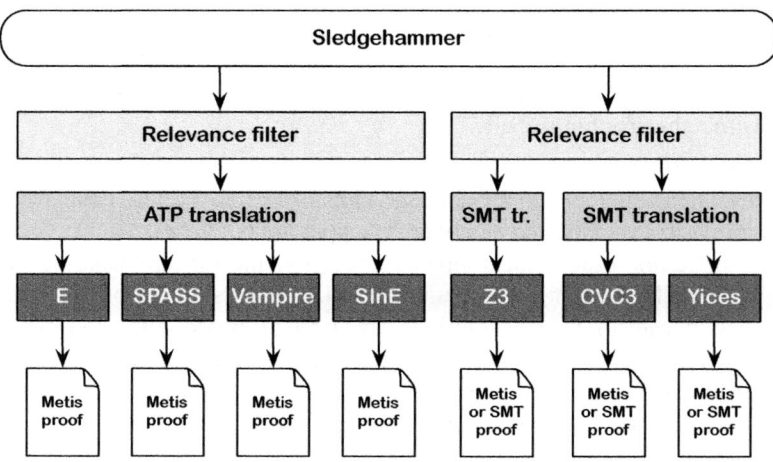

Fig. 1. Sledgehammer's extended architecture

Two instances of the relevance filter run in parallel, to account for different sets of built-in constants. The relevant facts and the conjecture are translated to the ATP or SMT version of first-order logic, and the resulting problems are passed to the provers. The translation for Z3 is done slightly differently than for CVC3 and Yices to take advantage of the former's support for nonlinear arithmetic.

4.1   Relevance Filtering

In the old architecture, the available lemmas were rewritten to conjunctive normal form (CNF) using a naive application of distributive laws before the relevance filter was invoked [28]. To avoid clausifying thousands of lemmas on each Sledgehammer invocation, the CNF clauses were kept in a cache. This design was technically incompatible with the (cache-unaware) *smt* method, and it was already unsatisfactory for ATPs, which include custom polynomial-time clausifiers [32].

We rewrote the relevance filter so that it operates on arbitrary HOL formulas, trying to simulate the old behavior. To mimic the penalty associated with Skolem constants in the CNF-based code, we keep track of polarities and detect quantifiers that give rise to Skolem constants.

The relevance filter gives more precise results if it ignores HOL constants that are translated to built-in constructs. For ATPs, this concerns equality, connectives, and quantifiers, as well as *let* and *if–then–else*. SMT solvers support a much larger set of built-in constructs, notably arithmetic operators. It was straightforward to generalize the filter code so that it performs its task appropriately for SMT solvers.

Observing that some provers cope better with large fact bases than others, we optimized the the maximum number of relevant facts to include in a problem independently for each prover (from a library of about 10 000 facts). The maxima we obtained are 150 for CVC3 and Yices and 250 for Z3. In comparison, the filter currently selects up to 250 facts for E, 150 for SPASS, 450 for Vampire, and 500 for SInE.

4.2   SMT Solver Invocation

In our first experiments, we simply invoked Z3 as an oracle with the monomorphized relevant facts, using the same translation as for the *smt* proof method. The results were disappointing. Several factors were to blame:

- The translation of hundreds of facts took many seconds.
- It took us a while to get the bugs out of our translation code. Syntax errors in many generated problems caused Z3 to give up immediately.
- Z3 often ran out of memory after a few seconds or, worse, crashed.

Latent issues both in our translation and in Z3 were magnified by the number of facts involved. Our previous experience with SMT solvers had involved only a handful of facts.

The bottleneck in the translation was monomorphization. Iterative expansion of a few hundred HOL formulas yielded thousands of monomorphic instances. We reduced the maximum number of iterations from 10 to 4, to great effect.

The syntax errors were typically caused by confusion between formulas and terms or the use of a partially applied built-in constant (both of which are legal in HOL). These were bugs in the *smt* proof method; we gradually eradicated them.

We reported the segmentation faults to the Z3 developers, who released an improved version. The bug was located in Z3's proof generation facility, which is disabled by default and hence not as well tested as the rest of the solver. To handle the frequent out-of-memory conditions, we modified Sledgehammer to retry aborted solver calls with half the facts. This simple change was enough to increase the success rate dramatically.

4.3   Proof Reconstruction

In case of success, Sledgehammer extracts the facts used in the SMT proof—the unsatisfiable core—and generates an *smt* proof method call with these facts supplied as arguments. For example:

by (*smt assms copyp0 sup_comm*)

The proof method invokes Z3 to re-find the proof, which it replays step by step. The Z3 proof can also be stored alongside the Isabelle formalization as a certificate to avoid invoking Z3 each time the proof is rechecked. Proof minimization can be done as for ATP proofs to reduce the number of facts.

To increase the success rate and reduce the dependency on external solvers or certificates, Sledgehammer first tries Metis for one second. If Metis succeeds, Sledgehammer generates a Metis call rather than an *smt* call. Metis will of course fail if the proof requires theories other than equality.

One of the less academically rewarding aspects of integrating third-party tools is the effort spent on solving mundane issues. Obtaining an unsatisfiable core from the SMT solvers turned out to be surprisingly difficult:

- CVC3 returns a full proof, but somehow the proof refers to all facts, whether they are actually needed or not, and there is no easy way to find out which facts are actually needed. We rely on Sledgehammer's proof minimizer and its binary algorithm to reduce the facts used to a reasonable number.
- Yices can output a minimal core, but for technical reasons only when its native input syntax is used rather than the standard SMT-LIB 1.2 format. We tried using off-the-shelf file format converters to translate SMT-LIB 1.2 to 2 then to Yices, but this repeatedly crashed. In the end, we settled for the same solution as for CVC3.
- For Z3, we could reuse our existing proof parser, which we need to reconstruct proofs. The proof format is fairly stable, although new releases often come with various minor changes.

4.4   Redistribution and Distribution

Our goal with Sledgehammer is to help as many Isabelle users as possible. Third-party provers should ideally be bundled with Isabelle and ready to be used without requiring configuration. Today, Isabelle includes E and SPASS executables for Linux, Mac OS X, and Windows; users can download Vampire (whose license forbids redistribution), but most simply run Vampire remotely on SystemOnTPTP.

For SMT solvers, the situation is similar. Only CVC3 allows redistribution and use by noncommercial and commercial users alike, and Z3 executables are not available for Mac OS X. With the Z3 developers' express permission, we set up a server in Munich in the style of SystemOnTPTP for running Z3 (as well as CVC3) remotely.

Remote servers are satisfactory for proof search, at least when they are up and running and the user has Internet access. They also help distribute the load: Unless the user's machine has eight processor cores, it would be reckless to launch four ATPs and three SMT solvers locally in parallel and expect the user interface to remain snappy.

4.5 Experiment: Generation of Weights and Triggers

SMT solvers work by incrementally building a model for the quantifier-free part of the problem. Quantifiers are instantiated at each iteration based on the set of active terms (ground terms which the current partial model can interpret). These instances are conjoined with the quantifier-free part of the problem, helping refine the model.

To help guide quantifier instantiation and avert an explosion in the number of instances generated, some SMT solvers support extralogical annotations on their quantifiers. We have done some experiments with weights and triggers, which so far have been somewhat inconclusive.

Weights. Weights are specific to Z3. The greater the weight of the quantifier, the fewer instantiations are allowed. The instantiations that are allowed are those by terms that became active early, because they are more likely to be relevant to the problem at hand.

Intuitively, there is an easy way for Sledgehammer to fill in the weights meaningfully. The iterative relevance filter yields a list of facts sorted by likely relevance. We can give a weight of 0 to the most relevant fact included, N to the least relevant fact, and interpolate in between. If $N = 0$, we obtain Z3's default behavior. We currently use $N = 10$ with a quadratic interpolation, which seems to help more than it harms.

Triggers. A trigger is a set of patterns that must all match some active term for the instantiation to take place. Patterns are usually subterms of the quantified formula. CVC3, Yices, and Z3 infer the triggers heuristically, but CVC3 and Z3 also provide a syntax for user-specified triggers.

We tried to rely on this mechanism to exploit the form of Isabelle/HOL lemmas. In particular, equations registered for use by the Isabelle simplifier typically define a function symbol applied to a constructor pattern in terms of a (possibly recursive) right-hand side. It then makes sense to take the entire left-hand side as the only trigger. When an instance of the left-hand side is active, the trigger enables the equation's instantiation.

In stark contrast with the SMT folklore that well chosen triggers are a prerequisite for success [29], we found that the SMT solvers can be relied on to infer acceptable triggers and that our scheme for equations is too limited to help much. Perhaps we should try to add support for other common syntactic forms, such as introduction and elimination rules, to obtain greater benefits. This remains for future work.

4.6 Example

A gratifying example arose on the Isabelle mailing list [30] barely one week after we had enabled SMT solvers in the development version of Sledgehammer. A new Isabelle user was experimenting with a simple arithmetic algebraic datatype:

datatype *arith* = *Z* | *Succ arith* | *Pred arith*

He had defined an inductive predicate *step* that takes two *arith* values and wanted to prove the following simple property but did not know how to proceed:

lemma *"step (Pred Z) m $\implies$ m = Z"*

Our colleague Tobias Nipkow helpfully supplied a structured Isabelle proof:

```
using assms
proof cases
  case s_pred_zero thus "m = Z" by simp
next
  case (s_pred m′)
  from 'step Z m′' have "False" by cases
  thus "m = Z" by blast
qed
```

The proof is fairly simple by interactive proving standards, but it nonetheless represents a few minutes' work to a seasoned user (and, as we saw, was too difficult for a novice). Our colleague then tried the development version of Sledgehammer and found a much shorter proof due to Z3:

```
by (smt arith.simps(2,4,5,8) step.simps)
```

Although it involves no theory reasoning beyond equality, the ATPs failed to find it within 30 seconds because of the presence of too many extraneous facts.

5 Evaluation

In their "Judgment Day" study, Böhme and Nipkow [9] evaluated Sledgehammer with E, SPASS, and Vampire on 1240 provable proof goals arising in seven representative formalizations from the Isabelle distribution and the *Archive of Formal Proofs*. To evaluate the SMT integration, we ran their benchmark suite with the latest versions of Sledgehammer on the same seven formalizations.[3] We also added two formalizations (*QE* and *S2S*) that rely heavily on arithmetic to exercise the SMT decision procedures.

The formalizations are listed below. The last two columns give the percentage of the (now) 1591 proof goals that come from each formalization and the features it contains, where A means arithmetic, I means induction and recursion, L means λ-abstractions, and S means sets.

Arrow	Arrow's impossibility theorem	L S	6.3%
FFT	Fast Fourier transform	A L	9.1%
FTA	Fundamental theorem of algebra	A	26.6%
Hoare	Completeness of Hoare logic with procedures	A I L	12.8%
Jinja	Type soundness of a subset of Java	I L	11.4%
NS	Needham–Schroeder shared-key protocol	I	6.2%
QE	DNF-based quantifier elimination	A L S	12.0%
S2S	Sum of two squares	A	8.1%
SN	Strong normalization of the typed λ-calculus	A I	7.2%

---

[3] Our test data set is available at http://www4.in.tum.de/~blanchet/cade2011-data.tgz.

	Arrow	FFT	FTA	Hoare	Jinja	NS	QE	S2S	SN	All	Uniq.
E 1.2	24%	15%	60%	42%	31%	31%	25%	39%	60%	40.2%	.1%
SPASS 3.7	34%	14%	57%	51%	32%	34%	**28%**	39%	60%	41.7%	.4%
Vampire 1.0	31%	**19%**	62%	49%	35%	**44%**	23%	48%	60%	44.2%	1.0%
SInE 0.4	23%	16%	55%	40%	31%	28%	20%	39%	**63%**	38.3%	.3%
CVC3 2.2	36%	18%	53%	51%	37%	29%	21%	57%	55%	41.8%	.1%
Yices 1.0.28	29%	18%	51%	51%	37%	31%	23%	**59%**	59%	41.7%	.3%
Z3 2.15	**48%**	18%	**62%**	**54%**	**47%**	42%	25%	58%	62%	**48.5%**	**2.6%**
ATPs	40%	21%	67%	55%	37%	45%	31%	55%	70%	49.9%	6.3%
SMT solvers	50%	23%	66%	65%	48%	42%	27%	66%	63%	52.4%	8.8%
All provers	55%	28%	73%	67%	48%	51%	41%	73%	72%	58.7%	–

Fig. 2. Success rates on all goals with proof reconstruction

	Arrow	FFT	FTA	Hoare	Jinja	NS	QE	S2S	SN	All	Uniq.
E 1.2	21%	11%	34%	26%	26%	19%	12%	9%	44%	23.2%	.2%
SPASS 3.7	29%	12%	31%	38%	27%	23%	**16%**	12%	**51%**	26.2%	.7%
Vampire 1.0	23%	**17%**	39%	36%	33%	**36%**	8%	19%	47%	29.0%	1.7%
SInE 0.4	18%	13%	28%	24%	26%	16%	9%	11%	**51%**	21.4%	.4%
CVC3 2.2	23%	13%	28%	36%	31%	18%	7%	25%	37%	24.3%	.1%
Yices 1.0.28	11%	13%	30%	40%	33%	19%	7%	26%	44%	25.4%	.4%
Z3 2.15	**35%**	13%	**41%**	**46%**	**46%**	34%	7%	**28%**	46%	**33.0%**	**4.3%**
ATPs	32%	18%	42%	42%	33%	38%	19%	26%	59%	33.8%	6.9%
SMT solvers	37%	17%	43%	54%	46%	34%	8%	33%	47%	35.8%	8.9%
All provers	42%	23%	50%	57%	46%	44%	23%	42%	61%	42.7%	–

Fig. 3. Success rates on "nontrivial" goals with proof reconstruction

We ran the provers for 30 seconds, which corresponds to the default time limit in Sledgehammer. Even though Sledgehammer runs asynchronously, most users prefer to wait for it to return, hoping to get a proof for free. Böhme and Nipkow [9] considered timeouts of 60 and 120 seconds, but these had a negligible impact on the success rate.

If a proof is found, proof search is followed by reconstruction with a 30-second time limit. We allotted an extra 30 seconds to CVC3 and Yices to account for the expensive black-box proof minimization. This might not be entirely fair, but it reflects a compromise between the real power of these solvers and what Isabelle users currently perceive. Moreover, users are normally patient when they know that a proof has been found and has reached the minimizer.

Figure 2 gives the success rates for each prover (or class of prover) on each formalization together with the unique contributions of each prover. Sledgehammer now solves 58.7% of the goals, compared with 49.9% without SMT. Much to our surprise, the best SMT solver, Z3, beats the best ATP, Vampire, with 48.5% versus 44.2%. Z3 also contributes by far the most unique proofs: 2.6% of the goals are proved only by it, a figure that climbs to 8.1% if we exclude CVC3 and Yices.

While it might be tempting to see this evaluation as a direct comparison of provers, recall that even provers of the same class (ATP or SMT solver) are not given the same

	Arrow	FFT	FTA	Hoare	Jinja	NS	QE	S2S	SN	All
Arithmetic	0%	49%	7%	9%	0%	0%	21%	51%	3%	12.9%
Metis	80%	24%	89%	77%	80%	92%	60%	29%	100%	75.9%

Fig. 4. Use of arithmetic in successful Z3 proofs and reconstructibility with Metis

	Arrow	FFT	FTA	Hoare	Jinja	NS	QE	S2S	SN	All
CVC3 2.2	0%	+2%	−1%	+3%	+2%	+1%	−9%	+12%	+4%	+.8%
Yices 1.0.28	0%	+3%	+2%	+4%	+1%	0%	−6%	+11%	+1%	+1.5%
Z3 2.15	−1%	−3%	+2%	−2%	+1%	0%	−13%	+8%	+2%	−.8%
SMT solvers	−1%	+1%	+3%	+2%	+1%	0%	−12%	+12%	+3%	+.9%

Fig. 5. Absolute success rate differences between SMT solver runs with and without arithmetic on all goals with proof reconstruction

number of facts or the same options. Sledgehammer is not so much a competition as a *combination* of provers.

About one third of the goals from the chosen Isabelle formalizations are "trivial" in the sense that they can be solved directly by standard Isabelle tactics invoked with no arguments. If we ignore these and focus on the "nontrivial" goals, which users are especially keen on seeing solved by Sledgehammer, the success rates are somewhat lower, as shown in Figure 3: The ATPs solve 33.8% of these harder goals, and SMT solvers increase the success rate to 42.7%.

We also evaluated the extent to which the SMT decision procedures (other than equality) contribute to the overall result. To this end, we inspected the successful Z3 proofs to determine the percentage of proofs that involve an arithmetic decision procedure. Theory-specific rewrite rules, which do not rely on any decision procedure, are not counted. Complementarily, we extracted the relevant facts from the Z3 proofs and passed them to Metis with a 30-second time limit. Figure 4 summarizes the results. For the formalizations under study, the vast majority of SMT proofs do not require any theory reasoning and can be reconstructed by a resolution prover.

These results prompted us to benchmark the SMT solvers with Isabelle's arithmetic constants left uninterpreted, effectively disabling theory reasoning. We expected a loss comparable to the use of arithmetic in Z3 proofs, but the actual loss is much smaller. For some formalizations, the SMT solvers' support for arithmetic is actually harmful, as shown in Figure 5. Tellingly, the formalization that relies the most on Isabelle's arithmetic decision procedure, *S2S*, is also the one for which SMT arithmetic helps the most, increasing the SMT solvers' success rate from 55% to 66% (compared with 55% for the ATPs).

Arithmetic decision procedures are therefore not the main reason why the SMT solvers collectively outperform the ATPs. A more important reason is that many proofs found by ATPs are type-unsound in higher-order logic and cannot be replayed; in contrast, the SMT translation is designed to be sound by exploiting SMT sorts. Moreover, Metis sometimes fails to rediscover an ATP proof within a reasonable time, whereas proof reconstruction for Z3 is typically faster and more reliable.

Looking at the test data more closely, we also noticed that SMT solvers performed better on higher-order problems, suggesting that the *smt* method's translation of λ-abstractions is better suited to the SMT solvers than combinators are to the ATPs. Remarkably, previous experiments found combinators superior to λ-lifting for ATPs [27]. We need to carry out new experiments to gain clarity on this point.

6 Conclusion

Sledgehammer has enjoyed considerable success since its inception in 2007 and has become indispensable to most Isabelle users, both novices and experts. It is possibly the only interface between interactive and automatic theorem provers to achieve such popularity. It owes its success to its ease of use: Sledgehammer is integral to Isabelle and works out of the box, using a combination of locally installed provers and remote servers. It can even be configured to run automatically on all newly entered conjectures.

To Isabelle users, the addition of SMT solvers as backends means that they now get more proofs without effort. The SMT solvers, led by Z3, compete advantageously with the resolution-based ATPs and Metis even on non-arithmetic problems. In our evaluation, they solved about 36% of the nontrivial goals, increasing Sledgehammer's success rate from 34% to 43% on these. Running the SMT solvers in parallel with the ATPs is entirely appropriate, for how is the user supposed to know which class of prover will perform best?

To users of SMT solvers, the Sledgehammer–SMT integration eases the transition from automatic proving in first-order logic to interactive proving in higher-order logic. Other tools, such as HOL-Boogie [8], assist in specific applications. Isabelle/HOL is powerful enough for the vast majority of hardware and software verification efforts, and its LCF-style inference kernel provides a trustworthy foundation.

Even the developers of SMT solvers profit from the integration: It helps them reach a larger audience, and proof reconstruction brings to light bugs in their tools, including soundness bugs, which might otherwise go undetected.[4]

While the evaluation and user feedback show that the integration is a resounding success, much can still be improved. Work is under way to reconstruct Z3 proofs involving arrays, bit vectors, and algebraic datatypes. The heuristics for trigger generation are simplistic and would probably benefit from more research. The encoding of HOL types, based on monomorphization, was never meant to cope with hundreds of facts and could also benefit from new ideas.

With the notable exceptions of triggers and weights, we treated the SMT solvers as black boxes. A tighter integration might prove beneficial, as has been observed with other verification tool chains (e.g., VCC/Boogie/Z3 [13] and PVS/SAL/Yices [37]), but it would also require much more work. Obtaining an unsatisfiable core from CVC3 and Yices would be a first small step in the right direction.

The main open question is the extent to which the improvements we obtained by adding support for SMT provers are due to the *smt* method's translation and proof reconstruction as opposed to the nature of SMT provers. To clarify this, we plan to carry out further experiments with SPASS's support for sorts and Z3's unsorted input format.

---

[4] Indeed, we discovered a soundness bug in Yices and another in Z3 while preparing this paper.

Acknowledgment. Tobias Nipkow made this work possible and encouraged us throughout. Nikolaj Bjørner promptly fixed a critical bug in Z3's proof generator, and Leonardo de Moura supplied a new Linux executable. Michał Moskal provided expert help on Z3 triggers. Mark Summerfield, Tjark Weber, and several anonymous reviewers provided useful comments on drafts of this paper. We thank them all.

References

1. Ahrendt, W., Beckert, B., Hähnle, R., Menzel, W., Reif, W., Schellhorn, G., Schmitt, P.H.: Integrating automated and interactive theorem proving. In: Bibel, W., Schmitt, P.H. (eds.) Automated Deduction—A Basis for Applications. Systems and Implementation Techniques, vol. II, pp. 97–116. Kluwer, Dordrecht (1998)
2. Andrews, P.B.: An Introduction to Mathematical Logic and Type Theory: To Truth Through Proof, 2nd edn. Applied Logic, vol. 27. Springer, Heidelberg (2002)
3. Backes, J., Brown, C.E.: Analytic tableaux for higher-order logic with choice. In: Giesl, J., Hähnle, R. (eds.) IJCAR 2010. LNCS (LNAI), vol. 6173, pp. 76–90. Springer, Heidelberg (2010)
4. Barrett, C., Tinelli, C.: CVC3. In: Damm, W., Hermanns, H. (eds.) CAV 2007. LNCS, vol. 4590, pp. 298–302. Springer, Heidelberg (2007)
5. Barsotti, D., Nieto, L.P., Tiu, A.: Verification of clock synchronization algorithms: Experiments on a combination of deductive tools. Formal Asp. Comput. 19(3), 321–341 (2007)
6. Benzmüller, C., Paulson, L.C., Theiss, F., Fietzke, A.: LEO-II—a cooperative automatic theorem prover for higher-order logic. In: Armando, A., Baumgartner, P., Dowek, G. (eds.) IJCAR 2008. LNCS (LNAI), vol. 5195, pp. 162–170. Springer, Heidelberg (2008)
7. Bezem, M., Hendriks, D., de Nivelle, H.: Automatic proof construction in type theory using resolution. J. Auto. Reas. 29(3-4), 253–275 (2002)
8. Böhme, S., Moskal, M., Schulte, W., Wolff, B.: HOL-Boogie—an interactive prover-backend for the Verifying C Compiler. J. Auto. Reas. 44(1-2), 111–144 (2010)
9. Böhme, S., Nipkow, T.: Sledgehammer: Judgement Day. In: Giesl, J., Hähnle, R. (eds.) IJCAR 2010. LNCS (LNAI), vol. 6173, pp. 107–121. Springer, Heidelberg (2010)
10. Böhme, S., Weber, T.: Fast LCF-style proof reconstruction for Z3. In: Kaufmann, M., Paulson, L.C. (eds.) ITP 2010. LNCS, vol. 6172, pp. 179–194. Springer, Heidelberg (2010)
11. Bradley, A.R., Manna, Z.: Property-directed incremental invariant generation. Formal Asp. Comput. 20, 379–405 (2008)
12. Claessen, K.: Equinox, a new theorem prover for full first-order logic with equality. Presentation at Dagstuhl Seminar on Deduction and Applications (2005)
13. Cohen, E., Dahlweid, M., Hillebrand, M.A., Leinenbach, D., Moskal, M., Santen, T., Schulte, W., Tobies, S.: VCC: A practical system for verifying concurrent C. In: Berghofer, S., Nipkow, T., Urban, C., Wenzel, M. (eds.) TPHOLs 2009. LNCS, vol. 5674, pp. 23–42. Springer, Heidelberg (2009)
14. Couchot, J.-F., Lescuyer, S.: Handling polymorphism in automated deduction. In: Pfenning, F. (ed.) CADE 2007. LNCS (LNAI), vol. 4603, pp. 263–278. Springer, Heidelberg (2007)
15. de Moura, L.M., Bjørner, N.: Z3: An efficient SMT solver. In: Ramakrishnan, C.R., Rehof, J. (eds.) TACAS 2008. LNCS, vol. 4963, pp. 337–340. Springer, Heidelberg (2008)
16. Dutertre, B., de Moura, L.: The Yices SMT solver (2006),
   http://yices.csl.sri.com/tool-paper.pdf
17. Erkök, L., Matthews, J.: Using Yices as an automated solver in Isabelle/HOL. In: Rushby, J., Shankar, N. (eds.) Automated Formal Methods, pp. 3–13 (2008)

18. Fontaine, P., Marion, J.-Y., Merz, S., Nieto, L.P., Tiu, A.: Expressiveness + automation + soundness: Towards combining SMT solvers and interactive proof assistants. In: Hermanns, H., Palsberg, J. (ed.) TACAS 2006. LNCS, vol. 3920, pp. 167–181. Springer, Heidelberg (2006)
19. Hoder, K., Voronkov, A.: Sine qua non for large theory reasoning. In: These proceedings (2011)
20. Hurd, J.: Integrating Gandalf and HOL. In: Bertot, Y., Dowek, G., Hirschowitz, A., Paulin, C., Théry, L. (eds.) TPHOLs 1999. LNCS, vol. 1690, pp. 311–321. Springer, Heidelberg (1999)
21. Hurd, J.: First-order proof tactics in higher-order logic theorem provers. In: Archer, M., Di Vito, B., Muñoz, C. (eds.) Design and Application of Strategies/Tactics in Higher Order Logics, number CP-2003-212448 in NASA Technical Reports, pp. 56–68 (2003)
22. Keller, C.: Cooperation between SAT, SMT provers and Coq. Presentation at the Synthesis. Verification and Analysis of Rich Models workshop (2011)
23. Klein, G., Nipkow, T., Paulson, L. (eds.): The Archive of Formal Proofs, http://afp.sf.net/
24. Korovin, K.: Instantiation-based automated reasoning: From theory to practice. In: Schmidt, R.A. (ed.) CADE-22. LNCS (LNAI), vol. 5663, pp. 163–166. Springer, Heidelberg (2009)
25. Leino, K.R.M., Rümmer, P.: A polymorphic intermediate verification language: Design and logical encoding. In: Esparza, J., Majumdar, R. (eds.) TACAS 2010. LNCS, vol. 6015, pp. 312–327. Springer, Heidelberg (2010)
26. McLaughlin, S., Barrett, C., Ge, Y.: Cooperating theorem provers: A case study combining HOL-Light and CVC Lite. Electr. Notes Theor. Comput. Sci. 144(2), 43–51 (2006)
27. Meng, J., Paulson, L.C.: Translating higher-order clauses to first-order clauses. J. Auto. Reas. 40(1), 35–60 (2008)
28. Meng, J., Paulson, L.C.: Lightweight relevance filtering for machine-generated resolution problems. J. Applied Logic 7(1), 41–57 (2009)
29. Moskal, M.: Programming with triggers. In: Dutertre, B., Strichman, O. (eds.) Satisfiability Modulo Theories (2009)
30. Nipkow, T.: Re: [isabelle] A beginner's questionu [sic], (November 26, 2010), https://lists.cam.ac.uk/pipermail/cl-isabelle-users/2010-November/msg00097.html
31. Nipkow, T., Paulson, L.C., Wenzel, M.T. (eds.): Isabelle/HOL: A Proof Assistant for Higher-Order Logic, LNCS, vol. 2283. Springer, Heidelberg (2002)
32. Nonnengart, A., Weidenbach, C.: Computing small clause normal forms. In: Robinson, A., Voronkov, A. (eds.) Handbook of Automated Reasoning, pp. 335–367. Elsevier, Amsterdam (2001)
33. Paulson, L.C., Blanchette, J.C.: Three years of experience with Sledgehammer, a practical link between automatic and interactive theorem provers. In: Sutcliffe, G., Ternovska, E., Schulz, S. (eds.) International Workshop on the Implementation of Logics (2010)
34. Paulson, L.C., Susanto, K.W.: Source-level proof reconstruction for interactive theorem proving. In: Schneider, K., Brandt, J. (eds.) TPHOLs 2007. LNCS, vol. 4732, pp. 232–245. Springer, Heidelberg (2007)
35. Ranise, S., Tinelli, C.: The SMT-LIB standard: Version 1.2 (2006), http://goedel.cs.uiowa.edu/smtlib/papers/format-v1.2-r06.08.30.pdf
36. Riazanov, A., Voronkov, A.: The design and implementation of Vampire. AI Comm. 15(2-3), 91–110 (2002)
37. Rushby, J.M.: Tutorial: Automated formal methods with PVS, SAL, and Yices. In: Hung, D.V., Pandya, P. (eds.) Software Engineering and Formal Methods, p. 262. IEEE, New York (2006)
38. Schulz, S.: System description: E 0.81. In: Basin, D., Rusinowitch, M. (eds.) IJCAR 2004. LNCS (LNAI), vol. 3097, pp. 223–228. Springer, Heidelberg (2004)

39. Siekmann, J., Benzmüller, C., Fiedler, A., Meier, A., Normann, I., Pollet, M.: Proof development with ΩMEGA: The irrationality of $\sqrt{2}$. In: Kamareddine, F. (ed.) Thirty Five Years of Automating Mathematics. Applied Logic, vol. 28, pp. 271–314. Springer, Heidelberg (2003)

40. Sutcliffe, G.: System description: SystemOnTPTP. In: McAllester, D. (ed.) CADE 2000. LNCS (LNAI), vol. 1831, pp. 406–410. Springer, Heidelberg (2000)

41. Sutcliffe, G., Chang, C., Ding, L., McGuinness, D., da Silva, P.P.: Different proofs are good proofs. In: McGuinness, D., Stump, A., Sutcliffe, G., Tinelli, C. (eds.) Workshop on Evaluation Methods for Solvers, and Quality Metrics for Solutions, pp. 1–10 (2010)

42. Urban, J.: MPTP 0.2: Design, implementation, and initial experiments. J. Auto. Reas. 37(1-2), 21–43 (2006)

43. Wampler-Doty, M.: A complete proof of the Robbins conjecture. In: Klein, G., Nipkow, T., Paulson, L. (eds.) The Archive of Formal Proofs (2010), http://afp.sf.net/entries/Robbins-Conjecture.shtml

44. Weidenbach, C.: Combining superposition, sorts and splitting. In: Robinson, A., Voronkov, A. (eds.) Handbook of Automated Reasoning, pp. 1965–2013. Elsevier, Amsterdam (2001)

45. Wenzel, M.: Type classes and overloading in higher-order logic. In: Gunter, E.L., Felty, A.P. (eds.) TPHOLs 1997. LNCS, vol. 1275, pp. 307–322. Springer, Heidelberg (1997)

46. Wenzel, M.: Parallel proof checking in Isabelle/Isar. In: Dos Reis, G., Théry, L. (eds.) Programming Languages for Mechanized Mathematics Systems, ACM Digital Library (2009)

Automated Cyclic Entailment Proofs in Separation Logic

James Brotherston[1], Dino Distefano[2], and Rasmus Lerchedahl Petersen[2]

[1] Dept. of Computing, Imperial College London
[2] Dept. of Computer Science, Queen Mary University of London

Abstract. We present a general automated proof procedure, based upon *cyclic proof*, for inductive entailments in separation logic. Our procedure has been implemented via a deep embedding of cyclic proofs in the HOL Light theorem prover. Experiments show that our mechanism is able to prove a number of non-trivial entailments involving inductive predicates.

1 Introduction

Separation logic [19] has recently become a very popular formalism for the verification of imperative, memory-manipulating programs. Proofs of programs in separation logic are based on the Hoare triples {P}C{Q} familiar from first-order approaches to verification. However, the pre- and post-conditions of triples may contain a special *separating conjunction* $*$, which allows the disjointness of portions of heap memory to be expressed: The formula $F * G$ denotes those heaps which can be separated into two disjoint parts satisfying F and G, respectively. This characteristic feature enables one to construct proofs that are highly modular, and thus separation logic scales well to large programs. Indeed, there are now several tools based upon separation logic that are capable of verifying code on an industrial scale [8,23,13].

In this paper, we address the issue of automatically proving *entailments* $F_1 \models F_2$ between formulas in separation logic. In proof systems and automated verification tools based on Hoare triples, the obligation to prove such entailments typically arises via the standard *rule of consequence*:

$$\frac{\{P'\}C\{Q'\}}{\{P\}C\{Q\}} \quad P \models P', Q' \models Q \ (\text{Consq})$$

This rule might be applied during a proof search to remove redundant information from the precondition P, or to convert P and Q into a format which matches a rule for the command C. Other activities in which entailments need to be proved include abstraction [12] and discharging the guards of conditional commands during symbolic execution. Thus, effective procedures for establishing entailments are at the foundation of automatic verification based on separation logic. Due to the intense use of dynamically-allocated data structure in real-world software (e.g., system code [23]), in practice, the pre- and postconditions occurring in separation logic proofs typically contain inductively defined predicates.

N. Bjørner and V. Sofronie-Stokkermans (Eds.): CADE 2011, LNAI 6803, pp. 131–146, 2011.

Thus any proof-theoretic approach to establishing entailments is essentially a problem of *inductive theorem proving*, which is known to present serious difficulties for automated search (see [7] for an overview). Moreover, in the case of separation logic, the induction hypotheses required for an inductive proof are often not even expressible in the fragments of the logic handled by automatic tools since they require unsupported operators like the spatial implication —∗.

Unfortunately, due to the current lack of off-the-shelf general theorem provers, most of the existing automated verification tools have to appeal to their own theorem prover for checking the validity of entailments. Because building them is a difficult and time-consuming activity, these provers tend to be rather *ad-hoc* and often do not provide support for inductive methods. Here, we present a prototype theorem prover for entailments of separation logic that uses *cyclic proof* to handle inductive theorems. Cyclic proof has recently been mooted as an alternative to the default approach of explicit inductive proof that offers potential advantages for automated proof search [4,6]. Cyclic proofs differ from explicit induction proofs in two main respects. First, explicit induction rules are replaced by simple "case split" rules for the inductively defined predicates. Second, proofs are allowed to contain cycles, and thus can be seen as infinite derivation trees. To ensure that such structures correspond to sound proofs, a global *soundness condition* is imposed on cyclic proofs guaranteeing the well-foundedness of all reasoning. The main attraction of cyclic proofs is that, unlike in standard induction proofs, the induction hypotheses are not supplied explicitly via the application of an induction rule. Instead, they are constructed implicitly via the discovery of a valid cyclic proof. This allows a much more exploratory approach to automated proof search.

Our theorem prover is implemented in HOL Light [15] and supports both fully automatic and interactive proof. The implementation of a cyclic proof system in HOL Light, or indeed any of the mainstream theorem provers, presents several non-trivial technical obstacles stemming from the fact that such provers take a *local* viewpoint of proofs, whereas cyclic proof is necessarily *global*. To overcome this mismatch, we employ a *deep embedding* of our formal cyclic proof system, i.e., a HOL Light representation in which cyclic proofs themselves are first-class objects. The main advantage of a fully explicit representation of this type is that we can easily impose the correct soundness conditions on proofs. Although we employ a fairly simple such condition in this paper, we can easily impose more general conditions in order to improve completeness at the expense of speed. We have evaluated our implementation on a series of examples, drawn from the literature. Although our prover is only a prototype, the results are encouraging for their coverage as well as their performance. Our implementation approach should also transfer to other, similar cyclic proof systems as described in [2].

The remainder of this paper is structured as follows. Section 2 introduces our separation logic fragment. Section 3 introduces our cyclic proof machinery. Section 4 describes the implementation of our proof procedure and evaluates its performance. Section 5 compares with related work and Section 6 concludes.

2   Syntax and Semantics

In this section we introduce the separation logic formulas that we shall consider throughout the paper, and their standard semantics with respect to a fixed heap model. We assume a fixed, infinite set $\mathcal{V}$ of first-order variables and a fixed finite set of predicate symbols, each with associated arity.

Definition 1 (Formulas). *Formulas* are given inductively by the grammar:

$$F ::= \top \mid \bot \mid x = y \mid x \neq y \mid \mathbf{emp} \mid x \mapsto y \mid x \overset{2}{\mapsto} y, z \mid F \vee F \mid F * F \mid P\mathbf{x}$$

where x, y range over $\mathcal{V}$, P ranges over predicate symbols and $\mathbf{x}$ ranges over tuples of variables of appropriate length to match the arity of P. We write $FV(F)$ to denote the set of variables occurring in formula F. We consider formulas up to associativity and commutativity of $*$ and $\vee$.

The fragment of separation logic considered here is relatively simple and does not include, for example, function symbols, plain conjunction ($\wedge$) or spatial implication ($-\!\!*$). These features are not typically employed in separation logic verification tools (in fact even $\vee$ is often removed as well) because the complexity rapidly becomes unmanageable. In fact, it has been shown that unrestricted separation logic is undecidable even in the purely propositional setting [5].

   The definitions of our predicate symbols are supplied by "inductive rule sets" in the style of [3,2], which are based on Martin-Löf's "productions" [16].

Definition 2 (Inductive rule set). An *inductive rule set* is a finite set of *inductive rules* each of the form $F \Rightarrow P\mathbf{x}$ where F and $P\mathbf{x}$ are formulas with P a predicate symbol.

From now on we assume a fixed inductive rule set Φ.

Semantics. Let L be an infinite set of *locations*, and V be a set of *values*. Then $H = L \rightharpoonup_{\text{fin}} V$, the set of all finite partial functions from L to V, is called the set of *heaps*. (We sometimes choose to work instead with heaps of the form $H = L \rightharpoonup_{\text{fin}} V \times V$, where a pair of values is stored at each location.) We write $\text{dom}(h)$ to denote the *domain* of the heap h, i.e., the set $\{l \in L \mid h(l) \text{ is defined}\}$. Composition of heaps, $h_1 \circ h_2$, is defined as the union of h_1 and h_2 if their domains are disjoint, and undefined otherwise. The *empty heap* e is the heap such that $e(l)$ is undefined for all $l \in L$. It is easy to see that $\langle H, \circ, e \rangle$ is a *separation algebra* (cf. [9]), i.e., a cancellative partial commutative monoid.

   The set of *stacks* is $S = \mathcal{V} \rightarrow L \cup V$, the set of total functions from first-order variables to locations or values (which are not necessarily disjoint). *Satisfaction* of a formula F by a stack s and heap h is denoted $s, h \models F$ and defined by structural induction on F in Figure 1. There, $[\![P]\!]$ is as usual a component of the least fixed point of a monotone operator constructed from the inductive definition set Φ; see [3,4] for details. We say the *entailment* $F_1 \models F_2$ holds if, for all stacks $s \in S$ and heaps $h \in H$, we have $s, h \models F_1$ implies $s, h \models F_2$.

$$
\begin{array}{rcl}
s, h \models \top & \Leftrightarrow & \text{always} \\
s, h \models \bot & \Leftrightarrow & \text{never} \\
s, h \models x = y & \Leftrightarrow & s(x) = s(y) \\
s, h \models x \neq y & \Leftrightarrow & s(x) \neq s(y) \\
s, h \models \mathbf{emp} & \Leftrightarrow & h = e \\
s, h \models x \mapsto y & \Leftrightarrow & \mathbf{dom}(h) = \{s(x)\} \text{ and } h(s(x)) = s(y) \\
s, h \models x \overset{2}{\mapsto} y, z & \Leftrightarrow & \mathbf{dom}(h) = \{s(x)\} \text{ and } h(s(x)) = (s(y), s(z)) \\
s, h \models P\mathbf{x} & \Leftrightarrow & (s(\mathbf{x}), h) \in [\![P]\!] \\
s, h \models F_1 \vee F_2 & \Leftrightarrow & s, h \models F_1 \text{ or } s, h \models F_2 \\
s, h \models F_1 * F_2 & \Leftrightarrow & \exists h_1, h_2 \in H. \; h = h_1 \circ h_2 \text{ and } s, h_1 \models F_1 \text{ and } s, h_2 \models F_2
\end{array}
$$

Fig. 1. Semantics of separation logic formulae. Note that the $\mapsto$ and $\overset{2}{\mapsto}$ predicates are interpreted only in heaps of type $L \rightharpoonup_{\text{fin}} V$ and $L \rightharpoonup_{\text{fin}} V \times V$ respectively.

3   Cyclic Proofs of Separation Logic Entailments

In this section we define a formal cyclic proof system for a class of separation logic entailment problems involving inductively defined predicates.

Our proof system employs *sequents* of the form $F \vdash G$ where F and G are separation logic formulas as given by Defn. 1. We write $F[\theta]$ for the result of applying a substitution $\theta : \mathcal{V} \to \mathcal{V}$ to the formula F, and extend substitution pointwise to tuples of variables. We give a set of basic proof rules for sequents in Figure 2. Note that we write a rule with a double-line between premise and conclusion to indicate that the premise and conclusion are interchangeable (so that a "double-line rule" effectively abbreviates two normal rules). We also comment that our rules have been chosen for simplicity and ease of implementation, rather than completeness and expressivity. In particular, there is no rule for rewriting with equalities; such rewriting techniques are out of the scope of the present paper, which concentrates on inductive techniques.

To the proof rules in Figure 2 we add simple *unfolding* rules for the inductive predicates in the definition set Φ. In order to formulate these, it is essential to know which variables occur free in our inductive rules, so that they can be instantiated correctly. We write an annotated inductive rule $F \overset{\mathbf{z}}{\Rightarrow} P\mathbf{x}$, where $\mathbf{z}$ is a tuple of distinct variables, to indicate that $FV(F) \cup \{\mathbf{x}\} = \{\mathbf{z}\}$.

Definition 3 (Unfolding rules). To any predicate symbol P we associate a finite number of *right-unfolding* rules and a single *left-unfolding* rule, constructed from its inductive definition in the inductive rule set Φ. First, for each inductive rule $F \overset{\mathbf{z}}{\Rightarrow} P\mathbf{x}$ there is a right-unfolding rule for P:

$$
\frac{G \vdash H * F[\mathbf{y}/\mathbf{z}]}{G \vdash H * P\mathbf{x}[\mathbf{y}/\mathbf{z}]} \; (PR)
$$

where $\mathbf{y}$ is any tuple of variables of the same length as $\mathbf{z}$. (Note that $\{\mathbf{x}\} \subseteq \{\mathbf{z}\}$ by definition, so that in $P\mathbf{x}[\mathbf{y}/\mathbf{z}]$ all of the variables in $\mathbf{x}$ are uniformly replaced by arbitrary variables from $\mathbf{y}$.)

$$\frac{}{F \vdash F}\,(\mathrm{Id}) \qquad \frac{}{\bot * F \vdash G}\,(\bot\mathrm{L}) \qquad \frac{}{F \vdash \top}\,(\top\mathrm{R}) \qquad \frac{}{F \vdash x = x}\,(=\mathrm{R})$$

$$\frac{}{x = y * x \neq y * F \vdash G}\,(=\mathrm{L}) \qquad \frac{}{x \mapsto y * x \mapsto z * F \vdash G}\,(\mapsto)$$

$$\frac{}{x \overset{2}{\mapsto} y_1, y_2 * x \overset{2}{\mapsto} z_1, z_2 * F \vdash G}\,(\overset{2}{\mapsto}) \qquad \frac{F \vdash H \quad H \vdash G}{F \vdash G}\,(\mathrm{Cut})$$

$$\frac{F \vdash G}{\mathbf{emp} * F \vdash G}\,(\mathrm{empL}) \qquad \frac{F \vdash G}{F \vdash G * \mathbf{emp}}\,(\mathrm{empR}) \qquad \frac{F_1 \vdash G_1 \quad F_2 \vdash G_2}{F_1 * F_2 \vdash G_1 * G_2}\,(*)$$

$$\frac{F_1 * F \vdash G \quad F_2 * F \vdash G}{(F_1 \vee F_2) * F \vdash G}\,(\vee\mathrm{L}) \qquad \frac{F \vdash G_i * G}{F \vdash (G_1 \vee G_2) * G}\,i \in \{1,2\}(\vee\mathrm{R})$$

Fig. 2. Basic proof rules. A rule written with a double-line between premise and conclusion indicates that the premise and conclusion are interchangeable.

The left-unfolding, or *case-split* rule for P has the following general schema:

$$\frac{\text{case premises}}{G * P\mathbf{v} \vdash H}\,(\mathrm{Case}\ P)$$

where, for each inductive rule of the form $F \overset{\mathbf{z}}{\Rightarrow} P\mathbf{x}$, there is a *case premise*:

$$G[(\mathbf{x}[\mathbf{y}/\mathbf{z}])/\mathbf{v}] * F[\mathbf{y}/\mathbf{z}] \vdash H[(\mathbf{x}[\mathbf{y}/\mathbf{z}])/\mathbf{v}]$$

where the variables $\mathbf{y}$ are *fresh*, i.e. $y \notin FV(G * P\mathbf{v}) \cup FV(H)$ for all $y \in \{\mathbf{y}\}$. We observe that the complicated-seeming variable instantiation here essentially works in two stages. First, the variables $\mathbf{z}$ appearing in the inductive rule $F \overset{\mathbf{z}}{\Rightarrow} P\mathbf{x}$ are replaced by the fresh variables $\mathbf{y}$, giving us a "fresh version" of the rule, $F[\mathbf{y}/\mathbf{z}] \overset{\mathbf{y}}{\Rightarrow} P\mathbf{x}[\mathbf{y}/\mathbf{z}]$. Second, to obtain the case premise we uniformly replace the variables $\mathbf{v}$ appearing in the formula to be unfolded, $P\mathbf{v}$, with the freshly instantiated variables $\mathbf{x}[\mathbf{y}/\mathbf{z}]$ appearing in the conclusion of the inductive rule[1].

Example 1 (List segment). Define the inductive predicate $\mathtt{ls}$ by:

$$\mathbf{emp} \overset{x}{\Rightarrow} \mathtt{ls}\,x\,x \qquad x \mapsto x' * \mathtt{ls}\,x'\,z \overset{x,x',z}{\Rightarrow} \mathtt{ls}\,x\,z$$

(Note the variable annotations.) The formula $\mathtt{ls}\,x\,y$ denotes a singly-linked list segment whose first cell is pointed to by x and whose last cell contains y. The right-unfolding rules for $\mathtt{ls}$ are:

$$\frac{G \vdash H * \mathbf{emp}}{G \vdash H * \mathtt{ls}\,y\,y}\,(\mathtt{ls}R_1) \qquad \frac{G \vdash H * y \mapsto y' * \mathtt{ls}\,y'\,v}{G \vdash H * \mathtt{ls}\,y\,v}\,(\mathtt{ls}R_2)$$

---

[1] We could write this premise more simply as $G * \mathbf{v} = \mathbf{x}[\mathbf{y}/\mathbf{z}] * F[\mathbf{y}/\mathbf{z}] \vdash H$. However, our formulation above allows us to do without rules for equality on the left.

The case-split rule for ls is:

$$\frac{\begin{array}{c} G[y/v, y/v'] * \mathbf{emp} \vdash H[y/v, y/v'] \\ G[y/v, y'/v'] * y \mapsto y'' * \mathbf{ls}\, y''\, y' \vdash H[y/v, y'/v'] \end{array}}{G * \mathbf{ls}\, v\, v' \vdash H} \text{(Case ls)}$$

where y, y', y'' are suitably fresh. Note that both v and v' are replaced by the *same* fresh variable y in the first premise, because the corresponding inductive rule $\mathbf{emp} \overset{x}{\Rightarrow} \mathbf{ls}\, x\, x$ only has a single free variable x.

Example 2 (Binary trees). Define the inductive predicate btr by:

$$\mathbf{emp} \overset{x}{\Rightarrow} \mathbf{btr}\, x \qquad x \overset{2}{\mapsto} y, z * \mathbf{btr}\, y * \mathbf{btr}\, z \overset{x,y,z}{\Rightarrow} \mathbf{btr}\, x$$

The formula btr x denotes a binary tree whose first cell is pointed to by x. The right-unfolding rules for btree are:

$$\frac{G \vdash H * \mathbf{emp}}{G \vdash H * \mathbf{btr}\, v} \text{(btr}R_1) \qquad \frac{G \vdash H * v \overset{2}{\mapsto} v_1, v_2 * \mathbf{btr}\, v_1 * \mathbf{btr}\, v_2}{G \vdash H * \mathbf{btr}\, v} \text{(btr}R_2)$$

The case-split rule for btr (where y, y_1, y_2 are suitably fresh) is:

$$\frac{\begin{array}{c} G[y/v] * \mathbf{emp} \vdash H[y/v] \\ G[y/v] * y \overset{2}{\mapsto} y_1, y_2 * \mathbf{btr}\, y_1 * \mathbf{btr}\, y_2 \vdash H[y/v] \end{array}}{G * \mathbf{btr}\, v \vdash H} \text{(Case btr)}$$

Our proof system allows proofs to be *cyclic*: that is, our proofs are derivation trees with "back edges", subject to a syntactic, global condition ensuring soundness. The following definitions are adapted from their analogues in [3].

Definition 4 (Pre-proof). A *bud* in a derivation tree $\mathcal{D}$ is a sequent occurrence in $\mathcal{D}$ to which no proof rule has been applied (i.e., it is not the conclusion of any proof rule instance in $\mathcal{D}$). A *companion* for a bud B is a sequent occurrence C in $\mathcal{D}$ of which B is a substitution instance, i.e. $C = B[\theta]$ for some substitution θ. A *pre-proof* of a sequent S is given by $(\mathcal{D}, \mathcal{R})$, where $\mathcal{D}$ is a derivation tree whose root is S and $\mathcal{R}$ is a function assigning a companion to every bud of $\mathcal{D}$.

A *path* in a pre-proof is a sequence of sequent occurrences $(F_i \vdash G_i)_{i \geq 0}$ such that, for all $i \geq 0$, it holds that either $F_{i+1} \vdash G_{i+1}$ is a premise of the rule instance in $\mathcal{D}$ with conclusion $F_i \vdash G_i$, or $F_{i+1} \vdash G_{i+1} = \mathcal{R}(F_i \vdash G_i)$.

Definition 5 (Trace). Let $(F_i \vdash G_i)_{i \geq 0}$ be a path in a pre-proof $\mathcal{P}$. A *trace following* $(F_i \vdash G_i)_{i \geq 0}$ is a sequence $(A_i)_{i \geq 0}$ such that, for all $i \geq 0$, A_i is a subformula occurrence of the form $P\mathbf{x}$ in the formula F_i, and either:

(i) A_{i+1} is the subformula occurrence in F_{i+1} corresponding to A_i in F_i (defined in the obvious way analogous to [3,4]), or

(ii) $F_i \vdash G_i$ is the conclusion of an instance of a case-split rule (Case P), A_i is the formula $P\mathbf{v}$ unfolded by the rule and A_{i+1} is a subformula of the formula $F[\mathbf{y}/\mathbf{z}]$ obtained by the unfolding, in which case i is said to be a *progress point* of the trace.

We remark that, in particular, condition (i) means that formulas can only be traced through the left-hand premise of an instance of (Cut) and not its right-hand premise. An *infinitely progressing trace* is a (necessarily infinite) trace having infinitely many progress points.

Definition 6 (Cyclic proof). A pre-proof $\mathcal{P}$ is a *cyclic proof* if it satisfies the *global trace condition*: for every infinite path $(F_i \vdash G_i)_{i \geq 0}$ in $\mathcal{P}$, there is an infinitely progressing trace following some tail $(F_i \vdash G_i)_{i \geq n}$ of the path.

Theorem 7 (Soundness). *If there is a cyclic proof of $F \vdash G$, then $F \models G$.*

Proof. (Sketch) The proof runs along the lines given in [3,6,4]. Briefly, suppose for contradiction that there is a cyclic proof $\mathcal{P}$ of $F \vdash G$ but $F \not\models G$, so that for some stack s and heap h we have $s, h \models F$ but $s, h \not\models G$. Then, by local soundness of the proof rules, we would be able to construct an infinite path $(F_i \vdash G_i)_{i \geq 0}$ in $\mathcal{P}$ (with $F_0 \vdash G_0 = F \vdash G$) such that $F_i \not\models G_i$ for all $i \geq 0$. Since $\mathcal{P}$ is a cyclic proof, there exists an $n \geq 0$ and an infinitely progressing trace following $(F_i \vdash G_i)_{i \geq n}$. It is a standard fact that the least fixed point interpretation of the inductive predicates can be generated by an ordinal-indexed chain of *approximants* (cf. [1]). The fact, guaranteed by the trace condition, that some occurrence of an inductive predicate is unfolded infinitely often using the case-split rules then induces an infinite decreasing chain of the ordinals indexing this chain of approximants, which contradicts their well-foundedness.   □

Example 3 (cf. [3]). The following is a pre-proof of $\mathtt{ls}\, x\, x' * \mathtt{ls}\, x'\, y \vdash \mathtt{ls}\, x\, y$.

$$
\cfrac{
  \cfrac{
    \cfrac{\ }{\mathtt{ls}\, x\, y \vdash \mathtt{ls}\, x\, y}\ \text{(Id)}
  }{\mathbf{emp} * \mathtt{ls}\, x\, y \vdash \mathtt{ls}\, x\, y}\ \text{(empL)}
  \qquad
  \cfrac{
    \cfrac{
      \cfrac{\ }{x \mapsto z \vdash x \mapsto z}\ \text{(Id)}
      \quad
      \cfrac{(\dagger)\ \underline{\mathtt{ls}\, z\, x'} * \mathtt{ls}\, x'\, y \vdash \mathtt{ls}\, z\, y}{}
    }{x \mapsto z * \underline{\mathtt{ls}\, z\, x'} * \mathtt{ls}\, x'\, y \vdash x \mapsto z * \mathtt{ls}\, z\, y}\ (*)
  }{x \mapsto z * \underline{\mathtt{ls}\, z\, x'} * \mathtt{ls}\, x'\, y \vdash \mathtt{ls}\, x\, y}\ (\mathtt{lsR_2})
}{(\dagger)\ \underline{\mathtt{ls}\, x\, x'} * \mathtt{ls}\, x'\, y \vdash \mathtt{ls}\, x\, y}\ \text{(Case ls)}
$$

The pairing of a suitable companion with the only bud in this pre-proof is denoted by $(\dagger)$. A trace from the companion to the bud is denoted by the underlined formulas, with a progress point at the displayed application of (Case ls).

We remark that the standard inductive proof of $\mathtt{ls}\, x\, x' * \mathtt{ls}\, x'\, y \vdash \mathtt{ls}\, x\, y$ is by induction on $\mathtt{ls}\, x\, x'$ using the induction hypothesis $\mathtt{ls}\, x'\, y \twoheadrightarrow \mathtt{ls}\, x\, y$, where $\twoheadrightarrow$ is the multiplicative implication of separation logic. Not only is this induction hypothesis not a subformula of the goal sequent, but it is not even expressible in our formula language (or that of most available verification tools).

4   Implementation of the Cyclic Prover

The proof system described in Section 3 has been implemented in HOL Light as a *deep embedding*, meaning that proofs as well as sequents are represented explicitly in our implementation. Thus we provide HOL datatypes for formulas (with a sequent being represented as a pair of formulas) and pre-proofs, with the proof rules captured by a HOL relation on sequents.

The main obstacles when implementing a cyclic prover all stem from the fact that the activities of constructing cycles and verifying the soundness condition are *global* operations on proof trees, whereas (like most theorem provers) HOL Light's internal view of proofs is inherently *local*. Thus, while one can typically implement a proof system simply by encoding each proof rule, we have to explicitly represent (portions of) pre-proofs in order to allow us to identify suitable companions for buds and to ensure that the resulting pre-proof satisfies the soundness condition that all infinite paths have infinitely progressing traces.

Our solution is to first tag each occurrence of an inductive predicate in our sequents, in order to assist in the construction of traces. We then augment each node with information about the current branch and any progress points in the traces along it. This gives us enough explicit information in a proof tree to enable the formation of "downlinks" from buds to companions, and to ensure the soundness condition on cyclic proofs. The next subsections describe the various components of the implementation.

4.1   Representation of Pre-proofs

As with the proof system in Section 3, the entire implementation is parameterized by a set of inductive definitions, so an OCaml datatype for inductive definitions has been designed and a list of such is a parameter to the whole implementation.

The type `formula` is implemented as a HOL datatype following Definition 1 except for atomic formulas of the form $P\mathbf{x}$, which have the constructor `Ind : num → inductive → formula`. The datatype `inductive` is generated from the input list of inductive definitions and simply has an entry $P\mathbf{x}$ for each inductive predicate. The argument to `Ind` of type `num` is a tag used to track occurrences so that traces can be established; Section 4.2 describes how traces are constructed using predicate tags. When searching for a cyclic proof, unique tags are assigned to all inductive predicates of the root node.

In the implemented system, the nodes of the proof tree are "augmented sequents" containing extra information about the proof tree, written as

$$(\alpha, \pi) : F \vdash G$$

(where F and G are formulas). The component α is called the *ancestry* of the current node. It records the entire branch from the root of the proof tree to the node, in the form of a (finite) list of entailments $F_1 \vdash G_1, \ldots, F_n \vdash G_n$, with $F_n \vdash G_n$ being the root of the tree. We write $F \vdash G :: \alpha$ for the ancestry obtained by adding $F \vdash G$ to the beginning of the list α, and write α_n for the nth element of α (if it exists). The component $\pi \in \mathbb{N}$, called the *progress pointer*, is the smallest natural number n such that α_n is the conclusion of a case-split rule (denoting the closest progress point below the current node in the sense of Definition 5). If no such n exists (so that no case-split rules are applied below the current node), we set $\pi = |\alpha| + 1$, so that π points past the end of the ancestry.

The general transformation from the rules of Figure 2 to rules using augmented sequents in the implemented system is the following:

$$\frac{S_1 \ \ldots \ S_n}{S} \quad \Longrightarrow \quad \frac{(S :: \alpha, \pi+1) : S_1 \ \ldots \ (S :: \alpha, \pi+1) : S_n}{(\alpha, \pi) : S}$$

I.e., when applying a rule backwards, the sequent in the conclusion of the rule is added to the ancestry of each of its premises. The progress pointer is incremented, because the distance from the current node to the nearest conclusion of a case-split rule has increased by one (reading the rule from conclusion to premise).

Naturally, the case-split rules are exceptions. When a case-split rule is applied, the progress pointer is set to 1 in each of its premises. So, for example, the implemented version of the case-split rule (Case $\mathtt{ls}$) looks like this:

$$\frac{((G * \mathtt{ls}_i \, v \, v' \vdash H) :: \alpha, 1) : G[y/v, y/v'] * \mathbf{emp} \vdash H[y/v, y/v']}{(\alpha, \pi) : G * \mathtt{ls}_i \, v \, v' \vdash H}$$
$$\frac{((G * \mathtt{ls}_i \, v \, v' \vdash H) :: \alpha, 1) : G[y/v, y'/v'] * y \mapsto y'' * \mathtt{ls}_i \, y'' \, y' \vdash H[y/v, y'/v']}{}$$

where the subscript i on $\mathtt{ls}$ denotes the tag assigned to the atomic formula occurrence; note that the subformula $\mathtt{ls} \, y'' \, y'$ in the second premise, obtained by unfolding $\mathtt{ls} \, v \, v'$ in the conclusion, inherits the tag i, in keeping with the rules for forming traces in Definition 5.

The axiom rule (Id) is the other exception because, since tags are only relevant for the purpose of constructing traces, they should be ignored when applying (Id). We define a binary predicate $\mathtt{matches}$ on formulas to implement equality up to change of tags, whence $F \, \mathtt{matches} \, G$ holds if F and G are equal when all their tags are erased. The implemented form of (Id) is then as follows:

$$\frac{F \ \mathtt{matches} \ F'}{(\alpha, \pi) : F \vdash F'} \ (\mathtt{c\_Id})$$

Finally, we need to add a rule that allows us to form cycles. The ancestry information alone is enough to form cycles, but the progress pointer allows us to only form cycles which contain at least one progress point: In order to find a companion for $(\alpha, \pi) : F \vdash G$, it suffices to find a substitution θ and an n such that $n > \pi$, α_n is defined and $\alpha_n = (F \vdash G)[\theta]$. However, because traces only involve predicates occurring on the left of sequents, it suffices that G and the right hand side of α_n are equal up to predicate tags. Thus, the proof rule for link formation in the implemented system is

$$\frac{|\alpha| > n > \pi \quad \exists \theta. \ \alpha_n = (F \vdash G')[\theta] \quad G \ \mathtt{matches} \ G'[\theta]}{(\alpha, \pi) : F \vdash G} \ (\mathtt{c\_downlink})$$

where $|\alpha|$ is the length of the ancestry. This rule ensures that if we can form a downlink from B to C then there is a progressing trace on the finite path $C \ldots B$ in the proof tree (and this trace has identical values at C and B).

4.2   Soundness of the Implementation

We now describe how the soundness of the implemented system follows from the soundness of the system in Section 3. First, we observe that there is a map $\mathcal{E}$ from proofs in the implemented system to pre-proofs in the system from Section 3. That is, for any proof tree T in the implemented system, $\mathcal{E}(T) = (\mathcal{D}, \mathcal{R})$, where:

- $\mathcal{D}$ is the derivation tree (in the proof system of section 3) obtained by stripping the ancestry, progress pointer and predicate tags from each node of T and turning every node occurring as the conclusion of an instance of (c_downlink) into a bud of $\mathcal{D}$;
- $\mathcal{R}$ is a function from the buds of $\mathcal{D}$ to suitable companions, built from the applications of (c_downlink) in the obvious way.

The main theorem of this section is that for every proof P in the implemented system, the pre-proof $\mathcal{E}(P)$ is actually a cyclic proof:

Theorem 8 (Soundness of the implementation). *If there is a proof of* $([], 1) : F \vdash G$ *in the implemented system, then* $F \models G$.

Proof. (Sketch) Given a proof P of $([], 1) : F \vdash G$, we show that $\mathcal{E}(P) = (\mathcal{D}, \mathcal{R})$ is a cyclic proof. $\mathcal{E}(P)$ is clearly a pre-proof by construction, so it just remains to show that it satisfies the global soundness condition of Defn. 6. Essentially, the argument is that our tagging of inductive predicates and the conditions on the "downlink" rule (c_downlink) ensure that there is a "trace manifold" for $\mathcal{E}(P)$, which implies the global soundness condition (see [2], ch. 7).

Let $(S_i)_{i \geq 0}$ be an infinite path in $\mathcal{E}(P)$. There must exist a tail $(S_i)_{i \geq n}$ of this path that traverses some strongly connected component $\mathcal{C}$ of $\mathcal{E}(P)$, which must be constructed from finite paths of the form $\mathcal{R}(B) \ldots B$ from companions to buds. Specifically, there is a non-empty (finite) set $\mathbf{B}$ of buds which are visited infinitely often on $(S_i)_{i \geq n}$. Choose $B \in \mathbf{B}$ such that $\mathcal{R}(B)$ is as close as possible to the root of $\mathcal{D}$. By inspection of the (c_downlink) rule, there is some tagged atomic formula $P_i \mathbf{x}$ occurring in both $\mathcal{R}(B)$ and B whose case-split rule is applied on the path $\mathcal{R}(B) \ldots B$. There must be an infinitely progressing trace following $(S_i)_{i \geq n}$, with all predicates tagged by i. A trace must exist because all tags on the left of sequents must be identical to apply (c_downlink) and our tagging discipline for other rules follows the method for constructing traces in Defn. 5. (In particular, if a tagged predicate is deleted along a path then that tag cannot be restored further up the tree.) Moreover, this trace is infinitely progressing because our choice of $\mathcal{R}(B)$ to be the lowermost companion in $\mathcal{C}$ visited infinitely often ensures that the path $(S_i)_{i \geq n}$ passes infinitely often through the case-split rule that unrolls a predicate tagged by i. □

We note that the soundness condition used in the implemented system is much simpler than the global trace condition of the formal system (Defn. 6), and is almost certainly incomplete. More sophisticated soundness conditions could be implemented at the expense of speed. We note also that our implementation, and its soundness, does not significantly depend on specific features of the fragment of separation logic considered in this paper, and should adapt to other cyclic proof systems employing a similar soundness condition (see [2], ch. 5).

4.3   Automated Proof Search

Split entailments. To better manage the sizes of the generated proofs, the entailment relation has been split into two: the augmented entailment $(\alpha, \pi) : P \vdash Q$ and a basic one $P \vdash_{basic} Q$ which is not augmented (and so $\vdash_{basic}$ is actually a subset of $\vdash$). The idea is to relay all reasoning using the associativity, commutativity and unit of $*$ to $\vdash_{basic}$. Such rules as (**empR**) are then found in this lightweight entailment rather than in the augmented one.

For the augmented entailment to make use of lightweight entailment rules such as (**empR**), we provide cut rules to inject $\vdash_{basic}$-reasoning into our proofs:

$$\frac{P \vdash_{basic} R \quad (\alpha, \pi) : R \vdash Q}{(\alpha, \pi) : P \vdash Q} \text{ (basicL)} \qquad \frac{(\alpha, \pi) : P \vdash R \quad R \vdash_{basic} Q}{(\alpha, \pi) : P \vdash Q} \text{ (basicR)}$$

It is important that $\vdash_{basic}$ does not interfere with the predicate tags, and so it is limited to reorganizing terms. Its id-rule, for instance, does not use the `matches`-predicate, and there is no cut rule. It can be shown that this careful re-factoring of the entailment relation does not change the truth of Theorem 8.

Tactics. Our prover is a collection of HOL tactics arranged into layers:

1. There is a tactic for each rule of the implemented proof system, and tactics are generated for the unfolding rules given by the inductive definitions, as described in section 3. The left rules introduce fresh variables and perform the (potentially unifying) substitutions, while the right rules introduce existential metavariables for any extra exposed variables.

   Additionally, a rule for link formation is implemented that searches through the ancestry for sequents of which the current node is a substitution instance and if one is found, applies (`c_downlink`).

2. Since a rule might not be directly applicable until some rearrangements have been performed, specialized tactics are using $\vdash_{basic}$-reasoning to set up rule applications. For the right-unfolding rules, this amounts to bringing the conclusion to the front on the right hand side.

3. "Advancing" rule applications. Right-unfolding rules, for instance, typically expose new state on the right side. An *advancing* version of such a rule will try to match this on the left hand side (resolving existential metavariables if necessary) and invoke a tactic to eliminate common state; the entire rule application fails if no state can be disposed of.

Elimination of common state is implemented using $\vdash_{basic}$-reasoning to bring both sides to similar forms and then using the rules ($*$) and a version of (c_Id) which resolves existential metavariables.

With these tactics at hand, one can conveniently use the system interactively or implement an automatic tactic. We implemented a backtracking proof search which applies any rule it can, from a prioritized list of rule sets:

1. $\{(\text{c\_Id}), \text{link formation}\}$ 2. advancing right rules   3. case-split rules

The other rules are only invoked as part of auxiliary reasoning for the rules in these groups.

4.4 Experimental Performance

Table 2 presents a list of lemmas that have been proven automatically by our cyclic prover, while Table 1 shows the definitions of the inductive predicates appearing in Table 2. The implementation was tested on a MacBook with a 2.4 GHz Intel Core Duo and 2 GB of 667 MHz DDR2 SDRAM running Mac OS 10.5.8. We also proved a more sophisticated lemma interactively, making use of Lemma 3 from Table 2:

Example 4. The following is a cyclic proof of $\text{RList}\, x\, y \vdash \text{List}\, x\, y$, where R and L below abbreviate RList and List from Table 1, respectively.

$$\dfrac{\dfrac{\dfrac{}{x \mapsto y \vdash x \mapsto y}\,(\text{Id})}{x \mapsto y \vdash Lxy}\,(LR_1) \qquad \dfrac{\dfrac{\dfrac{}{z \mapsto y \vdash z \mapsto y}\,(\text{Id}) \qquad (\dagger)\,\underline{Rxz} \vdash Lxz}{z \mapsto y * \underline{Rxz} \vdash z \mapsto y * Lxz}\,(*) \qquad \dfrac{\vdots}{z \mapsto y * Lxz \vdash Lxy}\,(\text{Lemma 3})}{z \mapsto y * \underline{Rxz} \vdash Lxy}\,(\text{Cut})}{(\dagger)\,\underline{Rxy} \vdash Lxy}\,(\text{Case } R)$$

It seems certain that our theorem prover would benefit from remembering earlier proven lemmas and allowing the automatic tactic to use these, as is provided e.g. by the lemma application mechanism in [17].

Most of the lemmas in Table 2 were proven with a bound of 3 on the depth of backtracking. Lemmas 10 through 12 required higher bounds, due to the mutual recursion (5, 7 and 5 respectively), and a few of the tree lemmas required a bound of 4 (lemmas 13, 14 and 16). The relatively low bound needed to prove lemmas is due to the split entailment relations.

5 Related Work

There is a substantial body of work in the literature that relates to our own work in a variety of ways.

Tuerk's Holfoot [20] is a general framework for separation logic, implemented in HOL, which has automatically proven properties of several interesting pointer

Table 1. Definitions of predicates

Predicate	Definition
RList (nonempty list segment)	$x \mapsto y \Rightarrow \text{RList } x\ y$ $\text{RList } x\ y * y \mapsto z \Rightarrow \text{RList } x\ z$
List (nonempty list segment)	$x \mapsto z \Rightarrow \text{List } x\ z$ $\text{List } z\ y * x \mapsto z \Rightarrow \text{List } x\ y$
ListE / ListO (nonempty list segment of even / odd length)	$x \mapsto z \Rightarrow \text{ListO } x\ z$ $\text{ListO } z\ y * x \mapsto z \Rightarrow \text{ListE } x\ y$ $\text{ListE } z\ y * x \mapsto z \Rightarrow \text{ListO } x\ y$
PeList (list segment)	$\mathbf{emp} \Rightarrow \text{PeList } x\ x$ $\text{PeList } z\ y * x \mapsto z \Rightarrow \text{PeList } x\ y$
DLL (doubly linked list segment)	$\mathbf{emp} \Rightarrow \text{DLL } a\ a\ b\ b$ $\text{DLL } x\ b\ c\ a * a \overset{2}{\mapsto} x,d \Rightarrow \text{DLL } a\ b\ c\ d$
SLL (singly linked list segment in binary heap)	$\mathbf{emp} \Rightarrow \text{SLL } a\ a$ $\text{SLL } x\ b * a \overset{2}{\mapsto} x,d \Rightarrow \text{SLL } a\ b$
BSLL (reverse SLL)	$\mathbf{emp} \Rightarrow \text{BSLL } c\ c$ $\text{BSLL } c\ x * x \overset{2}{\mapsto} a,d \Rightarrow \text{BSLL } c\ d$
BinTree (binary tree)	$\mathbf{emp} \Rightarrow \text{BinTree } a$ $\text{BinTree } b * \text{BinTree } c * a \overset{2}{\mapsto} b,c \Rightarrow \text{BinTree } a$
BinTreeSeg (binary tree segment)	$\mathbf{emp} \Rightarrow \text{BinTreeSeg } a\ a$ $\text{BinTreeSeg } c\ b * \text{BinTree } d * a \overset{2}{\mapsto} c,d \Rightarrow \text{BinTreeSeg } a\ b$ $\text{BinTree } c * \text{BinTreeSeg } d\ b * a \overset{2}{\mapsto} c,d \Rightarrow \text{BinTreeSeg } a\ b$
BinListFirst (list in cell 1 of binary heap)	$\mathbf{emp} \Rightarrow \text{BinListFirst } a$ $\text{BinListFirst } b * a \overset{2}{\mapsto} b,c \Rightarrow \text{BinListFirst } a$
BinListSecond (list in cell 2 of binary heap)	$\mathbf{emp} \Rightarrow \text{BinListSecond } a$ $\text{BinListSecond } c * a \overset{2}{\mapsto} b,c \Rightarrow \text{BinListSecond } a$
BinPath (path in binary heap)	$\mathbf{emp} \Rightarrow \text{BinPath } a\ a$ $\text{BinPath } c\ b * a \overset{2}{\mapsto} c,d \Rightarrow \text{BinPath } a\ b$ $\text{BinPath } c\ b * a \overset{2}{\mapsto} d,c \Rightarrow \text{BinPath } a\ b$

manipulating programs. However, Holfoot does not currently support cyclic proof, and we hope that our work may be useful for bringing this technique into such a general verification framework. Similar remarks apply to jStar [13].

Nguyen and Chin [17] describe an extension of an entailment checking technique introduced in earlier work [18] employing a fold/unfold mechanism for user defined inductive predicates. This extension is a mechanism that automatically proves and applies lemmas provided by the user. This mechanism employs a simple version of cyclic proof tailored to their specific verification system; when proving the lemmas, the theorem prover may apply a "smaller" instance of the lemma itself, with recursive lemma application carried out on the root node of inductive predicates. While the emphasis of that paper is in the application of lemmas, the emphasis of our work is rather on the definition and implementation of cyclic proof as well as in proving the soundness of our system. Here we have focused on developing a general cyclic entailment checker which could eventually become an off-the-shelf prover for verification tools or theorem provers.

Table 2. Experimental results

Lemma	Time (secs)	Proven
1	2.37	$x \mapsto y * \text{RList } y\ z \vdash \text{RList } x\ z$
2	2.37	$\text{RList } x\ z * \text{RList } z\ y \vdash \text{RList } x\ y$
3	2.56	$z \mapsto y * \text{List } x\ z \vdash \text{List } x\ y$
4	2.45	$\text{List } z\ y * \text{List } x\ z \vdash \text{List } x\ y$
5	2.78	$z \mapsto y * \text{PeList } x\ z \vdash \text{PeList } x\ y$
6	1.96	$\text{PeList } z\ y * \text{PeList } x\ z \vdash \text{PeList } x\ y$
7	3.54	$\text{DLL } u\ v\ x\ y \vdash \text{SLL } u\ v$
8	3.82	$\text{DLL } u\ v\ x\ y \vdash \text{BSLL } x\ y$
9	8.86	$\text{DLL } w\ v\ x\ z * \text{DLL } u\ w\ z\ y \vdash \text{DLL } u\ v\ x\ y$
10	5.44	$\text{ListO } z\ y * \text{ListO } x\ z \vdash \text{ListE } x\ y$
11	11.2	$\text{ListE } x\ z * \text{ListE } z\ y \vdash \text{ListE } x\ y$
12	5.57	$\text{ListO } z\ y * \text{ListE } x\ z \vdash \text{ListO } x\ y$
13	4.40	$\text{BinListFirst } x \vdash \text{BinTree } x$
14	4.43	$\text{BinListSecond } x \vdash \text{BinTree } x$
15	4.21	$\text{BinPath } z\ y * \text{BinPath } x\ z \vdash \text{BinPath } x\ y$
16	7.00	$\text{BinPath } x\ y \vdash \text{BinTreeSeg } x\ y$
17	8.78	$\text{BinTreeSeg } z\ y * \text{BinTreeSeg } x\ z \vdash \text{BinTreeSeg } x\ y$
18	8.61	$\text{BinTreeSeg } x\ y * \text{BinTree } y \vdash \text{BinTree } x$

In addition, we have the flexibility to easily tune the expressivity of our prover w.r.t. speed by implementing a more general soundness condition (which can be supplied parametrically to the system).

Chang *et al.* [11,10] propose a shape analysis guided by data structure invariants (provided by the programmer) that describe inductive predicates, called *invariant checkers*. While their emphasis is on defining expressive and precise shape analyses for a large variety of data structures, our emphasis here is on solving entailment questions which could be used to assist such analyses. We believe that our automated cyclic proof engine could be used to support or enhance various operations performed in their shape analysis (e.g. approximation testing, proving termination of fixed point computation, widening, etc.)

There are also a number of provers based upon infinite descent / cyclic proof that are oriented towards proving inductive theorems of arithmetic; we mention by way of example the Coq implementation of Voicu and Li [21], and the standalone QUODLIBET system of Wirth [22]. Our system differs from these works in that it is specialised towards separation logic (and thus aims to assist the analyses provided by automated program verification tools).

Finally, there is a large body of work on automated theorem proving using explicit induction; we mention IsaPlanner [14] as one contemporary such tool that employs Bundy's *rippling* technique to remove differences between the hypotheses of an induction and its goal. We think it far from unlikely that these techniques might usefully transfer to the setting of cyclic proof.

6   Conclusions and Future Work

In this paper we have introduced a sound automatic entailment checker for separation logic with inductive predicates based on cyclic proofs, focusing particularly on the soundness of our method and on the careful description of implementation details. The entailment checker has been implemented in HOL Light and has shown significant potential by proving a number of non-trivial lemmas for a range of inductive predicates corresponding to popular data structures. Thus our procedure represents a relevant first step towards the construction of off-the-shelf theorem provers based on separation logic. Our approach also adapts to other cyclic proof systems employing a similar soundness condition.

The automatic entailment checking procedure introduced in this paper opens up several avenues for future work, and in the future we plan to enhance its expressivity and effectiveness in a number of different directions. One direction is to experiment with weakening the soundness condition in order to admit more sophisticated cyclic proofs. Such a generalisation will necessitate more sophisticated tactics for our automated search procedure. Another direction is to extend the expressivity of our formulae by adding features such as quantifiers and arithmetic operations. In doing so it would also be natural to investigate the possibility of integrating our procedure with SMT solvers and arithmetic provers. Finally, we plan to explore the integration of our prover with automatic verification tools such as Holfoot [20] or jStar [13]. In particular, it would be interesting to see how our tool performs on the entailment questions those systems generate.

Acknowledgments. We thank Thomas Tuerk and Peter O'Hearn for intensive discussions, and Huu Hai Nguyen and Wei-Ngan Chin for providing us with sample lemmas to add to our experiments. We acknowledge the support of EPSRC and the Royal Academy of Engineering.

References

1. Aczel, P.: An introduction to inductive definitions. In: Barwise, J. (ed.) Handbook of Mathematical Logic, pp. 739–782. North-Holland, Amsterdam (1977)
2. Brotherston, J.: Sequent Calculus Proof Systems for Inductive Definitions. PhD thesis, University of Edinburgh (November 2006)
3. Brotherston, J.: Formalised inductive reasoning in the logic of bunched implications. In: Riis Nielson, H., Filé, G. (eds.) SAS 2007. LNCS, vol. 4634, pp. 87–103. Springer, Heidelberg (2007)
4. Brotherston, J., Bornat, R., Calcagno, C.: Cyclic proofs of program termination in separation logic. In: Proceedings of POPL-35, pp. 101–112. ACM, New York (2008)
5. Brotherston, J., Kanovich, M.: Undecidability of propositional separation logic and its neighbours. In: Proceedings of LICS-25, pp. 137–146. IEEE, New York (2010)
6. Brotherston, J., Simpson, A.: Sequent calculi for induction and infinite descent. Journal of Logic and Computation (2010)

7. Bundy, A.: The automation of proof by mathematical induction. In: Handbook of Automated Reasoning, vol. I, ch. 13, pp. 845–911. Elsevier Science, Amsterdam (2001)

8. Calcagno, C., Distefano, D., O'Hearn, P., Yang, H.: Compositional shape analysis by means of bi-abduction. In: Proceedings of POPL-36, pp. 289–300 (2009)

9. Calcagno, C., O'Hearn, P., Yang, H.: Local action and abstract separation logic. In: Proceedings of LICS-22, pp. 366–378. IEEE, Los Alamitos (2007)

10. Evan Chang, B.-Y., Rival, X.: Relational inductive shape analysis. In: POPL 2008, pp. 247–260 (2008)

11. Chang, B.-Y.E., Rival, X., Necula, G.C.: Shape analysis with structural invariant checkers. In: Riis Nielson, H., Filé, G. (eds.) SAS 2007. LNCS, vol. 4634, pp. 384–401. Springer, Heidelberg (2007)

12. Distefano, D., O'Hearn, P., Yang, H.: A local shape analysis based on separation logic. In: Hermanns, H. (ed.) TACAS 2006. LNCS, vol. 3920, pp. 287–302. Springer, Heidelberg (2006)

13. Distefano, D., Parkinson, M.: jStar: Towards practical verification for Java. In: Proceedings of OOPSLA, pp. 213–226. ACM, New York (2008)

14. Dixon, L., Fleuriot, J.D.: Higher order rippling in ISAPLANNER. In: Slind, K., Bunker, A., Gopalakrishnan, G.C. (eds.) TPHOLs 2004. LNCS, vol. 3223, pp. 83–98. Springer, Heidelberg (2004)

15. Harrison, J.: HOL light: An overview. In: Berghofer, S., Nipkow, T., Urban, C., Wenzel, M. (eds.) TPHOLs 2009. LNCS, vol. 5674, pp. 60–66. Springer, Heidelberg (2009)

16. Martin-Löf, P.: Haupstatz for the intuitionistic theory of iterated inductive definitions. In: Proc. Second Scandinavian Logic Symposium, pp. 179–216 (1971)

17. Nguyen, H.H., Chin, W.-N.: Enhancing program verification with lemmas. In: Gupta, A., Malik, S. (eds.) CAV 2008. LNCS, vol. 5123, pp. 355–369. Springer, Heidelberg (2008)

18. Nguyen, H.H., David, C., Qin, S.C., Chin, W.-N.: Automated verification of shape and size properties via separation logic. In: Cook, B., Podelski, A. (eds.) VMCAI 2007. LNCS, vol. 4349, pp. 251–266. Springer, Heidelberg (2007)

19. Reynolds, J.C.: Separation logic: A logic for shared mutable data structures. In: Proceedings of 17th LICS (2002)

20. Tuerk, T.: A formalisation of smallfoot in HOL. In: Berghofer, S., Nipkow, T., Urban, C., Wenzel, M. (eds.) TPHOLs 2009. LNCS, vol. 5674, pp. 469–484. Springer, Heidelberg (2009)

21. Voicu, R., Li, M.: Descente infinie proofs in Coq. In: Proceedings of the 1st Coq Workshop, Technische Universität München (2009)

22. Wirth, C.-P.: Descente Infinie + Deduction. Logic Journal of the IGPL 12(1), 1–96 (2004)

23. Yang, H., Lee, O., Berdine, J., Calcagno, C., Cook, B., Distefano, D., O'Hearn, P.W.: Scalable shape analysis for systems code. In: Gupta, A., Malik, S. (eds.) CAV 2008. LNCS, vol. 5123, pp. 385–398. Springer, Heidelberg (2008)

Reducing Higher-Order Theorem Proving to a Sequence of SAT Problems

Chad E. Brown

Saarland University, Saarbrücken, Germany

Abstract. We describe a complete theorem proving procedure for higher-order logic that uses SAT-solving to do much of the heavy lifting. The theoretical basis for the procedure is a complete, cut-free, ground refutation calculus that incorporates a restriction on instantiations. The refined nature of the calculus makes it conceivable that one can search in the ground calculus itself, obtaining a complete procedure without resorting to meta-variables and a higher-order lifting lemma. Once one commits to searching in a ground calculus, a natural next step is to consider ground formulas as propositional literals and the rules of the calculus as propositional clauses relating the literals. With this view in mind, we describe a theorem proving procedure that primarily generates relevant formulas along with their corresponding propositional clauses. The procedure terminates when the set of propositional clauses is unsatisfiable. We prove soundness and completeness of the procedure. The procedure has been implemented in a new higher-order theorem prover, Satallax, which makes use of the SAT-solver MiniSat. We also describe the implementation and give some experimental results.

Keywords: higher-order logic, simple type theory, higher-order theorem proving, abstract consistency, SAT solving.

1 Introduction

There are a number of distinct aspects of automated theorem proving. First, there is the usual combinatorial explosion already associated with search in the propositional case. Second, there is the problem of finding the correct instantiations for quantifiers. The instantiation problem appears in the first-order case. A third issue that appears in the higher-order case is how one builds in certain basic mathematical properties (e.g., extensionality and choice).

In this paper we give a complete theorem proving procedure for higher-order logic with extensionality and choice. The procedure separates the first issue from the second and third. We start from a complete ground calculus which already builds in extensionality and choice as well as certain restrictions on instantiations. Given a set of formulas to refute, the ground calculus can be used to suggest a sequence of relevant formulas which may be involved in a refutation. The procedure generates propositional clauses corresponding to the the meaning of these relevant formulas. When the set of propositional clauses is unsatisfiable

N. Bjørner and V. Sofronie-Stokkermans (Eds.): CADE 2011, LNAI 6803, pp. 147–161, 2011.

(in the propositional sense), then the original set of higher-order formulas is unsatisfiable (in the higher-order Henkin model sense). Conversely, when the original set of higher-order formulas is unsatisfiable, then an unsatisfiable set of propositional clauses will eventually be generated.

Such a procedure has been implemented in the new higher-order theorem prover Satallax[1]. The first implementation of Satallax was in Steel Bank Common Lisp. This earlier version, Satallax 1.4, competed in the higher-order division of CASC in 2010 [10]. Satallax 1.4 was able to prove 120 out of 200 problems, coming in second to LEO-II [4] which proved 125 out of 200 problems. The latest version of Satallax, Satallax 2.0, is implemented in Objective Caml. The SAT-solver MiniSat [6] (coded in C++) is used to determine propositional unsatisfiability.

2   Preliminaries

We begin with a brief presentation of Church's simple type theory with a choice operator. For more details see a similar presentation in [3]. Simple types (σ, τ) are given inductively: $o|\iota|\sigma\sigma$. Types $\sigma\tau$ correspond to functions from σ to τ. Terms s, t are generated inductively $x|c|st|\lambda x.s$ where x ranges over variables and c ranges over the logical constants $\bot, \rightarrow, \forall_\sigma, =_\sigma, *$ and ε_σ. A name is either a variable or a logical constant. A decomposable name is either a variable or ε_σ for some σ. We use δ to range over decomposable names.

Each variable has a corresponding type σ, and for each type there is a countably infinite set of variables of this type. Likewise each logical constant has a corresponding type: $\bot : o$, $\rightarrow: ooo$, $\forall_\sigma : (\sigma o)o$, $=_\sigma: \sigma\sigma o$, $* : \iota$ and $\varepsilon_\sigma : (\sigma o)\sigma$. The constant ε_σ is a choice operator at type σ. The constant $*$ plays the role of a "default" element of the nonempty type ι. Types can be assigned to (some) terms in the usual way. From now on we restrict ourselves to typed terms and let Λ_σ be the set of terms of type σ. A *formula* is a term $s \in \Lambda_o$.

We adopt common notational conventions: stu means $(st)u$, $s =_\sigma t$ (or $s = t$) means $=_\sigma st$, $s \rightarrow t$ means $\rightarrow st$, $\neg s$ means $s \rightarrow \bot$, $\top$ means $\neg\bot$, $s \neq_\sigma t$ (or $s \neq t$) means $\neg(s =_\sigma t)$, $\forall x.s$ means $\forall_\sigma \lambda x.s$ and $\varepsilon x.s$ means $\varepsilon_\sigma \lambda x.s$. Binders have as large a scope as is consistent with given parenthesis. For example, in $\forall x.px \rightarrow qx$ the occurrence of x in qx is bound by the $\forall$. The set $\mathcal{V}t$ of *free variables of t* is defined as usual.

An *accessibility context* $(\mathcal{C})$ is a term with a hole $[]_\sigma$ of the form $[]s_1 \cdots s_n$, $\neg([]s_1 \cdots s_n)$, $([]s_1 \cdots s_n) \neq_\iota s$ or $s \neq_\iota ([]s_1 \cdots s_n)$. We write $\mathcal{C}[s]$ for the term one obtains by putting s into the hole. A term s is *accessible* in a set A of formulas iff there is an accessibility context $\mathcal{C}$ such that $\mathcal{C}[s] \in A$.

Let $[s]$ denote a $\beta\eta$-normal form of s that makes a canonical choice of bound variables. That is, for any $s, t \in \Lambda_\sigma$, $[s] = [t]$ iff s and t are $\alpha\beta\eta$-equivalent. (In the implementation, de Bruijn indices are used.) A term s is *normal* if $[s] = s$.

A *substitution* is a type preserving partial function from variables to terms. If θ is a substitution, x is a variable, and s is a term that has the same type

---
[1] Satallax is available at `satallax.com`

as x, we write θ_s^x for the substitution that agrees everywhere with θ except $\theta_s^x x = s$. For each substitution θ let $\hat{\theta}$ be the usual extension of θ to all terms in a capture-avoiding manner.

A *frame* $\mathcal{D}$ is a typed collection of nonempty sets such that $\mathcal{D}_o = \{0, 1\}$ and $\mathcal{D}_{\sigma\tau}$ is a set of total functions from $\mathcal{D}_\sigma$ to $\mathcal{D}_\tau$. An *assignment* $\mathcal{I}$ into $\mathcal{D}$ is a mapping from variables and logical constants of type σ into $\mathcal{D}_\sigma$. An assignment $\mathcal{I}$ is *logical* if it interprets each logical constant to be an element satisfying the corresponding logical property. For example, if $\mathcal{I}$ is logical, then $\mathcal{I}\bot = 0$. An assignment $\mathcal{I}$ is an *interpretation* if it can be extended in the usual way to be a total function $\hat{\mathcal{I}}$ mapping each Λ_σ into $\mathcal{D}_\sigma$. A *Henkin model* $(\mathcal{D}, \mathcal{I})$ is a frame $\mathcal{D}$ and a logical interpretation $\mathcal{I}$ into $\mathcal{D}$. We say formula s is *satisfied* by a Henkin model $(\mathcal{D}, \mathcal{I})$ if $\hat{\mathcal{I}}s = 1$. A set A of formulas is satisfied by a Henkin model if each formula in A is satisfied by the model.

Let A be a set of formulas. A term s is discriminating in A iff there is a term t such that $s \not=_\iota t \in A$ or $t \not=_\iota s \in A$. For each set A of formulas and each type σ we define a nonempty universe $\mathcal{U}_\sigma^A \subseteq \Lambda_\sigma$ as follows.

- Let $\mathcal{U}_o^A = \{\bot, \neg\bot\}$.
- Let $\mathcal{U}_\iota^A$ be the set of discriminating terms in A if there is some discriminating term in A.
- Let $\mathcal{U}_\iota^A = \{*\}$ if there are no discriminating terms in A.
- Let $\mathcal{U}_{\sigma\tau}^A = \{[s] | s \in \Lambda_{\sigma\tau}, \mathcal{V}s \subseteq \mathcal{V}A\}$.

When the set A is clear in context, we write $\mathcal{U}_\sigma$.

We call a finite set of normal formulas a *branch*. A cut-free tableau calculus for higher-order logic with extensionality is given in [5]. The calculus is complete with respect to Henkin models without choice. The details of the completeness proof indicated that one can restrict instantiations for quantifiers on base types to terms occurring on one side of a disequation. This restriction is shown complete for the first-order case in [5]. The calculus is extended to include choice in [3] and the restriction on instantiations is proven complete in the higher-order case. The proof of completeness makes use of abstract consistency. A set Γ of branches is an *abstract consistency class* if it satisfies all the conditions in Figure 1. This definition differs slightly from the one in [3] because we are using $\rightarrow$ instead of $\neg$ and $\vee$. With obvious modifications to account for this difference, Theorem 2 in [3] implies that every $A \in \Gamma$ (where Γ is an abstract consistency class) is satisfiable by a Henkin model. We state this here as the *Model Existence Theorem*.

Theorem 1 (Model Existence Theorem). *Let Γ be an abstract consistency class. Each $A \in \Gamma$ is satisfiable by a Henkin model.*

3   Mapping into SAT

We next describe a simple mapping from higher-order formulas into propositional literals and clauses. The essential idea is to abstract away the semantics of all logical connectives except negation.

$\mathcal{C}_{\perp}$　$\perp$ is not in A.

$\mathcal{C}_{\neg}$　If $\neg s$ is in A, then s is not in A.

$\mathcal{C}_{\neq}$　$s \neq_\iota s$ is not in A.

$\mathcal{C}_{\rightarrow}$　If $s \rightarrow t$ is in A, then $A \cup \{\neg s\}$ or $A \cup \{t\}$ is in Γ.

$\mathcal{C}_{\neg\rightarrow}$　If $\neg(s \rightarrow t)$ is in A, then $A \cup \{s, \neg t\}$ is in Γ.

$\mathcal{C}_{\forall}$　If $\forall_\sigma s$ is in A, then $A \cup \{[st]\}$ is in Γ for every $t \in \mathcal{U}_\sigma^A$.

$\mathcal{C}_{\neg\forall}$　If $\neg\forall_\sigma s$ is in A, then $A \cup \{\neg[sx]\}$ is in Γ for some variable x.

$\mathcal{C}_{\mathrm{MAT}}$　If $\delta s_1 \ldots s_n$ is in A and $\neg\delta t_1 \ldots t_n$ is in A,
　　　then $n \geq 1$ and $A \cup \{s_i \neq t_i\}$ is in Γ for some $i \in \{1, \ldots, n\}$.

$\mathcal{C}_{\mathrm{DEC}}$　If $\delta s_1 \ldots s_n \neq_\iota \delta t_1 \ldots t_n$ is in A,
　　　then $n \geq 1$ and $A \cup \{s_i \neq t_i\}$ is in Γ for some $i \in \{1, \ldots, n\}$.

$\mathcal{C}_{\mathrm{CON}}$　If $s =_\iota t$ and $u \neq_\iota v$ are in A,
　　　then either $A \cup \{s \neq u, t \neq u\}$ or $A \cup \{s \neq v, t \neq v\}$ is in Γ.

$\mathcal{C}_{\mathrm{BQ}}$　If $s =_o t$ is in A, then either $A \cup \{s, t\}$ or $A \cup \{\neg s, \neg t\}$ is in Γ.

$\mathcal{C}_{\mathrm{BE}}$　If $s \neq_o t$ is in A, then either $A \cup \{s, \neg t\}$ or $A \cup \{\neg s, t\}$ is in Γ.

$\mathcal{C}_{\mathrm{FQ}}$　If $s =_{\sigma\tau} t$ is in A, then $A \cup \{[\forall x.sx =_\tau tx]\}$ is in Γ
　　　for some $x \in \mathcal{V}_\sigma \setminus (\mathcal{V}s \cup \mathcal{V}t)$.

$\mathcal{C}_{\mathrm{FE}}$　If $s \neq_{\sigma\tau} t$ is in A, then $A \cup \{\neg[\forall x.sx =_\tau tx]\}$ is in Γ
　　　for some $x \in \mathcal{V}_\sigma \setminus (\mathcal{V}s \cup \mathcal{V}t)$.

$\mathcal{C}_\varepsilon$　If $\varepsilon_\sigma s$ is accessible in A, then either $A \cup \{[s(\varepsilon s)]\}$ is in Γ or
　　　there is some $x \in \mathcal{V}_\sigma \setminus \mathcal{V}s$ such that $A \cup \{[\forall x.\neg(sx)]\}$ is in Γ.

Fig. 1. Abstract consistency conditions (must hold for every $A \in \Gamma$)

Let Atom be a countably infinite set of propositional *atoms*. For each atom a, let $\bar{a}$ denote a distinct negated atom. A *literal* is an atom or a negated atom. Let Lit be the set of all literals. Let $\bar{\bar{a}}$ denote a. A *clause* is a finite set of literals, which we write as $l_1 \sqcup \cdots \sqcup l_n$. A *propositional assignment* is a mapping Φ from Atom to $\{0, 1\}$. We extend any such Φ to literals by taking $\Phi(\bar{a}) = 1 - \Phi(a)$. We say an assignment Φ *satisfies a clause* $\mathcal{C}$ if there is some literal $l \in \mathcal{C}$ such that $\Phi l = 1$. An assignment Φ *satisfies a set* $\mathcal{S}$ of clauses if Φ satisfies $\mathcal{C}$ for all $\mathcal{C} \in \mathcal{S}$.

Let $\lfloor . \rfloor$ be a function mapping Λ_o into Lit such that $\lfloor \neg s \rfloor = \overline{\lfloor s \rfloor}$, $\lfloor s \rfloor = \lfloor \lfloor s \rfloor \rfloor$, and if $\lfloor s \rfloor = \lfloor t \rfloor$, then $\mathcal{I}s = \mathcal{I}t$ in every Henkin model $(\mathcal{D}, \mathcal{I})$.

Remark 1. In the implementation, $\lfloor s \rfloor = \lfloor t \rfloor$ whenever s and t are the same up to $\beta\eta$ and the removal of double negations. Under some flag settings, symmetric equations $u = v$ and $v = u$ are assigned the same literal.

We say Φ is a *pseudo-model* of A if $\Phi\lfloor s \rfloor = 1$ for all $s \in A$. We say an assignment Φ is *Henkin consistent* if there is a Henkin model $(\mathcal{D}, \mathcal{I})$ such that $\Phi\lfloor s \rfloor = \hat{\mathcal{I}}s$ for all $s \in \Lambda_o$.

4　States and Successors

Definition 1. *A quasi-state Σ is a 5-tuple $(\mathfrak{F}_p^\Sigma, \mathfrak{F}_a^\Sigma, \mathfrak{U}_p^\Sigma, \mathfrak{U}_a^\Sigma, \mathfrak{C}^\Sigma)$ where $\mathfrak{F}_p^\Sigma$ and $\mathfrak{F}_a^\Sigma$ are finite sets of normal formulas, $\mathfrak{U}_p^\Sigma$ and $\mathfrak{U}_a^\Sigma$ are finite sets of normal* *terms, and* $\mathfrak{C}^\Sigma$ *is a finite set of clauses. We call formulas in* $\mathfrak{F}_p^\Sigma$ *passive formulas, formulas in* $\mathfrak{F}_a^\Sigma$ *active formulas, terms in* $\mathfrak{U}_p^\Sigma$ *passive instantiations and terms in* $\mathfrak{U}_a^\Sigma$ *active instantiations.*

Given a quasi-state Σ, we define the following notation:

$$\mathfrak{F}^\Sigma := \mathfrak{F}_p^\Sigma \cup \mathfrak{F}_a^\Sigma \qquad \mathfrak{U}^\Sigma := \mathfrak{U}_p^\Sigma \cup \mathfrak{U}_a^\Sigma \qquad \mathfrak{U}_{p,\sigma}^\Sigma := \mathfrak{U}_p^\Sigma \cap \Lambda_\sigma \qquad \mathfrak{U}_{a,\sigma}^\Sigma := \mathfrak{U}_a^\Sigma \cap \Lambda_\sigma$$

During the procedure, we will only consider quasi-states that satisfy certain invariants. Such a quasi-state will be called a *state*. Before giving the technical definition of a state, we consider two simple examples. In these examples we will refer to the quasi-states as *states*, as they will always satisfy the relevant properties.

Each step of the search process will pass from one state to a successor state. The passive formulas and passive instantiations of a successor state will always include all the passive formulas and passive instantiations of the previous state. Likewise, all the clauses of the previous state will be clauses of the successor state. Often we obtain a successor state by moving an active formula (instantiation) to the set of passive formulas (instantiations). We will refer to this as *processing* the formula (instantiation).

Example 1. Let $p, q : o$ be variables. Suppose we wish to refute the branch with two formulas: p and $\forall q.p \to q$. We begin with a state Σ_0 with $\mathfrak{F}_p^{\Sigma_0} = \emptyset$, $\mathfrak{F}_a^{\Sigma_0} = \{p, \forall q.p \to q\}$, $\mathfrak{U}_p^{\Sigma_0} = \{\bot, \top\}$, $\mathfrak{U}_a^{\Sigma_0} = \emptyset$ and $\mathfrak{C}^{\Sigma_0}$ contains exactly the two unit clauses $\lfloor p \rfloor$ and $\lfloor \forall q.p \to q \rfloor$. We will refute this branch in one step. In particular, we process the formula $\forall q.p \to q$ by moving it from being active to passive and by applying all the instantiations of type o in $\mathfrak{U}_p^{\Sigma_0}$. This results in a state Σ_1 in which $\mathfrak{F}_p^{\Sigma_1} = \{\forall q.p \to q\}$, $\mathfrak{F}_a^{\Sigma_1} = \{p, p \to \bot, p \to \top\}$, $\mathfrak{U}_p^{\Sigma_1} = \mathfrak{U}_p^{\Sigma_0}$, $\mathfrak{U}_a^{\Sigma_1} = \mathfrak{U}_a^{\Sigma_0}$ and $\mathfrak{C}^{\Sigma_1}$ contains the two unit clauses from $\mathfrak{C}^{\Sigma_0}$ as well as the two clauses $\lceil \forall q.p \to q \rceil \sqcup \lfloor p \to \bot \rfloor$ and $\lceil \forall q.p \to q \rceil \sqcup \lfloor p \to \top \rfloor$. Note that $\lfloor p \to \bot \rfloor$ is the same as $\lceil p \rceil$. Clearly there is no propositional assignment satisfying the clauses in $\mathfrak{C}^{\Sigma_1}$. This completes the refutation. The two states can be displayed as in Figure 2.

	$\mathfrak{F}_p$	$\mathfrak{F}_a$	$\mathfrak{U}_p$	$\mathfrak{U}_a$	$\mathfrak{C}$
Σ_0		$p, \forall q.p \to q$	$\bot, \top$		$\lfloor p \rfloor$ $\lfloor \forall q.p \to q \rfloor$
Σ_1	$\forall q.p \to q$	$\cancel{\forall q.p \to q}$ $p \to \bot, p \to \top$			$\lceil \forall q.p \to q \rceil \sqcup \lceil p \rceil$ $\lceil \forall q.p \to q \rceil \sqcup \lfloor p \to \top \rfloor$

Fig. 2. States from Example 1

Example 2. Let $p : \iota o$ and $x : \iota$ be variables. Suppose we wish to prove the following basic property of the choice operator ε_ι: $\forall x.px \to p(\varepsilon_\iota p)$. The refutation will proceed in seven steps taking us from an initial state Σ_0 (corresponding to assuming the negation) to a state Σ_7 such that $\mathfrak{C}^{\Sigma_7}$ is propositionally unsatisfiable. The states Σ_i for $i \in \{0, \ldots, 7\}$ are indicated in Figure 3. In the first step we process $\neg\forall x.px \to p(\varepsilon p)$ by choosing a fresh variable $y : \iota$ and including the new formula $\neg(py \to p(\varepsilon p))$ and a clause relating the literals corresponding to the two formulas. The resulting state is Σ_1. We obtain Σ_2 by processing $\neg(py \to p(\varepsilon p))$ and obtaining two new formulas py and $\neg p(\varepsilon p)$ and two new clauses. We obtain Σ_3 by processing py. In general, processing such a formula involves mating it with all passive formulas of the form $\neg pt$. Since there are no such *passive* formulas (in particular, $\neg p(\varepsilon p)$ is active), Σ_3 only differs from Σ_2 in that py has been made passive. We obtain Σ_4 by processing $\neg p(\varepsilon p)$. This involves mating it with the passive formula py to obtain the formula $y \neq \varepsilon p$ and adding a new clause. (The reader should note that the new clause in Σ_4 will not be used to show the final set of clauses is propositionally unsatisfiable.) To obtain Σ_5 we process $y \neq \varepsilon p$. Since y and εp are discriminating terms in the set of passive formulas of Σ_5, we add them to the set of active instantiations. Also, since εp is accessible in $\mathfrak{F}_p^{\Sigma_5}$, we include the formulas $\forall x.\neg px$ and $p(\varepsilon p)$ as well as a clause corresponding to the meaning of the choice operator ε. We obtain Σ_6 by processing $\forall x.\neg px$. In principle, this means instantiating with all passive instantiations of type ι, but we have no *passive* instantiations of this type. Finally, we obtain Σ_7 by processing the instantiation y. Since y has type ι, we will use it as an instantiation for the passive formula $\forall x.\neg px$. As a consequence, we add the formula $\neg py$ and a corresponding clause. At this point, the clauses are propositionally unsatisfiable and we are done.

	$\mathfrak{F}_p$	$\mathfrak{F}_a$	$\mathfrak{U}_p$	$\mathfrak{U}_a$	$\mathfrak{C}$
Σ_0		$\neg\forall x.px \to p(\varepsilon p)$			$\overline{\lfloor\forall x.px \to p(\varepsilon p)\rfloor}$
Σ_1	$\neg\forall x.px \to p(\varepsilon p)$	$\neg\forall x.px \to p(\varepsilon p)$ $\neg(py \to p(\varepsilon p))$			$\lfloor\forall x.px \to p(\varepsilon p)\rfloor \sqcup \overline{\lfloor py \to p(\varepsilon p)\rfloor}$
Σ_2	$\neg(py \to p(\varepsilon p))$	$\neg(py \to p(\varepsilon p))$ $py, \neg p(\varepsilon p)$			$\lfloor py \to p(\varepsilon p)\rfloor \sqcup \lfloor py\rfloor$ $\lfloor py \to p(\varepsilon p)\rfloor \sqcup \overline{\lfloor p(\varepsilon p)\rfloor}$
Σ_3	py	py			
Σ_4	$\neg(p(\varepsilon p))$	$\neg p(\varepsilon p)$ $y \neq \varepsilon p$			$\overline{\lfloor py\rfloor} \sqcup \lfloor p(\varepsilon p)\rfloor \sqcup \lfloor y = \varepsilon p\rfloor$
Σ_5	$y \neq \varepsilon p$	$y \neq \varepsilon p$ $\forall x.\neg px, p(\varepsilon p)$	$y, \varepsilon p$		$\lfloor p(\varepsilon p)\rfloor \sqcup \lfloor\forall x.\neg px\rfloor$
Σ_6	$\forall x.\neg px$	$\forall x.\neg px, p(\varepsilon p)$			
Σ_7		$\neg py$	y	y	$\overline{\lfloor\forall x.\neg px\rfloor} \sqcup \lfloor py\rfloor$

Fig. 3. States from Example 2

Definition 2. *A quasi-state* $\Sigma = (\mathfrak{F}_p^{\Sigma}, \mathfrak{F}_a^{\Sigma}, \mathfrak{U}_p^{\Sigma}, \mathfrak{U}_a^{\Sigma}, \mathfrak{C}^{\Sigma})$ *is a state if the conditions in Figure 4 hold and for every clause C in $\mathfrak{C}^{\Sigma}$ and every literal $l \in C$, either $l = \lfloor s\rfloor$ for some $s \in \mathfrak{F}^{\Sigma}$ or $l = \overline{\lfloor s\rfloor}$ for some $s \in \mathfrak{F}_p^{\Sigma}$.*

$S_\bot$ If $\bot$ is in $\mathfrak{F}_p$, then $\overline{\lfloor\bot\rfloor}$ is in $\mathfrak{C}$.

$S_{\neq}$ If $s\neq_\iota s$ is in $\mathfrak{F}_p$, then $\lfloor s=s\rfloor$ is in $\mathfrak{C}$.

$S_{\to}$ If $s\to t$ is in $\mathfrak{F}_p$ and t is not $\bot$, then $\{\neg s,t\}\subseteq\mathfrak{F}$ and $\overline{\lfloor s\to t\rfloor}\sqcup\lfloor\neg s\rfloor\sqcup\lfloor t\rfloor$ is in $\mathfrak{C}$.

$S_{\neg\to}$ If $\neg(s\to t)$ is in $\mathfrak{F}_p$, then $\{s,\neg t\}\subseteq\mathfrak{F}$, $\lfloor s\to t\rfloor\sqcup\lfloor s\rfloor$ and $\lfloor s\to t\rfloor\sqcup\lfloor\neg t\rfloor$ are in $\mathfrak{C}$.

$S_{\forall}$ If $\forall_\sigma s$ is in $\mathfrak{F}_p$ and $t\in\mathfrak{U}_{p,\sigma}$, then $[st]\in\mathfrak{F}$ and $\overline{\lfloor\forall_\sigma s\rfloor}\sqcup\lfloor st\rfloor$ is in $\mathfrak{C}$.

$S_{\neg\forall}$ If $\neg\forall_\sigma s$ is in $\mathfrak{F}_p$, then there is some variable x of type σ such that $\neg[sx]\in\mathfrak{F}$ and $\lfloor\forall_\sigma s\rfloor\sqcup\overline{\lfloor sx\rfloor}$ is in $\mathfrak{C}$.

S_{MAT} If $\delta s_1\ldots s_n$ and $\neg\delta t_1\ldots t_n$ are in $\mathfrak{F}_p$ where $n\geq 1$, then $s_i\neq t_i$ is in $\mathfrak{F}$ for each $i\in\{1,\ldots,n\}$ and $\overline{\lfloor\delta s_1\ldots s_n\rfloor}\sqcup\lfloor\delta t_1\ldots t_n\rfloor\sqcup\lfloor s_1\neq t_1\rfloor\sqcup\cdots\sqcup\lfloor s_n\neq t_n\rfloor$ is in $\mathfrak{C}$.

S_{DEC} If $\delta s_1\ldots s_n\neq_\iota\delta t_1\ldots t_n$ is in $\mathfrak{F}_p$ where $n\geq 1$, then $s_i\neq t_i$ is in $\mathfrak{F}$ for each $i\in\{1,\ldots,n\}$ and $\lfloor\delta s_1\ldots s_n=\delta t_1\ldots t_n\rfloor\sqcup\lfloor s_1\neq t_1\rfloor\sqcup\cdots\sqcup\lfloor s_n\neq t_n\rfloor$ is in $\mathfrak{C}$.

S_{CON} If $s=_\iota t$ and $u\neq_\iota v$ are in $\mathfrak{F}_p$, then $\{s\neq u,t\neq u,s\neq v,t\neq v\}\subseteq\mathfrak{F}$ and the following four clauses are in $\mathfrak{C}$:

$$\lfloor s=t\rfloor\sqcup\lfloor u=v\rfloor\sqcup\lfloor s\neq u\rfloor\sqcup\lfloor s\neq v\rfloor,\qquad \lfloor s=t\rfloor\sqcup\lfloor u=v\rfloor\sqcup\lfloor s\neq u\rfloor\sqcup\lfloor t\neq v\rfloor$$
$$\lfloor s=t\rfloor\sqcup\lfloor u=v\rfloor\sqcup\lfloor t\neq u\rfloor\sqcup\lfloor s\neq v\rfloor,\qquad \lfloor s=t\rfloor\sqcup\lfloor u=v\rfloor\sqcup\lfloor t\neq u\rfloor\sqcup\lfloor t\neq v\rfloor$$

S_{BQ} If $s=_o t$ is in $\mathfrak{F}_p$, then $\{s,t,\neg s,\neg t\}\subseteq\mathfrak{F}$ and $\overline{\lfloor s=t\rfloor}\sqcup\lfloor s\rfloor\sqcup\lfloor\neg t\rfloor$ and $\overline{\lfloor s=t\rfloor}\sqcup\lfloor\neg s\rfloor\sqcup\lfloor t\rfloor$ are in $\mathfrak{C}$.

S_{BE} If $s\neq_o t$ is in $\mathfrak{F}_p$, then $\{s,t,\neg s,\neg t\}\subseteq\mathfrak{F}$ and $\lfloor s=t\rfloor\sqcup\lfloor s\rfloor\sqcup\lfloor t\rfloor$ and $\lfloor s=t\rfloor\sqcup\lfloor\neg s\rfloor\sqcup\lfloor\neg t\rfloor$ are in $\mathfrak{C}$.

S_{FQ} If $s=_{\sigma\tau}t$ is in $\mathfrak{F}_p$, then there is some $x\in\mathcal{V}_\sigma\setminus(\mathcal{V}s\cup\mathcal{V}t)$ such that $[\forall x.sx=_\tau tx]$ is in $\mathfrak{F}$ and $\overline{\lfloor s=t\rfloor}\sqcup\lfloor\forall x.sx=tx\rfloor$ is in $\mathfrak{C}$.

S_{FE} If $s\neq_{\sigma\tau}t$ is in $\mathfrak{F}_p$, then there is some $x\in\mathcal{V}_\sigma\setminus(\mathcal{V}s\cup\mathcal{V}t)$ such that $[\neg\forall x.sx=_\tau tx]$ is in $\mathfrak{F}$ and $\lfloor s=t\rfloor\sqcup\lfloor\neg\forall x.sx=tx\rfloor$ is in $\mathfrak{C}$.

S_ε If $\varepsilon_\sigma s$ is accessible in $\mathfrak{F}_p$, then there is some $x\in\mathcal{V}_\sigma\setminus\mathcal{V}s$ such that $[s(\varepsilon s)]$ and $[\forall x.\neg(sx)]$ are in $\mathfrak{F}$ and $\lfloor s(\varepsilon s)\rfloor\sqcup\lfloor\forall x.\neg(sx)\rfloor$ is in $\mathfrak{C}$.

Fig. 4. Conditions on a quasi-state $\Sigma=(\mathfrak{F}_p,\mathfrak{F}_a,\mathfrak{U}_p,\mathfrak{U}_a,\mathfrak{C})$

We say a propositional assignment Φ satisfies a state Σ if Φ satisfies $\mathfrak{C}^\Sigma$. We say Σ is *propositionally satisfiable* if there is a Φ such that Φ satisfies Σ. Otherwise, we say Σ is *propositionally unsatisfiable*. Furthermore, we say Σ is *Henkin satisfiable* if there is a Henkin consistent propositional assignment satisfying $\mathfrak{C}^\Sigma$. Note that checking whether Σ is propositionally satisfiable is simply a SAT-problem.

A variable x is *fresh* for a state Σ if x is not free in any $s\in\mathfrak{F}^\Sigma\cup\mathfrak{U}^\Sigma$.

Given a branch A, an *initial state* Σ for A is a state with $A\subseteq\mathfrak{F}^\Sigma$, and $\mathfrak{C}^\Sigma=\{\lfloor s\rfloor\,|\,s\in A\}$. (We require $A\subseteq\mathfrak{F}^\Sigma$ rather than $A\subseteq\mathfrak{F}_a^\Sigma$ to allow for the possibility that some formulas in A are passive rather than active in an initial state. In practice, this could result from some preprocessing of formulas in A.) To see that for any branch A there is an initial state, consider Σ with $\mathfrak{F}_p^\Sigma=\emptyset$, $\mathfrak{F}_a^\Sigma=A$, $\mathfrak{U}_p^\Sigma=\emptyset$, $\mathfrak{U}_a^\Sigma=\emptyset$ and $\mathfrak{C}^\Sigma=\{\lfloor s\rfloor\,|\,s\in A\}$.

Definition 3. *We say a state Σ' is a* successor *of a state Σ (and write $\Sigma\to\Sigma'$) if $\mathfrak{F}_p^\Sigma\subseteq\mathfrak{F}_p^{\Sigma'}$, $\mathfrak{F}_a^\Sigma\subseteq\mathfrak{F}_a^{\Sigma'}$, $\mathfrak{U}_p^\Sigma\subseteq\mathfrak{U}_p^{\Sigma'}$, $\mathfrak{U}_a^\Sigma\subseteq\mathfrak{U}_a^{\Sigma'}$, $\mathfrak{C}^\Sigma\subseteq\mathfrak{C}^{\Sigma'}$, and if Σ is Henkin satisfiable, then Σ' is Henkin satisfiable.*

Note that the successor relation is reflexive and transitive. Also, soundness of the procedure is built into the definition of the successor relation.

Proposition 1 (Soundness). *Let A be a branch. If there is a propositionally unsatisfiable Σ' such that $\Sigma_A \to \Sigma'$, then A is unsatisfiable.*

Proof. Assume $(\mathcal{D}, \mathcal{I})$ is a Henkin model of A. Choose Φ such that $\Phi\lfloor s \rfloor = \hat{\mathcal{I}}s$ for each $s \in A$. Clearly, Φ demonstrates that Σ_A is Henkin satisfiable. On the other hand, since Σ' is propositionally unsatisfiable, it is Henkin unsatisfiable. This contradicts the definition of $\Sigma_A \to \Sigma'$.

A strategy which chooses a successor state for each propositionally satisfiable state will yield a sound procedure. One such strategy is to interleave two kinds of actions: (1) process active formulas and instantiations while making the minimal number of additions of formulas and clauses consistent with the invariants in Figure 4 and (2) generate new active instantiations. To ensure soundness, when processing a formula $\neg \forall_\sigma s$ a procedure should choose a fresh variable x, add $\neg \lfloor sx \rfloor$ to $\mathfrak{F}_a$ and add $\lfloor \forall_\sigma s \rfloor \sqcup \overline{\lfloor sx \rfloor}$ to $\mathfrak{C}$.

If a strategy does not lead to a propositionally unsatisfiable state, then it will give a finite or infinite path of states. If the strategy is fair, this path will satisfy certain fairness properties. In this case, we can use the path to prove the original branch is satisfiable. That is, we can conclude that every fair strategy is complete.

Definition 4. *Let $\alpha \in \omega \cup \{\omega\}$. An α-path (or, simply path) is an α-sequence $\overline{\Sigma} = (\Sigma_i)_{i < \alpha}$ of propositionally satisfiable states such that $\Sigma_i \to \Sigma_{i+1}$ for each i with $i + 1 < \alpha$. We say a type σ is a quantified type on the path if there exist $i < \alpha$ and s such that $\forall_\sigma s \in \mathfrak{F}^{\Sigma_i}$. Such a path is fair if the following conditions hold:*

1. *For all $i < \alpha$ and $s \in \mathfrak{F}_a^{\Sigma_i}$ there is some $j \in [i, \alpha)$ such that $s \in \mathfrak{F}_p^{\Sigma_j}$.*
2. *If σ is a quantified type, then for all $i < \alpha$, $A \subseteq \mathfrak{F}^{\Sigma_i}$ and $t \in \mathcal{U}_\sigma^A$ there is some $j \in [i, \alpha)$ such that $t \in \mathfrak{U}_p^{\Sigma_j}$.*

Given a branch A_0, we will start with an initial state Σ_0 for A_0. Our theorem proving procedure will construct a sequence of successor states in such a way that, unless some state is propositionally unsatisfiable, the sequence will be a fair path. In order to prove completeness of this procedure, it is enough to prove that if there is a fair path starting from Σ_0, then A_0 is satisfiable. This result will be Theorem 2 given at the end of this section.

For the remainder of this section we assume a fixed α and fair α-path $\overline{\Sigma}$.

Definition 5. *Let $i < \alpha$ be given. We say a branch A is i-supported if $A \subseteq \mathfrak{F}^{\Sigma_i}$ and there is a pseudo-model Φ of A satisfying Σ_i. We say a branch A is i-consistent if A is j-supported for all $j \in [i, \alpha)$.*

Lemma 1. *Let $i < \alpha$ and $j \in [i, \alpha)$ be given. If A is j-supported and $A \subseteq \mathfrak{F}^{\Sigma_i}$, then A is i-supported.*

Proof. This follows from $\mathfrak{C}^{\Sigma_i} \subseteq \mathfrak{C}^{\Sigma_j}$.

Let Γ be the set of all branches A such that A is i-consistent for some $i < \alpha$. We will prove Γ is an abstract consistency class.

Lemma 2. *Let A be an j-consistent branch. Let $A_1, \ldots, A_n$ be branches such that $A \subseteq A_l \subseteq \mathfrak{F}^{\Sigma_j}$ for each $l \in \{1, \ldots, n\}$. Either there is some $l \in \{1, \ldots, n\}$ such that A_l is j-consistent or there is some $k \in [j, \alpha)$ such that A_l is not k-supported for each $l \in \{1, \ldots, n\}$.*

Proof. Assume none of $A_1, \ldots, A_n$ is j-consistent. Let $k_1, \cdots, k_n \in [j, \alpha)$ be such that A_l is not k_l-supported for each $l \in \{1, \ldots, n\}$. Let k be the maximum of $k_1, \ldots, k_n$. By Lemma 1 each A_l is not k-supported.

Lemma 3. *Γ is an abstract consistency class.*

Proof. We verify a representative collection of cases.

$\mathcal{C}_\perp$ Suppose $\perp \in A$ and A is i-consistent. By fairness there is some $j \in [i, \alpha)$ such that $\perp \in \mathfrak{F}_p^{\Sigma_j}$. By $\mathcal{S}_\perp$ the unit clause $\lfloor \perp \rfloor$ is in $\mathfrak{C}^{\Sigma_j}$. This contradicts A being j-supported.

$\mathcal{C}_\neg$ Suppose $\neg s$ and s are in A. Since no propositional assignment Φ can have $\Phi \lfloor \neg s \rfloor = 1$ and $\Phi \lfloor s \rfloor = 1$, A cannot be i-consistent for any i.

$\mathcal{C}_\rightarrow$ Suppose $s \rightarrow t$ is in an i-consistent branch A. If t is $\perp$, then $A \cup \{\neg s\}$ is the same as A and so $A \cup \{\neg s\}$ is i-consistent. Assume t is not $\perp$. Since A is i-consistent, we know $A \subseteq \mathfrak{F}^{\Sigma_i}$ and so $s \rightarrow t \in \mathfrak{F}^{\Sigma_i}$. By fairness there is some $j \in [i, \alpha)$ such that $s \rightarrow t \in \mathfrak{F}_p^{\Sigma_j}$. By $\mathcal{S}_\rightarrow$ we know $\{\neg s, t\} \subseteq \mathfrak{F}^{\Sigma_j}$ and $\lfloor s \rightarrow t \rfloor \sqcup \lfloor s \rfloor \sqcup \lfloor t \rfloor$ is in $\mathfrak{C}^{\Sigma_j}$. Note that $A \cup \{\neg s\} \subseteq \mathfrak{F}^{\Sigma_k}$ and $A \cup \{t\} \subseteq \mathfrak{F}^{\Sigma_k}$ for every $k \in [j, \alpha)$. Assume neither $A \cup \{\neg s\}$ nor $A \cup \{t\}$ is j-consistent. By Lemma 2 there is some $k \in [j, \alpha)$ such that neither $A \cup \{\neg s\}$ nor $A \cup \{t\}$ is k-supported. Since A is i-consistent, A is k-supported and has some pseudo-model Φ satisfying Σ_k. Since $\lfloor s \rightarrow t \rfloor \sqcup \lfloor s \rfloor \sqcup \lfloor t \rfloor$ is in $\mathfrak{C}^{\Sigma_k}$ and $\Phi \lfloor s \rightarrow t \rfloor = 1$, we must have $\Phi \lfloor s \rfloor = 0$ or $\Phi \lfloor t \rfloor = 1$. Thus Φ witnesses that either $A \cup \{\neg s\}$ or $A \cup \{t\}$ is k-supported, contradicting our choice of k. Hence either $A \cup \{\neg s\}$ or $A \cup \{t\}$ must be j-consistent.

$\mathcal{C}_{\neg\rightarrow}$ Suppose $\neg(s \rightarrow t)$ is in an i-consistent branch A. Since A is i-consistent, we know $\neg(s \rightarrow t) \in \mathfrak{F}^{\Sigma_i}$. By fairness there is some $j \in [i, \alpha)$ such that $\neg(s \rightarrow t) \in \mathfrak{F}_p^{\Sigma_j}$. By $\mathcal{S}_{\neg\rightarrow}$ we know $\{s, \neg t\} \subseteq \mathfrak{F}^{\Sigma_j}$, and both $\lfloor s \rightarrow t \rfloor \sqcup \lfloor s \rfloor$ and $\lfloor s \rightarrow t \rfloor \sqcup \lfloor t \rfloor$ are in $\mathfrak{C}^{\Sigma_j}$. We prove $A \cup \{s, \neg t\}$ is j-consistent. Let $k \in [j, \alpha)$ be given. Since A is i-consistent, it has some pseudo-model Φ satisfying Σ_k. Since $\Phi \lfloor \neg(s \rightarrow t) \rfloor = 1$, we must have $\Phi \lfloor s \rfloor = 1$ and $\Phi \lfloor \neg t \rfloor = 1$. Hence Φ is a pseudo-model of $A \cup \{s, \neg t\}$ and so $A \cup \{s, \neg t\}$ is k-supported. Therefore, $A \cup \{s, \neg t\}$ is j-consistent.

$\mathcal{C}_\forall$ Let A be an i-consistent branch such that $\forall_\sigma s \in A$ and $t \in \mathcal{U}_\sigma^A$. Note that $\forall_\sigma s \in A \subseteq \mathfrak{F}^{\Sigma_i}$ witnesses that σ is a quantified type on the path. By fairness there is some $j \in [i, \alpha)$ such that $\forall s \in \mathfrak{F}_p^{\Sigma_j}$ and $t \in \mathfrak{U}_p^{\Sigma_j}$. By $\mathcal{S}_\forall$ $\lfloor st \rfloor \in \mathfrak{F}^{\Sigma_j}$ and $\lfloor \forall_\sigma s \rfloor \sqcup \lfloor st \rfloor$ is in $\mathfrak{C}^{\Sigma_j}$. We prove A is j-consistent. Let $k \in [j, \alpha)$ be given. Since A is i-consistent, it has some pseudo-model Φ satisfying Σ_k. Since $\Phi\lfloor\forall s\rfloor = 1$ and $\overline{\lfloor\forall_\sigma s\rfloor} \sqcup \lfloor st\rfloor$ is in $\mathfrak{C}^{\Sigma_j}$, we must have $\Phi\lfloor st\rfloor = 1$ and so $A \cup \{[st]\}$ is k-supported. (We know $\lfloor[st]\rfloor = \lfloor st\rfloor$ as a property of $\lfloor\cdot\rfloor$.)

$\mathcal{C}_{\neg\forall}$ Let A be an i-consistent branch such that $\neg\forall_\sigma s \in A$. By fairness there is some $j \in [i, \alpha)$ such that $\neg\forall s \in \mathfrak{F}_p^{\Sigma_j}$. By $\mathcal{S}_{\neg\forall}$ there is some variable x such that $\neg[sx] \in \mathfrak{F}^{\Sigma_j}$ and $\lfloor\forall_\sigma s\rfloor \sqcup \overline{\lfloor sx\rfloor}$ is in $\mathfrak{C}^{\Sigma_j}$. Let $k \in [j, \alpha)$ be given. Let Φ be a pseudo-model of A satisfying Σ_k. Since $\Phi\lfloor\neg\forall s\rfloor = 1$ we must have $\Phi\lfloor\neg(sx)\rfloor = 1$ and so $A \cup \{\neg[sx]\}$ is k-supported.

$\mathcal{C}_{\text{CON}}$ Suppose $s =_\iota t$ and $u \neq_\iota v$ are in an i-consistent branch A. By fairness there is some $j \in [i, \alpha)$ such that $s =_\iota t$ and $u \neq_\iota v$ are $\mathfrak{F}_p^{\Sigma_j}$. By $\mathcal{S}_{\text{CON}}$ $\{s \neq u, t \neq u, s \neq v, t \neq v\} \subseteq \mathfrak{F}^{\Sigma_j}$ and the following four clauses are in $\mathfrak{C}^{\Sigma_j}$:
$$\overline{\lfloor s = t\rfloor} \sqcup \lfloor u = v\rfloor \sqcup \lfloor s \neq u\rfloor \sqcup \lfloor s \neq v\rfloor, \quad \overline{\lfloor s = t\rfloor} \sqcup \lfloor u = v\rfloor \sqcup \lfloor s \neq u\rfloor \sqcup \lfloor t \neq v\rfloor$$
$$\overline{\lfloor s = t\rfloor} \sqcup \lfloor u = v\rfloor \sqcup \lfloor t \neq u\rfloor \sqcup \lfloor s \neq v\rfloor, \quad \overline{\lfloor s = t\rfloor} \sqcup \lfloor u = v\rfloor \sqcup \lfloor t \neq u\rfloor \sqcup \lfloor t \neq v\rfloor$$
Assume neither $A \cup \{s \neq u, t \neq u\}$ nor $A \cup \{s \neq v, t \neq v\}$ is j-consistent. By Lemma 2 there is some $k \in [j, \alpha)$ such that neither $A \cup \{s \neq u, t \neq u\}$ nor $A \cup \{s \neq v, t \neq v\}$ is k-supported. Let Φ be a pseudo-model of A satisfying Σ_k. Note that $\Phi\lfloor s = t\rfloor = 1$ and $\Phi\lfloor u = v\rfloor = 0$. By examining the four clauses above, it is clear that we must either have $\Phi\lfloor s \neq u\rfloor = 1$ and $\Phi\lfloor t \neq u\rfloor = 1$ or have $\Phi\lfloor s \neq v\rfloor = 1$ and $\Phi\lfloor t \neq v\rfloor = 1$, a contradiction.

Theorem 2 (Model Existence). *Let A_0 be a branch and $\overline{\Sigma}$ be a fair α-path such that Σ_0 is an initial state for Σ_{A_0}. Then A_0 is satisfiable.*

Proof. By Theorem 1 it is enough to prove A_0 is 0-consistent. Let $j \in [0, \alpha)$ be given. Clearly $A_0 \subseteq \mathfrak{F}^{\Sigma_0} \subseteq \mathfrak{F}^{\Sigma_j}$. Let Φ satisfy Σ_j. For each $s \in A_0$, the unit clause $\lfloor s\rfloor$ is in $\mathfrak{C}^{\Sigma_j}$ and so $\Phi\lfloor s\rfloor = 1$.

5   Implementation

A procedure along the lines described above has been implemented in a theorem prover named Satallax. There are some minor differences from the abstract description. One difference is that double negations are eliminated during normalization in the implementation (e.g., the normal form of $p(\lambda x.\neg\neg x)$ is $p(\lambda x.x)$). Another difference is that there is no default constant $*$ of type ι. If there are no discriminating terms of type ι, then either a variable or the term $\varepsilon_\iota x.\bot$ is used as an instantiation of type ι. Also, there may be base types other than ι.

The first version of Satallax was written in Steel Bank Common Lisp. In this earlier version, MiniSat was restarted and sent all the clauses generated so far whenever propositional satisfiability was to be tested. The latest version of Satallax is implemented in Objective Caml. A foreign function interface allows Satallax to call MiniSat functions (coded in C++) in order to add new clauses to the current set of clauses and to test for satisfiability of the current set of clauses. This is a much more efficient way of using MiniSat.

Problems are given to Satallax as a TPTP file in THF format [11]. Such a file may include axioms and optionally a conjecture. The conjecture, if given, is negated and treated as an axiom. Logical constants that occur in axioms are rewritten in favor of the basic logical constants $\perp$, $\rightarrow$, $=_\sigma$, $\forall_\sigma$ and ε_σ. Also, all definitions are expanded and the terms are $\beta\eta$-normalized. (De Bruijn indices are used to deal with α-convertibility.) If the normalized axiom s is of the particular form $\forall px.px \rightarrow p(ep)$ or $\forall p.(\neg\forall x.\neg px) \rightarrow p(ep)$ where e is a constant of type $(\sigma o)\sigma$ for some σ, then e is registered as a choice operator of type σ and the axiom s is omitted from the initial branch. Every other normalized axiom is an initial assumption. The choice rule can be applied with every name registered as a choice operator.

There are about a hundred flags that can be set in order to control the order in which the search space is explored. A collection of flag settings is called a *mode*. Currently, there are a few hundred modes in Satallax. A particular mode can be chosen via a command line option. Otherwise, a default schedule of modes is used and each of the modes on the schedule is given a certain amount of time to try to refute the problem.

If the flag SPLIT_GLOBAL_DISJUNCTIONS is set to TRUE, then Satallax will decompose the topmost logical connectives including the topmost disjunctions. This is likely to result in a set of subgoals which can be solved independently. This is an especially good idea if, for example, the conjecture is a conjunction. It is, of course, a bad idea if there are many disjunctive axioms.

Once the initial branch is determined, the state is initialized to include a unit clause for each member and the set of active formulas is initialized to be the initial branch. The terms $\perp$ and $\neg\perp$ are added as passive instantiations. Additionally, if the flag INITIAL_SUBTERMS_AS_INSTANTIATIONS is set to TRUE, then all subterms of the initial branch are added as passive instantiations. During the search, discriminating terms of type ι are added as active instantiations. If there is a quantifier at a function type $\sigma\tau$, a process of enumerating normal terms of type $\sigma\tau$ is started. Of course, this enumeration process is the least directed part of the search procedure.

At each stage of the search there are a number of options for continuing the search. An example of an option is processing a particular active formula. Another option might be to work on enumerating instantiations of a given type. The different search options are put into a priority queue as they are generated. (The priority queue is modified to ensure every option is eventually considered.) Many flags control the priority given to different options.

The successor relation on states was defined very generally. In particular, it does not rule out adding more formulas, instantiations and clauses than the ones suggested by the invariants on states. These additions may be very useful, but they are not necessary for completeness. A simple example is that, if the flag INSTANTIATE_WITH_FUNC_DISEQN_SIDES is set to TRUE, the terms s and t are added as active instantiations whenever an active formula $s \neq_{\sigma\tau} t$ is processed.

One of the most useful extensions implemented in Satallax is, under certain flag settings, to generate higher-order clauses with higher-order literals to be matched against formulas as the formulas are processed. This is the only time Satallax uses existential variables. Such higher-order clauses are only used when every existential variable in the clause has a strict occurrence in some literal. (A strict occurrence is essentially a pattern occurrence which is not below another existential variable [8].) We also allow for equational literals which can be used to perform some equational inference. Rather than give a full description of this extension, we give one example. Suppose we process a formula $\forall f \forall x \forall y. mf(cxy) = c(fx)(mfy)$ where $m : (\iota\iota)\iota\iota$, $c : \iota\iota\iota$, $f : \iota\iota$, and $x, y : \iota$. In addition to processing this in the usual way (applying all passive instantiations of type $\iota\iota$), we can create a higher-order unit clause $mF(cXY) = c(FX)(mFY)$ where F, X and Y are existential variables. The first and last occurrences of F are strict. The first occurrence of X is strict. Both occurrences of Y are strict. Now, when processing a new formula s, Satallax uses higher-order pattern matching to check if s is of the form $C[mt(cuv)]$ for some t, u and v. If so, a propositional clause

$$\overline{\lfloor \forall f \forall x \forall y. mf(cxy) = c(fx)(mfy) \rfloor} \sqcup \overline{\lfloor C[mt(cuv)] \rfloor} \sqcup \lfloor C[c(tu)(mtv)] \rfloor$$

is added to the set of clauses and the formula $[C[c(tu)(mtv)]]$ is added to the set of active formulas to be processed later.

6   Results and Examples

TPTP v5.1.0 contains 2798 problems in THF0 format. Among these, 343 are known to be satisfiable. (Satallax 2.0 terminates on many of these problems, recognizing them as satisfiable.) For 1790 of the remaining 2455 problems (73%), there is some mode that Satallax 2.0 can use to prove the theorem (or show the assumptions are unsatisfiable) within a minute. For one other problem there is a mode that proves the theorem in 96 seconds. A strategy schedule running 36 modes for just over 10 minutes can solve each of the 1791 problems.

One reason for the success of Satallax is that it can solve some problems by brute force. An example of this is the first-order theorem SEV106^5 from the TPTP. This is a Ramsey-style theorem about graphs and cliques. We assume there are at least six distinct individuals and that there is a symmetric relation (i.e., an undirected graph) on individuals. There must be three distinct individuals all of whom are related or all of whom are unrelated. Since we are assuming there are six distinct individuals, we quickly have six corresponding discriminating terms. Satallax uses all six of these (blindly) as instantiations for the existential quantifiers, leading to 6^3 instantiations. Using mode MODE1 Satallax generates over 8000 propositional clauses which MiniSat can easily recognize as unsatisfiable. In most examples only a handful of the clauses are the cause of unsatisfiability. In this example a 284 clauses are used to show unsatisfiability.

Two higher-order examples from the TPTP that Satallax can solve are SYO378^5 and SYO379^5. These examples were created in TPS to illustrate the concept of quantificational depth, discussed at the end of [1]. Let $c : \iota$ be a variable and define $d_0 := \lambda x : \iota.x = c$, $d_1 := \lambda y : \iota o.y = d_0 \wedge \exists x.yx$ and $d_2 := \lambda z : (\iota o)o.z = d_1 \wedge \exists y.zy$ (where $s \wedge t$ means $\neg(s \rightarrow \neg t)$ and $\exists x.s$ means $\neg \forall x.\neg s$). One of the examples is $\exists y.d_1 y$ and the other is $\exists z.d_2 z$. A high-level proof is simply to note that $d_0 c$, $d_1 d_0$ and $d_2 d_1$ are all provable. However, if we expand all definitions, then these instantiations are no longer so easy to see. Fortunately, if the flag INSTANTIATE_WITH_FUNC_DISEQN_SIDES is set to TRUE, then d_0 and d_1 will appear as the side of a disequation and Satallax will include them as instantiations early. Verifying the instantiations work is not difficult. There are modes that can solve these problems within a second.

We also discuss two particularly interesting examples that are not yet in the TPTP. In both examples we use variables $f, g : \iota\iota$ and $x, y : \iota$.

$$(\forall y. \exists x. fx = y) \rightarrow \exists g. \forall x. (f(gx)) = x \tag{1}$$

Formula (1) means every surjective function f has a right inverse g.

$$(\forall x \forall y. fx = fy \rightarrow x = y) \rightarrow \exists g. \forall x. (g(fx)) = x \tag{2}$$

Formula (2) means every injective function f has a left inverse g.

In both examples (1) and (2) Satallax must enumerate potential instantiations of type $\iota\iota$ for g. Some of the instantiations (e.g., $\lambda x.x$, f and $\lambda x.f(fx)$) are unhelpful and only serve to make the search space large. In both cases the instantiation used in the refutation is $\lambda y. \varepsilon x. fx = y$. An equivalent instantiation, $\lambda y. \varepsilon x. y = fx$, is also generated. (While it seems likely that such an equivalent instantiation could be discarded without sacrificing completeness, there is no currently known meta-theoretic result to justify this intuition.)

Satallax can prove (1) using mode MODE219 in under 6 seconds. In the process it generates 29 higher-order instantiations (candidates for g) and 17776 propositional clauses. It turns out that only 6 of these clauses are required to determine propositional unsatisfiability. Satallax can prove (2) using mode MODE218 in about a minute. In the process it generates 24 candidates for g and 117650 propositional clauses. Only 10 of the clauses are needed.

7   Related Work

Smullyan introduced the notion of abstract consistency in 1963 [9]. One of Smullyan's applications of abstract consistency is to justify reducing first-order unsatisfiability of a set M to propositional unsatisfiability of an extended set $R \cup M$. The procedure described in this paper and implemented in Satallax was developed without Smullyan's application in mind. Nevertheless, one can consider the procedure to be both an elaboration of Smullyan's idea as well as an extension to the higher-order case.

A different instantiation-based method Inst-Gen is described in [7]. Inst-Gen generates ground instances of first-order clauses and searches by interacting with a SAT-solver. This method is implemented in the first-order prover iProver [7]. Note that iProver is also coded in Objective Caml and uses MiniSat via a foreign function interface. Two differences between the Inst-Gen method and the method in this paper should be noted. First, Inst-Gen assumes the problem is in clausal normal form. We do not make this assumption. As is well known, a substitution into a higher-order clause may lead to the need for further clause normalization. Second, Inst-Gen assumes an appropriate ordering on closures (clauses with substitutions). This ordering leads to important restrictions on inferences that can significantly improve the performance of Inst-Gen. We do not make use of any such ordering. In fact, a straightforward attempt to find such an ordering for the higher-order case is doomed to failure. This can be briefly indicated by an example. Suppose we define a closure to be a pair $C \cdot \theta$ of an atomic formula C and a substitution θ. The basic condition of a closure ordering $\succ$ (see [7]) is that $C \cdot \sigma \succ D \cdot \tau$ whenever $C\sigma = D\tau$ and $C\theta = D$ for some "proper instantiator" θ. In the higher-order case, we would consider equality of normal forms instead of strict syntactic equality. Consider two atomic formulas $C := p(\lambda xy.fxy)$ and $D := p(\lambda yx.fxy)$ where p, f, x and y are variables of appropriate types. Consider the substitution $\theta p := \lambda fxy.p(\lambda yx.fxy)$. Clearly $C\theta$ is β-equivalent to D and $D\theta$ is β-equivalent to C. An appropriate ordering (assuming θ would be considered a "proper instantiator") would need to have $C \cdot \emptyset \succ D \cdot \emptyset \succ C \cdot \emptyset$ where $\emptyset$ plays the identity substitution.

Regarding higher-order theorem provers, two well-known examples are Tps [2] and LEO-II [4]. Automated search in Tps is based on expansion proofs while search in LEO-II is based on a resolution calculus. Both Tps and LEO-II make use of existential variables which are partially instantiated during search. LEO-II was the first higher-order prover to take a cooperative approach. LEO-II makes calls to a first-order theorem prover to determine if the current set of higher-order clauses maps to an unsatisfiable set of first-order clauses.

8   Conclusion

We have given an abstract description of a search procedure for higher-order theorem proving. The key idea is to start with a notion of abstract consistency which integrates a restriction on instantiations. We gave a notion of a state which consists of finite sets of formulas, instantiations and propositional clauses. The invariants in the definition of a state correspond to the abstract consistency conditions. We have given a successor relation on states. Any fair strategy for choosing successors (until the set of propositional clauses is unsatisfiable) will give a complete theorem prover.

We have also described the implementation of this procedure as a higher-order theorem prover Satallax. A version of Satallax last year proved to be competitive in the higher-order division of CASC in 2010 [10]. The latest implementation (a complete reimplementation in Objective Caml) is more closely integrated with the SAT-solver MiniSat [6]. The new implementation will compete in the higher-order division of CASC in 2011.

Satallax is still new and there is a lot of room for improvement and further research. One of the areas where much more research is needed involves generating *useful* higher-order instantiations.

Acknowledgements. Thanks to Andreas Teucke whose ongoing work on translating Satallax refutations to Coq proof terms has led to the consideration of some interesting examples, including the Ramsey-style theorem described in Section 6. Thanks also to Gert Smolka for his support and stimulating conversations.

References

1. Andrews, P.B., Bishop, M., Brown, C.E.: System description: TPS: A theorem proving system for type theory. In: McAllester, D. (ed.) CADE 2000. LNCS, vol. 1831, pp. 164–169. Springer, Heidelberg (2000)
2. Andrews, P.B., Brown, C.E.: TPS: A hybrid automatic-interactive system for developing proofs. Journal of Applied Logic 4(4), 367–395 (2006)
3. Backes, J., Brown, C.E.: Analytic Tableaux for Higher-Order Logic with Choice. In: Giesl, J., Hähnle, R. (eds.) IJCAR 2010. LNCS, vol. 6173, pp. 76–90. Springer, Heidelberg (2010)
4. Benzmüller, C.E., Paulson, L.C., Theiss, F., Fietzke, A.: LEO-II - A cooperative automatic theorem prover for classical higher-order logic. In: Armando, A., Baumgartner, P., Dowek, G. (eds.) IJCAR 2008. LNCS (LNAI), vol. 5195, pp. 162–170. Springer, Heidelberg (2008)
5. Brown, C.E., Smolka, G.: Analytic tableaux for simple type theory and its first-order fragment. Logical Methods in Computer Science 6(2) (June 2010)
6. Eén, N., Sörensson, N.: An extensible sat-solver. In: Giunchiglia, E., Tacchella, A. (eds.) SAT 2003. LNCS, vol. 2919, pp. 333–336. Springer, Heidelberg (2004)
7. Korovin, K.: iProver – an instantiation-based theorem prover for first-order logic (System description). In: Armando, A., Baumgartner, P., Dowek, G. (eds.) IJCAR 2008. LNCS (LNAI), vol. 5195, pp. 292–298. Springer, Heidelberg (2008)
8. Pfenning, F., Schürmann, C.: Algorithms for equality and unification in the presence of notational definitions. In: Altenkirch, T., Naraschewski, W., Reus, B. (eds.) TYPES 1998. LNCS, vol. 1657, pp. 179–193. Springer, Heidelberg (1999)
9. Smullyan, R.M.: A unifying principle in quantification theory. Proceedings of the National Academy of Sciences, U.S.A 49, 828–832 (1963)
10. Sutcliffe, G.: The 5th IJCAR Automated Theorem Proving System Competition - CASC-J5. AI Communications 24(1), 75–89 (2011)
11. Sutcliffe, G., Benzmüller, C.: Automated Reasoning in Higher-Order Logic using the TPTP THF Infrastructure. Journal of Formalized Reasoning 3(1), 1–27 (2010)

Experimenting with Deduction Modulo*

Guillaume Burel

Énsiie/Cédric, 1 square de la résistance, 91025 Évry cedex, France
guillaume.burel@ensiie.fr
http://www.ensiie.fr/~guillaume.burel/

Abstract. Deduction modulo is a generic framework to describe proofs
in a theory better than using raw axioms. This is done by presenting
the theory through rules rewriting terms and propositions. In CSL 2010,
LNCS 6247, p.155–169, we gave theoretical justifications why it is possible to embed a proof search method based on deduction modulo, namely
Ordered Polarized Resolution Modulo, into an existing prover. Here, we
describe the implementation of these ideas, starting from iProver. We test
it by confronting Ordered Polarized Resolution Modulo and other proof-
search calculi, using benchmarks extracted from the TPTP Library. For
the integration of rewriting, we also compare several implementation
techniques, based for instance on discrimination trees or on compilation.
These results reveal that deduction modulo is a promising approach to
handle proof search in theories in a generic but efficient way.

Since proofs are rarely searched for without context, there is a strong need to
be able to handle theories efficiently in theorem provers. For instance, proofs of
software correction often need some flavor of arithmetic, or theories defining the
data structures of the program such as chained lists. Several approaches exist
to go in this direction. The first one is to design a procedure dedicated to the
theory in which the proof is searched for. This would provide provers that are
really adapted to the theory, but it would have the drawbacks of not exploiting
the fact that theories are often built upon well-understood logics, and of being
difficult to extend. In particular, combination of provers built independently
for different theories would be virtually impossible. On the opposite, a second
approach would be to present the theory using axioms, and to use a general-
purpose theorem prover. While this method is very flexible, it is in most of the
cases not efficient enough to be applied. Therefore, provers searching in theories
use an in-between approach: existing general-purpose provers are combined with
methods specific to the theory. SMT provers are based on this modus operandi:
a prover for propositional logic (a SAT solver) is combined with a procedure
specific to the theory, for instance the simplex method for linear arithmetic.
SMT provers are really efficient, and are used at industrial level. Nevertheless,
they suffer from the following weaknesses: they cannot prove general results,
since they are restricted to ground inputs (some of them use heuristics for non-
ground inputs, and there are attempts to combine first-order prover with decision

---

* This work was begun while the author was a post-doc fellow at the Max-Planck-
Institute for Informatics in Saarbrücken, Germany.

N. Bjørner and V. Sofronie-Stokkermans (Eds.): CADE 2011, LNAI 6803, pp. 162–176, 2011.
© Springer-Verlag Berlin Heidelberg 2011

procedures, but they are often restricted to linear arithmetic); as they handle each theory in a specific way, it is difficult to combine different theories in them, although progress has been done in that direction in the latter years, in particular thanks to the application of the Nelson-Oppen method. A solution to overcome these drawbacks is to design a framework that can be adapted to any kind of deductive system, and that handle all theories in a uniform and yet effective way. Deduction modulo [10] can be seen as such a framework. It consists in presenting a theory as a congruence over propositions, and in applying the inference rules of deductive systems modulo this congruence. The congruence is often defined by means of a rewriting system over terms and propositions. Proof-search methods derived from deduction modulo consists roughly in adding narrowing (not merely rewriting) to an existing method such as resolution or tableaux.

The study of deduction modulo has lead to strong theoretical results: any first-order theory can be presented as a rewriting system [6]; in particular, there are presentations of Peano's arithmetic [12] and Zermelo's set theory [11] with good proof-theoretical properties; it is also possible to encode higher-order systems such as Church's simple type theory or functional pure type systems as first-order theories modulo a rewriting system [9,7]; arbitrary proof-length reductions can be achieved by working modulo a rewriting system instead of using an axiomatic presentation [5]. Nevertheless, there was no experimental results supporting the claim that deduction modulo improves indeed proof search. This was due to the fact that no implementation of proof-search methods based on deduction modulo had been developed. In [4], we have shown that integrating a resolution method based on deduction modulo into an actual prover based on ordered resolution is sound and complete, and that the given-clause algorithm, which is in most of the cases the main loop of such a prover, can be used to ease the integration. We have applied the ideas of this paper into the prover called iProver, developed by Korovin at the University of Manchester [14]. The implementation is available as a patch to iProver v.0.7 on the webpage http://www.ensiie.fr/~guillaume.burel/empty_tools.html.en. Here, we give the details of our implementation, and we show that using deduction modulo improves indeed proof search compared to using axioms. To do so, we choose as benchmarks problems of the TPTP library [17] that use axiom sets. Since we have to design by hand a rewriting system with good properties for each of the axiom sets, this has been done only for five of them. We also compared different ways of implementing the rewriting system. Since rewriting rules are known in advance, compiling them proved to be more efficient as soon as big terms needs to be normalized. An easy but efficient way to compile the rewriting rules is to translate them as an OCaml program that is dynamically linked to the prover.

In the next section, we present deduction modulo, and in particular the resolution calculus that has been integrated into iProver. We then detail all the technicalities of this integration in Section 2. The results of the benchmarks used to test the implementation, given in Section 3, show that deduction modulo improves the search for proofs in theories, and open perspectives given in the conclusion.

1   Deduction Modulo

1.1   Extending Deductive Systems with Rewriting

We use standard definitions for terms, predicates, propositions (with connectives $\neg, \Rightarrow, \wedge, \vee$ and quantifiers $\forall, \exists$), substitutions, term rewriting rules and term rewriting. In deduction modulo, term rewriting and narrowing is extended to propositions by congruence on the proposition structure. In addition, there are also proposition rewriting rules whose left hand side is an atomic proposition and whose right hand side can be any proposition. Such rules can also be applied to non-atomic propositions by congruence on the proposition structure. It can be useful to distinguish whether a proposition rewriting rule can be applied at a positive position or a negative one. To this end, proposition rewriting rules are tagged with a polarity and then called polarized rewriting rules. A proposition A is rewritten positively into a proposition B $(A \longrightarrow {}^{+}B)$ if it is rewritten by a positive rule at a positive position or by a negative rule at a negative position. It is rewritten negatively $(A \longrightarrow {}^{-}B)$ if it is rewritten by a positive rule at a negative position or by a negative rule at a positive position. *Term* rewriting rules are considered as both positive and negative. $\xrightarrow{*}{}^{\pm}$ is the reflexive transitive closure of $\longrightarrow {}^{\pm}$. $s \overset{\mathfrak{p},\sigma}{\rightsquigarrow} t$ denotes that s can be narrowed to t at position $\mathfrak{p}$ with substitution σ, i.e. there exists a rewriting rule $l \to r$ such that $\sigma(s_{|\mathfrak{p}}) = \sigma l$ and $t = \sigma(s[r]_{\mathfrak{p}})$.

In deduction modulo [10], the inference rules of an existing system such as the sequent calculus are applied modulo the congruence associated with the rewriting system (term rewriting rules and proposition rewriting rules). This leads for instance to the sequent calculus modulo. In polarized deduction modulo, polarities of rewriting rules are also considered. For instance, the left and right rules for the implication in the sequent calculus become

$$\Rightarrow\vdash \frac{\Gamma \vdash A, \Delta \qquad \Gamma, B \vdash \Delta}{\Gamma, C \vdash \Delta} \; C \xrightarrow{*}{}^{-} A \Rightarrow B \qquad\qquad \vdash\Rightarrow \frac{\Gamma, A \vdash B, \Delta}{\Gamma \vdash C, \Delta} \; C \xrightarrow{*}{}^{+} A \Rightarrow B$$

Proof-search methods can be derived from deduction modulo. Since variables may need to be instantiated before being rewritten, we need to perform narrowing instead of merely rewriting. In other words, we need unification instead of pattern matching. There are basically two families of proof-search methods based on deduction modulo, one extending the resolution method (ENAR [10], PRM [8]), and one extending the tableau method (TaMed [3]). In each case, the idea is to add a narrowing inference rule to the existing method.

1.2   Ordered Polarized Resolution Modulo

In [4], we show that it is easily possible to integrate deduction modulo into a resolution-based prover. To do so, we designed a calculus, called Ordered Polarized Resolution Modulo (OPRM$_{\mathcal{R}}^{\succ}$), and recalled in Fig. 1. Note that the ordering $\succ$ does not need to be compatible with the rewriting system $\mathcal{R}$. We proved that OPRM$_{\mathcal{R}}^{\succ}$ is complete whenever the rewriting system fulfils a criterion, namely the admissibility of the cut rule in the sequent calculus modulo.

$$\text{Resolution } \frac{P \vee C \qquad \neg Q \vee D}{\sigma(C \vee D)} \; ^{a,\,b,\,c} \qquad\qquad \text{Factoring } \frac{L \vee K \vee C}{\sigma(L \vee C)} \; ^{d}$$

$$\text{Ext. Narr.}^{-} \frac{P \vee C}{\sigma(D \vee C)} \; ^{a,\,b}, \, Q \rightarrow^{-} D \qquad \text{Ext. Narr.}^{+} \frac{\neg Q \vee D}{\sigma(C \vee D)} \; ^{a,\,c}, \, P \rightarrow^{+} \neg C$$

$$\text{Ext. Narr.}^{t} \frac{L \vee C}{\sigma(L' \vee C)} \quad L \text{ maximal in } L \vee C, \, L \overset{\mathsf{p},\sigma}{\leadsto} L' \text{ by a term rewriting rule, } L_{|\mathsf{p}} \notin \mathcal{V}$$

^{a} $\sigma = mgu(P, Q)$ $\qquad\quad$ ^{b} P maximal in $P \vee C$ $\qquad\qquad$ ^{c} $\neg Q$ maximal in $\neg Q \vee D$
^{d} L and K maximal in $L \vee K \vee C$, $\sigma = mgu(L, K)$

Fig. 1. Inference rules of the OPRM$_{\mathcal{R}}^{\succ}$

We also proved that adding some simplification rules does not break this completeness. In particular, it is possible to eliminate strict subsumptions, and to normalize the clauses w.r.t. the term rewriting system. On the contrary, we gave a counter-example showing that removing tautology clauses can break the completeness. In the following, we assume that all considered rewriting systems have this cut-admissibility property. This implies in particular the confluence of the term rewriting systems.

This calculus can be easily integrated into a prover based on resolution with selection and on the given-clause algorithm by using the following remark of Dowek [8]: having a polarized rewriting rule $P \rightarrow^{-} C$, where C is in clausal normal form, is the same as adding a clause $\underline{\neg P} \vee C$ where $\neg P$ is selected, apart from the fact that this clause should not be narrowed itself. Similarly, $P \rightarrow^{+} \neg C$ behave the same as $\underline{P} \vee C$. These clauses corresponding to the polarized rewriting rules are called *one-way clauses* by Dowek. To prevent such clauses to be resolved one by each other, they can be directly put into the set of active clauses in the given-clause algorithm.

2   Technical Details

2.1   iProver

iProver [14] is a first-order theorem prover developed by Korovin. It is mainly based on the Inst-Gen method: to prove that a set of clauses is satisfiable, they are made ground by instantiating all their variables with a dummy constant and passed to a SAT-solver. If the SAT-solver answers that the ground clauses are unsatisfiable, so are the original ones. If not, new instances of clauses are generated using some inference rule called Inst-Gen. In this paper, we are not really concerned with this method, although it would be interesting to study its combination with the deduction modulo framework. However, in iProver, the Inst-Gen method is combined with a resolution-based prover. We have integrated the OPRM$_{\mathcal{R}}^{\succ}$ into this part of iProver.

Since we do not use the Inst-Gen method, the choice of iProver may seem rather strange. It results from the following points:

– The most efficient provers today (Vampire [15], E [16], Spass [18], ...) are based on superposition, not only on resolution with selection. Of course, one may argue that superposition is an extension of ordered resolution with selection. Designing a calculus combining superposition and deduction modulo should not be difficult, starting from the $\text{OPRM}_{\mathcal{R}}^{\succ}$. However, proving the completeness of such a calculus seems rather difficult. Indeed, as for resolution modulo, this completeness will not hold without the cut admissibility of the rewriting system. However, the standard technique to prove the completeness of superposition, namely by saturation, does not appear to be linked with cut-free proofs. The question whether one can combine the restriction of superposition with narrowing without losing completeness is therefore still open.

There is also a more technical difficulty concerning superposition-based provers. The treatment of literals by superposition is not symmetric w.r.t. their polarity: inference rules for negative literals are not the same as for positive ones, and selected literals in a clause must contain at least a negative literal if they are different from the maximal literals of the clause. Implementations of superposition exploit this asymmetry. However, we want to add one-way clauses into the prover. In these clauses, a positive literal can be selected, and it needs not to be the maximal literal w.r.t. some ordering. Just selecting this positive literal and putting the clause directly into the set of active clauses made the prover incomplete in the experimentation that we made using E, probably due to the reasons cited above.

– In the CASC-J5 competition, the first prover not based on superposition is iProver. Of course, its efficiency is largely due to the Inst-Gen method and the call to an efficient SAT-solver (namely MiniSat). Nevertheless, the data structures developed in iProver, for instance its discrimination trees, contribute to its performance, and these structures are used both by the Inst-Gen and by the resolution prover.

– iProver is written in a functional language with pattern matching, namely OCaml. Although some may argue that it can therefore not achieve the same level of performance as a prover hacked in a low-level language like C, it reveals itself to be useful in our case. Indeed, it is really easy to reflect rewriting rules into a language with pattern matching. It is therefore possible to automatically transform the input rewriting system into a program that normalizes the clauses w.r.t. it, to *compile* that program and to load it to normalize clauses. As we will see thereafter, since rewriting is compiled, this leads to real improvement in the proofs in which heavy computation is needed.

2.2   Input Files

In practice, we do not want to write a specific parser for the polarized rewriting rules. Instead, we choose to change the semantics of the TPTP format whenever the new `--modulo` command-line argument is set to true. In that case, any formula whose role is `axiom` is understood as a rewriting rule. (It is still possible to have raw axioms by using e.g. the `hypothesis` role.) If the clause consists only of one positive literal whose main symbol is an equality, this is understood as a term rewriting rule. For instance, `cnf(plus_def_o, axiom, plus(X,o) = X)`. is interpreted as the term rewriting rule $plus(X, o) \rightarrow X$. If the literal is negative, or its main symbol is not the equality, or there are more than one literal, the clause is understood as a one-way clause whose first literal is the selected one. For example,

```
cnf(all_m, axiom, ~ e(lappl(all,X)) | e(lappl(X,Y)) ).
cnf(all_p, axiom, e(lappl(all,X)) | ~ e(lappl(X,h(X))) ).
```

are interpreted as the one-way clauses $\neg\epsilon(\dot{\forall} @ X) \lor \epsilon(X @ Y)$ and $\epsilon(\dot{\forall} @ X) \lor \neg\epsilon(X @ h(X))$ which correspond to the polarized rewriting rules $\epsilon(\dot{\forall} @ X) \rightarrow^{-} \forall Y. \epsilon(X @ Y)$ and $\epsilon(\dot{\forall} @ X) \rightarrow^{+} \neg\neg\epsilon(X @ h(X))$ (see [8]). The special case of the reflexivity axiom $X = X$ is also treated as a one-way clause and not as a rewriting rule.

2.3   Clause Generation by Narrowing

To perform the Ext. Narr.$^{-}$ (resp. Ext. Narr.$^{+}$) inference rule, we add a rewriting rule $P \rightarrow^{-} C$ (resp. $P \rightarrow^{+} \neg C$) as a one-way clause $\underline{\neg P} \lor C$ (resp. $\underline{P} \lor C$). To this end, we need to select $\neg P$ (resp. P) in the clause, and put the clause directly into the set of active clauses, before the main loop of the given-clause algorithm is performed. Then, applying Resolution with one of these one-way clauses simulates Ext. Narr.$^{\pm}$. In iProver, selected literals in a clause are just a list of literals that is attached to the clause. Selecting a literal in a clause consists therefore simply in calling `assign_res_sel_lits` with the singleton list containing the left-hand side of the rule. Inserting the clause in the active set is done as it would be for a normal clause: adding the clause into the unification index (using the selected literal) and tagging the clause as active.

Implementing the Ext. Narr.^{t} in iProver is more difficult. Indeed, iProver does not have a special inference rule such as paramodulation to handle equality. If equalities are present, iProver only add the axioms that define equality in the current signature. Therefore, we need to add a paramodulation inference rule ourselves. Fortunately, some data structures to do so were already present for the resolution inference rule. For instance, active clauses are indexed using a non-perfect discrimination tree [13]. To add narrowing by a term rewriting rule, we add a new index, `rewrite_index_ref`. Only term rewriting rules are added into this index. Given a term t, the index will provide all candidate rewriting rules, i.e., only rules whose left-hand side can possibly be unified with t. Then, for all candidates $l \rightarrow r$, one tries to unify l with t, and if it is the case, one returns $\sigma(r)$ where σ is the substitution computed during the unification. However, this is not sufficient, since term narrowing should perform at any depth in the term t. Therefore, we implemented a data structure for contexts, allowing one to go inside terms, and if a term cannot be narrowed at one position $\mathfrak{p}$, narrowing is tried on all position directly below $\mathfrak{p}$. Note that by doing so, all clauses that could be generated by Ext. Narr.^{t} are not, since we do not go below a position if narrowing was successful. However, we generally assume that the term rewriting system is sufficiently well-formed (in particular, as stated above, it is assumed to be confluent) so that it does not break the completeness of the prover.

2.4   Simplifications

As recalled before, some simplifications that are compatible with standard ordered resolution break the completeness of OPRM$_{\mathcal{R}}^{\succ}$. For instance, tautologies cannot be eliminated. Because they break the completeness, or we do not know if they preserve it, we have to switch off the following options of iProver: `--instantiation_flag`, `--schedule`, `--prep_prop_sim`, `--ground_splitting`, `--res_to_prop_solver`, `--res_orphan_elimination`; `--res_lit_sel` is set to `kbo_max`. There is no flag in iProver to turn off tautology elimination, so we changed the source code to prevent their elimination whenever the new `--modulo` flag is set to `true`.

In OPRM$_{\mathcal{R}}^{\succ}$, clauses can be narrowed using the term rewriting system, hence generating new clauses, but we have shown that they can also be normalized, *i.e*, replaced by their normal form. Indeed, adding the demodulation simplification rule (C is simplified to D if $C \longrightarrow D$ by the term rewriting system) does not break the completeness, and repeatedly applying this simplification eventually leads to a normal form of the term, assuming it exists.

There are several way to perform the normalization of the clauses. We compared the following ones, that can be selected using the `--normalization_type` parameter:

none. No simplification is performed, clauses have to be rewritten using Ext. Narr.^{t}, generating new clauses.

interp. Rewriting rules are translated into OCaml closures performing the pattern matching: by structural induction on the left-hand side of the rule, a function is built that matches its arguments w.r.t. the left-hand side and returns a substitution:

```
let rec term_to_subst = function
| Term.Fun(f, f_args, _) -> (function
    Term.Fun(g, g_args, _) when f = g ->
      List.fold_left2
        (fun sub t1 t2 -> merge_subst (term_to_subst t1 t2) sub)
        (Subst.create ()) f_args g_args
  | _ -> raise No_match)
| Term.Var(var,_) ->
    let sub = Subst.create () in
    fun t -> Subst.add var t sub
```

If this function is successful, the obtained substitution is applied to the right-hand side. If not, one tries another rewriting rule. If no rewriting rules can be applied at that position, one tries the same method below in the term.

dtree. Thanks to the implementation of Ext.Narr.^{t}, there is already a data structure that helps in retrieving rewriting rules whose left-hand side can be unified with some term. Since pattern-matching is stronger than unification (if a term matches a pattern, then the term and the pattern can be unified), the same structure can be used to get candidates for matching. Here also, one needs to test rewriting deeply in the term.

pipe. Rewriting rules are known statically once the input file is parsed, since OPRM$^\succ_{\mathcal{R}}$ does not generate new rewriting rules. Therefore, they can be compiled to improve their efficiency. A simple way to compile them is to translate them into a OCaml program using pattern matching. For instance, the rules $f(X, g(X)) \to h(X)$ and $f(h(X), Y) \to Y$ are translated into the code

```
let match_term = function
  Fun("f",[x0; Fun("g",[x1])]) when x0 = x1 -> Fun("h",[x0])
| Fun("f",[Fun("h",[x0]); y0]) -> y0
| _ -> raise No_match
```

This translation is fully automated. Then, there is no need to implement an efficient pattern-matching algorithm, since it is the one of OCaml that will be used. This `match_term` function is added into an OCaml source file `pipe_iprover.ml`. There, it is called by a tree-traversal that tries to apply it at each position of the term. Note that it is easy for the user to change the rewriting strategy, since one only has to change the traversal in `pipe_iprover.ml` before launching iProver. The file contains a main loop that does the following: it waits a term on the standard input, normalizes it and put the result on the standard output. This file is then compiled, and the resulting program is run. iProver then communicates with it through UNIX pipes. Terms are expected to be passed using the marshalling function of OCaml. This implies that the version of OCaml used for compiling iProver must be the same as the one for compiling `pipe_iprover.ml`.

plugin. As for pipe, an OCaml program is compiled, but it is loaded using the dynamic loading library Dynlink of OCaml, which is available for native compilation since version 3.11 for most platforms: the `match_term` function is added into a file `plugin_iprover.ml` which is compiled as a dynamic library and loaded. The main function of the compiled plug-in changes only a reference to a normalization function, pointing it to the function that does the normalization using `match_term`. iProver has just to use the new reference to get the normalization function. Here again, the normalization strategy can be easily modified by the user by changing `plugin_iprover.ml`.

size_based. Compilation costs time. It is therefore not clear that the two previous options are more efficient, in particular when only small terms are rewritten. This last normalization method decides to launch the compilation (plugin style) only when a term whose size reaches some threshold needs to be normalized. For smaller term, the dtree method is used. The threshold can be changed using the `--normalization_size` command-line parameter.

3 Benchmarks

3.1 Comparison with Other Calculi

We first test whether $\mathrm{OPRM}_{\mathcal{R}}^{\succ}$ really improves proof search compared to standard ordered resolution with selection using "normal" axioms. As we need to switch off some simplifications in order $\mathrm{OPRM}_{\mathcal{R}}^{\succ}$ to be complete, we compare it to the following calculi:

Ordered resolution, same restrictions as OPRM: in this case, the same options are given to iProver as when $\mathrm{OPRM}_{\mathcal{R}}^{\succ}$ is tried, the only difference is that the `--modulo` flag is switched off, the axioms being therefore considered as normal clauses instead of rewriting rules.

Ordered resolution, default options of iProver: in this case, the default options of iProver are used; only the Inst-Gen prover is turned off.

Full iProver: iProver is launched with its default options; in particular, the Inst-Gen prover is combined with the resolution prover.

We may also have compared it to another prover, in particular a prover based on superposition such as SPASS or E. Notwithstanding, this seems unfair, since the resolution prover of iProver is written in OCaml whereas other provers are written in C, and contain a lot of low-level optimizations, leading to more efficient executables.

To perform a benchmark, we need a set of problems to test. We therefore need some theories, and some problems related to these theories. The TPTP library [17] provides a number of axiom sets, each of them used in several problems. We could have tried to consider each of these axiom sets as a theory. The main difficulty is that for each of them, we have to define an equivalent rewriting system for which cut admissibility holds, in order to guarantee the completeness of $\mathrm{OPRM}_{\mathcal{R}}^{\succ}$. There exists a procedure that transforms a set of axioms into a rewriting system with this property [6]. However, first, this procedure may not terminate, and second, it never was implemented, although we did write some prototype which showed us that the procedure produces systems that are too big to be usable. We therefore had to design rewriting systems and prove their cut admissibility by hand. Consequently, we only tried five theories, named after their TPTP v4.0.0 axiom-set files. We tested all the problems of the TPTP library that use these axiom sets. The rewriting systems we designed to present these theories are given at `http://www.ensiie.fr/~guillaume.burel/empty_tools.html.en`. We considered **ANA001**, axioms defining the analysis (limits) for continuous functions, **BOO001**, axioms defining a ternary boolean algebra (boolean algebra with a ternary multiplication function), **FLD001**, axioms defining ordered fields, **SET001** and **SET002**, axioms defining a weak set theory using resp. predicates or function symbols to define unions, intersections, differences and complements. We ran each problem with a time-out of 60 s: first using the rewriting system in $\mathrm{OPRM}_{\mathcal{R}}^{\succ}$, second using the axiom set of the TPTP in resolution with the same restriction as $\mathrm{OPRM}_{\mathcal{R}}^{\succ}$, third in resolution with default options and fourth using iProver in its whole. All tests were performed under Linux 2.6 on a four-core Intel® Core™ i3 CPU M330 at 2.13GHz.

Table 1. Comparison of Different Calculi on Problems Extracted from the TPTP Library. #: number of solved problems; %: percentage in the problem set corresponding to the theory; $\bar{t}$: average time to find a proof for the solved problems.

	ANA001		BOO001		FLD001		SET001		SET002		Total	
	# (%)	$\bar{t}$	# (%)	$\bar{t}$	# (%)	$\bar{t}$	# (%)	$\bar{t}$	# (%)	$\bar{t}$	# (%)	$\bar{t}$
OPRM	3 (75)	11.41	3 (100)	0.01	40 (29)	0.95	15 (100)	0.01	8 (100)	0.01	69 (42)	1.05
restricted resolution	0 (0)	NA	0 (0)	NA	23 (17)	2.85	15 (100)	4.05	5 (63)	8.06	43 (26)	3.88
default resolution	1 (25)	25.34	1 (33)	25.46	40 (29)	13.55	15 (100)	0.96	7 (88)	22.99	64 (39)	12.00
full iProver	1 (25)	0.18	1 (33)	0.42	42 (31)	4.69	15 (100)	0.17	7 (88)	7.11	66 (40)	3.79

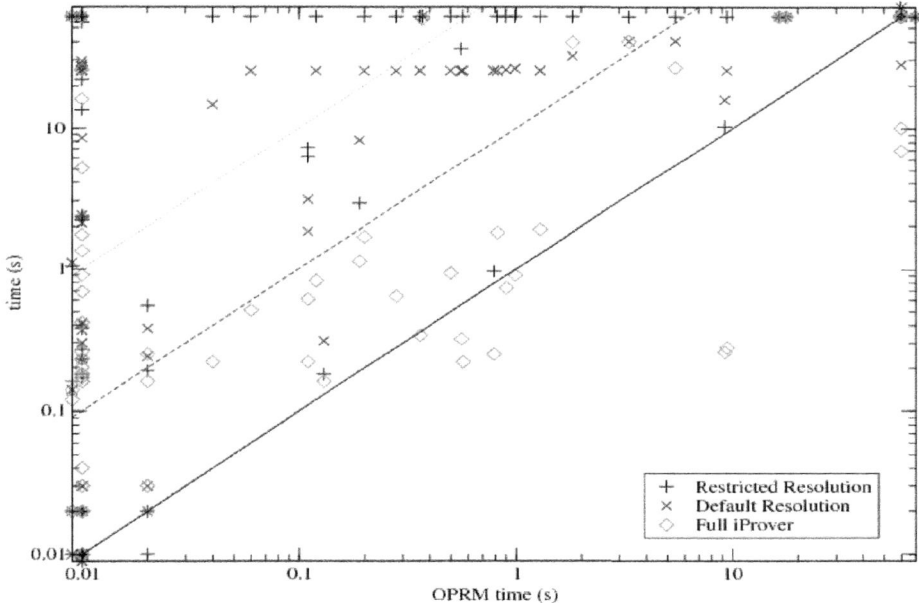

Fig. 2. Comparison of Different Calculi on Problems Extracted from the TPTP Library. The x-axis gives the time taken by $\mathrm{OPRM}^{\succ}_{\mathcal{R}}$, the y-axis by the other calculus.

The results are summarized in Table 1 and represented graphically in Figure 2. The time taken for a given problem by $\mathrm{OPRM}^{\succ}_{\mathcal{R}}$ is compared to the time taken by the other calculi. Since the scale is logarithmic, for all points above the dashed line, $\mathrm{OPRM}^{\succ}_{\mathcal{R}}$ is 10 times faster than the other calculus, and for all points above the dotted line, 100 times faster. As we can see, $\mathrm{OPRM}^{\succ}_{\mathcal{R}}$ is always at least as efficient as restricted or default resolution, and in most of the cases at least 10 times better. This was expected, because having proved the cut admissibility for the considered rewriting system implies that the theory is consistent, and the prover does not try to find a contradiction in the theory. A more surprising result is that using iProver in its whole is only rarely much better than using $\mathrm{OPRM}^{\succ}_{\mathcal{R}}$. This means that the gain of using $\mathrm{OPRM}^{\succ}_{\mathcal{R}}$ relative to using ordered resolution is comparable to the gain obtained by combining it with the Inst-Gen method (including the use of an efficient SAT-solver).

3.2 Comparison of Rewriting Implementations

In this section, we want to compare the different techniques that can be used to perform the normalization of the clauses w.r.t. the term rewriting system. To have a better control of the required amount of normalization, we do not rely on "real" problems of the TPTP, but on three families of problems crafted by hand. We first use tests requiring only normalization. The first one consists of proving that $n + n = 2 \times n$ in Peano's arithmetic, i.e., given $\underline{n} \stackrel{\text{def}}{=} s^n(o)$, we have to prove $\underline{n} + \underline{n} = s(s(o)) \times \underline{n}$ modulo the rewriting system

$$s(X) + Y \rightarrow s(X + Y) \qquad\qquad o + Y \rightarrow Y \qquad X = X \rightarrow^+ \neg\bot$$
$$s(X) \times Y \rightarrow (X \times Y) + Y \qquad\qquad o \times Y \rightarrow o$$

The second one consists in proving the same theorems, but using Church's integers in a λ-calculus with explicit substitutions. This calculus, similar to λ_v [1], is defined using binary operators for application $(\cdot @ \cdot)$ and substitution $(\cdot[\cdot])$, unary operators for lambda abstraction (λ), unit substitution $(/)$ and substitution lifting $(\Uparrow)$, De Bruijn indexes represented by 1 and sc, and the shifting substitution $\uparrow$. Then, given $\overline{n} \stackrel{\text{def}}{=} \lambda(\lambda(sc(1) @ (\cdots (sc(1) @ 1))))$, we have to prove $(+ @ \overline{n}) @ \overline{n} = (\times @ \overline{2}) @ \overline{n}$ modulo the rewriting system

$$\lambda(A) @ B \rightarrow A[/B] \qquad\qquad (A @ B)[S] \rightarrow A[S] @ B[S] \qquad\qquad 1[/A] \rightarrow A$$
$$(\lambda(A))[S] \rightarrow \lambda(A[\Uparrow S]) \qquad\qquad sc(N)[/A] \rightarrow N \qquad\qquad 1[\Uparrow S] \rightarrow 1$$
$$sc(N)[\Uparrow S] \rightarrow N[S][\uparrow] \qquad\qquad sc(N)[\uparrow] \rightarrow sc(sc(N)) \qquad\qquad 1[\uparrow] \rightarrow sc(1)$$
$$X = X \rightarrow^+ \neg\bot \qquad\qquad\qquad \times \rightarrow \lambda(\lambda(sc(1) @ 1))$$
$$+ \rightarrow \lambda(\lambda(\lambda(\lambda((sc(sc(sc(1))) @ (sc(sc(1)) @ sc(1)) @ 1)))))$$

Arguably, these tests do not reflect reals proofs, since they consists only of normalization, and no inference is performed. To have a test mixing both normalization and inference, we used an encoding of instances of the Syracuse conjecture, i.e., given an n, we tried to prove that by dividing n by 2 if n is even, and multiplying it by 3 and adding 1 if it is odd, and reiterating the process, 1 is reached eventually. This was encoded by proving $syracuse(\underline{n})$ modulo:

$$syracuse(X) \rightarrow^+ \neg\neg syracuse'(X, parity(X)) \qquad parity(s(o)) \rightarrow false$$
$$syracuse(s(o)) \rightarrow^+ \neg\bot \qquad\qquad\qquad\qquad parity(o) \rightarrow true$$
$$syracuse'(X, true) \rightarrow^+ \neg\neg syracuse(\tfrac{1}{2}(X)) \qquad \tfrac{1}{2}(s(s(X))) \rightarrow s(\tfrac{1}{2}(X))$$
$$syracuse'(X, false) \rightarrow^+ \neg\neg syracuse(\times 3 + 1(X)) \qquad \tfrac{1}{2}(s(o)) \rightarrow o$$
$$parity(s(s(X))) \rightarrow parity(X) \qquad\qquad\qquad \tfrac{1}{2}(o) \rightarrow o$$
$$\times 3 + 1(s(X)) \rightarrow s(s(s(\times 3 + 1(X)))) \qquad\qquad \times 3 + 1(o) \rightarrow s(o)$$

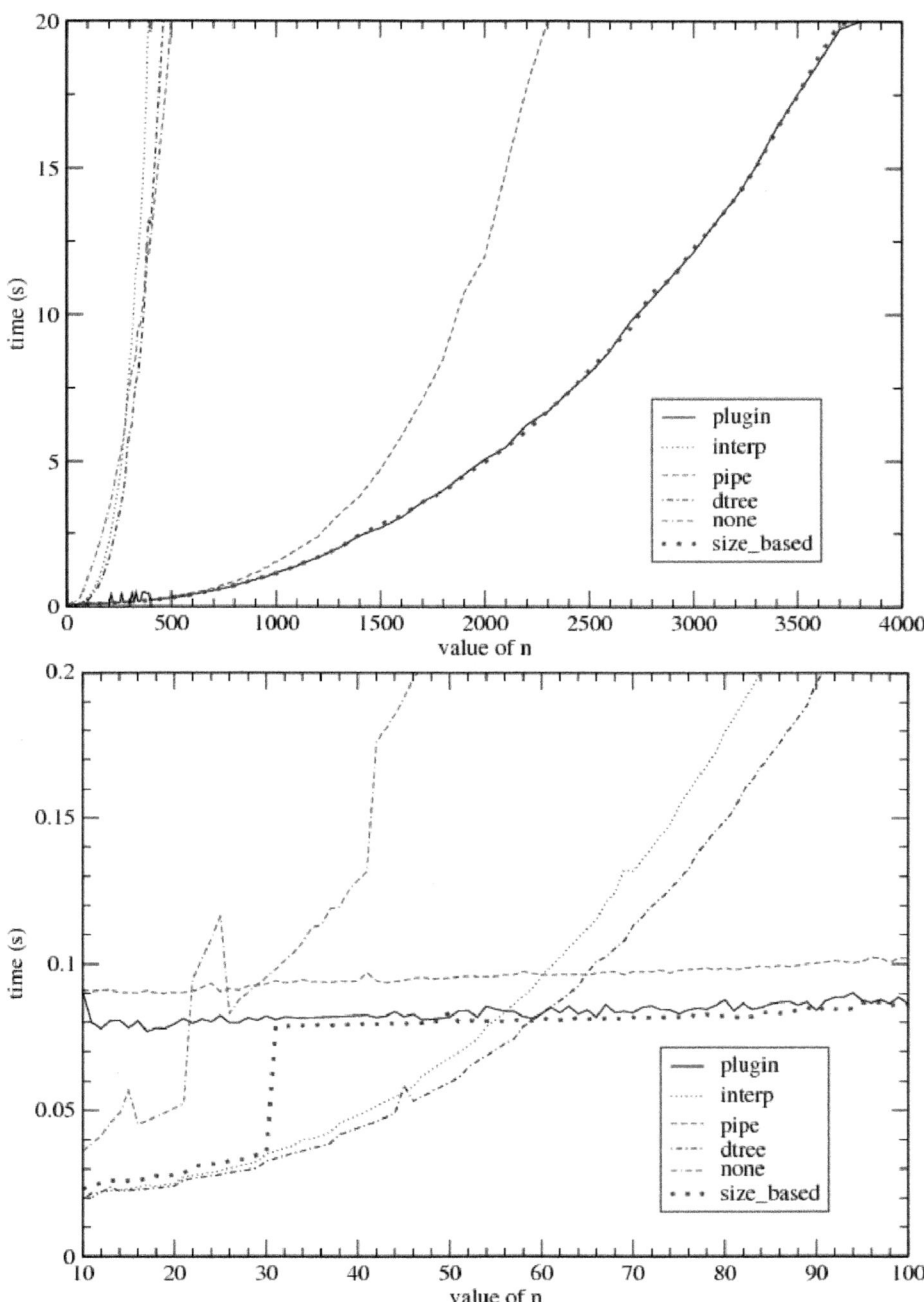

Fig. 3. Comparison of different techniques for implementing normalization: Proving that $n + n = 2 \times n$ in Peano's arithmetic. Values of n from 10 to 4000, and zoom from 10 to 100.

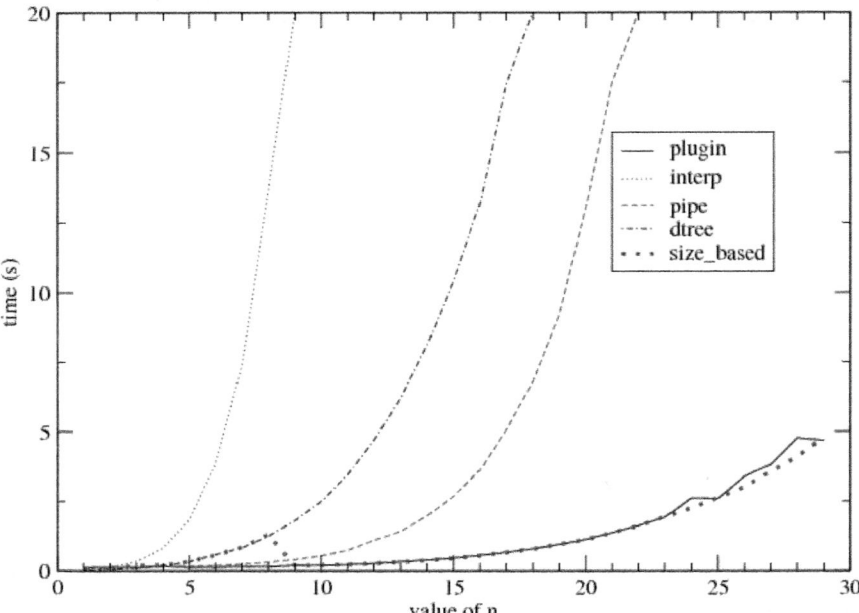

Fig. 4. Comparison of different techniques for implementing normalization: Proving that $n + n = 2 \times n$ with Church's integers

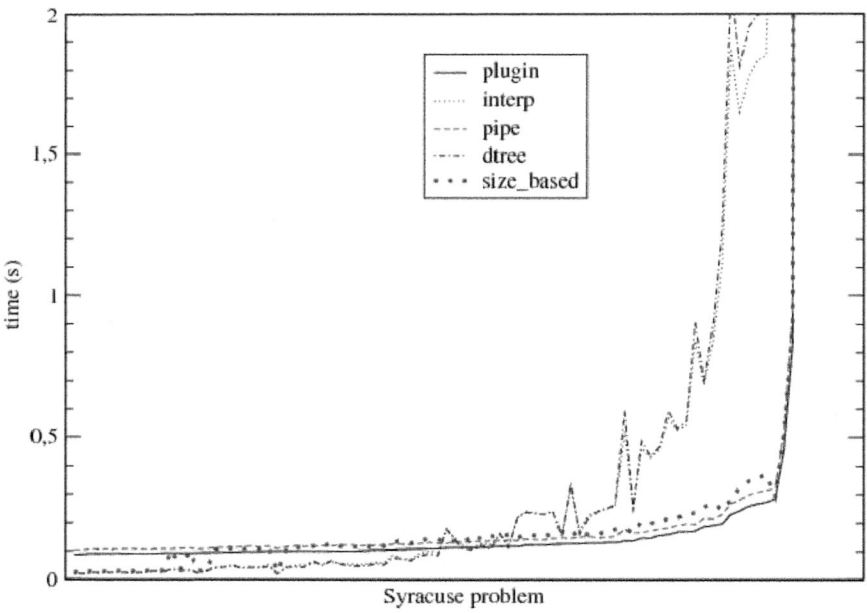

Fig. 5. Comparison of different techniques for implementing normalization: Instances of the Syracuse conjecture

The results are represented in Figures 3 to 5. As expected, compilation of the rewriting rules leads to much better results when heavy computation is needed. We also note that using Unix pipes degrades performance for large terms, compared to using a plug-in. The invocation of the OCaml compiler costs time. There is a threshold of approximately 0.07 s in Peano's arithmetic and for the Syracuse problem. Using the size_based method seems a fair choice, since it behaves, as expected, like dtree on small inputs and like plugin on large ones. However, the term-size threshold for launching compilation depends on the problem: it should be set greater for Peano's arithmetic, and smaller for Church's integers. This is due to the fact that normalizing a term of a given size requires more applications of the rewriting system for Church's integers than in Peano's arithmetic, so that the gain obtained by compiling the rules is greater for the formers. The rewriting systems of these tests are not meant to be good at reasoning about arithmetic, their purpose is to compare the different normalization techniques; the difference that were enlightened for these tests should occur for any rewriting system.

4   Conclusion

The benchmarks presented in the previous section demonstrate that using a rewriting system instead of axioms improves proof search, and that compiling the rewriting system is efficient as soon as big terms are rewritten. One could argue that one should not have used raw axioms, but a saturated set of clauses instead. There are two remarks to be made: A saturated set of clauses, if viewed as one-way clauses, can be seen as a rewriting system with cut admissibility. Conversely, the one-way clauses corresponding to a rewriting system with the cut admissibility does *not* need to be saturated w.r.t. the inference rules of the system to guarantee the completeness; they are therefore less numerous, and the completeness does not depend on the clause ordering.

A point that strongly needs to be studied is the automatic transformation of an axiomatic presentation into an equivalent rewriting system with cut admissibility. As mentioned above, a procedure exists, but its implementation showed that it would be impractical. A way to improve it would be to work on the remark above, namely that saturated set of clauses can be seen as cut-admitting rewriting systems. Note that once the set is saturated w.r.t. some ordering, it can be used with another ordering without breaking the completeness.

Another issue is to study whether extending superposition with narrowing preserves completeness. If not, we should search extra criteria that would imply it. This is crucial since we plan to integrate deduction modulo into today's most efficient first-order provers such as Vampire, E, or SPASS.

Last, compiling rewriting rules to improve first-order provers is not a new idea, but it was put aside because the compilation time is too long when the compiler needs to be called for each new rewriting rule generated by the system. Here, such a problem is not present, since rewriting rules are known in advance, *i.e.* once the input has been read. Moreover, our approach for the compilation of the rewriting rules is reminiscent of the normalization by evaluation technique [2].

To really have NbE, we should translate not only the rewriting rules into OCaml programs, but also the terms to be normalized themselves. It is not clear whether this would really improve proof search, but it should be tested.

References

1. Benaissa, Z., Briaud, D., Lescanne, P., Rouyer-Degli, J.: $\lambda\upsilon$, a calculus of explicit substitutions which preserves strong normalisation. Journal of Functional Programming 6(5), 699–722 (1996)
2. Berger, U., Eberl, M., Schwichtenberg, H.: Normalization by evaluation. In: Möller, B., Tucker, J.V. (eds.) NADA 1997. LNCS, vol. 1546, pp. 117–137. Springer, Heidelberg (1998)
3. Bonichon, R., Hermant, O.: A semantic completeness proof for taMeD. In: Hermann, M., Voronkov, A. (eds.) LPAR 2006. LNCS (LNAI), vol. 4246, pp. 167–181. Springer, Heidelberg (2006)
4. Burel, G.: Embedding deduction modulo into a prover. In: Dawar, A., Veith, H. (eds.) CSL 2010. LNCS, vol. 6247, pp. 155–169. Springer, Heidelberg (2010)
5. Burel, G.: Efficiently simulating higher-order arithmetic by a first-order theory modulo. Logical Methods in Computer Science 7(1:3), 1–31 (2011)
6. Burel, G., Kirchner, C.: Regaining cut admissibility in deduction modulo using abstract completion. Information and Computation 208(2), 140–164 (2010)
7. Cousineau, D., Dowek, G.: Embedding pure type systems in the lambda-pi-calculus modulo. In: Della Rocca, S.R. (ed.) TLCA 2007. LNCS, vol. 4583, pp. 102–117. Springer, Heidelberg (2007)
8. Dowek, G.: Polarized resolution modulo. In: Calude, C.S., Sassone, V. (eds.) IFIP TCS. IFIP AICT., vol. 323, pp. 182–196. Springer, Heidelberg (2010)
9. Dowek, G., Hardin, T., Kirchner, C.: HOL-$\lambda\sigma$. Mathematical Structures in Computer Science 11(1), 1–25 (2001)
10. Dowek, G., Hardin, T., Kirchner, C.: Theorem proving modulo. Journal of Automated Reasoning 31(1), 33–72 (2003)
11. Dowek, G., Miquel, A.: Cut elimination for Zermelo's set theory (2006); available on authors' web page
12. Dowek, G., Werner, B.: Arithmetic as a theory modulo. In: Giesl, J. (ed.) RTA 2005. LNCS, vol. 3467, pp. 423–437. Springer, Heidelberg (2005)
13. Graf, P. (ed.): Term Indexing. LNCS (LNAI), vol. 1053. Springer, Heidelberg (1996)
14. Korovin, K.: iProver – an instantiation-based theorem prover for first-order logic (System description). In: Armando, A., Baumgartner, P., Dowek, G. (eds.) IJCAR 2008. LNCS (LNAI), vol. 5195, pp. 292–298. Springer, Heidelberg (2008)
15. Razianov, A., Voronkov, A.: The design and implementation of Vampire. AI Communications 15(2-3), 91–110 (2002)
16. Schulz, S.: System description: E 0.81. In: Basin, D., Rusinowitch, M. (eds.) IJCAR 2004. LNCS (LNAI), vol. 3097, pp. 223–228. Springer, Heidelberg (2004)
17. Sutcliffe, G.: The TPTP Problem Library and Associated Infrastructure: The FOF and CNF Parts, v3.5.0. Journal of Automated Reasoning 43(4), 337–362 (2009)
18. Weidenbach, C., Dimova, D., Fietzke, A., Kumar, R., Suda, M., Wischnewski, P.: SPASS version 3.5. In: Schmidt, R.A. (ed.) CADE. LNCS, vol. 5663, pp. 140–145. Springer (2009)

Heaps and Data Structures:
A Challenge for Automated Provers

Sascha Böhme[1] and Michał Moskal[2]

[1] Technische Universität München
boehmes@in.tum.de
[2] Microsoft Research Redmond
michal.moskal@microsoft.com

Abstract. Software verification is one of the most prominent application areas for automatic reasoning systems, but their potential improvement is limited by shortage of good benchmarks. Current benchmarks are usually large but shallow, require decision procedures, or have soundness problems. In contrast, we propose a family of benchmarks in first-order logic with equality which is scalable, relatively simple to understand, yet closely resembles difficult verification conditions stemming from real-world C code. Based on this benchmark, we present a detailed comparison of different heap encodings using a number of SMT solvers and ATPs. Our results led to a performance gain of an order of magnitude for the C code verifier VCC.

1 Introduction

Among the applications of automatic provers, software verification is one of the most prominent and challenging driving forces [15]. Successful automatic code verifiers triggered and influenced the development of previously unseen improvements in reasoning systems. Yet, there is ample space for further advances, both in code verifiers and their underlying reasoning systems.

In practice, the development of automatic provers is usually driven by benchmarks (see [3, 28] for large collections), taken from examples of existing applications. Current benchmarks stemming from the program verification world, large in size as they may be, are typically shallow (i.e., their solution touches only a small fraction of the search space), sometimes have consistency problems in their axiomatizations, and in many cases do not fall into the domain of an entire class of strong automatic provers. Shallowness is due to the prevalent use of model checkers in program verification, whose applications rarely cover deep problems. Inconsistencies in axiomatizations remain frequently unnoticed, due to the "reliably" incomplete quantifier reasoning of the applied provers (interestingly, the provers still correctly discover bugs in programs). Inapplicability of provers is caused by the lack of support for specific theories, especially for integer arithmetic, which is frequently required by benchmarks. Thus, there is a demand for new and complex benchmarks with the potential to initiate further improvements in the world of automatic provers and code verifiers.

We consider two classes of automatic provers relevant for verifying complex code. The first class is that of resolution-based provers such as E [27], SPASS [30] or Vampire [26], which we will refer to as atomatic theorem provers (ATPs). They are powerful

N. Bjørner and V. Sofronie-Stokkermans (Eds.): CADE 2011, LNAI 6803, pp. 177–191, 2011.

in logical reasoning, but lack decision procedures for theories such as arithmetic. The second class is formed by satisifiability modulo theories (SMT) solvers, e.g., CVC3 [4], Yices [13] and Z3 [11]. They combine SAT solvers with decision procedures for various theories (e.g., equality and linear arithmetic) and quantifier instantiation heuristics.

1.1   The Quest for Fast Automated Provers

Automatic code verifiers demand an interactive feedback-driven style of verifying code: The user annotates the code and invokes the verifier, which, in turn, asks the automatic back-end prover to check the verification condition (VC) corresponding to the annotated code. In almost all cases, the initial annotation does not comply with the code and the user has to modify either of them and run the verifier again. Only after typically several repetitions of this feedback loop, the verifier will be satisfied. Especially for complex code (in particular in the domain of data structures), annotations are usually extensive and hence mostly added in small steps, requiring tens or hundreds of iterations.

Clearly, the response time of the code verifier (and, in particular, of the automatic prover running in the back-end) is of crucial importance to its adoption. In the Hypervisor verification project [18], for example, we have found verification times per entity (VCs corresponding to single C functions in that case) of over 30 seconds to be severely impeding productivity. Considerably longer return times made it virtually impossible to progress with verification. In fact, verification turnaround times (followed by fickleness of quantifier instantiation heuristics guiding the underlying SMT solver and difficulty in understanding verification errors) were reported as the main limiting factor during the Hypervisor verification project.

1.2   The Challenge

Verifying dynamic data structures is one of the challenges in code verification. This was also true for the aforementioned Hypervisor verification project (consisting of about 100,000 lines of C code), which used the VCC [8] verifier. In part, this might be due to the heavy methodology imposed by the verifier. However, we found some evidence that Dafny [19], a verifier for a type-safe language, performs much better than VCC on equivalent benchmarks of complex data structures. We suspected the heap encoding to be the culprit here. To confirm our guess, we have developed a series of benchmark programs and tested them against several different heap encodings (Sect. 2), including versions of VCC's and Dafny's heap models. These initial benchmarks have shown the VCC model to be much less efficient, but have also shown surprising differences between superficially similar heap encodings. Some of these results carried over to prototypical re-implementations of the heap encoding in VCC, but others did not.

Consequently, we devised a benchmark family of multiply-linked lists (Sect. 3) as an archetypical example of a recursive data structure. We implemented and specified the benchmarks in Boogie [2], a minimal intermediate verification language used by Dafny and VCC, among other verifiers. The axiomatization required is tiny, giving good guarantees of soundness, and does not require arithmetic. We have also reimplemented the multiply-linked list benchmarks, or *multi-list* benchmarks for short, in VCC and Dafny (both of which have large background axiomatizations using arithmetic).

1.3   Contributions

We propose a new family of benchmarks for both automatic code verifiers and auto-matic provers, named multi-lists (Sect. 3). These benchmarks can be arbitrarily scaled in two dimensions (showing trends instead of only scattered data-points), chopped into pieces (one per assertion), and run against any of the six heap encodings we consider (none of which is novel, but see Sect. 2). This gives a wealth of benchmarks, which, we believe, will be found useful by the community and will foster improvements of automatic provers.

Using our benchmarks, we compare several ATPs and SMT solvers (Sect. 4). This is the first comprehensive comparison of how well different heap encodings perform on different reasoning systems. The experiments also show that the proposed benchmarks are relevant in that our results using the rather low-level Boogie system carry over to VCC and Dafny and, moreover, behave comparable to benchmarks of real-world data structures. Since the benchmarks respond, under changes of the heap encoding and options to the back-end prover (Z3 in our case), similarly in all considered code verifiers (Boogie, VCC and Dafny), we believe that our results also apply to other verification systems.

2   Heap Encodings

It is customary to represent the heap as a mapping from indices to values and to provide functions read() and write() for accessing and updating it. Below we summarize the read-over-write axioms to characterize these functions [7]. Here, as well as in the rest of the paper, we use the syntax of the Boogie [2] intermediate verification language. The predicate disjoint() abstracts from the disequality test between two indices.

axiom ($\forall$ H, p, v $\bullet$ read(write(H, p, v), p) = v);
axiom ($\forall$ H, p, q, v $\bullet$ disjoint(p, q) $\Rightarrow$ read(write(H, p, v), q) = read(H, q));

Throughout this section, we assume a language with a two-tiered heap, i.e., where heap access and update require a pointer and a field. Note that this assumption is a gen-eralization of plain pointer-indexed heaps, because a pseudo-field can always artificially be constructed, if necessary. Moreover, we use (unbounded) integers to represent values stored on the heap, an over-approximation of real memory. Our assumptions apply to many languages such as Java, C#, or Dafny, just to name a few. Applying such a model to C is also possible, but requires additional work (Sect. 2.1).

Two-tiered heaps can be modeled in (at least) the following six logically equivalent ways (we abbreviate each heap model name by a short Boogie representation and refer to heap models by their abbreviation later on):

Linear heap H[dot(p,f)] . The heap is addressed by pointers only. It corresponds to the model sketched above with pointer disequality instantiating the disjointness pred-icate. Pointer-field pairs are coerced to pointers by means of the free constructor dot() axiomatized with its projections base() and field():

axiom ($\forall$ p, f $\bullet$ base(dot(p,f)) = p $\wedge$ field(dot(p,f)) = f);
axiom ($\forall$ p $\bullet$ dot(base(p), field(p)) = p);

State-based linear heap H[dot2(p,f)] . In some language formalizations (see Sect. 2.1 for more details), the above projections base() and field() only exist for certain pointers in certain states. We model that by making them dependent on the heap:

axiom ($\forall$ H, p, f • base(H, dot2(p, f)) = p $\land$ field(H, dot2(p, f)) = f);
axiom ($\forall$ H, p • dot2(base(H, p), field(H, p)) = p);

Synchronous heap H[p,f] . The heap is simultaneously accessed by pointer and field. Its axiomatization is as follows:

axiom ($\forall$ H, p, f, v • read(write(H, p, f, v), p, f) = v);
axiom ($\forall$ H, p, q, f, g, v • p $\neq$ q $\land$ f $\neq$ g $\Rightarrow$
read(write(H, p, f, v), q, g) = read(H, q, g));

Two-dimensional heap H[p][f] and H[f][p] . The heap is laid out in two dimensions, each addressed by either pointer or field. The only difference between H[p][f] and H[f][p] is the way values are obtained: For H[p][f], the heap is first addressed by a pointer and then by a field; for H[f][p], this is vice versa. Its axiomatization consists of two pairs of read-over-write axioms where disjointness is disequality of pointers and fields, respectively. For example, the heap model H[p][f] is axiomatized as follows:

axiom ($\forall$ H, p, h • read(write(H, p, h), p) = h);
axiom ($\forall$ H, p, q, h • p $\neq$ q $\Rightarrow$ read(write(H, p, h), q) = read(H, q));
axiom ($\forall$ h, f, v • read'(write'(h, f, v), f) = v);
axiom ($\forall$ h, f, g, v • f $\neq$ g $\Rightarrow$ read'(write'(h, f, v), g) = read'(h, g));

Field heaps F[p] . Instead of a single heap, there are several distinct heaps, one for each field. For each such heap, there are distinct functions read() and write(), axiomatized using read-over-write axioms with pointer disequality as disjointness predicate.

To clarify the description of each of these encodings, let us consider an example program—a sequence of assignments—and its translation into each of the described heap encodings. In the translations, the heap, which is only implicit in the program, gets explicit, which results in ordinary assignments turned into explicit heap assignments. The different instances of the heaps are numbered starting from 0 (the index of the initial heap).

Program (without explicit heap)

p.f := 3; p.g := p.f;

Linear heap H[dot(p,f)] (similar for H[dot2(p,f)])

H1 := write(H0, dot(p, f), 3); H2 := write(H1, dot(p, g), read(H1, dot(p, f)));

Synchronous heap H[p,f]

H1 := write(H0, p, f, 3); H2 := write(H1, p, g, read(H1, p, f));

Two-dimensional heap H[p][f]

H1 := write(H0, p, write'(read(H0, p), f, 3));
H2 := write(H1, p, write'(read(H1, p), g, read'(read(H1, p), f)));

Two-dimensional heap H[f][p]

H1 := write(H0, f, write'(read(H0, f), p, 3));
H2 := write(H1, g, write'(read(H1, g), p, read'(read(H1, f), p)));

Field heaps F[p]

F1 := write(F0, p, 3); G1 := write(G0, p, read(F1, p));

2.1 Type-Safe C

In general, C does not comply with our initial assumptions of a two-tiered heap. Instead, C heap is understood as a linear heap of bytes addressed solely by pointers. Even the access to structure fields is reduced to plain pointers using address arithmetic. Moreover, individually addressable entities spanning more than one byte each (e.g., integer values or floating point numbers) may overlap on the heap. Verifying complex data structure algorithms in such a setting is out of reach, because complex invariants will be hidden by layers of pointer arithmetic and numerous disjointness checks.

Fortunately, most C programs are written in a nearly type-safe manner, avoiding unrestricted casting and pointer arithmetic most of the time. This type-safety intuition led to the memory model implemented in the current version of VCC [9], which we will refer to as VCC2 from now on. This model maintains, throughout the execution of a program, a set of *valid pointers* and an invariant stating that they do not address overlapping portions of memory unless required by the type system. For instance, C's type system mandates that fields of a structure overlap with the entire structure, but not with each other. Each valid pointer p has a unique *embedding*, i.e., another valid pointer to the structure in which p is directly contained, as well as a unique field that identifies p within its embedding. The definition of the embedding and the field of a pointer depend on the current set of valid pointers. Hence, the heap model underlying VCC2 can be approximated by H[dot2(p,f)], although the actual axioms include premises about p being valid which slows down reasoning.

Along with our experiments (Sect. 4), we created a new memory model for VCC, dubbed VCC3, which separates the concepts of pointers from that of fields and is amenable to most of the heap models presented in Sect. 2 (except for F[p]), as it makes the embedding state-independent. The key idea is to treat C pointers as *fat pointers* for specification purposes, i.e., entities consisting of another fat pointer (to the embedding) and a field. For simple type-safe field accesses, there is just one field object per field of a source-level structure, corresponding exactly to our assumption about two-tiered heaps. VCC3 restricts memory accesses to a set of valid pointers, in much the same way as in the VCC2 model. Valid pointers occupy disjoint memory locations, and thus separate writes to valid pointers do not interfere. The details, in particular pointer arithmetic, arrays and casted pointers, are tricky, and will be described in an upcoming paper.

3 Multiply-Linked List Benchmark Family

Algorithms modifying data structures are among the most complex verification challenges. A simple, yet already sufficiently hard problem is inserting an element into a

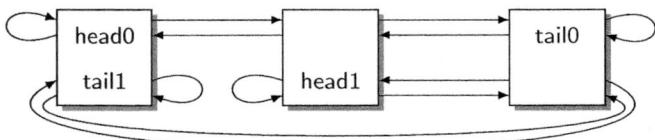

Fig. 1. An example of a generalized list with degree 2. The labels in the nodes mark the heads and tails of the two link sequences.

doubly-linked list. We render this problem even harder by generalizing the list datatype into a multiply-linked list, or *multi-list* for short. Instead of one bi-directional link (consisting of pointers next and prev per node) between two nodes, we allow n such links and call n the degree of the multi-list. Consequently, the nodes of a list are not only connected by one sequence of links, but there are n sequences, each imposing a (potentially different) order on the list nodes. Figure 1 gives an example of a multi-list with degree 2 and consisting of three nodes.

For specifying multi-lists, we assume that the following types and functions are already specified. Their exact semantics is given by the choice of the underlying heap model (Sect. 2). Here, we turned the heap into a global variable to make the specification more readable. Moreover, we require a function read_ptr() which reads and coerces heap values into pointers and a function of_ptr() which coerces pointers back into integers.

---

type heap; **type** ptr; **type** field;
var H: heap;
function read(H: heap, p: ptr, f: field): **int**;
procedure write(p: ptr, f: field, v: **int**) **modifies** H;
function read_ptr(H: heap, p: ptr, f: field): ptr;
function of_ptr(p: ptr): **int**;

All of the previously described heap models except for F[p] can easily provide semantics to these declarations. For field heaps, we provide several global heaps (one for each field) as well as copies of the heap-accessing functions.

A multi-list is characterized by its nodes, represented as a set nodes of pointers, as well as n head and n tail nodes, one head and tail for each link sequence (e.g., head0 and tail0 for the first link sequence). The predicate is_node() tests pointers for membership in a multi-list. We require the following properties (collectively referred to as the invariant of a multi-list) to be fulfilled for valid multi-lists (with examples for the first link sequence).

- Heads and tails are nodes of the list.

    ---
    is_node(H, list, read_ptr(H, list, head0)) $\wedge$ is_node(H, list, read_ptr(H, list, tail0))

- Each node's predecessors and successors are again nodes of the list.

    ($\forall$ p: Pointer • is_node(H, list, p) $\Rightarrow$
        read_ptr(H, list, next0) $\neq$ null $\wedge$ is_node(H, list, read_ptr(H, p, next0)) $\wedge$
        read_ptr(H, list, prev0) $\neq$ null $\wedge$ is_node(H, list, read_ptr(H, p, prev0)))

- All heads are their own predecessors, tails are their own successors.

read_ptr(H, read_ptr(H, list, head0), prev0) = read_ptr(H, list, head0) ∧
read_ptr(H, read_ptr(H, list, tail0), next0) = read_ptr(H, list, tail0)

– Each inner node connects bi-directionally with its predecessor and successor. An inner node's successor and predecessor is always distinct from the node.

(∀ p: Pointer • is_node(H, list, p) ∧ p ≠ read_ptr(H, list, tail0) ⇒
    read_ptr(H, read_ptr(H, p, next0), prev0) = p ∧
    read_ptr(H, p, next0) ≠ p) ∧
(∀ p: Pointer • is_node(H, list, p) ∧ p ≠ read_ptr(H, list, head0) ⇒
    read_ptr(H, read_ptr(H, p, prev0), next0) = p ∧
    read_ptr(H, p, prev0) ≠ p)

– Each node of the list contains m data fields, and every such data field fulfills an abstract property good_val(). We abbreviate this entire condition by the predicate node_valid().

Given a multi-list with these properties, insertion of a new node into the multi-list works as follows. First, the data fields of the new node are set in such a way that they then adhere to the predicate good_val(). Second, for each link sequence of the list, the new node is, based on nondeterministic choice, prepended to the head node or appended at the tail node. A nondeterministic choice may either be implemented as a random decision or simply by testing the (arbitrary) value of extra boolean arguments to the insertion function. Finally, the new node is added to the set nodes of the list. The verification condition for this function essentially corresponds to showing that the multi-list invariant also holds for the extended multi-list.

The purpose of nondeterministic choice is to simulate multiple paths, typical for data structure operations (e.g., red-black tree rotations have four cases). The number of paths is exponential in the number of links, but some provers may reuse parts of the proof between paths. Note that if the VC generator splits the paths before passing them to the prover, this will result in highly symmetric VCs—exponentially many in the number of links–being generated. Therefore, we also consider cases without nondeterministic choice, where we prepend to each list.

To better illustrate the mutual pointer updates, we give here the code which prepends a new node p in front of the head of the first link sequence (head0) of the multi-list d.

```
call write(p, next0, read(H, d, head0));
call write(p, prev0, of_ptr(p));
assume node_valid(H, read_ptr(H, d, head0));
call write(read_ptr(H, d, head0), prev0, of_ptr(p));
call write(d, head0, of_ptr(p));
assert node_valid(H, read_ptr(H, read_ptr(heap, d, head0), next0));
```

The case of $n = 1$ and $m = 1$ corresponds to a doubly-linked list with one data item per node. We consider cases where the degree of a mult-list $n \leq 3$ and the number of data fields $m \leq 10$ practically relevant, e.g., tree datatypes with several data fields fall well into this category with respect to the effort needed to verify corresponding functionality. For studying the impact of the coefficients n and m, we will also consider greater values in our experiments. It is clear that the burden on automatic provers increases drastically

Table 1. Automated provers used in the experiments and their configuration. $Z3_{+3p}$ is Z3 (version 2.18), but invoked with the configuration used by Boogie.

Automated prover	Configuration
E 1.2	−l5 −tAutoDev
SPASS 3.7	−Auto −PGiven=0 −PProblem=0 −Splits=0 −FullRed=0 −DocProof −VarWeight=3
Vampire 0.6 (r903)	−−mode casc
CVC3 2011-01-27	
Fx7 r1074	−o:MaxInstRounds=30,MaxQuantIters=2000
Yices 1.0.29	
Z3 2.18	AUTO_CONFIG=false
$Z3_{+3p}$ 2.18	CASE_SPLIT=3 DELAY_UNITS=true SORT_AND_OR=false QI_EAGER_THRESHOLD=100 RESTART_STRATEGY=0 RESTART_FACTOR=1.5 AUTO_CONFIG=false

by increasing n. This is far the less the case when increasing m. Hence, scaling n yields a good coarse-grained criterion, whereas scaling m provides smooth, fine-grained trends.

We use the naming scheme n/m to refer to the multi-list insertion benchmark with n link sequences and m data fields. Benchmarks without nondeterministic choice are indicated by a minus superscript (e.g., $3/9^-$).

4   Experiments

We compare seven different automatic provers as well as all heap models described in Sect. 2 (our benchmarks and results can be obtained from http://research. microsoft.com/~moskal/multilist.aspx). We used the ATPs E [27], SPASS [30], and Vampire [26], and we applied the SMT solvers CVC3 [4], Fx7 [22], Yices [13], and Z3 [11]. See Table 1 for the exact prover versions and their configurations. The configurations for the ATPs are the same as used in the most recent version of Isabelle/HOL [25], namely Isabelle2011, which was our best guess as to how to configure them. CVC3 and Yices do not seem to offer options that could be relevant. Fx7 is the historical entry from SMTCOMP 2007, run with the same options as in the competition. The results for Z3 should be taken with a grain of salt as its auto-configuration features fail due to a bug in the current version. This, however, does not affect the $Z3_{+p}$ and $Z3_{+p3}$ configurations, which were used in more extensive experiments described later (starting with Sect. 4.2).

4.1   Comparing ATPs with SMT Solvers

We used benchmarks $1/1^-$ and $2/2^-$, and generated one proof obligation per assertion. The check of the multi-list invariant at the end was split into separate assertions, one per conjunct. This yields 33 proof obligations per model. Table 2 summarizes the results of this experiment.

Table 2. Number of assertions solved and, in subscript, the average time of successful proofs in seconds for multi-list benchmarks $1/1^-$ and $2/2^-$. The timeout was set to 600 seconds, and the tests run on a 2.8 GHz Windows 7 PC.

Model	CVC3	E	Fx7	SPASS	Vampire	Yices	Z3	Z3$_{+p}$	Total
H[dot2(p,f)]	2 $_{.04}$	4 $_{.09}$	2 $_{2.04}$	5 $_{112.99}$	20 $_{2.08}$	2 $_{.08}$	3 $_{187.68}$	33 $_{.43}$	203 $_{9.09}$
H[p][f]	9 $_{37.92}$	5 $_{.15}$	16 $_{44.09}$	6 $_{35.46}$	20 $_{11.67}$	27 $_{9.19}$	2 $_{.03}$	32 $_{.43}$	249 $_{10.58}$
H[dot(p,f)]	12 $_{27.09}$	4 $_{.09}$	24 $_{22.64}$	9 $_{19.47}$	20 $_{1.64}$	31 $_{52.16}$	26 $_{20.34}$	33 $_{.37}$	291 $_{12.33}$
H[p,f]	11 $_{3.23}$	9 $_{3.76}$	27 $_{21.59}$	9 $_{50.67}$	25 $_{6.31}$	32 $_{3.80}$	33 $_{1.58}$	33 $_{.29}$	311 $_{5.83}$
H[f][p]	9 $_{.49}$	11 $_{.59}$	33 $_{9.37}$	10 $_{21.69}$	22 $_{1.91}$	33 $_{1.06}$	33 $_{1.64}$	33 $_{.12}$	316 $_{2.45}$
F[p]	18 $_{.07}$	15 $_{22.03}$	33 $_{1.02}$	23 $_{17.83}$	33 $_{1.21}$	33 $_{.04}$	33 $_{.04}$	33 $_{.04}$	353 $_{2.43}$
Total	61 $_{11.60}$	48 $_{7.76}$	135 $_{16.14}$	62 $_{32.84}$	140 $_{3.91}$	158 $_{12.80}$	130 $_{9.23}$	197 $_{.28}$	1723 $_{6.68}$

Among all models, F[p] is the most efficient: Most VCs are proved with this model, and mostly even in the shortest average time. However, it is unclear how to implement this model when field names are not known statically, which is the case for virtually all C programs. Second best in terms of proved VCs is H[f][p] for nearly all systems, followed by H[p,f] (only for Vampire, the order of these two models is swapped). Note that both H[f][p] and H[p,f] do not suffer from implementation problems as F[p]. We will see similar results in more complex benchmarks run by Z3 in Sect. 4.3 below.

The general trend is that SMT solvers are faster and solve more problems than ATPs, but Vampire is competitive, when presented with fragmented VCs, with the leading SMT solvers used in their default configurations. As we will see in the next section, it does not perform so well when one VC per problem is generated. Reasoning with quantifiers is a field in which ATPs usually excel SMT solvers, but when we manually supply additional hints on quantified formulas, in the form of patterns, SMT solvers easily outperform ATPs (see, e.g., Z3$_{+p}$ in the last column of Table 2).

4.2 Guiding SMT Solver with Patterns

A pattern [24] for a quantified formula $\forall \bar{x}.\,\psi$ is a set of terms $\{t_0, \ldots, t_n\}$, typically subterms of ψ. The solver can instantiate ψ with the substitution σ by adding a tautology $(\forall \bar{x}.\,\psi) \Rightarrow \sigma(\psi)$ to the logical context. It will do so if $\sigma(t_0), \ldots, \sigma(t_n)$ have an interpretation in the currently considered partial ground model.

Patterns are the standard approach for handling quantifiers in SMT solvers. All solvers used in our evaluation come with their own inference algorithms to automatically derive patterns. Except for Yices, all considered SMT solvers also provide syntax to manually add patterns to problems, effectively overriding the solver's internal pattern inference and providing direct user control over how solvers perform quantifier instantiations. While patterns are sometimes dismissed as a poor man's substitute for proper quantifier reasoning methods, they are often used to effectively program a custom decision procedure in the SMT solver [10,23]. Moreover, they give SMT solvers significant edge over ATPs in software verification scenarios.

Table 3 summarizes runs of ATPs as well as different SMT solvers with (indicated by the suffix $_{+p}$) or without pattern annotations. As opposed to Table 2, the benchmarks

Table 3. Number of benchmarks solved by different systems. Systems not mentioned in the table timeout on all benchmarks. Benchmarks: $1/1^-$, $1/10^-$, $2/2^-$, $2/10^-$, $3/3^-$, $1/1$, $1/10$, $2/2$, $2/10$, and $3/3$.

Model	CVC3$_{+p}$	Fx7	Fx7$_{+p}$	Vampire	Yices	Z3	Z3$_{+p}$	Z3$_{+p3}$	Total
H[p][f]	2 $_{69.61}$	0	7 $_{53.83}$	0	1 $_{4.92}$	0	6 $_{3.62}$	9 $_{29.52}$	34 $_{26.15}$
H[dot2(p,f)]	3 $_{34.78}$	0	5 $_{69.96}$	0	0	0	7 $_{53.66}$	10 $_{2.04}$	35 $_{24.96}$
H[dot(p,f)]	6 $_{150.85}$	2 $_{153.15}$	4 $_{18.89}$	0	1 $_{79.26}$	2 $_{294.07}$	10 $_{40.18}$	10 $_{1.47}$	45 $_{53.06}$
H[p,f]	3 $_{178.28}$	2 $_{94.47}$	7 $_{27.90}$	0	2 $_{43.21}$	6 $_{126.86}$	8 $_{13.07}$	10 $_{.60}$	48 $_{39.19}$
H[f][p]	6 $_{97.21}$	6 $_{180.64}$	10 $_{17.65}$	0	6 $_{28.11}$	6 $_{30.69}$	6 $_{12.87}$	10 $_{.18}$	60 $_{37.95}$
F[p]	7 $_{11.25}$	10 $_{29.01}$	10 $_{9.25}$	3 $_{7.65}$	10 $_{.27}$	10 $_{13.27}$	10 $_{.24}$	10 $_{.10}$	80 $_{7.80}$
Total	27 $_{86.87}$	20 $_{93.46}$	43 $_{29.45}$	3 $_{7.65}$	20 $_{17.10}$	24 $_{69.42}$	47 $_{20.92}$	59 $_{5.25}$	302 $_{29.58}$

Table 4. The first row shows that Z3 can solve 153 benchmarks both with and without patterns in average time per benchmark of 18.12 seconds and 0.70 seconds, respectively. There are 91 benchmarks that Z3 timeouts on (labelled T/O), and which Z3$_{+p}$ solves in an average time of 10.25 seconds, and the single benchmark that Z3$_{+p}$ timeouts on is solved by Z3 in 92.67 seconds. If we add up the three columns for each prover, Z3$_{+p}$ is 35.1 times faster (another approach would be to ignore timeouts and divide 18.12 by 0.70; this yields results in the same ballpark).

Prover	Common	Unique	T/O	Prover	Common	Unique	T/O	Ratio
Z3	153 $_{18.12}$	1 $_{92.67}$	91 $_{600.00}$	Z3$_{+p}$	153 $_{.70}$	91 $_{10.25}$	1 $_{600.00}$	35.1
CVC3	61 $_{11.60}$	0	164 $_{600.00}$	CVC3$_{+p}$	61 $_{.54}$	164 $_{26.49}$	0	22.6
Fx7	155 $_{26.12}$	0	86 $_{600.00}$	Fx7$_{+p}$	155 $_{1.81}$	86 $_{15.35}$	0	34.8
Z3$_{+p}$	244 $_{4.26}$	0	13 $_{600.00}$	Z3$_{+p3}$	244 $_{.28}$	13 $_{19.45}$	0	27.6

are not split by assertion, but each is given as one VC to the solvers. We see that, when provided with explicit patterns, Z3 is clearly the most successful and fastest solver.

Boogie runs Z3 with specific options (see Table 1), indicated by the suffix $_{+p3}$. Separate experiments showed that among these options, which configure Z3's SAT solver and quantifier heuristics, CASE_SPLIT=3 is most important. This causes Z3 not to use the common SAT case-split selection strategy (based on variable activity), but to try to satisfy the formula from left to right. Our results show that this configuration outperforms all provers, even the standard configuration of Z3.

To compare the relative performance impact of patterns and case-split selection we compared the cumulative run times of solvers when solving the proof obligations of Table 2 and those of Table 3 in all six heap encodings (($33 + 10$) × 6 encodings = 258 benchmarks). When only one solver of the pair could solve the benchmark, we took the time of the other to be 600 seconds (the timeout value). Table 4 summarizes the findings. The pattern speedups for Z3, CVC3 and Fx7 are roughly 1.5 order of magnitude, and would be larger had we decided to penalize timeouts more. Moreover, Z3$_{+p3}$ is 27.8 times faster than Z3$_{+p}$. Thus, a custom case-split selection strategy gives another 1.5 order of magnitude over just using patterns.

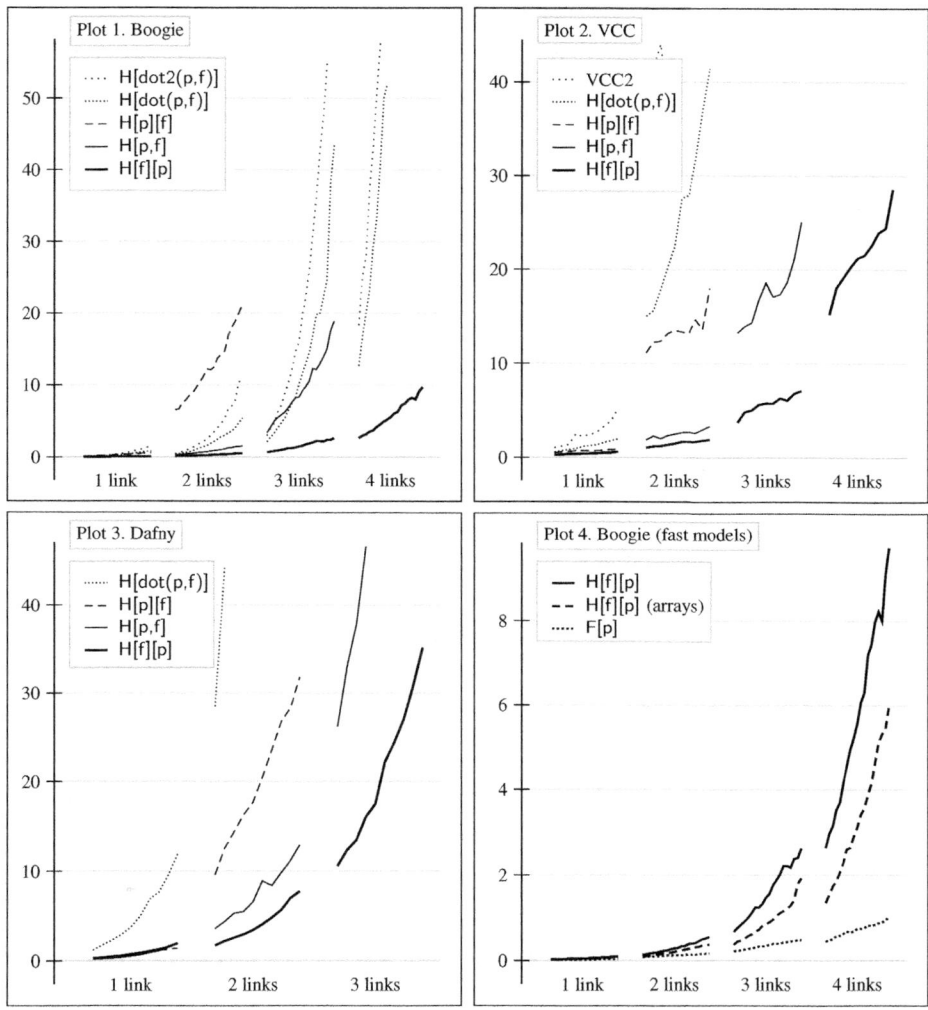

Fig. 2. Multi-list benchmark using different heap encodings and different programming languages. The x axis shows the complexity of the benchmark in order $1/1$, $1/2$, ..., $1/20$, $2/1$, ..., $2/20$, ..., $4/20$. The y axis shows the median runtime (in seconds) of Z3 run with 6 different random seeds.

4.3 Scaling Up

We subsequently compared different heap encodings in different languages using the fastest solver from the previous section: $Z3_{+p3}$, i.e., Z3 using patterns and the options used by Boogie. Plots 1, 2, and 3 in Fig. 2 show run times of our benchmarks in Boogie, VCC, and Dafny. We were unable to supply some of the pattern annotations to Dafny, which explains its poor performance relative to VCC. Still, it shows similar trends. We omitted all timed-out data points. We see similar results in terms of order, in particular the H[f][p] representation is always the fastest, and collapsing p and f into a single entity, especially using VCC2's dot2() function, performs very badly. This similarity gives us some confidence that experiments with other models would also carry over from Boogie to different verification systems.

Plot 4 shows the results of experiments with representations which are not implemented in VCC3, namely the F[p] and H[f][p] with the built-in array theory [12]. The F[p] representation brings about an order of magnitude speedup over H[f][p]. It is, however, known to be tricky to handle soundly and modularly: Often the accessed field is not known statically. Additionally, functions generally need to be allowed to write freshly allocated objects, which means they potentially write all fields in the heap, and thus modeling function calls reduces the benefits of F[p]. One can use different splits of the heap into field components in different functions, and maintain some consistency invariants between them, which is something we want to explore in the future.

The array decision procedure shows some speedup, but except for the biggest benchmark it is small (within 20%). It does so by avoiding certain instantiations of read-over-write axioms, which can lead to incompleteness when patterns are used to guide instantiations of user-provided axioms. Thus, in the context of VCC, using it is unlikely to be a good idea.

4.4   Interpretation of the Results

The two linear models, H[dot2(p,f)] and H[dot(p,f)], perform poorly because the prover needs to instantiate several axioms to prove disjointness of heap accesses. This is particularly painful when there are also a lot of other axioms to instantiate (i.e., in VCC or Dafny), and the prover will often instantiate those other axioms first. Especially the dot2() axioms are complicated, much more than the dot() axioms.

As for H[f][p] compared with H[p,f] or H[p][f], consider a write to x.a and subsequent reads of y.b and z.c. To find that writing x.a did not clobber the value of y.b in H[f][p], the prover can establish $a \neq b$, which is usually immediate, and moreover if $b = c$ then the value of z.c will be known without further quantifier instantiations. Similar reasoning holds for H[p][f] and $x \neq y$, but the pointer comparison usually involves complex reasoning (e.g., x was valid at some point, whereas y was not). Finally, in H[p,f] the prover can prove disjointness of either fields or pointers, but there is no reuse of instantiations for different heap accesses.

Difficult benchmarks typically have many invariants quantifying over pointers. For example, proving each of the quantified invariants in our artificial benchmark introduces a new Skolem constant n_{sk} and in turn $n_{sk}.\text{prev}_i$, $n_{sk}.\text{next}_i$, etc. Thus, difficult benchmarks are likely to use many more pointers than fields, making the reuse in H[f][p] much more significant.

The H[p][f] behaves surprisingly poorly. Initially we thought it was a Z3-specific problem (it seems to be generating very large conflict clauses in this case, which talk about distinctness of pointers), but it obviously also occurs in other provers.

4.5   Checking Real-World Verification Examples

Table 5 lists results of applying VCC with different heap encodings on verification of common data structures stemming from the VACID-0 benchmark suite [20]: binomial heaps, doubly-linked lists, and red-black trees. VCC3 (using the H[f][p] model) shows,

Table 5. Detailed comparison of different heap models in VCC3 against each other and VCC2. Times are median for 6 runs with different random seeds, given in seconds.

Testcase	VCC2		VCC3		Ratio
Heap.c: Heap_adm	0.14	±0.01	0.10	±0.00	1.3×
Heap.c: extractMin	15.55	±4.40	7.95	±1.63	2.0×
Heap.c: heapSort	7.11	±3.84	0.27	±0.01	26.4×
Heap.c: heapSortTestHarness	1.03	±0.11	0.14	±0.00	7.6×
Heap.c: init	0.14	±0.00	0.10	±0.00	1.4×
List.c: InitializeListHead	0.20	±0.01	0.14	±0.00	1.5×
List.c: InsertHeadList	8.12	±0.64	1.02	±0.05	8.0×
List.c: InsertTailList	8.45	±0.69	0.95	±0.07	8.9×
List.c: IsListEmpty	0.10	±0.00	0.07	±0.00	1.4×
List.c: RemoveEntryList	4.64	±0.23	0.53	±0.03	8.8×
List.c: RemoveHeadList	4.75	±0.12	0.49	±0.03	9.6×
List.c: RemoveTailList	4.12	±0.12	0.52	±0.07	8.0×
List.c: _LIST_MANAGER_adm	0.22	±0.01	0.15	±0.01	1.5×
RedBlackTrees.c: Tree_adm	0.59	±0.01	0.40	±0.01	1.5×
RedBlackTrees.c: left_rotate	108.40	±22.74	12.90	±4.43	8.4×
RedBlackTrees.c: right_rotate	97.06	±14.07	13.44	±0.77	7.2×
RedBlackTrees.c: tree_find	0.14	±0.00	0.13	±0.01	1.0×
RedBlackTrees.c: tree_init	0.13	±0.00	0.11	±0.00	1.2×
RedBlackTrees.c: tree_insert	94.17	±9.53	3.14	±0.24	30.0×
RedBlackTrees.c: tree_lookup	0.12	±0.00	0.08	±0.00	1.5×

in comparison with the current model of VCC (VCC2), about an order of magnitude of speedup on non-trivial functions.

We also conducted comparisons of heap models for the VACID-0 benchmarks. Due to overheads of the VCC axiomatizations, the differences between the heap encodings are not as dramatic as with our artificial multi-list benchmarks. Nevertheless, we found similar trends as in the other experiments, with H[f][p] being the best model. Thus, we consider the multi-list benchmark to be representative for real-world benchmarks.

5 Related Work

Many existing program verifiers support the selection of automatic back-end provers [2, 14, 17, 16], but so far, none has reported a thorough comparison between the automatic provers. Notably Jahob [31] uses both ATPs (E and SPASS) and SMT solvers (CVC3 and Z3) as background provers, among others.

None of the presented heap models is novel, and in fact, most of them are standard in program verifiers. For example, the state-based linear heap is used by VCC [9], the synchronous heap is underlying Dafny's memory model [19], and field heaps, due to [6, 5], are used by Jahob [31].

Challenges for program verifiers have been posed before [20], but we know of only one further proposal [1] of scalable benchmarks to evaluate the behaviour of automatic provers.

6   Conclusion

We have proposed a scalable and challenging benchmark taken from the domain of data structures, and tested it on a number of heap encodings and verification systems (Boogie, VCC and Dafny). The experiments gave similar results in terms of tendency (i.e., indicating a clear order of encodings with respect to performance) for the three systems. Additionally, testing realistic C benchmarks with a subset of the heap encodings yielded similar results. We thus believe that the multi-list benchmark is a good representative of benchmarks stemming from modular software verification, while being simple (no arithmetic required and no soundness problems) and scalable.

We have confirmed the folklore that splitting the heap by fields performs best, but have also put concrete numbers on that claim. We have also tested the performance impact of using a dedicated decision procedure for the array theory.

We have found that the performance of ATPs is comparable with that of SMT systems when software verification problems are provided without any additional hints and in small fragments. This may be particularly useful for parts of VCs without explicitly engineered patterns, such as those coming from the user of the verification tool. Processing the bigger chunks of the VC at once will likely be needed, if ATPs are to meet the performance requirements of today's verification demands.

Pattern annotations give SMT solvers a huge advantage over ATPs (at least 1.5 orders of magnitude). It would be very desirable for the ATPs to take advantage of these (e.g., via hints [29] as implemented in Otter [21]), maybe to guide term ordering heuristics. Similarly, a custom case split strategy further improves Z3's performance by 1.5 orders of magnitude.

References

1. Armando, A., Bonacina, M.P., Ranise, S., Schulz, S.: New results on rewrite-based satisfiability procedures. ACM Transactions on Computational Logic 10(1) (2009)
2. Barnett, M., Chang, B.-Y.E., DeLine, R., Jacobs, B., M. Leino, K.R.: Boogie: A modular reusable verifier for object-oriented programs. In: de Boer, F.S., Bonsangue, M.M., Graf, S., de Roever, W.-P. (eds.) FMCO 2005. LNCS, vol. 4111, pp. 364–387. Springer, Heidelberg (2006)
3. Barrett, C., Stump, A., Tinelli, C.: The Satisfiability Modulo Theories Library, SMT-LIB (2010), http://www.SMT-LIB.org
4. Barrett, C.W., Tinelli, C.: CVC3. In: Damm, W., Hermanns, H. (eds.) CAV 2007. LNCS, vol. 4590, pp. 298–302. Springer, Heidelberg (2007)
5. Bornat, R.: Proving pointer programs in Hoare Logic. In: Backhouse, R., Oliveira, J.N. (eds.) MPC 2000. LNCS, vol. 1837, pp. 102–126. Springer, Heidelberg (2000)
6. Burstall, R.M.: Some techniques for proving correctness of programs which alter data structures. Machine Intelligence 7, 23–50 (1972)
7. Cartwright, R., Oppen, D.: The logic of aliasing. Acta Informatica 15, 365–384 (1981)
8. Cohen, E., Dahlweid, M., Hillebrand, M., Leinenbach, D., Moskal, M., Santen, T., Schulte, W., Tobies, S.: VCC: A practical system for verifying concurrent C. In: Berghofer, S., Nipkow, T., Urban, C., Wenzel, M. (eds.) TPHOLs 2009. LNCS, vol. 5674, pp. 23–42. Springer, Heidelberg (2009)

9. Cohen, E., Moskal, M., Tobies, S., Schulte, W.: A precise yet efficient memory model for C. ENTCS 254, 85–103 (2009)
10. Condit, J., Hackett, B., Lahiri, S.K., Qadeer, S.: Unifying type checking and property checking for low-level code. In: POPL, pp. 302–314. ACM, New York (2009)
11. de Moura, L., Bjørner, N.S.: Z3: An efficient SMT solver. In: Ramakrishnan, C.R., Rehof, J. (eds.) TACAS 2008. LNCS, vol. 4963, pp. 337–340. Springer, Heidelberg (2008)
12. de Moura, L.M., Bjørner, N.: Generalized, efficient array decision procedures. In: Formal Methods in Computer-Aided Design, pp. 45–52. IEEE, Los Alamitos (2009)
13. Dutertre, B., de Moura, L.: The Yices SMT solver (2006), http://yices.csl.sri.com/tool-paper.pdf
14. Filliâtre, J.-C.: Why: a multi-language multi-prover verification tool. Research Report 1366, LRI, Université Paris Sud (March 2003)
15. Hoare, C.A.R.: The verifying compiler: A grand challenge for computing research. Journal of the ACM 50(1), 63–69 (2003)
16. James, P., Chalin, P.: Faster and more complete extended static checking for the Java Modeling Language. Journal of Automated Reasoning 44, 145–174 (2010)
17. Kuncak, V.: Modular Data Structure Verification. PhD thesis, EECS Department, Massachusetts Institute of Technology (February 2007)
18. Leinenbach, D., Santen, T.: Verifying the microsoft hyper-V hypervisor with VCC. In: Cavalcanti, A., Dams, D.R. (eds.) FM 2009. LNCS, vol. 5850, pp. 806–809. Springer, Heidelberg (2009)
19. Leino, K.R.M.: Dafny: An automatic program verifier for functional correctness. In: Clarke, E.M., Voronkov, A. (eds.) LPAR-16 2010. LNCS, vol. 6355, pp. 348–370. Springer, Heidelberg (2010)
20. Leino, K.R.M., Moskal, M.: VACID-0: Verification of Ample Correctness of Invariants of Data-structures. In: VSTTE (2010)
21. McCune, W.: OTTER 3.3 Reference Manual. Mathematics and Computer Science Division, Argonne National Laboratory, Technical Memorandum No. 263 (2003)
22. Moskal, M.: Fx7 or in software, it is all about quantifiers. Satisfiability Modulo Theories Competition (2007)
23. Moskal, M.: Programming with triggers. In: SMT 2009, pp. 20–29. ACM, New York (2009)
24. Nelson, G.: Techniques for program verification. Technical Report CSL-81-10, Xerox PARC (1981)
25. Nipkow, T., Paulson, L.C., Wenzel, M.: Isabelle/HOL–Isabelle/HOL – A Proof Assistant for Higher-Order Logic. LNCS, vol. 2283. Springer, Heidelberg (2002)
26. Riazanov, A., Voronkov, A.: The design and implementation of Vampire. AI Comm. 15(2-3), 91–110 (2002)
27. Schulz, S.: System description: E 0.81. In: Basin, D., Rusinowitch, M. (eds.) IJCAR 2004. LNCS (LNAI), vol. 3097, pp. 223–228. Springer, Heidelberg (2004)
28. Sutcliffe, G.: The TPTP problem library and associated infrastructure. Journal of Automated Reasoning 43(4), 337–362 (2009)
29. Veroff, R.: Using hints to increase the effectiveness of an automated reasoning program: Case studies. Journal of Automated Reasoning 16, 223–239 (1996)
30. Weidenbach, C., Dimova, D., Fietzke, A., Kumar, R., Suda, M., Wischnewski, P.: SPASS version 3.5. In: Schmidt, R.A. (ed.) CADE-22. LNCS, vol. 5663, pp. 140–145. Springer, Heidelberg (2009)
31. Zee, K., Kuncak, V., Rinard, M.C.: Full functional verification of linked data structures. In: Programming Language Design and Implementation, pp. 349–361. ACM, New York (2008)

Optimized Query Rewriting for OWL 2 QL

Alexandros Chortaras[*], Despoina Trivela, and Giorgos Stamou

School of Electrical and Computer Engineering,
National Technical University of Athens,
Zografou 15780, Athens, Greece
{achort,gstam}@cs.ntua.gr, despoina@image.ntua.gr

Abstract. The OWL 2 QL profile has been designed to facilitate query answering via query rewriting. This paper presents an optimized query rewriting algorithm which takes advantage of the special characteristics of the query rewriting problem via first-order resolution in OWL 2 QL and computes efficiently the rewriting set of a user query, by avoiding blind and unnecessary inferences, as well as by reducing the need for extended subsumption checks. The evaluation shows that in several cases the algorithm achieves a significant improvement and better practical scalability if compared to other similar approaches.

Keywords: query answering, query rewriting, OWL 2 QL, DL-Lite.

1 Introduction

The use of ontologies in data access allows for semantic query answering, i.e. for answering user queries expressed in terms of terminologies linked to some data [4,7]. Queries typically have the form of *conjunctive queries* (CQ) and terminologies the form of ontologies. Unfortunately, the problem of answering CQs in terms of ontologies axiomatized in expressive Description Logics suffers from high worst-case complexity. The obvious way to overcome this obstacle and develop practical systems is to reduce the expressivity of the ontology language; otherwise either soundness or completeness have to be sacrificed.

Late research in description logics has introduced DL-Lite$_R$, a DL ontology representation language that underpins the OWL 2 QL profile [1]. In DL-Lite$_R$, the CQ answering problem is tractable from the data point of view. Sound and complete CQ answering systems for DL-Lite$_R$ can follow a strategy that splits the procedure in two steps [7,1,8]: the query *rewriting*, in which the CQ is expanded into a union of CQs (UCQ), and the *execution* of the UCQ over the database. Apart from having the advantage of using the mature relational database technology, rewriting can be based on first order resolution-based reasoning algorithms [6], which are widely studied in the literature [2]. The main

---

[*] The work of this paper has been partially funded by EuropeanaConnect. Best Practice Network in the eContentplus Programme of the European Community. (ECP-2008-DILI-528001) www.europeanaconnect.eu.

N. Bjørner and V. Sofronie-Stokkermans (Eds.): CADE 2011, LNAI 6803, pp. 192–206, 2011.
© Springer-Verlag Berlin Heidelberg 2011

restriction is that for large terminologies and/or large queries the exponential complexity in the query size may result in a very large number of rewritings.

Several CQ answering algorithms for DL-Lite$_R$ have been proposed in the literature. In [3,9], the rewriting strategy is based on reformulating the conjuncts of the query according to the taxonomic information of the ontology. Although the strategy is effective, some of the ontology axioms must be rewritten in terms of auxiliary roles, which may increase the ontology size. This restriction is relaxed in [6], which proposes a resolution-based rewriting strategy, called RQR. However, the non goal-oriented saturation strategy may get tangled in long inference paths leading either to unnecessary or non function free rewritings. Such rewritings are discarded in the end, but their participation in the inference process and the increased number of required subsumption checks degrades significantly performance. Another strategy is proposed in [8] which, instead of computing a set of CQs, builds a non-recursive datalog program, deferring thus the main source of complexity to the database system. A different approach is used in [5], which partially materializes the data in order to facilitate the rewriting process.

In this paper we improve on the pure query rewriting approach and introduce a new query rewriting algorithm called Rapid, which is optimized for queries posed over DL-Lite$_R$ ontologies. Its efficiency is owed to the goal-oriented organization of the resolution process. Instead of applying exhaustively the resolution rule, it exploits the query structure and performs a restricted sequence of inferences that lead directly to rewriting sets with, hopefully, no unnecessary rewritings. In this way, we avoid a large number of blind inference paths which can be the cause of scalability issues, as well as the production of many unnecessary rewritings (that are subsumed by others) and the need to remove them by performing extended query subsumption checks, i.e. very costly operations. For simplicity, we restrict our study to user queries in which all body variables are reachable from a head variable through a role sequence. Although this assumption excludes some queries, e.g. 'boolean queries', it has little impact in practice, since such queries are not common in a typical semantic query answering system.

The effectiveness of the algorithm is demonstrated in its practical evaluation, which shows clearly an optimized performance, especially in the most problematic cases of large queries or large terminologies.

2   Preliminaries

A DL-Lite$_R$ *ontology* is a tuple $\langle \mathcal{T}, \mathcal{A} \rangle$, where $\mathcal{T}$ is the *terminology* and $\mathcal{A}$ the assertional knowledge. Formally, $\mathcal{T}$ is a set of axioms of the form $C_1 \sqsubseteq C_2$ or $R_1 \sqsubseteq R_2$, where C_1, C_2 are concept descriptions and R_1, R_2 role descriptions, employing atomic concepts, atomic roles and individuals. $\mathcal{A}$ is a finite set of *assertions* of the form $A(a)$ or $R(a, b)$, where a, b are individuals, A an atomic concept and R an atomic role. A DL-Lite$_R$ concept can be either atomic or $\exists R.\top$. If it appears in the RHS, we assume that it may also be of the form $\exists R.A$. Negations of concepts can be used only in the RHS of subsumption axioms. A DL-Lite$_R$ role is either an atomic role R or its inverse R^-.

A CQ Q has the form $\mathbf{A} \leftarrow \{\mathbf{B}_i\}_{i=1}^n$ (the sequence is a conjunction), where atom $\mathbf{A}$ is the *head* and atoms $\mathbf{B}_i$ the *body* of Q. We assume that $\mathbf{B}_i$s are distinct and denote the set of $\mathbf{B}_i$s by body Q, and $\mathbf{A}$ by head Q. A CQ Q is *posed* over an ontology $\langle \mathcal{T}, \mathcal{A} \rangle$ if the predicates of all atoms $\mathbf{B} \in$ body Q are entities of $\mathcal{T}$ and have arities 1 or 2, if the entity is a concept or a role, respectively. Hence, $\mathbf{B}$ is a *concept atom* $B(t)$ or a *role atom* $B(t, s)$. terms $\mathbf{B}$ (vars $\mathbf{B}$, cons $\mathbf{B}$) are the sets of terms (variables, constants) that appear in $\mathbf{B}$. For a set of atoms $\mathcal{B}$ we have that terms $\mathcal{B} = \bigcup_{\mathbf{B} \in \mathcal{B}}$ terms $\mathbf{B}$, for a CQ Q that terms $Q =$ terms $(\{$head $Q\} \cup$ body $Q)$, and similarly for vars Q and cons Q. An atom or CQ is *function free* if it contains no functional terms. User queries are always function free.

A term $t \in$ terms Q, where Q is a function free CQ is called *distinguished* if it appears in head Q, and *non distinguished* otherwise; *bound* if it is either a constant, or a distinguished variable, or a variable that appears at least twice in body Q, and *unbound* otherwise; and *disconnected* if there is a disconnected subgraph (V', E') of the graph (terms Q, $\{\{t, s\} \mid R(t, s)$ or $R(s, t) \in$ body $Q\})$ such that $t \in V'$ and set V' contains no distinguished term. We denote the set of bound terms, and distinguished, bound and unbound variables of Q by terms$^{\mathsf{B}} Q$, vars$^{\mathsf{D}} Q$, vars$^{\mathsf{B}} Q$ and vars$^{\mathsf{UB}} Q$, respectively. As noted in the introduction, we will assume that the user query Q is *connected*, i.e. it contains no disconnected terms. For simplicity and wlog we can also assume that Q contains no distinguished constants and that all its distinguished variables appear also in body Q.

A tuple of constants $\boldsymbol{a}$ is a *certain answer* of a CQ Q posed over the ontology $\mathcal{O} = \langle \mathcal{T}, \mathcal{A} \rangle$ iff $\Xi(\mathcal{O}) \cup \{Q\} \models C(\boldsymbol{a})$, where C is the predicate of head Q and $\Xi(\mathcal{O})$ the standard clausification of $\mathcal{O}$ into first order clauses. Each axiom of $\mathcal{O}$ adds either one or two clauses as shown in Table 1, and each axiom that contains an existential quantifier introduces a distinct function. The set that contains all answers of Q over $\mathcal{O}$ is denoted by cert $(Q, \mathcal{O})$. It has been proved [7,1] that for any CQ Q and DL-Lite$_R$ ontology $\mathcal{O}$, there is a set $\mathcal{Q}$ of function free CQs (called query rewritings) such that cert$(Q, \langle \mathcal{T}, \mathcal{A} \rangle) = \bigcup_{Q' \in \mathcal{Q}}$ cert$(Q', \langle \emptyset, \mathcal{A} \rangle)$. The set of these rewritings may be computed by saturating Q and $\Xi(\mathcal{O})$ using first order resolution. We denote derivability under the first order resolution rule by $\vdash_{\mathcal{R}}$.

Table 1. Translation of DL-Lite$_R$ axioms into clauses of $\Xi(\mathcal{O})$ (reproduced from [6])

Axiom	Clause		Axiom	Clause
$A \sqsubseteq B$	$B(x) \leftarrow A(x)$			
$P \sqsubseteq S$	$S(x, y) \leftarrow P(x, y)$		$P \sqsubseteq S^-$	$S(x, y) \leftarrow P(y, x)$
$P^- \sqsubseteq S^-$	$S(x, y) \leftarrow P(x, y)$		$P^- \sqsubseteq S$	$S(x, y) \leftarrow P(y, x)$
$\exists P \sqsubseteq A$	$A(x) \leftarrow P(x, y)$		$\exists P^- \sqsubseteq A$	$A(x) \leftarrow P(y, x)$
$A \sqsubseteq \exists P$	$P(x, f_P^A(x)) \leftarrow A(x)$		$A \sqsubseteq \exists P^-$	$P(f_{P^-}^A(x), x) \leftarrow A(x)$
$A \sqsubseteq \exists P.B$	$P(x, f_{P.B}^A(x)) \leftarrow A(x)$ $B(f_{P.B}^A(x)) \leftarrow A(x)$		$A \sqsubseteq \exists P^-.B$	$P(f_{P^-.B}^A(x), x) \leftarrow A(x)$ $B(f_{P^-.B}^A(x)) \leftarrow A(x)$

Formally, a function free CQ Q' is a *rewriting* of a CQ Q posed over ontology $\mathcal{O}$, iff Q and Q' have the same head predicate and $\Xi(\mathcal{O}) \cup \{Q\} \models Q'$. Nevertheless, not all possible rewritings are needed for the complete computation of cert $(Q, \mathcal{O})$, since some of them may be equivalent or subsumed by others. We say that a CQ Q *subsumes* a CQ Q' (or Q' *is subsumed by* Q) and write $Q \rhd Q'$, iff there is a substitution θ such that $\mathrm{head}\,(Q\theta) = \mathrm{head}\,Q'$ and $\mathrm{body}\,(Q\theta) \subseteq \mathrm{body}\,Q'$. If Q and Q' are mutually subsumed, they are *equivalent*. If $\mathcal{Q}$ is a set of CQs and for some CQ Q there is a $Q' \in \mathcal{Q}$ equivalent to Q, we write $Q \,\hat{\in}\, \mathcal{Q}$. We define also the operation $\mathcal{Q} \,\hat{\cup}\, \{Q\} = \mathcal{Q} \cup \{Q\}$ if $Q \,\hat{\notin}\, \mathcal{Q}$, and $\mathcal{Q} \,\hat{\cup}\, \{Q\} = \mathcal{Q}$ otherwise. A set $\mathrm{rewr}\,(Q, \mathcal{O})$ is a *rewriting set* of the CQ Q over $\mathcal{O}$ iff for each rewriting Q' of Q over $\mathcal{O}$, either $Q' \,\hat{\in}\, \mathrm{rewr}\,(Q, \mathcal{O})$ or there is a $Q'' \in \mathrm{rewr}\,(Q, \mathcal{O})$ such that $Q'' \rhd Q'$. Given a CQ Q, let Q' be the CQ $\mathrm{head}\,Q \leftarrow \{\mathbf{B}\}_{\mathbf{B}\in\mathcal{B}}$ for some $\mathcal{B} \subseteq \mathrm{body}\,Q$. If $\mathcal{B}$ is a minimal subset of $\mathrm{body}\,Q$ such that $Q \rhd Q'$, Q' is called *condensed* or a *condensation* of Q, and is denoted by $\mathrm{cond}\,Q$. Since a CQ is equivalent to its condensation, we can find $\mathrm{cert}\,(Q, \mathcal{O})$ by computing a rewriting set of Q that contains only condensed rewritings and that contains no two rewritings Q, Q' such that $Q \rhd Q'$. Hence, we say that Q' is a *core rewriting* of a CQ Q over $\mathcal{O}$, iff it is a rewriting of Q over O, it is condensed, and there is no (non equivalent) rewriting Q'' of Q over $\mathcal{O}$ such that $Q'' \rhd Q'$. The *core rewriting set* $\mathrm{rewr}^{\mathsf{C}}\,(Q, \mathcal{O})$ of Q over $\mathcal{O}$ is the set of all the core rewritings of Q over $\mathcal{O}$.

3   The Rapid Algorithm

Rapid computes $\mathrm{rewr}^{\mathsf{C}}\,(Q, \mathcal{O})$ for a user query Q in an efficient way. Its structure is similar to that of RQR, but it introduces several optimizations and organizes some tasks differently in order to reduce the inferences that lead to rewritings that will eventually be discarded because they are not function free or subsumed by others. The strategy of Rapid is based on the distinguishing property of the bound variables, namely that whenever a CQ Q is used as the main premise in a resolution rule in which an atom $\mathbf{A} \in \mathrm{body}\,Q$ unifies with the head of the side premise and the mgu θ contains a binding v/t for some variable $v \in \mathrm{vars}^{\mathsf{B}}\,Q$, the application of θ affects several atoms of Q apart from $\mathbf{A}$. This is not the case if $v \in \mathrm{vars}^{\mathsf{UB}}\,Q$, since unbound variables appear only once in Q. The main premise in the resolution rules in Rapid is always the user query or a rewriting of it.

Rapid consists of the following steps: (1) The *clausification* step, in which O is transformed into $\Xi(\mathcal{O})$. (2) The *shrinking* step, in which the clauses of $\Xi(\mathcal{O})$ are selectively used as side premises in resolution rule applications in order to compute rewritings which differ from the user query Q in that they do not contain one or more variables in $\mathrm{vars}^{\mathsf{B}}\,Q$, because the application of the resolution rule led to their unification with a functional term which subsequently was eliminated. (3) The *unfolding* step, which uses the results of the previous step to compute the remaining rewritings of Q, by applying the resolution rule without that the bound variables of the main premise are affected. In principle, only unbound variables are eliminated or introduced at this step. However, some bound variables of the main premise may also be eliminated, not through the introduction and subsequent elimination of functional terms, but while condensing the conclusion. Obviously, the same can also happen at the shrinking step. (4) The *subsumption check* step, in which non core rewritings are removed. This step is in principle the same as in RQR, but is more efficient in two ways: First, the previous steps produce much fewer rewritings that are subsumed by others, and second not every pair of rewritings has to be checked for subsumption, because, as we will see, some sets of rewritings that are produced at the unfolding step are guaranteed not to contain rewritings that are subsumed by others.

Notwithstanding this general description, Rapid does not implement the shrinking and unfolding steps by applying directly the resolution rule. Instead, a shrinking and unfolding inference rule are defined, which combine a series of several successful resolution rule application steps into one. In this way, the resolution rule is used only if it eventually leads to a function free and hopefully also a core rewriting, and a large number of unnecessary inferences is avoided.

3.1   Atom Unfolding Sets

The closure of $\Xi(\mathcal{O})$ under the FOL resolution rule contains clauses of the form

$$A(x) \leftarrow B(x), \qquad A(x) \leftarrow B(x,y), \quad A(x,y) \leftarrow B(x,y),$$
$$A(x,f(x)) \leftarrow B(x), \qquad\qquad\qquad A(x,f(x)) \leftarrow B(x,y),$$
$$A(g(x),f(g(x))) \leftarrow B(x), \qquad\qquad A(g(x),f(g(x))) \leftarrow B(x,y),$$
$$A(g(h(x)),f(g(h(x)))) \leftarrow B(x), \ \dots \quad A(g(h(x)),f(g(h(x)))) \leftarrow B(x,y), \ \dots$$

as well as the respective clauses with the role atom arguments inverted. We note that in the clauses of the first two rows, the non functional terms of the head appear also in the body. Based on this remark, and given that in the unfolding step we want that the bound variables do not unify with functional terms but be preserved in the conclusion, we define the unfolding of an atom as follows:

Definition 1. *Let* **A** *be a function free atom and* T *a non empty subset of* terms **A**. *Atom* **B**θ' *is an* unfolding *of* **A** *w.r.t.* T *iff* $\Xi(\mathcal{O}) \vdash_{\mathcal{R}}$ **A**$\theta \leftarrow$ **B** *for some substitution* θ *on a subset of* vars **A** $\setminus T$ *to functional terms, where* θ' *is a renaming of* vars **B** $\setminus T$ *such that for* $v \in$ vars **B** $\setminus T$ *we have that* $v\theta' \notin$ vars **A**.

Essentially, **B**θ' is an unfolding of **A** w.r.t. T if it is the body of a clause inferrable from $\Xi(\mathcal{O})$ that has in its head an atom **A**$'$ (of the same predicate as **A**), and both **B** and **A**$'$ contain unaltered all terms in T (which should contain the bound terms in **A**). Since the variable renaming θ' contains no essential information, we define the *unfolding set* of atom **A** for T w.r.t. $\Xi(\mathcal{O})$ as the set $\mathcal{D}(\mathbf{A};T) = \{\mathbf{B} \mid \Xi(\mathcal{O}) \cup \{\mathbf{A}\} \vdash_{\mathcal{J}(T)} \mathbf{B}\}$, where $\mathcal{J}(T)$ are the inference rules shown in Fig. 1, in the form $\frac{\mathbf{A}\ C}{\mathbf{B}}$. Given T, **A** (the main premise) and a clause $C \in \Xi(\mathcal{O})$ (the side premise), by applying the respective rule we get atom **B** (the conclusion). We also define the set $\hat{\mathcal{D}}(\mathbf{A};T) = \mathcal{D}(\mathbf{A};T) \cup \{\mathbf{A}\}$. By using Table 2, which lists all possible cases, it is easy to prove that given **A** and $T \neq \emptyset$ we have that $\Xi(\mathcal{O}) \vdash_{\mathcal{R}}$ **A**$\theta \leftarrow$ **B** iff **B**$\theta' \in \mathcal{D}(\mathbf{A};T)$, for θ, θ' as defined in Def. 1.

3.2   Atom Function Sets

As we have already seen, the closure of $\Xi(\mathcal{O})$ contains clauses of the form $A(x,f(x)) \leftarrow B(x)$, $A(f(x),x) \leftarrow B(x)$ and $A(f(x)) \leftarrow B(x)$, as well as of

T	rule	T	rule
$\{t\}$	$\dfrac{A(t) \quad A(x) \leftarrow B(x)}{B(t)}$		
$\{t\}$	$\dfrac{A(t) \quad A(x) \leftarrow P(x,y)}{P(t,z)}$	$\{t\}$	$\dfrac{A(t) \quad A(x) \leftarrow P(y,x)}{P(z,t)}$
$\{t\}$	$\dfrac{P(t,v) \quad P(x,f(x)) \leftarrow B(x)}{B(t)}$	$\{t\}$	$\dfrac{P(v,t) \quad P(f(x),x) \leftarrow B(x)}{B(t)}$
$\{t\},\{s\}$ or $\{t,s\}$	$\dfrac{P(t,s) \quad P(x,y) \leftarrow R(x,y)}{R(t,s)}$	$\{t\},\{s\}$ or $\{t,s\}$	$\dfrac{P(t,s) \quad P(x,y) \leftarrow R(y,x)}{R(s,t)}$

Fig. 1. The $\mathcal{J}(T)$ inference rules

Table 2. All possible cases for $\mathbf{A}$, $\mathbf{B}$, T, θ and θ' in Def. 1

$\mathbf{A}$	T	$\mathbf{B}\theta'$	$\mathbf{A}\theta \leftarrow \mathbf{B}$	θ	θ'
$A(t)$	$\{t\}$	$B(t)$	$A(t) \leftarrow B(t)$	$\emptyset$	$\emptyset$
$A(t)$	$\{t\}$	$P(t,y)\ /\ P(y,t)$	$A(t) \leftarrow P(t,z)\ /\ \leftarrow P(z,t)$	$\emptyset$	$\{z/y\}$
$P(t,v)$	$\{t\}$	$B(t)$	$P(t,f(t)) \leftarrow B(t)$	$\{v/f(t)\}$	$\emptyset$
$P(t,v)$	$\{t\}$	$R(t,y)\ /\ R(y,t)$	$P(t,f(t)) \leftarrow R(t,z)\ /\ \leftarrow R(z,t)$	$\{v/f(t)\}$	$\{z/y\}$
$P(t,t')$	$\{t\}$	$R(t,t')\ /\ R(t',t)$	$P(t,t') \leftarrow R(t,t')\ /\ \leftarrow R(t',t)$	$\emptyset$	$\emptyset$
$P(v,t)$	$\{t\}$	$B(t)$	$P(f(t),t) \leftarrow B(t)$	$\{v/f(t)\}$	$\emptyset$
$P(v,t)$	$\{t\}$	$R(t,y)\ /\ R(y,t)$	$P(f(t),t) \leftarrow R(t,z)\ /\ \leftarrow R(z,t)$	$\{v/f(t)\}$	$\{z/y\}$
$P(t',t)$	$\{t\}$	$R(t',t)\ /\ R(t,t')$	$P(t',t) \leftarrow R(t',t)\ /\ \leftarrow R(t,t')$	$\emptyset$	$\emptyset$
$P(t,s)$	$\{t,s\}$	$R(t,s)\ /\ R(s,t)$	$P(t,s) \leftarrow R(t,s)\ /\ \leftarrow R(s,t)$	$\emptyset$	$\emptyset$

the form $A(g(x), f(g(x))) \leftarrow B(x)$ and $A(g(x), f(g(x))) \leftarrow B(x,y)$. Unlike in the unfolding case, now we are interested in the behavior of the functional term $f(x)$, which appears in the head but not in the body, because if $f(x)$ appears in the body of some rewriting, it may be possible to eliminate it by using such clauses. Let funcs $\Xi(\mathcal{O})$ be the set of all functions in $\Xi(\mathcal{O})$. According to Table 1, each DL-Lite$_R$ axiom that has an existential quantifier in the RHS introduces a distinct function f. Hence, each function $f \in$ funcs $\Xi(\mathcal{O})$ is uniquely associated with the concept A that appears in the LHS of the axiom that introduces f. Let cn f denote the concept associated with f. We define the set of all functions that may appear in the place of a bound variable v of an atom $\mathbf{A}$ when resolving any of its unfoldings with a non function free clause in $\Xi(\mathcal{O})$ as follows:

Definition 2. *Let $\mathbf{A}$ be a function free atom, T a non empty subset of* terms $\mathbf{A}$ *and v a variable in* vars $\mathbf{A} \cap T$. *The function set $\mathcal{F}_v(\mathbf{A};T)$ of all functions associated with $\mathbf{A}$ in variable v w.r.t. T is defined as follows:*

$$\mathcal{F}_v(\mathbf{A};T) = \begin{aligned} &\{f \mid B(v) \in \hat{\mathcal{D}}(\mathbf{A};T) \text{ and } B(f(x)) \leftarrow (\text{cn } f)(x) \in \Xi(\mathcal{O})\} \cup \\ &\{f \mid B(v,t) \in \hat{\mathcal{D}}(\mathbf{A};T) \text{ and } B(f(x),x) \leftarrow (\text{cn } f)(x) \in \Xi(\mathcal{O})\} \cup \\ &\{f \mid B(t,v) \in \hat{\mathcal{D}}(\mathbf{A};T) \text{ and } B(x,f(x)) \leftarrow (\text{cn } f)(x) \in \Xi(\mathcal{O})\}. \end{aligned}$$

It follows that, given a $T \neq \emptyset$ which represents the set of bound terms in $\mathbf{A}$, (a) if $\mathbf{A} \equiv A(v,t)$ then $f \in \mathcal{F}_v(\mathbf{A};T)$ iff $\Xi(\mathcal{O}) \vdash_{\mathcal{R}} A(f(t),s) \leftarrow (\text{cn } f)(t)$, (b) if $\mathbf{A} \equiv A(t,v)$ then $f \in \mathcal{F}_v(\mathbf{A};T)$ iff $\varXi(\mathcal{O}) \vdash_{\mathcal{R}} A(s,f(t)) \leftarrow (\mathsf{cn}\,f)(t)$, where in both cases $s = t$ if $t \in T$ otherwise either $s = t$, or $s = g(f(t))$ for some function g, and (c) if $\mathbf{A} \equiv A(v)$ then $f \in \mathcal{F}_v(\mathbf{A};T)$ iff $\varXi(\mathcal{O}) \vdash_{\mathcal{R}} A(f(t)) \leftarrow (\mathsf{cn}\,f)(t)$.

Example 1. Define the ontology $\mathcal{O} = \{B \sqsubseteq A, \exists R \sqsubseteq A, S \sqsubseteq R^-, C \sqsubseteq \exists R.A,$ $\exists T^- \sqsubseteq C, D \sqsubseteq \exists S\}$, hence $\varXi(\mathcal{O}) = \{A(x) \leftarrow B(x), A(x) \leftarrow R(x,y), R(x,y) \leftarrow S(y,x), R(x,f_1(x)) \leftarrow C(x), A(f_1(x)) \leftarrow C(x), C(x) \leftarrow T(y,x), S(x,f_2(x)) \leftarrow D(x)\}$. Below we show the unfolding and function sets for the atoms $A(x)$, $C(x)$, $R(x,y)$ and $S(x,y)$ and some sets T. E.g. for $T = \{y\}$, main premise $R(x,y)$ and side premise $R(x,y) \leftarrow S(y,x)$, from Fig. 1 we get $S(y,x)$. Then (given that $x \notin T$), for main premise $S(y,x)$ and side premise $S(x,f_2(x)) \leftarrow D(x)$ we get $D(y)$. Because $R(x,f_1(x)) \leftarrow C(x) \in \varXi(\mathcal{O})$, we get that $\mathcal{F}_y(R(x,y);\{y\}) = \{f_1\}$.

$\mathbf{A};T$	$A(x);\{x\}$	$C(x);\{x\}$	$R(x,y);\{x\}$	$R(x,y);\{y\}$	$R(x,y);\{x,y\}$	$S(x,y);\{x\}$
	$B(x)$	$T(z_3,x)$	$S(y,x)$	$S(y,x)$	$S(y,x)$	$D(x)$
	$R(x,z_1)$		$C(x)$	$D(y)$		
$\mathcal{D}(\mathbf{A};T)$	$S(z_1,x)$		$T(z_4,x)$			
	$C(x)$					
	$T(z_2,x)$					
$\mathcal{F}_x(\mathbf{A};T)$	$\{f_1,f_2\}$	$\emptyset$	$\{f_2\}$	$\emptyset$	$\{f_2\}$	$\emptyset$
$\mathcal{F}_y(\mathbf{A};T)$	$-$	$-$	$\emptyset$	$\{f_1\}$	$\{f_1\}$	$-$

3.3   Query Shrinking

The shrinking step computes rewritings that can be inferred from the user query Q by eliminating one or more of its bound variables through their unification with a functional term. Given that the rewritings in $\mathsf{rewr}\,(Q,\mathcal{O})$ are function free, if a function is introduced in some rewriting during the standard resolution-based inference process, subsequently it must be eliminated. However, we know that each function appears in at most two clauses of $\varXi(\mathcal{O})$, both of which have as body the atom $(\mathsf{cn}\,f)(x)$. Now, $f(x)$ can be introduced in a CQ only if some inference led to the substitution of a bound variable v by $f(x)$. Hence, in order for $f(x)$ to be eliminated, all atoms in which $f(x)$ has been introduced must contain f in their function sets, for the appropriate argument. Moreover, if Q contains the terms say $R(x,v)$ and $R(v,y)$ and v is eliminated this way by unifying with $f(x)$, given the form of $\varXi(O)$, variables x and y must be unified. If in place of x, y there are constants, these should coincide in order for the inference to be possible. This is the intuition behind the following shrinking inference rule:

Definition 3. *Let Q be a CQ and v a non distinguished bound variable of Q. Write Q in the form $\mathbf{A} \leftarrow \mathbf{B}_1,\ldots,\mathbf{B}_k,\mathbf{C}_1,\ldots,\mathbf{C}_n$, where $\mathbf{B}_i$ are the atoms in body Q that contain v, and $\mathbf{C}_i$ the remaining atoms. Let also $\mathcal{C} = \bigcup_{i=1}^k \mathsf{cons}\,\mathbf{B}_i$ and $\mathcal{X} = \bigcup_{i=1}^k (\mathsf{vars}^{\mathsf{B}}\,Q \cap \mathsf{vars}\,\mathbf{B}_i) \setminus v$. The shrinking rule $\mathcal{S}$ on Q is as follows:*

$$\frac{\mathbf{A} \leftarrow \mathbf{B}_1,\ldots,\mathbf{B}_k,\mathbf{C}_1,\ldots,\mathbf{C}_n \qquad f \in \bigcap_{i=1}^k \mathcal{F}_v(\mathbf{B}_i; \mathsf{terms}^{\mathsf{B}}\,Q \cap \mathsf{terms}\,\mathbf{B}_i) \wedge |\mathcal{C}| \leq 1}{\mathsf{cond}\,(\mathbf{A}\theta \leftarrow (\mathsf{cn}\,f)(t), \mathbf{C}_1\theta,\ldots,\mathbf{C}_n\theta)}$$

where $\theta = \bigcup_{x \in \mathcal{X}} \{x/t\}$, and $t = a$ if $\mathcal{C} = \{a\}$ otherwise t is a variable $\notin \mathsf{vars}\, Q$.

The shrinking rule changes the structure of Q, in the sense that it eliminates a bound variable, and hence the atoms that contained it. Moreover, all variables in $\mathcal{X}$ are also merged into one. It is easy to prove that $\mathcal{S}$ is a sound inference rule, i.e. if $\Xi(\mathcal{O}) \cup \{Q\} \vdash_{\mathcal{S}} Q'$ then $\Xi(\mathcal{O}) \cup \{Q\} \models Q'$, for any CQ Q'.

3.4   Query Unfolding

Let $\mathcal{S}^*(Q)$ be the closure of $\mathsf{cond}\, Q$ under application of the inference rule $\mathcal{S}$, for any CQ Q. By construction, $\mathcal{S}^*(Q)$ contains a 'representative' for all query structures that can result from Q by eliminating one or more variables in $\mathsf{vars}^{\mathsf{B}}\, Q$ by using functional terms. This representative can be considered as a 'top' query, in the sense that in can produce several more CQs with no further structural changes due to bindings of bound variables with functional terms. Hence, the remaining rewritings can be obtained by computing, for each $Q' \in \mathcal{S}^*(Q)$, all CQs that can be inferred from Q' by replacing one or more of its atoms by one of their unfoldings. In this way we can eventually compute all rewritings of Q. This can be achieved by applying the following unfolding inference rule:

Definition 4. *Let Q be the CQ $\mathbf{A} \leftarrow \mathbf{B}_1, \ldots, \mathbf{B}_n$. The* unfolding rule $\mathcal{U}$ *on Q is defined as follows:*

$$\frac{\mathbf{A} \leftarrow \mathbf{B}_1, \ldots, \mathbf{B}_n \qquad \mathbf{C} \in \mathcal{D}(\mathbf{B}_i; \mathsf{terms}^{\mathsf{B}}\, Q \cap \mathsf{terms}\, \mathbf{B}_i)}{\mathsf{cond}\,(\mathbf{A} \leftarrow \mathbf{B}_1, \ldots, \mathbf{B}_{i-1}, \mathbf{C}\gamma, \mathbf{B}_{i+1}, \ldots, \mathbf{B}_n)}$$

where γ is a renaming of $\mathsf{vars}\, \mathbf{C} \setminus \mathsf{vars}^{\mathsf{B}}\, Q$ such that $x\gamma \notin \bigcup_{j=1, j \neq i}^{n} \mathsf{vars}\, \mathbf{B}_j$ for all $x \in \mathsf{vars}\, \mathbf{C} \setminus \mathsf{vars}^{\mathsf{B}}\, Q$.

It follows immediately that $\mathcal{U}$ is a sound inference rule, i.e. if $\Xi(\mathcal{O}) \cup \{Q\} \vdash_{\mathcal{U}} Q'$ then $\Xi(\mathcal{O}) \cup \{Q\} \models Q'$. Rule $\mathcal{U}$ replaces one atom of Q by one of its unfoldings, and can be applied iteratively on the conclusion in order to produce more rewritings. In order to facilitate the optimization of such a sequential application of the $\mathcal{U}$ rule on some rewriting, we define the *combined unfolding rule* $\mathcal{W}$ which can replace in one step more than one atoms of Q by one of their unfoldings. In this way, any unfolding of Q can be obtained in one step.

Definition 5. *An* unfolding *of CQ $Q : \mathbf{A} \leftarrow \mathbf{B}_1, \ldots, \mathbf{B}_n$, is the conclusion of any application of the following* combined unfolding rule $\mathcal{W}$:

$$\frac{\mathbf{A} \leftarrow \mathbf{B}_1, \ldots, \mathbf{B}_n \qquad \mathbf{C}_i \in \hat{\mathcal{D}}(\mathbf{B}_i; \mathsf{terms}^{\mathsf{B}}\, Q \cap \mathsf{terms}\, \mathbf{B}_i) \text{ for } i = 1 \ldots n}{\mathsf{cond}\,(\mathbf{A} \leftarrow \mathbf{C}_1\gamma_1, \ldots, \mathbf{C}_n\gamma_n)}$$

where γ_i is a renaming of $\mathsf{vars}\, \mathbf{C}_i \setminus \mathsf{terms}^{\mathsf{B}}\, Q$ such that $x\gamma_i \notin \bigcup_{j=1, j \neq i}^{n} \mathsf{vars}\,(\mathbf{C}_j\gamma_j)$ for all $x \in \mathsf{vars}\, \mathbf{C}_i \setminus \mathsf{terms}^{\mathsf{B}}\, Q$.

Let $\mathcal{W}^*(Q)$ be the closure of $\mathsf{cond}\, Q$ under application of the inference rule $\mathcal{W}$, for any CQ Q. The strategy by which Rapid computes the core rewriting set of a user query Q is justified by the following theorem:

Theorem 1. *Let Q be a connected CQ over a DL-Lite$_R$ ontology $\mathcal{O}$. We have that if $Q' \in \bigcup_{Q'' \in \mathcal{S}^*(Q)} \mathcal{W}^*(Q'')$ then $Q' \,\hat{\in}\, \text{rewr}(Q, \mathcal{O})$ (soundness), and that if $Q' \in \text{rewr}^C(Q, \mathcal{O})$ then $Q' \,\hat{\in}\, \bigcup_{Q'' \in \mathcal{S}^*(Q)} \mathcal{W}^*(Q'')$ (completeness).*

Proof (Sketch). Soundness follows from the soundness of the $\mathcal{S}$ and $\mathcal{W}$ rules. For completeness, if Q' is the final conclusion of a sequence of resolutions with main premises $Q, Q_1, \ldots, Q_{l-1}$, we must show that there is a sequence of shrinking rule applications with main premises $Q, Q_1^s, \ldots, Q_{l_s-1}^s$ and final conclusion $Q_{l_s}^s$, and a sequence of unfolding rule applications with main premises $Q_{l_s}^s, Q_1^u, \ldots, Q_{l_u-1}^u$ and final conclusion Q'. $Q_1, \ldots, Q_{l-1}$ may contain functional terms of the form $f_1(\cdots f_k(t))$ for $k > 0$ (k is called depth*). Since Q and Q' are both function free, any functional terms eventually are eliminated. The result can be proved by induction on the maximum depth d of the intermediate CQs $Q_1, \ldots, Q_{l-2}$, by showing that the sequence of resolutions that led to the introduction of a functional term of depth d can be rearranged so that only functional terms of depth 1 are introduced. Because the shrinking rule considers by definition all functional terms that may be introduced at any step of the resolution process, it can be applied first, thus giving rise to the shrinking rule application sequence, on whose final conclusion the unfolding rule is then applied, in order to get Q'.*

Note that if we wanted to lift the restriction to connected queries, we should take into account atoms containing only unbound variables. Such a variable may unify with a functional term and give its place to a new unbound variable. Hence, we should allow empty sets T in Def. 1 and include the appropriate rules in $\mathcal{J}(T)$, e.g. rule $\frac{A(t)\, A(f(x)) \leftarrow B(x)}{B(z)}$ for $T = \emptyset$, which 'replaces' variable t by z.

4   Implementation

The implementation of Rapid includes additional optimizations at the unfolding step that reduce the number of non core rewritings that are produced and hence the need for extended subsumption checks. Rapid (Algorithm 3) uses procedures SHRINK and UNFOLD (Algorithms 1 and 2). SHRINK computes the closure $\mathcal{S}^*(Q)$ by iteratively applying the shrinking rule. Each rewriting produced by SHRINK is processed by UNFOLD, which computes two disjoint sets of rewritings. We will now discuss their contents and explain the optimizations that have been used.

If we apply exhaustively the $\mathcal{W}$ rule on a CQ Q in order to get $\mathcal{W}^*(Q)$, we may end up with many rewritings subsumed by others. Since this is undesired, we have two options: to compute all rewritings and then remove the subsumed ones, or else try to apply $\mathcal{W}$ in a cleverer way, so as to get only non subsumed rewritings, or at least as few as possible. Because the subsumption check operation is very costly, we choose the second option, i.e. we have to solve the following problem: Given a CQ Q of the form $\mathbf{A} \leftarrow \mathbf{B}_1, \ldots, \mathbf{B}_n$, find the CQs that are conclusions of all possible applications of $\mathcal{W}$ on Q and are not subsumed by others. For convenience, define $\mathcal{B}_i = \hat{\mathcal{D}}(\mathbf{B}_i; \text{terms}^B\, Q \cap \text{terms}\, \mathbf{B}_i)$, so that we have the sequence of the possibly non disjoint unfolding sets $\mathcal{B}_1, \ldots, \mathcal{B}_n$. For simplicity, we can drop

Algorithm 1 The query shrinking procedure

---

procedure SHRINK(CQ Q, ontology $\mathcal{O}$)
    $\mathcal{Q}_r \leftarrow \{Q\}$
    for all unconsidered $Q' \in \mathcal{Q}_r$ **do**
        mark Q' as considered
        for all $v \in \mathsf{vars}^\mathsf{B}\,Q' \setminus \mathsf{vars}^\mathsf{D}\,Q'$ **do**
            $\mathcal{F} \leftarrow \mathsf{funcs}\,\Xi(\mathcal{O})$; $\mathcal{X} \leftarrow \emptyset$; $\mathcal{C} \leftarrow \emptyset$; $\mathcal{A} \leftarrow \emptyset$
            for all $\mathbf{B} \in \mathsf{body}\,Q'$ **do**
                if $v \in \mathsf{vars}\,\mathbf{B}$ **then**
                    $\mathcal{F} \leftarrow \mathcal{F} \cap \mathcal{F}_v(\mathbf{B}; \mathsf{terms}^\mathsf{B}\,Q' \cap \mathsf{terms}\,\mathbf{B})$
                    $\mathcal{X} \leftarrow \mathcal{X} \cup (\mathsf{vars}^\mathsf{B}\,Q' \cap \mathsf{vars}\,\mathbf{B})$; $\mathcal{C} \leftarrow \mathcal{C} \cup \mathsf{cons}\,\mathbf{B}$
                else
                    $\mathcal{A} \leftarrow \mathcal{A} \cup \{\mathbf{B}\}$
                end if
            end for
            if $|\mathcal{C}| > 1$ **then**
                continue
            else if $|\mathcal{C}| = \{a\}$ **then**
                $t \leftarrow a$
            else
                $t \leftarrow$ a new variable not in $\mathsf{vars}\,Q'$
            end if
            $\theta \leftarrow \bigcup_{x \in \mathcal{X}} \{x/t\}$
            $\mathcal{Q}_r \leftarrow \mathcal{Q}_r \,\hat{\bigcup}_{f \in \mathcal{F}} \{\mathsf{cond}\,(\mathsf{head}\,Q'\theta \leftarrow (\mathsf{cf}\,f)(t), \{\mathbf{B}\theta\}_{\mathbf{B} \in \mathcal{A}})\}$
        end for
    end for
    return $\mathcal{Q}_r$
end procedure

---

the substitutions γ_i that appear in the definition of $\mathcal{W}$ by assuming that if a member of a set $\mathcal{B}_j$ has been obtained by an inference that introduced a new variable, this variable does not appear elsewhere in $\bigcup_{i=1}^n \mathcal{B}_i$. If the sets $\mathcal{B}_i$ are not disjoint, simply taking all possible combinations of their elements so as to form the unfoldings of Q, will certainly result in rewritings subsumed by others.

For any $\mathbf{B} \in \bigcup_{i=1}^n \mathcal{B}_i$, define the set $\mathsf{ind}\,\mathbf{B} = \{j \mid \mathbf{B} \in \mathcal{B}_j\}$ of the indices of all the unfolding sets that contain $\mathbf{B}$. We call the set $\mathcal{A} = \{\mathbf{A}_1, \ldots, \mathbf{A}_k\}$ with $k \leq n$ a *selection* for Q iff (a) $\bigcup_{i=1}^k \mathsf{ind}\,\mathbf{A}_i = \mathbb{N}_n$ (where $\mathbb{N}_n \doteq \{1, \ldots, n\}$), and (b) $\mathsf{ind}\,\mathbf{A}_i \setminus \mathsf{ind}\,\mathbf{A}_j \neq \emptyset$ for all $i, j \in \mathbb{N}_k$, i.e. if $\mathcal{A}$ contains at least one atom from each unfolding set and no two sets $\mathsf{ind}\,\mathbf{A}_i$ overlap fully. Clearly, a selection corresponds to an unfolding of Q, in particular to $\mathsf{head}\,Q \leftarrow \mathbf{A}_1, \ldots, \mathbf{A}_k$. However, we are interested in *minimal selections*, which correspond to non subsumed rewritings. We call a selection $\mathcal{A}$ for Q minimal, iff there is no selection $\mathcal{A}'$ for Q such that $\mathcal{A}' \subset \mathcal{A}$, i.e. if in addition to the above we have that $\mathsf{ind}\,\mathbf{A}_i \setminus \left(\bigcup_{j=1, j \neq i}^k \mathsf{ind}\,\mathbf{A}_j \right) \neq \emptyset$ for all $i \in \mathbb{N}_k$, i.e. if all the atoms $\mathbf{A}_i$ need to be present in $\mathcal{A}$ in order for $\bigcup_{i=1}^k \mathsf{ind}\,\mathbf{A}_i = \mathbb{N}_n$ to hold. If this were not the case for some $\mathbf{A}_i$, we could form the selection $\mathcal{A}' = \{\mathbf{A}_1, \ldots, \mathbf{A}_{j-1}, \mathbf{A}_{j+1}, \mathbf{A}_k\} \subset \mathcal{A}$, hence $\mathcal{A}$ would not be minimal.

Algorithm 2 The query unfolding procedure

procedure UNFOLD(CQ Q of the form $\mathbf{A} \leftarrow \mathbf{B}_1, \ldots, \mathbf{B}_n$, ontology $\mathcal{O}$)
   $\mathcal{Q} \leftarrow \emptyset;\ \hat{\mathcal{Q}} \leftarrow \emptyset$
   for $i = 1 \ldots n$ **do**
      $\mathcal{B}_i \leftarrow \hat{\mathcal{D}}(\mathbf{B}_i; \mathsf{terms}^\mathsf{B}\, Q) \cap \mathsf{terms}\, \mathbf{B}_i);\ \hat{\mathcal{B}}_i \leftarrow \emptyset$
   end for
   for $i = 1 \ldots n$ **and for all** role atoms $\mathbf{A} \in \mathcal{B}_i$ **do**
      for $j = 1 \ldots n, j \neq i$ **and for all** role atoms $\mathbf{A}' \in \mathcal{B}_j$ **do**
         if $\exists \theta$ on vars $\mathbf{A}' \setminus \mathsf{vars}^\mathsf{B}\, Q$ such that $\mathbf{A}'\theta = \mathbf{A}$ **then**
            $\hat{\mathcal{B}}_j \leftarrow \hat{\mathcal{B}}_j \cup \{\mathbf{A}\}$
         end if
      end for
   end for
   for all selections $\mathbf{C}_1, \ldots, \mathbf{C}_k$ from $\mathcal{B}_1 \cup \hat{\mathcal{B}}_1, \ldots, \mathcal{B}_n \cup \hat{\mathcal{B}}_n$ **do**
      if $\mathsf{ind}\, \mathbf{C}_i \setminus \bigcup_{j=1 \ldots k, j \neq i} \mathsf{ind}\, \mathbf{C}_j \neq \emptyset$ for all i **then**
         if $\exists j$ such that $\mathbf{C}_i \in \hat{\mathcal{B}}_j$ for some i **then**
            $\hat{\mathcal{Q}} \leftarrow \hat{\mathcal{Q}} \,\hat{\cup}\, \{Q\}$
         else
            $\mathcal{Q} \leftarrow \mathcal{Q} \,\hat{\cup}\, \{Q\}$
         end if
      end if
   end for
   return $[\mathcal{Q}, \hat{\mathcal{Q}}]$
end procedure

The unfolding step in Rapid computes efficiently the minimal selections for a CQ Q by finding the common elements of the unfolding sets $\mathcal{B}_i$ and enforcing the above conditions. Although the set of unfoldings obtained by the minimal selections for Q contains no subsumed rewrittings, in general, the same will not hold for the union of the unfoldings of two distinct CQs Q_1 and Q_2 obtained at the shrinking step. The need for subsumption checks remains, however their number is much less, since the unfoldings of Q_1 have to be checked only against the unfoldings of Q_2 and vice versa, and not also against the unfoldings of Q_1.

The computation of the minimal selections as described above takes into account the equality between the elements of the unfolding sets, but not subsumption relations. However, an unfolding set $\mathcal{B}_i$ may contain an atom with an unbound variable that unifies with an atom of another set $\mathcal{B}_j$ that contains only bound variables. In order to address this issue we compute all such bindings in advance and include the respective atoms in the sets $\hat{\mathcal{B}}_i$, defined for this purpose. In particular, if for some $i, j \in \mathbb{N}_n$ we have that $\mathbf{A} \in \mathcal{B}_i$, $\mathbf{A}' \in \mathcal{B}_j$ and there is a substitution θ on vars $\mathbf{A}' \setminus \mathsf{vars}^\mathsf{B}\, Q$ such that $\mathbf{A}'\theta = \mathbf{A}$, we add $\mathbf{A}$ to $\hat{\mathcal{B}}_j$. We call the minimal selections for Q that contain an atom that appears in some $\hat{\mathcal{B}}_j$ *impure*. Their inclusion in the result does not affect soundness, since we have only replaced an unbound variable of $\mathbf{A}'$ by a bound variable of $\mathbf{A}$. However, an impure selection may result in an unfolding that subsumes or is subsumed by an unfolding given by another minimal selection for Q. For this reason, UNFOLD

Algorithm 3 The Rapid algorithm

procedure RAPID(connected CQ Q, ontology $\mathcal{O}$)
    $Q_f = \emptyset$
    for all $Q_s \in$ SHRINK$(Q, \mathcal{O})$ **do**
        $[\mathcal{Q}, \hat{\mathcal{Q}}] \leftarrow$ UNFOLD$(Q_s, \mathcal{O})$; $Q_t \leftarrow \emptyset$
        for all $Q' \in \mathcal{Q}$ **do**
            if cond Q' coincides with Q' **then**
                $Q_t \leftarrow Q_t \cup \{Q'\}$
            else
                $Q_f \leftarrow Q_f \cup \{\{\text{cond } Q'\}\}$
            end if
        end for
        $Q_f \leftarrow Q_f \cup \{Q_t\} \cup \bigcup_{Q' \in \hat{\mathcal{Q}}} \{\{\text{cond } Q'\}\}$
    end for
    return CHECKSUBSUMPTION(Q_f)
end procedure

---

distinguishes between the two sets of unfoldings and returns them in the sets $\mathcal{Q}$ and $\hat{\mathcal{Q}}$, which contain the unfoldings resulting from the pure and impure minimal selections, respectively.

The final step of Rapid is the check for subsumed rewritings within the results of UNFOLD. The check is done after first grouping the results into sets that are known not to contain subsumed rewritings. These are the sets of pure unfoldings returned by UNFOLD, excluding the unfoldings that do not coincide with their condensations. The condensation of each such query, as well as each impure unfolding forms a separate set. These sets are processed by CHECKSUBSUMPTION which checks for subsumption across sets only. We also note that UNFOLD applies rule $\mathcal{W}$ only on its input Q and not iteratively also on the conclusions. This does not affect completeness, because at the application of $\mathcal{W}$ bound terms may become unbound or eliminated only at the condensation step; this is the last step of the $\mathcal{W}$ rule, hence no rewriting is lost. However, it may be the case that an unbound variable v of such a conclusion, which was bound in Q, unifies with a functional term of a clause in $\Xi(\mathcal{O})$ and hence is eventually eliminated. If this is the case, variable v would have been eliminated also earlier at an application of the shrinking rule, hence again completeness is not affected. The algorithm terminates because when computing the unfolding sets or applying the $\mathcal{S}$ rule, atoms or clauses equivalent to already computed ones are not considered again.

Example 2. Consider the CQ $Q(x) \leftarrow A(x), R(x, y), A(y), S(x, z)$ posed over the ontology of Ex. 1. We have $\mathsf{vars}^D Q = \{x\}$, $\mathsf{vars}^B Q = \{x, y\}$ and $\mathsf{vars}^{UB} Q = \{z\}$. From Ex. 1 we know that $\mathcal{F}_y(R(x, y); \{x, y\}) \cap \mathcal{F}_y(A(y); \{y\}) = \{f_1\}$ and given that cn $f_1 = C$, the SHRINK procedures returns the rewritings $Q_1 : Q(x) \leftarrow A(x), R(x, y), A(y), S(x, z)$ (the initial CQ) and $Q_2 : Q(x) \leftarrow A(x), C(x), S(x, z)$, which are subsequently processed by the UNFOLD procedure. We have that $\mathsf{vars}^B Q_1 = \{x, y\}$ and $\mathsf{vars}^B Q_2 = \{x\}$. The sets $\mathcal{B}_i$ and $\hat{\mathcal{B}}_i$ for Q_1 and Q_2 are shown below (for convenience unbound variables have been replaced by $*$).

i	1	2	3	4
$\mathcal{B}_i$	$A(x)$ $B(x)$ $R(x,*)$ $S(*,x)$ $C(x)$ $T(*,x)$	$R(x,y)^{\{1,2\}}$ $S(y,x)^{\{1,2\}}$	$A(y)$ $B(y)$ $R(y,*)$ $S(*,y)$ $C(y)$ $T(*,y)$	$S(x,*)$ $D(x)$
$\hat{\mathcal{B}}_i$	$R(x,y)^{\{1,2\}}$ $S(y,x)^{\{1,2\}}$			

i	1	2	3
$\mathcal{B}_i$	$A(x)$ $B(x)$ $R(x,*)$ $S(*,x)$ $C(x)^{\{1,2\}}$ $T(*,x)^{\{1,2\}}$	$C(x)^{\{1,2\}}$ $T(*,x)^{\{1,2\}}$	$S(x,*)$ $D(x)$
$\hat{\mathcal{B}}_i$			

E.g. we add $R(x,y)$ to $\hat{\mathcal{B}}_1$ because $\mathcal{B}_1$ contains $R(x,*)$ which subsumes $R(x,y)$ in $\mathcal{B}_2$. For the atoms $\mathbf{A}$ for which $|\text{ind}\,\mathbf{A}| > 1$ the tables show the sets $\text{ind}\,\mathbf{A}$ in superscript. Since in both Q_1 and Q_2, for all atoms $\mathbf{A}$ in $\mathcal{B}_2$ we have $\text{ind}\,\mathbf{A} = \{1,2\}$, Rapid computes no unfoldings with atoms that appear only in $\mathcal{B}_1$, because they are subsumed (e.g. for Q_2 the CQ $Q(x) \leftarrow A(x), C(x), S(x,z)$ is subsumed by $Q(x) \leftarrow C(x), S(x,z)$). So, we get $24\,(= 2 \cdot 6 \cdot 2)$ rewritings from Q_1 and $4\,(= 2 \cdot 2)$ from Q_2. The unfoldings of Q_1 are all impure (they contain atoms in $\hat{\mathcal{B}}_1$) while those of Q_2 are all pure. All of them are finally checked for subsumption, but the check within the set of the unfoldings of Q_2 is skipped because we know that it contains no subsumed rewritings. Finally, we get 28 core rewritings.

5   Evaluation

We evaluated Rapid by comparing it with Requiem, the implementation of RQR. We used the same datasets as in [6], namely the V, S, U, A, P5, UX, AX, P5X ontologies. (V models European history, S European financial institutions, and A information about abilities, disabilities and devices. U is a DL-Lite$_R$ version of the LUBM benchmark ontology. P5 is synthetic and models graphs with paths of length 5. UX, AX and P5X are obtained by rewriting U, A and P5 without qualified existential restrictions). The results (for a Java implementation on a 3GHz processor PC) are shown in Table 3. T_A is the rewriting computation time without the final subsumption check step, and T_R the total time including this step. Similarly, R_A is the size of the (non core) rewriting set when omitting the subsumption check step, and R_F the size of the core rewriting set. As expected, both systems compute the same number of core rewritings.

The results show clearly the efficiency of Rapid. It is always faster and in several cases the improvement is very significant. The efficiency is more evident if we compare the results before and after the subsumption check step. In most cases, the number of rewritings discarded as subsumed in this step is small. Hence, by omitting it we would still get a 'good' result, but gain possibly a lot in time. The subsumption check step is very expensive, although our optimizations significantly reduced its cost too. The most striking case is ontology AX and query 5, in which Rapid completes the computation of the 32,921 core rewritings in less than 1 min, while Requiem needs about 2 hours. Moreover, Rapid needs only to 2.1 sec to compute a set containing only 35 non core rewritings and

Table 3. Evaluation results. *The greedy modality provided by the Requiem system applies forward query subsumption, dependency graph pruning and greedy unfolding.

$\mathcal{O}$	Q	Rapid				Requiem (greedy modality*)			
		T_A	T_F	R_A	R_F	T_A	T_F	R_A	R_F
	1	.001	.001	15	15	.001	.001	15	15
	2	.001	.001	10	10	.001	.001	10	10
V	3	.001	.001	72	72	.016	.016	72	72
	4	.015	.015	185	185	.031	.062	185	185
	5	.016	.016	30	30	.001	.015	30	30
	1	.001	.001	6	6	.001	.001	6	6
	2	.001	.001	2	2	.031	.062	160	2
S	3	.001	.001	4	4	.187	.515	480	4
	4	.001	.001	4	4	.406	1.047	960	4
	5	.001	.001	8	8	5.594	17.984	2,880	8
	1	.001	.001	2	2	.001	.001	2	2
	2	.001	.001	1	1	.031	.047	148	1
U	3	.001	.001	4	4	.047	.109	224	4
	4	.001	.001	2	2	.625	2.031	1,628	2
	5	.001	.001	10	10	2.187	7.781	2,960	10
	1	.001	.001	27	27	.031	.047	121	27
	2	.001	.001	54	50	.031	.047	78	50
A	3	.016	.016	104	104	.047	.063	104	104
	4	.031	.031	320	224	.078	.156	304	224
	5	.062	.078	624	624	.188	.610	624	624
	1	.001	.001	6	6	.001	.001	6	6
	2	.001	.001	10	10	.015	.015	10	10
P5	3	.001	.001	13	13	.047	.047	13	13
	4	.015	.015	15	15	.688	.688	15	15
	5	.015	.015	16	16	16.453	16.453	16	16
	1	.001	.001	14	14	.001	.001	14	14
	2	.001	.001	25	25	.031	.031	77	25
P5X	3	.015	.031	112	58	.125	.297	390	58
	4	.062	.109	561	179	2.453	7.375	1,953	179
	5	.344	1.313	2,805	718	1:10.141	3:48.690	9,766	718
	1	.001	.001	5	5	.001	.001	5	5
	2	.001	.001	1	1	.031	.078	240	1
UX	3	.001	.001	12	12	.391	1.125	1,008	12
	4	.001	.001	5	5	5.187	19.375	5,000	5
	5	.015	.125	25	25	15.125	57.672	8,000	25
	1	.001	.001	41	41	.047	.063	132	41
	2	.093	.140	1,546	1,431	.703	2.781	1,632	1,431
AX	3	.297	.672	4,466	4,466	6.484	29.109	4,752	4,466
	4	.219	.625	4,484	3,159	5.282	23.516	4,960	3,159
	5	2.140	43.374	32,956	32,921	27:04.006	1:56:21.585	76,032	32,921

then some 40 seconds to detect them, while Requiem computes 43,111 non core rewritings and needs 1.5 hours to detect and remove them.

We comment on two cases that illustrate best the efficiency of the shrinking and unfolding steps in Rapid. In ontology $P5$, where query i asks for nodes from which paths of length i start, the performance of Rapid is essentially unaffected by the query size, unlike Requiem which is not scalable. This is due to the efficiency of the shrinking inference rule, which fires only if it leads to a useful, function free rewriting. In RQR, resolution is performed exhaustively, leading to a large number of non function free rewritings that are eventually discarded. In ontology U, the superior performance of Rapid is due to the efficiency of the unfolding step, in particular to the non computation of subsumed unfoldings. In query 5, at the end of the unfolding step Rapid has computed only 8 rewritings, which are the final core rewritings. In contrast, Requiem computes 2,880, which need to be checked for subsumption. In the general case the superior performance of Rapid is due to the combined efficiency of the shrinking and unfolding steps.

Before concluding this section we should note, however, that Requiem, being an $\mathcal{EL}$ reasoner, is not optimized for DL-Lite$_R$. Nevertheless, in [6] which compares Requiem with CGLLR, an implementation of the authors of the PerfectRef algorithm, Requiem shows already a better performance.

6   Conclusions

We have presented Rapid, a new algorithm for the efficient computation of the core rewriting set of connected queries posed over DL-Lite$_R$ ontologies. Rapid optimizes the inference process by replacing the application of the first order resolution rule by specialized shrinking and unfolding rules, which save the algorithm from many unnecessary rewritings, subsumption checks and blind inference paths. The experimental evaluation of Rapid showed a significant performance benefit if compared to RQR, which in several practical cases can alleviate the exponential behavior. The specialized inference rules differentiate Rapid from pure resolution-based algorithms, however it remains committed to the computation of set of rewritings (i.e. of a UCQ), unlike recent approaches [8] which compute non recursive datalog programs, deferring thus the complexity to the underlying database system. The performance benefit that may result from computing and executing a non recursive datalog program instead of a rewriting set equivalent to a UCQ largely depends on the way relational engines deal with such datalog programs and needs to be better explored. Another interesting direction for future work is to apply the idea to more expressive DLs, like $\mathcal{ELHI}$.

References

1. Artale, A., Calvanese, D., Kontchakov, R., Zakharyaschev, M.: The DL-Lite family and relations. J. of Artificial Intelligence Research 36, 1–69 (2009)
2. Bachmair, L., Ganzinger, H.: Resolution theorem proving. In: Handbook of Automated Reasoning (in 2 volumes), vol. 1, pp. 19–99. Elsevier, MIT Press (2001)
3. Calvanese, D., De Giacomo, G., Lembo, D., Lenzerini, M., Rosati, R.: Tractable reasoning and efficient query answering in description logics: The DL-Lite family. J. of Automated Reasoning 39, 385–429 (2007)
4. Glimm, B., Horrocks, I., Lutz, C., Sattler, U.: Conjunctive query answering for the description logic SHIQ. J. of Artificial Intelligence Research 31, 157–204 (2008)
5. Kontchakov, R., Lutz, C., Toman, D., Wolter, F., Zakharyaschev, M.: The combined approach to query answering in DL-Lite. In: Procs. of KR 2010, pp. 247–357 (2010)
6. Pérez-Urbina, H., Horrocks, I., Motik, B.: Efficient query answering for OWL 2. In: Bernstein, A., Karger, D.R., Heath, T., Feigenbaum, L., Maynard, D., Motta, E., Thirunarayan, K. (eds.) ISWC 2009. LNCS, vol. 5823, pp. 489–504. Springer, Heidelberg (2009)
7. Poggi, A., Lembo, D., Calvanese, D., De Giacomo, G., Lenzerini, M., Rosati, R.: Linking data to ontologies. J. on Data Semantics 10, 133–173 (2008)
8. Rosati, R., Almatelli, A.: Improving query answering over DL-Lite ontologies. In: Procs. of KR 2010, pp. 290–300 (2010)
9. Stocker, M., Smith, M.: Owlgres: A scalable OWL reasoner. In: Procs. of OWLED 2008. CEUR-WS.org, vol. 432 (2008)

Sort It Out with Monotonicity
Translating between Many-Sorted and Unsorted First-Order Logic

Koen Claessen, Ann Lillieström, and Nicholas Smallbone

Chalmers University of Technology, Gothenburg, Sweden
{koen,annl,nicsma}@chalmers.se

Abstract. We present a novel analysis for sorted logic, which determines if a given sort is *monotone*. The domain of a monotone sort can always be extended with an extra element. We use this analysis to significantly improve well-known translations between unsorted and many-sorted logic, making use of the fact that it is cheaper to translate monotone sorts than non-monotone sorts. Many interesting problems are more naturally expressed in many-sorted first-order logic than in unsorted logic, but most existing highly-efficient automated theorem provers solve problems only in unsorted logic. Conversely, some reasoning tools, for example model finders, can make good use of sort-information in a problem, but most problems today are formulated in unsorted logic. This situation motivates translations in both ways between many-sorted and unsorted problems. We present the monotonicity analysis and its implementation in our tool *Monotonox*, and also show experimental results on the TPTP benchmark library.

1 Introduction

Many problems are more naturally expressed in many-sorted first-order logic than in unsorted logic, even though their expressive power is equivalent. However, none of the major automated theorem provers for first-order logic can deal with sorts. Most problems in first-order logic are therefore expressed in unsorted logic.[1] However, some automated reasoning tools (such as model finders) could greatly benefit from sort information in problems.

This situation motivates the need for translations between sorted and unsorted first-order logic: (1) users want to express their problems in sorted logic, whereas many tools only accept unsorted logic; (2) some tool developers want to work with sorted logic, whereas the input problems are mostly expressed in unsorted logic. For example, a model finder for a sorted logic has more freedom than for an unsorted logic: it can find domains of different sizes for different sorts, and apply symmetry reduction for each sort separately.

In this paper, we describe automated ways of translating back and forth between many-sorted and unsorted first-order logic. We use a novel *monotonicity*

---

[1] Indeed, only recently was a collection of many-sorted first-order problems added to the TPTP [11].

N. Bjørner and V. Sofronie-Stokkermans (Eds.): CADE 2011, LNAI 6803, pp. 207–221, 2011.

analysis to improve on well-known existing translations. In short, a sort is *monotone* in a problem if, for any model, the domain of that sort can be made larger without affecting satisfiability. The result of the translation for monotone sorts turns out to be much simpler than for non-monotone sorts. The monotonicity analysis and the translations are implemented in a tool called Monotonox.

To explain the problem we solve, and how monotonicity helps us, we will use the following running example.

Example 1 (monkey village). There exists a village of monkeys, with a supply of bananas. Every monkey must have at least two bananas to eat. A banana can not be shared among two monkeys. To model this situation we introduce two sorts, one of monkeys and one of bananas. We need a predicate owns $\in$ *monkey* $\times$ *banana* $\to o$ that says which monkey owns each banana, and Skolem functions banana$_1$ and banana$_2$ $\in$ *monkey* $\to$ *banana* to witness the fact that each monkey has two bananas. We use the following four axioms:

$$\forall M \in monkey.\, \mathsf{owns}(M, \mathsf{banana}_1(M)) \tag{1}$$

$$\forall M \in monkey.\, \mathsf{owns}(M, \mathsf{banana}_2(M)) \tag{2}$$

$$\forall M \in monkey.\, \mathsf{banana}_1(M) \neq \mathsf{banana}_2(M) \tag{3}$$

$$\forall M_1, M_2 \in monkey, B \in banana.\, (\mathsf{owns}(M_1, B) \wedge \mathsf{owns}(M_2, B) \\ \implies M_1 = M_2) \tag{4}$$

We use a simple but standard many-sorted first-order logic, in which sorts α have a non-empty domain $D(\alpha)$, all symbols have exactly one sort, there are no subsorts, and equality is only allowed between terms of the same sort.

If we want to use a standard reasoning tool for unsorted logic (for example a model finder) to reason about the monkey village, we need to translate the problem into unsorted logic. Automated reasoning folklore [12] suggests three alternatives:

Sort predicates. The most commonly used method is to introduce a new unary predicate P_α for every sort α that is used in the sorted formula [6]. All quantification over a sort α is translated into unsorted quantification bounded by the predicate P_α. Furthermore, for each function or constant symbol in the problem, we have to introduce an extra axiom stating the result sort of that symbol. For example, the first axiom of example 1 translates to

$$\forall M.\, (\mathsf{P}_{monkey}(M) \to \mathsf{owns}(M, \mathsf{banana}_1(M)))$$

and we have to add axioms like $\forall M.\, \mathsf{P}_{banana}(\mathsf{banana}_1(M))$ for each function symbol. Moreover, to rule out the possibility of empty sorts, we sometimes need to introduce axioms of the form $\exists X.\, \mathsf{P}_\alpha(X)$.

Although conceptually simple, this translation introduces a lot of clutter which affects most theorem provers negatively: one extra predicate symbol for each sort, one axiom for each function symbol, and one extra literal for each variable in each clause.

Sort functions. An alternative translation introduces a new function symbol f_α for each sort α. The translation applies f_α to any subterm of sort α in the sorted problem. The aim is to have the image of f_α in the unsorted problem be the domain of α in the sorted problem; f_α thus maps any arbitrary domain element into a member of the sort α. For example, using sort functions, the first axiom of example 1 translates to

$$\forall M.\, \mathsf{owns}(f_{monkey}(M), f_{banana}(\mathsf{banana}_1(f_{monkey}(M))))$$

No additional axioms are needed. Thus, this translation introduces a lot less clutter than the previous translation. Still, the performance of theorem provers is affected negatively, and it depends on the theorem prover as well as the problem which translation works best in practice.

Sort erasure. The translation which introduces least clutter of all simply *erases* all sort information from a sorted problem, resulting in an unsorted problem. However, while the two earlier mentioned translations preserve satisfiability of the problems, sort erasure does not, and is in fact unsound. Let us see what happens to the monkey village example. Erasing all the sorts, we get

$$\forall M.\, \mathsf{owns}(M, \mathsf{banana}_1(M))$$
$$\forall M.\, \mathsf{owns}(M, \mathsf{banana}_2(M))$$
$$\forall M.\, \mathsf{banana}_1(M) \neq \mathsf{banana}_2(M)$$
$$\forall M_1, M_2, B.\, (\mathsf{owns}(M_1, B) \wedge \mathsf{owns}(M_2, B) \rightarrow M_1 = M_2)$$

This new problem *has no finite model*, even though the sorted problem does! The reason is that, if the domain we choose has finite size k, we are forced to have k monkeys and k bananas. But a village of k monkeys must have $2k$ bananas, so this is impossible unless the domain is infinite (or empty, which we disallow). So, sort erasure does not preserve finite satisfiability, as shown by the example. In fact, it does not even preserve satisfiability.

Related work. The choice seems to be between translations that are sound, but introduce clutter, and a translation that introduces no clutter but is unsound. Automated theorem provers for unsorted first-order logic have been used to reason about formulae in Isabelle [8,9]. The tools apply sort erasure, and investigate the proof to see if it made use of unsound reasoning. If that happens they can use a sound but inefficient translation as a fall-back. A similar project using AgdaLight [1] uses sort erasure but, following [12], proposes that the theorem prover be restricted to not use certain rules (i.e. paramodulation on variables), leading to a sound (but possibly incomplete) proof procedure.

Monotonicity has been studied for higher-order logic [2] to help with pruning the search space when model finding. While the intention there is the same as ours and there are similarities between the approaches, the difference in logics changes the problem dramatically. For example, we infer that any formula without $=$ is monotone, which is not true in higher-order logic. Monotonicity is also related to the ideas of stable infiniteness and smoothness [10] in combining theories in SMT; it would be interesting to investigate this link further.

This paper. We give an alternative to choosing between clutter and unsoundness. We propose an analysis that indicates which sorts are safe to erase, leaving ideally only a few sorts left that need to be translated using one of the first two methods.

The problem with sort erasure is that it forces all sorts to use the same domain. If the domains all had the same size to start with, there is no problem. But if the sorted formula only has models where some domains have different sizes than others, the sort erasure makes the formula unsatisfiable. We formulate this observation in the following lemma:

Lemma 1. *The following statements about a many-sorted first-order formula φ are equivalent:*

1. *There is an unsorted model with domain D for the sort-erased version of φ.*
2. *There is a model of φ where the size of each domain is $|D|$.*

Proof. (sketch) The interesting case relies on the observation that, if there is a sorted model in which all domains have the same size, then there also is a model in which all the domains are identical, from which it is trivial to construct an unsorted model.   □

Our main contribution is a *monotonicity inference* calculus that identifies the so-called *monotone* sorts in a problem. If all sorts in a satisfiable sorted problem are monotone, then it is guaranteed that there will always be models for which all domains have the same size, in which case sort erasure is sound. The sorts that cannot be shown monotone will have to be made monotone first by introducing sort predicates or functions, but for these sorts only.

2   Monotonicity Calculus for First-Order Logic

Monotonox exploits *monotonicity* in the formula we are translating to produce a more efficient translation than the naive one. The purpose of this section is to explain what monotonicity is and how to infer it in a formula; section 3 explains how we use this information in Monotonox.

Before tackling monotonicity in a sorted setting, we first describe it in an unsorted one. We do this just because the notation gets in the way of the ideas when we have sorts.

2.1   Monotonicity in an Unsorted Setting

We start straight away with the definition of monotonicity. Monotonicity is a semantic property rather than a syntactic property of the formula.

Definition 1 (monotonicity, unsorted). *An unsorted formula φ is* monotone *if, for all $n \in \mathbb{N}$, whenever φ is satisfiable over domains of size n, it is also satisfiable over domains of size $n + 1$.*

An immediate consequence is that if a monotone formula is satisfiable over a finite domain, it is also satisfiable over all bigger finite domains.

Remark 1. Several common classes of formulae are monotone:

- Any unsatisfiable formula is monotone because it trivially satisfies our definition. The same goes for any formula that has no finite models.
- Any valid formula is monotone because it has a model no matter what the domain is.
- A formula that does not use = is monotone, as we will see later.

What about a non-monotone formula? The simplest example is $\forall X, Y. X = Y$, which is satisfied if the domain contains a single element but not if it contains two. We will see later that equality is the single source of nonmonotonicity in formulae.

Monotonicity allows us to take a model of a formula and get from it a model over a bigger domain. Although it is not obvious from our definition, this is even the case if we want to get an infinite model.

Lemma 2 (monotonicity extends to infinite domains). *φ is monotone iff, for every pair of domains D and D' such that $|D| \leq |D'|$, if φ is satisfiable over D then φ is satisfiable over D'.*

Proof. (sketch) If φ is monotone and has a finite model then it has models of unbounded size; by compactness it has an infinite model. The lemma follows from this property and Löwenheim-Skolem.   □

Monotonicity is not decidable. We can see from remark 1 that monotonicity is related to satisfiability, so we should not expect it to be decidable. Indeed it is not.[2] This does not mean we should give up on inferring monotonicity, just that we cannot *always* infer that a formula is monotone. The calculi we present later only answer "yes" if a formula is monotone but may answer "no" for a monotone formula too.

2.2   Monotonicity in a Many-Sorted Setting

Everything above generalises to sorted formulae, with the complication that we now have to talk about a formula being monotone in a particular sort. Informally, φ is monotone in the sort α if, given a model of φ, we can add elements to the domain of α while preserving satisfiability.

We use the notation $D(\alpha)$ for the domain of sort α. The formal definition mimics the one from the last section:

Definition 2 (monotonicity, sorted). *A sorted formula φ is monotone in the sort α if, whenever φ is satisfiable over D, and we are given D' such that*

---

[2] The proof works by encoding a given Turing machine by a formula that has a finite model of size k iff the Turing machine halts in exactly k steps. Thus if the Turing machine halts then the formula has a finite model at exactly one domain size and is therefore not monotone; if the Turing machine does not halt then the formula is finitely unsatisfiable and therefore monotone.

- $|D(\alpha)|$ is finite, and $|D(\alpha)| + 1 = |D'(\alpha)|$, and
- $D'(\beta) = D(\beta)$ for all $\beta \neq \alpha$,

then φ is satisfiable over D'.

Once again, we only consider taking a finite domain and adding a single element to it. The lemma from the last section still holds:

Lemma 3 (monotonicity extends to infinite domains (sorted)). φ is monotone in α iff, whenever φ is satisfiable over D, and we are given D' such that

- $|D'(\alpha)| \geq |D(\alpha)|$, and
- $D'(\beta) = D(\beta)$ for all $\beta \neq \alpha$,

then φ is satisfiable over D'.

The key insight of Monotonox is that *sort erasure is safe if the formula is monotone* in all sorts:

Theorem 1 (monotone formulae preserve satisfiability under erasure). *If φ is a many-sorted monotone formula, then φ and its sort-erasure are equisatisfiable.*

Proof. By lemma 1, it is enough to show that from a model of φ we can construct a model where all domains are the same size. By lemma 3 we can do this by extending all the domains to match the size of the biggest domain. □

Remark 2. Notice that this construction preserves finite satisfiability, which is important when we are going to use a finite model finder on the problem.

Going back to our monkeys example, the formula is monotone in the sort *banana* (you can always add a banana to the model) but not in the sort *monkey* (if we have k monkeys and $2k$ bananas, we may not add another monkey without first adding two bananas). In section 3.2 we will see that this means we only need to introduce a sort predicate for the sort *monkey*.

2.3 A Simple Calculus for Monotonicity Inference

We now present two calculi for inferring monotonicity of a formula. In both calculi we assume that the formula is in CNF.

Our first calculus is based on the key observation that any formula that does not use equality is monotone. To see why, suppose we have a model over domain D of a formula φ, and we want to add a new element to D while preserving satisfiability. We can do this by taking an existing domain element $e \in D$ and making the new element e' behave identically to e, so that for all unary predicates P, $P(e)$ is true iff $P(e')$ is true, and for all unary functions f, $f(e) = f(e')$, and similarly for predicates and functions of higher arities. If the formula does not use equality, e and e' cannot be distinguished. Thus, the addition of a new domain element preserves satisfiability of the formula.

On the other hand, with equality present, the addition of a new element to the domain may make a previously satisfiable formula unsatisfiable. For example, $\forall X, Y. X = Y$ has a model with domain size 1, but it is not satisfiable for any larger domain size. We cannot make the new domain element behave the same as the old domain element because equality can distinguish them.

However, not all occurrences of equality have this problem. The following examples of equality literals are all monotone:

1. Negative equality (by increasing the size of the domain, more terms may become unequal but previously unequal terms will not become equal).
2. Equality where neither side is a variable (i.e. both sides are functions or constants, possibly with variable arguments). This is because, by using the strategy above for extending the domain with a new element, no function ever returns the new element, so the new element is never tested for equality.
3. Equality over a sort α is monotone in any sort β different to α. (The satisfiability of $t_1 = t_2$, where t_1 and t_2 have sort α is unaffected by the addition of new elements to the domain of β).

Thus, the only problematic literal for monotonicity in the sort α is positive equality over α where either side of the equality is a variable.

Safe terms. We call a term *safe* in a sort α if, whenever we add a new element to the domain of α, the term never evaluates to this element. If the terms occurring on each side of an equality literal are both safe, the satisfiability of the literal is unaffected by the addition of new domain elements. Since positive equality literals are the only possible sources of nonmonotonicity, we can infer monotonicity of a formula by showing that all arguments of positive equality literals are safe. By the examples above, a term is safe in the sort α if it is not a variable, or it has a sort different to α. The simple calculus exploits these facts with the following rules:

1. $\varphi_1 \lor \varphi_2$ is monotone in α iff φ_1 and φ_2 are monotone in α.
2. $\varphi_1 \land \varphi_2$ is monotone in α iff φ_1 and φ_2 are monotone in α.
3. Any non-equality literal is monotone in any sort α.
4. $t_1 \neq t_2$ is monotone in any sort α.
5. $t_1 = t_2$ is monotone in α if t_1 and t_2 are safe in α, i.e., are not variables or are not of sort α.

Let us try out the simple calculus on the hungry monkeys in Example 1. The formula is monotone in *monkey* iff all of its clauses are monotone in *monkey*, and similarly for *banana*. Clauses (1) and (2) are monotone in both sorts, because the clauses do not contain equality. (3) is monotone in both sorts, because the clause does not contain positive equality. (4) is monotone in *banana*, because there is no equality between *banana* elements. The calculus does not let us infer monotonicity of *monkey* in this clause, because of the occurrence of an equality literal with two variables of sort *monkey*. Thus, the formula is monotone in *banana*, but not in *monkey*. This is consistent with our previous observation that we can add more *banana* elements without affecting satisfiability, but this is not the case for *monkey* elements.

2.4 Improved Calculus

There are many cases when our first calculus is not able to prove monotonicity. For example, suppose we change the problem so that some monkeys are not hungry and do not need bananas:

Example 2.

$$\forall M \in monkey. \, (\mathsf{hungry}(M) \implies \mathsf{owns}(M, \mathsf{banana}_1(M))) \tag{5}$$

$$\forall M \in monkey. \, (\mathsf{hungry}(M) \implies \mathsf{owns}(M, \mathsf{banana}_2(M))) \tag{6}$$

$$\forall M \in monkey. \, (\mathsf{hungry}(M) \implies \mathsf{banana}_1(M) \neq \mathsf{banana}_2(M)) \tag{7}$$

$$\forall M_1, M_2 \in monkey, B \in banana.$$
$$((\mathsf{hungry}(M_1) \wedge \mathsf{hungry}(M_2) \wedge \mathsf{owns}(M_1, B) \wedge \mathsf{owns}(M_2, B) \tag{8}$$
$$\implies M_1 = M_2)$$

It is not hard to see that, given a model of the axioms, we can always add an extra monkey, by making that monkey not be hungry. Thus, the above formula is monotone in *monkey*. However, our simple calculus can not infer this, because of the use of positive equality between two variables of sort *monkey* in (8). In this section we remedy the problem by extending the calculus.

In the simple calculus, the strategy for extending a model while preserving finite satisfiability was to pick an existing element e in the domain, and let any new domain element "mimic" e. This strategy does not work for clause (8) in Example 2: if we happen to pick an e such that $\mathsf{hungry}(e)$ is true, then this strategy will add an extra hungry monkey to the domain, which does not preserve finite satisfiability. In our improved calculus we can make use of alternative strategies for extending the model, which allows us to infer monotonicity in cases such as this.

Extension rules. In the improved calculus, we nominate some predicates to be *"true-extended"* and some to be *"false-extended"* in each sort α. If a predicate is neither true-extended nor false-extended, we say that it is *"copy-extended"*. When extending the model with a new domain element e', if a predicate P is true-extended, we make P return true whenever any of its arguments is e'; likewise if it is false-extended we make it return false if any of its arguments is e'. Copy-extended predicates behave as in the simple calculus.

Guard literals. We say that a literal $P(\ldots)$ in a clause C *guards* an occurrence of a variable $X \in \alpha$ in C if X is one of the arguments of that literal and P is true-extended in α. Similarly, a literal $\neg P(\ldots)$ in C with X among its arguments guards occurrences of X in C if P is false-extended in α. We call the literal $P(\ldots)$ or $\neg P(\ldots)$ in this case a *guard literal*. The idea is that when X is instantiated with the new domain element, the guard literal is true, hence satisfiability of the clause is preserved. This allows us to infer that a clause involving positive equality between variables is monotone, if those variables are guarded. For example, in the clause (8) in Example 2, the two variables M_1 and

M_2 occurring in the equality literal are guarded by the predicate hungry, which we can make false for any new elements of sort *monkey* that we add.

Furthermore, $X \neq t$ guards X if t is not a variable: the clause $X \neq t \vee \varphi[X]$ is equivalent to $X \neq t \vee \varphi[t]$, in which X does not appear unsafely.[3]

Contradictory extensions. When considering formulae, things get more problematic: if we add an axiom

$$\forall M \in monkey.\ \mathsf{hungry}(M) \tag{9}$$

to the formula in Example 2, we cannot add non-hungry monkeys to the domain, so the problem is no longer monotone in the sort *monkey*. For the clause (8) to be monotone, M_1 and M_2 must be guarded, which means that the predicate hungry must be false-extended. But extending hungry with false will not preserve satisfiability of the clause (9).

The new extension rules thus require some caution. If a predicate P is false-extended, then any occurrence of a variable X in the literal $P(\ldots)$ needs guarding just like it does in an equality literal $X = t$. Likewise, if P is true-extended, any occurrence of a variable X in the literal $\neg P(\ldots)$ needs guarding. This is illustrated in Example 3:

Example 3

$$\forall X.\ (P(X) \Longrightarrow X = t) \tag{10}$$
$$\forall X.\ (Q(X) \Longrightarrow P(X)) \tag{11}$$

(10) requires P to be false-extended, because the occurrence of X in the positive equality literal needs guarding. But if $P(X)$ is false whenever X is instantiated with a new domain element, then Q must be false-extended in order to satisfy (11).

An occurrence of a variable X is problematic if it occurs in a literal of one of the following forms:

 - $X = t$ or $t = X$
 - $P(\ldots, X, \ldots)$ where P is false-extended
 - $\neg P(\ldots, X, \ldots)$ where P is true-extended

In that case, we need to guard X for the formula to be monotone in X's sort.

The improved calculus infers monotonicity of a formula in α iff there is a consistent extension of predicates that guards all such variable occurrences.

2.5   Monotonicity Inference Rules of the Improved Calculus

Notation. In the following, we shall use the abbreviation K to denote a function from predicates to the extension methods $\{\mathsf{true}, \mathsf{false}, \mathsf{copy}\}$. We call such a K a *context*. Furthermore, we use the notation $K \rhd_\alpha \varphi$ to mean that φ is monotone in the sort α, given the context K.

---

[3] This even holds if X is a subterm of t.

Formulae. A formula φ is monotone with context K in the sort α iff all of its clauses are monotone with K in α:

$$\frac{K \rhd_\alpha C_1 \quad \cdots \quad K \rhd_\alpha C_n}{K \rhd_\alpha C_1 \wedge \ldots \wedge C_n}$$

Clauses. In the rule for clauses, we must also consider the set Γ of variables that are guarded in the clause. We write $\Gamma, K \rhd_\alpha l$ if l is monotone with K in α, given that the variables in Γ are guarded. A clause is monotone with context K in the sort α if all of its literals are monotone with K in α, given Γ:

$$\frac{\Gamma = \bigcup_{i=1}^n \mathsf{guarded}(K, l_i) \qquad \Gamma, K \rhd_\alpha l_1 \quad \cdots \quad \Gamma, K \rhd_\alpha l_n}{K \rhd_\alpha l_1 \vee \ldots \vee l_n}$$

where $\mathsf{guarded}(K, l)$ is defined as

$\mathsf{guarded}(K, P(t_1 \ldots t_n)) = \{X \,\|\, X \in \{t_1 \ldots t_n\}, X \text{ is a variable}\}$ if $K(P) = \mathsf{true}$,
$\mathsf{guarded}(K, \neg P(t_1 \ldots t_n)) = \{X \,\|\, X \in \{t_1 \ldots t_n\}, X \text{ is a variable}\}$ if $K(P) = \mathsf{false}$,
$\mathsf{guarded}(K, X \neq t) = \{X\}$ if X is a variable and t is not,
$\mathsf{guarded}(K, l) = \emptyset$ otherwise.

Literals. We have the following rules for monotonicity inference of literals:

$$\frac{}{\Gamma, K \rhd_\alpha t \neq_\beta u} \text{ (1)} \qquad \frac{\beta \neq \alpha}{\Gamma, K \rhd_\alpha t =_\beta u} \text{ (2)} \qquad \frac{\mathsf{safe}(\Gamma, t, \alpha) \quad \mathsf{safe}(\Gamma, u, \alpha)}{\Gamma, K \rhd_\alpha t =_\alpha u} \text{ (3)}$$

$$\mathsf{safe}(\Gamma, t, \alpha) = \begin{cases} t \in \Gamma & \text{if } t \text{ is a variable of sort } \alpha, \\ \mathsf{true} & \text{otherwise.} \end{cases}$$

(1) Negative equality is always monotone. (2) Equality in a sort β is monotone in any sort α that is different to β. (3) Equality between two terms is monotone if the terms are non-variables, or are guarded in the clause.

$$\frac{\mathsf{safe}(\Gamma, t_1, \alpha) \quad \cdots \quad \mathsf{safe}(\Gamma, t_n, \alpha)}{\Gamma, K \rhd_\alpha P(t_1, \ldots, t_n)} \text{ (4)} \qquad \frac{\mathsf{safe}(\Gamma, t_1, \alpha) \quad \cdots \quad \mathsf{safe}(\Gamma, t_n, \alpha)}{\Gamma, K \rhd_\alpha \neg P(t_1, \ldots, t_n)} \text{ (5)}$$

(4,5) A predicate literal is monotone in α if all of its variable arguments of sort α are guarded in the clause in which the literal occurs.

$$\frac{K(P) \in \{\mathsf{true}, \mathsf{copy}\}}{\Gamma, K \rhd_\alpha P(t_1, \ldots, t_n)} \text{ (6)} \qquad \frac{K(P) \in \{\mathsf{false}, \mathsf{copy}\}}{\Gamma, K \rhd_\alpha \neg P(t_1, \ldots, t_n)} \text{ (7)}$$

(6) A positive occurrence of a predicate is monotone if the predicate is true-extended or copy-extended. (7) A negative occurrence of a predicate is monotone if the predicate is false-extended or copy-extended.

It is not immediately clear how to implement the above rules, since there is no obvious way to infer the context K. We see in section 3.1 that we can do this using a SAT-solver.

2.6 NP-Completeness of the Improved Calculus

The improved calculus allows us to infer monotonicity in more cases. However, inferring monotonicity with it is NP-complete. We show NP-hardness by reducing CNF-SAT to a problem of inferring monotonicity in the calculus.

Given any propositional formula φ_{SAT} in CNF, we construct a formula φ_{MON} such that φ_{SAT} is satisfiable iff φ_{MON} is monotone. The idea is that a context that makes φ_{SAT} monotone corresponds to a satisfying assignment for φ_{SAT}.

For each positive literal l in φ_{SAT}, we introduce a unary predicate P_l in φ_{MON}. For negative literals $\neg l$, we define $P_{\neg l}(X)$ as $\neg P_l(X)$. We equip φ_{MON} with a single constant c. We translate each clause $(l_1 \vee ... \vee l_n)$ of φ_{SAT} into the following clause in φ_{MON}:

$$\forall X.\, P_{l_1}(X) \vee ... \vee P_{l_n}(X) \vee X = \mathsf{c}$$

Our calculus proves this clause monotone exactly when our context extends at least one of $P_{l_1}, .., P_{l_n}$ by true. Thus if we find a context that makes φ_{MON} monotone we may extract a satisfying assignment for φ_{SAT} by doing the following for each positive literal l of φ_{SAT}:

- If P_l is extended by true then let l be true.
- If P_l is extended by false then let l be false.
- If P_l is extended by copy then choose an arbitrary value for l.

The same method takes us from a satisfying assignment of φ_{SAT} to a context that makes φ_{MON} monotone.

3 Monotonox: Sorted to Unsorted Logic and Back Again

We have implemented the monotonicity calculus as part of our tool Monotonox. This section first shows how the calculus is implemented and then how monotonicity is exploited in translating between sorted and unsorted first-order logic.

3.1 Monotonicity Inference with Monotonox

We show in this section how to use a SAT-solver to implement the monotonicity calculus. The use of a SAT-solver is a reasonable choice, as we have seen previously that monotonicity inference in our calculus is NP-hard.

We encode the problem of inferring monotonicity of a formula φ as a SAT-problem, where a satisfying assignment corresponds to a context in our calculus.

We construct for each predicate P in φ two literals, p_T and p_F. The idea is that if p_T is assigned true, then P should be true-extended. If p_F is assigned true, then P should be false-extended. If both p_T and p_F are assigned false, then P should be copy-extended. Our task is to construct a propositional formula with these literals, that is satisfiable iff φ is monotone according to our calculus.

Formulae. The SAT-encoding of a formula φ is the conjunction of SAT-encodings of the clauses of φ and the constraint that each predicate may not be extended by both true and false:

$$\mathsf{monotone}((C_1 \wedge .. \wedge C_n), \alpha) = \bigwedge_{i=1}^{n} \mathsf{monotone}(C_i, \alpha) \wedge \bigwedge_{P_i \in \varphi} \neg p_{i_F} \vee \neg p_{i_T}$$

Clauses. The SAT-encoding of a clause C is the conjunction of SAT-encodings of the literals of C.

$$\mathsf{monotone}((l_1 \vee .. \vee l_n), \alpha) = \bigwedge_{i=1}^{n} \mathsf{monotone}((l_1 \vee .. \vee l_n), l_i, \alpha)$$

Literals. The SAT-encoding of a literal may depend on the clause in which it occurs. In a positive equality literal, both of the terms must be safe. A negative equality literal is trivially monotone. An occurrence of a predicate is monotone if the predicate is extended in an appropriate way or its arguments are safe.

$$\mathsf{monotone}(C, l, \alpha) = \begin{cases} \mathsf{safe}(C, t_1, \alpha) \wedge \mathsf{safe}(C, t_2, \alpha) & \text{if } l \text{ is } t_1 = t_2, \\ \mathsf{true} & \text{if } l \text{ is } t_1 \neq t_2, \\ \neg p_F \vee \bigwedge_{i=1}^{n} \mathsf{safe}(C, t_i, \alpha) & \text{if } l \text{ is } P(t_1, \ldots, t_n), \\ \neg p_T \vee \bigwedge_{i=1}^{n} \mathsf{safe}(C, t_i, \alpha) & \text{if } l \text{ is } \neg P(t_1, \ldots, t_n), \end{cases}$$

A term t is safe in a clause if it is not a variable of the sort considered for monotonicity, or it is guarded by any of the literals in the clause.

$$\mathsf{safe}((l_1 \vee .. \vee l_n), t, \alpha) = \begin{cases} \bigvee_{i=1}^{n} \mathsf{guards}(l_i, t) & \text{if } t \text{ is a variable of sort } \alpha \\ \mathsf{true} & \text{otherwise} \end{cases}$$

A literal l guards a variable X according to the rules that we discussed in section 2.4.

$$\mathsf{guards}(l, X) = \begin{cases} p_T & \text{if } l \text{ is of the form } P(\ldots, X, \ldots), \\ p_F & \text{if } l \text{ is of the form } \neg P(\ldots, X, \ldots), \\ \mathsf{true} & \text{if } l \text{ is of the form } X \neq f(\ldots) \text{ or } f(\ldots) \neq X, \\ \mathsf{false} & \text{otherwise.} \end{cases}$$

If there is a satisfying assignment of the SAT-formula $\mathsf{monotone}(\varphi, \alpha)$, then there is a consistent extension of the predicates of φ (a context) that makes φ monotone in α, and vice versa. Monotonox uses MiniSat [5] to find out whether a satisfying assignment exists for each sort.

3.2   Translating Sorted to Unsorted Logic

To translate from a sorted problem to an unsorted problem, we use the principle that *monotone sorts can simply be erased*, but non-monotone sorts need to be encoded using, for example, a sort predicate. Thus our algorithm is as follows:

1. Analyse the formula to discover which sorts are monotone.
2. For each non-monotone sort, transform the formula by introducing a sort predicate or a sort function (according to the user's choice)—but do not erase the sort yet.
3. Erase all the sorts at once.

It makes no difference *which* method we use to encode the non-monotone sorts—predicates, functions or something else. We can in principle use sort predicates for some sorts and sort functions for others.

We justify the algorithm as follows: by adding sort predicates or functions for all the non-monotone sorts, we have transformed the input formula into an equisatisfiable formula *which is also monotone*.[4] Once we have this monotone formula then erasing all the sorts preserves satisfiability (theorem 1).

An example. Suppose we take the first axiom of our running example, $\forall M \in$ *monkey*. $\mathsf{owns}(M, \mathsf{banana}_1(M))$. As discussed, we know that the sort *banana* is monotone but the sort *monkey* is not. Thus we need to introduce a sort predicate or function for only the sort *monkey*. If we introduce a sort function—while still keeping the formula sorted—the new formula we obtain is $\forall M \in$ *monkey*. $\mathsf{owns}(\mathsf{f}_{monkey}(M), \mathsf{banana}_1(\mathsf{f}_{monkey}(M)))$.

Having done this, it is enough to erase the sorts from the formula (step 3 of the algorithm) and we obtain an unsorted formula which is equisatisfiable over each domain size to the original sorted formula, namely:

$$\forall M. \mathsf{owns}(\mathsf{f}_{monkey}(M), \mathsf{banana}_1(\mathsf{f}_{monkey}(M)))$$

3.3   Translating Unsorted to Sorted Logic

The translation from unsorted to sorted formulae makes use of the same machinery, only in the reverse direction: given an unsorted problem ϕ, if we find a well-sorted problem ψ such that (1) erasing the sorts in ψ gives us back ϕ, and (2) all sorts in ψ are monotone, then (theorem 1) ϕ and ψ are equisatisfiable.

The problem is finding the sorted problem ψ. We can use an existing algorithm [4], that we call *sort unerasure* here, for this. Sort unerasure computes the *maximal typing* of an unsorted problem. It starts by creating unique sorts for all variable occurrences in the problem, and for all argument positions of predicate and function symbols, and for all results of function symbols. Then, it computes equivalence classes of sorts that should be equal to each other in order for the problem to be well-sorted, in the following way. Everywhere in the problem, whenever we apply a function symbol or predicate symbol P to a term t, we force the sort of the corresponding argument position of P to be in the same equivalence class as the result sort of t. Using a union/find algorithm, we get an algorithm that is close to linear time in complexity.

---

[4] In the case of sort predicates, our second calculus can infer monotonicity by false-extending the sort predicate; in the case of sort functions, our first calculus also can because no variable appears directly as the argument of an equality literal.

To sum up, the translation goes in three steps:

1. Compute candidate sorts for all symbols occurring in the problem (using sort unerasure), and create the corresponding sorted problem.
2. Use Monotonox to find out if all sorts in the resulting problem are monotone. If they are, we are done.
3. If there exists any sort that cannot be shown monotone, then give up. We simply return the unsorted problem as a sorted problem with one sort.

In practice, there is more we can do in step 3 than giving up. One has to constrain the sorted formula so that (1) the domains of all non-monotone sorts have the same size, and (2) no monotone sort's domain can be bigger than a non-monotone sort's domain. A finite model finder can easily implement these constraints; when theorem-proving, one can enforce size constraints between sorts by adding to the problem an injective function from the smaller sort to the bigger sort.

4   Results

The TPTP library [11] has recently been extended with many-sorted (so-called TFF) problems. Unfortunately, only 26 of these problems have more than one sort.[5] They break down as follows: 11 have no non-ground positive equality, which means that they are trivially monotone. Monotonox proves a further 5 monotone. 4 are monotone only because they have no finite models, a situation which we cannot detect but plan to in the future. 6 are truly not monotone.

Translating from unsorted to many-sorted logic, we applied sort unerasure to all 13610 unsorted TPTP problems,[6] finding 6380 problems with more than one sort, to which we applied our monotonicity inference. The results are as follows.

	Total problems	Total sorts	Monotone sorts	Other sorts[7]	Affected problems[8]	Monotone problems[9]
CNF problems						
Simple calculus	2598	19908	12317	7591	2446	592
Improved calculus			12545	7363	2521	726
Full first-order problems						
Simple calculus	3782	91843	85025	6818	3154	1034
Improved calculus			88645	3198	3715	1532

Running times. None of the tests above took more than a few seconds. Monotonicity inference was not more expensive than the sort unerasure algorithm.

---

[5] TFF adds both sorts and arithmetic to TPTP; the vast majority of the problems so far only test arithmetic, so only have one sort.

[6] Excluding the so-called SYN problems that just test syntax.

[7] Sorts that we couldn't infer monotone (including sorts that are truly not monotone).

[8] Problems where at least one sort was inferred monotone.

[9] Problems where all sorts were inferred monotone.

5   Conclusions and Future Work

We have introduced the concept of *monotonicity*, and applied it to the problem of translating between many-sorted and unsorted first-order logic. Detecting monotonicity of a sort is not decidable, but we have introduced two algorithms approximating the answer, one linear in the size of the problem, and one improved algorithm solving an NP-complete problem using a SAT-solver. Our results show that the improved algorithm detects many cases of monotonicity, and that the NP-completeness is not a problem in practice.

For future work, we plan to integrate our previous work on finite unsatisfiability detection [3] with monotonicity detection—any sort which must have an infinite domain is monotone. We expect this method to improve monotonicity detection for typical problems that have been translated from higher-order logics with recursive datatypes, such as lists. Moreover, we are working on generalising guards to arbitrary literals.

Finally, we plan to use the translation from unsorted to many-sorted logic to populate the typed section of the TPTP benchmark library.

References

1. Abel, A., Coquand, T., Norell, U.: Connecting a logical framework to a first-order logic prover. In: Gramlich [7], pp. 285–301
2. Blanchette, J.C., Krauss, A.: Monotonicity inference for higher-order formulas. In: Giesl, J., Hähnle, R. (eds.) IJCAR 2010. LNCS, vol. 6173, pp. 91–106. Springer, Heidelberg (2010)
3. Claessen, K., Lillieström, A.: Automated inference of finite unsatisfiability. Journal of Automated Reasoning (2011),
   http://dx.doi.org/10.1007/s10817-010-9216-8,
   doi: 10.1007/s10817-010-9216-8
4. Claessen, K., Sörensson, N.: New Techniques that Improve MACE-style Finite Model Finding. In: Proc. of Workshop on Model Computation, MODEL (2003)
5. Eén, N., Sörensson, N.: An extensible SAT-solver. In: Giunchiglia, E., Tacchella, A. (eds.) SAT 2003. LNCS, vol. 2919, pp. 502–518. Springer, Heidelberg (2004)
6. Enderton, H.B.: A Mathematical Introduction to Logic, ch. 4.3 (Many-Sorted Logic), 2nd edn. Academic Press, New York (2001)
7. Gramlich, B. (ed.): FroCos 2005. LNCS (LNAI), vol. 3717. Springer, Heidelberg (2005)
8. Meng, J., Paulson, L.C.: Translating higher-order clauses to first-order clauses. Journal of Automated Reasoning 40(1), 35–60 (2008)
9. Paulson, L.C.: A generic tableau prover and its integration with Isabelle. Journal of Universal Computer Science 5(3), 73–87 (1999)
10. Ranise, S., Ringeissen, C., Zarba, C.G.: Combining data structures with nonstably infinite theories using many-sorted logic. In: Gramlich [7], pp. 48–64
11. Sutcliffe, G.: The TPTP problem library and associated infrastructure: The FOF and CNF parts, v3.5.0. Journal of Automated Reasoning 43(4), 337–362 (2009)
12. Wick, C.A., McCune, W.: Automated reasoning about elementary point-set topology. Journal of Automated Reasoning 5(2), 239–255 (1989)

Exploiting Symmetry in SMT Problems

David Déharbe[1], Pascal Fontaine[2],
Stephan Merz[2], and Bruno Woltzenlogel Paleo[3,*]

[1] Universidade Federal do Rio Grande do Norte, Natal, RN, Brazil
david@dimap.ufrn.br
[2] University of Nancy and INRIA, Nancy, France
{Pascal.Fontaine,Stephan.Merz}@inria.fr
[3] Technische Universität Wien
bruno.wp@gmail.com

Abstract. Methods exploiting problem symmetries have been very successful in several areas including constraint programming and SAT solving. We here recast a technique to enhance the performance of SMT-solvers by detecting symmetries in the input formulas and use them to prune the search space of the SMT algorithm. This technique is based on the concept of (syntactic) invariance by permutation of constants. An algorithm for solving SMT by taking advantage of such symmetries is presented. The implementation of this algorithm in the SMT-solver veriT is used to illustrate the practical benefits of this approach. It results in a significant improvement of veriT's performances on the SMT-LIB benchmarks that places it ahead of the winners of the last editions of the SMT-COMP contest in the QF_UF category.

1 Introduction

While the benefit of symmetries has been recognized for the satisfiability problem of propositional logic [15], for constraint programming [9], and for finite model finding [4,7,11], SMT solvers (see [3] for a detailed account of techniques used in SMT solvers) do not yet fully exploit symmetries. Audemard et al. [1] use symmetries as a simplification technique for SMT-based model-checking, and the SMT solver HTP [14] uses some symmetry-based heuristics, but current state-of-the-art solvers do not exploit symmetries to decrease the size of the search space.

In the context of SMT solving, a frequent source of symmetries is when some terms take their value in a given finite set of totally symmetric elements. The idea here is very simple: given a formula G invariant by all permutations of some uninterpreted constants $c_0, \ldots, c_n$, for any model $\mathcal{M}$ of G, if term t does not contain these constants and $\mathcal{M}$ satisfies $t = c_i$ for some i, then there should be a model in which t equals c_0. While checking for unsatisfiability, it is thus sufficient to look for models assigning t and c_0 to the same value. This simple idea is very

---

* This work was partly supported by the ANR DeCert project and the INRIA-CNPq project SMT-SAVeS.

N. Bjørner and V. Sofronie-Stokkermans (Eds.): CADE 2011, LNAI 6803, pp. 222–236, 2011.

effective, especially for formulas generated by finite instantiations of quantified problems. We have implemented our technique in a moderately efficient SMT solver (veriT [5]), and with this addition it outperforms the winners of recent editions of the SMT-COMP [2] contest in the QF_UF category. This indicates that detecting symmetries, automatically or based on hints in the input, can be important for provers to reduce the search space that they have to consider, just as some constraint solvers already take symmetry information into account.

Outline. We first introduce notations, then define symmetries and give the main theorem that allows us to reduce the search space. We recast an algorithm to exploit such symmetries in the context of SMT-solvers. Next, the classical pigeonhole problem is analyzed from the perspective of symmetries. Finally, some experimental results, based on the SMT-LIB, are provided and discussed.

2   Notations

A many-sorted first-order language is a tuple $\mathcal{L} = \langle \mathcal{S}, \mathcal{V}, \mathcal{F}, \mathcal{P}, d \rangle$ such that $\mathcal{S}$ is a countable non-empty set of disjoint sorts (or types), $\mathcal{V}$ is the (countable) union of disjoint countable sets $\mathcal{V}_\tau$ of variables of sort τ, $\mathcal{F}$ is a countably infinite set of function symbols, $\mathcal{P}$ is a countably infinite set of predicate symbols, and d assigns a sort in $\mathcal{S}^+$ to each function symbol $f \in \mathcal{F}$ and a sort in $\mathcal{S}^*$ to each predicate symbol $p \in \mathcal{P}$. Nullary predicates are propositions, and nullary functions are constants. The set of predicate symbols is assumed to contain a binary predicate $=_\tau$ for every sort $\tau \in \mathcal{S}$; since the sort of the equality can be deduced from the sort of the arguments, the symbol $=$ will be used for equality of all sorts. Terms and formulas over the language $\mathcal{L}$ are defined in the usual way.

An interpretation for a first-order language $\mathcal{L}$ is a pair $\mathcal{I} = \langle D, I \rangle$ where D assigns a non-empty domain D_τ to each sort $\tau \in \mathcal{S}$ and I assigns a meaning to each variable, function, and predicate symbol. As usual, the identity is assigned to the equality symbol. By extension, an interpretation $\mathcal{I}$ defines a value $\mathcal{I}[t]$ in D_τ for every term t of sort τ, and a truth value $\mathcal{I}[\varphi]$ in $\{\top, \bot\}$ for every formula φ. A model of a formula φ is an interpretation $\mathcal{I}$ such that $\mathcal{I}[\varphi] = \top$. The notation $\mathcal{I}_{s_1/r_1,\dots,s_n/r_n}$ stands for the interpretation that agrees with $\mathcal{I}$, except that it associates the elements r_i of appropriate sort to the symbols s_i.

For convenience, we will consider that a theory is a set of interpretations for a given many-sorted language. The theory corresponding to a set of first-order axioms is thus naturally the set of models of the axioms. A theory may leave some predicates and functions uninterpreted: a predicate symbol p (or a function symbol f) is uninterpreted in a theory $\mathcal{T}$ if for every interpretation $\mathcal{I}$ in $\mathcal{T}$ and for every predicate q (resp., function g) of suitable sort, $\mathcal{I}_{p/q}$ belongs to $\mathcal{T}$ (resp., $\mathcal{I}_{f/g} \in \mathcal{T}$). It is assumed that variables are always uninterpreted in any theory, with a meaning similar to uninterpreted constants. Given a theory $\mathcal{T}$, a formula φ is $\mathcal{T}$-satisfiable if it has a model in $\mathcal{T}$. Two formulas are $\mathcal{T}$-equisatisfiable if one formula is $\mathcal{T}$-satisfiable if and only if the other is. A formula φ is a logical consequence of a theory $\mathcal{T}$ (noted $\mathcal{T} \models \varphi$) if every interpretation in $\mathcal{T}$ is a model of φ. A formula φ is a $\mathcal{T}$-logical consequence of a formula ψ, if every model

$\mathcal{M} \in \mathcal{T}$ of ψ is also a model of φ; this is noted $\psi \models_{\mathcal{T}} \varphi$. Two formulas ψ and φ are $\mathcal{T}$-logically equivalent if they have the same models in $\mathcal{T}$.

3   Defining Symmetries

We now formally introduce the concept of formulas invariant w.r.t. permutations of uninterpreted symbols and study the $\mathcal{T}$-satisfiability problem of such formulas. Intuitively, the formula φ is invariant w.r.t. permutations of uninterpreted symbols if, modulo some syntactic normalization, it is left unchanged when the symbols are permuted. Formally, the notion of permutation operators depends on the theory $\mathcal{T}$ for which $\mathcal{T}$-satisfiability is considered, because only uninterpreted symbols may be permuted.

Definition 1. *A permutation operator P on a set $\mathcal{R} \subseteq \mathcal{F} \cup \mathcal{P}$ of uninterpreted symbols of a language $\mathcal{L} = \langle \mathcal{S}, \mathcal{V}, \mathcal{F}, \mathcal{P}, d \rangle$ is a sort-preserving bijective map from $\mathcal{R}$ to $\mathcal{R}$, that is, for each symbol $s \in \mathcal{R}$, the sorts of s and $P[s]$ are equal. A permutation operator homomorphically extends to an operator on terms and formulas on the language $\mathcal{L}$.*

As an example, a permutation operator on a language containing the three constants c_0, c_1, c_2 of identical sort, may map c_0 to c_1, c_1 to c_2 and c_2 to c_0.

To formally define that a formula is invariant by a permutation operator *modulo some rewriting*, the concept of $\mathcal{T}$-preserving rewriting operator is introduced.

Definition 2. *A $\mathcal{T}$-preserving rewriting operator R is any transformation operator on terms and formulas such that $\mathcal{T} \models t = R[t]$ for any term, and $\mathcal{T} \models \varphi \Leftrightarrow R[\varphi]$ for any formula φ. Moreover, for any permutation operator P, for any term and any formula, $R \circ P \circ R$ and $R \circ P$ should yield identical results.*

The last condition of Def. 2 will be useful in Lemma 6. Notice that R must be idempotent, since $R \circ P \circ R$ and $P \circ R$ should be equal for all permutation operators, including the identity permutation operator.

To better motivate the notion of a $\mathcal{T}$-preserving rewriting operator, consider a formula containing a clause $t = c_0 \lor t = c_1$. Obviously this clause is symmetric if t does not contain the constants c_0 and c_1. However, a permutation operator on the constants c_0 and c_1 would rewrite the formula into $t = c_1 \lor t = c_0$, which is not syntactically equal to the original one. Assuming the existence of some ordering on terms and formulas, a typical $\mathcal{T}$-preserving rewriting operator would reorder arguments of all commutative symbols according to this ordering. With appropriate data structures to represent terms and formulas, it is possible to build an implementation of this $\mathcal{T}$-preserving rewriting operator that runs in linear time with respect to the size of the DAG or tree that represents the formula.

Definition 3. *Given a $\mathcal{T}$-preserving rewriting operator R, a permutation operator P on a language $\mathcal{L}$ is a symmetry operator of a formula φ (a term t) on the language $\mathcal{L}$ w.r.t. R if $R[P[\varphi]]$ and $R[\varphi]$ (resp., $R[P[t]]$ and $R[t]$) are identical.*

Notice that, given a permutation operator P and a linear time $\mathcal{T}$-preserving rewriting operator R satisfying the condition of Def. 3, it is again possible to check in linear time if P is a symmetry operator of a formula w.r.t. R. In the following, we will assume a fixed rewriting operator R and say that P is a symmetry operator if it is a symmetry operator w.r.t. R.

Symmetries could alternatively be defined semantically, stating that a permutation operator P is a symmetry operator if $P[\varphi]$ is $\mathcal{T}$-logically equivalent to φ. The above syntactical symmetry implies of course the semantical symmetry. But the problem of checking if a permutation operator is a semantical symmetry operator has the same complexity as the problem of unsatisfiability checking. Indeed, consider the permutation P such that $P[c_0] = c_1$ and $P[c_1] = c_0$, and a formula ψ defined as $c = c_0 \wedge c \neq c_1 \wedge \psi'$ (where c, c_0 and c_1 do not occur in ψ'). To check if the permutation operator P is a semantical symmetry operator of ψ, it is necessary to check if formulas ψ and $P[\psi]$ are logically equivalent, which is only the case if ψ' is unsatisfiable.

Definition 4. *A term t (a formula φ) is* invariant *w.r.t. permutations of uninterpreted constants $c_0, \ldots, c_n$ if any permutation operator P on $c_0, \ldots, c_n$ is a symmetry operator of t (resp. φ).*

The main theorem follows: it allows one to introduce a symmetry breaking assumption in a formula that is invariant w.r.t. permutations of constants. This assumption will decrease the size of the search space.

Theorem 5. *Consider a theory $\mathcal{T}$, uninterpreted constants $c_0, \ldots, c_n$, a formula φ that is invariant w.r.t. permutations of $c_i, \ldots, c_n$, and a term t that is invariant w.r.t. permutations of $c_i, \ldots, c_n$. If $\varphi \models_{\mathcal{T}} t = c_0 \vee \ldots \vee t = c_n$, then φ is $\mathcal{T}$-satisfiable if and only if*

$$\varphi' =_{\mathrm{def}} \varphi \wedge (t = c_0 \vee \ldots \vee t = c_i)$$

is also $\mathcal{T}$-satisfiable. Clearly, φ' is invariant w.r.t. permutations of $c_{i+1}, \ldots, c_n$.

Proof: Let us first prove the theorem for $i = 0$.

Assume that $\varphi \wedge t = c_0$ is $\mathcal{T}$-satisfiable, and that $\mathcal{M} \in \mathcal{T}$ is a model of $\varphi \wedge t = c_0$; $\mathcal{M}$ is also a model of φ, and thus φ is $\mathcal{T}$-satisfiable.

Assume now that φ is $\mathcal{T}$-satisfiable, and that $\mathcal{M} \in \mathcal{T}$ is a model of φ. By assumption there exists some $j \in \{0, \ldots, n\}$ such that $\mathcal{M} \models t = c_j$, hence $\mathcal{M} \models \varphi \wedge t = c_j$. In the case where $j = 0$, $\mathcal{M}$ is also a model of $\varphi \wedge t = c_0$. If $j \neq 0$, consider the permutation operator P that swaps c_0 and c_j. Notice (this can be proved by structural induction on formulas) that, for any formula ψ, $\mathcal{M} \models \psi$ if and only if $\mathcal{M}_{c_0/d_j, c_j/d_0} \models P[\psi]$, where d_0 and d_j are respectively $\mathcal{M}[c_0]$ and $\mathcal{M}[c_j]$. Choosing $\psi =_{\mathrm{def}} \varphi \wedge t = c_j$, it follows that $\mathcal{M}_{c_0/d_j, c_j/d_0} \models P[\varphi \wedge t = c_j]$, and thus $\mathcal{M}_{c_0/d_j, c_j/d_0} \models P[\varphi] \wedge t = c_0$ since t is invariant w.r.t. permutations of $c_0, \ldots, c_n$. Furthermore, since φ is invariant w.r.t. permutations of $c_0, \ldots, c_n$, $R[P[\varphi]]$ is φ for the fixed $\mathcal{T}$-preserving rewriting operator. Since R is $\mathcal{T}$-preserving, $\mathcal{M}_{c_0/d_j, c_j/d_0} \models P[\varphi]$ if and only if $\mathcal{M}_{c_0/d_j, c_j/d_0} \models R[P[\varphi]]$, that is, if and only if $\mathcal{M}_{c_0/d_j, c_j/d_0} \models \varphi$. Finally $\mathcal{M}_{c_0/d_j, c_j/d_0} \models \varphi \wedge t = c_0$, and $\mathcal{M}_{c_0/d_j,c_j/d_0}$ belongs to $\mathcal{T}$ since c_0 and c_j are uninterpreted. The formula $\varphi \wedge t = c_0$ is thus $\mathcal{T}$-satisfiable.

For the general case, notice that $\varphi'' =_{\text{def}} \varphi \wedge \neg(t = c_0 \vee \ldots \vee t = c_{i-1})$ is invariant w.r.t. permutations of $c_i, \ldots, c_n$, and $\varphi'' \models_{\mathcal{T}} t = c_i \vee \ldots \vee t = c_n$. By the previous case (applied to the set of constants $c_i, \ldots, c_n$ instead of $c_0, \ldots, c_n$), φ'' is $\mathcal{T}$-equisatisfiable to $\varphi \wedge \neg(t = c_0 \vee \ldots \vee t = c_{i-1}) \wedge t = c_i$. Formulas φ and

$$\big(\varphi \wedge \neg(t = c_0 \vee \ldots \vee t = c_{i-1})\big) \vee \big(\varphi \wedge (t = c_0 \vee \ldots \vee t = c_{i-1})\big)$$

are $\mathcal{T}$-logically equivalent. Since $A \vee B$ and $A' \vee B$ are $\mathcal{T}$-equisatisfiable whenever A and A' are $\mathcal{T}$-equisatisfiable, φ is $\mathcal{T}$-equisatisfiable to

$$\big(\varphi \wedge \neg(t = c_0 \vee \ldots \vee t = c_{i-1}) \wedge t = c_i\big) \vee \big(\varphi \wedge (t = c_0 \vee \ldots \vee t = c_{i-1})\big).$$

This last formula is $\mathcal{T}$-logically equivalent to

$$\varphi \wedge (t = c_0 \vee \ldots \vee t = c_{i-1} \vee t = c_i)$$

and thus the theorem holds.   □

Checking if a permutation is syntactically equal to the original term or formula can be done in linear time. And checking if a formula is invariant w.r.t. permutations of given constants is also linear: only two permutations have to be considered instead of the $n!$ possible permutations.

Lemma 6. *A formula φ is invariant w.r.t. permutations of constants $c_0, \ldots, c_n$ if both permutation operators*

- P_{circ} *such that* $P_{\text{circ}}[c_i] = c_{i-1}$ *for* $i \in \{1, \ldots, n\}$ *and* $P_{\text{circ}}[c_0] = c_n$,
- P_{swap} *such that* $P_{\text{swap}}[c_0] = c_1$ *and* $P_{\text{swap}}[c_1] = c_0$

are symmetry operators for φ.

Proof: First notice that any permutation operator on $c_0, \ldots, c_n$ can be written as a product of P_{circ} and P_{swap}, because the group of permutations of $c_0, \ldots, c_n$ is generated by the circular permutation and the swapping of c_0 and c_1. Any permutation P of $c_0, \ldots, c_n$ can then be rewritten as a product $P_1 \circ \cdots \circ P_m$, where $P_i \in \{P_{\text{circ}}, P_{\text{swap}}\}$ for $i \in \{1, \ldots, m\}$. It remains to prove that any permutation operator $P_1 \circ \cdots \circ P_m$ is indeed a symmetry operator. This is done inductively. For $m = 1$ this is trivially true. For the inductive case, assume $P_1 \circ \cdots \circ P_{m-1}$ is a symmetry operator of φ, then

$$\begin{aligned}
R[(P_1 \circ \ldots \circ P_m)[\varphi]] &\equiv R[P_m[(P_1 \circ \cdots \circ P_{m-1})[\varphi]]] \\
&\equiv R[P_m[R[(P_1 \circ \cdots \circ P_{m-1})[\varphi]]]] \\
&\equiv R[P_m[\varphi]] \\
&\equiv R[\varphi]
\end{aligned}$$

where $\equiv$ stands for syntactical equality. The first equality simply expands the definition of the composition operator $\circ$, the second comes from the definition of the $\mathcal{T}$-preserving rewriting operator R, the third uses the inductive hypothesis, and the last uses the fact that P_m is either P_{circ} or P_{swap}, that is, also a symmetry operator of φ. $\square$

4   SMT with Symmetries: An Algorithm

Algorithm 1 applies Theorem 5 in order to exhaustively add symmetry breaking assumptions on formulas. First, a set of sets of constants is guessed (line 1) from the formula φ by the function *guess_permutations*; each such set of constants $\{c_0, \ldots, c_n\}$ will be successively considered (line 2), and invariance of φ w.r.t. permutations of $\{c_0, \ldots, c_n\}$ will be checked (line 3). Notice that function *guess_permutations*(φ) gives an approximate solution to the problem of partitioning constants of φ into classes $\{c_0, \ldots, c_n\}$ of constants such that φ is invariant by permutations. If the $\mathcal{T}$-preserving rewriting operator R is given, then this is a decidable problem. However we have a feeling that, while the problem is still polynomial (it suffices to check all permutations with pairs of constants), only providing an approximate solution is tractable. Function *guess_permutations* should be such that a small number of tentative sets are returned. Every tentative set will be checked in function *invariant_by_permutations* (line 3); with appropriate data structures the test is linear with respect to the size of φ (as a corollary of Lemma 6).

As a concrete implementation of function *guess_permutations*(φ), partitioning the constants in classes that all give the same values to some functions $f(\varphi, c)$

```
1  P := guess_permutations(φ);
2  foreach {c₀, ..., cₙ} ∈ P do
3  │   if invariant_by_permutations(φ, {c₀, ..., cₙ}) then
4  │   │   T := select_terms(φ, {c₀, ..., cₙ}) ;
5  │   │   cts := ∅ ;
6  │   │   while T ≠ ∅ ∧ |cts| ≤ n do
7  │   │   │   t := select_most_promising_term(T, φ) ;
8  │   │   │   T := T \ {t} ;
9  │   │   │   cts := cts ∪ used_in(t, {c₀, ..., cₙ}) ;
10 │   │   │   let c ∈ {c₀, ..., cₙ} \ cts;
11 │   │   │   cts := cts ∪ {c};
12 │   │   │   if cts ≠ {c₀, ..., cₙ} then
13 │   │   │   │   φ := φ ∧ (⋁_{cᵢ∈cts} t = cᵢ);
14 │   │   │   end
15 │   │   end
16 │   end
17 end
18 return φ;
```

Algorithm 1. A symmetry breaking preprocessor

works well in practice, where the functions f compute syntactic information that is unaffected by permutations, i.e. $f(\varphi, c)$ and $f(P[\varphi], P[c])$ should yield the same results. Obvious examples of such functions are the number of appearances of c in φ, or the maximal depth of c within an atom of φ, etc. The classes of constants could also take into account the fact that, if φ is a large conjunction, with $c_0 \neq c_1$ as a conjunct (c_0 and c_1 in the same class), then it should have $c_i \neq c_j$ or $c_j \neq c_i$ as a conjunct for every pair of different constants c_i, c_j contained in the class of c_0 and c_1. In veriT we use a straightforward detection of clusters $c_0, \ldots, c_n$ of constants such that there exists an inequality $c_i \neq c_j$ for every $i \neq j$ as a conjunct in the original formula φ.

Line 3 checks the invariance of formula φ by permutation of $c_0, \ldots, c_n$. In veriT, function $invariant\_by\_permutations(\varphi, \{c_0, \ldots, c_n\})$ simply builds, in linear time, the result of applying a circular permutation of $c_0, \ldots, c_n$ to φ, and the result of applying a permutation swapping two constants (for instance c_0 and c_1). Both obtained formulas, as well as the original one, are normalized by a rewriting operator sorting arguments of conjunctions, disjunctions, and equality according to an arbitrary term ordering. The three formulas should be syntactically equal (this is tested in constant time thanks to the maximal sharing of terms in veriT) for $invariant\_by\_permutations(\varphi, \{c_0, \ldots, c_n\})$ to return true.

Lines 4 to 15 concentrate on breaking the symmetry of $\{c_0, \ldots, c_n\}$. First a set of terms

$$T \subseteq \{t \mid \varphi \models t = c_0 \vee \ldots \vee t = c_n\}$$

is computed. Again, function $select\_terms(\varphi, \{c_0, \ldots, c_n\})$ returns an approximate solution to the problem of getting all terms t such that $t = c_0 \vee \ldots \vee t = c_n$; an omission in T would simply restrict the choices for a good candidate on line 7, but would not jeopardize soundness. Again, this is implemented in a straightforward way in veriT.

The loop on lines 6 to 15 introduces a symmetry breaking assumption on every iteration (except perhaps on the last iteration, where a subsumed assumption would be omitted). A candidate symmetry-breaking term $t \in T$ is chosen by the call $select\_most\_promising\_term(T, \varphi)$. The efficiency of the SMT solver is very sensitive to this selection function. If the term t is not important for unsatisfiability, then the assumption would simply be useless. In veriT, the selected term is the most frequent constant-free term (i.e. the one with the highest number of clauses in which it appears), or, if no constant-free terms remains, the one with the largest ratio of the number of clauses in which the term appears over the number of constants that will be required to add to cts on line 11; so actually, $select\_most\_promising\_term$ also depends on the set cts.

Function $used\_in(t, \{c_0, \ldots, c_n\})$ returns the set of constants in term t. If the term contains constants in $\{c_0, \ldots, c_n\} \setminus cts$, then only the remaining constants can be used. On line 10, one of the remaining constants c is chosen non-deterministically: in principle, any of these constants is suitable, but the choice may take into account accidental features that influence the decision heuristics of the SMT solver, such as term orderings.

Finally, if the symmetry breaking assumption $\bigvee_{c_i \in cts} t = c_i$ is not subsumed (i.e. if $cts \neq \{c_0, \ldots, c_n\}$), then it is conjoined to the original formula.

Theorem 7. *The formula φ obtained after running Algorithm 1 is $\mathcal{T}$-satisfiable if and only if the original formula φ_0 is $\mathcal{T}$-satisfiable.*

Proof: If the obtained φ is $\mathcal{T}$-satisfiable then φ_0 is $\mathcal{T}$-satisfiable since φ is a conjunction of φ_0 and other formulas (the symmetry breaking assumptions).

Assume that φ_0 is $\mathcal{T}$-satisfiable, then φ is $\mathcal{T}$-satisfiable, as a direct consequence of Theorem 5. In more details, in lines 6 to 15, φ is always invariant by permutation of constants $\{c_0, \ldots, c_n\} \setminus cts$, and more strongly, on line 13, φ is invariant by permutations of constants in cts as defined in line 9. In lines 4 to 15 any term $t \in T$ is such that $\varphi \models_{\mathcal{T}} t = c_0 \vee \ldots \vee t = c_n$. On lines 10 to 14, t is invariant with respect to permutations of constants in cts as defined in line 9. The symmetry breaking assumption conjoined to φ in line 13 is, up to the renaming of constants, the symmetry breaking assumption of Theorem 5 and all conditions of applicability of this theorem are fulfilled. □

5   SMT with Symmetries: An Example

A classical problem with symmetries is the pigeonhole problem. Most SMT or SAT solvers require exponential time to solve this problem; these solvers are strongly linked with the resolution calculus, and an exponential lower bound for the length of resolution proofs of the pigeon-hole principle was proved in [10]. Polynomial-length proofs are possible in stronger proof systems, as shown by Buss [6] for Frege proof systems. An extensive survey on the proof complexity of pigeonhole principles can be found in [13]. Polynomial-length proofs are also possible if the resolution calculus is extended with symmetry rules (as in [12] and in [17]).

We here recast the pigeonhole problem in the SMT language and show that the preprocessing introduced previously transforms the series of problems solved in exponential time with standard SMT solvers into a series of problems solved in polynomial time. This toy problem states that it is impossible to place $n + 1$ pigeons in n holes. We introduce n uninterpreted constants $h_1, \ldots, h_n$ for the n holes, and $n + 1$ uninterpreted constants $p_1, \ldots, p_{n+1}$ for the $n + 1$ pigeons. Each pigeon is required to occupy one hole:

$$p_i = h_1 \vee \ldots \vee p_i = h_n$$

It is also required that distinct pigeons occupy different holes, and this is expressed by the clauses $p_i \neq p_j$ for $1 \leq i < j \leq n + 1$. One can also assume that the holes are distinct, i.e., $h_i \neq h_j$ for $1 \leq i < j \leq n$, although this is not needed for the problem to be unsatisfiable.

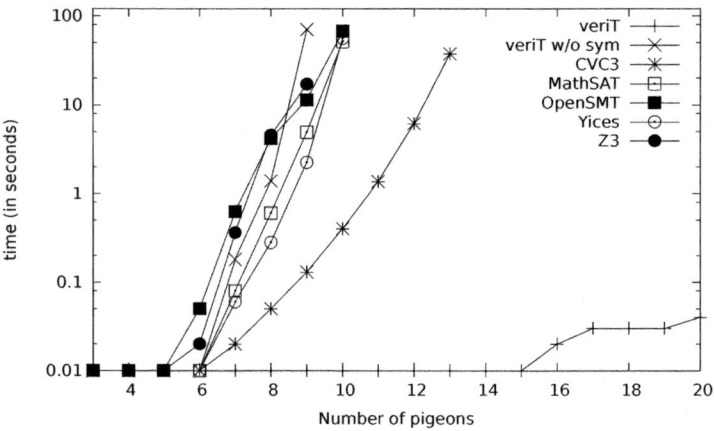

Fig. 1. Some SMT solvers and the pigeonhole problem

The generated set of formulas is invariant by permutations of the constants $p_1, \ldots, p_{n+1}$, and also by permutations of constants $h_1, \ldots, h_n$; very basic heuristics would easily guess this invariance. However, it is not obvious from the presentation of the problem that $h_i = p_1 \vee \ldots \vee h_i = p_{n+1}$ for $i \in [1..n]$, so any standard function *select_terms* in the previous algorithm will fail to return any selectable term to break the symmetry; this symmetry of $p_1, \ldots, p_{n+1}$ is not directly usable. It is however most direct to notice that $p_i = h_1 \vee \ldots \vee p_i = h_n$; *select_terms* in the previous algorithm would return the set of $\{p_1, \ldots, p_{n+1}\}$. The set of symmetry breaking clauses could be

$$p_1 = h_1$$
$$p_2 = h_1 \vee p_2 = h_2$$
$$p_3 = h_1 \vee p_3 = h_2 \vee p_3 = h_3$$
$$\vdots$$
$$p_{n-1} = h_1 \vee \ldots \vee p_{n-1} = h_{n-1}$$

or any similar set of clauses obtained from these with by applying a permutation operator on $p_1, \ldots, p_{n+1}$ and a permutation operator on $h_1, \ldots, h_n$. Without need for any advanced theory propagation techniques[1], $(n + 1) \times n/2$ conflict clauses of the form $p_i \neq h_i \vee p_j \neq h_i \vee p_j \neq p_i$ with $i < j$ suffice to transform the problem into a purely propositional problem. With the symmetry breaking clauses, the underlying SAT solver then concludes (in polynomial time) the unsatisfiability of the problem using only Boolean Constraint Propagation.

Without the symmetry breaking clauses, the SAT solver will have to investigate all $n!$ assignments of n pigeons in n holes, and conclude for each of those assignments that the pigeon $n + 1$ cannot find any unoccupied hole.

---

[1] Theory propagation in veriT is quite basic: only equalities deduced from congruence closure are propagated. $p_i \neq h_i$ would never be propagated from $p_j = h_i$ and $p_i \neq p_j$.

The experimental results, shown in Figure 1, support this analysis: all solvers (including veriT without symmetry heuristics) time out[2] on problems of relatively small size, although CVC3 performs significantly better than the other solvers. Using the symmetry heuristics allows veriT to solve much larger problems in insignificant times. In fact, the modified version of veriT solves every instance of the problem with as many as 30 pigeons in less than 0.15 seconds.

6   Experimental Results

In the previous section we showed that detecting and breaking symmetries can sometimes decrease the solving time from exponential to polynomial. We now investigate its use on more realistic problems by evaluating its impact on SMT-LIB benchmarks.

Consider a problem on a finite domain of a given cardinality n, with a set of arbitrarily quantified formulas specifying the properties for the elements of this domain. A trivial way to encode this problem into quantifier-free first-order logic, is to introduce n constants $\{c_1, \ldots, c_n\}$, add constraints $c_i \neq c_j$ for $1 \leq i < j \leq n$, Skolemize the axioms and recursively replace in the Skolemized formulas the remaining quantifiers $Qx.\varphi(x)$ by conjunctions (if Q is $\forall$) or disjunctions (if Q is $\exists$) of all formulas $\varphi(c_i)$ (with $1 \leq i \leq n$). All terms should also be such that $t = c_1 \vee \ldots \vee t = c_n$. The set of formulas obtained in this way is naturally invariant w.r.t. permutations of $c_1, \ldots, c_n$. So the problem in its most natural encoding contains symmetries that should be exploited in order to decrease the size of the search space. The QF_UF category of the SMT library of benchmarks actually contains many problems of this kind.

Figure 2 presents a scatter plot of the running time of veriT on each formula in the QF_UF category. The x axis gives the running times of veriT without the symmetry breaking technique presented in this paper, whereas the times reported on the y axis are the running times of full veriT. It clearly shows a global improvement; this improvement is even more striking when one restricts the comparison to unsatisfiable instances (see Figure 3); no significant trend is observable on satisfiable instances only. We understand this behavior as follows: for some (not all) satisfiable instances, adding the symmetry breaking clauses "randomly" influences the decision heuristics of the SAT solver in such a way that it sometimes takes more time to reach a satisfiable assignment; in any way, if there is a satisfiable assignment, then all permutations of the uninterpreted constants (i.e. the ones for which the formula is invariant) are also satisfiable assignments, and there is no advantage in trying one rather than an other. For unsatisfiable instances, if terms breaking the invariance play a role in the unsatisfiability of the problem, then adding the symmetry breaking clauses always reduces the number of cases to consider, potentially by a factor of $n^n/n!$ (where n is the number of constants), and have a negligible impact if the symmetry breaking terms play no role in the unsatisfiability.

---

[2] The timeout was set to 120 seconds, using Linux 64 bits on Intel(R) Xeon(R) CPU E5520 at 2.27GHz, with 24 GBytes of memory.

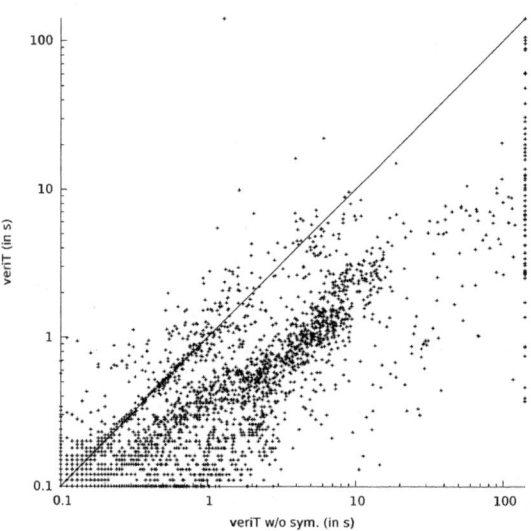

Fig. 2. Efficiency in solving individual instances: veriT vs. veriT without symmetries on all formulas in the QF_UF category. Each point represents a benchmark, and its horizontal and vertical coordinates represent the time necessary to solve it (in seconds). Points on the rightmost and topmost edges represent a timeout.

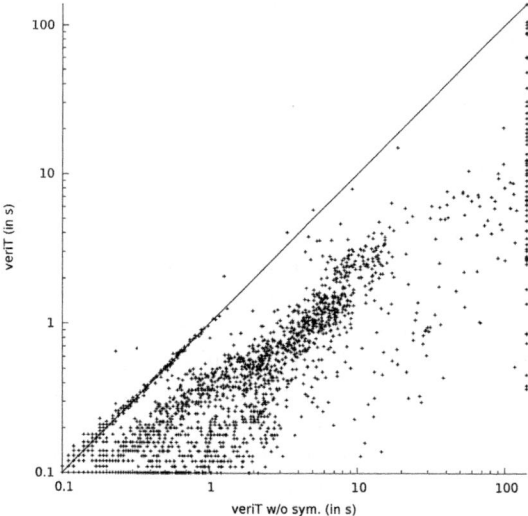

Fig. 3. Efficiency in solving individual instances: veriT vs. veriT without symmetries on the unsatisfiable instances of the QF_UF category

Table 1. Some SMT solvers on the QF_UF category

	Nb. of instances		Instances within time range (in s)						Total time	
	success	timeout	0-20	20-40	40-60	60-80	80-100	100-120	T	T'
veriT	6633	14	6616	9	2	1	3	2	3447	5127
veriT w/o sym.	6570	77	6493	33	14	9	12	9	10148	19388
CVC3	6385	262	6337	20	12	7	5	4	8118	29598
MathSAT	6547	100	6476	49	12	6	3	1	5131	7531
openSMT	6624	23	6559	43	13	6	1	2	5345	8105
Yices	6629	18	6565	32	23	5	1	3	4059	6219
Z3	6621	26	6542	33	23	15	4	4	6847	9967

To compare with the state-of-the-art solvers, we selected all competing solvers in SMT-COMP 2010, adding also Z3 (for which we took the most recent version running on Linux we could find, namely version 2.8), and Yices (which was competing as the 2009 winner). The results are presented in Table 1. Columns T and T' are the total time, in seconds, on the QF_UF library, excluding and including timeouts, respectively. It is important to notice that these results include the whole QF_UF library of benchmarks, that is, with the diamond benchmarks. These benchmarks require some preprocessing heuristic [16] which does not seem to be implemented in CVC3 and MathSAT. This accounts for 83 timeouts in CVC3 and 80 in MathSAT. According to this table, with a 120 seconds timeout, the best solvers on QF_UF without the diamond benchmarks are (in decreasing order) veriT with symmetries, Yices, MathSAT, openSMT, CVC3. Exploiting symmetries allowed veriT to jump from the second last to the first place of this ranking. Within 20 seconds, it now solves over 50 benchmarks more than the next-best solver.

Figure 4 presents another view of the same experiment; it clearly shows that veriT is always better (in the number of solved instances within a given timeout) than any other solver except Yices, but it even starts to be more successful that Yices when the timeout is larger than 3 seconds. Scatter plots of veriT against the solvers mentioned above give another comparative view; they are available in Appendix A of the full version of this paper [8].

Table 2 presents a summary of the symmetries found in the QF_UF benchmark category. Among 6647 problems, 3310 contain symmetries tackled by our method. For 2698 problems, the symmetry involves 5 constants; for most of them, 3 symmetry breaking clauses were added.

The technique presented in this paper is a preprocessing technique, and, as such, it is applicable to the other solvers mentioned here. We conducted an experiment on the QF_UF benchmarks augmented with the symmetry breaking clauses. We observed the same kind of impressive improvement for all solvers. The most efficient solvers solve all but very few instances (diamond benchmarks excluded): within a time limit of 120s and on the whole library, Yices only fails for one formula, CVC for 36, and the others fails for 3 or 4 formulas. We also observe a significant decrease in cumulative times, the most impressive being Yices solving the full QF_UF library but one formula in around 10 minutes.

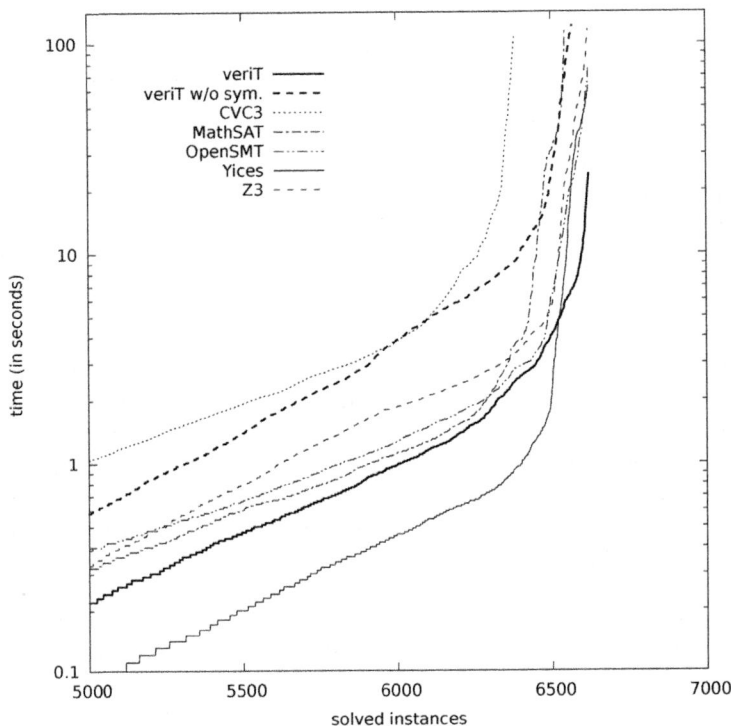

Fig. 4. Number of solved instances of QF_UF within a time limit, for some SMT solvers

Table 2. Symmetries detected for the QF_UF category: n_{sym} indicates the number of constants involved in the symmetry, n_c the number of symmetry breaking clauses

n_c \ n_{sym}	2	3	4	5	6	7	8	9	10	11
1	2									
2		12		8						
3			24	2668						
4				22	92	3				
5					122	166				
6						156				
7							17			
8								11		
9									5	
10										2
Total	2	12	24	2698	214	325	17	11	5	2

Scatter plots exhibiting the improvements are available in Appendix B of the full version of this paper.

7   Conclusion

Symmetry breaking techniques have been used very successfully in the areas of constraint programming and SAT solving. We here present a study of symmetry breaking in SMT. It has been shown that the technique can account for an exponential decrease of running times on some series of crafted benchmarks, and that it significantly improves performances in practice, on the QF_UF category of the SMT library, a category for which the same solver performed fastest in 2009 and 2010. It may be argued that the heuristic has only be shown to be effective on the pigeonhole problem and competition benchmarks in the QF_UF category. However, we believe that in their most natural encoding many concrete problems contain symmetries; provers in general and SMT solvers in particular should be aware of those symmetries to avoid unnecessary exponential blowup. We are particularly interested in proof obligations stemming from verification of distributed systems; in this context many processes may be symmetric, and this should translate to symmetries in the corresponding proof obligations.

Although the technique is applicable in the presence of quantifiers and interpreted symbols, it appears that symmetries in the other SMT categories are somewhat less trivial, and so, require more clever heuristics for guessing invariance, as well as more sophisticated symmetry breaking tools. This is left for future work. Also, our technique is inherently non-incremental, that is, symmetry breaking assumptions should be retrieved, and checked against new assertions when the SMT solver interacts in an incremental manner with the user. This is not a major issue, but it certainly requires a finer treatment within the SMT solver than simple preprocessing.

The veriT solver is open sourced under the BSD license and is available on http://www.veriT-solver.org.

Acknowledgements. Experiments presented in this paper were carried out using the Grid'5000 experimental testbed, being developed under the INRIA ALADDIN development action with support from CNRS, RENATER and several universities as well as other funding bodies (see https://www.grid5000.fr). We would like to thank the anonymous reviewers for their helpful comments and suggestions.

References

1. Audemard, G., Cimatti, A., Kornilowicz, A., Sebastiani, R.: Bounded model checking for timed systems. In: Peled, D., Vardi, M.Y. (eds.) FORTE 2002. LNCS, vol. 2529, pp. 243–259. Springer, Heidelberg (2002)
2. Barrett, C., de Moura, L., Stump, A.: SMT-COMP: Satisfiability Modulo Theories Competition. In: Etessami, K., Rajamani, S.K. (eds.) CAV 2005. LNCS, vol. 3576, pp. 20–23. Springer, Heidelberg (2005)

3. Barrett, C., Sebastiani, R., Seshia, S.A., Tinelli, C.: Satisfiability modulo theories. In: Biere, A., Heule, M.J.H., van Maaren, H., Walsh, T. (eds.) Handbook of Satisfiability. Frontiers in Artificial Intelligence and Applications, ch.26, vol. 185, pp. 825–885. IOS Press, Amsterdam (2009)

4. Baumgartner, P., Fuchs, A., de Nivelle, H., Tinelli, C.: Computing finite models by reduction to function-free clause logic. J. Applied Logic 7(1), 58–74 (2009)

5. Bouton, T., Caminha B. de Oliveira, D., Déharbe, D., Fontaine, P.: veriT: An open, trustable and efficient SMT-solver. In: Schmidt, R.A. (ed.) CADE-22. LNCS, vol. 5663, pp. 151–156. Springer, Heidelberg (2009)

6. Buss, S.R.: Polynomial size proofs of the propositional pigeonhole principle. Journal of Symbolic Logic 52, 916–927 (1987)

7. Claessen, K., Sörensson, N.: New techniques that improve MACE-style finite model finding. In: Proceedings of the CADE-19 Workshop: Model Computation - Principles, Algorithms, Applications (2003)

8. Déharbe, D., Fontaine, P., Merz, S., Woltzenlogel Paleo, B.: Exploiting symmetry in SMT problems (2011), http://www.loria.fr/~fontaine/Deharbe6b.pdf

9. Gent, I.P., Petrie, K.E., Puget, J.-F.: Symmetry in Constraint Programming. In: Rossi, F., van Beek, P., Walsh, T. (eds.) Handbook of Constraint Programming. Foundations of Artificial Intelligence, vol. 2, pp. 329–376. Elsevier, Amsterdam (2006)

10. Haken, A.: The intractability of resolution. Theoretical Computer Science 39, 297–308 (1985)

11. Jia, X., Zhang, J.: A powerful technique to eliminate isomorphism in finite model search. In: Furbach, U., Shankar, N. (eds.) IJCAR 2006. LNCS (LNAI), vol. 4130, pp. 318–331. Springer, Heidelberg (2006)

12. Krishnamurthy, B.: Short proofs for tricky formulas. Acta Inf. 22, 253–275 (1985)

13. Razborov, A.A.: Proof complexity of pigeonhole principles. In: Conference on Developments in Language Theory (DLT), pp. 100–116. Springer, Heidelberg (2002)

14. Roe, K.: The heuristic theorem prover: Yet another SMT modulo theorem prover. In: Ball, T., Jones, R.B. (eds.) CAV 2006. LNCS, vol. 4144, pp. 467–470. Springer, Heidelberg (2006)

15. Sakallah, K.A.: Symmetry and satisfiability. In: Biere, A., Heule, M., van Maaren, H., Walsh, T. (eds.) Handbook of Satisfiability. Frontiers in Artificial Intelligence and Applications, vol. 185, pp. 289–338. IOS Press, Amsterdam (2009)

16. Strichman, O., Seshia, S.A., Bryant, R.E.: Deciding separation formulas with SAT. In: Brinksma, E., Larsen, K.G. (eds.) CAV 2002. LNCS, vol. 2404, pp. 265–279. Springer, Heidelberg (2002)

17. Szeider, S.: The complexity of resolution with generalized symmetry rules. Theory Comput. Syst. 38(2), 171–188 (2005)

Compression of Propositional Resolution Proofs via Partial Regularization*

Pascal Fontaine, Stephan Merz, and Bruno Woltzenlogel Paleo

University of Nancy and INRIA, Nancy, France
{Pascal.Fontaine,Stephan.Merz,Bruno.WoltzenlogelPaleo}@inria.fr

Abstract. This paper describes two algorithms for the compression of propositional resolution proofs. The first algorithm, `RecyclePivots-WithIntersection`, performs partial regularization, removing an inference η when it is redundant in the sense that its pivot literal already occurs as the pivot of another inference located below in the path from η to the root of the proof. The second algorithm, `LowerUnits`, delays the resolution of (both input and derived) unit clauses, thus removing (some) inferences having the same pivot but possibly occurring also in different branches of the proof.

1   Introduction

Propositional satisfiability (SAT) solving has made enormous progress during the recent decade, and powerful decision procedures are being used in many different contexts, such as hardware and software verification, knowledge representation, and diagnostic applications (see [3] for a thorough presentation of techniques and applications of SAT solving). SAT solving also forms the backbone for automated reasoning over more expressive logics, such as in SMT (satisfiability modulo theories) solving (see [2] for a detailed account of techniques used in SMT solvers). For many applications, it is not enough to just obtain a yes/no answer to the decision problem, but one is also interested in a justification of the verdict, that is, a model satisfying the original formula, or a proof showing that no such model exists. For example, in the context of proof carrying code [7], the code producer must provide a proof that will be checked by the code consumer. In the context of SAT solving, it is well understood how decision procedures can be adapted to construct a resolution proof while performing proof search. However, proofs output by SAT solvers can be huge (millions of learned clauses and tens or hundreds of megabytes for typical benchmark cases), and techniques for obtaining small proofs become of interest. Producing a proof of minimum size is an NP-hard problem, so it is important to find heuristics of low (preferably linear) complexity that achieve interesting reductions in practical cases. Going beyond trivial optimizations, such as eliminating inferences that do not contribute to the final conclusion, one frequently observes that the same clause (or the same pivot literal) is used more than once within a proof, and even along

---

* This work was partly supported by the ANR DeCert project.

N. Bjørner and V. Sofronie-Stokkermans (Eds.): CADE 2011, LNAI 6803, pp. 237–251, 2011.
© Springer-Verlag Berlin Heidelberg 2011

a single branch in a proof. Although it is not a priori the case that multiple uses of a clause (or pivot) are actually redundant or that their elimination results in a shorter proof, we concentrate in this work on identifying such cases and on corresponding transformations of proofs. Our algorithms are generalizations of similar techniques proposed in the literature [1,5,9]. We show that our techniques yield provably better results than previous algorithms, while their implementation is no more complex. A more detailed comparison with existing work appears in Section 7. We have implemented our algorithms and we presented experimental validations on standard benchmarks in Section 6.

2   The Resolution Calculus

A *literal* is an atomic formula or a negated atomic formula. A *clause* is a set of literals, $\perp$ denotes the *empty clause*. We write $\bar{\ell}$ to denote the dual of ℓ and $|\ell|$ for the atom underlying the literal ℓ (i.e., $\bar{p} = \neg p$, $\overline{\neg p} = p$, and $|p| = |\neg p| = p$ for an atomic formula p).

Definition 1. *A resolution inference is an instance of the following rule:*

$$\frac{\Gamma_1 \cup \{\ell\} \qquad \Gamma_2 \cup \{\bar{\ell}\}}{\Gamma_1 \cup \Gamma_2} \, |\ell|$$

The clauses $\Gamma_1 \cup \{\ell\}$ and $\Gamma_2 \cup \{\bar{\ell}\}$ are the inference's premises and $\Gamma_1 \cup \Gamma_2$ (the resolvent of the premises) is its conclusion. The literal ℓ ($\bar{\ell}$) is the left (right) resolved literal, and $|\ell|$ is the resolved atom or pivot. □

A *(resolution) proof* of a *clause* κ from a set of clauses C is a directed acyclic graph (dag): the *input nodes* are *axiom inferences* (without premises) whose conclusions are elements of C, the *resolvent nodes* are resolution inferences, and the proof has a node with conclusion κ. The dag contains an edge from a node η_1 to a node η_2 if and only if a premise of η_1 is the conclusion of η_2. In this case, η_1 is a *child* of η_2, and η_2 is a *parent* of η_1. A node with no children is a *root*. A *(resolution) refutation* of C is a resolution proof of $\perp$ from C. For the sake of brevity, given a node η, we say *clause η* or *η's clause* meaning the conclusion clause of η, and *(sub)proof η* meaning the (sub)proof having η as its only root. The resolvent of κ_1 and κ_2 with pivot p can be denoted as $\kappa_1 \odot_p \kappa_2$. When the pivot is uniquely defined or irrelevant, we omit it and write simply $\kappa_1 \odot \kappa_2$. In this way, the set of clauses can be seen as an algebra with a commutative operator $\odot$ whose properties have been investigated in [6]; and terms in the corresponding term algebra denote resolution proofs in a notation style that is more compact and more convenient for describing resolution proofs than the usual graph notation.

Example 2. Consider the proof ψ shown below:

$$\cfrac{\eta_1 \quad \cfrac{\eta_2 : a, c, \neg b \quad \cfrac{\eta_1 : \neg a \quad \eta_3 : a, b}{\eta_4 : b} \, a}{\cfrac{\eta_5 : a, c}{\eta_6 : c} \, a} b \qquad \cfrac{\eta_4 \quad \cfrac{\eta_7 : a, \neg b, \neg c}{\eta_8 : a, \neg c} \, b \quad \eta_1}{\eta_9 : \neg c} \, a}{\psi : \perp} c$$

The node η_4 has pivot a, left (right) resolved literal $\neg a$ (a). Its conclusion is $\{b\}$ and its premises are the conclusions of its parents: the input nodes η_1 ($\{\neg a\}$) and η_3 ($\{a, b\}$). It has two children (η_5 and η_8). ψ can be compactly represented by the following proof term:

$$(\underbrace{\{\neg a\}}_{\eta_1} \odot (\{a, c, \neg b\} \odot \underbrace{(\eta_1 \odot \{a, b\})}_{\eta_4})) \odot ((\eta_4 \odot \{a, \neg b, \neg c\}) \odot \eta_1).$$

3   Redundant Proofs

A proof ψ of κ is considered *redundant* iff there exists another proof ψ' of κ' such that $\kappa' \subseteq \kappa$ (i.e. κ' subsumes κ) and $|\psi'| < |\psi|$ where $|\varphi|$ is the number of nodes in φ. The definition below describes two patterns of local redundancy: proofs matching them (modulo commutativity of $\odot$) can be easily compressed.

Definition 3 (Local Redundancy). *A proof containing a subproof of the shapes (here omitted pivots indicate that the resolvents must be uniquely defined)*

$$(\eta \odot \eta_1) \odot (\eta \odot \eta_2) \quad or \quad \eta \odot (\eta_1 \odot (\eta \odot \eta_2))$$

is locally redundant. Indeed, both of these subproofs can be equivalently replaced by the shorter subproof $\eta \odot (\eta_1 \odot \eta_2)$. □

Example 4. The proofs below are two of the simplest examples of locally redundant proofs.

$$\cfrac{\cfrac{\eta : \neg a \qquad \eta_1 : a, b}{b}\,a \qquad \cfrac{\eta \qquad \eta_2 : a, \neg b}{\neg b}\,a}{\psi_1 : \bot}\,b$$

$$\cfrac{\eta : \neg a \qquad \cfrac{\eta_1 : a, b \qquad \cfrac{\eta \qquad \eta_2 : a, \neg b}{\neg b}\,a}{b}}{\psi_2 : \bot}\,a$$

Both proofs can be rewritten to the shorter proof below:

$$\cfrac{\eta : \neg a \qquad \cfrac{\eta_1 : a, b \qquad \eta_2 : a, \neg b}{a}\,b}{\psi_3 : \bot}\,a$$

Note that, by locally permuting the lowermost inference with pivot a and the inference with pivot b, the proof ψ_2 can be transformed into ψ_1. This indicates that the two patterns given in Def. 3 can be seen as different manifestations of the same underlying phenomenon. They appear differently in resolution proofs because the resolution calculus enforces a sequential order of inferences even when the order actually does not matter. □

In the case of local redundancy, the pairs of redundant inferences having the same pivot occur close to each other in the proof. However, redundant inferences can also occur far apart in the proof. One could attempt to remove global redundancies by repeatedly permuting inferences until the redundant inferences appear next to each other. However this approach is intrinsically inefficient because many permutations must be considered and intermediate resolvents must be recomputed after every permutation.

The following definition generalizes Def. 3 by considering inferences with the same pivot that occur within different contexts. We write $\psi[\eta]$ to denote a *proof-context* $\psi[\_]$ with a single placeholder replaced by the subproof η.

Definition 5 ((Global) Redundancy). *A proof*

$$\psi[\psi_1[\eta \odot_p \eta_1] \odot \psi_2[\eta \odot_p \eta_2]] \quad or \quad \psi[\psi_1[\eta \odot_p (\eta_1 \odot \psi_2[\eta \odot_p \eta_2])]]$$

is potentially (globally) redundant. Furthermore, it is (globally) redundant if it can be rewritten to one of the following shorter proofs:

$$\psi[\eta \odot_p (\psi_1[\eta_1] \odot \psi_2[\eta_2])] \quad or \quad \eta \odot_p \psi[\psi_1[\eta_1] \odot \psi_2[\eta_2]] \quad or \quad \psi[\psi_1[\eta_1] \odot \psi_2[\eta_2]].$$

Example 6. Consider the following proof ψ.

$$
\cfrac{\cfrac{\cfrac{\eta : p, q \qquad \eta_1 : \neg p, r}{q, r}\, p \qquad \eta_3 : \neg q}{r}\, q \qquad \cfrac{\cfrac{\eta \qquad \eta_2 : \neg p, s, \neg r}{q, s, \neg r}\, p \qquad \eta_3}{s, \neg r}\, q}{\psi : s}\, r
$$

It corresponds to the proof term $((\eta \odot_p \eta_1) \odot \eta_3) \odot ((\eta \odot_p \eta_2) \odot \eta_3)$, which is an instance of the first pattern appearing in Def. 5, hence ψ is potentially globally redundant. However, ψ is not globally redundant: the replacement terms according to Def. 5 contain $(\eta_1 \odot \eta_3) \odot (\eta_2 \odot \eta_3)$, which does not correspond to a proof. In particular, neither η_1 nor η_2 can be resolved with η_3, as they do not contain the literal q.   □

The second pattern of potentially globally redundant proofs appearing in Def. 5 is related to the well-known notion of *regularity* [10]. Informally, a proof is irregular if there is a path from a node to the root of the proof such that a literal is used more than once as a pivot in this path.

Definition 7 (Irregularity). *A proof of the form* $\psi[\eta \odot_p (\eta_1 \odot \psi'[\eta' \odot_p \eta_2])]$ *is irregular.*   □

The *regular resolution calculus* is the resolution calculus restricted so that irregular proofs are disallowed. Although it is still complete, it does not p-simulate the unrestricted resolution calculus [10]: there are unsatisfiable formulas whose shortest regular resolution refutations are exponentially longer than their shortest unrestricted resolution refutations.

4   Algorithm LowerUnits

A closer inspection of Example 6 shows that it relies on η's clause containing two literals: its literal q had to be resolved within the proof-contexts $\psi_1[\_]$ and $\psi_2[\_]$, and hence η could not be moved outside the contexts. It is easy to see that a potentially redundant proof is always redundant in case the redundant node contains a unit clause.

Theorem 8. *Let φ be a potentially redundant proof, and η be the redundant node. If η's clause is a unit clause, then φ is redundant.*

Proof. Consider first a proof of the form $\psi[\psi_1[\eta \odot \eta_1] \odot \psi_2[\eta \odot \eta_2]]$ and let ℓ be the only literal of η's clause. Then the clause $\psi_1[\eta_1] \odot \psi_2[\eta_2]$ contains the literal $\bar{\ell}$. Two cases can be distinguished, depending on whether the literal $\bar{\ell}$ gets propagated to the root of $\psi[\_]$:

1. In all paths from $\psi_1[\eta_1] \odot \psi_2[\eta_2]$ to the root of $\psi[\_]$, $\bar{\ell}$ gets resolved out: then, the clause $\psi[\psi_1[\eta_1] \odot \psi_2[\eta_2]]$ is equal to the clause $\psi[\psi_1[\eta \odot \eta_1] \odot \psi_2[\eta \odot \eta_2]]$, and hence the original proof can be rewritten to $\psi[\psi_1[\eta_1] \odot \psi_2[\eta_2]]$.
2. In some paths from $\psi_1[\eta_1] \odot \psi_2[\eta_2]$ to the root of $\psi[\_]$, $\bar{\ell}$ does not get resolved out: in this case, the clause of $\psi[\psi_1[\eta_1] \odot \psi_2[\eta_2]]$ is equal to the clause of $\psi[\psi_1[\eta \odot \eta_1] \odot \psi_2[\eta \odot \eta_2]]$ with the additional literal $\bar{\ell}$. Consequently, the clause $\eta \odot (\psi[\psi_1[\eta_1] \odot \psi_2[\eta_2]])$ is equal to the clause $\psi[\psi_1[\eta \odot \eta_1] \odot \psi_2[\eta \odot \eta_2]]$, and hence the original proof can be rewritten to $\eta \odot (\psi[\psi_1[\eta_1] \odot \psi_2[\eta_2]])$.

In both cases, since the rewriting to one of the three shorter proofs described in Definition 5 is possible, the proof is redundant. The case for potentially redundant proofs of the form $\psi[\psi_1[\eta \odot_p (\eta_1 \odot \psi_2[\eta \odot_p \eta_2])]]$ is analogous. $\square$

The `LowerUnits` (LU) algorithm targets exactly the class of global redundancy stemming from multiple resolutions with unit clauses. The algorithm takes its name from the fact that, when this rewriting is done and the resulting proof is displayed as a dag, the unit node η appears lower (i.e., closer to the root) than it used to appear in the original proof.

A naive implementation exploiting Theorem 8 would require the proof to be traversed and fixed after each unit node is lowered. It is possible, however, to do better by first collecting and removing all the unit nodes in a single traversal, and afterwards fixing the whole proof in a single second traversal. Finally, the collected and fixed unit nodes have to be reinserted at the bottom of the proof (cf. Algorithms 1 and 2).

Care must be taken with cases when a unit node η' occurs above in the subproof that derives another unit node η. In such cases, η depends on η'. Let ℓ be the single literal of the unit clause of η'. Then any occurrence of $\bar{\ell}$ in the subproof above η will not be cancelled by resolution inferences with η' anymore. Consequently, $\bar{\ell}$ will be propagated downwards when the proof is fixed and will appear

---

input : A proof ψ
output: A proof ψ' with no global redundancy with unit redundant node

1 (unitsQueue, ψ_b) $\leftarrow$ collectUnits(ψ);
2 $\psi_f \leftarrow$ fix(ψ_b);
3 fixedUnitsQueue $\leftarrow$ fix(unitsQueue);
4 $\psi' \leftarrow$ reinsertUnits(ψ_f, fixedUnitsQueue) ;
5 **return** ψ';

Algorithm 1. `LowerUnits`

---

input : A proof ψ

output: A pair containing a queue of all unit nodes (unitsQueue) that are used
more than once in ψ and a broken proof ψ_b

1 $\psi_b \leftarrow \psi$;
2 traverse ψ_b bottom-up and **foreach** *node η in ψ_b* **do**
3   **if** *η is unit and η has more than one child* **then**
4   add η to unitsQueue;
5   remove η from ψ_b;
6   **end**
7 **end**
8 **return** (unitsQueue, ψ_b);

Algorithm 2. CollectUnits

in the clause of η. Difficulties with such dependencies can be easily avoided if
we reinsert the upper unit node η' after reinserting the unit node η (i.e. after
reinsertion, η' must appear below η, to cancel the extra literal $\overline{\ell}$ from η's clause).
This can be ensured by collecting the unit nodes in a queue during a bottom-up
traversal of the proof and reinserting them in the order they were queued.

The algorithm for fixing a proof containing many roots performs a top-down
traversal of the proof, recomputing the resolvents and replacing broken nodes
(e.g. nodes having deletedNodeMarker as one of their parents) by their surviving
parents (e.g. the other parent, in case one parent was deletedNodeMarker).

When unit nodes are collected and removed from a proof of a clause κ and the
proof is fixed, the clause κ' in the root node of the new proof is not equal to κ
anymore, but contains (some of) the duals of the literals of the unit clauses that
have been removed from the proof. The reinsertion of unit nodes at the bottom
of the proof resolves κ' with the clauses of (some of) the collected unit nodes, in
order to obtain a proof of κ again.

---

input : A proof ψ_f (with a single root) and a queue q of root nodes

output: A proof ψ'

1 $\psi' \leftarrow \psi_f$;
2 **while** q $\neq \emptyset$ **do**
3    $\eta \leftarrow$ first element of q;
4   q $\leftarrow$ tail of q;
5   **if** *η is resolvable with root of ψ'* **then**
6       $\psi' \leftarrow$ resolvent of η with the root of ψ' ;
7   **end**
8 **end**
9 **return** ψ';

Algorithm 3. ReinsertUnits

Example 9. When applied to the proof ψ shown in Example 2, the algorithm LU collects the nodes η_4 and η_1, and replaces them by `deletedNodeMarker` (DNM):

$$\cfrac{\text{DNM} \quad \cfrac{\cfrac{\text{DNM} \quad \cfrac{\eta_3 : a, b}{\eta_4 : \text{DNM}}\ a}{\eta_2 : a, c, \neg b \qquad\qquad \eta_5 : a, c}\ b}{\eta_6 : c}\ a \qquad \cfrac{\text{DNM} \quad \cfrac{\eta_7 : a, \neg b, \neg c}{\eta_8 : a, \neg c}\ b}{\eta_9 : \neg c}\ \text{DNM}\ a}{\psi : \bot}\ c$$

Fixing removes the DNMs. The derived unit clause η_4 is replaced by η_3, since its other parent was a DNM. And the proof ψ becomes:

$$\cfrac{\eta_2 : a, c, \neg b \qquad \eta_7 : a, \neg b, \neg c}{\psi : a, \neg b}\ c$$

Finally, the collected units η_4 (now replaced by η_3) and η_1 can be reinserted in the bottom of the proof, resulting in $((\eta_2 \odot \eta_7) \odot \eta_3) \odot \eta_1$:

$$\cfrac{\cfrac{\cfrac{\eta_2 : a, c, \neg b \qquad \eta_7 : a, \neg b, \neg c}{\psi : a, \neg b}\ c \qquad \eta_3(\eta_4) : a, b}{\psi' : a}\ b \qquad \eta_1 : \neg a}{\psi'' : \bot}\ a$$

$\square$

For efficiency reasons, modern SAT solvers tend to use unit clauses eagerly: once a unit clause is found, it is used to simplify all other clauses. While this is clearly a good heuristic during proof search, unit resolutions can be delayed once a proof is found, since the number of resolution steps can then be significantly reduced. This effect is illustrated by a toy example in the proof of Theorem 10 below. While modern SAT solvers can produce a linear-size proof for this particular example, it nevertheless illustrates the undesirable effects that eager unit resolution may have on proof size.

Theorem 10. *There is a sequence of unsatisfiable clause sets S_n for which the shortest refutations φ_n obtained via eager unit resolution grow quadratically (i.e. $|\varphi_n| \in \Omega(n^2)$) while the compressed proofs $\mathsf{LU}(\varphi_n)$ grow only linearly (i.e. $|\mathsf{LU}(\varphi_n)| \in O(n)$).*

Proof. Consider the clause set S_n below:

$$\kappa_1 = \neg p_1 \quad \kappa_2 = p_1, \neg p_2 \quad \kappa_3 = p_1, p_2, \neg p_3 \quad \cdots \quad \kappa_{n+1} = p_1, p_2, p_3, \ldots, p_n$$

By *eager unit resolution*, κ_1 is firstly resolved with all other n clauses. Then the unit resolvent of κ_1 and κ_2 is resolved with all resolvents of κ_1 and κ_i $(3 \le i \le n+1)$ and so on... The kth iteration of unit resolution generates $n+1-k$ resolvents. One of these is the unit clause $\kappa_{k+1}^u = \neg p_{k+1}$ which is then resolved in the next iteration. It is easy to see that this refutation φ_n has length $\frac{n^2+n}{2}$. The compressed proof $\mathsf{LU}(\varphi_n)$, shown below, has length equal to n only.

$$(\kappa_1 \odot (\ldots \odot (\kappa_{n-1} \odot (\kappa_n \odot \kappa_{n+1}))\ldots))$$

$\square$

5   Algorithm `RecyclePivotsWithIntersection`

Our second algorithm, `RecyclePivotsWithIntersection` (RPI), aims at compressing irregular proofs. It can be seen as a simple but significant modification of the `RecyclePivots` (RP) algorithm described in [1], from which it derives its name. Although in the worst case full regularization can increase the proof length exponentially [10], these algorithms show that many irregular proofs can have their length decreased if a careful partial regularization is performed.

Consider an irregular proof of the form $\psi[\eta \odot_p \psi'[\eta' \odot_p \eta'']]$ and assume, without loss of generality, that $p \in \eta$ and $p \in \eta'$. Then, if $\eta' \odot_p \eta''$ is replaced by η'' within the proof-context $\psi'[\,]$, the clause $\eta \odot_p \psi'[\eta'']$ subsumes the clause $\eta \odot_p \psi'[\eta' \odot_p \eta'']$, because even though the literal $\neg p$ of η'' is propagated down, it gets resolved against the literal p of η later on below in the proof. More precisely, even though it might be the case that $\neg p \in \psi'[\eta'']$ while $\neg p \notin \psi'[\eta' \odot_p \eta'']$, it is necessarily the case that $\neg p \notin \eta \odot_p \psi'[\eta' \odot_p \eta'']$ and $\neg p \notin \eta \odot_p \psi'[\eta'']$.

Although the remarks above suggest that it is safe to replace $\eta' \odot_p \eta''$ by η'' within the proof-context $\psi'[\,]$, this is not always the case. If a node in $\psi'[\,]$ has a child in $\psi[\,]$, then the literal $\neg p$ might be propagated down to the root of the proof, and hence, the clause $\psi[\eta \odot_p \psi'[\eta'']]$ might not subsume the clause $\psi[\eta \odot_p \psi'[\eta' \odot_p \eta'']]$. Therefore, it is only safe to do the replacement if the literal $\neg p$ gets resolved in all paths from η'' to the root or if it already occurs in the root clause of the original proof $\psi[\eta \odot_p \psi'[\eta' \odot_p \eta'']]$.

These observations lead to the idea of traversing the proof in a bottom-up manner, storing for every node a set of *safe literals* that get resolved in all paths below it in the proof (or that already occurred in the root clause of the original proof). Moreover, if one of the node's resolved literals belongs to the set of safe literals, then it is possible to regularize the node by replacing it by one of its parents (cf. Algorithm 4).

The regularization of a node should replace a node by one of its parents, and more precisely by the parent whose clause contains the resolved literal that is safe. After regularization, all nodes below the regularized node may have to

---

input : A proof ψ
output: A possibly less-irregular proof ψ'

1 $\psi' \leftarrow \psi$;
2 traverse ψ' bottom-up and **foreach** *node η in ψ'* **do**
3 │ **if** *η is a resolvent node* **then**
4 │ │   setSafeLiterals(η) ;
5 │ │   regularizeIfPossible(η)
6 │ **end**
7 **end**
8 $\psi' \leftarrow$ fix(ψ') ;
9 **return** ψ';

Algorithm 4. `RecyclePivotsWithIntersection`

```
input  : A node η
output: nothing (but the proof containing η may be changed)
1  if η.rightResolvedLiteral ∈ η.safeLiterals then
2  │    replace left parent of η by deletedNodeMarker ;
3  │    mark η as regularized
4  else if η.leftResolvedLiteral ∈ η.safeLiterals then
5  │    replace right parent of η by deletedNodeMarker ;
6  │    mark η as regularized
7  end
```

Algorithm 5. `regularizeIfPossible`

be fixed. However, since the regularization is done with a bottom-up traversal, and only nodes below the regularized node need to be fixed, it is again possible to postpone fixing and do it with only a single traversal afterwards. Therefore, instead of replacing the irregular node by one of its parents immediately, its other parent is replaced by `deletedNodeMarker`, as shown in Algorithm 5. Only later during fixing, the irregular node is actually replaced by its surviving parent (i.e. the parent that is not `deletedNodeMarker`).

The set of safe literals of a node η can be computed from the set of safe literals of its children (cf. Algorithm 6). In the case when η has a single child ς, the safe literals of η are simply the safe literals of ς together with the resolved literal p of ς belonging to η (p is safe for η, because whenever p is propagated down the proof through η, p gets resolved in ς). It is important to note, however, that if ς has been marked as regularized, it will eventually be replaced by η, and hence p should not be added to the safe literals of η. In this case, the safe literals of η

```
input  : A node η
output: nothing (but the node η gets a set of safe literals)
1  if η is a root node with no children then
2  │    η.safeLiterals ← η.clause
3  else
4  │    foreach η' ∈ η.children do
5  │    │    if η' is marked as regularized then
6  │    │    │    safeLiteralsFrom(η') ← η'.safeLiterals ;
7  │    │    else if η is left parent of η' then
8  │    │    │    safeLiteralsFrom(η') ← η'.safeLiterals ∪ { η'.rightResolvedLiteral } ;
9  │    │    else if η is right parent of η' then
10 │    │    │    safeLiteralsFrom(η') ← η'.safeLiterals ∪ { η'.leftResolvedLiteral } ;
11 │    │    end
12 │    end
13 │    η.safeLiterals ← ⋂_{η'∈η.children} safeLiteralsFrom(η')
14 end
```

Algorithm 6. `setSafeLiterals`

```
    input : A node η
    output: nothing (but the node η gets a set of safe literals)
 1  if η is a root node with no children then
 2  |    η.safeLiterals ← ∅
 3  else
 4  |    if η has only one child η' then
 5  |    |    if η' is marked as regularized then
 6  |    |    |    η.safeLiterals ← η'.safeLiterals ;
 7  |    |    else if η is left parent of η' then
 8  |    |    |    η.safeLiterals ← η'.safeLiterals ∪ { η'.rightResolvedLiteral } ;
 9  |    |    else if η is right parent of η' then
10  |    |    |    η.safeLiterals ← η'.safeLiterals ∪ { η'.leftResolvedLiteral } ;
11  |    |    end
12  |    else
13  |    |    η.safeLiterals ← ∅
14  |    end
15  end
```

Algorithm 7. `setSafeLiterals` for `RecyclePivots`

should be exactly the same as the safe literals of ς. When η has several children, the safe literals of η w.r.t. a child ς_i contain literals that are safe on all paths that go from η through ς_i to the root. For a literal to be safe for all paths from η to the root, it should therefore be in the intersection of the sets of safe literals w.r.t. each child.

The RP and the RPI algorithms differ from each other mainly in the computation of the safe literals of a node that has many children. While RPI returns the intersection as shown in Algorithm 6, RP returns the empty set (cf. Algorithm 7). Additionally, while in RPI the safe literals of the root node contain all the literals of the root clause, in RP the root node is always assigned an empty set of literals. (Of course, this makes a difference only when the proof is not a refutation.) Note that during a traversal of the proof, the lines from 5 to 10 in Algorithm 6 are executed as many times as the number of edges in the proof. Since every node has at most two parents, the number of edges is at most twice the number of nodes. Therefore, during a traversal of a proof with n nodes, lines from 5 to 10 are executed at most $2n$ times, and the algorithm remains linear. In our prototype implementation, the sets of safe literals are instances of Scala's `mutable.HashSet` class. Being mutable, new elements can be added efficiently. And being HashSets, membership checking is done in constant time in the average case, and set intersection (line 12) can be done in $O(k.s)$, where k is the number of sets and s is the size of the smallest set.

Example 11. When applied to the proof ψ shown in Example 2, the algorithm RPI assigns $\{a, c\}$ and $\{a, \neg c\}$ as the safe literals of, respectively, η_5 and η_8. The safe literals of η_4 w.r.t. its children η_5 and η_8 are respectively $\{a, c, b\}$ and $\{a, \neg c, b\}$, and hence the safe literals of η_4 are $\{a, b\}$ (the intersection of $\{a, c, b\}$

and $\{a, \neg c, b\}$). Since the right resolved literal of η_4 (a) belongs to η_4's safe literals, η_4 is correctly detected as a redundant node and hence regularized: η_4 is replaced by its right parent η_3. The resulting proof is shown below:

$$\frac{\eta_2 : a, c, \neg b \qquad \eta_3 : a, b}{\frac{\eta_5 : a, c}{\eta_6 : c}}$$

$$\frac{\eta_3 \qquad \frac{\eta_7 : a, \neg c, \neg b}{\eta_8 : a, \neg c}}{\eta_9 : \neg c} \qquad \eta_1}$$

$$\psi : \bot$$

$$(\underbrace{\{\neg a\} \odot (\{a, c, \neg b\} \odot \{a, b\})}_{\eta_1})) \odot ((\underbrace{\eta_3 \odot \{\neg b, \neg c, a\}}_{\eta_3}) \odot \eta_1)$$

RP, on the other hand, assigns $\emptyset$ as the set of safe literals for η_4. Therefore, it does not detect that η_4 is a redundant irregular node, and then $\mathrm{RP}(\varphi) = \varphi$. □

Theorem 12. *For any proof φ, $|\mathrm{RPI}(\varphi)| \leq |\mathrm{RP}(\varphi)|$.*

Proof. For every node η in φ, let S_{RPI}^{η} (resp., S_{RP}^{η}) be the set of safe literals for η computed by RPI and RP. It is easy to see that $S_{\mathrm{RPI}}^{\eta} \supseteq S_{\mathrm{RP}}^{\eta}$ for all η. Therefore, RPI detects and eliminates more redundancies than RP. □

The better compression of RPI does not come for free, as computing an intersection of sets is more costly than assigning the empty set. For a node η with k children, k sets must be intersected and the size of each set is in the worst case in $O(h)$, where h is the length of the shortest path from η to a root.

6   Experimental Evaluation

In order to evaluate these algorithms, we implemented prototypes[1] of RP, RPI, and LU in the high-level programming language Scala [8] and applied them, as well as the two possible sequential compositions of LU and RPI, to 98 refutations of standard unsatisfiable benchmark problems[2]. These refutations[3] were generated by the CDCL-based SAT-solver included in veriT [4]. For each proof ψ and each algorithm α, we measured[4] the time $t(\alpha, \psi)$ taken by α to compress ψ and the lengths of ψ and $\alpha(\psi)$, and we calculated the obtained compression $((|\psi| - |\alpha(\psi)|)/|\psi|)$ and the compression speed $((|\psi| - |\alpha(\psi)|)/t(\alpha, \psi))$.

The scatter plot shown in the left side of Figure 1 confirms that RPI always compresses more than RP, as predicted by Theorem 12. Furthermore, it shows that RPI often compressed much more than RP. The comparison becomes even more favorable when RPI is followed by LU, as shown in the right-hand figure.

---

[1] Source code available at http://code.google.com/p/proof-compression/

[2] The benchmarks were: (1) unsatisfiable problems of the SatRace 2010 competition solved by veriT in less than 30s and stemming from verification of software ("Babic" and "Nec" benchmarks) and hardware ("IBM" and "Manolios"); (2) smaller problems of the Sat-Lib DIMACS benchmarks ("AIM", "Dubois", "JNH", "BF", "Pret", "SSA", described in www.cs.ubc.ca/~hoos/SATLIB/benchm.html)

[3] Proofs in www.logic.at/people/bruno/Experiments/2011/LU-RPI/Proofs.zip

[4] The raw data of the experiments is available at https://spreadsheets.google.com/ccc?key=0Al709ihGgKdndG1yWm5kNXIzNHppNXdOZGQwTE01V0E&hl=en.

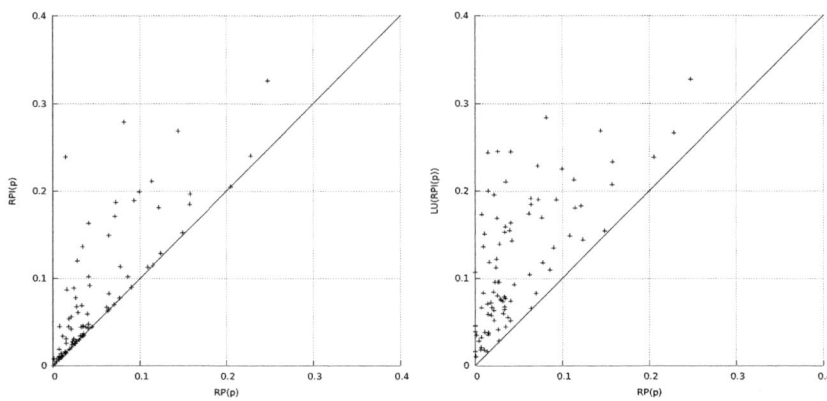

Fig. 1. Comparing RP and RPI, resp. RPI followed by LU

Even though our implementations are just prototypes and the experiments were executed on a modest computer (2.8GHz Intel Core 2 Duo processor with only 2GB of RAM (1067MHz DDR3) available for the Java Virtual Machine), we were pleased to see that the algorithms presented an acceptable and scalable performance. The proofs generated by veriT contained up to millions of derived clauses and were up to 100MB big (in the size of the text file) in a minimalistic proof format[5]. They included all intermediate clauses that had been learned during the execution of veriT, even those that were not used to derive the final empty clause. Before applying the compression algorithms, we removed these unused clauses, but the pruned proofs were still up to more than half a million clauses long and up to about 20MB big. The execution times of all algorithms varied between less than 100 miliseconds for the smaller proofs, less than 10 seconds for the majority of the much bigger proofs of the SatRace benchmarks, and 7.5 minutes in the worst case (for a highly redundant proof with more than half a million clauses).

Figure 2 shows the compression (top) and compression speed (bottom) for the examples from the SatRace. The top figure suggests a trend where longer proofs are more redundant and allow for more compression. This might be due to the fact that the SAT solver backtracks and restarts more often for harder problems that generate longer proofs.

The bottom figure shows that compression speeds of the RPI and RP algorithms are very similar, although RPI took significantly more time than RP for some examples. In cases where the compression rates are comparable, the execution times are similar as well. When RPI took more time than RP, it achieved correspondingly better compression. This indicates that computing the intersections is worthwhile in practice. Finally, note that LU is usually the fastest algorithm in terms of compression speed.

---

[5] This format is closely related to the resolution proof terms used in this paper and is quite compact: (1) only the parents of a derived clause must be indicated explicitly; (2) a clause only needs an explicit name/number if it has more than one child.

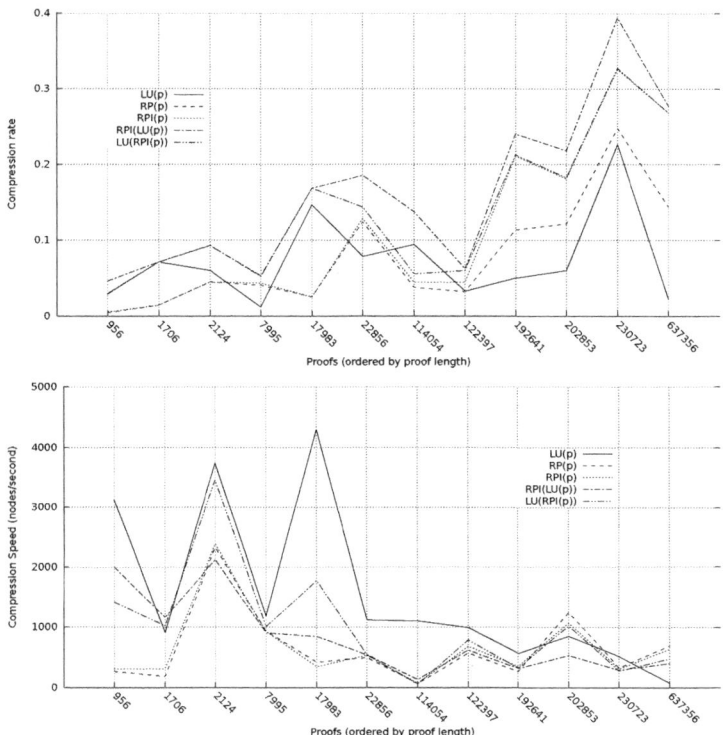

Fig. 2. Compression and compression speed for the SatRace examples

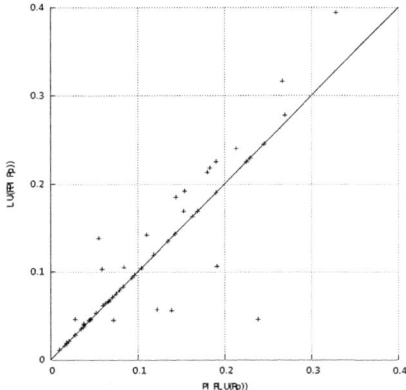

The compression achieved by applying both LU and RPI is usually less than the sum of the compressions achieved by each algorithm alone. This is so because certain redundancies are eliminated by both algorithms. Moreover, the scatter plot above shows that the order in which LU and RPI are applied matters.

7   Related Work and Ideas for Future Work

One of the kinds of local redundancy was considered in our previous work [6], where we also proposed *resolution hypergraphs* as a possible non-linear notation for resolution proofs, making it easier to identify and address non-local redundancies. Although in principle more general than the techniques described here, they do not scale to large proofs, because resolution hypergraphs can be exponentially larger than the proofs they represent.

The same kind of local redundancy was also mentioned by Simone et al. [9], as the local proof rewriting rule $A1'$. They address global redundancies by having another local proof rewriting rule ($A2$) that performs inference permutations when possible. As we have argued before, this approach is inherently inefficient, since too many permutations would have to be considered in order to eliminate all global redundancies. They also consider other interesting local proof rewriting rules that eliminate redundancies not considered in this paper. It would be worthwhile to generalize these other kinds of local redundancy by defining their global counterparts too; it might then be possible to adapt the global techniques described in this paper to these other kinds of redundancy.

Besides RP, Bar-Ilan et al. [1] also defined the RecycleUnits algorithm, which replaces one of the parents of a resolvent with a resolved literal ℓ by a unit clause containing ℓ, if such a unit clause exists somewhere else in the proof. Although this algorithm eliminates some kinds of redundancy, it generates redundancies of the kind handled by LU. Therefore it would be helpful to always execute LU after RecycleUnits, or to combine both algorithms more tightly: instead of replacing a parent by the unit, the resolvent can be replaced by the other parent, and the unit can be queued to be reinserted at the bottom of the proof.

Cotton [5] proposes to split a refutation ψ into a proof ψ_p of the unit clause containing the atom p and a proof $\psi_{\neg p}$ of unit clause containing the literal $\neg p$. This is done by deleting one of the parents of every resolvent with pivot p. A new refutation ψ', possibly shorter than ψ, is then obtained by resolving ψ_p and $\psi_{\neg p}$. Since in ψ' there is now only one resolvent with pivot p, all potential redundancies with pivot p are removed with this splitting technique. Consequently, in principle this splitting technique could subsume all other techniques previously described, including the ones in this paper. However, since not all potential redundancies are actual redundancies, ψ' might actually be longer than ψ. This problem is atenuated by heuristically choosing a promising literal p to split, and iterating until the next proof ψ' becomes longer than the current proof ψ. The techniques that globally identify precisely which potential redundancies are actual redundancies, such as those presented in [1] and here should scale better, since they do not need to iterate an undefined number of times and fix the proof after every iteration.

While this paper focused on regularization of proofs, trying to compress proofs by introducing irregularities is also an interesting possibility to be investigated in future work, since exponential compression might be achieved in the best cases.

8   Conclusions

The use of proof contexts makes for a clear transition from local to global transformations of proofs, and in particular helped us generalize certain kinds of local redundancies to global ones. In this way, we designed two algorithms that eliminate these global redundancies more efficiently than previous ones. Our experiments seem to indicate that we can expect reductions of around 20% for large proofs, beyond what is possible just by pruning irrelevant inferences. Since these reductions essentially come for free and proof checking can be costly (for example when it is performed by the trusted kernel of an interactive proof assistant or when it has to be repeated many times by different proof consumers such as in a PCC scenario), we believe that it is worthwhile to implement our techniques when proof size matters.

References

1. Bar-Ilan, O., Fuhrmann, O., Hoory, S., Shacham, O., Strichman, O.: Linear-time reductions of resolution proofs. Hardware and Software: Verification and Testing, 114–128 (2009)
2. Barrett, C., Sebastiani, R., Seshia, S.A., Tinelli, C.: Satisfiability Modulo Theories. Frontiers in Artificial Intelligence and Applications, vol. 185, pp. 825–885. IOS Press, Amsterdam (2009)
3. Biere, A., Heule, M.J.H., van Maaren, H., Walsh, T. (eds.): Handbook of Satisfiability. Frontiers in Artificial Intelligence and Applications, vol. 185. IOS Press, Amsterdam (2009)
4. Bouton, T., de Oliveira, D. C.B., Déharbe, D., Fontaine, P.: veriT: An open, trustable and efficient SMT-solver. In: Schmidt, R.A. (ed.) CADE-22. LNCS, vol. 5663, pp. 151–156. Springer, Heidelberg (2009)
5. Cotton, S.: Two techniques for minimizing resolution proofs. In: Strichman, O., Szeider, S. (eds.) SAT 2010. LNCS, vol. 6175, pp. 306–312. Springer, Heidelberg (2010)
6. Fontaine, P., Merz, S., Woltzenlogel Paleo, B.: Exploring and Exploiting Algebraic and Graphical Properties of Resolution. In: 8th International Workshop on Satisfiability Modulo Theories (Part of FLoC - Federated Logic Conferences) (2010)
7. Necula, G.C.: Proof-carrying code. In: Proceedings of the 24th ACM SIGPLAN-SIGACT Symposium on Principles of Programming Languages, POPL 1997, pp. 106–119. ACM, New York (1997)
8. Odersky, M., Spoon, L., Venners, B.: Programming in Scala. Artima Press (2008)
9. Simone, S., Brutomesso, R., Sharygina, N.: An efficient and flexible approach to resolution proof reduction. In: 6th Haifa Verification Conference (2010)
10. Tseitin, G.: On the complexity of proofs in propositional logics. In: Siekmann, J., Wrightson, G. (eds.) Automation of Reasoning: Classical Papers in Computational Logic, vol. 2, pp. 1967–1970. Springer, Heidelberg (1983)

Dynamic Behavior Matching: A Complexity Analysis and New Approximation Algorithms

Matthew Fredrikson[1], Mihai Christodorescu[2], and Somesh Jha[1]

[1] University of Wisconsin – Madison
[2] IBM Research – Hawthorne, NY

Abstract. A number of advances in software security over the past decade have foundations in the *behavior matching* problem: given a specification of software behavior and a concrete execution trace, determine whether the behavior is exhibited by the execution trace. Despite the importance of this problem, precise descriptions of algorithms for its solution, and rigorous analyses of their complexity, are missing in the literature. In this paper, we formalize the notion of behavior matching used by the software security community, study the complexity of the problem, and give several algorithms for its solution, both exact and approximate. We find that the problem is in general not efficiently solvable, i.e. *behavior matching is NP-Complete*. We demonstrate empirically that our approximation algorithms can be used to efficiently find accurate solutions to real instances.

1 Introduction

The prevalence of malicious software, and the inability of traditional protection mechanisms to stop it, has led security researchers and practitioners to develop behavior-based techniques [2, 3, 6, 11, 12, 13, 15, 16, 17, 18, 19]. Unlike the syntax-based techniques used for years to detect the presence of known malicious code, behavior-based techniques observe the actions of potentially-malicious code, and attempt to match then against pre-defined specifications of malicious behavior. Conventional thinking suggests that this is a better way to detect threats, as it is much more difficult for malicious code developers to obfuscate the behavior of their software than it is to obfuscate its syntax in memory. Experimental results and practical experience have supported these claims [2, 12, 13].

This has made the technical problem of matching behavior specifications to run-time program behavior important. However, when one surveys the literature in this area [2, 6, 12, 16, 17, 18], one finds that formal descriptions of algorithms for this operation are largely missing. Furthermore, given the reported performance characteristics of existing matching techniques [2, 12, 16, 18], it seems to be widely assumed that behavior matching can be done efficiently, e.g. accounts of 3%-5% overhead on baseline program runtime are common. So, when we implemented a behavior matching algorithm for a project last winter [9], we did not expect to encounter any performance problems. To our surprise, we found

N. Bjørner and V. Sofronie-Stokkermans (Eds.): CADE 2011, LNAI 6803, pp. 252–267, 2011.

that matching simple behavior graphs against pre-recorded traces of short (120 second) executions either exhausted available memory resources, or took several days to complete.

This led us to examine our algorithm in an effort to determine the cause of its apparent high complexity. We determined that in order to correctly match our behavioral specifications to realistic traces, backtracking on the potential mappings between specification components and trace entries was needed. Furthermore, we could not envision a scenario in which the algorithms discussed in the literature would *not* need to perform a similar kind of backtracking. This prompted us to perform the study reported in this paper: a detailed formal examination of the inherent complexity of the problem posed by matching behavior specifications to concrete execution traces, and a study of potential algorithms, exact and approximate, for doing so. This paper makes the following contributions:

- We present a general formulation of behavior matching that encompasses the most prevalent accounts in the literature (Section 2), and use it to show that behavior matching is an NP-Complete problem under the conservative assumption that one allows equality dependencies between events in the behavior specification (Section 2). Furthermore, our formulation is sufficiently generic to apply to arbitrary software behaviors, and thus relevant to specification needs in problems outside of security, such as runtime verification.
- We give two exact algorithms for performing behavior matching: one in direct terms of our formalism, and one from a reduction to SAT that allows practitioners to benefit from recent advances in SAT-solving technology (Section 3).
- We also present two approximation algorithms for behavior matching. One algorithm allows the user to bound the probability of false positives for a small trade-off in runtime complexity, and the other runs in time linear in the size of the trace.

The rest of this paper is organized as follows. Section 2 formulates the problem of behavior matching, and gives our main complexity result. Section 3 presents several algorithms for solving behavior matching instances. Section 5 discusses related work, and Section 6 provides concluding remarks.

2   Definitions and Problem Statement

First, we discuss the notion of software behavior that defines the basis of the matching problem. Any propositions we state have corresponding proofs in the technical report [8]. All of our formalisms make use of *terms* [1] $T(\Sigma, V)$, which denotes the set of all terms over the signature Σ of function symbols and V of variables. We also make use of the projection function $\pi_i(\cdot)$, which takes a tuple and returns its ith component.

Intuitively, dynamic behavior matching seeks to determine whether an observed *execution trace*, or sequence of observable facts emitted by a program, "fits" a pre-defined *behavior specification*, which can be thought of as a set of observable facts together with dependencies that describe necessary relations between the facts. In previous work, the dependencies generally encode either equality [11, 17], or some predicate over the data in the facts (e.g. SubStr [9] or taint [13]). In our work, the "fits" relation is made precise as a mapping between the facts in the specification and the facts in the trace, that properly accounts for the dependencies in the specification. This characterization naturally gives rise to a graphical structure, which is the basis for our notion of specification, called the *behavior graph* (Definition 1). This definition is meant to encompass as many of the relevant notions of behavior from the related work as possible, without introducing features that would make the matching problem more complex. In other words, it should be possible to translate our specifications into other formalisms found in the literature.

Definition 1. Behavior Graph. *A behavior graph* $\mathbf{G}$ *is a 5-tuple* $(A, E, a_0, \alpha, \beta)$, *where*

- A *is a set of states, and* $a_0 \in A$ *is an initial state.*
- $E \subseteq A \times A$ *is a set of directed edges between states such that* (A, E) *is a DAG.*
- $\alpha : A \to T(\Sigma, V)$ *is a total mapping from each state to a* Σ-terms *over* V.
- $\beta : E \to (V \to T(\Sigma, V))$ *is a total mapping from each edge to* $T(\Sigma, V)$-*substitutions.*

The signature Σ used in α and β corresponds to a set of observable events in the system. α maps states in $\mathbf{G}$ to observable events, with variables from V ($V \cap \Sigma = \varnothing$) allowing variation in the substructure of events. β serves to constrain the *dependencies* between the states connected by $e \in E$. For example, if $\beta((a, b)) = [v_1 = v_2 + 1]$, then the behavior graph has the equality constraint $v_1 = v_2 + 1$ on the edge (a, b).

As an example, much of the existing literature is concerned with *system calls* and *taint tracking*. This work can be represented in our framework by treating each system call as a function symbol in Σ, and introducing a symbol taint[(2)] such that taint(x, y) denotes that fact that x matches the taint label of y. Labels are constant symbols, and represent data provenance, which can correspond to a number of system entities such as network connections, memory regions, and files. An example of this is given in Example 1.

Example 1. Download-then-Execute. The behavior graph given by:

- $A = \{s_0, s_1\}$, $E = \{(s_0, s_1)\}$, $a_0 = s_0$, $\beta = \{(s_0, s_1) \mapsto [l_2 \mapsto l_1]\}$
- $\alpha = \{s_0 \mapsto \text{download}(\text{taint}(x, l_1)), s_1 \mapsto \text{execute}(\text{taint}(y, l_2))\}$

corresponds to the download-then-execute behavior. It is depicted in the following diagram:

$$\boxed{s_0 : \text{download}(\text{taint}(x, l_1))} \xrightarrow{\;[l_2 \mapsto l_1]\;} \boxed{s_1 : \text{execute}(\text{taint}(y, l_2))}$$

In this figure, the label on the edge corresponds to the β-constraint, and the labels on states to the corresponding α-labels. Note the β-constraint $[l_2 \mapsto l_1]$

between the two states, which states that the taint label in the second state must be equal to that in the first, effectively requiring that the data that is executed have the same *taint label* as the data that was downloaded.

Now we define an *execution trace*, the other relevant data in the behavior matching problem. An execution trace is a sequence of ground terms, as there are no unknowns about events that have already occurred in the execution of a program.

Definition 2. Execution Trace. *An execution trace $\mathbf{T} \in T(\Sigma, \varnothing)^*$ is a finite-length sequence of ground Σ-terms that may contain repetitions , where we use* Range($\mathbf{T}$) *to denote the set of terms in the sequence and* $\mathbf{T}(i)$ *to the ith element. Each term in $\mathbf{T}$ corresponds to a concrete observation about the execution of some program, with the interpretation that for $i < j$, $\mathbf{T}(i)$ occurs before $\mathbf{T}(j)$ in the program execution.*

The most common type of trace for behavior matching in the security literature is that obtained by letting Σ denote system calls and their arguments, often with meta-symbols for additional functionalities such as provenance and taint tracking, timing information, etc.

We now come to the primary definition of this section – behavior matching. Behavior matching is a problem defined in terms of a behavior graph and an execution trace; the goal is to determine whether the execution trace exhibits the behavior specified in the behavior graph. To simplify notation, in what follows we write $\beta_{x,y}$ to denote $\beta(x, y)$ and ρ^x_y for $\pi_x(\rho(y))$.

Definition 3. Behavior Matching. *Given a behavior graph $\mathbf{G} = (A, E, a_0, \alpha, \beta)$ and execution trace $\mathbf{T}$, we say that $\mathbf{G}$ matches $\mathbf{T}$, written $\mathbf{G} \models \mathbf{T}$, iff there exists a total function $\rho : A \to \mathbb{Z}^+ \times (V \to T(\Sigma, V))$ such that:*

1. $\rho_{a_0} = (i, \sigma)$, *where* $\sigma(\alpha(a_0)) = \mathbf{T}(i)$.
2. *For each* $(a, a') \in E$:

$$\rho^2_{a'}(\rho^2_a(\beta_{a,a'}(\alpha(a')))) = \mathbf{T}(\rho^1_{a'})$$

   Intuitively,
   - $\beta_{a,a'}(\alpha(a'))$ *is the term associated with the latter state a', with dependencies instantiated according to $\beta_{a,a'}$.*
   - *Each application of ρ^2_a and $\rho^2_{a'}$ specializes the dependencies according to the trace terms to which ρ associates a and a', respectively.*
3. *If $i < j$ and $\rho_a = (i, \sigma), \rho_{a'} = (j, \sigma')$, then a must be an ancestor of a' in (A, E). Intuitively ρ maps states in $\mathbf{G}$ to terms in $\mathbf{T}$ that obey the temporal constraints introduced by the edges in $\mathbf{G}$.*
4. *For any $a, a' \in A$, $\rho^1_a \neq \rho^1_{a'}$, i.e. ρ cannot map two states to the same trace element.*

We call ρ a *witness* of the matching between $\mathbf{G}$ and $\mathbf{T}$. Intuitively, ρ maps a path through $\mathbf{G}$ to a sequence of ground terms in $\mathbf{T}$, while satisfying all temporal and data dependencies stipulated by the edges in $\mathbf{G}$.

Note that at times we abuse notation slightly by taking substitutions over terms, even though they are technically defined over variables; this is taken to mean the extension of the substitution over all free variables in the term. Also notice that in Definition 3, ρ must be a total mapping over A: all states in $\mathbf{G}$ must map to a term in $\mathbf{T}$ for the witness to be valid. Some researchers work with behavior graphs that have so-called "or-edge sets", which allow a matching trace to cover a path over one edge in the set, instead of all of them. This style of disjunctive behavior graph can be simulated with multiple graphs from Definition 1, one behavior matching instance per graph.

Example 2. The sequence

$$\texttt{download}(\texttt{taint}(/\texttt{tmp}/\texttt{data}, l_1)), \texttt{open}(\texttt{taint}(/\texttt{tmp}/\texttt{data}, l_1)),$$
$$\texttt{execute}(\texttt{taint}(/\texttt{tmp}/\texttt{data}, l_1))$$

matches the behavior graph from Example 1, with a witness that unifies the first and third terms in the trace with the behavior graph:

$$\left\{ s_0 \mapsto (1, [x \mapsto /\texttt{tmp}/\texttt{data}, l_1 \mapsto l_1]), s_1 \mapsto (3, [y \mapsto /\texttt{tmp}/\texttt{data}, l_2 \mapsto l_1]) \right\}$$

Example 3. The sequence

$$\texttt{download}(\texttt{taint}(/\texttt{tmp}/\texttt{data}, l_1)), \texttt{open}(\texttt{taint}(/\texttt{tmp}/\texttt{data}, l_1)),$$
$$\texttt{execute}(\texttt{taint}(/\texttt{bin}/\texttt{bash}, l_2))$$

does not match the behavior graph from Example 1. Looking to Definition 3, we see that the only way to unify $\alpha(s_0)$ with a term in the trace is

$$\sigma = [x \mapsto /\texttt{tmp}/\texttt{data}, l_1 \mapsto l_1]$$

So $\rho(s_0) = (1, [x \mapsto /\texttt{tmp}/\texttt{data}, l_1 \mapsto l_1])$. This gives us

$$\rho_{s_0}^1(\beta_{s_0, s_1}(\alpha(s_1))) = \texttt{execute}(\texttt{taint}(y, l_1))$$

There is no substitution that can unify this term with $\texttt{execute}(\texttt{taint}(/\texttt{bin}/\texttt{bash}, l_2))$, because of the mismatched taint labels.

We now move on to define two notions of behavior matching that specify different aspects of accuracy. Intuitively, soundness relates to false negatives, or the ability of an algorithm to correctly identify a matching execution trace when it is present, and completeness relates to false positives, or the ability of an algorithm to correctly identify traces that do not match a given graph.

Definition 4. Sound and Complete Matching Algorithm. *A matching algorithm* $\mathbf{A}$ *is a decision procedure for Definition 3. An algorithm* $\mathbf{A}$ *is a* sound matching algorithm *iff given a behavior graph* $\mathbf{G}$ *and trace* $\mathbf{T}$, $\mathbf{G} \models \mathbf{T} \Rightarrow \mathbf{A}(\mathbf{T}, \mathbf{G}) = \mathsf{True}$. *It is a* complete matching algorithm *iff* $\mathbf{A}(\mathbf{G}, \mathbf{T}) = \mathsf{True} \Rightarrow \mathbf{G} \models \mathbf{T}$.

Next, we discuss one of the central results of this work, which is that the inherent complexity of the behavior matching problem makes it intractable for most settings. To our knowledge, this is the first result of its kind for the problem.

Proposition 1. *Sound and complete behavior matching, with plain equality constraints between states, is NP-complete.*

By *plain* equality constraints, we are referring to dependencies that map a variable to another variable, without involving additional term structure. The proof [8] shows that checking a witness against a trace is a polynomial operation, and reduces instances of sub-DAG isomorphism (previously shown to be NP-Complete [20]) to behavior matching. The reduction treats nodes and edges in each of the DAGs as though they are events in Σ. For the larger of the DAGs, all of the structure is encoded in constant symbols, and the reduction views it as an execution trace. The reduction encodes the structure of the smaller of the two DAGs as dependence relations, and produces a corresponding behavior graph. Notice that the reduction only uses simple equality dependencies in the behavior graph; this implies that even the most simple dependencies arising in behavior graphs can lead to intractable instances of the problem. An example reduction on small graphs is given in Example 4.

Example 4. Consider the subgraph isomorphism problem given in Figure 1(a), where we would like to determine whether the three-node graph is isomorphic to a subgraph of the four-node graph. We reduce this to the instance of behavior matching given in Figure 1(b). Beginning and ending sentinels, s and f respectively, are added to the trace. In the reduction of the smaller graph to a behavior graph, nodes are represented by states that have corresponding $n(x)$ terms under α, and edges to states with $e(x_1, x_2)$ terms. Data dependencies are introduced to reflect the fact that the arguments of the terms on edge states must match the arguments of the corresponding node-state endpoints, as shown on the edges of the behavior graph in Figure 1 (b). The matching problem has a witness:

$$\left\{ \begin{array}{l} \rho(s_0) = (1, \varnothing), \rho(s_6) = (10, \varnothing), \\ \rho(s_1) = (2, [x_1 \mapsto o_1]), \rho(s_4) = (5, [x_6 \mapsto o_2]), \\ \rho(s_5) = (7, [x_7 \mapsto o_3]), \rho(s_2) = (2, [x_2 \mapsto o_1, x_3 \mapsto o_2]), \\ \rho(s_3) = (4, [x_4 \mapsto o_1, x_5 \mapsto o_3]) \end{array} \right\}$$

This mapping gives an isomorphism for the original subgraph isomorphism problem: the top three nodes in each graph map to each other.

3   Algorithms

In this section, we detail several solutions for solving instances of the behavior matching problem. We begin with an exact algorithm, and conclude our discussion with two sound approximation algorithms.

Preliminaries. All of our algorithms are built from a shared collection of entities and primitives, which vary in detail among different algorithms:

- $\mathcal{F}$, the *frontier set*, which represents the current state of the matching operation. Different algorithms will place different sorts of elements in $\mathcal{F}$, but we always use Γ to refer to the sort of elements in $\mathcal{F}$. The frontier set is analogous

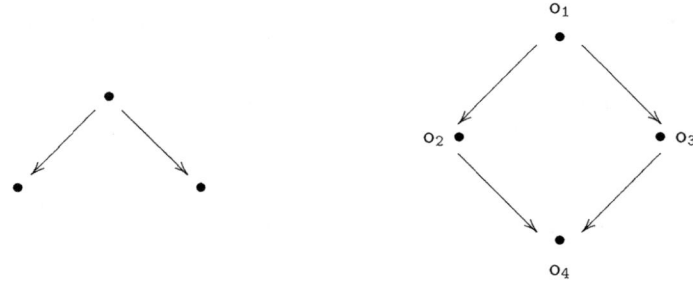

(a) Sub-DAG isomorphism instance.

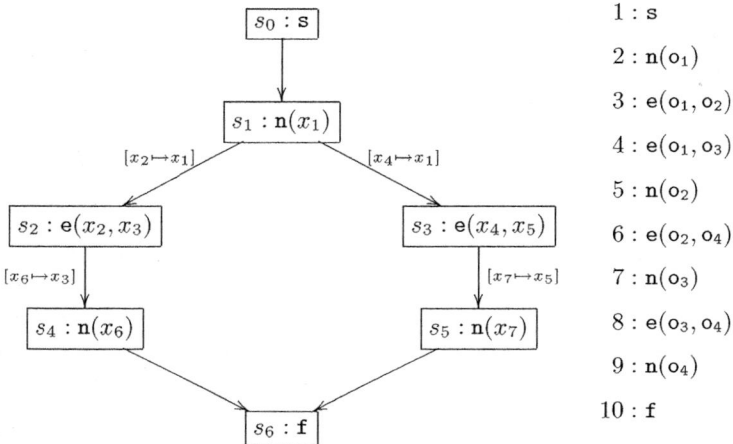

$1 : \mathsf{s}$

$2 : \mathsf{n}(o_1)$

$3 : \mathsf{e}(o_1, o_2)$

$4 : \mathsf{e}(o_1, o_3)$

$5 : \mathsf{n}(o_2)$

$6 : \mathsf{e}(o_2, o_4)$

$7 : \mathsf{n}(o_3)$

$8 : \mathsf{e}(o_3, o_4)$

$9 : \mathsf{n}(o_4)$

$10 : \mathsf{f}$

(b) Corresponding reduction to behavior matching.

Fig. 1. Sub-DAG isomorphism to behavior matching reduction

to a similar notion used in classic algorithms for matching NFAs [10], which consists of the set of states that the matching as reached at a given time.

- Test : $A \times \mathbb{Z}^+ \times \Gamma \mapsto \{\mathsf{True}, \mathsf{False}\}$, returns true if and only if the given frontier element (3rd argument) can be extended by matching the given state (1st argument) to the trace element at the given index (2nd argument).
- Update : $\mathcal{P}(\Gamma) \times A \times \mathbb{Z}^+ \times \Gamma \mapsto \mathcal{P}(\Gamma)$, updates the given frontier set (1st argument) to reflect an extension to the given frontier element (4th argument) by a mapping between the state/indexed trace term pair (2nd and 3rd arguments), returning a new frontier.

These primitives are used in Algorithm 1 (explained below), and are later modified to obtain approximation algorithms.

A Sound and Complete Algorithm. Algorithm 1 presents a sound and complete behavior matching algorithm. This property is a result of the definitions

Algorithm 1. Exact behavior matching

```
 1: Input: Behavior graph G = (A, E, a₀, α, β), execution trace T
 2: // Each element in the frontier maps states to trace terms and substitutions
 3: Γ = A ↦ (ℤ⁺, V ↦ T(Σ, V))
 4: // Test(·, ·, ·) Applies the dependence requirement for each edge (s′, s) on s
 5: Test(s, i, w) ≡ ∃σ.(∀(s′, s) ∈ E.σ(w²_{s′})(β_{s′,s}(α(s)))) = T(i))
 6: // Update(·, ·, ·, ·) extends witness w with a mapping from s to T(i)
 7: Update(F, s, i, w) = F ∪ {w¹[s ↦ (i, σ)]} where σ matches α(s) to T(i)
 8: F ← ∅
 9: for 0 ≤ i ≤ |T| do
10:    for w ∈ F do
11:       for each next matchable state s on frontier element w do
12:          // Test dependencies with predecessors in current derivation
13:          if Test(s, i, w) = True then
14:             // Extend frontier with matching term and updated derivation
15:             F ← Update(F, s, i, w)
16:             if w is a complete mapping then
17:                return (True, w)
18:             end if
19:          end if
20:       end for
21:    end for
22:    // If current trace term matches the initial state of G, update frontier
23:    if Test(s, i, ∅) = True then
24:       F ← Update(F, a₀, i, ∅)
25:    end if
26: end for
27: return False
```

on lines 2 – 7, which specify the core primitives of the algorithm. The first definition is of Γ, the sort of element found in $\mathcal{F}$. Γ corresponds to mappings from states in **G** to pairs of trace indices and substitutions (e.g. *partial witnesses*). The substitution in this pair unifies the term associated with the state with the trace element indexed by the first component. For example, if $\gamma \in \Gamma$, then $\mathbf{T}(\gamma_a^1)$ matches $\gamma_a^2(\alpha(a))$. By defining Γ in this way, the algorithm can build a full set of possible partial witnesses as it enumerates a trace, and return a complete witness if a match exists; no approximation is necessary. Notice the correspondence between this definition of Γ (and thus $\mathcal{F}$) to the frontier used in traditional NFA matching: partial witnesses represent possible intermediate states as **G** is matched with **T**.

The second definition is of Test, on line 5. This definition is a formal restatement of the dependence relation stated in Definition 3. When Test(s, i, w) is applied, all predecessors of s in **G** are checked, according to the mappings in the given witness w, for satisfaction of the dependence requirement stated in Definition 3. The expression is True iff the requirement holds for all predecessors of s. The final definition, Update$(\mathcal{F}, s, i, w)$, extends the witness w with a mapping from state s to trace element $\mathbf{T}(i)$, and the substitution σ that makes it possible. Notice that this definition of $\mathcal{F}$ does not drop or replace elements, but only adds new elements that are extensions of existing ones. This is equivalent to allowing the algorithm to backtrack, and is the source of the algorithm's complexity. If partial witnesses were dropped once their frontiers were all matched, it would make the algorithm "greedy", as backtracking would become impossible. However, it would also make the algorithm unsound, as it would open up the possibility for a trace to "trick" the algorithm into going down a particular path, which never leads to a full witness, and then pursuing an alternate matching path from midway through the original path. The corresponding technical report [8] describes this issue in more depth.

The rest of Algorithm 1 works by scanning the behavior trace $\mathbf{T}$ from beginning to end, one element at a time. For each trace element, each frontier element is enumerated (line 10), and an attempt is made to match the trace term to a term corresponding to the next matchable states of the frontier element (line 13). When the algorithm starts, the frontier is empty, so the matching on line 23 attempts to pair trace terms with the initial state in $\mathbf{G}$. If the initial-state matching succeeds, then the frontier is updated (line 24) to reflect this partial matching. In subsequent iterations, an attempted match between the latest trace term $\mathbf{T}(i)$ and each element in the frontier (line 15) is made, and if successful, the frontier is extended (line 15). This is continued until a complete witness is constructed, at which point the algorithm returns True (line 17).

Proposition 2. *The worst-case complexity of Definition 1 is $O(|A|MD^{|\mathbf{T}|})$ in time and $O(D^{|\mathbf{T}|})$ in space, where D is the maximal out-degree for any state in a given behavior graph $\mathbf{G}$ and execution trace $\mathbf{T}$, and M is the maximum time needed to match terms in $T(\Sigma, V)$.*

The operation of reference in Proposition 2 is the term matching between terms on states in $\mathbf{G}$ and events in $\mathbf{T}$. Note that because our term alphabet is finite, there is a hard upper bound on term size, and thus on the complexity of term matching. The technical report has a proof of soundess and completeness for Definition 1, as well as a proof of Proposition 2.

Sound Approximation Algorithms. The worst-case time and space complexity of Algorithm 1 make it a poor fit for many applications, particularly those involving long-running applications. In this section, we discuss approximation algorithms that mitigate this issue. We are only interested in sound approximation algorithms that never fail to detect a matching trace, but may spuriously decide that a benign trace matches a behavior graph. This property maintains the crucial guarantee that the algorithm will detect all attacks defined by the behavior graphs. We view this as the most important property that a behavior matching algorithm can possess, provided that the false positive rate is not unreasonably high.

The first approximation algorithm is obtained by re-defining the primitives $\mathcal{F}$, Test, and Update in Algorithm 1; the formal definitions of the primitives for this approximation algorithm are given in the technical report [8]. It performs matching by maintaining a memory, for each state in **G**, of terms from **T** that may be matched to that particular state. If at any point a substitution exists that matches a frontier element to a trace element, the algorithm considers each predecessor s' of s, and checks the memory for each one to determine whether previous trace terms satisfy the dependencies needed to match $\mathbf{T}(i)$ to $\alpha(s)$. If so, then the frontier is updated with the new matching between s and $\mathbf{T}(i)$, and the next trace event is considered.

The imprecision in this algorithm comes from the fact that the frontier does not record partial witnesses, but instead only *local* history with respect to each states in **G**. This means that Test might consult substitutions that would belong to multiple distinct partial witnesses in the exact algorithm, thus incorrectly concluding that all dependence constraints are satisfied when a single witness that satisfies all constraints does not exist. While this can lead to false positives, note that if a true witness does exist, then Test will effectively find it, so there can be no false negatives. This is related to existential abstraction, which describes the relationship between these approximate primitives, and the exact ones listed in Algorithm 1.

The next proposition guarantees that the amount of work required by the algorithm on receiving a new trace element is at most linear in the size of the behavior graph, length of the execution trace, and maximum term size of Σ.

Proposition 3. *When the approximate primitives are used in Algorithm 1, each iteration of the main loop is $O(iM|A|)$, where i is the current index into $\mathbf{T}$ and M is the maximum time needed to match terms in $T(\Sigma, V)$.*

Note that Proposition 3 implies that the algorithm has a worst-case time complexity that is linear in $|\mathbf{T}||A|$. The worst-case space complexity is $O(|\mathbf{T}|)$, as the frontier requires exactly one entry for each trace term.

We now present an approximation algorithm that uses Bloom filters [4] to record possible matchings between states in **G** and terms in **T**. Intuitively, a set of Bloom filters is kept for each argument of each term in the image of α. As trace terms are matched to states, the corresponding substitutions for arguments are added to the filters, and later consulted when dependencies are matched. This algorithm has linear complexity with a very low coefficient (see Proposition 4), but at the cost of increased false positives due to the overapproximation of the Bloom filters. We represent the domain of Bloom filters by the symbol $\mathcal{B}$. The algorithm is obtained by substituting the following primitives in Algorithm 1:

- $\Gamma = (A \mapsto (\mathbb{Z}^+ \mapsto \mathcal{P}(\mathcal{B})), A)$. The first component of an element in Γ is a mapping from states to a different set of mappings, that contain an over-approximation for each term argument previously bound to the state. Note that the structure used for this overapproximation (the range of the mapping $\mathbb{Z}^+ \mapsto \mathcal{P}(\mathcal{B})$) is a set of Bloom filters, rather than a single Bloom filter. We override the default Bloom filter union operation to add a new filter to this set when the probability of encountering a false positive in the filter exceeds ϕ. Similarly, the membership query operation must be overridden to check *all filters in the set* to maintain soundness.

- Test(s, i, w) returns True whenever:

$$\forall(s', s) \in E. \ \forall 0 \leq j \leq \text{arity}(\alpha(s')). \exists f \in w^1_{s'}(j).$$
$$[\text{args}(\alpha(s'), j) \mapsto f](\beta_{s',s}(\alpha(s))) \text{ matches } \mathbf{T}(i)$$

In other words, the Bloom filters associated with all predecessors of s are checked for elements that satisfy the needed dependencies.

- Update,

$$\text{Update}(\mathcal{F}, s, i, w) = \mathcal{F} - \{w\}\cup$$
$$(w^1[s \mapsto \delta_s], w^2 \cup \{a : (a, s) \in E\})$$

where

$$\delta_s(k) = w^1_k \cup \text{args}(\alpha(s), k)$$

In other words, all of the Bloom filters associated with s are updated to reflect the arguments of $\mathbf{T}(i)$, and the old w is removed from $\mathcal{F}$.

We note that it is not strictly necessary to use a *set* of Bloom filters for each argument, particularly when the length of the inputs are known in advance, and the parameters of the Bloom filter can be configured to avoid false positives. This has the benefit of producing a constant-time algorithm in the size of the input trace. In many cases, however, it is not possible to determine a bound on trace length in advance. By using an unbounded set of Bloom filters to represent each argument, the algorithm overcomes the risk of encountering an explosion of false positives when the trace length exceeds the parameters of each individual Bloom filter. This is accomplished by overriding the union and membership query operations over filters in the definition of Test and Update, essentially tracking the number of entries inserted into each filter, and creating a new one when the probability of encountering a false positive rises above a user-specified value ϕ. When the history is consulted to establish a dependence, each of these filters must be checked to maintain soundness, and the number of the filters is a linear function of $|\mathbf{T}|$, thus the linear complexity in trace length.

Proposition 4. *The number of Bloom filters needed to maintain a false positive rate of at most ϕ is $O\left(-2|\mathbf{T}|k/2(b-1)\ln(1 - \phi^{1/k}) + k\right)$, where k is the number of hash functions used in the Bloom filters, and b is the number of bits.*

Proposition 4 tells us that the complexity of the algorithm grows very slowly in the length of $\mathbf{T}$. Recall that the algorithm's complexity depends on $|\mathbf{T}|$ only insofar as the number of Bloom filters needed to maintain a false positive rate of no more than ϕ must be checked each time a new trace element is encountered. Proposition 4 tells us that this dependence is linear, with the given coefficient. Because the logarithm function has an asymptote at zero towards negative infinity, $-k/(b-1)\ln(1 - \phi^{\frac{1}{k}})$ shrinks rather well in b and k, leaving the linear coefficient quite small. For example, devoting one megabyte of memory to the Bloom filter ($b = 8,388,608$) and using $k = 100$ hash functions, the coefficient is approximately 2×10^{-6} for a false positive rate of no more than 1%. Needless to say, this is an impressive performance characteristic for a small amount of memory and imprecision.

4   Experimental Results

We performed experiments to determine the run-time characteristics of each of the algorithms presented in Section 3, in addition to the false positive rates of the approximation algorithms. We also implemented a reduction of behavior matching to SAT constraints (details in the technical report [8]), in order to evaluate the feasibility of using an off-the-shelf solver [7] for real instances of the problem. Our results are encouraging:

- The approximation algorithms perform significantly better than the exact algorithm; on our set, they performed 17.3 and 21.6 times faster (for the first and second approximation algorithms discussed, respectively), on average.
- The false positive rate of the approximation algorithms is not excessive: 7.3% and 9.1%.
- The SAT constraints corresponding to our data set are quickly solved by modern solvers, requiring 0.18 seconds to solve an instance, on average. However, generating the constraints generally requires a substantial amount of time and space: we observed on average 65.6 seconds and approximately 10^6 constraints for 120 second execution traces.

These results demonstrate the practical value of our algorithms.

We collected behavior traces from 70 applications (both known malware and common desktop applications), and matched them against ten behavior graphs mined from a repository of behavior data using simulated annealing [9]. The behavior traces are composed of system call events, along with detailed data and annotations about the arguments of each event; for an in-depth account of our behavior collection mechanism, consult our previous work [9, 13]. We ran all experiments on a quad-core workstation, with 8 gigabytes of main memory. For experiments involving Bloom filters, we utilized the pybloom library, with a low false positive probability ($\phi = 1\%$) and a moderate number of bits ($b = 4,000$).

The first noteworthy result we obtained is that the exact behavior matching algorithm presented in Definition 1 is significantly slower than both approximation algorithms, as well as the reduction to SAT constraints. On average, the precise algorithm required 31.35 seconds to complete, compared to 1.84 and 1.47 for the first and second algorithms discussed, respectively. The runtime overhead, which in this case corresponds to the amount of time taken by the algorithm taken as a percentage of the trace execution time,of the exact algorithm amounts to 26%, compared 1.5% and 1.2% for the approximation algorithms. Furthermore, 2% of the instances given to the precise algorithm timed out after 45 minutes. This confirms our suggestion that existing algorithms for behavior matching, which are purported to resemble Algorithm 1, have much higher complexity than previously thought.

Of the reduction to SAT, we found that while the instances can generally be solved quickly (more quickly than all of our algorithms, in fact), the constraint systems for an instance also grow quickly, and take a non-trivial amount of time to generate. In other words, the reduction to SAT is not yet suitable for run-time behavior matching, but may be ideally suited to off-line forensic analysis where exact solutions are required. We solved instances of SAT constraints using MINISAT [7], which required on average 0.18 seconds to complete. We take this result as indication that it is common to encounter behavior matching instances that are "easy" in some sense. The running time of constraint generation on our dataset is distributed bimodally, with means at 16.6 seconds (87% of samples) and 883.7 seconds (6% of samples), and 7% timing out after 1 hour. This means that for the "easy" cases, the runtime overhead of constraint generation is approximately 14%, but for the "hard" cases, it is approximately 733%. The number of clauses in the constraint system has a similar bimodal distribution, with means at 6.7×10^5 (89% of samples) and 1.1×10^7 (4% of samples) clauses. If we assume that each clause takes 5 bytes of memory (a conservative underapproximation), then this means that on average, running an application for 120 seconds generates 3 megabytes of constraint data for easy cases, and 52 megabytes for hard cases; clearly, even for easy cases this does not scale to long-running applications.

Finally, we studied the false positive rates of the approximation algorithms, using the results of our precise algorithms (both Algorithm 1 and the SAT reduction) as ground truth. We found the rates to be reasonable: 7.36%, 9.13% for the first and second algorithms discussed, respectively. For the exceptionally low overhead produced by these methods (1.5% and 1.2%), we assert that this is an acceptable trade-off.

5   Related Work

Several abstractions with similarities to behavior graphs have been previously studied. Neven *et al.* studied both register and pebble automata [14] (RA and PA, respectively), which are two generalizations of traditional FSA to infinite alphabets. They conclude that PA is a more natural extension of FSA to infinite alphabets, but we do not see a way to encode a behavior graph as either formalism. The main issue is the bounded number of pebbles (or registers), which must be used to calculate dependencies; because a graph state may need to be temporarily matched to an unbounded number of trace events, the bounded number of pebbles (or registers) will cause the matching algorithm to drop history.

Another related formalism that has recieved attention is tree automata [5], which operate over ranked alphabets. Behavior graphs cannot be reduced to traditional finite-state tree automata for two reasons: dependencies between subterms cannot be represented, and the set of initial states in the automaton must be finite, whereas the execution traces that serve as inputs are unbounded, and would therefore require an infinite set of possible initial states. Extensions of tree automata involving dependence relations between subterms have been studied ([5] Chapter 4), but not their extension to infinite-state automata, which would be required for direct application to the problem of behavior matching.

Behavior matching has seen mention in the system security literature frequently in recent years. Perhaps the most compelling account is due to Kolbitsch *et al.* [12]. In this work, the authors describe behavior specifications that are nearly identical to those formalized in this paper, with nearly arbitrary data dependencies between events. An algorithm for matching execution traces to these specifications is alluded to, but a precise description of this algorithm is not given, much less an analysis of its complexity. The same notion of behavior and matching seems to be operative in other work by the same authors [2, 6]. However, the technique is pitched as *efficient* throughout the work, and reported overheads typically range around 5%. Given the strong connection between our notion of behavior matching and that presented by Kolbitsch *et al.*, these results diverge significantly from the theoretical results presented in this paper, as well as the observed performance characteristics of the sound and complete algorithm.

Sekar and Uppuluri [17] discuss the use of *extended finite-state automata* (EFSA) in intrusion detection. EFSA bear resemblance to the behavior graphs discussed in this paper insofar as they allow general data dependencies (including equality), but the authors do not attempt to formalize the computational model that these dependences may adopt. An algorithm for run-time matching of EFSA is given, and the authors claim that the amount of work on receiving an event is $O(N)$, where N is the number of states in the EFSA. This conflicts with our results. However, this claim is given without proof, and seems to be predicated on the assumption that the algorithm needs only remember a bounded number of possible matching configurations (the authors state this assumption in the description of their algorithm). This indicates that their algorithm is a greedy version of Definition 1, and therefore unsound; this conclusion is backed by the complexity results presented in Section 3.

Tokhtabayev *et al.* describe a behavior matching scheme based on colored Petri nets [18]. The formalism used to describe behaviors shares nearly all of its salient features with our notion of behavior, including complex data dependencies. The performance overheads they report fall below 5%, but the complexity of their matching algorithm is not discussed, and a formal description of the algorithm is not given due to "limitations." There are several other accounts of behavior matching involving data dependencies in the security literature [9, 11, 13, 15, 16, 21] that use notions of behavior for various ends. There is also work that formalizes software behaviors in terms of events without accounting for data dependencies [3]; this work is interesting in contrast to ours, the simpler notion of behavior may be more suitable for certain applications.

6   Conclusion

In this paper, we presented a formulation of behavior matching that encompasses most of those seen in the literature, and demonstrated the problem is NP-Complete. We proceeded to give two exact algorithms for solving the problem, presented two approximation algorithms, and demonstrated that they can be used to find accurate solutions to real instances of behavior matching. In the future, it will be important to determine whether real applications of behavior matching can be made to fit into a tractable subclass of the general problem presented here.

Acknowledgments. We would like to thank Eric Bach, Drew Davidson, Bill Harris, and Thomas Reps for their helpful comments. The first author of this work is supported by a Microsoft Research PhD Fellowship. A portion of this work was supported by the DARPA CRASH program.

References

[1] Baader, F., Nipkow, T.: Term rewriting and all that. Cambridge University Press, Cambridge (1998)

[2] Bayer, U.: Large-Scale Dynamic Malware Analysis. PhD thesis, Technical University of Vienna (2009)

[3] Beaucamps, P., Gnaedig, I., Marion, J.-Y.: Behavior abstraction in malware analysis. Runtime Verification (2010)

[4] Bloom, B.H.: Space/time trade-offs in hash coding with allowable errors. Communications of the ACM 13 (1970)

[5] Comon, H., Dauchet, M., Gilleron, R., Löding, C., Jacquemard, F., Lugiez, D., Tison, S., Tommasi, M.: Tree automata techniques and applications (2007) (release October 12, 2007)

[6] Comparetti, P.M., Salvaneschi, G., Kirda, E., Kolbitsch, C., Kruegel, C., Zanero, S.: Identifying dormant functionality in malware programs. In: Proceedings of the IEEE Symposium on Security and Privacy (2010)

[7] En, N., Srensson, N.: An extensible SAT-solver. In: SAT (2004)

[8] Fredrikson, M., Christodorescu, M., Jha, S.: Dynamic behavior matching: A complexity analysis and new approximation algorithms. Technical report (2011), http://www.cs.wisc.edu/~mfredrik/matching-tr.pdf

[9] Fredrikson, M., Christodorescu, M., Jha, S., Sailer, R., Yang, X.: Synthesizing near-optimal specifications of malicious behavior. In: Proceedings of the IEEE Symposium of Security and Privacy (2010)

[10] Hopcroft, J.E., Ullman, J.D.: Introduction to Automata Theory, Languages, and Computation. Adison-Wesley Publishing Company, Reading (1979)

[11] Jacob, G., Debar, H., Filiol, E.: Malware behavioral detection by attribute-automata using abstraction from platform and language. In: Recent Advances in Intrusion Detection (2009)

[12] Kolbitsch, C., Comparetti, P.M., Kruegel, C., Zhou, X., Wang, X.: Efficient and effective malware detection at the end host. In: Proceedings of the Usenix Security Symposium (2009)

[13] Martignoni, L., Stinson, E., Fredrikson, M., Jha, S., Mitchell, J.C.: A layered architecture for detecting malicious behaviors. In: Lippmann, R., Kirda, E., Trachtenberg, A. (eds.) RAID 2008. LNCS, vol. 5230, pp. 78–97. Springer, Heidelberg (2008)

[14] Neven, F., Schwentick, T., Vianu, V.: Finite state machines for strings over infinite alphabets. ACM Transactions on Computational Logic 5 (2004)

[15] Park, Y., Reeves, D., Mulukutla, V., Sundaravel, B.: Fast malware classification by automated behavioral graph matching. In: Proceedings of the Workshop on Cyber Security and Information Intelligence Research (2010)

[16] Park, Y.-J., Zhang, Z., Chen, S.: Run-time detection of malware via dynamic control-flow inspection. In: Proceedings of the IEEE Conference on Application-specific Systems, Architectures and Processors (2009)

[17] Sekar, R., Uppuluri, P.: Synthesizing fast intrusion prevention/detection systems from high-level specifications. In: Proceedings of the Usenix Security Symposium (1999)

[18] Tokhtabayev, A.G., Skormin, V.A., Dolgikh, A.M.: Expressive, efficient and obfuscation resilient behavior based IDS. In: Gritzalis, D., Preneel, B., Theoharidou, M. (eds.) ESORICS 2010. LNCS, vol. 6345, pp. 698–716. Springer, Heidelberg (2010)

[19] Wang, X., Jhi, Y.-C., Zhu, S., Liu, P.: Behavior based software theft detection. In: Proceedings of the ACM Conference on Computer and Communications Security, CCS (2009)

[20] Werth, T., Wrlein, M., Dreweke, A., Fischer, I., Philippsen, M.: Dag mining for code compaction. In: Cao, L., Yu, P.S., Zhang, C., Zhang, H. (eds.) Data Mining for Business Applications (2009)

[21] Zhao, C., Kong, J., Zhang, K.: Program behavior discovery and verification: A graph grammar approach. IEEE Transactions on Software Engineering 36 (2010)

A Connection-Based Characterization of Bi-intuitionistic Validity

Didier Galmiche and Daniel Méry

LORIA - Université Henri Poincaré
Campus Scientifique BP 239
Vandœuvre-lés-Nancy, France

Abstract. We give a connection-based characterization of validity in propositional bi-intuitionistic logic in terms of specific directed graphs called R-graphs. Such a characterization is well-suited for deriving labelled proof-systems with counter-model construction facilities. We first define the notion of bi-intuitionistic R-graph from which we then obtain a connection-based characterization of propositional bi-intuitionistic validity and derive a sound and complete free-variable labelled sequent calculus that admits cut-elimination and also variable splitting.

1 Introduction

Bi-intuitionistic logic Bilnt is a conservative extension of intuitionistic logic that introduces a new connective $\prec$, called exclusion (also called co-implication or subtraction), which is dual to the implication connective $\rightarrow$. It was first studied by Rauszer that gives a Hilbert calculus with Kripke and algebraic semantics [11] and more recently by Crolard from the perspective of bicartesian closed categories with coexponents and the underlying type system with applications to type theory [2,3]. An interesting aspect of Bilnt lies in the duality between implication and exclusion which motivates the definition of proof systems that work as programming languages in which values and continuations are handled in a symmetric way. From a proof-theoretic point of view, a strong focus has been put on the achievement of cut-free proof-systems since cut-elimination in Gentzen-style (shallow) sequent calculi is particularly difficult to obtain. In this perspective some cut-free calculi for Bilnt have been proposed from sequent structures like nested sequents [6] or display inference rules [10]. Another solution makes use of Negri's general methodology for designing labelled sequent calculi in modal logics [7] in order to provide a cut-free labelled sequent calculus where labels correspond to worlds in Kripke structures [9].

In this paper we give the first connection-based characterization of propositional bi-intuitionistic validity in terms of bi-intuitionistic R-graphs. Let us note that similar structures have been defined in the case of BI or separation logics [5,4] in order to characterize validity. Our characterization is well-suited for deriving labelled proof-systems with counter-model construction facilities which, compared with the existing labelled proof-systems [9], easily integrate

N. Bjørner and V. Sofronie-Stokkermans (Eds.): CADE 2011, LNAI 6803, pp. 268–282, 2011.

free-variables and variable splitting [1]. The main contributions of this work are: the definition of bi-intuitionistic R-graphs; a connection-based characterization of validity in propositional Bilnt; a new sound and complete free-variable labelled sequent calculus that includes variable splitting and has the cut-elimination property; an algorithm for solving admissibility constraints and thus deriving a connection-based method.

2   Bi-intuitionistic Propositional Logic

The language of Bilnt consists of a countable set $\mathcal{V}$ of propositional letters $P, Q \dots$ and the logical symbols $\bot$, $\vee$, $\wedge$, $\rightarrow$ and $\prec$. Formulas are inductively built from propositional letters as follows:

$$A ::= P \mid \bot \mid A \vee A \mid A \wedge A \mid A \rightarrow A \mid A \prec A.$$

We write $\mathcal{F}$ to denote the set of all formulas of Bilnt. Negation $\neg A$ is defined as syntactic sugar for $A \rightarrow \bot$ and is therefore not considered as primitive in our setting. Similarly, the conjunctive unit $\top$ is defined as a shorthand for $P \rightarrow P$. Bi-intuitionistic logic Kripke semantics is a straightforward extension of that of intuitionistic logic.

Definition 1. *A* Kripke model *is a triple* $\mathcal{M} = \langle M, \sqsubseteq, \llbracket \cdot \rrbracket \rangle$, *where* M *is a set of worlds,* $\sqsubseteq$ *is a partial order on* M *and* $\llbracket \cdot \rrbracket$ *is a function from worlds to sets of propositional letters satisfying the following* Kripke monotonicity *condition: if* $P \in \llbracket m \rrbracket$ *and* $m \sqsubseteq n$ *then* $P \in \llbracket n \rrbracket$.
The Kripke forcing relation $\models$ *is defined as the least relation between worlds and formulas such that:*

- $m \models \bot$ *never;*
- $m \models P$ *iff* $P \in \llbracket m \rrbracket$;
- $m \models A \vee B$ *iff* $m \models A$ *or* $m \models B$;
- $m \models A \wedge B$ *iff* $m \models A$ *and* $m \models B$;
- $m \models A \rightarrow B$ *iff for all* $n \in M$ *such that* $m \sqsubseteq n$, $n \not\models A$ *or* $n \models B$;
- $m \models A \prec B$ *iff for some* $n \in M$ *such that* $n \sqsubseteq m$, $n \models A$ *and* $n \not\models B$.

Kripke monotonicity lifts from propositional letters to formulas as in intuitionistic logic. As usual, a formula A is *satisfied in* $\mathcal{M}$ iff $m \models A$ for all worlds m in M, *satisfiable* if it is satisfied in some Kripke model $\mathcal{M}$, and *valid* if it is satisfied in all Kripke models. Figure 1 depicts the standard (Dragalin-style) multi-conclusioned sequent calculus for Bilnt which can be found in [9]. We observe that the rules for the exclusion connective $\prec$ simply behave as duals for the ones dealing with the inclusion $\rightarrow$. However, the price to pay for the easy dual formulation is that the calculus does not admit cut-elimination.

3   Indexing Formulas

In this section, we recall some basic terminology of connection-based characterizations of validity as we shall heavily rely on it in the forthcoming sections.

$$\frac{}{\Gamma, \bot \vdash \Delta}$$

$$\frac{\Gamma \vdash \Delta}{\Gamma \vdash \bot, \Delta} \bot_{\mathrm{R}}$$

$$\frac{}{\Gamma, A \vdash A, \Delta} \text{ ax}$$

$$\frac{\Gamma \vdash A, \Delta \quad \Gamma, A \vdash \Delta}{\Gamma \vdash \Delta} \text{ cut}$$

$$\frac{\Gamma, A, B \vdash \Delta}{\Gamma, A \wedge B \vdash \Delta} \wedge_{\mathrm{L}}$$

$$\frac{\Gamma \vdash A, \Delta \quad \Gamma \vdash B, \Delta}{\Gamma \vdash A \wedge B, \Delta} \wedge_{\mathrm{R}}$$

$$\frac{\Gamma, A \vdash \Delta \quad \Gamma, B \vdash \Delta}{\Gamma, A \vee B \vdash \Delta} \vee_{\mathrm{L}}$$

$$\frac{\Gamma \vdash A, B, \Delta}{\Gamma \vdash A \vee B, \Delta} \vee_{\mathrm{R}}$$

$$\frac{\Gamma, A \to B \vdash A, \Delta \quad \Gamma, B \vdash \Delta}{\Gamma, A \to B \vdash \Delta} \to_{\mathrm{L}}$$

$$\frac{\Gamma, A \vdash B}{\Gamma \vdash A \to B, \Delta} \to_{\mathrm{R}}$$

$$\frac{\Gamma \vdash A, \Delta \quad \Gamma, B \vdash A \prec B, \Delta}{\Gamma \vdash A \prec B, \Delta} \prec_{\mathrm{R}}$$

$$\frac{A \vdash B, \Delta}{\Gamma, A \prec B \vdash \Delta} \prec_{\mathrm{L}}$$

Fig. 1. Dragalin-style sequent calculus for Bilnt

A *signed formula* is a pair (C, S), written C^{s}, where C is a Bilnt formula and $\mathrm{S} \in \{+, -\}$ is a *sign*. Depending on its principal connective and sign, a signed formula is given a *principal type (ptype)* α or β. If α (respectively β) is the principal type of a signed formula C, then, its left subformula A is of *secondary type (stype)* α_1 (respectively β_1) and its right subformula B is of *secondary type* α_2 (respectively β_2). Signed formulas the principal connective of which belongs to the set $\{\to, \prec\}$ also admit an additional *intuitionistic type (itype)* ϕ, $\overline{\phi}$, ψ or $\overline{\psi}$. The following tables describe how signs, principal, secondary and intuitionistic types are inductively determined.

α	α_1	α_2	β	β_1	β_2		*itype*
$(A \wedge B)^+$	A^+	B^+	$(A \wedge B)^-$	A^-	B^-	$(A \to B)^+$	ϕ
$(A \vee B)^-$	A^-	B^-	$(A \vee B)^+$	A^+	B^+	$(A \to B)^-$	ψ
$(A \to B)^-$	A^+	B^-	$(A \to B)^+$	A^-	B^+	$(A \prec B)^+$	$\overline{\psi}$
$(A \prec B)^+$	A^+	B^-	$(A \prec B)^-$	A^-	B^+	$(A \prec B)^-$	$\overline{\phi}$

For readability, we often simply speak of the type of a signed formula each time the context makes it clear what type (ptype, stype or itype) is actually intended; we also write "*t*-formula" as a shorthand for "formula of type *t*". Moreover, given a (plain) formula C and a subformula A in C, the (principal, secondary or intuitionistic) type of A in C is defined as the type of the signed formula A^{s} in C^- that (syntactically) corresponds to A.

Let Φ and Ψ be two disjoint and denumerable sets of symbols respectively called variable and constant symbols. We shall use the letters ranging from a to d (possibly subscripted) to denote constant symbols. Similarly, we shall use the letters from x to z to denote variable symbols. For convenience, let us also

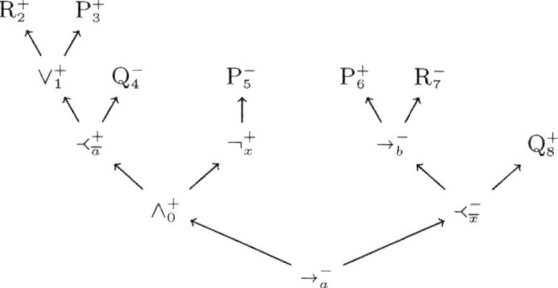

Fig. 2. Indexed formula tree

assume that Ψ always contains the particular symbol ϵ and that if s is a constant (respectively variable) symbol, then so is $\bar{s}$.

Given a formula C, an *indexed formula* can be obtained from C by assigning a unique index (often called "position" in the matrix terminology) to each subformula encountered along a depth first exploration of C^- (w.r.t. the syntactic structure of C) in such a way that ψ- and $\bar{\psi}$-subformulas are indexed with constant symbols in Ψ, ϕ- and $\bar{\phi}$-subformulas are indexed with variable symbols in Φ, all other subformulas being indexed with natural numbers.

Assuming strict total orders $<_\Phi, <_\Psi, <_\mathbb{N}$ on $\Phi, \Psi, \mathbb{N}$, assignments can be made deterministic so as to obtain a one-to-one correspondence between formulas and indexed formulas. We interpret $<_\Phi$ and $<_\Psi$ as lexicographic orders and $<_\mathbb{N}$ as the usual strict order on natural numbers; therefore, each time we have to choose an index for a (sub)formula, we always pick the first symbol in Φ, Ψ or $\mathbb{N}$ (w.r.t. $<_\Phi, <_\Psi, <_\mathbb{N}$) that has not already been used as an index. We write $\mathcal{F}(C, i)$ (respectively $\mathcal{S}f(C, i)$) to denote the unique subformula (respectively signed subformula) associated to the index i in a formula C (or signed formula C^s depending on the context).

For example, indexing $C = (((R \vee P) \prec Q) \wedge \neg P) \rightarrow ((P \rightarrow R) \prec Q)$ we get the indexed (signed) formula

$$(((R_2^+ \vee_1^+ P_3^+) \prec_{\bar{a}}^+ Q_4^-) \wedge_0^+ \neg_x^- P_5^-) \rightarrow_a^- ((P_6^+ \rightarrow_b^- R_7^-) \prec_{\bar{x}}^- Q_8^+).$$

Since indexes are in a one-to-one correspondence with (signed) formulas, we shall sometimes use indexes in places where (signed) formulas would normally be expected (and vice-versa).

A *formula tree* for a formula C is a representation of its corresponding indexed formula as a syntax tree. A formula tree induces a strict partial ordering $\ll$ on indexes, called the *domination ordering*, which is such that the index of the root is the least element and if $i \ll j$ then i is encountered before j on a path from the root to j. If i is a non-atomic index in C (*i.e.*, if $\mathcal{F}(C, i)$ is a non-atomic formula) then the two indexes j and k such that $\mathcal{F}(C, j)$ and $\mathcal{F}(C, k)$ are the immediate (left and right) subformulas of $\mathcal{F}(C, i)$ are called *dual* and we write $j \triangle k = i$. Figure 2 shows the formula tree associated with $(((R \vee P) \prec Q) \wedge \neg P) \rightarrow ((P \rightarrow R) \prec Q)$.

In the standard sequent calculus of Figure 1, contraction is internalized by the repetition of the principal formula $A \to B$ (respectively $A \prec B$) in the left (respectively right) premiss of the $\to_L$ (respectively $\prec_R$) rule so that there is no need for an explicit contraction rule. In a connection-based setting contraction is usually handled via the notion of *multiplicity*. Given a formula C of Bilnt, a multiplicity for C is a function $\mu()$ which assigns a natural number to each ϕ- or $\overline{\phi}$-subformula A in C. The formula $\mu(C)$ is then defined as the formula obtained from C by replacing every subformula A in C such that $\mu(A) = n$ with the subformula $A \wedge A \wedge \ldots \wedge A$, where the connective $\wedge$ occurs exactly n times. For example, if $C = (P \to Q) \to (R \prec S)$, $\mu(P \to Q) = 1$ and $\mu(R \prec S) = 2$, then $\mu(C) = ((P \to Q) \wedge (P \to Q)) \to ((R \prec S) \wedge (R \prec S) \wedge (R \prec S))$. Intuitively, a multiplicity function encodes the number of copies that would be allowed (via contraction) for each ϕ- or $\overline{\phi}$-formula in a sequent-style derivation.

For convenience, when dealing with indexed formulas, we use superscripted indexes to distinguish between the copies of ϕ- and $\overline{\phi}$-formulas. For the previous example, if we assume that x is the index of $R \prec S$ in C, then $\mu(R \prec S) = 2$ implies that x^1 and x^2 should respectively be the indexes of the first and second additional copies of $R \prec S$ in $\mu(C)$. The previous notions are fairly common to most connection-based characterizations of validity. If we were to follow the standard recipe for such characterizations, the next step would be the introduction of the key notions of (atomic) matrix paths, connections and spanning sets together with admissible substitutions leading to irreflexive reduction orderings. However, we shall not follow the standard approach for the upcoming sections and rather introduce the concept of R-graphs since it allows us to reformulate all the standard notions on the same graphical structure. Moreover, R-graphs can easily be turned into Kripke models when dealing with non valid formulas.

4   Bi-intuitionistic R-Graphs

From a very general point of view, R-graphs for a given logic are directed graphs in which vertices are meant to represent worlds in the underlying Kripke semantics of the logic [5]. Let us first define the general notion of R-graph before restricting it to match the bi-intuitionistic case.

Definition 2 (R-graph). *A R-graph (RG) is a directed graph $G(V, E)$ with vertices V and edges E. The vertices are named with elements of $\Psi \cup \Phi$. Moreover, V is required to contain a distinguished vertex ϵ called the ϵ-vertex, every vertex u is associated with a set $\mathcal{F}(G, u)$ of signed formulas the elements of which are referred to as the tags of u, and every edge e is tagged with a letter $\mathcal{T}(G, e)$ from the set $\mathcal{T} = \{\psi, \phi, \overline{\psi}, \overline{\phi}, \sigma, \kappa\}$ of edge-tags.*

A vertex named with a constant symbol (respectively variable symbol) is called a ψ-vertex (respectively ϕ-vertex). The set of ψ-vertices (respectively ϕ-vertices) is written V^Ψ (respectively V^Φ). We use the letters u, v and w to range over arbitrary vertices and we write $u[\tau]v$ to denote the edge, tagged with the letter $\tau \in \mathcal{T}$, that goes from u to v; we then call this edge a τ-edge and say that u

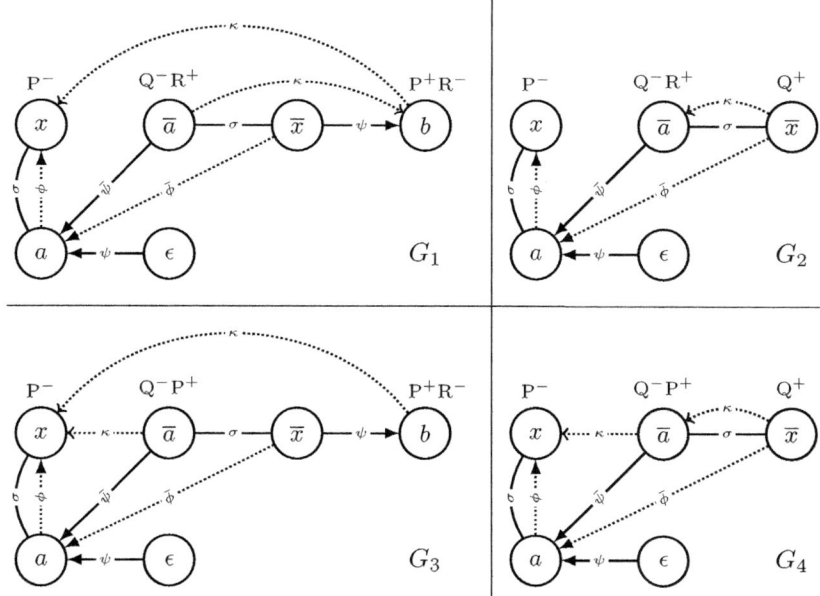

Fig. 3. Bi-intuitionistic R-graphs

and v respectively are its *source* and *target*. Given a subset $T \subseteq \mathcal{T}$, the set of all τ-edges such that $\tau \in T$ is written E^T.

Definition 3 (Bi-intuitionistic RG). *A R-graph $G(V, E)$ is a bi-intuitionistic R-graph (biRG) if it satisfies the following structural conditions:*

- *every ψ-edge has a ψ-vertex as its target;*
- *every $\bar{\psi}$-edge has a ψ-vertex as its source;*
- *every ϕ-edge has a ϕ-vertex as its target;*
- *every $\bar{\phi}$-edge has a ϕ-vertex as its source;*
- *every σ-edge induces a "bidirectional" link between a ϕ-vertex and a ψ-vertex, more formally, $u[\sigma]v \in E$ iff $v[\sigma]u \in E$, with either $u \in V^\Psi$ and $v \in V^\Phi$, or $u \in V^\Phi$ and $v \in V^\Psi$;*
- *every κ-edge $u[\kappa]v$ is a link between two (arbitrary) vertices such that there exists at least one formula occurring positively (with a "+" sign) in $\mathcal{F}(G, u)$ and negatively (with a "−" sign) in $\mathcal{F}(G, v)$.*

Figure 3 gives some examples of bi-intuitionistic R-graphs. We shall explain in the next section how such graphs can be associated with formulas and discuss them in more details.

5   R-Graph Reductions

Standard matrix characterizations heavily rely on the notion of (atomic) matrix paths through a given formula C. In our setting, such atomic matrix paths are replaced with the notion of irreducible R-graphs.

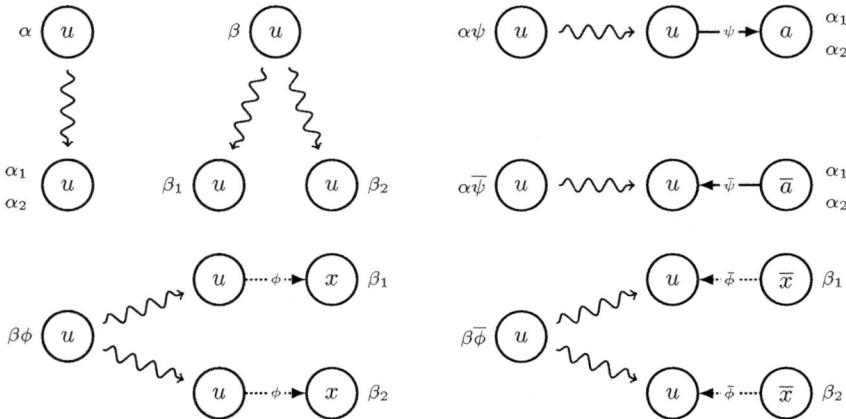

a (resp. $\bar{a}$, x, $\bar{x}$) is the index of the $\alpha\psi$- (resp. $\alpha\bar{\psi}$-, $\beta\phi$-, $\beta\bar{\phi}$-) formula under reduction.

Fig. 4. Reduction rules

Given a Bilnt formula A, a *(biRG-)reduction through* A is a sequence $\mathcal{R} = R_0\rho_1 \ldots \rho_{i-1}\rho_i \ldots$ in which R_0 is a collection (of biRGs) containing the single biRG $G_0(V_0, E_0)$, where $V_0 = \{\epsilon\}$, $E_0 = \emptyset$ and $\mathcal{F}(G_0, \epsilon) = \{A^-\}$, and each ρ_i is a reduction step that transforms the collection R_{i-1} inherited from the previous reduction step into a new collection R_i by applying one of the reduction rules given in Fig. 4.

In order to apply a reduction rule to a biRG $G(V, E)$, one first needs to choose a vertex u in V and a signed formula A^s in $\mathcal{F}(G, u)$.

- If A^s has principal type α and has no intuitionistic type, $G(V, E)$ is reduced to the new biRG $G_1(V_1, E_1)$ such that $V_1 = V$, $E_1 = E$, $\mathcal{F}(G_1, v) = \mathcal{F}(G, v)$ for all $v \neq u$ and $\mathcal{F}(G_1, u) = \mathcal{F}(G, u) \cup \{\alpha_1(A^s), \alpha_2(A^s)\}$, where $\alpha_1(A^s)$ and $\alpha_2(A^s)$ respectively are the first and second signed subformulas of A^s (of secondary type α_1 and α_2).
- If A^s has principal type β and has no intuitionistic type, $G(V, E)$ is reduced to two new biRGs $G_1(V_1, E_1)$, $G_2(V_2, E_2)$ such that for $i \in \{1, 2\}$, $V_i = V$, $E_i = E$, $\mathcal{F}(G_i, v) = \mathcal{F}(G, v)$ for all $v \neq u$ and $\mathcal{F}(G_i, u) = \mathcal{F}(G, u) \cup \{\beta_i(A^s)\}$.

The previous reduction rules are the reformulation of the standard α and β matrix-path reduction rules. The next two reduction rules are specific to Bilnt and depend on the index (a, $\bar{a}$, x or $\bar{x}$) and intuitionistic type of the signed formula under reduction (principal formula).

- If A^s has principal type α and has intuitionistic type ψ (respectively $\bar{\psi}$), $G(V, E)$ is reduced to the new biRG $G_1(V_1, E_1)$ such that $V_1 = V \cup \{a\}$ and $E_1 = E \cup \{u[\psi]a\}$ (respectively $V_1 = V \cup \{\bar{a}\}$ and $E_1 = E \cup \{\bar{a}[\bar{\psi}]u\}$). Moreover, $\mathcal{F}(G_1, v) = \mathcal{F}(G, v)$ for all $v \neq a$ (respectively $v \neq \bar{a}$), and $\mathcal{F}(G_1, a) = \{\alpha_1(A^s), \alpha_2(A^s)\}$ (respectively $\mathcal{F}(G_1, \bar{a}) = \{\alpha_1(A^s), \alpha_2(A^s)\}$).

- If A^s has principal type β and has intuitionistic type ϕ (respectively $\overline{\phi}$), $G(V, E)$ is reduced to two new biRGs $G_1(V_1, E_1)$, $G_2(V_2, E_2)$ such that for $i \in \{1, 2\}$, $V_i = V \cup \{x\}$ and $E_i = E \cup \{u[\phi]x\}$ (respectively $V_i = V \cup \{\overline{x}\}$ and $E_i = E \cup \{\overline{x}[\overline{\phi}]u\}$). Moreover, $\mathcal{F}(G_i, v) = \mathcal{F}(G, v)$ for all $v \neq x$ (respectively $v \neq \overline{x}$) and $\mathcal{F}(G_i, x)$ (respectively $\mathcal{F}(G_i, \overline{x})) = \{A^s\} \cup \{\beta_i(A^s)\}$.

Let us remark that we have chosen to prevent the reduction rules from discarding their principal formula from the tags of u (although we shall forget about them in graphical representations to increase readability). This is not a strict requirement but it makes the counter-model construction process (*e.g.*, the saturation relation) easier to define.

Definition 4 (irreducibility). *A biRG is* irreducible *if it is stable under the reduction rules; it is* reducible *otherwise. Accordingly, a collection R of biRGs is* irreducible *if and only if all biRGs in R are irreducible.*

Let $\mathcal{R}$ be a reduction through A, we say that $\mathcal{R}$ is *finished* if and only if for some natural number n, the collection R_n in $\mathcal{R}$ is irreducible and for all R_m in $\mathcal{R}$ such that $m < n$, R_m is not irreducible. We then say that n is the length of the reduction $\mathcal{R}$. Since we consider formulas indexed w.r.t. a given multiplicity, an inspection of the reduction rules of Figure 4 shows that all finished reductions through A lead to the same irreducible biRG-collection denoted R_f and called the *final* biRG-collection through A. Every biRG in R_f is then called an irreducible biRG through A.

If one forgets about the σ- and κ-edges, Figure 3 gives examples of irreducible biRGs[1] through $(((R_2^+ \vee_1^+ P_3^+) \prec_{\overline{a}}^+ Q_4^-) \wedge_0^+ \neg_x^- P_5^-) \to_a^- ((P_6^+ \to_b^- R_7^-) \prec_{\overline{x}}^- Q_8^+)$.

6   Validity through R-Graphs

Before stating our connection-based characterization of Bilnt validity, we need to define the notions of slice, concrete path and admissible R-graphs.

Definition 5 (slice). *Let $G(V, E)$ be a biRG and S be a subset of V, the S-slice of G is defined as the smallest (w.r.t. the number of vertices and edges) biRG $G^S(V^S, E^S)$ such that $S \subseteq V^S$ and for all vertices $u \in V^S$ and $v \in V$,*

- *if $v[\tau]u \in E$ and $\tau \in \{\psi, \phi, \sigma\}$, then $v \in V^S$ and $v[\tau]u \in E^S$;*
- *if $u[\tau]v \in E$ and $\tau \in \{\overline{\psi}, \overline{\phi}, \sigma\}$, then $v \in V^S$ and $u[\tau]v \in E^S$.*

The purpose of a slice is to capture only the essential information, *i.e.*, the minimal portion of a biRG, that is necessary to establish the validity of a Bilnt formula. Let us remark that in the construction of a slice $\overline{\psi}$- and $\overline{\phi}$-edges are traversed forward, from their source to their target, while ψ- and ϕ-edges are traversed backward, from their target to their source.

---

[1] For readability, non-atomic signed formulas are not mentioned in the vertex tags.

Definition 6 (path). *Given two vertices u, v in a biRG $G(V, E)$, a path in G from u to v is a sequence $u_0 \tau_1 u_1 \ldots u_{p-1} \tau_p u_p$ such that $u_0 = u$, $u_p = v$ and for all $1 \leqslant i \leqslant p$, u_i is a vertex in V, τ_i is an edge-tag in $\mathcal{T}$ and there exists a τ_i-edge $u_{i-1}[\tau_i]u_i$ in E. A cycle is a path such that the initial and terminal vertices are the same, i.e., $u_0 = u_p$.*

Given a subset T of $\mathcal{T}$, a T-path is a path $P = u_0 \tau_1 u_1 \ldots u_{p-1} \tau_p u_p$ such that for all $1 \leqslant i \leqslant p$, $\tau_i \in T$. In particular, when $T = \{\psi, \bar{\psi}, \sigma\}$, P is called a *concrete path* (in the graphical representation, a path using only solid edges). T-cycles and concrete cycles are defined accordingly. Using the previous notions, we define the relation ($\_\_ \blacktriangleright \_$) such that $Gu \blacktriangleright v$ holds if and only if $u = v$ or there exists at least one concrete path from u to v in G.

Definition 7 (admissibility). *A biRG $G(V, E)$ is admissible if and only if*

- *all concrete cycles in G are σ-cycles that contain at most one ψ-vertex and*
- *for all τ-edges $u[\tau]v$ in E such that $\tau \in \{\phi, \bar{\phi}\}$, $Gu \blacktriangleright v$ (in other words, there is a concrete path in G from u to v).*

Definition 8 (consistency). *A biRG $G(V, E)$ is inconsistent if and only if $(\exists u \in V)(\bot^+ \in \mathcal{F}(G, u))$; it is consistent otherwise.*

Definition 9 (complementarity). *A biRG $G(V, E)$ is complementary if and only if there is at least one κ-edge $u[\kappa]v$ in E such that the slice $G^{\{u,v\}}$ is admissible and $G^{\{u,v\}}u \blacktriangleright v$ (there is a concrete path in the slice from u to v).*

A collection of biRGs is inconsistent (respectively admissible) if it contains at least one biRG which is inconsistent (respectively admissible). On the contrary, a collection is *complementary* if all of its biRGs are complementary.

6.1   Characterization of Validity

Starting with the final biRG-collection R_f through a Bilnt formula A, we define the notions of σ- and κ-bindings.

A local σ-binding for a biRG $G(V, E)$ is a function σ that extends $G(V, E)$ by inserting σ-links (bidirectional σ-edges) in E. More formally, $\sigma(G(V, E)) = G_\sigma(V_\sigma, E_\sigma)$ such that $V_\sigma = \sigma(V) = V$ and $E_\sigma = \sigma(E) = E \cup \Sigma$, where σ is a set of σ-links between vertices of V^Φ and vertices of V^Ψ. Let us remark that a local σ-binding is completely determined by Σ.

Given two collections $R = \{G_1, \ldots, G_n\}$ and $S = \{\sigma_1, \ldots, \sigma_n\}$ such that for all $1 \leqslant i \leqslant n$, σ_i is a local σ-binding for the biRG G_i, the global σ-binding $\overline{\sigma}$ for R (induced by S) is defined as $\overline{\sigma}(G_i) = \sigma_i(G_i)$ for all $1 \leqslant i \leqslant n$. A global σ-binding induces a relation $\sqsubset$ on $\Psi \times \Phi$ such that $a \sqsubset x$ if there is a σ-link $a[\sigma]x$ in $\overline{\sigma}(G_i)$ for some $1 \leqslant i \leqslant n$. A local σ-binding σ is admissible for a biRG G if $\sigma(G)$ is admissible. A global σ-binding $\overline{\sigma}$ is admissible for a biRG-collection R if for all G in R, $\overline{\sigma}(G)$ is admissible. Local and global κ-bindings are defined accordingly w.r.t. the structural conditions required for κ-edges in Definition 3.

Definition 10 (bi-intuitionistic validity). *A* Bilnt *formula* A *is biRG-valid if and only if there exists some multiplicity μ, a (global) σ-binding $\overline{\sigma}$ and a (global) κ-binding $\overline{\kappa}$ for the final biRG-collection R_f of irreducible biRGs through $\mu(A)$ such that:*

1. *For all (not necessarily distinct) biRGs $G_1(V_1, E_1), G_2(V_2, E_2)$ in $\overline{\sigma} \circ \overline{\kappa}(R_f)$ and all ϕ-vertices x in $V_1 \cap V_2$, if $x[\sigma]u \in E_1$ and $x[\sigma]v \in E_2$ then $u = v$.*
2. *For all consistent biRGs $G(V, E)$ in $\overline{\sigma} \circ \overline{\kappa}(R_f)$, $G(V, E)$ is complementary.*
3. *The* reduction ordering $\lhd = (\ll \cup \sqsubset)^+$ *induced by $\overline{\sigma}$, where $(\cdot)^+$ stands for transitive closure, is irreflexive.*

Using the previous definition and the irreducible biRGs of Figure 3, it is easy to see that $(((R_2 \vee_1 P_3) \prec_{\overline{a}} Q_4) \wedge_0 \neg_x P_5) \rightarrow_a ((P_6 \rightarrow_b R_7) \prec_{\overline{x}} Q_8)$ is biRG-valid. Let us now discuss the soundness and completeness of the characterization.

6.2 Soundness and Completeness of the Characterization

Definition 10 can be used to extract a labelled calculus the rules of which generate bi-intuitionistic R-graphs. Such a calculus is depicted in Fig. 5 and generates one biRG per branch in a derivation, which is induced by the edges (written as side conditions) introduced along that branch by the inference rules $\rightarrow_L$, $\rightarrow_R$, $\rightarrow_L$ and $\rightarrow_R$. A labelled formula A[v] on the left- (respectively right-) hand side of a labelled sequent simply means that A^+ (respectively A^-) appears in the tags of the vertex u.

Moreover, the notion of global σ-binding gives rise to the more standard notion of global substitution, *i.e.*, $\sigma(x) = a$ iff there is a σ-link between x and a in some irreducible biRG associated with some irreducible initial sequent[2] of a derivation. Similarly, there is a κ-edge from u and v in the irreducible biRG associated with an irreducible initial sequent s of a derivation iff there are some labelled formulas A[u] and A[v] occurring on the left-hand and right-hand side of s respectively. An example of a derivation in that labelled calculus is given in Sect. 8, where variable splitting is discussed.

Theorem 1. *Let* A *be a* Bilnt *formula.* A *is biRG-valid iff* A *is valid in the Kripke semantics.*

Proof. The soundness and completeness proofs rely on the labelled calculus given in Fig. 5. The soundness proof follows the standard pattern of proving that every inference rule of the calculus preserves a standard notion of realizability in Bilnt Kripke models. The completeness proof proceeds by counter-model construction from any admissible, consistent and saturated R-graph in the final collection of a finished reduction through A.

---

[2] A sequent that contains only atomic formulas.

$$\dfrac{}{\Gamma, A[u] \vdash A[u], \Delta}\ \text{ax} \qquad\qquad \dfrac{}{\Gamma, \bot[u] \vdash \Delta}\ \bot_{\text{L}}$$

$$\dfrac{\Gamma, A[u], B[u] \vdash \Delta}{\Gamma, (A \wedge B)[u] \vdash \Delta}\ \wedge_{\text{L}} \qquad\qquad \dfrac{\Gamma \vdash A[u], \Delta \quad \Gamma \vdash B[u], \Delta}{\Gamma \vdash (A \wedge B)[u], \Delta}\ \wedge_{\text{R}}$$

$$\dfrac{\Gamma, A[u] \vdash \Delta \quad \Gamma, B[u] \vdash \Delta}{\Gamma, (A \vee B)[u] \vdash \Delta}\ \vee_{\text{L}} \qquad\qquad \dfrac{\Gamma \vdash A[u], B[u], \Delta}{\Gamma \vdash (A \vee B)[u], \Delta}\ \vee_{\text{R}}$$

$$\dfrac{\Gamma \vdash A[x], \Delta \quad \Gamma, B[x] \vdash \Delta}{\Gamma, (A \to B)[u] \vdash \Delta}\ u[\phi]x \qquad\qquad \dfrac{\Gamma, A[a] \vdash B[a], \Delta}{\Gamma \vdash (A \to B)[u], \Delta}\ u[\psi]a$$

$$\dfrac{\Gamma \vdash A[\overline{x}], \Delta \quad \Gamma, B[\overline{x}] \vdash \Delta}{\Gamma \vdash (A \prec B)[u], \Delta}\ \overline{x}[\overline{\phi}]u \qquad\qquad \dfrac{\Gamma, A[\overline{a}] \vdash B[\overline{a}], \Delta}{\Gamma, (A \prec B)[u] \vdash \Delta}\ \overline{a}[\overline{\psi}]u$$

Fig. 5. Labelled calculus for Bilnt

6.3   Counter-Model Construction

We first need to define a saturation relation which plays the same role for biRGs as Hintikka collections for sets of formulas in intuitionistic logic.

Definition 11 (saturation). *Let $G(V, E)$ be a biRG. The saturation relation (on $G(V, E)$) is defined as the smallest relation between vertices and signed formulas such that:*

- *Base case: for all A in $\{\bot\} \cup \mathcal{V}$,*
    - $Gu \Vdash A^+$ *iff* $(\exists v \in V)(Gv \blacktriangleright u$ *and* $A^+ \in \mathcal{F}(G, v))$;
    - $Gu \Vdash A^-$ *iff* $(\exists v \in V)(Gu \blacktriangleright v$ *and* $A^- \in \mathcal{F}(G, v))$;
- *Induction:*
    - $Gu \Vdash (A \wedge B)^+$ *iff* $Gu \Vdash A^+$ *and* $Gu \Vdash B^+$;
    - $Gu \Vdash (A \wedge B)^-$ *iff* $Gu \Vdash A^-$ *or* $Gu \Vdash B^-$;
    - $Gu \Vdash (A \vee B)^+$ *iff* $Gu \Vdash A^+$ *or* $Gu \Vdash B^+$;
    - $Gu \Vdash (A \vee B)^-$ *iff* $Gu \Vdash A^-$ *and* $Gu \Vdash B^-$;
    - $Gu \Vdash (A \to B)^+$ *iff* $(\forall v \in V)(if\ Gu \blacktriangleright v$ *and* $Gv \Vdash A^+$ *then* $Gv \Vdash B^+)$;
    - $Gu \Vdash (A \to B)^-$ *iff* $(\exists v \in V)(Gu \blacktriangleright v$ *and* $Gv \Vdash A^+$ *and* $Gv \Vdash B^-)$;
    - $Gu \Vdash (A \prec B)^+$ *iff* $(\exists v \in V)(Gv \blacktriangleright u$ *and* $Gv \Vdash A^+$ *and* $Gv \Vdash B^-)$;
    - $Gu \Vdash (A \prec B)^-$ *iff* $(\forall v \in V)(if\ Gv \blacktriangleright u$ *and* $Gv \Vdash A^+$ *then* $Gv \Vdash B^+)$.

$G(V, E)$ is saturated *if and only if* $(\forall u \in V)(\forall C^s \in \mathcal{F}(G, u))(Gu \Vdash C^s)$.

Let us illustrate how to extract counter-models from saturated biRGs with a short example, the formula $D = Q \to ((\neg(P \prec Q) \prec P) \vee P)$. Up to σ- and κ-edges, the collection of irreducible biRGs through D is as follows:

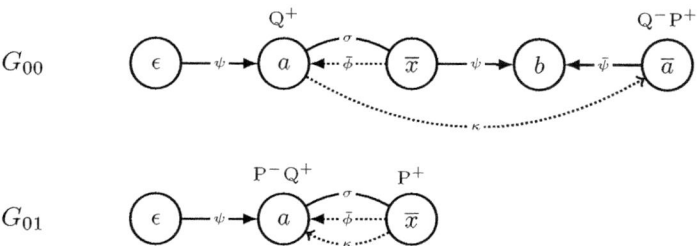

Both biRGs G_{00} and G_{01} are admissible and consistent, but only G_{00} is not complementary. Moreover, it happens that G_{00} is also saturated. In order to turn G_{00} into a counter-model of D, we first calculate the quotient of G_{00} by the equivalence generated by the σ-edges which leads to the following set of vertex-classes: $V = \{\dot{\epsilon}, \dot{a}, \dot{b}, \dot{\overline{a}} \mid \dot{\epsilon} = \{\epsilon\}, \dot{a} = \dot{\overline{x}} = \{a, \overline{x}\}, \dot{b} = \{b\}, \dot{\overline{a}} = \{\overline{a}\}\}$. Then, we consider V as a set of worlds and define an accessibility relation $\sqsubseteq$ between worlds of V as follows: $(\forall m, n \in V)(m \sqsubseteq n$ iff $(\exists m' \in m)(\exists n' \in n)(Gm' \blacktriangleright n'))$. Finally, we define the forcing relation by setting the following interpretation: $(\forall P \in \mathcal{V})(\forall m \in V)(P \in m$ iff $(\exists m' \in m)(P^+ \in \mathcal{F}(G, m')))$, which leads to following bi-intuitionistic Kripke model:

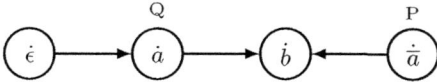

It is not difficult to generalize the previous example so as to extract a counter-model from any consistent, admissible and saturated biRG that cannot be made complementary in any way (under any σ- and κ-bindings).

7   Solving Admissibility Constraints

In plain intuitionistic logic, we could use prefixes instead of labels and resort to T-string (prefix) unification to solve prefix constraints [8]. However we cannot do that in the case of Bilnt because a prefix essentially is a way to encode the path to a given node in a Kripke tree. Since the Kripke semantics of Bilnt deals with graphs instead of trees, there can be several distinct paths to a given node and taking care of that using prefixes (by encoding both successors and predecessors) would break the T-string property of such prefixes, which in turns prevents the use of T-string unification.

Given an admissible σ-binding, it is not difficult to check whether κ-edges are covered by a concrete path or not, the problem is to find such σ-bindings. A trivial but particularly inefficient solution would be to enumerate all possible σ-bindings and check whether they are admissible or not. As a first step toward more efficient solutions, we now sketch an algorithm that only enumerates admissible σ-bindings for a given biRG (which is a slice determined by a κ-edge) that also preserves the acyclicity of the underlying reduction ordering $\lhd$. For that, we first need the notion of *walk* through a biRG which is similar to the notion of path described in Definition 6 except that in a walk $\bar{\phi}$- and $\bar{\psi}$-edges must be crossed backward from their target to their source and σ-edges can only be crossed from their ψ-vertex to their ϕ-vertex. T-walks are defined accordingly as walks that only cross τ-edges such that $\tau \in T$ and, whenever $T = \{\psi, \bar{\psi}, \sigma\}$, a T-walk is called a concrete walk.

Let u be an arbitrary vertex in a biRG, we define $A_T^n(u)$ (resp. $B_T^n(u)$) as the set of all ψ-vertices that can be reached from u (resp. from which u can be reached) by a T-walk of length n. The two sets $S_T^n(u)$ and $P_T^n(u)$ are defined analogously using the notion T-path instead of T-walk. In particular, for all $F \in \{S, P, A, B\}$, $F_T^0(u) = \{u\}$ if u is a ψ-vertex and $\emptyset$ otherwise. For readability, we forget the T subscript whenever $T = \{\phi, \bar{\phi}, \psi, \bar{\psi}\}$. Finally, let $F(u) = \bigcup_{i \in \mathbb{N}} F^i(u)$ and let $t \in \{\phi, \bar{\phi}\}$ denote an intuitionistic type and u, v be two vertices, we then define the set $M_t(u, v)$ as $M_t(u) - A(v)$ with $M_\phi = S$ and $M_{\bar{\phi}} = P$.

Our solving algorithm relies on two particular objects $R(u)$ and $D(u)$ that are computed for all ϕ-vertices u in the biRG $G(V, E)$ under consideration. In the initial step, $R(u) = B_t^1(u)$ and $D(u) = M_t(R(u), u)$ for all $u \in V^\Phi$. Intuitively, $D(u)$ (called the *domain* of u) is meant to represent all suitables instantiations for u (*i.e.*, ψ-vertices that would be suitable targets for a σ-link the source of which is u) and $R(u)$ (called the *root* of u) initially is the vertex responsible for the introduction of u in the biRG reduction process. In a second step, all ϕ-edges are partially ordered in a list $X = x_1, \ldots, x_n$ so that if $i < j$ and $x_i \propto x_j$ then $x_j \not\propto x_i$, where $\propto$ is the following notion of *variable dependency*: let x and y be two ϕ-vertices, we say that x *depends on* y, and we write $x \propto y$, if and only if $x \in D(y)$. Intuitively, if x depends on y then y should be bound before x because some ψ-vertices may only become admissible for x after y gets bound to some specific ψ-vertex. The third step finally consists of the actual enumeration: for each ϕ-vertex $u = x_i$ in X, select a ψ-vertex c in $D(u)$ (then assuming the addition of a σ-link $u[\sigma]c$) and apply the corresponding rule of Figure 6, more precisely perform

```
applyRule := selectRule(u,c,v) ; R(v),D(v) := applyRule(u,c,v)
```

on all $v = x_j$ in X such that $j > i$. If all ϕ-vertices in X can be bound then we have an admissible σ-binding and we just check whether the κ-edge we are interested in (*i.e.*, the one that determines the slice which corresponds to the biRG we are working on) is covered by a concrete path. If so, we are done, otherwise, we must backtrack and perform a distinct selection of ψ-vertices until a solution is found or all possible choices have been exhausted.

8   Variable Splitting

In this section we briefly discuss how the technique of variable splitting recently developed for prefixes [1] can be adapted to our R-graph based setting. Let us illustrate the main ideas with a short example. With a multiplicity $\mu(x) = \mu((P \to P) \to P) = 0$, it is not possible to prove the validity of the formula for which a derivation in the labelled calculus of Figure 5 is given below (indexes are indicated as subscripts).

Rule	$\texttt{selectRule}(u,c,v)$	$\texttt{applyRule}(u,c,v)$
Bind	$R(v) = u$	$c,\ D(v) \cup M_t(c,v)$
Narrow	$c \in A(v)$	$R(v),\ D(v) - A(u)$
Widen	$c = R(v) \wedge (c \neq R(u) \vee itype(u) = itype(v))$	$R(v),\ D(v) \cup M_t(u,v)$

Fig. 6. Solving rules given that $v \neq u$ and $itype(v) = t$

$$\cfrac{\cfrac{\overline{P_{2[d]} \vdash P_{3[d]}}\ ax}{\vdash (P_2 \to P_3)_{d[x]}}\ x[\psi]d \qquad \cfrac{\cfrac{P_{4[x]}, Q_{6[b]} \vdash P_{7[b]}}{P_{4[x]} \vdash (Q_6 \to P_7)_{b[a]}}\ a[\psi]b \qquad \cfrac{P_{4[x]}, R_{8[c]} \vdash P_{9[c]}}{P_{4[x]} \vdash (R_8 \to P_9)_{c[a]}}\ a[\psi]c}{P_{4[x]} \vdash ((Q_6 \to P_7)_b \wedge (R_8 \to P_9)_c)_{5[a]}}\ \wedge_R}{\cfrac{((P_2 \to P_3)_d \to P_4)_{x[a]} \vdash ((Q_6 \to P_7)_b \wedge (R_8 \to P_9)_c)_{5[a]}}{(((P_2 \to P_3)_d \to P_4)_x \to ((Q_6 \to P_7)_b \wedge (R_8 \to P_9)_c)_5)_{a[\epsilon]}}\ \epsilon[\psi]a}\ a[\phi]x$$

The first initial sequent[3] requires $\sigma_1 = \{x/c\}$ while the second one requires $\sigma_2 = \{x/b\}$. The conflict on x thus makes it impossible to compute a global substitution from the two local substitutions σ_1 and σ_2. A first solution would be to increase multiplicity in order to have one copy x^1 of the variable x so as to set $\sigma_1 = \{x/c\}$ and $\sigma_2 = \{x^1/b\}$. The price to pay for this solution is an unnecessary longer derivation because, in this example, assigning two distinct values to the variable x would not harm soundness. The problem actually lies in the fact that the labelled calculus is *variable sharing*: the same ϕ- or $\overline{\phi}$-formula occurring in distinct branches leads to the introduction of the same variable in all branches since we use the index of that formula as the introduced variable.

Variable sharing leads to full permutability of the rules, but also results in potentially longer derivations. Had we allowed the $\to_L$ and $\prec_R$ rules to introduce a fresh copy of the variable associated to its principal ϕ- or $\overline{\phi}$-formula for each of its occurrences in distinct branches of a derivation, expanding the β-formula $(Q \to P) \wedge (R \to P)$ before the ϕ-formula $(P \to P) \to P$ in our example would have resulted in the introduction of the variable x in the branch corresponding to the first premiss of $\wedge_L$ and of a fresh copy x^1 in the branch corresponding to the second premiss of $\wedge_R$. However, such a *variable pure* formulation of our labelled calculus would break full permutability: β-formulas need to be expanded before ϕ- and $\overline{\phi}$-formulas to enable as many copies of each variable as possible.

Variable splitting is a technique developed for variable sharing calculi that allows a (shared) variable to be assigned a specific value in each distinct branch it occurs in, which enables the computation of local substitutions and helps keeping derivations shorter. Let A be a Bilnt formula. A *splitting set* for A is a set of dual-free indexes of secondary type β_1 or β_2 which is downward closed w.r.t. the tree ordering $\ll$. In order to enable variable splitting for our labelled calculus, we replace variables with *colored variables*, *i.e.*, pairs x^X where x is a variable occurring as an index in A and X is a splitting set for A. Substitutions

---

[3] Indexing initial sequents of the derivation from right to left.

are replaced with *colored substitutions* accordingly. A colored substitution σ induces a *splitting ordering* which is the least relation between β- and ϕ- or $\overline{\phi}$-indexes such that if $\sigma(x^X) \neq \sigma(x^Y)$, then there are dual indexes $i \in X$ and $j \in Y$ such that $(i \triangle j) \prec x$. Intuitively, a splitting ordering encodes the fact that β-formulas should be expanded before ϕ- or $\overline{\phi}$-formulas (in a variable pure setting).

The last thing to do is to take into account the new splitting ordering in the characterization of biRG-validity of Definition 10, which is done by redefining the reduction ordering so that $\lhd = (\ll \cup \sqsubset \cup \prec)^+$. The sets $\{c\}$ and $\{b\}$ are splitting sets for the derivation given previously. Accordingly, the two initial sequents can now give rise to two distinct colored substitutions $\sigma_1 = \{x^{\{c\}}/c\}$ and $\sigma_2 = \{x^{\{b\}}/b\}$ from which we get $(b \triangle c) = 5$, $5 \prec x$, $b \sqsubset x$ and $c \sqsubset x$. The induced reduction ordering $\lhd = (\ll \cup \sqsubset \cup \prec)^+$ is easily checked irreflexive.

References

1. Antonsen, R., Waaler, A.: A labelled system for IPL with variable splitting. In: Pfenning, F. (ed.) CADE 2007. LNCS (LNAI), vol. 4603, pp. 132–146. Springer, Heidelberg (2007)
2. Crolard, T.: Substractive logic. Theoretical Computer Science 254(1-2), 151–185 (2001)
3. Crolard, T.: A formulae-as-types interpretation of substractive logic. Journal of Logic and Computation 14(4), 529–570 (2004)
4. Galmiche, D., Méry, D.: Characterizing provability in bI's pointer logic through resource graphs. In: Sutcliffe, G., Voronkov, A. (eds.) LPAR 2005. LNCS (LNAI), vol. 3835, pp. 459–473. Springer, Heidelberg (2005)
5. Galmiche, D., Méry, D.: Resource graphs and countermodels in resource logics. Electronic Notes in Theoretical Computer Science 125(3), 117–135 (2005)
6. Goré, R., Postniece, L., Tiu, A.: Cut-elimination and proof-search for Bi-intuitionistic logic using nested sequents. In: Advances in Modal Logic, vol. 7, pp. 43–66. College Publications, London (2008)
7. Negri, S.: Proof analysis in modal logic. J. of Philos. Logic 34(5-6), 507–554 (2005)
8. Otten, J., Kreitz, C.: T-string-unification: unifying prefixes in non classical proof methods. In: Miglioli, P., Moscato, U., Ornaghi, M., Mundici, D. (eds.) TABLEAUX 1996. LNCS (LNAI), vol. 1071, pp. 244–260. Springer, Heidelberg (1996)
9. Pinto, L., Uustalu, T.: Proof search and counter-model construction for bi-intuitionistic propositional logic with labelled sequents. In: Giese, M., Waaler, A. (eds.) TABLEAUX 2009. LNCS (LNAI), vol. 5607, pp. 295–309. Springer, Heidelberg (2009)
10. Postniece, L.: Deep inference in bi-intuitionistic logic. In: Ono, H., Kanazawa, M., de Queiroz, R. (eds.) WoLLIC 2009. LNCS, vol. 5514, pp. 320–334. Springer, Heidelberg (2009)
11. Rauszer, C.: An algebraic and Kripke-style approach to a certain extension of intuitionistic logic. Dissertationes Mathematicae 168 (1980)

Automated Reasoning in $\mathcal{ALCQ}$ via SMT

Volker Haarslev[1], Roberto Sebastiani[2], and Michele Vescovi[2]

[1] CSE, Concordia University, Montreal,
haarslev@cse.concordia.ca
[2] DISI, Università di Trento
{rseba,vescovi}@disi.unitn.it

Abstract. Reasoning techniques for qualified number restrictions (QNRs) in Description Logics (DLs) have been investigated in the past but they mostly do not make use of the arithmetic knowledge implied by QNRs. In this paper we propose and investigate a novel approach for concept satisfiability in acyclic $\mathcal{ALCQ}$ ontologies. It is based on the idea of encoding an $\mathcal{ALCQ}$ ontology into a formula in Satisfiability Modulo the Theory of Costs (SMT($\mathcal{C}$)), which is a specific and computationally much cheaper subcase of Linear Arithmetic under the Integers, and to exploit the power of modern SMT solvers to compute every concept-satisfiability query on a given ontology. We implemented and tested our approach, which includes a very effective individuals-partitioning technique, on a wide set of synthesized benchmark formulas, comparing the approach with the main state-of-the-art DL reasoners available. Our empirical evaluation confirms the potential of the approach.

1 Introduction

Description logics (DLs) form one of the major foundations of the semantic web and its web ontology language (OWL). In fact, OWL 2, a recent W3C recommendation, is a syntactic variant of a very expressive DL that supports reasoning with so-called *qualified number restrictions* (QNRs). A sound and complete calculus for reasoning with the DL $\mathcal{ALCQ}$ that adds QNRs to the basic DL $\mathcal{ALC}$ was first proposed in [9]. For example, this calculus decides the satisfiability of an $\mathcal{ALCQ}$ concept $(\geq 5\, s.C \sqcap \geq 5\, s.D \sqcap \leq 2\, s.E)$ by trying to find a model with fillers for the role s such that at least 5 fillers are instances of C, at least 5 fillers are instances of D, and at most 2 fillers are instances of E. It satisfies the at-least restrictions by creating 10 fillers for S, 5 of which are instances of C and 5 are instances of D. A concept choose rule non-deterministically assigns E or $\neg E$ to these fillers. In case the at-most restriction $(\leq 2\, s.E)$ is violated a merge rule non-deterministically merges pairs of fillers for s that are instances of E [9]. Searching for a model in such an arithmetically uninformed way can become very inefficient especially when bigger numbers occur in QNRs or several QNRs interact. To the best of our knowledge this calculus still serves as reference in most tableau-based OWL reasoners (e.g., Pellet [15], FaCT++ [16]) for implementing reasoning about QNRs. The only exception is Racer [7] where conceptual QNR reasoning is based on an algebraic approach [8] that integrates integer linear programming with DL tableau methods.

The work presented in this paper was inspired by two recent novel approaches, combined with the progress in satisfiability modulo theory (SMT) solving techniques. First,

N. Bjørner and V. Sofronie-Stokkermans (Eds.): CADE 2011, LNAI 6803, pp. 283–298, 2011.

$\perp^{\mathcal{I}} = \emptyset, \top^{\mathcal{I}} = \Delta^{\mathcal{I}}, (\neg C)^{\mathcal{I}} = \Delta^{\mathcal{I}} \setminus C^{\mathcal{I}}, (C \sqcap D)^{\mathcal{I}} = C^{\mathcal{I}} \cap D^{\mathcal{I}}, (C \sqcup D)^{\mathcal{I}} = C^{\mathcal{I}} \cup D^{\mathcal{I}},$
$(\exists r.C)^{\mathcal{I}} = \{x \in \Delta^{\mathcal{I}} \mid \text{there exists } y \in \Delta^{\mathcal{I}} \text{ s.t. } (x, y) \in r^{\mathcal{I}} \text{ and } y \in C^{\mathcal{I}}\},$
$(\forall r.C)^{\mathcal{I}} = \{x \in \Delta^{\mathcal{I}} \mid \text{for all } y \in \Delta^{\mathcal{I}} \text{ s.t. } (x, y) \in r^{\mathcal{I}} \text{ then } y \in C^{\mathcal{I}}\},$
$(\geq nr.C)^{\mathcal{I}} = \{x \in \Delta^{\mathcal{I}} \mid |FIL(r, x) \cap C^{\mathcal{I}}| \geq n\},$
$(\leq mr.C)^{\mathcal{I}} = \{x \in \Delta^{\mathcal{I}} \mid |FIL(r, x) \cap C^{\mathcal{I}}| \leq m\}, C \sqsubseteq D \text{ is satisfied iff } C^{\mathcal{I}} \subseteq D^{\mathcal{I}}$

Fig. 1. Syntax and semantics of $\mathcal{ALCQ}$ ($n \geq 1$ and $m \geq 0$)

[13,14] explored the idea of performing automated reasoning tasks in DLs by encoding problems into Boolean formulas and by exploiting the power of modern SAT techniques. In particular, the experiments in [13] showed that, in practice and despite the theoretical worst-case complexity limits, this approach could handle most or all the $\mathcal{ALC}$ satisfiablity problems which also the other approaches could handle, with performances which were comparable with, and often better than, those of state-of-the-art tools. Second, a revised and extended algebraic approach was presented for $\mathcal{SHQ}$ [6] and $\mathcal{SHOQ}$ [4]. These approaches represent knowledge about interacting QNRs as systems of linear inequations where numerical variables represent cardinalities of sets of domain elements (e.g., role fillers) divided into mutually disjoint decompositions. On a set of synthetic QNR benchmarks these algebraic approaches demonstrated a superior performance for most test cases [6,5].

The main idea of this paper is thus to encode an $\mathcal{ALCQ}$ ontology into a formula in Satisfiability Modulo the Theory of Costs (SMT($\mathcal{C}$)) [3], which is a specific and computationally much cheaper subcase of Linear Arithmetic under the Integers ($\mathcal{LA}(\mathbb{Z})$), and to exploit the power of modern SMT solvers to compute every concept-satisfiability query on a given ontology. We have implemented and tested our approach (called $\mathcal{ALCQ}2SMT_{\mathcal{C}}$) that includes a very effective individuals-partitioning technique on a wide set of synthesized benchmark formulas and compared it with main state-of-the-art OWL reasoners. Our empirical evaluation demonstrates the potential of our approach and, compared with the tested OWL reasoners, demonstrates a significantly better performance in the case of benchmarks having multiple/balanced sources of complexity.

2 Background

2.1 The Description Logic $\mathcal{ALCQ}$

The logic $\mathcal{ALCQ}$ extends the well-known logic $\mathcal{ALC}$ by adding *qualified number restrictions* (QNRs). In more details, the *concept descriptions* in $\mathcal{ALCQ}$ (namely $\hat{C}, \hat{D}, \dots$) are inductively defined through the constructors listed in Figure 1, starting from the non-empty and pair-wise disjoint sets of *concept names* N_C (denoted by the letters $A, B, C, \dots$) and *role names* N_R (denoted by the letters $r, s, \dots$). It allows for negations, conjunctions/disjunctions, existential/universal restrictions and, indeed, QNRs. An $\mathcal{ALCQ}$ *TBox* (or *ontology*) is a finite set of general concept inclusion (GCI) axioms as defined in Figure 1.

Given a TBox $\mathcal{T}$, we denote with $BC_{\mathcal{T}}$ the set of the *basic concepts* for $\mathcal{T}$, i.e. the smallest set of concepts containing: (i) the top and the bottom concepts $\top$ and $\perp$; (ii) all the concepts of $\mathcal{T}$ in the form C and $\neg C$ where C is a concept name in N_C. We denote the basic concepts in $\mathsf{BC}_\mathcal{T}$ with the letters $C, D, \dots$ (thus, C may represent a concept $\neg C'$ with $C' \in \mathsf{BC}_\mathcal{T}$), whilst we use $\hat{C}, \hat{D}, \dots$ for complex concepts, i.e. $\hat{C}, \hat{D} \notin \mathsf{BC}_\mathcal{T}$. Our approach is currently restricted to *acyclic* (or *unfoldable*) TBoxes. We call a TBox $\mathcal{T}$ *acyclic* if there exist no cyclic dependencies between its concept names, i.e., named concepts are neither defined directly or indirectly in terms of themselves through the axioms in $\mathcal{T}$.

Semantics. The semantics of $\mathcal{ALCQ}$ is defined in terms of *interpretations*. An interpretation $\mathcal{I}$ is a couple $\mathcal{I} = (\Delta^\mathcal{I}, \cdot^\mathcal{I})$, where $\Delta^\mathcal{I}$ is the domain (i.e. a non-empty set of individuals), and $\cdot^\mathcal{I}$ is the interpretation function which maps each concept name (atomic concept) $A \in N_C$ to a set $A^\mathcal{I} \subseteq \Delta^\mathcal{I}$ and maps each role name (atomic role) r to a binary relation $r^\mathcal{I} \subseteq \Delta^\mathcal{I} \times \Delta^\mathcal{I}$. In Figure 1 the inductive extensions of $\cdot^\mathcal{I}$ to arbitrary concept descriptions are defined, where n and m are positive integer values and $FIL(r, x)$ is the set of the r-fillers of the individual $x \in \Delta^\mathcal{I}$ for the role $r \in N_R$ and is defined as $FIL(r, x) = \{y \in \Delta^\mathcal{I} | (x, y) \in r^\mathcal{I}\}$. An interpretation $\mathcal{I}$ is a *model* of a given TBox $\mathcal{T}$ if and only if the conditions given in Figure 1 are respected for every axiom in $\mathcal{T}$; when this is the case, the TBox $\mathcal{T}$ is said to be *consistent*. A concept $\hat{C}$ is said to be *satisfiable* wrt. $\mathcal{T}$ if and only if there exists a model $\mathcal{I}$ of $\mathcal{T}$ with $\hat{C}^\mathcal{I} \neq \emptyset$, i.e. there exists an individual $x \in \Delta^\mathcal{I}$ as an instance of $\hat{C}$, i.e. such that $x \in \hat{C}^\mathcal{I}$.

Normal Form. We assume wlog. that all $\mathcal{ALCQ}$ concept descriptions are in *negative normal form* (NNF), i.e. negation signs only occurs in front of concept names (see [17] for details). Then, for the sake of an easier exposition, we restrict our attention to those $\mathcal{ALCQ}$ TBoxes in which all axioms are in the following normal form:

$$C \sqsubseteq D \qquad \sqcap_i C_i \sqsubseteq D \qquad C \sqsubseteq \sqcap_i D_i \qquad \Re r.C \sqsubseteq D \qquad C \sqsubseteq \Re r.D \qquad (1)$$

with $\Re \in \{\forall, \geq n, \leq m\}$ s.t. $n, m \geq 1$, and $C, C_i, D, D_i \in \mathsf{BC}_\mathcal{T}$.[1] Every given TBox $\mathcal{T}$ can be turned into a normalized TBox $\mathcal{T}'$ (where all concept description in $\mathcal{T}'$ are in NNF) that is a conservative extension of $\mathcal{T}$ by introducing new concept names. The transformation of a TBox $\mathcal{T}$ into $\mathcal{T}'$ can be done in linear time, and the size of $\mathcal{T}'$ is linear wrt. the size of $\mathcal{T}$. We call every non-conjunctive and non-disjunctive concept description occurring in the concept inclusions of $\mathcal{T}'$ a *normal concept* of a normalized TBox $\mathcal{T}'$; we call $\mathsf{NC}_{\mathcal{T}'}$ the set of all the normal concepts of $\mathcal{T}'$. For more details we refer the reader to [17].

2.2 Satisfiablity Modulo Theory with Cost Functions

Satisfiability Modulo (the) Theory $\mathcal{T}$, $SMT(\mathcal{T})$, is the problem of deciding the satisfiability of a (typically) ground formula under a background theory $\mathcal{T}$. Most state-of-the art SMT solvers are based on the *lazy SMT schema*: in a nutshell, a SAT solver is used to search for a truth assignment μ to the atomic subformulas of the input ground formula φ, s.t. μ tautologically entails φ and μ is found consistent in $\mathcal{T}$ by the $\mathcal{T}$-*solver*. (We refer the reader to, e.g., [12] for details and further references.)

---

[1] In particular, we avoid redundant existential and at-most restrictions that are replaced by their following equivalents: $\exists r.C \implies \geq 1 r.C$ and $\leq 0 r.C \implies \forall r.nnf(\neg C)$.

The work in [3] addresses the problem of the satisfiability in some theory $\mathcal{T}$ of a formula φ augmented with a set of *cost functions* $\{cost_1, ..., cost_N\}$ s.t., for every i:

$$cost_i = \sum_{j=1}^{N_i} \textit{if-then-else}(A_{ij}, c_{ij}, 0), \quad lb_i < cost_i \leq ub_i, \tag{2}$$

A_{ij} being Boolean atoms occurring in φ, and N_i, lb_i, ub_i, c_{ij} being integer values ≥ 0. (Intuitively, in (2) $cost_i = \sum_j A_{ij} c_{ij}$ s.t. $A_{ij} \in \{0, 1\}$.) The problem can be encoded into SMT($\mathcal{T} \cup \mathcal{LA}(\mathbb{Z})$). However, [3] remarked the inefficiency of such solution, which does not fully exploit the fact that the values of $cost_i$ derive deterministically from the truth values of all the A_{ij}'s. They proposed instead a specific *theory of costs* $\mathcal{C}$, which is much simpler and computationally much cheaper than $\mathcal{LA}(\mathbb{Z})$, and developed a specific very-fast $\mathcal{T}$-solver for $\mathcal{C}$. In a nutshell, $\mathcal{C}$ consists of: (i) a collection of integer variables $cost_1, \ldots, cost_N$, that we call *cost variables*, denoting the output of the cost functions in (2); (ii) an interpreted predicate BC "*bound cost*" s.t. BC($cost_i, c$) is true iff $cost_i$ is upper-bounded by the integer value c; (i.e., iff $cost_i \leq c$); (iii) an interpreted predicate IC "*incur cost*" s.t. IC($cost_i, c_{ij}, j$) is true if the j-th element of sum (2) is c_{ij}, false if it is 0. Thus, φ is satisfiable in $\mathcal{T}$ under the cost constraints (2) iff the formula

$$\varphi \wedge \bigwedge_{i=1}^{N} (\text{BC}(cost_i, ub_i) \wedge \neg\text{BC}(cost_i, lb_i) \wedge \bigwedge_{j=1}^{N_i} (A_{ij} \leftrightarrow \text{IC}(cost_i, c_{ij}, j))) \tag{3}$$

is satisfiable in $\mathcal{T} \cup \mathcal{C}$. A specific $\mathcal{T}$-solver for $\mathcal{C}$ works simply by adding the value c_{ij} [resp. 0] to the current minimum value of $cost_i$ and 0 [resp. c_{ij}] to its current maximum when IC($cost_i, c_{ij}, j$) (i.e. A_{ij}) is assigned to true [resp. false], and by checking if such minimum [resp. maximum] value of $cost_i$ is smaller or equal than ub_i [resp. greater or equal than lb_i]. We refer the reader to [3] for details and further references.

3 Concept Satisfiability via SMT with Costs

3.1 Encoding $\mathcal{ALCQ}$ into SMT($\mathcal{C}$)

The encoding we propose simulates the construction of an interpretation $\mathcal{I}$ by introducing new individuals, assigning individuals to the interpretations of concepts in $\mathcal{T}$, and counting their occurrences in the interpretations. We represent uniquely *individuals* in $\Delta^{\mathcal{I}}$ by means of *labels* σ, represented as non-empty sequences of positive integer values and role names in N_R. A label σ can be either the label 1 or in the form $\sigma'.r.n$, with σ' another label, $r \in N_R$ and $n \geq 1$. With a small abuse of notation, hereafter we may say "the individual σ" meaning "the individual labeled by σ". Moreover, we call *instantiated concept* a pair $\langle \sigma, C \rangle$, s.t. $\sigma \in \Delta^{\mathcal{I}}$ and C is an $\mathcal{ALCQ}$ normal concept of $\mathcal{T}$, representing the fact that the σ is an instance of C in the interpretation $\mathcal{I}$, i.e. $\sigma \in C^{\mathcal{I}}$.

We define $A_{\langle \ , \ \rangle}$ an injective function which maps one instantiated concept $\langle \sigma, C \rangle$ s.t. C is not in the form $\neg C'$, into a Boolean variable $A_{\langle \sigma, C \rangle}$ that we call *concept variable*. The so-called *concept literal* $L_{\langle \sigma, C \rangle}$, denotes $\neg A_{\langle \sigma, C' \rangle}$ if C is in the form $\neg C'$, $A_{\langle \sigma, C \rangle}$ otherwise. The truth value of $L_{\langle \sigma, C \rangle}$ states whether the instantiation relation between σ and C [resp. $\neg C$] holds, i.e. if $\langle \sigma, C \rangle$ [resp. $\langle \sigma, \neg C \rangle$] is an existing instantiated concept in $\mathcal{I}$. We conventionally assume that $A_{\langle \sigma, \perp \rangle}$ is $\perp$. Notice also that $\langle \sigma, \top \rangle$

means $\sigma \in \Delta^{\mathcal{I}}$, i.e. that if $A_{\langle \sigma, \top \rangle}$ is assigned to true then σ exists in $\Delta^{\mathcal{I}}$. We informally say that σ (meaning $\langle \sigma, \top \rangle$) or $\langle \sigma, C \rangle$ is "enabled" when the respective literal is assigned to true.

We define indiv a function which maps one instantiated concept $\langle \sigma, \Re r.C \rangle$, such that $\Re \in \{\geq n, \leq m\}$ and C is a basic concept (since we are considering concepts in normal form), into a cost variable $\mathrm{indiv}_{\sigma.r}^{C}$ in the Theory of Costs, that we call *individuals cost variable*. Notice that indiv is not injective since the same cost variable $\mathrm{indiv}_{\sigma.r}^{C}$ is "shared" among all the instantiated concepts which refer both to the same σ and to QNRs involving the same r and C. However, notice also that $\langle \sigma, \Re r.C \rangle$ and $\langle \sigma, \Re r.\neg C \rangle$ are mapped to different cost variables. The final value of the individuals cost variable $\mathrm{indiv}_{\sigma.r}^{C}$ represents the number of individuals which are in relation with the individual σ via the role r and are in the interpretation of C, in other words the final value of $\mathrm{indiv}_{\sigma.r}^{C}$ exactly represents the cardinality of $FIL(r, \sigma) \cap C^{\mathcal{I}}$.

Our encoding works by means of the following principles:

- GCIs are represented via Boolean implications between instantiated concepts.
- Every at-least restriction $\langle \sigma, \geq nr.C \rangle$ is handled by introducing exactly n individuals $\sigma.r.i$ associated to C. The existence of individuals is forced by binding each of them to an incur cost of value 1 for $\mathrm{indiv}_{\sigma.r}^{C}$, and then fixing a lower-bound for $\mathrm{indiv}_{\sigma.r}^{C}$.
- When both at-least and at-most restrictions coexist wrt. σ, the encoding allows for sharing individuals separately introduced by distinct at-least restrictions. At-most restrictions are handled by fixing upper-bounds for the respective cost variables.
- It mimics the construction of a labeled tableaux with the difference of the above exposed sharing of individuals which generalizes the merging of pairs of fillers to satisfy at-most QNR.

Definition 1 ($\mathcal{ALCQ}2SMT_{\mathcal{C}}(\mathcal{T})$ **encoding**). *Let $\mathcal{T}$ be an acyclic $\mathcal{ALCQ}$ TBox in normal form. Wlog., we represent every axiom $\hat{C} \sqsubseteq \hat{D}$ of $\mathcal{T}$ as $\sqcap_i \hat{C}_i \sqsubseteq \sqcup_j \hat{D}_j$ where $i, j \geq 1$ and $i = 1$ (resp. $j = 1$), with $\hat{C}_1$ (resp. $\hat{D}_1$) a normal concept, for every normal form (1) except for the second (resp. the third) one. The SMT($\mathcal{C}$) encoding $\mathcal{ALCQ}2SMT_{\mathcal{C}}(\mathcal{T})$ for $\mathcal{T}$ is defined as the sextuple $\langle \Sigma^{\mathcal{T}}, \mathcal{I}_{-}^{\mathcal{T}}, \mathcal{I}_{+}^{\mathcal{T}}, A_{\langle \, , \, \rangle}, \mathrm{indiv}, \varphi^{\mathcal{T}} \rangle$, where:*

- *$\Sigma^{\mathcal{T}}$ is the set of all the possible individuals introduced;*
- *$\mathcal{I}_{-}^{\mathcal{T}}, \mathcal{I}_{+}^{\mathcal{T}}$ represent respectively the set of the implicant (i.e. left-side) and implied (i.e. right-side) instantiated concepts that must be encoded accordingly to their side;*
- *$A_{\langle \, , \, \rangle}$ and indiv are the functions defined above;*
- *$\varphi^{\mathcal{T}}$ is a CNF formula on propositional- and $\mathcal{C}$-literals encoding $\mathcal{T}$ into SMT($\mathcal{C}$). We represent $\varphi^{\mathcal{T}}$ as the set of its clauses.[2]*

The sets $\Sigma^{\mathcal{T}}, \mathcal{I}_{-}^{\mathcal{T}}, \mathcal{I}_{+}^{\mathcal{T}}$ and $\varphi^{\mathcal{T}}$ are incrementally defined as the minimum sets s.t.:

1. **Initialization.** *$1 \in \Sigma^{\mathcal{T}}, \langle 1, \top \rangle \in \mathcal{I}_{-}^{\mathcal{T}}, \langle 1, \top \rangle \in \mathcal{I}_{+}^{\mathcal{T}}$ and $(A_{\langle 1, \top \rangle}) \in \varphi^{\mathcal{T}}$.*
2. **Axioms initialization.** *If $\hat{C} \sqsubseteq \hat{D} \in \mathcal{T}$, then $\{\langle 1, C_i \rangle \mid \hat{C} = \sqcap_i C_i\} \subseteq \mathcal{I}_{-}^{\mathcal{T}}$.*

---

[2] For better readability we often represent the clauses of $\varphi^{\mathcal{T}}$ as implications.

3. **Axioms expansion.** If $\sigma \in \Sigma^{\mathcal{T}}$, $\sqcap_i C_i \sqsubseteq \sqcup_j D_j \in \mathcal{T}$, $\{\langle \sigma, C_i \rangle \mid \hat{C} = \sqcap_i C_i\} \subseteq \mathcal{I}_-^{\mathcal{T}} \cup \mathcal{I}_+^{\mathcal{T}}$, then

$$\{\langle \sigma, D_j \rangle \mid \hat{D} = \sqcup_j D_j\} \subseteq \mathcal{I}_+^{\mathcal{T}},$$
$$(\bigwedge_i L_{\langle \sigma, C_i \rangle}) \to (\bigvee_j L_{\langle \sigma, D_j \rangle}) \in \varphi^{\mathcal{T}}. \tag{4}$$

4. **Handle left-side QNRs.** If $\sigma \in \Sigma^{\mathcal{T}}$, $\langle \sigma, \Re'.r.C' \rangle \in \mathcal{I}_+^{\mathcal{T}}$ with $\Re' \in \{\geq n', \leq m', \forall\}$, then

$$\{\langle \sigma, \Re r.C \rangle \mid \Re r.C \sqsubseteq \hat{D} \in \mathcal{T}\} \subseteq \mathcal{I}_-^{\mathcal{T}}, \Re \in \{\geq n, \leq m, \forall\}.$$

5. **At-least restrictions: introduce individuals.** If $\sigma \in \Sigma^{\mathcal{T}}$, $\langle \sigma, \geq nr.C \rangle \in \mathcal{I}_+^{\mathcal{T}}$ then

$$\{\sigma.r.k_i^C \mid i = 1, \ldots, n\} \subset \Sigma^{\mathcal{T}},$$
$$\{\langle \sigma.r.k_i^C, C \rangle \mid i = 1, \ldots, n\} \cup \{\langle \sigma.r.k_i^C, \top \rangle \mid i = 1, \ldots, n\} \subset \mathcal{I}_-^{\mathcal{T}},$$
$$\{\mathsf{IC}(\mathrm{indiv}_{\sigma.r}^C, 1, k_i^C) \to L_{\langle \sigma.r.k_i^C, C \rangle} \mid i = 1, \ldots, n\} \subset \varphi^{\mathcal{T}}, \tag{5}$$
$$\{\mathsf{IC}(\mathrm{indiv}_{\sigma.r}^C, 1, k_i^C) \to A_{\langle \sigma.r.k_i^C, \top \rangle} \mid i = 1, \ldots, n\} \subset \varphi^{\mathcal{T}}, \tag{6}$$

where $k_1^C \geq 1$, $k_{i+1}^C = k_i^C + 1$ and $k_i^C \neq k_j^D$ for every $\langle \sigma, \geq n'r.D \rangle \in \mathcal{I}_+^{\mathcal{T}}$ with $C \neq D$ and $i = 1, \ldots, n$, $j = 1, \ldots, n'$. We assume consecutive values for all the $\sigma.r.j$.[3]

6. **At-least restrictions: fix lower bounds.** If $\sigma \in \Sigma^{\mathcal{T}}$, $\langle \sigma, \geq nr.C \rangle \in \mathcal{I}_+^{\mathcal{T}}$, then

$$((A_{\langle \sigma, \geq nr.C \rangle} \wedge A_{\langle \sigma, \top \rangle}) \to \neg \mathsf{BC}(\mathrm{indiv}_{\sigma.r}^C, n-1)) \in \varphi^{\mathcal{T}}, \tag{7}$$

if $\sigma \in \Sigma^{\mathcal{T}}$, $\langle \sigma, \geq nr.C \rangle \in \mathcal{I}_-^{\mathcal{T}}$, then

$$((\neg \mathsf{BC}(\mathrm{indiv}_{\sigma.r}^C, n-1) \wedge A_{\langle \sigma, \top \rangle}) \to A_{\langle \sigma, \geq nr.C \rangle}) \in \varphi^{\mathcal{T}}. \tag{8}$$

7. **Coexisting at-least/at-most: sharing individuals.** If $\sigma \in \Sigma^{\mathcal{T}}$, $\langle \sigma, \leq mr.E \rangle \in \mathcal{I}_+^{\mathcal{T}}$, $\langle \sigma, \geq nr.C \rangle \in \mathcal{I}_+^{\mathcal{T}}$, $\langle \sigma, \geq n'r.D \rangle \in \mathcal{I}_+^{\mathcal{T}}$, with $C \neq D$, then

$$\{\langle \sigma.r.k_i^C, D \rangle \mid i = 1, \ldots, n\} \cup \{\langle \sigma.r.k_i^D, C \rangle \mid i = 1, \ldots, n'\} \subset \mathcal{I}_-^{\mathcal{T}},$$
$$\{\mathsf{IC}(\mathrm{indiv}_{\sigma.r}^D, 1, k_i^C) \to L_{\langle \sigma.r.k_i^C, D \rangle} \mid i = 1, \ldots, n\} \cup$$
$$\{\mathsf{IC}(\mathrm{indiv}_{\sigma.r}^C, 1, k_i^D) \to L_{\langle \sigma.r.k_i^D, C \rangle} \mid i = 1, \ldots, n'\} \subset \varphi^{\mathcal{T}}, \tag{9}$$
$$\{\mathsf{IC}(\mathrm{indiv}_{\sigma.r}^D, 1, k_i^C) \to A_{\langle \sigma.r.k_i^C, \top \rangle} \mid i = 1, \ldots, n\} \cup$$
$$\{\mathsf{IC}(\mathrm{indiv}_{\sigma.r}^C, 1, k_i^D) \to A_{\langle \sigma.r.k_i^D, \top \rangle} \mid i = 1, \ldots, n'\} \subset \varphi^{\mathcal{T}}. \tag{10}$$

8. **At-most restrictions: count individuals.** If $\sigma \in \Sigma^{\mathcal{T}}$, $\langle \sigma, \leq mr.C \rangle \in \mathcal{I}_+^{\mathcal{T}}$ then

$$\{\langle \sigma.r.j, C \rangle \mid \sigma.r.j \in \Sigma^{\mathcal{T}}\} \subset \mathcal{I}_-^{\mathcal{T}},$$
$$\{(L_{\langle \sigma.r.j, C \rangle} \wedge A_{\langle \sigma.r.j, \top \rangle}) \to \mathsf{IC}(\mathrm{indiv}_{\sigma.r}^C, 1, j) \mid \sigma.r.j \in \Sigma^{\mathcal{T}}\} \subset \varphi^{\mathcal{T}}. \tag{11}$$

---

[3] Hence, either $k_1^C = 1$ or $k_1^C = k_{n'}^D + 1$ for some $\langle \sigma, \geq n'r.D \rangle \in \mathcal{I}_+^{\mathcal{T}}$

9. **At-most restrictions: fix upper bounds.** If $\sigma \in \Sigma^T$, $\langle \sigma, \leq mr.C \rangle \in \mathcal{I}_+^T$, then

$$((A_{\langle \sigma, \leq mr.C \rangle} \wedge A_{\langle \sigma, \top \rangle}) \rightarrow \mathsf{BC}(\mathsf{indiv}_{\sigma.r}^C, m)) \in \varphi^T, \tag{12}$$

if $\sigma \in \Sigma^T$, $\langle \sigma, \leq mr.C \rangle \in \mathcal{I}_-^T$, then

$$((\mathsf{BC}(\mathsf{indiv}_{\sigma.r}^C, m) \wedge A_{\langle \sigma, \top \rangle}) \rightarrow A_{\langle \sigma, \leq mr.C \rangle}) \in \varphi^T. \tag{13}$$

10. **Universal restrictions.** if $\sigma \in \Sigma^T$, $\langle \sigma, \forall r.C \rangle \in \mathcal{I}_+^T$, then

$$\{ \langle \sigma.r.j, C \rangle \mid \sigma.r.j \in \Sigma^T \} \subset \mathcal{I}_-^T$$
$$\{ ((A_{\langle \sigma, \forall r.C \rangle} \wedge A_{\langle \sigma.r.j, \top \rangle}) \rightarrow L_{\langle \sigma.r.j, C \rangle}) \mid \sigma.r.j \in \Sigma^T \} \subset \varphi^T, \tag{14}$$

if $\sigma \in \Sigma^T$, $\langle \sigma, \forall r.C \rangle \in \mathcal{I}_-^T$, then

$$((\mathsf{BC}(\mathsf{indiv}_{\sigma.r}^{\neg C}, 0) \wedge A_{\langle \sigma, \top \rangle}) \rightarrow A_{\langle \sigma, \forall r.C \rangle}) \in \varphi^T. \tag{15}$$

Importantly, at the effect of the encoding, left-side at-most (and universal) restrictions behave as right-side at-least restrictions, and vice versa. Thus, for instance, the instantiated concept $\langle \sigma, \leq n - 1r.C \rangle \in \mathcal{I}_-^T$ [resp. $\langle \sigma, \forall r.\neg C \rangle \in \mathcal{I}_-^T$, $n \stackrel{def}{=} 1$] must be handled by the encoding as if it were the instantiated concept $\langle \sigma, \geq nr.C \rangle \in \mathcal{I}_+^T$. In order to simplify the exposition, in Definition 1 and afterwards, we generically refer to at-least/at-most restrictions (respectively to the instantiated concepts $\langle \sigma, \geq nr.C \rangle /$ $\langle \sigma, \leq mr.C \rangle$) meaning the right-side ones, but implicitly including left-side at-most (or universal)/at-least restrictions, respectively. The interested reader can find in [17] the complete $\mathcal{ALCQ}2SMT_C$ encoding and some encoding examples.

The following facts concerning $\mathcal{ALCQ}2SMT_C$ hold. (We refer the reader to [17] for the formal proofs.)

Theorem 1. *An $\mathcal{ALCQ}$ acyclic TBox T in normal form is consistent if and only if the SMT(C)-formula φ^T of $\mathcal{ALCQ}2SMT_C(T)$ (Definition 1) is satisfiable.*

Theorem 2. *Given an $\mathcal{ALCQ}$ acyclic TBox T in normal form and the encoding $\mathcal{ALCQ}2SMT_C(T) = \langle \Sigma^T, \mathcal{I}_-^T, \mathcal{I}_+^T, A_{\langle \, , \, \rangle}, \mathsf{indiv}, \varphi^T \rangle$ of Definition 1, every $C \in \mathsf{BC}_T$ is satisfiable wrt. T iff $\varphi^T \wedge L_{\langle 1, C \rangle}$ is satisfiable.*

We remark on some facts about the encoding of Definition 1:

- Point 4. is necessary to force the encoding of axioms having on the left-hand side restrictions wrt. the role r, when other restrictions wrt. r are involved. Such kind of axioms can create cycles in TBoxes (we remark that our encoding ensures termination for acyclic TBoxes).
- In all the clauses of type (5), (6), (9), (10) and (5), (11), every IC-literal has cost value 1 and the same index of the bound individual. This ensures that IC-literals referring to distinct individuals/cost variables are represented by distinct atoms.
- Due to the theory C clauses (7) and (12), are those concretely ensuring the numerical satisfiability of both at-least and at-most restrictions. In order to be satisfied: (i) a clause of type (7) forces some IC-literals to be assigned to true (thus (5), (9) work

in only one direction); (ii) a clause of type (12), instead, bounds the number of IC-literals that can be enabled (motivating the opposite direction of (11)). Clauses (8) and (13) instead enforce the application of an axiom having a left-side QNRs if it is numerically satisfied.

Notice that if, for the same σ, r and C, more than one restriction satisfies the conditions of point 5. with different values of n (being n^* the highest of these values), then only exactly n^* new individuals and n^* clauses (5) and (6) are in φ^T. In contrast, one distinct clause (7) is in φ^T for every different value of n (the same holds for the clauses (12) in case of different values of m wrt. the same σ, r and C).

$\mathcal{ALCQ}$ with general TBoxes has the finite tree model property [11], thus every satisfiable $\mathcal{ALCQ}$ concept is satisfiable in a finite interpretation (in this case of worst-case exponential size) which has the shape of a tree. Intuitively the individuals in Σ^T form a super-tree of all such models. Let $\mathcal{N}$ represent the sum of the values occurring in the QNRs of T: a very coarse upper bound to the cardinality of Σ^T is $\Theta(|T|^{\mathcal{N}})$, in fact the number of nested restrictions is bounded by the number of axioms of T while $\mathcal{N}$ bounds the number of branches in the tree for every nesting level. The size of φ^T is, instead, bounded by $\Theta(|T|^{2\mathcal{N}})$ because for every individual and every concept of T a fixed number of clauses can be introduced. In [17] we define a terminating queue-based algorithm building $\mathcal{ALCQ}2SMT_\mathcal{C}$ by means of expansion rules which mimic Definition 1. Since we are restricted to acyclic TBoxes it is ensured that our encoding algorithm terminates even without introducing blocking techniques [1], in particular, the proposed algorithm is polynomial in the size of the SMT($\mathcal{C}$) formula produced.

4   Partitioning Individuals

One potential drawback of the basic $\mathcal{ALCQ}2SMT_\mathcal{C}$ is the high number of individuals introduced, that is linear wrt. the values occurring in the at-least restrictions. This number can increase exponentially when nested restrictions must be encoded, significantly impacting on the size and on the hardness of the resulting SMT($\mathcal{C}$) formula. However, similarly to the hybrid approach of [6,4], we can cope with this problem by encoding groups of individuals having identical properties (instead of using single ones) and by using only one "proxy" individual as representative of the group. We aim at partitioning the individuals introduced in Definition 1 on the basis of the following considerations:[4]

- Individuals are naturally pre-partitioned in groups wrt. r and the predecessor σ.
- If, given σ, r, no at-most restriction exists, all the fillers $\sigma.r.k_i^C$ referring to one at-least restriction can be represented by one single proxy individual.
- Otherwise, the $\sum_j n_j$ distinct individuals introduced by some $\langle \sigma, \geq n_j r.C_j \rangle$ can still be partitioned, but the partitioning must allow for representing possible intersections between the $C_j^{\mathcal{I}}$.

---

[4] Notice that here we present a *different* partitioning that avoids the a-priori exponential number of partitions in [6,4] (wrt. the number of coexisting QNRs). In our case, we consider the whole set of individuals necessary to trivially satisfy all the coexisting at-least restrictions, then, only on the basis of the numbers involved in QNRs, we compute a partitioning of such a set, where the target of our approach is to decide which partitions of individuals belong to a concept interpretation.

In the latter case not all possible cardinalities of the intersections must be considered. Instead, it is sufficient to distinguish between the empty intersection and some "limit" cases depending on the values occurring in the QNRs. To sum up, given σ, r, we can compute a partitioning of the individuals referring to σ and r by taking into account the values of the restrictions which concern σ and r.

Example 1. Suppose that it is necessary to encode the restrictions: $\langle \sigma, \geq 10r.C \rangle$ and $\langle \sigma, \geq 1000r.D \rangle$. The basic $\mathcal{ALCQ}2SMT_{\mathcal{C}}$ encoding would introduce 1010 distinct individuals. Applying the idea explained above, instead, we could divide these 1010 individuals in, e.g., three partitions of respectively 10, 990 and again 10 individuals. If, for example, also $\langle \sigma, \leq 1005r.\top \rangle$ must be encoded, then the last 10 individuals could be further divided into two distinct partitions. This partitioning allows for representing the cases in which 0, 5, 10, 15, 20, 990, 995, 1000, 1005 or 1010 of these individuals exist in $\Delta^{\mathcal{I}}$ (being part or not of $C^{\mathcal{I}}$ and/or $D^{\mathcal{I}}$). Even if not exhaustive these combinations are enough to represent the significant cases concerning satisfiability.

4.1 Smart Partitioning

In order to handle partitions of individuals we extend $\mathcal{ALCQ}2SMT_{\mathcal{C}}$ with *cumulative labels* and *proxy individuals*. Given a normal/cumulative label σ' and a role r, a *cumulative label* $\sigma'.r.(i \rightarrow j)$ represents a group of consecutive individuals by means of the range of integer values $i \rightarrow j$, with $i \leq j$, thus it represents a set of individuals whose cardinality is $j - i + 1$. When $i = j$ we can both write $\sigma'.r.(i \rightarrow i)$ and $\sigma'.r.i$. With a small abuse of notation, in the following we call *proxy individual* any $\sigma.r.(i \rightarrow j)$, meaning both: (i) the cumulative label representing the set of individuals $\sigma.r.i, \sigma.r.i+1, \ldots, \sigma.r.j$ and (ii) that $\sigma.r.(i \rightarrow j)$ can be one/any of these individuals acting as proxy for all the other individuals of the set.

The idea is to compute a *"smart" partitioning* of the individuals to be encoded into $\mathcal{ALCQ}2SMT_{\mathcal{C}}$. With *"smart"* we mean a "safe but as small as possible" partitioning, i.e. with "a small" number of partitions but "safely" preserving the semantics of the problem, so that the cardinality of the computed partitions allow for representing every relevant case wrt. satisfiability. We formally define our smart partitioning:

Definition 2. *Let $\mathcal{T}$ being an acyclic $\mathcal{ALCQ}$ TBox in normal form. Given $\mathcal{ALCQ}2SMT_{\mathcal{C}}(\mathcal{T})$ (Definition 1), $\sigma \in \Sigma^{\mathcal{T}}$ and $r \in N_R$ we define the arrays:*[5]

$$\mathcal{N}^{\geq}_{\sigma.r} \overset{def}{=} \{\, n_i \mid \langle \sigma, \geq n_i r.C_i \rangle \in \mathcal{I}^{\mathcal{T}}_+ \,\}_i\,^{6} \quad and$$

$$\mathcal{N}^{\leq}_{\sigma.r} \overset{def}{=} \{\, m_j \mid \langle \sigma, \leq m_j r.D_j \rangle \in \mathcal{I}^{\mathcal{T}}_+ \,\}_j.$$

From $\mathcal{N}^{\geq}_{\sigma.r}$ and $\mathcal{N}^{\leq}_{\sigma.r}$, respectively, we define the integer values:

$$N^{\geq}_{\sigma.r} \overset{def}{=} \Sigma_{n_i \in \mathcal{N}^{\geq}_{\sigma.r}}\, n_i \quad and \quad N^{\leq}_{\sigma.r} \overset{def}{=} \Sigma_{m_j \in \mathcal{N}^{\leq}_{\sigma.r}}\, m_j.$$

---

[5] With *array* we mean that equal n_i [resp. m_j] values repeat in $\mathcal{N}^{\geq}_{\sigma.r}$ [resp. $\mathcal{N}^{\leq}_{\sigma.r}$] as many times as they occur in the involved QNRs.

[6] $\langle \sigma, \forall r.C_i \rangle \in \mathcal{I}^{\mathcal{T}}_-$ must be considered like $\langle \sigma, \leq 0r.\neg C_i \rangle \in \mathcal{I}^{\mathcal{T}}_-$, while $\langle \sigma, \leq n_i{-}1r.C_i \rangle \in \mathcal{I}^{\mathcal{T}}_-$ must be considered like $\langle \sigma, \geq n_i r.C_i \rangle \in \mathcal{I}^{\mathcal{T}}_+$ and vice versa.

We define the set $\mathcal{P}_{\sigma.r} \overset{def}{=} \mathcal{P}^{\geq}_{\sigma.r} \cup \mathcal{P}^{\leq}_{\sigma.r}$ *as the* smart partitioning *for the* $N^{\geq}_{\sigma.r}$ *individuals of* $\Sigma^{\mathcal{T}}$ *in the form* $\sigma.r.k$, *where:*

$$\mathcal{P}^{\geq}_{\sigma.r} \overset{def}{=} \{\, n_S \mid S \in 2^{N^{\geq}_{\sigma.r}}, \; n_S = \Sigma_{n_k \in S}\, n_k \,\} \quad and$$

$$\mathcal{P}^{\leq}_{\sigma.r} \overset{def}{=} \{\, m_S \mid S \in 2^{N^{\leq}_{\sigma.r}}, \; m_S = \Sigma_{m_k \in S}\, m_k \,\}.^{7}$$

Finally, we define $p_i \in \mathcal{P}_{\sigma.r}$ *the* i-*th sorted element of* $\mathcal{P}_{\sigma.r}$, *so that* $p_i < p_{i+1}$. *We have in particular:* $p_1 = 0$ *and* $p_{|\mathcal{P}_{\sigma.r}|} = \max\{N^{\geq}_{\sigma.r}, N^{\leq}_{\sigma.r}\}$.

As $\mathcal{P}^{\geq}_{\sigma.r}, \mathcal{P}^{\leq}_{\sigma.r}, \mathcal{P}_{\sigma.r}$ are sets, equal values are uniquely represented in them. Given σ, r, and assuming to include in each partition consecutive individuals among $\sigma.r.1, ..., \sigma.r.N^{\geq}_{\sigma.r}$, then $\mathcal{P}_{\sigma.r}$ is the set containing the indexes of the last individual of all the partitions. Hence, partitions can be represented by the proxy individuals $\sigma.r.(p_{j-1}+1 \rightarrow p_j)$, with $j > 1$. For instance, notice that the partitionings shown in Example 1 are computed in accordance with Definition 2. We remark that Definition 2 defines a *safe* [8] partitioning, in fact:

- it takes into account all the values in QNRs for σ, r;
- it considers all the possible sums of the values n_i [resp. m_j] for all the at-least [resp. at-most] restrictions, which allows for representing all the possible lower-bounds [resp. upper-bounds] in case of disjoint concept interpretations;
- the union of $\mathcal{P}^{\geq}_{\sigma.r}, \mathcal{P}^{\leq}_{\sigma.r}$ represents the combination of lower- and upper-bounds;
- by sorting all the possible sums and by using the distance between these values (a partition ranges from $p_{j-1}+1$ to p_j) as the cardinality of the partitions, it allows for representing all the possible intersecting concept interpretations.

We remark that partitioning makes our approach independent from the magnitude/offset of the values occurring in QNRs.

4.2 Exploit Smart Partitioning in $\mathcal{ALCQ}2SMT_{\mathcal{C}}$

Using partitions and proxy individuals does not affect the $\mathcal{ALCQ}2SMT_{\mathcal{C}}$ encoding, because the Theory of Costs allows for arbitrary incur costs. We can enhance Definition 1 by taking advantage of smart partitioning as follows. First we assume that the sets $\Sigma^{\mathcal{T}}, \mathcal{I}^{\mathcal{T}}_{-}, \mathcal{I}^{\mathcal{T}}_{-}$ and the functions $A_{\langle \, , \, \rangle}$, indiv are defined consistently with the use of proxy individuals. Second, assuming to compute the partitioning $\mathcal{P}_{\sigma.r}$ of Definition 2 for every σ, r, we modify $\mathcal{ALCQ}2SMT_{\mathcal{C}}$ as follows:

- The n clauses of the types (5) and (6) at point 5. are replaced by the following:

$$\{\, \mathsf{IC}(\mathrm{indiv}^{C}_{\sigma.r},\, cost_j,\, idx_j) \rightarrow L_{\langle \sigma_{proxy_j},\, C \rangle} \mid p_j \in \mathcal{P}_{\sigma.r},\, 0<p_j\leq n \,\} \subset \varphi^{\mathcal{T}},$$

$$\{\, \mathsf{IC}(\mathrm{indiv}^{C}_{\sigma.r},\, cost_j,\, idx_j) \rightarrow A_{\langle \sigma_{proxy_j},\, \top \rangle} \mid p_j \in \mathcal{P}_{\sigma.r},\, 0<p_j\leq n \,\} \subset \varphi^{\mathcal{T}},$$

$$cost_j = p_j - p_{(j-1)},\; idx_j = k^{C}_1 + p_{(j-1)},\; \sigma_{proxy_j} = \sigma.r.k^{C}_1 + p_{(j-1)} \rightarrow k^{C}_1 + p_j - 1.$$

---

[7] Being 2^{X} the power set for the set/array X.

[8] I.e. it preserves the semantics of the problem wrt. satisfiability.

- Clauses (9), (10) at point 7. are modified accordingly.
- The clauses (11) defined at point 8. must take into account the use of proxy individuals and of incur costs potentially bigger than 1. Hence they are replaced by:

$$\{(L_{\langle \sigma.r.(i \to j),\, C \rangle} \wedge A_{\langle \sigma.r.(i \to j),\, \top \rangle}) \to \mathsf{IC}(\mathsf{indiv}^C_{\sigma.r},\, j-i+1,\, i) \mid \sigma.r.(i \to j) \in \Sigma^T \}.$$

- Clauses (14) at point 10. are modified in the same way, handling proxy individuals.

We make the following observations:

- If, for σ, r, the conditions of point 7. of Definition 1 do not hold (e.g. no at-most restriction exists), then an even more efficient partitioning requires only the following two clauses for every $\langle \sigma, \geq nr.C \rangle$:

$$\mathsf{IC}(\mathsf{indiv}^C_{\sigma.r}, n, k^C_1) \to L_{\langle \sigma.r.(k^C_1 \to k^C_1 + n-1),\, C \rangle}, \in \varphi^T,$$
$$\mathsf{IC}(\mathsf{indiv}^C_{\sigma.r}, n, k^C_1) \to A_{\langle \sigma.r.(k^C_1 \to k^C_1 + n-1),\, \top \rangle} \in \varphi^T.$$

- Otherwise, if the conditions of point 7. hold, then φ^T contains all the clauses:

$$\{ \mathsf{IC}(\mathsf{indiv}^C_{\sigma.r}, p_j - p_{j-1}, p_{j-1}+1) \to L_{\langle \sigma.r.(p_{j-1}+1 \to p_j),\, C \rangle} \mid p_j \in \mathcal{P}_{\sigma.r}, j > 1\} \cup$$
$$\{ \mathsf{IC}(\mathsf{indiv}^C_{\sigma.r}, p_j - p_{j-1}, p_{j-1}+1) \to A_{\langle \sigma.r.(p_{j-1}+1 \to p_j),\, \top \rangle} \mid p_j \in \mathcal{P}_{\sigma.r}, j > 1\}$$

for every $\langle \sigma, \geq nr.C \rangle$, as consequence of point 5. and of the sharing of (proxy) individuals performed at point 7.

An exponential-time algorithm computing the smart partitioning $\mathcal{P}_{\sigma.r}$ (Definition 2) for every given individual σ and the role r is presented in [17]. Taken as input the arrays $\mathcal{N}^{\geq}_{\sigma.r}$ and $\mathcal{N}^{\leq}_{\sigma.r}$, the algorithm is shown to have worst-case complexity $O(2^{\max |\mathcal{N}^{\geq}_{\sigma.r}|, |\mathcal{N}^{\leq}_{\sigma.r}|})$.

5 Empirical Evaluation

We have implemented the encoder $\mathcal{ALCQ}$2SMT in C++; *smart partitioning* (§4) can be enabled optionally (denoted with S.P. hereafter). In combination with $\mathcal{ALCQ}$2SMT, we have used MATHSAT (v. 3.4.1) [2] that is the SMT-solver including the Theory of Costs [3]. We have evaluated the effectiveness of our novel approach by performing an empirical test session on about 700 synthesized[9] and parameterized $\mathcal{ALCQ}$-concept satisfiability problems adapted from [6], plus more. In order to compare with the available state-of-the-art reasoners we have executed the following tools on every test case: FACT++ (v. v1.4.0) [16], PELLET (v. 2.1.1) [15], and RACER (RacerPro 1-9-0) [7].

All the results presented in this section have been obtained on a 64bit biprocessor dual-core IntelXeon2.66GHz machine, with 16GB of RAM. We set a 1000 seconds timeout for every concept satisfiability query. We also fixed a bound of 1GB of disk space for the SMT($\mathcal{C}$) encoding output from $\mathcal{ALCQ}$2SMT. When reporting the results

---

[9] Due to lack of space we refer the reader to Section 6.1 in [6] for a discussion on why real-world ontologies are not yet available as suitable QNR benchmarks.

for one $\mathcal{ALCQ}$2SMT+MathSat configuration (either including S.P. or not), every CPU time reported is the sum of both the $\mathcal{ALCQ}$2SMT encoding and the MathSat solving time (both including the loading and parsing of the respective input problem).[10]

Importantly, with all test problems, all tools under examination (including both the variants of $\mathcal{ALCQ}$2SMT+MathSat) agreed on the expected un/satisfiability results when terminating within the timeout, with the exception of Pellet which incorrectly returned "sat" on some nested_restr_unsat problems.

Test Description. For our empirical evaluation, we have made use of synthesized test cases adapted from those in [6].The benchmark problems of [6] focus on concept expressions containing only QNRs and define different sets of indexed problems, increasingly stressing on different sources of complexity at the increase of the index i. Since the values occurring in QNRs are one of the sources of complexity which can strongly affect the performance of reasoning for some tools, wrt. the original test cases of [6] we further parameterized such values making them depend on a parameter n. Below we list the sources of complexity of the reasoning in $\mathcal{ALCQ}$considered in [6] with the relative test set names, the ranges of the indexes i and the values chosen for n in our empirical evaluation:[11]

1. the size of the values occurring in QNRs (test cases: incr_lin_sat/unsat$_i$ with i=1–100; incr_exp_sat/unsat$_i$ with i=1–6, *satisfiable/unsatisfiable*);
2. the number of QNRs (test cases: restr_num$_i(n)$ with i =1–100, $n = 1, \underline{5}, 50$, *satisfiable*);
3. effect of backtracking (number of disjoint concepts) (test cases: backtracking$_i(n)$ with i=1–20, $n=1, 2, \underline{3}, 10$, *unsatisfiable*);
4. the ratio between the number of at-least restrictions and the number of at-most restrictions (test cases: restr_ratio$_i(n)$ with i=0–14, $n=1, \underline{5}$, *satisfiable*);
5. the satisfiability versus the unsatisfiability of the input concept expression (test cases: sat_unsat$_i(n)$ with $i=1, 2, 4, 6, \ldots, 24, n=1, \underline{10}$, *half-and-half*).

For the sake of fairness of the comparison, we introduced two novel groups of problems which we believe can stress the main limitations of our approach wrt. the competitors. These groups stress two sources of complexity which were not considered in [6]:

6. the variability of the values occurring in QNRs, i.e. in every restriction occurs a unique value (test cases: var_restr_num$_i(n)$ with i=1–100, $n=100$, *satisfiable*);
7. the number of nested QNRs (test cases: nested_restr_sat/unsat$_i(n)$, with i=1–20, $n=5, 50$, *satisfiable/unsatisfiable*).

For a much more detailed description and the exact TBoxes we refer the reader to [6,17].

Results. We compare $\mathcal{ALCQ}$2SMT+MathSat against the other state-of-the-art reasoners Racer, FaCT++ and Pellet. In Figures 2 and 3 we plot, as representative, the results in the most challenging test cases for every benchmark category. (More plots and all the detailed results can be found in [17].) We notice the following facts about $\mathcal{ALCQ}$2SMT+MathSat S.P.:

---

[10] To make the experiments reproducible, all the plots in full size, the tools, the problems, and the results are available at http://disi.unitn.it/~rseba/cade11/tests.tar.gz.

[11] The benchmark of [6] are defined for $\mathcal{SHQ}$ but we have adapted them to $\mathcal{ALCQ}$ by flattening all the role hierarchies to the only role r. The value of n originally used in [6] is underlined.

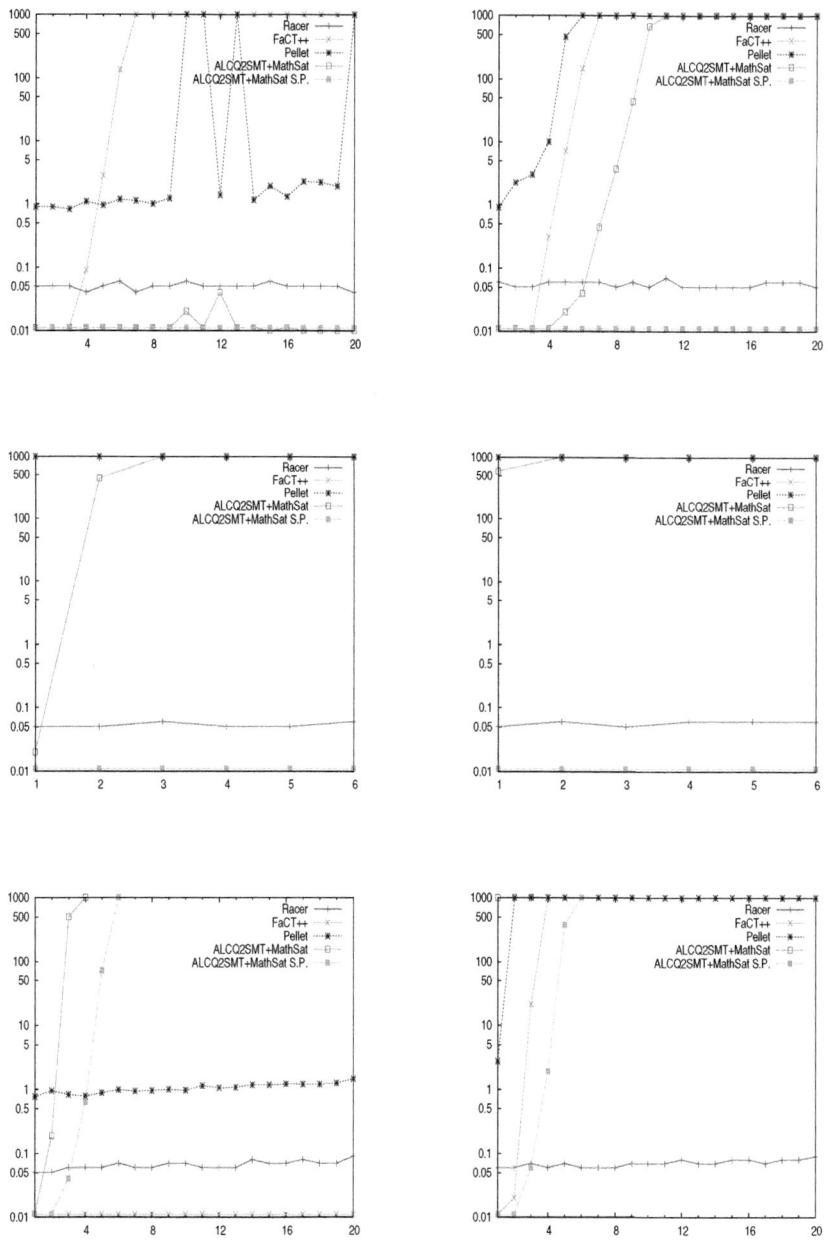

Fig. 2. Tools comparison. From left to right: `sat`, `unsat` problems; 1st row: `incr_lin`; 2nd row: `incr_exp`; 3rd row: `nested_restr`, $n = 5$. X axis: test case index; Y axis: CPU time (sec).

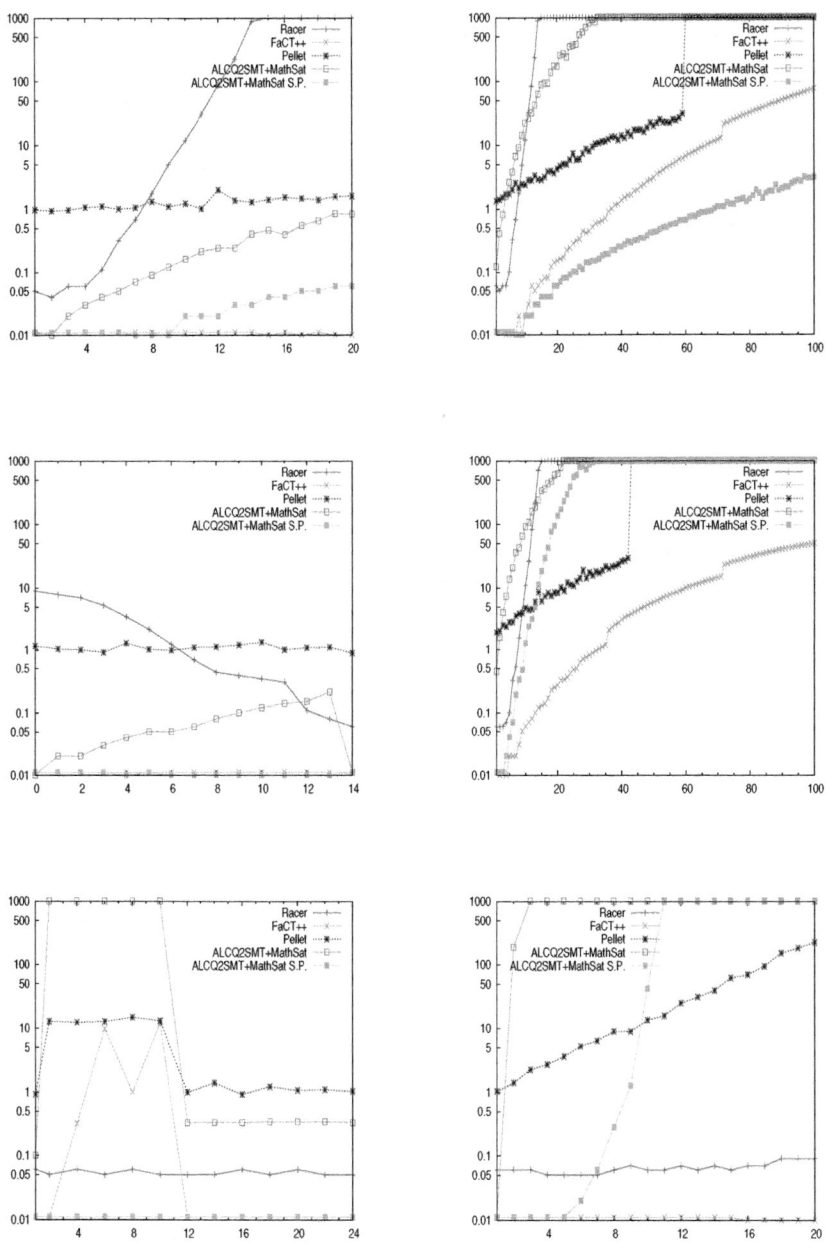

Fig. 3. Tools comparison. From let to right: 1st row: $\mathtt{restr\_num}_i(5)$, $\mathtt{restr\_num}_i(50)$; 2nd row: $\mathtt{restr\_ratio}_i(5)$, $\mathtt{var\_restr\_num}_i(100)$. 3rd row: $\mathtt{sat\_unsat}_i(10)$, $\mathtt{backtracking}_i(10)$. X axis: test case index; Y axis: CPU time (sec).

- in all tests, it performs uniformly much better than plain $\mathcal{ALCQ}$2SMT+MATHSAT;
- with RACER it is the best performer in the incr_lin and incr_exp (sat/unsat) categories (Fig. 2 rows 1,2), solving all problems in negligible time;
- in the nested_restr_sat it is the worst performer, but in nested_restr_unsat it performs better than FACT++ and PELLET (Fig. 2 row 3); [12]
- with FACT++ it is the best performer in the restr_num$_i$(5) and restr_ratio$_i$(5) categories (Fig. 3 rows 1,2 left), solving all problems in negligible time;
- it is the absolute best scorer in restr_num$_i$(50) test set (Fig. 3 row 1 right);
- in the var_restr_num category it performs worse than FACT++ and PELLET, but better than RACER[13] (Fig. 3 row 2 right);
- with RACER it is the best performer in the sat_unsat category (Fig. 3 row 3 left), solving all problems in negligible time;
- it is the worst performer on the backtracking problems (Fig. 3 row 3 right).

Looking into the data we notice a few more facts. First, the size of the encoded problems of $\mathcal{ALCQ}$2SMT –for both the basic and the S.P. variants– never exceed the 1GB-file-size limit, except for the nested_restr test cases with $i \geq 5$ and $i \geq 7$, respectively. (In fact, nested QNRs exponentially affect the size of our encoding.) In general, the encoded problems present a very low number of cost variables, which depends on the number of the QNRs in the input problem, and a possibly huge number of Boolean variables and clauses, which depend on the number of (proxy-) individuals introduced. Second, in the vast majority of the input problems the encoding required by $\mathcal{ALCQ}$2SMT is negligible ($\leq 10^{-2}$s); with S.P. it is significant only with the nested_restr and var_restr_num benchmarks (still $\leq$ 4s for the hardest problems).

Discussion. The performances of $\mathcal{ALCQ}$2SMT+MATHSAT S.P. wrt. other state-of-the-art reasoners range from some cases where it is much less efficient (backtracking, nested_restr_sat and var_restr_num) up to problems in which it significantly outperforms other tools (incr, sat_unsat and restr_num). Notice that we have specifically designed the nested_restr and var_restr_num problems in order to enforce the exponentiality of the encoding and to maximally inhibit smart partitioning, respectively. The backtracking problems, instead, have been designed in [6] to test the capability of performing dependency-directed backtracking [10]. Since the encoding is decoupled from the search, our approach cannot benefit of this optimization.

$\mathcal{ALCQ}$2SMT+MATHSAT S.P. instead performs extremely well in those benchmarks presenting multiple/balanced sources of complexity. Moreover, the size of the encoding is not the main complexity issue for our approach, which is very effective also on large or really complex problems (e.g., MATHSAT scales up to problems with more than 10^5 Boolean variables and clauses, and 10^4 cost variables, in the nested_restr benchmarks). Finally, smart partitioning is extremely effective, being able to drastically (and exponentially) reduce the size of the output SMT($\mathcal{C}$) problems, up to three

---

[12] Notice that that PELLET gave wrong "sat" results on nested_restr_unsat problems.

[13] RACER's implementation of the algebraic approach [8] is best-case exponential wrt. the number of QNRs.

orders of magnitude in the extreme `rest_num` and `nested_restr` cases wrt. basic $\mathcal{ALCQ}$2SMT (it exponentially impacts also in the number of cost variables in case of nested QNRs). The empirical evaluation clearly confirms that partitioning makes our approach independent from the magnitude/offset of the values occurring in QNRs.

References

1. Baader, F., Calvanese, D., McGuinness, D., Nardi, D., Patel-Schneider, P.F. (eds.): The Description Logic Handbook: Theory, Implementation, and Applications (2003)
2. Bruttomesso, R., Cimatti, A., Franzén, A., Griggio, A., Hanna, Z., Nadel, A., Palti, A., Sebastiani, R.: MathSAT 4 SMT Solver. In: Gupta, A., Malik, S. (eds.) CAV 2008. LNCS, vol. 5123, pp. 547–560. Springer, Heidelberg (2008)
3. Cimatti, A., Franzén, A., Griggio, A., Sebastiani, R., Stenico, C.: Satisfiability Modulo the Theory of Costs: Foundations and Applications. In: Esparza, J., Majumdar, R. (eds.) TACAS 2010. LNCS, vol. 6015, pp. 99–113. Springer, Heidelberg (2010)
4. Faddoul, J., Haarslev, V.: Algebraic Tableau Reasoning for the Description Logic $\mathcal{SHOQ}$. Journal of Applied Logic, Special Issue on Hybrid Logics 8(4) (2010)
5. Faddoul, J., Haarslev, V.: Optimizing Algebraic Tableau Reasoning for $\mathcal{SHOQ}$: First Experimental Results. In: Proc. of DL, Waterloo, Canada, May 4-7 (2010)
6. Farsiniamarj, N., Haarslev, V.: Practical reasoning with qualified number restrictions: A hybrid abox calculus for the description logic $\mathcal{SHQ}$. J. AI Communications 23(2-3) (2010)
7. Haarslev, V., Möller, R.: RACER System Description. In: Goré, R.P., Leitsch, A., Nipkow, T. (eds.) IJCAR 2001. LNCS (LNAI), vol. 2083, p. 701. Springer, Heidelberg (2001)
8. Haarslev, V., Timmann, M., Möller, R.: Combining Tableaux and Algebraic Methods for Reasoning with Qualified Number Restrictions. In: Proc. of DL 2001 (2001)
9. Hollunder, B., Baader, F.: Qualifying Number Restrictions in Concept Languages. In: Proc. of KR, Boston, USA (1991)
10. Horrocks, I., Sattler, U., Tobies, S.: Practical reasoning for very expressive description logics. Logic Journal of the IGPL 8(3) (2000)
11. Lutz, C., Areces, C., Horrocks, I., Sattler, U.: Keys, Nominals, and Concrete Domains. Journal of Artificial Intelligence Research, JAIR 23(1) (2005)
12. Sebastiani, R.: Lazy Satisfiability Modulo Theories. Journal on Satisfiability, Boolean Modeling and Computation, JSAT 3, 141–224 (2007)
13. Sebastiani, R., Vescovi, M.: Automated Reasoning in Modal and Description Logics via SAT Encoding: the Case Study of $K(m)/\mathcal{ALC}$-satisfiability. JAIR 35(1) (2009)
14. Sebastiani, R., Vescovi, M.: Axiom pinpointing in lightweight description logics via horn-SAT encoding and conflict analysis. In: Schmidt, R.A. (ed.) CADE-22. LNCS, vol. 5663, pp. 84–99. Springer, Heidelberg (2009)
15. Sirin, E., Parsia, B., Grau, B.C., Kalyanpur, A., Katz, Y.: Pellet: A practical OWL-DL reasoner. Journal of Web Semantics 5(2) (2007)
16. Tsarkov, D., Horrocks, I.: faCT++ description logic reasoner: System description. In: Furbach, U., Shankar, N. (eds.) IJCAR 2006. LNCS (LNAI), vol. 4130, pp. 292–297. Springer, Heidelberg (2006)
17. Vescovi, M., Sebastiani, R., Haarslev, V.: Automated Reasoning on TBoxes with Qualified Number Restrictions via SMT. Tech. Rep. DISI-11-001, Università di Trento (April 2011), http://disi.unitn.it/~rseba/cade11/techrep.pdf

Sine Qua Non for Large Theory Reasoning

Kryštof Hoder and Andrei Voronkov[*]

University of Manchester, Manchester, UK

Abstract. One possible way to deal with large theories is to have a good selection method for relevant axioms. This is confirmed by the fact that the largest available first-order knowledge base (the Open CYC) contains over 3 million axioms, while answering queries to it usually requires not more than a few dozen axioms. A method for axiom selection has been proposed by the first author in the Sumo INference Engine (SInE) system. SInE has won the large theory division of CASC in 2008. The method turned out to be so successful that the next two years it was used by the winner as well as by several other competing systems. This paper contains the presentation of the method and describes experiments with it in the theorem prover Vampire.

1 Introduction

First-order theorem provers traditionally were designed for working with relatively small collections of input formulas, for example, those based on a small axiomatisation of a class of algebras, or some axiomatisation of a set theory. Recently, several very large first-order axiomatisations and problems using these axiomatisations have become available. Problems of this kind usually come either from knowledge-base reasoning over large ontologies (such as SUMO [6] and CYC [4]) or from reasoning over large mathematical libraries (such as MIZAR [9]). Solving these problems usually involves reasoning in theories that contain thousands to millions of axioms, of which only a few are going to be used in proofs we are looking for.

Reasoning with very large theories expressed in first-order logic requires radical redesign of theorem provers. For example, a quadratic time preprocessing algorithm (such algorithms were routinely used in the past) may become prohibitively expensive when the input contains a million formulas.

The first-order problems we will discuss in this paper consist of a very large (thousands to millions) set Ax of *axioms*, plus a small number of additional *assumptions* $A_1, \ldots, A_n$ and a *conjecture* G, sometimes also called a *goal*. We have to prove the conjecture from the axioms and assumptions. Since the set of additional assumptions is normally small (and often empty), it will be convenient for us to assume that we have a large set of axioms and a single goal $A_1 \wedge \ldots \wedge A_n \rightarrow G$. When we discuss complexity of algorithms in this paper, we assume that all axioms and the goal are *small*, for example, have a size (number of symbols, connectives and quantifiers) bound by a constant.

If the conjecture is provable from the axioms, then it is normally provable from a very small subset of these axioms. For example, some of the CYC problems mentioned

---

[*] This work and the second author are partially supported by an EPSRC grant.

N. Bjørner and V. Sofronie-Stokkermans (Eds.): CADE 2011, LNAI 6803, pp. 299–314, 2011.
© Springer-Verlag Berlin Heidelberg 2011

above contain over 3,000,000 axioms, and all of these problems have proofs involving only less than 20 axioms. If we only use the axioms occurring in such a proof instead of all axioms, a proof will be found by any modern theorem prover in essentially no time.

Provided that only a tiny subset T of axioms is sufficient for finding a proof, one can try to select a small subset $S \subseteq$ Ax of axioms, which is likely to contain T, and search for a proof using a standard first-order theorem prover on the subset S instead of Ax. It is common that the subset S we are trying to select consists of the axioms *most relevant* to the goal. This paper describes an algorithm for axiom selection. The first version of the algorithm was originally introduced by the first author and implemented in the system SInE. The version and options described here are implemented in the theorem prover Vampire [3].

This paper is structured as follows. In Section 2 we discuss the problem of selecting axioms relevant to a goal and the natural idea of *symbol-based selection*. Based on this discussion, in Subsection 2.2 we introduce a definition of *trigger-based selection*, which captures a special case of symbol-based selection. In Section 3 we present the Sine selection algorithm as a trigger-based selection algorithm. In Section 4 we discuss possible variations of this algorithm obtained by changing the trigger relation to overcome potential shortcomings of Sine selection. We also describe the Vampire parameters that can be used to invoke these variations.

Section 5 presents experimental results carried out over TPTP problems with large axiomatisations. It shows the effect of various parameter values on the size of the selected set of axioms, the number of iterations of the algorithm, and on the ability to solve hard TPTP problems. Section 6 describes the use of our selection method in the recent CASC competitions. In Section 7 we briefly overview other algorithms used for selection of relevant axioms and other related work.

2 Symbol-Based Selection

2.1 Idea: Relevance

When one thinks of selecting axioms relevant to a goal, perhaps the most natural idea is to use *symbol-based selection*. By a symbol we mean any predicate or function symbol (including constants) apart from equality $=$. Symbol-based selection means that axioms are selected based on symbols occurring in them. Let us call two symbols *neighbours* if either they occur in the same axiom. Let us also call two symbols s_1, s_2 *relevant* if (s_1, s_2) belongs to the reflexive and transitive closure of the neighbour relation. We will say that a symbol is *relevant* (to the goal) if it is relevant to a symbol occurring in the goal. Likewise, we say that an *axiom is relevant* if it contains at least one relevant symbol. Note that in an axiom containing at least one relevant symbol, all symbols will be relevant too.

One possible way of axiom selection is to use all relevant axioms. However, for all benchmark suites available to us, the set of relevant symbols is usually the set of all or nearly all axioms. This is mostly due to the use of very general relations having occurrences in many axioms: as soon as any such relation is relevant, all axioms containing this relation become relevant. We will refer to symbols having occurrences in many axioms as to *common symbols*. Typical examples of common symbols are "instance-of" and "subclass" relations in ontologies: many ontologies consists almost exclusively of axioms using these two relations (or similar relations, such as "subsumes"). Therefore, any selection procedure that tries to avoid selecting nearly all axioms should solve the problem of common symbols.

Another idea for selecting fewer axioms is not to use the full reflexive and transitive closure of the neighbour relation but only a subset thereof, for example by only allowing to make n steps of the computation of the transitive closure, for some (small) positive integer n. Let us formalise the relevancy relation, so that we can refine it later. More precisely, we will deal with two relevancy relations, one for symbols and another for axioms.

1. If s is a symbol occurring in the goal, then s is 0-step relevant.
2. If s is k-step relevant and occurs in an axiom A, then A is $k + 1$-step relevant.
3. A is k-step relevant and s occurs in A, then s is k-step relevant, too.

Clearly, a symbol or an axiom is relevant, if it is k-relevant for some $k \geq 0$. This definition implies also that a k-relevant symbol or axiom is m-relevant for every $m \geq k$.

One can use this inductive definition to select either the set of all k-relevant, for some fixed k, axioms, or the set of all relevant axioms. To compute the latter, we can mark all relevant axioms until the inductive step does not select any new axiom. Moreover, it is easy to implement this algorithm in the time linear in the size of the set of all axioms.

Even better, assuming that the set of all axioms is fixed (which is a natural assumption for applications), by preprocessing the set of axioms one can compute the set of relevant (or k-step relevant) axioms in the time *linear in the size of the computed set*. To this end, it is sufficient to index the set of all pairs (s, A) such that s is a symbol occurring in an axiom A (of course, A can be represented as a reference in the index). This index can be implemented by storing for every symbol the set of axioms in which it occurs. Let us show that such an algorithm is indeed linear in the size of the computed set. To this end, let us consider the set of pairs (s, A) inspected by this algorithm. Note that for every such pair, A will be included in the output. We use an assumption that the size of every axiom is bound by a constant; therefore the number of symbols occurring in a single axiom is also bound by a constant c. This implies that, for a given axiom A, pairs of the form (s, A) can be inspected at most c times. This shows that if axioms of the total size n were selected, the runtime of the algorithm is in the worst case $O(c \cdot n)$, where c is the maximal number of symbols occurring in an axiom.

Note that using k-step relevance instead of relevance does not solve the problem of common relations, since they can already become relevant for very small values of k.

2.2 General Scheme

We will introduce a class of symbol-based selection algorithms that generalise and refine the idea of symbol-based selection. The only deviation from the previous definition is to add extra conditions for an axiom to be relevant. We will achieve this by introducing a trigger relation as follows. Suppose that we have a relation $trigger(s, A)$ between symbols and axioms, such that this relation holds only if s occurs in A. If this relation holds, we will also say that s *triggers* A.

Definition 1 (trigger-based selection)

1. *If s is a symbol occurring in the goal, then s is 0-step triggered.*
2. *If s is k-step triggered and s triggers A, then A is $k + 1$-step triggered.*
3. *A is k-step triggered and s occurs in A, then s is k-step triggered, too.*

An axiom or a symbol is called triggered *if it is k-triggered for some $k \geq 0$.*

It is easy to see that the introduction of the trigger relation can solve the problem of common symbols. One can simply postulate that s triggers A only if s is not a common symbol. Or, to be on a safe side, one can say that a common symbol s triggers A only if all symbols of A are common. This would avoid excluding axioms like

$$subclass(x, y) \wedge subclass(y, z) \rightarrow subclass(x, z)$$

(transitivity of the subclass relation) or

$$instanceof(x, y) \wedge subclass(y, z) \rightarrow instanceof(x, z).$$

It is not hard to argue that if the set of all symbols s such that s triggers axiom A can be computed in the time linear in the size of A, then the set T of all triggered (as well as all k-step triggered) axioms can be computed in time linear in the size of T. This is achieved by keeping a mapping from symbols to the sets of axioms which they trigger.

3   The Sine Selection

3.1   Idea

The Sine selection algorithm is a special case of trigger-based selection. It uses a trigger relation that tries to reflect, in a certain way, the hard-to-formalise notions "s_2 *is defined using s_1*" or "s_1 *is more general than s_2*" on symbols.

It is not unreasonable to assume that large knowledge bases contain large hierarchical collections of definitions, where more general terms are defined using less general terms. It is not easy to extract such definitions, since they can take various forms. It is also not easy to formalise the relation "more general". As a simple approximation to "more general" one can consider the relation "more common": a symbol s_2 is considered more common than s_1 if s_1 occurs in more axioms than s_2. Then, as a potential approximation to "s_2 *is defined in terms of s_1*" we can consider the relation "s_1, s_2 *occur in the same axiom A and s_2 is a least common symbol in A.*" This is, essentially, the definition of the trigger function for the Sine selection.

Definition 2 (Trigger relation for the Sine selection). *Let us denote by* $occ(s)$ *the number of axioms in which the symbol s appears. Then we define the relation trigger as follows: trigger*(s, A) *iff for all symbols* s' *occurring in A we have* $occ(s) \leq occ(s')$. *In other words, an axiom is only triggered by the least common symbols occurring in it.*

3.2 Examples

Example 3 (Sine selection). In this example we will denote variables by capital letters. The example illustrates the Sine selection and also a typical reason why it is, in general, incomplete. Consider the following set of axioms:

```
subclass(X,Y) ∧ subclass(Y,Z) → subclass(X,Z)
subclass(petrol,liquid)
¬subclass(stone,liquid)
subclass(beverage,liquid)
subclass(beer,beverage)
subclass(guinness,beer)
subclass(pilsner,beer)
```

The following table gives, for every symbol s, the number of axioms in which it occurs.

s	$occ(s)$
subclass	7
liquid	3
beer	3
beverage	2
petrol	1
stone	1
guinness	1
pilsner	1

Using the occurrence table, we can compute the trigger relation as follows:

axiom	symbols
subclass(X,Y) ∧ subclass(Y,Z) → subclass(X,Z)	subclass
subclass(petrol,liquid)	petrol
¬subclass(stone,liquid)	stone
subclass(beverage,liquid)	beverage
subclass(beer,beverage)	beverage
subclass(guinness,beer)	guinness
subclass(pilsner,beer)	pilsner

Consider the goal `subclass(beer,liquid)`. This goal is a logical consequence of these axioms. However, the symbols from the goal `subclass`, `beer`, and `liquid` only trigger the first axiom. The selection will terminate with only the first axiom selected, which is insufficient to prove the goal.   □

Consider another example. This example illustrates how (small) changes in the input set of axioms can influence selection.

Example 4. Let us remove the last axiom from the axioms of Example 3. This changes the function *occ* as follows:

s	$occ(s)$
subclass	6
liquid	3
beer	2
beverage	2
petrol	1
stone	1
guinness	1

This also changes the trigger relation as follows:

axiom	symbols
subclass(X,Y) ∧ subclass(Y,Z) → subclass(X,Z)	subclass
subclass(petrol,liquid)	petrol
¬subclass(stone,liquid)	stone
subclass(beverage,liquid)	beverage
subclass(beer,beverage)	beverage,beer
subclass(guinness,beer)	guinness

Consider the same goal subclass(beer,liquid) as in Example 3. Now the symbols from the goal subclass, beer, and liquid trigger the first axiom as before plus the axiom subclass(beer,beverage). This results in adding beverage to the list of triggered symbols. As a consequence, this addition triggers the axiom subclass(beverage,liquid). This triggers no new symbols (since beverage was already triggered before), and so selection terminates with the following subset of selected axioms

```
subclass(X,Y) ∧ subclass(Y,Z) → subclass(X,Z)
subclass(beverage,liquid)
subclass(beer,beverage)
```

This collection of axioms is sufficient to prove the goal, contrary to Example 3. Moreover, it is the minimal set of axioms sufficient to prove this goal.   □

This example also illustrates that removing some axioms from the input set can result in selecting more axioms than before the removal.

3.3 The Selection Algorithm in More Detail

The algorithm runs in two phases. The first phase is goal-independent and only preprocesses the set of all axioms. In this phase we do the following:

1. count, for each symbol, the number of axioms in which it occurs;
2. store the set of pairs (s, A) such that s triggers A.

Note that this phase can be implemented in the time linear in the size of the set of axioms. It can be done by two traversals of the axioms (computing the trigger relation needs the number of occurrences).

In the second phase (which depends on the goal) we build the set of all triggered (or k-triggered, if k is given) axioms using the stored trigger relation. If the trigger relation is indexed on the first argument, the time complexity of the second phase is linear in the size of the resulting set of selected axioms and independent of the overall number of theory axioms. After the selection, the goal and the selected axioms are passed to a first-order theorem prover.

Separating the two steps of the algorithm provides an efficient way to treat collections of problems that share a large number of theory axioms. After preprocessing the shared theory axiomatisation, only the second phase is run on each of the problems, which allows us to avoid repeated execution of the first phase.

4   Variations

To turn the Sine selection on, one uses Vampire with the option

```
--sine_selection on
```

(the default value of this option is off). In the previous versions of Vampire we had two values: axioms and included instead of on. The value axioms considered as axioms the formulas marked as such in the TPTP language. The value included considered as axioms formulas coming from included files.[1] However, the value included is fragile since simple preprocessing of the input can change which formulas are included. In addition it turned out not to be good in practice, so in the current version we replaced these two values by a single one.

In the rest of this section we consider several variations of Sine selection. Each of these variations is implemented in Vampire as a parameter whose value can be set by the user. We present experimental evaluation of these parameters in Section 5.

4.1   Tolerance

Since our selection algorithm is incomplete, we introduced parameters changing the trigger function in various ways. One obvious problem with the selection is that it is very fragile with the respect to the number of axioms in which a symbol occurs, as already illustrated in Examples 3 and 4. Indeed, suppose a symbol s_1 occurs in (say) 7 axioms while s_2 occurs in 8 axioms. One can argue that s_1 and s_2 are, essentially, equally common. However, s_1 can trigger an axiom in which both s_1 and s_2 occur, while s_2 cannot trigger it.

To cope with this problem, we introduced a parameter called *tolerance*. The value of this parameter is a real number $t \geq 1$. It changes the trigger relation as follows.

Definition 5 (Trigger relation with tolerance). *Given the tolerance $t \geq 1$, define the relation trigger as follows: $trigger(s, A)$ iff for all symbols s' occurring in A we have $occ(s) \leq t \cdot occ(s')$.*

Compare this definition with Definition 2.

---

[1] The TPTP language classifies the input formulas into axioms, additional assumptions (hypotheses) and conjectures. Formulas can also be included from files using the TPTP directive include().

Example 6 (Sine selection with tolerance). Consider the set of axioms and the goal of Example 3. Assume the tolerance value is 1.5. This changes the trigger relation for two of the axioms as follows:

axiom	symbols
subclass(X,Y) ∧ subclass(Y,Z) → subclass(X,Z)	subclass
subclass(petrol,liquid)	petrol
¬subclass(stone,liquid)	stone
subclass(beverage,liquid)	beverage,liquid
subclass(beer,beverage)	beer,beverage
subclass(guinness,beer)	guinness
subclass(pilsner,beer)	pilsner

For the same goal `subclass(beer,liquid)`, the set of selected axioms becomes

```
subclass(X,Y) ∧ subclass(Y,Z) → subclass(X,Z)
subclass(beverage,liquid)
subclass(beer,beverage)
```

This set is sufficient to prove the goal.   □

Note that the set of selected axioms is monotonic with regard to the value of tolerance: if we increase the value, all previously selected axioms will also be selected. For large enough values of tolerance, the set of selected axioms is simply the set of all relevant axioms in the sense of Section 2.1, because axioms become triggered by all the symbols that occur in them. For example, in Example 3 all axioms become selected when $t \geq 3$ and each symbol triggers all axioms in which it occurs when $t \geq 7$.

Having a fixed value of the tolerance parameter, we may perform axiom selection using the two-phase algorithm described in section 3.3. However, a likely scenario is that we will want to run several proof attempts with different values of the tolerance parameter. Using the basic two-phase algorithm, we would have to run the first phase of the algorithm for each value of the tolerance parameter. At the cost of a slight increase in the complexity, the algorithm may be modified, so that the first phase is run only once, allowing selection with arbitrary tolerance values. During the first phase, instead of storing a mapping from every symbol s to the set of axioms triggered by s, we store a mapping from s to the list of all pairs $(A_1, t_1), \ldots, (A_m, t_m)$ such that s triggers A_i if $t \geq t_i$. This list is ordered by the values of the t_i's. Ordering such lists can take $n \cdot log(n)$ time, so the complexity of the first phase slightly increases. However, the complexity of the second phase does not change: it is still linear in the size of selected axioms, since we only inspect the sublist of $(A_1, t_1), \ldots, (A_m, t_m)$ corresponding to the trigger relation.

To change the value of tolerance from the default value 1 to t, one uses Vampire with the option

```
--sine_tolerance t
```

4.2   Depth Limit

One can restrict the number of steps in computing the set of selected axioms so that it computes the set of all d-step triggered axioms. To this end, one can run Vampire with the option

`--sine_depth` d

The default value of `sine_depth` in Vampire is ∞. Evidently, the set of selected axioms is monotonic with regard to d: if we increase the value, all previously selected axioms will be selected, too.

4.3   Generality Threshold

The last modification of Vampire is based on the following idea: if a symbol s occurs in few axioms, then it triggers any axiom in which it occurs, even if the axiom contains symbols with fewer occurrences. To implement this, we fix some positive integer value $g \geq 1$ (called generality threshold) and modify the trigger relation as follows.

Definition 7 (Trigger relation with generality threshold). *Given the generality threshold* $g \geq 1$, *define the relation trigger as follows: trigger(s, A) iff either* $occ(s) \leq g$ *or for all symbols s' occurring in A we have* $occ(s) \leq occ(s')$.

To turn the generality threshold in Vampire on, one can run Vampire with the option

`--sine_generality_threshold` g

The default value is 0 and the set of selected axioms is, evidently, monotonic with regard to g. If we set g to a large enough number, for example, the number of all axioms, then (similarly to setting a large value of the tolerance parameter) all the relevant axioms will be selected.

To use both a tolerance value t and a generality threshold value g, one should define the trigger relation as the union of the corresponding trigger relations. Namely, $trigger(s, A)$ iff either $occ(s) \leq g$ or for all symbols s' occurring in A we have $occ(s) \leq t \cdot occ(s')$.

5   Experiments

All experiments described in this section were carried out using a cluster of 64-bit quad core Dell servers having 12 GB RAM each.[2] Each of the runs used only one core and we never ran more than 3 tests in parallel on one computer to achieve the best performance.

The experiments were run on three benchmark suites taken from the TPTP library [11]. The library contains three different classes of very large problems:[3]

1. problems from the SUMO ontology [6]: CSR075 to CSR109.
2. problems from the CYC knowledge base [4]; CSR025 to CSR074.
3. problems from the Mizar library [9]: ALG214 to ALG234, CAT021 to CAT037, GRP618 to GRP653, LAT282 to LAT380, SEU406 to SEU451, and TOP023 to TOP048.

---

[2] The cluster was donated to our group by the Royal Society.
[3] These classes correspond to categories of the LTB division in the CASC competition [12].

Table 1. Average problem size information

problems	axioms	atoms	predicates	functions
SUMO	298,420	323,170	20	24,430
CYC	3,341,990	5,328,216	204,678	1,050,014
Mizar	44,925	332,143	2,328	6,115

Table 2. Selected formulas of CYC problems depending on the depth, tolerance and generality threshold

	$t = 1.0$		$t = 1.2$		$t = 1.5$		$t = 2.0$		$t = 3.0$		$t = 5.0$	
$d = 1$	29	1.17	35	1.09	41	1.05	47	1.02	60	1.02	72	1.01
$d = 2$	142	1.25	287	1.07	442	1.03	607	1.01	1027	1.00	1476	1.00
$d = 3$	505	1.32	937	1.13	1451	1.07	2484	1.02	5311	1.01	10482	1.01
$d = 4$	1784	1.41	3232	1.20	5716	1.10	11603	1.02	29963	1.01	69015	1.01
$d = 5$	4432	1.57	8870	1.27	16806	1.13	37599	1.03	110186	1.02	249192	1.04
$d = 7$	10698	2.16	25607	1.50	56337	1.21	150277	1.06	431875	1.09	832935	1.10
$d = \infty$	36356	28.37	495360	3.33	1310965	1.34	1562064	1.20	1822427	1.12	2057597	1.07

Each of these classes contains several different axiomatisations. To evaluate the size of the set of selected axioms and the number of iterations we only considered the largest axiomatisations in each class (that is, SUMO problems with the suffix +3, CYC problems with the suffix +6, and Mizar problems with the suffix +4. Table 1 contains information about sizes of these problems.

5.1 Generality Threshold

Table 2 shows how the number of selected formulas depends on the generality threshold. We considered the smallest possible value $g = 0$ and a sufficiently large value $g = 16$. In every column of the table we show on the left the number of axioms selected when $g = 0$ and on the right the number of axioms selected when $g = 16$ divided by the value on the left. The numbers are average over all CYC problems. One can see from the table that the largest increase (by the factor of 28.37) was achieved when the depth was unlimited and tolerance equal to 1. Predictably, when the tolerance grows, the percentage of additional axioms selected by the generality threshold value becomes smaller, since some axioms selected due to the large value of generality threshold become selected due to the high tolerance.

Our results have also shown that all the problems Vampire could solve, could also be solved with the value $g = 0$, so for the rest of this section we will focus on the remaining two options (depth and tolerance) and only consider the results obtained when the generality threshold was not used, that is, when $g = 0$. Therefore, the conclusion we can draw is that, although the generality threshold parameter is intended to cope with the problem of common relations, in practice it can be replaced by other parameters.

5.2 Selected Formulas

Table 2 shows the average numbers of selected axioms for the CYC problems, and table 3 shows these numbers for the Mizar and SUMO problems. Note that the numbers

Table 3. The number of selected formulas for the Mizar (left) and SUMO (right) problems

$d\backslash t$	1.0	1.2	1.5	2.0	3.0	5.0	$d\backslash t$	1.0	1.2	1.5	2.0	3.0	5.0
1	4903	4911	4921	4936	4973	5038	1	12	13	14	16	21	28
2	5296	5395	5553	5823	6427	7743	2	70	82	115	158	272	654
3	6118	6451	7068	8280	10841	16337	3	188	230	372	762	1950	5980
4	6893	7556	9001	12176	18300	28878	4	316	470	942	3021	8720	23440
5	7432	8517	11165	16945	26842	37284	5	540	979	2417	8179	22644	52241
7	7897	9991	15788	26203	36507	41443	7	1027	2708	8517	24445	54958	97481
∞	8047	15987	28353	35345	39389	41762	∞	1116	8361	26959	57322	82379	107926

Table 4. The minimal, average and maximal number of steps required to build the set of all triggered axioms as a function of tolerance

suite		$t = 1.0$	$t = 1.2$	$t = 1.5$	$t = 2.0$	$t = 3.0$	$t = 5.0$
	min	4	7	36	25	29	23
CYC	avg	19.3	102.7	44.3	29.9	33.0	25.1
	max	47	135	60	41	37	27
	min	6	7	19	15	14	10
Mizar	avg	9.5	27.5	25.4	19.7	15.0	12.3
	max	15	61	33	23	18	14
	min	3	5	4	6	13	11
SUMO	avg	7.3	15.3	20.8	19.8	16.6	12.6
	max	17	35	39	25	23	15

for the Mizar problems are essentially different from the SUMO and CYC problems. The number of selected Mizar axioms is large (over 4,000) even when the depth limit is set to 1, while it is relatively small for the CYC and SUMO problems. This is related to the fact that the Mizar problems usually have complex goals containing several assumptions and many symbols, while for the CYC and SUMO problems the goal is simple and usually is just an atomic formula with very few symbols. This is also one of the reasons why Mizar problems are much harder for all theorem provers using the Sine selection.

5.3 Number of Iterations

The next question we are interested in is the number of steps required by Sine selection to compute the set of all triggered relations. Table 4 contains statistics about the number of iterations. To our surprise, in some cases this number is very large (135 for CYC problems, 61 for Mizar problems, and 39 for SUMO problems). There is also no obvious pattern on how this parameter depends on the value of tolerance.

5.4 Essential Parameters

For experiments described in this subsection we considered all (not only largest) SUMO, CYC and Mizar problems.

Since our main aim is to automatically prove (hard) theorems, the most important questions related to the use of Sine selection are the following:

Table 5. Problems solved with and without Sine selection

atoms	only with Sine	only without Sine	together
10,000	243	64	721
20,000	217	10	542
40,000	208	7	464
80,000	187	3	373
160,000	138	1	243
320,000	80	1	168
640,000	50	0	100
1,280,000	50	0	50
rating 1	232	25	402

1. How powerful is the selection method?
2. Which of the parameters (and ranges of values for these parameters) are essential in practice?

The first question cannot be answered in a simple way. On the one hand, we have strong evidence that the method is very powerful. To support this, consider Table 5. It shows the number of all the TPTP 4.0.1 CYC, Mizar, and SUMO problems solved with some Sine selection and without it, depending on the size of the problem measured as the number of atoms in it. The last row shows these numbers for the problems having TPTP rating 1. A problem has TPTP rating 1 if it was previously unsolved by all provers, including the previous versions of Vampire. For example, among the problems having 80,000 or more atoms, 373 problems were solved by Vampire all together. 138 problems could only be solved with the help of Sine selection, while only 3 problems out of 373 could not be solved with Sine selection.

When a problem is not solved, we do not know why Vampire (or any other prover) fails to prove it. This can be for at least the following three reasons, of which two are directly related to the power of our selection method:

1. the set of selected axioms can be insufficient to prove the goal;
2. the set of selected axioms is too large, which prevents theorem provers from success;
3. the problem is very hard even for small sets of axioms sufficient to prove the goal.

Let us now investigate which parameters and their values are essential for Vampire. As we pointed out, it turned out that the generality threshold parameter can be dropped without any effect on the set of problems solved by Vampire. It turned out that both the tolerance and depth limit are very essential. To show this, we used our database of proofs found by Vampire, which was generated using about 70 CPU years of run time and now contains about 575,000 results, of which over 43,000 are related to the mentioned benchmark suite.

We selected problems having less than 10 solutions in the database. The reason to use the number of solutions as a criterion was that problems with few solutions are believed to be harder. Also, such problems can be solved only with a small subset of possible values for the various Vampire parameters.

Table 6. The sine depth range for solved hard problems

range	CYC	Mizar	SUMO
1 − 1		16	
1 − 2		10	
1 − 3		5	
1 − 4		3	
1 − 5		2	
1 − 10		1	
1 − ∞	15	107	6
2 − 2		21	
2 − 3		12	
2 − 4		3	
2 − 5		6	
2 − 7		1	
2 − 10		1	
2 − ∞	21	39	4
3 − 3		1	
3 − 4		1	
3 − ∞	6	1	1
4 − 4		1	
4 − ∞	6		
5 − ∞	3		
10 − ∞	3		1
total	51	231	12

Table 7. The sine tolerance range for solved hard problems

range	CYC	Mizar	SUMO
1.0 − 1.0		3	
1.0 − 1.2		4	
1.0 − 1.5		12	1
1.0 − 2.0		17	
1.0 − 3.0		19	
1.0 − 5.0	49	155	11
1.2 − 1.5		2	
1.2 − 2.0		1	
1.2 − 3.0		1	
1.2 − 5.0	2	1	
1.5 − 5.0		1	
2.0 − 2.0		1	
2.0 − 3.0		7	
2.0 − 5.0		1	
3.0 − 5.0		3	
5.0 − 5.0		2	
total	51	231	12

This selection resulted in 51 CYC problems, 231 Mizar problems and 12 SUMO problems. For each of these problems we checked which parameter values solve these problems. More precisely, we took their known solutions, changed the depth and tolerance parameters and checked which of the changes still solve the problem. The results are summarised in Tables 6 and 7. The table cells show the number of problems which can be solved by the given range of values. We do a projection on the possible values of the parameter that is not present in the table (tolerance in the case of Table 6 and depth limit in Table 7). For example, the third row in Table 7 means that there were 12 selected Mizar problems and 1 selected SUMO problem that could be solved with some values of the depth limit and only with the values of tolerance between 1.0 and 1.5.

Let us first analyse the depth limit in Table 6. For the evaluation we used the following values of depth limit: 1, 2, 3, 4, 5, 7, 10 and ∞. The first observation is that this parameter is, indeed, very important. For example, there were 39 Mizar problems that could be solved with only one value of this parameter (1, 2, 3 or 4). For both CYC and SUMO collections setting the depth to ∞ is always a good strategy. On the contrary, only 147 out of 231 solved Mizar problems (and only 30 of 64 the largest Mizar problems) could be solved with this setting.

Next, let us analyse the tolerance in Table 7. For the evaluation we used the following values of tolerance: 1.0, 1.2, 1.5, 2.0, 3.0, 4.0, and 5.0. It turned out that this parameter is also very important. However, the behaviour of solutions depending on this parameter is more stable than for the depth parameter: only 6 Mizar problems could be solved with exactly one value of the tolerance and 155 Mizar problems out of 231 were solved with all the values we tried. Among the largest hard Mizar problems, only 36 out of 64 were solved with all the tried values of tolerance. 11 out of 12 SUMO problems and 49 out of 51 CYC problems could be solved with any value of the tolerance and all CYC problems could be solved with the value 1.2 or higher.

6 Competition Performance

Our axiom selection algorithm was used by several systems participating in the Large Theory (LTB) division of recent CASC competitions.

The Sine selection was introduced in 2008, at the CASC-J4 [10] competition. The only participant that used our algorithm was the SInE theorem prover. It has won the division by solving 88 out of 150 problems, which was 12 problems ahead of the second best participant.

In 2009, at the CASC-22 [12] competition, four out of seven participants were using our selection algorithm, and these four participants ended up at the first four positions, solving 69 to 35 problems out of 100, while the best participant not using our algorithm solved only 18 problems.

In 2010, at the CASC-J5 competition, five out of seven systems were using our algorithm as the only axiom selection algorithm, including the winner (Vampire). The second best ranked system (Currahee) used our selection algorithm as one of possible selection algorithms.

7 Related Work

In our algorithm we maintain the set of selected axioms (starting from goal), and select new axioms that are relevant to the goal step by step. The lightweight relevance filtering algorithm [5] shares this approach, but instead of a trigger relation, which is used by our algorithm, it selects an axiom if certain percentage of its symbols appears in the already selected axioms. This method also penalizes common symbols—the more often a symbol appears in the problem, the less impact its appearance in an axiom has.

Several other algorithms use some measure of distance in a graph of axioms, in order to determine which axioms are relevant to the goal. The contextual relevance filtering [1] and the syntactic relevance measure [13] compute the weighted graph between axioms with weights based on the number of shared symbols (taking into account their commonness). The latter does not use the distance from conjecture to select relevant axioms, but to order them for further (semantic) processing. The relevance restriction strategy described in [7] connects two clauses in the graph if they have unifiable literals. The paper also examines the suitability of different graph distance measures.

Semantic algorithms are another group of axiom selection algorithms that use a model of currently selected axioms to guide the selection of new ones. To this group belong the Semantic Relevance Axiom Selection System [13] and the algorithm for semantic selection of premises [8].

Yet another approach is taken in the latent semantic analysis [1], which uses a technique for analysing relationships between documents. Each formula is considered to be a document, and formulas with strong relationship toward the goal are selected. The MaLARea system [16] uses machine learning on previous proofs in the theory to estimate which theory axioms are likely to contribute to proofs of new problems.

In [15] the benefit of our axiom selection algorithm for reasoning on the Mizar Mathematical Library [14] is examined.

8   Conclusion

We defined the Sine selection used in the theorem prover Vampire and several other theorem provers to select axioms potentially relevant to the goal. We formalised the Sine selection as a family of *trigger-based selection algorithms*. We showed that all the existing axiom selection parameters in Vampire can be formalised as a special case of such algorithms.

We also discussed, using extensive experiments over all TPTP problems with large axiomatisations, the effect of various parameter values on the size of the selected set of axioms, the number of iterations of the algorithm, and solutions of hard TPTP problems.

We also added a new mode to Vampire to make others able to experiment with our axiom selection. If Vampire is run in a new *axiom selection mode*, it does not try to prove the problem but only selects axioms according to the user-given options and outputs the selected axioms and the goal in the TPTP format. This mode can be invoked by using `vampire --mode axiom_selection`.

Acknowledgements

The authors would like to thank Josef Urban for helpful suggestions, and for his support and supervision of the first author during the first year of the work on the Sine algorithm.

References

1. Roederer, A., Puzis, Y., Sutcliffe, G.: divvy: An ATP meta-system based on axiom relevance ordering. In: Schmidt, R.A. (ed.) CADE-22. LNCS, vol. 5663, pp. 157–162. Springer, Heidelberg (2009)
2. Armando, A., Baumgartner, P., Dowek, G. (eds.): IJCAR 2008. LNCS (LNAI), vol. 5195. Springer, Heidelberg (2008)
3. Hoder, K., Kovács, L., Voronkov, A.: Interpolation and symbol elimination in vampire. In: Giesl, J., Hähnle, R. (eds.) IJCAR 2010. LNCS, vol. 6173, pp. 188–195. Springer, Heidelberg (2010)
4. Lenat, D.B.: CYC: A large-scale investment in knowledge infrastructure. Communications of the ACM 38(11), 33–38 (1995)
5. Meng, J., Paulson, L.C.: Lightweight relevance filtering for machine-generated resolution problems. J. Applied Logic 7(1), 41–57 (2009)
6. Niles, I., Pease, A.: Towards a standard upper ontology. In: FOIS, pp. 2–9 (2001)
7. Plaisted, D.A., Yahya, A.H.: A relevance restriction strategy for automated deduction. Artif. Intell. 144(1-2), 59–93 (2003)
8. Pudlak, P.: Semantic selection of premises for automated theorem proving. In: Sutcliffe, G., Urban, J., Schulz, S. (eds.) ESARLT. CEUR Workshop Proceedings, vol. 257, pp. 27–44. (2007) CEUR-WS.org
9. Rudnicki, P. (ed.): An overview of the mizar project, pp. 311–332. University of Technology, Bastad (1992)

10. Sutcliffe, G.: CASC-J4 the 4th IJCAR ATP system competition. In: Armando (ed.) [2], pp. 457–458
11. Sutcliffe, G.: The tptp problem library and associated infrastructure. J. Autom. Reasoning 43(4), 337–362 (2009)
12. Sutcliffe, G.: The cade-22 automated theorem proving system competition - casc-22. AI Commun. 23(1), 47–59 (2010)
13. Sutcliffe, G., Puzis, Y.: Srass - a semantic relevance axiom selection system. In: Pfenning, F. (ed.) CADE 2007. LNCS (LNAI), vol. 4603, pp. 295–310. Springer, Heidelberg (2007)
14. Urban, J.: Mptp 0.2: Design, implementation, and initial experiments. J. Autom. Reasoning 37(1-2), 21–43 (2006)
15. Urban, J., Hoder, K., Voronkov, A.: Evaluation of automated theorem proving on the mizar mathematical library. In: Fukuda, K., van der Hoeven, J., Joswig, M., Takayama, N. (eds.) ICMS 2010. LNCS, vol. 6327, pp. 155–166. Springer, Heidelberg (2010)
16. Urban, J., Sutcliffe, G., Pudlák, P., Vyskocil, J.: Malarea sg1- machine learner for automated reasoning with semantic guidance. In: Armando (ed.) [2], pp. 441–456.

Predicate Completion for non-Horn Clause Sets

Matthias Horbach

University of New Mexico
Albuquerque, U.S.A.
horbach@mpi-inf.mpg.de

Abstract. The standard semantics of a logical program described by a set of predicative Horn clauses is minimal model semantics. To reason about negation in this context, Clark proposed to enrich the description in such a way that all Herbrand models but the minimal one are excluded. This *predicate completion* is used in explicit negation as failure, and also for example by Comon and Nieuwenhuis in inductive theorem proving.

In this article, I extend predicate completion to a class of non-Horn clause sets. These may have several minimal models and I show how predicate completion with respect to a ground total reduction ordering singles out the same model as the model construction procedure by Bachmair and Ganzinger.

1 Introduction

In logic programs given by predicative Horn clauses, usually mainly positive information is explicitly encoded, e.g. in the form $\to P(a)$ and $P(a) \to Q(b)$. Negative information, in this case that the ground atoms $P(b)$ and $Q(a)$ are supposed not to hold, is implicit: They do not hold because any attempt at deriving them from the program fails. This *negation as failure* is the standard semantics of negation for logic programs. To capture it explicitly, Clark [3] introduced the idea of *predicate completion*, i.e. of enriching the program with a formula containing explicit information on which ground atoms should not hold. For the example above and the predicate Q, this could be done using the formula $\forall x.(Q(x) \Leftrightarrow (x = b \wedge P(a)))$, which can be derived locally from $P(a) \to Q(b)$, i.e. using only the clause that directly describes Q. From a semantic perspective, the goal of predicate completion is to distinguish the unique minimal model of the program, thereby identifying negation as failure and first-order negation.

Clark's idea was later cast by Comon and Nieuwenhuis [6] into an algorithm that expresses the completion not by a formula (which may contain both existential and universal quantifiers) but by additional Horn clauses, i.e. an extended logic program. The precondition for this algorithm is that the original clauses are *universally reductive*, i.e. the head of each clause must contain all its variables.

Apart from the obvious application in logic programming [18], predicate completion has long been in use in several areas of artificial intelligence, including knowledge representation [14], default reasoning [16] and planning [8]. Comon and Nieuwenhuis [6] shifted the focus towards automated deduction by using

N. Bjørner and V. Sofronie-Stokkermans (Eds.): CADE 2011, LNAI 6803, pp. 315–330, 2011.

predicate completion to harvest the power of first-order reasoners for minimal model reasoning in a more general context.

In spite of an abundance of possible applications for example in non-Horn databases and non-Horn logic programming [15], extensions of predicate completion (in the sense of a completion taking the form of first-order clauses) beyond universally reductive predicative Horn clauses are scarce. Reiter [17] and later Togashi et al. [19] proved that predicate completion is possible for non-Horn clauses where every predicate occurs only positively or only negatively and where no two positive atom occurrences in the same clause are unifiable. I showed [9] how to extend predicate completion in a different direction by for the first time allowing non-predicative elements, namely *ultimate periodicity equations* of the form $s^n(x) \simeq s^m(x)$, which includes reasoning about quotients of the naturals. The general problem of predicate completion for arbitrary (even predicative) clauses is not solvable because minimal model validity is undecidable.

In this article, I will present a predicate completion algorithm for clause sets consisting of (i) universally reductive predicative clauses that need not be Horn, and of (ii) ultimate periodicity equations. I will prove that the algorithm does indeed compute a completion, i.e. a clause set with a unique Herbrand model. Where predicate completion for Horn clause sets describes the unique minimal model, I will show that predicate completion can be used to distinguish the different minimal models of a non-Horn set. Indeed, given a ground total reduction ordering, predicate completion singles out the same model as the classical model construction procedure by Bachmair and Ganzinger [1].

2   Preliminaries

I build on the notions of [1, 4] and shortly recall the most important concepts.

Terms, Formulas and Clauses. Let X be an infinite set of variables. A *signature* $\Sigma = (S, P, F, \tau)$ consists of three finite sets S, P, F of *sorts*, *predicate symbols* and *function symbols* such that S and F are non-empty and X, P and F are disjoint, and a mapping τ that assigns to every variable in X a sort, to every symbol in P a tuple of sorts and to every symbol in F a non-empty tuple of sorts. Assignments $\tau(P) = (S_1, \ldots, S_n)$ and $\tau(f) = (S_1, \ldots, S_n, S)$ for $P \in P$, $f \in F$ and $n \geq 0$ are written as $P : S_1, \ldots, S_n$ and $f : S_1, \ldots, S_n \to S$. I assume that there are infinitely many variables and at least one term of each sort.

Let $T(F, X)$ be the set of all well-sorted *terms* over F and X defined as usual. Let $T(F)$ be the set of all *ground terms* over F. To improve readability, a list $t_1, \ldots, t_n$ of terms is often written as $\vec{t}$, and the n-fold application $f(\ldots(f(t))\ldots)$ of a unary function symbol f to a term t is written as $f^n(t)$.

A *predicative atom* over Σ is a well-sorted expression $P(t_1, \ldots, t_n)$, where $P : S_1, \ldots, S_n$ is a predicate symbol and $t_1 : S_1, \ldots, t_n : S_n$ are terms of the corresponding sorts. An *equation* (or *disequation*, respectively) is a multiset of two terms of the same sort, written as $t \simeq t'$ (or $t \not\simeq t'$). An *atom* is either a predicative atom or an equation or one of the symbols $\top, \bot$ (true and false). A *literal* is an atom or a disequation or a negated predicative atom. *Formulas* are constructed from atoms by the constructors $\exists x., \forall x., \wedge, \vee$ and $\neg$. The notation $\exists \vec{x}.\phi$ is a shorthand notation for $\exists x_1. \cdots \exists x_n.\phi$, and analogously for $\forall \vec{x}.\phi$. In both cases, $\vec{x}$ may be empty. *Equational formulas* are formulas that do not contain predicative atoms. A formula is in *negation normal form* if the symbol $\neg$ appears only in literals. By pushing down all negations and eliminating double negations, each formula can be transformed into an equivalent negation normal form.

The set of variables occurring freely in a formula ϕ is denoted by $\mathrm{var}(\phi)$. The expression $\phi|_p$ denotes the subformula at position p, and $\phi[\psi]_p$ denotes the result of replacing $\phi|_p$ by ψ. For terms t, $\mathrm{var}(t)$, $t|_p$ and $t[t']_p$ are defined analogously.

A *clause* is a pair of multisets of predicative or equational atoms, written $\Gamma \to \Delta$, interpreted as the conjunction of all atoms in the *antecedent* Γ implying the disjunction of all atoms in the *succedent* Δ. A clause is *Horn* if Δ contains at most one atom. It is *predicative* if all atoms in Γ and Δ are predicative.

Rewrite Systems. A *rewrite rule* is a pair (l, r) of two terms of the same sort or of two formulas, written $l \to r$, such that all variables in r also occur in l. A set of rewrite rules is called a *rewrite system*. For a given rewrite system R, a term (or formula) t *rewrites* to a term (or formula) t', written $t \to_R t'$, if $t|_p = l\sigma$ and $t' = t[r\sigma]_p$, for some rule $l \to r$ in R, position p in t, and substitution σ. A term (or formula) t is called *irreducible* or a *normal form* if there is no term (or formula) t' such that $t \to_R t'$.

A rewrite system R is *terminating* if there is no infinite chain $t_1 \to_R t_2 \to_R \cdots$; it is *convergent* if it is terminating and every term rewrites to a unique normal form.

Substitutions. A *substitution* σ is a map from X to $\mathcal{T}(\mathcal{F}, X)$ that maps each variable to a term of the same sort and acts as the identity map on all but a finite number of variables. A substitution is identified with its homomorphic extensions to terms and atoms, and with its capture-free extension to formulas. The application to a term t (or a formula ϕ) of a substitution σ mapping variables $\vec{x} = x_1, \ldots, x_n$ to terms $\vec{t} = t_1, \ldots, t_n$ is written as $t\sigma$ or $t\{\vec{x} \mapsto \vec{t}\}$ (or as $\phi\sigma$ or $\phi\{\vec{x} \mapsto \vec{t}\}$).

Orderings. A (strict) partial ordering $\succ$ on a set T is a binary relation that is antisymmetric ($t_1 \succ t_2$ implies $t_2 \nsucc t_1$) and transitive ($t_1 \succ t_2$ and $t_2 \succ t_3$ implies $t_1 \succ t_3$). A partial ordering $\succ$ on a set T can be extended to a partial ordering $\succ^{mul}$ on multisets over T, i.e. maps from T into the non-negative integers, as follows: $M \succ^{mul} N$ if $M \neq N$ and whenever there is a $t \in T$ such that $N(t) \succ M(t)$ then $M(t') \succ N(t')$ for some $t' \succ t$. It can be extended to a partial ordering $\succ^{lex}$ on n-tuples over T as follows: $(t_1, \ldots, t_n) \succ^{lex} (t'_1, \ldots, t'_n)$ if there is an index $1 \le i \le n$ such that $t_j = t'_j$ for all $1 \le j < i$ and $t_i \succ t'_i$.

Any ordering $\succ$ on terms over Σ lifts to equational atoms over a signature as its multiset extension. As usual, a predicative atom $P(\vec{t})$ can be regarded as an equational atom $f_P(\vec{t}) \simeq c_{\text{true}}$ over a suitably adapted signature where c_{true} is $\succ$-minimal. By abuse of notation, I will usually not discriminate between an ordering on atoms and the underlying ordering on terms.

A *reduction ordering* is a partial ordering on terms (or atoms) that is well-founded (i.e. there is no infinite chain $t_1 \succ t_2 \succ \ldots$), has the subterm property

($t_1 \succ t_2$ whenever t_2 is a strict subterm of t_1) and is stable under substitutions ($t_1 \succ t_2$ implies $t_1\sigma \succ t_2\sigma$ for all t_1, t_2 and all substitutions σ).

Any partial ordering $\succ$ on atoms is extended to clauses in the following way: Consider clauses as multisets of occurrences of atoms. The occurrence of an atom A in the antecedent is identified with the multiset $\{A, A\}$; the occurrence of an atom A in the succedent is identified with the multiset $\{A\}$. Now $\succ$ is lifted to atom occurrences as its multiset extension, and to clauses as the multiset extension of this ordering on atom occurrences.

An occurrence of an atom A is *maximal* in a clause C if there is no occurrence of an atom in C that is strictly greater with respect to $\succ$ than the occurrence of A. It is *strictly maximal* in C if there is no other occurrence of an atom in C that is equal to or greater than the occurrence of A with respect to $\succ$. A clause $C = \Gamma \to \Delta, A$ is *universally reductive* if A is a strictly maximal occurrence in C and all variables that occur in C also occur in A.

Inferences, Redundancy and Derivations. An *inference rule* is a relation on clauses. An *inference calculus* is a set of inference rules.

A ground clause C is called *redundant* with respect to a set N of clauses if there are ground instances $C_1, \ldots, C_k$ of clauses in N such that $C \succ C_i$ for all i and $C_1, \ldots, C_k \models C$. A non-ground clause is redundant if all its ground instances are redundant.

Given an inference calculus, a ground inference $(C'_1, \ldots, C'_n, C)$ is *redundant* with respect to N if some C'_i is redundant, or if the conclusion is redundant with respect to ground instances smaller than the maximal C'_i. A non-ground inference is redundant if all its ground instances are redundant. A clause set N is *saturated* with respect to a calculus if every inference with premises in N is redundant with respect to N. An inference calculus is *(refutationally) complete* if every unsatisfiable saturated clause set contains the empty clause.

Herbrand Interpretations and Perfect Models. A *Herbrand interpretation* $\mathcal{I}$ over the signature Σ is a set of ground atoms over Σ that is closed under rewriting with the rewrite system consisting of all rules $t \to t'$ and $t' \to t$ such that $t \simeq t' \in \mathcal{I}$ (i.e. $\simeq$ is interpreted as a congruence in $\mathcal{I}$). A Herbrand interpretation $\mathcal{I}$ is a *model* of a set N of clauses if for every ground instance $\Gamma \to \Delta$ of a clause in N it holds that $\Gamma \subseteq \mathcal{I}$ implies $\Delta \cap \mathcal{I} \neq \emptyset$.

The unique *minimal model* with respect to set inclusion of a satisfiable set N of Horn clauses is denoted by $\mathcal{I}_N$. For non-Horn clause sets, there may be more than one minimal model. Let $\succ$ be a well-founded reduction ordering that is total on ground terms and let $\succ^{\mathcal{I}}$ be the multiset extension of the inverse relation of $\succ$. Among the minimal models of a clause set N (with respect to set inclusion), there is a unique one that is minimal with respect to $\succ^{\mathcal{I}}$. This model is called the *perfect model* of N with respect to $\succ$ and denoted by $\mathcal{I}_N^{\succ}$.

Bachmair and Ganzinger [1] introduced the construction of a special Herbrand interpretation that under certain conditions yields the perfect model:

Definition 1. *Let N be a clause set and $\succ$ a well-founded ordering on ground clauses. By induction over $\succ$, define atom sets $\mathrm{Prod}(C), R(C)$ as follows:*

Let Prod(C) = {A}, if C = Γ → Δ, A is a ground instance of a clause C′ ∈ N such that (i) A is a strictly maximal occurrence of an atom in C, (ii) A is not an element of R(C) and not reducible[1] by any equation in R(C), (iii) Γ ⊆ R(C), and (iv) Δ ∩ R(C) = ∅. Otherwise Prod(C) = ∅. In both cases, R(C) = ⋃_{C≻C′} Prod(C′).
Finally define an interpretation $\mathcal{I}_{N,\succ}$ by $\mathcal{I}_{N,\succ} = \bigcup_C Prod(C)$.

Lemma 2. *If N is consistent and saturated with respect to a complete inference system and ≻ is a well-founded reduction ordering that is total on ground terms, then $\mathcal{I}_{N,\succ}$ coincides with the perfect model $\mathcal{I}_N^\succ$.*

3   Predicate Completion

When an interpretation is given as a minimal model $\mathcal{I}_N$ of a clause set N, it is often of interest to enrich N to a set $N′$ in such a way that $N′$ does not have any Herbrand models other than $\mathcal{I}_N$, for example to derive negative facts for $\mathcal{I}_N$. The key to this enrichment is the so-called *completion* of predicates [3]: For each predicate P, the set $N′$ must describe for which arguments P does *not* hold in $\mathcal{I}_N$.

Example 3. If $N_{\mathrm{Even}} = \{\mathrm{Even}(0); \mathrm{Even}(x) \to \mathrm{Even}(s(s(x)))\}$ describes the even numbers over the single-sorted signature $\Sigma_{\mathrm{Even}} = (\{\mathrm{Even}\}, \{s, 0\})$, with Even : Nat, s : Nat → Nat and 0 : Nat, then $\mathrm{Even}(s^n(0))$ holds in the minimal model $\mathcal{I}_{N_{\mathrm{Even}}}$ if, and only if, n is an even number. Let $N′_{\mathrm{Even}}$ contain N_{Even} and the additional clauses $\mathrm{Even}(s(0)) \to$ and $\mathrm{Even}(s(s(x))) \to \mathrm{Even}(x)$. Then $\mathcal{I}_{N_{\mathrm{Even}}}$ is the only Herbrand model of $N′_{\mathrm{Even}}$ over Σ_{Even}, because Even holds for every even number, the first new clause makes it not hold on 1, and repeated inferences with the second new clause show that Even does not hold for any odd number.

In the predicative Horn case, the completion $N′$ of a clause set N is supposed to satisfy $N′ \models A \Leftrightarrow N \models A$ and $N′ \models \neg A \Leftrightarrow N \not\models A$ for every ground atom A, according to the idea of negation as failure. In terms of the unique minimal model $\mathcal{I}_N$, this means that $\mathcal{I}_N$ is the only Herbrand model of $N′$. Using this semantic approach if N is not Horn, it is natural to call $N′$ a *completion* if one of the minimal models of N is the only Herbrand model of $N′$.

3.1   The Predicate Completion Algorithm PC

For predicative clause sets N, ≃ is interpreted as syntactic equality in $\mathcal{I}_N$. Comon and Nieuwenhuis [6, Section 7.3] used this fact to develop a predicate completion procedure for predicative and universally reductive Horn clause sets. In [9] (and not in [6]), the correctness of the procedure was proved and the procedure was enhanced to also encompass equations of the form $s^l(x) \simeq s^k(x)$.

I will now present an extension of this algorithm that can deal with predicative non-Horn clauses that are universally reductive.

---

[1] A ground term t is *reducible* by an equation $u \simeq u′$ where $u′ \not\succ u$ if u is unifiable with any subterm of t. A ground equation $t \simeq t′$ where $t′ \not\succ t$ is reducible if t is reducible; a predicative atom $P(t_1, \ldots, t_n)$ is reducible if one of the t_i is.

Definition 4 (Ultimately Periodic Interpretation). *Let $\Sigma=(\mathcal{S},\mathcal{P},\mathcal{F},\mathcal{X},\tau)$ be a signature. Let $S_1,\ldots,S_n$ be n different sorts such that all ground terms of sort S_i are of the form $s_i^m(0_i)$ for two function symbols $s_i,0_i$. A finite set $E = \{s_1^{l_1}(x)\simeq s_1^{k_1}(x),\ldots,s_n^{l_n}(x)\simeq s_n^{k_n}(x)\}$ of equations between terms in $S_1,\ldots,S_n$ with $l_i > k_i$ for all i is called a* set of ultimate periodicity equations. *Each sort S_i is called* ultimately periodic *of type (k_i,l_i). All other sorts are called* free.

Let $\succ$ be a well-founded reduction ordering that is total on ground terms and let N be a finite set of predicative and universally reductive clauses such that $N \cup E$ is satisfiable. The perfect model $\mathcal{I}_{N\cup E}^{\succ}$ of $N \cup E$ with respect to $\succ$ is called an ultimately periodic interpretation.

Definition 5 (Predicate Completion). *Let $\Sigma = (\mathcal{S},\mathcal{P},\mathcal{F},\mathcal{X},\tau)$ be a signature and $\mathcal{I}_{N\cup E}^{\succ}$ an ultimately periodic interpretation over Σ as in Definition 4. The* predicate completion algorithm PC *for $N \cup E$ and $\succ$ works as follows:*

(i) *For every $P \in \mathcal{P}$, let $N_P \subseteq N$ be the set of clauses in N of the form $\Gamma \to \Delta, P(\vec{t})$, where $P(\vec{t})$ is a strictly maximal literal occurrence. Combine all these clauses into the single formula $\forall \vec{x}.(\phi_P \to P(\vec{x}))$ where*

$$\phi_P = \exists \vec{y}. \bigvee_{\Gamma \to \Delta, P(\vec{t}) \in N_P} (x_1 \simeq t_1 \wedge \ldots \wedge x_n \simeq t_n \wedge \bigwedge_{A \in \Gamma} A \wedge \bigwedge_{B \in \Delta} \neg B) ,$$

the y_i are the variables appearing in N_P, and the x_j are fresh variables.
(ii) *Transform $\neg\phi_P$ into an equivalent formula ϕ_P' that does not contain any universal quantifiers.*
(iii) *Write the formula $\forall \vec{x}.(\phi_P' \to \neg P(\vec{x}))$ as a finite set N_P' of clauses.*
(iv) *Let N' be the union of $N \cup E$ and all sets N_P', $P \in \mathcal{P}$.*

The idea of the algorithm was already introduced by Clark [3], who considered only pure predicative Horn clauses. He executed steps (ii) and (iii) by hand and did not discuss the question if they can be automatized. Steps (i) and (iv) are only finite syntactic transformations, and step (i) can be executed because all clauses in N with non-empty succedent have a unique strictly maximal positive literal occurrence. So the critical steps are (ii) and (iii): It is neither obvious that the universal quantifiers can be eliminated from $\neg\phi_P$, nor is it obvious that, once the universal quantifiers are gone, the result can be written as a finite set of clauses.

3.2   Disunification-Based Quantifier Elimination

The transformation of $\neg\phi_P$ into an equivalent formula without universal quantifiers in step (ii) can be performed using a quantifier elimination procedure given by a set of rewrite rules. A basic version of this procedure was introduced by Comon and Lescanne [5] under the name *disunification* and I stick to this terminology.

The disunification procedure DisU that I will employ is given in Figures 1–3. It is terminating [9, Theorem 18] and correct in the sense that rewrite steps

Formulae are always kept normalized with respect to these rules.

Propagation of Negation:

$\neg\top \;\rightarrowtail\; \bot$ $\qquad \neg(\phi \vee \phi') \;\rightarrowtail\; \neg\phi \wedge \neg\phi'$ $\qquad \neg(\exists x.\phi) \;\rightarrowtail\; \forall x.\neg\phi$

$\neg\bot \;\rightarrowtail\; \top$ $\qquad \neg(\phi \wedge \phi') \;\rightarrowtail\; \neg\phi \vee \neg\phi'$ $\qquad \neg(\forall x.\phi) \;\rightarrowtail\; \exists x.\neg\phi$

$\qquad\qquad\qquad\qquad\qquad\qquad\qquad\qquad\qquad\qquad\qquad\qquad\qquad\quad \neg\neg\phi \rightarrowtail \phi$

Propagation of Truth and Falsity:

$\top \wedge \phi \;\rightarrowtail\; \phi$ $\qquad \top \vee \phi \rightarrowtail \top$ $\qquad \exists x.\top \;\rightarrowtail\; \top$

$\bot \wedge \phi \;\rightarrowtail\; \bot$ $\qquad \bot \vee \phi \rightarrowtail \phi$ $\qquad \exists x.\bot \;\rightarrowtail\; \bot$

$\phi \wedge \top \;\rightarrowtail\; \phi$ $\qquad \phi \vee \top \;\rightarrowtail\; \top$ $\qquad \forall x.\top \;\rightarrowtail\; \top$

$\phi \wedge \bot \;\rightarrowtail\; \bot$ $\qquad \phi \vee \bot \;\rightarrowtail\; \bot$ $\qquad \forall x.\bot \;\rightarrowtail\; \bot$

Quantifier Accumulation:

P1: $\forall \vec{x}.\phi[\forall \vec{y}.\phi']_p \rightarrow \forall \vec{x}, \vec{y}.\phi[\phi']_p$

P2: $\exists \vec{x}.\phi[\exists \vec{y}.\phi']_p \rightarrow \exists \vec{x}, \vec{y}.\phi[\phi']_p$

if $\vec{x}$ and $\vec{y}$ are not empty in P1,P2 and there is none of the symbols $\neg, \forall, \exists$ between the two melted quantifiers; if a variable of $\vec{y}$ occurs in $\phi[\top]_p$, it is renamed to avoid capturing.

Fig. 1. DisU: Normalization Rules

preserve the set of satisfying variable assignments with respect to every Herbrand interpretation $\mathcal{I}$ that interprets $\simeq$ as E-equality, i.e. $\mathcal{I} \models t \simeq t'$ if, and only if, $t =_E t'$ [9, Theorem 6].

To prove that the universal quantifiers can in fact be eliminated from $\neg\phi_P$, I will examine an invariant that holds for $\neg\phi_P$ (Lemma 7), is preserved during the application of DisU (Lemma 8), and holds only for such normal forms that do not contain universal quantifiers (Lemma 9).

In this section, I always implicitly assume a set E of ultimate periodicity equations to be given.

Invariant 6. *Let $\phi\!\downarrow$ be the normal form of a formula ϕ under the Normalization rules, Decomposition, Periodic Decomposition and Distribution of Figures 1–3. Consider the following properties of ϕ:*

(1) No subformula of $\phi\!\downarrow$ of the form $\forall \vec{x}.\phi'$, where the top symbol of ϕ' is not a universal quantifier, contains a quantifier.

(2) Universally quantified variables occur in $\phi\!\downarrow$ only in predicative literals or in disequations $t[x] \not\simeq t'$ where all variables in t' are free or existentially quantified.

For every predicative literal occurrence A_x in $\phi\!\downarrow$ containing a universally quantified variable x, there is a subformula of $\phi\!\downarrow$ of the form $A_x \vee B_x \vee \phi_x$ where B_x is a disequation containing x.

This invariant was introduced for the Horn case in [9]. The proofs of Lemmas 8 and 9 are identical to those in [9].

Lemma 7 (Invariant Holds Initially). *Let N be a set of universally reductive clauses and let ϕ_P be defined as in Definition 5. Then Invariant 6 holds for $\neg\phi_P$.*

Decomposition, Clash, and Occurrence Check:

D1: $f(u_1, \ldots, u_n) \simeq f(u'_1, \ldots, u'_n) \to u_1 \simeq u'_1 \wedge \ldots \wedge u_n \simeq u'_n$

D2: $f(u_1, \ldots, u_n) \not\simeq f(u'_1, \ldots, u'_n) \to u_1 \not\simeq u'_1 \vee \ldots \vee u_n \not\simeq u'_n$

C1: $f(u_1, \ldots, u_m) \simeq g(u'_1, \ldots, u'_n) \to \bot$ if $f \neq g$

C2: $f(u_1, \ldots, u_m) \not\simeq g(u'_1, \ldots, u'_n) \to \top$ if $f \neq g$

O1: $t \simeq u[t] \to \bot$ if $u[t] \neq t$

O2: $t \not\simeq u[t] \to \top$ if $u[t] \neq t$

if $f(u_1, \ldots, u_n)$, t and $u[t]$ belong to a free sort

Quantifier Elimination:

Q1: $\exists \vec{x}.\phi_1 \vee \phi_2 \to (\exists \vec{x}.\phi_1) \vee (\exists \vec{x}.\phi_2)$ if $\vec{x} \cap \mathrm{var}(\phi_1, \phi_2) \neq \emptyset$

Q2: $\forall \vec{x}.\phi_1 \wedge \phi_2 \to (\forall \vec{x}.\phi_1) \wedge (\forall \vec{x}.\phi_2)$ if $\vec{x} \cap \mathrm{var}(\phi_1, \phi_2) \neq \emptyset$

Q3: $\exists \vec{x}, x.\phi \to \exists \vec{x}.\phi$ if $x \notin \mathrm{var}(\phi)$

Q4: $\forall \vec{x}, x.\phi \to \forall \vec{x}.\phi$ if $x \notin \mathrm{var}(\phi)$

Q5: $\forall \vec{x}, x.x \not\simeq t \vee \phi \to \forall \vec{x}.\phi\{x \mapsto t\}$ if $x \notin \mathrm{var}(t)$

Q6: $\exists \vec{x}, x.x \simeq t \wedge \phi \to \exists \vec{x}.\phi\{x \mapsto t\}$ if $x \notin \mathrm{var}(t)$

Q7: $\forall \vec{z}, \vec{x}.y_1 \simeq t_1 \vee \ldots \vee y_n \simeq t_n \vee \phi \to \forall \vec{z}.\phi$

Q8: $\exists \vec{z}, \vec{x}.y_1 \not\simeq t_1 \wedge \ldots \wedge y_n \not\simeq t_n \wedge \phi \to \exists \vec{z}.\phi$

if in Q7 and Q8 $y_i \neq t_i$ and $\mathrm{var}(y_i, t_i) \cap \vec{x} \neq \emptyset$ for all i and $\mathrm{var}(\phi) \cap \vec{x} = \emptyset$ and the sorts of all variables in $\vec{x}$ contain infinitely many ground terms (in particular, all t_i are of a free sort).

Q1 and Q2 also require that no redex for P1 or P2 is created.

Finite Sort Reduction:

S1: $\forall \vec{x}, x.\phi \to \forall \vec{x}.\phi\{x \mapsto t_1\} \wedge \ldots \wedge \phi\{x \mapsto t_n\}$

S2: $\exists \vec{x}, x.\phi \to \exists \vec{x}.\phi\{x \mapsto t_1\} \vee \ldots \vee \phi\{x \mapsto t_n\}$

if the sort S of x is free and finite and $t_1, \ldots, t_n$ are the finitely many ground terms in S.

Distribution:

N1: $\forall \vec{x}.\phi[\phi_0 \vee (\phi_1 \wedge \phi_2)]_p \to \forall \vec{x}.\phi[(\phi_0 \vee \phi_1) \wedge (\phi_0 \vee \phi_2)]_p$

N2: $\exists \vec{x}.\phi[\phi_0 \wedge (\phi_1 \vee \phi_2)]_p \to \exists \vec{x}.\phi[(\phi_0 \wedge \phi_1) \vee (\phi_0 \wedge \phi_2)]_p$

if ϕ_0, ϕ_1, ϕ_2 are quantifier-free, $\mathrm{var}(\phi_1) \cap \vec{x} \neq \emptyset$, ϕ_1 is not a conjunction in N1 and not a disjunction in N2 and does not contain a redex for N1 or N2, and there is no negation and no quantifier in ϕ along the path p.

Explosion:

Ex1: $\exists \vec{x}.\phi \to \bigvee_{f \in \mathcal{F}'} \exists \vec{x}, \vec{x}_f.y \simeq f(\vec{x}_f) \wedge \phi\{y \mapsto f(\vec{x}_f)\}$

if y is free in ϕ and $\forall \vec{x}'.\phi'$, respectively, no other rule except Ex2 can be applied, there is in ϕ a literal $y \simeq t$ or $y \not\simeq t$ where t contains a universally quantified variable, and $\vec{x}$ is non-empty or $\phi = \forall \vec{x}'.\phi'$. If y is of sort S, then $\mathcal{F}' \subseteq \mathcal{F}$ is the set of function symbols of sort $S_1, \ldots, S_n \to S$.

Ex2: $\forall \vec{x}.\phi \to \bigwedge_{f \in \mathcal{F}'} \forall \vec{x}, \vec{x}_f.y \not\simeq f(\vec{x}_f) \vee \phi\{y \mapsto f(\vec{x}_f)\}$

if y is free in ϕ, no other rule can be applied, there is in ϕ a literal $y \simeq t$ or $y \not\simeq t$ where t contains an existentially quantified variable, and $\vec{x}$ is non-empty. If y is of sort S, then $\mathcal{F}' \subseteq \mathcal{F}$ is the set of function symbols of sort $S_1, \ldots, S_n \to S$.

Fig. 2. DisU: Rules for both Free and Ultimately Periodic Sorts

Periodic Reduction:

PR: $A[s^l(t)]_p \rightarrow A[s^k(t)]_p$

if A is an atom and $s^l(t)$ belongs to an ultimately periodic sort of type (k, l).

Periodic Decomposition:

$$\text{PD1: } s(t) \simeq s(t') \rightarrow \begin{cases} t \simeq t' & \text{if } t \text{ and } t' \text{ are ground} \\ t \simeq s^{k-1}(0) \vee t \simeq s^{l-1}(0) & \text{if } t \text{ is not ground} \\ & \text{and } s(t') = s^k(0) \\ t \simeq t' & \text{if } t \text{ is not ground} \\ & \text{and } t' \text{ is ground} \\ & \text{and } s(t') \neq s^k(0) \\ t \simeq t' \vee (t \simeq s^{k-1}(0) \wedge t' \simeq s^{l-1}(0)) & \\ \quad \vee (t \simeq s^{l-1}(0) \wedge t' \simeq s^{k-1}(0)) & \text{if } t, t' \text{ are not ground} \end{cases}$$

$$\text{PD2: } s(t) \not\simeq s(t') \rightarrow \begin{cases} t \not\simeq t' & \text{if } t \text{ and } t' \text{ are ground} \\ t \not\simeq s^{k-1}(0) \wedge t \not\simeq s^{l-1}(0) & \text{if } t \text{ is not ground} \\ & \text{and } s(t') = s^k(0) \\ t \not\simeq t' & \text{if } t \text{ is not ground} \\ & \text{and } t' \text{ is ground} \\ & \text{and } s(t') \neq s^k(0) \\ t \not\simeq t' \wedge (t \not\simeq s^{k-1}(0) \vee t' \not\simeq s^{l-1}(0)) & \\ \quad \wedge (t \not\simeq s^{l-1}(0) \vee t' \not\simeq s^{k-1}(0)) & \text{if } t, t' \text{ are not ground} \end{cases}$$

if $s(t)$ belongs to an ultimately periodic sort of type (k, l) and $s(t) \simeq s(t')$ (or $s(t) \not\simeq s(t')$) is irreducible by PR. For $k = 0$, the atom $\perp$ replaces $t \simeq s^{k-1}(0)$ and $\top$ replaces $t \not\simeq s^{k-1}(0)$.

Periodic Clash Test:

PC1: $s(t) \simeq 0 \rightarrow \begin{cases} t \simeq s^{l-1}(0) & \text{if } k = 0 \text{ and } t \text{ is not ground} \\ \perp & \text{if } k > 0 \text{ or } t \text{ is ground} \end{cases}$

PC2: $s(t) \not\simeq 0 \rightarrow \begin{cases} t \not\simeq s^{l-1}(0) & \text{if } k = 0 \text{ and } t \text{ is not ground} \\ \top & \text{if } k > 0 \text{ or } t \text{ is ground} \end{cases}$

if $s(t)$ belongs to an ultimately periodic sort of type (k, l) and $s(t) \simeq 0$ (or $s(t) \not\simeq 0$) is irreducible by PR.

Periodic Occurrence:

PO1: $x \simeq s^n(x) \rightarrow \begin{cases} x \simeq s^k(0) \vee \ldots \vee x \simeq s^{l-1}(0) & \text{if } l - k \text{ divides } n \\ \perp & \text{if } l - k \text{ does not divide } n \end{cases}$

PO2: $x \not\simeq s^n(x) \rightarrow \begin{cases} x \not\simeq s^k(0) \wedge \ldots \wedge x \not\simeq s^{l-1}(0) & \text{if } l - k \text{ divides } n \\ \top & \text{if } l - k \text{ does not divide } n \end{cases}$

if x and $s^n(x)$ belong to an ultimately periodic sort of type (k, l) and $n > 0$.

Periodic Sort Reduction:

PS1: $\forall \vec{x}, x.\phi \rightarrow \forall \vec{x}.\phi\{x \mapsto 0\} \wedge \ldots \wedge \phi\{x \mapsto s^{l-1}(0)\}$

PS2: $\exists \vec{x}.x.\phi \rightarrow \exists \vec{x}.\phi\{x \mapsto 0\} \vee \ldots \vee \phi\{x \mapsto s^{l-1}(0)\}$

if x belongs to an ultimately periodic sort of type (k, l) and x occurs in ϕ.

Fig. 3. DisU: Rules for Ultimately Periodic Sorts

Proof. The normal form $(\neg\phi_P)\!\downarrow$ of $\neg\phi_P$ is

$$(\neg\phi_P)\!\downarrow = \forall\vec{y}. \bigwedge_{\Gamma\to\Delta,P(\vec{t})\in N_P} (x_1\not\simeq t_1 \vee \ldots \vee x_n\not\simeq t_n \vee \bigvee_{A\in\Gamma} \neg A \vee \bigvee_{B\in\Delta} B) .$$

Part (1) of the invariant holds because there are no nested quantifiers in $(\neg\phi_P)\!\downarrow$. Part (2) holds because all clauses in N are universally reductive, and so every variable that occurs in a predicative literal $\neg A$ or B also occurs in one of the disequations $x_i\not\simeq t_i$ in the same conjunct of $(\neg\phi_P)\!\downarrow$.

Lemma 8 (Invariant is Preserved). *Let $\phi \twoheadrightarrow_{DisU} \phi'$. If ϕ satisfies Invariant 6 then so does ϕ'.*

Lemma 9 (Normal Forms Without Universal Quantifiers). *Every normal form ϕ with respect to $DisU$ that fulfills Invariant 6 is free of universal quantifiers.*

Corollary 10 (Universal Quantifier Elimination). *Let N be universally reductive, let ϕ_P be defined as in Definition 5 and let ϕ'_P be a normal form of $\neg\phi_P$ with respect to $DisU$. Then ϕ'_P does not contain any universal quantifiers.*

Proof. Straightforward combination of the preceding Lemmas 7, 8, and 9.

3.3   Solved Form Computation

To address the second issue of transforming the formula $\forall\vec{x}.(\phi'_P \to \neg P(\vec{x}))$ into a set of clauses, I will make use of the fact that certain normal forms with respect to $DisU$ can be transformed into a particularly simple form:

Definition 11 (Solved Forms). *Let $\mathcal{I}$ be an ultimately periodic interpretation. A formula ϕ is a solved form with respect to $\mathcal{I}$ if $\phi = \top$, $\phi = \bot$, or ϕ is a disjunction $\phi = \phi_1 \vee \ldots \vee \phi_m$ and each ϕ_j is of the shape*

$$\phi_j = \exists\vec{y}.x_{i_1}\simeq t_1 \wedge\ldots\wedge x_{i_n}\simeq t_n \wedge A_1 \wedge\ldots\wedge A_k \wedge\neg B_1 \wedge\ldots\wedge\neg B_{k'} \wedge z_1\not\simeq t'_1 \wedge\ldots\wedge z_l\not\simeq t'_l ,$$

where $x_{i_1}, \ldots, x_{i_n}$ occur only once in ϕ_j, the A_i and B_i are predicative atoms, the z_i are variables and $z_i \neq t'_i$, and ϕ_j is irreducible by Periodic Reduction.

The motivation for choosing this particular form is that, if the formula ϕ'_P appearing in the predicate completion procedure (Definition 5) can be transformed into a solved form, the formula $\forall\vec{x}.(\phi'_P \to \neg P(\vec{x}))$ is equivalent to a finite clause set: Either the formula is equivalent to

- $\top$, i.e. to the empty clause set (for $\phi'_P = \bot$), or to
- $\forall x.\neg P(\vec{x})$, i.e. to the singleton clause set $\{P(\vec{x}) \to\}$ (for $\phi'_P = \top$), or to
- $\forall\vec{x}.\bigwedge_j(\phi'_j \to \neg P(\vec{x}))$, and each conjunct can equivalently be written as a clause of the form
  $A_1, \ldots, A_k, P(\vec{x})\{x_{i_1} \mapsto t_1, \ldots, x_{i_n} \mapsto t_n\} \to B_1, \ldots, B_k, z_1\simeq t'_1, \ldots, z_l\simeq t'_l .$

Quantifier Elimination:

Q1: $\exists \vec{x}.\phi_1 \vee \phi_2 \twoheadrightarrow (\exists \vec{x}.\phi_1) \vee (\exists \vec{x}.\phi_2)$ if $\vec{x} \cap \text{var}(\phi_1, \phi_2) \neq \emptyset$

Q6: $\exists \vec{x}, x.x \simeq t \wedge \phi \twoheadrightarrow \exists \vec{x}.\phi\{x \mapsto t\}$ if $x \notin \text{var}(t)$

All formulas are kept normalized with respect to Q1.

Distribution:

N2': $\phi_0 \wedge (\phi_1 \vee \phi_2) \twoheadrightarrow (\phi_0 \wedge \phi_1) \vee (\phi_0 \wedge \phi_2)$

Replacement and Merging:

R : $\exists \vec{x}.x \simeq t \wedge \phi \twoheadrightarrow \exists \vec{x}.x \simeq t \wedge \phi\{x \mapsto t\}$ if x is free and $x \notin \text{var}(t)$

and if $t \in \mathcal{X}$ then $t \in \text{var}(\phi)$

M: $x \simeq t_1 \wedge x \simeq t_2 \twoheadrightarrow x \simeq t_1 \wedge t_1 \simeq t_2$ if t_1 is not a variable

and $|t_1| \leq |t_2|$

Fig. 4. Solved Form Conversion Rules

The transformation into a solved form is again performed using a rewrite system:

Definition 12 (SF). *Let E be a set of ultimate periodicity equations. The* Solved Form Transformation Algorithm SF *for E consists of the Normalization rules of Figure 1, the (regular and periodic) Decomposition, Clash and Occurrence rules as well as Periodic Reduction from Figures 2 and 3 and the rules of Figure 4.*

This calculus is an extension of a corresponding calculus used by Comon and Delor [4, Section 6.3] for the predicative Horn case.

Lemma 13 (SF Produces Solved Forms). *Let $\phi = \bigvee_{i \in I} \exists \vec{x}_i.\phi_i$ be a formula where the ϕ_i are quantifier-free conjunctions. If ϕ is a normal form with respect to SF, then ϕ is a solved form.*

Proof. Because of the Decomposition and Clash rules, each equational literal must be of the form $x \simeq t$ or $x \not\simeq t$. So each disjunct is of the form

$$\exists \vec{y}.x_{i_1} \simeq t_1 \wedge \ldots \wedge x_{i_n} \simeq t_n \wedge A_1 \wedge \ldots \wedge A_k \wedge \neg B_1 \wedge \ldots \wedge \neg B_{k'} \wedge z_1 \not\simeq t'_1 \wedge \ldots \wedge z_l \not\simeq t'_l$$

where the x_i, y_i and z_i are variables and the A_i and B_i are predicative atoms. Because of Q6, the x_i must be free variables. Moreover, each x_i occurs only once: Either t_i is not a free variable and x occurs only once because of R and O1, or t_i is a free variable, in which case R guarantees that one of x_i and t_i occurs only once; by symmetry, this variable is without loss of generality x_i. Finally, $z_i \neq t'_i$ is guaranteed by O2.

Lemma 14 (Termination of SF). *Let $\phi = \bigvee_{i \in I} \exists \vec{x}_i.\phi_i$ be a formula where the ϕ_i are quantifier-free conjunctions. Then SF terminates on ϕ.*

Proof. SF terminates because it is decreasing for a well-founded strict ordering $\succ_{\text{SF}}$ on formulas of the given form. To define this ordering, let $I_{\text{SF}}(\bigvee_{i \in I} \exists \vec{x}_i.\phi_i)$, where ϕ_i is quantifier-free, be the multiset

$$\{(I_1(\exists \vec{x}_i.\phi_i), I_2(\exists \vec{x}_i.\phi_i), I_3(\exists \vec{x}_i.\phi_i), I_4(\exists \vec{x}_i.\phi_i), I_5(\exists \vec{x}_i.\phi_i)) \mid i \in I\} \ ,$$

where the five components of each tuple are defined as follows:

(i) $I_1(\exists \vec{x}_i.\phi_i)$ is the number of variables in $\vec{x}_i$.

(ii) $I_2(\exists \vec{x}_i.\phi_i)$ is the number of variables in ϕ_i that are not solved; a variable x in ϕ_i is *solved* if $\phi_i = x \simeq t \wedge \phi_i'$ and x occurs only once in ϕ_i.

(iii) $I_3(\exists \vec{x}_i.\phi_i)$ is a term over the set $\mathcal{F}_3 = \{\vee, \wedge, g, f, a, \top, \bot\}$ of function symbols, inductively defined by

 - $I_3(\exists \vec{x}_i.\phi_i) = I_3(\phi_i)$
 - $I_3(\psi_1 \vee \psi_3) = I_3(\psi_1) \vee I_3(\psi_3)$
 - $I_3(\psi_1 \wedge \psi_3) = I_3(\psi_1) \wedge I_3(\psi_3)$
 - $I_3(t_1 \simeq t_3) = I_3(t_1 \not\simeq t_3) = g(f^{\max\{|t_1|,|t_3|\}}(a))$ if t_1 and t_3 are not ground
   $I_3(t_1 \simeq t_3) = I_3(t_1 \not\simeq t_3) = f^{\max\{|t_1|,|t_3|\}}(a)$ if t_1 and t_3 are ground,
   $I_3(t_1 \simeq t_3) = I_3(t_1 \not\simeq t_3) = g(f^{|t_1|}(a))$ if t_1 is not ground and t_3 is ground
 - $I_3(P(\vec{t})) = I_3(\neg P(\vec{t})) = a$ if P is a predicate symbol.
 - $I_3(\top) = \top$ and $I_3(\bot) = \bot$

(iv) $I_4(\exists \vec{x}_i.\phi_i)$ is the number of redexes for PR in $\exists \vec{x}_i.\phi_i$.

(v) $I_5(\exists \vec{x}_i.\phi_i)$ is the number of redexes for M in $\exists \vec{x}_i.\phi_i$.

Terms over $\mathcal{F}_3$ are ordered by the associative path ordering $\succ_3$ (cf. [2]) extending the strict ordering $g \succ f \succ a \succ \wedge \succ \vee \succ \top \succ \bot$. Every rule application reduces the formula with respect to this ordering.

Proposition 15 (Equivalence to Solved Forms). *Let $\mathcal{I}_{N \cup E}^{\succ}$ be an ultimately periodic interpretation and let ϕ be a formula in negation normal form that does not contain any universal quantifiers. Then ϕ can be transformed into an equivalent solved form.*

Proof. Using Q1, N2' and the rule $(\exists x.\psi_1) \wedge \psi_2 \twoheadrightarrow \exists x.(\psi_1 \wedge \psi_2)$, where x is renamed if it occurs in ψ_2 to avoid capturing (this rule is well-known to be correct for any interpretation), ϕ can be transformed into a disjunction of formulas of the form $\exists \vec{x}. \bigwedge L_i$ with literals L_i.

By the preceding Lemmas 13 and 14, the calculus SF transforms this formula into a solved form. The algorithm preserves the solutions of a formula with respect to every interpretation where equality is interpreted as E-equality: The correctness of the all rules except Replacement and Merging follows from the correctness of DisU (the correctness of N2 is independent of the constraint on the context) and the correctness of the remaining two rules is obvious because they replace equals by equals. If ϕ is irreducible by DisU, then it is in particular irreducible by Finite and Periodic Sort Reduction and does not contain any bound variables of a finite free or ultimately periodic sort. Since the transformation algorithm does not introduce any new quantifier symbols, this invariant is preserved throughout the transformation.

Corollary 16. *Let $\mathcal{I}_{N \cup E}^{\succ}$ be an ultimately periodic interpretation. Then the formula $\forall \vec{x}.(\neg \phi_P \rightarrow \neg P(\vec{x}))$ from Definition 5 corresponds to a finite set of clauses that can be computed using the algorithm PC.*

This property is only true because of the special form that ϕ_P takes for ultimately periodic models. For example, the clause set $N = \{Q(y) \rightarrow P\}$ yields $\phi_P = \exists y.Q(y)$, and the resulting formula $(\forall y.\neg Q(y)) \rightarrow \neg P$ cannot be written as an equivalent finite clause set if y is of an infinite sort.

Example 17 (Completion of the Even Predicate). As a simple example assume that the Even predicate is not given as in Example 3 but by the non-Horn clause set $N = \{\text{Even}(0); \text{Even}(x) \rightarrow \text{Even}(s(x)), \text{Even}(s(s(x)))\}$. Because the last literal is maximal in the second clause with respect to any reduction ordering, ϕ_{Even} is given by $\phi_{\text{Even}} = x{\simeq}0 \vee \exists y.(y{\simeq}s(s(x)) \wedge \text{Even}(y) \wedge \neg\text{Even}(s(y)))$.

If no equation is present, the above algorithms lead to the completion $N' = N \cup \{\text{Even}(s(0)) \rightarrow; \text{Even}(s(s(x))) \rightarrow \text{Even}(x); \text{Even}(s(x)), \text{Even}(s(s(x))) \rightarrow\}$. With respect to the equation $E = \{s(s(0)){\simeq}0\}$, the computed completion is $N' = N \cup \{\text{Even}(s(0)), \text{Even}(0) \rightarrow; \text{Even}(s(0)) \rightarrow \text{Even}(0)\}$.

3.4   Predicate Completion and Unique Herbrand Models

Comon and Nieuwenhuis showed that the minimal model of a satisfiable universally reductive and predicative Horn clause set is the unique Herbrand model of its completion [6, Lemma 47]. In the presence of equality, this means:

Lemma 18 (Completions of Horn Clause Sets). *Let N be a satisfiable universally reductive predicative Horn clause set over Σ and let N' be the result of applying predicate completion to N. Then the minimal model of N (with respect to set inclusion) is the unique Herbrand model of N' over Σ in which $\simeq$ is interpreted as syntactic equality (i.e. $t_1{\simeq}t_2$ holds if, and only if, $t_1{=}t_2$).*

I will now show that this result also extends to ultimately periodic interpretations. Non-Horn clause sets may have more than one minimal model, a simple example being $\{\rightarrow P, Q\}$ with minimal models $\{P\}$ and $\{Q\}$. If the model construction by Bachmair and Ganzinger (Definition 1) is applicable, one of them can be distinguished using this construction (Lemma 2). Completion singles out exactly the same interpretation:

Theorem 19 (Completions of Universally Reductive Saturated Clause Sets). *Let $\succ$ be a well-founded strict reduction ordering that is total on ground terms. Let $N \cup E$ as in Definition 4 be saturated with respect to a refutationally complete calculus and let $\mathcal{M}$ be a Herbrand model of the completion N' of $N \cup E$. If $\simeq$ is interpreted in $\mathcal{M}$ as E-equality (i.e. $\mathcal{M} \models t_1{\simeq}t_2$ if, and only if, $t_1{=}_E t_2$), then $\mathcal{M}$ equals $\mathcal{I}^{\succ}_{N \cup E}$.*

Proof. Because $N \cup E$ is saturated, $\mathcal{I}^{\succ}_{N \cup E}$ is a minimal model of $N \cup E$ with respect to set inclusion (Lemma 2) and $\mathcal{M}$ cannot be a strict subset of $\mathcal{I}^{\succ}_{N \cup E}$.

Assume, contrary to the proposition, that $\mathcal{M} \setminus \mathcal{I}^{\succ}_{N \cup E} \neq \emptyset$ and let $P(\vec{s}) \in \mathcal{M} \setminus \mathcal{I}^{\succ}_{N \cup E}$ be minimal with respect to $\succ$. Because $\mathcal{M}$ is a model of the completion and the algorithms DisU and SF are correct, the formula $\forall \vec{x}.P(\vec{x}) \rightarrow \phi_P$ holds in $\mathcal{M}$. In particular, $\mathcal{M} \models \phi_P\{\vec{x} \mapsto \vec{s}\}$. This formula has the following shape:

$$\phi_P\{\vec{x} \mapsto \vec{s}\} = \exists \vec{y}. \bigvee\nolimits_{\Gamma \to \Delta, P(\vec{t}) \in N_P} (s_1 {\simeq} t_1 \wedge \ldots \wedge s_n {\simeq} t_n \wedge \bigwedge\nolimits_{A \in \Gamma} A \wedge \bigwedge\nolimits_{B \in \Delta} \neg B)$$

Because the equality predicate is interpreted as E-equality, each of the disjuncts can only hold in $\mathcal{M}$ if $\vec{s} =_E \vec{t}$. The remaining literals are by definition strictly smaller (with respect to $\succ$) than $P(\vec{t})$ and hence also strictly smaller than $P(\vec{s})$. By minimality of $P(\vec{s})$, they all hold in $\mathcal{M}$ if, and only if, they hold in $\mathcal{I}_{N \cup E}^{\succ}$. Because $\simeq$ is interpreted as E-equality on non-predicative terms in $\mathcal{I}_{N \cup E}^{\succ}$ as well, it follows that $\mathcal{I}_{N \cup E}^{\succ} \models \phi_P\{\vec{x} \mapsto \vec{s}\}$. Because $\mathcal{I}_{N \cup E}^{\succ} \models N$, the formula $\forall \vec{x}. \phi_P \to P(\vec{x})$ also holds in $\mathcal{I}_{N \cup E}^{\succ}$. This implies $\mathcal{I}_{N \cup E}^{\succ} \models P(\vec{s})$, which contradicts the choice of $P(\vec{s})$. Hence $\mathcal{M} \subseteq \mathcal{I}_N^{\succ}$, i.e. $\mathcal{M} = \mathcal{I}_N^{\succ}$.

Note that this means that $\mathcal{I}_{N \cup E}^{\succ}$ agrees with all Herbrand models of N' over Σ on the validity of predicative atoms (and formulas), i.e. validity in the minimal model and in all Herbrand models coincide:

Corollary 20. *Let Σ be a signature and let $\succ$ be a well-founded strict reduction ordering that is total on ground terms. Moreover, let $N \cup E$ as in Definition 4 be saturated with respect to a refutationally complete calculus and let ϕ be a predicative formula. Then $\mathcal{I}_{N \cup E}^{\succ} \models \phi$ if, and only if, $\mathcal{M} \models \phi$ for every Herbrand model $\mathcal{M}$ of $N \cup E$.*

So PC indeed computes a completion. This is especially interesting because it is in many cases easier to prove properties of all Herbrand models of a clause set than to prove properties of a unique model (cf. [7, 6, 12]).

4   Conclusion

I have presented the disunification-based predicate completion algorithm PC for ultimately periodic interpretations, i.e. for the minimal models of sets of universally reductive clauses and equations $s^n(x) {\simeq} s^m(x)$, and generalized a unique model result for predicate completion to saturated non-Horn clause sets. This extends work by Comon et al. [5, 4, 6] on disunification and predicate completion for Horn clauses and work of Ludwig and Hustadt [13] and myself [9] on ultimately periodic interpretations and provides the first predicate completion for a reasonably large class of non-Horn problems.

Predicate completion yields a detailed description of the perfect model, which is interesting for all superposition-based reasoning. Immediately possible concrete applications of predicate completion for ultimately periodic interpretations include saturation-based theorem proving for distinguished models: Ultimately periodic interpretations appear naturally as minimal models of formula sets in propositional linear time temporal logic [13], and recently developed algorithms for inductive theorem proving [12, 11] also rely on predicate completion for the examined models. In all these cases, first-order provers can now be employed for minimal model reasoning.

The presented algorithms have been implemented in the tool SPASS-FD [10]. Both the implementation and a collection of examples are available online at cs.unm.edu/~horbach/software/.

Next research steps will include a further inspection of in how far more expressive equational theories can be incorporated. The restriction to universally reductive clauses will not vanish in the foreseeable future, because it is inherent to all algorithms that complete each predicate separately.

Acknowledgements. This work was supported by the German Transregional Collaborative Research Center SFB/TR 14 AVACS and by the German Academic Exchange Service (DAAD).

References

[1] Bachmair, L., Ganzinger, H.: Rewrite-based equational theorem proving with selection and simplification. J. of Logic and Computation 4(3), 217–247 (1994)

[2] Bachmair, L., Plaisted, D.A.: Associative path orderings. In: Jouannaud, J.-P. (ed.) RTA 1985. LNCS, vol. 202, pp. 241–254. Springer, Heidelberg (1985)

[3] Clark, K.L.: Negation as failure. In: Gallaire, H., Minker, J. (eds.) Logic and Data Bases, pp. 293–322. Plenum Press, New York (1977)

[4] Comon, H., Delor, C.: Equational formulae with membership constraints. Information and Computation 112(2), 167–216 (1994)

[5] Comon, H., Lescanne, P.: Equational problems and disunification. Journal of Symbolic Computation 7(3-4), 371–425 (1989)

[6] Comon, H., Nieuwenhuis, R.: Induction = I-Axiomatization + First-Order Consistency. Information and Computation 159(1/2), 151–186 (2000)

[7] Ganzinger, H., Stuber, J.: Inductive theorem proving by consistency for first-order clauses. In: Rusinowitch, M., Remy, J.-L. (eds.) CTRS 1992. LNCS, vol. 656, pp. 226–241. Springer, Heidelberg (1993)

[8] Gelfond, M., Lifschitz, V.: Representing action and change by logic programs. Journal of Logic Programming 17(2/3&4), 301–321 (1993)

[9] Horbach, M.: Disunification for ultimately periodic interpretations. In: Clarke, E.M., Voronkov, A. (eds.) LPAR-16 2010. LNCS (LNAI), vol. 6355, pp. 290–311. Springer, Heidelberg (2010)

[10] Horbach, M.: System description: SPASS-FD. In: Bjørner, N., Sofronie-Stokkermans, V. (eds.) CADE 2011. LNCS (LNAI), vol. 6803, pp. 315–321. Springer, Heidelberg (2011)

[11] Horbach, M., Weidenbach, C.: Decidability results for saturation-based model building. In: Schmidt, R. (ed.) CADE-22. LNCS (LNAI), vol. 5663, pp. 404–420. Springer, Heidelberg (2009)

[12] Horbach, M., Weidenbach, C.: Superposition for fixed domains. ACM Transactions on Computational Logic 11(4), 27:1–27:35 (2010)

[13] Ludwig, M., Hustadt, U.: Resolution-based model construction for PLTL. In: Lutz, C., Raskin, J.-F. (eds.) TIME 2009, pp. 73–80. IEEE Computer Society, Los Alamitos (2009)

[14] McCarthy, J.: Applications of circumscription to formalizing common sense knowledge. Artificial Intelligence 28, 89–116 (1986)

[15] Nie, X.: non-Horn clause logic programming. Artificial Intelligence 92(1-2), 243–258 (1997)

[16] Reiter, R.: A logic for default reasoning. Artificial Intelligence 13(1-2), 81–132 (1980)

[17] Reiter, R.: Circumscription implies predicate completion (sometimes). In: Waltz, D.L. (ed.) AAAI, pp. 418–420. AAAI Press, Menlo Park (1982)

[18] Stuckey, P.J.: Constructive negation for constraint logic programming. In: LICS, pp. 328–339. IEEE Computer Society, Los Alamitos (1991)

[19] Togashi, A., Hou, B.-H., Noguchi, S.: Generalized predicate completion. In: Ramani, S., Anjaneyulu, K., Chandrasekar, R. (eds.) KBCS 1989. LNCS, vol. 444, pp. 286–295. Springer, Heidelberg (1990)

System Description: SPASS-FD

Matthias Horbach

University of New Mexico, Albuquerque, U.S.A.
horbach@cs.unm.edu

Abstract. Using a constrained superposition calculus and a disunification procedure, it is possible to employ superposition-based first-order reasoners for reasoning not only about all models of a first-order theory, but also about all models over a specific finite domain and often as well about the perfect models of the theory (or the unique minimal model in case of a Horn theory). Both of these problems are second-order problems.

In this paper, I describe the tool SPASS-FD, an extension of the first-order prover SPASS that equips SPASS with disunification as well as with fixed domain and minimal model theorem proving capabilities.

1 Introduction

Saturation-based calculi such as superposition [11] can be instantiated to decision procedures for many decidable fragments of first-order logic. Superposition provers are state of the art in first-order theorem proving, i.e. in deciding whether a given set of clauses has a model. Often however, any model is not good enough: When describing real-world systems, the domain of the admissible models is usually predefined as the Herbrand universe over the symbols appearing in the description. Moreover, the system description will mostly state what the system can do, leaving what it cannot do implicit: The intended semantics of the description is a minimal model (or closed world) semantics. For formal reasoning about the system, the implicit information about the minimal model has to be recovered.

Originally, this line of thought was developed to handle negation in logic programming [2]. In automated theorem proving, it can be used for example to reason about the so-called contexts in the model evolution calculus [1], or about models described by sets of atoms with exceptions [5], about rewrite systems, or in general for any kind of inductive problems.

Aiming at the long-standing goal to harvest the power of first-order reasoning for this setting [4], Horbach and Weidenbach [10,8] developed a superposition-based algorithm that allows for fixed domain reasoning with a saturation-based first-order prover. Later, this was extended using predicate completion [2,4,6] to systems for minimal model reasoning that decide, e.g., validity of queries with one quantifier alternation for the above-mentioned contexts [9,8,6].

The tool SPASS-FD is an implementation on top of the automated theorem prover SPASS [15] of (i) the calculi for saturation-based reasoning with respect

N. Bjørner and V. Sofronie-Stokkermans (Eds.): CADE 2011, LNAI 6803, pp. 331–337, 2011.

to fixed domains and minimal models as described in [8] (including the decision procedure for contexts), and (ii) the underlying disunification procedure from [6]. SPASS provides a powerful superposition-based saturation machinery, which makes this prover well-suited as a basis for the implementation. SPASS-FD can be downloaded from `cs.unm.edu/~horbach/software/`.

2 Theoretical Background

Disunification and Predicate Completion. *Disunification* [3,6] is an extension of the idea of unification from equations to arbitrary equational formulas. Technically, it is a rewrite system for quantifier elimination in the empty theory.

The most obvious use of disunification is as a decision procedure for satisfiability of equational formulas. A second and for the current application even more important one is *predicate completion* [2,7], where a set N of clauses is extended to a set N' such that N' has only one Herbrand model, namely one of the minimal models of N. Predicate completion is one of the main tools to connect first-order, fixed domain and minimal model reasoning [4,6]. It is restricted to so-called universally reductive clauses, which are either purely negative or contain a unique maximal positive literal (with respect to a given ordering) that is not equational and contains all variables of the clause.

Fixed Domain and Minimal Model Reasoning. Superposition is an established decision procedure for a variety of first-order logic theories represented by sets of clauses. A satisfiable theory, saturated by superposition, implicitly defines a minimal term-generated model for the theory. Unfortunately, checking consistency of existential properties with respect to a saturated theory directly leads to a modification of the Herbrand domain, as new Skolem functions are introduced. At the core of the fixed domain reasoning algorithm of SPASS-FD thus lies a superposition calculus that avoids Skolemization by using an explicit representation of existential variables [10]. To this end, clauses are extended by constraints that restrict the instantiations of the existential variables for a clause. For example, a formula $\exists u.\forall y.P(u,y) \land \neg P(a,a)$ corresponds to constrained clauses $u \simeq x \,\|\, \to P(x,y)$ and $u \simeq x \,\|\, P(a,a) \to$. Resolving these two clauses and unifying their constraints leads to an empty clause with constraint $u \simeq a$, signifying that $u \mapsto a$ does not satisfy the initial clauses. In this setting, a contradiction is formed by a set of constrained empty clauses that together exclude all possible ground instantiations of the existential variables. This property, called *coverage*, can be expressed as unsatisfiability of an equational formula over the empty theory and can hence be decided by disunification.

Analogous to the first-order case, a saturated clause set is not covering iff it has a Herbrand model [10]. When the initial clause set is completed, the only remaining Herbrand model is the minimal model. Hence techniques for reasoning about fixed domain properties can be also used for minimal model reasoning. This turns the previously mentioned constrained superposition calculus into a decision procedure for several classes of minimal model problems [8,9,6].

Reasoning about Equational Literals. Predicate completion as well as minimal model reasoning quickly becomes undecidable in the presence of an equational theory. An important exception are equations of the form $s^n(x) \simeq s^m(x)$. Interpretations where such equations hold are called *ultimately periodic*. They occur e.g. as the models of predicative linear time linear logic. An extension of the aforementioned algorithms to encompass ultimate periodicity equations [6] is also integrated in SPASS-FD.

It is furthermore possible to allow arbitrary disequations in constraints. This makes it possible to write completions in such a way that the non-constraint part of every clause is predicative [8].

3   Implementation

The tool SPASS-FD is an implementation of the aforementioned algorithms on top of SPASS [15] and, as SPASS, is written in plain C. The main advantage of using SPASS as a basis is that this reasoner is specialized on saturation-based theorem proving and already places efficiently implemented data types at the disposal for its modules. The additions made by SPASS-FD are mostly orthogonal to the other SPASS modules and can be used in conjunction with them. They are activated by specifying the command line option -PComp=1. Because the current version of SPASS does not yet support constraints, constraints are represented by antecedent literals with the special predicate symbols ExVars (signifying instantiations of the existential variables) and CDis

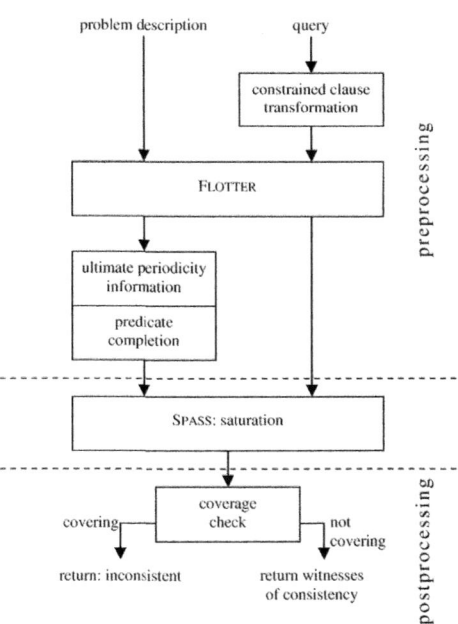

Fig. 1. Structure of SPASS-FD

(for constraint disequations), i.e. a constrained clause $v_1 \simeq t_1, \ldots, v_n \simeq t_n$, $s_1 \not\simeq s'_1, \ldots, s_m \not\simeq s'_m \parallel \Gamma \rightarrow \Delta$ is modeled internally by a regular clause of the form $\mathrm{ExVars}(t_1, \ldots, t_n), \mathrm{CDis}(s_1, s'_1), \ldots, \mathrm{CDis}(s_m, s'_m), \Gamma \rightarrow \Delta$.

For easy reference, a graphical overview of the general structure of SPASS-FD is presented in Figure 1.

Preprocessing. SPASS-FD takes as its input a file in dfg syntax or tptp syntax containing a problem description and a query of the form $\exists^* \forall^* \phi$. The input (except the query) is as usual processed by FLOTTER, the clause normal form generator of SPASS, and the ultimate periodicity information is extracted. The input clauses, which must all be universally reductive, are then partitioned with respect to the predicate of their maximal positive atom. For each such predicate P, a formula ϕ_P is created that describes which ground instances of P hold. Disunification is then used to compute a normalization of $\neg\phi_P$, from which the completion clauses are extracted in a straightforward way and added to the input.

In parallel, existential variables in the query formula are replaced by ExVars literals and the resulting query is also processed by FLOTTER. The input clauses, their completion, and the transformed query are then handed on to saturation.

As an example, consider the following input file, a problem taken from [8]:

```
begin_problem(X).                         end_of_list.
list_of_descriptions.
name({*Atom with Exceptions*}).           list_of_formulae(conjectures).
author({*Matthias Horbach*}).             formula(exists([x],P(s(x),x))).
status(satisfiable).                      end_of_list.
description({*Simple Example*}).
end_of_list.                              list_of_settings(SPASS).
                                          {*
list_of_symbols.                          set_flag(PComp,1).
functions[(s,1),(0,0)].                   set_flag(Select,0).
predicates[(P,2), (Pp,2), (Pn,2)].        set_flag(Sorts,0).
end_of_list.                              set_precedence(P,Pp,Pn).
                                          set_DomPred(P,Pn,Pp).
list_of_formulae(axioms).                 *}
formula(forall([x,y],Pp(x,s(y)))).        end_of_list.
formula(forall([x],Pn(s(x),s(x)))).
formula(forall([x,y],implies(             end_problem.
    Pp(x,y),or(Pn(x,y),P(x,y)))))).
```

This input is transformed by the SPASS-FD preprocessing step into the following clause set, consisting of a representation of the problem description (clauses 1–3), the converted query (clause 4), and the computed completion (clauses 5–10):[1]

```
Input Problem:                            6 P(U,V)* Pn(U,V) -> .
1   -> Pp(U,s(V))*.                       7 Pn(s(U),V)* CDis(V,s(U)) -> .
2   -> Pn(s(U),s(U))*.                     8 Pn(0,U)* -> .
3 Pp(U,V) -> P(U,V)* Pn(U,V).             9 Pp(U,0)* -> .
4 ExVars(U) -> P(s(U),U)*.                10 CDis(U,U)* -> .
5 P(U,V)* -> Pp(U,V).
```

Saturation. The actual saturation relies completely on the given machinery of SPASS. To deter literals with the predicates ExVars and CDis from interfering with the saturation process, they are artificially kept minimal in the superposition ordering. To avoid the accumulation of multiple ExVars literals, the code of

---

[1] This presentation is condensed. The actual output by SPASS-FD is slightly more verbose.

resolution inferences in SPASS has been changed such that, on top of the unification of the resolved literals, ExVars literals are also unified during each inference step. This is the only change to the actual saturation machinery of SPASS.

In the example, SPASS derives the following clauses, where, e.g., Res:4.1,5.0 indicates that the clause is the result of a resolution inference between clauses 4 and 5:

```
11[Res:4.1,5.0] ExVars(U) -> Pp(s(U),U)*.
12[Res:11.1,9.0] ExVars(0)* -> .
13[Res:4.1,6.1] ExVars(U) Pn(s(U),U)* -> .
```

Postprocessing. If saturation terminates, then the resulting constrained empty clauses are checked for coverage, again using disunification. If they are covering, the query $\exists^*\forall^*\phi$ does not hold in the minimal model of the input; otherwise a representation of those instances witnessing that it does hold is returned.

In the example, the only constrained empty clause that was derived is clause 12: $u{\simeq}0 \,\|\, \square$. Consequently, the final coverage check yields that the conjecture holds for all other instantiations of the existential variable:

```
Conjecture holds in the minimal model of the axioms
      for the following instances: (not (equal U (0)))
```

4   Testing and Optimizations

In the superposition component of SPASS-FD, mainly straightforward optimizations have been implemented, like the addition of a clause $CDis(x,x) \to$ (corresponding to $x{\not\simeq}x \,\|\, false$) that directly makes all clauses with unsatisfiable constraints redundant. On the other hand, two strong optimizations in SPASS must be deactivated: Splitting changes the minimal model and the especially efficient algorithms for reasoning about sort theories [14] interferes with the semantics of constrained clauses containing ExVars and CDis literals. The latter can be remedied by an explicit integration of constraints into SPASS, which is planned for future releases.

I represent ultimate periodicity equations $s^k(0){\simeq}s^l(0)$ using a globally accessible data structure that provides constant-time access to the values k and $l-k$, the constructors s and 0 and the regularly needed terms $s^{k-1}(0)$ and $s^{l-1}(0)$.

Formulas are represented using the term module of SPASS. I adapted the data structures to grant instant access to regularly needed information like parent links and normalization markers that make the non-local changes during normalization (e.g. by replacements like $x{\simeq}t \wedge \phi \rightsquigarrow x{\simeq}t \wedge \phi[x \mapsto t]$) tractable. For disunification, which is both code-wise the biggest and computation-wise the most expensive part of the implementation, the nondeterminism of the used algorithm allows for a wide variety of normalization strategies. Motivated by performance increases on the tested examples, I made the following design decisions:

Formulas are traversed in a depth search pattern to allow for fast propagation of occurrences of the atoms true or false, which often considerably reduces the size of the formula. Formulas are not kept locally in conjunctive normal form, a prerequisite of previous algorithms. Rules that tend to increase formula size (e.g. Sort Reduction, Distribution and Explosion) are only applied to otherwise normalized subformulas.

To the best of my knowledge, there has so far only been one publicly available implementation of disunification [12], which relies on an early inefficient variant of the algorithm and is not maintained any more. It also only works for Horn clauses, a restriction that does not apply for SPASS-FD. The algorithms for disunification and predicate completion over ultimately periodic models and non-Horn clauses and the algorithm for fixed domain reasoning have not been implemented before. In particular, no benchmarks for these problems exist. Instead, SPASS-FD was tested in the following ways:

- The implementation of the disunification and predicate completion procedures has been tested on and optimized with the help of problems in the TPTP library [13].
- The extension for ultimately periodic interpretations and the overall minimal model reasoning has been tested on hand-crafted problems.
- The decision procedure for contexts has been tested on randomly generated examples.

Collections of the respective problem files are available from the system's homepage.

5   Conclusion

SPASS-FD enriches SPASS by predicate completion and a constrained superposition calculus for existential variables. It is thus the first implementation of saturation-based minimal model reasoning and in particular of all decision procedures from [8] and [6] for queries with a quantifier alternation. Until recently, these procedures only existed for Horn clause sets. However, a newly developed extension of predicate completion to universally reductive non-Horn clause sets [7] is also implemented in SPASS-FD.

Currently, an extension of constrained superposition to arbitrary equational clauses [10] is under construction, as are more involved decision procedures based thereon [9]. A version using proper constraints for full modularity will appear once those are officially supported by SPASS, and the same holds for real multi-sorting.

Acknowledgments. This work was supported by the German Transregional Collaborative Research Center SFB/TR 14 AVACS and by the German Academic Exchange Service DAAD.

References

1. Baumgartner, P., Tinelli, C.: The model evolution calculus. In: Baader, F. (ed.) CADE 2003. LNCS (LNAI), vol. 2741, pp. 350–364. Springer, Heidelberg (2003)
2. Clark, K.L.: Negation as failure. In: Gallaire, H., Minker, J. (eds.) Logic and Data Bases, pp. 293–322. Plenum Press, New York (1977)
3. Comon, H., Lescanne, P.: Equational problems and disunification. Journal of Symbolic Computation 7(3-4), 371–425 (1989)
4. Comon, H., Nieuwenhuis, R.: Induction = I-axiomatization + first-order consistency. Information and Computation 159(1/2), 151–186 (2000)
5. Fermüller, C.G., Pichler, R.: Model representation via contexts and implicit generalizations. In: Nieuwenhuis, R. (ed.) CADE 2005. LNCS (LNAI), vol. 3632, pp. 409–423. Springer, Heidelberg (2005)
6. Horbach, M.: Disunification for ultimately periodic interpretations. In: Clarke, E.M., Voronkov, A. (eds.) LPAR-16 2010. LNCS (LNAI), vol. 6355, pp. 290–311. Springer, Heidelberg (2010)
7. Horbach, M.: Predicate completion for non-Horn clause sets. In: Bjørner, N., Sofronie-Stokkermans, V. (eds.) CADE 2011. LNCS (LNAI), vol. 6803, pp. 299–314. Springer, Heidelberg (2011)
8. Horbach, M., Weidenbach, C.: Decidability results for saturation-based model building. In: Schmidt, R.A. (ed.) CADE-22. LNCS (LNAI), vol. 5663, pp. 404–420. Springer, Heidelberg (2009)
9. Horbach, M., Weidenbach, C.: Deciding the inductive validity of $\forall\exists^*$ queries. In: Grädel, E., Kahle, R. (eds.) CSL 2009. LNCS, vol. 5771, pp. 332–347. Springer, Heidelberg (2009)
10. Horbach, M., Weidenbach, C.: Superposition for fixed domains. ACM Transactions on Computational Logic 11(4), 27:1–27:35 (2010)
11. Nieuwenhuis, R., Rubio, A.: Paramodulation-based theorem proving. In: Handbook of Automated Reasoning, ch.7, vol. I, pp. 371–443. Elsevier, Amsterdam (2001)
12. Peltier, N.: System description: An equational constraints solver. In: Kirchner, C., Kirchner, H. (eds.) CADE 1998. LNCS (LNAI), vol. 1421, pp. 119–123. Springer, Heidelberg (1998)
13. Sutcliffe, G.: The TPTP problem library and associated infrastructure. Journal of Automomated Reasoning 43(4), 337–362 (2009)
14. Weidenbach, C.: Towards an automatic analysis of security protocols in first-order logic. In: Ganzinger, H. (ed.) CADE 1999. LNCS (LNAI), vol. 1632, pp. 378–382. Springer, Heidelberg (1999)
15. Weidenbach, C., Dimova, D., Fietzke, A., Kumar, R., Suda, M., Wischnewski, P.: SPASS version 3.5. In: Schmidt, R.A. (ed.) CADE-22. LNCS, vol. 5663, pp. 140–145. Springer, Heidelberg (2009)

Cutting to the Chase Solving Linear Integer Arithmetic

Dejan Jovanović[1] and Leonardo de Moura[2]

[1] New York University
[2] Microsoft Research

Abstract. We describe a new algorithm for solving linear integer programming problems. The algorithm performs a DPLL style search for a feasible assignment, while using a novel cut procedure to guide the search away from the conflicting states.

1 Introduction

One of the most impressive success stories of computer science in industrial applications was the advent of linear programming algorithms. Linear programming (LP) became feasible with the introduction of Dantzig simplex algorithm. Although the original simplex algorithm targets problems over the rational numbers, in 1958 Gomory [12] introduced an elegant extension to the integer case (ILP). He noticed that, whenever the simplex algorithm encounters a non-integer solution, one can eliminate this solution by deriving a plane, that is implied by the original problem, but does not satisfy the current assignment. Incrementally adding these *cutting planes*, until an integer solution is found, yields an algorithm for solving linear programs over the integers. Cutting planes have been studied thoroughly both as an abstract proof system [4], and as a practical pre-processing step for hard structured problems. For such problems, one can exploit the structure by adding cuts tailored for the problem, such as the clique cuts, or the covering cuts [20], which can reduce the search space dramatically.

The main idea behind the algorithm of Gomory, i.e to combine a model searching procedure, with a conflict resolution procedure – a procedure that can derive new facts in order to eliminate a conflicting candidate solution – is in fact quite general. Somewhat later, for example, in the field of automated reasoning, there was a similar development with equally impressive end results. Solvers for the Boolean satisfiability problem (SAT), although a canonical NP-complete problem, have seen a steady improvement over the years, culminating in thrilling advances in the last 10 years. It has become a matter of routine to use a SAT solver on problems with millions of variables and constraints. Of course, there are many ingredients that make a modern SAT solver efficient, but one of the most appealing ones, is the combination of two different approaches to solving a problem. One is a backtracking search for a satisfying assignment, in the style of DPLL [7]. The other, is a search for a resolution refutation of the problem, as in the DP algorithm [8]. To combine these two [19] first noticed that, once a conflict

N. Bjørner and V. Sofronie-Stokkermans (Eds.): CADE 2011, LNAI 6803, pp. 338–353, 2011.
© Springer-Verlag Berlin Heidelberg 2011

has been encountered, we can derive a clause that explains the conflict, i.e. the *search is guiding the resolution*. As with the Gomory cuts, the explanation clause eliminates the current assignment, forcing a backtrack, and eliminating an (often substantial) part of the search tree. In the other direction, [17] introduced the so called VSIDS heuristic that adjusts the variable selection heuristic so that it prefers the variables involved in the resolution of conflicts, i.e. *the resolution is guiding the search*. This approach to solving SAT problems is commonly called Conflict-Directed Clause Learning (CDCL) and is employed by most modern SAT solvers. Apart from CDCL, there are many other important techniques that have become standard such as fast restarts[17], and fast indexing schemes for unit propagation [17].

In this paper, we propose a new CDCL-like procedure for solving arbitrary ILP problems. Our procedure, inspired by recent algorithms for solving linear real arithmetic [16,14,6], has all the important theoretical and practical ingredients that have made CDCL based SAT solvers so successful, including: model search complemented with the generation of resolvents explaining the conflicts; propagation rules enabling reduction of the search space and early detection of conflicts; resolvents learned during analysis of conflicts enable non-chronological backtracking; all resolvents generated during the search are valid, i.e. implied by the input formula, and not conditioned by any decisions; decisions (case-splits) are not based on a fixed variable order, thus enabling dynamic reordering heuristics; and cutting-plane inequalities (resolvents) learned during the search can be removed, allowing for flexible memory management by keeping the constraint database limited.

Another contribution of our paper is a that our procedure *guarantees termination*. We describe two arguments that imply termination. First, we propose a simple heuristic for deciding when a cutting-planes based approach does not terminate, recognizing variables contributing to the divergence. Then, we show that, in such a case, one can isolate a finite number of small cores that are inconsistent with the corresponding current partial models. These cores comprise of two inequalities and at most one divisibility constraint. Finally, we apply Cooper's quantifier elimination procedure to derive a resolvent that will *block* a particular core from ever happening again, which in turn implies termination. And, as a matter of practical importance, our resolvents do not involve disjunctions and are expressed only with valid inequalities and divisibility constraints.

2   Preliminaries

As usual, we denote the set of integers as $\mathbb{Z}$. We assume a finite set of variables X ranging over $\mathbb{Z}$. We use x, y, z, k to denote variables in X, a, b, c, d to denote coefficients in $\mathbb{Z}$, and p, q, r and s for linear polynomials over X with coefficients in $\mathbb{Z}$. In the work that follows, all polynomials are assumed to be in sum-of-monomials normal form $a_1 x_1 + \cdots + a_n x_n + c$. Given a polynomial $p = a_1 x_1 + \ldots + a_n x_n + c$, and a coefficient b, we use bp to denote the polynomial $(a_1 b) x_1 + \ldots + (a_n b) x_n + (bc)$.

Inequalities. We use I and J to denote inequalities $a_n x_n + \cdots + a_1 x_1 + c \leq 0$. We rewrite $p < 0$ as $p + 1 \leq 0$, and $p = 0$ as $p \leq 0 \wedge -p \leq 0$. We use $\mathsf{coeff}(p, x)$ ($\mathsf{coeff}(I, x)$) to denote the coefficient of x in the linear polynomial p (inequality I), where $\mathsf{coeff}(p, x) = 0$ if x does not occur in p (I). We say an inequality I is *tightly-propagating* for a variable x if $\mathsf{coeff}(I, x) \in \{-1, 1\}$.

Divisibility Constraints. In addition to inequalities, we also consider divisibility constraints of the form $d \mid a_1 x_1 + \cdots + a_n x_n + c$, where d is a non-zero integer constant. We denote divisibility constraints with the (possibly subscripted) letter D.

   Finally, given a set of constraints C and a constraint I, we use $C \vdash_{\mathbb{Z}} I$ to denote that I is implied by C in the theory of linear integer arithmetic.

3   The Abstract Search Procedure

We describe our procedure as an abstract transition system in the spirit of Abstract DPLL [18,15]. The states are pairs of the form $\langle M, C \rangle$, where M is a sequence of *bound refinements*, and C is a set of constraints. We use $[\![]\!]$ to denote the empty sequence. In this section we assume that all constraints in C are inequalities. Bound refinements can be either *decisions* or *implied bounds*. Decided lower and upper bounds are decisions we make during the search, and we represent them in M as $x \geq b$ and $x \leq b$. On the other hand, lower and upper bounds that are implied in the current state by an inequality I, are represented as $x \geq_I b$ and $x \leq_I b$. We say a sequence M is *non-redundant* if, for all variables x, the bound refinements in M are monotone, i.e. all the lower (upper) bounds are increasing (decreasing), and M does not contain the same bound for x, decided or implied.

   Let $\mathsf{lower}(x, M)$ and $\mathsf{upper}(x, M)$ denote the best, either decided or implied, lower and upper bounds for x in M, where we assume the usual values of $-\infty$ and ∞, when the corresponding bounds do not exist. A sequence M is *consistent* if there is no x such that $\mathsf{lower}(x, M) > \mathsf{upper}(x, M)$. We lift the best lower and upper bound functions to linear polynomials using identities such as: $\mathsf{lower}(p + q, M)$ is $\mathsf{lower}(p, M) + \mathsf{lower}(q, M)$ when variables in p and q are disjoint[1], $\mathsf{lower}(b, M) = b$, and $\mathsf{lower}(ax, M)$ is $a(\mathsf{lower}(x, M))$ if $a > 0$, and $a(\mathsf{upper}(x, M))$ otherwise.

Definition 1. *We say a sequence M is* well-formed *(wf) with respect to a set of constraints C when M is non-redundant, consistent and M is either an empty sequence or it starts with a wf prefix M', i.e. $M = [\![M', \gamma]\!]$, where the bound refinement γ is either*

   $-\; x \geq_I b$, *with* $I \equiv (-x + q \leq 0)$, $C \vdash_{\mathbb{Z}} I$, *and* $b \leq \mathsf{lower}(q, M')$; *or*

---

[1] In general, when estimating bounds of polynomials, for a consistent sequence M it holds that, if $\mathsf{lower}(p, M)$ and $\mathsf{lower}(q, M)$ are defined, then $\mathsf{lower}(p + q, M) \geq \mathsf{lower}(p, M) + \mathsf{lower}(q, M)$.

- $x \leq_I b$, with $I \equiv (x - q \leq 0)$, $C \vdash_{\mathbb{Z}} I$, and $b \geq upper(q, M')$; or
- $x \geq b$, where M' contains $x \leq_I b$ for some I; or
- $x \leq b$, where M' contains $x \geq_I b$ for some I.

Intuitively, in a well-formed sequence, every decision $x \geq b$ ($x \leq b$) amounts to *deciding* a value for x that is equal to the best upper (lower) bound. We say that a state $\langle M, C \rangle$ is well-formed if M is well-formed with respect to C. Note that, when refining a bound, we allow a bound b that is *not necessarily the most precise one* with respect to I. Although going against intuition, the reason for this flexibility will become apparent later.

Given an implied lower (upper) bound refinement $x \geq_I b$ ($x \leq_I b$) and an inequality $ax + p \leq 0$, the function resolve combines (if possible) the tight inequality $I \equiv \pm x + q \leq 0$ with $ax + p \leq 0$. If the combination is not applicable, resolve just returns $p \leq 0$. It is defined as

$$\begin{aligned} \mathsf{resolve}(x \geq_I b, ax + p \leq 0) \\ \mathsf{resolve}(x \leq_I b, ax + p \leq 0) \end{aligned} = \begin{cases} |a|q + p \leq 0 & \text{if } a \times \mathsf{coeff}(I, x) < 0 , \\ ax + p \leq 0 & \text{otherwise} . \end{cases}$$

We also define the function $\mathsf{bound}(I, x, M)$ that, given an inequality I and a sequence M returns the bound that I implies on x, with respect to M, i.e

$$\mathsf{bound}(ax + p \leq 0, x, M) = \begin{cases} -\left\lceil \frac{\mathsf{lower}(p, M)}{a} \right\rceil & \text{if } a > 0 , \\ -\left\lfloor \frac{\mathsf{lower}(p, M)}{a} \right\rfloor & \text{if } a < 0 . \end{cases}$$

Lemma 1. *Given[2] a well-formed state $\langle M, C \rangle$, with $M = [\![M', \gamma]\!]$, such that γ is an implied bound, $p \leq 0$ an inequality, and $q \leq 0 \equiv \mathsf{resolve}(\gamma, p \leq 0)$ then*

$$C \vdash_{\mathbb{Z}} (p \leq 0) \quad \text{implies} \quad C \vdash_{\mathbb{Z}} (q \leq 0) ,$$
$$\mathsf{lower}(q, M') \geq \mathsf{lower}(p, M) .$$

Example 1. In the statement of Lemma 1, we only get to keep $\mathsf{lower}(q, M') \geq \mathsf{lower}(p, M)$ because all of the implied bounds were justified by tightly-propagating inequalities. If we would allow non-tight justifications, this might not hold. Consider, for example, a state $\langle M, C \rangle$ where

$$C = \{\overbrace{-x \leq 0}^{I}, \overbrace{-3y + x + 2 \leq 0}^{J}\} , \qquad M = [\![x \geq_I 0, \; y \geq_J 1]\!] ,$$

and the inequality $1 + 6y \leq 0$. Then, we have that

$$\mathsf{lower}(1 + 6y, M) = 7 \text{ and } \mathsf{resolve}(y \geq_J 1, \; 1 + 6y \leq 0) = 2x + 5 \leq 0 .$$

So, after performing resolution on y using a non-tight inequality J, the inequality became weaker since i.e $\mathsf{lower}(2x + 5, [\![x \geq_I 0]\!]) = 5 \ngeq 7$.

---

[2] The proofs of all lemmas and theorems are included in a separate technical report.

The predicate $\mathsf{improves}(I, x, M)$ is true if the inequality $I \equiv ax+p \leq 0$ implies a better bound for x in M, but does not make M inconsistent. It is defined as

$$\mathsf{improves}(I, x, M) = \begin{cases} \mathsf{lower}(x, M) < \mathsf{bound}(I, x, M) \leq \mathsf{upper}(x, M), & \text{if } a < 0, \\ \mathsf{lower}(x, M) \leq \mathsf{bound}(I, x, M) < \mathsf{upper}(x, M), & \text{if } a > 0, \\ \text{false}, & \text{otherwise.} \end{cases}$$

3.1 Deriving Tight Inequalities

Since we require that all the implied bound refinements in M are justified by tightly propagating inequalities, we now show, given an inequality $\pm ax + p \leq 0$ such that $\mathsf{improves}(\pm ax+p \leq 0, x, M)$ holds, how to deduce a tightly propagating inequality that can justify the bound implied by $\pm ax + p \leq 0$.

The deduction is described using an auxiliary transition system. The states of this system are tuples of the form

$$\langle M', \pm ax + as \oplus r \rangle \;,$$

where $a > 0$, s and r are polynomials, M' is a prefix of the initial M, and we keep the invariant that

$$C \vdash_{\mathbb{Z}} \pm ax + as + r \leq 0, \quad \mathsf{lower}(as + r, M) \geq \mathsf{lower}(p, M) \;.$$

The initial state for tightening $\pm ax + p \leq 0$ is $\langle M, \pm ax \oplus p \rangle$ and the transition rules are as follows.

Consume
$$\langle M, \pm ax + as \oplus aky + r \rangle \qquad \Longrightarrow \quad \langle M, \pm ax + as + aky \oplus r \rangle$$
where $x \neq y$.

Resolve-Implied
$$\langle [\![M, \gamma]\!], \pm ax + as \oplus p \rangle \qquad \Longrightarrow \quad \langle M, \pm ax + as \oplus q \rangle$$
where γ is an implied bound and $q \leq 0 \equiv \mathsf{resolve}(\gamma, p \leq 0)$

Decided-Lower
$$\langle [\![M, y \geq b]\!], \pm ax + as \oplus cy + r \rangle \Longrightarrow \quad \langle M, \pm ax + as + aky \oplus r + (ak - c)q \rangle$$
where $y \leq_I b$ in M, with $I \equiv y + q \leq 0$, and $k = \lceil c/a \rceil$.

Decided-Lower-Neg
$$\langle [\![M, y \geq b]\!], \pm ax + as \oplus cy + r \rangle \Longrightarrow \quad \langle M, \pm ax + as \oplus cq + r \rangle$$
where $y \leq_I b$ in M, with $I \equiv y - q \leq 0$, and $c < 0$.

Decided-Upper
$$\langle [\![M, y \leq b]\!], \pm ax + as \oplus cy + r \rangle \Longrightarrow \quad \langle M, \pm ax + as + aky \oplus r + (c - ak)q \rangle$$
where $y \geq_I b$ in M, with $I \equiv -y + q \leq 0$, and $k = \lfloor c/a \rfloor$.

Decided-Upper-Pos
$$\langle [\![M, y \leq b]\!], \pm ax + as \oplus cy + r \rangle \Longrightarrow \quad \langle M, \pm ax + as \oplus cq + r \rangle$$
where $y \geq_I b$ in M, with $I \equiv -y + q \leq 0$, and $c > 0$.

Round (and terminate)
$$\langle M, \pm ax + as \oplus b \rangle \qquad \Longrightarrow \quad \pm x + s + \lceil b/a \rceil \leq 0$$

We use tight(I, x, M) to denote the tightly propagating inequalities derived using some strategy for applying the transition rules above.

Example 2. Given a well-formed state $\langle M_4, C \rangle$, where

$$C = \{\underbrace{-y \leq 0}_{I_1}, \underbrace{-x + 2 \leq 0}_{I_2}, \underbrace{-y + 7 + x \leq 0}_{I_3}, \underbrace{-3z + 2y - 5x \leq 0}_{I_4}\}$$

$$M_4 = [\![\ y \geq_{I_1} 0,\ x \geq_{I_2} 2,\ y \geq_{I_3} 9,\ x \leq 2\ ]\!]$$

We denote with M_1, M_2, M_3 the prefixes of M_4. In M_4, we have that bound$(I_4, z, M_4) = 3$, that is, I_4 is implying a lower bound of z in the current state. We now derive a tight inequality that justifies this lower bound.

$\langle M_4, -3z \oplus 2y - 5x \rangle$
$\Longrightarrow$ Decided-Upper-Pos
    $x \leq 2$ is a decided bound, M contains implied bound $x \geq_{I_2} 2$.
    We make the coefficient of x divisible by 3 by adding $-x + 2 \leq 0$.
$\langle M_3, -3z - 6x \oplus 2y + 2 \rangle$
$\Longrightarrow$ Resolve-Implied
    We eliminate y by adding two times $-y + 7 + x \leq 0$.
$\langle M_2, -3z - 6x \oplus 2x + 16 \rangle$
$\Longrightarrow$ Resolve-Implied
    We eliminate x in $2x + 16$ by adding two times $-x + 2 \leq 0$.
$\langle M_1, -3z - 6x \oplus 20 \rangle$
$\Longrightarrow$ Round
$-z - 2x + 7 \leq 0$

The tightly propagating inequality $-z - 2x + 7 \leq 0$ implies the same lower bound bound$(-z - 2x + 7 \leq 0, z, M) = 3$ for z.

Lemma 2. *Given a well-formed state $\langle M, C \rangle$ and an implied inequality I, i.e. such that $\langle M, C \rangle \vdash_{\mathbb{Z}} I$, and improves$(I, x, M)$ the procedure for deriving tightly-propagating inequalities terminates with a tight-inequality J such that $\langle M, C \rangle \vdash_{\mathbb{Z}} J$ and*

- *if I improves the lower bound on x, then bound$(I, x, M) \leq$ bound(J, x, M),*
- *if I improves the upper bound on x, then bound$(I, x, M) \geq$ bound(J, x, M).*

Note that in the statement above, it is does not necessarily hold that improves(J, x, M), as the improves predicate requires the new bound to be consistent, and the derived inequality might in fact imply a stronger bound.

3.2   Main Procedure

We are now ready to define our main transition system: Cutting to the Chase. In the following system of rules, if a propagation rule can derive a new implied bound $x \geq_I b$ or $x \leq_I b$, the tightly propagating inequality I is computed eagerly. This simplification clarifies the presentation but, due to the allowance of Definition 1, we can use them as just placeholders and compute them on demand, which is what we do in our implementation.

Decide

$$\langle M, C \rangle \implies \langle [\![M, x \geq b]\!], C \rangle \qquad \textbf{if } \mathsf{lower}(x, M) < b = \mathsf{upper}(x, M)$$

$$\langle M, C \rangle \implies \langle [\![M, x \leq b]\!], C \rangle \qquad \textbf{if } \mathsf{lower}(x, M) = b < \mathsf{upper}(x, M)$$

Propagate

$$\langle M, C \cup \{J\} \rangle \implies \langle [\![M, x \geq_I b]\!], C \cup \{J\} \rangle \textbf{ if } \begin{cases} \mathsf{improves}(J, x, M), \\ I = \mathsf{tight}(J, x, M), \\ b = \mathsf{bound}(J, x, M). \end{cases}$$

$$\langle M, C \cup \{J\} \rangle \implies \langle [\![M, x \leq_I b]\!], C \cup \{J\} \rangle \textbf{ if } \begin{cases} \mathsf{improves}(J, x, M), \\ I = \mathsf{tight}(J, x, M), \\ b = \mathsf{bound}(J, x, M). \end{cases}$$

Forget

$$\langle M, C \cup \{J\} \rangle \implies \langle M, C \rangle \qquad \textbf{if } C \vdash_{\mathbb{Z}} J, \text{ and } J \notin C$$

Conflict

$$\langle M, C \rangle \implies \langle M, C \rangle \vdash p \leq 0 \qquad \textbf{if } p \leq 0 \in C, \mathsf{lower}(p, M) > 0$$

Learn

$$\langle M, C \rangle \vdash I \implies \langle M, C \cup I \rangle \vdash I \qquad \textbf{if } I \notin C$$

Resolve

$$\langle [\![M, \gamma]\!], C \rangle \vdash I \implies \langle M, C \rangle \vdash \mathsf{resolve}(\gamma, I) \quad \textbf{if } \gamma \text{ is an implied bound.}$$

Unsat

$$\langle [\![M, \gamma]\!], C \rangle \vdash b \leq 0 \implies \mathsf{unsat} \qquad \textbf{if } b > 0$$

Backjump

$$\langle [\![M, \gamma, M']\!], C \rangle \vdash J \implies \langle [\![M, x \geq_I b]\!], C \rangle \quad \textbf{if } \begin{cases} \gamma \text{ is a decided bound} \\ \mathsf{improves}(J, x, M), \\ I = \mathsf{tight}(J, x, M), \\ b = \mathsf{bound}(J, x, M). \end{cases}$$

$$\langle [\![M, \gamma, M']\!], C \rangle \vdash J \implies \langle [\![M, x \leq_I b]\!], C \rangle \quad \textbf{if } \begin{cases} \gamma \text{ is a decided bound} \\ \mathsf{improves}(J, x, M), \\ I = \mathsf{tight}(J, x, M), \\ b = \mathsf{bound}(J, x, M). \end{cases}$$

Theorem 1 (Soundness). *For any derivation sequence $\langle [\![ ]\!], C_0 \rangle \implies S_1 \implies \cdots \implies S_n$, If S_n is of the form $\langle M_n, C_n \rangle$, then C_0 and C_n are equisatisfiable. If S_n is of the form $\langle M_n, C_n \rangle \vdash I$, then C_0 implies I, and C_0 and C_n are equisatisfiable. Moreover, $\langle M_n, C_n \rangle$ is well-formed.*

Example 3. Consider the set of inequalities C

$$\{\underbrace{-x \leq 0}_{I_1}, \underbrace{6x - 3y - 2 \leq 0}_{I_2}, \underbrace{-6x + 3y + 1 \leq 0}_{I_3}\}$$

Now we show C to be unsatisfiable using our abstract transition system.

$\langle [\![\,]\!], C \rangle$
$\Longrightarrow$ Propagate x using I_1
$\langle [\![x \geq_{I_1} 0]\!], C \rangle$
$\Longrightarrow$ Decide x
$\langle [\![x \geq_{I_1} 0, \ x \leq 0]\!], C \rangle$
$\Longrightarrow$ Propagate y using I_3
$\langle [\![x \geq_{I_1} 0, \ x \leq 0, \ y \leq_J -1]\!], C \rangle$, where $J = \mathsf{tight}(I_3, y, [\![x \geq_{I_1} 0, x \leq 0]\!])$
$\qquad \langle [\![x \geq_{I_1} 0, \ x \leq 0]\!], 3y \oplus -6x + 1 \rangle$
$\qquad \Longrightarrow$ Consume
$\qquad \langle [\![x \geq_{I_1} 0, \ x \leq 0]\!], 3y - 6x \oplus 1 \rangle$
$\qquad \Longrightarrow$ Round
$\qquad J \equiv y - 2x + 1 \leq 0$
$\Longrightarrow$ Conflict using I_2
$\langle [\![x \geq_{I_1} 0, \ x \leq 0, \ y \leq_J -1]\!], C \rangle \vdash 6x - 3y - 2 \leq 0$
$\Longrightarrow$ Resolve $\mathsf{resolve}(y \leq_J -1, 6x - 3y - 2 \leq 0) = (3(-2x+1) + 6x - 2 \leq 0)$
$\langle [\![M, x \leq 0]\!], C \rangle \vdash 1 \leq 0$
$\Longrightarrow$ Unsat
unsat

Slack Introduction. Given a state $S = \langle M, C \rangle$, we say variable x is *unbounded* at S if $\mathsf{lower}(x, M) = -\infty$, $\mathsf{upper}(x, M) = \infty$. We also say x is *stuck* at S if it is unbounded and Propagate cannot be used to deduce a lower or upper bound for x. A state S is *stuck* if all unbounded variables in S are stuck, and no inequality in C is false in M. That is, there is no possible transition for a stuck state S. Before we describe how we avoid stuck states, we make the observation that for every finite set of inequalities C, there is an equisatisfiable set C' such that every variable x in C', $(-x \leq 0) \in C'$. The idea is to replace every occurrence of x in C with $x^+ - x^-$, and add the inequalities $-x^+ \leq 0$ and $-x^- \leq 0$. Instead of using this eager preprocessing step, we use a lazy approach, where *slack variables* are dynamically introduced. Suppose, we are in a stuck state $\langle M, C \rangle$, then we simply select an unbounded variable x, add a fresh *slack* variable $x_s \geq 0$, and add new inequalities to C that "bound" x in the interval $[-x_s, x_s]$. This idea is captured by the following rule:

Slack-Intro

$$\langle M, C \rangle \Longrightarrow \langle M, C \cup \{x - x_s \leq 0, -x - x_s \leq 0, -x_s \leq 0\} \rangle \ \text{if} \ \begin{cases} \langle M, C \rangle \ \text{is stuck} \\ x_s \ \text{is fresh} \end{cases}$$

Note that it is sound to reuse a slack variable x_s used for "bounding" x, to bound y, and we actually do that in our implementation.

3.3   Termination

We say a set of inequalities C is a *finite problem* if for every variable x in C, there are two integer constants a and b such that $\{x - a \leq 0, -x + b \leq 0\} \subseteq C$. We say a set of inequalities C is an *infinite problem* if it is not finite. That is, there is a variable x in C such that there are no values a and b such that

$\{x - a \leq 0, -x + b \leq 0\} \subseteq C$. We say an inequality is *simple* if it is of the form $x - a \leq 0$ or $-x + b \leq 0$. Let Propagate-Simple be a rule such as Propagate, but with an extra condition requiring J to be a simple inequality. We say a strategy for applying the Cutting to the Chase rules is *reasonable* if a rule R different from Propagate-Simple is applied only if Propagate-Simple is not applicable. Informally, a *reasonable* strategy is preventing the generation of derivations where simple inequalities $\{x - a \leq 0, -x + b \leq 0\}$ are ingored and C is essentialy treated as an infinite problem.

Theorem 2 (Termination). *Given a finite problem C, and a* reasonable *strategy, there is no infinite derivation sequence starting from $\langle [\![ ]\!], C_0 \rangle$.*

3.4   Relevant Propagations

Unlike in SAT and Pseudo-Boolean solvers, Propagate rules cannot be applied to exhaustion for infinite problems. If C is unsatisfiable, the propagation rules may remain applicable indefinitely.

Example 4. Consider the followin set of (unsatisfiable) constraints

$$C = \{\overbrace{-x + y + 1 \leq 0}^{I}, \overbrace{-y + x \leq 0}^{J}, \overbrace{-y \leq 0}^{K}\} \ .$$

Starting from the initial state $\langle [\![y \geq 0]\!], C \rangle$, it is possible to generate the following infinite sequence of states by only applying the Propagate rule.

$$\langle [\![ ]\!], C \rangle \implies \langle [\![y \geq_K 0]\!], C \rangle \implies \langle [\![y \geq_K 0, x \geq_I 1]\!], C \rangle$$
$$\implies \langle [\![y \geq_K 0, x \geq_I 1, y \geq_J 1]\!], C \rangle \implies$$
$$\langle [\![y \geq_K 0, x \geq_I 1, y \geq_J 1, x \geq_I 2]\!], C \rangle \implies \ldots$$

Let $\mathsf{nb}(x, M)$ denote the number of lower and upper bounds for x in M. Given a state $S = \langle M, C \rangle$, we say a new lower bound $x \geq_I b$ is δ-*relevant* at S if

1. $\mathsf{upper}(x, M) \neq +\infty$, or
2. $\mathsf{lower}(x, M) = -\infty$, or
3. $\mathsf{lower}(x, M) + \delta |\mathsf{lower}(x, M)| < b$ and $\mathsf{nb}(x, M) < \mathsf{Max}$.

If x has a upper bound, then any lower bound is δ-relevant because x becomes bounded, and termination is not an issue for bounded variables. If x does not already have lower bound, then any new lower bound $x \geq_I b$ is relevant. Finally, the third case states that the magnitude of the improvement must be significant and the number of bound improvements for x in M must be smaller than Max. In theory, to prevent non-termination during bound propagation we only need the cutoff Max. The condition $\mathsf{lower}(x, M) + \delta |\mathsf{lower}(x, M)| < b$ is used for pragmatical reasons, and is inspired by an approach used in [1]. The idea is to block any bound improvement for x that is *insignificant* with respect to the already known bound for x.

Even when only δ-relevant propagations are performed, it is still possible to generate an infinite sequence of transitions. The key observation is that Backjump is essentially a propagation rule, that is, it backtracks M, but it also adds a new improved bound for some variable x. It is easy to construct non-terminating examples, where Backjump is used to generate an infinite sequence of non δ-relevant bounds.

We propose a simple heuristic to deal with the termination problem. It is based on the observation that if we generate a non δ-relevant bound for x, then the problem is probably unsatisfiable, and x is in the unsatisfiable core. Thus, when selecting variables for the rule Decide we should give preference to variables that we computed non δ-relevant bounds for.

4   Strong Conflict Resolution

In this section, we extend our procedure to be able to handle divisibility constraints, by adding propagation, solving and consistency checking rules into our system. Then we show how to ensure that our procedure terminates even in cases when some variables are unbounded.

Solving divisibility constraints. We will add one proof rule to the proof system, in order to help us keep the divisibility constraints in a normal form. As Cooper originally noticed in [5], given two divisibility constraints, we can always eliminate a variable from one of them, obtaining equivalent constraints.

$$\text{DIV-SOLVE} \quad \frac{d_1 \mid a_1x + p_1, d_2 \mid a_2x + p_2}{\begin{array}{c} d_1d_2 \mid dx + \alpha(d_2p_1) + \beta(d_1p_2) \\ d \mid a_2p_1 - a_1p_2 \end{array}} \quad \text{if} \quad \boxed{\begin{array}{c} d = \gcd(a_1d_2, a_2d_1) \\ \alpha(a_1d_2) + \beta(a_2d_1) = d \end{array}}$$

We use the above proof rule in our transition system to enable such normalization when needed.

Solve-Div

$$\langle M, C \rangle \quad \Longrightarrow \quad \langle M, C' \rangle \qquad \text{if} \quad \begin{cases} D_1, D_2 \in C, \\ (D_1', D_2') = \text{DIV-SOLVE}(D_1, D_2), \\ C' = C \setminus \{D_1, D_2\} \cup \{D_1', D_2'\}. \end{cases}$$

Unsat-Div

$$\langle M, C \cup \{(d \mid a_1x_1 + \cdots + a_nx_n + c)\} \rangle \quad \Longrightarrow \quad \text{unsat} \quad \text{if } gcd(d, a_1, \ldots, a_n) \nmid c$$

Propagation. With divisibility constraints as part of our problem, we can now achieve even more powerful propagation of bounds on variables. We say a variable x is *fixed* in the state $S = \langle M, C \rangle$ if $\mathsf{upper}(x, M) = \mathsf{lower}(x, M)$. Similarly a polynomial p is fixed if all its variables are fixed. To clarify the presentation, for fixed variables and polynomials we write $\mathsf{val}(x, M)$ and $\mathsf{val}(p, M)$ as a shorthand for $\mathsf{lower}(x, M)$ and $\mathsf{lower}(p, M)$.

Let $\langle M, C \rangle$ be a well-formed state, and $D, I \in C$ be a divisibility constraint and a tight inequality

$$D \equiv d \mid ax + p \ , \qquad\qquad I \equiv -x + q \leq 0 \ ,$$

with $a > 0$, $d > 0$, and $x \geq_I b \in M$. Assume, additionally, that p is fixed, i.e. assume that $\mathsf{val}(p, M) = k$.

In order to satisfy the divisibility constraint we then must have an integer z such that $dz = ax + p \geq aq + p$. Since all the variables in $aq + p$ are either assigned or implied, we can now use our system for deriving tight inequalities to deduce $-z + r \leq 0$ that would bound z in this state. Moreover substituting the solution for z, that is on the bound of the inequality, when substituted for x, would also satisfy the divisibility constraint. Using this, since $dz = ax + p$, we can deduce an inequality $-dax - dp + dr \leq 0$ which will guarantee that the bound on x satisfies the divisibility constraint. And, we can also use our procedure to convert this constraint into a tightly propagating one. Similar reasoning can be applied for the upper bound inequalities. We denote, as a shorthand, the result of this whole derivation with $\mathsf{div\text{-}derive}(I, D, x, M)$. We can now use the derivation above to empower propagation driven by divisibility constraints, as summarize below.

Propagate-Div

$$\langle M, C \rangle \;\; \Longrightarrow \;\; \langle [\![M, x \geq_I c]\!], C \cup \{ I \} \rangle \qquad\qquad \textbf{if} \;\; \begin{cases} D \equiv d \mid ax + p \in C, \\ x \geq_J b \in M, \\ I = \mathsf{div\text{-}derive}(J, D, x, M) \\ \mathsf{improves}(I, x, M) \\ c = \mathsf{bound}(I, x, M) \end{cases}$$

Eliminating Conflicting Cores. For sets of constraints containing unbounded variables, there is no guarantee that the procedure described in the previous section will terminate, even if learned inequalities (cuts) are not deleted using the Forget rule. In this section, we describe an extension based on Cooper's quantifier elimination procedure that guarantees termination.

Let U be a subset of the variables in X. We say U is the set of *unbounded* variables. Let $\prec$ be a total order over the variables in X such that for all variables $x \in X \setminus U$ and $y \in U$, $x \prec y$. We say a variable x is *maximal* in a constraint C containing x if for all variables y different from x in C, $y \prec x$. For now, we assume U contains all unbounded variables in the set of constraints C, and $\prec$ is fixed. Later, we describe how to dynamically change U and $\prec$ without compromising termination.

A *interval conflicting core* for variable x at state $S = \langle M, C \rangle$ is a set $\{ -ax + p \leq 0, \ bx - q \leq 0 \}$ such that p and q are fixed at S, and $\mathsf{bound}(-ax + p \leq 0, x, M) > \mathsf{bound}(bx - q \leq 0, x, M)$. A *divisibility conflicting core* for variable x at state S is a set $\{ -ax + p \leq 0, \ bx - q \leq 0, \ (d \mid cx + s) \}$ such that p, q and s are fixed, and for all values k in the interval $[\mathsf{bound}(-ax + p \leq 0, x, M), \mathsf{bound}(bx - q \leq 0, x, M)]$, $(d \nmid ck + \mathsf{val}(s, M))$. We do not consider cores containing more than one divisibility constraint because rule Solve-Div can be used to eliminate all but one of them. From hereafter, we assume a core is always of the form $\{-ax + p \leq 0, \; bx - q \leq 0, \; (d \mid cx + r)\}$, since we can include the redundant divisibility constraint $(1 \mid x)$ to any interval conflicting core. We say x is a *conflicting variable* at state S if there is a interval or divisibility conflicting core for x. The variable x is the *minimal conflicting variable* at S if there is no $y \prec x$ such that y is also a conflicting variable at S. Let x be a minimal conflicting variable at state $S = \langle M, C \rangle$ and $D = \{-ax + p \leq 0, \; bx - q \leq 0, \; (d \mid cx + r)\}$ be a conflicting core for x, then a *strong resolvent* for D is a set R of inequality and divisibility constraints equivalent to

$$\exists x. \, -ax + p \leq 0 \wedge bx - q \leq 0 \wedge (d \mid cx + r)$$

The key property of R is that in any state $\langle M', C' \rangle$ such that $R \subset C'$, x is not the minimal conflicting variable or D is not a conflicting core.

We compute the resolvent R using Cooper's left quantifier elimination procedure. It can be summarized by the rule

$$\textsc{Cooper-Left} \; \frac{(d \mid cx + s), \; -ax + p \leq 0, \; bx - q \leq 0}{\begin{array}{c} 0 \leq k \leq m, \; bp - aq + bk \leq 0, \\ a \mid k + p, \; ad \mid ck + cp + as \end{array}}$$

where k is a fresh variable and $m = \mathsf{lcm}(a, \frac{ad}{\gcd(ad,c)}) - 1$. The fresh variable k is bounded so it does not need to be included in U. We extend the total order $\prec$ to k by making k the minimal variable. For the special case, where $(d \mid cx + s)$ is $(1 \mid x)$, the rule above simplifies to

$$\frac{-ax + p \leq 0, \; bx - q \leq 0}{0 \leq k < a, \; bp - aq + bk \leq 0, \; a \mid p + k}$$

The rule Cooper-Left is biased to lower bounds. We may also define the Cooper-Right rule that is based on Cooper's right quantifier elimination procedure and is biased to upper bounds. We use $\mathsf{cooper}(D)$ to denote a procedure that computes the strong resolvent R for a conflicting core D. Now, we extend our procedure with a new rule for introducing resolvents for minimal conflicting variables.

Resolve-Cooper

$$\langle M, C \rangle \implies \langle M, C \cup \mathsf{cooper}(D) \rangle \quad \text{if} \quad \begin{cases} x \in U, \\ x \text{ is the minimal conflicting variable,} \\ D \text{ is a conflicting core for } x. \end{cases}$$

Note in addition to fresh variables, Resolve-Cooper rule also introduces new constraints without resorting to the Learn rule. We will show that this can not happen indefinitely, as the rule can only be applied a finite number of times.

Now we are ready to present and prove a simple and flexible strategy that will guarantee termination of our procedure even in the unbounded case.

Definition 2 (Two-layered strategy). *We say a strategy is two-layered for an initial state* $\langle [\![]\!], C_0 \rangle$ *if*

1. *it is reasonable (i.e., gives preference to the* Propagate-Simple *rules);*
2. *the* Propagate *rules are limited to* δ-*relevant bound refinements;*
3. *the* Forget *rule is never used to eliminate resolvents introduced by* Resolvent-Cooper*;*
4. *only applies the* Conflict *rule if* Resolve-Cooper *is not applicable.*

Theorem 3 (Termination). *Given a set of constraints C, there is no infinite derivation sequence starting from $S_0 = \langle [\![]\!], C \rangle$ that uses a two-layered strategy and U contains all unbounded variables in C.*

As an improvement, we note that we do not need to fix ordering $\prec$ at the beginning. It *can* be modified but, in this case, termination is only guaranteed if we eventually stop modifying it. Moreover, we can start applying the strategy with $U = \emptyset$. Then, far any non-δ-relevant bound refinement $\gamma(x)$, produced by the Backjump rules, we add x to the set U. Moreover, a variable x can be removed from U whenever a lower and upper bound for x can be deduced, and they do not depend on any decided bounds (variable becomes bounded).

5   Experimental Evaluation

We implemented the procedure described in a new solver cutsat. Implementation is a straightforward translation of the presented ideas, with very limited propagation, but includes heuristics from the SAT community such as dynamic ordering based on conflict activity, and Luby restarts. When a variable is to be decided, and we have an option to choose between the upper and lower bound, we choose the value that could satisfy most constraints. The solver source code, binaries used in the experiments, and all the accompanying materials are available at the authors website[3].

In order to evaluate our procedure we took a variety of already available integer problems from the literature, but we also crafted some additional ones. We include the problems that were used in [10] to evaluate their new simplex-based procedure that incorporates a new way of generating cuts to eliminate rational solutions. These problems are generated randomly, with all variables unbounded. This set of problems, which we denote with dillig, was reported hard for modern SMT solvers. We also include a reformulation of these problems, so that all the variables are bounded, by introducing slack variables, which we denote as slack. Next, we include the pure integer problems from the MIPLIB 2003 library [2], and we denote this problem set as miplib2003. The original problems are all very hard optimization instances, but, since we are dealing with the decision problem only, we have removed the optimization constraints and turned them into feasibility problems.[4] We include PB problems from the 2010 pseudo-Boolean

---

[3] http://cs.nyu.edu/~dejan/cutsat/
[4] All of the problems have a significant Boolean part, and 13 (out of 16) problems are pure PB problems.

competition that were submitted and selected in 2010, marked as pb2010, and problems encoding the pigeonhole principle using cardinality constraints, denoted as pigeons. The pigeonhole problems are known to have no polynomial Boolean resolution proofs, and will therefore be hard for any solver that does not use cutting planes. And finally, we include a group of crafted benchmarks encoding a tight n-dimensional cone around the point whose coordinates are the first n prime numbers, denoted as primes. In these benchmarks all the variables are bounded from below by 0. We include the satisfiable versions, and the unsatisfiable versions which exclude points smaller than the prime solution.

In order to compare to the state-of-the art we compare to three different types of solvers. We compare to the current best integer SMT solvers, i.e yices 1.0.29 [11], z3 2.15 [9], mathsat5 [13] and mathsat5+cfp that simulates the algorithm from [10]. On all 0-1 problems in our benchmark suite, we also compare to the sat4j [3] PB solver, one of the top solvers from the PB competition, and a version sat4j+cp that is based on cutting planes. And, as last, we compare with the two top commercial MIP solvers, namely, gurobi 4.0.1 and cplex 12.2, and the open source MIP solver glpk 4.38. The MIP solvers have largely been ignored in the theorem-proving community, as it is claimed that, due to the use of floating point arithmetic, they are not sound.

Table 1. Experimental results

problems	miplib2003 (16)		pb2010 (81)		dillig (250)		slacks (250)		pigeons (19)		primes (37)	
cutsat	722.78	12	1322.61	46	4012.65	223	2722.19	152	0.15	19	5.08	37
smt solvers	time(s)	solved	time(s)	solved	time(s)	solved	time(s)	solved	time(s)	solved	time(s)	solved
mathsat5+cfp	575.20	11	2295.60	33	**2357.18**	**250**	160.67	98	0.23	19	1.26	37
mathsat5	**89.49**	11	1224.91	38	3053.19	245	**3243.77**	**177**	0.30	19	**1.03**	**37**
yices	226.23	8	57.12	37	5707.46	159	7125.60	134	**0.07**	**19**	0.64	32
z3	532.09	9	**168.04**	**38**	885.66	171	589.30	115	0.27	19	11.19	23
pb solvers												
sat4j	**22.34**	**10**	**798.38**	**67**	0.00	0	0.00	0	110.81	8	0.00	0
sat4j+cp	28.56	10	349.15	60	0.00	0	0.00	0	**4.85**	**19**	0.00	0
mip solvers												
glpk	242.67	12	1866.52	46	4.50	248	0.08	10	**0.09**	**19**	**0.44**	**37**
cplex	53.86	**15**	1512.36	58	8.65	250	8.76	248	0.51	19	3.47	37
gurobi	**28.96**	**15**	**1332.53**	**58**	**5.48**	**250**	**8.12**	**248**	0.21	19	0.80	37

All tests were conducted on an Intel Pentium E2220 2.4 GHz processor, with individual runs limited to 2GB of memory and 600 seconds. The results of our experimental evaluation are presented in Table 1. The rows are associated with the individual solvers, and columns separate the problem sets. For each problem set we write the number of problems that the solver managed to solve within 600 seconds, and the cumulative time for the solved problems. We mark with bold the results that are best in a group of solvers, and we underline the results that are best among all solvers.

Compared to the SMT solvers, cutsat performs surprisingly strong, particularly being a prototype implementation. It outperforms or is the same as other smt solvers, except mathsat5 on all problem sets. Most importantly, it outperforms even mathsat5 on the real-world miplib2003 and pb2010 problem sets. The random dillig problems seem to be attainable by the solvers that implement the procedure from [10], but the same solvers surprisingly fail to solve the same problems with the slack reformulation (slacks).

Also very noticeable, the commercial MIP solvers outperform all the SMT solvers and cutsat by a big margin.

6   Conclusion

We proposed a new approach for solving ILP problems. It has all key ingredients that made CDCL-based SAT solver successful. Our solver justifies propagation steps using tightly-propagating inequalities that guarantee that any conflict detected by the search procedure can be resolved using only inequalities. We presented an approach to integrate Cooper's quantifier elimination algorithm in a model guided search procedure. Our first prototype is already producing encouraging results.

We see many possible improvements and extensions to our procedure. A solver for Mixed Integer-Real problems is the first natural extension. One basic idea would be to make the real variables bigger than the integer variables in the variable order $\prec$, and use Fourier-Moztkin resolution (instead of Cooper's procedure) to explain conflicts on rational variables. Integrating our solver with a Simplex-based procedure is another promising possibility. The idea is to use Simplex to check whether the current state or the search is feasible in the rational numbers or not. In principle, our solver can be integrated with a SMT solver based on DPLL(T). For example, it is straightforward to extract proofs/lemmas from unsatisfiable problems. On the other hand, there are many technical problems that need to be addressed. One radical, but appealing possibility, would be to use our solver instead of a SAT solver as the main search engine in a SMT solver.

Acknowledgements. We would like to thank Ken McMillan for reading an early draft and providing useful feedback, and Alberto Griggio for providing us with a custom version of mathsat5.

References

1. Achterberg, T.: SCIP: Solving constraint integer programs. PhD thesis, TU Berlin (2007)
2. Achterberg, T., Koch, T., Martin, A.: MIPLIB 2003. Operations Research Letters 34(4), 361–372 (2006)
3. Berre, D.L., Parrain, A.: The Sat4j library, release 2.2 system description. Journal on Satisfiability, Boolean Modeling and Computation 7, 59–64 (2010)
4. Chvátal, V.: Edmonds polytopes and a hierarchy of combinatorial problems. Discrete Mathematics 4(4), 305–337 (1973)
5. Cooper, D.: Theorem proving in arithmetic without multiplication. Machine Intelligence 7(91-99), 300 (1972)

6. Cotton, S.: Natural domain SMT: A preliminary assessment. In: Chatterjee, K., Henzinger, T.A. (eds.) FORMATS 2010. LNCS, vol. 6246, pp. 77–91. Springer, Heidelberg (2010)
7. Davis, M., Logemann, G., Loveland, D.: A machine program for theorem-proving. Communications of the ACM 5(7), 397 (1962)
8. Davis, M., Putnam, H.: A computing procedure for quantification theory. Journal of the ACM (JACM) 7(3), 201–215 (1960)
9. de Moura, L., Bjørner, N.S.: Z3: An Efficient SMT Solver. In: Ramakrishnan, C.R., Rehof, J. (eds.) TACAS 2008. LNCS, vol. 4963, pp. 337–340. Springer, Heidelberg (2008)
10. Dillig, I., Dillig, T., Aiken, A.: Cuts from proofs: A complete and practical technique for solving linear inequalities over integers. In: Bouajjani, A., Maler, O. (eds.) CAV 2009. LNCS, vol. 5643, pp. 233–247. Springer, Heidelberg (2009)
11. Dutertre, B., de Moura, L.: A Fast Linear-Arithmetic Solver for DPLL(T). In: Ball, T., Jones, R.B. (eds.) CAV 2006. LNCS, vol. 4144, pp. 81–94. Springer, Heidelberg (2006)
12. Gomory, R.E.: Outline of an algorithm for integer solutions to linear programs. Bulletin of the American Mathematical Society 64(5), 275–278 (1958)
13. Griggio, A.: A practical approach to SMT(LA(Z)). In: SMT Workshop (2010)
14. Korovin, K., Tsiskaridze, N., Voronkov, A.: Conflict resolution. In: Gent, I.P. (ed.) CP 2009. LNCS, vol. 5732, Springer, Heidelberg (2009)
15. Krstic, S., Goel, A.: Architecting Solvers for SAT Modulo Theories: Nelson-Oppen with DPLL. In: FroCos (2007)
16. McMillan, K.L., Kuehlmann, A., Sagiv, M.: Generalizing DPLL to richer logics. In: Bouajjani, A., Maler, O. (eds.) CAV 2009. LNCS, vol. 5643, pp. 462–476. Springer, Heidelberg (2009)
17. Moskewicz, M.W., Madigan, C.F., Zhao, Y., Zhang, L., Malik, S.: Chaff: engineering an efficient SAT solver. In: DAC (2001)
18. Nieuwenhuis, R., Oliveras, A., Tinelli, C.: Solving SAT and SAT Modulo Theories: From an abstract DPLL procedure to DPLL(T). J. ACM 53(6), 937–977 (2006)
19. Silva, J.P.M., Sakallah, K.A.: GRASP – a new search algorithm for satisfiability. In: ICCAD (1997)
20. Wolsey, L.A., Nemhauser, G.L.: Integer and combinatorial optimization. Wiley, New York (1999)

A Hybrid Method for Probabilistic Satisfiability

Pavel Klinov and Bijan Parsia

University of Manchester, Manchester M139PL, UK
{pklinov,bparsia}@cs.man.ac.uk

Abstract. Determining satisfiability of sets of formula formulated in a Nilsson style probabilistic logic (PSAT) by reduction to a system of linear (in)equations has been extensively studied, esp. in the propositional setting. The basic technique for coping with the potentially exponentially large (in terms of the formulae) linear system is column generation, which has been successful (in various forms) in solving problems of around 1000 formulae. Common to existing techniques is that the column generation model explicitly encodes all classical, i.e., non-probabilistic, knowledge. In this paper we introduce a straightforward but new hybrid method for PSAT that makes use of a classical solver in the column generation process. The benefits of this technique are twofold: first, we can, in practice, accommodate inputs with significantly larger classical parts, and thus which are overall larger, and second, we can accommodate inputs with supra-propositional classical parts, such as propositionally complete description logics. We validate our approach with an extensive series of experiments which show that our technique is competitive with traditional non-hybrid approaches in spite of scaling the expressivity of the classical part to the description logic $\mathcal{SROIQ}$.

Keywords: column generation, probabilistic satisfiability.

1 Introduction

Nilsson-style probabilistic logics [13] have been known for the intractability of probabilistic inference. Reasoning procedures are typically implemented via reduction to linear programming but it is well known that the corresponding linear programs are exponentially large in the size of the knowledge base. Thus, scalability is very limited. Over the last two decades there have been several attempts to use column generation to overcome that issue which eventually led to solving the probabilistic satisfiability problem (PSAT) for 800–1000 propositional probabilistic formulas [7,2,16,3]. The results have been encouraging but a few gaps remained unfilled. First, it has been unclear if the standard reduction plus column generation approach could be generalized to handle PSAT for more expressive logics, e.g., probabilistic description logics such as P-$\mathcal{SROIQ}$ [12]. Second, the scalability of the algorithms has been strongly limited by the number of propositional formulas not involving any probabilities (classical formulas).

In this paper we present a new PSAT algorithm for P-$\mathcal{SROIQ}$ (and thus, for propositional probabilistic satisfiability), a range of optimization techniques,

N. Bjørner and V. Sofronie-Stokkermans (Eds.): CADE 2011, LNAI 6803, pp. 354–368, 2011.

and an empirical evaluation of our implementation in Pronto,[1] our reasoner for a probabilistic extension of the DL $\mathcal{SROIQ}$ (named P-$\mathcal{SROIQ}$) [12]. Differently from the previous approaches the algorithm is *hybrid*, i.e., it separates classical reasoning (mainly SAT solving) from linear and integer programming.

Pronto is the first reasoner for a Nilsson-style probabilistic DL with scalability is comparable to (and often better than) the scalability of propositional solvers. In particular, it can solve propositional PSATs of similar size but i) can also handle probabilistic statements over arbitrary (i.e. non-propositional) $\mathcal{SROIQ}$ expressions and ii) can efficiently deal with KBs containing large bodies of non-probabilistic knowledge *in addition to* roughly 1000 probabilistic statements. This stands in stark contrast to existing propositional probabilistic solvers which, aside from not being able to handle the greater expressivity of the classical portion, are quite limited in the amount of classical knowledge they can handle.

2 Probabilistic Logic P-$\mathcal{SROIQ}$

P-$\mathcal{SROIQ}$ [12] is a probabilistic generalization of the DL $\mathcal{SROIQ}$ [5]. It provides means for expressing probabilistic relationships between arbitrary $\mathcal{SROIQ}$ concepts and a certain class of probabilistic relationships between classes and individuals. Any $\mathcal{SROIQ}$ ontology can be used as a basis for a P-$\mathcal{SROIQ}$ ontology which facilitates transition from classical to probabilistic ontologies.

The syntactic constructs of P-$\mathcal{SROIQ}$ [12] include those of $\mathcal{SROIQ}$ [5] together with *conditional constraints*. Conditional constraints are expressions of the form $(D|C)[l, u]$ where D, C are $\mathcal{SROIQ}$ concept expressions (called *conclusion* and *evidence* respectively) and $[l, u] \subseteq [0, 1]$ is a closed real-valued interval. Unconditional constraints are a special case of conditional ones when the evidence class is $\top$. A probabilistic TBox (PTBox) is a pair $PT = (\mathcal{T}, \mathcal{P})$ where $\mathcal{T}$ is a classical $\mathcal{SROIQ}$ TBox and P is a finite set of conditional constraints. (For current purposes, we neglect discussion of PABoxes which are not distinctive with respect to PSAT.)

A possible world I is a subset of the set of *basic concepts* Φ (not necessarily atomic, see [12]) such that the set of axioms $\{\{o\} \sqsubseteq C | C \in I\} \cup \{\{o\} \sqsubseteq \neg C | C \notin I\}$ is satisfiable for a fresh individual o (in other words, possible worlds correspond to *realizable* concept types). A basic concept C occurs *positively* in a possible world I if $C \in I$, otherwise it occurs *negatively*. The set of all possible worlds with respect to Φ, also called the index set, is denoted as $\mathcal{I}_\Phi$. A world I satisfies a basic concept C denoted as $I \models C$ if C occurs positively in I. Satisfiability of basic concepts is inductively extended to boolean concept expressions in the standard way, e.g., $I \models C \sqcap D$ if $I \models C$ and $I \models D$. We assume a *linear order* (fixed across all worlds of a PTBox) of basic concepts in Φ. Since Φ is a finite set we can denote the i-th basic concept in Φ by C_i. For a given possible world I we use the notation I_i to denote either C_i if C_i occurs positively in I or $\neg C_i$ if it occurs negatively.

---

[1] http://www.cs.manchester.ac.uk/~klinovp/research/pronto

A world I is said to be a model of a TBox axiom $\alpha = C \sqsubseteq D$ denoted as $I \models \alpha$ if $\eta \cup \{\{o\} \sqsubseteq C | C \in I\} \cup \{\{o\} \sqsubseteq \neg C | C \notin I\}$ is satisfiable for a new individual o. A world I is a model of a $\mathcal{SROIQ}$ TBox $\mathcal{T}$ denoted as $I \models \mathcal{T}$ if it is a model of all axioms of $\mathcal{T}$. A world I that satisfies a TBox $\mathcal{T}$ exists iff $\mathcal{T}$ has a model $(\Delta^{\mathcal{I}}, \cdot^{\mathcal{I}})$ [12].

A probabilistic interpretation Pr is a function $Pr : \mathcal{I}_\Phi \rightarrow [0, 1]$ such that $\sum_{I \in \mathcal{I}_\Phi} Pr(I) = 1$. Pr is said to *satisfy* a $\mathcal{SROIQ}$ TBox $\mathcal{T}$ denoted as $Pr \models \mathcal{T}$ if $\forall I \in \mathcal{I}_\Phi, Pr(I) > 0 \Rightarrow I \models \mathcal{T}$. The probability of a concept C, denoted as $Pr(C)$, is defined as $\sum_{I \models C} Pr(I)$. $Pr(D|C)$ is used as an abbreviation for $Pr(C \sqcap D)/Pr(C)$ given $Pr(C) > 0$. A probabilistic interpretation Pr satisfies a conditional constraint $(D|C)[l, u]$, denoted as $Pr \models (D|C)[l, u]$, if $Pr(C) = 0$ or $Pr(D|C) \in [l, u]$. A PTBox $PT = (\mathcal{T}, \mathcal{P})$ is called *satisfiable* if there exists an interpretation that satisfies $\mathcal{T}$ and all constraints in $\mathcal{P}$.

The probabilistic satisfiability problem (PSAT) is the problem of deciding if a PTBox $(\mathcal{T}, \mathcal{P})$ has a model Pr. It is decidable and its complexity class is N2ExpTime-complete, i.e. the same as the complexity of reasoning in $\mathcal{SROIQ}$ [8]. We refer to [12] for a more detailed presentation of P-$\mathcal{SROIQ}$.

3 The Probabilistic Satisfiability Algorithm

A PTBox $PT = (\mathcal{T}, \mathcal{P})$ is satisfiable iff the following system of linear inequalities is *feasible*, i.e., admits a solution (by generalization from propositional PSAT [3]):

$$\sum_{I \models C_i} l_i x_I \leq \sum_{I \models D_i \sqcap C_i} x_I \leq \sum_{I \models C_i} u_i x_I, \text{ for each } (D_i|C_i)[l_i, u_i] \in \mathcal{P} \qquad (1)$$

$$\sum_{I \in \mathcal{I}_\Phi} x_I = 1 \text{ and all } x_I \geq 0$$

where $\mathcal{I}_\Phi$ is the set of all possible worlds for the set of concepts Φ in $\mathcal{T}$. Observe, that $\mathcal{I}_\Phi$ is exponential in the size of Φ so it is not practical to try to explicitly generate this system and then check whether it has a solution.

One successful approach to dealing with linear systems having an exponential number variables is *column generation*. It is based on a fundamental property of linear programming: any feasible program always has an optimal solution in which only a linear number of variables have non-zero values. Column generation exploits this property by trying to avoid an explicit representation of variables (columns) which will not have positive values in the solution.

Consider the standard form of a linear program (2). Any linear program, e.g., the system (1), is reducible to this form by adding extra (i.e., *slack*) variables.

$$\max z = cx \qquad (2)$$
$$\text{s.t. } Ax = b \text{ and } x \geq 0$$

Let A denote a $m \times n$ matrix of linear coefficients of (2). At every step of the simplex algorithm, A is represented as a combination (B, N) where B and N are submatrices of the *basic* and *non-basic* variables, respectively. Values of non-basic variables are fixed to zero, and the solver proceeds by replacing one basic variable by a non-basic one until the optimal solution is found. Variables are represented as indexed columns of A. The index of a non-basic column which enters the basis is determined according to the following expression [3]:

$$j \in \{1, \ldots, |N|\} \text{ s.t. } c_j - u^T A^j \text{ is maximal} \qquad (3)$$

where c_j is the objective coefficient for the new variable and u^T is the current dual solution of (2). The expression $c_j - u^T A^j$ is called the *reduced cost*. At each iteration the column with the highest positive reduced cost is selected. If no such column exists, the program is at an optimum and the simplex algorithm stops.

If the size of N is exponential, as is the case for the program (1), one should compute the index of the entering column according to (3) without examining all columns in N. This is done using the column generation technique in which (3) is treated as an optimization problem with the following objective function:

$$max \ (c_j - \sum_{i=1}^{m+1} u_i a_i^j), \ A^j = (a_i^j) \in \{0, 1\}^{m+1} \qquad (4)$$

where a_i^j are variables representing linear coefficients of the entering column.

Successful column generation depends on the following criteria: i) there exists an efficient algorithm for the optimization problem (4), and ii) an optimal solution of the program can be found without generation of an excessive number of columns. This number characterizes *convergence* of the algorithm.

for s **do**
   p
end

ace and clarity, we explain a simplified version of the algorithm which decides PSAT for PTBoxes of the form $(\mathcal{T}\{(C_i|\top)[p_i, p_i]\})$, i.e., where probabilistic statements are unconditional constraints over concept names with point-valued probabilities.[2] We first rewrite the simplified version of the linear system (1) as the following linear program:

---

[2] The generalization is straightforward, if somewhat cumbersome. In particular, handling conditional constraints merely requires a somewhat more complicated (6) (i.e., mapping of columns to concept expressions). The columns are no longer binary, e.g., the ith component could be one of $\{0, 1 - l_i, -l_i, u_i, u_i - 1\}$ which map, respectively, to $\{\neg C_i, D_i \sqcap C_i, \neg D_i \sqcap C_i, D_i \sqcap C_i, \neg D_i \sqcap C_i\}$. However, each column can still be validated by checking satisfiability of a conjunctive concept expression (i.e., a possible world) using a $\mathcal{SROIQ}$ reasoner. Allowing arbitrary concept expressions in constraints is a simple matter of introducing fresh names and adding corresponding definitional axioms to $\mathcal{T}$. Our implementation, Pronto, decides PSAT for arbitrary PTBoxes.

$$\max \sum_{I \in I_\Phi} x_I \qquad (5)$$

$$\text{s.t.} \sum_{I \models C_i} x_I = p_i \times \sum_{I \in I_\Phi} x_I, \text{ for each } (C_i | \top)[p_i, p_i] \in \mathcal{P}$$

$$\sum_{I \in I_\Phi} x_I \leq 1 \text{ and all } x_I \geq 0$$

This program has the optimal objective value of 1 if and only if the system (1) is feasible. The advantage of using this program is that it is feasible even if the PTBox is not satisfiable which facilitates use of the column generation technique.

The algorithm follows the basic column generation procedure. It first constructs so called *restricted master problem* (RMP) which is a subprogram of (5) with a restricted set of variables. Next the algorithm enters the main column generation loop during which it tries to generate an improving column and, if it has been generated, adds it to the linear program. The algorithm breaks out of the loop when no improving column can be generated. Finally, it checks the optimal value of the final RMP and returns Yes if it is equal to 1. The central role in the algorithm is played by the procedure generating new improving columns.

3.1   Possible World Generation

Consider a_i^j, the i-th coefficient of some column A^j for the PSAT program (5). The column corresponds to some possible world $I^j = \{C_i\}$, therefore $a_i^j = 1$ implies that C_i occurs positively in I^j while $a_i^j = 0$ implies that it occurs negatively. We represent I^j as a *conjunctive* concept expression in $\mathcal{SROIQ}$ using a fixed linear ordering of concept names $\{C_i\}$ in Φ. We define the following function η which maps columns, i.e. binary vectors, to conjunctions of concepts from Φ:

$$\eta(A^j) = \bigsqcap X_i, \text{ where } X_i = \begin{cases} C_i, & \text{if } a_i^j = 1 \\ \neg C_i, & \text{if } a_i^j = 0 \end{cases} \qquad (6)$$

X_i are literals that denote either a basic concept or its negation.

Soundness of the PSAT algorithm strongly depends on whether every solution of the optimization problem (4), which is added as a column to the RMP, corresponds to a concept expression that is satisfiable w.r.t. $\mathcal{T}$, i.e. is a *possible world*. If this condition is true then soundness trivially follows because one may enumerate the set of all solutions (since the set of possible worlds is finite), so (5) will be equivalent to the original linear system (1). *Completeness* requires that every possible world for the given PTBox corresponds to some solution of (4). Therefore, for ensuring both soundness and completeness it is crucial to construct a set of constraints $\mathcal{H}$ for the problem (4) such that its set of solutions is in one-to-one correspondence with the set of all possible worlds $\mathcal{I}_\Phi$.

In what follows we will call columns which correspond to satisfiable expressions *valid* and the others *invalid*. More formally, given a $\mathcal{SROIQ}$ TBox $\mathcal{T}$, a column A^j is valid if $\mathcal{T} \nvDash \eta(A^j) \sqsubseteq \bot$ and is invalid otherwise. Validity can easily be ensured in the propositional case where each C_i is a clause. One possibility is to employ a well known formulation of SAT as a mixed-integer linear program (MILP) [4]. For example, if $C_i = c_1 \vee \neg c_2 \vee c_3$ then (4) will have the constraint $a_i = x_{c1} + (1 - x_{c2}) + x_{c3}$ where all variables are binary. In that case soundness and completeness follow from the reduction of SAT to MILP.

In the case of an expressive language, such as $\mathcal{SROIQ}$, there appears to be no easy way of determining the set of constraints $\mathcal{H}$ (it may not be polynomial in the size of $\mathcal{T}$). Informally, $\mathcal{H}$ must capture every entailment, such as $\mathcal{T} \models C_i \sqcap, \ldots, \sqcap C_j \sqsubseteq \bot$ in order to prevent generation of any column A^j such that $C_i \sqcap, \ldots, \sqcap C_j$ is a subexpression of $\eta(A^j)$. All such entailments can be computed in a naive way by checking satisfiability of all conjunctions $C_i \sqcap, \ldots, \sqcap C_j$ over Φ but this is no better than constructing the full linear system (1). Instead, Pronto implements a novel *hybrid, iterative* procedure to compute $\mathcal{H}$ (Algorithm 1).

Algorithm 1. Possible world generation algorithm

Input: PTBox $PT = (\mathcal{T}, \mathcal{P})$, current dual solution u^T of (5)
Output: New column A^j or *null*
1 $IP_{ColGen} \leftarrow$ initialize the integer program (4) using u^T and $\mathcal{P}$
2 $\mathcal{H} \leftarrow \emptyset$
3 **while** $A^j \neq null$ **do**
4 $\quad$ Solve IP_{ColGen} subject to $\mathcal{H}$ to optimality
5 $\quad$ $A^j \leftarrow$ some optimal solution of IP_{ColGen}
6 $\quad$ **if** $A^j \neq null$ **then**
7 $\quad\quad$ **if** $satisfiable(\eta(A^j), \mathcal{T})$ **then**
8 $\quad\quad\quad$ **return** A^j
9 $\quad\quad$ **end**
10 $\quad\quad$ $\mathcal{H} \leftarrow \mathcal{H} \cup$ inequalities that exclude A^j
11 $\quad$ **end**
12 **end**
13 **return** *null*

The key steps are 5 and 8. On step 5 the algorithm invokes a $\mathcal{SROIQ}$ reasoner (e.g., Pellet [15]) to determine if the computed column corresponds to a *possible* world. If yes, the column is valid and returned. If no, the current set of constraints $\mathcal{H}$ needs to be extended to exclude A^j from the set of solutions to (4). To explicate this step we first define the notion of the minimal unsatisfiable core for an unsatisfiable conjunctive concept expression.

Definition 1 (Unsatisfiable Core). *Given a TBox $\mathcal{T}$ and unsatisfiable (w.r.t. $\mathcal{T}$) concept expression $\bigsqcap X_i$ represented as a set of conjuncts $X = \{X_i\}$, a minimal unsatisfiable subexpression (MUS) is a subset $X' = \{X_i'\} \subseteq \{X_i\}$ such that $\bigsqcap X_i$ is unsatisfiable w.r.t. $\mathcal{T}$ and any $X'' = \{X_i''\} \subset \{X_i'\}$ is satisfiable w.r.t. $\mathcal{T}$. The unsatisfiable core (UC) of $\bigsqcap X_i$ is the set of all its MUSes.*

Observe that it is sufficient to add a constraint that rules out *any* of the MUSes to exclude the current column from the set of solutions to (4).

Next, we show how to translate MUSes into linear inequalities. A MUS is a set of conjuncts $\{X_i'\}$ each of which corresponds to a binary variable (observe that η, as defined in (6), is a bijective function). By a slight abuse of notation we write $a_i = \eta^{-1}(X_i')$ to denote the variable that corresponds to C_i. Then given a MUS $X' = \{X_i'\}_{i=1}^k$ we add the following linear constraint:

$$\sum_{i=1}^k a_i \leq k - 1, \text{ where } a_i = \begin{cases} \eta^{-1}(X_i'), & X_i' = C_i \\ 1 - \eta^{-1}(X_i'), & X_i = \neg C_i \end{cases} \tag{7}$$

If a conjunctive concept contains $\bigsqcap X_i$ as a subexpression then all binary expressions b_i, i.e. either a_i or $1 - a_i$ depending on whether X_i is a positive or a negative literal, are equal to 1. Therefore $\sum_{i=1}^k a_i = k$ where k is the size of $\{X_i\}$. Constraining $\sum_{i=1}^k b_i$ to be less or equal to $k - 1$ is equivalent to requiring at least one b_i to be equal to 0. According to the definition of η this is equivalent to removing of at least one conjunct from X' which makes it satisfiable. Therefore, each of the constraints (7) is sufficient to exclude all columns, which correspond to concept expressions containing X', from the set of solutions to (4). The algorithm does so on step 8 by computing the unsatisfiable core, transforming each of the MUSes into a linear inequality according to (7), and adding it to $\mathcal{H}$. Observe that the new inequalities do not exclude any columns *not* containing X' thus ensuring completeness.

We call algorithm 1 "hybrid" because it combines invocations of LP solver (to optimize (5)), MILP and $\mathcal{SROIQ}$ solvers (to optimize (4) and check satisfiability of concept expressions respectively). It is *iterative* because during the possible world generation phase it iteratively tightens the set of solutions to (4) until either a valid column is found or provably no such column exists. We conclude with a short example demonstrating our iterative technique:

Example 1. Consider a PTBox where $\mathcal{T} = \{A \sqsubseteq \exists R.C, B \sqsubseteq \exists R.\neg C, \geq 2R.\top \sqsubseteq D\}$ and $\mathcal{P}$ contains some probabilistic constraints over the ordered signature $\Phi = \{A, B, D\}$. Algorithm 1 starts out with an empty set of linear constraints for (4). The list of binary variables for (4) is (x_A, x_B, x_D). Assume that at some iteration the algorithm generates the following column: $A^j = (1, 1, 0, 1)$ (the last component of any column is always equal to 1 because of the normalization row in (5)). Then $\eta(A^j) = A \sqcap B \sqcap \neg D$.

Observe that $\mathcal{T} \models \eta(A^j) \sqsubseteq \bot$. Any instance o of $A \sqcap B$ must have two R-successors (domain elements which are connected to $o^{\mathcal{I}}$ by $R^{\mathcal{I}}$). They are necessarily distinct because one is an instance of C and another is an instance of $\neg C$. Therefore, o is an instance of $\geq 2R.\top$ and consequently is an instance of D. This is a contradiction with $\neg D$ in $\eta(A^j)$. The unsatisfiable core of $\eta(A^j)$ is $\{A, B, \neg D\}$. This MUS is converted into the following linear inequality $x_D \geq x_A + x_B - 1$ which is then added to the binary program (4). As a result, no invalid column containing *this* MUS will be computed on subsequent iterations.

Theorem 1 (Soundness, Correctness, and Termination). *The column generation algorithm for solving PSAT in P-$\mathcal{SROIQ}$ which uses Algorithm 1 to generate columns is sound, complete, and N2ExpTime-complete.*

Proof. The proofs are straightforward (see the technical report [10]).

A naive implementation will exhibit quite poor performance simply due to the overhead of switching between the solver and the reasoner, not to mention that classical SAT tests can be expensive. A reasonable implementation can mitigate these issues by pulling larger chunks of classical knowledge into the solver at a time. For example, a large portion of real ontologies is propositional. In fact, we need not limit our attention to asserted knowledge. Virtually all modern DL reasoners can efficiently construct the so called *classification hierarchy* by finding all subsumptions between concept names that are logically entailed by the TBox. These entailments are essentially propositional and can be absorbed. In the extreme case all propositional knowledge (asserted or inferred) can be absorbed into the program (4). However, the algorithm tries to find a trade-off between eager absorption (which can exhaust memory) and lazy generation of inequalities (which requires extra concept satisfiability checks). The balance depends on available memory vs. the number of absorbable axioms.

Another issue with a naive implementation of Algorithm 1 is that computing unsatisfiability cores may appear impractical for certain concept expressions and TBoxes. This may especially happen for long expressions which contain MUSes with little or no overlap. It is known the model diagnosis theory [14] that finding all minimal unsatisfiable sets may require a number of SAT tests that is exponential in the total size of all sets. To address this issue the algorithm imposes a time limit on the procedure that computes the UC. If at least one MUS has been found but finding others exceeds the timeout the procedure is interrupted. The found MUSes are then converted to linear inequalities and the algorithm moves on as if the full UC was computed.

4   Evaluation

Our implementation, Pronto, is written in Java and compiled using Sun JDK 1.6. All evaluation tests have been performed on a PC with 2GHz CPU, 2GB of RAM, Sun JRE 1.6.0_07 running under Windows XP SP3. The only JVM option that was used for performance tuning was -Xmx to allow the reasoner use the maximal available amount of memory. All of the evaluation tests presented below use wall time as the main measure of performance ("Total Time"). We also also record the number of generated columns (to track convergence speed) and total column generation time ("CG Total").

Due to the lack of existing probabilistic knowledge bases, all of our experiments have to involve a generated component. For each experimental configuration (i.e., each row in Tables 1-4), we generated 5 distinct test cases and report the average. While we experimented with generation larger number of cases, the variance between cases was so low and the cost of generating and running additional cases was high, the benefit of additional cases was low.

4.1   Random Propositional Knowledge Bases

In order to compare our algorithm with existing approaches in the propositional
literature, we have followed the methodology for generating random knowledge
bases which was described by Jaumard et al. [6] and later used in [1,3]. Since
those solvers are not publicly available, the comparison primarily rests on solving
similarly sized problems and in tracking the columns generated. The number of
concept names was kept fixed to 200 since it is the largest number of atoms
in [3]. We generated the required number of disjunctive expressions and then
assigned probability intervals in the satisfiability preserving way (see [10] for
details). The length of each expression is randomly varied between 1 and 4
literals. The polarity of each literal is also random. Note that while the input
does not have a separate set of classical axioms, the interactions between the
classical structure of the clauses effectively introduces such. It is easy to see
that naming the disjunctive expressions using equivalence axioms is satisfiability
preserving (and, effectively, is what our implementation does internally).

The results are presented in Table 1. As reported in [3] the previously developed propositional PSAT algorithm on average generated about 3300 columns
for collections of 800 clauses over 200 atoms. Our algorithm generates about 10
times fewer columns (we do not compare the total time to abstract away from
the hardware differences). Even more importantly our algorithm does not seem
to exhibit a super-polynomial growth in the number of generated columns which
is the case with Hansen's. One possible reason for that is that we use exact
optimization methods for computing each improving column while Hansen and
Perron use the variable neighborhood heuristics to optimize non-linear 0-1 programs. In fact, the number of columns increases only very gently, most probably
because of the fixed signature size. At the same time the experiment reveals
that the average time it takes to generate a column may increase exponentially.
Since the number of variables in the column generation model, i.e. the MILP
program (4), depends only on the signature size and therefore stays constant,
this suggests that the program becomes harder for some other reason. We leave
tuning of this program to future work.

Given this good performance, it is surprising that a hybrid approach has not
been considered in the literature before. Our speculation is that the increase
in implementation complexity and the obvious overhead potential of communication between the components made hybrid methods unattractive. Of course,
they are forced upon us by the expressive and large classical parts we must deal
with, but this experiment shows that they do well even in the propositional case.

Table 1. PSAT performance on random propositional clauses

# atoms	# clauses	Time(s)	CG Total (s)	# columns
200	250	27.32	18.46	164.6
200	500	102.43	61.73	228.2
200	750	263.06	140.79	264.6
200	1000	396.8	185.22	274.6

4.2   Probabilistic Extensions of Real Ontologies

While there are hundreds to thousands of publicly available OWL (i.e., $\mathcal{SROIQ}$) ontologies of varying size, logical expessivity, and axiom sophistication, none of these have a probabilistic part. For our experiments, we selected six ontologies:[3] The NCI Anatomy Ontology (NCI), the Subcellular Anatomy Ontology (SAO), the Process Ontology, the Sequence Ontology with Composite Terms (SO-XP), the Teleost Anatomy Ontology (TAO), and the Cell Type ontology. None of these ontologies is propositional or small and simple enough to consider their propositionalization and are varied enough to give a reasonable feel for robustness. The probabilistic parts of test PTBoxes are produced by a random generation process that takes a probabilistic signature as an argument. Common to all cases, we fix the number of unconditional statements to 10% of the size probabilistic part. We need to have some unconditional part for two reasons: First, it is necessary for realism; in our modelling experience, a small ratio of unconditional constraints likely common modeling pattern in P-$\mathcal{SROIQ}$, e.g., to represent probabilistic facts, or beliefs, about a specific individual [9]. Second, and relatedly, it is necessary to avoid *trivial* satisfiability. If all constraints are conditional, then we can obtain a vacuous model by assigning zero probability to all evidence concepts. This is undesirable from both a modeling perspective (that is, unrealistic) and does not engage the reasoning algorithm at all. As from modeling realism, we settle on 10% because in preliminary experiments wherein we varied the percentage of unconditionals from 10%-50% there was no significant performance differences (see [10] for details).

Ultimately it is the probability intervals attached to constraints that determine whether the resulting PTBox will be satisfiable or not. It has been reported that satisfiable KBs are typically harder for PSAT algorithms [16,3] so, we want to focus on (nontrivial) satisfiable problems. Unfortunately, random assignment of probabilities to generated constraints is likely to result in an unsatisfiable PTBox, provided that it contains unconditional statements [6,16,3]. Therefore, we use a standard technique based on generation of probabilistic interpretations which can then be used to assign probabilities to statements [6]. In that case satisfiability is guaranteed because satisfying interpretations (models) have been constructed explicitly. Its main advantage is that it works with any probabilistic KB, propositional or not, and does not impose any restrictions on its structure (such as cycle disallowance). The main disadvantage is that large cases become prohibitively more difficult to generate. For the current evaluation it has been implemented in the following steps: First, two sets of possible worlds $\mathcal{I}_\Phi^1, \mathcal{I}_\Phi^2$ of size $k \geq 2 \times |\mathcal{P}|$ are generated for a PTBox $(\mathcal{T}, \mathcal{P})$ with probabilistic signature Φ. Second, probabilistic interpretations Pr_1, Pr_2 are defined by generating two sequences of k random numbers summing to 1 which represent probabilities of possible worlds in $\mathcal{I}_\Phi^1$ and $\mathcal{I}_\Phi^2$. Third, the lower probability l (resp. the upper probability u) for each constraint $(D|C)[l,u]$ in $\mathcal{P}$ is determined as the smallest (resp. the largest) of values $Pr_i(D|C)$ ($i \in \{1,2\}$).

---

[3] All ontologies are available from: `http://bit.ly/cade-2011-ontologies`

Against these common factors, we explore three basic scenarios: (1) where the probabilistic signature is fixed, but the number of axioms with regard to that signature grows; (2) where the number of probabilistic axioms is fixed, but the probabilistic signature grows; and (3) where both the probabilistic signature and number of probabilistic axioms grows, but the ratio between them stays fixed. In addition to isolating the key factors (signature and axiomatization level), each scenario corresponds to a reasonable set of ontologies: (1) corresponds to increasing probabilistic axiomatization of a given subpart of the classical ontology. For example, a formalization of the risk factors for a given disease (e.g., breast cancer) would focus on a fairly fixed subset of something like the NCI Oncology Ontology, though the number of probabilistic axioms would increase as additional risk factors and their interaction were modeled. (2) corresponds to a variety of situations wherein we have roughly the same amount of probabilistic knowledge, but it touches a varying amount of the ontology. Considering risk relations, it is not uncommon for different domains to have more (or less) scattered risk factors: compare the risk of mortality due to breast cancer vs. risk of mortality due to all causes. Finally, (3) corresponds to cases where the modeler aims to increase the probabilistic "coverage" of the ontology, that is, wherein they aim to say *something* about the probabilistic relations over increasing amounts of the terms in the ontology. Obviously, each scenario, and the particular way we realize it, is artificial, but they are reasonably motivated and, in aggregate, capture a wide variety of probabilistic ontologies.

To realize (1) (Table 2), the probabilistic signature size is fixed at 250 concept names while the number of PTBox constraints varies from 250 to 1000. To realize (2) (Table 3) , the PTBox size was kept fixed at 500 constraints while the signature size was varied from 100 to 500. To realize (3) (Table 4), the number of constraints was varied between 250 and 1000 as in the first experiment but signature's size was kept at 50% of the PTBox size.

Summary. The first, and the major, conclusion that can be made from the evaluation results is that the algorithm is *robust*, i.e. it behaves quite well on satisfiable PTBoxes with varying parameters. No combination of the main parameters causes it to hit the worst case. It robustly scales to 1000 probabilistic statements defined over 500 concepts from large, expressive real ontologies.

The second observation is that PTBoxes built over the SAO and the SO-XP ontologies tend to be harder for the algorithm than the rest. The difference is especially visible in Table 3 and Table 4, i.e. where signature size varies. While the total number of generated columns is approximately the same, it is substantially harder to generate a column when signature size is over approximately 200 concepts (for the SO-XP ontology) and 300 concepts (for the SAO ontologies). The explanation for this is that in these ontologies is most concepts, which are randomly selected from the TBox, are highly connected by subsumption or disjointness relationships. These relationships need to be captured in the MILP model. However, if the number of the relationships is high not all corresponding linear inequalities will be created when exploiting

Table 2. PSAT times for PTBoxes with probabilistic signatures of 250 concept names

Ontology	Language	TBox size	PTBox size	Total time (s)	CG Total (s)	# columns
NCI	$\mathcal{ALE}+$	5423	250	151.33	22.6	99
			500	240.06	95.12	190.6
			750	314.92	125.68	241.8
			1000	440.35	163.43	306
SAO	$\mathcal{SHIN}$	2499	250	77.94	65.35	123.2
			500	160.48	134.17	246.2
			750	321.2	242.82	404.2
			1000	525.55	344.49	526
Process	$\mathcal{SHOF}$	2007	250	46.73	28.58	97.2
			500	124.73	91.16	180.4
			750	211.78	132.4	248.6
			1000	337.5	166.71	300.4
SO-XP	$\mathcal{SHI}$	1928	250	129.18	89.32	130.4
			500	206.11	151.67	198.2
			750	319.47	227.03	251.8
			1000	524.95	350.67	318.4
TAO	$\mathcal{EL}+$	3406	250	43.64	22.41	95.6
			500	127.42	90.15	182.4
			750	205.36	124.1	240.8
			1000	326.16	164.38	310.2
Cell Type	$\mathcal{EL}+$	1263	250	65.96	34.33	98
			500	138.12	91.3	182.2
			750	219.59	126.65	244.2
			1000	336.54	162.48	300.2

the concept hierarchy in order to prevent memory exhaustion.[4] Consequently, invalid column candidates are more likely to be generated and require a computationally intensive search for the unsatisfiable cores. This effect can be mitigated by either increasing the amount of available memory or employing a more intelligent approach to compute the initial set of inequalities for the MILP model.

The third outcome is that the number of columns generated by Algorithm 1 does not seem to grow exponentially with either size of the PTBox or size of the probabilistic signature. This suggests that the PSAT algorithm may well scale beyond 1000 conditional constraints. We have not yet extended the experiments beyond 1000 since it is extremely time consuming to generate *satisfiable* probabilistic KBs of that size over complex ontologies because it requires computing a high number of possible worlds.

5 Conclusion

In many cases, the vast majority of inequalities for the column generation model are generated by absorption. Note that since we absorb a distinguished set

---

[4] Given the available RAM (2GB) we set the limit of the height of the MILP model to 15,000 inequalities—enough to capture all subsumptions from the Process, T-A and Cell Type ontologies, but not for the SAO or SO-XP. The problem is especially visible for the SO-XP for which Algorithm 1 computed more than 100 invalid columns for an average PTBox of 500 constraints and 500 concepts in the signature.

Table 3. PSAT times for PTBoxes with 500 probabilistic statements

Ontology	Language	TBox size	Sig. size	Total time (s)	CG Total (s)	# columns
NCI	$\mathcal{ALE}+$	5423	100	139.56	71.83	145.4
			200	201.66	82.72	169.6
			300	258.94	89.25	202.6
			400	304.98	84.88	224
			500	365.23	93.44	249.2
SAO	$\mathcal{SHIN}$	2499	100	179.35	153.15	306
			200	158.56	133.4	246
			300	165.47	138	232.6
			400	252.37	221.93	212
			500	415.24	382.17	197
Process	$\mathcal{SHOF}$	2007	100	95.71	73.47	146.6
			200	119.17	89.6	175.6
			300	134.28	97.44	188.8
			400	158.02	111.54	211
			500	180.3	124.05	234.8
SO-XP	$\mathcal{SHI}$	1928	100	118.69	89.45	152
			200	178.3	132.59	186.4
			300	266.66	203.28	208.4
			400	330.62	250.81	224.6
			500	468.64	370.46	252.8
TAO	$\mathcal{EL}+$	3406	100	91.91	68.91	139.8
			200	107.78	76.64	156.2
			300	124.89	84.02	193.6
			400	139.68	88.61	224.4
			500	160.15	95.94	258
Cell Type	$\mathcal{EL}+$	1263	100	96.53	69.03	141.6
			200	126.55	85.96	172.4
			300	155.55	101.11	198.4
			400	170.59	105.81	200.4
			500	218.77	139.25	252.6

of entailments (i.e., the atomic subsumptions and disjointnesses), even a KB with complete absorption is hybrid: the classical reasoner performs a good deal of the computation, in these cases, in the first round. This holds even in pure propositional cases. Not computing all MUSs is indispensable for dealing with hard TBoxes for which computing all unsatisfiable subexpressions of a conjunctive concept expression is highly intractable (mostly due to their large number). In particular, the PSAT algorithm runs out of memory on PTBoxes with 1000 constraints over the SAO and the SO-XP ontologies if this technique is off. Normal column generation tweaking, e.g., various *stabilization* techniques (omitted for space reasons but see [10]) is needed for acceptable convergence. Without reasonable stabilization the algorithm generates more than 5,000 columns for PTBoxes with a weak classical part. The PSAT algorithm is very memory intensive: First, it makes heavy use of the $\mathcal{SROIQ}$ reasoning algorithms which have exponential memory requirements. Second, it may require a non-polynomial number of linear inequalities to capture the TBox structure in the MILP model (4).

The key obstacle to further improvements in scalability is the size and hardness of the MILP model (4) used to generate columns for the PSAT algorithm.

Table 4. PSAT times for PTBoxes with varying number of statements & concepts

Ontology	Language	TBox size	PTBox size	Total time (s)	CG Total (s)	# columns
NCI	$\mathcal{ALE}+$	5423	250	100.21	32.79	83.4
			500	239.45	93.89	186.4
			750	429.13	157.37	301.4
			1000	745.15	231.62	418.4
SAO	$\mathcal{SHIN}$	2499	250	77.1	68.41	129.4
			500	178.16	149.29	276.4
			750	375.3	300.02	341.2
			1000	1360.21	1176.05	425.4
Process	$\mathcal{SHOF}$	2007	250	50.98	39.39	88.6
			500	119.92	87.02	176.4
			750	240.94	144.42	275.2
			1000	479.69	236.42	404.8
SO-XP	$\mathcal{SHI}$	1928	250	61.31	40.31	76
			500	197.05	144.17	189
			750	449.49	323.31	307.6
			1000	921.57	644.28	423.4
TAO	$\mathcal{EL}+$	3406	250	50.24	37.13	89.4
			500	125.76	89.38	179.8
			750	252.52	149.5	287.8
			1000	544.71	238.09	431.8
Cell Type	$\mathcal{EL}+$	1263	250	57.22	39.18	89.2
			500	137.89	91.66	182.6
			750	283.45	158.88	296.4
			1000	487.68	220.32	384.2

The time it takes to solve it (CG Total) is the only performance measure that appears to grow non-polynomially with the size of probabilistic KBs.[5] Approximate approaches to solving it do not promise substantial improvements because the time it takes to obtain *some*, not even a near-optimal, solution also grows non-polynomially. This suggests that required are ways to decompose this model into smaller sub-models which, in turn, leads to a wider research question of decomposing (or *modularizing*) probabilistic knowledge bases. Our results guarantee that even decomposing a KB onto even a small number of relatively large, i.e. around 1000 constraints, modules can lead to a dramatic increase of scalability. We have demonstrated this in practice on the CADIAG-2 propositional knowledge base which has over 20,000 statements, a majority of which are probabilistic. Due to the particular structure of CADIAG-2, we were able to perform an ad hoc partitioning and verify the satisfiability of a repaired version [11].

The experiments we have conducted establish two key points: First, a column generation based hybrid procedure for PSAT is competitive with the traditional non-hybrid approaches, even when using a solver not tuned for propositional SAT. It has the inherent advantages of being more robust with respect to the amount of non-probabilistic knowledge as well as its expressivity.

Second, our implementation is a computationally reasonable tool for modelers seeking to add probabilistic statements to large existing ontologies. Worst case

---

[5] Another measure is the difference between Total time and CG Total which is the time spent on optimizing the main linear program (1). However, since LP is a `PTime` problem it could be improved by tuning the program or using `PTime` methods to solve it, e.g., interior-point algorithms.

complexity considerations preclude strong promises in the face of novel input, however, it is evident that we have reason to believe that even if the current optimizations fail at some point that, as with classical DL reasoners, new ones can be found.

References

1. Hansen, P., Jaumard, B.: Probabilistic satisfiability. In: Handbook of Defeasible Reasoning and Uncertainty Management Systems, Algorithms for Uncertainty and Defeasible Reasoning, vol. 5, pp. 321–367. Kluwer, Dordrecht (2000)
2. Hansen, P., Jaumard, B., Nguetsé, G.B.D., de Aragão, M.P.: Models and algorithms for probabilistic and Bayesian logic. In: International Joint Conference on Artificial Intelligence, pp. 1862–1868 (1995)
3. Hansen, P., Perron, S.: Merging the local and global approaches to probabilistic satisfiability. International Journal of Approximate Reasoning 47(2), 125–140 (2008)
4. Hooker, J.N.: Quantitative approach to logical reasoning. Decision Support Systems 4, 45–69 (1988)
5. Horrocks, I., Kutz, O., Sattler, U.: The even more irresistible $\mathcal{SROIQ}$. In: KR, pp. 57–67 (2006)
6. Jaumard, B., Hansen, P., de Aragão, M.P.: Column generation methods for probabilistic logic. In: IPCOC, pp. 313–331 (1990)
7. Jaumard, B., Hansen, P., de Aragão, M.P.: Column generation methods for probabilistic logic. INFORMS Journal on Computing 3(2), 135–148 (1991)
8. Kazakov, Y.: SRIQ and SROIQ are harder than SHOIQ. In: KR, pp. 274–284 (2008)
9. Klinov, P., Parsia, B.: Probabilistic modeling and OWL: A user oriented introduction into P-$\mathcal{SHIQ}$(D). In: OWLED (2008)
10. Klinov, P., Parsia, B.: Practical reasoning in Probabilistic Description Logic. Tech.rep., University of Manchester (2011), http://www.cs.man.ac.uk/~klinovp/pubs/2011/psroiq-eval-report.pdf
11. Klinov, P., Parsia, B., Picado-Muiño, D.: The consistency of the medical expert system CADIAG-2: A probabilistic approach. Journal of Information Technology Research 4(1), 1–20 (2011)
12. Lukasiewicz, T.: Expressive probabilistic description logics. Artificial Intelligence 172(6-7), 852–883 (2008)
13. Nilsson, N.J.: Probabilistic logic. Artificial Intelligence 28(1), 71–87 (1986)
14. Reiter, R.: A theory of diagnosis from first principles. Artificial Intelligence 32, 57–95 (1987)
15. Sirin, E., Parsia, B., Grau, B.C., Kalyanpur, A., Katz, Y.: Pellet: A practical OWL-DL reasoner. Journal of Web Semantics 5(2), 51–53 (2007)
16. de Souza Andrade, P.S., da Rocha, J.C.F., Couto, D.P., da Costa Teves, A., Cozman, F.G.: A toolset for propositional probabilistic logic. In: Encontro Nacional de Inteligencia Artificial, pp. 1371–1380 (2007)

Solving Systems of Linear Inequalities by Bound Propagation

Konstantin Korovin[*] and Andrei Voronkov[**]

The University of Manchester

Abstract. In this paper we introduce a new method for solving systems of linear inequalities. The algorithm incorporates many state-of-the-art techniques from DPLL-style reasoning. We prove soundness, completeness and termination of the method.

1 Introduction

There are several well-known methods for linear programming and solving systems of linear inequalities over the rational or real numbers. These are the Fourier-Motzkin variable elimination method, simplex, the interior point method (see, [7] for an overview), a recent conflict resolution method [2] and the GDPLL method [5]. In this paper we introduce a new method. Interestingly, this method is rather different from the previously known methods in that it incorporates ideas recently developed in the SAT solving community: namely, DPLL [1], unit propagation, dynamic variable ordering, lemma learning and backjumping [4], see also [6] for the state-of-the-art exposition of DPLL related techniques.

The method works by assigning values to variables and using the assigned values to derive bounds on other variables, using *bound propagation*. The process of assigning values either terminates with a solution, or results in inconsistent bounds derived by bound propagation. In the latter case we learn a new inequality, which we call a *collapsing inequality*, which is also used to derive a bound on a variable excluding a previously done assignment. After that we either obtain inconsistent bounds, which means that the system is unsatisfiable or change the assignment to conform to the new bound. The algorithm incorporates many ideas developed in SAT solving, such as clause learning, backjumping and dynamic variable ordering. Another interesting property of the algorithm is that the number of inequalities at each stage can be kept linear in the number of variables and the number of input inequalities.

For those familiar with DPLL, the informal description of the method above may look familiar. However, there are fundamental differences between the two methods. Firstly, it turns out that bound propagation can be non-terminating, so we have to impose some restrictions on it. Secondly, unlike propositional DPLL, there exists an infinite possible number of bounds and values for a variable, so making an algorithm that terminates is highly non-trivial.

---

[*] Supported by a Royal Society University Research Fellowship.
[**] Partially supported by an EPSRC grant.

N. Bjørner and V. Sofronie-Stokkermans (Eds.): CADE 2011, LNAI 6803, pp. 369–383, 2011.

The rest of this paper is organised as follows. Section 2 introduces definitions related to systems of linear inequalities. We define notions of bound (on a variable), context as a set of bounds, and inference rules of resolution and bound-resulting resolution on linear inequalities. We also introduce bound propagation as a sequence of bound-resulting resolution inferences. Section 3 introduces a fundamental notion of *collapsing inequality*. We give an algorithm for extracting collapsing inequalities from resolution proofs. We show that, in the case of bound propagation, the extracted collapsing inequality can be used to collapse a bound propagation derivation into a single inference by bound-resulting resolution.

In Section 4 we introduce our algorithm for solving systems of linear inequalities using bound propagation and other rules. Section 5 gives an example of how this algorithm works. In Section 6 we show soundness, completeness and termination of the algorithm. Proofs that did not fit can be found in the full version of this paper [3].

2   Preliminaries

We will denote variables by x, rational constants by c and *positive* rational constants by d, maybe with indices. We call a *literal* a variable x or its negation $-x$ and denote literals by l. Literals of the forms x and $-x$ are said to be *complementary*. A literal complementary to a literal l will be denoted by $\bar{l}$. Note that every linear inequality can be written in the form

$$d_1 l_1 + \cdots + d_n l_n + c \geq 0. \tag{1}$$

where the variables of the l_i's are pairwise different. Note that all the constants d_i's are positive by our choice of notation. We say that inequality (1) *contains* literals $l_1, \ldots, l_n$. An inequality is called *trivial* if it contains no variables. It is straightforward to adapt all our considerations to systems also containing strict inequalities and equalities, which for simplicity we do not consider in this paper.

We define an *assignment* σ over a set of variables X as a mapping from X to the set of real numbers $\mathbb{R}$, i.e. $\sigma : X \to \mathbb{R}$.

For a linear term q over X, denote by $q\sigma$ the value of q after replacing all variables $x \in X$ by the corresponding values $\sigma(x)$. An assignment σ is called a *solution of a linear inequality* $q \geq 0$ if $q\sigma \geq 0$ is true; it is a *solution of a system* of linear inequalities if it is a solution of every inequality in the system. If σ is a solution of a linear inequality I (or a system $\mathcal{L}$ of such inequalities), we also say that σ *satisfies* I (respectively, $\mathcal{L}$), denoted by $\sigma \models$ I (respectively, $\sigma \models \mathcal{L}$), otherwise we say that σ *violates* I (respectively, $\mathcal{L}$). A system of linear inequalities is said to be *satisfiable* if it has a solution.

We will denote inequalities as I, J, G, possibly with indexes and the corresponding linear terms as I, J, G respectively, so I $= (I \geq 0)$, J $= (J \geq 0)$ and so on. Two linear inequalities are *equivalent* if one can be obtained from another by multiplying by a positive constant. When we deal with linear inequalities, we will not distinguish equivalent linear inequalities. That is, we assume that the order of linear terms $d_i l_i$ in a linear expression is irrelevant and that we can multiply the inequality by any positive rational. We also assume that a trivial inequality is either $-1 \geq 0$ or $0 \geq 0$.

For an inequality I, let $var(\text{I})$ denote the set of all variables with non-zero coefficients in I. Similarly, for a system of inequalities $\mathcal{L}$, let $var(\mathcal{L})$ denote the set

Table 1. Correspondence between the SAT terminology and our terminology

SAT	this paper
variable	variable
literal	literal
clause	linear inequality
unit clause	bound
resolution	resolution
unit-resulting resolution	bound-resulting resolution
unit propagation	bound propagation

$\cup_{I \in \mathcal{L}} var(I)$. We say that a system of inequalities $\mathcal{L}$ *implies* an inequality I, if every solution to $\mathcal{L}$ is also a solution to I. We say that an inequality I is a *non-negative linear combination* of inequalities $I_1, \ldots, I_k$, if I is of the form $\alpha_1 I_1 + \cdots + \alpha_k I_k \geq 0$ where $\alpha_i \geq 0$ for $1 \leq i \leq k$, in this case we also write $I = \alpha_1 I_1 + \cdots + \alpha_k I_k$. It is easy to see that any non-negative linear combination of inequalities from $\mathcal{L}$ is implied by $\mathcal{L}$. An inequality I of the form $d_1 l_1 + \cdots + d_n l_n + c \geq 0$ *improves* an inequality I' if either I is $-1 \geq 0$ or I' is of the form $d_1 l_1 + \cdots + d_n l_n + c' \geq 0$ and $c' \geq c$.

Lemma 2.1. If an inequality I improves I' then I implies I'.

Proof. Let I be of the form $d_1 l_1 + \cdots + d_n l_n + c \geq 0$. If I is $-1 \geq 0$ then the lemma trivially holds. Assume I is not $-1 \geq 0$ and I' is of the form $d_1 l_1 + \cdots + d_n l_n + c' \geq 0$, where $c' \geq c$. Then $I' = I + (c' - c \geq 0)$, hence I implies I'.   ❏

Definition 2.2. *(Bounds).* A *bound on a literal* l is an inequality of the form $l + c \geq 0$. A pair of bounds $l + c_1 \geq 0$ and $\bar{l} + c_2 \geq 0$ on two complementary literals is *contradictory* if $c_1 + c_2 < 0$, in this case we will also say that $l + c_1 \geq 0$ *contradicts* $\bar{l} + c_2 \geq 0$. A *bound* is either a bound on a literal, or a trivial inequality. Trivial inequalities will also be called *trivial bounds*. A bound $l + c_1 \geq 0$ is said to *strictly improve* a bound $l + c_2 \geq 0$ if $c_2 > c_1$.   ❏

Definition 2.3. *(Context).* Let B be a finite set of non-trivial bounds. B is called a *context* if it contains no contradictory pair of bounds. A bound b is called *redundant* in B if some bound in B strictly improves b. We say that a *bound* b *contradicts to a context* B if some bound in B contradicts b.   ❏

By our definition contexts are always satisfiable. It is easy to see that a bound b is implied by a context B if and only if either $b \in B$ or b is redundant in B.

Our aim now is to introduce an inference system on linear inequalities. This inference system will have inference rules similar to those used in the resolution calculus. To emphasise the analogy to the resolution calculus we will use terminology similar to the one used in the theory of resolution.

For the readers familiar with the resolution calculus for propositional logic and the DPLL method we define a correspondence between the notions introduced in this paper and those used in propositional satisfiability in Table 1.

Definition 2.4 *(Resolution).* Let I_1, I_2 be linear inequalities such that I_1 has the form $d_1 x + I'_1 \geq 0$ and I_2 has the form $-d_2 x + I'_2 \geq 0$ for some variable x. We say that the linear inequality

$$d_2 I_1' + d_1 I_2' \geq 0$$

is a *resolvent of* I_1 *and* I_2 *upon* x. We consider resolvent as a symmetric relation, that is, a resolvent of I_1 and I_2 upon x is also a resolvent of I_2 and I_1 upon x. *Resolution* is the inference rule deriving a resolvent from two linear inequalities.   ❑

For example, consider two clauses $x_1 + 2x_2 + x_3 + 3 \geq 0$ and $-2x_1 - 3x_2 + 5 \geq 0$. Then their resolvent upon x_1 is $x_2 + 2x_3 + 11 \geq 0$ and their resolvent upon x_2 is $-x_1 + 3x_3 + 19 \geq 0$. Note that any resolvent of two inequalities is a consequence of these inequalities. Also note that resolution is compatible with equivalence on linear inequalities. That is if we replace inequalities in the premise of a resolution inference by equivalent inequalities then the conclusion of the new inference will be equivalent to the conclusion of the original inference.

Any application of resolution to a bound b and a linear inequality I eliminates a variable from I in the following sense: the variables of the resolvent are the variables of I minus the variable of b. Thus, if we repeatedly apply resolution to a linear inequality of n variables $x_1, \ldots, x_n$ and bounds on variables $x_2, \ldots, x_n$, all variables except x_1 in I will be eliminated and we will obtain a bound on x_1. We will formalise such repeated applications of resolution to a linear inequality and a sequence of bounds in the following definition.

Definition 2.5 *(Bound-Resulting Resolution).* Consider any linear inequality I of the form (1). Let b_i be bounds of the form $\bar{l}_i + c_i \geq 0$, where $i = 2, \ldots, n$, on literals complimentary to literals in I. Then one can derive (by a sequence of resolution inferences) from $b_2, \ldots, b_n$ and I the following bound b on l_1:

$$l_1 + (c + d_2 c_2 + \ldots + d_n c_n)/d_1 \geq 0.$$

We will say that b is obtained by *bound-resulting resolution* from $b_2, \ldots, b_n$ and I.

Likewise, let b_i be bounds of the form $\bar{l}_i + c_i \geq 0$, where $i = 1, \ldots, n$, on literals complimentary to literals in I. Then one can derive (by a sequence of resolution inferences) from $b_1, \ldots, b_n$ and I the following trivial inequality:

$$c + d_1 c_1 + d_2 c_2 + \ldots + d_n c_n \geq 0.$$

In this case we will also say that this trivial inequality is obtained by *bound-resulting resolution* from $b_1, \ldots, b_n$ and I.   ❑

We can consider resolution and bound-resulting resolution as inference rules and put together sequences of resolution steps to form a *derivation*, that is, a tree consisting of inferences. For example, the following

$$\frac{\dfrac{x_4 - 1 \geq 0 \quad x_3 - x_4 + 1 \geq 0}{x_3 \geq 0} \qquad -x_2 \geq 0 \quad x_4 - 1 \geq 0 \quad x_1 + x_2 - x_3 - x_4 \geq 0}{x_1 - 1 \geq 0}$$

$$(2)$$

is a derivation of the bound $x_1 - 1 \geq 0$ from two bounds $x_4 - 1 \geq 0$ and $-x_2 \geq 0$ and two inequalities $x_3 - x_4 + 1 \geq 0$ and $x_1 + x_2 - x_3 - x_4 \geq 0$. This derivation uses two bound propagation inferences.

By repeated applications of bound-resulting resolution we can repeatedly derive new bounds. Such repeated applications are formalised in the following definition.

Definition 2.6 *(Bound Propagation).* Let B be a context and $\mathcal{L}$ a system of linear in-equalities. A *bound propagation* from B and $\mathcal{L}$ is a sequence of bounds $b_1, \ldots, b_n$, such that

1. $n > 0$.
2. For all k such that $1 \leq k \leq n$, the bound b_k is not implied by $B \cup \{b_1, \ldots, b_{k-1}\}$.
3. For all k such that $1 \leq k \leq n$, the bound b_k is obtained by bound-resulting resolu-tion from $B \cup \{b_1, \ldots, b_{k-1}\}$ and an inequality in $\mathcal{L}$.

We will also use this definition in the case when b_n is a trivial inequality.   ❏

By collecting all inferences in a tree one can regard bound propagation as a derivation of the bound (or a trivial inequality) b_n from B and $\mathcal{L}$.

3 Collapsing Inequalities

In the DPLL procedure unit propagation always terminates since there is only a finite number of literals that can be derived. In the case of linear equalities the number of bounds is infinite, which may result in bound propagation of unrestricted length, deriv-ing better and better bounds. This is illustrated by the following example.

Example 3.1. Consider the context $\{x_1 \geq 0\}$ and the following two linear inequalities

$$x_2 - x_1 \geq 0 \tag{3}$$
$$x_1 - x_2 - 1 \geq 0 \tag{4}$$

Using $x_1 \geq 0$ and (3) one can derive a new bound $x_2 \geq 0$, from which, using (4) one can derive an improved bound $x_1 - 1 \geq 0$ on x_1. In a similar way from $x_1 - 1 \geq 0$ one can derive in two steps $x_1 - 2 \geq 0$, then $x_1 - 3 \geq 0$ etc.   ❏

In this section we will analyse bound propagation. First, we will show that any deriva-tion consisting of bound propagation steps using a collection of inequalities can be collapsed into a single bound-resulting resolution inference by adding a new inequality, called a *collapsing inequality*.

To explain the idea of collapsing inequalities consider derivation (2). It uses two inferences to derive the bound $x_1 - 1 \geq 0$ from the context $B = \{x_4 - 1 \geq 0, -x_2 \geq 0\}$. It also derives the bound $x_3 \geq 0$ on the variable x_3. If we resolve the inequalities $x_1 + x_2 - x_3 - x_4 \geq 0$ and $x_3 - x_4 + 1 \geq 0$ used in the derivation upon the variable x_3 we obtain a new inequality $x_1 + x_2 - 2x_4 + 1 \geq 0$. This inequality has the following interesting property: we can obtain the bound $x_1 - 1 \geq 0$ from the context B using a single inference

$$\frac{x_4 - 1 \geq 0 \quad -x_2 \geq 0 \quad x_1 + x_2 - 2x_4 + 1 \geq 0}{x_1 - 1 \geq 0}.$$

Thus, the new inequality $x_1 + x_2 - 2x_4 + 1 \geq 0$ makes derivation (2) *collapse* into a single inference.

Let us prove a general result on collapsing inequalities and then show how to extract collapsing inequalities from resolution and bound-resulting resolution proofs. We will use Farkas's Theorem stated in the following form.

Theorem 3.2 (Farkas). Let $\mathcal{L}$ be a system of linear inequalities. If $\mathcal{L}$ implies a linear inequality I then there is a linear non-negative combination of inequalities from $\mathcal{L}$ improving I. ❑

For a proof we refer to [7].

Theorem 3.3 (Collapsing Inequalities). Let $\mathcal{L}_1$ and $\mathcal{L}_2$ be two systems of linear inequalities such that $\mathcal{L}_1 \cup \mathcal{L}_2$ implies a linear inequality I. Then there exist two linear inequalities I_1 and I_2 such that

1. $\mathcal{L}_1$ implies I_1 and $\mathcal{L}_2$ implies I_2;
2. the system $\{I_1, I_2\}$ implies I.

Proof. By Theorem 3.2, if $\mathcal{L}_1 \cup \mathcal{L}_2$ implies a linear inequality I then there is a nonnegative linear combination of inequalities from $\mathcal{L}_1 \cup \mathcal{L}_2$ which implies I. This combination can be represented in the form

$$\alpha_1 J_1 + \cdots + \alpha_k J_k + \beta_1 G_1 + \cdots + \beta_m G_m,$$

where $J_i \in \mathcal{L}_1, \alpha_i \geq 0$ for $1 \leq i \leq k$ and $G_i \in \mathcal{L}_2, \beta_i \geq 0$ for $1 \leq i \leq m$.

We define $I_1 = \alpha_1 J_1 + \cdots + \alpha_k J_k$ and $I_2 = \beta_1 G_1 + \cdots + \beta_m G_m$. It is straightforward to check that I_1 and I_2 satisfy conditions 1–2 of the theorem. ❑

We will call inequalities I_1 and I_2 satisfying the conditions of Theorem 3.3 *collapsing* for I w.r.t. $\mathcal{L}_1$ and $\mathcal{L}_2$ respectively.

Let us show how to effectively extract collapsing inequalities from resolution proofs.

Theorem 3.4. Let $\mathcal{L}_1$ and $\mathcal{L}_2$ be two systems of linear inequalities and Π be a resolution (or a bound-resulting resolution) derivation of an inequality I from inequalities in $\mathcal{L}_1 \cup \mathcal{L}_2$. Then inequalities I_1 and I_2, collapsing for I w.r.t. $\mathcal{L}_1$ and $\mathcal{L}_2$ respectively, can be constructed in time polynomial in the size of Π.

Proof. Since any bound-resulting resolution derivation can be considered as a special case of a resolution derivation, we will only prove this theorem for resolution derivations.

The proof is by induction on the depth of Π. We will prove a slightly stronger, yet equivalent statement: our construction will also imply $I = I_1 + I_2$.

Base case. Suppose Π has I as the (only) leaf, then $I \in \mathcal{L}_1 \cup \mathcal{L}_2$. If $I \in \mathcal{L}_1$ then we define $I_1 \stackrel{\text{def}}{=} I$ and $I_2 \stackrel{\text{def}}{=} (0 \geq 0)$. The case $I \in \mathcal{L}_2$ is similar.

Inductive case. Let I be a conclusion of an inference in Π with premises J and G:

$$\frac{\begin{array}{cc} \Pi_1 & \Pi_2 \\ J & G \end{array}}{I}.$$

By the induction hypothesis, we can construct pairs of collapsing inequalities J_1, J_2 for Π_1 and G_1, G_2 for Π_2. Since I is obtained by resolution from J and G, we have that $I = \alpha J + \beta G$ for some coefficients $\alpha > 0$ and $\beta > 0$. Define $I_1 \stackrel{\text{def}}{=} \alpha J_1 + \beta G_1$ and $I_2 \stackrel{\text{def}}{=} \alpha J_2 + \beta G_2$. By the induction hypothesis, $\mathcal{L}_1$ implies $\{J_1, G_1\}$, hence $\mathcal{L}_1$ implies I_1. Likewise, we have $\mathcal{L}_2$ implies I_2. By the induction hypothesis we also have $J = J_1 + J_2$ and $G = G_1 + G_2$. It remains to prove $I_1 + I_2 = I$. To this end, note that $I_1 + I_2 = (\alpha J_1 + \beta G_1) + (\alpha J_2 + \beta G_2) = \alpha(J_1 + J_2) + \beta(G_1 + G_2) = \alpha J + \beta G = I$.

Let us note that with additional bookkeeping we can obtain an explicit representation for the collapsing inequalities I_1 and I_2 as non-negative combinations of inequalities from $\mathcal{L}_1$ ($\mathcal{L}_2$ respectively).   ❏

Let us now consider bound-resulting resolution inferences between a context B and a set of inequalities $\mathcal{L}$.

Theorem 3.5. Let b be a (possibly trivial) bound derived from a context B and a set $\mathcal{L}$ of linear inequalities by bound propagation. Then there exists a linear inequality I such that

1. $\mathcal{L}$ implies I, and
2. either (i) I is $-1 \geq 0$, or (ii) there is a bound b′ improving b which can be derived from B and I by a single bound-resulting resolution inference.

Moreover, the bound b' and inequality I can be constructed in time polynomial in the size of the derivation by bound propagation.   ❏

For the proof we refer to the full version of this paper. Let us only note that we can take I to be a collapsing inequality for b w.r.t. $\mathcal{L}$, which by Theorem 3.4, can be computed in polynomial time from the bound-resulting resolution proof of b.

4   Bound Propagation Algorithm

In this section we introduce the bound propagation algorithm for solving systems of linear inequalities, called BPA. BPA will be presented using a system of derivation (transition) rules which are applied to states of BPA. A *state* is a triple $(S, \mathcal{L}, \epsilon)$ where S is a sequence of annotated bounds, called *bound stack*, $\mathcal{L}$ is a system of inequalities and ϵ is either the empty set or a set consisting of one bound, called *conflicting bound*. We denote a state $(S, \mathcal{L}, \epsilon)$ as $S \parallel \mathcal{L}, \epsilon$ and in the case when $\epsilon = \emptyset$ as $S \parallel \mathcal{L}$. The bounds in S are annotated with information reflecting on how the bounds were introduced. Each bound b in S is either:

– a *decision bound*, denoted b^d, or
– a *propagation bound*, denoted as b^p.

We say that a bound b in S is *below* a bound b′ in S if b occurs before b′ (in the order of their occurrences in S), in this case b′ is also called *above* b. In other words, we consider the stack as growing upwards.

Every propagation bound in the stack will be obtained by bound propagation from bounds below it and linear inequalities in $\mathcal{L}$. Consider a bound stack S. Let b be a propagation bound in the stack. We refer to the corresponding bound-resulting resolution derivation of b from bounds below it as Π_b. Based on Theorems (3.4–3.5) we can calculate a collapsing inequality from Π_b, which we call *the collapsing inequality for b under S* and denote by CI_b, such that (i) CI_b is implied by $\mathcal{L}$ and (ii) a bound improving b can be derived by a single bound-resulting resolution inference from CI_b and decision bounds in S below b.

An *initial state* of BPA is a state of the form $S_0 \parallel \mathcal{L}_0$ where S_0 is the empty sequence, and $\mathcal{L}_0$ is the system of inequalities we want to solve. Let us state invariants on BPA states which will be preserved by BPA derivations. These invariants either trivially follow from the BPA rule definitions or will be proved later. Consider a BPA state $S \parallel \mathcal{L}, \epsilon$ which is obtained from an initial state by a sequence of applications of BPA derivation rules.

Invariant 1. The set of all bounds in S is consistent. In other words, we can consider S as a context.

We call a sequence consisting of a pair of bounds $\langle x - c \geq^d 0, -x + c \geq^d 0 \rangle$ a *decision pair* on x with the *decision value c*. To simplify the notation we will also write such a decision pair as x^c. If a stack contains a decision pair on x, we will call x a *decision variable* of this stack.

Invariant 2. S is of the form $U_0 \, x_1^{c_1} \, U_1 \ldots x_k^{c_k} \, U_k$ where $k \geq 0$ and (i) all $x_1^{c_1}, \ldots, x_k^{c_k}$ are decision pairs, (ii) each U_i contains no decision bounds for $0 \leq i \leq k$, (iii) for any variable x there is at most one decision pair on x in S. We say that bounds in U_i are implied bounds of the *decision level i* for $0 \leq i \leq k$, and the *decision level* of S is k.

Denote a restriction of the stack S to bounds below a decision pair x^c as $S_{<x^c}$ (including x^c as $S_{\leq x^c}$), or simply $S_{<l}$ ($S_{\leq l}$, respectively) when we are not concerned with the decision value and $var(l) = x$.

Invariant 3. Any propagation bound b in S is not implied by the set of the bounds below b.

Let us note that Invariants (2, 3) imply that if S contains a decision pair on a variable x then there are no bounds on x above this decision pair.

A bound b is called *decision-derived* from an inequality I and a stack S if either (i) both I and b are $-1 \geq 0$, or (ii) I is of the form $l + I \geq 0$, where all variables in I are decision variables in $S_{\leq l}$, and b either coincides with I, or is obtained by a single bound-resulting resolution inference from I and decision bounds in $S_{<l}$.

With each decision pair x^c in S we associate a pair of sets $BCI_x = \langle US_x, LS_x \rangle$ called a *bounding collapsing interval* on x with the following properties. The set LS_x (respectively, US_x) is either empty or consists of a single inequality L_x (respectively, U_x) of the form $x + I \geq 0$ ($-x + I \geq 0$, respectively), where all variables in I are decision variables in $S_{<x}$. We denote by lb_x the bound on x decision-derived from L_x and S, called the *lower collapsing bound* on x and similarly by ub_x the bound on x decision-derived from U_x and S, called the *upper collapsing bound* on x.

Invariant 4. For any decision pair x^c in S with the associated bounding collapsing pair BCI_x, inequalities in BCI_x are implied by $\mathcal{L}$.

For example, consider a system of inequalities $\mathcal{L}$:

$$-y + x - 2z + 3 \geq 0$$
$$y - x - 3z + 1 \geq 0$$
$$z \geq 0$$

and a stack

$$S = \langle z \geq^p 0, x^1, y^2 \rangle.$$

Assume that with the first decision pair we associated a bounding collapsing pair consisting of empty sets, and with the second the pair $\langle \{-y + x + 3 \geq 0\}, \{y - x + 1 \geq 0\} \rangle$. Invariant 4 is satisfied since both $-y + x + 3 \geq 0$ and $y - x + 1 \geq 0$ are implied by $\mathcal{L}$. Note that the assignment $\{y \mapsto 2\}$ satisfies the corresponding upper and lower collapsing bounds $ub_y = (-y + 4 \geq 0)$ and $lb_y = (y \geq 0)$.

Invariant 5. If ϵ consists of a conflicting bound b then b contradicts to a decision bound in S. With each conflicting bound b we associate a *conflicting collapsing inequality* $\mathtt{CCI_b}$ satisfying the following. Conflicting collapsing inequality $\mathtt{CCI_b}$ is implied by $\mathcal{L}$, and b is the bound decision-derived from $\mathtt{CCI_b}$ and S.

We define the *bound-propagation depth* of bounds in a bound-propagation derivation w.r.t. S inductively as follows. If a bound b is a decision bound in S or a bound in $\mathcal{L}$ then the bound propagation depth of b is $bpd(b) = 0$. If a bound b is obtained by a bound-resulting resolution inference from bounds $b_1, \ldots, b_k$ and an inequality in $\mathcal{L}$ then the bound-propagation depth of b is $bpd(b) = \max\{bpd(b_i) \mid 1 \leq i \leq k\} + 1$.

Invariant 6. We restrict bound-propagation depth of propagation bounds in S by an a priory fixed constant denoted $D \geq 0$.

During backjumping (rules (LBBC) and (UBBC)) we can resolve collapsing inequalities. In order to show that the number of such resolvents is finite we need a notion of the resolution rank.

The resolution rank of inequalities is defined by induction as follows. The set of inequalities of rank 0, denoted RI_0, consists of all inequalities in $\mathcal{L}$ together with all collapsing inequalities obtained from bound-propagation derivations of depth $\leq D + 1$, from $\mathcal{L}$ and a set of bounds. Assume that RI_k is defined then RI_{k+1} consists of all inequalities in RI_k together with all inequalities obtained by a single resolution inference from inequalities in RI_k.

Lemma 4.1. For any (finite) set of inequalities $\mathcal{L}$ and any non-negative integers D and k, the set RI_k is finite. ❑

The proof is given in [3].

Invariant 7. Consider the conflicting collapsing inequality $\mathtt{CCI_b}$ associated with a conflicting bound b of the form $l + c \geq 0$. Denote the number of all variables in $\mathcal{L}$ as $|var(\mathcal{L})|$ and the number of decision variables in $S_{\leq l}$ as $|var_d(S_{\leq l})|$. Then $\mathtt{CCI_b} \in RI_{|var(\mathcal{L})| - |var_d(S_{\leq l})|}$. Similarly, if x^c is a decision variable in S then $BCI_x \in RI_{|var(\mathcal{L})| - |var_d(S_{\leq x})|}$.

We define a *contradictory* BPA state as a special state denoted as $\perp$. Now we define the BPA derivation rules. When defining the rules, we assume by induction, that all invariants above are satisfied on the BPA states to which the rules are applied. Initial BPA states trivially satisfy the invariants.

Bound Propagation (BP)

$$S \parallel \mathcal{L} \Rightarrow_{BP} S\, b^p \parallel \mathcal{L}, \text{ where}$$

1. b is in $\mathcal{L}$, or obtained by bound propagation from S and $\mathcal{L}$,
2. $bpd(\mathrm{b}) \leq D$,
3. b is consistent with S,
4. b is not implied by S.

Decide (D)

$$S \parallel \mathcal{L} \Rightarrow_D S\,x^c \parallel \mathcal{L}, \text{ where}$$

1. x^c is a decision pair $\langle x - c \geq^d 0, -x + c \geq^d 0 \rangle$, such that
2. x is a variable in $\mathcal{L}$,
3. x is not a decision variable in S,
4. bounds $x - c \geq 0$ and $-x + c \geq 0$ are consistent with S and at least one bound in x^c is not implied by S.

In the Decide rule above, we associate with the introduced decision pair x^c a bounding collapsing pair $BCI_x = \langle US_x, LS_x \rangle$ where US_x and LS_x are defined as follows. If there is no lower bound on x in S then LS_x is the empty set. Otherwise, let $x - c' \geq 0$ be a lower bound on x in S which is not implied by any other bound in S. Note that $x - c' \geq 0$ is a propagation bound, since by conditions on the applicability of Decide, x is not a decision variable in S. Therefore $x - c' \geq 0$ is derived from $\mathcal{L}$ and decision bounds in S by bound propagation (of depth $\leq D$). We define $LS_x = \{CI_{(x-c' \geq 0)}\}$. The set US_x is defined similarly.

Conflicting Bound (CB)

$$S \parallel \mathcal{L} \Rightarrow_{CB} S \parallel \mathcal{L}, \{\mathrm{b}\}, \text{ where}$$

1. $(-1 \geq 0)$ is obtained by bound-resulting resolution from S and $\mathcal{L}$,
2. $CI_{(-1 \geq 0)}$ is the collapsing inequality for $(-1 \geq 0)$ under S, and
3. b is decision-derived from $CI_{(-1 \geq 0)}$ and S.

In the Conflicting Bound rule above, we associate with the bound b the conflicting collapsing inequality $CCI_\mathrm{b} = CI_{(-1 \geq 0)}$.

Contradiction ($\perp$)

$$S \parallel \mathcal{L}, \{-1 \geq 0\} \Rightarrow_\perp \perp$$

The next set of rules deals with the case when the conflicting bound b is a lower bound, i.e., of the form $x + c \geq 0$, these rules are (LBBV) and (LBBC). The case when the conflicting bound is of the form $-x + c \geq 0$ is similar and the corresponding rules are (UBBV) and (UBBC).

Lower Bound Backjump Value (LBBV)

$$V\,x^u U \parallel \mathcal{L}, \{x + c \geq 0\} \Rightarrow_{LBBV} V\,x^v \parallel \mathcal{L}, \text{ where}$$

1. $CCI_{(x+c \geq 0)}$ is of the form $x + I \geq 0$,

2. $x + c \geq 0$ is consistent with the upper bound ub_x,
3. define $BCI'_x = \langle US_x, \{\text{CCI}_{(x+c \geq 0)}\} \rangle$,
4. x^v is consistent with ub'_x and lb'_x corresponding to BCI'_x.

In the (LBBV) rule above, with the new decision pair x^v we associate the bounding collapsing pair BCI'_x.

We use the following notation. Consider two inequalities of the form $\text{I} = (x + I \geq 0)$ and $\text{J} = (-x + J \geq 0)$. Then the resolvent of I and J on x will be denoted as $\text{I} \otimes_x \text{J}$.

Lower Bound Backjump Conflict (LBBC)

$$V x^u U \parallel \mathcal{L}, \{x + c \geq 0\} \Rightarrow_{LBBC} V \parallel \mathcal{L}, \{\text{b}\}, \text{ where}$$

1. $\text{CCI}_{(x+c \geq 0)}$ is of the form $x + I \geq 0$,
2. $x + c \geq 0$ is inconsistent with the upper bound ub_x,
3. b is decision-derived from $\text{CCI}_{(x+c \geq 0)} \otimes_x U_x$.

In the (LBBC) rule above, with the new decision conflicting bound b we associate the conflicting collapsing inequality $\text{CCI}_{(x+c \geq 0)} \otimes_x U_x$.

The rules (UBBV) and (UBBC) below are defined similarly to (LBBV) and (LBBC).

Upper Bound Backjump Value (UBBV)

$$V x^u U \parallel \mathcal{L}, \{-x + c \geq 0\} \Rightarrow_{UBBV} V x^v \parallel \mathcal{L}, \text{ where}$$

1. $\text{CCI}_{(-x+c \geq 0)}$ is of the form $-x + I \geq 0$,
2. $-x + c \geq 0$ is consistent with the lower bound lb_x,
3. define $BCI'_x = \langle \{\text{CCI}_{(-x+c \geq 0)}\}, LS_x \rangle$,
4. x^v is consistent with ub'_x and lb'_x corresponding to BCI'_x.

In the (UBBV) rule above, with the new decision pair x^v we associate the bounding collapsing pair BCI'_x.

Upper Bound Backjump Conflict (UBBC)

$$V x^u U \parallel \mathcal{L}, \{-x + c \geq 0\} \Rightarrow_{UBBC} V \parallel \mathcal{L}, \{\text{b}\}, \text{ where}$$

1. $\text{CCI}_{(-x+c \geq 0)}$ is of the form $-x + I \geq 0$,
2. $-x + c \geq 0$ is inconsistent with the lower bound lb_x,
3. b is decision-derived from $\text{CCI}_{(-x+c \geq 0)} \otimes_x L_x$.

In the (UBBC) rule above, with the new decision conflicting bound b we associate the conflicting collapsing inequality $\text{CCI}_{(-x+c \geq 0)} \otimes_x L_x$.

A *BPA transition* is a transition by one of the BPA rules above, denoted as $\Rightarrow$. A *BPA derivation* is a sequence of BPA transitions starting from an initial state.

Let us remark on some properties of the BPA derivations. First we note that the set of inequalities $\mathcal{L}$ is never changed during the BPA derivations. Secondly, the number of inequalities at each state is linear in the number of variables and the number of input inequalities. Indeed, the only inequalities in a state are the input inequalities, inequalities in bounding collapsing pairs, which are at most double in the number of variables and at most one conflicting collapsing inequality. Thirdly, the order of variables is not fixed and can be dynamically changed during the BPA derivations. Fourthly, we can note that bounding collapsing pairs are used only during backjumping rules. Therefore in an implementation instead of computing BCI's for each decision variable, we can compute BCI's on demand during backjumping.

5   Example

We use a simplified notation for bounds: upper bounds of the form $-x - c \geq 0$ will be denoted as $-x \geq c$ and lower bounds of the form $x - c \geq 0$ as $x \geq c$.

Let us apply our BPA algorithm to the following set of inequalities $\mathcal{L}$.

$$x_0 - 2x_1 - 1 \geq 0 \tag{5}$$
$$x_0 + 2x_1 - 1 \geq 0 \tag{6}$$
$$-x_0 + x_1 \geq 0 \tag{7}$$

We have the following possible BPA derivation.

$$
\begin{array}{lll}
\| \mathcal{L} & \Rightarrow_D & \\
\langle x_0^0 \rangle \| \mathcal{L} & \Rightarrow_{BP}^{(6)} & \\
\langle x_0^0, x_1 \geq^p 1/2 \rangle \| \mathcal{L} & \Rightarrow_{CB}^{(5)} & (\mathrm{CCI}_{(x_0 \geq 1)} = (x_0 \geq 1)) \\
\langle x_0^0, x_1 \geq^p 1/2 \rangle \| \mathcal{L}, \{x_0 \geq 1\} & \Rightarrow_{LBBV} & (BCI' = \langle \emptyset, \{x_0 \geq 1\} \rangle) \\
\langle x_0^1 \rangle \| \mathcal{L} & \Rightarrow_{BP}^{(7)} & \\
\langle x_0^1, x_1 \geq^p 1 \rangle \| \mathcal{L} & \Rightarrow_{CB}^{(5)} & (\mathrm{CCI}_{(-x_0 \geq 1)} = (-x_0 \geq 1)) \\
\langle x_0^1, x_1 \geq^p 1 \rangle \| \mathcal{L}, \{-x_0 \geq 1\} & \Rightarrow_{UBBC} & (\mathrm{CCI}_{(-x_0 \geq 1)} \otimes_x (x_0 \geq 1) = (-1 \geq 0)) \\
\| \mathcal{L}, \{-1 \geq 0\} & \Rightarrow_\perp \perp &
\end{array}
$$

Let us informally explain the derivation steps. There are no bounds in $\mathcal{L}$ available for bound propagation, therefore only the Decide rule is applicable to the initial state, which adds decision bounds $x_0 \geq^d 0$ and $-x_0 \geq^d 0$ to the bound stack. With this decision pair we associate the empty bounding collapsing interval ($BCI_{x_0} = \langle \emptyset, \emptyset \rangle$). Now, the Bound Propagation rule is applicable resulting in a propagation bound $x_1 \geq^p 1/2$, derived from the decision bound $-x_0 \geq^d 0$ and inequality (6). Next, the contradictory bound $-1 \geq 0$ is derivable by bound-resulting resolution from bounds $-x_0 \geq^d 0$, $x_1 \geq^p 1/2$ and inequality (5) (transition $\Rightarrow_{CB}$).

We construct a collapsing inequality for this bound as in the proof of Theorem 3.4, in this case $\mathrm{CI}_{(-1 \geq 0)} = (x_0 \geq 1)$. Let us note that $x_0 \geq 1$ is implied by $\mathcal{L}$ (without using any decision bounds) and all variables in $x_0 \geq 1$ are decision variables in our bound stack. From $x_0 \geq 1$ we decision-derive the conflicting bound b, which in this case coincides with $x_0 \geq 1$. We associate with b the conflicting collapsing inequality $\mathrm{CCI}_{(x_0 \geq 1)} = (x_0 \geq 1)$.

By Invariant 5, the conflicting bound b contradicts to one of the decision bounds, in this case $-x_0 \geq^d 0$. Next we backjump to the decision that contradicts to b and try to modify the decision value within the bounding collapsing interval, such that the new decision bounds would not contradict to the conflicting inequality (transition $\Rightarrow_{LBBV}$). This is possible by taking a decision value for x_0 satisfying the new lower collapsing bound $lb'_{x_0} = (x_0 \geq 1)$, which is decision-derived from the new collapsing interval $BCI' = \langle \emptyset, \text{CCI}_{(x_0 \geq 1)} \rangle$. The new stack consists of the decision bounds $x_0 \geq^d 1$ and $-x_0 \geq^d -1$.

We apply the Bound Propagation rule adding $x_1 \geq^p 1$ to the stack. Next, the contradictory bound $-1 \geq 0$ is derivable and we analyse it as above. In this case it is not possible to modify the value of the decision variable x_0 in such a way as to satisfy both the conflicting inequality and collapsing bounds on x_0. This results in application of the (UBBC) rule which resolves the conflicting inequality ($\text{CCI}_{(-x_0 \geq 1)} = (-x_0 \geq 1)$) with the corresponding inequality from the bounding collapsing interval ($L_{x_0} = (x_0 \geq 1)$). The resulting conflicting collapsing inequality is $\text{CCI}_{(-x_0 \geq 1)} \otimes_{x_0} L_{x_0} = (-1 \geq 0)$. The corresponding conflicting bound is also $(-1 \geq 0)$.

After this step, the only applicable rule is the Contradiction rule. Note that conflicting collapsing inequalities are implied by $\mathcal{L}$, and therefore at the last step we have $\mathcal{L}$ implies $-1 \geq 0$, i.e., $\mathcal{L}$ is indeed unsatisfiable.

6 Correctness of BPA

Lemma 6.1. In any BPA derivation $\mathbb{S}_0 \Rightarrow \cdots \Rightarrow \mathbb{S}_n \Rightarrow \cdots$, all states $\mathbb{S}_0, \ldots, \mathbb{S}_n, \ldots$ satisfy Invariants (1–7).

Proof. We prove this lemma by induction on the length of the BPA derivation. Initial states satisfy the invariants since at these states the stack is empty and there are no conflicting bounds. Assume that the invariants hold for states $\mathbb{S}_0, \ldots, \mathbb{S}_{n-1}$. Let us show that the invariants also hold for $\mathbb{S}_n = S \parallel \mathcal{L}, \epsilon$.

Invariants (1–3) trivially follow from the definition of the BPA derivation rules.

Invariant (4) states that for any decision pair x^c in S, inequalities in BCI_x are implied by $\mathcal{L}$. This follows from the fact that inequalities in BCI_x are either collapsing inequalities for $\mathcal{L}$, or obtained from collapsing inequalities by a sequence of resolution inferences in both cases these inequalities are implied by $\mathcal{L}$.

Let us show that Invariant (5) holds at the state $\mathbb{S}_n$. First, let us note the conflicting collapsing inequality CCI_b is either a collapsing inequality w.r.t. $\mathcal{L}$, or obtained from collapsing inequalities by a sequence of resolution inferences, in both cases CCI_b is implied by $\mathcal{L}$. Now we show that the conflicting bound b contradicts to a decision bound in S. The only non-trivial cases are when $\mathbb{S}_n$ is obtained by one of the BPA rules (CB), (LBBC) or (UBBC). First we consider the (CB) rule. If b is of the form $-1 \geq 0$ then obviously b is itself contradictory. Assume that b is of the form $l + c \geq 0$ and b is decision-derived from $\text{CI}_{(-1 \geq 0)}$ of the form $l + I \geq 0$, where all variables in $\text{CI}_{(-1 \geq 0)}$ are decision variables. Let $\bar{l} + c' \geq 0$ be the decision bound in S which is used in the single bound-resulting inference deriving $-1 \geq 0$ from $\text{CI}_{(-1 \geq 0)}$. It is easy to see that b is contradictory with $\bar{l} + c' \geq 0$ and hence Invariant (5) is satisfied. Now we consider the (LBBC) rule. We have $\mathbb{S}_{n-1}$ is of the form $V x^u U \parallel \mathcal{L}, \{x + c \geq 0\}$ and $\mathbb{S}_n$ is of the form $V \parallel \mathcal{L}, \{b\}$. From the conditions on applicability of (LBBC) we have $x + c \geq 0$ is inconsistent with the upper bound ub_x on x and b is decision-derived from $\mathrm{CCI}_{(x+c \geq 0)} \otimes_x U_x$. We have $\mathrm{CCI}_{(x+c \geq 0)}$ is of the form $x + I \geq 0$, U_x is of the form $-x + U \geq 0$. The bound $(x + c \geq 0)$ is decision-derived from $\mathrm{CCI}_{(x+c \geq 0)}$ and inconsistent with the bound ub_x, decision-derived from U_x. Therefore, $\mathrm{CCI}_{(x+c \geq 0)} \otimes_x U_x$ is inconsistent with decision bounds in V. Since b is decision-derived from $\mathrm{CCI}_{(x+c \geq 0)} \otimes_x U_x$, b is inconsistent with a decision bound in V. The case of the (UBBC) rule is similar. Therefore Invariant (5) holds at the state $\mathbb{S}_n$.

Invariant 6 holds by conditions in the definition of the (BP) rule.

Let us show that Invariant 7 holds at $\mathbb{S}_n$. We need to consider the case when $\mathbb{S}_n$ is obtained by one of the following BPA rules: (D), (CB), (LBBV), (UBBV), (LBBC) and (UBBC). Note that by Invariant 6, bound propagation depth of all bounds in S is less or equal to D. Consider the (D) rule. In this case, all inequalities in BCI_x are collapsing inequalities obtained from bound propagation derivations of depth $\leq D$. Therefore inequalities in BCI_x are in RI_0 and Invariant 6 is satisfied. Consider the (CB) rule. The bound propagation depth of the derived $(-1 \geq 0)$ is less or equal to $D + 1$. Hence, $\mathrm{CCI}_b = \mathrm{CI}_{(-1 \geq 0)}$ is in RI_0 and Invariant 6 is satisfied. In the case of the rules (LBBV) and (UBBV) one of the bounding inequalities is replaced by a conflicting collapsing inequality which is by induction assumed to be of the required resolution rank. Now we consider the case of the rule (LBBC). We have $\mathbb{S}_{n-1}$ is of the form $V x^u U \parallel \mathcal{L}, \{x + c \geq 0\}$ and $\mathbb{S}_n$ is of the form $V \parallel \mathcal{L}, \{b\}$. Denote $S' = V x^u U$. Let the conflicting bound b be of the form $l + c' \geq 0$ where $var(l)$ is a decision variable in V. The conflicting collapsing inequality associated with b is $\mathrm{CCI}_{(x+c \geq 0)} \otimes_x U_x$. By the induction hypothesis, $\mathrm{CCI}_{(x+c) \geq 0}$ and U_x are in $RI_{|var(\mathcal{L})| - |var_d(S'_{\leq x})|}$. Hence, $\mathrm{CCI}_{(x+c \geq 0)} \otimes_x U_x \in RI_{|var(\mathcal{L})| - |var_d(S'_{\leq x})| + 1}$. Since $V_{\leq l}$ contains at least one decision variable less than $S'_{\leq x}$, namely x, we have $|var(\mathcal{L})| - |var_d(S'_{\leq x})| + 1 \leq |var(\mathcal{L})| - |var_d(V_{\leq l})|$. Therefore, $\mathrm{CCI}_{(x+c \geq 0)} \otimes_x U_x \in RI_{|var(\mathcal{L})| - |var_d(V_{\leq l})|}$ and Invariant 6 is satisfied. The case of the rule (UBBC) is similar. $\qed$

Theorem 6.2 (Termination). Any BPA derivation terminates. $\qed$

The proof is given in [3].

Theorem 6.3 (Soundness). If a BPA derivation terminates in a contradictory state $\perp$ then the initial system of inequalities $\mathcal{L}$ is unsatisfiable.

Proof Let us note that the system of inequalities $\mathcal{L}$ does not change during BPA derivations. A BPA derivation can result in the contradictory state $\perp$ only by applying the Contradiction rule ($\perp$). We have that the last step in such derivation is of the form $S \parallel \mathcal{L}, \{-1 \geq 0\} \Rightarrow_\perp \perp$. But in this case the conflicting collapsing inequality associated with $-1 \geq 0$ is contradictory, i.e., $\mathrm{CCI}_{(-1 \geq 0)} = (-1 \geq 0)$. By Invariant 5, $\mathrm{CCI}_{(-1 \geq 0)}$ is implied by $\mathcal{L}$, and therefore $\mathcal{L}$ is unsatisfiable. $\qed$

Before stating the Completeness theorem let us observe the following. Any BPA derivation that finishes at a state with a conflicting bound, i.e., of the form $S \parallel \mathcal{L}, \{b\}$, can be extended by applying one of the following rules: ($\perp$), (LBBV), (LBBC), (UBBV) or (UBBC).

Theorem 6.4 (Completeness). Consider a BPA derivation $\| \mathcal{L} \Rightarrow \mathbb{S}_1 \Rightarrow \cdots \Rightarrow \mathbb{S}_n$ such that $\mathbb{S}_n$ is a non-contradictory state of the form $S \| \mathcal{L}$ and neither the Decide rule (D) nor the Conflicting Bound rule (CB) is applicable to $\mathbb{S}_n$. Then the initial system of inequalities $\mathcal{L}$ is satisfiable.

Proof. Since the Decide rule is not applicable at the state $\mathbb{S}_n = S \| \mathcal{L}$, for any variable x in $\mathcal{L}$, x is either (i) a decision variable in S, or (ii) there are two implied bounds in S of the form $x - c \geq 0$ and $-x + c \geq 0$, called *value-implying bounds*. In the latter case we call c the *implied value* of x in S. Let us note that by Invariant 1, S is consistent. Therefore each variable has a unique decision or implied value. Define an assignment σ, mapping each variable into the corresponding decision/implied value. Let us show that σ satisfies each inequality in $\mathcal{L}$. Assume otherwise, and let I be an inequality in $\mathcal{L}$ which is not satisfied by σ. It is easy to see that in this case $(-1 \geq 0)$ can be obtained by a bound-resulting resolution inference from I and the bounds in S, resolving all literals in I with the corresponding decision/value-implying bounds in S. Therefore the Conflicting Bound rule is applicable to the state $S \| \mathcal{L}$, contradicting to our assumption. ☐

7 Conclusions

We presented a new method for solving systems of linear inequalities. The method incorporates DPLL-style techniques such as backjumping, lemma learning and bound propagation, which can be seen as an analogue of unit propagation in DPLL. Unlike unit propagation, bound-propagation can easily lead to non-termination if applied naively. We showed that our method is sound, complete and terminating.

References

1. Davis, M., Logemann, G., Loveland, D.W.: A machine program for theorem-proving. Commun. ACM 5(7), 394–397 (1962)
2. Korovin, K., Tsiskaridze, N., Voronkov, A.: Conflict resolution. In: Gent, I.P. (ed.) CP 2009. LNCS, vol. 5732, pp. 509–523. Springer, Heidelberg (2009)
3. Korovin, K., Voronkov, A.: Solving systems of linear inequalities by bound propagation, full version (2011), http://www.cs.man.ac.uk/~korovink/my_pub/
4. Marques-Silva, J.P., Sakallah, K.A.: GRASP: a search algorithm for propositional satisfiability. IEEE Trans. Computers 48(5), 506–521 (1999)
5. McMillan, K.L., Kuehlmann, A., Sagiv, M.: Generalizing DPLL to richer logics. In: Bouajjani, A., Maler, O. (eds.) CAV 2009. LNCS, vol. 5643, pp. 462–476. Springer, Heidelberg (2009)
6. Nieuwenhuis, R., Oliveras, A., Tinelli, C.: Solving SAT and SAT modulo theories: From an abstract Davis–Putnam–Logemann–Loveland procedure to DPLL. J. ACM 53(6), 937–977 (2006)
7. Schrijver, A.: Theory of Linear and Integer Programming. John Wiley and Sons, West Sussex (1998)

On Transfinite Knuth-Bendix Orders

Laura Kovács[1,*], Georg Moser[2], and Andrei Voronkov[3]

[1] TU Vienna
[2] Institute of Computer Science, University of Innsbruck
[3] University of Manchester

Abstract. In this paper we discuss the recently introduced *transfinite* Knuth-Bendix orders. We prove that any such order with finite subterm coefficients and for a finite signature is equivalent to an order using ordinals below ω^ω, that is, finite sequences of natural numbers of a fixed length. We show that this result does not hold when subterm coefficients are infinite. However, we prove that in this general case ordinals below ω^{ω^ω} suffice. We also prove that both upper bounds are tight. We briefly discuss the significance of our results for the implementation of first-order theorem provers and describe relationships between the transfinite Knuth-Bendix orders and existing implementations of extensions of the Knuth-Bendix orders.

1 Introduction

The Knuth-Bendix order (KBO for short) is the most common order used in first-order theorem provers. It is implemented in all commonly used resolution theorem provers: Vampire [15,19], E [16], Otter [21], Spass [20], and in the equational theorem prover Waldmeister [4]. Recently, Ludwig and Waldmann [11] introduced a modification of KBO, called *transfinite KBO* (*TKBO* for short), which can use arbitrary ordinals below ϵ_0 instead of natural numbers as symbols weights and subterm coefficients (we give all the necessary definitions in Section 3).

The TKBO can be more expressive than the KBO. However, the increase in expressiveness comes at the cost of a more complex implementation since one has to implement ordinals and two operations on them: the natural sum and the natural product. The natural product is especially hard to implement. One can get rid of the natural product by requiring that subterm coefficients are finite.

This paper is organised as follows. Section 2 gives a brief introduction into ordinals. In Section 3 we define the KBO and the TKBO. Our two main results are proved in Sections 4 and 6, as follows. In Section 4 we show that every instance of the TKBO on finite signatures with finite subterm coefficients is equivalent to a TKBO using ordinals below ω^ω, that is, sequences of natural numbers of a fixed length. Moreover, in Section 6 we prove that every instance

---

* The first author is supported by an FWF Hertha Firnberg Research grant (T425-N23). The second author is partially supported by FWF (P20133-N15). The third author is partially supported by EPSRC. This research was partly supported by the FWF National Research Network RiSE (S11410-N23).

N. Bjørner and V. Sofronie-Stokkermans (Eds.): CADE 2011, LNAI 6803, pp. 384–399, 2011.
© Springer-Verlag Berlin Heidelberg 2011

of the TKBO (with unrestricted subterm coefficients) is equivalent to a TKBO using ordinals below ω^{ω^ω}, that is, sequences of sequences of natural numbers. In Section 5 we show that these results cannot be significantly improved. Note that ordinals below ω^ω are relatively easy to implement. For example, such orders have been implemented in Vampire long ago. In Section 7 we discuss the use of KBO and TKBO in theorem provers and termination tools.

2   Preliminaries

We assume basic knowledge of set-theory, in particular of ordinals [5]. We write $>$ to denote the standard order on ordinals, and $<$ to denote the inverse of $>$. Recall that any ordinal $\alpha \neq 0$ can be uniquely represented in *Cantor normal form*, that is, written as a finite sum

$$\omega^{\alpha_1} + \cdots + \omega^{\alpha_n} ,$$

where $\alpha_1 \geqslant \cdots \geqslant \alpha_n$. Here $\geqslant$ denotes the usual total order on ordinals. We allow the sum in the above equation to be empty, that is, $0 = \omega^{\alpha_1} + \cdots + \omega^{\alpha_n}$ for $n = 0$.

For ordinals below ϵ_0, the Cantor normal form gives a basis for their syntactic representation: any such ordinal can be written in this form by recursively writing the exponents of ω in the same form. For every ordinal α, the set of ordinals strictly less than α is denoted by $\mathcal{O}(\alpha)$. Note that $\mathcal{O}(\alpha) = \alpha$, however we will use $\mathcal{O}(\alpha)$ when we consider α as a set rather than an element of an ordered collection. We will simply write $\mathcal{O}$ when $\alpha = \epsilon_0$, that is, $\mathcal{O}$ is the set of all ordinals strictly below ϵ_0. Recall, that ϵ_0 is the smallest solution of the equation $\alpha = \omega^\alpha$.

In the sequel we assume that all ordinals are represented using their Cantor normal form.

To motivate the definitions of *natural sum* and *natural product* given below, we recall that the standard ordinal addition $+$ and ordinal multiplication $\cdot$ are not commutative. Moreover, $\cdot$ does not right-distribute over $+$.

For $\alpha = \omega^{\alpha_1} + \cdots + \omega^{\alpha_n}$ and $\beta = \omega^{\alpha_{n+1}} + \cdots + \omega^{\alpha_{n+m}}$, we define the *natural sum* $\alpha \oplus \beta$ as $\omega^{\alpha_{\pi(1)}} + \cdots + \omega^{\alpha_{\pi(n+m)}}$, where π is any permutation of the indices $\{1, \ldots, n+m\}$ such that $\alpha_{\pi(1)} \geqslant \alpha_{\pi(2)} \geqslant \cdots \geqslant \alpha_{\pi(n+m)}$. Note that this definition includes the case that β is zero; so we have $\alpha \oplus 0 = 0 \oplus \alpha = \alpha$. Likewise, we define the *natural product* $\odot$ of ordinals in $\mathcal{O}$, as follows. For $\alpha = \omega^{\alpha_1} + \cdots + \omega^{\alpha_n}$ and $\beta = \omega^{\beta_1} + \cdots + \omega^{\beta_m}$, we define

$$\alpha \odot \beta = \bigoplus_{i=1}^{n} \bigoplus_{j=1}^{m} \left(\omega^{\alpha_i \oplus \beta_j} \right) .$$

Remark 2.1. The natural sum and product defined above are respectively called the *Hessenberg addition* and the *Hessenberg product* in [11].

We write $\alpha \cdot n$ as an abbreviation of $\underbrace{\alpha + \cdots + \alpha}_{n \text{ times}}$. Further, we identify the natural numbers with the ordinals below ω. For example, we write 3 instead of $\omega^0 + \omega^0 + \omega^0$.

The following lemma is an immediate consequence of the above given definitions.

Lemma 2.2. Let α, β, and γ be ordinals in $\mathcal{O}$. Then the following properties hold.

1. $\alpha \oplus \beta = \beta \oplus \alpha$.
2. $\alpha \odot \beta = \beta \odot \alpha$.
3. $\alpha \odot (\beta \oplus \gamma) = \alpha \odot \beta \oplus \alpha \odot \gamma$.
4. If $\alpha > \beta$, then $\alpha \oplus \gamma > \beta \oplus \gamma$. If, in addition, $\gamma > 0$, then $\alpha \odot \gamma > \beta \odot \gamma$. $\square$

3   Transfinite KBO

In what follows, we assume that $\mathcal{F}$ is a *finite signature*. We denote by $\mathbb{N}$ the set of natural numbers.

Definition 3.1. Let $\mathcal{F}$ be a signature. A *weight function* for $\mathcal{F}$ is a function $\mathsf{w} : \mathcal{F} \to \mathcal{O}$. A *subterm coefficient function* for $\mathcal{F}$ is a partial function $\mathsf{s} : \mathcal{F} \times \mathbb{N} \to \mathcal{O}$ such that for every $f \in \mathcal{F}$ and every $n > 0$, if n is less than or equal to the arity of f, then $\mathsf{s}(f, n)$ is defined and $\mathsf{s}(f, n) > 0$. A *precedence relation* on $\mathcal{F}$ is any (strict) total order on $\mathcal{F}$. $\square$

Definition 3.2 (order basis). An *order basis* is a tuple $(\mathsf{w}, \mathsf{s}, \gg, w_0)$ where:

1. w is a weight function for $\mathcal{F}$;
2. s is a subterm coefficient function for $\mathcal{F}$;
3. $\gg$ is a precedence relation on $\mathcal{F}$;
4. $w_0 \in \mathbb{N}$ and $w_0 > 0$;
5. for every constant $c \in \mathcal{F}$, we have $\mathsf{w}(c) \geqslant w_0$;
6. if $f \in \mathcal{F}$ is a unary function symbol and $\mathsf{w}(f) = 0$, then f is the greatest element in $\mathcal{F}$ w.r.t. $\gg$. $\square$

We will extend weight functions to variables and assume that $\mathsf{w}(x) = w_0$ for every variable x.

Given an order basis $(\mathsf{w}, \mathsf{s}, \gg, w_0)$, we define the *weight* of terms as follows.

Definition 3.3 (weight). Let t be a term. The *weight* of t, denoted by $weight(t)$, is defined inductively as follows.

1. If t is a variable, then $weight(t) \stackrel{\text{def}}{=} w_0$.
2. $weight(f(t_1, \ldots, t_n)) \stackrel{\text{def}}{=} \mathsf{w}(f) \oplus (\mathsf{s}(f, 1) \odot weight(t_1))$
$$\oplus \cdots$$
$$\oplus (\mathsf{s}(f, n) \odot weight(t_n)) \,.$$
$\square$

In the sequel we will often assume that we have a fixed order basis $(\mathsf{w}, \mathsf{s}, \gg, w_0)$.

The notion of the weight of a term is central for this paper. We will therefore introduce some notation and prove essential properties of term weights.

We will use the standard notion of a *position* in a term, and a *subterm* at a given position [2]. Any position is a sequence of positive integers. The empty position is denoted by ϵ.

Definition 3.4 (coefficient). Let t be a term and let p be a position in t. The *coefficient* of p in t, denoted by $coeff(p, t)$, is an ordinal defined inductively as follows.

1. $coeff(\epsilon, t) \stackrel{\text{def}}{=} 1$.
2. $coeff(i.p, f(t_1, \ldots, t_n)) \stackrel{\text{def}}{=} \mathsf{s}(f, i) \odot coeff(p, t_i)$. ❏

Let t be a term. We denote by $\mathcal{V}ar(t)$ the set of all variables of t, by $\mathsf{Pos}(t)$ the set of positions in t, and by $\mathsf{Pos}_\mathcal{V}(t)$ the set of variable positions in t. If p is a position in t, we denote by $top_p(t)$ the symbol (that is, a function symbol or a variable) of t at the position p. Let x be a variable. The set of positions of x in t is denoted by $\mathsf{Pos}_\mathcal{V}(x, t)$. We call the *variable coefficient* of x in t, denoted by $vcoeff(x, t)$, the ordinal $\bigoplus_{p \in \mathsf{Pos}_\mathcal{V}(x,t)} coeff(p, t)$.

Let us give a useful characterisation of weights of terms using *coeff*.

Lemma 3.5. For every term t we have

$$weight(t) = \bigoplus_{p \in \mathsf{Pos}(t)} coeff(p, t) \odot \mathsf{w}(top_p(t)).$$

Proof. By straightforward induction on the depth of t. ❏

Definition 3.6 (TKBO). Let $B = (\mathsf{w}, \mathsf{s}, \gg, w_0)$ be an order basis. The *instance of a transfinite Knuth-Bendix order induced by B*, denoted by $\succ_B$, is defined as follows. For all terms s, t, we have $s \succ_B t$ if the following conditions hold:

1. $\mathcal{V}ar(s) \supseteq \mathcal{V}ar(t)$;
2. for all $x \in \mathcal{V}ar(t)$,
$$vcoeff(x, s) \geqslant vcoeff(x, t) ; \tag{†}$$

3. either
   (a) $weight(s) > weight(t)$, or
   (b) $weight(s) = weight(t)$, and one of the following alternatives hold:
       i. t is a variable, and $s = f^n(t)$ for some unary function symbol f and $n > 0$;
       ii. $s = f(s_1, \ldots, s_n)$, $t = f(t_1, \ldots, t_n)$, and there exists $i \in \{1, \ldots, n\}$ such that $s_i \succ_B t_i$ and $s_j = t_j$ for all $1 \leqslant j < i$.
       iii. $s = f(s_1, \ldots, s_n)$, $t = g(t_1, \ldots, t_m)$, and $f \gg g$. ❏

We will sometimes simply write "a TKBO" instead of "an instance of a TKBO".

For every function whose range is a set of ordinals, we say that the function is *finite* if every value of this function is an ordinal below ω, that is, an element of $\mathbb{N}$. The *standard Knuth-Bendix order* (KBO) is a special case of the TKBO when the weight function is finite and the subterm coefficient function always returns 1. The TKBO is thus more expressive than the KBO, as it allows the use of infinite weight functions and arbitrary finite and infinite subterm coefficient functions.

We recall the following fact about the TKBO from [11].

Proposition 3.7. For any order basis B, the induced TKBO $\succ_B$ is a simplification order. That is, $\succ_B$ is monotone, closed under substitutions, well-founded, and extends the subterm relation. ❏

We will now give two lemmas formulating sufficient conditions for equality and inequality of instances of the TKBO.

In the sequel we will assume that $B = (\mathsf{w}, \mathsf{s}, \gg, w_0)$ and $B' = (\mathsf{w}', \mathsf{s}', \gg', w_0')$ are two order bases. Denote by *weight* and *weight'* the term weight functions defined respectively by B and B'. Likewise, denote by *coeff* and *coeff'* the coefficients, and by *vcoeff* and *vcoeff'* the variable coefficients defined respectively by B and B'.

Lemma 3.8. Suppose that (i) $\gg$ coincides with $\gg'$; (ii) for every two terms s and t and variable $x \in \mathcal{V}ar(t)$ we have $vcoeff(x, s) \geqslant vcoeff(x, t)$ iff $vcoeff'(x, s) \geqslant vcoeff'(x, t)$; and (iii) for every two terms s and t we have $weight(s) > weight(t)$ iff $weight'(s) > weight'(t)$.
    Then $\succ_B$ coincides with $\succ_{B'}$.

Proof. Immediate by Definition 3.6. ❏

Lemma 3.9. Suppose there exist two terms s and t such that $weight(s) > weight(t)$ and $weight'(t) > weight'(s)$.
    Then $\succ_B$ does not coincide with $\succ_{B'}$.

Proof. Let s, t be terms satisfying the conditions of the lemma. Take a fresh variable x and denote by u and v the terms obtained by replacing all variables in, respectively, s and t by x. Then $\mathcal{V}ar(u) = \mathcal{V}ar(v) = \{x\}$. Furthermore, as the weights of all variables are the same, we have $weight(u) = weight(s) > weight(t) = weight(v)$. Similarly, we conclude $weight'(v) > weight'(u)$.

Consider now the two possible cases. If $vcoeff(x, u) \geqslant vcoeff(x, v)$, we have $u \succ_B v$, but $weight'(v) > weight'(u)$ makes $u \succ_{B'} v$ impossible, so the two orderings do not coincide. Likewise, if $vcoeff(x, v) > vcoeff(x, u)$, we have $v \succ_{B'} u$, but $weight(u) > weight(v)$ makes $v \succ_B u$ impossible, so the two orderings do not coincide, too. ❏

4   TKBOs with Finite Subterm Coefficient Functions

In this section we consider TKBOs with *finite subterm coefficient functions*. Throughout this section we thus assume that $B = (\mathsf{w}, \mathsf{s}, \gg, w_0)$ is an order basis such that s is finite. The aim of this section is to prove that for every such basis, $\succ_B$ is equivalent to a TKBO using ordinals less than ω^ω. To this end, we will define a new basis $B' = (\mathsf{w}', \mathsf{s}, \gg, w_0')$ which agrees with B on the subterm coefficient function and the precedence relation, and show that B' induces the same transfinite Knuth-Bendix order as B.

Definition 4.1 (Γ_B). Let α be an ordinal such that $\alpha = \omega^{\alpha_1} + \cdots + \omega^{\alpha_n}$. Then we define $\Gamma(\alpha) \stackrel{\text{def}}{=} \{\alpha_1, \ldots, \alpha_n\}$. The collection of ordinals Γ_B is defined as $\Gamma_B \stackrel{\text{def}}{=} \Gamma(w_0) \cup \bigcup_{f \in \mathcal{F}} \Gamma(\mathsf{w}(f))$. ❏

In other words, Γ_B is the set of exponents used in w_0 and in the weights of symbols in $\mathcal{F}$. Since $\mathcal{F}$ is finite, clearly the set Γ_B is finite and totally ordered by $>$. This property is used in the next definition.

Definition 4.2 (rank function). We define a *rank function* $\phi \colon \Gamma_B \to \mathbb{N}$ as follows:

$$\phi(\alpha) \overset{\text{def}}{=} \max\{\phi(\beta) + 1 \mid \alpha > \beta, \beta \in \Gamma_B\} \,,$$

where we assume that $\max \varnothing \overset{\text{def}}{=} 0$. In other words, $\phi(\alpha)$ is the number of ordinals in Γ_B strictly smaller than α. Note that ϕ is only defined on elements of Γ_B. $\square$

The next lemma is a direct consequence of the previous definitions.

Lemma 4.3 (ϕ is monotone). Let $\alpha, \beta \in \Gamma_B$. Then $\alpha \geqslant \beta$ (respectively, $\alpha > \beta$) if and only if $\phi(\alpha) \geqslant \phi(\beta)$ (respectively, $\phi(\alpha) > \phi(\beta)$). $\square$

Note that, if $0 \in \Gamma_B$, then $\phi(0) = 0$. Likewise, if $i \in \mathbb{N} \cap \Gamma_B$, then $\phi(i) \leqslant i$.

Let us also make a trivial but useful observation on how to compare two weights given in Cantor normal form.

Lemma 4.4. Let

$$\alpha = \omega^{\alpha_1} + \ldots + \omega^{\alpha_k},$$
$$\beta = \omega^{\beta_1} + \ldots + \omega^{\beta_m}$$

be two non-zero ordinals in Cantor normal form. Then $\alpha > \beta$ if and only if $(\alpha_1, \ldots, \alpha_k) > (\beta_1, \ldots, \beta_m)$, where the sequences of ordinals are compared lexicographically. $\square$

We now define a new weight function w' and an ordinal w_0'.

Definition 4.5. Let $f \in \mathcal{F}$ and $\mathsf{w}(f) = \omega^{\alpha_1} + \cdots + \omega^{\alpha_n}$. Then we define

$$\mathsf{w}'(f) \overset{\text{def}}{=} \omega^{\phi(\alpha_1)} + \cdots + \omega^{\phi(\alpha_n)} \,.$$

Likewise, if $w_0 = \omega^{\alpha_1} + \cdots + \omega^{\alpha_n}$, then we define $w_0' \overset{\text{def}}{=} \omega^{\phi(\alpha_1)} + \cdots + \omega^{\phi(\alpha_n)}$. $\square$

Due to Lemma 4.3, note that the above expressions for $\mathsf{w}'(f)$ and w_0' are in Cantor normal form. Using Definition 4.5, we define $B' \overset{\text{def}}{=} (\mathsf{w}', \mathsf{s}, \gg, w_0')$.

Lemma 4.6. B' is an order basis.

Proof. Properties (1)-(3) of Definition 3.2 of order basis are obvious. Property (5) is derived by using Lemma 4.4 in conjunction with Lemma 4.3 on the monotonicity of ϕ. To prove property (6), take an arbitrary $f \in \mathcal{F}$. Let $\mathsf{w}(f) = \omega^{\alpha_1} + \cdots + \omega^{\alpha_n}$. Then $\mathsf{w}'(f) = \omega^{\phi(\alpha_1)} + \cdots + \omega^{\phi(\alpha_n)}$. Evidently, $\mathsf{w}(f) = 0$ holds if and only if $n = 0$, and likewise for $\mathsf{w}'(f) = 0$. Therefore, $\mathsf{w}(f) = 0$ if and only if $\mathsf{w}'(f) = 0$. From this property (6) follows immediately. By replacing f with w_0 is this proof, we obtain a proof of property (4). $\square$

Lemma 4.7. Let t be a term and $weight(t) = \omega^{\alpha_1} + \ldots + \omega^{\alpha_k}$. Then $weight'(t) = \omega^{\phi(\alpha_1)} + \ldots + \omega^{\phi(\alpha_k)}$. As a consequence, $weight'(t) < \omega^{\omega}$.

Proof. Straightforward from Lemma 3.5. ❏

Lemma 4.8. For all terms s, t of the signature $\mathcal{F}$, we have $s \succ_B t$ if and only if $s \succ_{B'} t$.

Proof. Use Lemma 3.8. Since properties (i) and (ii) of Lemma 3.8 are trivially satisfied, it suffices to prove for any two terms s and t, we have $weight(s) > weight(t)$ iff $weight'(s) > weight'(t)$.

Assume $weight(s) > weight(t)$. Let $weight(s) = \omega^{\alpha_1} + \ldots + \omega^{\alpha_k}$ and $weight(t) = \omega^{\beta_1} + \ldots + \omega^{\beta_m}$. By Lemma 4.4 we have

$$(\alpha_1, \ldots, \alpha_k) > (\beta_1, \ldots, \beta_m). \tag{1}$$

By Lemma 4.7 we have $weight'(s) = \omega^{\phi(\alpha_1)} + \ldots + \omega^{\phi(\alpha_k)}$ and $weight'(t) = \omega^{\phi(\beta_1)} + \ldots + \omega^{\phi(\beta_m)}$. Applying Lemma 4.3 on monotonicity of ϕ to (1) we obtain $(\phi(\alpha_1), \ldots, \phi(\alpha_k)) > (\phi(\beta_1), \ldots, \phi(\beta_m))$, which by Lemma 4.4 gives $weight'(s) > weight'(t)$. ❏

Lemmas 4.8 and 4.6 imply one of our main results for the case of finite weight coefficients.

Theorem 4.9. Every instance of a TKBO with finite weight coefficients is equivalent to an instance using weights in $\mathcal{O}(\omega^\omega)$. ❏

5 Lower Bounds on Ordinals

In Section 4 we showed that for a basis with finite subterm coefficients the induced TKBO $\succ_B$ is equivalent to a TKBO using ordinals less than ω^ω. In Subsection 5.1 of this section we will show that this result is essentially optimal. Then in Subsection 5.2 we prove a similar lower bound of ω^{ω^ω} for the general case.

To prove these results we will use *ordering constraints* (in the sequel simply *constraints*), that is, expressions $s \sqsupset t$, where s and t are terms. We say that an order $>$ *satisfies* such a constraint if $s > t$. The way we use constraints is the following. Suppose we have a family F of orders and an order $>$. Suppose also that $>$ satisfies a set S of constraints and each order in F violates at least one of the constraints in S. Then we can conclude that $>$ does not belong to F.

5.1 Finite Term Coefficients

Throughout this subsection we assume finite subterm coefficients. In this subsection a, b, c will denote constants; f, g, maybe with indices, unary function symbols; and h a binary function symbol.

We will now define, for every natural number k, a satisfiable set of constraints that can only be satisfied when the weight of one of the symbols is at least ω^k.

Example 5.1. Let $k \in \mathbb{N}$, $\mathcal{F} = \{c, h, f_0, \ldots, f_k\}$. Consider the set consisting of all the constraints $f_i(x) \sqsupset h(x, x)$, where $0 \leqslant i \leqslant k$, and the constraints $f_{i+1}(c) \sqsupset f_i^n(c)$, where $0 \leqslant i < k$ and $n \geqslant 0$. ❏

Lemma 5.2. There exists a TKBO $>$ with finite subterm coefficients satisfying all constraints of Example 5.1. Moreover, for every TKBO satisfying these constraints, we have $\mathsf{w}(f_i) \geqslant \omega^i$ for all $1 \leqslant i \leqslant k$.

Proof. To satisfy the constraints, we define the weights and subterm coefficients of h and c to be 1, the subterm coefficients of each f_i to be 2 and the weight of f_i to be ω^i, for all $0 \leqslant i \leqslant k$. We arbitrarily fix the value of w_0. It is not hard to argue that $weight(f_i^n(c)) < \omega^{i+1} < weight(f_{i+1}(c))$, so all the constraints $f_{i+1}(c) \sqsupset f_i^n(c)$ are satisfied. It is also easy to see that the constraints $f_i(x) \sqsupset h(x,x)$ are satisfied too.

For the second part, take any TKBO $\succ$ that satisfies all constraints of Example 5.1. First, we note that $f_i(x) \succ h(x,x)$ and condition (2) of the TKBO imply

$$\mathsf{s}(f_i,1) = vcoeff(x, f_i(x)) \geqslant vcoeff(x, h(x,x)) = \mathsf{s}(h,1) \oplus \mathsf{s}(h,2) \geqslant 2.$$

Therefore, the subterm coefficient of every f_i is not less than 2. This implies that for every term t we have $weight(f_i^n(t)) \geqslant 2^n \odot weight(t) \oplus 2^{n-1} \odot \mathsf{w}(f_i)$. As $weight(f_{i+1}(c)) \geqslant weight(f_i^n(c))$, we then have

$$\mathsf{w}(f_{i+1}) \oplus \mathsf{s}(f_{i+1},1) \odot \mathsf{w}(c) = weight(f_{i+1}(c)) \geqslant$$
$$weight(f_i^n(c)) \geqslant 2^n \odot \mathsf{w}(c) \oplus 2^{n-1} \odot \mathsf{w}(f_i).$$

Thus, we proved that for all natural numbers $n \geqslant 1$ we have

$$\mathsf{w}(f_{i+1}) \oplus \mathsf{s}(f_{i+1},1) \odot \mathsf{w}(c) \geqslant 2^n \odot \mathsf{w}(c) \oplus 2^{n-1} \odot \mathsf{w}(f_i). \tag{2}$$

Consider the case $i = 0$. In this case (2) implies

$$\mathsf{w}(f_1) \oplus \mathsf{s}(f_1,1) \odot \mathsf{w}(c) \geqslant 2^n \odot \mathsf{w}(c).$$

Since $\mathsf{s}(f_1,1)$ is finite, we have $\mathsf{w}(f_1) \geqslant (2^n - \mathsf{s}(f_1,1)) \odot \mathsf{w}(c)$ for all sufficiently large n. This implies $\mathsf{w}(f_1) \geqslant \omega$. Let us now prove $\mathsf{w}(f_{i+1}) \geqslant \omega^{i+1}$ for all $i = 1, \ldots, k-1$ by induction on i. To this end, note that for sufficiently large n we have $2^n \odot \mathsf{w}(c) > \mathsf{s}(f_{i+1},1) \odot \mathsf{w}(c)$. Hence, for sufficiently large n, inequality (2) implies

$$\mathsf{w}(f_{i+1}) \geqslant 2^{n-1} \odot \mathsf{w}(f_i).$$

The induction hypothesis gives $\mathsf{w}(f_i) \geqslant \omega^i$, so

$$\mathsf{w}(f_{i+1}) \geqslant 2^{n-1} \odot \mathsf{w}(f_i) \geqslant 2^{n-1} \odot \omega^i.$$

Since this holds for all sufficiently large n, we finally conclude $\mathsf{w}(f_{i+1}) \geqslant \omega^{i+1}$. ❏

The next theorem is a direct consequence of Lemma 5.2.

Theorem 5.3. For every natural number $k > 0$ there exists a TKBO $>$ with finite subterm coefficients satisfying the following conditions: (i) all function symbols have weights less than ω^{k+1}, and (ii) $>$ is not equivalent to any TKBO with finite subterm coefficients in which all function symbols have weights less than ω^k. ❏

Let us emphasise that the constraints defined in Example 5.1 are based on *finite* signatures.

5.2 Arbitrary Weight Coefficients

In the remaining part of this section we prove lower bounds for the case when *arbitrary subterm coefficient functions* are used. To this end, we use the condition (†) of Definition 3.6 to force higher ordinals as lower bounds.

Example 5.4. Consider the finite signature $\mathcal{F} = \{g, h, f_1\}$. We define the following set S_1 of constraints: $f_1(x) \sqsupset g^n(x)$ for all $n \geq 0$, and $g(x) \sqsupset h(x, x)$. ❑

We show that S_1 can only be satisfied when infinite subterm coefficient functions are used. More precisely, we show that the constraints of this example force $\mathsf{s}(f_1, 1) \geq \omega$.

Lemma 5.5. S_1 is satisfiable. For every TKBO satisfying S_1, we have $\mathsf{s}(f_1, 1) \geq \omega$.

Proof. To satisfy S_1, we set $\mathsf{w}(g) = 2$, and $\mathsf{w}(f_1) = \mathsf{w}(h) = w_0 = 1$. We also set $\mathsf{s}(f_1, 1) = \omega$, $\mathsf{s}(g, 1) = 2$, and $\mathsf{s}(h, 1) = \mathsf{s}(h, 2) = 1$.

Let us prove the second part of the lemma. Take any TKBO $>$ satisfying S_1. Property (†) of Definition 3.6 applied to $g(x) > h(x, x)$ implies $\mathsf{s}(g, 1) \geq 2$. Then $f_1(x) > g^n(x)$ implies $\mathsf{s}(f_1, 1) \geq 2^n$ for all n, hence $\mathsf{s}(f_1, 1)$ is infinite. ❑

Example 5.4 shows that we can force infinite values for the subterm coefficient functions. The next example uses ideas of Example 5.1 to define, for every positive integer k, constraints over a finite signature that require the use of subterm coefficient functions greater than ω^{ω^k}.

Example 5.6. Let $\mathcal{F} = \{g, h, f_1, \ldots, f_k, a, b\}$. Consider the set S_2 of constraints obtained from S_1 by adding, for every $1 \leq i < k$ and $n \geq 0$, the constraints $f_{i+1}(x) \sqsupset f_i^n(x)$, plus a single constraint $a \sqsupset f_k(b)$. ❑

Lemma 5.7. S_2 is satisfiable. For every TKBO satisfying S_2, we have $\mathsf{s}(f_i, 1) \geq \omega^{\omega^{i-1}}$ for all $1 \leq i \leq k$, and $weight(a) \geq \omega^{\omega^{k-1}}$.

Proof. To prove satisfiability, we arbitrarily fix the the constants a and b, and change the order basis of the proof of Lemma 5.5 by changing the weights of f_i as follows: $\mathsf{w}(f_i) = 1$ and $\mathsf{s}(f_i, 1) = \omega^{\omega^i}$, for all i. To verify that S_2 requires $\mathsf{s}(f_i, 1) \geq \omega^{\omega^{i-1}}$ for all i, we proceed inductively as before. Finally, $weight(a) \geq \omega^{\omega^{k-1}}$ follows from $weight(b) \geq 1$. ❑

The next theorem is a direct consequence of Lemma 5.7.

Theorem 5.8. For every positive integer k there exists a TKBO satisfying the following conditions: (i) all terms have weights less than $\omega^{\omega^{k+1}}$, and (ii) this TKBO is not equivalent to any TKBO in which terms have weights less than ω^{ω^k}. ❑

6 TKBOs with Unrestricted Subterm Coefficient Functions

Throughout this section we assume that $B = (\mathsf{w}, \mathsf{s}, \gg, w_0)$ is an order basis. We will show, using a modification of the construction used in Definition 4.5, that an *arbitrary TKBO* is equivalent to a TKBO using only ordinals less than ω^{ω^ω}. To do so, we first define an analogue of Γ_B given in Definition 4.1 as follows.

Definition 6.1. Let α be an ordinal such that $\alpha = \omega^{\alpha_1} + \cdots + \omega^{\alpha_n}$, where $\alpha_i = \omega^{\beta_{i1}} + \cdots + \omega^{\beta_{im_i}}$ for each $i \in \{1, \ldots, n\}$. We define $\Delta(\alpha) \stackrel{\text{def}}{=} \{\beta_{11}, \ldots, \beta_{1m_1}, \ldots, \beta_{n1}, \ldots, \beta_{nm_n}\}$. Further, the collection of ordinals Δ_B is defined as:

$$\Delta_B \stackrel{\text{def}}{=} \Delta(w_0) \cup \bigcup_{f \in \mathcal{F}} \Delta(\mathsf{w}(f)) \cup \bigcup_{f \in \mathcal{F}, i \in \mathbb{N}} \Delta(\mathsf{s}(f, i)) . \qquad \square$$

In other words, Δ_B is the set of exponents of the exponents used in w_0, in the weights of symbols in $\mathcal{F}$, and in the subterm coefficient functions. Clearly, Δ_B is finite and totally ordered by $>$. Without loss of generality, we assume that $0 \in \Delta_B$.

We next refine the definition of the mapping ϕ given in Definition 4.2.

Definition 6.2. We define a rank function $\psi \colon \Delta_B \to \mathbb{N}$ as follows:

$$\psi(\alpha) \stackrel{\text{def}}{=} \max\{\psi(\beta) + 1 \mid \alpha > \beta, \beta \in \Delta_B\} ,$$

where we set $\max \varnothing \stackrel{\text{def}}{=} 0$. $\qquad \square$

Using the function ψ, below we define an ordinal basis $B' = (\mathsf{w}', \mathsf{s}', \gg, w_0')$ using only ordinals in $\mathcal{O}(\omega^{\omega^\omega})$, and then prove that it defines a TKBO equivalent to B. To this end, we will first develop some results about ordinals.

Definition 6.3. Denote by $\mathcal{O}_B$ the set of all ordinals having the form

$$\omega^{\omega^{\beta_{11}} + \cdots + \omega^{\beta_{1m_1}}} + \cdots + \omega^{\omega^{\beta_{n1}} + \cdots + \omega^{\beta_{nm_n}}} + \omega k + m . \qquad (3)$$

where for all $1 \leqslant i \leqslant n$, $1 \leqslant j \leqslant m_i$, $\beta_{ij} \in \Delta_B$. Note that the set $\mathcal{O}_B$ is closed under $\oplus$ and $\odot$. We define an *ordinal mapping* γ with the domain $\mathcal{O}_B$ as follows. For every ordinal α of the form (3) we have

$$\gamma(\alpha) \stackrel{\text{def}}{=} \omega^{\omega^{\psi(\beta_{11})} + \cdots + \omega^{\psi(\beta_{1m_1})}} + \cdots + \omega^{\omega^{\psi(\beta_{n1})} + \cdots + \omega^{\psi(\beta_{nm_n})}} + \omega k + m . \qquad \square$$

The following lemma is the key for all proofs of this section.

Lemma 6.4. The mapping γ defines an isomorphic embedding of the ordered algebra of ordinals $\mathcal{O}_B$ into $\mathcal{O}$, that is, for every pair (α_1, α_2) of ordinals we have
$$\gamma(\alpha_1 \oplus \alpha_2) = \gamma(\alpha_1) \oplus \gamma(\alpha_2),$$
$$\gamma(\alpha_1 \odot \alpha_2) = \gamma(\alpha_1) \odot \gamma(\alpha_2),$$
$$\alpha_1 \geqslant \alpha_2 \text{ iff } \gamma(\alpha_1) \geqslant \gamma(\alpha_2). \qquad \square$$

The proof of this lemma is straightforward and left to the reader.

Using γ, we can now define the order base B' which will give us the required order.

Definition 6.5. Define the order basis $B' = (\mathsf{w}', \mathsf{s}', \gg, w'_0)$ having the same precedence relation $\gg$ as B, as follows. Let $f \in \mathcal{F}$. Then $\mathsf{w}'(f) \overset{\text{def}}{=} \gamma(\mathsf{w}(f))$. Further, let i be a positive integer less than or equal to the arity of f. Then $\mathsf{s}'(f, i) \overset{\text{def}}{=} \gamma(\mathsf{s}(f, i))$. Finally, we let $w'_0 \overset{\text{def}}{=} \gamma(w_0)$. ❏

As usual, we will respectively denote by *coeff'*, *vcoeff'*, and *weight'* the functions *coeff*, *vcoeff*, and *weight* induced by B'. The following result is then straightforward.

Lemma 6.6. B' is an order basis. For all terms t, we have $weight'(t) < \omega^{\omega^\omega}$. ❏

It remains to prove that B' defines the same order as B. To this end, we will use Lemma 6.4.

Lemma 6.7. Let t be a term, x be a variable, and p a position in s. Then we have the following.

1. $coeff'(p, t) = \gamma(coeff(p, t))$;
2. $vcoeff'(v, t) = \gamma(vcoeff(v, t))$;
3. $weight'(t) = \gamma(weight(t))$.

Proof. (1) is immediate by the definition of *coeff* and Lemma 6.4. (2) is immediate by the definition of *vcoeff*, (1) and Lemma 6.4. (3) is immediate by the definition of *weight*, (1) and Lemma 6.4. ❏

Lemma 6.8. For all s, t, we have $s \succ_B t$ if and only if $s \succ_{B'} t$.

Proof. Immediate by the definition of TKBO and Lemmas 6.4 and 6.7. ❏

Lemma 6.8 implies the main result of this paper given below.

Theorem 6.9. Every instance of a TKBO is equivalent to an instance using weights in $\mathcal{O}(\omega^{\omega^\omega})$. ❏

7   Notes on Implementation and Applications

Knuth-Bendix orders have two main applications: automatic proofs of termination and first-order theorem proving. In termination tools, one automatically seeks orders that orient a given set of rewrite rules. For that purpose one can use the ordering algorithm of Korovin and Voronkov [7] to decide whether a given set of rules is compatible with a KBO – see also related results by Zankl et al. in [22].

The transfinite KBO has not been used for this purpose so far. The standard KBO ordering problem can be reduced to a problem of finding weights of symbols and precedences satisfying some conditions that turn out to be decidable (and even solvable in polynomial time). For transfinite KBOs the problem is much

Table 1. Performance of the TKBO in Vampire on Hard Problems

Order	Solvable only by such orders	30 seconds difference	10 seconds difference
KBO	163	32	110
TKBO	342	59	190

more complex, since subterm coefficients create non-linear inequalities and there is no clear way of searching for ordinals instead of numbers. Our results shed some light on the problem and essentially show that it is sufficient to search for "small" ordinals only, but it is not clear also how the search for such small ordinals can be implemented. This can be a subject of future work.

It is interesting that simple variants of the transfinite KBO have been implemented in theorem provers before paper [11] describing them appeared. The theorem prover Otter [21] allowed for arbitrary finite subterm coefficient functions. The resulting instances of the KBO were not transfinite since the weights were always finite. We do not know exactly when such subterm coefficient functions first appeared in Otter, but they were available already in 1994 (see [13], sections 5.4 and 8.1).

Later in 2004 such orders were implemented in Vampire and immediately abandoned. The reason was that the use of weight coefficient 2 resulted in integer arithmetic overflows. We asked Bill McCune [12] whether he observed a similar behavior in Otter. He replied that Otter uses ordinary C "int"s (that were 32 bits at the time), yet he "have never noticed it, and no one has ever complained about it". He also pointed out that Otter's weighting is used only for very simple things, mainly for slight adjustments to the default weight (symbol count).

Since integer overflow results in incorrect ordering comparisons, using weight coefficients greater than 1 requires the use of arbitrary precision integers. We decided not to use such weight coefficients in Vampire for efficiency reasons. Indeed, theorem provers sometimes make millions of KBO comparisons in a short time, and these comparisons may take considerable time [10]. Therefore, modern theorem provers use a linear KBO comparison algorithm of [10]. Using arbitrary-precision integers incurs potential performance degradation both in time and space.

Nonetheless, a simple special case of TKBO was implemented in Vampire [15,19] in 1996, and already used in the version of 1999, winning CASC-16 [17]. In Vampire, comparison of atoms is done in the following way. Each predicate symbol is assigned, in addition to the precedence and weight, a *level*, which is a non-negative integer. When we compare two atoms $p(s_1, \ldots, s_m)$ and $q(t_1, \ldots, t_n)$, we first compare the levels of p and q. If the level of p is greater, we decide $p(s_1, \ldots, s_m) \succ q(t_1, \ldots, t_n)$. If we compare two atoms having predicates of the same level, we apply the ordinary KBO. One can see that this way of ordering atoms corresponds to using a TKBO where the weight of a predicate symbol p is $\omega \cdot l + w$, where l is the level and w the weight of p. This ordering scheme is also convenient for the following reason: the use of orders in superposition-based provers normally requires that equalities be smaller than non-equality atoms. We achieve this by assigning equality level 0 and using positive levels for all other

Table 2. Use of Strategies in the CASC Version of Vampire

Category	TKBO	KBO
CNF, non-Horn, with equality (NEQ)	35	28
CNF, Horn, with equality (HEQ)	7	9
CNF, non-Horn, without equality (NNE)	16	3
First-order, with equality (FEQ)	145	79
First-order, without equality (FNE)	10	4
Total	213	123

predicates. This means that Vampire uses a special case of the TKBO with ordinals below ω^2 and subterm coefficient always set to 1. We will now present some statistics showing that the use of such ordinals is essential in Vampire's performance.

Hard problems. We have a database containing results of running various proving strategies of Vampire on TPTP problems [18]. We selected all problems solvable by Vampire and belonging to categories having predicate symbols different from equality (otherwise, the use of levels makes no difference). There are 8019 such problems. This set of problems contains many very hard problems: 652 problems, for example, have the TPTP rating greater than 0.91 which, in most cases, means that these problems are solvable by only one theorem prover.

The database contains results of 1,351,630 test runs of Vampire on these problems. Most of the runs use 60 seconds time limits, but there are other runs ranging from 30 seconds to 3 minutes time limits. It is common in theorem proving that solvable problems are solved by at least one strategy in a very short time (a few seconds) but there are many exceptions.

Table 1 shows the number of problems on which KBO is considerably better than TKBO and vice versa. It turned out that there are 342 problems solvable only by TKBO and 163 problems solvable only by KBO. That is, the 163 problems solvable only by the KBO could not be solved using a TKBO where the subterm coefficient function is not set to 1 and the weight function is not finite. We also considered problems solvable both by the KBO and the TKBO but on which the difference between the best KBO and TKBO results is more than 30 seconds (10 seconds). It turned out that on such problems the TKBO also behaves considerably better than the KBO.

Use of strategies in the CASC version of Vampire. Since 1999, Vampire won 23 World Champion titles in various divisions of CASC. The 2010 version won in three divisions. Given a problem, Vampire runs on it a sequence of strategies, depending on the syntactic class of the problem. For each class of problems (i.e. category) we selected a collection of proving strategies that turned out to be the best on this class in our test runs before the competition. Each strategy uses exactly one instance of the KBO or the TKBO.

Table 2 summarises the number of strategies using, respectively, the KBO and the TKBO. It turns out that the number of strategies using the TKBO is almost double the number of strategies using the KBO. The difference is especially big on problems without equality.

Note that Vampire does not implement the full TKBO with ordinals below ω^2 since function symbols only have finite weights. Nonetheless, Vampire was probably the first first-order prover using a TKBO with infinite ordinals in CASC. The usage of limited forms of the TKBO in Vampire suggests that other forms of the TKBO may turn out to be useful for solving hard problems. The TKBO with finite subterm coefficients turned out to be also very useful in [1] for proving algebraic problems by combining resolution theorem proving with quantifier elimination over real closed fields.

Our theoretical results show that one does not need very complex ordinals to obtain arbitrarily complex instances of the TKBO. However, we think it is unrealistic to expect TKBOs with arbitrary subterm coefficients to be used in first-order theorem provers since the overhead of implementing ordinals in $\mathcal{O}$ and especially their natural product is too high. Moreover, as we pointed out, even the use of finite subterm coefficient functions requires arbitrary precision integers. However, implementing TKBOs with ordinals below ω^k for small k (sequences of k non-negative integers ordered lexicographically) and subterm coefficients set to 1 seems relatively inexpensive and requires more experiments to be understood. We believe it makes sense to make experiments in this area since in practice in first-order provers KBO behaves much better than LPO. For example, Waldmeister [4] selects LPO only on a small handful of problems (Waldmeister implements both kinds of orderings and is known for its extensive experiments with finding best orderings and strategies).

One potential use of instances of the TKBO below ω^k would be to assign large weights to symbols "close" to the goal. The theorem prover E [16] has a similar strategy (though based on finite ordinals only); likewise, Vampire chooses the level of a predicate symbol based on the "distance" between the symbol and symbols occurring in the goal. However, to the best of our knowledge nobody so far used TKBO instances in which function (not predicate) symbols have infinite weights. Checking whether a potential gain from using TKBOs outweighs performance overhead arising from their use is an interesting subject for future work.

Yet another potential use of the TKBO is automated termination proofs of sets of rewrite rules that are currently outside the scope of termination tools. Such set R is given for example as an early formalisation of the battle of Hydra and Hercules [6]. The system R, introduced in [3], withstands any attempt so far in proving its termination automatically. The reason is that the termination proof necessarily needs interpretations into $\mathcal{O}$ [14]. Due to our results we cannot hope to define generalisations of TKBO that are compatible with R. Even if we would allow for ordinal weights greater or equal to ϵ_0, our result imply that we cannot use this additional power. However, the TKBO may be successfully applied on restrictions.

It is also worth noting that the use of a TKBO with ordinals below ω^3 was essential in the applications of Vampire in interpolation [9] and loop invariant generation [8].

8 Conclusion

We proved two main results related to the use of transfinite Knuth-Bendix orders with finite signatures. First, we proved that any such order with finite subterm coefficients is equivalent to an order using ordinals below ω^ω, that is, finite sequences of natural numbers of a fixed length. Second, we proved that any such order is equivalent to an order using ordinals below ω^{ω^ω}. We also proved that the ω^ω and ω^{ω^ω} bounds are tight. Our results show that transfinite Knuth-Bendix orders based on arbitrarily complex ordinals below ϵ_0 can be replaced by such orders using simpler ordinals. For example, when searching for an instance of the TKBO ordering a rewrite rule system, it is enough to search only for such instances using ordinals below ω^{ω^ω}.

We also discuss application and implementation issues of extensions of the Knuth-Bendix orders in first-order theorem provers.

Acknowledgements. We thank reviewers, including Uwe Waldmann, for pointing out technical problems in the previous version of the paper.

References

1. Akbarpour, B., Paulson, L.C.: MetiTarski: An Automatic Theorem Prover for Real-Valued Special Functions. J. of Automated Reasoning 44(3), 175–205 (2010)
2. Baader, F., Nipkow, T.: Term Rewriting and All That. Cambridge University Press, Cambridge (1998)
3. Dershowitz, N., Jouannaud, J.P.: Rewrite Systems, pp. 245–319 (1990)
4. Gaillourdet, J.-M., Hillenbrand, T., Löchner, B., Spies, H.: The New Waldmeister Loop at Work. In: Proc. of CADE, pp. 317–321 (2003)
5. Jech, T.: Set Theory. Springer, Heidelberg (2002)
6. Kirby, L., Paris, J.: Accessible Independence Results for Peano Arithmetic. Bulletin London Mathematical Society 4, 285–293 (1982)
7. Korovin, K., Voronkov, A.: Orienting Equalities with the Knuth-Bendix Order. In: Proc. of LICS, pp. 75–84 (2003)
8. Kovacs, L., Voronkov, A.: Finding Loop Invariants for Programs over Arrays Using a Theorem Prover. In: Chechik, M., Wirsing, M. (eds.) FASE 2009. LNCS, vol. 5503, Springer, Heidelberg (2009)
9. Kovács, L., Voronkov, A.: Interpolation and symbol elimination. In: Schmidt, R.A. (ed.) CADE-22. LNCS, vol. 5663, pp. 199–213. Springer, Heidelberg (2009)
10. Löchner, B.: Things to Know when Implementing KBO. J. of Automated Reasoning 36(4), 289–310 (2006)
11. Ludwig, M., Waldmann, U.: An extension of the knuth-bendix ordering with LPO-like properties. In: Dershowitz, N., Voronkov, A. (eds.) LPAR 2007. LNCS (LNAI), vol. 4790, pp. 348–362. Springer, Heidelberg (2007)
12. McCune, B.: Private Communication (September 2004)
13. McCune, W.W.: OTTER 3.0 Reference Manual and Guide. Technical Report ANL-94/6, Argonne National Laboratory (January 1994)
14. Moser, G.: The Hydra Battle and Cichon's Principle. AAECC 20(2), 133–158 (2009)

15. Riazanov, A., Voronkov, A.: The Design and Implementation of Vampire. AI Communications 15(2-3), 91–110 (2002)
16. Schulz, S.: System Description: E 0.81. In: Proc. of IJCAR, pp. 223–228 (2004)
17. Sutcliffe, G.: The CADE-16 ATP System Competition. J. of Automated Reasoning 24(3), 371–396 (2000)
18. Sutcliffe, G.: The TPTP Problem Library and Associated Infrastructure. The FOF and CNF Parts, v3.5.0. J. of Automated Reasoning 43(4), 337–362 (2009)
19. Vampire's homepage, http://www.vprover.org/
20. Weidenbach, C., Schmidt, R.A., Hillenbrand, T., Rusev, R., Topic, D.: System description: SPASS version 3.0. In: Pfenning, F. (ed.) CADE 2007. LNCS (LNAI), vol. 4603, pp. 514–520. Springer, Heidelberg (2007)
21. Wos, L.: Milestones for Automated Reasoning with Otter. Int. J. on Artificial Intelligence Tools 15(1), 3–20 (2006)
22. Zankl, H., Hirokawa, N., Middeldorp, A.: KBO orientability. JAR 43(2), 173–201 (2009)

Scala to the Power of Z3:
Integrating SMT and Programming

Ali Sinan Köksal, Viktor Kuncak, and Philippe Suter⋆

École Polytechnique Fédérale de Lausanne (EPFL), Switzerland
`firstname.lastname@epfl.ch`

Abstract. We describe a system that integrates the SMT solver Z3 with
the Scala programming language. The system supports the use of the
SMT solver for checking satisfiability, unsatisfiability, as well as solution
enumeration. The embedding of formula trees into Scala uses the host
type system of Scala to prevent the construction of certain ill-typed constraints. The solution enumeration feature integrates into the iteration
constructions of Scala and supports writing non-deterministic programs.
Using Z3's mechanism of theory extensions, our system also helps users
construct custom constraint solvers where the interpretation of predicates and functions is given as Scala code. The resulting system preserves the productivity advantages of Scala while simplifying tasks such
as combinatorial search.

1 Introduction

Satisfiability Modulo Theories (SMT) solvers have in the past few years become
very powerful tools. Their efficient search heuristics have made them applicable
to a wide variety of problems. However, they are still primarily used by *expert*
users that have substantial understanding of constraint solvers, their languages
and interfaces. Our aim is to make SMT solving accessible to a wider audience
by integrating it into a familiar programming language.

This paper presents Scala^{Z3}, a library to bring the power of the SMT solver
Z3 [3] to users of the Scala programming language [4]. We identify two types of
clients for our system:

- general programmers, who are not necessarily familiar with SMT, but who
  may want to use constraint solving as a library;
- SMT power users, who can use it in a way similar to how they would in C,
  yet will still benefit from a concise language with a strong type system.

2 Implicit Computation Using Z3

Our system enables programmers to state the properties that the values should
satisfy instead of how to compute them. In that sense, it supports a form of
implicit computation. We illustrate this approach through several examples.

⋆ Alphabetical author order. Philippe Suter was supported by the Swiss NSF Grant
200021_120433.

N. Bjørner and V. Sofronie-Stokkermans (Eds.): CADE 2011, LNAI 6803, pp. 400–406, 2011.

Mixing searching with solving. Consider the following satisfiability problem: *Find three integers* x, y, z *such that* $x > 0$, $y > x$, $2x + 3y \leq 40$, $x \cdot z = 3y^2$, *and* y *is prime?* We know of no decidable logic in which this problem can be naturally expressed. As an alternative to applying a decision procedure, we can search for a solution. Using the system we present in this paper, we can concisely program the search in Scala as follows:

```
val results = for(
    (x,y) ← findAll((x: Val[Int], y: Val[Int]) ⇒ x > 0 && y > x && x * 2 + y * 3 ≤ 40);
    if(isPrime(y));
    z ← findAll((z: Val[Int]) ⇒ z * x === 3 * y * y))
        yield (x, y, z)
```

This for-comprehension constructs an iterator of integer triples. The iterator ranges over all solutions (in general, it can be infinite, here there are 8 solutions). The for-comprehension interleaves invocations of the SMT solver Z3 —the calls to findAll— and applications of Scala functions —here isPrime, whose definition we omit. Because findAll works by lazily generating a stream, Z3 is only invoked as more values are requested. For instance, if we only wish to check whether a solution exists, we can test results.isEmpty and only one solution will be computed. Similarly, when y is not prime, the inner constraint is not dispatched to the solver. Note that this constraint is, despite its appearance, in linear arithmetic, since x and y are known at the time of its construction. Note that the only constructs that a Scala programmer needs to learn to use the above example is the findAll function, and the Val[_] type constructor. The remaining constructs are a standard part of Scala [4].

N-Queens puzzle. We consider now the problem of solving the N-Queens puzzle: *In how many ways can* N *queens be placed on an* $N \times N$ *checkerboard such that they do not attack each other?* The following program encodes the problem using integer arithmetic and invokes the solver to count the number of solutions:

```
val z3 = new Z3Context("MODEL" → true)
val N = 8
val cols = (0 until N) map { _ ⇒ IntVar() } // column vars
val diffCnstr = Distinct(cols : _*) // all queens on distinct cols
val boundsCnstr = for (c ← cols) yield (c ≥ 0 && c < N) // cols are within bounds
val diagonalsCnstr = // no two queens on same diagonal
    for (i ← 0 until N; j ← 0 until i) yield
        ((cols(i) − cols(j) !== i − j) && (cols(i) − cols(j) !== j − i))

z3.assertCnstr(diffCnstr)
boundsCnstr map (z3.assertCnstr(_))
diagonalsCnstr map (z3.assertCnstr(_))
println(z3.checkAndGetAllModels.size) // prints 92
```

In this example, we use Scala^{Z3} with the same degree of control we would have with the native interface: we build the context explicitly, push constraints, etc. We start by declaring a list of Z3 constants; the i-th constant representing the (integer) column value of the queen that will be placed on row i. We then specify the constraints, stating that each queen is on a different column, row and diagonal. Finally we assert these three constraints in the current context, and invoke the solver to retrieve the stream of all solutions that satisfy the constructed formulas. Most variables in this program are of the type Tree yet type inference allows us to keep this transparent. Thanks to operator overloading, the meaning of the constraints is clear from the code.[1]

Calendar computation. Implicit computations are useful not only as a form of constraint solving, but also in cases where writing code that matches a precise specification may be hard; in such cases we can sometimes replace explicit code by an implicit definition. Our next example shows how we can use Scala^{Z3} to compute date differences while accounting for leap years.[2] The following program takes as input a number of days totalDays and computes the year and the day in the year that correspond to totalDays since January 1st, 1980.

```
val totalDays = 10593
val originYear = 1980

val (year, day) = choose((year: Val[Int], day: Val[Int]) ⇒ {
    def leapYearsUntil(y : Tree[IntSort]) = (y − 1) / 4 − (y − 1) / 100 + (y − 1) / 400

    totalDays === (year − originYear) * 365
        + leapYearsUntil(year) − leapYearsUntil(originYear) + day &&
    day > 0 && day ≤ 366
})

println(year + ", " + day) // prints 2008, 366
```

Note that we defined a helper method leapDaysUntil which produces a tree expressing the number of leap years between year 1 and y. This is possible because this auxiliary definition doesn't affect the type of the predicate used in the call to choose. We can then use this method in our predicate to express conveniently the number of total days between January 1st, 1980 and the day specified by year and day.

3   Design and Implementation

Scala^{Z3} is implemented as a Scala library that connects to Z3's C interface through the Java Native Interface [2], and consists of just over 5,000 lines of a combination of Scala, Java, and C code. Although it is possible to use Scala^{Z3} as a simple Scala view of the C or OCaml interface of Z3, there are several features that enable more productive combinations of the two systems.

---

[1] We use the operators === and !== to construct ASTs because == and != can only return booleans in Scala.

[2] A piece of code that incorrectly performed this computation is famously responsible for a bug that caused thousands of portable media devices to freeze in 2008.

```
abstract class Tree[+A >: Bottom <: Top]

sealed trait Top
trait IntSort extends Top
trait BoolSort extends Top
trait BVSort extends Top
trait ... extends Top
trait SetSort extends Top
trait Bottom extends IntSort with BoolSort with BVSort with ... with SetSort
```

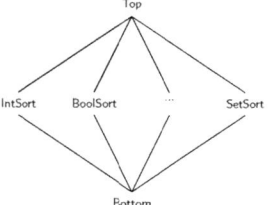

Fig. 1. Soft typing system for the domain specific language

Domain specific language. There are two possible representations of Z3 abstract syntax trees (ASTs) in Scala[Z3]. The most basic is a Z3AST class that encapsulates a C pointer to the internal representation. This is used by all functions that are direct mappings to the C interface. The other representation encodes Z3 ASTs into typed Scala syntax trees. These trees can be combined using operators with which programmers are familiar, such as &&, +, as well as numerical constants, for instance. The examples throughout this paper are all written using this domain specific language (DSL), which is enabled by adding the import statement **import** z3.scala.dsl._.

The representations are mutually compatible, and through the mechanism of *implicit conversions* [4, Chapter 21], the Scala compiler automatically inserts calls to conversion functions where needed. The DSL trees are *typed* using a soft-typing approach to prevent the construction of some ill-typed terms. Figure 1 shows the type system, which relies on Scala generic types and multiple inheritance. For instance, the < operator defined on trees of integer sort has the following signature:

def <(that: Tree[_ <: IntSort]): Tree[BoolSort]

This declaration indicates that < expects an operand of a type equal to (or a subtype of) Tree[IntSort] and returns a tree of type Tree[BoolSort]. Because Z3ASTs are by nature untyped and should be usable in combination with the DSL, they are converted to trees of type Tree[Bottom]. Because trees are covariant in their type parameter, such trees can be used in place of any type. In these cases, the library performs a runtime check to ensure that the types match, so as to avoid triggering an error in the Z3 native library.

High-level model navigation. One key feature of the system is the ability to evaluate the model of a Z3 constant as a Scala type. This is achieved by a generic method whose signature is:

def evalAs[T](ast: Z3AST)(**implicit** extr: (Z3Model, Z3AST) ⇒ Option[T]): Option[T]

It returns an Option type because the model may not define a value for the desired tree. The definition refers to an *implicit* parameter extr. Implicit parameters are parameters that can be omitted at the call-site, and that will be filled according to objects that are marked as implicit in the scope. Here, extr is the function responsible for building a value of the proper Scala type from a Z3 model and constant. How this is done depends on the requested type. Scala^{Z3} thus defines such functions for base types, and Scala's mechanism for resolving implicits automatically inserts the right definitions according to the type T. Because implicit resolution is done at compile-time, invocations of evalAs with unsupported types result in a compile error. Experienced users can also extend this mechanism by writing their own extractors, for instance to automatically build algebraic data types such as lists or trees from models. Scala^{Z3} also provides methods to recover models of uninterpreted function symbols or arrays, and to wrap them in an object that can then be used as a Scala function.

The choose, find and findAll constructs. These three constructs are defined as part of the domain specific language. choose attempts to find one assignment to a constraint, and throws an exception if it could not, while find returns an Option type using None to describe failures. findAll enumerates all models, as in the introductory example. They all take a predicate that describes the constraint as an argument. The particularity of these functions is that all the interaction with Z3 is completely transparent. Similarly to evalAs, choose and findAll rely on implicit arguments to build Z3 trees of the right kind and to retrieve values from the models. Additionally, the type constructor Val[_] encapsulates more implicit conversion functions to build ASTs from it. The complete signature for (the one argument version of) findAll is as follows:

```
def findAll[T](predicate : Val[T] ⇒ Tree[BoolSort])
              (implicit cons : T ⇒ Tree[Bottom],
                        extr : (Z3Model, Z3AST) ⇒ T) : Iterator[T]
```

In the implementation, an iterator is constructed by maintaining the Z3 context and successively pushing the negation of the previous model as a new constraint when the next model is requested. Since iterators are standard in Scala, we can use all the usual higher-order constructs on the result, including for instance map, filter or for-comprehensions.

4   Theory Plugins

Z3 supports user-defined *theory plugins*; users can integrate their decision procedure into Z3's DPLL engine by specifying callbacks that are invoked by Z3 on events such as context pushes and pops, newly propagated equalities, etc. We now give two examples of how this mechanism can be exploited through Scala^{Z3}.

Theory plugin for sets with cardinality constraints. We implemented a decision procedure for Boolean Algebra with Presburger Arithmetic, a logic that supports sets with cardinality constraints,[3] as a full-fledged theory extension to Z3 using Scala^{Z3} [5]. The details of the implementation are too complex to be presented here, but we shortly illustrate here some of the programming language aspects that we believe simplified this development. Scala is also an object-oriented language, and following that paradigm, user-defined theory plugins are

---

[3] Z3 natively supports sets, but without the cardinality operator.

created by subclassing a class Z3Theory defined as part of Scala^{Z3}. A definition such as the following is all that is needed to add a theory solver to Z3's DPLL engine:

```
class BAPATheory(val z3: Z3Context) extends Z3Theory(z3, "Sets with cardialities") {
  // User−defined sorts, constant values and functions:
  val setSort = mkTheorySort("setSort")
  val emptySet = mkTheoryValue("empty", setSort)
  // Declares a unary function from sets to integers:
  val cardinality = mkTheoryFuncDecl("card.", setSort, z3.mkIntSort)

  // This method is automatically called when a new term enters the logical context:
  override def newApp(ast: Z3AST) : Unit = ast.getKind match {
    case Z3AppAST('cardinality', arg) ⇒ processCard(arg)
    case _ ⇒ ...
}}
```

The interaction with Z3 is done by overriding the right methods, like newApp in the example above, which replace the callback functions used by the C interface. Theory plugins typically need to manipulate many abstract syntax trees communicated from Z3. To simplify such tasks, Scala^{Z3} defines *extractors*, which are functions that can be used in pattern-matching expressions [1]. The newApp method contains an example, where with a single line of code we test whether a Z3 tree corresponds to an application of the cardinality function and at the same time bind the variable args to its argument.

Procedural attachments. Scala^{Z3} provides special support for *procedural attachment* extensions. Procedural attachments are a special kind of theory plugins where the interpretation of ground terms is provided as executable functions. To illustrate their use, consider the code below, where we define two predicates and one function over strings:

```
val z3 = new Z3Context()
// Defines a new theory of strings with two predicates and one function symbol.
val strings = new ProceduralAttachment[String](z3) {
  val oddLength = predicate(s ⇒ s.length % 2 == 1)
  val isSubstr = predicate((s1,s2) ⇒ s2.contains(s1))
  val concat = function((s1,s2) ⇒ s1 + s2)
}
```

From this declaration, Scala^{Z3} constructs a Z3 theory plugin for a new sort representing strings and creates the proper predicate and function symbols. It also registers callbacks such that any ground term built over string constants is 1) translated back into Scala, 2) evaluated using the function definitions passed by the user, 3) converted back into Z3 trees. A usage example follows:

```
import strings._
val s1, s2 = variable
z3.assertCnstr(s1 === "hello" && (s2 === "world" || s2 === "moon")
  && oddLength(concat(s2, s1)) && isSubstr("low", concat(s1,s2)))
println(z3.check) // unsatisfiable
```

The import statement brings into scope not only the predicate and function symbols, which can then be used as part of the domain specific language, but also helper functions such as variable, which creates a Z3 tree for a variable representing a string, as well as an implicit conversion function which converts any string into a tree node representing its constant value. As a result, the constraints can be expressed very naturally. Using Z3's DPLL engine to assign truth values to literals, the system concludes that the constraints cannot be satisfied. Procedural attachment theories are in general not complete and may return *unknown* when some variables never become ground. They remain very useful extensions, though, for instance when all variables are known to range over a finite domain.

5   Conclusions

We have demonstrated that it is possible and fruitful to smoothly integrate a modern programming language and a powerful SMT solver. Our system enables users to dynamically construct constraints, while supporting the syntax of the underlying programming language. It enables combinatorial search that combines Z3's constraint solving with explicit tests and enumeration in the programming language, as well as the creation of custom theory solvers based on executable functions.

We have found a number of uses for Scala^{Z3} in our research group, including several program verification tools under development, as well as a new theory plugin for Z3 [5]. We have also recently received interest from other groups to use and contribute to Scala^{Z3}. Our implementation is freely available at:

http://lara.epfl.ch/w/ScalaZ3

We hope that the community will join the effort in enhancing the implementation further. The current version includes mappings for all Z3 operations (including manipulation of abstract data types, arrays and bitvectors, for instance), so expert users can already use it as a substitute for the C interface. Among the particularly desirable future extensions are: high-level support for further data types, parallel invocation of Z3 instances, and reconstruction of proof objects.

References

1. Emir, B., Vetta, A., Williams, J.: Matching objects with patterns. In: Ernst, E. (ed.) ECOOP 2007. LNCS, vol. 4609, pp. 273–298. Springer, Heidelberg (2007)
2. Liang, S.: The Java Native Interface: Programmer's Guide and Specification. Addison-Wesley, London (1999)
3. de Moura, L., Bjørner, N.S.: Z3: An efficient SMT solver. In: Ramakrishnan, C.R., Rehof, J. (eds.) TACAS 2008. LNCS, vol. 4963, pp. 337–340. Springer, Heidelberg (2008)
4. Odersky, M., Spoon, L., Venners, B.: Programming in Scala: a comprehensive step-by-step guide. Artima Press (2008)
5. Suter, P., Steiger, R., Kuncak, V.: Sets with cardinality constraints in satisfiability modulo theories. In: Jhala, R., Schmidt, D. (eds.) VMCAI 2011. LNCS, vol. 6538, pp. 403–418. Springer, Heidelberg (2011)

Efficient General Unification for XOR with Homomorphism

Zhiqiang Liu and Christopher Lynch[*]

Clarkson University, Potsdam, NY 13699, USA
{liuzh,clynch}@clarkson.edu

Abstract. General E-unification is an important tool in cryptographic protocol analysis, where the equational theory E represents properties of the cryptographic algorithm, and uninterpreted function symbols represent other functions. Some important properties are XOR, Abelian groups, and homomorphisms over them. Polynomial time algorithms exist for unification in those theories. However, the general E-unification problem in these theories is NP-complete, and existing algorithms are highly nondeterministic. We give a mostly deterministic set of inference rules for solving general E-unification modulo XOR with (or without) a homomorphism, and prove that it is sound, complete and terminating. These inference rules have been implemented in Maude, and are being incorporated into the Maude NPA. They are designed in such a way so that they can be extended to an Abelian group with a homomorphism.

1 Introduction

In symbolic cryptographic protocol analysis, messages are represented as terms. Actions of principals involved in the protocol are represented with rules, indicating that if a principal receives a message with a given pattern then the principal will send out a message based on the message received. Abilities of malicious intruders are represented by rules indicating how an intruder can manipulate data, where variables in the pattern indicate that the principal will accept any message of that type. A goal state represents an attack, and an analyzer decides whether the goal state is reachable. Generally, the analysis involves working back from the goal state to initial states. If this is possible, then an attack exists. Initial methods of cryptographic protocol analysis were based on the free algebra model[8]. In this method of analysis, two messages are the same only if they are represented by the same term. In this case, during the search back from the goal, a message pattern representing a received message will be compared against a message pattern representing a sent message. Syntactic unification is used to compare them against each other and find the intersection of the patterns.

However, the free algebra model is not precise enough to model properties of cryptographic algorithms[6]. For example, cryptographic algorithms may involve XOR operations, and therefore two messages may be equivalent in the theory

---

[*] Both authors are supported by NSF Grant CNS 09-05378.

N. Bjørner and V. Sofronie-Stokkermans (Eds.): CADE 2011, LNAI 6803, pp. 407–421, 2011.

of XOR but not syntactically equivalent. Abelian groups are also important, because they can model products, such as the product of exponents in Diffie Hellman. Another common property of cryptographic algorithms is a homomorphisms over an XOR or an Abelian group operator. For example, RSA, has the property $m_1{}^e m_2{}^e = (m_1 m_2)^e$, where raising to the power of e is a homomorphism, and the product of the messages forms an Abelian group. Unfortunately, the free algebra approach fails to detect attacks in protocols using cryptographic algorithms with these properties. Therefore, to conduct a more precise analysis, unification must be performed modulo these equational theories.

In conclusion, unification algorithms for the theory of XOR (with homomorphism) and Abelian groups (with homomorphism) are essential for cryptographic protocol analysis. It is important that these algorithms are efficient. Efficient unification algorithms have been developed for these theories[4,7]. However, cryptographic protocol analysis also must deal with uninterpreted function symbols. So it is important to have unification algorithms for these theories in combination with uninterpreted function symbols. When uninterpreted function symbols occur in combination with these theories, the complete set of unifiers is not always a singleton, but it is finite. It is crucial that the unification algorithm creates a complete set of unifiers that is as small as possible. If this set is too large, the search space of searching for an attack quickly blows up and cryptographic protocol analysis becomes infeasible.

The goal then is to build equational unification algorithms for these theories that are both efficient and create a small complete set of unifiers. There are two standard techniques for dealing with these equational theories in combination with uninterpreted function symbols. Let us consider the theory of exclusive OR in particular, because the other theories suffer from the same issues. One way to deal with XOR with uninterpreted function symbols is to create an efficient algorithm to solve XOR unification, and an efficient syntactic unification algorithm for uninterpreted function symbols and then to apply a standard combination algorithm to combine the theories[1]. The second technique is to create a convergent equational theory and apply Narrowing to solve the unification problem[5]. Both of these methods are highly nondeterministic. They are not very efficient in practice, but worse they build a highly redundant complete set of unifiers.

In this paper, we try to overcome these problems by devising a set of inference rules that is simple, easy to implement, very deterministic in practice, and produces a small complete set of unifiers. We can compare our work to [10]. That work is based on the combination method, and also has the goal of an efficient unification algorithm for XOR unification. We think our inference rules are simpler and easily extended to other equational theories.

We have developed a sound, complete and terminating set of inference rules for XOR with homomorphism, along with uninterpreted function symbols. We have implemented our inference rules in Maude[3], and they are being incorporated into the NRL protocol analyzer[6]. These inference rules also apply to XOR without homomorphism. We have designed them in such a way that they can be extended to Abelian groups.

2 Basic Definitions

Here we give some basic terminology which we will use in the following sections. Let $\mathbb{V}$ be a set of variables, and $\mathbb{F}$ be a finite set of function symbols, where a constant is a function with 0 arguments. We say t is a term if $t \in \mathbb{V}$, or t has the form $f(t_1, t_2, \cdots, t_n)$, where $f \in \mathbb{F}$, t_i is a term.

We use $\mathbb{T}$ to denote the set of all terms. If t is a term, we use $Sym(t)$ to denote the multi-set of symbols occurring in t. We use $Vars(t)$ to denote the set of variables occurring in t, here t can be a term, or a set of terms. $Top(t)$ denotes the top symbol of term t. i.e. $Top(f(t_1, t_2, \cdots, t_n)) = f$. If t is a variable x, $Top(x) = x$. Let t be a term and S be a set of terms. $Top(t; S)$ denotes the set of all terms in S which have top symbol $Top(t)$.

The following are standard definitions[2].

A *substitution* σ is a mapping from $\mathbb{V}$ to the set of terms, which can be represented explicitly by a set of bindings of variables, i. e. $\{x_1 \longmapsto t_1, x_2 \longmapsto t_2, \cdots, x_n \longmapsto t_n\}$ represents the substitution which maps x_i to t_i for $i = 1, 2, \cdots, n$ and which maps y to y if $y \neq x_i$ for all $i = 1, 2, \cdots, n$. When we apply σ to a term t, we denote the result as $t\sigma$. If t is a variable x_i, $x_i\sigma = t_i$; if t has the form $f(s_1, s_2, \cdots, s_n)$, then $t\sigma = f(s_1\sigma, s_2\sigma, \cdots, s_n\sigma)$. The *composition* of two substitutions σ and θ, denoted $\sigma\theta$ is defined by $t(\sigma\theta) = (t\sigma)\theta$ for each term.

A set of *identities* E is a subset of $\mathbb{T} \times \mathbb{T}$. We write identities in the form $s \approx t$. An *equational theory* $=_E$ is induced by a set of identities E and it is the least congruence relation (i.e. reflexive, symmetric, transitive and monotonic) on $\mathbb{T}$ that is closed under substitution and contains E.

If two terms, t and s, are equal with respect to a theory E, we write it as $t =_E s$.

Definition 1 (*E*-unification problem, *E*-unifier, *E*-unifiable). *For a given signature $\mathfrak{F}$ and a set of identities E, an E-**unification problem** over $\mathfrak{F}$ is a finite multiset of equations*

$$\Gamma = \{s_1 =^?_E t_1, s_2 =^?_E t_2, \cdots, s_n =^?_E t_n\}$$

*between terms. A substitution σ such that $s_i\sigma =_E t_i\sigma$, $i = 1, 2, \cdots, n$ is called an E-**unifier** or a **solution** of Γ. $U_E(\Gamma)$ is the set of all E-unifiers of Γ. A unification problem Γ is called E-**unifiable** iff $U_E(\Gamma) \neq \emptyset$. If E is the empty theory, we call the E-unification problem a **syntactic unification problem**.*

Let $\Gamma = \{t_1 =^? s_1, \cdots, t_n =^? s_n\}$, we use $\mathbb{V}_\Gamma$ to denote the set of variables in Γ. And for $\sigma = \{x_1 \longmapsto t_1, x_2 \longmapsto t_2, \cdots, x_n \longmapsto t_n\}$, we call the set of equations $\{x_1 =^? t_1, x_2 =^? t_2, \cdots, x_n =^? t_n\}$ the *solved form*, which we will denote by $[\sigma]$

For an E-unification problem Γ, two substitutions σ and θ are called *equal* with respect to Γ, denoted by $\sigma = |^E_\Gamma \theta$, if $x\sigma =_E x\theta$ for every variable in Γ. A substitution σ is *more general modulo E with respect to Γ* than another substitution θ, denoted $\sigma \leq |^E_\Gamma \theta$ if there exists a substitution τ, such that for every variable x in Γ, $x\sigma\tau =_E x\theta$. Note that the relation $\leq$ is a quasi-ordering,

i. e. reflexive and transitive. We will omit Γ or E where Γ or E is clear from the context.

Definition 2 (Complete Set of E-Unifiers). *A **complete set of E-unifiers** of an E-unification problem Γ is a set C of idempotent E-unifiers of Γ such that for each $\theta \in U_E(\Gamma)$ there exists $\sigma \in C$ with $\sigma \leq_E \theta|_{\mathbb{V}_\Gamma}$. We call a complete set C of E-unifiers minimal if two distinct elements are incomparable w.r.t. $\leq_E$, i.e. if $\sigma \leq_E \theta$ and $\sigma, \theta \in C$ then $\sigma = \theta$.*

A minimal complete set of unifiers for the syntactic unification problem Γ has only one element if it is not empty. We use $mgu(\Gamma)$ to denote this unifier. Without loss of generality, we suppose all variables in $mgu(\Gamma)$ are in $\mathbb{V}_\Gamma$.

For some equational theory E, we will call two E-unification problems *equivalent modulo E* if they have the same set of unifiers modulo theory E.

Definition 3 (Conservative Extension). *Let E be an equational theory, we say a multi-set of equations Γ' is a **conservative E-extension** of another multi-set of equations Γ, if any solution of Γ' is also a solution of Γ and any solution of Γ can be extended to a solution of Γ', which means for any solution σ of Γ, there exists θ whose domain is the variables in $Vars(\Gamma')/Vars(\Gamma)$ such that $\sigma\theta$ is a solution of Γ'.*

If $s\theta \neq t\theta$ syntactically, we say the substitution θ satisfies the disequation $s \neq^? t$.

3   Exclusive OR with Homomorphism

In this section, we will consider the theory of Exclusive OR and Homomorphism, together, we use **EXH** to denote this theory.

3.1   Basic Notation

Here the signature $\mathbb{F}$ is composed of $\{0, \oplus, h\} \cup \mathbb{F}'$, where 0 is a constant, $\oplus$ a binary symbol, h a unary function symbol and $\mathbb{F}'$ a collection of uninterpreted function symbols, with the following properties:

- $(x \oplus y) \oplus z \approx x \oplus (y \oplus z)$ [Associativity];
- $x \oplus y \approx y \oplus x$ [Commutativity];
- $x \oplus 0 \approx x$ [Existence of Unity];
- $x \oplus x \approx 0$ [Nilpotence];
- $h(x \oplus y) \approx h(x) \oplus h(y)$ [Homomorphism of h] .

We say a term t is *pure*, if $\oplus \notin Sym(t)$ and h does not occur under the top symbol of t. We call a term *h-term* if the top function symbol of this term is h. In a set of equations Γ, a *free* variable is the variable which does not occur under a uninterpreted function symbol or in h-term. A term t is in PURE SUM form if t has the form $t_1 \oplus t_2 \oplus \cdots t_n$, and: (i) for every i, t_i is a pure term, (ii) in $\{t_1, \cdots, t_n\}$, there is at most one h-term and (iii) $n > 0$. We say an equation $\mathbf{S} =^? 0$ is in PURE SUM form, if $\mathbf{S}$ is a PURE SUM.

Because of the properties of Exclusive OR, we only consider equations of the form $s =^? 0$ where s is a term. So for convenience, we will write an **EXH**-unification problem as $\{s_1 =^? 0, s_2 =^? 0, \cdots s_n =^? 0\}$, where each s_i is a term.

3.2   Rewriting System $\mathfrak{R}_{EXH}$

Before we introduce our inference system, we give a convergent rewriting system $\mathfrak{R}_{EXH}$ for **EXH** modulo associativity and commutativity:

- $x \oplus x \rightarrow 0$;
- $x \oplus 0 \rightarrow x$;
- $h(x) \oplus h(y) \rightarrow h(x \oplus y)$;
- $h(0) \rightarrow 0$;

Here we omit the extensions of $x \oplus x \rightarrow 0$ and $h(x) \oplus h(y) \rightarrow h(x \oplus y)$.

In our inference system, all terms will get reduced by $\mathfrak{R}_{EXH}$ modulo **AC**. So unless stated, all the terms are in reduced form by $\mathfrak{R}_{EXH}$.

Lemma 4. *Any set of equations Γ can be purified to be a set of equations Γ' in* PURE SUM *form, which is a conservative extension of Γ.*

Proof. We use the following inference rule, which we call **Purify**, to prove this:

$$\frac{\Gamma \cup \{S \oplus t[s] =^? 0\}}{\Gamma \cup \{S \oplus t[x] =^? 0\} \cup \{x \oplus s =^? 0\}}$$

where Γ is a set of equations, S a term, t a pure term, s a proper subterm of t, with $Top(s) \in \{\oplus, h\}$, and x is a fresh variable.

Purification (the exhaustive application of **Purify**) on a unification problem Γ will halt in a PURE SUM Γ', which is a conservation extension of Γ.   □

Without difficulty, we have the following lemma:

Lemma 5. *Let Γ and Γ' be two unification problems, where Γ' is the result of applying **Purify** on Γ. Then Γ' is Conservative Extension of Γ.*

From now on, we will assume that every equation has the form $\mathbf{S} =^? 0$, where $\mathbf{S}$ is a PURE SUM. In the following sections, we will use Γ to denote a set of equations, $\mathbf{S}$ to denote a PURE SUM, s, t, s_i, t_i to denote pure terms, x, x_i, y, y_i, v, v_i, etc. to denote variables, σ, θ to denote substitutions.

3.3   Inference System $\mathfrak{I}_{EXH}$

For efficiency and convenience, in our inference procedure, we will use a triple $\Gamma \| \Delta \| \Lambda$, where $\|$s are used to separate these three sets. In $\Gamma \| \Delta \| \Lambda$, Γ is a unification problem, a set of the form $\{S_1 =^? 0, S_2 =^? 0, \cdots, S_n =^? 0\}$, where each S_i is a PURE SUM. Δ is a set of disequations, and Λ is a set of equations. Every disequation in Δ has the form $f(s_1, \cdots, s_n) \oplus f(t_1, \cdots, t_n) \neq^? 0$ or $0 \neq^? 0$, where f is an uninterpreted symbol from Γ and s_i, t_i are terms. Δ is used to track non-deterministic choices in our inference system. Every time we make a choice, we will add a disequation into Δ. Some equation will be added to Λ if a variable in Γ was solved during the inference procedure. All the equations in Λ

will have the form $x =^? S$ where x is a *solved variable*, which means that x does not occur in Γ. Δ and Λ are both empty initially.

For convenience, we call Γ an *equation set*, Δ a *disequation set*, Λ a *solved equation set* and $\Gamma\|\Delta\|\Lambda$ a *set triple*. We say a substitution θ satisfies the set triple $\Gamma\|\Delta\|\Lambda$, if θ satisfies every equation in Γ and Λ, and every disequation in Δ, and write that relation as $\theta \vDash \Gamma\|\Delta\|\Lambda$. Similarly, we call $\Gamma\|\Lambda$ a *set pair*, and a substitution θ satisfies the set pair $\Gamma\|\Lambda$ if θ satisfies every equation in Γ and Λ. We use **Fail** to be a special set triple with no solution.

$\mathfrak{I}_{EXH}$ contains four *necessary rules*: Trivial, Variable Substitution, N-Decomposition and Annulization; and six *auxiliary rules* used for efficiency. Trivial, Variable Substitution, Annulization and the auxiliary rules are deterministic, and N-Decomposition is nondeterministic. In our inference procedure, there are three priorities for applying rules. The rules with the highest priority are Trivial, Variable Substitution and the auxiliary rules. They will be applied whenever they can be applied. The rule with the second highest priority is N-Decomposition. The rule with lowest priority is Annulization. Rules can only be applied if no rules with higher priority can be applied.

If $\Gamma = \emptyset$, then Λ is a solution. Exhaustively applying the inference rules to $\Gamma\|\emptyset\|\emptyset$ yields a complete set of **EXH**-unifiers of Γ.

In this section, we introduce the necessary rules.

Trivial
$$\frac{\Gamma \cup \{0 =^? 0\}\|\Delta\|\Lambda}{\Gamma\|\Delta\|\Lambda}$$

Variable Substitution
$$\frac{(\Gamma \cup \{x \oplus \mathbf{S} =^? 0\})\|\Delta\|\Lambda}{(\Gamma\sigma)\|(\Delta\sigma)\|\Lambda\sigma \cup \{x =^? \mathbf{S}\}}$$

where $\sigma = [x \longmapsto \mathbf{S}]$. Here we need the conditions: x is free in $\Gamma \cup x \oplus \mathbf{S} =^? 0$ and either (i) S has no h-term, or (ii) all equations of the form $x \oplus T =^? 0$ in Γ contain an h-term; Note: (a)If $\mathbf{S}$ is empty, then we set $\sigma = [x \longmapsto 0]$. (b) If the resulting equation set is not pure[1], Purification is immediately applied to the conclusion of the inference.

If we do not check the first condition (i), the procedure may not terminate.

Example 31. *Find the solution of* $\{x \oplus f(z) =^? 0, x \oplus y \oplus z =^? 0\}$.

If we solve x *first, we get* $[x \to f(z)]$ *and* $\{f(z)\oplus y\oplus z =^? 0\}$. *At this time,* y *is the only free variable, so we solve* y *and get the answer* $[x \to f(z), y \to z\oplus f(z)]$. *If we had chosen* y *first, we would get the same result.*

The next inference rule N-Decomposition is nondeterministic. When we apply N-Decomposition, we get two new independent problems, whose combined solutions are the solutions of the original problem. We will use $\bigvee$ to separate these two problems.

---

[1] This can only happen by application of the rewrite rule $h(x) \oplus h(y) \to h(x \oplus y)$

N-Decomposition

If $f(s_1, s_2, \cdots, s_m) \oplus f(t_1, t_2, \cdots, t_m) \neq^? 0 \notin \Delta$,

$$\frac{\Gamma \cup \{\mathbf{S} \oplus f(s_1, s_2, \cdots, s_m) \oplus f(t_1, t_2, \cdots, t_m) =^? 0\} \| \Delta \| \Lambda}{(\Gamma\sigma \cup \{\mathbf{S} =^? 0\}\sigma) \| (\Delta\sigma) \| (\Lambda\sigma \cup [\sigma]) \qquad \bigvee \qquad \Gamma_1' \| \Delta_1' \| \Lambda}.$$

where (i) $\sigma = mgu(s_1 =^? t_1, s_2 =^? t_2, \cdots, s_m =^? t_m)$ (ii) $\Gamma_1' = \Gamma \cup \{\mathbf{S} \oplus f(s_1, s_2, \cdots, s_m) \oplus f(t_1, t_2, \cdots, t_m) =^? 0\}$. (iii) $\Delta_1' = \Delta \cup \{f(s_1, s_2, \cdots, s_m) \oplus f(t_1, t_2, \cdots, t_m) \neq^? 0\}$

Example 32

$$\Gamma = \{x \oplus f(y) \oplus f(z) =^? 0, y \oplus f(x) \oplus f(w) =^? 0\}$$

We can do nothing via Variable Substitution, so choose two of the pure terms in one equation to apply the N-Decomposition rule.

$$\{x \oplus f(y) \oplus f(z) =^? 0, y \oplus f(x) \oplus f(w) =^? 0\} \| \emptyset \| \emptyset$$
$$\Longrightarrow (N\text{-}Decomposition)$$
$$\{x =^? 0, z \oplus f(x) \oplus f(w) =^? 0\} \| \emptyset \| \{y =^? z\}$$
$$\bigvee \Gamma_1 \| \Delta_1 \| \emptyset$$
$$\overset{*}{\Rightarrow} (several\ steps\ by\ Variable\ Substitution)$$
$$\emptyset \| \emptyset \| \{x =^? 0, y =^? f(0) \oplus f(w), z =^? f(0) \oplus f(w)\} \bigvee \Gamma_1 \| \Delta_1 \| \emptyset$$

where

$$\Gamma_1 = \{x \oplus f(y) \oplus f(z) =^? 0, y \oplus f(x) \oplus f(w) =^? 0\}$$
$$\Delta_1 = \{f(y) \oplus f(z) \neq^? 0\}$$

Here we get one solution $\sigma_1 = [x \longmapsto 0, y \longmapsto f(0) \oplus f(w), x \longmapsto f(0) \oplus f(w)]$ and another equation set Γ_1 and disequation set Δ_1. We apply N-Decomposition to $\Gamma_1 \| \Delta_1 \| \emptyset$, and use a similar procedure to get the second solution $\sigma_2 = [x \longmapsto f(0) \oplus f(z), y \longmapsto 0, w \longmapsto f(0) \oplus f(z)]$ (We will prove that the Δ can be thrown away at the end). So σ_1 and σ_2 are two solutions to this problem. The third branch fails, because no inference rule can be applied to it.

The fourth rule is based on the homomorphism property $h(0) =_{EXH} 0$:

Annulization

$$\frac{(\Gamma \cup \{\mathbf{S} \oplus h(t) =^? 0\}) \| \Delta \| \Lambda}{(\Gamma \cup \{\mathbf{S} =^? 0\} \cup \{t =^? 0\}) \| \Delta \| \Lambda}$$

if (i) no other rules can be applied, and (ii)there are no uninterpreted function symbol on the top in Γ and $\mathbf{S}^2$, Here $\mathbf{S}$ may be empty.

Now we give an example of how to apply Annulization. For convenience we will ignore Δ and Λ.

---

[2] If there are uninterpreted function symbols and no other rules apply then there is no solution.

Example 33

$$\Gamma = \{x \oplus h(y) =^? 0, y \oplus h(z) =^? 0, z \oplus h(x) =^? 0\}$$

In Γ, no variables are pure and N-Decomposition cannot be applied. We can only apply Annulization: in three steps, get $x = 0, y = 0, z = 0$. So the solution is $[x \rightarrow 0, y \rightarrow 0, z \rightarrow 0]$.

3.4   Termination, Soundness and Completeness

In this subsection, we will give the proof of the termination, soundness and completeness of our inference system.

Before giving the proof, we define directed conservative extension:

Definition 6 (Directed Conservative Extension). *Let $\Gamma\|\Delta\|\Lambda$ and $\Gamma'\|\Delta'\|\Lambda'$ be set triples. $\Gamma'\|\Delta'\|\Lambda'$ is called a **directed conservative extension** of $\Gamma\|\Delta\|\Lambda$ if for any substitution θ, such that $\theta \vDash \Gamma\|\Delta\|\Lambda$, then there exists σ, whose domain is the variables in $Vars(\Gamma' \cup \Lambda')/Vars(\Gamma \cup \Lambda)$, such that $\theta\sigma \vDash \Gamma'\|\Delta'\|\Lambda'$.*

This is one direction of conservative extension, but with respect to triples not only Γ. We will used it to prove the inference rules never lose any solutions.

Next, we give some notation and definitions about an abstract inference rule called *Simplifier*, which covers all our concrete auxiliary rules, given later.

We give two mappings here: P and μ. We call $P : \mathcal{P}(\Gamma) \rightarrow \{True, False\}$ a *property* of Γ. and $\mu : \mathcal{P}(\Gamma\|\Delta\|\Lambda) \rightarrow \mathbf{N}$ a *measurement* of $\Gamma\|\Delta\|\Lambda$, where $\mathbf{N}$ is a well-ordered set.

Definition 7 (Preservative rules and Simplifiers)
Let E be an equational theory. Let I be an inference rule of the following form:

$$\frac{\Gamma\|\Delta\|\Lambda}{\Gamma'\|\Delta'\|\Lambda'}$$

*If $\Gamma\|\Delta\|\Lambda$ has the same set of solutions as $\Gamma'\|\Delta'\|\Lambda'$ and every solution of $\Gamma'\|\Lambda'$ is a solution of $\Gamma\|\Lambda$, and $\Gamma'\|\Delta'\|\Lambda'$ is a directed conservative extension of $\Gamma\|\Delta\|\Lambda$, we say I is E-**equation preservative**. If for some property P, $P(\Gamma')$ is true whenever $P(\Gamma)$ is true, we say I is P-**preservative**. If μ is a measurement such that $\mu(\Gamma\|\Delta\|\Lambda) > \mu(\Gamma'\|\Delta'\|\Lambda')$, we say I is μ-**reducing**. If I is E-Equation Preservative, P-preservative and μ-reducing, we say I is a (P, E, μ)-**Simplifier**.*

*If P, E and μ are clear, we will write it as **simplifier**.*

Termination. We give four well-founded orderings for proving termination:

Let Γ be a set of equations then $Vars(\Gamma) = \{x | x$ occurs in some equation in $\Gamma\}$, and $|Vars(\Gamma)|$ is a well-founded ordering.

Recall that $Sym(\Gamma)$ is the multiset of all symbols occurring in Γ. Obviously, the standard ordering of $|Sym(\Gamma)|$ based on natural numbers is a well-founded ordering on the set of equations sets.

From the definition of Δ, we see that Δ only contains disequations of the form $s \oplus t \neq^? 0$ where s and t have the same top function symbol. So we let $Par(\Delta)$ be $\{(t, s) : t \oplus s \neq^? 0 \in \Delta\}$ and $Par(\Gamma)$ be $\{(t, s) : t, s \in \Gamma$ and t has the same top function symbol as $s\}$.

We use $Par(\Gamma/\Delta)$ to denote $Par(\Gamma) - Par(\Delta)$. Since the number of terms in Γ is finite, $|Par(\Gamma/\Delta)|$ is a well-founded ordering. This ordering is used to count all possible disequations that could be placed in Δ by N-Decomposition, not including the ones that are already there.

We also need a well-founded ordering $H(\Gamma)$, which is the number of h-terms in Γ.

We then define the measure of $\Gamma\|\Delta\|\Lambda$ as the lexicographically ordered quadruple $\mathbb{M}_{EXH}(\Gamma, \Delta, \Lambda) = (H(\Gamma), |Vars(\Gamma)|, |Sym(E)|, |Par(\Gamma/\Delta)|)$. Obviously, this measure is well founded because the four arguments are well-founded.

For two set triples, $\Gamma\|\Delta\|\Lambda$ and $\Gamma'\|\Delta'\|\Lambda'$, we use $\Gamma\|\Delta\|\Lambda \Rightarrow_{\mathfrak{I}_{EXH}} \Gamma'\|\Delta'\|\Lambda'$ to mean we can obtain $\Gamma'\|\Delta'\|\Lambda'$ from $\Gamma\|\Delta\|\Lambda$ by applying a rule with the following form from $\mathfrak{I}_{EXH}$ once. Note that for N-Decomposition, $\Gamma'\|\Delta'\|\Lambda'$ could represent either of the choices. We let $\Gamma\|\Delta\|\Lambda \overset{*}{\Rightarrow}_{\mathfrak{I}_{EXH}} \Gamma'\|\Delta'\|\Lambda'$ mean that $\Gamma'\|\Delta'\|\Lambda'$ can be obtained by applying zero or more rules from $\mathfrak{I}_{EXH}$.

Given this measurement, $\mathbb{M}_{EXH}(\Gamma, \Delta, \Lambda)$ is reduced by every inference rule.

Lemma 8. *Let $\Gamma\|\Delta\|\Lambda$ and $\Gamma'\|\Delta'\|\Lambda'$ be two triple sets, such that $\Gamma\|\Delta\|\Lambda \Rightarrow_{\mathfrak{I}_{EXH}} \Gamma'\|\Delta'\|\Lambda'$, Then, $\mathbb{M}_{EXH}(\Gamma, \Delta, \Lambda) > \mathbb{M}_{EXH}(\Gamma', \Delta', \Lambda')$*

Theorem 9. *For any triple set $\Gamma\|\Delta\|\Lambda$, there is a triple set $\Gamma'\|\Delta'\|\Lambda'$ such that $\Gamma\|\Delta\|\Lambda \overset{*}{\Rightarrow}_{\mathfrak{I}_{EXH}} \Gamma'\|\Delta'\|\Lambda'$ and no rules in $\mathfrak{I}_{EXH}$ can be applied on $\Gamma'\|\Delta'\|\Lambda'$.*

Let us estimate how many steps we need to solve a unification problem in the worst case.

The purification procedure is linear with respect to the size of the unification problem.

For Variable Substitution, assume after purification from the original unification problem, we have m equations and n h-terms, where m is smaller than the size of the original unification problem. Every time we apply Variable Substitution, some equation will be removed from Γ. Because N-Decomposition and Annulization will not add any new equations, the only possibility that new equations are added is from the purification after Variable Substitution. In this case, the newly added equations will not contain any h-terms and the number of new equations will be one less than the current number of h-terms. So in the worst case, we need to apply Variable Substitution at most $m + (n-1)(n-2)/2$ times, where $(n-1)(n-2)/2$ is the number of newly added equations.

For N-Decomposition, in the worst case we might need to compare all the possible uninterpreted function terms. Assume we have k different function terms. Because our rules never increase the size of the set of uninterpreted function terms, at most we need to compare $k(k-1)/2$ times, which means at most we need to apply N-Decomposition $k(k-1)/2$ times.

We apply Annulization at most n times, where n is the number of h-terms.

So the upper bound of inference steps we might apply is non-deterministically quadratic with respect to the size of the problem. Because applying every inference rule is in polynomial time, our algorithm is bounded by non-deterministic polynomial time.

Soundness and Completeness. The following theorem justifies disregarding Δ at the end of the inference procedure.

Theorem 10. *For any two set triples $\Gamma\|\Delta\|\Lambda$ and $\Gamma'\|\Delta'\|\Lambda'$, satisfying $\Gamma\|\Delta\|\Lambda \overset{*}{\Rightarrow}_{\Im_{EXH}} \Gamma'\|\Delta'\|\Lambda'$, if there is a solution θ, satisfying $\theta \models \Gamma'\|\Lambda'$, then $\theta \models \Gamma\|\Lambda$.*

In the rest of this section, we show that the inference rules never lose any solutions.

Lemma 11. *Let $\Gamma\|\Delta\|\Lambda$ be a set triple, if there exists another set triple $\Gamma'\|\Delta'\|\Lambda'$, such that $\Gamma\|\Delta\|\Lambda \Rightarrow_{\Im_{EXH}} \Gamma'\|\Delta'\|\Lambda'$ via a deterministic rule except Annulization, then $\Gamma'\|\Delta'\|\Lambda'$ is a directed conservative extension of $\Gamma\|\Delta\|\Lambda$.*

Before we give the next lemma, we define a function called *Lay* which will count the layers of a term, when the term is represented as a tree

Definition 12. *If t is reduced, then $\mathbf{Lay}(t)$ has the following value:*

- $\mathbf{Lay}(t) = 0$, *if t is a constant or variable.*
- $\mathbf{Lay}(f(t_1, t_2, \cdots, t_n)) = \max\{Lay(t_1), Lay(t_2), \cdots, Lay(t_n)\} + 1$, *where f is an uninterpreted symbol.*
- $\mathbf{Lay}(t_1 \oplus t_2 \oplus \cdots \oplus t_n) = \max\{Lay(t_1), Lay(t_2), \cdots, Lay(t_n)\}$.
- $\mathbf{Lay}(h(t)) = 1 + Lay(t)$.

Lemma 13. *Let $\Gamma\|\Delta\|\Lambda$ be a set triple, if there exists another set triple $\Gamma'\|\Delta'\|\Lambda'$, such that $\Gamma\|\Delta\|\Lambda \Rightarrow_{\Im_{EXH}} \Gamma'\|\Delta'\|\Lambda'$ via Annulization, then $\Gamma'\|\Delta'\|\Lambda'$ is a directed conservative extension of $\Gamma\|\Delta\|\Lambda$.*

Proof. In the procedure of applying Annulization, we will not generate new variables, so it is enough to show for any substitution θ, $\theta \models \Gamma'\|\Delta'\|\Lambda'$ whenever $\theta \models \Gamma\|\Delta\|\Lambda$.

Since Annulization is applicable, every equation has the form

$$x_{i1} \oplus x_{i2} \oplus \cdots \oplus x_{in} \oplus h(t_i) =^? 0$$

where none of the x_{ij}'s are free. Annulization sets all the h-terms to zero. From the rule, we know Annulization will not change Δ. So it is enough to show there is no solution θ, such that for some $h(t_i)$, $(h(t_i)\theta \downarrow) \neq 0$.

Suppose there is a ground reduced substitution θ and there exists an h-term $h(t_j)$, such that $(h(t_j)\theta) \downarrow \neq 0$. Suppose θ is $\{x_1 \longmapsto T_1, x_2 \longmapsto T_2, \cdots x_n \longmapsto T_n, y_1 \longmapsto S_1, y_2 \longmapsto S_2, \cdots, y_l \longmapsto S_l\}$, where each x_i is a non-free variable and y_i is a free variable in Γ. Without loss of generality, we suppose $Lay(T_1) \geq Lay(T_2) \geq \cdots \geq Lay(T_n)$.

We claim that $Lay(T_1)$ is not zero. If it is, then all $Lay(T_i)$ are zero, which means all the T_i are variables or constants. Then for the equation $x_{j1} \oplus x_{j2} \oplus \cdots \oplus x_{jn} \oplus h(t_j) =^? 0$, where $(h(t_j)\theta) \downarrow \neq 0$, we have:

$$x_{j1} \oplus x_{j2} \oplus \cdots \oplus x_{jn} \oplus h(t_j)\theta$$
$$= a_{j1} \oplus a_{j2} \oplus \cdots \oplus a_{jn} + h(t_j)\theta$$

where a_{ji} are constants or variables. There is no way to cancel $h(t_j)\theta$ if $h(t)\theta \downarrow \neq 0$. This equation cannot be true.

So $Lay(T_1)$ is not zero. Since x_1 occurs in t_i in the equation $x_{i1} \oplus x_{i2} \oplus \cdots \oplus x_{im} \oplus h(t_i) =^? 0$, where x_{ij}'s are not free variables, if we want to cancel $h(t_i)\theta$, we need another variable $x_{ij}\theta$ cancel it because there are no other h-terms in it. Suppose $x_{i1} \oplus x_{i2} \oplus \cdots \oplus x_{ik}$ can cancel $h(t_i)\theta$. Then we have $(x_{i1} \oplus x_{i2} \oplus \cdots \oplus x_{ik})\theta = h(t_i)\theta + T$. So $Lay((x_{i1} \oplus x_{i2} \oplus \cdots \oplus x_{ik})\theta) = \max\{Lay(t_{i1}), Lay(t_{i2}), \cdots, Lay(t_{ik})\} = Lay(h(t_i)) > Lay(x_1\theta) = Lay(T_1)$, which is a contradiction.

So in this case there is no solution θ, such that for some $h(t)$, $(h(t)\theta \downarrow) \neq 0$. Therefore the statement is true.   □

Lemma 14. *Let $\Gamma\|\Delta\|\Lambda$ be a set triple. If there exists another set triple $\Gamma'\|\Delta'\|\Lambda'$, such that $\Gamma\|\Delta\|\Lambda \Rightarrow_{\mathfrak{I}_{EXH}} \Gamma'\|\Delta'\|\Lambda'$ via N-Decomposition, then $\Gamma'\|\Delta'\|\Lambda'$ is a directed conservative extension of $\Gamma\|\Delta\|\Lambda$.*

Proof. In the procedure of applying N-Decomposition, we will not generate new variables, so it is enough to show that if there exists another two set triples $\Gamma'\|\Delta'\|\Lambda'$ and $\Gamma''\|\Delta''\|\Lambda''$, such that $\Gamma\|\Delta\|\Lambda \Rightarrow_{\mathfrak{I}_{EXH}} \Gamma'\|\Delta'\|\Lambda'$ and $\Gamma\|\Delta\|\Lambda \Rightarrow_{\mathfrak{I}_{EXH}} \Gamma''\|\Delta''\|\Lambda''$ via N-Decomposition, then for any substitution θ, either $\theta \vDash \Gamma'\|\Delta'\|\Lambda'$ or $\theta \vDash \Gamma''\|\Delta''\|\Lambda''$, whenever $\theta \vDash \Gamma\|\Delta\|\Lambda$.

We have two cases if we can apply N-Decomposition.

Case 1: Γ has an equation of the form

$$\mathbf{S} \oplus f(s_1, s_2, \cdots, s_m) \oplus f(t_1, t_2, \cdots, t_m) =^? 0$$

which has a solution θ, such that $f(s_1, s_2, \cdots, s_m)\theta = f(t_1, t_2, \cdots, t_m)\theta$.

Recall what σ is in N-Decomposition. Let $x\sigma = r$ where x is in the domain of σ. Then $x =^? r \in [\sigma]$. Because $\theta \vDash f(s_1, s_2, \cdots, s_m) =^? f(t_1, t_2, \cdots, t_m)$, we have $\theta \vDash [\sigma]$. So $x\sigma\theta = r\theta = x\theta$. For every variable y in Γ which is not in the domain of σ, $y\sigma\theta = y\theta$, which means $\theta \vDash (\Gamma\sigma \cup \{\mathbf{S} =^? 0\})\|\Delta\sigma\|(\Lambda\sigma \cup [\sigma])$.

Case 2: Γ has an equation of the form

$$\mathbf{S} \oplus f(s_1, s_2, \cdots, s_m) \oplus f(t_1, t_2, \cdots, t_m) =^? 0$$

and a solution θ, such that $f(s_1, s_2, \cdots, s_m)\theta \neq f(t_1, t_2, \cdots, t_m)\theta$, there is no deterministic rule to be applied and $f(s_1, s_2, \cdots, s_m) \oplus f(t_1, t_2, \cdots, t_m) \neq^? 0 \notin \Delta$.

We can apply N-Decomposition(the second choice) and add $f(s_1, s_2, \cdots, s_m) \oplus f(t_1, t_2, \cdots, t_m) \neq^? 0$ into the disequation set. It is trivially true that

$$\theta \vDash \Gamma \| \Delta \cup \{ f(s_1, s_2, \cdots, s_m) \oplus f(t_1, t_2, \cdots, t_m) \neq^? 0 \} \| \Lambda. \qquad \square$$

Lemma 15. *Let $\Gamma \| \Delta \| \Lambda$ be a set triple. If there is not another set triple $\Gamma' \| \Delta' \| \Lambda'$, such that $\Gamma \| \Delta \| \Lambda \Rightarrow_{\mathfrak{I}_{EXH}} \Gamma' \| \Delta' \| \Lambda'$, then $\Gamma \| \Delta \| \Lambda$ has no solution.*

Proof. Because there are no rules applicable including Annulization, there is some uninterpreted function symbol occurring as top function symbol, i.e. some equation has the form:

$$x_{i1} \oplus \cdots \oplus x_{ik} \oplus \mathbf{S} \oplus f(s_1, s_2, \cdots, s_m) =^? 0$$

where each x_{ij} is a non-free variable in Γ, and $\mathbf{S}$ contains no pure variables.

Assume there are no rules to apply to $\Gamma \| \Delta \| \Lambda$ and θ is a ground reduced substitution, which is $\{ x_1 \longmapsto T_1, x_2 \longmapsto T_2, \cdots x_n \longmapsto T_n, y_1 \longmapsto S_1, y_2 \longmapsto S_2, \cdots, y_l \longmapsto S_l \}$, where each x_i is a non-free variable and each y_i is a free variable in Γ. Without loss of generality, we suppose $Lay(T_1) \geq Lay(T_2) \geq \cdots \geq Lay(T_n)$.

Here, we claim that $Lay(T_1)$ is not zero. If it is, then all $Lay(T_i)$s are zero. Then the equation

$$x_{i1} \oplus \cdots \oplus x_{ik} \oplus \mathbf{S} \oplus f(s_1, s_2, \cdots, s_m) =^? 0$$

becomes

$$a_{i1} \oplus \cdots \oplus a_{ik} \oplus \mathbf{S}\theta \oplus f(s_1, s_2, \cdots, s_m)\theta = 0$$

where a_i are constants or variables. Because this equation is true, we need the inverse of $f(s_1, s_2, \cdots, s_m)\theta$ to cancel it. If there is some f-term, e.g. $f(t_1, t_2, \cdots, t_m)\theta$ in $\mathbf{S}\theta$ which can cancel it, then because here we have no rules to apply, $f(t_1, t_2, \cdots t_m) \oplus f(s_1, s_2, \cdots, s_m) \neq 0 \in \Delta$, which means $f(t_1, t_2, \cdots t_m)\theta \neq f(s_1, s_2, \cdots, s_m)\theta$. So this equation can not be zero.

Thus $Lay(T_1)$ is not zero.

Because no rules in $\mathfrak{I}_{EXH}$ can be applied and from Variable Substitution's conditions, there are no free variable in Γ. Since x_1 is not a free variable, x_1 must occur under some uninterpreted function symbol or h-term. So we have two cases:

Case A: x_1 occurs under some uninterpreted function symbol. Suppose this equation is $\mathbf{S} \oplus t =^? 0$ where $x_1 \in t$ and $Top(t)$ is an uninterpreted function symbol or t is an h-term of the form $h(f(t_1, t_2, \cdots, t_n))$. Then if we want to cancel $x_1\theta$, we need another variable $x\theta$ to cancel it because there is no other t' in $\mathbf{S}$ with f on the top to cancel it or else N-Decomposition could be applied.

Suppose this x is some x_i, then $x_i\theta = t[x_1]\theta + T$. Then $Lay(x_i\theta) = Lay(T_i) = Lay(t[x_1]\theta + T) \geq Lay(t[x_1]\theta) > Lay(x_1\theta) = Lay(T_1)$, which is a contradiction with $Lay(T_1)$ is the biggest during all the T_i's.

Case B: x_1 occurs only in an h-term. If it is under some uninterpreted function symbol in this h-term, we know there is no solution from the analysis of Case A. So we can suppose this equation is $\mathbf{S} \oplus h(x_1) =^? 0$. Because $Lay(T_1) \neq 0$, we can suppose $T_1 = t_1 \oplus T_2'$, where $Lay(T_1) = Lay(t_1) \geq Lay(T'2)$ and t_1 is not a sum. Because only one h-term is in this equation and $h(s) + h(t) = h(s + t)$, we need another variable x to has the contribution to cancel $h(t_1)$. we claim that no variable can cancel $h(t_1)$.

If some non-free variable x_i can cancel $h(t_1)$, then $x_i\theta = h(t_1) + R$. So $Lay(T_i) = Lay(x_i\theta) = Lay(h(t_1) + R) \geq Lay(h(T_1)) > Lay(T_1)$ which is a contradiction.

In summary, if there is no rule we can apply for some triple, there is no solution for this triple.   □

Then by combining Lemma 11, Lemma 13, Lemma 14 and Lemma 15 we get:

Lemma 16. *Let $\Gamma\|\Delta\|\Lambda$ be a set triple. If there exists another set triple $\Gamma'\|\Delta'\|\Lambda'$, such that $\Gamma\|\Delta\|\Lambda \Rightarrow_{\mathfrak{I}_{EXH}} \Gamma'\|\Delta'\|\Lambda'$, then $\Gamma'\|\Delta'\|\Lambda'$ is a directed conservative extension of $\Gamma\|\Delta\|\Lambda$. If there is no such set triple, then $\Gamma\|\Delta\|\Lambda$ has no solution.*

Then by induction via Lemma 16, we get:

Theorem 17. *Let $\Gamma\|\Delta\|\Lambda$ be a set triple. If there exists another set triple $\Gamma'\|\Delta'\|\Lambda'$, such that $\Gamma\|\Delta\|\Lambda \stackrel{+}{\Rightarrow}_{\mathfrak{I}_{EXH}} \Gamma'\|\Delta'\|\Lambda'$, then $\Gamma'\|\Delta'\|\Lambda'$ is a directed conservative extension of $\Gamma\|\Delta\|\Lambda$. If there is no such set triple, then $\Gamma\|\Delta\|\Lambda$ has no solution.*

We have proved our inference system $\mathfrak{I}_{EXH}$ is terminating, sound and complete.

3.5 Auxiliary Rules for Improving Efficiency

For efficiency, we add some other inference rules to our system. These auxiliary rules are all Simplifiers.

Dis-Trivial

$$\frac{\Gamma\|(\Delta \cup \{0 \neq^? 0\})\|\Lambda}{\mathbf{Fail}}.$$

Clash

$$\frac{(\Gamma \cup \{\mathbf{S} \oplus f(t_{11}, \cdots, t_{1n}) \oplus \cdots \oplus f(t_{m1}, t_{m2}, \cdots, t_{mn}) =^? 0\})\|\Delta\|\Lambda}{\mathbf{Fail}}.$$

if there is neither a pure variable nor a term with uninterpreted function symbol f as top symbol in $\mathbf{S}$, and m is odd.

Clash-Annul

$$\frac{(\Gamma \cup \{\mathbf{S} \oplus h(t) =^? 0\})\|\Delta\|\Lambda}{(\Gamma \cup \{\mathbf{S} =^? 0\} \cup \{t =^? 0\})\|\Delta\|\Lambda}.$$

if there is no pure variable in **S**.

Occur Check

$$\frac{(\varGamma \cup \{x_1 \oplus x_2 \oplus \cdots \oplus x_n \oplus t_1 \oplus t_2 \oplus \cdots \oplus t_m =^? 0\}) \| \varDelta \| \varLambda}{\textbf{Fail}}.$$

where, $i > 0$, and for all x_i, there exists a term t_j with an uninterpreted function symbol on the top of it, such that:

1. $x_i \in Vars(t_j)$;
2. $|Top(t_j; \{t_1, t_2, \cdots, t_m\})|$ is odd; and
3. x_i occurs in every term in $Top(t_j; \{t_1, t_2, \cdots, t_m\})$.

Occur Check-Annul

$$\frac{(\varGamma \cup \{x \oplus \mathbf{S} \oplus h(t) =^? 0\}) \| \varDelta \| \varLambda}{(\varGamma \cup \{t =^? 0\} \cup \{\mathbf{S} =^? 0) \| \varDelta \| \varLambda\}}.$$

if no pure variable in **S** and x occurs in t.

Decomposition

If all the pure variables x_i in **S** occur in some term s_j (or t_j) and no top symbol of a pure term of **S** is uninterpreted function symbol f, then:

$$\frac{(\varGamma \cup \{\mathbf{S} \oplus f(s_1, s_2, \cdots s_m) \oplus f(t_1, t_2, \cdots t_m) =^? 0\}) \| \varDelta \| \varLambda}{(\varGamma_1 \sigma) \| (\varDelta \sigma) \| (\varLambda \sigma \cup \{[\sigma]\})}$$

where $\varGamma_1 = \varGamma \cup (\{\mathbf{S} =^? 0\})$, where $\sigma = mgu(s_1 =^? t_1, s_2 =^? t_2, \cdots, s_m =^? t_m)$.

4   Conclusion and Future Work

We introduced inference rules for general E-unification problems modulo XOR with homomorphism. We proved these inference rules to be sound, complete and terminating. We also introduced auxiliary rules to avoid applying N-Decomposition, and to make the inference system more efficient. These inference rules also apply to XOR without homomorphism. In this case, the Variable Substitution rule becomes simpler, because the conditions involving the h symbols are trivially true, N-Decomposition remains the same, and Annulization never applies. The auxiliary rules are the same, but Clash-Annul and Occur-Check-Annul no longer apply.

XOR is an important theory in cryptographic protocols, and that is the focus of our research. The algorithms are simple to implement, have already been implemented in Maude, and are being incorporated in the Maude NPA. The inference rules have the benefit that the N-Decomposition rule is not applied often, so the inference system is mostly deterministic. This makes the algorithm more efficient and the complete set of unifiers smaller.

The theory of Abelian groups, especially with homomorphism, is also an important theory in cryptographic protocols. That is our next extension of this theory. For future work, we will also combine it with convergent rewrite theories like cancellation.

References

1. Baader, F., Schulz, K.U.: Unification in the union of disjoint equational theories: Combining decision procedures. In: Kapur, D. (ed.) CADE 1992. LNCS, vol. 607, pp. 50–65. Springer, Heidelberg (1992)
2. Baader, F., Snyder, W.: Unification theory. In: Robinson, Voronkov (eds.) [9], pp. 445–532.
3. Clavel, M., Durán, F., Eker, S., Lincoln, P., Martí-Oliet, N., Bevilacqua, V., Talcott, C. L. (eds.): All About Maude - A High-Performance Logical Framework. LNCS, vol. 4350. Springer, Heidelberg (2007)
4. Brady, B., Lankford, D., Butler, G.: Abelian group unification algorithms for elementary terms. Contemporary Mathematics 29, 193–199 (1984)
5. Dershowitz, N., Plaisted, D.A.: Rewriting. In: Robinson, Voronkov (eds.) [9], pp. 535–610.
6. Escobar, S., Meadows, C., Meseguer, J.: Maude-npa: Cryptographic protocol analysis modulo equational properties. In: Aldini, A., Barthe, G., Gorrieri, R. (eds.) FOSAD. LNCS, vol. 5705, pp. 1–50. Springer, Heidelberg (2007)
7. Guo, Q., Narendran, P., Wolfram, D.A.: Unification and matching modulo nilpotence. In: McRobbie, M.A., Slaney, J.K. (eds.) CADE 1996. LNCS, vol. 1104, pp. 261–274. Springer, Heidelberg (1996)
8. Meadows, C.: Formal verification of cryptographic protocols: A survey. In: Pieprzyk, J., Safavi-Naini, R. (eds.) ASIACRYPT 1994. LNCS, vol. 917, pp. 135–150. Springer, Heidelberg (1995)
9. Robinson, J.A., Voronkov, A. (eds.): Handbook of Automated Reasoning (in 2 volumes). Elsevier, MIT Press, Amsterdam (2001)
10. Tuengerthal, M., Küsters, R., Turuani, M.: Implementing a unification algorithm for protocol analysis with xor. In: CoRR, abs/cs/0610014 (2006)

A Dependency Pair Framework for Innermost Complexity Analysis of Term Rewrite Systems[*]

Lars Noschinski[1], Fabian Emmes[2], and Jürgen Giesl[2]

[1] Institut für Informatik, TU Munich, Germany
[2] LuFG Informatik 2, RWTH Aachen University, Germany

Abstract. We present a modular framework to analyze the innermost runtime complexity of term rewrite systems automatically. Our method is based on the dependency pair framework for termination analysis. In contrast to previous work, we developed a *direct* adaptation of successful termination techniques from the dependency pair framework in order to use them for complexity analysis. By extensive experimental results, we demonstrate the power of our method compared to existing techniques.

1 Introduction

In practice, termination is often not sufficient, but one also has to ensure that algorithms terminate in *reasonable* (e.g., polynomial) *time*. While termination of term rewrite systems (TRSs) is well studied, only recently first results were obtained which adapt termination techniques in order to obtain polynomial complexity bounds automatically, e.g., [2,3,4,5,7,9,15,16,19,20,21,23,27,28]. Here, [3,15,16] consider the *dependency pair (DP) method* [1,10,11,14], which is one of the most popular termination techniques for TRSs.[1] Moreover, [28] introduces a related modular approach for complexity analysis based on relative rewriting.

Techniques for automated innermost termination analysis of term rewriting are very powerful and have been successfully used to analyze termination of programs in many different languages (e.g., Java [25], Haskell [12], Prolog [26]). Hence, by adapting these termination techniques, the ultimate goal is to obtain approaches which can also analyze the complexity of programs automatically.

In this paper, we present a fresh adaptation of the DP framework for *innermost runtime complexity analysis* [15]. In contrast to [3,15,16], we follow the original DP framework closely. This allows us to directly adapt the several termination techniques ("processors") of the DP framework for complexity analysis. Like [28], our method is modular. But in contrast to [28], which allows to investigate *derivational complexity* [17], we focus on innermost runtime complexity. Hence, we can inherit the modularity aspects of the DP framework and benefit from its transformation techniques, which increases power significantly.

---

[*] Supported by the DFG grant GI 274/5-3.
[1] There is also a related area of *implicit computational complexity* which aims at characterizing complexity classes, e.g., using type systems [18], bottom-up logic programs [13], and also using termination techniques like dependency pairs (e.g., [20]).

N. Bjørner and V. Sofronie-Stokkermans (Eds.): CADE 2011, LNAI 6803, pp. 422–438, 2011.
© Springer-Verlag Berlin Heidelberg 2011

After introducing preliminaries in Sect. 2, in Sect. 3 we adapt the concept of *dependency pairs* from termination analysis to so-called *dependency tuples* for complexity analysis. While the *DP framework* for termination works on *DP problems*, we now work on *DT problems* (Sect. 4). Sect. 5 adapts the "processors" of the DP framework in order to analyze the complexity of DT problems. We implemented our contributions in the termination analyzer AProVE. Due to the results of this paper, AProVE was the most powerful tool for innermost runtime complexity analysis in the *International Termination Competition* 2010. This is confirmed by our experiments in Sect. 6, where we compare our technique empirically with previous approaches. All proofs can be found in [24].

2   Runtime Complexity of Term Rewriting

See e.g. [6] for the basics of term rewriting. Let $\mathcal{T}(\Sigma, \mathcal{V})$ be the set of all terms over a signature Σ and a set of variables $\mathcal{V}$ where we just write $\mathcal{T}$ if Σ and $\mathcal{V}$ are clear from the context. The *arity* of a function symbol $f \in \Sigma$ is denoted by $\mathrm{ar}(f)$ and the size of a term is $|x| = 1$ for $x \in \mathcal{V}$ and $|f(t_1, \ldots, t_n)| = 1 + |t_1| + \ldots + |t_n|$. The *derivation height* of a term t w.r.t. a relation $\rightarrow$ is the length of the longest sequence of $\rightarrow$-steps starting with t, i.e., $\mathrm{dh}(t, \rightarrow) = \sup\{ n \mid \exists t' \in \mathcal{T}, t \rightarrow^n t' \}$, cf. [17]. Here, for any set $M \subseteq \mathbb{N} \cup \{\omega\}$, "$\sup M$" is the least upper bound of M. Thus, $\mathrm{dh}(t, \rightarrow) = \omega$ if t starts an infinite sequence of $\rightarrow$-steps.

As an example, consider $\mathcal{R} = \{\mathsf{dbl}(0) \rightarrow 0,\ \mathsf{dbl}(\mathsf{s}(x)) \rightarrow \mathsf{s}(\mathsf{s}(\mathsf{dbl}(x)))\}$. Then $\mathrm{dh}(\mathsf{dbl}(\mathsf{s}^n(0)), \rightarrow_{\mathcal{R}}) = n + 1$, but $\mathrm{dh}(\mathsf{dbl}^n(\mathsf{s}(0)), \rightarrow_{\mathcal{R}}) = 2^n + n - 1$.

For a TRS $\mathcal{R}$ with *defined symbols* $\Sigma_d = \{\mathrm{root}(\ell) \mid \ell \rightarrow r \in \mathcal{R}\}$, a term $f(t_1, \ldots, t_n)$ is *basic* if $f \in \Sigma_d$ and $t_1, \ldots, t_n$ do not contain symbols from Σ_d. So for $\mathcal{R}$ above, the basic terms are $\mathsf{dbl}(\mathsf{s}^n(0))$ and $\mathsf{dbl}(\mathsf{s}^n(x))$ for $n \in \mathbb{N}$, $x \in \mathcal{V}$. The *innermost runtime complexity function* $\mathrm{irc}_{\mathcal{R}}$ maps any $n \in \mathbb{N}$ to the length of the longest sequence of $\xrightarrow{i}_{\mathcal{R}}$-steps starting with a basic term t with $|t| \leq n$. Here, "$\xrightarrow{i}_{\mathcal{R}}$" is the innermost rewrite relation and $\mathcal{T}_B$ is the set of all basic terms.

Definition 1 ($\mathrm{irc}_{\mathcal{R}}$ [15]). *For a TRS $\mathcal{R}$, its innermost runtime complexity function* $\mathrm{irc}_{\mathcal{R}} : \mathbb{N} \rightarrow \mathbb{N} \cup \{\omega\}$ *is* $\mathrm{irc}_{\mathcal{R}}(n) = \sup\{ \mathrm{dh}(t, \xrightarrow{i}_{\mathcal{R}}) \mid t \in \mathcal{T}_B, |t| \leq n \}$.

If one only considers evaluations of basic terms, the (runtime) complexity of the dbl-TRS is linear ($\mathrm{irc}_{\mathcal{R}}(n) = n - 1$ for $n \geq 2$). But if one also permits evaluations starting with $\mathsf{dbl}^n(\mathsf{s}(0))$, the complexity of the dbl-TRS is exponential.

When analyzing the complexity of *programs*, one is typically interested in (innermost) evaluations where a defined function like dbl is applied to data objects (i.e., terms without defined symbols). Therefore, *(innermost) runtime complexity* corresponds to the usual notion of "complexity" for programs [5,4]. So for any TRS $\mathcal{R}$, we want to determine the *asymptotic complexity* of the function $\mathrm{irc}_{\mathcal{R}}$.

Definition 2 (Asymptotic Complexities). *Let* $\mathfrak{C} = \{\mathcal{P}ol_0, \mathcal{P}ol_1, \mathcal{P}ol_2, \ldots, ?\}$ *with the order* $\mathcal{P}ol_0 \sqsubset \mathcal{P}ol_1 \sqsubset \mathcal{P}ol_2 \sqsubset \ldots \sqsubset ?$. *Let* $\sqsubseteq$ *be the reflexive closure of* $\sqsubset$. *For any function* $f : \mathbb{N} \rightarrow \mathbb{N} \cup \{\omega\}$ *we define its complexity* $\iota(f) \in \mathfrak{C}$ *as follows:* $\iota(f) = \mathcal{P}ol_k$ *if* k *is the smallest number with* $f(n) \in \mathcal{O}(n^k)$ *and* $\iota(f) = ?$ *if there is no such* k. *For any TRS* $\mathcal{R}$, *we define its complexity* $\iota_{\mathcal{R}}$ *as* $\iota(\mathrm{irc}_{\mathcal{R}})$.

So the dbl-TRS $\mathcal{R}$ has linear complexity, i.e., $\iota_{\mathcal{R}} = \mathcal{P}ol_1$. As another example, consider the following TRS $\mathcal{R}$ where "m" stands for "minus".

Example 3.

$$\begin{aligned}
\mathsf{m}(x,y) &\to \mathsf{if}(\mathsf{gt}(x,y),x,y) & \mathsf{gt}(0,k) &\to \mathsf{false} & \mathsf{p}(0) &\to 0 \\
\mathsf{if}(\mathsf{true},x,y) &\to \mathsf{s}(\mathsf{m}(\mathsf{p}(x),y)) & \mathsf{gt}(\mathsf{s}(n),0) &\to \mathsf{true} & \mathsf{p}(\mathsf{s}(n)) &\to n \\
\mathsf{if}(\mathsf{false},x,y) &\to 0 & \mathsf{gt}(\mathsf{s}(n),\mathsf{s}(k)) &\to \mathsf{gt}(n,k)
\end{aligned}$$

Here, $\iota_{\mathcal{R}} = \mathcal{P}ol_2$ (e.g., $\mathsf{m}(\mathsf{s}^n(0),\mathsf{s}^k(0))$ starts evaluations of quadratic length).

3 Dependency Tuples

In the DP method, for every $f \in \Sigma_d$ one introduces a fresh symbol $f^\sharp$ with $\mathrm{ar}(f) = \mathrm{ar}(f^\sharp)$. For a term $t = f(t_1,\ldots,t_n)$ with $f \in \Sigma_d$ we define $t^\sharp = f^\sharp(t_1,\ldots,t_n)$ and let $\mathcal{T}^\sharp = \{\, t^\sharp \mid t \in \mathcal{T}, \mathrm{root}(t) \in \Sigma_d \,\}$. Let $\mathcal{P}os(t)$ contain all positions of t and let $\mathcal{P}os_d(t) = \{\, \pi \mid \pi \in \mathcal{P}os(t), \mathrm{root}(t|_\pi) \in \Sigma_d \,\}$. Then for every rule $\ell \to r$ with $\mathcal{P}os_d(r) = \{\pi_1,\ldots,\pi_n\}$, its *dependency pairs* are $\ell^\sharp \to r|_{\pi_1}^\sharp, \ldots, \ell^\sharp \to r|_{\pi_n}^\sharp$.

While DPs are used for termination, for complexity we have to regard all defined functions in a right-hand side *at once*. Thus, we extend the concept of *weak dependency pairs* [15, 16] and only build a single *dependency tuple* $\ell \to [r|_{\pi_1}^\sharp, \ldots, r|_{\pi_n}^\sharp]$ for each $\ell \to r$. To avoid handling tuples, for every $n \geq 0$, we introduce a fresh *compound symbol* COM_n of arity n and use $\ell^\sharp \to \mathrm{COM}_n(r|_{\pi_1}^\sharp, \ldots, r|_{\pi_n}^\sharp)$.

Definition 4. *[Dependency Tuple] A* dependency tuple *is a rule of the form* $s^\sharp \to \mathrm{COM}_n(t_1^\sharp,\ldots,t_n^\sharp)$ *for* $s^\sharp, t_1^\sharp,\ldots,t_n^\sharp \in \mathcal{T}^\sharp$. *Let* $\ell \to r$ *be a rule with* $\mathcal{P}os_d(r) = \{\pi_1,\ldots,\pi_n\}$. *Then* $DT(\ell \to r)$ *is defined[2] to be* $\ell^\sharp \to \mathrm{COM}_n(r|_{\pi_1}^\sharp,\ldots,r|_{\pi_n}^\sharp)$. *For a TRS* $\mathcal{R}$, *let* $DT(\mathcal{R}) = \{DT(\ell \to r) \mid \ell \to r \in \mathcal{R}\}$.

Example 5. For the TRS $\mathcal{R}$ from Ex. 3, $DT(\mathcal{R})$ is the following set of rules.

$$\mathsf{m}^\sharp(x,y) \to \mathrm{COM}_2(\mathsf{if}^\sharp(\mathsf{gt}(x,y),x,y),\mathsf{gt}^\sharp(x,y)) \quad (1)$$
$$\mathsf{p}^\sharp(0) \to \mathrm{COM}_0 \quad (4)$$
$$\mathsf{if}^\sharp(\mathsf{true},x,y) \to \mathrm{COM}_2(\mathsf{m}^\sharp(\mathsf{p}(x),y),\mathsf{p}^\sharp(x)) \quad (2)$$
$$\mathsf{p}^\sharp(\mathsf{s}(n)) \to \mathrm{COM}_0 \quad (5)$$
$$\mathsf{if}^\sharp(\mathsf{false},x,y) \to \mathrm{COM}_0 \quad (3)$$
$$\mathsf{gt}^\sharp(0,k) \to \mathrm{COM}_0 \quad (6)$$
$$\mathsf{gt}^\sharp(\mathsf{s}(n),0) \to \mathrm{COM}_0 \quad (7)$$
$$\mathsf{gt}^\sharp(\mathsf{s}(n),\mathsf{s}(k)) \to \mathrm{COM}_1(\mathsf{gt}^\sharp(n,k)) \quad (8)$$

For termination, one analyzes *chains* of DPs, which correspond to sequences of function calls that can occur in reductions. Since DTs represent *several* DPs, we now obtain *chain trees*. (This is analogous to the *path detection* in [16]).

Definition 6. *[Chain Tree] Let* $\mathcal{D}$ *be a set of DTs and* $\mathcal{R}$ *be a TRS. Let* T *be a (possibly infinite) tree whose nodes are labeled with both a DT from* $\mathcal{D}$ *and a substitution. Let the root node be labeled with* $(s^\sharp \to \mathrm{COM}_n(\ldots) \mid \sigma)$. *Then* T *is a* $(\mathcal{D},\mathcal{R})$-chain tree *for* $s^\sharp\sigma$ *if the following holds for all nodes of* T: *If a node is labeled with* $(u^\sharp \to \mathrm{COM}_m(v_1^\sharp,\ldots,v_m^\sharp) \mid \mu)$, *then* $u^\sharp\mu$ *is in normal form w.r.t.* $\mathcal{R}$. *Moreover, if this node has the children* $(p_1^\sharp \to \mathrm{COM}_{m_1}(\ldots) \mid \tau_1),\ldots,(p_k^\sharp \to$

---

[2] To make $DT(\ell \to r)$ unique, we use a total order $<$ on positions where $\pi_1 < \ldots < \pi_n$.

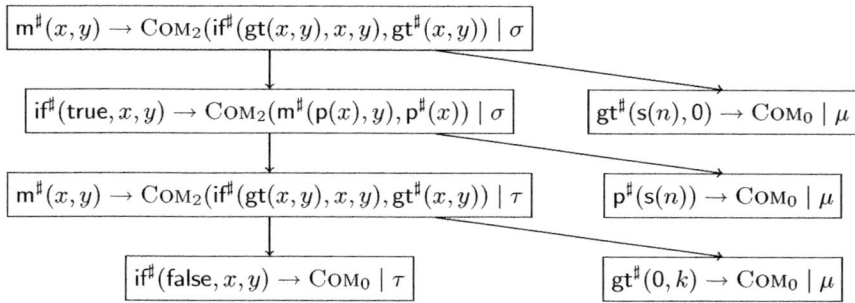

Fig. 1. Chain Tree for the TRS from Ex. 3

$\text{COM}_{m_k}(\ldots) \mid \tau_k)$, *then there are pairwise different* $i_1, \ldots, i_k \in \{1, \ldots, m\}$ *with* $v_{i_j}^\sharp \mu \xrightarrow{i}_{\mathcal{R}}^* p_j^\sharp \tau_j$ *for all* $j \in \{1, \ldots, k\}$. *A path in the chain tree is called a chain.*[3]

Example 7. For the TRS $\mathcal{R}$ *from Ex. 3 and its DTs from Ex. 5, the tree in Fig. 1 is a* $(DT(\mathcal{R}), \mathcal{R})$-*chain tree for* $\mathsf{m}^\sharp(\mathsf{s}(0), 0)$. *Here, we use substitutions with* $\sigma(x) = \mathsf{s}(0)$ *and* $\sigma(y) = 0$, $\tau(x) = \tau(y) = 0$, *and* $\mu(n) = \mu(k) = 0$.

For any term $s^\sharp \in \mathcal{T}^\sharp$, we define its *complexity* as the maximal number of nodes in any chain tree for $s^\sharp$. However, sometimes we do not want to count *all* DTs in the chain tree, but only the DTs from some subset $\mathcal{S}$. This will be crucial to adapt termination techniques for complexity, cf. Sect. 5.2 and 5.4.

Definition 8 (Complexity of Terms, $Cplx_{\langle \mathcal{D}, \mathcal{S}, \mathcal{R} \rangle}$**).** *Let* $\mathcal{D}$ *be a set of dependency tuples,* $\mathcal{S} \subseteq \mathcal{D}$, $\mathcal{R}$ *a TRS, and* $s^\sharp \in \mathcal{T}^\sharp$. *Then* $Cplx_{\langle \mathcal{D}, \mathcal{S}, \mathcal{R} \rangle}(s^\sharp) \in \mathbb{N} \cup \{\omega\}$ *is the maximal number of nodes from* $\mathcal{S}$ *occurring in any* $(\mathcal{D}, \mathcal{R})$-*chain tree for* $s^\sharp$. *If there is no* $(\mathcal{D}, \mathcal{R})$-*chain tree for* $s^\sharp$, *then* $Cplx_{\langle \mathcal{D}, \mathcal{S}, \mathcal{R} \rangle}(s^\sharp) = 0$.

Example 9. For $\mathcal{R}$ *from Ex. 3, we have* $Cplx_{\langle DT(\mathcal{R}), DT(\mathcal{R}), \mathcal{R} \rangle}(\mathsf{m}^\sharp(\mathsf{s}(0), 0)) = 7$, *since the maximal tree for* $\mathsf{m}^\sharp(\mathsf{s}(0), 0)$ *in Fig. 1 has 7 nodes. In contrast, if* $\mathcal{S}$ *is* $DT(\mathcal{R})$ *without the* $\mathsf{gt}^\sharp$-*DTs (6) – (8), then* $Cplx_{\langle DT(\mathcal{R}), \mathcal{S}, \mathcal{R} \rangle}(\mathsf{m}^\sharp(\mathsf{s}(0), 0)) = 5$.

Thm. 10 shows how dependency tuples can be used to approximate the derivation heights of terms. More precisely, $Cplx_{\langle DT(\mathcal{R}), DT(\mathcal{R}), \mathcal{R} \rangle}(t^\sharp)$ is an upper bound for t's derivation height, provided that t is in *argument normal form*.

Theorem 10 (*Cplx* bounds Derivation Height). *Let* $\mathcal{R}$ *be a TRS. Let* $t = f(t_1, \ldots, t_n) \in \mathcal{T}$ *be in* argument normal form, *i.e., all* t_i *are normal forms w.r.t.* $\mathcal{R}$. *Then we have* $dh(t, \xrightarrow{i}_{\mathcal{R}}) \leq Cplx_{\langle DT(\mathcal{R}), DT(\mathcal{R}), \mathcal{R} \rangle}(t^\sharp)$. *If* $\mathcal{R}$ *is confluent, we have* $dh(t, \xrightarrow{i}_{\mathcal{R}}) = Cplx_{\langle DT(\mathcal{R}), DT(\mathcal{R}), \mathcal{R} \rangle}(t^\sharp)$.

Note that DTs are much closer to the original DP method than the *weak DPs* of [15, 16]. While weak DPs also use compound symbols, they only consider the

---

[3] These *chains* correspond to the *"innermost chains"* in the DP framework [1, 10, 11]. To handle *full* (i.e., not necessarily innermost) runtime complexity, one would have to adapt Def. 6 (e.g., then $u^\sharp \mu$ would not have to be in normal form).

topmost defined function symbols in right-hand sides of rules. Hence, [15, 16] does not use DP concepts when defined functions occur nested on right-hand sides (as in the m- and the first if-rule) and thus, it cannot fully benefit from the advantages of the DP technique. Instead, [15, 16] has to impose several restrictions which are not needed in our approach, cf. Footnote 8. The close analogy of our approach to the DP method allows us to adapt the termination techniques of the DP framework in order to work on DTs (i.e., in order to analyze $Cplx_{\langle DT(\mathcal{R}),DT(\mathcal{R}),\mathcal{R}\rangle}(t^\sharp)$ for all basic terms t of a certain size). Using Thm. 10, this yields an upper bound for the complexity $\iota_\mathcal{R}$ of the TRS $\mathcal{R}$, cf. Thm. 14. Note that there exist non-confluent TRSs[4] where $Cplx_{\langle DT(\mathcal{R}),DT(\mathcal{R}),\mathcal{R}\rangle}(t^\sharp)$ is exponentially larger than $dh(t, \xrightarrow{i}_\mathcal{R})$ (in contrast to [15, 16], where the step from TRSs to weak DPs does not change the complexity). However, our main interest is in TRSs corresponding to "typical" (confluent) *programs*. Here, the step from TRSs to DTs does not "lose" anything (i.e., one has equality in Thm. 10).

4   DT Problems

Our goal is to find out automatically how large $Cplx_{\langle \mathcal{D},\mathcal{S},\mathcal{R}\rangle}(t^\sharp)$ could be for basic terms t of size n. To this end, we will repeatedly replace the triple $\langle \mathcal{D}, \mathcal{S}, \mathcal{R}\rangle$ by "simpler" triples $\langle \mathcal{D}', \mathcal{S}', \mathcal{R}'\rangle$ and examine $Cplx_{\langle \mathcal{D}',\mathcal{S}',\mathcal{R}'\rangle}(t^\sharp)$ instead.

This is similar to the DP framework where termination problems are represented by so-called DP problems (consisting of a set of DPs and a set of rules) and where DP problems are transformed into "simpler" DP problems repeatedly. For complexity analysis, we consider "DT problems" instead of "DP problems" (our "DT problems" are similar to the "complexity problems" of [28]).

Definition 11 (DT Problem). *Let $\mathcal{R}$ be a TRS, $\mathcal{D}$ a set of DTs, $\mathcal{S} \subseteq \mathcal{D}$. Then $\langle \mathcal{D}, \mathcal{S}, \mathcal{R}\rangle$ is a DT problem and $\mathcal{R}$'s canonical DT problem is $\langle DT(\mathcal{R}),DT(\mathcal{R}),\mathcal{R}\rangle$.*

Thm. 10 showed the connection between the derivation height of a term and the maximal number of nodes in a chain tree. This leads to the definition of the *complexity of a DT problem* $\langle \mathcal{D}, \mathcal{S}, \mathcal{R}\rangle$. It is defined as the asymptotic complexity of the function $irc_{\langle \mathcal{D},\mathcal{S},\mathcal{R}\rangle}$ which maps any number n to the maximal number of $\mathcal{S}$-nodes in any $(\mathcal{D}, \mathcal{R})$-chain tree for $t^\sharp$, where t is a basic term of at most size n.

Definition 12 (Complexity of DT Problems). *For a DT problem $\langle \mathcal{D}, \mathcal{S}, \mathcal{R}\rangle$, its complexity function is $irc_{\langle \mathcal{D},\mathcal{S},\mathcal{R}\rangle}(n) = \sup\{ Cplx_{\langle \mathcal{D},\mathcal{S},\mathcal{R}\rangle}(t^\sharp) \mid t \in \mathcal{T}_B, |t| \leq n \}$. We define the complexity $\iota_{\langle \mathcal{D},\mathcal{S},\mathcal{R}\rangle}$ of the DT problem as $\iota(irc_{\langle \mathcal{D},\mathcal{S},\mathcal{R}\rangle})$.*

Example 13. Consider $\mathcal{R}$ from Ex. 3 and let $\mathcal{D} = DT(\mathcal{R}) = \{(1),\ldots,(8)\}$. For $t \in \mathcal{T}_B$ with $|t| = n$, the maximal chain tree for $t^\sharp$ has approximately n^2 nodes, i.e., $irc_{\langle \mathcal{D},\mathcal{D},\mathcal{R}\rangle}(n) \in \mathcal{O}(n^2)$. Thus, $\langle \mathcal{D}, \mathcal{D}, \mathcal{R}\rangle$'s complexity is $\iota_{\langle \mathcal{D},\mathcal{D},\mathcal{R}\rangle} = \mathcal{P}ol_2$.

Thm. 14 shows that to analyze the complexity of a TRS $\mathcal{R}$, it suffices to analyze the complexity of its canonical DT problem: By Def. 2, $\iota_\mathcal{R}$ is the complexity of

---

[4] Consider the TRS $f(s(x)) \to f(g(x))$, $g(x) \to x$, $g(x) \to a(f(x))$. Its runtime complexity is linear, but for any $n > 0$, we have $Cplx_{\langle DT(\mathcal{R}),DT(\mathcal{R}),\mathcal{R}\rangle}(f^\sharp(s^n(0))) = 2^{n+1} - 2$.

the runtime complexity function $irc_{\mathcal{R}}$ which maps n to the length of the longest innermost rewrite sequence starting with a basic term of at most size n. By Thm. 10, this length is less than or equal to the size $Cplx_{\langle DT(\mathcal{R}), DT(\mathcal{R}), \mathcal{R}\rangle}(t^{\sharp})$ of the maximal chain tree for any basic term t of at most size n, i.e., to $irc_{\langle DT(\mathcal{R}), DT(\mathcal{R}), \mathcal{R}\rangle}(n)$.

Theorem 14 (Upper bound for TRSs via Canonical DT Problems). *Let $\mathcal{R}$ be a TRS and let $\langle \mathcal{D}, \mathcal{D}, \mathcal{R}\rangle$ be the corresponding canonical DT problem. Then we have $\iota_{\mathcal{R}} \sqsubseteq \iota_{\langle \mathcal{D}, \mathcal{D}, \mathcal{R}\rangle}$ and if $\mathcal{R}$ is confluent, we have $\iota_{\mathcal{R}} = \iota_{\langle \mathcal{D}, \mathcal{D}, \mathcal{R}\rangle}$.*

Now we can introduce our notion of processors which is analogous to the "DP processors" for termination [10, 11] (and related to the "complexity problem processors" in [28]). A DT processor transforms a DT problem P to a pair (c, P') of an asymptotic complexity $c \in \mathfrak{C}$ and a DT problem P', such that P's complexity is bounded by the maximum of c and of the complexity of P'.

Definition 15 (Processor, $\oplus$). *A DT processor PROC is a function $\text{PROC}(P) = (c, P')$ mapping any DT problem P to a complexity $c \in \mathfrak{C}$ and a DT problem P'. A processor is sound if $\iota_P \sqsubseteq c \oplus \iota_{P'}$. Here, "$\oplus$" is the "maximum" function on $\mathfrak{C}$, i.e., for any $c, d \in \mathfrak{C}$, we define $c \oplus d = d$ if $c \sqsubseteq d$ and $c \oplus d = c$ otherwise.*

To analyze the complexity $\iota_{\mathcal{R}}$ of a TRS $\mathcal{R}$, we start with the canonical DT problem $P_0 = \langle DT(\mathcal{R}), DT(\mathcal{R}), \mathcal{R}\rangle$. Then we apply a sound processor to P_0 which yields a result (c_1, P_1). Afterwards, we apply another (possibly different) sound processor to P_1 which yields (c_2, P_2), etc. This is repeated until we obtain a *solved* DT problem (whose complexity is obviously $\mathcal{P}ol_0$).

Definition 16 (Proof Chain, Solved DT Problem). *We call a DT problem $P = \langle \mathcal{D}, \mathcal{S}, \mathcal{R}\rangle$ solved, if $\mathcal{S} = \varnothing$. A proof chain[5] is a finite sequence $P_0 \overset{c_1}{\leadsto} P_1 \overset{c_2}{\leadsto} \ldots \overset{c_k}{\leadsto} P_k$ ending with a solved DT problem P_k, such that for all $0 \leq i < k$ there exists a sound processor PROC_i with $\text{PROC}_i(P_i) = (c_{i+1}, P_{i+1})$.*

By Def. 15 and 16, for every P_i in a proof chain, $c_{i+1} \oplus \ldots \oplus c_k$ is an upper bound for its complexity ι_{P_i}. Here, the empty sum (for $i = k$) is defined as $\mathcal{P}ol_0$.

Theorem 17 (Approximating Complexity by Proof Chain). *Let $P_0 \overset{c_1}{\leadsto} P_1 \overset{c_2}{\leadsto} \ldots \overset{c_k}{\leadsto} P_k$ be a proof chain. Then $\iota_{P_0} \sqsubseteq c_1 \oplus \ldots \oplus c_k$.*

Thm. 14 and 17 now imply that our approach for complexity analysis is correct.

Corollary 18 (Correctness of Approach). *If P_0 is the canonical DT problem for a TRS $\mathcal{R}$ and $P_0 \overset{c_1}{\leadsto} \ldots \overset{c_k}{\leadsto} P_k$ is a proof chain, then $\iota_{\mathcal{R}} \sqsubseteq c_1 \oplus \ldots \oplus c_k$.*

---

[5] Of course, one could also define DT processors that transform a DT problem P into a complexity c and a *set* $\{P_1', \ldots, P_n'\}$ such that $\iota_P \sqsubseteq c \oplus \iota_{P_1'} \oplus \ldots \oplus \iota_{P_n'}$. Then instead of a proof chain one would obtain a proof tree.

5   DT Processors

In this section, we present several processors to simplify DT problems automatically. To this end, we adapt processors of the DP framework for termination.

The *usable rules processor* (Sect. 5.1) simplifies a problem $\langle \mathcal{D}, \mathcal{S}, \mathcal{R} \rangle$ by deleting rules from $\mathcal{R}$. The *reduction pair processor* (Sect. 5.2) removes DTs from $\mathcal{S}$, based on term orders. In Sect. 5.3 we introduce the *dependency graph*, on which the *leaf removal* and *knowledge propagation processor* (Sect. 5.4) are based. Finally, Sect. 5.5 adapts processors based on transformations like *narrowing*.

5.1   Usable Rules Processor

As in termination analysis, we can restrict ourselves to those rewrite rules that can be used to reduce right-hand sides of DTs (when instantiating their variables with normal forms). This leads to the notion of *usable rules*.[6]

Definition 19 (Usable Rules $\mathcal{U}_{\mathcal{R}}$ [1]). *For a TRS $\mathcal{R}$ and any symbol f, let $Rls_{\mathcal{R}}(f) = \{\ell \to r \mid \mathrm{root}(\ell) = f\}$. For any term t, $\mathcal{U}_{\mathcal{R}}(t)$ is the smallest set with*

- $\mathcal{U}_{\mathcal{R}}(x) = \varnothing$ *if* $x \in \mathcal{V}$ *and*
- $\mathcal{U}_{\mathcal{R}}(f(t_1, \ldots, t_n)) = Rls_{\mathcal{R}}(f) \ \cup \ \bigcup_{\ell \to r \in Rls_{\mathcal{R}}(f)} \mathcal{U}_{\mathcal{R}}(r) \cup \bigcup_{1 \le i \le n} \mathcal{U}_{\mathcal{R}}(t_i)$

For any set $\mathcal{D}$ of DTs, we define $\mathcal{U}_{\mathcal{R}}(\mathcal{D}) = \bigcup_{s \to t \in \mathcal{D}} \mathcal{U}_{\mathcal{R}}(t)$.

So for $\mathcal{R}$ and $DT(\mathcal{R})$ in Ex. 3 and 5, $\mathcal{U}_{\mathcal{R}}(DT(\mathcal{R}))$ contains just the gt- and the p-rules. The following processor removes non-usable rules from DT problems.[7]

Theorem 20 (Usable Rules Processor). *Let $\langle \mathcal{D}, \mathcal{S}, \mathcal{R} \rangle$ be a DT problem. Then the following processor is sound:* $\mathrm{Proc}(\langle \mathcal{D}, \mathcal{S}, \mathcal{R} \rangle) = (\mathcal{Pol}_0, \langle \mathcal{D}, \mathcal{S}, \mathcal{U}_{\mathcal{R}}(\mathcal{D}) \rangle)$.

So when applying the usable rules processor on the canonical DT problem $\langle \mathcal{D}, \mathcal{D}, \mathcal{R} \rangle$ of $\mathcal{R}$ from Ex. 3, we obtain $\langle \mathcal{D}, \mathcal{D}, \mathcal{R}_1 \rangle$ where $\mathcal{R}_1$ are the gt- and p-rules.

5.2   Reduction Pair Processor

Using orders is one of the most important methods for termination or complexity analysis. In the most basic approach, one tries to find a well-founded order $\succ$ such that every reduction step (strictly) decreases w.r.t. $\succ$. This proves termination and most reduction orders also imply some complexity bound, cf. e.g. [7, 17]. However, *direct* applications of orders have two main drawbacks: The obtained bounds are often far too high to be useful and there are many TRSs that cannot be oriented strictly with standard orders amenable to automation, cf. [28].

---

[6] The idea of applying *usable rules* also for complexity analysis is due to [15], which introduced a technique similar to Thm. 20.

[7] While Def. 19 is the most basic definition of *usable rules*, the processor of Thm. 20 can also be used with more sophisticated definitions of "usable rules" (e.g., as in [11]).

Therefore, the *reduction pair processor* of the DP framework only requires a strict decrease (w.r.t. $\succ$) for at least one DP, while for all other DPs and rules, a weak decrease (w.r.t. $\succsim$) suffices. Then the strictly decreasing DPs can be deleted. Afterwards one can use other orders (or termination techniques) to solve the remaining DP problem. To adapt the reduction pair processor for complexity analysis, we have to restrict ourselves to COM-*monotonic* orders.[8]

Definition 21 (Reduction Pair). *A reduction pair* $(\succsim, \succ)$ *consists of a stable monotonic quasi-order* $\succsim$ *and a stable well-founded order* $\succ$ *which are compatible (i.e.,* $\succsim \circ \succ \circ \succsim\ \subseteq\ \succ$ *). An order* $\succ$ *is* COM-*monotonic iff* $\mathrm{COM}_n(s_1^\sharp, ..., s_i^\sharp, ..., s_n^\sharp) \succ \mathrm{COM}_n(s_1^\sharp, ..., t^\sharp, ..., s_n^\sharp)$ *for all* $n \in \mathbb{N}$*, all* $1 \le i \le n$*, and all* $s_1^\sharp, ..., s_n^\sharp, t^\sharp \in \mathcal{T}^\sharp$ *with* $s_i^\sharp \succ t^\sharp$*. A reduction pair* $(\succsim, \succ)$ *is* COM-*monotonic iff* $\succ$ *is* COM-*monotonic.*

For a DT problem $(\mathcal{D}, \mathcal{S}, \mathcal{R})$, we orient $\mathcal{D} \cup \mathcal{R}$ by $\succsim$ or $\succ$. But in contrast to the processor for termination, if a DT is oriented strictly, we may not remove it from $\mathcal{D}$, *but only from* $\mathcal{S}$. So the DT is not counted anymore for complexity, but it may still be used in reductions.[9] We will improve this later in Sect. 5.4.

Example 22. This TRS $\mathcal{R}$ *shows why DTs may not be removed from* $\mathcal{D}$*.*[10]

$$\mathsf{f}(0) \to 0 \qquad \mathsf{f}(\mathsf{s}(x)) \to \mathsf{f}(\mathsf{id}(x)) \qquad \mathsf{id}(0) \to 0 \qquad \mathsf{id}(\mathsf{s}(x)) \to \mathsf{s}(\mathsf{id}(x))$$

Let $\mathcal{D} = DT(\mathcal{R}) = \{\mathsf{f}^\sharp(0) \to \mathrm{COM}_0, \ \mathsf{f}^\sharp(\mathsf{s}(x)) \to \mathrm{COM}_2(\mathsf{f}^\sharp(\mathsf{id}(x)), \mathsf{id}^\sharp(x)), \ \mathsf{id}^\sharp(0) \to \mathrm{COM}_0, \ \mathsf{id}^\sharp(\mathsf{s}(x)) \to \mathrm{COM}_1(\mathsf{id}^\sharp(x))\}$, where $\mathcal{U}_\mathcal{R}(\mathcal{D})$ are just the id-rules. For the DT problem $\langle \mathcal{D}, \mathcal{S}, \mathcal{U}_\mathcal{R}(\mathcal{D}) \rangle$ with $\mathcal{S} = \mathcal{D}$, there is a linear polynomial interpretation $[\cdot]$ that orients the first two DTs strictly and the remaining DTs and usable rules weakly: $[0] = 0, [\mathsf{s}](x) = x + 1, [\mathsf{id}](x) = x, [\mathsf{f}^\sharp](x) = x + 1, [\mathsf{id}^\sharp](x) = 0, [\mathrm{COM}_0] = 0, [\mathrm{COM}_1](x) = x, [\mathrm{COM}_2](x, y) = x + y$. If one would remove the first two DTs from $\mathcal{D}$, there is another linear polynomial interpretation that orients the remaining DTs strictly (e.g., by $[\mathsf{id}^\sharp](x) = x + 1$). Then, one would falsely conclude that the whole TRS has linear runtime complexity.

Hence, the first two DTs should only be removed from $\mathcal{S}$, not from $\mathcal{D}$. This results in $\langle \mathcal{D}, \mathcal{S}', \mathcal{U}_\mathcal{R}(\mathcal{D}) \rangle$ where $\mathcal{S}'$ consists of the last two DTs. These DTs can occur quadratically often in reductions with $\mathcal{D} \cup \mathcal{U}_\mathcal{R}(\mathcal{D})$. Hence, when trying to orient $\mathcal{S}'$ strictly and the remaining DTs and usable rules weakly, we have to use a quadratic polynomial interpretation (e.g., $[0] = 0, [\mathsf{s}](x) = x + 2, [\mathsf{id}](x) = x, [\mathsf{f}^\sharp](x) = x^2, [\mathsf{id}^\sharp](x) = x + 1, [\mathrm{COM}_0] = 0, [\mathrm{COM}_1](x) = x, [\mathrm{COM}_2](x, y) = x + y)$.

---

[8] In [15] "COM-monotonic" is called "safe". Note that our reduction pair processor is much closer to the original processor of the DP framework than [15]. In the main theorem of [15], all (weak) DPs have to be oriented strictly in one go. Moreover, one even has to orient the (usable) rules strictly. Finally, one is either restricted to non-duplicating TRSs or one has to use orderings $\succ$ that are monotonic on *all* symbols.

[9] This idea is also used in [28]. However, [28] treats derivational complexity instead of (innermost) runtime complexity, and it operates directly on TRSs and not on DPs or DTs. Therefore, [28] has to impose stronger restrictions (it requires $\succ$ to be monotonic on *all* symbols) and it does not use other DP- resp. DT-based processors.

[10] An alternative such example is shown in [8, Ex. 11].

Hence, now we (correctly) conclude that the TRS has quadratic runtime complexity (indeed, $\mathrm{dh}(\mathsf{f}(\mathsf{s}^n(0)), \overset{\mathrm{i}}{\to}_{\mathcal{R}}) = \frac{(n+1)\cdot(n+2)}{2}$ *).*

So when applying the reduction pair processor to $\langle \mathcal{D}, \mathcal{S}, \mathcal{R} \rangle$, we obtain $(c, \langle \mathcal{D}, \mathcal{S} \setminus \mathcal{D}_{\succ}, \mathcal{R} \rangle)$. Here, $\mathcal{D}_{\succ}$ are the strictly decreasing DTs from $\mathcal{D}$ and c is an upper bound for the number of $\mathcal{D}_{\succ}$-steps in innermost reductions with $\mathcal{D} \cup \mathcal{R}$.

Theorem 23 (Reduction Pair Processor). *Let* $P = \langle \mathcal{D}, \mathcal{S}, \mathcal{R} \rangle$ *be a DT problem and* $(\succsim, \succ)$ *be a* Com*-monotonic reduction pair. Let* $\mathcal{D} \subseteq \succsim \cup \succ$, $\mathcal{R} \subseteq \succsim$, *and* $c \sqsupseteq \iota(\mathrm{irc}_{\succ})$ *for the function* $\mathrm{irc}_{\succ}(n) = \sup\{\, \mathrm{dh}(t^{\sharp}, \succ) \mid t \in \mathcal{T}_B, |t| \le n \,\}$.[11] *Then the following processor is sound:* $\mathrm{Proc}(\langle \mathcal{D}, \mathcal{S}, \mathcal{R} \rangle) = (c, \langle \mathcal{D}, \mathcal{S} \setminus \mathcal{D}_{\succ}, \mathcal{R} \rangle)$.

To automate Thm. 23, we need reduction pairs $(\succsim, \succ)$ where an upper bound c for $\iota(\mathrm{irc}_{\succ})$ is easy to compute. This holds for reduction pairs based on *polynomial interpretations* with coefficients from $\mathbb{N}$ (which are well suited for automation). For Com-monotonicity, we restrict ourselves to *complexity polynomial interpretations (CPIs)* $[\cdot]$ where $[\mathrm{Com}_n](x_1, ..., x_n) = x_1 + ... + x_n$ for all $n \in \mathbb{N}$. This is the "smallest" polynomial which is monotonic in $x_1, ..., x_n$. As Com_n only occurs on right-hand sides of inequalities, $[\mathrm{Com}_n]$ should be as small as possible.

Moreover, a *CPI* interprets constructors $f \in \Sigma \setminus \Sigma_d$ by polynomials $[f](x_1, ..., x_n) = a_1 x_1 + ... + a_n x_n + b$ where $b \in \mathbb{N}$ and $a_i \in \{0, 1\}$. This ensures that the mapping from constructor ground terms $t \in \mathcal{T}(\Sigma \setminus \Sigma_d, \varnothing)$ to their interpretations is in $\mathcal{O}(|t|)$, cf. [7,17]. Note that the interpretations in Ex. 22 were *CPIs*.

Thm. 24 shows how such interpretations can be used[12] for the processor of Thm. 23. Here, as an upper bound c for $\iota(\mathrm{irc}_{\succ})$, one can simply take $\mathcal{P}ol_m$, where m is the maximal degree of the polynomials in the interpretation.

Theorem 24 (Reduction Pair Processor with Polynomial Interpretations). *Let* $P = \langle \mathcal{D}, \mathcal{S}, \mathcal{R} \rangle$ *be a DT problem and let* $\succsim$ *and* $\succ$ *be induced by a CPI* $[\cdot]$. *Let* $m \in \mathbb{N}$ *be the maximal degree of all polynomials* $[f^{\sharp}]$, *for all* $f^{\sharp}$ *with* $f \in \Sigma_d$. *Let* $\mathcal{D} \subseteq \succsim \cup \succ$ *and* $\mathcal{R} \subseteq \succsim$. *Then the following processor is sound:* $\mathrm{Proc}(\langle \mathcal{D}, \mathcal{S}, \mathcal{R} \rangle) = (\mathcal{P}ol_m, \langle \mathcal{D}, \mathcal{S} \setminus \mathcal{D}_{\succ}, \mathcal{R} \rangle)$.

Example 25. This TRS [1] illustrates Thm. 24, where $\mathsf{q}(x, y, y)$ *computes* $\lfloor \frac{x}{y} \rfloor$.

$$\mathsf{q}(0, \mathsf{s}(y), \mathsf{s}(z)) \to 0 \quad \mathsf{q}(\mathsf{s}(x), \mathsf{s}(y), z) \to \mathsf{q}(x, y, z) \quad \mathsf{q}(x, 0, \mathsf{s}(z)) \to \mathsf{s}(\mathsf{q}(x, \mathsf{s}(z), \mathsf{s}(z)))$$

---

[11] As noted by [22], this can be weakened by replacing $\mathrm{dh}(t^{\sharp}, \succ)$ with $\mathrm{dh}(t^{\sharp}, \succ \cap \overset{\mathrm{i}}{\to}_{\mathcal{D}/\mathcal{R}})$, where $\to_{\mathcal{D}/\mathcal{R}} = \to_{\mathcal{R}}^* \circ \to_{\mathcal{D}} \circ \to_{\mathcal{R}}^*$ and $\overset{\mathrm{i}}{\to}_{\mathcal{D}/\mathcal{R}}$ is the restriction of $\to_{\mathcal{D}/\mathcal{R}}$ where in each rewrite step with $\to_{\mathcal{R}}$ or $\to_{\mathcal{D}}$, the arguments of the redex must be in $(\mathcal{D} \cup \mathcal{R})$-normal form, cf. [3]. Such a weakening is required to use reduction pairs based on path orders where a term $t^{\sharp}$ may start $\succ$-decreasing sequences of arbitrary (finite) length.

[12] Alternatively, our reduction pair processor can also use matrix interpretations [8,19, 21,23,27], polynomial path orders (POP* [3]), etc. For POP*, we would extend $\mathfrak{C}$ by a complexity $\mathcal{P}ol_*$ for polytime computability, where $\mathcal{P}ol_n \sqsubset \mathcal{P}ol_* \sqsubset ?$ for all $n \in \mathbb{N}$.

The dependency tuples $\mathcal{D}$ of this TRS are

$$\mathsf{q}^\sharp(0,\mathsf{s}(y),\mathsf{s}(z)) \to \mathrm{COM}_0 \quad (9) \qquad \mathsf{q}^\sharp(\mathsf{s}(x),\mathsf{s}(y),z) \to \mathrm{COM}_1(\mathsf{q}^\sharp(x,y,z)) \quad (10)$$

$$\mathsf{q}^\sharp(x,0,\mathsf{s}(z)) \to \mathrm{COM}_1(\mathsf{q}^\sharp(x,\mathsf{s}(z),\mathsf{s}(z))) \quad (11)$$

As the usable rules are empty, Thm. 20 transforms the canonical DT problem to $\langle \mathcal{D}, \mathcal{D}, \varnothing \rangle$. Consider the CPI $[0] = 0$, $[\mathsf{s}](x) = x{+}1$, $[\mathsf{q}^\sharp](x,y,z) = x{+}1$, $[\mathrm{COM}_0] = 0$, $[\mathrm{COM}_1](x) = x$. With the corresponding reduction pair, the DTs (9) and (10) are strictly decreasing and (11) is weakly decreasing. Moreover, the degree of $[\mathsf{q}^\sharp]$ is 1. Hence, the reduction pair processor returns $(\mathcal{P}ol_1, \langle \mathcal{D}, \{(11)\}, \varnothing \rangle)$. Unfortunately, no reduction pair based on CPIs orients (11) strictly and both (9) and (10) weakly. So for the moment we cannot simplify this problem further.

5.3 Dependency Graph Processors

As in the DP framework for termination, it is useful to have a finite representation of (a superset of) all possible chain trees.

Definition 26 (Dependency Graph). *Let $\mathcal{D}$ be a set of DTs and $\mathcal{R}$ a TRS. The $(\mathcal{D}, \mathcal{R})$-dependency graph is the directed graph whose nodes are the DTs in $\mathcal{D}$ and there is an edge from $s \to t$ to $u \to v$ in the dependency graph iff there is a chain tree with an edge from a node $(s \to t \mid \sigma_1)$ to a node $(u \to v \mid \sigma_2)$.*

Every $(\mathcal{D}, \mathcal{R})$-chain corresponds to a path in the $(\mathcal{D}, \mathcal{R})$-dependency graph. While dependency graphs are not computable in general, there are several techniques to compute over-approximations of dependency graphs for termination, cf. e.g. [1]. These techniques can also be applied for $(\mathcal{D}, \mathcal{R})$-dependency graphs.

Example 27. For the TRS $\mathcal{R}$ from Ex. 3, we obtain the following $(\mathcal{D}, \mathcal{R}_1)$-dependency graph, where $\mathcal{D} = DT(\mathcal{R})$ and $\mathcal{R}_1$ are the gt- and p-rules.

For termination analysis, one can regard strongly connected components of the graph separately and ignore nodes that are not on cycles. This is not possible for complexity analysis: If one regards the DTs $\mathcal{D}' = \{(1),(2)\}$ and $\mathcal{D}'' = \{(8)\}$ on the two cycles of the graph separately, then both resulting DT problems $\langle \mathcal{D}', \mathcal{D}', \mathcal{R}_1 \rangle$ and $\langle \mathcal{D}'', \mathcal{D}'', \mathcal{R}_1 \rangle$ have linear complexity. However, this allows no conclusions on the complexity of $\langle \mathcal{D}, \mathcal{D}, \mathcal{R}_1 \rangle$ (which is quadratic). Nevertheless, it is possible to remove DTs $s \to t$ that are leaves (i.e., $s \to t$ has no successors in the dependency graph). This yields $\langle \mathcal{D}_1, \mathcal{D}_1, \mathcal{R}_1 \rangle$, where $\mathcal{D}_1 = \{(1),(2),(8)\}$.

Theorem 28 (Leaf Removal Processor). *Let $\langle \mathcal{D}, \mathcal{S}, \mathcal{R} \rangle$ be a DT problem and let $s \to t \in \mathcal{D}$ be a leaf in the $(\mathcal{D}, \mathcal{R})$-dependency graph. Then the following processor is sound:* $\mathrm{PROC}(\langle \mathcal{D}, \mathcal{S}, \mathcal{R} \rangle) = (\mathcal{P}ol_0, \langle \mathcal{D} \setminus \{s \to t\}, \mathcal{S} \setminus \{s \to t\}, \mathcal{R} \rangle)$.

5.4   Knowledge Propagation

In the DP framework for termination, the reduction pair processor removes "strictly decreasing" DPs. While this is unsound for complexity analysis (cf. Ex. 22), we now show that by an appropriate *extension* of DT problems, one can obtain a similar processor also for complexity analysis.

Lemma 29 shows that we can estimate the complexity of a DT if we know the complexity of all its *predecessors* in the dependency graph.

Lemma 29 (Complexity Bounded by Predecessors). *Let $\langle \mathcal{D}, \mathcal{S}, \mathcal{R} \rangle$ be a DT problem and $s \to t \in \mathcal{D}$. Let $Pre(s \to t) \subseteq \mathcal{D}$ be the predecessors of $s \to t$, i.e., $Pre(s \to t)$ contains all DTs $u \to v$ where there is an edge from $u \to v$ to $s \to t$ in the $(\mathcal{D}, \mathcal{R})$-dependency graph. Then $\iota_{\langle \mathcal{D}, \{s \to t\}, \mathcal{R} \rangle} \sqsubseteq \iota_{\langle \mathcal{D}, Pre(s \to t), \mathcal{R} \rangle}$.*

Example 30.   Consider the TRS from Ex. 25. By usable rules and reduction pairs, we obtained $\langle \mathcal{D}, \{(11)\}, \varnothing \rangle$ for $\mathcal{D} = \{(9), (10), (11)\}$. The leaf re-

$$\circlearrowleft$$
$$\boxed{\mathsf{q}^\sharp(\mathsf{s}(x), \mathsf{s}(y), z) \to \mathrm{COM}_1(\mathsf{q}^\sharp(x, y, z))\ (10)}$$
$$\boxed{\mathsf{q}^\sharp(x, 0, \mathsf{s}(z)) \to \mathrm{COM}_1(\mathsf{q}^\sharp(x, \mathsf{s}(z), \mathsf{s}(z)))\ (11)}$$

moval processor yields $\langle \mathcal{D}', \{(11)\}, \varnothing \rangle$ with $\mathcal{D}' = \{(10), (11)\}$. Consider the the $(\mathcal{D}', \varnothing)$-dependency graph above. We have $\iota_{\langle \mathcal{D}', \{(11)\}, \varnothing \rangle} \sqsubseteq \iota_{\langle \mathcal{D}', \{(10)\}, \varnothing \rangle}$ by Lemma 29, since (10) is the only predecessor of (11). Thus, the complexity of $\langle \mathcal{D}', \{(11)\}, \varnothing \rangle$ does not matter for the overall complexity, if we can guarantee that we have already taken the complexity of $\langle \mathcal{D}', \{(10)\}, \varnothing \rangle$ into account.

Therefore, we now extend the definition of DT problems by a set $\mathcal{K}$ of DTs with "known" complexity, i.e., the complexity of the DTs in $\mathcal{K}$ has already been taken into account. So a processor only needs to estimate the complexity of a set of DTs correctly if their complexity is higher than the complexity of the DTs in $\mathcal{K}$. Otherwise, the processor may return an arbitrary result. To this end, we introduce a "subtraction" operation $\ominus$ on complexities from $\mathfrak{C}$.

Definition 31 (Extended DT Problems, $\ominus$). *For $c, d, \in \mathfrak{C}$, let $c \ominus d = c$ if $d \sqsubset c$ and $c \ominus d = \mathcal{P}ol_0$ if $c \sqsubseteq d$. Let $\mathcal{R}$ be a TRS, $\mathcal{D}$ a set of DTs, and $\mathcal{S}, \mathcal{K} \subseteq \mathcal{D}$. Then $\langle \mathcal{D}, \mathcal{S}, \mathcal{K}, \mathcal{R} \rangle$ is an extended DT problem and $\langle DT(\mathcal{R}), DT(\mathcal{R}), \varnothing, \mathcal{R} \rangle$ is the canonical extended DT problem for $\mathcal{R}$. We define the complexity of an extended DT problem to be $\gamma_{\langle \mathcal{D}, \mathcal{S}, \mathcal{K}, \mathcal{R} \rangle} = \iota_{\langle \mathcal{D}, \mathcal{S}, \mathcal{R} \rangle} \ominus \iota_{\langle \mathcal{D}, \mathcal{K}, \mathcal{R} \rangle}$ and also use γ instead of ι in the soundness condition for processors. So on extended DT problems, a processor with $\mathrm{PROC}(P) = (c, P')$ is sound if $\gamma_P \sqsubseteq c \oplus \gamma_{P'}$. An extended DT problem $\langle \mathcal{D}, \mathcal{S}, \mathcal{K}, \mathcal{R} \rangle$ is solved if $\mathcal{S} = \varnothing$.*

So for $\mathcal{K} = \varnothing$, the definition of "complexity" for extended DT problems is equivalent to complexity for ordinary DT problems, i.e., $\gamma_{\langle \mathcal{D}, \mathcal{S}, \varnothing, \mathcal{R} \rangle} = \iota_{\langle \mathcal{D}, \mathcal{S}, \mathcal{R} \rangle}$. Cor. 32 shows that our approach is still correct for extended DT problems.

Corollary 32 (Correctness). *If P_0 is the canonical extended DT problem for a TRS $\mathcal{R}$ and $P_0 \overset{c_1}{\leadsto} \ldots \overset{c_k}{\leadsto} P_k$ is a proof chain, then $\iota_{\mathcal{R}} = \gamma_{P_0} \sqsubseteq c_1 \oplus \ldots \oplus c_k$.*

Now we introduce a processor which makes use of $\mathcal{K}$. It moves a DT $s \to t$ from $\mathcal{S}$ to $\mathcal{K}$ whenever the complexity of all predecessors of $s \to t$ in the dependency graph has already been taken into account.[13]

Theorem 33 (Knowledge Propagation Processor). *Let $\langle \mathcal{D}, \mathcal{S}, \mathcal{K}, \mathcal{R} \rangle$ be an extended DT problem, $s \to t \in \mathcal{S}$, and $Pre(s \to t) \subseteq \mathcal{K}$. Then the following processor is sound:* $\text{PROC}(\langle \mathcal{D}, \mathcal{S}, \mathcal{K}, \mathcal{R} \rangle) = (\mathcal{P}ol_0, \langle \mathcal{D}, \mathcal{S} \backslash \{s \to t\}, \mathcal{K} \cup \{s \to t\}, \mathcal{R} \rangle)$.

Before we can illustrate this processor, we need to adapt the previous processors to *extended* DT problems. The adaption of the usable rules and leaf removal processors is straightforward. But now the reduction pair processor does not only delete DTs from $\mathcal{S}$, but moves them to $\mathcal{K}$. The reason is that the complexity of these DTs is bounded by the complexity value $c \in \mathfrak{C}$ returned by the processor. (Of course, the special case of the reduction pair processor with polynomial interpretations of Thm. 24 can be adapted analogously.)

Theorem 34 (Processors for Extended DT Problems). *Let $P = \langle \mathcal{D}, \mathcal{S}, \mathcal{K}, \mathcal{R} \rangle$ be an extended DT problem. Then the following processors are sound.*

- *The usable rules processor:* $\text{PROC}(P) = (\mathcal{P}ol_0, \langle \mathcal{D}, \mathcal{S}, \mathcal{K}, \mathcal{U}_{\mathcal{R}}(\mathcal{D}) \rangle)$.
- *The leaf removal processor* $\text{PROC}(P) = (\mathcal{P}ol_0, \langle \mathcal{D} \backslash \{s \to t\}, \mathcal{S} \backslash \{s \to t\}, \mathcal{K} \backslash \{s \to t\}, \mathcal{R} \rangle)$, *if $s \to t$ is a leaf in the $(\mathcal{D}, \mathcal{R})$-dependency graph.*
- *The reduction pair processor:* $\text{PROC}(P) = (c, \langle \mathcal{D}, \mathcal{S} \backslash \mathcal{D}_\succ, \mathcal{K} \cup \mathcal{D}_\succ, \mathcal{R} \rangle)$, *if $(\succsim, \succ)$ is a COM-monotonic reduction pair, $\mathcal{D} \subseteq \succsim \cup \succ$, $\mathcal{R} \subseteq \succsim$, and $c \sqsupseteq \iota(\text{irc}_\succ)$ for the function $\text{irc}_\succ(n) = \sup\{ \text{dh}(t^\sharp, \succ) \mid t \in \mathcal{T}_B, |t| \leq n \}$.*

Example 35. Reconsider the TRS $\mathcal{R}$ for division from Ex. 25. Starting with its canonical extended DT problem, we now obtain the following proof chain.

$$
\begin{array}{llll}
& \langle \{(9), (10), (11)\}, & \{(9), (10), (11)\}, & \varnothing, & \mathcal{R} \rangle \\
\overset{\mathcal{P}ol_0}{\leadsto} & \langle \{(10), (11)\}, & \{(10), (11)\}, & \varnothing, & \mathcal{R} \rangle & \text{(leaf removal)} \\
\overset{\mathcal{P}ol_0}{\leadsto} & \langle \{(10), (11)\}, & \{(10), (11)\}, & \varnothing, & \varnothing \rangle & \text{(usable rules)} \\
\overset{\mathcal{P}ol_1}{\leadsto} & \langle \{(10), (11)\}, & \{(11)\}, & \{(10)\}, & \varnothing \rangle & \text{(reduction pair)} \\
\overset{\mathcal{P}ol_0}{\leadsto} & \langle \{(10), (11)\}, & \varnothing, & \{(10), (11)\}, \varnothing \rangle & \text{(knowledge propag.)}
\end{array}
$$

For the last step we use $Pre((11)) = \{(10)\}$, cf. Ex. 30. The last DT problem is solved. Thus, $\iota_{\mathcal{R}} \sqsubseteq \mathcal{P}ol_0 \oplus \mathcal{P}ol_0 \oplus \mathcal{P}ol_1 \oplus \mathcal{P}ol_0 = \mathcal{P}ol_1$, i.e., $\mathcal{R}$ has linear complexity.

5.5 Transformation Processors

To increase power, the DP framework for termination analysis has several processors which *transform* a DP into new ones (by "narrowing", "rewriting", "instantiation", or "forward instantiation") [11]. We now show how to adapt such processors for complexity analysis. For reasons of space, we only present the narrowing processor (the other processors can be adapted in a similar way).

---

[13] In particular, this means that nodes without predecessors (i.e., "roots" of the dependency graph that are not in any cycle) can always be moved from $\mathcal{S}$ to $\mathcal{K}$.

For an extended DT problem $\langle \mathcal{D}, \mathcal{S}, \mathcal{K}, \mathcal{R} \rangle$, let $s \to t \in \mathcal{D}$ with $t = \text{COM}_n(t_1,$
$\ldots, t_i, \ldots, t_n)$. If there exists a (variable-renamed) $u \to v \in \mathcal{D}$ where t_i and u have
an mgu μ and both $s\mu$ and $u\mu$ are in $\mathcal{R}$-normal form, then we call μ a *narrowing*
substitution of t_i and define the corresponding *narrowing result* to be $t_i\mu$.

Moreover, if $s \to t$ has a successor $u \to v$ in the $(\mathcal{D}, \mathcal{R})$-dependency graph
where t_i and u have no such mgu, then we obtain additional narrowing substitutions and narrowing results for t_i. The reason is that in any possible reduction
$t_i\sigma \xrightarrow{i}{}^*_\mathcal{R} u\tau$ in a chain, the term $t_i\sigma$ must be rewritten at least one step before it
reaches $u\tau$. The idea of the narrowing processor is to already perform this first
reduction step directly on the DT $s \to t$. Whenever a subterm $t_i|_\pi \notin \mathcal{V}$ of t_i
unifies with the left-hand side of a (variable-renamed) rule $\ell \to r \in \mathcal{R}$ using an
mgu μ where $s\mu$ is in $\mathcal{R}$-normal form, then μ is a *narrowing substitution* of t_i
and the corresponding *narrowing result* is $w = t_i[r]_\pi\mu$.

If $\mu_1, \ldots, \mu_d$ are all narrowing substitutions of t_i with the corresponding narrowing results $w_1, \ldots, w_d$, then $s \to t$ can be replaced by $s\mu_j \to \text{COM}_n(t_1\mu_j, \ldots,$
$t_{i-1}\mu_j, w_j, t_{i+1}\mu_j, \ldots, t_n\mu_j)$ for all $1 \le j \le d$.

However, there could be a t_k (with $k \ne i$) which was involved in a chain
(i.e., $t_k\sigma \xrightarrow{i}{}^*_\mathcal{R} u\tau$ for some $u \to v \in \mathcal{D}$ and some σ, τ), but this chain is no longer
possible when instantiating t_k to $t_k\mu_1, \ldots, t_k\mu_d$. We say that t_k is *captured* by μ_1,
$\ldots, \mu_d$ if for each narrowing substitution ρ of t_k, there is a μ_j that is more general
(i.e., $\rho = \mu_j \rho'$ for some substitution ρ'). The narrowing processor has to add
another DT $s \to \text{COM}_m(t_{k_1}, \ldots, t_{k_m})$ where $t_{k_1}, \ldots, t_{k_m}$ are all terms from $t_1,$
$\ldots, t_n$ which are not captured by the narrowing substitutions $\mu_1, \ldots, \mu_d$ of t_i.

This leads to the following processor. For any sets $\mathcal{D}, \mathcal{M}$ of DTs, $\mathcal{D}[s \to t \,/\, \mathcal{M}]$
denotes the result of replacing $s \to t$ by the DTs in $\mathcal{M}$. So if $s \to t \in \mathcal{D}$, then
$\mathcal{D}[s \to t \,/\, \mathcal{M}] = (DT \setminus \{s \to t\}) \cup \mathcal{M}$ and otherwise, $\mathcal{D}[s \to t \,/\, \mathcal{M}] = \mathcal{D}$.

Theorem 36 (Narrowing Processor). *Let $P = \langle \mathcal{D}, \mathcal{S}, \mathcal{K}, \mathcal{R} \rangle$ be an extended*
DT problem and let $s \to t \in \mathcal{D}$ with $t = \text{COM}_n(t_1, \ldots, t_i, \ldots, t_n)$. Let $\mu_1, \ldots, \mu_d$
be the narrowing substitutions of t_i with the corresponding narrowing results
$w_1, \ldots, w_d$, where $d \ge 0$. Let $t_{k_1}, \ldots, t_{k_m}$ be the terms from $t_1, \ldots, t_n$ that are
not captured by $\mu_1, \ldots, \mu_d$, where $k_1, \ldots, k_m$ are pairwise different. We define

$$\begin{aligned}
\mathcal{M} = \ &\{s\mu_j \to \text{COM}_n(t_1\mu_j, \ldots, t_{i-1}\mu_j, w_j, t_{i+1}\mu_j, \ldots, t_n\mu_j) \mid 1 \le j \le d\} \\
&\cup \{s \ \ \to \text{COM}_m(t_{k_1}, \ldots, t_{k_m})\}.
\end{aligned}$$

Then the following processor is sound: $\text{PROC}(P) = (\mathcal{P}ol_0, \langle \mathcal{D}', \mathcal{S}', \mathcal{K}', \mathcal{R} \rangle)$, *where*
$\mathcal{D}' = \mathcal{D}[s \to t \,/\, \mathcal{M}]$ and $\mathcal{S}' = \mathcal{S}[s \to t \,/\, \mathcal{M}]$. $\mathcal{K}'$ results from $\mathcal{K}$ by removing $s \to t$
and all DTs that are reachable from $s \to t$ in the $(\mathcal{D}, \mathcal{R})$-dependency graph.[14]

---

[14] We cannot define $\mathcal{K}' = \mathcal{K}[s \to t \,/\, \mathcal{M}]$, because the narrowing step performed on
$s \to t$ does not necessarily correspond to an *innermost* reduction. Hence, there can
be $(\mathcal{D}', \mathcal{R})$-chains that correspond to non-innermost reductions with $\mathcal{D} \cup \mathcal{R}$. So there
may exist terms whose maximal $(\mathcal{D}', \mathcal{R})$-chain tree is larger than their maximal
$(\mathcal{D}, \mathcal{R})$-chain tree and thus, $\iota_{\langle \mathcal{D}', \mathcal{K}[s \to t/\mathcal{M}], \mathcal{R} \rangle} \sqsupseteq \iota_{\langle \mathcal{D}, \mathcal{K}, \mathcal{R} \rangle}$. But we need $\iota_{\langle \mathcal{D}', \mathcal{K}', \mathcal{R} \rangle} \sqsubseteq$
$\iota_{\langle \mathcal{D}, \mathcal{K}, \mathcal{R} \rangle}$ in order to guarantee the soundness of the processor, i.e., to ensure that
$\gamma_{\langle \mathcal{D}, \mathcal{S}, \mathcal{K}, \mathcal{R} \rangle} = \iota_{\langle \mathcal{D}, \mathcal{S}, \mathcal{R} \rangle} \ominus \iota_{\langle \mathcal{D}, \mathcal{K}, \mathcal{R} \rangle} \sqsubseteq \iota_{\langle \mathcal{D}', \mathcal{S}', \mathcal{R} \rangle} \ominus \iota_{\langle \mathcal{D}', \mathcal{K}', \mathcal{R} \rangle} = \gamma_{\langle \mathcal{D}', \mathcal{S}', \mathcal{K}', \mathcal{R} \rangle}$.

Example 37. To illustrate the narrowing processor, consider the following TRS.

$$\mathsf{f}(\mathsf{c}(n,x)) \rightarrow \mathsf{c}(\,\mathsf{f}(\mathsf{g}(\mathsf{c}(n,x))),\,\mathsf{f}(\mathsf{h}(\mathsf{c}(n,x)))\,) \qquad \mathsf{g}(\mathsf{c}(0,x)) \rightarrow x \qquad \mathsf{h}(\mathsf{c}(1,x)) \rightarrow x$$

So f operates on "lists" of 0s and 1s, where g removes a leading 0 and h removes a leading 1. Since g's and h's applicability "exclude" each other, the TRS has linear (and not exponential) complexity. The leaf removal and usable rules processors yield the problem $\langle\,\{(12)\},\,\{(12)\},\,\varnothing,\,\{\mathsf{g}(\mathsf{c}(0,x)) \rightarrow x,\,\mathsf{h}(\mathsf{c}(1,x)) \rightarrow x\}\,\rangle$ *with*

$$\mathsf{f}^\sharp(\mathsf{c}(n,x)) \rightarrow \mathrm{COM}_4(\,\mathsf{f}^\sharp(\mathsf{g}(\mathsf{c}(n,x))),\,\mathsf{g}^\sharp(\mathsf{c}(n,x)),\,\mathsf{f}^\sharp(\mathsf{h}(\mathsf{c}(n,x))),\,\mathsf{h}^\sharp(\mathsf{c}(n,x))\,). \quad (12)$$

The only narrowing substitution of $t_1 = \mathsf{f}^\sharp(\mathsf{g}(\mathsf{c}(n,x)))$ *is* $[n/0]$ *and the corresponding narrowing result is* $\mathsf{f}^\sharp(x)$. *However,* $t_3 = \mathsf{f}^\sharp(\mathsf{h}(\mathsf{c}(n,x)))$ *is not captured by the substitution* $[n/0]$, *since* $[n/0]$ *is not more general than* t_3's *narrowing substitution* $[n/1]$. *Hence, the DT (12) is replaced by the following two new DTs:*

$$\mathsf{f}^\sharp(\mathsf{c}(0,x)) \rightarrow \mathrm{COM}_4(\,\mathsf{f}^\sharp(x),\,\mathsf{g}^\sharp(\mathsf{c}(0,x)),\,\mathsf{f}^\sharp(\mathsf{h}(\mathsf{c}(0,x))),\,\mathsf{h}^\sharp(\mathsf{c}(0,x))\,) \quad (13)$$
$$\mathsf{f}^\sharp(\mathsf{c}(n,x)) \rightarrow \mathrm{COM}_1(\,\mathsf{f}^\sharp(\mathsf{h}(\mathsf{c}(n,x)))\,) \quad (14)$$

Another application of the narrowing processor replaces (14) by $\mathsf{f}^\sharp(\mathsf{c}(1,x)) \rightarrow \mathrm{COM}_1(\mathsf{f}^\sharp(x)).$[15] *Now* $\iota_\mathcal{R} \sqsubseteq \mathcal{P}ol_1$ *is easy to show by the reduction pair processor.*

Example 38. Reconsider the TRS of Ex. 3. The canonical extended DT problem is transformed to $\langle \mathcal{D}_1, \mathcal{D}_1, \varnothing, \mathcal{R}_1\rangle$, where $\mathcal{D}_1 = \{(1), (2), (8)\}$ and $\mathcal{R}_1$ are the gt- and p-rules, cf. Ex. 27. In $\mathsf{m}^\sharp(x,y) \rightarrow \mathrm{COM}_2(\mathsf{if}^\sharp(\mathsf{gt}(x,y),x,y),\mathsf{gt}^\sharp(x,y))$ (1), one can narrow $t_1 = \mathsf{if}^\sharp(\mathsf{gt}(x,y),x,y).$ Its narrowing substitutions are $[x/0,y/k],$ $[x/\mathsf{s}(n),y/0],$ $[x/\mathsf{s}(n),y/\mathsf{s}(k)].$ Note that $t_2 = \mathsf{gt}^\sharp(x,y)$ is captured, as its only narrowing substitution is $[x/\mathsf{s}(n),y/\mathsf{s}(k)].$ So (1) can be replaced by*

$$\mathsf{m}^\sharp(0,k) \rightarrow \mathrm{COM}_2(\mathsf{if}^\sharp(\mathsf{false},0,k),\mathsf{gt}^\sharp(0,k)) \quad (15)$$
$$\mathsf{m}^\sharp(\mathsf{s}(n),0) \rightarrow \mathrm{COM}_2(\mathsf{if}^\sharp(\mathsf{true},\mathsf{s}(n),0),\mathsf{gt}^\sharp(\mathsf{s}(n),0)) \quad (16)$$
$$\mathsf{m}^\sharp(\mathsf{s}(n),\mathsf{s}(k)) \rightarrow \mathrm{COM}_2(\mathsf{if}^\sharp(\mathsf{gt}(n,k),\mathsf{s}(n),\mathsf{s}(k)),\mathsf{gt}^\sharp(\mathsf{s}(n),\mathsf{s}(k))) \quad (17)$$
$$\mathsf{m}^\sharp(x,y) \rightarrow \mathrm{COM}_0 \quad (18)$$

The leaf removal processor deletes (15), (18) and yields $\langle \mathcal{D}_2, \mathcal{D}_2, \varnothing, \mathcal{R}_1\rangle$ *with* $\mathcal{D}_2 = \{(16), (17), (2), (8)\}.$ *We replace* $\mathsf{if}^\sharp(\mathsf{true},x,y) \rightarrow \mathrm{COM}_2(\mathsf{m}^\sharp(\mathsf{p}(x),y),\mathsf{p}^\sharp(x))$ *(2) by*

$$\mathsf{if}^\sharp(\mathsf{true},0,y) \rightarrow \mathrm{COM}_2(\mathsf{m}^\sharp(0,y),\mathsf{p}^\sharp(0)) \quad (19)$$
$$\mathsf{if}^\sharp(\mathsf{true},\mathsf{s}(n),y) \rightarrow \mathrm{COM}_2(\mathsf{m}^\sharp(n,y),\mathsf{p}^\sharp(\mathsf{s}(n))) \quad (20)$$

by the narrowing processor. The leaf removal processor deletes (19) and the usable rules processor removes the p-rules from $\mathcal{R}_1$. *This yields* $\langle \mathcal{D}_3, \mathcal{D}_3, \varnothing, \mathcal{R}_2\rangle,$

---

[15] One can also simplify (13) further by narrowing. Its subterm $\mathsf{g}^\sharp(\mathsf{c}(0,x))$ has no narrowing substitutions. This (empty) set of narrowing substitutions captures $\mathsf{f}^\sharp(\mathsf{h}(\mathsf{c}(0,x)))$ and $\mathsf{h}^\sharp(\mathsf{c}(0,x))$ which have no narrowing substitutions either. Since $\mathsf{f}^\sharp(x)$ is not captured, (13) can be transformed into $\mathsf{f}^\sharp(\mathsf{c}(0,x)) \rightarrow \mathrm{COM}_1(\mathsf{f}^\sharp(x)).$

where $\mathcal{D}_3 = \{(16),(17),(20),(8)\}$ and $\mathcal{R}_2$ are the gt-rules. By the polynomial interpretation $[0] = [\mathsf{true}] = [\mathsf{false}] = [\mathsf{p}^\sharp](x) = 0$, $[\mathsf{s}](x) = x+2$, $[\mathsf{gt}](x,y) = [\mathsf{gt}^\sharp](x,y) = x$, $[\mathsf{m}^\sharp](x,y) = (x+1)^2$, $[\mathsf{if}^\sharp](x,y,z) = y^2$, all DTs in $\mathcal{D}_3$ are strictly decreasing and all rules in $\mathcal{R}_2$ are weakly decreasing. So the reduction pair processor yields $\langle \mathcal{D}_3, \mathcal{D}_3, \varnothing, \mathcal{R}_2\rangle \overset{Pol_2}{\leadsto} \langle \mathcal{D}_3, \varnothing, \mathcal{D}_3, \mathcal{R}_2\rangle$. As this DT problem is solved, we obtain $\iota_\mathcal{R} \sqsubseteq Pol_0 \oplus \ldots \oplus Pol_0 \oplus Pol_2 = Pol_2$, i.e., $\mathcal{R}$ has quadratic complexity.

6   Evaluation and Conclusion

We presented a new technique for innermost runtime complexity analysis by adapting the termination techniques of the DP framework. To this end, we introduced several processors to simplify "DT problems", which gives rise to a flexible and modular framework for automated complexity proofs. Thus, recent advances in termination analysis can now also be used for complexity analysis.

To evaluate our contributions, we implemented them in the termination prover APROVE and compared it with the complexity tools CaT 1.5 [28] and TCT 1.6 [2]. We ran the tools on 1323 TRSs from the *Termination Problem Data Base* used in the *International Termination Competition* 2010.[16] As in the competition, each tool had a timeout of 60 seconds for each example. The left half of the table compares CaT and APROVE. For instance, the first row means that APROVE showed constant complexity for 209 examples. On those examples, CaT proved linear complexity in 182 cases and failed in 27 cases. So in the light gray part of the table, APROVE gave more precise results than CaT. In the medium gray part, both tools obtained equal results. In the dark gray part, CaT was more precise than APROVE. Similarly, the right half of the table compares TCT and APROVE.

		CaT						TCT					
		Pol_0	Pol_1	Pol_2	Pol_3	no result	$\sum$	Pol_0	Pol_1	Pol_2	Pol_3	no result	$\sum$
APROVE	Pol_0	-	182	-	-	27	209	10	157	-	-	42	209
	Pol_1	-	187	7	-	76	270	-	152	1	-	117	270
	Pol_2	-	32	2	-	83	117	-	35	-	-	82	117
	Pol_3	-	6	-	-	16	22	-	5	-	-	17	22
	no result	-	27	3	1	674	705	-	22	3	-	680	705
	$\sum$	0	434	12	1	876	1323	10	371	4	0	938	1323

So APROVE showed polynomial innermost runtime for 618 of the 1323 examples (47 %). (Note that the collection also contains many examples whose complexity is not polynomial.) In contrast, CaT resp. TCT proved polynomial innermost runtime for 447 (33 %) resp. 385 (29 %) examples. Even a "combined tool" of CaT and TCT (which always returns the better result of these two tools) would only show polynomial runtime for 464 examples (35 %). Hence, our contributions represent a significant advance. This also confirms the results of the *Termination Competition 2010*, where APROVE won the category of innermost runtime

---

[16] See http://www.termination-portal.org/wiki/Termination_Competition.

complexity analysis.[17] AProVE also succeeds on Ex. 3, 25, and 37, whereas CaT and TCT fail. (Ex. 22 can be analyzed by all three tools.) For details on our experiments (including information on the exact DT processors used in each example) and to run our implementation in AProVE via a web interface, we refer to http://aprove.informatik.rwth-aachen.de/eval/RuntimeComplexity/.

Acknowledgments. We are grateful to the CaT and the TCT team for their support with the experiments and to G. Moser and H. Zankl for many helpful comments.

References

1. Arts, T., Giesl, J.: Termination of term rewriting using dependency pairs. Theoretical Computer Science 236, 133–178 (2000)
2. Avanzini, M., Moser, G., Schnabl, A.: Automated Implicit Computational Complexity Analysis (System Description). In: Armando, A., Baumgartner, P., Dowek, G. (eds.) IJCAR 2008. LNCS (LNAI), vol. 5195, pp. 132–138. Springer, Heidelberg (2008)
3. Avanzini, M., Moser, G.: Dependency Pairs and Polynomial Path Orders. In: Treinen, R. (ed.) RTA 2009. LNCS, vol. 5595, pp. 48–62. Springer, Heidelberg (2009)
4. Avanzini, M., Moser, G.: Closing the gap between runtime complexity and polytime computability. In: Proc. RTA 2010. LIPIcs, vol. 6, pp. 33–48 (2010)
5. Avanzini, M., Moser, G.: Complexity Analysis by Graph Rewriting. In: Blume, M., Kobayashi, N., Vidal, G. (eds.) FLOPS 2010. LNCS, vol. 6009, pp. 257–271. Springer, Heidelberg (2010)
6. Baader, F., Nipkow, T.: Term Rewriting and All That. Cambridge U. Pr., Cambridge (1998)
7. Bonfante, G., Cichon, A., Marion, J.-Y., Touzet, H.: Algorithms with polynomial interpretation termination proof. J. Functional Programming 11(1), 33–53 (2001)
8. Endrullis, J., Waldmann, J., Zantema, H.: Matrix interpretations for proving termination of term rewriting. J. Automated Reasoning 40(2-3), 195–220 (2008)
9. Geser, A., Hofbauer, D., Waldmann, J., Zantema, H.: On tree automata that certify termination of left-linear term rewriting systems. Information and Computation 205(4), 512–534 (2007)
10. Giesl, J., Thiemann, R., Schneider-Kamp, P.: The Dependency Pair Framework: Combining Techniques for Automated Termination Proofs. In: Baader, F., Voronkov, A. (eds.) LPAR 2004. LNCS (LNAI), vol. 3452, pp. 301–331. Springer, Heidelberg (2005)
11. Giesl, J., Thiemann, R., Schneider-Kamp, P., Falke, S.: Mechanizing and improving dependency pairs. Journal of Automated Reasoning 37(3), 155–203 (2006)
12. Giesl, J., Raffelsieper, M., Schneider-Kamp, P., Swiderski, S., Thiemann, R.: Automated termination proofs for Haskell by term rewriting. ACM Transactions on Programming Languages and Systems 33(2) (2011)
13. Givan, R., McAllester, D.A.: Polynomial-time computation via local inference relations. ACM Transactions on Computational Logic 3(4), 521–541 (2002)

---

[17] In contrast to CaT and TCT, AProVE did not participate in any other complexity categories as it cannot analyze derivational or non-innermost runtime complexity.

14. Hirokawa, N., Middeldorp, A.: Automating the dependency pair method. Information and Computation 199(1,2), 172–199 (2005)

15. Hirokawa, N., Moser, G.: Automated Complexity Analysis Based on the Dependency Pair Method. In: Armando, A., Baumgartner, P., Dowek, G. (eds.) IJCAR 2008. LNCS (LNAI), vol. 5195, pp. 364–379. Springer, Heidelberg (2008)

16. Hirokawa, N., Moser, G.: Complexity, Graphs, and the Dependency Pair Method. In: Cervesato, I., Veith, H., Voronkov, A. (eds.) LPAR 2008. LNCS (LNAI), vol. 5330, pp. 652–666. Springer, Heidelberg (2008)

17. Hofbauer, D., Lautemann, C.: Termination proofs and the length of derivations. In: Dershowitz, N. (ed.) RTA 1989. LNCS, vol. 355, pp. 167–177. Springer, Heidelberg (1989)

18. Hofmann, M.: Linear types and non-size-increasing polynomial time computation. In: Proc. LICS 1999, pp. 464–473. IEEE Press, Los Alamitos (1999)

19. Koprowski, A., Waldmann, J.: Max/plus tree automata for termination of term rewriting. Acta Cybernetica 19(2), 357–392 (2009)

20. Marion, J.-Y., Péchoux, R.: Characterizations of polynomial complexity classes with a better intensionality. In: Proc. PPDP 2008, pp. 79–88. ACM Press, New York (2008)

21. Moser, G., Schnabl, A., Waldmann, J.: Complexity analysis of term rewriting based on matrix and context dependent interpretations. In: Proc. FSTTCS 2008. LIPIcs, vol. 2, pp. 304–315 (2008)

22. Moser, G.: Personal communication (2010)

23. Neurauter, F., Zankl, H., Middeldorp, A.: Revisiting Matrix Interpretations for Polynomial Derivational Complexity of Term Rewriting. In: Fermüller, C.G., Voronkov, A. (eds.) LPAR-17. LNCS, vol. 6397, pp. 550–564. Springer, Heidelberg (2010)

24. Noschinski, L., Emmes, F., Giesl, J.: A dependency pair framework for innermost complexity analysis of term rewrite systems. Technical Report AIB-2011-03, RWTH Aachen (2011), http://aib.informatik.rwth-aachen.de

25. Otto, C., Brockschmidt, M., von Essen, C., Giesl, J.: Automated termination analysis of Java Bytecode by term rewriting. In: Proc. RTA 2010. LIPIcs, vol. 6, pp. 259–276 (2010)

26. Schneider-Kamp, P., Giesl, J., Ströder, T., Serebrenik, A., Thiemann, R.: Automated termination analysis for logic programs with cut. In: Proc. ICLP 2010, Theory and Practice of Logic Programming, vol.10(4-6), pp. 365–381 (2010)

27. Waldmann, J.: Polynomially bounded matrix interpretations. In: Proc. RTA 2010. LIPIcs, vol. 6, pp. 357–372 (2010)

28. Zankl, H., Korp, M.: Modular complexity analysis via relative complexity. In: Proc. RTA 2010. LIPIcs, vol. 6, pp. 385–400 (2010)

Static Analysis of Android Programs

Étienne Payet[1] and Fausto Spoto[2]

[1] LIM-IREMIA, Université de la Réunion, France
[2] Dipartimento di Informatica, Università di Verona, Italy

Abstract. Android is a programming language based on Java and an operating system for mobile or embedded devices. It features an extended event-based library and dynamic inflation of graphical views from declarative XML layout files. A static analyzer for Android programs must consider such features, for correctness and precision. This article is a description of how we extended the Julia system, based on abstract interpretation, to run formally correct analyses of Android programs. We have analyzed with Julia the Android sample applications by Google and a few larger open-source programs. Julia has found, automatically, bugs and flaws both in the Google samples and in the open-source programs.

1 Introduction

Android is a main actor in the operating system market for mobile or embedded devices. It is an operating system for such devices and a programming language, based on Java, with an extended event-based library for mobile applications. Any Java compiler can compile Android applications, but the resulting Java bytecode must be translated into a final, very optimized, *Dalvik* bytecode.

Static analysis of Android applications is important as quality and reliability are keys to success on the Android market (http://www.android.com/market). The company Klocwork (http://www.klocwork.com) has already extended its analysis tools from Java to Android, obtaining the only static analysis for Android that we are aware of, currently limited in power and incorrect: if the analyzed program contains a bug, it will often miss it. Nevertheless, this shows that industry recognizes the importance of the static analysis of Android code.

Julia is a static analyzer for Java bytecode programs that do not use reflection nor multithreading, based on abstract interpretation [1]. It ensures, automatically, that the analyzed applications do not contain a large set of programming bugs. It applies non-trivial whole-program, interprocedural and semantical static analyses, including classcast, dead code, nullness and termination analysis. It comes with a correctness guarantee, as typical in the abstract interpretation community: if the application contains a bug, of a kind considered by the analyzer, then Julia reports it. This makes the result of the analyses more significant. However, its application to Android is not immediate and we had to solve many problems before Julia could analyze Android programs in a correct and precise way. This article presents those problems and our solutions. The resulting system analyzes non-trivial Android programs with high degree

N. Bjørner and V. Sofronie-Stokkermans (Eds.): CADE 2011, LNAI 6803, pp. 439–445, 2011.

of precision and finds bugs in third-party code. Our experimental results are available at `http://julia.scienze.univr.it/runs/android/results.html`. This paper does not describe in detail the static analyses provided by Julia, already published elsewhere, but only their adaptation to Android. Our analyzer is a commercial product (`http://www.juliasoft.com`). It can be freely used through the web interface at `http://julia.scienze.univr.it`, whose maximal analysis size has been limited.

The analysis of Android programs is non-trivial since we must consider some specific features of Android, both for correctness and precision of analysis. First of all, Julia analyzes Java bytecode while Android applications are shipped in Dalvik bytecode. Eclipse (`http://www.eclipse.org`) is the standard development environment for Android at the moment. It can export Android applications in jar format *i.e.*, in Java bytecode. Hence we have generated the jar files of our experiments from Eclipse. Another problem is that Julia starts the analysis of a program from its main method while Android programs start from many event handlers, executed by a single thread. Hence, we had to modify Julia so that it starts the analysis from all such handlers, considering them as potentially concurrent entry points. Layout classes, such as *views*, *menus* and *preferences*, contain most or even all the code of an Android application, including its business logic. A complex problem is that, in Android, user interfaces are specified declaratively by XML files. This means that the code is not completely available in bytecode format, but is rather *inflated*, at runtime, from XML layout files into actual bytecode, by using Java reflection. Moreover, the link between XML inflated code and the explicit application code introduces casts and potential null pointer exceptions. Finally, a real challenge is the size of the libraries: Android programs use both the `java.*` and the new `android.*` hierarchies. Their classes must be analyzed along with the programs, which easily leads to analyze 10,000 methods and more.

2   Android Basics

Android applications are written in Java and made out of *activities*, or event-driven user interfaces. Programs do not have a single entry point but can rather use parts of other Android applications on-demand and ask services by calling their event handlers, directly or through the operating system.

An XML *manifest file* registers the components of an application. Other XML files describe the visual layout of the activities. Activities *inflate* layout files into visual objects (a hierarchy of *views*), through an *inflater* provided by the Android library. This means that library or user-defined views are not explicitly created by `new` statements but rather inflated through reflection. Library methods such as `findViewById` access the inflated views. As an example, consider the activity in Fig. 1, from the Google distribution of Android 2.1. The `onCreate` event handler gets called when the activity is first created, after its constructor has been implicitly invoked by the Android system. The `setContentView` library method calls the layout inflator. Its integer parameter uniquely identifies the XML layout file shown in Fig. 2. From line 3 of this file, it is clear

```
1   public class LunarLander extends Activity {
2     private LunarView mLunarView;
3     @Override
4     protected void onCreate(Bundle savedInstanceState) {
5       super.onCreate(savedInstanceState);
6       // tell system to use the layout defined in our XML file
7       setContentView(R.layout.lunar_layout);
8       // get handles to the LunarView from XML
9       mLunarView = (LunarView) findViewById(R.id.lunar);
10      // give the LunarView a handle to a TextView
11      mLunarView.setTextView((TextView) findViewById(R.id.text));
12    }
13  }
```

Fig. 1. A portion of the source code Android file `LunarLander.java`

```
1   <FrameLayout xmlns:android="http://schemas.android.com/apk/res/android"
2       android:layout_width="match_parent" android:layout_height="match_parent">
3     <com.example.android.lunarlander.LunarView android:id="@+id/lunar"
4       android:layout_width="match_parent" android:layout_height="match_parent"/>
5     <RelativeLayout
6       android:layout_width="match_parent" android:layout_height="match_parent" >
7       <TextView android:id="@+id/text"
8         android:text="@string/lunar_layout_text_text"
9         android:visibility="visible"
10        android:layout_width="wrap_content" android:layout_height="wrap_content"
11        android:layout_centerInParent="true" android:gravity="center_horizontal"
12        android:textColor="#88ffffff"         android:textSize="24sp"/>
13    </RelativeLayout>
14  </FrameLayout>
```

Fig. 2. The XML layout file `lunar_layout.xml`

that the view identified as `lunar` at line 9 of Fig. 1 belongs to the user-defined view class `com.example.android.lunarlander.LunarView`. The cast at line 9 in Fig. 1 is hence correct. Constants `R.layout.lunar_layout` and `R.id.lunar` are automatically generated at compile-time from the XML layout file names and from the view identifiers that they contain, respectively. The user can call `setContentView` many times and everywhere in the code; he can pass the value of any integer expression to it and to `findViewById`, although the usual approach is to pass the compiler-generated constants. This declarative construction of objects also applies to preferences (graphical application options) and menus.

3   Our Set of Static Analyses

We describe here the analyses that we let Julia apply to Android programs. None of these analyses is a simple syntactical check, but they all exploit semantical, whole-program and inter-procedural information about the program.

Equality Checks. Java programmers can compare objects with a pointer identity check `==` and with a programmatic check `.equals`. In most cases, the latter is preferred but `==` can be used for efficient comparisons. The use of

== and .equals on the same class type is a symptom of a potential bug. This check controls such situations, using the precise class analysis of Julia.

Classcast Checks. The XML layout inflation used in Android has introduced situations where casts are unavoidable. Julia applies its class analysis to prove casts correct. We had to consider the idiosyncracies of the Android library to keep this class analysis precise for the Android casts (see Sect. 4).

Static Update Checks. The modification of a static field from inside a constructor or an instance method is legal but a symptom of a possible bug or, at least, of bad programming style. We check when that situation occurs inside the reachable code by exploiting the precise class analysis of Julia.

Dead Code Checks. Dead code is a method or constructor never invoked in the program and hence *useless*. The identification of dead code is complex in object-oriented programs, as method call targets are resolved at runtime. The class analysis of Julia comes to help, by providing a static over-approximation of the run-time resolved targets. Android complicates this problem, as event handlers are called by the system, implicitly, and some constructors are invoked, implicitly, during the XML layout inflation.

Method Redefinition Checks. A programmer might use, mistakenly, slightly different names (differences in case) or argument types (differences in the package portion) for the redefining and redefined methods. He might also use an inconsistent policy while calling super, forgetting some of those calls. This check controls such situations.

Nullness Checks. *Dereferences* occur when an instance field or an array is accessed, an instance method is called or threads synchronize. If they occur on null, a run-time exception is raised. Julia performs a very precise nullness analysis for Java [4]. Android complicates the problem, because of the XML layout inflation and of the use of the onCreate event handler to perform tasks that, in Java, are normally done in constructors. Hence the precision of the nullness analysis of Julia, applied to Android code, is not so high as for Java. We had to improve it by considering these specific features (Sect. 5).

Termination Checks. A non-terminating program is often considered incorrect. Julia performs termination analysis of Java code [6], and has won the latest international competition of termination analysis for Java bytecode on July 2010. The application of its termination analysis to Android code is challenging because of the size of the Java and Android libraries together.

4   Class Analysis for Android

Before the analysis of a program, the latter must be available and its boundaries clear. Object-oriented languages use dynamic lookup of method implementations in method calls, on the basis of the run-time class of their *receiver*. Hence, the exact control-flow graph of a program is not even computable. An over-approximation can be computed, where each method call is decorated with a superset of its actual run-time targets. *Class analysis* computes, for each program variable, field or method return value, a superset of the class types of the objects that it might contain at run-time [5]. Julia uses an improvement of the very precise class analysis defined in [3], to build a constraint graph whose nodes are the variables, fields and method return values in the program. Arcs link these nodes and mimick the propagation of data in the program. The new statements inject class types in the graph, that propagate along the arcs. Since the control-flow graph of the program is not yet available when the class analysis starts, the latter *extracts* the program on-demand, from its main method, during the same propagation of the class types. This is problematic for Android programs, that do not have a single main entry point, but many event handlers, that the system calls when a specific event occurs. They are syntactically identified as implementations overriding some method in the android.* hierarchy. Class analysis must hence start from all event handlers and use, at their beginning, a worst-case assumption about the state of the system.

This does not solve the problem of class analysis for Android programs yet. As we said above, new statements inject class types in the constraint graph. But it turns out that Android uses reflection to *inflate* (instantiate) graphical views from the strings found in the XML layout files. In general, class analyses are incorrect for reflection. Here, we want to stick on Julia's precise class analysis and we want it to work on Android code.

The first step in that direction has been to instrument the code of the library class android.view.LayoutInflater, that performs the inflation. We replace reflection, there, with a non-deterministic execution of new statements, for all view classes reported in the layout files of the application. This makes the class analysis of Julia correct *w.r.t.* layout inflation, but we have a problem of precision with the return value of the Android method findViewById, which retrieves the inflated views from constant identifiers. Thus, the second step has been to use explicit knowledge on the view identifiers. We introduced new nodes $views(x)$ in the constraint graph, one for each view identifier x occurring in the XML layout files. Node $views(x)$ contains a superset of the class types of the views labelled as x. Note that the same identifier x can be used for many views in the same or different layout files and this is why, in general, we need a set. Node $views(x)$ is used for the return value of the findViewById(R.id.x) calls. Moreover, we build the arc {$name$ | x identifies a view of class $name$ in some layout file} $\rightarrow$ $views(x)$ to inject into $views(x)$ all class types explicitly bound to the identifier x. We let (very unusual) calls findViewById(exp), for an expression exp that is not, syntactically, a constant view identifier, keep their normal approximation for the return value, containing all views referenced in the XML layout files. This same technique is used also for menus and preferences, that work similarly.

5   Nullness Analysis for Android

Julia includes one of the most precise correct nullness analyses for Java. A basic analysis is strengthened with others, to get a high degree of precision [4]. We can apply it to Android, without any modification. The results are precise, with some exceptions that we describe below, together with our solutions.

An extensively used programming pattern in Android consists in calling the
setContentView method to inflate an XML layout file and the findViewById
method to retrieve the inflated views. The nullness analysis of Julia, without any
improvement, issues spurious warnings complaining about the possible nullness
of the views returned by findViewById. This is because Julia is not so clever
to understand that setContentView inflates an XML layout file where a view,
associated with an identifier, exists, so that a subsequent call to findViewById,
with that same identifier, does not yield null.

The nullness analysis of Julia includes, already, an *expression non-nullness*
analysis that computes, at each program point, sets of expressions that are locally non-null. For instance, this analysis knows that if a check this.foo(x)
!= null succeeds, then the expression this.foo(x) is non-null, *if foo does not
modify any field or array read by foo itself.* This local non-nullness is lost as soon
as the subsequent code modifies a field or array read by foo. To check these conditions, Julia embeds a side-effect analysis of method calls. We exploited this analysis to embed specific knowledge on the setContentView method. Namely, after
a call to setContentView(R.layout.*file*), we let the expression non-nullness
analysis add non-null expressions findViewById(R.id.z), for every identifier
z of a view reported in *file*.xml. These expressions remain non-null as long as
no field or array is modified, that is read by findViewById (for instance, by a
setId or another setContentView), but this is the standard way of working of
our expression non-nullness analysis, so we had to change nothing for that.

This work removes some spurious warnings, but it is not completely satisfactory. When an Android activity is first created, the onCreate event handler
gets called, *before* any other event handler of the activity. The problem is that
Android engineers have introduced onCreate to put code that, in Java, would
normally go into constructors. This comes with some drawback: Julia does not
spot these fields as globally non-null, although they do behave as such. Our
solution has been to instrument the code of activities and give them an extra
constructor that calls the standard constructor of the activity, normally empty,
and then the onCreate event handler, passing a null Bundle, exactly as it happens at activity start-up. Activities have two constructors now: the standard
one, typically never used directly, and this extra one, that Julia uses to simulate
the creation of the activity. They are syntactically distinguished by adding extra,
dummy parameters to the instrumented constructor. This solves our problem:
the instrumented constructor is now the only constructor called, directly, in the
program, to create the activity.

6   Termination Analysis for Android

Our termination analysis for Android is basically the same that we apply to
Java [6]. It builds linear constraints on the size of the program variables. This
results in a constraint logic program whose termination is proved by the Bin-
Term tool. For efficiency, Julia uses zones [2] for the linear approximation. It
can also use polyhedra, but their cost is much higher and we have not experienced significant improvements in precision. BinTerm uses polyhedra anyway.

For extra precision, we have defined the size of Android *cursors* as the number of elements that must yet be scanned before reaching their end. This lets Julia prove termination of the typical loops of Android code, where a cursor over a database is used to scan its elements.

We observe that our tool proves termination of loops and recursive methods. Most Android programs might diverge if the user or the system keep interacting with their event handlers. Our work does not consider this case of non-termination, which is typically always possible.

7   Conclusion

This is the first static analysis framework for Android programs, based on a formal basis such as abstract interpretation. It can analyze real third-party Android applications, without any user annotation of the code, yielding formally correct results in a few minutes and on standard hardware. So, it is ready for a first industrial use. Formal correctness means that programs such as VoiceRecognition in the table at `http://julia.scienze.univr.it/runs/android/results.html` are proved to be bug-free, *w.r.t.* the classes of bugs considered by Julia.

References

1. Cousot, P., Cousot, R.: Abstract Interpretation: A Unifed Lattice Model for Static Analysis of Programs by Construction or Approximation of Fixpoints. In: Proc. of the 4th Symposium on Principles of Programming Languages (POPL 1977), pp. 238–252. ACM Press, New York (1977)
2. Miné, A.: A New Numerical Abstract Domain Based on Difference-Bound Matrices. In: Danvy, O., Filinski, A. (eds.) PADO 2001. LNCS, vol. 2053, pp. 155–172. Springer, Heidelberg (2001)
3. Palsberg, J., Schwartzbach, M.I.: Object-Oriented Type Inference. In: Paepcke, A. (ed.) Proc. of the 6th International ACM Conference on Object-Oriented Programming, Systems, Languages and Applications (OOPSLA 1991). ACM SIGPLAN Notices, vol. 26(11), pp. 146–161. ACM Press, New York (1991)
4. Spoto, F.: Precise null-Pointer Analysis. Software and Systems Modeling 10(2), 219–252 (2011)
5. Spoto, F., Jensen, T.: Class Analyses as Abstract Interpretations of Trace Semantics. ACM Transactions on Programming Languages and Systems (TOPLAS) 25(5), 578–630 (2003)
6. Spoto, F., Mesnard, F., Payet, É.: A Termination Analyzer for Java Bytecode Based on Path-Length. ACM Transactions on Programming Languages and Systems (TOPLAS) 32(3), 70 pages (2010)

Stochastic Differential Dynamic Logic for Stochastic Hybrid Programs*

André Platzer

Carnegie Mellon University, Computer Science Department, Pittsburgh, PA, USA
aplatzer@cs.cmu.edu

Abstract. Logic is a powerful tool for analyzing and verifying systems, including programs, discrete systems, real-time systems, hybrid systems, and distributed systems. Some applications also have a stochastic behavior, however, either because of fundamental properties of nature, uncertain environments, or simplifications to overcome complexity. Discrete probabilistic systems have been studied using logic. But logic has been chronically underdeveloped in the context of stochastic hybrid systems, i.e., systems with interacting discrete, continuous, and stochastic dynamics. We aim at overcoming this deficiency and introduce a dynamic logic for stochastic hybrid systems. Our results indicate that logic is a promising tool for understanding stochastic hybrid systems and can help taming some of their complexity. We introduce a compositional model for stochastic hybrid systems. We prove adaptivity, càdlàg, and Markov time properties, and prove that the semantics of our logic is measurable. We present compositional proof rules, including rules for stochastic differential equations, and prove soundness.

1 Introduction

Logic has been used very successfully for verifying several classes of system models, including programs [24], discrete systems, real-time systems [4], hybrid systems [20], distributed systems, and distributed hybrid systems [21]. This gives us confidence in the power of logic. Not all aspects of real systems can be represented faithfully by these models, however. Some systems are inherently uncertain, either because of fundamental properties of nature, because they operate in an uncertain environment, or because deterministic models are simply too complex. Such systems have a stochastic dynamics. Nondeterministic overapproximations may be too inaccurate for a meaningful analysis, e.g., because a worst-case analysis would let bad environment actions happen always, which is very unlikely. Discrete probabilistic systems have been studied using logic. Yet, complex systems are driven by joint discrete, continuous, and stochastic dynamics. Logic has been chronically underdeveloped in the context of these stochastic hybrid systems.

---

* This material is based upon work supported by the National Science Foundation by NSF CAREER Award CNS-1054246, NSF EXPEDITION CNS-0926181, CNS-0931985, CNS-1035800, by ONR N00014-10-1-0188 and DARPA FA8650-10C-7077.

N. Bjørner and V. Sofronie-Stokkermans (Eds.): CADE 2011, LNAI 6803, pp. 446–460, 2011.
© Springer-Verlag Berlin Heidelberg 2011

Classical logic is about boolean truth and yes/no answers. That is why it is tricky to use logic for systems with stochastic effects. Logic has reached out into probabilistic extensions at least for discrete programs [13,14,6] and for first-order logic over a finite domain [25]. Logic has been used for the purpose of specifying system properties in model checking finite Markov chains [27] and probabilistic timed automata [17]. Stochastic hybrid systems, instead, are a domain where logic and especially proof calculi have so far been more conspicuous by their absence. Given how successful logic has been elsewhere, we want to change that.

Stochastic hybrid systems [2,3,9] are systems with interacting discrete, continuous, and stochastic dynamics. There is not just one canonical way to add stochastic behavior to a system model. Stochasticity might be restricted to the discrete dynamics, as in piecewise deterministic Markov decision processes, restricted to the continuous and switching behavior as in switching diffusion processes [8], or allowed in many parts as in so-called General Stochastic Hybrid Systems; see [2,3] for an overview. Several different forms of combinations of probabilities with hybrid systems and continuous systems have been considered, both for model checking [7,12,3] and for simulation-based validation [18,28].

We develop a very different approach. We consider logic and theorem proving for stochastic hybrid systems[1] to transfer the success that logic has had in other domains. Our approach is partially inspired by probabilistic PDL [14] and by barrier certificates for continuous dynamics [23]. We follow the arithmetical view that Kozen identified as suitable for probabilistic logic [14].

Classical analysis is provably inadequate [11] for analyzing even simple continuous stochastic processes. We heavily draw on both stochastic calculus and logic. It is not possible to present all mathematical background exhaustively here. But we provide basic definitions and intuition and refer to the literature for details and proofs of the main results of stochastic calculus [10,19,11].

Our most interesting contributions are:

1. We present the new model of stochastic hybrid programs (SHPs) and define a compositional semantics of SHP executions in terms of stochastic processes.
2. We prove that the semantic processes are adapted, have almost surely càdlàg paths, and that their natural stopping times are Markov times.
3. We introduce a new logic called stochastic differential dynamic logic (Sd$\mathcal{L}$) for specifying and verifying properties of SHPs.
4. We define a semantics and prove that it is measurable such that probabilities are well-defined and probabilistic questions become meaningful.
5. We present proof rules for Sd$\mathcal{L}$ and prove their soundness.
6. We identify the requirements for using Dynkin's formula for proving properties using the infinitesimal generator of stochastic differential equations.

Sd$\mathcal{L}$ makes the rich semantical complexity and deep theory of stochastic hybrid systems accessible in a simple syntactic language. This makes the verification of stochastic hybrid systems possible with elementary syntactic proof principles.

---

[1] Note that there is a model called Stochastic Hybrid Systems [9]. We do not mean this specific model in the narrow sense but refer to stochastic hybrid systems as the broader class of systems that share discrete, continuous, and stochastic dynamics.

2   Preliminaries: Stochastic Processes

We fix a dimension $d \in \mathbb{N}$ for the Euclidean state space $\mathbb{R}^d$ equipped with its *Borel σ-algebra* $\mathcal{B}$, i.e., the σ-algebra generated by all open subsets. A *σ-algebra* on a set Ω is a nonempty set $\mathcal{F} \subseteq 2^\Omega$ that is closed under complement and countable union. We axiomatically fix a *probability space* $(\Omega, \mathcal{F}, P)$ with a σ-algebra $\mathcal{F} \subseteq 2^\Omega$ of events on space Ω and a probability measure P on $\mathcal{F}$ (i.e., $P : \mathcal{F} \to [0,1]$ is countable additive with $P \geq 0, P(\Omega) = 1$). We assume the probability space has been completed, i.e., every subset of a null set (i.e., $P(A) = 0$) is measurable. A property holds *P-almost surely* (*a.s.*) if it holds with probability 1. A *filtration* is a family $(\mathcal{F}_t)_{t \geq 0}$ of σ-algebras that is increasing, i.e., $\mathcal{F}_s \subseteq \mathcal{F}_t$ for all $s < t$. Intuitively, $\mathcal{F}_t$ are the events that can be discriminated at time t. We always assume a filtration $(\mathcal{F}_t)_{t \geq 0}$ that has been completed to include all null sets and that is right-continuous, i.e., $\mathcal{F}_t = \bigcap_{u > t} \mathcal{F}_u$ for all t. We generally assume the compatibility condition that $\mathcal{F}$ coincides with the σ-algebra $\mathcal{F}_\infty := \sigma \left(\bigcup_{t \geq 0} \mathcal{F}_t \right)$, i.e., the σ-algebra generated by all $\mathcal{F}_t$.

For a σ-algebra Σ on a set D and the Borel σ-algebra $\mathcal{B}$ on $\mathbb{R}^d$, function $f : D \to \mathbb{R}^d$ is *measurable* iff $f^{-1}(B) \in \Sigma$ for all $B \in \mathcal{B}$ (or, equivalently, for all open $B \subseteq \mathbb{R}^d$). An $\mathbb{R}^d$-valued *random variable* is an $\mathcal{F}$-measurable function $X : \Omega \to \mathbb{R}^d$. All sets and functions definable in first-order logic over real arithmetic are Borel-measurable. A *stochastic process* X is a collection $\{X_t\}_{t \in T}$ of $\mathbb{R}^d$-valued random variables X_t indexed by some set T for time. That is, $X : T \times \Omega \to \mathbb{R}^d$ is a function such that for all $t \in T$, $X_t = X(t, \cdot) : \Omega \to \mathbb{R}^d$ is a random variable. Process X is *adapted* to filtration $(\mathcal{F}_t)_{t \geq 0}$ if X_t is $\mathcal{F}_t$-measurable for each t. That is, the process does not depend on future events. We consider only adapted processes (e.g., using the completion of the natural filtration of a process or the completion of the optional σ-algebra for $\mathcal{F}$ [10]). A process X is *càdlàg* iff its *paths* $t \mapsto X_t(\omega)$ (for each $\omega \in \Omega$) are càdlàg a.s., i.e., right-continuous ($\lim_{s \searrow t} X_s(\omega) = X_t(\omega)$) and left limits ($\lim_{s \nearrow t} X_s(\omega)$) exist.

We further need an e-dimensional *Brownian motion* W (i.e., W is a stochastic process starting at 0 that is almost surely continuous and has independent increments that are normally distributed with mean 0 and variance equal to the time difference). Brownian motion is mathematically extremely complex. Its paths are almost surely continuous everywhere but differentiable nowhere and of unbounded variation. Intuitively, W can be understood as the limit of a random walk. We denote the Euclidean vector norm by $|x|$ and use the Frobenius norm $|\sigma| := \sqrt{\sum_{i,j} \sigma_{ij}^2}$ for matrices $\sigma \in \mathbb{R}^{d \times e}$.

3   Stochastic Differential Equations

We consider stochastic differential equations [19,11] to describe stochastic continuous system dynamics. They are like ordinary differential equations but have an additional diffusion term that varies the state stochastically. Stochastic differential equations are of the form $dX_t = b(X_t)dt + \sigma(X_t)dW_t$. We consider Itō stochastic differential equations, whose solutions are defined by the stochastic

Itō integral [19,11], which is again a stochastic process. Like in an ordinary differential equation, the drift coefficient $b(X_t)$ determines the deterministic part of how X_t changes over time as a function of its current value. As a function of X_t, the diffusion coefficient $\sigma(X_t)$ determines the stochastic influence by integration with respect to the Brownian motion

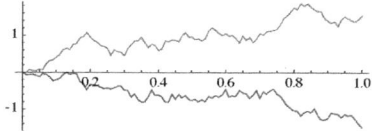

Fig. 1. Sample paths with $b = 1$ (top) and $b = 0$ (bottom), $\sigma = 1$

process W_t. See Fig. 1 for two sample paths. Ordinary differential equations are retained for $\sigma = 0$. We focus on the time-homogenous case, where b and σ are time-independent, because time could be added as an extra state variable.

Definition 1 (Stochastic differential equation). *A stochastic process* $X : [0, \infty) \times \Omega \to \mathbb{R}^d$ *solves the (Itō) stochastic differential equation*

$$dX_t = b(X_t)dt + \sigma(X_t)dW_t \tag{1}$$

with $X_0 = Z$, *if* $X_t = Z + \int b(X_t)dt + \int \sigma(X_t)dW_t$, *where* $\int \sigma(X_t)dW_t$ *is an Itō integral process [19,11].*

For simplicity, we always assume $b : \mathbb{R}^d \to \mathbb{R}^d$ and $\sigma : \mathbb{R}^d \to \mathbb{R}^{d \times e}$ to be measurable and locally Lipschitz-continuous:

$$\forall N \exists C \forall x, y : |x|, |y| \leq N \Rightarrow |b(x) - b(y)| \leq C|x - y|, |\sigma(x) - \sigma(y)| \leq C|x - y|$$

As an integral of an a.s. continuous process, solution X has almost surely continuous paths [19]. A.s. continuous solution X is pathwise unique [11, Ch 4.5]. Process X is a strong Markov process for each initial value x [19, Theorem 7.2.4].

4   Stochastic Hybrid Programs

As a system model for stochastic hybrid system, we introduce stochastic hybrid programs (SHPs). SHPs combine stochastic differential equations for describing the stochastic continuous system dynamics with program operations to describe the discrete switching, jumps, and discrete stochastic choices. These primitive dynamics can be combined programmatically in flexible ways. All basic terms in stochastic hybrid programs and stochastic differential dynamic logic are polynomial terms built over real-valued variables and rational constants. Our approach is sound for more general settings, but first-order real arithmetic is decidable [26].

Syntax. *Stochastic hybrid programs (SHPs)* are formed by the following grammar (where x_i is a variable, x a vector of variables, θ a term, b a vector of terms, σ a matrix of terms, H is a quantifier-free first-order real arithmetic formula, $\lambda, \nu \geq 0$ are rational numbers):

$$\alpha ::= x_i := \theta \mid x_i := * \mid ?H \mid dx = bdt + \sigma dW \& H \mid \lambda \alpha \oplus \nu \beta \mid \alpha; \beta \mid \alpha^*$$

Assignment $x_i := \theta$ deterministically assigns term θ to variable x_i instantaneously. *Random assignment* $x_i := *$ randomly updates variable x_i, but unlike in classical dynamic logic [24], we assume a probability distribution for x. As one example for a probability distribution, we consider uniform distribution in the interval $[0,1]$, but other distributions can be used as long as they are computationally tractable, e.g., definable in first-order real arithmetic.

Most importantly, $dx = bdt + \sigma dW \,\&\, H$ represents a stochastic continuous evolution along a stochastic differential equation, restricted to the evolution domain region H, i.e., the stochastic process will not continue when it leaves H. We assume that $dx = bdt + \sigma dW$ satisfies the assumptions of stochastic differential equations according to Def. 1. In particular, the dimensions of the vectors x, b, matrix σ, and (vectorial) Brownian motion W fit together and b, σ are globally Lipschitz-continuous (which is first-order definable for polynomial terms and, thus, decidable by quantifier elimination [26]).

Test $?H$ represents a stochastic process that fails (disappears into an absorbing state) if H is not satisfied yet continues unmodified otherwise. *Linear combination* $\lambda\alpha \oplus \nu\beta$ evolves like α in λ percent of the cases and like β otherwise. We simply assume $\lambda + \nu = 1$. *Sequential composition* $\alpha; \beta$ and *repetition* α^* work similarly to dynamic logic [24], except that they combine SHPs.

Stochastic Process Semantics. The semantics of a SHP is the stochastic process that it generates. The semantics $[\![\alpha]\!]$ of a SHP α consists of a function $[\![\alpha]\!] : (\Omega \to \mathbb{R}^d) \to ([0, \infty) \times \Omega \to \mathbb{R}^d)$ that maps any $\mathbb{R}^d$-valued random variable Z describing the initial state to a stochastic process $[\![\alpha]\!]^Z$ together with a function $(\![\alpha]\!) : (\Omega \to \mathbb{R}^d) \to (\Omega \to \mathbb{R})$ that maps any $\mathbb{R}^d$-valued random variable Z describing the initial state to a stopping time $(\![\alpha]\!)^Z$ indicating when to stop $[\![\alpha]\!]^Z$. Often, an $\mathcal{F}_0$-measurable random variable Z or deterministic state is used to describe the initial state. We assume independence of Z from subsequent stochastic processes like Brownian motions occurring in the definition of $[\![\alpha]\!]^Z$.

For an $\mathbb{R}^d$-valued random variable Z, we denote by $\hat{Z}$ the stochastic process $\hat{Z} : \{0\} \times \Omega \to \mathbb{R}^d; (0, \omega) \mapsto \hat{Z}_0(\omega) := Z(\omega)$ that is stuck at Z. We write $\hat{x}$ for the random variable Z that is a deterministic state $Z(\omega) := x$ for all $\omega \in \Omega$. We write $[\![\alpha]\!]^x$ and $(\![\alpha]\!)^x$ for $[\![\alpha]\!]^Z$ and $(\![\alpha]\!)^Z$ then.

In order to simplify notation, we assume that all variables are uniquely identified by an index, i.e., the only occurring variables are $x_1, x_2, \ldots, x_d$. We write $Z(\omega) \models H$ if state $Z(\omega)$ satisfies first-order real arithmetic formula H and $Z(\omega) \not\models H$ otherwise. In the semantics we will use a family of random variables $\{U_i\}_{i \in I}$ that are distributed uniformly in $[0, 1]$ and independent of other U_j and all other random variables and stochastic processes in the semantics. Hence, U satisfies $P(\{\omega \in \Omega : U(\omega) \le s\}) = \int_{-\infty}^{s} \mathcal{I}_{[0,1]} dt$ with the usual extensions to other Borel subsets. To describe this situation, we just say that "$U \sim \mathcal{U}(0, 1)$ is i.i.d. (independent and identically distributed)", meaning that U is furthermore independent of all other random variables and stochastic processes in the semantics. We denote the *characteristic function* of a set S by $\mathcal{I}_S$, which is defined by $\mathcal{I}_S(x) := 1$ if $x \in S$ and $\mathcal{I}_S(x) := 0$ otherwise.

Definition 2 (Stochastic hybrid program semantics). *The semantics of SHP α is defined by $[\![\alpha]\!] : (\Omega \to \mathbb{R}^d) \to ([0,\infty) \times \Omega \to \mathbb{R}^d); Z \mapsto [\![\alpha]\!]^Z = ([\![\alpha]\!]_t^Z)_{t \geq 0}$ and $(\!|\alpha|\!) : (\Omega \to \mathbb{R}^d) \to (\Omega \to \mathbb{R}); Z \mapsto (\!|\alpha|\!)^Z$. These functions are inductively defined for random variable Z by*

1. *$[\![x_i := \theta]\!]^Z = \hat{Y}$ where $Y(\omega)_i = [\![\theta]\!]^{Z(\omega)}$ and $Y_j = Z_j$ for all $j \neq i$. Further, $(\!|x_i := \theta|\!)^Z = 0$.*

2. *$[\![x_i := *]\!]^Z = \hat{U}$ where $U_j = Z_j$ for all $j \neq i$ and $U_i \sim \mathcal{U}(0,1)$ is i.i.d. and $\mathcal{F}_0$-measurable. Further, $(\!|x_i := *|\!)^Z = 0$.*

3. *$[\![?H]\!]^Z = \hat{Z}$ on the event $\{Z \models H\}$ and $(\!|?H|\!)^Z = 0$ (on all events $\omega \in \Omega$). Note that $[\![?H]\!]^Z$ is not defined on the event $\{Z \not\models H\}$.*

4. *$[\![dx = bdt + \sigma dW \,\&\, H]\!]^Z$ is the process $X : [0,\infty) \times \Omega \to \mathbb{R}^d$ that solves the (Itō) stochastic differential equation $dX_t = [\![b]\!]^{X_t} dt + [\![\sigma]\!]^{X_t} dB_t$ with $X_0 = Z$ on the event $\{Z \models H\}$, where B_t is a fresh e-dimensional Brownian motion if σ has e columns. We assume that Z is independent of the σ-algebra generated by $(B_t)_{t \geq 0}$. Further, $(\!|dx = bdt + \sigma dW \,\&\, H|\!)^Z = \inf\{t \geq 0 : X_t \notin H\}$. Note that X is not defined on the event $\{Z \not\models H\}$.*

5. *$[\![\lambda\alpha \oplus \nu\beta]\!]^Z = \mathcal{I}_{U \leq \lambda}[\![\alpha]\!]^Z + \mathcal{I}_{U > \lambda}[\![\beta]\!]^Z = \begin{cases} [\![\alpha]\!]^Z & \text{on the event } \{U \leq \lambda\} \\ [\![\beta]\!]^Z & \text{on the event } \{U > \lambda\} \end{cases}$*

   $(\!|\lambda\alpha \oplus \nu\beta|\!)^Z = \mathcal{I}_{U \leq \lambda}(\!|\alpha|\!)^Z + \mathcal{I}_{U > \lambda}(\!|\beta|\!)^Z$
   where $U \sim \mathcal{U}(0,1)$ is i.i.d. and $\mathcal{F}_0$-measurable.

6. *$[\![\alpha; \beta]\!]_t^Z = \begin{cases} [\![\alpha]\!]_t^Z & \text{on } \{t < (\!|\alpha|\!)^Z\} \\ [\![\beta]\!]_{t-(\!|\alpha|\!)^Z}^{[\![\alpha]\!]_{(\!|\alpha|\!)^Z}^Z} & \text{on } \{t \geq (\!|\alpha|\!)^Z\} \end{cases}$ and $(\!|\alpha; \beta|\!)^Z = (\!|\alpha|\!)^Z + (\!|\beta|\!)^{[\![\alpha]\!]_{(\!|\alpha|\!)^Z}^Z}$*

7. *$[\![\alpha^*]\!]_t^Z = [\![\alpha^n]\!]_t^Z$ on the event $\{(\!|\alpha^n|\!)^Z > t\}$ and $(\!|\alpha^*|\!)^Z = \lim_{n \to \infty} (\!|\alpha^n|\!)^Z$ where $\alpha^0 \equiv ?true$, $\alpha^1 \equiv \alpha$, and $\alpha^{n+1} \equiv \alpha; \alpha^n$.*

For Case 7, note that $(\!|\alpha^n|\!)^Z$ is monotone in n, hence the limit $(\!|\alpha^*|\!)^Z$ exists and is finite if the sequence is bounded. The limit is ∞ otherwise. Note that $[\![\alpha^*]\!]_t^Z$ is independent of the choice of n on the event $\{(\!|\alpha^n|\!)^Z > t\}$ (but not necessarily independent of n on the event $\{(\!|\alpha^n|\!)^Z \geq t\}$, because α might start with a jump after α^n). Observe that $[\![\alpha^*]\!]_t^Z$ is not defined on the event $\{\forall n \, (\!|\alpha^n|\!)^Z \leq t\}$, which happens, e.g., for Zeno executions violating divergence of time. It would still be possible to give a semantics in this case, e.g., at $t = (\!|\alpha^n|\!)^Z$, but we do not gain much from introducing those technicalities.

In the semantics of $[\![\alpha]\!]^Z$, time is allowed to end. We explicitly consider $[\![\alpha]\!]_t^Z$ as not defined for a realization ω if a part of this process is not defined, because of failed tests in α. The process may be explicitly not defined when $t > (\!|\alpha|\!)^Z$. Explicitly being not defined can be viewed as being in a special absorbing state that can never be left again, as in killed processes. The stochastic process $[\![\alpha]\!]^Z$ is only intended to be used until time $(\!|\alpha|\!)^Z$. We stop using $[\![\alpha]\!]^Z$ after time $(\!|\alpha|\!)^Z$.

A *Markov time* (a.k.a. stopping time) is a non-negative random variable τ such that $\{\tau \leq t\} \in \mathcal{F}_t$ for all t. For a Markov time τ and a stochastic process X_t, the following process is called *stopped process* X^τ

$$X_t^\tau := X_{t \sqcap \tau} = \begin{cases} X_t & \text{if } t < \tau \\ X_\tau & \text{if } t \geq \tau \end{cases} \quad \text{where} \quad t \sqcap \tau := \min\{t, \tau\}$$

A class $\mathcal{C}$ of processes is *stable under stopping* if $X \in \mathcal{C}$ implies $X^\tau \in \mathcal{C}$ for every Markov time τ. Right continuous adapted processes, and processes satisfying the strong Markov property are stable under stopping [5, Theorem 10.2].

Most importantly, we show that the semantics is well-defined. We prove that the natural stopping times $(\!|\alpha|\!)^Z$ are actually Markov times so that it is meaningful to stop process $[\![\alpha]\!]^Z$ at $(\!|\alpha|\!)^Z$ and useful properties of $[\![\alpha]\!]^Z$ inherit to the stopped process $[\![\alpha]\!]^Z_{t \sqcap (\!|\alpha|\!)^Z}$. Furthermore, we show that the process $[\![\alpha]\!]^Z$ is adapted (does not look into the future) and càdlàg, which will be important to define a semantics for formulas. We give a proof of the following theorem in [22].

Theorem 3 (Adaptive càdlàg process with Markov times). *For each SHP α and any $\mathbb{R}^d$-valued random variable Z, $[\![\alpha]\!]^Z$ is an a.s. càdlàg process and adapted (to the completed filtration $(\mathcal{F}_t)_{t \geq 0}$ generated by Z and the constituent Brownian motion $(B_s)_{s \leq t}$ and uniform U processes) and $(\!|\alpha|\!)^Z$ is a Markov time (for $(\mathcal{F}_t)_{t \geq 0}$). In particular, the end value $[\![\alpha]\!]^Z_{(\!|\alpha|\!)^Z}$ is again $\mathcal{F}_{(\!|\alpha|\!)^Z}$-measurable.*

Note in particular, that the event $\{(\!|\alpha^n|\!)^Z \geq t\}$ is $\mathcal{F}_t$-measurable, thus, by [10, Prop 1.2.3], the event $\{(\!|\alpha^n|\!)^Z > t\}$ in Case 7 of Def. 2 is $\mathcal{F}_t$-measurable. As a corollary to Theorem 3, $[\![\alpha]\!]^Z$ is progressively measurable [10, Prop 1.1.13].

5   Stochastic Differential Dynamic Logic

For specifying and analyzing properties of SHPs, we introduce *stochastic differential dynamic logic* Sd$\mathcal{L}$.

Syntax. *Function terms of stochastic differential dynamic logic* Sd$\mathcal{L}$ *are formed by the grammar (F is a primitive measurable function definable in first-order real arithmetic, e.g., the characteristic function $\mathcal{I}_S$ of a measurable set S*

$$0 \equiv \mathcal{I}_\emptyset$$
$$1 \equiv \mathcal{I}_{\mathbb{R}^d}$$
$$\neg f \equiv 1 - f$$
$$A \wedge B \equiv AB$$
$$A \vee B \equiv A + B - AB$$
$$A \rightarrow B \equiv 1 - A + AB$$
$$\texttt{if}(H)\,\{\alpha\}\texttt{else}\{\beta\} \equiv \frac{1}{2}(?H; \alpha) \oplus \frac{1}{2}(?\neg H; \beta)$$
$$\texttt{while}(H)\,\{\alpha\} \equiv (?H; \alpha)^*; ?\neg H$$
$$[\alpha]f \equiv \neg\langle\alpha\rangle\neg f$$

Fig. 2. Common Sd$\mathcal{L}$ and SHP abbreviations

definable in first-order real arithmetic, B is a boolean combination of such characteristic functions using operators $\wedge, \vee, \neg, \rightarrow$ from Fig. 2, λ, ν are rational numbers):

$$f, g \ ::= \ F \mid \lambda f + \nu g \mid B f \mid \langle \alpha \rangle f$$

These are for linear $(\lambda f + \nu g)$ or boolean product (Bf) combinations of terms. Term $\langle \alpha \rangle f$ represents the supremal value of f along the process belonging to α. The syntactic abbreviations in Fig. 2 can be useful. Formulas of Sd$\mathcal{L}$ are simple, because Sd$\mathcal{L}$ function terms are powerful. Sd$\mathcal{L}$ formulas express equational and inequality relations between Sd$\mathcal{L}$ function terms f, g. They are of the form:

$$\phi \ ::= \ f \leq g \mid f = g$$

Measurable Semantics. The semantics of classical logics maps an interpretation to a truth-value. This does not work for stochastic logic, because the state evolution of SHPs contained in Sd$\mathcal{L}$ formulas is stochastic, not deterministic. Instead, we define the semantics of an Sd$\mathcal{L}$ function term as a random variable.

Definition 4 (Sd$\mathcal{L}$ semantics). *The semantics $[\![f]\!]$ of a function term f is a function $[\![f]\!] : (\Omega \rightarrow \mathbb{R}^d) \rightarrow (\Omega \rightarrow \mathbb{R})$ that maps any $\mathbb{R}^d$-valued random variable Z describing the current state to a random variable $[\![f]\!]^Z$. It is defined by*

1. $[\![F]\!]^Z = F^\ell(Z)$, *i.e.,* $[\![F]\!]^Z(\omega) = F^\ell(Z(\omega))$ *where function F denotes F^ℓ*
2. $[\![\lambda f + \nu g]\!]^Z = \lambda [\![f]\!]^Z + \nu [\![g]\!]^Z$
3. $[\![Bf]\!]^Z = [\![B]\!]^Z * [\![f]\!]^Z$, *i.e., multiplication* $[\![Bf]\!]^Z(\omega) = [\![B]\!]^Z(\omega) * [\![f]\!]^Z(\omega)$
4. $[\![\langle \alpha \rangle f]\!]^Z = \sup\{[\![f]\!]^{[\alpha]_t^Z} : 0 \leq t \leq (\![\alpha]\!)^Z\}$

When Z is not defined (results from a failed test), then $[\![f]\!]^Z$ is not defined. To avoid partiality, we assume the convention $[\![f]\!]^Z := 0$ when Z is not defined.

If f is a characteristic function of a measurable set, then $[\![\langle \alpha \rangle f]\!]^Z$ corresponds to a random variable that reflects the supremal f value that α can reach at least once during its evolution until stopping time $(\![\alpha]\!)^Z$ when starting in a state corresponding to random variable Z. Then $P([\![\langle \alpha \rangle f]\!]^Z = 1)$ is the probability with which α reaches f at least once and $E([\![\langle \alpha \rangle f]\!]^Z)$ is the expected value, given Z. This includes the special case where Z is a deterministic state $Z(\omega) := x$ for all $\omega \in \Omega$. But first, we prove that these quantities are well-defined probabilities at all. Note that well-definedness of the definition in case 4 uses Theorem 3.

Cases 1–3 of Def. 4 are as in [14] with the notable exception of case 4, which we define as a supremum, not an integral. The reason is that we are interested in probabilistic worst-case verification, not in average-case verification. For discrete programs, it is often sufficient to consider the input-output behavior, so that Kozen did not need to consider the temporal evolution of the program over time, only its final (probabilistic) outcome [14]. In stochastic hybrid systems, the temporal evolution is highly relevant, in addition to the stochastic behavior. When averaging over time, the system state may be very probably good (the integral of the error is small). But, still, it could be very likely that the system exhibits a bug at some state during a run. In this case, we would still want to declare such a system as broken, because, when using it, it will very likely get us into trouble. Stochastic average-case analysis is interesting for performance analysis. But for safety verification, supremal stochastic analysis is more relevant, because a system that is very probably broken at some time, is still too broken to be used safely. We thus consider stochastic dynamics with worst-case temporal behavior, i.e., our semantics performs stochastic averaging (in the sense of probability) among different behaviors, but considers supremal worst-case probability over time. The logic Sd$\mathcal{L}$ is intended to be used (among other things) to prove bounds on the probability that a system fails at some point at all.

A car that, on average over all times of its use, has a low crash rate, but still has a high probability of crashing at least once during the first ride would not be safe. This is one example where stochastic hybrid systems exhibit new interesting characteristics that we do not see in discrete systems.

We show that the semantics is well-defined. We prove that $[\![f]\!]^Z$ is, indeed, a random variable, i.e., measurable. Without this, probabilistic questions about the value of formulas would not be well-defined, because they are not measurable with respect to the probability space $(\Omega, \mathcal{F}, P)$ and the Borel σ-algebra on $\mathbb{R}$.

Theorem 5 (Measurability). *For any $\mathbb{R}^d$-valued random variable Z, the semantics $[\![f]\!]^Z$ of function term f is a random variable (i.e., $\mathcal{F}$-measurable).*

We give a proof of this theorem in [22].

Corollary 6 (Pushforward measure). *For any $\mathbb{R}^d$-valued random variable Z and function term f, probability measure P induces the pushforward measure*

$$S \mapsto P(([\![f]\!]^Z)^{-1}(S)) = P(\{\omega \in \Omega : [\![f]\!]^Z(\omega) \in S\}) = P([\![f]\!]^Z \in S)$$

which defines a probability measure on $\mathbb{R}$. Hence, for each Borel-measurable set S, the probability $P([\![f]\!]^Z \in S)$ is well-defined.

We say that $f \leq g$ is *valid* if it holds for all $\mathbb{R}^d$-valued random variables Z:

$$\vDash f \leq g \quad \text{iff} \quad \text{for all } Z, \ [\![f]\!]^Z \leq [\![g]\!]^Z, \text{ i.e., } ([\![f]\!]^Z)(\omega) \leq ([\![g]\!]^Z)(\omega) \text{ for all } \omega \in \Omega$$

Validity of $f = g$ is defined accordingly, hence, $\vDash f = g$ iff $\vDash f \leq g$ and $\vDash g \leq f$. As consequence relation on formulas, we use the *(global) consequence relation* that we define as follows (similarly when some of the formulas are $f_i = g_i$):

$$f_1 \leq g_1, \ldots, f_n \leq g_n \vDash f \leq g$$
$$\text{iff } \vDash f_1 \leq g_1, \ldots, \vDash f_n \leq g_n \text{ implies } \vDash f \leq g$$

Also $f_1 \leq g_1, \ldots, f_n \leq g_n \vDash f \leq g$ holds *pathwise* if it holds for each $\omega \in \Omega$.

6   Stochastic Calculus

In this section, we review important results from stochastic calculus [10,19,11] that we use in our proof calculus. To indicate the probability law of process X

starting at $X_0 = x$ a.s., we write P^x instead of P. By E^x we denote the expectation operator for probability law P^x. That is $E^x(f(X_t)) := \int_\Omega f(X_t(\omega))dP^x(\omega)$ for each Borel-measurable function $f : \mathbb{R}^d \to \mathbb{R}$. A very important concept is the infinitesimal generator that captures the average rate of change of a process.

Definition 7 (Infinitesimal generator). *The* (infinitesimal) *generator of an a.s. right continuous strong Markov process (e.g., solution from Def. 1) is the operator A that maps a function $f : \mathbb{R}^d \to \mathbb{R}$ to function $Af : \mathbb{R}^d \to \mathbb{R}$ defined as*

$$Af(x) := \lim_{t \searrow 0} \frac{E^x f(X_t) - f(x)}{t}$$

We say that Af is defined if this limit exists for all $x \in \mathbb{R}^d$. The generator can be used to compute the expected value of a function when following the process until a Markov time without solving the SDE.

Theorem 8 (Dynkin's formula [19, Theorem 7.4.1],[5, p. 133]). *Let X_t an a.s. right continuous strong Markov process (e.g., solution from Def. 1). If $f \in C^2(\mathbb{R}^d, \mathbb{R})$ has compact support and τ is a Markov time with $E^x \tau < \infty$, then*

$$E^x f(X_\tau) = f(x) + E^x \int_0^\tau Af(X_s)ds$$

Dynkin's formula is very useful, but only if we can compute the generator and its integral. The generator A gives a stochastic expression. It has been shown, however, that it is equal to a deterministic expression called the differential generator under fairly mild assumptions:

Theorem 9 (Differential generator [19, Theorem 7.3.3]). *For a solution X_t from Def. 1, if $f \in C^2(\mathbb{R}^d, \mathbb{R})$ is compactly supported, then Af is defined and*

$$Af(x) = Lf(x) := \sum_i b_i(x)\frac{\partial f}{\partial x_i}(x) + \frac{1}{2}\sum_{i,j}(\sigma(x)\sigma(x)^*)_{i,j}\frac{\partial^2 f}{\partial x_i \partial x_j}(x)$$

A stochastic process Y that is adapted to a filtration $(\mathcal{F}_t)_{t\geq 0}$ is a *supermartingale* iff $E|Y_t| < \infty$ for all $t \geq 0$ and

$$E(Y_t \mid \mathcal{F}_s) \leq Y_s \quad \text{for all } t \geq s \geq 0$$

Proposition 10 (Doob's maximal martingale inequality [10, Theorem I.3.8]). *If $f(X_t)$ is a càdlàg supermartingale with respect to the filtration generated by $(X_t)_{t\geq 0}$ and $f \geq 0$ on the evolution domain of X_t, then for all $\lambda > 0$:*

$$P\left(\sup_{t\geq 0} f(X_t) \geq \lambda \mid \mathcal{F}_0\right) \leq \frac{Ef(X_0)}{\lambda}$$

7   Proof Calculus

Now that we have a model, logic, and semantics for stochastic hybrid systems, we investigate reasoning principles that can be used to prove logical properties of

$$\langle x := \theta \rangle f = f_x^\theta \quad \text{if admissible substitution replacing } x \text{ with } \theta \qquad (\langle := \rangle)$$

$$\langle ?H \rangle f = H f \qquad (\langle ? \rangle)$$

$$\langle \alpha; \beta \rangle f \leq \langle \alpha \rangle (f \sqcup \langle \beta \rangle f) \quad (\leq \langle \alpha \rangle (f + \langle \beta \rangle f) \text{ if } 0 \leq f) \qquad (\langle ; \rangle)$$

$$\langle \alpha; \beta \rangle f \leq \langle \alpha \rangle \langle \beta \rangle f \quad \text{if } \vDash f \leq \langle \beta \rangle f \text{ or } \beta \text{ continuous at } 0 \text{ a.s.} \qquad (\langle ; \rangle')$$

$$\langle \alpha \rangle (\lambda f) = \lambda \langle \alpha \rangle f \qquad (\langle \rangle \lambda)$$

$$\langle \alpha \rangle (\lambda f + \nu g) \leq \lambda \langle \alpha \rangle f + \nu \langle \alpha \rangle g \qquad (\langle \rangle +)$$

$$0 \leq B = BB \leq 1 \quad \text{if } B \text{ boolean from characteristic functions} \qquad (\mathcal{I})$$

$$0 \leq f \vDash 0 \leq \langle \alpha \rangle f \qquad (pos)$$

$$f \leq g \vDash \langle \alpha \rangle f \leq \langle \alpha \rangle g \qquad (mon)$$

$$\overline{H} \to f \leq \lambda \vDash \langle dx = b \, dt + \sigma dW \,\&\, H \rangle f \leq \lambda \quad (\lambda \in \mathbb{Q}) \qquad (mon')$$

$$\langle \alpha \rangle g \leq g \vDash \langle \alpha^* \rangle g \leq g \qquad (ind)$$

Fig. 3. Pathwise proof rules for Sd$\mathcal{L}$

stochastic hybrid systems. First we present proof rules that are sound pathwise, i.e., satisfy the global consequence relation pathwise for each $\omega \in \Omega$. By $\sqcup$ we denote the binary maximum operator. It can either be added into the language or approximated conservatively by $+$ as in rule $\langle ; \rangle$. Operator $\sqcup$ coincides with $\vee$ for values in $\{0,1\}$, e.g., built using operators $\wedge, \vee, \neg, \langle \alpha \rangle$ from characteristic functions. As a supremum, $\langle \alpha \rangle B$ only takes on values $\{0,1\}$ if B does.

Theorem 11 (Pathwise sound). *The proof rules in Fig. 3 are globally sound pathwise.*

For a proof see [22]. For $\langle ; \rangle'$, β is a.s. continuous at 0 if, on all paths, the first primitive operation that is not a test is a stochastic differential equation, not a (random) assignment. Our rules generalize to the case of probabilistic assumptions. Note that formula $\overline{H} \to f \leq \lambda$ in mon' is equivalent to $\overline{H}f \leq \overline{H}\lambda$ but easier to read. If f is continuous, rule mon' is sound when replacing the topological closure $\overline{H}$ (which is computable by quantifier elimination) by H, because the inequality is weak.

Next we show proof rules that do not hold pathwise, but still in distribution.

Theorem 12 (Sound in distribution). *Rule $\langle \oplus \rangle$ is sound in distribution.*

$$P(\langle \lambda \alpha \oplus \nu \beta \rangle f \in S) = \lambda P(\langle \alpha \rangle f \in S) + \nu P(\langle \beta \rangle f \in S) \qquad (\langle \oplus \rangle)$$

For a proof see [22]. How to prove properties about random assignment $x_i := *$ depends on the distribution for the random assignment. For a uniform distribution in $[0,1]$, e.g., we obtain the following proof rule that is sound in distribution:

$$P(\langle x_i := * \rangle f \in S) = \int_0^1 \mathcal{I}_{\langle x_i := r \rangle f \in S} \, dr \qquad (\langle * \rangle)$$

The integrand is measurable for measurable S by Corollary 6. The rule is applicable when f has been simplified enough using other proof rules such that the integral can be computed after using $\langle := \rangle$ to simplify the integrand.

Theorem 13 (Soundness for stochastic differential equations). *If function* $f \in C^2(\mathbb{R}^d, \mathbb{R})$ *has compact support on* H *(which holds for all* $f \in C^2(\mathbb{R}^d, \mathbb{R})$ *if* H *represents a bounded set), then the proof rule* $\langle ' \rangle$ *is sound for* $\lambda > 0, p \geq 0$

$$(\langle ' \rangle) \quad \frac{\langle \alpha \rangle (H \rightarrow f) \leq \lambda p \quad H \rightarrow f \geq 0 \quad H \rightarrow Lf \leq 0}{P(\langle \alpha \rangle \langle dx = bdt + \sigma dW \,\&\, H \rangle f \geq \lambda) \leq p}$$

Proof. Since f has compact support on H, it has a $C^2(\mathbb{R}^d, \mathbb{R})$ modification with compact support on $\mathbb{R}^d$ that still satisfies the premises of $\langle ' \rangle$, because all properties of f in the premises assume H. To simplify notation, we write $f(x)$ for $\llbracket f \rrbracket^x$. Let X_t be the stochastic process $\llbracket dx = bdt + \sigma dW \,\&\, H \rrbracket^Z$. Let $\check{X}_t$ be X_t restricted to H, i.e., the stopped process $\check{X}_t := X_{t \sqcap (\llbracket dx = bdt + \sigma dW \,\&\, H \rrbracket)^Z}$, which is stopped at a Markov time by Theorem 3. The stopped process $\check{X}_t$, thus, inherits càdlàg and strong Markov properties from X_t; see, e.g., [5, Theorem 10.2]. If Af is defined and continuous and bounded on H [5, Ch 11.3][15, Ch I.3,I.4], then the infinitesimal generator of $\check{X}_t$ agrees with the generator of X_t on H (and is zero otherwise). This is the case, since $f \in C^2(\mathbb{R}^d, \mathbb{R})$ has compact support (thus bounded as continuous), because Af is then defined and $Af = Lf$ by Theorem 9, hence, Lf is continuous, because b, σ are continuous by Def. 1.

All premises of rule $\langle ' \rangle$ still hold when assuming the topological closure $\overline{H}$ instead of H, because the functions f and Lf are continuous and the conditions are weak inequalities, thus, closed. Consider any $x \in \mathbb{R}^d$ and any time $s \geq 0$. The deterministic time s is a (very simple) Markov time with $E^x s = s < \infty$. Since f is compactly supported, Theorem 8 is applicable and implies that

$$E^x f(\check{X}_s) = f(x) + E^x \int_0^s Af(\check{X}_r) dr \tag{2}$$

Now $Lf \leq 0$ on $\overline{H}$ by the third premise. Hence, $Af \leq 0$ on $\overline{H}$, because $Lf = Af$ (on $\overline{H}$) by Theorem 9, as $f \in C^2(\mathbb{R}^d, \mathbb{R})$ has compact support. Because X and $\check{X}$ have a.s. continuous paths *and* are not defined on the event $\{Z \not\models H\}$, we know that $\check{X}_s$ stays in the closure $\overline{H}$ a.s. Thus, $Af(\check{X}_s) \leq 0$ a.s., hence, $\int_0^s Af(\check{X}_r) dr \leq 0$ a.s., thus, $E^x \int_0^s Af(\check{X}_r) dr \leq 0$. Then (2) implies $E^x f(\check{X}_s) \leq f(x)$ for all x.

Because the filtration is right-continuous and $f \in C(\mathbb{R}^d, \mathbb{R})$ is compactly supported (hence bounded), the strong Markov property [10, Prop 2.6.7] for $\check{X}_t$ implies for all $t \geq s \geq 0$ that P^x-a.s.: $E^x(f(\check{X}_t)|\mathcal{F}_s) = E^{\check{X}_s} f(\check{X}_{t-s}) \leq f(\check{X}_s)$. The inequality holds, since $E^x f(\check{X}_s) \leq f(x)$ for all x, s. Thus, $f(\check{X}_t)$ is a supermartingale with respect to $\check{X}_t$, because it is adapted to the filtration of $\check{X}_t$ (as $f \in C^2(\mathbb{R}^d, \mathbb{R})$) and $E^x |f(\check{X}_t)| < \infty$ for all t since $f \in C^2(\mathbb{R}^d, \mathbb{R})$ has compact support. Further, $f(\check{X}_t)$ inherits continuity from $\check{X}_t$ (which follows from X_t), since f is continuous.

Thus, by the second premise, Proposition 10 is applicable. Consider any initial state $Y := \llbracket \alpha \rrbracket_t^Z$ for $\check{X}$. Thus, $P\left(\sup_{t \geq 0} f(\check{X}_t) \geq \lambda \,|\, \mathcal{F}_0\right) \leq \frac{Ef(Y)}{\lambda}$ by Proposition 10 (filtration at $\check{X}_0$ is $\mathcal{F}_0$). On event $\{Y \not\models H\}$, $\check{X}$ is not defined and nothing to show. On $\{Y \models H\}$, $f(Y) \leq \lambda p$ is *valid* where relevant by the first premise. This implies the conclusion, as $\llbracket \langle dx = bdt + \sigma dW \,\&\, H \rangle f \rrbracket^Y = \sup_{t \geq 0} f(\check{X}_t)$. $\square$

The implications in the premises can be understood like that in *mon'*. Let H be given by first-order real arithmetic formulas. If f is polynomial and, thus, $f \in C^2(\mathbb{R}^d, \mathbb{R})$, then the second and third premise of $\langle' \rangle$ are in first-order real arithmetic, hence decidable. Note that our proof rules can be generalized to probabilistic assumptions by the rule of partition and then combined.

The proof shows that it is enough to assume the first premise holds only a.s. From the proof we see that it would be sufficient to replace the third premise of $\langle' \rangle$ with $\int_0^s Lf(X_r)dr \leq 0$. This is a weaker condition, because it does not require $Lf \leq 0$ always, but only "on average". But this condition is computationally more involved, because the integral needs to be computed first. For polynomial expressions, this is not too difficult, but still increases the polynomial degree.

A simple two-dimensional example is the following for $H \equiv x^2 + y^2 < 10$:

$$P(\langle ?x^2+y^2 \leq \frac{1}{3}; x := \frac{x}{2}; dx = \frac{-x}{2}dt - ydW, dy = \frac{-y}{2}dt + xdW \,\&\, H\rangle x^2+y^2 \geq 1) \leq \frac{1}{3}$$

which can be proven easily using $\langle;\rangle', \langle;\rangle, \langle?\rangle, \langle:=\rangle, \langle'\rangle$, since $f \equiv x^2 + y^2 \geq 0$ and

$$Lf = \frac{1}{2}\left(-x\frac{\partial f}{\partial x} - y\frac{\partial f}{\partial y} + y^2\frac{\partial^2 f}{\partial x^2} - 2xy\frac{\partial^2 f}{\partial x \partial y} + x^2\frac{\partial^2 f}{\partial y^2}\right) \leq 0$$

8   Related Work

Our approach is partially inspired by the work of Kozen, who studied 3 semantics of programs with random number generators [13] and probabilistic PDL [14]. We generalize from discrete systems to stochastic hybrid systems. To reflect the new challenges, we have departed from probabilistic PDL. Kozen uses a measure semantics. We choose a semantics that is based on stochastic processes, because the temporal behavior of SHPs is more crucial than that of abstract discrete programs. Sd$\mathcal{L}$ further uses a supremal semantics that is more interesting for stochastic worst-case verification than the integral semantics assumed in [14].

The comparison to a first-order dynamic logic for deterministic programs with random number generators [6] is similar. They axiomatize relative to first-order analysis with arithmetic, enriched with frequencies and random number generators. They do not show how this logic could be handled (incompletely).

Our approach for stochastic differential equations is inspired by barrier certificates [23]. We extend this work by identifying the assumptions that are required for soundness of using Dynkin-type arguments for stochastic differential equations. They propose to use global generators for switching diffusion processes (which cannot reset variables). We use logic and compositional proofs for SHPs.

Probabilities and logic have also been used in AI, e.g., [25]. Markov logic networks are a combination of Markov networks and first-order logic and resembles logic programming with weights for probabilities. They are restricted to finite domains, which is not the case in stochastic hybrid systems.

Model checking has been used for discrete probabilistic systems like finite Markov chains, e.g., [27], and probabilistic timed automata [17]. Assume-guarantee model checking is a challenge for discrete probabilistic automata, with recent successes for finite automata assumptions [16]. We use a compositional proof approach based on logic and consider stochastic hybrid systems.

Statistical model checking has been suggested for validating stochastic hybrid systems [18] and later refined for discrete-time hybrid systems with a probabilistic simulation function [28] based on corresponding discrete probabilistic techniques [27]. They did not show measurability and do not support stochastic differential equations [28]. Validation by simulation is generally unsound, but the probability of giving a wrong answer can sometimes be bounded [27,28].

Fränzle et al. [7] show first pieces for continuous-time bounded model checking of probabilistic hybrid automata (no stochastic differential equations).

Bujorianu and Lygeros [2] show strong Markov and càdlàg properties for a class of systems known as General Stochastic Hybrid Systems. They also study an interesting concatenation operator. For an overview of model checking techniques for various classes of stochastic hybrid systems, we refer to [3]. Most verification techniques for stochastic hybrid systems use discretizations, approximations, or assume discrete time, bounded horizon [12,3,1,9]. We consider the continuous-time behavior and develop compositional logic and theorem proving.

9   Conclusions

We introduce the first verification logic for stochastic hybrid systems along with a compositional model of stochastic hybrid programs. We prove theoretical properties that are important for well-definedness and measurability and we develop a compositional proof calculus. Our logic makes the complexity of stochastic hybrid systems accessible in logic with simple syntactic proof principles.

Our results indicate that $Sd\mathcal{L}$ is a promising starting point for the study of logic for stochastic hybrid systems. Extensions include nondeterminism.

Acknowledgements. I thank the anonymous referees for their good comments and Steve Marcus and Sergio Pulido Niño for helpful discussions.

References

1. Abate, A., Prandini, M., Lygeros, J., Sastry, S.: Probabilistic reachability and safety for controlled discrete time stochastic hybrid systems. Automatica 44(11), 2724–2734 (2008)
2. Bujorianu, M.L., Lygeros, J.: Towards a general theory of stochastic hybrid systems. In: Blom, H.A.P., Lygeros, J. (eds.) Stochastic Hybrid Systems: Theory and Safety Critical Applications. Lecture Notes Contr. Inf., vol. 337, pp. 3–30. Springer, Heidelberg (2006)
3. Cassandras, C.G., Lygeros, J. (eds.): Stochastic Hybrid Systems. CRC, Boca Raton (2006)
4. Dutertre, B.: Complete proof systems for first order interval temporal logic. In: LICS, pp. 36–43. IEEE Computer Society, Los Alamitos (1995)
5. Dynkin, E.B.: Markov Processes. Springer, Heidelberg (1965)
6. Feldman, Y.A., Harel, D.: A probabilistic dynamic logic. J. Comput. Syst. Sci. 28(2), 193–215 (1984)

7. Fränzle, M., Teige, T., Eggers, A.: Engineering constraint solvers for automatic analysis of probabilistic hybrid automata. J. Log. Algebr. Program. 79(7), 436–466 (2010)
8. Ghosh, M.K., Arapostathis, A., Marcus, S.I.: Ergodic control of switching diffusions. SIAM J. Control Optim. 35(6), 1952–1988 (1997)
9. Hu, J., Lygeros, J., Sastry, S.: Towards a theory of stochastic hybrid systems. In: Lynch, N.A., Krogh, B.H. (eds.) HSCC 2000. LNCS, vol. 1790, pp. 160–173. Springer, Heidelberg (2000)
10. Karatzas, I., Shreve, S.: Brownian Motion and Stochastic Calculus. Springer, Heidelberg (1991)
11. Kloeden, P.E., Platen, E.: Numerical Solution of Stochastic Differential Equations. Springer, New York (2010)
12. Koutsoukos, X.D., Riley, D.: Computational methods for verification of stochastic hybrid systems. IEEE T. Syst. Man, Cy. A 38(2), 385–396 (2008)
13. Kozen, D.: Semantics of probabilistic programs. J. Comput. Syst. Sci. 22(3), 328–350 (1981)
14. Kozen, D.: A probabilistic PDL. J. Comput. Syst. Sci. 30(2), 162–178 (1985)
15. Kushner, H.J. (ed.): Stochastic Stability and Control. Academic Press, New York (1967)
16. Kwiatkowska, M.Z., Norman, G., Parker, D., Qu, H.: Assume-guarantee verification for probabilistic systems. In: Esparza, J., Majumdar, R. (eds.) TACAS 2010. LNCS, vol. 6015, pp. 23–37. Springer, Heidelberg (2010)
17. Kwiatkowska, M.Z., Norman, G., Sproston, J., Wang, F.: Symbolic model checking for probabilistic timed automata. Inf. Comput. 205(7), 1027–1077 (2007)
18. Bevilacqua, V., Sharykin, R.: Specification and analysis of distributed object-based stochastic hybrid systems. In: Hespanha, J.P., Tiwari, A. (eds.) HSCC 2006. LNCS, vol. 3927, pp. 460–475. Springer, Heidelberg (2006)
19. Øksendal, B.: Stochastic Differential Equations: An Introduction with Applications. Springer, Heidelberg (2007)
20. Platzer, A.: Differential-algebraic dynamic logic for differential-algebraic programs. J. Log. Comput. 20(1), 309–352 (2010)
21. Platzer, A.: Quantified differential dynamic logic for distributed hybrid systems. In: Dawar, A., Veith, H. (eds.) CSL 2010. LNCS, vol. 6247, pp. 469–483. Springer, Heidelberg (2010)
22. Platzer, A.: Stochastic differential dynamic logic for stochastic hybrid systems. Tech. Rep. CMU-CS-11-111, School of Computer Science, Carnegie Mellon University, Pittsburgh, PA (2011)
23. Prajna, S., Jadbabaie, A., Pappas, G.J.: A framework for worst-case and stochastic safety verification using barrier certificates. IEEE T. Automat. Contr. 52(8), 1415–1429 (2007)
24. Pratt, V.R.: Semantical considerations on Floyd-Hoare logic. In: FOCS, pp. 109–121. IEEE, Los Alamitos (1976)
25. Richardson, M., Domingos, P.: Markov logic networks. Machine Learning 62(1-2), 107–136 (2006)
26. Tarski, A.: A Decision Method for Elementary Algebra and Geometry, 2nd edn. University of California Press, Berkeley (1951)
27. Younes, H.L.S., Kwiatkowska, M.Z., Norman, G., Parker, D.: Numerical vs. statistical probabilistic model checking. STTT 8(3), 216–228 (2006)
28. Zuliani, P., Platzer, A., Clarke, E.M.: Bayesian statistical model checking with application to Simulink/Stateflow verification. In: Johansson, K.H., Yi, W. (eds.) HSCC, pp. 243–252. ACM, New York (2010)

Reasoning in the OWL 2 Full Ontology Language Using First-Order Automated Theorem Proving

Michael Schneider[1],[*] and Geoff Sutcliffe[2]

[1] FZI Research Center for Information Technology, Germany
[2] University of Miami, USA

Abstract. OWL 2 has been standardized by the World Wide Web Consortium (W3C) as a family of ontology languages for the Semantic Web. The most expressive of these languages is OWL 2 Full, but to date no reasoner has been implemented for this language. Consistency and entailment checking are known to be undecidable for OWL 2 Full. We have translated a large fragment of the OWL 2 Full semantics into first-order logic, and used automated theorem proving systems to do reasoning based on this theory. The results are promising, and indicate that this approach can be applied in practice for effective OWL reasoning, beyond the capabilities of current Semantic Web reasoners.

Keywords: Semantic Web, OWL, First-order logic, ATP.

1 Introduction

The Web Ontology Language OWL 2 [16] has been standardized by the World Wide Web Consortium (W3C) as a family of ontology languages for the Semantic Web. OWL 2 includes OWL 2 DL [10], the OWL 2 RL/RDF rules [9], as well as OWL 2 Full [12]. The focus of this work is on reasoning in OWL 2 Full, the most expressive of these languages. So far, OWL 2 Full has largely been ignored by the research community, and no reasoner has been implemented for this language.

OWL 2 Full does not enforce any of the numerous syntactic restrictions of the description logic-style language OWL 2 DL. Rather, OWL 2 Full treats arbitrary RDF graphs [7] as valid input ontologies, and can safely be used with weakly structured RDF data as is typically found on the Web. Further, OWL 2 Full provides for reasoning outside the scope of OWL 2 DL and the OWL 2 RL/RDF rules, including sophisticated reasoning based on meta-modeling. In addition, OWL 2 Full is semantically fully compatible with RDFS [5] and also with the OWL 2 RL/RDF rules, and there is even a strong semantic correspondence [12] with OWL 2 DL, roughly stating that any OWL 2 DL conclusion can be reflected in OWL 2 Full. This makes OWL 2 Full largely interoperable with the other OWL 2 languages, and allows an OWL 2 Full reasoner to be combined with

[*] Partially supported by the projects *SEALS* (European Commission, EU-IST-2009-238975) and *THESEUS* (German Federal Ministry of Economics and Technology, FK OIMQ07019).

N. Bjørner and V. Sofronie-Stokkermans (Eds.): CADE 2011, LNAI 6803, pp. 461–475, 2011.

most existing OWL reasoners to provide higher syntactic flexibility and semantic expressivity in reasoning-enabled applications.

Due to its combination of flexibility and expressivity, OWL 2 Full is computationally undecidable with regard to consistency and entailment checking [8]. While there cannot be any complete decision procedure for OWL 2 Full, the question remains to what extent practical OWL 2 Full reasoning is possible. This paper presents the results of a series of experiments about reasoning in OWL 2 Full using first-order logic (FOL) theorem proving. A large fragment of the OWL 2 Full semantics has been translated into a FOL theory, and automated theorem proving (ATP) systems have been used to do reasoning based on this theory. The primary focus of these experiments was on the question of what can be achieved at all; a future study may shift the focus to efficiency aspects.

The basic idea used in this work is not new. An early application of this approach to a preliminary version of RDF and a precursor of OWL was reported by Fikes et al. [2]. That work focused on identifying technical problems in the original language specifications, rather than on practical reasoning. Hayes [4] provided fairly complete translations of RDF(S) and OWL 1 Full into Common Logic, but did not report on any reasoning experiments. This gap was filled by Hawke's reasoner *Surnia* [3], which applied an ATP system to an FOL axiomatisation of OWL 1 Full. For unknown reasons, however, Surnia performed rather poorly on reasoning tests [17]. Comparable studies have been carried out for ATP-based OWL DL reasoning, as for *Hoolet* [15], an OWL DL reasoner implemented on top of a previous version of the Vampire ATP system (http://www.vprover.org). The work of Horrocks and Voronkov [6] addresses reasoning over large ontologies, which is crucial for practical Semantic Web reasoning. Finally, [1] reports on some historic knowledge representation systems using ATP for description logic-style reasoning, such as *Krypton* in the 1980s.

All these previous efforts are outdated, in that they refer to precursors of OWL 2 Full, and appear to have been discontinued after publication. The work reported in this paper refers to the current specification of OWL 2 Full, and makes a more extensive experimental evaluation of the FOL-based approach than any previous work. Several aspects of OWL 2 Full reasoning have been studied: the degree of language coverage of OWL 2 Full; semantic conclusions that are characteristic specifically of OWL 2 Full; reasoning on large data sets; and the ability of first-order systems to detect non-entailments and consistent ontologies in OWL 2 Full. The FOL-based results have been compared with the results of a selection of well-known Semantic Web reasoners, to determine whether the FOL-based approach is able to add significant value to the state-of-the-art in Semantic Web reasoning.

This paper is organized as follows: Section 2 provides an introduction to the technologies used in this paper. Section 3 describes the FOL-based reasoning approach. Section 4 describes the evaluation setting, including the test data, the reasoners, and the computers used in the experiments. The main part of the paper is Section 5, which presents the results of the experiments. Section 6 concludes, and gives an outlook on possible future work.

2   Preliminaries

2.1   RDF and OWL 2 Full

OWL 2 Full is specified as the language that uses the OWL 2 RDF-Based Semantics [12] to interpret arbitrary RDF graphs. RDF graphs are defined by the RDF Abstract Syntax [7]. The OWL 2 RDF-Based Semantics is defined as a semantic extension of the RDF Semantics [5].

According to the RDF Abstract Syntax, an *RDF graph* G is a set of RDF triples: $G = \{t_1, \ldots, t_n\}$. Each *RDF triple* t is given as an ordered ternary tuple $t = s\,p\,o$ of *RDF nodes*. The RDF nodes s, p, and o are called the *subject*, *predicate*, and *object* of the triple t, respectively. Each RDF node is either a *URI*, a (plain, language-tagged or typed) *literal*, or a *blank node*.

The *RDF Semantics* is defined on top of the RDF Abstract Syntax as a model theory for arbitrary RDF graphs. For an *interpretation* I and a *domain* U, a URI denotes an individual in the domain, a literal denotes a concrete data value (also considered a domain element), and a blank node is used as an existentially quantified variable indicating the existence of some domain element. The meaning of a triple $t = s\,p\,o$ is a truth value of the relationship $\langle I(s), I(o) \rangle \in \mathrm{IEXT}(I(p))$, where IEXT is a mapping from domain elements that are *properties* to associated binary relations. The meaning of a graph $G = \{t_1, \ldots, t_n\}$ is a truth value determined by the conjunction of the meaning of all the triples, taking into account the existential semantics of blank nodes occurring in G. If an RDF graph G is true under an interpretation I, then I *satisfies* G. An RDF graph G is *consistent* if there is an interpretation I that satisfies G. An RDF graph G *entails* another RDF graph H if every interpretation I that satisfies G also satisfies H.

Whether an interpretation satisfies a given graph is primarily determined by a collection of model-theoretic *semantic conditions* that constrain the mapping IEXT. There are different sets of model-theoretic semantic conditions for the different semantics defined by the RDF Semantics specification. For example, the semantics of class subsumption in *RDFS* is defined mainly by the semantic condition defined for the RDFS vocabulary term `rdfs:subClassOf`:

$$\langle c, d \rangle \in \mathrm{IEXT}(I(\texttt{rdfs:subClassOf})) \Rightarrow c, d \in IC \wedge \mathrm{ICEXT}(c) \subseteq \mathrm{ICEXT}(d)$$

where "c" and "d" are universally quantified variables. Analogous to the mapping IEXT, the mapping ICEXT associates *classes* with subsets of the domain. The two mappings are responsible for the *metamodeling capabilities* of RDFS and its semantic extensions: Although the quantifiers in the RDFS semantic conditions range over exclusively domain elements, which keeps RDFS in the realm of first-order logic, the associations provided by the two mappings allow domain elements (properties and classes) to indirectly refer to sets and binary relations. This enables a limited but useful form of higher order-style modeling and reasoning.

The *OWL 2 RDF-Based Semantics*, i.e. the semantics of OWL 2 Full, extends the RDF Semantics specification by additional semantic conditions for the OWL-specific vocabulary terms, such as `owl:unionOf` and `owl:disjointWith`.

2.2   FOL, the TPTP Language, and ATP

The translation of the OWL 2 Full semantics is to classical untyped first-order logic. The concrete syntax is the TPTP language [14], which is the de facto standard for state-of-the-art ATP systems for first-order logic. The ATP systems used in the evaluation were taken from their web sites (see Section 4.3) or from the archives of the 5th IJCAR ATP System Competition, CASC-J5 (http://www.tptp.org/CASC/J5/). Most of the systems are also available online as part of the SystemOnTPTP service (http://www.tptp.org/cgi-bin/SystemOnTPTP/).

3   Approach

Each of the model-theoretic semantic conditions of the OWL 2 Full semantics is translated into a corresponding FOL axiom. The result is an axiomatization of OWL 2 Full. The RDF graphs to reason about are also converted into FOL formulae. In the case of *consistency checking* there is a single RDF graph that is converted into a FOL axiom, for which satisfiability needs to be checked. In the case of *entailment checking*, there is a premise graph that is converted into a FOL axiom, and a conclusion graph that is converted into a FOL conjecture. The FOL formulae (those representing the input RDF graphs and those building the FOL axiomatization of the OWL 2 Full semantics) are passed to an ATP system, which tries to prove the conclusion or establish consistency.

We apply a straight-forward *translation of the semantic conditions*, making use of the fact that all semantic conditions have the form of FOL formulae. A semantic relationship of the form "$\langle s, o \rangle \in \mathrm{IEXT}(p)$" that appears within a semantic condition is converted into an atomic FOL formula of the form "iext(p, s, o)". Likewise, a relationship "$x \in \mathrm{ICEXT}(c)$" is converted into "icext(c, x)". Apart from this, the basic logical structure of the semantic conditions is retained. For example, the semantic condition specifying RDFS class subsumption shown in Section 2.1 is translated into

$$\forall c, d : [\, \mathrm{iext}(\texttt{rdfs:subClassOf}, c, d) \Rightarrow$$
$$(\,\mathrm{ic}(c) \wedge \mathrm{ic}(d) \wedge \forall x : (\mathrm{icext}(c, x) \Rightarrow \mathrm{icext}(d, x))\,)\,]$$

The *translation of RDF graphs* amounts to converting the set of triples "$s\,p\,o$" into a conjunction of corresponding "iext(p, s, o)" atoms. A *URI* occurring in an RDF graph is converted into a constant. An *RDF literal* is converted into a function term, with a constant for the literal's lexical form as one of its arguments. Different functions are used for the different kinds of literals: function terms for *plain literals* have arity 1; function terms for *language-tagged literals* have a constant representing the language tag as their second argument; function terms for *typed literals* have a constant for the datatype URI as their second argument. For each *blank node*, an existentially quantified variable is introduced, and the scope of the corresponding existential quantifier is the whole conjunction of the "iext" atoms. For example, the RDF graph

```
_:x rdf:type foaf:Person .
_:x foaf:name "Alice"^^xsd:string .
```

which contains the blank node "`_:x`", the typed literal ""`"Alice"^^xsd:string`",
and the URIs "`rdf:type`", "`foaf:Person`", and "`foaf:name`", is translated into
the FOL formula

$$\exists x : [\ \mathrm{iext}(\mathtt{rdf:type}, x, \mathtt{foaf:Person}) \wedge$$
$$\mathrm{iext}(\mathtt{foaf:name}, x, \mathrm{literal_{typed}}(\mathtt{Alice}, \mathtt{xsd:string})) \ ]$$

4 Evaluation Setting

This section describes the evaluation setting: the OWL 2 Full axiomatization,
the test cases, the reasoners, and the computing resources. *Supplementary material* including the axiomatizations, test data, raw results, and the software
used for this paper can be found online at: `http://www.fzi.de/downloads/`
`ipe/schneid/cade2011-schneidsut-owlfullatp.zip`.

4.1 The FOL Axiomatization and RDF Graph Conversion

Following the approach described in Section 3, most of the normative semantic
conditions of the OWL 2 Full semantics have been converted into the corresponding FOL axioms, using the TPTP language [14]. The main omission is that most
of the semantics concerning *reasoning on datatypes* has not been treated, as we
were only interested in evaluating the "logical core" of the language. All other
language features of OWL 2 Full were covered in their full form, with a restriction
that was sufficient for our tests: while OWL 2 Full has many size-parameterized
language features, for example the intersection of arbitrarily many classes, our
axiomatization generally supports these language feature schemes only up to a
size of 3. The resulting FOL axiomatization consists of 558 formulae. The axiom set is fully first-order with equality, but equality accounts for less than 10%
of the atoms. The first-order ATP systems used (see Section 4.3) convert the
formulae to clause normal form. The resultant clause set is non-Horn. Almost
all the clauses are range-restricted, which can result in reasoning that produces
mostly ground clauses.

In addition, a converter from RDF graphs to FOL formulae was implemented.
This allowed the use of RDF-encoded OWL test data in the experiments, without
time consuming and error prone manual conversion.

4.2 Test Data

Two complementary test suites were used for the experiments: one test suite
to evaluate the degree of language coverage of OWL 2 Full, and another suite
consisting of characteristic conclusions for OWL 2 Full reasoning. For scalability
experiments a large set of RDF data was also used.

The Language Coverage Test Suite. For the language coverage experiments, the test suite described in [13] was used.[1] The test suite was created specifically as a conformance test suite for OWL 2 Full and its main sub languages, including RDFS and the OWL 2 RL/RDF rules. The test suite consists of one or more test cases for each of the semantic conditions of the OWL 2 RDF-Based Semantics, i.e., the test suite provides a systematic coverage of OWL 2 Full at a specification level. Most of the test cases are positive entailment and inconsistency tests, but there are also a few negative entailment tests and positive consistency tests. The complete test suite consists of 736 test cases. A large fraction of the test suite deals with datatype reasoning. As the FOL axiomatization has almost no support for datatype reasoning, only the test cases that cover the "logical core" of OWL 2 Full were used. Further, only the positive entailment and inconsistency tests were used. The resultant test suite has 411 test cases.

OWL 2 Full-characteristic Test Cases. In order to investigate the extent of the reasoning possible using the FOL axiomatization, a set of test cases that are characteristic conclusions of OWL 2 Full was created. "Characteristic" means that the test cases represent OWL 2 Full reasoning that cannot normally be expected from either OWL 2 DL reasoning or from reasoners implementing the OWL 2 RL/RDF rules. The test suite consists of 32 tests, with 28 entailment tests and 4 inconsistency tests. There are test cases probing semantic consequences from meta-modeling, annotation properties, the unrestricted use of complex properties, and consequences from the use of OWL vocabulary terms as regular entities (sometimes called "syntax reflection").

Bulk RDF Data. For the scalability experiments, a program that generates RDF graphs of arbitrary size ("bulk RDF data") was written. The data consist of RDF triples using URIs that do not conflict with the URIs in the test cases. Further, no OWL vocabulary terms are used in the data sets. This ensures that adding this bulk RDF data to test cases does not affect the reasoning results.

4.3   Reasoners

This section lists the different reasoning systems that were used in the experiments. The idea behind the selection was to have a small number of representative systems for (i) first-order proving, (ii) first-order model finding, and (iii) OWL reasoning. Details of the ATP systems can be found on their web sites, and (for most) in the system descriptions on the CASC-J5 web site. The OWL reasoners were tested to provide comparisons with existing state of the art Semantic Web reasoners. Unless explicitly stated otherwise, the systems were used in their default modes.

---

[1] There is an official W3C test suite for OWL 2 at `http://owl.semanticweb.org/page/OWL_2_Test_Cases` (2011-02-09). However, it does not cover OWL 2 Full sufficiently well, and was not designed in a systematic way that allows easy determination of which parts of the language specification are not supported by a reasoner.

Systems for first-order theorem proving

- **Vampire 0.6** (http://www.vprover.org). A powerful superposition-based ATP system, including strategy scheduling.
- **Vampire-SInE 0.6** A variant of Vampire that always runs the SInE strategy (http://www.cs.man.ac.uk/~hoderk/sine/desc/) to select axioms that are expected to be relevant.
- **iProver-SInE 0.8** (http://www.cs.man.ac.uk/~korovink/iprover). An instantiation-based ATP system, using the SInE strategy, and including strategy scheduling.

Systems for first-order model finding

- **Paradox 4.0** (http://www.cse.chalmers.se/~koen/code/). A finite model finder, based on conversion to propositional form and the use of a SAT solver.
- **DarwinFM 1.4.5** (http://goedel.cs.uiowa.edu/Darwin). A finite model finder, based on conversion to function-free first-order logic and the use of the Darwin ATP system.

Systems for OWL reasoning

- **Pellet 2.2.2** (http://clarkparsia.com/pellet). An OWL 2 DL reasoner that implements a tableaux-based decision procedure.
- **HermiT 1.3.2** (http://hermit-reasoner.com). An OWL 2 DL reasoner that implements a tableaux-based decision procedure.
- **FaCT++ 1.5.0** (http://owl.man.ac.uk/factplusplus). An OWL 2 DL reasoner that implements a tableaux-based decision procedure.
- **BigOWLIM 3.4** (http://www.ontotext.com/owlim). An RDF entailment-rule reasoner that comes with predefined rule sets. The OWL 2 RL/RDF rule set (owl2-rl) was used. The commercial "BigOWLIM" variant of the reasoning engine was applied, because it provides inconsistency checking.
- **Jena 2.6.4** (http://jena.sourceforge.net). A Java-based RDF framework that supports RDF entailment-rule reasoning and comes with predefined rule sets. The most expressive rule set, OWL_MEM_RULE_INF, was used.
- **Parliament 2.6.9** (http://parliament.semwebcentral.org). An RDF triple store with some limited OWL reasoning capabilities. Parliament cannot detect inconsistencies in ontologies.

4.4   Evaluation Environment

Testing was done on computers with a 2.8GHz Intel Pentium 4 CPU, 2GB memory, running Linux FC8. A 300s CPU time limit was imposed on each run.

5   Evaluation Results

This section presents the results of the following reasoning experiments: a *language coverage analysis*, to determine the degree of conformance to the language specification of OWL 2 Full; *"characteristic" OWL 2 Full reasoning* experiments to determine the extent to which distinguishing OWL 2 Full reasoning is possible; some basic *scalability testing*; and several *model finding experiments* to determine whether first-order model finders can be used in practice for the recognition of non-entailments and consistent ontologies. The following markers are used in the result tables to indicate the outcomes of the experiments:

- *success ('+')*: a test run that provided the correct result.
- *wrong ('−')*: a test run that provided a wrong result, e.g., when a reasoner claims that an entailment test case is a non-entailment.
- *unknown ('?')*: a test run that did not provide a result, e.g., due to a processing error or time out.

This section also presents comparative evaluation results for the OWL reasoners listed in Section 4.3. This illustrates the degree to which OWL 2 Full reasoning can already be achieved with existing OWL reasoners, and the added value of our reasoning approach compared to existing Semantic Web technology. This means, for example, that an OWL 2 DL reasoner will produce a wrong result if it classifies an OWL 2 Full entailment test case as a non-entailment. However, this negative evaluation result refers to only the level of conformance with respect to OWL 2 Full reasoning, i.e., the reasoner may still be a compliant implementation of OWL 2 DL.

5.1   Language Coverage

This experiment used the FOL axiomatization with the 411 test cases in the language coverage suite described in Section 4.2. The results of the experiment are shown in Table 1. iProver-SInE succeeded on 93% of the test cases, and Vampire succeeded on 85%. It needs to be mentioned that the results were not perfectly stable. Over several runs the number of successes varied for iProver-SInE between 382 and 386. This is caused by small variations in the timing of strategy changes within iProver-SInE's strategy scheduling.

Figure 1 shows the runtime behavior of the two systems, with the times for successes sorted into increasing order. Both systems take less than 1s for the majority of their successes. Although Vampire succeeded on less cases than iProver-SInE, it is typically faster in the case of a success.

Table 1. Language coverage: ATPs with OWL 2 Full axiom set

Reasoner	Success	Wrong	Unknown
Vampire	349	0	62
iProver-SInE	383	0	28

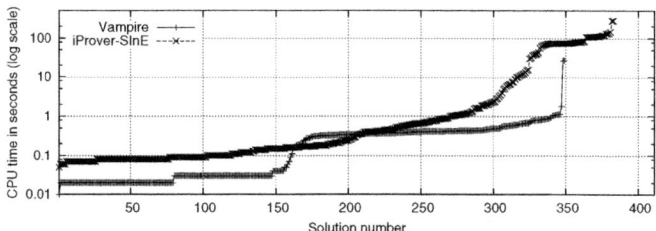

Fig. 1. Language coverage: ordered system times of ATPs

An analysis of the 28 test cases for which both Vampire and iProver-SInE did not succeed revealed that 14 of them require support for OWL 2 Full language features not covered by the FOL axiomatization, including certain forms of datatype reasoning and support for the RDF container vocabulary [5]. A future version of the axiomatization will encode these parts of the OWL 2 Full semantics, which might lead to improved results. For each of the remaining 14 test cases, subsets of axioms sufficient for a solution were hand-selected from the FOL axiomatization. These axiom sets were generally very small, with up to 16 axioms, and in most cases less than 10 axioms. iProver-SInE succeeded on 13 of these 14 test cases. The remaining test case is a considerably complex one, involving the semantics of qualified cardinality restrictions. It was solved by Vampire. Thus, all test cases were solved except for the 14 that are beyond the current axiomatization.

For comparison, the OWL reasoners listed in Section 4.3 were also tested. The results are shown in Table 2. The OWL 2 DL reasoners Pellet and HermiT both succeeded on about 60% of the test cases. A comparison of the individual results showed that the two reasoners succeeded mostly on the same test cases. Interestingly, although most of the test cases are formally invalid OWL 2 DL ontologies, reasoning rarely resulted in a processing error. Rather, in ca. 40% of the cases, the reasoners wrongly reported a test case to be a non-entailment or a consistent ontology. The third OWL 2 DL reasoner, FaCT++, signaled a processing error more often, and succeeded on less than 50% of the test cases.

The OWL 2 RL/RDF rule reasoner BigOWLIM succeeded on roughly 70% of the test cases. Although the number of successful tests was larger than for all the OWL 2 DL reasoners, there was a considerable number of test cases for which the OWL 2 DL reasoners were successful but not BigOWLIM, and vice versa. The Jena OWL reasoner, which is an RDF entailment rule reasoner like BigOWLIM, succeeded on about only 30% of the test cases, which is largely due to missing support for OWL 2 features. Finally, Parliament succeeded on only 14 of the test cases. In particular, it did not solve any of the inconsistency test cases. The low success rate reflects the style of "light-weight reasoning" used in many reasoning-enabled RDF triple stores.

Table 2. Language coverage: OWL reasoners

Reasoner	Success	Wrong	Unknown
Pellet	237	168	6
HermiT	246	157	8
FaCT++	190	45	176
BigOWLIM	282	129	0
Jena	129	282	0
Parliament	14	373	24

Table 3. Characteristic conclusions: OWL reasoners PE=Pellet, HE=HermiT, FA=FaCT++, BO=BigOWLIM, JE=Jena, PA=Parliament

	01	02	03	04	05	06	07	08	09	10	11	12	13	14	15	16	17	18	19	20	21	22	23	24	25	26	27	28	29	30	31	32
PE	+	+	+	−	−	−	−	−	+	+	−	−	−	−	−	+	−	−	−	−	+	+	−	−	−	−	+	−	−	?	−	−
HE	+	?	+	−	−	?	−	+	+	+	−	−	−	−	−	+	−	−	−	−	+	+	−	−	+	?	+	−	−	?	−	−
FA	+	?	?	?	?	?	−	?	+	−	−	−	−	?	+	?	−	−	−	+	+	?	?	?	?	+	−	?	?	−	−	?
BO	+	−	−	+	−	−	−	+	+	−	−	+	+	−	−	+	−	−	+	+	−	−	−	−	−	−	−	−	−	−	−	−
JE	+	−	−	−	−	+	+	+	−	−	+	−	−	−	−	−	−	+	−	−	−	−	+	−	−	+	−	−	−	−	−	+
PA	+	−	−	−	−	−	−	+	+	−	−	?	−	−	−	−	−	−	−	−	?	−	−	−	−	−	−	−	−	?	?	−

5.2   Characteristic OWL 2 Full Conclusions

The test suite of characteristic OWL 2 Full conclusions focuses on semantic consequences that are typically beyond the scope of OWL 2 DL or RDF rule reasoners. This is reflected in Table 3, which presents the results for the OWL reasoning systems. The column numbers correspond to the test case numbers in the test suite. In general, the OWL reasoners show significantly weaker performance on this test suite than on the language coverage test suite. Note that the successful test cases for the OWL 2 DL reasoners (Pellet, HermiT and FaCT++) have only little overlap with the successful test cases for the RDF rule reasoners (BigOWLIM and Jena). Parliament succeeded on only two test cases.

The first two rows of Table 4 show that the ATP systems achieved much better results than the OWL reasoners, using the complete OWL 2 Full axiomatization. iProver-SInE succeeded on 28 of the 32 test cases, and Vampire succeeded on 23. As was done for the language coverage test cases, small subsets of axioms sufficient for each of the test cases were hand-selected from the FOL axiomatization. As the last two rows of Table 4 show, both ATP systems succeeded on all these simpler test cases.

Figure 2 shows the runtime behavior of the two systems. For the complete axiomatization, Vampire either succeeds in less than 1s or does not succeed. In contrast, iProver's performance degrades more gracefully. The reasoning times using the small-sufficient axiom sets are generally up to several magnitudes lower than for the complete axiomatization. In the majority of cases they are below 1s.

Table 4. Characteristic conclusions: ATPs with complete and small axiom sets. VA/c=Vampire/complete, IS/c=iProver-SInE/complete, VA/s=Vampire/small, IS/s=iProver-SInE/small.

	01	02	03	04	05	06	07	08	09	10	11	12	13	14	15	16	17	18	19	20	21	22	23	24	25	26	27	28	29	30	31	32
VA/c	+	+	+	+	+	+	+	+	+	+	?	+	?	?	+	+	+	+	+	+	?	?	?	+	+	?	+	?	?	+	+	+
IS/c	+	+	+	+	+	+	+	+	+	+	+	+	?	?	+	+	+	+	+	+	?	?	+	+	+	+	+	+	+	+	+	+
VA/s	+	+	+	+	+	+	+	+	+	+	+	+	+	+	+	+	+	+	+	+	?	+	+	+	+	+	+	+	+	+	+	+
IS/s	+	+	+	+	+	+	+	+	+	+	+	+	+	+	+	+	+	+	+	+	+	+	+	+	+	+	+	+	+	+	+	+

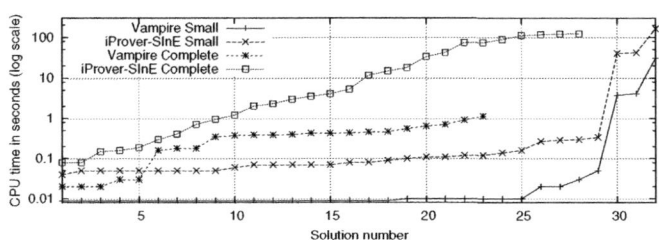

Fig. 2. Characteristic conclusions: ordered system times of ATPs

5.3 Scalability

The Semantic Web consists of huge data masses, but single reasoning results presumably often depend on only a small fraction of that data. As a basic test of the ATP systems' abilities to ignore irrelevant background axioms, a set of one million "bulk RDF axioms" (as described in Section 4.2) was added to the test cases of characteristic OWL 2 Full conclusions. This was done using the complete FOL axiomatization, and also the small-sufficient sets of axioms for each test case.

Table 5 shows the results. The default version of Vampire produced very poor results, as is shown in the first and fourth rows of the table. (Strangely, Vampire had two more successes with the complete axiomatization than with the small-sufficient axiom sets. That can be attributed to differences in the strategies selected for the different axiomatizations.) In contrast, as shown in the second, third, fifth and sixth rows, the version of Vampire-SInE and iProver-SInE did much better. The use of the SInE strategy for selecting relevant axioms clearly helps.

Figure 3 shows the runtime behavior of the systems. The bulk axioms evidently add a constant overhead of about 20s to all successes, which is believed to be taken parsing the large files. In an application setting this might be done only once at the start, so that the time would be amortized over multiple reasoning tasks. The step in iProver's performance at the 20th problem is an artifact of strategy scheduling.

Table 5. Scalability: ATPs with complete and small axiom sets, 1M RDF triples. VA/c=Vampire/complete, VS/c=Vampire-SInE/complete, IS/c=iProver-SInE/complete, VA/s=Vampire/small, VS/s=Vampire-SInE/small, IS/s=iProver-SInE/small.

	01	02	03	04	05	06	07	08	09	10	11	12	13	14	15	16	17	18	19	20	21	22	23	24	25	26	27	28	29	30	31	32
VA/c	+	+	+	?	?	?	?	?	?	?	?	?	?	?	+	?	?	?	?	?	?	?	?	?	?	?	?	?	?	?	?	?
VS/c	+	+	+	+	?	+	?	?	+	?	?	?	+	+	?	+	+	?	+	+	?	?	+	?	?	?	+	?	?	?	+	+
IS/c	+	+	+	+	+	+	+	+	+	+	+	+	?	?	+	+	+	+	+	+	?	?	+	+	+	+	+	+	+	+	+	+
VA/s	+	?	+	?	?	?	?	?	?	?	?	?	?	?	?	?	?	?	?	?	?	?	?	?	?	?	?	?	?	?	?	?
VS/s	+	+	+	+	+	+	?	+	+	+	+	+	?	+	+	+	?	+	+	?	?	+	+	+	+	+	?	+	+	?	+	?
IS/s	+	+	+	+	+	+	+	+	+	+	+	+	?	+	+	+	+	+	+	+	+	+	+	+	+	+	+	+	+	+	+	+

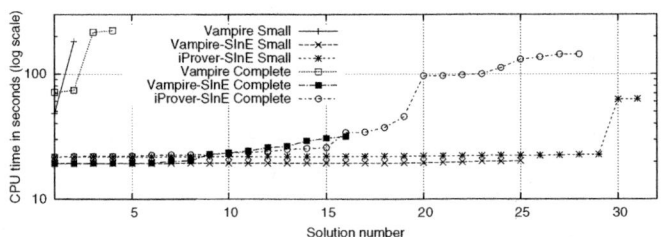

Fig. 3. Scalability: ordered system times of ATPs, 1M RDF triples

The bulk axioms were designed to have no connection to the FOL axiomatization or the RDF graphs. As such, simple analysis of inference chains from the conjecture [11] would be sufficient to determine that the bulk axioms could not be used in a solution. This simplistic approach is methodologically an appropriate way to start testing robustness against irrelevant axioms, and potentially not too far off the reality of Semantic Web reasoning. However, future work using axioms that are not so obviously redundant would properly exercise the power of the SInE approach to axiom selection.

5.4 Model Finding

This section presents the results from experiments concerning the detection of non-entailments and consistent ontologies w.r.t. OWL 2 Full and two of its sub languages: ALCO Full [8] and RDFS [5]. ALCO Full is interesting because it is a small fragment of OWL 2 Full that is known to be undecidable [8]. RDFS is interesting because it is a minimally meaningful language that shares the main characteristics of OWL 2 Full. The RDFS axioms included the "extensional" semantic extension, as non-normatively defined in Section 4.2 of [5]. Similarly, the original definition of ALCO Full was extended to include extensional RDFS. No report is given for the OWL reasoners, as only the OWL 2 DL reasoners have model-finding capabilities, and not for any of the three languages considered here.

Table 6. Model Finding: ATPs with ALCO Full and RDFS axiom sets. The black entries indicate positive entailments or inconsistent ontologies. PA/A=Paradox/ALCO Full, PA/R=Paradox/RDFS, DF/R=DarwinFM/RDFS.

	01	02	03	04	05	06	07	08	09	10	11	12	13	14	15	16	17	18	19	20	21	22	23	24	25	26	27	28	29	30	31	32
PA/A	■	■	■	■	+	+	+	+	+	■	■	+	?	■	■	+	+	+	+	+	?	?	?	?	+	?	?	?	+	■	+	?
PA/R	■	+	+	+	+	+	+	+	+	+	+	+	+	+	+	+	+	+	+	+	+	+	+	+	+	+	+	+	+	+	+	+
DF/R	■	+	+	+	+	+	+	+	+	+	+	+	+	+	+	+	+	+	+	+	+	+	+	+	+	+	+	+	+	+	+	+

Consistency checking for an RDF graph G w.r.t. some ontology language L corresponds to consistency checking for the combination of a complete axiomatization of L and the FOL translation of G. Hence, a minimum requirement is to confirm that the FOL axiomatization of OWL 2 Full is consistent. Unfortunately, for the OWL 2 Full axiomatization no model finder was able to confirm consistency.[2]

For the ALCO Full axioms, Paradox found a finite model of size 5 in ca. 5s CPU time, while DarwinFM timed out. Paradox was then used on the characteristic OWL 2 Full test cases, with the OWL 2 Full axiomatization replaced by the ALCO Full axioms. As ALCO Full is a sub language of OWL 2 Full, 24 of the 32 test cases are either non-entailments or consistent ontologies, out of which 15 were correctly recognized by Paradox. iProver-SInE was used to confirm that the remaining 8 test cases are positive entailments or inconsistent ontologies. The results are shown in the first row of Table 6.

For the RDFS axioms, analogous experiments were done. Paradox found a finite model of the axioms, of size 1, in about 1s. The consistency was confirmed by DarwinFM in less than 1s. With the OWL 2 Full axiomatization replaced by the RDFS axioms, 29 of the 32 characteristic test cases are non-entailments or consistent ontologies. Paradox and Darwin confirmed all of these, mostly in ca. 1s, with a maximum time of ca. 2s. iProver-SInE confirmed that the remaining 3 test cases are positive entailments or inconsistent ontologies. These results are shown in the second and third rows of Table 6.

An interesting observation made during the model finding experiments was that *finite* model finders were effective, e.g., the results of Paradox and DarwinFM above. In contrast, other model finders such as iProver-SAT (a variant of iProver tuned for model finding) and Darwin (the plain Model Evolution core of DarwinFM) were less effective, e.g., taking 80s and 37s respectively to confirm the satisfiability of the RDFS axiom set.

6   Conclusions and Future Work

This paper has described how first order ATP systems can be used for reasoning in the OWL 2 Full ontology language, using a straight-forward translation of the

---

[2] This raised the question of whether our positive entailment reasoning results were perhaps due to an inconsistent axiomatization. However, none of the theorem provers was able to establish inconsistency. In addition, the model finders confirmed the consistency of all the small-sufficient axiom sets mentioned in Section 5.2. Hence, it is at least ensured that those positive reasoning results are achievable from consistent subsets of the OWL 2 Full axiomatization.

underlying model theory into a FOL axiomatization. The results were obtained from two complementary test suites, one for language coverage analysis and one for probing characteristic conclusions of OWL 2 Full. The results indicate that this approach can be applied in practice for effective OWL reasoning, and offers a viable alternative to current Semantic Web reasoners. Some scalability testing was done by adding large sets of semantically unrelated RDF data to the test case data. While the ATP systems that include the SInE strategy effectively ignored this redundant data, it was surprising that other ATP systems did not use simple reachability analysis to detect and ignore this bulk data – this suggests an easy way for developers to adapt their systems to such problems.

In contrast to the successes of the ATP systems proving theorems, model finders were less successful in identifying non-entailments and consistent ontologies w.r.t. OWL 2 Full. However, some successes were obtained for ALCO Full. Since ALCO Full is an undecidable sub-language of OWL 2 Full, there is hope that the failures were not due to undecidability but rather due to the large number of axioms. This needs to be investigated further. Model finding for RDFS worked quite efficiently, which is interesting because we do not know of any tool that detects RDFS non-entailments.

In the future we plan to extend the approach to datatype reasoning, which is of high practical relevance in the Semantic Web. It may be possible to take advantage of the typed first-order or typed higher-order form of the TPTP language to effectively encode the datatypes, and reason using ATP systems that take advantage of the type information. Another topic for further research is to develop techniques for identifying parts of the FOL axiomatization that are relevant to a given reasoning task. It is hoped that by taking into account OWL 2 Full specific knowledge, more precise axiom selection than offered by the generic SInE approach will be possible. An important area of development will be query answering, i.e., the ability to obtain explicit answers to users' questions. For future OWL 2 Full reasoners this will be a very relevant reasoning task, particularly with respect to the current extension of the standard RDF query language SPARQL towards "entailment regimes" (http://www.w3.org/TR/sparql11-entailment). This topic is also of growing interest in the ATP community, with a proposal being considered for expressing questions and answers in the TPTP language (http://www.tptp.org/TPTP/Proposals/AnswerExtraction.html).

References

1. Baader, F., McGuinness, D.L., Nardi, D., Patel-Schneider, P.F. (eds.): The Description Logic Handbook: Theory, Implementation, and Applications. Cambridge University Press, Cambridge (2003)
2. Fikes, R., McGuinness, D., Waldinger, R.: A First-Order Logic Semantics for Semantic Web Markup Languages. Tech. Rep. KSL-02-01, Knowledge Systems Laboratory, Stanford University, Stanford, CA 94305 (January 2002)
3. Hawke, S.: Surnia. Homepage (2003), http://www.w3.org/2003/08/surnia

4. Hayes, P.: Translating Semantic Web Languages into Common Logic. Tech. rep., IHMC Florida Institute for Human & Machine Cognition, 40 South Alcaniz Street, Pensacola, FL 32502 (July 18, 2005), http://www.ihmc.us/users/phayes/CL/SW2SCL.html
5. Hayes, P. (ed.): RDF Semantics. W3C Recommendation (February 10, 2004), http://www.w3.org/TR/rdf-mt/
6. Horrocks, I., Voronkov, A.: Reasoning Support for Expressive Ontology Languages Using a Theorem Prover. In: Dix, J., Hegner, S.J. (eds.) FoIKS 2006. LNCS, vol. 3861, pp. 201–218. Springer, Heidelberg (2006)
7. Klyne, G., Carroll, J.J. (eds.): Resource Description Framework (RDF): Concepts and Abstract Syntax. W3C Recommendation (February 10, 2004), http://www.w3.org/TR/rdf-concepts/
8. Motik, B.: On the Properties of Metamodeling in OWL. Journal of Logic and Computation 17(4), 617–637 (2007)
9. Motik, B., Grau, B.C., Horrocks, I., Wu, Z., Fokoue, A., Lutz, C. (eds.): OWL 2 Web Ontology Language: Profiles. W3C Recommendation (October 27, 2009), http://www.w3.org/TR/owl2-profiles/
10. Motik, B., Patel-Schneider, P.F., Parsia, B. (eds.): OWL 2 Web Ontology Language: Structural Specification and Functional-Style Syntax. W3C Recommendation (October 27, 2009), http://www.w3.org/TR/owl2-syntax/
11. Plaisted, D., Yahya, A.: A Relevance Restriction Strategy for Automated Deduction. Artificial Intelligence 144(1-2), 59–93 (2003)
12. Schneider, M. (ed.): OWL 2 Web Ontology Language: RDF-Based Semantics. W3C Recommendation (October 27, 2009), http://www.w3.org/TR/owl2-rdf-based-semantics/
13. Schneider, M., Mainzer, K.: A Conformance Test Suite for the OWL 2 RL/RDF Rules Language and the OWL 2 RDF-Based Semantics. In: Hoekstra, R., Patel-Schneider, P.F. (eds.) Proceedings of the 6th International Workshop on OWL: Experiences and Directions (OWLED 2009). CEUR Workshop Proceedings, vol. 529 (2009), http://ceur-ws.org/Vol-529/owled2009_submission_19.pdf
14. Sutcliffe, G.: The TPTP Problem Library and Associated Infrastructure. The FOF and CNF Parts, v3.5.0. Journal of Automated Reasoning 43(4), 337–362 (2009)
15. Tsarkov, D., Riazanov, A., Bechhofer, S., Horrocks, I.: Using Vampire to Reason with OWL. In: McIlraith, S.A., Plexousakis, D., van Harmelen, F. (eds.) ISWC 2004. LNCS, vol. 3298, pp. 471–485. Springer, Heidelberg (2004)
16. W3C OWL Working Group (ed.): OWL 2 Web Ontology Language: Document Overview. W3C Recommendation (October 27, 2009), http://www.w3.org/TR/owl2-overview/
17. W3C WebOnt OWL Working Group: OWL 1 Test Results (March 9, 2004), http://www.w3.org/2003/08/owl-systems/test-results-out

An Efficient Decision Procedure for Imperative Tree Data Structures[*]

Thomas Wies[1], Marco Muñiz[2], and Viktor Kuncak[3]

[1] Institute of Science and Technology (IST), Austria
wies@ist.ac.at
[2] University of Freiburg, Germany
muniz@informatik.uni-freiburg.de
[3] EPFL, Switzerland
viktor.kuncak@epfl.ch

Abstract. We present a new decidable logic called TREX for expressing constraints about imperative tree data structures. In particular, TREX supports a transitive closure operator that can express reachability constraints, which often appear in data structure invariants. We show that our logic is closed under weakest precondition computation, which enables its use for automated software verification. We further show that satisfiability of formulas in TREX is decidable in NP. The low complexity makes it an attractive alternative to more expensive logics such as monadic second-order logic (MSOL) over trees, which have been traditionally used for reasoning about tree data structures.

1 Introduction

This paper introduces a new decision procedure for reasoning about imperative manipulations of tree data structures. Our logic of trees with reachability expressions (TREX) supports reasoning about reachability in trees and a form of quantification, which enables its use for expressing invariants of tree data structures, including the tree property itself. Despite the expressive power of the logic, we exhibit a non-deterministic polynomial-time decision procedure for its satisfiability problem, showing that TREX is NP-complete. Our development is directly motivated by our experience with verifying tree data structures in the Jahob verification system [15, 18, 21] in which we used the MONA decision procedure [11] for MSOL over trees. Although MONA contributed great expressive power to our specification language and, in our experience, works well for programs that manipulate lists, there were many tree-manipulating programs whose verification failed due to MONA running out of resources. It was thus a natural goal to identify a logic that suits our needs, but can be decided much more efficiently.

There are other expressive logics supporting reachability but with lower complexity than MSOL [4, 7, 10, 20]. We did not find them suitable as a MONA alternative, for several reasons. First, we faced difficulties in the expressive power: some of the logics can only reason about sets but not individual objects, others have tree model property and thus cannot detect violations of the tree invariants. Moreover, the complexity

---

[*] An extended version of this paper including proofs of the key lemmas is available as a technical report [19].

N. Bjørner and V. Sofronie-Stokkermans (Eds.): CADE 2011, LNAI 6803, pp. 476–491, 2011.

of these logics is still at least EXPTIME, and their decision procedures are given in terms of automata-theoretic techniques or tableaux procedures, which can be difficult to combine efficiently with existing SMT solvers. Similarly, the logic of reachable patterns [20] is decidable through a highly non-trivial construction, but the complexity is at least NEXPTIME, as is the complexity of the Bernays-Schönfinkel Class with Datalog [5]. The logic [2] can express nested list structures of bounded nesting along with constraints on data fields and numerical constraints on paths, but cannot express constraints on arbitrary trees. On the other hand, TREX does not support reasoning on data fields; although such an extension is in principle possible. Other approaches generate induction scheme instances to prove transitive closure properties in general graphs [14]. While this strategy can succeed for certain examples, it gives neither completeness nor complexity guarantees, and suffers from the difficulties of first-order provers in handling transitive relations. Tree automata with size constraints can express properties such as the red-black tree invariant [8]. However, this work does not state the complexity of the reasoning task and the presented automata constructions appear to require running time beyond NP. Regular tree model checking with abstraction has yielded excellent results so far [3] and continues to improve, but has so far not resulted in a logic whose complexity is in NP, which we believe to be an important milestone.

The primary inspiration for our solution came from the efficient SMT-based techniques for reasoning about list structures [13], as well as the idea of viewing single-parent heaps as duals of lists [1]. However, there are several challenges in relying on this immediate inspiration. For integration with other decision procedures, as well as for modular reasoning with preconditions and postconditions, it was essential to obtain a logic and not only a finite-model property for the analysis of systems as in [1]. Furthermore, the need to support imperative updates on *trees* led to technical challenges that are very different than those of [13]. To address these challenges, we introduced a reachability predicate that is parametrized by a carefully chosen class of formulas to control the reachability relation. We show that the resulting logic of trees is closed under weakest preconditions with respect to imperative heap updates, which makes it suitable for expressing verification conditions in imperative programs. We devised a four-step decision procedure that contains formula transformations and ultimately reduces to a Ψ-local theory extension [9, 16]. Consequently, our logic can be encoded using a quantifier instantiation recipe within an SMT solver. We have encoded the axiomatization of TREX in Jahob and used Z3 [6] with a default instantiation strategy to verify tree and list manipulating programs. We have obtained verification times of around 1s, reducing the running times by two orders of magnitude compared to MONA.

Motivating Example. We next show how to use our decision procedure to verify functional correctness of a Java method that manipulates a binary tree data structure.

Fig. 1 shows a fragment of Java code for insertion into a binary search tree, factored out into a separate insertLeftOf method. In addition to Java statements, the example in Fig. 1 contains preconditions and postconditions, written in the notation of the Jahob verification system [12, 15, 17, 18, 21].

The search tree has fields (l, r) that form a binary tree, and field p, which for each node in the tree points to its parent (or null, if the node is the root of the tree). This property is expressed by the first class invariant using the special predicate ptree, which takes the

```
class Node {Node l, r, p;}
class Tree {
    private Node root;
    invariant "ptree p [l,r]"; invariant "p root = null";
    private specvar content :: objset;
    vardefs "content=={x. root ≠ null ∧ (x,root) ∈ {(x,y). p x = y}*}";
    public void insertLeftOf (Node pos, Node e)
        requires "pos ∈ content ∧ pos ≠ null ∧ l pos = null ∧
                    e ∉ content ∧ e ≠ null ∧ p e = null ∧ l e = null ∧ r e = null"
        modifies content,l,p
        ensures "content = old content ∪ {e}"
    { e.p = pos; pos.l = e; } }
```

Fig. 1. Fragment of insertion into a tree

parent field and a list of successor fields of the tree structure as arguments. The second invariant expresses that the field root points to the root node of the tree. The **vardefs** notation introduces the set content denoting the useful content of the tree. Note that if we are given a program that manipulates a tree data structure without explicit parent field then we can always introduce one as a specification variable that is solely used for the purpose of verification. This is possible because the parent field in a tree is uniquely determined by the successor fields.

The insertLeftOf method is meant to be invoked when the insertion procedure has traversed the tree and found a node pos that has no left child. The node e then becomes the new left child of pos. Our system checks that after each execution of the method insertLeftOf the specified class invariants still hold and that its postcondition is satisfied. The postcondition states that the node e has been properly inserted into the tree.

The full verification condition of method insertLeftOf can be expressed in our logic. Figure 2 shows one of the subgoals of this verification condition. It expresses that after execution of method insertLeftOf the heap graph projected to field p is still acyclic. This is a subgoal for checking that the ptree invariant is preserved by method insertLeftOf. Note that our logic supports field update expressions $upd(p, e, pos)$ so that we can express the verification condition directly in the logic. Note further that the precondition stating that the ptree invariant holds at entry to the method is not explicitly part of the verification condition. It is implicit in the semantics of our logic.

Our logic also supports reasoning about forward reachability $\langle l, r \rangle^*$ in the trees (i.e., transitive closure of the successor fields rather than the parent field) and quantification over sets of reachable objects. The latter is used, e.g., to prove the postcondition of method insertLeftOf stating that the node e was properly inserted and that no elements have been removed from the tree.

While we only consider a logic of *binary* trees in this paper; the generalization to trees of arbitrary finite arity is straightforward. In particular, an acyclic doubly-linked list is a special case of a tree with parent pointers, so reasoning about such structures is also supported by our decision procedure.

$$p(\text{root}) = \text{null} \wedge \text{root} \neq \text{null} \wedge \langle p \rangle^*(\text{pos}, \text{root}) \wedge \neg \langle p \rangle^*(e, \text{root}) \wedge$$
$$e \neq \text{null} \wedge p(e) = \text{null} \wedge l(e) = \text{null} \wedge r(e) = \text{null}$$
$$\rightarrow (\forall z. \langle \text{upd}(p, e, \text{pos}) \rangle^*(z, \text{null}))$$

Fig. 2. Verification condition expressing that, after execution of method insertLeftOf, the heap graph projected to field p is still acyclic

$$p(\text{root}) = \text{null} \wedge \text{root} \neq \text{null} \wedge \langle p \rangle^*(\text{pos}, \text{root}) \wedge \neg \langle p \rangle^*(e, \text{root}) \wedge e \neq \text{null} \wedge p(e) = \text{null} \wedge$$
$$l(e) = \text{null} \wedge r(e) = \text{null} \wedge \neg(\forall z. \langle p \rangle^*_{(x \neq e)}(z, \text{null}) \vee \langle p \rangle^*(z, e) \wedge \langle p \rangle^*_{(x \neq e)}(\text{pos}, \text{null}))$$

Fig. 3. Negated verification condition from Fig. 2 after function update elimination

2 Decision Procedure through an Example

We consider the negation of the verification condition shown in Figure 2, which is unsatisfiable in tree structures. Our decision procedure is described in Section 5 and proceeds in four steps.

The first step (Section 5.1) is to eliminate all function update expressions in the formula. The result of this step is shown in Figure 3. Our logic supports so called *constrained reachability expressions* of the form $\langle p \rangle^*_Q$ where Q is a binary predicate over dedicated variables x, y. The semantics of this predicate is that $\langle p \rangle^*_Q(u, v)$ holds iff there exists a p-path connecting u and v and between every consecutive nodes w_1, w_2 on this path, $Q(w_1, w_2)$ holds. Using these constrained reachability expressions we can reduce reachability expressions over updated fields to reachability expressions over the non-updated fields, as shown in the example. This elimination even works for updates of successor functions below forward reachability expressions of the form $\langle l, r \rangle^*$.

The second step (Section 5.2) eliminates all forward reachability constraints over fields l, r from the formula and expresses them in terms of the relation $\langle p \rangle^*$. Since there are no such constraints in our formula, we immediately proceed to Step 3.

The third step (Section 5.3) reduces the formula to a formula in first-order logic, whose finite models are exactly the models of the formula from the previous step, which is still expressed in TREX. For the purpose of the reduction, all occurrences of the reachability relation $\langle p \rangle^*$ are replaced by a binary predicate symbol P, which is then axiomatized using universally quantified first-order axioms so that $\langle p \rangle^*$ and P coincide in all finite models. All remaining reachability constraints are of the form $\langle p \rangle^*_Q$. We can express these constraints in terms of P by introducing a unary function bp_Q (called *break point function*) that maps each node u to the first p-reachable node v of u for which $Q(v, p(v))$ does not hold, i.e., $bp_Q(u)$ marks the end of the segment of nodes w that satisfy $\langle p \rangle^*_Q(u, w)$. The function bp_Q can be axiomatized in terms of P and Q. Figure 4 shows the resulting formula (including only the necessary axioms for proving unsatisfiability of the formula).

The fourth step (Section 5.4) computes prenex normal form and skolemizes remaining top-level existential quantifiers. Then we add additional axioms that ensure Ψ-locality of the universally quantified axioms in the formula obtained from Step 3.

$\mathsf{p}(\mathsf{root}) = \mathsf{null} \land \mathsf{root} \neq \mathsf{null} \land P(\mathsf{pos}, \mathsf{root}) \land \neg P(\mathsf{e}, \mathsf{root}) \land$
$\mathsf{e} \neq \mathsf{null} \land \mathsf{p}(\mathsf{e}) = \mathsf{null} \land \mathsf{l}(\mathsf{e}) = \mathsf{null} \land \mathsf{r}(\mathsf{e}) = \mathsf{null} \land$
$\neg(\forall z. P(z, \mathsf{null}) \land P(\mathsf{null}, bp_{(x \neq \mathsf{e})}(z)) \lor P(z, \mathsf{e}) \land P(\mathsf{pos}, \mathsf{null}) \land P(\mathsf{null}, bp_{(x \neq \mathsf{e})}(\mathsf{pos}))) \land$
$(\forall z. P(z, \mathsf{null})) \land (\forall z. P(z, z)) \land (\forall wz. P(w, z) \land P(z, w) \rightarrow z = w) \land$
$(\forall vwz. P(v, w) \land P(v, z) \rightarrow P(w, z) \lor P(z, w)) \land$
$(\forall wz. P(w, z) \rightarrow w = z \lor P(\mathsf{p}(w), z)) \land$
$(\forall z. P(z, bp_{(z \neq \mathsf{e})}(z))) \land (\forall z. bp_{(x \neq \mathsf{e})}(z) \neq \mathsf{e} \rightarrow bp_{(x \neq \mathsf{e})}(z) = \mathsf{null}) \land$
$(\forall wz. P(w, z) \land P(z, bp_{(x \neq \mathsf{e})}(w)) \rightarrow z \neq \mathsf{e} \lor z = bp_{(x \neq \mathsf{e})}(w)) \land \ldots$

Fig. 4. Negated verification condition from Figure 2 after the reduction step to first-order logic. Only the axioms that are necessary for proving unsatisfiability of the formula are shown.

The key property of the resulting formula is that its universal quantifiers can be instantiated finitely many times with terms syntactically derived from the terms within the formula. The result is an equisatisfiable quantifier-free formula, which can be handled by the SMT solver's congruence closure and the SAT solver.

3 Preliminaries

In the following, we define the syntax and semantics of formulas. We further recall the notions of partial structures and Ψ-local theories as defined in [9].

Sorted logic. We present our problem in sorted logic with equality. A *signature* Σ is a tuple (S, Ω), where S is a countable set of sorts and Ω is a countable set of function symbols f with associated arity $n \geq 0$ and associated sort $s_1 \times \cdots \times s_n \rightarrow s_0$ with $s_i \in S$ for all $i \leq n$. Function symbols of arity 0 are called *constant symbols*. In this paper we will only consider signatures with sorts $S = \{\mathsf{bool}, \mathsf{node}\}$ and the dedicated equality symbol $= \in \Omega$ of sort node $\times$ node $\rightarrow$ bool. Note that we generally treat predicate symbols of sort $s_1, \ldots, s_n$ as function symbols of sort $s_1 \times \ldots \times s_n \rightarrow \mathsf{bool}$. Terms are built as usual from the function symbols in Ω and (sorted) variables taken from a countably infinite set X that is disjoint from Ω. A term t is said to be *ground*, if no variable appears in t. We denote by $\mathsf{Terms}(\Sigma)$ the set of all ground Σ-terms.

A Σ-atom A is a Σ-term of sort bool. We use infix notation for atoms built from the equality symbol. A Σ-*formula* F is defined via structural recursion as either one of A, $\neg F_1$, $F_1 \land F_2$, or $\forall x : s. F_1$, where A is a Σ-atom, F_1 and F_2 are Σ-formulas, and $x \in X$ is a variable of sort $s \in S$. In formulas appearing in this paper we will only ever quantify over variables of sort node, so we typically drop the sort annotation. We use syntactic sugar for Boolean constants ($\top$, $\bot$), disjunctions ($F_1 \lor F_2$), implications ($F_1 \rightarrow F_2$), and existential quantification ($\exists x. F_1$). For a finite index set $\mathcal{I}$ and Σ-formulas F_i, for all $i \in \mathcal{I}$, we write $\bigwedge_{i \in \mathcal{I}} F_i$ for the conjunction of the F_i (respectively, $\top$ if $\mathcal{I}$ is empty) and similarly $\bigvee_{i \in \mathcal{I}} F_i$ for their disjunction. We further write $F[x_1 := t_1, \ldots, x_n := t_n]$ for the simultaneous substitutions of the free variables x_i appearing in F by the terms t_i. We define literals and clauses as usual. A clause C is called *flat* if no term that occurs in C below a predicate symbol or the symbol $=$ contains nested function symbols. A clause C is called *linear* if (i) whenever a variable occurs in two non-variable terms in C that do not start with a predicate or the equality symbol, the two terms are identical, and if (ii) no such term contains two occurrences of the same variable.

Total and partial structures. Given a signature $\Sigma = (S, \Omega)$, a *partial Σ-structure* α is a function that maps each sort $s \in S$ to a non-empty set $\alpha(s)$ and each function symbol $f \in \Omega$ of sort $s_1 \times \cdots \times s_n \to s_0$ to a partial function $\alpha(f) : \alpha(s_1) \times \cdots \times \alpha(s_n) \rightharpoonup \alpha(s_0)$. If α is understood, we write just t instead of $\alpha(t)$ whenever this is not ambiguous. We assume that all partial structures interpret the sort bool by the two-element set of Booleans $\{0, 1\}$. We therefore call $\alpha(\text{node})$ the *universe* of α and often identify $\alpha(\text{node})$ and α. We further assume that all structures α interpret the symbol $=$ by the equality relation on $\alpha(\text{node})$. A partial structure α is called *total structure* or simply *structure* if it interprets all function symbols by total functions. For a Σ-structure α where Σ extends a signature Σ_0 with additional sorts and function symbols, we write $\alpha|_{\Sigma_0}$ for the Σ_0-structure obtained by restricting α to Σ_0.

Given a total structure α and a *variable assignment* $\beta : X \to \alpha(S)$, the evaluation $[\![t]\!]_{\alpha,\beta}$ of a term t in α, β is defined as usual. For a ground term t we typically write just $[\![t]\!]_{\alpha}$. A quantified variable of sort s ranges over all elements of $\alpha(s)$. From the interpretation of terms the notions of satisfiability, validity, and entailment of atoms, formulas, clauses, and sets of clauses in total structures are derived as usual. In particular, we use the standard interpretations for propositional connectives of classical logic. We write $\alpha, \beta \models F$ if α satisfies F under β where F is a formula, a clause, or a set of clauses. Similarly, we write $\alpha \models F$ if F is valid in α. In this case we also call α a *model* of F. The interpretation $[\![t]\!]_{\alpha,\beta}$ of a term t in a partial structure α is as for total structures, except that if $t = f(t_1, \ldots, t_n)$ for $f \in \Omega$ then $[\![t]\!]_{\alpha,\beta}$ is undefined if either $[\![t_i]\!]_{\alpha,\beta}$ is undefined for some i, or $([\![t_1]\!]_{\alpha,\beta}, \ldots, [\![t_n]\!]_{\alpha,\beta})$ is not in the domain of $\alpha(f)$. We say that a partial structure α *weakly satisfies* a literal L under β, written $\alpha, \beta \models_w L$, if (i) L is an atom A and either $[\![A]\!]_{\alpha,\beta} = 1$ or $[\![A]\!]_{\alpha,\beta}$ is undefined, or (ii) L is a negated atom $\neg A$ and either $[\![A]\!]_{\alpha,\beta} = 0$ or $[\![A]\!]_{\alpha,\beta}$ is undefined. The notion of weak satisfiability is extended to clauses and sets of clauses as for total structures. A clause C (respectively, a set of clauses) is *weakly valid* in a partial structure α if α weakly satisfies α for all variable assignments β. We then call α a *weak partial model* of C.

Ψ-local theories. The following definition is a particular special case of the more general notion of Ψ-local theory extensions. For the general definitions of local theory extensions, respectively, Ψ-local theory extensions, we direct the reader to [9, 16].

Let $\Sigma = (S, \Omega)$ be a signature. A *theory* $\mathcal{T}$ for a signature Σ is simply a set of Σ-formulas. We consider theories $\mathcal{T}(\mathcal{K})$ defined as a set of Σ-formulas that are consequences of a given set of clauses $\mathcal{K}$. We call $\mathcal{K}$ the *axioms* of the theory $\mathcal{T}(\mathcal{K})$ and we often identify $\mathcal{K}$ and $\mathcal{T}(\mathcal{K})$. In the following, when we refer to a set of ground clauses G, we assume they are over the signature $\Sigma^c = (S, \Omega \cup \Omega_c)$ where Ω_c is a set of new constant symbols. For a set of clauses $\mathcal{K}$, we denote by $\text{st}(\mathcal{K})$ the set of all ground subterms that appear in $\mathcal{K}$. Let Ψ be a function associating with a set of (universally quantified) clauses $\mathcal{K}$ and a set of ground terms T a set $\Psi(\mathcal{K}, T)$ of ground terms such that (i) all ground subterms in $\mathcal{K}$ and T are in $\Psi(\mathcal{K}, T)$; (ii) for all sets of ground terms T, T' if $T \subseteq T'$ then $\Psi(\mathcal{K}, T) \subseteq \Psi(\mathcal{K}, T')$; (iii) Ψ is a closure operation, i.e., for all sets of ground terms T, $\Psi(\mathcal{K}, \Psi(\mathcal{K}, T)) \subseteq \Psi(\mathcal{K}, T)$. (iv) Ψ is compatible with any map h between constants, i.e., for any map $h : \Omega_c \to \Omega_c$, $\Psi(\mathcal{K}, \overline{h}(T)) = \overline{h}(\Psi(\mathcal{K}, T))$ where

$\overline{h}$ is the unique extension of h to terms. Let $\mathcal{K}[\Psi(\mathcal{K}, G)]$ be the set of instances of $\mathcal{K}$ in which all terms are in $\Psi(\mathcal{K}, \mathrm{st}(G))$, which here will be denoted by $\Psi(\mathcal{K}, G)$. We say that $\mathcal{K}$ is Ψ-local if it satisfies condition (Loc^Ψ):

(Loc^Ψ) For every finite set of ground clauses G, $\mathcal{K} \cup G \models \bot$ iff $\mathcal{K}[\Psi(\mathcal{K}, G)] \cup G$
has no weak partial model in which all terms in $\Psi(\mathcal{K}, G)$ are defined.

4   TREX: Logic of Trees with Reachability Expressions

We now formally define the formulas of our logic of trees with reachability expressions (TREX), whose satisfiability we study. For simplifying the exposition in the remainder of this paper, we restrict ourselves to binary trees. The decidability and complexity result carries over to trees of arbitrary finite arity in a straightforward manner.

Syntax of TREX formulas. Figure 5 defines the TREX formulas. A TREX formula is a propositional combination of atomic formulas. An atomic formula is either an equality between terms, a reachability expression, or a restricted quantified formula. A term t is either a constant $c \in \Gamma$ or a function term f applied to a term t. The set of constants Γ is an arbitrary countably infinite set of symbols disjoint from all other symbols used in the syntax of formulas. However, we assume that Γ contains the special constant symbol null. A function term is either one of the function symbols l, r (standing for the two successor functions of a tree), and p (standing for the parent function of a tree), or an update $\mathrm{upd}(f, t_1, t_2)$ of a function term f. In the latter case we call t_1 the *index* of the update and t_2 the *target*. A forward reachability expression relates two terms by a relation $\langle f_l, f_r \rangle_Q^*$ where f_l and f_r are the possibly updated successor functions and Q is a predicate built from boolean combinations of equalities between constants and the dedicated variables x and y. The syntactic restrictions on Q ensure that if one computes the disjunctive normal form of Q then the resulting formula will contain a disjunct that is a conjunction of disequalities between constants and variables. A backward reachability expression is similar but refers to the possibly updated parent function. We call the relations $\langle f_l, f_r \rangle_Q^*$ *descendant relations* and the relations $\langle f_p \rangle_Q^*$ *ancestor relations*. Finally, the formulas below restricted quantified formulas are almost like TREX formulas, except that the quantified variable may only appear at particular positions below function symbols and only as arguments of ancestor relations. For a predicate Q and terms t_1, t_2, we typically write $Q(t_1, t_2)$ for the formula $Q[x := t_1, y := t_2]$. Finally, we simply write p^* as a shorthand for $\langle \mathrm{p} \rangle_\top^*$.

Semantics of TREX formulas. TREX formulas are interpreted over finite forests of finite binary trees. We formally define these forests as first-order structures $\alpha_\mathcal{F}$ over the signature $\Sigma_\mathcal{F}$ of constant symbols Γ and the unary function symbols l, r and p. To this end define the set of *tree nodes* $\mathcal{N}$ as the set of strings consisting of the empty string ϵ and all strings over alphabet $\mathbb{N} \cup \{\mathrm{L}, \mathrm{R}\}$ that satisfy the regular expression $\mathbb{N} \cdot (\mathrm{L} \mid \mathrm{R})^*$, i.e., we enumerate the trees comprising a forest by attaching a natural number to the nodes in each tree. A *forest* $\alpha_\mathcal{F}$ is then a structure whose universe is a finite prefixed-closed subset of tree nodes. The interpretation of the special constant symbol null $\in \Gamma$ and the function symbols l, r, and p are determined by the universe of $\alpha_\mathcal{F}$ as in Figure 6. The remaining constant symbols in Γ may be interpreted by any tree node in $\alpha_\mathcal{F}$. Let $\mathcal{F}$ be the set of all forests and let $\mathcal{M}_\mathcal{F}$ be the set of all first-order structures over signature

$$F ::= A \mid F \wedge F \mid \neg F$$
$$A ::= t = t \mid \langle f_\mathsf{l}, f_\mathsf{r} \rangle_Q^*(t,t) \mid \langle f_\mathsf{p} \rangle_Q^*(t,t) \mid F_\forall$$
$$t ::= c \mid f(t)$$
$$f ::= f_\mathsf{l} \mid f_\mathsf{r} \mid f_\mathsf{p}$$
$$f_\mathsf{l} ::= \mathsf{upd}(f_\mathsf{l}, t, t) \mid \mathsf{l}$$
$$f_\mathsf{r} ::= \mathsf{upd}(f_\mathsf{r}, t, t) \mid \mathsf{r}$$
$$f_\mathsf{p} ::= \mathsf{upd}(f_\mathsf{p}, t, t) \mid \mathsf{p}$$
$$Q ::= v = c \rightarrow R \mid Q \wedge Q$$
$$R ::= t_R = t_R \mid R \wedge R \mid \neg R$$
$$t_R ::= v \mid c$$

$$F_\forall ::= \forall z.\, G_{\mathsf{in}}$$
$$G_{\mathsf{in}} ::= f(z) = t \rightarrow G_{\mathsf{in}} \mid F_{\mathsf{in}}$$
$$F_{\mathsf{in}} ::= A_{\mathsf{in}} \mid F_{\mathsf{in}} \wedge F_{\mathsf{in}} \mid \neg F_{\mathsf{in}}$$
$$A_{\mathsf{in}} ::= t_{\mathsf{in}} = t_{\mathsf{in}} \mid \langle f_\mathsf{p} \rangle_Q^*(t_{\mathsf{in}}, t_{\mathsf{in}})$$
$$t_{\mathsf{in}} ::= z \mid t$$

terminals:

$c \in \Gamma$ - constant symbol

$\mathsf{l}, \mathsf{r}, \mathsf{p}$ - function symbols

$v \in \{x, y\}$ - dedicated variable

$z \in X$ - variable

Fig. 5. Logic of trees with reachability TREX

$$\alpha_\mathcal{F}(\mathsf{null}) = \epsilon \qquad \alpha_\mathcal{F}(\mathsf{l})(n) = \begin{cases} n\mathrm{L} & \text{if } n\mathrm{L} \in \alpha_\mathcal{F} \\ \epsilon & \text{otherwise} \end{cases} \qquad \alpha_\mathcal{F}(\mathsf{r})(n) = \begin{cases} n\mathrm{R} & \text{if } n\mathrm{R} \in \alpha_\mathcal{F} \\ \epsilon & \text{otherwise} \end{cases}$$

$$\alpha_\mathcal{F}(\mathsf{p})(n) = \begin{cases} n' & \text{if } n = n's \text{ for some } s \in \mathbb{N} \cup \{\mathrm{L}, \mathrm{R}\} \text{ and } n' \in \alpha_\mathcal{F} \\ \epsilon & \text{otherwise} \end{cases}$$

Fig. 6. Semantics of functions and constants in the forest model

$\Sigma_\mathcal{F}$ that are isomorphic to some structure in $\mathcal{F}$. We extend the term *forest* to all the structures in $\mathcal{M}_\mathcal{F}$.

For defining the semantics of TREX formulas, let $\alpha_\mathcal{F} \in \mathcal{M}_\mathcal{F}$. We only explain the interpretation of terms, function terms, and reachability expressions in detail, the remaining constructs are interpreted as expected. The notions of satisfiability, entailment, etc. for TREX formulas are defined as in Section 3.

The interpretation of terms and function terms in $\alpha_\mathcal{F}$ under a variable assignment β recursively extend the interpretation of $\Sigma_\mathcal{F}$-terms as follows:

$$[\![f]\!]_{\alpha_\mathcal{F},\beta} \overset{\text{def}}{=} \alpha_\mathcal{F}(f), \text{ for } f \in \{\mathsf{l}, \mathsf{r}, \mathsf{p}\}$$
$$[\![\mathsf{upd}(f, t_1, t_2)]\!]_{\alpha_\mathcal{F},\beta} \overset{\text{def}}{=} [\![f]\!]_{\alpha_\mathcal{F},\beta}[[\![t_1]\!]_{\alpha_\mathcal{F},\beta} \mapsto [\![t_2]\!]_{\alpha_\mathcal{F},\beta}]$$
$$[\![f(t)]\!]_{\alpha_\mathcal{F},\beta} \overset{\text{def}}{=} [\![f]\!]_{\alpha_\mathcal{F},\beta}([\![t]\!]_{\alpha_\mathcal{F},\beta})$$

In order to define the semantics of reachability expressions compactly, we write $\langle Fn \rangle_Q^*(t_1, t_2)$ for either a forward reachability expression $\langle f_\mathsf{l}, f_\mathsf{r} \rangle_Q^*(t_1, t_2)$ or a backward reachability expression $\langle f_\mathsf{p} \rangle_Q^*(t_1, t_2)$. In the first case, the meta variable Fn denotes the set of function terms $\{f_\mathsf{l}, f_\mathsf{r}\}$ and in the second case the set $\{f_\mathsf{p}\}$. We also use the notation $\langle f, Fn \rangle_Q^*(t_1, t_2)$, which denotes: $\langle f_\mathsf{p} \rangle_Q^*(t_1, t_2)$ if $f = f_\mathsf{p}$ and $Fn = \emptyset$, and denotes $\langle f_\mathsf{l}, f_\mathsf{r} \rangle_Q^*(t_1, t_2)$ if $Fn = \{f_\mathsf{r}\}$ and $f = f_\mathsf{l}$ or $Fn = \{f_\mathsf{l}\}$ and $f = f_\mathsf{r}$. A reachability expression $\langle Fn \rangle_Q^*(t_1, t_2)$ expresses that the node defined by t_2 can be obtained from the node defined by t_1, by successively applying the functions defined by the function terms in Fn, where at each step Q holds between the current node and its image. Formally, we define the binary predicate $R_{Q,Fn}$ by the formula

$\left(\bigvee_{f \in Fn} f(x) = y \right) \wedge Q$ and interpret the reachability relation $\langle Fn \rangle_Q^*$ as the reflexive transitive closure of $R_{Q,Fn}$:

$$[\![\langle Fn \rangle_Q^*]\!]_{\alpha_{\mathcal{F}}, \beta} \overset{\text{def}}{=} \left\{ (u,v) \in \alpha_{\mathcal{F}} \times \alpha_{\mathcal{F}} \mid [\![R_{Q,Fn}]\!]_{\alpha_{\mathcal{F}}, \beta[x \mapsto u, y \mapsto v]} \right\}^*$$

The interpretation of $\langle Fn \rangle_Q^*(t_1, t_2)$ is then defined as expected.

Definition 1 (Satisfiability Problem for TREX). *The satisfiability problem for TREX asks whether, given a TREX formula F, there exists a forest $\alpha_{\mathcal{F}}$ that satisfies F.*

5   Decision Procedure for TREX

The logic TREX is a proper subset of MSOL over finite trees. Thus, decidability of the satisfiability problem for TREX follows from the decidability of MSOL over trees. In fact TREX formulas can be expressed in terms of MSOL formulas with at most two quantifier alternations, which gives a 2-EXPTIME upper-bound for the complexity. In the following, we show that the satisfiability problem for TREX is actually in NP.

For the remainder of this section we fix a TREX formula F_0. Our decision procedure proceeds in four steps. The first two steps eliminate function updates and forward reachability expressions from F_0, resulting in equisatisfiable TREX formulas F_1 and then F_2. In the third step the formula F_2 is reduced to a first-order formula F_3 that has the same finite models as the original formula F. We then use results on local theories [9, 16] to prove a small model property for the obtained formulas. This allows us to use an existing decision procedure to check satisfiability of F_3 in the final step of our algorithm and obtain NP completeness.

5.1   Elimination of Function Updates

We first describe the elimination of function updates from the input formula F_0. The algorithm that achieves this is as follows:

1. Flatten the index and target terms of function updates in F_0 by exhaustively applying the following rewrite rule:
   $$C[\text{upd}(f, i, t)] \rightsquigarrow C[\text{upd}(f, c_i, c_t)] \wedge c_i = i \wedge c_t = t$$
   where i, t are non-constant terms and $c_i, c_t \in \Gamma$ are fresh constant symbols
2. Eliminate function updates in reachability expressions by exhaustively applying the following rewrite rule:
   $$C[\langle \text{upd}(f, c_i, c_t), Fn \rangle_Q^*(t_1, t_2)] \rightsquigarrow C[H] \wedge \bigwedge_{f' \in Fn} c_{f'} = f'(c_i)$$
   where the $c_{f'}$ are fresh constant symbols and
   $$H \overset{\text{def}}{=} \langle f, Fn \rangle_R^*(t_1, t_2) \vee \langle f, Fn \rangle_R^*(t_1, c_i) \wedge \langle f, Fn \rangle_R^*(c_t, t_2) \wedge Q(c_i, c_t)$$
   $$R \overset{\text{def}}{=} Q \wedge (x = c_i \rightarrow \bigvee_{f' \in Fn} y = c_{f'})$$
3. Eliminate all remaining function updates by exhaustively applying the following rewrite rule:
   $$t_1 = C[\text{upd}(f, c_i, c_t)(t_2)] \rightsquigarrow t_2 = c_i \wedge t_1 = C[c_t] \vee t_2 \neq c_i \wedge t_1 = C[f(t_2)]$$

Note that the exhaustive application of the rule in each of the steps 1. to 3. is guaranteed to terminate. Thus, let F_1 be any of the possible normal form formulas obtained after exhaustive application of these rules to F_0.

Lemma 2. F_1 *is a TREX formula and is equisatisfiable with F_0.*

5.2 Elimination of Descendant Relations

We next describe the second step of our decision procedure, which eliminates all descendant relations from the formula F_1. The elimination is performed using the following rewrite rule:

$$\langle \mathsf{l}, \mathsf{r}\rangle^*_Q(s,t) \; \leadsto \; s = t \; \vee \; s \neq \mathsf{null} \wedge (\exists z.\, (\mathsf{l}(z) = t \vee \mathsf{r}(z) = t) \wedge \langle \mathsf{p}\rangle^*_{Q^{-1}}(z,s) \wedge Q(z,t))$$

where $Q^{-1} \stackrel{\mathrm{def}}{=} Q[x := y, y := x]$. Let F_2 be any of the normal form formulas obtained by exhaustively applying this rewrite rule to F_1.

Lemma 3. F_2 is a TREX formula and is equisatisfiable with F_1.

5.3 Reduction to First-Order Logic

In the third step of our decision procedure we reduce the formula F_2 obtained after the second step to a formula F_3 in first-order logic. The idea of the reduction is to provide a first-order axiomatization of the unconstrained ancestor relation p^* whose finite models are precisely the forests $\mathcal{M}_\mathcal{F}$ defined in Section 4. For this purpose we introduce a fresh binary predicate symbol P representing p^*. The axioms defining P are given in Figure 7. We can then axiomatize each constrained ancestor relation $\langle \mathsf{p}\rangle^*_Q$ in terms of p^*. To achieve thism we exploit that the relations $\langle \mathsf{p}\rangle^*_Q$ can be characterized as follows:

$$\forall xy.\, \langle \mathsf{p}\rangle^*_Q(x,y) \leftrightarrow \mathsf{p}^*(x,y) \wedge \mathsf{p}^*(y, bp_Q(x)) \tag{1}$$

where bp_Q is the function that maps a node x to the first ancestor z of x such that $Q(z, \mathsf{p}(z))$ does not hold (or null if such a node does not exist). We call bp_Q the *break point* function for $\langle \mathsf{p}\rangle^*_Q$. The intuition behind the above definition is that for $\langle \mathsf{p}\rangle^*_Q(x,y)$ to be true, the break point for the path of ancestor nodes of x must come after y has been reached (respectively, y itself is the break point of x). Note that this definition exploits the fact that forests are acyclic graphs. The axioms defining bp_Q are given in Figure 8.

Formally, the reduction of F_2 to a first-order logic formula F_3 is defined as follows: Let P be a fresh binary predicate symbol and let $F_{3,1}$ be the formula obtained by conjoining F_2 with the axioms shown in Figure 7. Let $\mathcal{Q}$ be the set of predicates Q appearing in reachability expressions $\langle \mathsf{p}\rangle^*_Q(t_1, t_2)$ in F_2. For each $Q \in \mathcal{Q}$, let bp_Q be a fresh unary function symbol. For each $Q \in \mathcal{Q}$, replace all occurrences of the form $\langle \mathsf{p}\rangle^*_Q(t_1, t_2)$ in F_2 by $P(t_1, t_2) \wedge P(t_2, bp_Q(t_1))$. Let the result be $F_{3,2}$. Finally, for each $Q \in \mathcal{Q}$, conjoin $F_{3,2}$ with the axioms shown in Figure 8. Let F_3 be the resulting formula and let Σ_P be the extension of the signature $\Sigma_\mathcal{F}$ with the symbols P, and bp_Q, for all $Q \in \mathcal{Q}$.

Lemma 4. For every finite Σ_P-model α of the axioms in Figure 7, $\alpha(P) = \alpha(\mathsf{p})^*$ and $\alpha|_{\Sigma_\mathcal{F}} \in \mathcal{M}_\mathcal{F}$.

Lemma 5. The TREX formula F_2 has a model in $\mathcal{M}_\mathcal{F}$ iff the Σ_P-formula F_3 has a finite Σ_P-model.

l-Child : $p(l(x)) = x \vee l(x) = \text{null}$	p-Loop : $p(x) = x \to x = \text{null}$
r-Child : $p(r(x)) = x \vee r(x) = \text{null}$	NullTerm : $P(x, \text{null})$
Parent : $l(p(x)) = x \vee r(p(x)) = x \vee p(x) = \text{null}$	Refl : $P(x, x)$
lr-Diff : $l(x) = y \wedge r(x) = y \to y = \text{null}$	Trans : $P(x, y) \wedge P(y, z) \to P(x, z)$
l-Root : $p(x) = \text{null} \wedge l(z) = x \to x = \text{null}$	AntiSym : $P(x, y) \wedge P(y, x) \to x = y$
r-Root : $p(x) = \text{null} \wedge r(z) = x \to x = \text{null}$	p-Step : $P(x, p(x))$
Total : $P(x, y) \wedge P(x, z) \to P(z, y) \vee P(y, z)$	p-Unfold : $P(x, y) \to x = y \vee P(p(x), y)$

Fig. 7. First-order axioms for the unconstrained ancestor relation p^* (represented by the binary predicate symbol P) and the functions l, r, and p in a forest

$$bp_Q\text{-Def1} : P(x, bp_Q(x)) \quad bp_Q\text{-Def2} : Q(bp_Q(x), p(bp_Q(x))) \to bp_Q(x) = \text{null}$$
$$bp_Q\text{-Def3} : P(x, y) \wedge P(y, bp_Q(x)) \to Q(y, p(y)) \vee y = bp_Q(x)$$

Fig. 8. First-order axioms defining the break point functions bp_Q

5.4 Ψ-Locality

Now let F_4 be the formula obtained by transforming F_3 into prenex normal from and skolemizing all existential quantifiers. Note that our syntactic restrictions on TREX formulas ensure that there are no alternating quantifiers appearing in the formulas F_0, F_1, F_2, and hence F_3. So skolemization only introduces additional Skolem constants, but no additional function symbols.

Let C be the set of clauses obtained by transforming F_4 into clausal normal form. Then partition C into sets of ground clauses G and non-ground clauses $\mathcal{K}_P$ in which all terms have been linearized and flattened. The idea is now to define a closure operator Ψ such that condition (Loc^Ψ) from Section 3 holds for the particular pair $\mathcal{K}_P, G$. To ensure that we can extend finite weak partial models of $\mathcal{K}_P[\Psi(\mathcal{K}_P, G)] \cup G$ to finite total models of $\mathcal{K}_P \cup G$, we have to make sure that $\Psi(\mathcal{K}_P, G)$ contains sufficiently many ground terms.

We will define Ψ such that in every finite weak partial model of $\mathcal{K}_P[\Psi(\mathcal{K}_P, G)] \cup G$, both P and the break point functions are already totally defined. However, for this we have to bound the possible values of the break point functions. In fact, each predicate $Q \in \mathcal{Q}$ bounds the possible values that bp_Q can take. Let $\Gamma(Q)$ be the set of constants appearing in Q and let α be a finite total model of $\mathcal{K}_P$, then for all $u \in \alpha$, $bp_Q(u)$ is one of null, c, $l(c)$, or $r(c)$ for some $c \in \Gamma(Q)$. Thus, for each predicate $Q \in \mathcal{Q}$ define the set of its potential break points $BP(Q)$ as follows. For sets of ground terms T and a k-ary function symbol f, let $f(T)$ be the set of all (properly sorted) ground terms $f(t_1, \ldots, t_k)$ for some $t_1, \ldots, t_k \in T$. Then define

$$BP(Q) \stackrel{\text{def}}{=} \Gamma(Q) \cup l(\Gamma(Q)) \cup r(\Gamma(Q)) \cup \{\text{null}\}$$

Let further $BP(\mathcal{Q})$ be the union of all sets $BP(Q)$ for $Q \in \mathcal{Q}$. This leads us to our first approximation Ψ_{bp} of Ψ. To this end let $f^i(T)$ be the set $f(T)$ restricted to the terms in which the function symbol f appears at most i times, and let $bp^-(T)$ be the set of

$$bp_Q\text{-Def4} : P(x,y) \land P(y, bp_Q(x)) \rightarrow bp_Q(x) = bp_Q(y)$$
$$bp_Q\text{-Def5} : \bigvee_{t \in BP(Q)} bp_Q(x) = t$$

Fig. 9. Additional first-order axioms for bounding the break point functions

$$fca\text{-Def1} : P(x, fca(x,y)) \qquad fca\text{-Def2} : P(y, fca(x,y))$$
$$fca\text{-Def3} : P(x,z) \land P(y,z) \rightarrow P(fca(x,y),z)$$
$$fca\text{-Def4} : fca(x,y) = w \land fca(x,z) = w \land fca(y,z) = w \rightarrow x = y \lor x = z \lor y = z \lor w = \text{null}$$

Fig. 10. Axioms defining the first common ancestor of two nodes in a forest

ground terms obtained by removing from each ground term in T all appearances of the function symbols $\{\, bp_Q \mid Q \in \mathcal{Q} \,\}$. Then define

$$\Psi_0(T) \overset{\text{def}}{=} T \cup \{\, \mathsf{p}(t) \mid t \in T, \exists t'. t = \mathsf{l}(t') \lor t = \mathsf{r}(t') \,\} \cup BP(\mathcal{Q}) \cup \mathsf{p}(BP(\mathcal{Q}))$$
$$\Psi_4(T) \overset{\text{def}}{=} T \cup \bigcup_{Q \in \mathcal{Q}} bp_Q(bp^-(T))$$
$$\Psi_5(T) \overset{\text{def}}{=} T \cup P(T)$$
$$\Psi_{bp}(\mathcal{K}, T) \overset{\text{def}}{=} \Psi_5 \circ \Psi_4 \circ \Psi_0(\mathsf{st}(\mathcal{K}) \cup T)$$

Let $\mathcal{K}_{bp}$ be the set of clauses obtained from $\mathcal{K}_P$ by adding the linearized and flattened clauses corresponding to the axioms shown in Figure 9. These additional axioms ensure that the interpretation of the break point functions in weak partial models of $\mathcal{K}_P$ are consistent with those in total models of $\mathcal{K}_P$.

However, the above definition is not yet sufficient to ensure Ψ-locality. Assume that a clause of the form $z = c \lor z = d$ appears in $\mathcal{K}_{bp}$ that results from a restricted quantified formula $\forall z.z = c \lor z = d$ in F_0. Then this clause imposes an upper bound of 2 on the cardinality of the models of F_4. We thus have to make sure that for any weak partial model of $\mathcal{K}_{bp}[\Psi_{bp}(\mathcal{K}_{bp}, G)] \cup G$, we can find a total model of the same cardinality. We can ensure that total models of matching cardinality exist by enforcing that every weak partial model already determines the *first common ancestor* of every pair of nodes. We axiomatize the first common ancestor of two nodes by introducing a fresh binary function symbol fca and then adding the axioms shown in Figure 10. Let Σ_{fca} be the signature Σ_P extended with the binary function symbol fca and let $\mathcal{K}_{fca}$ be the set of clauses obtained by adding to $\mathcal{K}_{bp}$ the linearized and flattened clauses corresponding to the axioms in Figure 10. Our second attempt at defining Ψ is then:

$$\Psi_3(T) \overset{\text{def}}{=} T \cup fca^1(T) \cup fca^2(T \cup fca^1(T))$$
$$\Psi_{fca}(\mathcal{K}, T) \overset{\text{def}}{=} \Psi_5 \circ \Psi_4 \circ \Psi_3 \circ \Psi_0(\mathsf{st}(\mathcal{K}) \cup T)$$

Unfortunately, the operator Ψ_{fca} is still not good enough to ensure Ψ-locality. Assume that a clause of the form $f(z) = t \rightarrow H$ appears in $\mathcal{K}_{fca}$ that resulted from a restricted quantified formula in F_0 of the form $\forall z. f(z) = t \rightarrow H$ and where f is either one of p, l, or r. Assume that $f = \mathsf{p}$. To ensure that this clause remains valid whenever we complete p to a total function in some weak partial model α, we have to ensure that we never have to define $\mathsf{p}(u) = t$, for any $u \in \alpha$ for which p is undefined. Consider first the case that in said model t is not null, then we can guarantee that we never have to define $\mathsf{p}(u) = t$ by making sure that α is already defined on the ground terms $\mathsf{p}(\mathsf{l}(t))$

Root1 : $P(x,y) \rightarrow P(y, root(x)) \lor y = \mathsf{null}$ Root2 : $root(x) = \mathsf{null} \leftrightarrow x = \mathsf{null}$
l-Leaf1 : $P(lleaf(x), x) \lor lleaf(x) = \mathsf{null}$ r-Leaf1 : $P(rleaf(x), x) \lor rleaf(x) = \mathsf{null}$
l-Leaf2 : $P(lleaf(x), \mathsf{l}(x))$ r-Leaf2 : $P(rleaf(x), \mathsf{r}(x))$
l-Leaf3 : $lleaf(lleaf(x)) = \mathsf{null}$ r-Leaf3 : $rleaf(rleaf(x)) = \mathsf{null}$
l-Leaf4 : $lleaf(rleaf(x)) = \mathsf{null}$ r-Leaf4 : $rleaf(rleaf(x)) = \mathsf{null}$
Leaves1 : $fca(lleaf(x), rleaf(x)) = x \lor lleaf(x) = \mathsf{null} \lor rleaf(x) = \mathsf{null}$
Leaves2 : $(lleaf(x) = \mathsf{null} \lor rleaf(x) = \mathsf{null}) \land fca(y, z) = x \rightarrow x = y \lor x = z \lor x = \mathsf{null}$
Leaves3 : $lleaf(x) = \mathsf{null} \land rleaf(x) = \mathsf{null} \land P(y, x) \rightarrow y = x \lor x = \mathsf{null}$

Fig. 11. Axioms for the auxiliary function symbols $root$, $lleaf$, and $rleaf$

and $\mathsf{p}(\mathsf{r}(t))$. This suggests that we should add the following additional ground terms to the set of ground terms generated by $\Psi_0(T)$:

$$\Psi_1(T) \stackrel{\mathrm{def}}{=} T \cup \{\,\mathsf{l}(t), \mathsf{p}(\mathsf{l}(t)), \mathsf{r}(t), \mathsf{p}(\mathsf{r}(t)) \mid (\mathsf{p}, t) \in Grd\,\}$$
$$\cup \{\,\mathsf{p}(t), \mathsf{l}(\mathsf{p}(t)), \mathsf{p}(\mathsf{l}(\mathsf{p}(t))) \mid (\mathsf{l}, t) \in Grd\,\}$$
$$\cup \{\,\mathsf{p}(t), \mathsf{r}(\mathsf{p}(t)), \mathsf{p}(\mathsf{r}(\mathsf{p}(t))) \mid (\mathsf{r}, t) \in Grd\,\}$$

where Grd is the set of all pairs (f, t) of function symbols and ground terms appearing in guards of clauses of the form $f(z) = t \rightarrow H$ in $\mathcal{K}_{fca}$.

If for some $(f, t) \in Grd$ the weak partial model α satisfies $t = \mathsf{null}$ then the situation is not quite so simple. We have to make sure that α already explicitly determines which nodes $u \in \alpha$ satisfy $f(u) = \mathsf{null}$, even if f is not defined on u. However, there is no finite set of ground terms T over the signature Σ_{fca} such that instantiation of $\mathcal{K}_{fca}$ with the terms in T will ensure this. To enable the construction of such a finite set of terms, we introduce auxiliary functions $root$, $lleaf$, and $rleaf$ that determine the root, a left child, and a right child of every node in a forest. More precisely, the semantics of these functions is as follows: for each $u \in \alpha$, $root(u)$ determines the root of the tree in α to which u belongs (i.e., in all total models α of $\mathcal{K}_{fca}$ and $u \in \alpha$, $\mathsf{p}(u) = \mathsf{null}$ iff $root(u) = u$). Similarly, $lleaf(u)$ is some leaf of the tree to which u belongs such that $lleaf(u)$ is descendant of $\mathsf{l}(u)$, or null if $\mathsf{l}(u)$ is null (i.e., in all total models α of $\mathcal{K}_{fca}$ and $u \in \alpha$, $\mathsf{l}(u) = \mathsf{null}$ holds iff $lleaf(u) = \mathsf{null}$). The semantics of $rleaf$ is analogous. Let Σ be the signature Σ_{fca} extended with fresh unary function symbols $root$, $lleaf$, and $rleaf$. The axioms capturing this semantics are given in Figure 11. We can then replace every clause $f(z) = t \rightarrow H$ in $\mathcal{K}_{fca}$ by the two clauses

$$f(z) = t \rightarrow t = \mathsf{null} \lor H \qquad \text{and} \qquad t = \mathsf{null} \land N_f(z) \rightarrow H$$

where $N_f(z)$ is $root(z) = z$ if f is p, $lleaf(z) = \mathsf{null}$ if f is l, and $rleaf(z) = \mathsf{null}$ if f is r. Let $\mathcal{K}$ be the resulting set of clauses extended with the linearized and flattened clauses obtained from the axioms in Figure 11. After this final rewriting step no non-ground occurrences of function symbols l, r, p remain in the clauses that resulted from quantified subformulas in the original formula F_0.

Lemma 6. *The formula F_3 has a finite Σ_P-model iff $\mathcal{K} \cup G$ has a finite Σ-model.*

The final definition of the closure operator Ψ is then as follows:

$$Roots(T) \stackrel{\text{def}}{=} root^1(T) \cup root(root^1(T))$$
$$Leaves(T) \stackrel{\text{def}}{=} lleaf^1(T \cup root^1(T)) \cup rleaf^1(T \cup root^1(T))$$
$$\Psi_2(T) \stackrel{\text{def}}{=} T \cup Roots(T) \cup Leaves(T) \cup lleaf(Leaves(T)) \cup rleaf(Leaves(T))$$
$$\Psi(\mathcal{K}, T) \stackrel{\text{def}}{=} \Psi_5 \circ \Psi_4 \circ \Psi_3 \circ \Psi_2 \circ \Psi_1 \circ \Psi_0(\text{st}(\mathcal{K}) \cup T)$$

One can easily check that Ψ satisfies the conditions (i) to (iv) on the closure operator of a Ψ-local theory, as defined in Section 3.

Lemma 7. *If there exists a weak partial model of $\mathcal{K}[\Psi(\mathcal{K}, G)] \cup G$ in which all terms in $\Psi(\mathcal{K}, G)$ are defined, then there exists a finite total model of $\mathcal{K} \cup G$.*

Lemma 7 implies that we can decide satisfiability of $\mathcal{K} \cup G$ using the decision procedure described in [9, Section 3.1]. Together with the previous Lemmas we conclude that the combination of the steps described in this section result in a decision procedure for the satisfiability problem of TREX.

Complexity. Note that the number of terms in $\Psi(\mathcal{K}, G)$ is polynomial in the size of $\mathcal{K} \cup G$. From the parametric complexity considerations for Ψ-local theories in [9, 16] follows that satisfiability of $\mathcal{K} \cup G$ can be checked in NP. Further note that all steps of the reduction, except for the elimination of function updates, increase the size of the formula at most by a polynomial factor. The case splits in the rewrite steps 2. and 3. of the function update elimination may cause that the size of the formula increases exponentially in the nesting depth of function updates in the original formula F_0. However, this exponential blowup can be easily avoided using standard techniques that are used, e.g., for efficient clausal normal form computation.

Theorem 8. *The satisfiability problem for TREX is NP-complete.*

Implementation and experiments. We started implementation of our decision procedure in the Jahob system. Our current prototype implements the first three steps of our decision procedure and already integrates with the verification condition generator of Jahob. Instead of manually instantiating the generated axioms, as described in the fourth step of our decision procedure, we currently give the generated axioms directly to the SMT solver and use triggers to encode some of the instantiation restrictions imposed by Ψ. While this implementation is not yet complete, we already successfully used it to verify implementations of operations on doubly-linked lists and a full insertion method on binary search trees (including the loop traversing the tree). The speedup obtained compared to using the MONA decision procedure is significant. For instance, using our implementation the verification of all 16 subgoals for the insert method takes about 1s in total. Checking the same subgoals using MONA takes 135s. We find these initial results encouraging and consistent with other success stories of using SMT solvers to encode NP decision procedures.

6   Conclusion

This paper introduced the logic TREX for reasoning about imperative tree data structures. The logic supports a transitive closure operator and a form of universal quantification. It is closed under propositional operations and weakest preconditions for heap manipulating statements. By analyzing the structure of partial and finite models, we exhibited a particular Ψ-local axiomatization of TREX, which implies that the satisfiability problem for TREX is in NP. It also yields algorithms for generating model representations for satisfiable formulas, respectively, proofs of unsatisfiability.

References

1. Balaban, I., Pnueli, A., Zuck, L.D.: Shape analysis of single-parent heaps. In: Cook, B., Podelski, A. (eds.) VMCAI 2007. LNCS, vol. 4349, pp. 91–105. Springer, Heidelberg (2007)
2. Bouajjani, A., Drăgoi, C., Enea, C., Sighireanu, M.: A logic-based framework for reasoning about composite data structures. In: Bravetti, M., Zavattaro, G. (eds.) CONCUR 2009. LNCS, vol. 5710, pp. 178–195. Springer, Heidelberg (2009)
3. Bouajjani, A., Habermehl, P., Rogalewicz, A., Vojnar, T.: Abstract regular tree model checking of complex dynamic data structures. In: Penkler, D., Reitenspiess, M., Tam, F. (eds.) SAS 2006. LNCS, vol. 4328, Springer, Heidelberg (2006)
4. Calvanese, D., di Giacomo, G., Nardi, D., Lenzerini, M.: Reasoning in expressive description logics. In: Handbook of Automated Reasoning. Elsevier, Amsterdam (2001)
5. Charatonik, W., Witkowski, P.: On the complexity of the bernays-schönfinkel class with datalog. In: Fermüller, C.G., Voronkov, A. (eds.) LPAR-17. LNCS, vol. 6397, pp. 187–201. Springer, Heidelberg (2010)
6. de Moura, L., Bjørner, N.S.: Z3: An efficient SMT solver. In: Ramakrishnan, C.R., Rehof, J. (eds.) TACAS 2008. LNCS, vol. 4963, pp. 337–340. Springer, Heidelberg (2008)
7. Genevès, P., Layaïda, N., Schmitt, A.: Efficient static analysis of XML paths and types. In: ACM PLDI (2007)
8. Habermehl, P., Iosif, R., Vojnar, T.: Automata-based verification of programs with tree updates. Acta Inf. 47, 1–31 (2010)
9. Ihlemann, C., Jacobs, S., Sofronie-Stokkermans, V.: On local reasoning in verification. In: Ramakrishnan, C.R., Rehof, J. (eds.) TACAS 2008. LNCS, vol. 4963, pp. 265–281. Springer, Heidelberg (2008)
10. Immerman, N., Rabinovich, A. M., Reps, T. W., Sagiv, M., Yorsh, G.: The boundary between decidability and undecidability for transitive-closure logics. In: Marcinkowski, J., Tarlecki, A. (eds.) CSL 2004. LNCS, vol. 3210, pp. 160–174. Springer, Heidelberg (2004)
11. Klarlund, N., Møller, A.: MONA Version 1.4 User Manual. BRICS Notes Series NS-01-1, Department of Computer Science, University of Aarhus (January 2001)
12. Kuncak, V.: Modular Data Structure Verification. PhD thesis, EECS Department, Massachusetts Institute of Technology (February 2007)
13. Lahiri, S., Qadeer, S.: Back to the future: revisiting precise program verification using SMT solvers. In: POPL (2008)
14. Lev-Ami, T., Immerman, N., Reps, T., Sagiv, M., Srivastava, S., Yorsh, G.: Simulating reachability using first-order logic with applications to verification of linked data structures. In: Nieuwenhuis, R. (ed.) CADE 2005. LNCS (LNAI), vol. 3632, pp. 99–115. Springer, Heidelberg (2005)
15. Podelski, A., Wies, T.: Counterexample-guided focus. In: ACM Symposium on the Principles of Programming Languages (POPL 2010), pp. 249–260. ACM, New York (2010)
16. Sofronie-Stokkermans, V.: Hierarchic reasoning in local theory extensions. In: Nieuwenhuis, R. (ed.) CADE 2005. LNCS (LNAI), vol. 3632, pp. 219–234. Springer, Heidelberg (2005)
17. Wies, T.: Symbolic Shape Analysis. PhD thesis, University of Freiburg (2009)
18. Wies, T., Kuncak, V., Lam, P., Podelski, A., Rinard, M.: Field constraint analysis. In: Proc. Int. Conf. Verification, Model Checking, and Abstract Interpratation (2006)

19. Wies, T., Muñiz, M., Kuncak, V.: On an efficient decision procedure for imperative tree data structures. Technical Report IST-2011-0005, EPFL-REPORT-165193, IST Austria, EPFL (2011)
20. Yorsh, G., Rabinovich, A.M., Sagiv, M., Meyer, A., Bouajjani, A.: A logic of reachable patterns in linked data-structures. J. Log. Algebr. Program. (2007)
21. Zee, K., Kuncak, V., Rinard, M.: Full functional verification of linked data structures. In: PLDI (2008)

AC Completion with Termination Tools*

Sarah Winkler and Aart Middeldorp

Institute of Computer Science, University of Innsbruck, Austria

Abstract. We present mascott, a tool for Knuth-Bendix completion modulo the theory of associative and commutative operators. In contrast to classical completion tools, mascott does not rely on a fixed AC-compatible reduction order. Instead, a suitable order is implicitly constructed during a deduction by collecting all oriented rules in a similar fashion as done in the tool Slothrop. This allows for convergent systems which cannot be completed using standard orders. We outline the underlying inference system and comment on implementation details such as the use of multi-completion, term indexing techniques, and critical pair criteria.

1 Introduction

Reasoning modulo an equational theory A is required in many practical problems. The generalization of the classical Knuth-Bendix completion algorithm to rewriting modulo A is well-known (see [3] for an overview). Like ordinary completion, completion modulo A critically depends on the choice of the A-compatible reduction order supplied as input. In this system description we show how the use of termination tools supporting termination modulo A can replace a fixed reduction order, in a similar fashion as proposed by the authors of the tool Slothrop [20]. Recent developments in the area of termination proving can thus be directly exploited to obtain convergent systems for theories which were difficult to complete before. Our method can be combined with the multi-completion approach proposed by Kondo and Kurihara [14]. For equational theories A consisting of AC axioms, this approach is implemented in our new tool mascott. Our contribution can thus be viewed as an extension of the completion tool mkb$_{\mathsf{TT}}$ [19,21] to AC theories. As an example, mascott successfully completes the following system (adapted from [17]) describing addition on natural numbers represented in binary:

$$\#0 \simeq \# \qquad (x+y)1 \simeq x0 + y1 \qquad \mathsf{triple}(x) \simeq x0 + x$$
$$(x+y)0 \simeq x0 + y0 \qquad x0 + y0 + \#10 \simeq x1 + y1$$

Here $+$ is an AC operator, 0 and 1 are unary operators in postfix notation, and $\#$ denotes the empty bit sequence. For example, $\#100$ represents the number 4 in binary. The following completed system is obtained when using (e.g.) AProVE [11] as a termination prover, but cannot be shown terminating by any

---

* The first author is supported by a DOC-fFORTE fellowship of the Austrian Academy of Sciences.

N. Bjørner and V. Sofronie-Stokkermans (Eds.): CADE 2011, LNAI 6803, pp. 492–498, 2011.
© Springer-Verlag Berlin Heidelberg 2011

standard AC-compatible simplification order:

$$\#0 \to \#$$
$$\mathsf{triple}(x) \to x0 + x$$
$$(x + \#)0 \to x0 + \#$$
$$(x + \#)1 \to x1 + \#$$
$$x0 + y0 \to (x + y)0$$
$$x0 + y0 + z \to (x + y)0 + z$$
$$x0 + y1 \to (x + y)1$$
$$x0 + y1 + z \to (x + y)1 + z$$
$$x1 + y1 \to (x + y + \#1)0$$
$$x1 + y1 + z \to (x + y + \#1)0 + z$$

Our tool mascott can be accessed via a simple web interface.[1] The sources and a binary are available as well. In the sequel we outline the underlying inference system, describe the implementation, and give some (preliminary) experimental results for mascott.

2   Inference System

We assume familiarity with term rewriting and Knuth-Bendix completion, and recall only some central notions. We consider a rewrite system R and a set of equations A. A term s rewrites to t in R modulo A, denoted by $s \to_{R/A} t$, whenever $s \leftrightarrow_A^* \cdot \to_R \cdot \leftrightarrow_A^* t$. The system R *terminates modulo* A whenever the relation $\to_{R/A}$ is well-founded. It is *convergent modulo* A if in addition for every conversion $s \leftrightarrow_{A \cup R}^* t$ there exist terms u and v such that $s \to_R^* u \leftrightarrow_A^* v \leftarrow_R^* t$. To check termination of R modulo A, A-compatible reduction orders $>$ satisfying $\leftrightarrow_A^* \cdot > \cdot \leftrightarrow_A^* \subseteq >$ can be used. Since the relation $\to_{R/A}$ is undecidable in general, one typically considers the rewrite system R_A consisting of all rules $s \to t$ such that $s \leftrightarrow_A^* \ell\sigma$ and $t = r\sigma$ for some rule $\ell \to r$ in R and substitution σ. We obviously have $\to_R \subseteq \to_{R_A} \subseteq \to_{R/A}$. Thus, if R is convergent modulo A then also R_A is convergent modulo A [3], and defines the same normal forms as R/A. Hence rewriting using rules in R_A constitutes a decidable way to compute with respect to R/A.

We confine our analysis to theories A for which minimal sets of complete unifiers are computable, and denote by $CP_A(R)$ the set of A-critical pairs among rules in R.[2] For a rule $\ell \to r$ and a variable-disjoint equation $u \simeq v$ in A such that a proper non-variable subterm $u|_p$ of u and ℓ are A-unifiable, $u[\ell]_p \to u[r]_p$ is an A-extended rule [18]. The set of A-extended rules of R is denoted by $EXT_A(R)$.

Our tool is based on a variant of the inference system $\mathcal{E}$ for extended completion developed by Bachmair [3, Chapter 3]. In order to get rid of a fixed reduction order and have termination checks as side conditions, the system was modified to resemble the calculus underlying Slothrop [20]. The inference rules thus operate on a set of equations E, a set of rewrite rules R partitioned into unprotected rules N and protected rules S, and a constraint system C. The resulting inference system $\mathcal{E}_{\mathsf{TT}}$ for completion modulo the theory A is depicted in Figure 1.

---

[1] http://cl-informatik.uibk.ac.at/software/mascott

[2] Although our tool is restricted to the theory of associative and commutative operators, the underlying inference system is presented for arbitrary theories A that satisfy the stated condition.

deduce	$$\dfrac{E, N, S, C}{E \cup \{s \simeq t\}, N, S, C}$$	if $s \leftrightarrow^*_{A \cup R} t$
extend	$$\dfrac{E, N, S, C}{E, N, S \cup \{s \to t\}, C}$$	if $s \simeq t \in EXT_A(R)$
orient	$$\dfrac{E \cup \{s \simeq t\}, N, S, C}{E, N \cup \{s \to t\}, S, C \cup \{s \to t\}}$$	if $C \cup \{s \to t\}$ terminates modulo A
protect	$$\dfrac{E, N \cup \{s \to t\}, S, C}{E, N, S \cup \{s \to t\}, C}$$	
delete	$$\dfrac{E \cup \{s \simeq t\}, N, S, C}{E, N, S, C}$$	if $s \leftrightarrow^*_A t$
simplify	$$\dfrac{E \cup \{s \simeq t\}, N, S, C}{E \cup \{s \simeq u\}, N, S, C}$$	if $t \to_{R/A} u$
compose	$$\dfrac{E, N \cup \{s \to t\}, S, C}{E, N \cup \{s \to u\}, S, C}$$	if $t \to_{R/A} u$
	$$\dfrac{E, N, S \cup \{s \to t\}, C}{E, N, S \cup \{s \to u\}, C}$$	if $t \to_{R/A} u$
collapse	$$\dfrac{E, N \cup \{t \to s\}, S, C}{E \cup \{u \simeq s\}, N, S, C}$$	if $t \leftrightarrow^{\leqslant p}_A t' \to^p_{\ell \to r} u$ for some rule $\ell \to r$ in R with $t \gg \ell$

Fig. 1. System $\mathcal{E}_{\mathsf{TT}}$ of extended completion with termination checks

Here $\gg$ is some well-founded order on terms such as the encompassment order[3] and the relation $\simeq$ is assumed to be symmetric.

A sequence $(E_0, \varnothing, \varnothing, \varnothing) \vdash (E_1, N_1, S_1, C_1) \vdash (E_2, N_2, S_2, C_2) \vdash \cdots$ of inference steps in $\mathcal{E}_{\mathsf{TT}}$ is called a *run*. Note that orient is the only inference rule which actually modifies the set C of constraint rules. Since an A-termination check is performed whenever a rule is added, all constraint systems C_n are terminating modulo A. Hence the transitive closure of the rewrite relation $\to^+_{C_n/A}$ is an A-compatible reduction order, so runs in $\mathcal{E}_{\mathsf{TT}}$ can be simulated in $\mathcal{E}$:

Lemma 1

1. For every finite run $(E_0, \varnothing, \varnothing, \varnothing) \vdash^* (E_n, N_n, S_n, C_n)$ in $\mathcal{E}_{\mathsf{TT}}$ there is a corresponding run $(E_0, \varnothing, \varnothing) \vdash^* (E_n, N_n, S_n)$ in $\mathcal{E}$ using the A-compatible reduction order $\to^+_{C_n/A}$.
2. Every run $(E_0, \varnothing, \varnothing) \vdash^* (E_n, N_n, S_n)$ in $\mathcal{E}$ using an A-compatible reduction order $>$ can be simulated in an $\mathcal{E}_{\mathsf{TT}}$ run $(E_0, \varnothing, \varnothing, \varnothing) \vdash^* (E_n, N_n, S_n, C_n)$ such that $C_n \subseteq >$ holds. $\qquad\square$

---

[3] In which s is greater than t if a subterm of s is an instance of t but not vice versa.

The straightforward induction proofs closely resemble the respective counter-parts for standard completion and are thus omitted. Since our implementation is restricted to the theory AC of associative and commutative operators in $\mathcal{F}_{AC}$, we will now focus on this setting. Let R^e denote the rewrite system containing R, extended with all rules of the form $f(\ell, x) \rightarrow f(r, x)$ such that $f \in \mathcal{F}_{AC}$, $\ell \rightarrow r \in R$ and x is a fresh variable.

Corollary 1. *If a non-failing finite $\mathcal{E}_{\mathsf{TT}}$ run $(E_0, \varnothing, \varnothing, \varnothing) \vdash^* (\varnothing, N_n, S_n, C_n)$ satisfies $CP_{AC}(R_n) \subseteq \bigcup_i E_i$ and $(R_n)^e \subseteq \bigcup_i S_i$ then $(R_n)_{AC}$ is convergent modulo AC.* □

3 Implementation

In this section we present some implementation details of mascott, which stands for <u>m</u>ulti-<u>a</u>ssociative/commutative <u>co</u>mpletion with <u>t</u>ermination <u>t</u>ools.

If an equation $s \simeq t$ can be oriented in both directions, the orient rule in $\mathcal{E}_{\mathsf{TT}}$ allows for a choice. In order not to restrict to one orientation, we adapted the multi-completion approach proposed by Kondo and Kurihara [14] to the setting of completion modulo a theory A. Similar to standard completion the obtained method can be described by an inference system operating on sets of nodes $\mathcal{N}$, which are defined as in [19], the difference being that a rewrite label R_i is now split into unprotected and protected labels (N_i, S_i). Figure 2 shows the inference rules orient and extend which are specific to completion modulo A.

As an example, on input $\{\mathsf{d}(\mathsf{s}(x)+y) \simeq \mathsf{d}(\mathsf{p}(\mathsf{s}(x))+y), \mathsf{p}(\mathsf{s}(\mathsf{s}(x))) \simeq \mathsf{s}(\mathsf{p}(\mathsf{s}(x)))\}$ with $+$ an AC symbol, any completion procedure using standard AC-compatible simplification orders orients the first equation from right to left, causing diver-gence of the procedure. In contrast, our tool keeps track of both orientations and immediately outputs the AC-convergent system obtained when orienting both rules from left to right.

The termination checks required in orient inference steps may be performed by an external tool supporting AC termination such as AProVE or muterm [1]. Alternatively, a modified version of $\mathsf{T}_{\mathsf{T}}\mathsf{T}_2$ [13] can be used internally, supporting AC-dependency pairs [10,17,2] and reduction pairs induced by polynomial or matrix interpretations. A criterion for AC-compatibility of polynomial interpre-tations was given in [5]. It is not difficult to check that matrix interpretations [7] are AC-compatible if every AC symbol f is interpreted as $f_\mathcal{M}(x, y) = Ax + By + b$ where the square matrices A and B satisfy $A = A^2 = B$ in addition to the usual constraint that the top-left entry of A is positive.

In order to limit the number of equational consequences, only *prime* critical pairs are computed [12]. For AC-unification, the algorithms proposed in [16,8] were used, in the latter case incorporating the SMT solver Yices to solve linear Diophantine equations. For rewriting, AC-discrimination trees allow for a fast pre-selection of matching rules [4].

The tool is equipped with a simple command-line interface. The termination prover is given as argument to the -tp option. It is supposed to take the name of

orient

$$\frac{\mathcal{N} \cup \{\, \langle s : t, (N_0, S_0), (N_1, S_1), E, C_0, C_1 \rangle \,\}}{\mathrm{split}_P(\mathcal{N}) \cup \{\, \langle s : t, (N_0 \cup R_{lr}, S_0), (N_1 \cup R_{rl}, S_1), E', C_0 \cup R_{lr}, C_1 \cup R_{rl} \rangle \,\}}$$

with $E_{lr}, E_{rl} \subseteq E$ such that $E_{lr} \cup E_{rl} \neq \varnothing$, $P = E_{lr} \cap E_{rl}$, $E' = E \setminus (E_{lr} \cup E_{rl})$, $C[N, p] \cup \{s \to t\}$ terminates modulo A for all $p \in E_{lr}$, $C[N, p] \cup \{t \to s\}$ terminates modulo A for all $p \in E_{rl}$, $R_{lr} = (E_{lr} \setminus E_{rl}) \cup \{p0 \mid p \in P\}$ and $R_{rl} = (E_{rl} \setminus E_{lr}) \cup \{p1 \mid p \in P\}$ where $\mathrm{split}_P(N)$ replaces every $p \in P$ in any label of a node in $\mathcal{N}$ by $p0$ and $p1$

extend

$$\frac{\mathcal{N}}{\mathcal{N} \cup \{\, \langle \ell' : r', (\varnothing, N_0 \cup S_0), (\varnothing, \varnothing), \varnothing, \varnothing, \varnothing \rangle \,\}}$$

if $\langle \ell : r, (N_0, S_0), \ldots \rangle \in \mathcal{N}$, $\ell' \to r' \in EXT_A\{\ell \to r\}$ and $N_0 \cup S_0 \neq \varnothing$

Fig. 2. Two inference rules for multi-completion modulo A

a file describing the termination problem in the TPDB[4] format and print YES on the first line of the output if termination modulo AC could be established. Our tool accepts two time limits: for the overall procedure (-t) and for each call to the termination prover (-T). The option -cp prime allows to apply primality as a critical pair criterion. Further options are -ct to print the completed system and -st to obtain some statistics. An example call might thus look as follows:

```
mascott -t 300 -T 1 -st -tp muterm binary_arithmetic.trs
```

4   Experiments

For our experiments we collected AC completion problems from a number of different sources and ran mascott with different termination provers as backends. All of the tests were performed on an Intel Core Duo running at a clock rate of 1.4 GHz with 2.8 GB of main memory.

The results are summarized in Table 1, where the superscripts attached to the problems indicate their source: a refers to [9], b refers to [17], and c is associated with [15]. The remaining examples were added by the authors. Columns (1) list the total time in seconds while columns (2) give the percentage of time spent on termination. The symbol ∞ marks a timeout of 300 seconds. For internal termination checks a termination strategy employing dependency pairs and matrix interpretations was used. As expected, this strategy is far less powerful than the techniques used by AProVE or muterm.

We also include a comparison with CiME [6], the only other current tool for AC completion that we are aware of, although this requires the specification of a concrete AC-RPO or AC-compatible polynomial interpretation by the user. For our experiments we supplied an appropriate order whenever possible, and in these cases CiME completed the given problems considerably faster. However, a suitable order does not always exist (as for the example mentioned in Section 3)

---

[4] Termination Problem Data Base, http://www.lri.fr/~marche/tpdb/

Table 1. Comparison of mascott using different termination backends and C*i*ME

| | mascott | | | | | | C*i*ME |
| | internal | | APorVE | | muterm | | |
	(1)	(2)	(1)	(2)	(1)	(2)	(1)
Abelian groups (AG)[a]	14.48	63	9.33	70	3.02	7	0.05
AG + homomorphism	169.62	87	73.87	84	30.20	15	0.05
arithmetic[a]	∞		24.58	47	35.03	8	?
AC-ring with unit[a]	∞		64.15	53	55.96	38	0.1
associative ring with unit[a]	∞		∞		163.96	71	0.1
binary arithmetic[b]	∞		78.36	89	23.94	20	?
commutative monoid[a]	0.5	2	0.7	95	0.03	32	0.01
example 5.4.2[c]	8.26	97	5.94	98	0.39	79	0.01
example from Section 3	∞		∞		0.74	91	?
ICS[a]	12.75	7	9.03	34	6.10	1	0.01
max[c]	∞		8.34	98	0.29	58	?
multisets over $\{0,1\}$	∞		117.11	96	9.76	52	?
nondeterministic machine[a]	∞		∞		∞		0.2
ring[a]	∞		224.99	75	125.88	67	0.07
ring with unit[a]	∞		201.11	76	81.94	62	0.1
semiring[a]	∞		24.90	75	12.35	45	0.1
semilattice[a]	10.12	4	5.66	12	5.33	1	0.01
sum	∞		7.58	98	0.33	54	?
completed systems	6		13		17		12
average time for success	33.54		58.60		42.71		0.07

or is not known (as for the binary addition example from the introduction or the arithmetic problem). In Table 1 the symbol ? marks these cases.

In line with previous work on AC completion, the use of critical pair criteria turned out to be highly beneficial. Restricting to so-called prime critical pairs increases performance on the examples from Table 1 by 40%. For example, without the criterion the theory of associative rings with unit cannot be completed within 300 seconds.

5 Conclusion

Apparently, mascott is the only tool for AC completion which is automatic in that it does not require a fixed reduction order as input. To the best of our knowledge, mascott is also the first AC completion tool not restricted to AC-RPO or AC-compatible polynomial interpretations as termination methods. Instead, all techniques developed for AC termination can be exploited, such as the dependency pair framework or matrix interpretations. Our tool is thus able to produce novel complete systems such as the one mentioned in the introduction.

References

1. Alarcón, B., Gutiérrez, R., Lucas, S., Navarro-Marset, R.: Proving termination properties with MU-TERM. In: Johnson, M., Pavlovic, D. (eds.) AMAST 2010. LNCS, vol. 6486, pp. 201–208. Springer, Heidelberg (2011)
2. Alarcón, B., Lucas, S., Meseguer, J.: A dependency pair framework for $A \vee C$-termination. In: Ölveczky, P.C. (ed.) WRLA 2010. LNCS, vol. 6381, pp. 35–51. Springer, Heidelberg (2010)
3. Bachmair, L.: Canonical Equational Proofs. Progress in Theoretical Computer Science. Birkhäuser (1991)
4. Bachmair, L., Chen, T., Ramakrishnan, I.V.: Associative-commutative discrimination nets. In: Gaudel, M.-C., Jouannaud, J.-P. (eds.) TAPSOFT 1993. LNCS, vol. 668, pp. 61–74. Springer, Heidelberg (1993)
5. Ben Cherifa, A., Lescanne, P.: Termination of rewriting systems by polynomial interpretations and its implementation. SCP 9(2), 137–159 (1987)
6. Contejean, E., Marché, C.: CiME: Completion modulo E. In: Ganzinger, H. (ed.) RTA 1996. LNCS, vol. 1103, pp. 416–419. Springer, Heidelberg (1996)
7. Endrullis, J., Waldmann, J., Zantema, H.: Matrix interpretations for proving termination of term rewriting. JAR 40(2-3), 195–220 (2008)
8. Fortenbacher, A.: An algebraic approach to unification under associativity and commutativity. JSC 3(3), 217–229 (1987)
9. Gehrke, W.: Detailed catalogue of canonical term rewrite systems generated automatically. Technical report, RISC Linz (1992)
10. Giesl, J., Kapur, D.: Dependency pairs for equational rewriting. In: Middeldorp, A. (ed.) RTA 2001. LNCS, vol. 2051, pp. 93–108. Springer, Heidelberg (2001)
11. Giesl, J., Schneider-Kamp, P., Thiemann, R.: AProVE 1.2: Automatic Termination Proofs in the Dependency Pair Framework. In: Furbach, U., Shankar, N. (eds.) IJCAR 2006. LNCS (LNAI), vol. 4130, pp. 281–286. Springer, Heidelberg (2006)
12. Kapur, D., Musser, D.R., Narendran, P.: Only prime superpositions need be considered in the Knuth-Bendix completion procedure. JSC 6(1), 19–36 (1988)
13. Korp, M., Sternagel, C., Zankl, H., Middeldorp, A.: Tyrolean Termination Tool 2. In: Treinen, R. (ed.) RTA 2009. LNCS, vol. 5595, pp. 295–304. Springer, Heidelberg (2009)
14. Kurihara, M., Kondo, H.: Completion for multiple reduction orderings. JAR 23(1), 25–42 (1999)
15. Kusakari, K.: AC-Termination and Dependency Pairs of Term Rewriting Systems. PhD thesis, JAIST (2000)
16. Lincoln, P., Christian, J.: Adventures in associative-commutative unification. JSC 8, 393–416 (1989)
17. Marché, C., Urbain, X.: Modular and incremental proofs of AC-termination. JSC 38(1), 873–897 (2004)
18. Peterson, G.E., Stickel, M.E.: Complete sets of reductions for some equational theories. JACM 28(2), 233–264 (1981)
19. Sato, H., Winkler, S., Kurihara, M., Middeldorp, A.: Multi-completion with termination tools (system description). In: Armando, A., Baumgartner, P., Dowek, G. (eds.) IJCAR 2008. LNCS (LNAI), vol. 5195, pp. 306–312. Springer, Heidelberg (2008)
20. Wehrman, I., Stump, A., Westbrook, E. M.: SLOTHROP: Knuth-Bendix completion with a modern termination checker. In: Pfenning, F. (ed.) RTA 2006. LNCS, vol. 4098, pp. 287–296. Springer, Heidelberg (2006)
21. Winkler, S., Sato, H., Middeldorp, A., Kurihara, M.: Optimizing mkbTT (system description). In: Proc. 21st RTA. LIPIcs, vol. 6, pp. 373–384 (2010)

CSI – A Confluence Tool*

Harald Zankl, Bertram Felgenhauer, and Aart Middeldorp

Institute of Computer Science, University of Innsbruck, 6020 Innsbruck, Austria

Abstract. This paper describes a new confluence tool for term rewrite systems. Due to its modular design, the few techniques implemented so far can be combined flexibly. Methods developed for termination analysis are adapted to prove and disprove confluence. Preliminary experimental results show the potential of our tool.

Keywords: term rewriting, confluence, automation.

1 Introduction

We describe a new automatic tool for (dis)proving confluence of first-order rewrite systems (TRSs for short). Our tool is developed in Innsbruck, the city at the confluence of the two rivers Sill and Inn, and abbreviated CSI. It is available from

$$\text{http://cl-informatik.uibk.ac.at/software/csi}$$

and supports two new techniques for disproving confluence and very few but recent techniques for establishing confluence. CSI is open-source, equipped with a strategy language, and accessible via a simple web interface.

We assume familiarity with term rewriting and confluence [3, 15]. The remainder of this paper is organized as follows. In Section 2 the main techniques supported by CSI are summarized. Implementation issues are addressed in Section 3 and Section 4 concludes with preliminary experimental results.

2 Techniques

Besides Knuth and Bendix' criterion [9] (joinability of critical pairs for terminating systems), CSI supports the techniques described below.

Non-Confluence To disprove confluence of a TRS $\mathcal{R}$ we consider peaks

$$t \ ^{\leqslant m}\!\!\leftarrow t_1 \leftarrow s \rightarrow u_1 \rightarrow^{\leqslant n} u \tag{1}$$

such that $t_1 = s[r_1\sigma]_p \leftarrow s[\ell_1\sigma]_p = s = s[\ell_2\sigma]_q \rightarrow s[r_2\sigma]_q = u_1$ with $\ell_1 \rightarrow r_1$, $\ell_2 \rightarrow r_2 \in \mathcal{R}$, $q \leqslant p$, and $p \in \mathcal{P}os(s[\ell_2]_q)$. This includes critical overlaps and some variable overlaps. In order to test non-joinability of t and u we consider ground

---

* This research is supported by FWF (Austrian Science Fund) project P22467.

N. Bjørner and V. Sofronie-Stokkermans (Eds.): CADE 2011, LNAI 6803, pp. 499–505, 2011.

instances of t and u. Let c_x be a fresh constant for every variable x and let $\hat{t}$ denote the result of replacing every variable in a term t by the corresponding constant. Since for terms s and w we have $s \to_{\mathcal{R}} w$ if and only if $\hat{s} \to_{\mathcal{R}} \hat{w}$, it follows that terms t and u are joinable if and only if $\hat{t}$ and $\hat{u}$ are joinable. In order to test non-joinability of $\hat{t}$ and $\hat{u}$ we overapproximate the sets of reducts for $\hat{t}$ and $\hat{u}$ and check if the intersection is empty.

The first approach is based on TCAP, which was introduced to obtain a better approximation of dependency graphs [7]. Let t be a term. The term $\mathrm{TCAP}(t)$ is inductively defined as follows. If t is a variable, $\mathrm{TCAP}(t)$ is a fresh variable. If $t = f(t_1, \ldots, t_n)$ then we let $u = f(\mathrm{TCAP}(t_1), \ldots, \mathrm{TCAP}(t_n))$ and define $\mathrm{TCAP}(t)$ to be u if u does not unify with the left-hand side of a rule in $\mathcal{R}$, and a fresh variable otherwise.

Lemma 1. *If $\hat{t}$ and $\hat{u}$ are joinable then $\mathrm{TCAP}(\hat{t})$ and $\mathrm{TCAP}(\hat{u})$ unify.* $\square$

In the sequel we use the result in its contrapositive form, i.e., whenever $\mathrm{TCAP}(\hat{t})$ and $\mathrm{TCAP}(\hat{u})$ are not unifiable then $\hat{t}$ and $\hat{u}$ are not joinable.

The following example motivates why replacing variables by constants is beneficial.

Example 2. Consider the TRS $\mathcal{R}$ consisting of the rules $\mathsf{f}(x, y) \to \mathsf{g}(x)$ and $\mathsf{f}(x, y) \to \mathsf{g}(y)$. Note that $\mathrm{TCAP}(\mathsf{g}(x)) = \mathsf{g}(x')$ and $\mathrm{TCAP}(\mathsf{g}(y)) = \mathsf{g}(y')$ are unifiable but since x and y are different normal forms it is beneficial to replace them by fresh constants such that unification fails. We have $\mathrm{TCAP}(\mathsf{g}(\mathsf{c}_x)) = \mathsf{g}(\mathsf{c}_x)$ is not unifiable with $\mathsf{g}(\mathsf{c}_y) = \mathrm{TCAP}(\mathsf{g}(\mathsf{c}_y))$.

The next example illustrates Lemma 1.

Example 3. Consider the TRS $\mathcal{R} = \{\mathsf{a} \to \mathsf{f}(\mathsf{a}, \mathsf{b}), \mathsf{f}(\mathsf{a}, \mathsf{b}) \to \mathsf{f}(\mathsf{b}, \mathsf{a})\}$ from [16] and the peak $\hat{t} = \mathsf{f}(\mathsf{f}(\mathsf{b}, \mathsf{a}), \mathsf{b}) \,{}^2{\leftarrow} \mathsf{f}(\mathsf{a}, \mathsf{b}) \to \mathsf{f}(\mathsf{b}, \mathsf{a}) = \hat{u}$. Since $\mathrm{TCAP}(\hat{t}) = \mathsf{f}(\mathsf{f}(\mathsf{b}, x), \mathsf{b})$ and $\mathrm{TCAP}(\hat{u}) = \mathsf{f}(\mathsf{b}, y)$ are not unifiable $\mathcal{R}$ is not confluent.

We remark that Lemma 1 subsumes the case that t and u are different normal forms or that t and u have different root symbols which do not occur at the root of any left-hand side in $\mathcal{R}$. The latter amounts to $t(\epsilon) \neq u(\epsilon)$ and $t(\epsilon) \neq \ell(\epsilon) \neq u(\epsilon)$ for all $\ell \to r \in \mathcal{R}$, which is the test performed in [2].

Our second approach is based on tree automata. Let $\mathcal{R}$ be a left-linear TRS and L a set of ground terms. A tree automaton $\mathcal{A} = (\mathcal{F}, Q, Q_f, \Delta)$ is *compatible* [6] with $\mathcal{R}$ and L if $L \subseteq \mathcal{L}(\mathcal{A})$ and for each $\ell \to r \in \mathcal{R}$ and state substitution $\sigma \colon \mathcal{V}\mathrm{ar}(\ell) \to Q$, $r\sigma \to^*_{\Delta} q$ whenever $\ell\sigma \to^*_{\Delta} q$. The extension to arbitrary TRSs that we use in our implementation is described in [10]. Here $\mathcal{L}(\mathcal{A})$ is the language accepted by a tree automaton $\mathcal{A}$. In the following $\to^*_{\mathcal{R}}(L)$ denotes the set $\{t \mid s \to^*_{\mathcal{R}} t \text{ for some } s \in L\}$.

Theorem 4. *Let $\mathcal{R}$ be a TRS, $\mathcal{A}$ a tree automaton, and L a set of ground terms. If $\mathcal{A}$ is compatible with $\mathcal{R}$ and L then $\to^*_{\mathcal{R}}(L) \subseteq \mathcal{L}(\mathcal{A})$.* $\square$

We overapproximate the sets of terms reachable from $\hat{t}$ and $\hat{u}$ using tree automata, i.e., we construct tree automata $\mathcal{A}_1$ and $\mathcal{A}_2$ (by *tree automata completion* [10]) such that $\rightarrow_{\mathcal{R}}^*(\{\hat{t}\}) \subseteq \mathcal{L}(\mathcal{A}_1)$ and $\rightarrow_{\mathcal{R}}^*(\{\hat{u}\}) \subseteq \mathcal{L}(\mathcal{A}_2)$ and conclude non-joinability of $\hat{t}$ and $\hat{u}$ if $\mathcal{L}(\mathcal{A}_1) \cap \mathcal{L}(\mathcal{A}_2) = \varnothing$, which is decidable.

Example 5. Consider Lévy's TRS $\mathcal{R}$ from [8]

$$\begin{array}{llll} \mathsf{f}(\mathsf{a},\mathsf{a}) \rightarrow \mathsf{g}(\mathsf{b},\mathsf{b}) & \mathsf{a} \rightarrow \mathsf{a}' & \mathsf{f}(\mathsf{a}',x) \rightarrow \mathsf{f}(x,x) & \mathsf{f}(x,\mathsf{a}') \rightarrow \mathsf{f}(x,x) \\ \mathsf{g}(\mathsf{b},\mathsf{b}) \rightarrow \mathsf{f}(\mathsf{a},\mathsf{a}) & \mathsf{b} \rightarrow \mathsf{b}' & \mathsf{g}(\mathsf{b}',x) \rightarrow \mathsf{g}(x,x) & \mathsf{g}(x,\mathsf{b}') \rightarrow \mathsf{g}(x,x) \end{array}$$

and $\hat{t} = \mathsf{f}(\mathsf{a}',\mathsf{a}') \ {}^*\!\!\leftarrow \mathsf{f}(\mathsf{a},\mathsf{a}) \rightarrow^* \mathsf{g}(\mathsf{b}',\mathsf{b}') = \hat{u}$. We have $\rightarrow_{\mathcal{R}}^*(\{\hat{t}\}) = \{\hat{t}\}$ and $\rightarrow_{\mathcal{R}}^*(\{\hat{u}\}) = \{\hat{u}\}$. Consequently $\rightarrow_{\mathcal{R}}^*(\{\hat{t}\}) \cap \rightarrow_{\mathcal{R}}^*(\{\hat{u}\}) = \varnothing$ and hence we conclude non-joinability of $\hat{t}$ and $\hat{u}$ which yields the non-confluence of $\mathcal{R}$. Note that $\mathrm{TCAP}(\hat{t}) = x$ and $\mathrm{TCAP}(\hat{u}) = y$ unify.

Order-Sorted Decomposition. Next we focus on a criterion that allows to decompose a TRS $\mathcal{R}$ into TRSs $\mathcal{R}_1 \cup \cdots \cup \mathcal{R}_n$ where $\mathcal{R}$ is confluent whenever all $\mathcal{R}_i$ are confluent. Order-sorted decomposition is a generalization of persistent decomposition [2, Definition 2] to ordered sorts. It is based on a result in [5].

Theorem 6. *Let $\mathcal{R}$ be a TRS and $\langle \mathcal{F}, \mathcal{V} \rangle$ an order-sorted signature with sorts $\mathcal{S}$ equipped with a strict order $\succ$. Assume that the following conditions hold:*

1. *$\mathcal{R}$ is compatible with $\mathcal{S}$, i.e., rules $\ell \rightarrow r \in \mathcal{R}$ are well-sorted, with variables bound strictly in ℓ and the sort of ℓ is $\succeq$ that of r.*
2. *If $\mathcal{R}$ is non-left-linear and duplicating then for $\ell \rightarrow r \in \mathcal{R}$, variables in r are bound strictly as well. Furthermore, if $r \in \mathcal{V}$ the sort of r must be maximal.*

If $\mathcal{R}$ is confluent on well-sorted terms then $\mathcal{R}$ is confluent on all terms. □

Each sort attachment satisfying the conditions of Theorem 6 gives rise to a decomposition of $\mathcal{R}$ into $\max \{ \mathcal{R} \cap \mathcal{T}_{\trianglelefteq\alpha}(\mathcal{F}, \mathcal{V}) \times \mathcal{T}_{\trianglelefteq\alpha}(\mathcal{F}, \mathcal{V}) \mid \alpha \in \mathcal{S} \}$, where $\mathcal{T}_{\trianglelefteq\alpha}(\mathcal{F}, \mathcal{V})$ denotes the subterms of terms of sort $\preceq \alpha$. Note that we can replace proper subterms $t|_p : \beta$ by any other terms with sort $\preceq \beta$. Hence $\mathcal{T}_{\trianglelefteq\alpha}(\mathcal{F}, \mathcal{V})$ is closed under adding terms of sort $\preceq$ that of any terms in $\mathcal{T}_{\trianglelefteq\alpha}(\mathcal{F}, \mathcal{V})$. As in the many-sorted persistence case, we can find a most general ordered sort attachment consistent with any given TRS efficiently. Start by assigning sort variables to the argument and result types of all function symbols and to the variables occurring in the rules, after renaming them to ensure that no two rules share any variables. The consistency conditions, except for the maximality condition for collapsing rules, translate to inequalities $\alpha \succeq \beta$ between these type variables. To solve a system of such constraints, consider the graph with sort variables as nodes and edges from α to β whenever there is a constraint $\alpha \succeq \beta$. Then assign a distinct sort to the variables of each strongly connected component of the graph, ordered strictly by the edges between the components. A maximality constraint on β can be enforced in a second pass that equates α and β whenever $\alpha \succ \beta$. This process is demonstrated in the example below.

Example 7. Consider the TRS

$$1: f(x, A) \to G(x) \quad 2: f(x, G(x)) \to B \quad 3: G(C) \to C \quad 4: F(x) \to F(G(x))$$

We start by assigning variables to the various sorts. Let x_i be the sort of x in rule i. Furthermore let $A : A$, $B : B$, $C : C$, $f : f_1 \times f_2 \to f$, $F : F_1 \to F$ and $G : G_1 \to G$. By well-sortedness we get constraints $f_1 \succeq x_1$, $f_2 \succeq A$ from the left-hand side of the first rule. By strictness of left-hand sides, we require that $x_1 \succeq f_1$. We get similar constraints from the other rules, noting that since the TRS is non-duplicating, we do not have strictness constraints on the right-hand sides. By relating the sorts of left-hand sides and right-hand sides, we obtain further constraints, namely $f \succeq G$, $f \succeq B$, $G \succeq C$ and $F \succeq F$. Denoting $\alpha \succeq \beta$ by an edge $\alpha \to \beta$, we obtain the following graph:

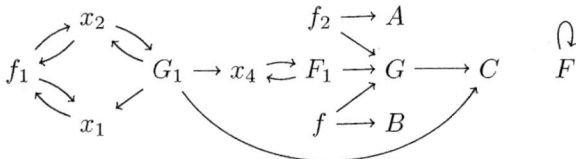

The strongly connected components are $8 = \{f_2\}$, $7 = \{A\}$, $6 = \{f\}$, $5 = \{B\}$, $4 = \{G_1, x_1, f_1, x_2\}$, $3 = \{F_1, x_4\}$, $2 = \{G\}$, $1 = \{C\}$, and $0 = \{F\}$, ordered by $8 \succ 7, 2$, $6 \succ 5, 2$, and $4 \succ 3 \succ 2 \succ 1$. The resulting signature is $A : 7$, $B : 5$, $C : 1$, $f : 4 \times 8 \to 6$, $F : 3 \to 0$, and $G : 4 \to 2$ giving rise to the decomposition into the TRSs $\{(1), (2), (3)\}$ and $\{(3), (4)\}$.

If we required maximality of the sort $2 = \{G\}$, then we would equate 2 and 3 (since $3 \succ 2$), and further with 4 (as $4 \succ 3$), 6 (as $6 \succ 2$) and 8 (as $8 \succ 2$), obtaining $8' = \{G, F_1, x_4, G_1, x_1, f_1, x_2, f, f_2\}$, ordered by $8' \succ 7, 5, 1$. The resulting signature is $A : 7$, $B : 5$, $C : 1$, $f : 8' \times 8' \to 8'$, $F : 8' \to 0$, and $G : 8' \to 8'$. Note that here no (non-trivial) decomposition is possible.

Decreasing Diagrams. The decreasing diagrams technique [12, 14] is a complete method for confluence on countable abstract rewrite systems. The next result employs decreasing diagrams for TRSs and follows immediately from [17, Corollary 3.16]. It also serves to demonstrate the design of our tool which typically implements one criterion by combining smaller pieces via a strategy language (cf. Section 3). Here $\mathcal{R}_d$ ($\mathcal{R}_{nd}$) denotes the (non)duplicating rules in a TRS $\mathcal{R}$.

Theorem 8. *A left-linear TRS $\mathcal{R}$ is confluent if $\mathcal{R}_d$ is terminating relative to $\mathcal{R}_{nd}$ and all critical peaks of $\mathcal{R}$ are decreasing with respect to the rule labeling.*   □

To exploit this theorem we need to solve relative termination problems. In [17] we show that relative termination techniques can additionally be used for labeling diagrams (also in combination with the rule labeling).

3   Implementation

CSI is implemented based on the open source termination tool T$_T$T$_2$ [11] and written in OCaml. As explained in the preceding section, several criteria from termination analysis are useful for confluence. Our tool is based on few techniques, but a *strategy language* (akin to the one to control T$_T$T$_2$) allows one to combine different criteria flexibly and to obtain a powerful tool. For a grammar of this strategy language, consult [11] or pass the option -h to the tool.

Automatic Mode. In its automatic mode CSI executes the strategy

    (KB || NOTCR || (((CLOSED || DD) | add)2*)! || sorted -order)*

Here identifiers in capital letters abbreviate combinations of techniques. We skip details for brevity. The command KB refers to Knuth and Bendix' criterion [9], NOTCR is a test for non-confluence as described in Section 2, and sorted -order aims for an order-sorted decomposition (cf. Section 2 and [5]). The operator || executes all those criteria in parallel—to make use of modern multi-core architectures—and the first substrategy that succeeds is used to make progress on the given problem. Since a successful call to sorted -order returns a list of problems, the trailing * ensures that the above strategy is iterated on all subproblems until no further progress can be achieved. Finally we describe the part that is still missing. CLOSED tests whether the critical pairs of a left-linear system are development closed [13] and DD implements decreasing diagrams (Section 2 and [17]). If these methods do not succeed the alternative | executes add, which adds new rules that might enable the other criteria to succeed ([17, Lemma 4.3 and Example 4.4]) while the postfix 2* executes the strategy inside parentheses at most two times, i.e., CLOSED || DD is run again, if some rules have been added. The outermost ! ensures that the strategy inside only succeeds if confluence could be (dis)proved.

Strategy Language. We elaborate on the strategy language to show the flexibility and modularity of our tool. In the strategy nonconfluence -steps 2 -tcap the flag -tcap tests non-joinability of terms with TCAP, as outlined in Section 2. With -steps values for m and n in the peak (1) on page 499 are set.

The criterion from Theorem 8 allows one to use the decreasing diagrams technique, provided some precondition is satisfied. To this end the composition operator ; is employed, where A;B executes B only if A succeeds. Given an input TRS $\mathcal{R}$, in the strategy

    cr -dup; matrix -dim 2*; rule_labeling; decreasing

the expression cr -dup generates the relative TRS $\mathcal{R}_d/\mathcal{R}_{nd}$, termination of which is attempted with matrix interpretations of dimension 2. If this succeeds the critical diagrams are labeled with the rule labeling [14], before a test for decreasingness is performed. We note that the strategy language allows to label incrementally combining different (relative termination) criteria [17]. Here a critical diagram is a critical peak $t \leftarrow s \rightarrow u$ together with joining sequences $t \rightarrow^* v \,{}^*\!\leftarrow u$. In the implementation for every critical peak we consider all joining sequences $t \rightarrow^{\leqslant n} \cdot \,{}^{\leqslant n}\!\leftarrow u$ for which there is no smaller n that admits a common reduct.

Table 1. Experiments

(a) 106 TRSs.			
	CSI	ACP	$\sum$
CR	61	64	67
not CR	20	18	21

(b) 99 TRSs.			
	CSI	ACP	$\sum$
CR	43	42	43
not CR	47	47	47

(c) 9 TRSs.			
	CSI	ACP	$\sum$
CR	6	2	6
not CR	2	2	2

Table 2. Performance difference on the three testbenches

system	CSI	ACP	status	system	CSI	ACP	status
BN98/ex6.5f	$\times(\infty)$	$\checkmark(0.4)$	$\neg$CR	Tiw02/ex1	$\checkmark(0.3)$	$\times(0.1)$	$\neg$CR
Der97/p204	$\times(6.6)$	$\checkmark(0.1)$	CR	Toy98/ex1	$\times(6.1)$	$\checkmark(0.1)$	CR
GL06/ex3	$\checkmark(0.6)$	$\times(0.2)$	CR	standards/AC	$\checkmark(2.7)$	$\times(0.1)$	CR
GOO96/R2p	$\times(6.3)$	$\checkmark(0.1)$	CR	standards/add_C	$\checkmark(4.0)$	$\times(0.1)$	CR
Gra96caap/ex2	$\times(3.0)$	$\checkmark(0.1)$	CR	Transformed_CS^a	$\checkmark(4.6)$	$\times(\infty)$	CR
OO03/ex1	$\checkmark(4.0)$	$\times(7.0)$	CR	ZFM11/ex1.1	$\checkmark(4.9)$	$\times(7.0)$	CR
OO03/ex2	$\times(6.3)$	$\checkmark(0.1)$	CR	ZFM11/ex3.18	$\checkmark(1.0)$	$\times(0.1)$	CR
Ohl94caap/ex5.12	$\checkmark(0.4)$	$\times(0.1)$	$\neg$CR	ZFM11/ex3.20	$\checkmark(2.1)$	$\times(0.5)$	CR
TO01/ex6	$\times(6.3)$	$\checkmark(0.1)$	CR	ZFM11/ex4.1	$\checkmark(0.9)$	$\times(0.1)$	CR

^{a} Transformed_CSR_04_PALINDROME_nokinds-noand_L

4 Evaluation

For experiments[1] we used the collection from [1] which consists of 106 TRSs from the rewriting literature dealing with confluence (Table 1(a)), the 99 TRSs from the 2010 edition of the termination competition which are non-terminating or not known to be terminating (Table 1(b)), and the TRSs from [5,17] (Table 1(c)). The time limit of 60 seconds was hardly ever reached.

In Table 1 we compare the automatic mode of our tool with ACP [2], a confluence prover that implements various techniques from the literature. On the testbench in Table 1(a) ACP can show more systems confluent than CSI but our tool is superior for non-confluence. The last column shows that on this testbench no tool subsumes the other one which is not the case for Tables 1(b)(c).

Table 2 elaborates on the differences of the tools' performance. Here a $\times$ indicates that the corresponding tool failed to analyze the status of the given TRS while a $\checkmark$ means that confluence (or non-confluence) could be determined. The numbers in parentheses refer to the time spent on this problem in seconds. The different blocks in Table 2 correspond to the different testbeds employed.

The rewriting toolkit CiME3 [4] also supports confluence analysis as one of its many features. This tool exploits Newman's Lemma, i.e., for a terminating TRS confluence coincides with local confluence (the latter can then effectively be

---

[1] Details are available from the CSI website.

checked [9]). While this test is also contained in ACP and CSI, the novel feature of C*i*ME3 is that it can (automatically) certify such confluence proofs in the proof assistant Coq.

To conclude we stress the main attractions of CSI: To the best of our knowledge it is the only tool that implements order-sorted decomposition of rewrite systems, it employs powerful criteria for disproving confluence, and due to the modular design it allows to combine different labeling functions for the decreasing diagrams technique.

References

1. Aoto, T.: Automated confluence proof by decreasing diagrams based on rule-labelling. In: Lynch, C. (ed.) RTA 2010. LIPIcs, vol. 6, pp. 7–16. Schloss Dagstuhl, Dagstuhl (2010)
2. Aoto, T., Yoshida, J., Toyama, Y.: Proving confluence of term rewriting systems automatically. In: Treinen, R. (ed.) RTA 2009. LNCS, vol. 5595, pp. 93–102. Springer, Heidelberg (2009)
3. Baader, F., Nipkow, T.: Term Rewriting and All That. Cambridge University Press, Cambridge (1998)
4. Contejean, E., Courtieu, P., Forest, J., Pons, O., Urbain, X.: Automated certified proofs with CiME3. In: Schmidt-Schauß, M. (ed.) RTA 2011. LIPIcs, vol. 10, pp. 21–30. Schloss Dagstuhl, Dagstuhl (2011)
5. Felgenhauer, B., Zankl, H., Middeldorp, A.: Proving confluence with layer systems (2011); submitted for publication
6. Genet, T.: Decidable approximations of sets of descendants and sets of normal forms. In: Nipkow, T. (ed.) RTA 1998. LNCS, vol. 1379, pp. 151–165. Springer, Heidelberg (1998)
7. Giesl, J., Thiemann, R., Schneider-Kamp, P.: Proving and disproving termination of higher-order functions. In: Gramlich, B. (ed.) FroCoS 2005. LNCS (LNAI), vol. 3717, pp. 216–231. Springer, Heidelberg (2005)
8. Huet, G.: Confluent reductions: Abstract properties and applications to term rewriting systems. JACM 27(4), 797–821 (1980)
9. Knuth, D., Bendix, P.: Simple word problems in universal algebras. In: Leech, J. (ed.) Computational Problems in Abstract Algebra, pp. 263–297. Pergamon Press, Oxford (1970)
10. Korp, M., Middeldorp, A.: Match-bounds revisited. I&C 207(11), 1259–1283 (2009)
11. Korp, M., Sternagel, C., Zankl, H., Middeldorp, A.: Tyrolean termination tool 2. In: Treinen, R. (ed.) RTA 2009. LNCS, vol. 5595, pp. 295–304. Springer, Heidelberg (2009)
12. van Oostrom, V.: Confluence by decreasing diagrams. TCS 126(2), 259–280 (1994)
13. van Oostrom, V.: Developing developments. TCS 175(1), 159–181 (1997)
14. van Oostrom, V.: Confluence by decreasing diagrams. In: Voronkov, A. (ed.) RTA 2008. LNCS, vol. 5117, pp. 306–320. Springer, Heidelberg (2008)
15. Terese: Term Rewriting Systems, vol. 55. Cambridge Tracts in Theoretical Computer Science. Cambridge University Press, Cambridge (2003)
16. Tiwari, A.: Deciding confluence of certain term rewriting systems in polynomial time. In: LICS 2002, pp. 447–457 (2002)
17. Zankl, H., Felgenhauer, B., Middeldorp, A.: Labelings for decreasing diagrams. In: Schmidt-Schauß, M. (ed.) RTA 2011. LIPIcs, vol. 10, pp. 377–392. Schloss Dagstuhl, Dagstuhl (2011)

Author Index